McGRAW-HILL'S

D0102656

12 SAT PRACTICE TESTS AND PSAT

SECOND EDITION

CHRISTOPHER BLACK

MARK ANESTIS

and the TUTORS of COLLEGE HILL COACHING™

McGraw-Hill

NewYork / Chicago /San Francisco / Lisbon / London / Madrid / Mexico City
Milan / New Delhi / San Juan / Seoul / Singapore / Sydney / Toronto

The McGraw·Hill Companies

Copyright © 2008, 2007 by The McGraw-Hill Companies, Inc. All rights reserved. Printed in the United States of America. Except as permitted under the United States Copyright Act of 1976, no part of this publication may be reproduced or distributed in any form or by any means, or stored in a data base or retrieval system, without the prior written permission of the publisher.

4 5 6 7 8 9 0 QWD/QWD 0 1 2 1 0 9

ISBN: 978-0-07-158317-6
MHID: 0-07-158317-3

Printed and bound by Quebecor/Dubuque.

McGraw-Hill books are available at special quantity discounts to use as premiums and sales promotions, or for use in corporate training programs. For more information, please write to the Director of Special Sales, McGraw-Hill Professional, Two Penn Plaza, New York, NY 10121-2298. Or contact your local bookstore.

SAT and PSAT are registered trademarks of the College Entrance Examination Board, which was not involved in the production of, and does not endorse, this product.

College Hill Coaching® is a registered trademark under the control of Christopher F. Black.

ABOUT THE AUTHORS

Christopher Black, M.A. is the founder and director of College Hill Coaching. He has been a consultant to the nation's leading educational publishers and software developers and is coauthor of *McGraw-Hill's SAT*.

Mark Anestis is the founder and director of The Learning Edge and coauthor of *McGraw-Hill's SAT*.

CONTENTS

CONTENTS

CHAPTER 1

WHAT YOU NEED TO KNOW ABOUT THE NEW SAT

Important Questions About a Tough Test

Why do colleges need to see my SAT scores? Aren't my grades and SAT Subject Test scores enough?

Many colleges use your SAT scores to help them assess your readiness to do tough college work. Although the SAT does not assess broad subject knowledge, it provides a universal benchmark that your high school transcript can't. It assess skills that are essential to success in a competitive liberal-arts college: written argumentation, critical reading, and mathematical analysis.

Competitive colleges need the SAT because course grades are, unfortunately, far from objective measures of your academic ability. Teachers rarely give out grades consistently and without bias. We all know that every school has easy graders and hard graders. Also, many teachers occasionally inflate or deflate grades for reasons unrelated to intellectual ability, like "effort" or personal preference. Even when objective standards are used, they vary widely from teacher to teacher and school to school. Achievement tests like AP exams and SAT Subject Tests are more objective, but they are designed to assess subject knowledge, which can be easily forgotten, rather than basic reasoning skills, which determine broader academic ability. Subject knowledge is effective only when it is incorporated into a meaningful and robust way of solving problems. The SAT, although not perfect, does a good job of measuring how well you reason under pressure, an important academic and life skill.

SAT-bashing has been a very popular pastime in the last 25 years or so, largely due to the "crack-the-test" SAT-prep franchises. Very few of their arguments against the SAT, however, hold any water. The fact is that more students take the SAT every year, and more colleges—not fewer—rely on the SAT every year.

Doesn't the SAT do a poor job of predicting first-year college grades?

SAT-bashers have long liked to claim that the SAT isn't valuable to colleges because it doesn't predict college grades very well. They miss two important points: first, smart college admissions officers don't *want* it to predict grades, and second, it correlates very well with something more important than grades—real success in academic fields like law, medicine, and the like.

As we just discussed, predicting grades is a wild-goose chase because grades are not objectively distributed: most any teacher can give out grades any way he or she wishes. Many students, as we all know, get good grades without having great intellectual ability. They just learn to "play the game" of school—seek the easy "A"s, suck up to teachers, and pad their transcripts.

Smart college admissions officers like the SAT because it often weeds the grade-grubbers out from the truly good thinkers. Rather than predicting your grades, your SAT scores indicate your ability to read critically, write cogently, solve math problems intelligently, and think under pressure. Thankfully, the SAT is not designed to predict how well you'll play the college grading game.

Doesn't the SAT just measure "test-taking skills"?

Although many large SAT-prep franchises try to convince students that taking the SAT has nothing to do with real academic skills, and that it's all about applying their test-taking "secrets," most of this is just hype. In fact the only way to see dramatic score improvements on the SAT is through smart practice in the reasoning skills at the core of the SAT. Real success on the SAT takes hard work and the right attitude. Treating the SAT like a joke is definitely *not* the right attitude.

The SAT isn't written by a monopoly of sadists who hate students and want to make college admissions as arduous as possible. The Educational Testing Service (ETS) writes the SAT at the request of the College Board, a nonprofit association of over 4,200 colleges whose goal is to promote high academic standards for students. More than likely, any college you apply to will be a member of the College Board.

The ETS changes the format and content of the SAT from time to time, based on the needs of the member colleges and universities. For instance, in 2002, educators at the University of California, unhappy with the writing skills of their incoming freshmen, suggested that the SAT incorporate an essay and eleminate some of the more "artificial" vocabulary-based questions so that it would better reflect actual college work. After much research, the ETS changed the SAT accordingly, and the most recent version of the SAT was implemented in 2005.

Why does so much ride on just one test?

It may seem unfair that a 4½ hour test is so important. Remember, though, that the SAT is not a one-shot, all-or-nothing affair. Your standardized test scores account for only about ⅕ to ⅓ of your college application, depending on where you apply. The other essential components include your grades, your curriculum, your essay, your recommendations, your special talents, and your extracurricular activities. Also, you can take the SAT many times, and colleges will consider only the top individual scores from all of your tests. In other words, if you take the SAT twice, and get scores of 460 Critical Reading, 530 Math and 500 Writing on the first test, and 540 Critical Reading, and 490 Math and 400 Writing on the second test, then your score is, for all practical purposes, 540 Critical Reading, 530 Math and 500 Writing. Colleges won't average the scores, or penalize you for being a bit inconsistent. They do this for their own benefit as well as yours: they fare better in the college rankings if they report higher scores!

The SAT is only "unfair" if you allow it to be by not taking it seriously. If, instead, you look at it as an opportunity to hone important academic reasoning skills, and prepare for it meaningfully, you'll find the process more rewarding and less nerve-racking.

Don't wealthy students who can afford expensive coaching have an unfair advantage?

Undoubtedly, the ability to afford the best coaching is an advantage. This should come as no surprise. Athletes and musicians certainly benefit from good personal coaching, and students are no different. This simply shows that the SAT is a test of ability, not race or any other innate quality. It is a test of reasoning skills, which can be learned. The right kind of training will pay off. If you follow the College Hill Method and take your preparation seriously, your efforts will be rewarded.

Is the SAT an intelligence test?

This isn't a simple question, so there's no simple answer. "Intelligence" can be used to refer to many different qualities, and certainly the SAT does not assess all of them. The common definition of intelligence as "an innate, general, and stable cognitive ability that determines one's ability to reason across a wide range of tasks" is outmoded and unhelpful. Most psychologists agree that humans possess many different "intelligences" that can improve or atrophy with use or disuse. These include musical intelligence, interpersonal intelligence, mechanical intelligence, verbal intelligence, mathematical intelligence, and analytical intelligence. The SAT measures only certain aspects of verbal, mathematical, and analytical intelligence.

When people ask whether the SAT is an "intelligence" test, usually they really mean: "Do my SAT scores put limits on how successful I can be?" The answer is: only if you misinterpret them. Rather than a measure of your innate "limits" for success, the SAT indicates your mastery of a few basic but essential academic skills. If you improve these skills, you will be more successful academically. Of course, academic success isn't the only kind of success. We can all find wonderful success stories about people who have become successful artists, politicians, and business leaders despite having low SAT scores. The SAT doesn't measure artistic, athletic, intrapersonal, or interpersonal skills, and these are often key elements to nonacademic success. You will find, however, that success in academic fields correlates quite highly (but not, of course, perfectly) with SAT scores.

Doesn't the College Board claim that you can't study for the SAT?

In fact, the College Board openly states that you can and should study for the SAT, because it assesses very learnable skills. It strongly encourages preparation by focusing on *academic* skills. In fact, for decades the College Board has published materials to help students study for the SAT.

The College Board's research does shows quite clearly, however, that just learning test-taking tricks doesn't help much. Only solid practice in fundamental reasoning skills produces dramatic score improvements.

Do I have to take the SAT?

Probably, but not necessarily. Consult the web sites of the colleges you are interested in to see if they require the SAT or SAT Subject Tests. Most competitive schools will require the SAT or a test like it (such as the ACT), but some colleges do not. Even if your college does not require the SAT, you should consider taking it anyway. If you do well, your scores can make your application much more attractive. If you don't, just don't send them.

Do the colleges see all of my SAT Scores?

It's very important to remember that no college will see any of your SAT scores until you *tell* the College Board to release them. You will be given the opportunity to release your scores to specific schools when you register for the test, but be cautious about doing this. Don't—I repeat, *don't*—release your scores until either you're satisfied with your entire score report or you have no other choice (such as when a deadline is approaching).

When you release your score report to a college, the report will contain all of the scores of the SATs and SAT Subject Tests that you have taken up to that point. But remember: if you have taken any test more than once, the college will consider only the top score among all of the results.

Do I have to take SAT Subject Tests?

The SAT Subject Tests are one-hour subject area tests. They are offered in most academic subjects, like mathematics, physics, chemistry, biology, literature, history, languages, and so on. Some colleges do not require you to submit any SAT Subject Test scores, while others may require you to submit up to three SAT Subject Test scores. (But you may submit more than three if you wish.) If you are planning to apply to highly competitive colleges, you should plan to take three or more.

If you believe you have academic strengths that are not shown by your class grades, the SAT Subject Tests are an excellent way to show colleges those strengths.

When should I take the SAT and SAT Subject Tests?

It's usually best to take the SAT Subject Test in June for any course you've finished successfully, so that the subject material is fresh in your mind. For instance, if you do well in freshman biology, take the SAT Subject Test in biology in June of your freshman year. Likewise, consider taking the Math Level I after completing algebra II successfully, the Math Level II after precalculus, etc. You will want to take any SAT Subject Test in a subject when you feel you are "at your peak" in that subject.

Learn which SAT Subject Tests your colleges require, and try to complete them by June of your junior year. You can take up to three SAT Subject Tests on any one test date. After you take the PSAT in October of your junior year, you can take the SAT in late January, late March (or early April), or early May of your junior year and in early November, early December, and late January of your senior year.

Most of our students take the SAT in March and May of their junior year and, only if necessary, again in October of their senior year. Remember, if you submit more than one set of SAT scores, most colleges will use only your top scores.

How do I register for the SAT or SAT Subject Tests?

Since the cost and terms of registration change from time to time, check the College Board web site, *www.collegeboard.com* for all the necessary information about registration. The site also contains all the information you need to apply for special accommodations for students with disabilities.

Are my SAT and SAT Subject Test scores the most important part of my college application?

In most cases, no, but these scores are becoming more important as college admissions become more selective. Without exception, high SAT scores will provide you with an admission advantage regardless of what kind of school you are applying to. Most colleges are also very interested in your high school curriculum, your high school grades, your essay, your teacher recommendations, your special talents or experiences, and your extracurricular activities.

Generally, the more selective a college is, the more important the personal factors are, such as extracurricular activities and special talents. Some large or specialized schools will weigh the SAT or ACT scores more heavily than others, and even declare a cutoff score for applicants. If you have any questions about how heavily a certain college weighs your SAT or ACT scores, call the admissions office and ask.

How is the SAT scored?

Each of the three SAT sections (Critical Reading, Math and Writing) is scored on a scale from 200 to 800. The median (50th percentile) score for each section is usually between 490 and 530.

Each scaled score is based on a raw score for that section. This raw score increases by 1 point for every correct answer, and decreases by ¼ point for every wrong answer (except for the "grid-in" math questions, for which there is no penalty for wrong answers). If you skip a question, your raw score remains the same.

Should I guess if I don't know the answer to a question?

Because of the wrong answer penalty described above, blind guessing on multiple-choice questions will likely harm your score in the short run. If you are guessing on no more than five questions, be conservative and guess only when you can eliminate two or more choices.

If you are guessing on more than ten questions, though, you can be more aggressive. Answer all of the questions on which you can eliminate at least one choice before guessing.

On grid-in math questions, guessing can't harm your score, but it may help. So, if you have any kind of guess, fill it in.

Can I take the SAT with extended time?

Some students with special needs can take the SAT with accommodations such as extended time. These accommodations are available only to students with

Test Dates	Test	Registration Deadline	Late Deadline
October 4, 2008	SAT & Subject Tests		
November 1, 2008	SAT & Subject Tests		
December 6, 2008	SAT & Subject Tests		
January 24, 2009	SAT & Subject Tests		
March 14, 2009	SAT only		
May 2, 2009	SAT & Subject Tests		
June 6, 2009	SAT & Subject Tests		

formal recommendations and are strictly proctored. If you have a learning disability that has been diagnosed by a psychologist and feel that special accommodations would benefit you, talk to your guidance counselor about how to qualify and register.

When will I receive my scores?

You can get your SAT or SAT Subject Test scores by phone or on the web about two weeks after you take the test. About ten days later, a written report will be mailed to you free of charge. Any schools to which you release your scores will receive them by mail at about the same time you do. If a college needs your scores sooner, you can "rush" them for a fee.

Can I get the actual test back when I receive my scores?

On some SAT administrations (usually those in October, January, and May), the College Board provides the Question and Answer Service (QAS) for a fee. This service provides you with a copy of the test booklet, a record of your answers, the answer key, scoring instructions, and information about the types and difficulty of each question. You may order this service when you register or up to five months after the date of the test. You may also order a copy of your answer sheet only for a smaller fee. You can find information about these services in your score report.

Are some SATs easier than others?

No. SATs are statistically "equated" so that one test should be, on average, just as difficult as any other. Many people think that, since the SAT is "graded on a curve," it is best to take the test when the "smart" kids are not taking the test, so the curve will be in your favor. They are wrong. The grading curves are determined ahead of time for each test. Don't let such misconceptions dictate when you take the test. Take it when you are best prepared for it.

CHAPTER 2

THE COLLEGE HILL METHOD

Smart Training for the SAT

What is the College Hill Method?

In the last few decades, the SAT-prep industry has been dominated by two general approaches: the "crack-the-test" approach and the "buckshot" approach. The "crack-the-test" approach assumes that acing the SAT (and tests like it) requires only memorizing a set of "proprietary" test-taking tricks. The "buckshot" approach assumes that acing the SAT requires memorizing scores and scores of "best strategies" for tackling every type of SAT question. (A shotgun sprays dozens of shotgun pellets over a wide area, hoping to hit something, in contrast to a rifle, which is far more accurate and efficient.)

Both approaches are occasionally somewhat helpful to students, but neither is close to an optimal approach. Just as sugar pills can give patients the feeling that they are getting better in the short run, yet cause serious harm in the long run by discouraging them from seeking real medical help, so do test-taking tricks give students a false sense of confidence. Worse, they often encourage poor thinking habits, which hurt students in college.

The "buckshot" approach also limits a student's potential on the SAT. Imagine any professional—a base ballplayer, for instance—training by simply memorizing standard procedures for every possible scenario that might arise. There are too many to count, so the effort is doomed from the start. Instead, real experts develop their expertise through active, structured and flexible knowledge, and robust general problem-solving skills that are particular to their field of expertise. A good baseball player learns to react to novel situations, to analyze situations on the fly, and to use his strengths flexibly. If a major-league hitter becomes too rigid and standardized in his approach, he will never be able to handle a new pitcher or a new hitting situation.

Since 2005, the SAT has raised its standards. It now includes a written essay, more reading passages, tougher math concepts, and questions about grammar and usage. It is, more than ever, an academic reasoning test, requiring creativity, analytical skill, insight, knowledge, logic, and genuine academic skills. Don't let the big SAT-prep franchises fool you: the test is less susceptible to their "tricks," and the colleges know it. Students who see very large score improvements on the SAT do it through smart practice and by systematically improving their creative problem-solving skills.

The College Hill Method, the focus of the successful McGraw-Hill SAT workbook series, is not focused on mere test-taking tricks or memorizing scores of procedures. Based on the work of Christopher Black, founder of College Hill Coaching in Greenwich, Connecticut, it focuses on two elements: structured core knowledge and robust, flexible problem-solving skills that apply to a wide array of problem situations.

Structured Core Knowledge

Structured core knowledge is the essential knowledge of the concepts, skills and relationships in a particular subject area. In mathematics, for instance, structured core knowledge includes the "basics" of such skills as adding, multiplying, dividing, and solving equations, but also includes a deep and fluent understanding of number relationships, operational equivalences (for instance, the fact that dividing by a number is the same as multiplying by its reciprocal, and that multiplication is commutative but raising to powers is not), and functional relationships(for instance, that squaring a positive number less than 1 makes it smaller). In reading and writing, structured core knowledge includes the "basics" of vocabulary and sentence-building skills, but also includes a deep and fluent understanding of the higher-order structure of words, sentences, paragraphs, long passages, and books, as well as an understanding of rhetorical strategies, etymology and literary devices.

In most game situations, chess masters instantly intuit the best move because of their vast structured core knowledge culled from actively analyzing hundreds of previous games. Similarly, good doctors can quickly diagnose their patients because of their vast structured core knowledge. With smart training, you will build your structured core knowledge of the SAT.

Robust problem-solving skills

Okay, so chess masters become masters by analyzing hundreds and hundreds of games. But how does this help you on the SAT? After all, you sure haven't taken hundreds of SATs before, and probably don't plan to in the near future.

But you *have* been reading, writing and doing math problems for many years, and if you have approached them mindfully, you have accumulated a great deal of structured core knowledge in those subject areas. The keys to success on the SAT are, first, *using* that structured core knowledge effectively on the SAT (rather than just applying standard test-taking tricks), and *building* your structured core knowledge through mindful problem-solving.

How do some people seem to learn so much more quickly than others? The key is in how they solve new problems. If you use mindful problem-solving skills, then every new problem reinforces old knowledge and builds new knowledge. Poor problem-solvers just apply a standardized procedure and move on to the next problem, hoping that they applied the procedure correctly. Good problem-solvers, on the other hand, mindfully employ the eight reasoning skills that we at College Hill Coaching summarize with the mnemonic MAPS CATCH: mapping, analyzing, finding patterns, simplifying, connecting to structured knowledge, considering alternatives, thinking logically, and checking work.

In this book, we don't have enough space to discuss the College Hill Method and MAPS CATCH in very much detail. It is discussed in more detail in books like *McGraw-Hill's SAT* and *Conquering the SAT Writing* and the upcoming *Brain Corps Training* series.

However, we can give you some important mindful questions to ask as you solve SAT problems that will help you to build your structured core knowledge:

- As you read critical reading passages, are you in control of how your eyes move through the page? Do you always know what to look for in a passage? Is your mind actively seeking to answer questions as you read and to "construct" a representation of what you read in your mind? Do you consolidate information as you read? Do you notice the structure of the passage as you read?
- As you write your essay, do you stay mindful of the central purpose of your essay? Do you think about different ways of phrasing and arranging your thoughts? Do you address the objections a reader might have to your points? Are you continually checking that your writing is clear and forceful to your reader?
- When solving a math problem, do you always represent the problem information in a way you can use, manipulate and check? Do you look for patterns or repetition in the problem so that you can simplify it? Do you consider the different approaches you could take to solving the problem? Do you have good strategies for checking your work?

Getting in the zone: mindful training for the SAT

SAT training is like marathon training. For one thing, those who finish happy are those who take their training seriously. Unfortunately, many students "train" to take the SAT merely by memorizing tricks and gimmicks for "cracking" the test. This is like training for a marathon merely by buying a pair of magic socks. The socks may give you a little bit of extra confidence, but they're not going to make a big difference. Second, the vast majority of marathon runners know that they don't have any chance of coming in first, but the good runners are happy just running their own race as best they can. They listen to their own bodies, rather than chasing the other runners around them. Similarly, good test takers don't pay attention to the students around them when they are taking a test. Instead, they know what they can do and what they can't do, and they don't stress out about not being able to answer every single question.

TRAIN YOUR BODY WITH YOUR MIND

There are two great reasons to combine a regimen of vigorous physical exercise with your preparation for the SAT. First, physical health yields mental benefits. Those who are in good physical shape can focus longer and think faster than those who don't exercise. Second, the task of getting your body in shape teaches you a lot about getting your mind in shape. When you are training to run a race like a marathon, for instance, you learn quickly that consistency pays off. Getting out there every day and logging miles is critical. Similarly, consistency pays off in SAT prep. If you set aside only one day a week to do your work, you won't see nearly as much benefit as if you had spread it out over the week. Also, physical training teaches you to listen to your body; you learn when it's okay to push yourself hard, and when you need to ease up. Similarly, good SAT training teaches you to listen to your mind; you learn which problems you can tackle easily, which are challenging but manageable, and which ones to skip. This will help you enormously on test day.

PRACTICE FOCUSING AND RELAXATION EXERCISES

Top athletes and performers often do focusing and relaxation exercises before they perform. These exercises help them to eliminate distractions and unnecessary tension so that they can do their best. You should practice these exercises, too. Here are some that work wonders.

I. FOCUSED BREATHING

Focused breathing is perhaps the oldest and most powerful technique for calming nerves and focusing the mind. It is also amazingly simple. Sit in an upright chair with your hands on your knees, or sit upright on the floor with your legs crossed. Close your eyes and focus your attention on your breathing. Do not alter your breathing at first, just notice it. After a few breaths, you will notice that it will become slower and deeper.

This deep breathing is the key to relaxation. When we are tense and anxious, our breathing becomes short and shallow, and the oxygen flow through the body is diminished.

Next, focus on gently controlling your breathing so that you extend both the in breath and the out breath. Your in breath should feel like you are filling your lungs completely with air. The out breath should be slow and controlled, and should produce a light, hollow, raspy sound at the back of your throat.

Do not hold your breath at any point. Your in breath should move smoothly into an out breath. After a few breaths like this, you will notice that your mind will begin to wander. You will think about other things, perhaps about responsibilities that you have, and your body will tense up briefly. Focus on "releasing" those thoughts from your mind in the same way that you are releasing the air from your lungs, and return your focus to the breath. This practice of noticing and releasing distractions is an essential part of focused breathing practice. It teaches you that these thoughts are normal, that you shouldn't get too anxious about them, and that you have control over them. You can "release" them from your mind.

After a few minutes of focused breathing, your body is relaxed and your mind is alert, so you are prepared to do your homework or take your test.

2. Systematic relaxation

Another amazingly simple practice for releasing tension is systematic relaxation. Sit in an upright chair, or lie on the floor. Close your eyes. Bring your attention to the muscles in your head and face. These are usually the first muscles to become tense when we are anxious. As your attention moves around your face to the different muscles, "see" these muscles in your mind's eye at the same time that you consciously relax them. When your face and head feel relaxed, move to your neck and shoulders.

Don't rush. Often, the tension in your muscles goes so deep that you must focus on it for a minute or so before that tension will release. Then move systematically down to your arms, your torso and back, your hips, your legs, and your feet. With each stage of relaxation, you should feel the tension flowing out of you like sand from a bag. After several minutes of systematic relaxation, your body is relaxed, but your mind is focused, so you are ready to do your work.

3. Yoga and mindful exercise

The problem with most exercise is that it is not mindful, and therefore can put more stress on your body than it should. If exercise to you means grunting out reps with a barbell, or running with music blasting from your earphones, then your exercise strategy may be more of an assault on your body and mind than a healthful practice.

Certain exercise disciplines have evolved over centuries to provide mindful, healthful practices. Yoga, for instance, is not just about bending and twisting your body into odd shapes. It is about pushing your body's strength, flexibility, and stamina to their limits in a mindful way, so that not only does your body become stronger and more flexible, but your mind develops a much deeper "body awareness" that is so essential to good health. T'ai Chi is also a great practice for developing body awareness, although it is generally not as physically demanding as yoga can be.

Learning these disciplines requires the help of an instructor. You can probably find such classes available at your local gym, or find some instruction tapes in the library or store. Incorporating these practices into your life can make you calmer and more prepared to handle life's problems.

Listen to your body

1. Don't slouch when you work—sit up!

Your brain is constantly receiving signals from your body. When studying or taking a test, you don't want those signals to interfere with your thinking. When you slouch in your seat, or slump over your desk, your body tells your brain that it's time to rest, not to think. If you want to stay alert, sit upright and lean slightly forward over your work. You will find that this position helps you to process information much more efficiently than if you are in a more relaxed position.

2. Look at your test head-on, not at an angle

You will find it much easier to read when your test book is facing you directly, rather than at an angle. As an exercise, try to read both ways. You will notice that your brain has to work harder to process the words when the book is at an angle. Don't make things harder than they need to be!

3. Take short breaks when you feel fatigued

Whenever you begin to feel fatigued from studying, take a five-minute break. But be strict—don't let your break get out of hand. Five minutes is enough time to get a snack or use the bathroom but not long enough to do much else. Don't take a break to watch your favorite show; you can do that after your homework is done. But a good short break can provide a great energy boost in the midst of your studying.

Eat smart and get your rest

Most high school students don't put nutrition and sleep near the top of their daily priorities. If you owned a $70,000 sports car, would you leave it out in hailstorms, neglect changing the oil or transmission fluid, and use only the cheapest gasoline? Obviously not. So don't think that your brain will work just fine even if you neglect its basic needs. Here are some simple tips to make sure that your mind and body are getting what they need.

1. Drink five glasses of water a day

Even though water contains no calories or vitamins, it is the most important part of a nutritious diet. Water vitalizes your cells by helping transport essential nutrients to them. It also helps to flush out the toxic by-products that can build up in your system. Even though soda and juice are mostly water, they add lots of other unnecessary stuff that your cells don't need. All of your vital systems require an ample supply of pure water to function well.

2. Take a good multivitamin supplement daily

Even if you eat three square meals a day, you still may not be getting some of the nutrients your body and brain need to work at their best. Just one multivitamin supplement can ensure that you won't miss any nutrients even if you miss a meal. But remember: many essential nutrients, like Vitamin C, are not produced by your body, and so should be consumed regularly throughout the day. Vitamin supplements are helpful, but they can't substitute for good general eating habits.

3. Eat protein with every meal

Protein, which is found in eggs, milk, fish, poultry, and meat, is essential to a good diet because it provides the "building blocks" for a healthy body. If you eat a lot of cereal and processed, packaged foods, you probably aren't getting enough protein. Egg whites, fish, chicken, lentils, tofu, and beans are the best sources of high-quality protein.

4. Eat whole grains and lots of vegetables

There is some evidence that food additives can be harmful to the functioning of your organs, and this includes your brain. Try to eliminate processed foods from your diet: packaged crackers, cookies and cakes, processed cheeses, soda, and so on, because the additives in these foods generally offset any nutritional value they have. America is fat largely because of processed foods. Instead, eat more salads and green vegetables, fruits, and whole grains.

Instead of sugary processed cereal in the morning, try yogurt with fruit and oatmeal. Instead of a fast-food hamburger or pizza, try a grilled chicken sandwich with lettuce and tomato (keep the sauces to a minimum). Cutting out processed food is not too hard, and your energy will skyrocket and you'll feel (and think) much better.

5. Treat sleep like an appointment

Whenever a student a walks into my office with bleary eyes, I don't need an explanation. I usually get one anyway: she was up until 2 a.m. the previous night because she needed to finish an assignment that she had to postpone because of a softball game, or because her friend had an emotional crisis. Now, I'm not going to tell you to quit sports or abandon your friends, but you must understand something critical about sleep: if you don't get enough, your problems will snowball. If you have to stay up late to finish an assignment, then you'll be too tired to pay attention in class the next day, and you'll need to study harder to catch up, so you'll stay up even later the next night, and so on.

Think of it this way: if you plan your schedule so that you get eight hours of rest instead of six, you will probably find that you make up those two hours with better focus, energy, and productivity each day. So treat your bedtime like it's an important appointment, and you'll find you'll be much happier and get more done every day.

Smart test-taking tips

1. Make your practice tests feel real

One essential part of SAT prep is taking realistic practice tests, like those in this book. When taking each practice SAT, try your best to replicate the experience of the actual test as much as possible:

- If you can't take the test in a proctored classroom, at least take it in some other "neutral" setting like a public library. If you absolutely must take it at home, take it at the dining room table and have a parent turn off the phones and time you on each section.
- Start your practice test in the morning since you'll probably start your official SAT between 8 and 9 am.
- If you are timing yourself, use a stopwatch that will beep when your time is up on each section.
- Take the test in one sitting, with only one or two 5-minute breaks.

It may help to build your test-taking stamina slowly. The SAT is a long test; the practice tests in this book are just under 4 hours in length, but the real SAT will take you over 4 hours. Just as marathoners don't start their training by running a full marathon, but instead work their way up to longer runs, you might want to take just a few sections at a time to start, building up gradually until, in the last few weeks before the SAT, you are taking full tests each week.

2. Get the oxygen flowing—exercise

To stay sharp, your brain needs a good supply of oxygen. So, a good aerobic exercise regimen can help your SAT preparation tremendously. If you don't already have a good exercise regime, get in the habit of doing at least 20 minutes of good aerobic exercise every day, preferably before you sit down to do your homework or take a practice test. This will get the oxygen flowing to your brain, relieve stress, and enhance your mental agility. But be careful—always check with your doctor before making dramatic changes in your physical activity level.

3. PREPARE YOUR STUDY AREA

When taking a practice test or just studying, preparing the area is important. Most students work inefficiently because they don't prepare their work space. Put yourself in a place where you can maintain mindful focus for an extended time. Do not study or take your tests on your bed. Your bed is a place for sleep, not study. When you recline, your brain becomes less alert. You can't study well if one part of your brain is sending sleep signals to the other parts! Instead, sit in a quiet area. Sit in an upright chair at a table or desk with good lighting. This makes it easier for your brain to absorb new information and solve new problems. Also, make sure that all the tools you will need are within easy reach: the test booklet, a calculator, and pencils with erasers.

4. TAKE CONTROL OF THE TEST

When you take the SAT, the test booklet is yours— mark it up freely. You get no points for neatness on the SAT. Jotting down notes, crossing off wrong answers, and marking up diagrams are essential to good test-takers.

Within any SAT section except the reading portion, the questions are in roughly ascending order of difficulty. But you can skip around as necessary—difficulty is a matter of opinion! Remember, your objective is to accumulate as many "raw points" as you possibly can, so don't get needlessly bogged down on any tough questions.

Be careful, though: if you skip around, make sure you keep extra careful track of your answers on the answer sheet!

> Write on the test when you need to. Mark up the diagrams on math problems, write in your own words in the Sentence Completion questions, and summarize each paragraph of the reading passages.
>
> *Alex Davidow (Syracuse '08, + 170 points CR)*

5. SET CLEAR GOALS

Head into each test with a well-formulated strategy for attacking the test. Have clear score goals in mind, and know what percentage of questions you will need to answer correctly to achieve those goals. The score conversion table below will tell you this. Remember that answering every question is a bad strategy unless you have a very realistic shot at breaking 700 per section. As a rule of thumb, remember that you need to get only about 50% (or $\frac{1}{2}$) of the questions right in order to break 500, about 67% (or $\frac{2}{3}$) of the questions right in order to break 600, and about 87.5% (or $\frac{7}{8}$) of the questions right in order to break 700. It's best to focus the majority of your time on just that percentage of questions you will need to break your score goal. This strategy gives you more time to check your work on each question, and minimizes the chance of making careless errors. Use your PSAT scores or your Diagnostic Test scores as a starting point. Then decide what score will make you happy. You should know what the median SAT scores are for the schools you'd like to apply to. Set aggressive goals as you train (our students always expect to improve their scores by 100 points or so on each section) but pick a realistic goal as you get closer to the test date, based on your performance on the practice tests. If you've been getting 400s on all sections of your practice tests, don't expect to get 600s on the real thing!

6. REVIEW INTELLIGENTLY

After you take the practice tests in this book, you may need to review particular academic skills. Our review book, *McGraw-Hill's SAT*, provides a comprehensive review of all of the skills tested on the SAT. Are the geometry questions particularly tough for you? If so, focus on Chapter 13, "Essential Geometry Skills." Was pre-algebra so long ago that you forget what the commutative law and remainders are? If so, Chapter 10, "Essential Pre-Algebra Skills," is a good place to start. Look carefully at any troublesome critical reading questions on your tests. What part was toughest? If it was the vocabulary, focus on Chapter 6, "How to Build an Impressive Vocabulary with MAPS-CATCH." If you struggled in analyzing the passages, or finding their main points, focus on Chapter 7, "Critical Reading Skills." If you missed more sentence completion questions than you'd like, work on Chapter 8, "Sentence Completion Skills." Look carefully at any troublesome writing questions on your tests. Did you find yourself struggling with the essay? If so, Chapters 15 and 16 will teach you how to approach the essay more effectively, as will *Conquering the SAT Writing*. If the rules of grammar sometimes seem overwhelming, work on Chapter 18, "Essential Grammar Skills," and Chapter 17, "Attacking the Grammar Questions."

SAT Score Conversion Table

Use this table to help you set your strategy for reaching your score goals. Beneath each section heading, find your score goal. Then find the "raw score" that corresponds to it. This is the number of points you need in total for that section. For instance, if your score goal is 500 on the critical reading section, you need a raw score of 29 points. This means that you must get *at least* 29 correct answers in total on all of the critical reading section. Since there are 67 critical reading questions in total, this allows plenty of room to skip the harder questions.

Remember, however, that a wrong answer on any multiple-choice question deducts ¼ point from your raw score. Therefore, it is important to answer more questions than the minimum required for your goal, so that you give yourself room for error. If your goal is 500 on the critical reading section, for instance, you should plan to answer at least 35 questions to allow for a few wrong answers.

Raw Score	Critical Reading Scaled Score	Math Scaled Score	Writing Scaled Score	Raw Score	Critical Reading Scaled Score	Math Scaled Score	Writing Scaled Score
67	800			32	520	550	610
66	800			31	510	550	600
65	790			30	510	540	580
64	780			29	500	530	570
63	760			28	490	520	560
62	750			27	490	530	550
61	730			26	480	510	540
60	720			25	480	500	530
59	700			24	470	490	520
58	700			23	460	480	510
57	690			22	460	480	500
56	680			21	450	470	490
55	670			20	440	460	480
54	660	800		19	440	450	470
53	650	790		18	430	450	460
52	650	760		17	420	440	450
51	640	740		16	420	430	440
50	630	720		15	410	420	440
49	620	710	800	14	400	410	430
48	620	700	800	13	400	410	420
47	610	680	800	12	390	400	410
46	600	670	790	11	380	390	400
45	600	660	780	10	370	380	390
44	590	650	760	9	360	370	380
43	590	640	740	8	350	360	380
42	580	630	730	7	340	350	370
41	570	630	710	6	330	340	360
40	570	620	700	5	320	330	350
39	560	610	690	4	310	320	340
38	550	600	670	3	300	310	320
37	550	590	660	2	280	290	310
36	540	580	650	1	270	280	300
35	540	580	640	0	250	260	280
34	530	570	630	−1	230	240	270
33	520	560	620	−2 or less	210	220	250

> Take Practice Tests in the library, where there are no distractions, and go over each of your practice SATs for a second time soon after you take them to help you to understand where and why you are going wrong.
>
> *Joia Ramchandani (MIT '07, 700 CR 770 M)*

7. PRACTICE, PRACTICE, PRACTICE!

Whatever strategies you want to use on the SAT, practice them on tests so that you don't spend energy re-thinking strategy during the real SAT. Don't get too focused on "point-counting" during the test. This will take your focus away from the real problems.

> Taking Practice Tests under real test conditions helps a lot!
>
> *Alex Davidow (Syracuse '08, +170 points CR)*

8. FAMILIARIZE YOURSELF WITH THE TEST FORMAT AND INSTRUCTIONS

One of the simplest ways to increase your chances of success on test day is to familiarize yourself with the format of the exam ahead of time. Know the format and instructions for each section of the SAT. This will save you time on the actual test. Why waste time reading the directions when you could memorize them beforehand? The rules won't change.

> Whenever you have the choice, turn off the TV and read a good book instead!
>
> *Elisha Barron (Yale '06, 800 CR 800 M)*

9. KNOW WHEN TO GUESS

The SAT is different from exams you take in the classroom because you get negative points for wrong answers. On a 100-question classroom math exam, if you answer 80 questions correctly and get 20 questions wrong, your score would be an 80. On the SAT, if you answer 80 questions correctly and get 20 questions wrong, your score would be a 75. Why? Because the

ETS includes a "wrong-answer penalty" to discourage random guessing. For 5-question multiple-choice questions, a correct answer is worth 1 "raw" point, a wrong answer costs you ¼ point, and an unanswered question costs you nothing. It's better to leave a question blank than it is to get it wrong. If you can eliminate two or more choices, however, you should probably make an educated guess. Work on your guessing strategy as you practice. When you take a Practice Test, write a "G" on the test booklet next to questions you guess on (not on the answer sheet). After the exam, check to see how many of those guesses you got right. If you consistently get more than 20% (or ⅕) of your guesses right, you are "beating the odds," and your guessing strategy is better than omitting those questions.

> Do some review almost every day rather than cramming it into just one or two days each week.
>
> *Joia Ramchandani (MIT '07, 700 CR 770 M)*

On SAT Day

1. THE NIGHT BEFORE—RELAX!

The night before the SAT, your studying should all be behind you; cramming at this point will probably do more harm than good. Relax, go see a movie, grab dinner with your friends, do whatever you need to do to reward your brain for its efforts over the previous months. As long as you get a good night's rest, you're allowed to have some fun the evening before the exam. For a truly peaceful slumber, lay out everything you need for test day the night before.

> Prepare in advance, but don't study the night before, just get a good night's sleep. And don't forget a good breakfast the next morning! (Even if you're nervous!)
>
> *Julie MacPherson (+130 points CR)*

2. GET YOUR STUFF TOGETHER

The night before the test, lay out everything you will need for the test on your night stand or kitchen table. Don't forget any of the following:
- Admission ticket
- Photo ID
- Several #2 pencils with erasers

- Calculator (with fresh batteries)
- Stopwatch
- A light snack, like a banana or granola bar
- Your brain
- Earplugs (if you need them to shut out distractions)
- Directions to the test site (if you haven't been there before)

Few things are as awful as having your calculator conk out ten minutes into your first math section, so put in fresh batteries the night before. Forgetting your ticket would be disastrous. And they rarely have a spare brain available if you happen to forget yours.

3. KNOW YOUR WAY

If you will be taking the SAT at an unfamiliar test site, make sure to get directions to the site well ahead of time. Drive (or take the bus or subway) to the test site at some point in the days before the test, so you can familiarize yourself with it. Even better, have someone else drive you to the test, but make sure that he or she knows the way, too. Leave yourself plenty of time to get to the test site by 8 am so that you don't stress out if you hit traffic or get a little lost.

4. BYOS—BRING YOUR OWN STOPWATCH

Your testing room will almost certainly have a clock, but it can be a big advantage to have your own stopwatch.(But make sure it doesn't make noise, or the proctor will confiscate it!) The best stopwatch is one that counts backwards from the time that you set.

Make sure you practice setting, starting, and stopping the watch before you get to the test site. This will help you to manage your time and avoid that annoying mental arithmetic you would have to do to tell how much time you have left. Practice using your stopwatch when taking your practice exams so that you feel comfortable using it.

> Bring a light snack for energy on SAT day to eat during one of the breaks.
>
> *Joia Ramchandani (MIT '07, 700 CR 770 M)*

5. DRESS WELL

Wear clothes that will keep you comfortable in any temperature. If it is late spring, bring an extra layer in case the room is too cold; if it is winter, wear layers so that you can remove clothing if you are too hot. Sometimes it seems as if NASA is using SAT testing rooms to test human endurance at extreme temperatures.

6. EAT A POWER BREAKFAST

Eat a good breakfast before the exam, with protein to give your brain the energy it will need. Oatmeal is a good option, or eggs and bacon. Try to stay away from sugary cereals and syrup. While eating, you may want to relax to some peaceful music, or you may want to "start your engine" by looking over an SAT critical reading passage or an interesting math problem to get your brain in the right mode.

7. GET THE EYE OF THE TIGER

Finally, head into the SAT with a positive attitude. If you go in with an "I don't want to be here" attitude, the SAT will eat you alive. Your attitude is critical to success on the SAT. Any negative energy will detract from your thinking power and cost you points. Positive energy serves as motivation and puts you into a sharper mindset, helping you to focus on the tough questions.

8. IT STARTS—FOCUS!

Good preparation will be wasted if you can't focus on test day. When you step into the classroom to take your SAT, you shouldn't be thinking about the things that could go wrong. Fight the urge to think about the sweet party you will go to that night, the argument that you had with your best friend the night before, or what you are going to have for lunch. Before the test begins, focus on relaxing and carrying out your game plan.

9. STAY ALERT DOWN THE STRETCH

The SAT is like a marathon, so pace yourself well. If you lose focus for the last section, it may cost you dearly. When you get near the end, don't think, "I'm almost out of here!" Focus by thinking, "Finish strong!" Keep yourself mentally sharp from beginning to end; don't allow yourself to let up until that final answer is filled in.

10. DON'T CHANGE YOUR ANSWER FOR DUMB REASONS

When should you change an answer and when should you leave it alone? The answer is simple: *only change your answer when you've reviewed the entire problem and discovered a mistake.* Don't change your answer for dumb reasons like, "This one can't be (A) because the last two answers were (A)!" or "It can't be that easy, it must be another answer!"

On your practice exams, whenever you change your answer, write a "Ch" next to the question in your test booklet. After you finish the exam, see how many of those changes were for the better. This will give you a better sense on test day of whether your checking strategy is an effective one.

11. WASTE NOT

Don't waste too much time on any one question. Some students lose 30–40 points on a section simply by being too stubborn to let a problem go. If a question is going to take too much time, circle the question number in the test booklet, skip it on your answer sheet, and come back to it later. If you return to the problem 10 or 15 minutes later, your refreshed brain may well see things more clearly and find a simple way to solve the problem!

12. DON'T GIVE THE RIGHT ANSWER TO THE WRONG QUESTION

Don't go so fast that you answer the wrong question when doing a math problem. Always re-read the question to make sure you are giving the answer to the question it asks! For example, in the question

$3x + 6 = 12$, what is the value of $3x$?

even bright students often solve for x and give the answer of 2. However, the question asked for the value of $3x$, which is 6. This is an example of giving the right answer to the wrong question. If you occasionally make this kind of mistake, get into the habit of underlining what the question wants you to find. This will help you to focus on answering the right question.

13. DON'T BLOW BUBBLES

Many SAT horror stories begin with a student putting answers in the wrong places on the answer sheet. To avoid this, practice using the answer sheets when taking your practice tests so that you get comfortable with them. Experiment with different methods of filling in your answer sheet. Some students like to slide the answer sheet from under the test booklet, revealing just one space at a time for each question. Others prefer to fill in the answer after every question, and some prefer to wait until they've answered all of the questions on a page (circling their answers on the test booklet before transferring them to the answer sheet). There is no one "best way" to do it; just find the approach that is best for you.

If you skip a problem, be extremely careful to skip that question on your answer sheet as well. A small erasable dash next to the question number on the answer sheet works well as a reminder.

14. FINISH STRONG

If you budget your time wisely, you should have plenty of time to do everything you need to do on the SAT, and that probably includes leaving some hard questions unanswered. But what should you do if suddenly time is running out and you have several questions left that you need to answer? First, make sure that you really do need to answer them; answering too many questions is a common mistake. If you really do need to rush a bit, at least rush wisely. First answer the questions that can be done quickly. For example, a "word-in-context" critical reading question can usually be answered much more quickly than a "main idea" question. If your time is running out, attack the simplest questions!

CHAPTER 3

ATTACKING THE SAT ESSAY

Know What They're Looking For

Why an essay?

The first section of your SAT is a 25-minute writing assignment designed to assess how well you can express your ideas in writing—that is, make an argument using clear and specific examples, solid reasoning and fluent language. It is not simply an assessment of "what you know," and it isn't a spelling or grammar test. Many colleges regard this as one of the most important elements of the SAT, because essays are often an important part of college evaluation.

The assignment will be to answer a very broad question about human values or behavior, such as *Is an individual person responsible, through his or her example, for the behavior of others?* There is no "right" or "wrong" answer to the question; you may present any point of view you wish.

Writing an argumentative essay is not like writing a story or a letter to a friend. On the SAT essay, your job is not to entertain but to *persuade*. You may be funny and creative if you wish, but your primary task is to *explain and support an interesting point of view*, not to impress someone with flowery language or cute observations.

A good persuasive essay respects the reader's intelligence, yet explains an argument carefully. Although you *can* assume that your readers are smart and well-read, you *cannot* assume that they think exactly as you do, or that they will fill in logical gaps for you. You must show your reasoning.

How long should it be?

Quality is much more important than quantity. Nevertheless, you should try to fill both of the pages you're given for the essay. Plan to write four paragraphs, and add a fifth if you have enough time and substance.

Most essays that get perfect scores are four or five paragraphs long. Very few top-scoring essays have fewer than four paragraphs. The scorers will evaluate your essay's organization, and this includes how effectively you use paragraphs.

The five essential qualities of a good persuasive essay

Your SAT essay will be scored by two SAT English teachers who are trained by the ETS. They are looking for the five basic elements that all good humanities professors expect of good writing

1. INTERESTING, RELEVANT, AND CONSISTENT POINT OF VIEW

Do you take a thoughtful and interesting position on the issue? Do you answer the question as it is presented? Do you maintain a consistent point of view?

2. GOOD REASONING

Do you define any necessary terms to make your reasoning clear? Do you explain the reasons for and implications of your thesis? Do you acknowledge and address possible objections to your thesis without sacrificing its integrity?

3. SOLID SUPPORT

Do you give relevant and *specific* examples to support your thesis? Do you explain how these examples support your thesis?

4. LOGICAL ORGANIZATION

Does every paragraph relate clearly to your thesis? Do you provide logical transitions between paragraphs? Do you have a clear introduction and conclusion? Does the conclusion provide thoughtful commentary, rather than mere repetition of the thesis?

5. EFFECTIVE USE OF LANGUAGE.

Do you use effective and appropriate vocabulary? Do you vary sentence length and structure effectively? Do you avoid needless repetition? Do you use parallelism, metaphor, personification, or other rhetorical devices to good effect? Do you use strong verbs? Do you avoid needlessly abstract language? Do you avoid cliché?

PRACTICE TEST 1

ANSWER SHEET

Last Name:_____   First Name:_____

Date:_____   Testing Location:_____

Directions for Test

- Remove these answer sheets from the book and use them to record your answers to this test.
- This test will require 3 hours and 20 minutes to complete. Take this test in one sitting.
- The time allotment for each section is written clearly at the beginning of each section. This test contains six 25-minute sections, two 20-minute sections, and one 10-minute section.
- This test is 25 minutes shorter than the actual SAT, which will include a 25-minute "experimental" section that does not count toward your score. That section has been omitted from this test.
- You may take one short break during the test, of no more than 10 minutes in length.
- You may only work on one section at any given time.
- You must stop ALL work on a section when time is called.
- If you finish a section before the time has elapsed, check your work on that section. You may NOT work on any other section.
- Do not waste time on questions that seem too difficult for you.
- Use the test book for scratchwork, but you will receive credit only for answers that are marked on the answer sheets.
- You will receive one point for every correct answer.
- You will receive no points for an omitted question.
- For each wrong answer on any multiple-choice question, your score will be reduced by ¼ point.
- For each wrong answer on any "numerical grid-in" question, you will receive no deduction.

When you take the real SAT, you will be asked to fill in your personal information in grids as shown below.

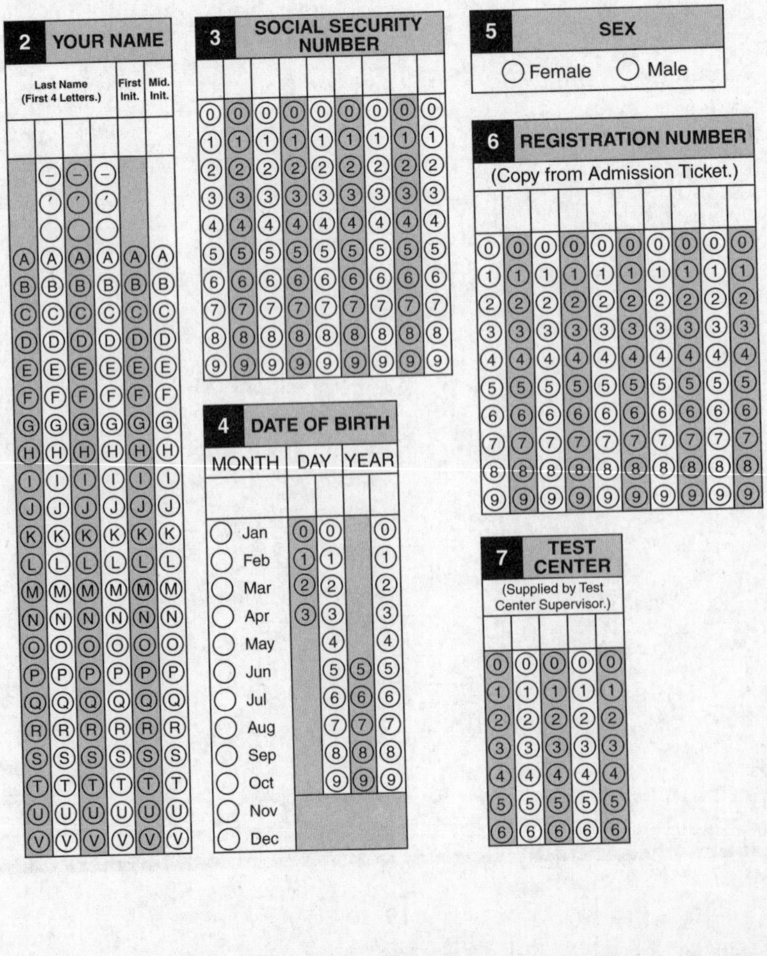

Start with number 1 for each new section. If a section has fewer questions than answer spaces, leave the extra answer spaces blank. Be sure to erase any errors or stray marks completely.

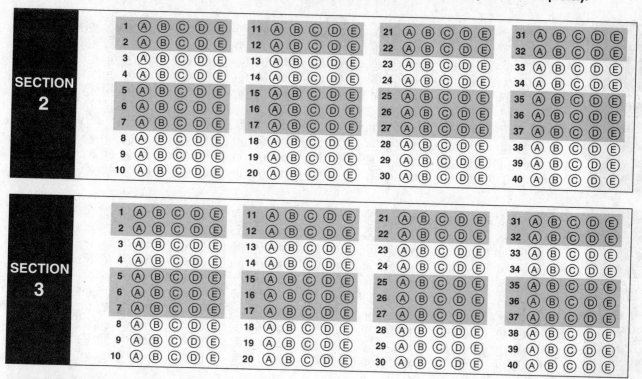

SECTION 2

SECTION 3

CAUTION Use the answer spaces in the grids below for Section 2 or Section 3 only if you are told to do so in your test book.

Student-Produced Responses

ONLY ANSWERS ENTERED IN THE CIRCLES IN EACH GRID WILL BE SCORED. YOU WILL NOT RECEIVE CREDIT FOR ANYTHING WRITTEN IN THE BOXES ABOVE THE CIRCLES.

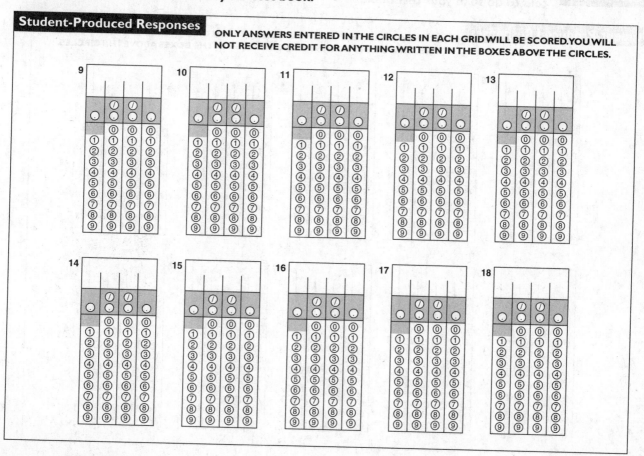

Start with number 1 for each new section. If a section has fewer questions than answer spaces, leave the extra answer spaces blank. Be sure to erase any errors or stray marks completely.

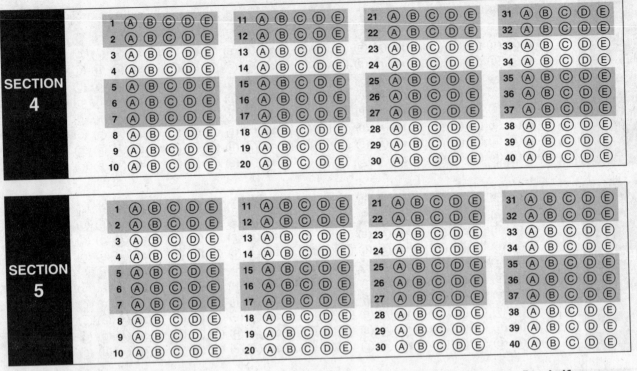

SECTION 4

SECTION 5

CAUTION Use the answer spaces in the grids below for Section 4 or Section 5 only if you are told to do so in your test book.

Student-Produced Responses ONLY ANSWERS ENTERED IN THE CIRCLES IN EACH GRID WILL BE SCORED. YOU WILL NOT RECEIVE CREDIT FOR ANYTHING WRITTEN IN THE BOXES ABOVE THE CIRCLES.

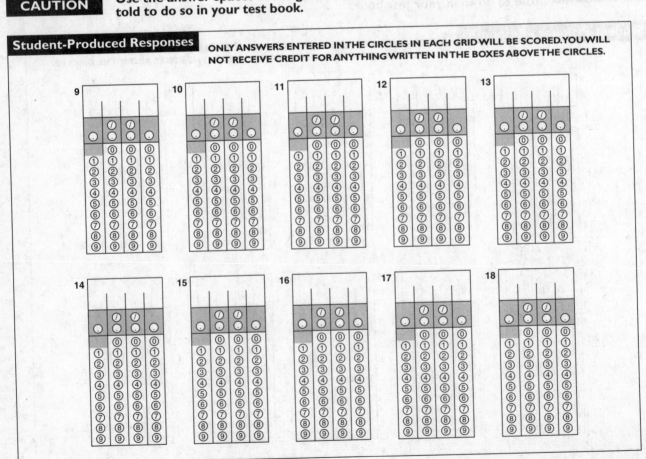

Start with number 1 for each new section. If a section has fewer questions than answer spaces, leave the extra answer spaces blank. Be sure to erase any errors or stray marks completely.

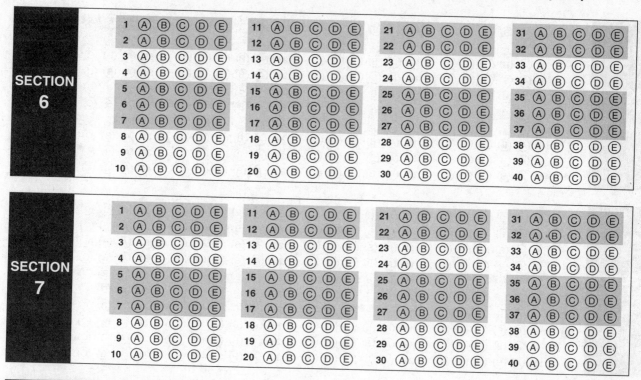

CAUTION | Use the answer spaces in the grids below for Section 6 or Section 7 only if you are told to do so in your test book.

Student-Produced Responses

ONLY ANSWERS ENTERED IN THE CIRCLES IN EACH GRID WILL BE SCORED. YOU WILL NOT RECEIVE CREDIT FOR ANYTHING WRITTEN IN THE BOXES ABOVE THE CIRCLES.

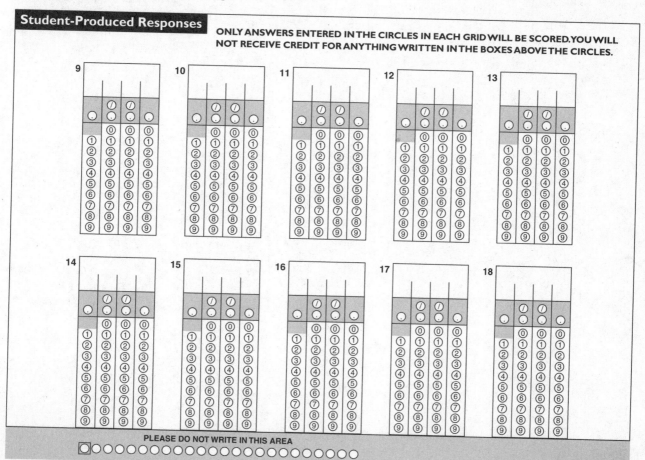

PLEASE DO NOT WRITE IN THIS AREA

Start with number 1 for each new section. If a section has fewer questions than answer spaces, leave the extra answer spaces blank. Be sure to erase any errors or stray marks completely.

SECTION 8

1 (A) (B) (C) (D) (E)	11 (A) (B) (C) (D) (E)	21 (A) (B) (C) (D) (E)	31 (A) (B) (C) (D) (E)
2 (A) (B) (C) (D) (E)	12 (A) (B) (C) (D) (E)	22 (A) (B) (C) (D) (E)	32 (A) (B) (C) (D) (E)
3 (A) (B) (C) (D) (E)	13 (A) (B) (C) (D) (E)	23 (A) (B) (C) (D) (E)	33 (A) (B) (C) (D) (E)
4 (A) (B) (C) (D) (E)	14 (A) (B) (C) (D) (E)	24 (A) (B) (C) (D) (E)	34 (A) (B) (C) (D) (E)
5 (A) (B) (C) (D) (E)	15 (A) (B) (C) (D) (E)	25 (A) (B) (C) (D) (E)	35 (A) (B) (C) (D) (E)
6 (A) (B) (C) (D) (E)	16 (A) (B) (C) (D) (E)	26 (A) (B) (C) (D) (E)	36 (A) (B) (C) (D) (E)
7 (A) (B) (C) (D) (E)	17 (A) (B) (C) (D) (E)	27 (A) (B) (C) (D) (E)	37 (A) (B) (C) (D) (E)
8 (A) (B) (C) (D) (E)	18 (A) (B) (C) (D) (E)	28 (A) (B) (C) (D) (E)	38 (A) (B) (C) (D) (E)
9 (A) (B) (C) (D) (E)	19 (A) (B) (C) (D) (E)	29 (A) (B) (C) (D) (E)	39 (A) (B) (C) (D) (E)
10 (A) (B) (C) (D) (E)	20 (A) (B) (C) (D) (E)	30 (A) (B) (C) (D) (E)	40 (A) (B) (C) (D) (E)

SECTION 9

1 (A) (B) (C) (D) (E)	11 (A) (B) (C) (D) (E)	21 (A) (B) (C) (D) (E)	31 (A) (B) (C) (D) (E)
2 (A) (B) (C) (D) (E)	12 (A) (B) (C) (D) (E)	22 (A) (B) (C) (D) (E)	32 (A) (B) (C) (D) (E)
3 (A) (B) (C) (D) (E)	13 (A) (B) (C) (D) (E)	23 (A) (B) (C) (D) (E)	33 (A) (B) (C) (D) (E)
4 (A) (B) (C) (D) (E)	14 (A) (B) (C) (D) (E)	24 (A) (B) (C) (D) (E)	34 (A) (B) (C) (D) (E)
5 (A) (B) (C) (D) (E)	15 (A) (B) (C) (D) (E)	25 (A) (B) (C) (D) (E)	35 (A) (B) (C) (D) (E)
6 (A) (B) (C) (D) (E)	16 (A) (B) (C) (D) (E)	26 (A) (B) (C) (D) (E)	36 (A) (B) (C) (D) (E)
7 (A) (B) (C) (D) (E)	17 (A) (B) (C) (D) (E)	27 (A) (B) (C) (D) (E)	37 (A) (B) (C) (D) (E)
8 (A) (B) (C) (D) (E)	18 (A) (B) (C) (D) (E)	28 (A) (B) (C) (D) (E)	38 (A) (B) (C) (D) (E)
9 (A) (B) (C) (D) (E)	19 (A) (B) (C) (D) (E)	29 (A) (B) (C) (D) (E)	39 (A) (B) (C) (D) (E)
10 (A) (B) (C) (D) (E)	20 (A) (B) (C) (D) (E)	30 (A) (B) (C) (D) (E)	40 (A) (B) (C) (D) (E)

1 ESSAY   ESSAY 1

ESSAY
Time—25 minutes

Write your essay on separate sheets of standard lined paper.

The essay gives you an opportunity to show how effectively you can develop and express ideas. You should, therefore, take care to develop your point of view, present your ideas logically and clearly, and use language precisely.

Your essay must be written on the lines provided on your answer sheet—you will receive no other paper on which to write. You will have enough space if you write on every line, avoid wide margins, and keep your handwriting to a reasonable size. Remember that people who are not familiar with your handwriting will read what you write. Try to write or print so that what you are writing is legible to those readers.

Important Reminders:

- **A pencil is required for the essay.** An essay written in ink will receive a score of zero.
- **Do not write your essay in your test book.** You will receive credit only for what you write on your answer sheet.
- **An off-topic essay will receive a score of zero.**

You have twenty-five minutes to write an essay on the topic assigned below.

Consider carefully the issue discussed in the following passage, then write an essay that answers the question posed in the assignment.

> The liberally educated person is one who is able to resist the easy and preferred answers, not because he is obstinate but because he knows others worthy of consideration.
>
> —Allan Bloom

Assignment: **What is one important "easy and preferred answer" that we should resist? That is, what dangerous misconception do people commonly hold?** Write an essay in which you answer this question and support your position logically with examples from literature, the arts, history, politics, science and technology, current events, or your experience or observation.

If you finish before time is called, you may check your work on this section only.
Do not turn to any other section of the test.

2 2 2 2 2 2

SECTION 2
Time—25 minutes
20 questions

Turn to Section 2 of your answer sheet to answer the questions in this section.

Directions: For this section, solve each problem and decide which is the best of the choices given. Fill in the corresponding circle on the answer sheet. You may use any available space for scratchwork.

Notes

1. The use of a calculator is permitted.

2. All numbers used are real numbers.

3. Figures that accompany problems in this test are intended to provide information useful in solving the problems. They are drawn as accurately as possible EXCEPT when it is stated in a specific problem that the figure is not drawn to scale. All figures lie in a plane unless otherwise indicated.

4. Unless otherwise specified, the domain of any function f is assumed to be the set of all real numbers x for which $f(x)$ is a real number.

Reference Information

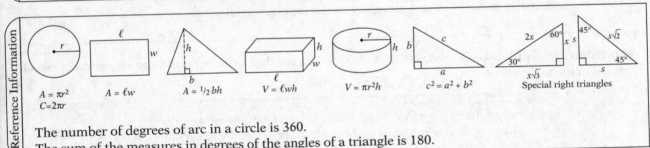

$A = \pi r^2$
$C = 2\pi r$
$A = \ell w$
$A = \frac{1}{2}bh$
$V = \ell wh$
$V = \pi r^2 h$
$c^2 = a^2 + b^2$
Special right triangles

The number of degrees of arc in a circle is 360.
The sum of the measures in degrees of the angles of a triangle is 180.

---

1. If $3(m + n) + 3 = 15$, then $m + n =$

(A) 2
(B) 3
(C) 4
(D) 5
(E) 6

2. If Elena reads at a rate of r pages per minute for a total of m minutes, which of the following represents the total number of pages that Elena reads?

(A) rm

(B) $\dfrac{r}{m}$

(C) $\dfrac{m}{r}$

(D) $\dfrac{60r}{m}$

(E) $\dfrac{60m}{r}$

GO ON TO THE NEXT PAGE

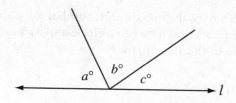

Note: Figure not drawn to scale.

3. In the figure above, if l is a line, $a + b = 120$ and $b + c = 100$, then what is the value of b?

    (A) 10
    (B) 20
    (C) 30
    (D) 40
    (E) 50

4. If $6^n \times 6^4 = 6^{12}$, then $n =$

    (A) 2
    (B) 3
    (C) 5
    (D) 6
    (E) 8

5. If $4x + b = x + 2$, what is b in terms of x?

    (A) $5x + 2$
    (B) $3x + 2$
    (C) $2 - x$
    (D) $2 - 3x$
    (E) $2 - 5x$

	RETAIL CAR PRICES			QUANTITY SOLD	
	Model A	Model B		Model A	Model B
1995	$15,000	$25,000	1995	200	100
2000	$20,000	$30,000	2000	220	150
2005	$25,000	$35,000	2005	200	200

6. The tables above show the retail prices of two car models and the quantities of those models sold at a particular car dealership in three different years. Based on these tables, how much greater was the total value of cars sold in 2005 than in 1995?

    (A) $5,500,000
    (B) $6,500,000
    (C) $9,000,000
    (D) $10,500,000
    (E) $12,000,000

7. An isosceles triangle has one angle with a measure greater than 95° and another with a measure of $x°$. Which of the following must be true?

    (A) $x > 85$
    (B) $x = 85$
    (C) $x = 42.5$
    (D) $x < 42.5$
    (E) $x > 42.5$

8. When m is divided by 7, the remainder is 2. What is the remainder when $4m$ is divided by 7?

    (A) 1
    (B) 2
    (C) 3
    (D) 4
    (E) 5

GO ON TO THE NEXT PAGE

9. If a is a multiple of 3 and b is an odd integer, then which of the following must be an odd integer?

   (A) $\dfrac{a}{b}$
   (B) ab
   (C) $a + b$
   (D) $2a + b$
   (E) $a + 2b$

10. The point (a, b) is reflected over the x-axis, and then the reflected point is reflected over the y-axis. If a and b are both positive, which of the following represents the coordinates of the point after the second reflection?

    (A) (a, b)
    (B) (b, a)
    (C) $(-a, -b)$
    (D) $(-b, -a)$
    (E) $(a, -b)$

11. A right circular cylinder with a radius of 1 and a height of 1 has a volume that is most nearly the same as the volume of a rectangular solid with dimensions

    (A) 1 by 1 by 1
    (B) 1 by 1 by 2
    (C) 1 by 1 by 3
    (D) 1 by 2 by 2
    (E) 1 by 2 by 3

12. If the nth term of a sequence is $3n^2 - n$, then how much greater is the 10th term than the 3rd term?

    (A) 242
    (B) 266
    (C) 281
    (D) 286
    (E) 290

13. What is the maximum number of points of intersection between a circle and a square that lie in the same plane?

    (A) 4
    (B) 6
    (C) 7
    (D) 8
    (E) 9

14. If $x < x^3 < x^2$, then which of the following must be true?

    (A) $x < -1$
    (B) $-1 < x < 0$
    (C) $0 < x < 1$
    (D) $x > 1$
    (E) x is not a real number

15. If $(m + n)^2 = 18$ and $mn = 4$, then what is the value of $m^2 + n^2$?

    (A) 10
    (B) 14
    (C) 18
    (D) 22
    (E) 26

16. An isosceles triangle has two sides of length 5 and 12. Which of the following could be the perimeter of this triangle?

    I. 22
    II. 29
    III. 30

    (A) II only
    (B) I and II only
    (C) I and III only
    (D) II and III only
    (E) I, II, and III

GO ON TO THE NEXT PAGE

2   2   2   2   2   2

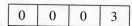

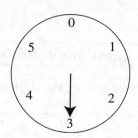

17. The figure above shows a digital counter above a dial counter showing the digits 0 through 5. Both counters are initially set to 0 and count upward together in increments of 1. For instance, when the digital counter reads 5 the dial counter also reads 5, but when the digital counter reads 6, the dial counter resets back to 0. What will the dial counter read when the digital counter reads 1000?

(A) 0
(B) 1
(C) 2
(D) 4
(E) 5

18. In a mixture of raisins and dates, the ratio by weight of raisins to dates is 7 to 3. How many pounds of raisins will there be in 7 pounds of this mixture?

(A) 2.1
(B) 2.3
(C) 2.8
(D) 3.0
(E) 4.9

19. If m and n are integers and $m = n - \dfrac{2}{n} - \dfrac{2}{n^2}$, then which of the following could be the value of m?

I.   −5
II. −3
III. −1

(A) II only
(B) II and III only
(C) I and II only
(D) I and III only
(E) I, II, and III

20. Each of the k girls in a club agreed to raise an equal amount of money to give to a charity to which the club had pledged a total of x dollars. If p more girls later join the club and also agree to raise an equal share of the pledged amount, how much <u>less</u> would each of the original club members have to raise, in dollars, than she had originally agreed to raise?

(A) $\dfrac{x}{k}$

(B) $\dfrac{x}{k+p}$

(C) $\dfrac{px}{k+p}$

(D) $\dfrac{x(k+p)}{k}$

(E) $\dfrac{px}{k(k+p)}$

If you finish before time is called, you may check your work on this section only. Do not turn to any other section of the test.

3   3   3   3   3   3

SECTION 3
Time—25 minutes
35 questions

Turn to Section 3 of your answer sheet to answer the questions in this section.

Directions: For each question in this section, select the best answer from among the choices given and fill in the corresponding circle on the answer sheet.

The following sentences test correctness and effectiveness of expression. Part of each sentence or the entire sentence is underlined; beneath each sentence are five ways of phrasing the underlined material. Choice A repeats the original phrasing; the other four choices are different. Select the choice that completes the sentence most effectively.

In making your selection, follow the requirements of standard written English; that is, pay attention to grammar, choice of words, sentence construction, and punctuation. Your selection should result in the most effective sentence—clear and precise, without awkwardness or ambiguity.

EXAMPLE:

The children <u>couldn't hardly believe their eyes</u>.

(A) couldn't hardly believe their eyes
(B) could hardly believe their eyes
(C) would not hardly believe their eyes
(D) couldn't nearly believe their eyes
(E) couldn't hardly believe his or her eyes

---

1. Andrews was one of the first executives to realize that employees are most productive when <u>he or she feels to be part of a family</u>.

(A) he or she feels to be part of a family
(B) they feel as if they are part of a family
(C) he or she feels part of a family
(D) it's more like a family for them
(E) feeling a part of a family is made possible

2. Several agents were dispatched to Europe <u>for the purpose of investigating</u> a lead that could potentially provide a break in the case.

(A) for the purpose of investigating
(B) to investigate on
(C) for the investigation of
(D) to investigate
(E) to investigate after

3. Although worried about the dangers of going into debt, <u>Helena's concern was more about the possibility of losing her business</u>.

(A) Helena's concern was more about the possibility of losing her business
(B) it was the possibility of losing her business that gave Helena more concern
(C) Helena was more concerned towards her business and the possibility of losing it
(D) the possibility of losing her business gave Helena more concern
(E) Helena was more concerned about the possibility of losing her business

4. Those who enjoy Marquez's <u>novels, being those who tend not to read</u> traditional fiction, preferring instead the intellectual challenge of magical realism.

(A) novels, being those who tend not to read
(B) novels, tending to be those who do not read
(C) novels tend not to read
(D) novels are the ones that tend not to be the ones reading
(E) novels being the ones tending not to read

GO ON TO THE NEXT PAGE

3   3   3   3   3   3

5. The reason the event was cancelled was not so much the poor weather <u>as the lack of interest</u>.

   (A) as the lack of interest
   (B) than the lack of interest
   (C) than because of the lack of interest
   (D) but rather the lack of interest
   (E) as it was lacking interest

6. The statute recently passed gives the chief of police sole authority to determine <u>about which duties qualify for overtime pay</u>.

   (A) about which duties qualify for overtime pay
   (B) regarding the qualifications of duties for overtime pay
   (C) whether overtime pay qualifies for certain duties or not
   (D) for those duties that qualify for overtime pay
   (E) which duties qualify for overtime pay

7. In baseball, the batter attempts to hit the ball within a ninety degree <u>quadrant, in cricket the batter can hit</u> the ball in any direction.

   (A) quadrant, in cricket the batter can hit
   (B) quadrant; but in cricket the batter can hit
   (C) quadrant, but the batter can hit in cricket
   (D) quadrant, but in cricket the batter can hit
   (E) quadrant; the batter in cricket hitting

8. Skeptical of the abilities of prophets to tell the future, <u>Athens was where significant numbers of philosophers began to value reason over revealed truths</u>.

   (A) Athens was where significant numbers of philosophers began to value reason over revealed truths
   (B) it was a significant number of philosophers that began to value reason over revealed truths
   (C) a significant number of philosophers in Athens began to value reason over revealed truths
   (D) the valuing of reason over revealed truths was begun by a significant number of philosphers in Athens
   (E) valuing of reason over revealed truths by philosophers in Athens was begun

9. As the investigation concludes, the debate over the origins of the scandal, the merits of the federal investigation, and <u>the legal authority of the prosecutor have</u> intensified greatly.

   (A) the legal authority of the prosecutor have
   (B) whether the prosecutor has legal authority has
   (C) the legal authority of the prosecutor has
   (D) what the legal authority of the prosecutor is has
   (E) the prosecutor's legal authority have

10. Excited by the prospect of starting her own business, <u>Kyra's first decision needed to be where she could rent office space</u>.

   (A) Kyra's first decision needed to be where she could rent office space
   (B) Kyra first had to decide where it was to rent office space
   (C) Kyra's first decision had to be regarding renting office space and where it would be
   (D) Kyra first had to decide where to rent office space
   (E) renting office space had to be what Kyra's first decision was about

GO ON TO THE NEXT PAGE

3   3   3   3   3   3

11. Elizabeth is a highly skilled teacher, in addition to being an outstanding pianist and composer, and these are talents she uses to get her students interested in music.

(A) Elizabeth is a highly skilled teacher, in addition to being an outstanding pianist and composer, and these are talents she uses to get her students interested in music.

(B) A highly skilled teacher, Elizabeth uses her outstanding talents as a pianist and composer to get her students interested in music.

(C) Getting her students interested in music, Elizabeth uses her outstanding talents as a pianist and a composer, making her a highly skilled teacher.

(D) Elizabeth being an outstanding pianist and composer and a highly skilled teacher, she uses these talents to get her students interested in music.

(E) To get her students interested in music, Elizabeth uses her outstanding talents as a pianist and composer, her being a highly skilled teacher.

The following sentences test your ability to recognize grammar and usage errors. Each sentence contains either a single error or no error at all. No sentence contains more than one error. The error, if there is one, is underlined and lettered. If the sentence contains an error, select the one underlined part that must be changed to make the sentence correct. If the sentence is correct, select choice E. In choosing answers, follow the requirements of standard written English.

EXAMPLE:

By the time <u>they reached</u> the halfway point
             A
<u>in the race</u>, <u>most of the runners</u> <u>hadn't hardly</u>
    B   C   D
begun to hit their stride. <u>No error</u>
                         E

Ⓐ Ⓑ Ⓒ ● Ⓔ

---

12. Yet to be discussed in the conference <u>is</u>
                                   A
more than a dozen <u>proposals</u> for changes
                B
<u>in</u> the procedural rules for <u>choosing</u>
C   D
new officers. <u>No error</u>
             E

13. Although the latest senatorial debate <u>focused</u>
                                   A
on the more <u>controversial</u> topics in the
              B
campaign, the candidates conducted

<u>themselves</u> much more <u>civil</u> than they
    C   D
had previously. <u>No error</u>
                E

14. <u>Having experienced</u> many realistic disaster
      A
drills in his months of training

<u>as a fire fighter</u>, Leon handled the disaster
       B
<u>calmly and effectively</u> and in fact is
       C
<u>credited</u> with saving several lives. <u>No error</u>
   D   E

15. While the Athenians <u>were outraged</u> by the
                      A
oppressive and unenlightened Spartans,

<u>but the</u> Spartans were <u>indignant</u> about
  B   C
the Athenians' indifference <u>to the gods</u>
                             D
and religious matters. <u>No error</u>
                    E

GO ON TO THE NEXT PAGE ⟩

3   3   3   3   3   3

16. If some of the hikers <u>had not took</u> the
                                    A
riskier but shorter route up the mountain,

<u>they</u> would probably not <u>have become</u> so
 B   C
<u>widely separated</u> by nightfall. <u>No error</u>
      D   E

17. Jason <u>was confused</u> by the theory, <u>about</u>
                  A   B
which many of his classmates often

referred, <u>because</u> it seemed to <u>be based</u>
             C   D
on an obviously false premise. <u>No error</u>
                                                E

18. The pace at <u>which</u> industrial and
                       A
communications technologies

<u>are progressing</u> in developing countries
      B
<u>are</u> so rapid that many governments
 C
cannot anticipate the harm these

technologies <u>may do</u> to the
                    D
environment. <u>No error</u>
                     E

19. Every living creature on earth <u>owe their</u>
                                                A
existence <u>to</u> the chemical properties of atoms
             B
<u>that were forged</u> in stars billions of miles
         C
away and billions of <u>years ago</u>. <u>No error</u>
                                 D   E

20. Having <u>such acute</u> senses of hearing, smell
                    A
<u>and sight</u>, zebras often <u>provide</u> early
      B   C
warning to <u>other grazers</u> that predators are
                   D
approaching. <u>No error</u>
                     E

21. Many students fail <u>to appreciate</u> <u>that</u> it is
                                A   B
much more difficult to teach someone

<u>how to write</u> good prose than <u>teaching</u>
       C   D
someone how to appreciate good prose

written by others. <u>No error</u>
                            E

22. Because the coach <u>was</u> so preoccupied <u>on</u>
                               A   B
developing and practicing trick plays, she

<u>did not spend</u> enough time <u>drilling</u> the
        C   D
fundamental skills. <u>No error</u>
                             E

23. <u>Without</u> our permission, our teacher
       A
assigned a new research topic to

<u>Jose and I</u> only two days before we
       B
<u>were</u> <u>to give</u> our presentation. <u>No error</u>
  C   D   E

24. Although statistical methods

<u>can rarely prove</u> causality, they can
       A
frequently <u>refute</u> theories by
              B
demonstrating that no correlation <u>exists</u>
                                               C
between <u>particular effects</u> and their
              D
presumed causes. <u>No error</u>
                          E

GO ON TO THE NEXT PAGE ➡

3   3   3   3   3   3

25. In the central courtyard <u>was</u> over a dozen
     A   B
     different <u>varieties of lilies</u>, meticulously
                        C
     maintained <u>by</u> the gardener. <u>No error</u>
                  D   E

26. Cara's <u>constant</u> improving race times
                A
     demonstrated that her new training <u>regimen</u>
                                          B
     had been <u>more effective</u> than even she
                    C
     <u>had hoped</u>. <u>No error</u>
        D   E

27. The devastation wrought by the hurricane

     <u>was</u> so <u>widespread</u> that officials
      A   B
     <u>had to suspend</u> many government services
          C
     for an <u>indecisive</u> amount of time. <u>No error</u>
               D   E

28. High in isoflavones, protein, and <u>also in</u>
                                          A
     fiber, soy beans <u>are</u> a flavorful food
                        B
     <u>with</u> many <u>healthful</u> benefits. <u>No error</u>
      C   D   E

29. The project on nuclear energy

     <u>that Jenna presented</u> to the science fair
              A
     committee <u>was</u> considered superior to
                  B
     <u>the other students</u>, and <u>so</u> she was awarded
          C   D
     the blue ribbon. <u>No error</u>
                         E

Directions: The following passage is an early draft of an essay. Some parts of the passage need to be rewritten.

Read the passage and select the best answers for the questions that follow. Some questions are about particular sentences or parts of sentences and ask you to improve sentence structure or word choice. Other questions ask you to consider organizations and development. In choosing answers, follow the requirements of standard written English.

Questions 30–35 are based on the following passage.

(1) Almost everyone knows about incentives and disincentives, even if they never actually heard the words. (2) People choose to do things because they perceive a benefit to doing them, or avoid things for which they perceive they will be punished. (3) That thing that makes them want to do it is called an incentive, and what makes them not want to do them would be a disincentive. (4) Business people are encouraged to make more money for the company through incentives like bonus pay and perks. (5) Students are constantly exposed to incentives like peer pressure, parental guilt and grades. (6) Peers use incentives to persuade others to become part of a group so that the group's influence can grow. (7) Parents use bribery or guilt to encourage you to behave in a way that makes them proud. (8) Teachers try to make their students do what they want by holding the gradebook that may determine their future.

(9) But what is surprising is that incentives don't always work in the way like they're supposed to. (10) For instance, in some schools they paid kids to read books one summer. (11) But people who studied such programs discovered that the kids ended up reading less in the long run, because paying them took the fun out of it. (12) Also, a day care center that imposed a 3 dollar an hour penalty on parents for picking up their kids late discovered that

GO ON TO THE NEXT PAGE

3   **3**   **3**   **3**   **3**   **3**

more parents, not fewer, started picking up their kids late. **(13)** This was because the parents no longer felt guilty because now they were paying the school for the extra service, but the penalty was cheap enough that they considered it a good deal. **(14)** The bottom line is that people who try to reward or punish things shouldn't assume that either rewards or punishments work the way they think they should.

30. In context, which of the following is the best revision of sentence 3 (reproduced below)?

    That thing that makes them want to do it is called an incentive, and what makes them not want to do them would be a disincentive.

    (A) It is an incentive making someone want to do something, and a disincentive making them not want to do it.
    (B) An incentive is what makes someone want to do something, and a disincentive is what makes someone want to avoid doing something.
    (C) Incentives make someone want to do things, but disincentives are the things making them not want to do it.
    (D) People are made to want to do something by incentives, and a disincentive is for not wanting to do it.
    (E) It is incentives that make people want to do something, disincentives on the other hand being what makes people want to avoid doing something.

31. Which of the following changes to sentence 7 would best improve the coherence of the first paragraph?

    (A) Change "you" to "their children."
    (B) Change "use" to "also use."
    (C) Begin the sentence with "Nevertheless."
    (D) Begin the sentence with "For instance."
    (E) Change "to behave" to "behaving."

32. Where is the best place to insert the following sentence?

    Incentives are used to influence people in many walks of life.

    (A) after sentence 2
    (B) after sentence 3
    (C) after sentence 4
    (D) after sentence 5
    (E) after sentence 6

33. Which of the following is the best version of sentence 9 (reproduced below)?

    But what is surprising is that incentives don't always work in the way like they're supposed to.

    (A) (as it is now)
    (B) It is the surprising fact that incentives don't always work like they're supposed to.
    (C) What is surprising, incentives don't always work like they should.
    (D) Incentives don't always work as they should, it is surprising.
    (E) Surprisingly, incentives don't always work as they should.

34. In context, what is the best version of the underlined portion of sentence 10 (reproduced below)?

    For instance, <u>in some schools they</u> paid kids to read books one summer.

    (A) in some schools where they
    (B) some schools are where they
    (C) some schools implemented programs that
    (D) programs in some schools were where they
    (E) in some school programs they

35. Which is the best sentence to insert between sentence 13 and sentence 14?

    (A) Examples such as this demonstrate that incentives can be very effective.
    (B) If the penalty had been greater, perhaps it would have had the desired effect.
    (C) Clearly, rewards are more effective in most situations than punishments.
    (D) Many schools have also implemented effective after-school reading programs.
    (E) I'm not sure what the school decided to do with the program, since it wasn't working.

STOP

If you finish before time is called, you may check your work on this section only. Do not turn to any other section of the test.

SECTION 4
Time—25 minutes
24 questions

Turn to Section 4 of your answer sheet to answer the questions in this section.

Directions: For each question in this section, select the best answer from among the choices given and fill in the corresponding circle on the answer sheet.

Each sentence below has one or two blanks, each blank indicating that something has been omitted. Beneath the sentence are five words or sets of words labeled A through E. Choose the word or set of words that, when inserted in the sentence, best fits the meaning of the sentence as a whole.

EXAMPLE:

Rather than accepting the theory unquestioningly, Deborah regarded it with -----.

(A) mirth
(B) sadness
(C) responsibility
(D) ignorance
(E) skepticism

---

1. Geological evidence suggests that the earth's magnetic polarity has switched back and forth many times over the millennia; such ------- in the magnetic field may affect the ability of our planet to ward off cosmic radiation.

   (A) intensifications
   (B) justifications
   (C) records
   (D) correlations
   (E) fluctuations

2. Recent studies have demonstrated that even birds are capable of making and using tools, but scientists disagree as to whether such behavior is learned or -------.

   (A) intelligent
   (B) impassive
   (C) innate
   (D) pragmatic
   (E) suspect

3. Although doctors have been thus far successful at ------- the spread of tuberculosis in the United States, they are nonetheless concerned that ------- strains of the disease may yet arise.

   (A) marginalizing . . innocuous
   (B) controlling . . virulent
   (C) obscuring . . indifferent
   (D) imperiling . . responsive
   (E) dismissing . . required

4. The lecturer admonished those who confused the carefully formulated ------- of the scientific method with the more wishful ------- of pseudoscience.

   (A) theories . . divergences
   (B) concessions . . estimates
   (C) hypotheses . . conjectures
   (D) paradigms . . restrictions
   (E) hunches . . proofs

GO ON TO THE NEXT PAGE

4   4   4   4   4   4

5. Unlike the first lecture, which was ------- and filled with irrelevant references, Ken's presentation was easy to understand and illustrated with ------- examples.

    (A) obscure . . vague
    (B) lucid . . pertinent
    (C) convoluted . . petty
    (D) concise . . esoteric
    (E) abstruse . . germane

6. Although Ian's argument seemed plausible at first, his opponent in the debate dismissed it as mere ------- and refuted it thoroughly.

    (A) sophistry
    (B) solicitousness
    (C) acumen
    (D) substantiation
    (E) resolution

7. Glen is considered one of the most ------- members of the group, having already read dozens of philosophical treatises and ------- researched all new developments in his discipline.

    (A) erudite . . assiduously
    (B) contrite . . painstakingly
    (C) cerebral . . hesitantly
    (D) stoic . . lackadaisically
    (E) argumentative . . generously

8. The establishment of international phone service in 1964 appeased those citizens of the tiny island who bemoaned the ------- of their community and longed for a greater connection to the world outside.

    (A) obstinacy
    (B) precociousness
    (C) obsequiousness
    (D) insularity
    (E) insinuation

The passages below are followed by questions based on their content. Answer the questions on the basis of what is <u>stated</u> or <u>implied</u> in the passage and in any introductory material that may be provided.

Questions 9–12 are based on the following passages.

PASSAGE 1

In polls, Kennedy is listed as one of the greatest presidents ever to serve. How is it
Line that a man who barely served 1,000 days and enacted few lasting policies, won no
5   wars and who was never much more popular than his Republican rival, could be perceived as greater than George Washington, James Madison, Thomas Jefferson or Ronald Reagan? The answer lies in the most consistent feature
10   of Baby Boomers, their narcissism. The president of the "Me generation" trumps all others, just as their war (Vietnam) is the measuring stick by which all modern wars are judged and their music (rock n' roll) continues
15   to dominate the air waves. History be damned; if it didn't happen between 1960 and 1980, it's irrelevant. If they didn't see it on television, it might as well not have happened. JFK was the first president to make effective use of
20   television.

PASSAGE 2

Kennedy was the first President to be born in the twentieth century and was very much a man of his time. He was restless, seeking, with a thirst of knowledge, and he had a
25   feeling of deep commitment, not only to the people of the United States, but to the peoples of the world. Many of the causes he fought for exist today because of what he did for the rights of minorities, the poor, the
30   very old and the very young. He never took

First paragraph: http://www.renewamerica.us/columns/cox/031124
Second paragraph: *http://www.studyworld.com/newsite/ReportEssay/Biography/ AmericanPresident%5CJFK_His_Life_and_Legacy-322663.htm*

GO ON TO THE NEXT PAGE →

anything for granted and worked for everything he owned. Perhaps Kennedy summed up his life best in his own inaugural speech: "Ask not what your country can do for you, but ask what you can do for your country."

9.　Unlike Passage 2, Passage 1 conveys a tone of

(A)　cynicism
(B)　hope
(C)　objectivity
(D)　fear
(E)　humor

10.　The question posed in lines 2–8 ("How is it ... Ronald Reagan?") suggests that the author of Passage 1 believes that

(A)　polls are unreliable gauges of real sentiments
(B)　Kennedy's policies are what made him so popular
(C)　Kennedy's high ranking is undeserved
(D)　Kennedy was a savvy politician
(E)　Kennedy himself was unconcerned with his own popularity

11.　Passage 2 mentions "the very old and the very young" (lines 29–30) in order to make the point that Kennedy

(A)　was elected by a very wide range of voters
(B)　focused more on political issues than on moral ones
(C)　was mourned by the entire nation
(D)　was adept at manipulating the media
(E)　supported policies that benefited divergent groups

12.　With which of the following statements would BOTH authors most likely agree?

(A)　American culture in the 60s and 70s was highly self-centered.
(B)　Polls are powerful tools for assessing popular sentiments.
(C)　Kennedy was one of the foremost advocates of minority rights.
(D)　Kennedy was one of the hardest working American presidents
(E)　Kennedy was in touch with the unique qualities of the era in which he governed.

Questions 13–24 are based on the following passages.

The following passages discuss American political dissent. The first passage, written in 1922 by H. L. Mencken, an American essayist, discusses real versus ideal government. The second, written in 1991 by Gordon S. Wood, a professor of history, discusses the basis of the American Revolution.

PASSAGE 1

All government, in its essence, is a conspiracy against the superior man: its one permanent
Line　object is to oppress him and cripple him. If it be aristocratic in organization, then it seeks
5　to protect the man who is superior only in law against the man who is superior in fact; if it be democratic, then it seeks to protect the man who is inferior in every way against both. One of its primary functions is to
10　regiment men by force, to make them as much alike as possible and as dependent upon one another as possible, to search out and combat originality among them. All it can see in an original idea is potential change,
15　and hence an invasion of its prerogatives. The most dangerous man, to any government, is the man who is able to think things out for himself, without regard to the prevailing superstitions and taboos. Almost inevitably

GO ON TO THE NEXT PAGE

Passage 1: From *A Mencken Chresthomathy* by H.L. Mencken, copyright 1916, 1918, 1919, 1920, 1924, 1926, 1927, 1929, 1932, 1934, 1942, 1949, by Alfred A. Knopf, a division of Random House, Inc. Used by permission of Alfred A. Knopf, a division of Random House, Inc.
Passage 2: From *The Radicalism of the American Revolution* by Gordon S. Wood, copyright © 1992 by Gordon S. Wood. Used by permission of Alfred A. Knopf, a division of Random House, Inc.

20 he comes to the conclusion that the
government he lives in is dishonest, insane
and intolerable, and so, if he is romantic, he
tries to change it. And even if he is not romantic
personally he is very apt to spread discontent
25 among those who are.

    There is seldom, if ever, any evidence that
the new government proposed would be any
better than the old one. On the contrary, all
the historical testimony runs the other way.
30 Political revolutions do not often accomplish
anything of genuine value; their one undoubted
effect is simply to throw out one gang of
thieves and put in another. After a revolution,
of course, the successful revolutionists
always
35 try to convince doubters that they have
achieved great things, and usually they hang
any man who denies it. But that surely
doesn't prove their case. In Russia, for many
years, the plain people were taught that
getting rid
40 of the Czar would make them all rich and
happy, but now that they have got rid of him
they are poorer and unhappier than ever
before. Even the American colonies gained
little by their revolt in 1776. For twenty-five
45 years after the Revolution they were in far
worse condition as free states as they would
have been as colonies. Their government was
more expensive, more inefficient, more
dishonest, and more tyrannical. It was only
50 the gradual material progress of the country
that saved them from starvation and collapse,
and that material progress was due, not to
the virtues of their new government, but to
the lavishness of nature. Under the British
55 hoof they would have got on just as well, and
probably a great deal better.

    The ideal government of all reflective men,
from Aristotle onward, is one which lets the
individual alone—one which barely escapes
60 being no government at all. This ideal, I
believe, will be realized in the world twenty or
thirty centuries after I have passed from these
scenes.

PASSAGE 2

    By the late 1760s and early 1770s a
65 potentially revolutionary situation existed in
many of the colonies. There was little evidence
of those social conditions we often associate
with revolution (and some historians have
desperately sought to find): no mass poverty,
70 no seething social discontent, no grinding
oppression. The colonists' growing prosperity
contributed to the unprecedented eighteenth-
century sense that people here and now were
capable of ordering their own reality.
75 Consequently, there was a great deal of
jealousy and touchiness everywhere, for what
could be made could be unmade; the people
were acutely nervous about their prosperity
and the liberty that seemed to make it possible.
80 Social changes, particularly since the
1740s, multiplied rapidly, and many
Americans struggled to make sense of what
was happening. These social changes were
complicated, and they are easily misinterpreted.
85 Luxury and conspicuous consumption by
very ordinary people were increasing. So, too,
was religious dissent of all sorts. But social
classes based on occupation or wealth did not
set themselves against one another, for no
90 classes in this modern sense yet existed.
The society was becoming more unequal,
but its inequalities were not the source of the
instability and anxiety. Indeed, it was the
pervasive equality of American society that was
95 causing the problems—even in aristocratic
South Carolina.

    Perhaps the society of no colony was more
unequal, more riven by discrepancies of rich
and poor, more dominated by an ostentatious
100 aristocracy than that of South Carolina.
"State and magnificence, the natural attendant
on great riches, are conspicuous among this
people," declared a wide-eyed New England
visitor in 1773. "In grandeur, splendour of
105 buildings, decorations, equipage, numbers,
commerce, shipping, and indeed in almost
everything, it far surpasses all I ever saw, or
ever expect to see in America." Yet, surprisingly,
in the opinion of Carolinian Christopher

GO ON TO THE NEXT PAGE ⇨

4   4   4   4   4   4

110 Gadsden, society in his colony was most
remarkable, not for its inequality, but for its
equality, for the prevalence in it of substantial
hardworking farmers and artisans.
These honest industrious white folk were
115 extraordinarily prosperous. Even "the poorest
of them (unless some very uncommon
instances indeed) but must find himself in a
very comfortable situation, especially when
he compares his condition with that of the
120 poor of other nations," or Gadsden might
have added, with that of the black slaves in
their own midst. The result, said Gadsden,
was that white society in South Carolina was
comparatively equal, "the distinctions ...
125 between the farmer and rich planter, the
mechanic and the rich merchant, being
abundantly more here, in imagination, than
reality."
    Yet because such equality and prosperity
130 were so unusual in the Western world, they
could not be taken for granted. Therefore any
possibility of oppression, any threat to the
colonists' hard-earned prosperity, any hint of
reducing them to the poverty of other nations,
135 nations, was especially frightening; for it
seemed likely to slide them back into the
traditional status of servants or slaves, into
the older world where labor was merely a
painful necessity and not a source of prosperity.

13.   As it is used in line 3, "object" most nearly means

(A)   disagreement
(B)   symbol
(C)   material thing
(D)   control
(E)   goal

14.   Passage 1 suggests that an "aristocratic" (line 4)
government is similar to a "democratic" (line 7)
government primarily in its

(A)   concern for commerce and private
enterprise
(B)   unpopularity among the common people
(C)   oppression of its most creative citizens
(D)   desire to implement fair and equitable
laws
(E)   promotion of new ideas

15.   The "historical testimony" (line 29) most likely
regards

(A)   the social effects of political revolutions
(B)   the causes of discontent that breeds
rebellion
(C)   the development of artistic movements
(D)   the origins of superstitions and taboos
(E)   the ascendancy of romantic sentiment

16.   Passage 1 suggests that the post-revolutionary
government of the American colonies eventually succeeded only because it

(A)   was more responsive to the people
(B)   enjoyed the benefit of natural resources
(C)   established a more rigid framework of
laws
(D)   was more efficient than the previous gov-
ernment
(E)   did not oppress its citizens

17.   The author of Passage 1 believes that the "ideal
government" (line 57) is characterized primarily by its

(A)   commitment to putting educated
citizens in power
(B)   efficient systems of industry
(C)   emphasis on law and order
(D)   unintrusiveness
(E)   support of broad social programs

18.   According to Passage 2, the "revolutionary
situation" (line 65) among the colonists
included

(A)   impoverishment
(B)   political persecution
(C)   envy
(D)   hopelessness
(E)   sharp class divisions

GO ON TO THE NEXT PAGE →

4   4   4   4   4   4

19. The author of Passage 2 suggests that "some historians" (line 68) believe that

(A) the situation in the American colonies prior to the revolution was not as dire as previously thought
(B) political upheaval is caused by social discontent
(C) American colonists had unprecedented power
(D) the American revolution was caused by jealousy
(E) colonial culture was highly traditional

20. As it is used in line 101, "state" most nearly means

(A) government
(B) pomp
(C) independence
(D) stage of physical development
(E) emotional condition

21. Christopher Gadsden refers to "the farmer and rich planter, the mechanic and the rich merchant" (lines 125–126) primarily as a means of highlighting

(A) the great range of occupations available in the colonies
(B) the fact that many kinds of citizens were willing to fight for their independence
(C) the profound discontent found throughout the colonies
(D) those who were most guilty of repressing their fellow colonists
(E) the relative lack of socioeconomic classes in South Carolina

22. With which of the following statements would the authors of BOTH passages most likely agree?

(A) The American Revolution is best characterized as a quest for religious freedom.
(B) Government is by its nature repressive.
(C) The transition to a democratic system of government dramatically benefited the American colonists.
(D) During and after the revolution, American colonists benefited from material prosperity.
(E) The post-revolutionary American government was unjust and tyrannical.

23. Passage 1 suggests that the American revolutionaries were inspired by

(A) impoverished conditions, while the author of Passage 2 suggests that they were inspired by class conflict
(B) lack of freedom, while the author of Passage 2 suggests that they were inspired by unjust taxation
(C) political idealism, while the author of Passage 2 suggests that they were inspired by fear of losing their wealth
(D) blind ideology, while the author of Passage 2 suggests that they were inspired by a lack of equality
(E) political repression, while the author of Passage 2 suggests that they were inspired by religious repression

24. Which of the following terms in Passage 2 is most similar in meaning to "hoof" in line 55 of Passage 1?

(A) "discontent" (line 70)
(B) "dissent" (line 87)
(C) "instability" (line 93)
(D) "magnificence" (line 101)
(E) "oppression" (line 132)

STOP

If you finish before time is called, you may check your work on this section only. Do not turn to any other section of the test.

5   **5**   **5**   **5**   **5**   **5**

SECTION 5
Time—25 minutes
18 questions

Turn to Section 5 of your answer sheet to answer the questions in this section.

Directions: This section contains two types of questions. You have 25 minutes to complete both types. For questions 1–8, solve each problem and decide which is the best of the choices given. Fill in the corresponding circle on the answer sheet. You may use any available space for scratchwork.

Notes

1. The use of a calculator is permitted.
2. All numbers used are real numbers.
3. Figures that accompany problems in this test are intended to provide information useful in solving the problems. They are drawn as accurately as possible EXCEPT when it is stated in a specific problem that the figure is not drawn to scale. All figures lie in a plane unless otherwise indicated.
4. Unless otherwise specified, the domain of any function f is assumed to be the set of all real numbers x for which $f(x)$ is a real number.

Reference Information

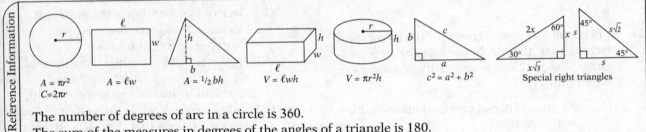

$A = \pi r^2$ $A = \ell w$ $A = \frac{1}{2}bh$ $V = \ell wh$ $V = \pi r^2 h$ $c^2 = a^2 + b^2$ Special right triangles
$C = 2\pi r$

The number of degrees of arc in a circle is 360.
The sum of the measures in degrees of the angles of a triangle is 180.

1. If $4m - 2 = m + 7$, what is the value of m?

    (A) 3.0
    (B) 4.5
    (C) 6.0
    (D) 7.5
    (E) 9.0

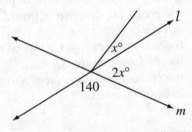

Note: Figure not drawn to scale.

2. In the figure above, l and m are lines. What is the value of x?

    (A) 10
    (B) 20
    (C) 30
    (D) 40
    (E) 80

GO ON TO THE NEXT PAGE

3. If $\frac{3}{8}$ of m is 48, what is $\frac{5}{8}$ of m?

(A) 80
(B) 64
(C) 60
(D) 40
(E) 30

4. Let a_n represent the nth term of a particular sequence. If $a_2 = 54$ and each term except the first
is equal to the previous term divided by 3, then
what is the first term that is NOT an integer?

(A) a_4
(B) a_5
(C) a_6
(D) a_7
(E) a_8

5. If $\sqrt{n} \times \sqrt{2}$ is an integer, which of the following
could *not* be the value of n?

(A) 2
(B) 8
(C) 12
(D) 18
(E) 32

6. Four of the six faces of a cube are painted black,
and the other two faces are painted white. What
is the *least* number of vertices on this cube that
could be shared by two or more black faces?

(A) eight
(B) seven
(C) six
(D) five
(E) four

7. If y varies directly as x, and if $y = 8$ when
$x = a$ and $y = 12$ when $x = a + 10$, what is
the value of a?

(A) 5
(B) 8
(C) 10
(D) 15
(E) 20

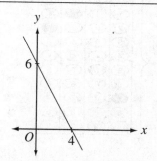

Note: Figure not drawn to scale.

8. The figure above shows the graph of the function $f(x) = ax + b$, where a and b are constants.
What is the slope of the graph of the function
$g(x) = -2f(x)$?

(A) -3

(B) $-\frac{4}{3}$

(C) $\frac{4}{3}$

(D) $\frac{3}{2}$

(E) 3

GO ON TO THE NEXT PAGE

5   **5**   **5**   **5**   **5**   **5**

Directions: For student-produced response questions 9–18, use the grids at the bottom of the answer sheet page on which you have answered questions 1–8.

Each of the remaining ten questions requires you to solve the problem and enter your answer by marking the circles in the special grid, as shown in the examples below. You may use any available space for scratchwork.

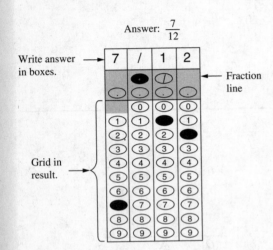

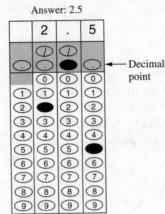

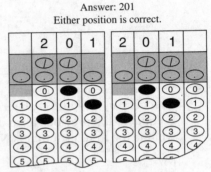

Note: You may start your answers in any column, space permitting. Columns not needed should be left blank.

• Mark no more than one circle in any column.

• Because the answer sheet will be machine-scored, **you will receive credit only if the circles are filled in correctly.**

• Although not required, it is suggested that you write your answer in the boxes at the top of the columns to help you fill in the circles accurately.

• Some problems may have more than one correct answer. In such cases, grid only one answer.

• No question has a negative answer.

• **Mixed numbers** such as $3\frac{1}{2}$ must be gridded as

3.5 or 7/2. (If [3 1 / 2] is gridded, it will be

interpreted as, $\frac{31}{2}$ not $3\frac{1}{2}$.)

• **Decimal Answers:** If you obtain a decimal answer with more digits than the grid can accommodate, it may be either rounded or truncated, but it must fill the entire grid. For example, if you obtain an answer such as 0.6666..., you should record your result as .666 or .667. **A less accurate value such as .66 or .67 will be scored as incorrect.**

Acceptable ways to grid $^2/_3$ are:

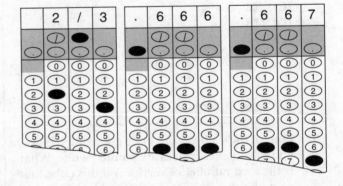

---

9. If $x + 9$ is 50% greater than x, then what is the value of x?

10. If a printer can print 5 pages in 20 seconds, then, at this rate, how many pages can it print in 5 minutes?

GO ON TO THE NEXT PAGE ⇒

5   5   5   5   5   5

11. If 5 is $x\%$ of 15, then what is $x\%$ of 60?

12. The measures of the four angles in a quadrilateral have a ratio of 2:3:6:7. What is the measure, in degrees, of the largest of these angles?

13. If a is $\frac{2}{5}$ of b, b is $\frac{1}{10}$ of c, and $c > 0$, then what is the value of $\frac{a}{c}$?

14. A rectangle and a triangle share the same base. If the area of the triangle is 6 times the area of the rectangle, and the height of the rectangle is 4, what is the height of the triangle?

15. The median of a set of 5 integers is 10. If the greatest of these integers is 5 times the least integer, and if all the integers are different, what is the greatest possible sum of the numbers in this set?

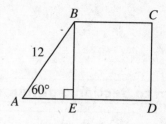

16. In the figure above, $BCDE$ is a square and $AB = 12$. What is the area of square $BCDE$?

17. Each term in a sequence, except for the first, is equal to the previous term times a positive constant, k. If the 3rd term of this sequence is 12 and the 5th term is 27, what is the first term?

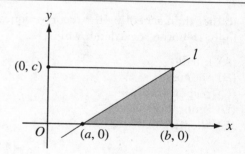

Note: Figure not drawn to scale.

18. In the figure above, $2b = 3c$ and the area of the shaded triangle is $\frac{2}{5}$ the area of the rectangle. What is the slope of line l?

STOP

If you finish before time is called, you may check your work on this section only. Do not turn to any other section of the test.

SECTION 6
Time—25 minutes
24 questions

Turn to Section 6 of your answer sheet to answer the questions in this section.

Directions: For each question in this section, select the best answer from among the choices given and fill in the corresponding circle on the answer sheet.

Each sentence below has one or two blanks, each blank indicating that something has been omitted. Beneath the sentence are five words or sets of words labeled A through E. Choose the word or set of words that, when inserted in the sentence, best fits the meaning of the sentence as a whole.

EXAMPLE:

Rather than accepting the theory unquestioningly, Deborah regarded it with -----.

(A) mirth
(B) sadness
(C) responsibility
(D) ignorance
(E) skepticism

Ⓐ Ⓑ Ⓒ Ⓓ ●

1. Although the party gained a clear majority in the election, its philosophy remained -------, never achieving a clear and consistent form.

   (A) versatile   (B) indisputable
   (C) homogenous   (D) nebulous
   (E) appealing

2. The astronomer was ------- the evidence she was receiving from the radio telescope, because the data did not ------- her theory regarding the mass of the distant galaxy.

   (A) concerned about . . refute
   (B) disappointed by . . substantiate
   (C) intimidated by . . ignore
   (D) chastened . . conceal
   (E) bolstered by . . exaggerate

3. Wildebeests are ------- creatures, often trekking over 1,000 miles in a typical year in search of food resources that shift according to the rainy season.

   (A) itinerant
   (B) indigenous
   (C) subdued
   (D) nocturnal
   (E) arboreal

4. Carlos has always been ------- the motivations of politicians, often insisting that even their most seemingly ------- initiatives are in fact based on selfish impulses.

   (A) skeptical of . . contemptible
   (B) sanguine about . . magnanimous
   (C) disparaging of . . callous
   (D) enthusiastic about . . immaterial
   (E) cynical about . . altruistic

5. Herbert was not ------- enough to be a good literary agent, often mistaking ------- prose for original and competent writing.

   (A) discerning . . derivative
   (B) gauche . . sublime
   (C) obstinate . . proficient
   (D) diligent . . innovative
   (E) servile . . pedestrian

GO ON TO THE NEXT PAGE

6   6   6   6   6   6

The passages below are followed by questions based on their content. Answer the questions on the basis of what is <u>stated</u> or <u>implied</u> in the passage and in any introductory material that may be provided.

Questions 6–7 are based on the following passage.

Geologists use radiological methods to deduce the age of mineral samples. These
Line methods rely on the fact that when a radioactive sample within a rock is first
5 formed it is nearly pure, but gradually decays into a more stable element. Since this decay occurs at a predictable rate, measuring the proportion of each type of element within a rock can tell scientists
10 how long it has been since that rock was formed. One problematic aspect of this dating method is that some of the stable element may have already been present when the mineral was formed, and therefore was
15 not the result of radioactive decay.

6.   The primary purpose of this passage is to

(A)   introduce a scientific controversy
(B)   refute a misconception
(C)   explain a technique
(D)   describe a historical fact
(E)   examine a theory

7.   According to the passage, radiological dating methods are most likely to yield inaccurate results when the radioactive mineral sample within a rock

(A)   is exceptionally old
(B)   comprises a large portion of the rock's mass
(C)   decays into a stable element at a consistent rate
(D)   originally contains samples of the element into which the radioactive element will decay
(E)   decays into a stable element that remains in the rock, rather than being released into the atmosphere

Questions 8–9 are based on the following passage.

The tragic hero with Shakespeare need not be "good," though generally he is "good"
Line and therefore at once wins sympathy in his error. But it is necessary that he should have
5 so much of greatness that in his error and fall we may be vividly conscious of the possibilities of human nature. Hence, in the first place, a Shakespearean tragedy is never, like some miscalled tragedies, depressing.
10 No one ever closes the book with the feeling that man is a poor mean creature. He may be wretched and he may be awful, but he is not small. His lot may be heart-rending and mysterious, but it is not contemptible. The
15 most confirmed of cynics ceases to be a cynic while he reads these plays.

8.   As it is used in line 13, "lot" most nearly means

(A)   parcel of land
(B)   great quantity
(C)   fate in life
(D)   motivation
(E)   friend

9.   The passage suggests that a "cynic" (line 16) is one who believes that

(A)   Shakespeare's plays are self-serving
(B)   human beings can be ignoble
(C)   heroes should be imbued with greatness
(D)   tragic heroes are worthy of sympathy
(E)   Shakespeare's characters are unrealistic

GO ON TO THE NEXT PAGE →

Each passage below is followed by questions based on its content. Answer the questions based on what is stated or implied in each passage and in any introductory material that may be provided.

Questions 10–16 pertain to the following passage.

The following is an excerpt from a short story, written by an American author in 1909, regarding the crew of a sailing ship.

She floated at the starting point of a long
journey, very still in an immense stillness,
Line   the shadows of her spars flung far to the
eastward by the setting sun. At that moment
5   I was alone on her decks. There was not a
sound in her—and around us nothing moved,
nothing lived, not a canoe on the water, not a
bird in the air, not a cloud in the sky. In this
breathless pause at the threshold of a long
10   passage we seemed to be measuring our
fitness for a long and arduous enterprise, the
appointed task of both our existences to be
carried out, far from all human eyes, with
only sky and sea for spectators and for
15   judges.
        There must have been some glare in the air
to interfere with one's sight, because it was
only just before the sun left us that my
roaming eyes made out beyond the highest
20   ridges of the principal islet of the group
something which did away with the
solemnity of perfect solitude. The tide of
darkness flowed on swiftly; and with tropical
suddenness a swarm of stars came out above
25   the shadowy earth, while I lingered yet, my
hand resting lightly on my ship's rail as if
on the shoulder of a trusted friend. But,
with all that multitude of celestial bodies
staring down at one, the comfort of quiet
30   communion with her was gone for good. And
there were also disturbing sounds by this
time—voices, footsteps forward; the steward

flitted along the main-deck, a busily
ministering spirit; a hand bell tinkled
35   urgently under the poop deck.
        I found my two officers waiting for me
near the supper table, in the lighted cuddy.
We sat down at once, and as I helped the
chief mate, I said:
40   "Are you aware that there is a ship anchored
inside the islands? I saw her mastheads
above the ridge as the sun went down."
        He raised sharply his simple face,
overcharged by a terrible growth of whisker,
45   and emitted his usual ejaculations:
        "Bless my soul, sir! You don't say so!"
        My second mate was a round-cheeked,
silent young man, grave beyond his years, I
thought; but as our eyes happened to meet I
50   detected a slight quiver on his lips. I looked
down at once. It was not my part to
encourage sneering on board my ship. It
must be said, too, that I knew very little of
my officers. In consequence of certain events
55   of no particular significance, except to
myself, I had been appointed to the
command only a fortnight before. Neither did
I know much of the hands forward. All these
people had been together for eighteen
60   months or so, and my position was that of
the only stranger on board. I mention this
because it has some bearing on what is to
follow. But what I felt most was my being a
stranger to the ship; and if all the truth must
65   be told, I was somewhat of a stranger to
myself. The youngest man on board (barring
the second mate), and untried as yet by a
position of the fullest responsibility, I was
willing to take the adequacy of the others for
70   granted. They had simply to be equal to their
tasks; but I wondered how far I should turn
out faithful to that ideal conception of one's
own personality every man sets up for
himself secretly.
75   Meantime the chief mate, with an almost
visible effect of collaboration on the part of
his round eyes and frightful whiskers, was
trying to evolve a theory of the anchored
ship. His dominant trait was to take all

GO ON TO THE NEXT PAGE

6   **6**   6   6   6   **6**

80   things into earnest consideration. He was of
a painstaking turn of mind. As he used to say,
he "liked to account to himself" for
practically everything that came in his way,
down to a miserable scorpion he had found
85   in his cabin a week before. The why and the
wherefore of that scorpion—how it got on
board and came to select his room rather
than the pantry (which was a dark place and
more what a scorpion would be partial to),
90   and how on earth it managed to drown itself
in the inkwell of his writing desk—had
exercised him infinitely. The ship within the
islands was much more easily accounted for,
and just as we were about to rise from table
95   he made his pronouncement. She was, he
doubted not, a ship from home lately arrived.
Probably she drew too much water to cross
the bar except at the top of spring tides.
Therefore she went into that natural harbor
100 to wait for a few days in preference to
remaining in an open roadstead.

10.   The tone of the first paragraph is primarily
one of

    (A)   reflective anticipation
    (B)   anxious dread
    (C)   unrestrained excitement
    (D)   detached analysis
    (E)   incomprehension

11.   The narrator mentions the "glare" (line 16) in
order to make the point that

    (A)   the sea around him was filled with
commotion
    (B)   his crew was not entirely reliable
    (C)   the ship was kept in very good
condition
    (D)   the weather was about to change
    (E)   he did not see the distant masthead
immediately

12.   The "certain events" mentioned in line 54
pertain to the means by which

    (A)   the crew was chosen for the voyage
    (B)   the mysterious ship came to be docked
nearby
    (C)   the second mate developed his grave
disposition
    (D)   the narrator was chosen as captain
    (E)   the hands came to know each other

13.   In lines 63–74 (But what I felt ... for himself
secretly") the narrator conveys primarily his

    (A)   skepticism about the ability of his
crewmen
    (B)   apprehensions about the mysterious ship
    (C)   excitement about the upcoming voyage
    (D)   lack of self-confidence
    (E)   pride in his accomplishments as such a
young age

14.   As it is used in line 78, the word "evolve" most
nearly means

    (A)   destroy
    (B)   frighten
    (C)   generate
    (D)   dominate
    (E)   turn around

15.   In the final paragraph, the chief mate is characterized primarily as being

    (A)   physically intimidating
    (B)   intelligent and erudite
    (C)   emotionally sensitive
    (D)   reserved and dull-witted
    (E)   meticulously thoughtful

16.   As it is used in line 92, "exercised" most nearly
means

    (A)   perplexed
    (B)   practiced
    (C)   strengthened
    (D)   eradicated
    (E)   weakened

GO ON TO THE NEXT PAGE

6   6   6   6   6   6

Questions 17–24 pertain to the following passage.

The following passage discusses the study of language acquisition, the means by which humans learn to speak and understand language.

Language acquisition is one of the central topics in cognitive science. Every theory of
Line cognition has tried to explain it; probably no other topic has aroused such controversy.
5   Possessing a language is the quintessentially human trait: all normal humans speak, no nonhuman animal does. Language is the main vehicle by which we know about other people's thoughts, and the two must be
10   intimately related. Every time we speak we are revealing something about language, so the facts of language structure are easy to come by; these data hint at a system of extraordinary complexity. Nonetheless,
15   learning a first language is something every child does successfully, in a matter of a few years and without the need for formal lessons. With language so close to the core of what it means to be human, it is not
20   surprising that children's acquisition of language has received so much attention. Anyone with strong views about the human mind would like to show that children's first few steps are steps in the right direction.
25   Is language simply grafted on top of cognition as a way of sticking communicable labels onto thoughts? Or does learning a language somehow mean learning to think in that language? A famous hypothesis, outlined
30   by Benjamin Whorf, asserts that the categories and relations that we use to understand the world come from our particular language, so that speakers of different languages conceptualize the world in different ways.
35   Language acquisition, then, would be learning to think, not just learning to talk.
        This is an intriguing hypothesis, but virtually all modern cognitive scientists believe it is false. Babies can think before they can talk. Cognitive
40   psychology has shown that people think not just in words but in images and abstract logical propositions. And linguistics has shown that

human languages are too ambiguous and schematic to use as a medium of internal
45   computation: when people think about "spring," surely they are not confused as to whether they are thinking about a season or something that goes "boing"—and if one word can correspond to two thoughts,
50   thoughts can't be words.
        But language acquisition has a unique contribution to make to this issue. As we shall see, it is virtually impossible to show how children could learn a language unless you
55   assume they have a considerable amount of nonlinguistic cognitive machinery in place before they start.
        All humans talk but no house pets or house plants do, no matter how pampered, so
60   heredity must be involved in language. But a child growing up in Japan speaks Japanese whereas the same child brought up in California would speak English, so the environment is also crucial. Thus there is no
65   question about whether heredity or environment is involved in language, or even whether one or the other is "more important." Instead, language acquisition might be our best hope of finding out how
70   heredity and environment interact. We know that adult language is intricately complex, and we know that children become adults. Therefore something in the child's mind must be capable of attaining that complexity. Any
75   theory that posits too little innate structure, so that its hypothetical child ends up speaking something less than a real language, must be false. The same is true for any theory that posits too much innate
80   structure, so that the hypothetical child can acquire English but not, say, Bantu or Vietnamese.
        And not only do we know about the output of language acquisition, we know a
85   fair amount about the input to it, namely, parents' speech to their children. So even if language acquisition, like all cognitive processes, is essentially a "black box," we know enough about its input and output to
90   be able to make precise guesses about its contents.

Excerpted from http://www.ecs.soton.ac.uk/~harnad/Papers/Py104/pinker.langacq.html

GO ON TO THE NEXT PAGE ⟶

The scientific study of language acquisition began around the same time as the birth of cognitive science, in the late
95 1950s. We can see now why that is not a coincidence. The historical catalyst was Noam Chomsky's review of Skinner's Verbal Behavior. At that time, Anglo-American natural science, social science, and philosophy
100 had come to a virtual consensus about the answers to the questions listed above. The mind consisted of sensorimotor abilities plus a few simple laws of learning governing gradual changes in an organism's behavioral
105 repertoire. Therefore language must be learned; it cannot be a module; and thinking must be a form of verbal behavior, since verbal behavior is the prime manifestation of "thought" that can be observed externally.
110 Chomsky argued that language acquisition falsified these beliefs in a single stroke: children learn languages that are governed by highly subtle and abstract principles, and they do so without explicit instruction or any
115 other environmental clues to the nature of such principles. Hence language acquisition depends on an innate, species-specific module that is distinct from general intelligence. Much of the debate in language
120 acquisition has attempted to test this once-revolutionary, and still controversial, collection of ideas. The implications extend to the rest of human cognition.

17. This passage as a whole is best described as

(A) a history of a new academic discipline
(B) a comparison of the traits of different species
(C) a discussion of a particular human ability
(D) biographical sketches of several scientists
(E) a refutation of an experimental method

18. The "data" mentioned in line 13 most likely include information regarding

(A) the literacy levels of different countries
(B) the best methods for teaching infants to speak
(C) the ability of primates and other mammals to communicate
(D) the structure of the human brain
(E) the intricacy of the expression of human language

19. The sentence "Anyone ... direction" (lines 22–24) indicates that

(A) Most parents are concerned about their children's ability to read and write correctly.
(B) Language theorists tend to focus on language acquisition more than later language development.
(C) Scientists are inclined to disregard evidence that suggests that nonhuman animals can use language.
(D) More should be done to help children who have difficulty learning language.
(E) Poor parenting usually leads to weak oral language skills in children.

20. The statement "Babies can think before they can talk" (line 39) is intended to show that

(A) learning to talk can sometimes be difficult
(B) verbal skill is not necessary to cognition
(C) psychologists should take into account the desires of infants
(D) speakers of different languages conceptualize the world in different ways
(E) all cognitive skills develop according to a rigid timeline

GO ON TO THE NEXT PAGE →

6   6   6   6   6   6

---

21. The statement "language acquisition might be our best hope" (lines 68–69) means that

(A) the ability to speak is a great asset to the survival of the human species
(B) studying how language is learned will help answer deeper questions about psychology
(C) the study of linguistics is helping to make cognitive science a more popular subject
(D) an individual who does not learn to speak will not develop cognitive skills
(E) cognitive science has been given little notice until now

22. The "structure" mentioned in line 75 pertains to

(A) the grammatical rules of a language
(B) the derivations of particular words
(C) cognitive machinery
(D) a person's linguistic environment
(E) a means of investigating scientific claims

23. In line 99, "natural science, social science and philosophy" are mentioned as examples of disciplines that

(A) mutually accepted a single theory of how language is acquired
(B) questioned the need to study cognitive science as a separate discipline
(C) regarded an understanding of language acquisition to be beyond the scope of the scientific method
(D) did not put enough resources into the study of language acquisition
(E) disagreed about the manner in which human languages should be studied

24. Which of the following would most likely agree with the statement that "it cannot be a module" (line 106)?

(A) Noam Chomsky
(B) modern cognitive scientists
(C) philosophers from pre-1950
(D) modern comparative linguists
(E) adults who are learning a new language

If you finish before time is called, you may check your work on this section only. Do not turn to any other section of the test.

SECTION 7
Time—20 minutes
16 questions

Turn to Section 7 of your answer sheet to answer the questions in this section.

Directions: For this section, solve each problem and decide which is the best of the choices given. Fill in the corresponding circle on the answer sheet. You may use any available space for scratchwork.

Notes

1. The use of a calculator is permitted.

2. All numbers used are real numbers.

3. Figures that accompany problems in this test are intended to provide information useful in solving the problems. They are drawn as accurately as possible EXCEPT when it is stated in a specific problem that the figure is not drawn to scale. All figures lie in a plane unless otherwise indicated.

4. Unless otherwise specified, the domain of any function f is assumed to be the set of all real numbers x for which $f(x)$ is a real number.

Reference Information

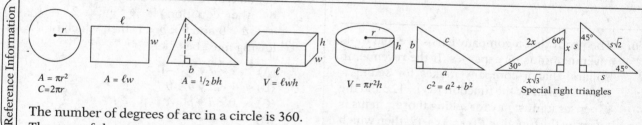

$A = \pi r^2$
$C = 2\pi r$

$A = \ell w$

$A = \frac{1}{2} bh$

$V = \ell wh$

$V = \pi r^2 h$

$c^2 = a^2 + b^2$

Special right triangles

The number of degrees of arc in a circle is 360.
The sum of the measures in degrees of the angles of a triangle is 180.

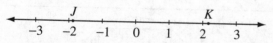

1. In the figure above, if the coordinates of points J and K are added together, this sum will be the coordinate of a point between

(A) –3 and –2
(B) –2 and –1
(C) 0 and 1
(D) 1 and 2
(E) 2 and 3

2. If $6x + 9y = 8$, then $2x + 3y =$

(A) $\dfrac{3}{8}$

(B) $\dfrac{4}{3}$

(C) 2

(D) $\dfrac{8}{3}$

(E) 3

3. Glenna had three boxes of pencils, each of which contained y pencils. She distributed these pencils by giving one to each student in her class, and had 9 pencils left over. If there are 21 students in Glenna's class, what is y?

(A) 3
(B) 4
(C) 6
(D) 8
(E) 10

GO ON TO THE NEXT PAGE

7   **7**   **7**   **7**   **7**   **7**

4. If an integer n is divisible by both 12 and 20, then it must also be divisible by

(A)   15
(B)   24
(C)   32
(D)   80
(E)   240

5. A container in the shape of a right circular cylinder contains 12 liters of liquid when it is filled to $\frac{3}{4}$ of its height. How many liters does it contain when it is completely filled?

(A)   18
(B)   16
(C)   15
(D)   10
(E)   9

6. The profit that a company earns is equal to its revenue minus its expenses. If the revenue, in dollars, that a company makes for selling x items is given by the function $R(x) = 12x$ and the expenses it must pay for selling those x items is given by the function $E(x) = 3x + 12$, then which of the following expresses the profit, in dollars, that the company earns for selling those x items?

(A) $P(x) = 15x + 12$
(B) $P(x) = 15x - 12$
(C) $P(x) = 9x + 12$
(D) $P(x) = 9x - 12$
(E) $P(x) = 12 - 9x$

7. The average (arithmetic mean) of x and y is m, where $m \neq 0$. What is the average (arithmetic mean) of x, y, and $2m$?

(A) m

(B) $\frac{4}{3}m$

(C) $\frac{3}{2}m$

(D) $\frac{5}{3}m$

(E) $2m$

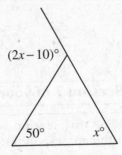

Note: Figure not drawn to scale.

8. In the figure above, what is the value of x?

(A)   30
(B)   40
(C)   50
(D)   60
(E)   70

9. For all real values of x and y, let $x \blacklozenge y$ be defined by the equation $x \blacklozenge y = 2 - xy$. If $-1 < a < 0$ and $0 < b < 1$, then which of the following must be true?

(A) $-2 < a \blacklozenge b < -1$
(B) $-1 < a \blacklozenge b < 0$
(C) $0 < a \blacklozenge b < 1$
(D) $1 < a \blacklozenge b < 2$
(E) $2 < a \blacklozenge b < 3$

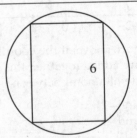

Note: Figure not drawn to scale.

10. The figure above shows a circle with an area of 25π square units. If each vertex of the rectangle is on the circle as shown, what is the area of the rectangle, in square units?

(A)   30
(B)   36
(C)   42
(D)   48
(E)   54

GO ON TO THE NEXT PAGE

7   **7**   **7**   **7**   **7**   **7**

11. Line l passes through the origin and is perpendicular to the line given by the equation $2x + y = 8$. Which of the following points is NOT on line l?

   (A) $(-4, -2)$
   (B) $(-1, 1)$
   (C) $(2, 1)$
   (D) $(4, 2)$
   (E) $(7, 3.5)$

12. If a and b are positive numbers, which of the following is equivalent to $a\%$ of $5b$?

   (A) $\dfrac{ab}{20}$

   (B) $\dfrac{ab}{5}$

   (C) $\dfrac{a}{20b}$

   (D) $\dfrac{a}{5b}$

   (E) $\dfrac{b}{20a}$

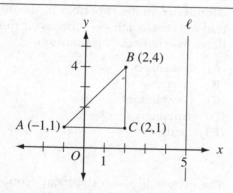

13. If the triangle in the figure above is reflected over line l, what will be the coordinates of the reflection of point A?

   (A) $(4, 1)$
   (B) $(6, 1)$
   (C) $(10, 1)$
   (D) $(11, 1)$
   (E) $(12, 1)$

14. How many positive 3-digit integers contain only odd digits?

   (A)   15
   (B)   75
   (C)   125
   (D)   225
   (E)   500

15. If k is a positive odd integer greater than 4, which of the following always represents the product of two even integers?

   (A) $k^2 - 4$
   (B) $k^2 + 4k - 5$
   (C) $k^2 + 5k + 6$
   (D) $k^2 + 3k - 10$
   (E) $k^2 + k - 20$

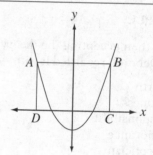

Note: Figure not drawn to scale.

16. The figure above shows the graph of the function $f(x) = x^2 - k$. Points A and B lie on the graph of the function and are the vertices of rectangle $ABCD$. If $AB = 6$ and the area of rectangle $ABCD$ is 20, what is the value of k?

   (A) $\dfrac{17}{3}$

   (B) $\dfrac{19}{3}$

   (C) $\dfrac{34}{3}$

   (D) $\dfrac{68}{3}$

   (E) $\dfrac{98}{3}$

STOP

If you finish before time is called, you may check your work on this section only. Do not turn to any other section of the test.

8   **8**   **8**   **8**   **8**   **8**

SECTION 8
Time—20 minutes
19 questions

Turn to Section 8 of your answer sheet to answer the questions in this section.

Directions: For each question in this section, select the best answer from among the choices given and fill in the corresponding circle on the answer sheet.

Each sentence below has one or two blanks, each blank indicating that something has been omitted. Beneath the sentence are five words or sets of words labeled A through E. Choose the word or set of words that, when inserted in the sentence, best fits the meaning of the sentence as a whole.

EXAMPLE:

Rather than accepting the theory unquestioningly, Deborah regarded it with -----.

(A) mirth
(B) sadness
(C) responsibility
(D) ignorance
(E) skepticism

---

1. As an advocate of -------, Gena has always believed that individuals who have been ------- deserve the opportunity to return to society as productive citizens.

    (A) tolerance .. revered
    (B) conservatism .. overlooked
    (C) rehabilitation .. incarcerated
    (D) perseverence .. championed
    (E) independence .. criticized

2. Early researchers discovered that quinine produced ------- responses such as sweating and shivering when ingested by healthy individuals, but actually ------- these effects in people who had malaria.

    (A) beneficial .. assuaged
    (B) physiological .. ameliorated
    (C) circumstantial .. exacerbated
    (D) premeditated .. rebuffed
    (E) communicable .. concentrated

3. Even his friends believed that Yuri was too submissive to his superiors in the office, and told him that such ------- behavior might even harm his chances of promotion.

    (A) headstrong
    (B) tolerable
    (C) complaisant
    (D) truculent
    (E) tactless

4. The efforts to ------- the local economy after the departure of the town's largest employer were ------- by the construction of a new arts center that would infuse the community with much-needed revenue.

    (A) revive .. facilitated
    (B) debilitate .. expedited
    (C) reform .. postponed
    (D) initiate .. tabled
    (E) preempt .. subsidized

GO ON TO THE NEXT PAGE →

5. As ------- the value of free trade, Bennett was often called upon to give speeches around the world extolling the virtues of unencumbered commerce.

   (A) an antagonist to
   (B) a stalwart of
   (C) a caviler about
   (D) a diviner of
   (E) a skeptic of

6. Federica expressed doubt about the existence of true altruism, claiming that no one makes a sacrifice without expecting it to be ------- in one form or another.

   (A) requited
   (B) repudiated
   (C) portended
   (D) rescinded
   (E) expropriated

GO ON TO THE NEXT PAGE →

8   8   8   8   8   8

The passages below are followed by questions based on their content; questions following a pair of related passages may also be based on the relationship between the paired passages. Answer the questions on the basis of what is <u>stated</u> or <u>implied</u> in the passage and in any introductory material that may be provided.

Questions 7–19 pertain to the following passage.

The following passage discusses Bohemianism, an unconventional and artistic lifestyle that had wide appeal in 19th century Europe and elsewhere.

Bohemia is a land-locked country in central Europe, once a province of the Holy Roman
Line   Empire and until 1918 ruled from Vienna by the Austrian Hapsburgs. Today it constitutes
5   a part of modern Czechoslovakia and its major city, Prague, forms the nation's capital.
    Bohemia is also another, less clearly defined country, a country of the mind. This Bohemia in fact derives from misconceptions
10   about the true Bohemia and, in the English-speaking world, such misconceptions go back as far as Shakespeare. The designation of Bohemia as the spiritual habitation of artists stemmed from a
15   different misconception about the real country, because it was also once thought to be the homeland of the gypsies—a notion that quite ignored the "Egyptian" origin of "gypsy."
20   In 1843, when Michael William Balfe's once famous opera *The Bohemian Girl* premiered in London, this meaning was still widely current. A Bohemian had come to mean any wandering or vagabond soul, who need not
25   have been associated with the arts. It was the malnourished Parisian poet, Henry Murger, who was responsible for clinching the term's special association with the life of artists.

    In November 1849 a dramatized version
30   of the Latin Quarter tales Murger had written for the journal *Le Corsaire* was staged at the Theatre des Varietes with the title *La Vie de Boheme*. So extraordinarily successful did this prove that the stories themselves were
35   collected as *Scenes de la Vie de Boheme*. The public's appetite had been whetted and a popular cult of the gypsy-artist was underway. Murger's volume of stories became the textbook for the artistic life throughout the
40   late nineteenth and early twentieth centuries.
    What were the basic elements of this Bohemia as it evolved under Murger? To start with, Bohemia belonged to the romantic movements which preached a doctrine of the
45   power of the individual imagination and came to adopt a secular religion of art.
    Like early Christianity it had its true believers and its heathens; the believers in this case being artists themselves, the elect of
50   the spirit, touched with the divine power of imagination, while the heathen were the commercial middle classes who had prospered and grown as a result of increased commodity production in the wake of the
55   Industrial Revolution.
    To the artists, these were people of no imagination who were only concerned with material things. As Philistines they virtually inhabited a different country from the
60   Bohemians, Murger's achievement was to define, quite persuasively, the boundaries of Bohemia in terms of a particular lifestyle. In his Bohemia, the production of art was in fact of less importance than the capacity
65   for art.
    Murger was also responsible for the term "Bohemian" becoming inseparably linked with the supposedly unconventional, outlandish behaviour of artists, yet it is
70   evident that he did not invent Bohemianism. Most of its ingredients had been in existence in Paris for at least two decades before he

GO ON TO THE NEXT PAGE →

started writing. Murger can thus be described
as a Bohemian of the second generation.
75   Bohemia had been a haven for the political
rebel and, as the 19th century drew to a
close, more than one French observer had
seen it as the breeding-ground of cynicism,
as the source of much potential danger.
80   "It is quite clear," Jules Claretie wrote,
indignantly, in 1888, "that every country has
its Bohemians. But they do not have the
influence over the rest of the nation which
they do in France—thanks to that poisonous
85   element in the French character which is
known as *la blague*—or cynicism." As
Augustin Challamel wrote in his *Souvenirs*:

Behind the "irregulars of the pen" came an
increasing number of Bohemians, affecting
90   the most profound disdain for what the
bourgeois called the "code of behaviour."
They posed as literary students, habitues
of the wine-bars, often of
places of ill-repute, breaking with the
95   customs of polite society, and believing, in
short, that everything is permissible to
men of intelligence...
Besides the false Romantic Byrons there
were some good men who fell into the
100   excesses of the literary revolution, and
practised debauchery and immorality.
Skeptical and materialistic, they elevated
poverty into a system.

There were others who showed an
105   active sympathy for the Bohemians.
Arsene Houssaye had generously
befriended Bohemian poets. Yet Arsene
Houssaye was far from blind: he was well
aware that Bohemia included many
110   impostors. "I don't believe in the good faith
of the literary Bohemian," he had written as
early as 1856. "His disordered life is only a
journey in search of sensations, of the
documents and observations he needs to
115   produce his work. The real Bohemian is the
one who has no communication with the
public."

7.   The overall purpose of this passage is to

(A)   analyze a historical period
(B)   define a broad cultural phenomenon
(C)   explain the merits of Henry Murger's work
(D)   evaluate several literary works of a
        particular genre
(E)   describe the culture of a particular region

8.   The "notion" (line 17) refers most directly to

(A)   a mistaken assumption
(B)   a bigoted point of view
(C)   a means of producing art
(D)   the celebration of a lifestyle
(E)   the inspiration for an opera

9.   The author uses the word "Egyptian" (line 18) in
order to

(A)   refute the perception that Bohemians are
        artists
(B)   compare African culture to European
        culture
(C)   indicate the true source of a particular term
(D)   refer to the origin of a style of art
(E)   acknowledge the culture that first
        studied Bohemia

10.   According to the passage, Henry Murger's
work is most notable for its ability to

(A)   reveal the historical inaccuracy of
        certain accounts
(B)   justify the biases of a social class
(C)   inspire a fascination with a particular
        lifestyle
(D)   revive the fortunes of a depressed industry
(E)   establish a new field of study

GO ON TO THE NEXT PAGE ⟩

11. In saying that Murger's stories became a "textbook" (line 39) the author means that these stories

(A) were the first to apply historical analysis to Bohemianism
(B) predicted the political upheaval that was to come in 19th and 20th century Europe
(C) provided a means of sustaining interest in Bohemianism
(D) warned against the social dangers of Bohemianism
(E) became a dry and lifeless depiction of a once vibrant movement

12. Murger was a "Bohemian of the second generation" (line 74) because he

(A) occasionally criticized the Bohemian lifestyle
(B) was an an observer of Bohemianism rather than a participant in it
(C) helped to transform Bohemianism from an artistic movement to a political one
(D) was not involved in the birth of Bohemianism
(E) could not maintain his romantic perspective on Bohemianism

13. In the sixth paragraph, lines 47–55, Bohemians are characterized primarily as being

(A) rebellious
(B) prosperous
(C) divinely selected
(D) traditionally pious
(E) insincere

14. The "people" (line 56) are

(A) early Christians
(B) the Bohemians
(C) artists of all types
(D) the ruling class
(E) the middle classes

15. Which of the following most accurately describes the difference between the Bohemians described by Jules Claretie and those described by Henry Murger?

(A) Claretie's Bohemians were optimistic, while Murger's Bohemians were cynical.
(B) Claretie's Bohemians are driven to acquire political power, while Murger's Bohemians have a need for secrecy.
(C) Claretie's Bohemians have no artistic talent, while Murger's Bohemians are artists with extraordinary skill.
(D) Claretie's Bohemians had very little social influence, while Murger's Bohemians shaped the culture of an entire nation.
(E) Claretie's Bohemians are a social blight, while Murger's Bohemians are uniquely creative and nonconformist.

16. Augustin Challamel's quotation (lines 88–103) indicates that he regards Bohemianism as being characterized by all of the following EXCEPT

(A) affectation
(B) violence
(C) iconoclasm
(D) arrogance
(E) depravity

GO ON TO THE NEXT PAGE →

17. The statement that Houssaye was "far from blind" (line 108) means that he

(A) understood the political benefits of Bohemianism
(B) did not hold the literary work of the Bohemians in high esteem
(C) did not have unquestioning sympathy for all Bohemians
(D) distrusted the social ambitions of Bohemians
(E) believed that Bohemians were too radical

18. Arsene Houssaye's attitude toward the Bohemians is best characterized as

(A) objectively analytical
(B) ambivalent
(C) morally outraged
(D) reverent
(E) mildly amused

19. Houssaye's quotation (lines 110–117) suggests that a "real Bohemian" is characterized primarily by his or her

(A) aloofness
(B) economic ambition
(C) respect for his or her literary audience
(D) comraderie with other Bohemians
(E) political idealism

STOP

If you finish before time is called, you may check your work on this section only. Do not turn to any other section of the test.

9   9   9   9   9   9

SECTION 9
Time—10 minutes
14 questions

Turn to Section 9 of your answer sheet to answer the questions in this section.

Directions: For each question in this section, select the best answer from among the choices given and fill in the corresponding circle on the answer sheet.

The following sentences test correctness and effectiveness of expression. Part of each sentence or the entire sentence is underlined; beneath each sentence are five ways of phrasing the underlined material. Choice A repeats the original phrasing; the other four choices are different. Select the choice that completes the sentence most effectively.

In making your selection, follow the requirements of standard written English; that is, pay attention to grammar, choice of words, sentence construction, and punctuation. Your selection should result in the most effective sentence—clear and precise, without awkwardness or ambiguity.

EXAMPLE:

The children <u>couldn't hardly believe their eyes</u>.

(A) couldn't hardly believe their eyes
(B) could hardly believe their eyes
(C) would not hardly believe their eyes
(D) couldn't nearly believe their eyes
(E) couldn't hardly believe his or her eyes

1. One way to improve student participation in the food drive <u>is by providing transportation for</u> those students who don't have cars.

(A) is by providing transportation for
(B) would be by providing transportation for
(C) is to provide transportation for
(D) is with transporting
(E) is to be providing transportation to

2. Political reporters often must choose between currying favor with powerful officials to get inside information <u>or to gather</u> information as an objective outsider.

(A) or to gather
(B) as opposed to gathering
(C) without gathering
(D) and to gather
(E) and gathering

3. Over 1,000 volunteers are available <u>to begin dispensing food and medicine after the order were given</u>.

(A) to begin dispensing food and medicine after the order were given
(B) if the order were given on the dispensing of food and medicine
(C) for beginning to dispense food and medicine once the order is given
(D) to begin dispensing food and medicine once the order is given
(E) once the giving of the order about dispensing food and medicine

GO ON TO THE NEXT PAGE

4. <u>With so many available</u>, an advisor should take time to help his or her students choose the courses that are best suited to them.

(A) With so many available
(B) Being that there are so many available
(C) So many courses being available
(D) With there being so many courses available
(E) Because there are so many courses available

5. Very few high schools have such well-maintained athletic facilities <u>as our local school does</u>.

(A) as our local school does
(B) than our local school
(C) compared to our local school
(D) like our local school
(E) like our local school does

6. Most scientists acknowledge <u>controlled studies to be most effective for</u> examining psychological hypotheses, but recognize that many such experiments are unethical to conduct on human subjects.

(A) controlled studies to be most effective for
(B) that controlled studies being most effective as
(C) controlled studies being most effective to
(D) that controlled studies are most effective for
(E) where controlled studies are most effective for

7. Although computer chips were once relatively large and expensive to manufacture, <u>they are now smaller and more affordable</u>.

(A) they are now smaller and more affordable
(B) it has become far smaller in recent years and they are more affordable
(C) their cost and size in recent years has decreased
(D) they have become less in terms of price and size in recent years
(E) it has become far smaller and more affordable in recent years

8. <u>To ignore</u> those who challenge your thesis is more insulting than attacking them outright.

(A) To ignore
(B) In ignoring
(C) Ignoring
(D) While ignoring
(E) When you ignore

9. The new wireless technology will allow doctors to diagnose patients, update files, and <u>let them access medical research without</u> leaving their homes.

(A) let them access medical research without
(B) to access medical research without the need for
(C) access medical research and not be
(D) to access medical research without
(E) access medical research without

GO ON TO THE NEXT PAGE

9   9   9   9   9   9

10. The director of the agency was concerned that the latest advertisements will not be regarded with the lightheartedness they were intended with.

(A) will not be regarded with the light-heartedness they were intended with

(B) would not be regarded with the light-heartedness with which they had been intended

(C) would not be regarded with the light-heartedness that they were regarded to be intended with

(D) will not be regarded with the light-heartedness regarding with which they were intended

(E) would not be regarded with the light-heartedness with which they were intended to be regarded to have

11. The anthropologist was interested in studying the Maori people, particularly their history, rituals, and social relationships.

(A) particularly their history, rituals, and social relationships

(B) to study particularly their history, rituals, and social relationships

(C) particularly the study of their history, rituals, and social relationships

(D) particularly of their history and rituals in addition to their social relationships

(E) particularly studying their history, rituals, and social relationships

12. Although he was not elected as the captain, Omar has become the team leader, him being the most vocal and respected player on the team.

(A) has become the team leader, him being

(B) is being the team leader because of his being

(C) is the team leader for being

(D) has become the team leader because he is

(E) has become the team leader for having been

13. Most students thought that the new parking policy was as restrictive, if not more, than the previous policy.

(A) as restrictive, if not more, than

(B) as restrictive, if not more, as

(C) perhaps as restrictive, but perhaps more restrictive, as

(D) as restrictive as, if not more, than

(E) as restrictive as, if not more restrictive than,

14. The total revenue generated by the three drug therapies that the company unveiled this summer are not likely to be as great as their newest drug.

(A) are not likely to be as great as their newest drug

(B) are not likely to be as great as that generated by their newest drug

(C) is not likely to be as great as that generated by their newest drug

(D) is not likely to be as great as that generated by its newest drug

(E) is not likely to be as great as its newest drug

STOP

If you finish before time is called, you may check your work on this section only. Do not turn to any other section of the test.

ANSWER KEY

Critical Reading

Section 4

	COR. ANS.	DIFF. LEV.		COR. ANS.	DIFF. LEV.
1.	E	2	13.	E	4
2.	C	2	14.	C	3
3.	B	3	15.	A	3
4.	C	3	16.	B	4
5.	E	3	17.	D	4
6.	A	3	18.	C	5
7.	A	4	19.	B	3
8.	D	5	20.	B	3
9.	A	5	21.	E	3
10.	C	3	22.	D	3
11.	E	3	23.	C	4
12.	E	4	24.	E	4

Number correct

Number incorrect

Section 6

	COR. ANS.	DIFF. LEV.		COR. ANS.	DIFF. LEV.
1.	D	1	13.	D	3
2.	B	3	14.	C	4
3.	A	2	15.	E	3
4.	E	3	16.	A	4
5.	A	4	17.	C	3
6.	C	3	18.	E	5
7.	D	3	19.	B	4
8.	C	4	20.	B	3
9.	B	3	21.	B	2
10.	A	2	22.	C	3
11.	E	4	23.	A	4
12.	D	3	24.	C	4

Number correct

Number incorrect

Section 8

	COR. ANS.	DIFF. LEV.		COR. ANS.	DIFF. LEV.
1.	C	2	11.	C	4
2.	B	2	12.	D	3
3.	C	2	13.	C	2
4.	A	3	14.	E	3
5.	B	4	15.	E	4
6.	A	5	16.	B	3
7.	B	2	17.	C	3
8.	A	4	18.	B	3
9.	C	4	19.	A	4
10.	C	3			

Number correct

Number incorrect

Math

Section 2

	COR. ANS.	DIFF. LEV.		COR. ANS.	DIFF. LEV.
1.	C	1	11.	C	3
2.	A	2	12.	B	3
3.	D	2	13.	D	3
4.	E	2	14.	B	3
5.	D	3	15.	A	4
6.	B	2	16.	A	3
7.	D	3	17.	D	4
8.	A	3	18.	E	4
9.	D	3	19.	B	5
10.	C	3	20.	E	5

Number correct

Number incorrect

Section 5

Multiple-Choice Questions

	COR. ANS.	DIFF. LEV.
1.	A	1
2.	B	2
3.	A	3
4.	C	4
5.	C	3
6.	C	3
7.	E	4
8.	E	5

Student-produced Response questions

	COR. ANS.	DIFF. LEV.
9.	18	1
10.	75	2
11.	20	3
12.	140	3
13.	1/25 or 0.4	3
14.	48	4
15.	106	3
16.	108	4
17.	16/3 or 5.33	4
18.	5/6 or .833	5

Number correct (9–18)

Number incorrect

Section 7

	COR. ANS.	DIFF. LEV.		COR. ANS.	DIFF. LEV.
1.	C	1	9.	E	4
2.	D	2	10.	D	3
3.	E	2	11.	B	3
4.	A	2	12.	A	4
5.	B	2	13.	D	4
6.	D	3	14.	C	4
7.	B	4	15.	B	4
8.	D	3	16.	A	5

Number correct

Number incorrect

Writing

Section 3

	COR. ANS.	DIFF. LEV.		COR. ANS.	DIFF. LEV.		COR. ANS.	DIFF. LEV.		COR. ANS.	DIFF. LEV.
1.	B	1	11.	B	4	21.	D	4	31.	A	3
2.	D	1	12.	A	2	22.	B	3	32.	B	4
3.	E	2	13.	D	1	23.	B	3	33.	E	3
4.	C	3	14.	E	4	24.	E	3	34.	C	3
5.	A	2	15.	B	3	25.	B	3	35.	B	3
6.	E	2	16.	A	3	26.	A	3			
7.	D	4	17.	B	2	27.	D	4			
8.	C	5	18.	C	3	28.	A	3			
9.	C	4	19.	A	3	29.	C	4			
10.	D	4	20.	E	4	30.	B	3			

Number correct

Number incorrect

Section 9

	COR. ANS.	DIFF. LEV.		COR. ANS.	DIFF. LEV.
1.	C	1	11.	A	3
2.	E	2	12.	D	3
3.	D	2	13.	E	4
4.	E	2	14.	D	4
5.	A	3			
6.	D	2			
7.	A	3			
8.	C	3			
9.	E	3			
10.	B	3			

Number correct

Number incorrect

NOTE: Difficulty levels are estimates of question difficulty that range from 1 (easiest) to 5 (hardest).

SCORE CONVERSION TABLE

How to score your test

Use the answer key on the previous page to determine your raw score on each section. Your raw score on each section except Section 4 is simply the number of correct answers minus ¼ of the number of wrong answers. On Section 4, your raw score is the sum of the number of correct answers for questions 1–8 minus ¼ of the number of wrong answers for questions 1–8 plus the total number of correct answers for questions 9–18. Next, add the raw scores from Sections 3, 4, and 7 to get your Math raw score, add the raw scores from Sections 2, 5, and 8 to get your Critical Reading raw score and add the raw scores from Sections 6 and 9 to get your Writing raw score. Write the three raw scores here:

Raw Critical Reading score: _____ Raw Math score: _____ Raw Writing score: _____

Use the table below to convert these to scaled scores.

Scaled scores: Critical Reading: _____ Math: _____ Writing: _____

Raw Score	Critical Reading Scaled Score	Math Scaled Score	Writing Scaled Score	Raw Score	Critical Reading Scaled Score	Math Scaled Score	Writing Scaled Score
67	800			32	520	570	610
66	800			31	510	560	600
65	790			30	510	550	580
64	780			29	500	540	570
63	770			28	490	530	560
62	750			27	490	520	550
61	740			26	480	510	540
60	730			25	480	500	530
59	720			24	470	490	520
58	700			23	460	480	510
57	690			22	460	480	500
56	680			21	450	470	490
55	670			20	440	460	480
54	660	800		19	440	450	470
53	650	800		18	430	450	460
52	650	780		17	420	440	450
51	640	760		16	420	430	440
50	630	740		15	410	420	440
49	620	730	800	14	400	410	430
48	620	710	800	13	400	410	420
47	610	710	800	12	390	400	410
46	600	700	790	11	380	390	400
45	600	690	780	10	370	380	390
44	590	680	760	9	360	370	380
43	590	670	740	8	350	360	380
42	580	660	730	7	340	350	370
41	570	650	710	6	330	340	360
40	570	640	700	5	320	330	350
39	560	630	690	4	310	320	340
38	550	620	670	3	300	310	320
37	550	620	660	2	280	290	310
36	540	610	650	1	270	280	300
35	540	600	640	0	250	260	280
34	530	590	630	−1	230	240	270
33	520	580	620	−2 or less	210	220	250

SCORE CONVERSION TABLE FOR WRITING COMPOSITE
[ESSAY + MULTIPLE CHOICE]

Calculate your writing raw score as you did on the previous page and grade your essay from a 1 to a 6 according to the standards that follow in the detailed answer key.

Essay score: _____ Raw Writing score: _____

Use the table below to convert these to scaled scores.

Scaled score: Writing: _____

Raw Score	Essay Score 0	Essay Score 1	Essay Score 2	Essay Score 3	Essay Score 4	Essay Score 5	Essay Score 6
−2 or less	200	230	250	280	310	340	370
−1	210	240	260	290	320	360	380
0	230	260	280	300	340	370	400
1	240	270	290	320	350	380	410
2	250	280	300	330	360	390	420
3	260	290	310	340	370	400	430
4	270	300	320	350	380	410	440
5	280	310	330	360	390	420	450
6	290	320	340	360	400	430	460
7	290	330	340	370	410	440	470
8	300	330	350	380	410	450	470
9	310	340	360	390	420	450	480
10	320	350	370	390	430	460	490
11	320	360	370	400	440	470	500
12	330	360	380	410	440	470	500
13	340	370	390	420	450	480	510
14	350	380	390	420	460	490	520
15	350	380	400	430	460	500	530
16	360	390	410	440	470	500	530
17	370	400	420	440	480	510	540
18	380	410	420	450	490	520	550
19	380	410	430	460	490	530	560
20	390	420	440	470	500	530	560
21	400	430	450	480	510	540	570
22	410	440	460	480	520	550	580
23	420	450	470	490	530	560	590
24	420	460	470	500	540	570	600
25	430	460	480	510	540	580	610
26	440	470	490	520	550	590	610
27	450	480	500	530	560	590	620
28	460	490	510	540	570	600	630
29	470	500	520	550	580	610	640
30	480	510	530	560	590	620	650
31	490	520	540	560	600	630	660
32	500	530	550	570	610	640	670
33	510	540	550	580	620	650	680
34	510	550	560	590	630	660	690
35	520	560	570	600	640	670	700
36	530	560	580	610	650	680	710
37	540	570	590	620	660	690	720
38	550	580	600	630	670	700	730
39	560	600	610	640	680	710	740
40	580	610	620	650	690	720	750
41	590	620	640	660	700	730	760
42	600	630	650	680	710	740	770
43	610	640	660	690	720	750	780
44	620	660	670	700	740	770	800
45	640	670	690	720	750	780	800
46	650	690	700	730	770	800	800
47	670	700	720	750	780	800	800
48	680	720	730	760	800	800	800
49	680	720	730	760	800	800	800

Detailed Answer Key

Section 1

The following essay received 12 points out of a possible 12. It demonstrates *clear and consistent mastery* in that it

- develops an insightful point of view on the topic
- demonstrates exemplary critical thinking
- uses very effective examples, reasons, and other evidence to support its thesis
- is consistently focused, coherent, and well-organized
- demonstrates skillful and effective use of language and sentence structure
- is largely (but not necessarily completely) free of grammatical and usage errors

> The liberally educated person is one who is able to resist the easy and preferred answers, not because he is obstinate but because he knows others worthy of consideration.
>
> —Allan Bloom

Assignment: **What is one important "easy and preferred answer" that we should resist? That is, what dangerous misconception do people commonly hold**? Write an essay in which you answer this question and support your position logically with examples from literature, the arts, history, politics, science and technology, current events, or your experience or observation.

SAMPLE STUDENT ESSAY

One of the most dangerous misconceptions that people hold today is the idea that our enemies are fundamentally different from us. It is easy, to a certain extent, to understand how such a belief comes about. Most human societies must kill in order to survive, but must at the same time prohibit particular kinds of killing. Throughout our history, humans have been meat-eaters, and so must kill and eat animals in order to thrive (the minority of vegetarians notwithstanding). Also, societies must often defend themselves against violent enemies, necessitating the occasional use of deadly force. On the other hand, civilized societies must prohibit most killing within their own ranks, so that their populations do not die out or suffer needlessly.

So how do humans deal with this dichotomy: the need to kill, at least occasionally, to survive, and the need to prohibit killing within its ranks? Simply, humans have developed the concepts of "us" and "them." It is okay to kill and eat animals because they do not have the value of humans. Perhaps, too, a society may justify the killing of animals by adopting a belief system that says that animals are gifts to humans from a divine being or beings.

In much the same way, humans are inclined to put their enemies in the category of "other," that is, less than human, or to believe that a divine being has given them permission to kill those enemies. Paradoxically, those religious systems are also very likely to have severe restrictions against killing other human beings. In practice, most cultures regard these as restrictions merely against killing "their own kind." However, this type of thinking is counterproductive to the goal of building more just and functional societies. If one society can easily categorize another as an "enemy" and thereby reduce its foes to the status of animal, then the concept of universal human rights is abolished.

We see the dangers inherent in denying the humanity of our enemies in the United States today. Although the American Constitution champions the concept of inalienable rights that are due to all human beings, the United States Senate is actively engaged in undermining those rights. The right of habeas corpus, that is, the right of a person in custody to seek a hearing to determine whether or not he or she is being held justly, is a cornerstone of the United States Constitution. It is regarded as a fundamental element of a just society. Yet the Senate is seeking to eliminate that right for foreign detainees captured in the "war on terror." In other words, the mere suspicion of terrorism—not proof, but suspicion—is evidently reason enough to reduce a human being to the status of an animal. This heinous distinction of "us" versus "them" will surely have dire consequences for the United States, who will rightfully be seen as being grossly hypocritical on the matter of human rights.

Even beyond the trampling of human rights, the "us" versus "them" distinction is not even as useful in wartime as it may seem at first glance, because to defeat our enemy, we must understand our enemy. If we begin with the assumption that your enemy lacks human intelligence, desires and motivations, then we risk severely underestimating his ability. Therefore, if the United States continues down this dangerous path, it runs the risk of losing not only the moral war but the actual war.

Reader's comments

This is an exceptionally well-reasoned and well-organized essay supporting the thesis that "it is a dangerous misconception to believe that our enemies are fundamentally different from us." The author demonstrates a strong understanding of the origins of a belief as well as its effects. The author consistently focuses on the dangers of reducing other human beings "to the status of animal," and uses the example of *habeas corpus* to excellent effect. The author also demonstrates strong facility and effective variety in diction and sentence structure. Its consistent critical reasoning and effective use of language merits a 12.

Section 2

1. C

$$3(m+n) + 3 = 15$$
Subtract 3: $\quad 3(m+n) = 12$
Divide by 3: $\quad m+n = 4$

---

2. A Recall the basic rate formula: *work = rate × time*. Since the rate is *r* pages per minute and the time is *m* minutes, the total amount of work is *rm* pages. It may also help you to give *r* and *m* simple numerical values, like 4 and 5, respectively, and calculate the numerical result, which is 20 pages, and confirm that choice (A) gives that result.

---

3. D Since there are 180° in a line, $a+b+c = 180$.

$$a+b = 120$$
$$\underline{b+c = 100}$$
Add equations: $\quad a + 2b + c = 220$
Subtract: $\quad \underline{-(a+b+c = 180)}$
$$b = 40$$

Alternately, you can solve for *a* and *c* separately:

$$a+b+c = 180$$
$$\underline{b+c = 100}$$
Subtract equations: $\quad a = 80$
$$a+b+c = 180$$
$$\underline{a+b = 120}$$
Subtract equations: $\quad c = 60$
Substitute into $\quad a+b+c = 180$
$$80 + b + 60 = 180$$
Simplify: $\quad 140 + b = 180$
Subtract 140: $\quad b = 40$

---

4. E

$$6^n \times 6^4 = 6^{12}$$
Simplify: $\quad 6^{n+4} = 6^{12}$
Equate exponents: $\quad n + 4 = 12$
Subtract 4: $\quad n = 8$

---

5. D This question simply requires you to solve for *b*.

$$4x + b = x + 2$$
Subtract 4x: $\quad b = -3x + 2$
Commute: $\quad b = 2 + -3x = 2 - 3x$

---

6. B In 1995, 200 cars valued at $15,000 and 100 cars valued at $25,000 were sold, for a total value of (200)($15,000) + (100)($25,000) = $5,500,000. In 2005, 200 cars valued at $25,000 and 200 cars valued at $35,000 were sold, for a total value of (200)($25,000) + (200)($35,000) = $12,000,000. The difference is $12,000,000 – $5,500,000 = $6,500,000.

---

7. D An isosceles triangle always contains two angles of equal measure. One of the angles has a measure greater than 95°, but neither of the other angles can measure more than 95°, because the sum of all three angles must be exactly 180°. The only way for this to be true is for the other two angles to be equal. If you choose a value of, say, 96° for the largest angle (of course, any value between 95° and 180° will do), and say that the others each measure *x* degrees, then

$$x + x + 96 = 180$$
Subtract 96: $\quad 2x = 84$
Divide by 2: $\quad x = 42$

Now notice that the only choice that is true is (D) $x < 42.5$.

---

8. A If *m* gives a remainder of 2 when divided by 7, then *m* must be 2 more than a multiple of 7. Choose any such value for *m*, like 2, 9, or 16. Then simply multiply this number by 4 and calculate the remainder when it is divided by 7. In each case, the result is the same: 4(2) = 8, 4(9) = 36, and 4(16) = 64 all give a remainder of 1 when divided by 7.

---

9. D You might start by choosing simple values for *a* and *b*, like 6 and 5. (Always make sure that any numbers you choose satisfy the conditions in the problem—in this case, that *a* is a multiple of 3 and *b* is odd.) With these values, only choices (C) 6 + 5 = 11 and (D) 2(6) + 5 = 17 yield odd numbers, so the others can be eliminated. Trying new values like *a* = 3 and *b* = 7 shows that only choice (D) must always be odd. Alternately, you may notice that 2*a* must always be even, since it is a multiple of 2. When an even number is added to an odd number, *b*, the result must always be odd, so 2*a* + *b* will always be odd.

---

10. C When a point is reflected over the *x*-axis, it keeps its *x*-coordinate, but "negates" its *y*-coordinate. When it is reflected over the *y*-axis, it keeps its *y*-coordinate but negates its *x*-coordinate. The reflections look like this:

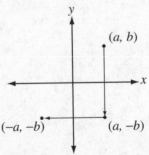

Therefore, the final position is $(-a, -b)$.

11. **C** The formula for the volume of a right cylinder is given in the Reference Information on the first page of every math section: $V = \pi r^2 h$. (Remember that a "right" cylinder is simply a cylinder in which the sides are perpendicular to the bases.) Therefore, a cylinder with radius 1 and height 1 has a volume of $\pi(1)^2(1) = \pi \approx 3.14$. The formula for the volume of a rectangular solid, which is also given in the Reference Information, is $V = lwh$. Therefore, the volumes of the boxes described in the choices are (A) 1, (B) 2, (C) 3, (D) 4 and (E) 6. The closest to π is (C) 3.

12. **B** Since the nth term is $3n^2 - n$, then the 3rd term is $3(3)^2 - 3 = 24$ and the 10th term is $3(10)^2 - 10 = 290$, and $290 - 24 = 266$.

13. **D** As this diagram shows, the maximum number of points of intersection is 8.

14. **B** Examining sample values from among the choices should make it clear that the inequality is only true when x takes a value between -1 and 0. For instance, if $x = -.5$, then $x^2 = (-.5)^2 = .25$ and $x^3 = (-.5)^3 = -.125$, and therefore $x < x^3 < x^2$.

15. **A** Simply "expand" and FOIL the expression to get $(m + n)^2 = (m + n)(m + n) = m^2 + 2mn + n^2$
Now simply substitute the values of the expressions that you are given. $(m + n)^2 = m^2 + 2mn + n^2$

Substitute:	$18 = m^2 + 2(4) + n^2$
Subtract 8:	$10 = m^2 + n^2$

16. **A** An isosceles triangle has two equal sides. If two of the sides have lengths of 5 and 12, then the only possible triangle is a 12–12–5 triangle. A 5–5–12 triangle is impossible, because the sum of any two sides of a triangle must be greater than the third side. (If you don't immediately see why, then just take three sticks and cut them to lengths of 5 in., 5 in. and 12 in., then try to construct a triangle with them. It can't be done!) Therefore the only possible perimeter of this triangle is $12 + 12 + 5 = 29$.

17. **D** Since the dial is cyclical and contains only the six digits 0–5, it indicates the remainder when the digital counter reading is divided by 6. If the digital counter reads 1000, then the dial will indicate the remainder when 1000 is divided by 6. You can find this remainder through long division, or you can use your calculator. $1000 \div 6 = 166.66 \ldots$, and $6 \times .66 \ldots = 4$, so the dial reads 4.

18. **E** Since the ratio by weight of raisins to dates is 7 to 3, then 10 pounds of the mix would contain 7 pounds of raisins and 3 pounds of dates. In other words, 7/10 of the mix, by weight, is raisins. Therefore, in 7 pounds of the mix $(7/10)(7) = 4.9$ pounds is raisins.

19. **B** The key fact in this problem is that m and n must be integers. Start by considering simple integer values for n. Notice that if $n = 1$, then $m = 1 - 2/1 - 2/1 = -3$, which is an integer. Notice, also, that if n is greater than 1 or less than -1, then $2/n^2$ will not be an integer, and so m will not be an integer. The only other integer value of n that corresponds to an integer value of m is $n = -1$, which means $m = -1 - 2/(-1) - 2/(-1)^2 = -1 + 2 - 2 = -1$, which is an integer.
Therefore, the only possible values of m are -3 and -1.

20. **E** You can approach this question numerically or algebraically. To take the numerical approach, consider simple values for k, x, and p. For instance, $k = 3$, $x = 12$, and $p = 1$. This means that 3 girls originally agreed to split \$12, and so should have contributed \$4 apiece. But then 1 more girl joined and so the \$12 would have been split 4 ways, or \$3 apiece, a savings of \$1 per girl. Now plug the values in to each choice and see which gives a value of 1. The only choice that works is (E).
Alternately, you can take the algebraic approach. If k girls must raise a total of x dollars, then each must raise x/k dollars. If p more girls join, then $k + p$ girls must raise x dollars, or $x/(k + p)$ apiece. Now calculate the difference:
$$\frac{x}{k} - \frac{x}{k+p} = \frac{x(k+p)}{k(k+p)} - \frac{kx}{k(k+p)} = \frac{kx+px-kx}{k(k+p)} = \frac{px}{k(k+p)}$$

Section 3

1. **B** Since the pronoun here refers to *employees*, it should be the plural *they* rather than the singular *he* or *she*. Choice (D) uses the plural pronoun *them*, but it also uses the pronoun *it*, which lacks a clear antecedent.

2. **D** The phrase *for the purpose of investigating* is awkward and unidiomatic. The standard idiom is *to investigate*. The phrases *investigate on* and *investigate after* are also unidiomatic.

3. **E** The sentence begins with a modifying phrase based on the participle *worried*. The subject of this participle must be the subject of the main clause, but the subject of the main clause is *Helena's concern*. It is illogical to suggest that a *concern* is *worried*. The only logical subject of this participle is *Helena*, which is the subject in (C) and (E). Choice (C) is incorrect, however, because it is awkward and contains the unidiomatic phrase *concerned towards*.

4. **C** The original sentence lacks a verb. Both (C) and (D) correct this problem, but (C) is far more concise and effective.

5. **A** The original sentence is the most concise, idiomatic, and effective.

6. **E** The phrase *determine about* is unidiomatic, as are *determine regarding* and *determine for*. The sentence is most effective if the needless preposition is simply eliminated. Choice (C) is grammatically sound, but it is logically nonsensical, since *pay* cannot *qualify for duties*.

7. **D** The original sentence contains a comma splice. Clearly, the two clauses contrast each other, so the conjunction *but* is clearly appropriate. Choice (B) is incorrect because the conjunction *but* cannot be used with a semicolon. Choice (C) is wrong because the phrase *in cricket* is misplaced.

8. **C** The modifying phrase that begins the sentence must modify the subject of the main clause. But the subject of the main clause is *Athens*, which cannot be *skeptical*. The only logical subject is *philosophers*, which is provided only by choice (C).

9. **C** The subject of the sentence is the singular noun *debate*, so the verb *have* is conjugated incorrectly, and should be changed to *has*. The sentence also contains a list which requires parallel phrasing: *the origins* and *the merits* should be combined with *the legal authority*. The only choice that corrects both problems is choice (C).

10. **D** The participle *excited* modifies the subject of the main clause of the sentence, but it is illogical to say that a *decision* is *excited*. The only logical subject is *Kyra*, but (B) is awkward and unidiomatic, so the best choice is clearly (D).

11. **B** The three ideas in the original sentence are co-ordinated awkwardly. An effective complex sentence must coordinate the ideas logically and concisely.

Choice (B) is concise, logical and effective. The participial phrases are very awkward in choice (C), the list in choice (D) is awkward and not parallel, and the gerund phrase at the end of choice (E) is awkward and illogical.

12. **A** The subject *proposals* is plural, therefore the verb should be changed to *are*.

13. **D** The modifier *civil* modifies the verb *conducted*, and therefore should be the adverb *civilly*.

14. **E** The original sentence is correct.

15. **B** The conjunction *but* is redundant, and should be eliminated, because the sentence already uses the contrasting conjunction *while*.

16. **A** The correct past participle of *to take* is *taken*, not *took*.

17. **B** The preposition *about* is unidiomatic. One refers *to* a theory, not *about* a theory.

18. **C** The main subject of the sentence is the singular noun *pace*, so the verb should be changed to *is*.

19. **A** The phrase *every living creature* is singular, so the phrase in (A) should be changed to *owes its*.

20. **E** The original sentence is correct.

21. **D** The comparison in the sentence is not parallel. How hard it is *to teach* one thing should be compared to how hard it is *to teach* another thing. Therefore choice (D) should be changed from *teaching* to *to teach*.

22. **B** The pronoun *on* is unidiomatic. The correct idiom is *preoccupied with*.

23. **B** Since the phrase *Jose and I* is the object of the preposition *to*, it must take the objective case *Jose and me*.

24. **E** The original sentence is correct.

25. **B** The subject of the sentence is *varieties*, so the verb should be changed to *were*.

26. **A** If Cara's race times are improving, they cannot be *constant*. This word should be changed to the adverb *constantly*, because it modifies the adjective *improving*.

27. **D** The word *indecisive* means *unable to make a decision*. Its use in this context is illogical. An amount of time cannot be *indecisive*, but it can be *indefinite*.

28. **A** The first two items in the list are simple nouns, so to maintain parallelism the phrase in choice (A) should be eliminated.

29. **C** The comparison between the *project* to *the other students* is illogical, so the phrase in (C) should be changed to *those of the other students*.

30. **B** The sentence is defining two terms, and choice (B) does so most effectively and concisely. Choice (A) uses the pronoun *it* without a clear antecedent, and uses two awkward participial phrases. Choice (C) is wordy and uses the pronoun *it* without a clear antecedent. Choices (D) and (E) are both unparallel and awkward.

31. **A** Since the paragraph is talking about general trends in behavior, the subjects and objects of discussion should all be in the third person. The pronoun *you* is therefore inappropriate and should be changed to *their children*.

32. **B** This sentence is best inserted after sentence 3 because it is a logical introduction to a discussion of specific uses of incentives, which is presented in sentences 4 through 8.

33. **E** The original sentence is wordy and uses the unidiomatic phrase *in the way like*. The most effective and idiomatic option is (E). Choice (B) is needlessly wordy, and choices (C) and (D) contain runons.

34. **C** The pronoun *they* has no clear antecedent in the original phrasing. The same error is repeated in choices (A), (B), (D), and (E). Choice (C), although not the most concise, is the most effective and grammatically correct.

35. **B** The inserted sentence follows a sentence discussing the reasons that a particular incentive program was ineffective, and precedes the concluding sentence of the passage. Therefore, the most effective sentence to insert here provides a concluding thought to the discussion of the incentive program, which choice (B) does. Since the paragraph discusses the reasons for the program's ineffectiveness, sentences (A) and (D) are illogical. Since the passage does not discuss the relative value of rewards and punishments, choice (C) is inappropriate. Sentence (E) does not convey any relevant information to the discussion at all.

Section 4

1. **E** Saying that *the earth's magnetic polarity has switched back and forth* is equivalent to saying that this polarity has *fluctuated* (varied irregularly). *correlations* = relationships between two variables

2. **C** The sentence indicates that scientists *disagree* about an issue. One position on the issue is that this particular bird behavior *is learned*. The opposing view must be that this behavior is *not* learned, and therefore was simply instinctive. Choice (C) *innate* means *present at birth*. *impassive* = lacking emotion; *pragmatic* = concerned with practical matters

3. **B** Since doctors try to cure diseases, it would be considered a success for them to *stop or slow* the spread of tuberculosis. They would be concerned, however, about *dangerous* strains arising. *marginalizing* = rendering irrelevant; *innocuous* = harmless; *virulent* = dangerous; *obscuring* = hiding from view; *indifferent* = uncaring; *imperiling* = putting in danger

4. **C** The first missing word represents something that is *carefully formulated* and is found in the scientific method, while the second missing word represents something that is *wishful* and found in *pseudoscience* (fake science). Since *concessions* (reluctant agreements) and *hunches* (intuitive guesses) are not part of the scientific method, choices (B) and (E) can be eliminated. Since *divergences* (departures from norms) and *restrictions* are not integral to pseudoscience and are not *wishful*, choices (A) and (D) can be eliminated. *conjectures* = guesses; *paradigms* = a set of assumptions and methods for solving problems or construing reality

5. **E** Since the two lectures are contrasted using parallel language, and since the first lecture is viewed negatively and the second positively, the first missing word must be the opposite of *easy to understand*, and the second missing word must be the opposite of *irrelevant*. *obscure* = little-known; *vague* = unclear; *lucid* = clear; *pertinent* = relevant; *convoluted* = confusing; *petty* = concerned with trivial matters; *concise* = brief and to the point; *esoteric* = intended to be understood only by a select group; *abstruse* = difficult to understand; *germane* = relevant

6. **A** Ian's argument was *thoroughly refuted*, although it *seemed plausible at first*. Therefore it was an example of *sophistry* (plausible but fallacious argumentation). *solicitousness* = anxious concern or eagerness; *acumen* = keen skill; *substantiation* = verifiable support for a claim; *resolution* = commitment

7. **A** One who has *read dozens of philosophical treatises* is clearly *well-read*, and such a person would likely have *thoroughly* researched new developments. *erudite* = well-educated; *assiduously* = with vigor and attention to detail; *contrite* = remorseful; *cerebral* = thoughtful and intelligent; *stoic* = deliberately unemotional; *lackadaisically* = inattentively and without energy

8. **D** Someone who seeks *a greater connection to the world outside* would likely *bemoan* (lament) the *insularity* (social isolation) of an island community. The *establishment of international phone service* would likely *appease* (ease the concerns of) those citizens. *obstinacy* = stubbornness; *precociousness* = characterized by early maturity; *obsequiousness* = servility; *insinuation* = subtle implication

9. **A** Passage 1 conveys a cynical tone in criticizing the *narcissism* (line 10) of the Baby Boomers and by mocking their self-centered point of view: *History be damned; if it didn't happen between 1960 and 1980, it's irrelevant* (lines 15–17). Passage 2 does not convey any such cynicism, and is in fact a uniformly positive depiction of Kennedy.

10. **C** This question is posed incredulously, implying that Kennedy should not *be perceived as greater than George Washington*. Therefore, the author believes that Kennedy's high ranking in polls is undeserved.

11. **E** This sentence discusses the good work that Kennedy did for *the rights of minorities, the poor, the very old and the very young*, thereby indicating that Kennedy supported policies that benefited divergent groups.

12. **E** Both passages agree that Kennedy was in touch with the unique qualities of the era in which he governed. Passage 1 states that he *was the first president to make effective use of television* (lines 18–20) and was held in high esteem by the Baby Boomers, and Passage 2 states that he was *very much a man of his time* (lines 22–23) and fought for the rights of many people who were suffering during that era.

13. **E** In saying that government's *one permanent object is to oppress* superior people, the author means that government's *goal* is to oppress them.

14. **C** The passage indicates that an *aristocratic* (line 4) government works *against the man who is superior in fact* (line 6), and that a *democratic* (line 7) government works against *both* those who are superior in law and those who are superior in fact. It then goes on to say that governments *combat originality* (line 13) among their citizens.

15. **A** In saying that *the historical testimony runs the other way* (line 29), the author is saying that this testimony contradicts the idea that *the new government would be any better than the old one* (lines 27–28). Therefore, such testimony must be about the effect of revolutions in trying to create better societies.

16. **B** Passage 1 states *that material progress was due, not to the virtues of their new government, but to the lavishness of nature* (lines 52–54). In other words, the government succeeded by the benefit of natural resources.

17. **D** The author of Passage 1 states that the ideal government *lets the individual alone* (lines 58–59) and is therefore characterized by its unintrusiveness.

18. **C** Passage 2 contends that the *revolutionary situation* did not include any *mass poverty ... seething social discontent* or *grinding oppression* (lines 69–71). It did, however, include *a great deal of jealousy* (line 78).

19. **B** These historians *desperately sought to find...mass poverty...seething social discontent...* and *grinding oppression* in order to explain the causes of the American Revolution. Therefore, they believed that political upheaval is caused by social discontent.

20. **B** In saying that *state and magnificence, the natural attendant on great riches, are conspicuous among this people*, the visitor is saying that the citizens of South Carolina conspicuously flaunt their wealth through ceremonious pomp. The word *state* most nearly means *pomp*.

21. **E** The quotation from Gadsden makes the point that *white society in South Carolina was comparatively equal* (lines 123–124). The distinctions among *the farmer and rich planter, the mechanic and the rich merchant ...* do not exist in reality.

22. **D** Both authors would agree that American colonists benefited from material prosperity. Passage 1 states that *material progress [in the colonies] was due, not to the virtues of their new government, but to the lavishness of nature* (lines 52–54), and Passage 2 states that *the colonists' growing prosperity contributed to [their sense that they] were capable of ordering their own reality* (lines 71–74).

23. **C** Passage 1 states that *almost inevitably [the citizen] comes to the conclusion that the government he lives in is dishonest, insane and intolerable, and so, if he is romantic, he tries to change it* (lines 19–23). In other words, those who change the government, the revolutionaries, are motivated by romanticism or political idealism. Passage 2 states that the revolutionaries

were motivated by *jealousy and touchiness everywhere* (line 76). The revolutionaries *were acutely nervous about their prosperity and the liberty that seemed to make it possible* (lines 78–79). In other words, they were concerned about losing their wealth.

24. E In saying that American colonists lived *under the British hoof* (lines 54–55), the author of Passage 1 is saying that the British were guilty of *oppressing* the colonists. Therefore, *hoof* is being used as a metaphor for *oppression*.

Section 5

1. A

$$4m - 2 = m + 7$$

Subtract m: $3m - 2 = 7$

Add 2: $3m = 9$

Divide by 3: $m = 3$

2. B Since l is a line, and the measure of a straight angle is 180°,

$$140 + 2x = 180$$

Subtract 140: $2x = 40$

Divide by 2: $x = 20$

3. A

$$\frac{3}{8} \text{ of } m \text{ is } 48$$

Translate: $\frac{3}{8}m = 48$

Multiply by 5/3: $\left(\frac{5}{3}\right)\frac{3}{8}m = \left(\frac{5}{3}\right)48$

Simplify: $\frac{5}{8}m = 80$

4. C Since each term is the previous term divided by 3, $a_2 = 54$, $a_3 = 18$, $a_4 = 6$, $a_5 = 2$, $a_6 = 2/3$. Therefore the first term that is not an integer is a_6.

5. C $\sqrt{n} \times \sqrt{2} = \sqrt{2n}$ is an integer only when $2n$ is a perfect square. The only choice that is not half of a perfect square is (C) 12. You should check to see that the other four choices are half of a perfect square, and so make $\sqrt{2n}$ an integer.

6. C The only way to prevent any of the vertices from touching at least two black faces is to paint the cube so that the two white faces are adjacent, as in the diagram below. (All unseen faces are black.)

Notice that here the two vertices that are circled touch only one black face. All of the others touch at least two black faces. Since there are 8 vertices in all, the minimum number of vertices that could be shared by two or more black faces is $8 - 2 = 6$.

7. E If y varies directly as x, then $y = kx$ for some constant k. Another way to express this relationship is to say $y/x = k$, that is, the ratio of y to x is always the same value.

Therefore, $\dfrac{8}{a} = \dfrac{12}{a+10}$

Cross-multiply: $8a + 80 = 12a$

Subtract $8a$: $80 = 4a$

Divide by 4: $20 = a$

8. E The original function is a line containing the points $(0, 6)$ and $(4, 0)$. Notice that the slope of the line (*rise/run*) or $(y_2 - y_1)/(x_2 - x_1)$ is $(0 - 6)/(4 - 0) = -6/4 = -3/2$. If the function is multiplied by -2, the slope is also multiplied by -2, and $(-3/2)(-2) = 3$.

9. 18 The number that is 50% greater than x is $(x + .5x) = 1.5x$. If $x + 9$ is 50% greater than x,

$$x + 9 = 1.5x$$

Subtract x: $9 = .5x$

Multiply by 2: $18 = x$

10. 75 Since 60 seconds = 1 minute, there are $5(60) = 300$ seconds in 5 minutes. Recall the basic rate formula: *work = rate × time*.

$$\frac{5 \text{ pages}}{20 \text{ seconds}} \times 300 \text{ seconds} = \frac{1500}{20} \text{pages} = 75 \text{ pages}$$

11. 20

     5 is $x\%$ of 15

Translate: $5 = x\%(15)$

Multiply by 4: $20 = x\%(60)$

12. 140 Since the measures of the four angles in a quadrilateral must have a sum of 360°, and the ratio of these angles is 2:3:6:7, then

$$2x + 3x + 6x + 7x = 360$$

Simplify: $18x = 360$

Divide by 18: $x = 20$

Therefore the four angles have measures of $2(20) = 40°$, $3(20) = 60°$, $6(20) = 120°$, and $7(20) = 140°$.

13. 1/25 or .04 You can approach this question numerically or algebraically. To approach it numerically, choose simple values for a, b, and c that satisfy the conditions. For instance, if you choose $c = 100$, then since b is 1/10 of c, $b = (1/10)(100) = 10$, and since a is 2/5 of b, $a = (2/5)(10) = 4$. Therefore, $a/c = 4/100 = 1/25$ or .04. To approach it algebraically, notice that you can express both a and c in terms of b. Since a is 2/5 of

b, $a = (2/5)b$, and since b is 1/10 of c, $c = 10b$. Therefore

$$\frac{a}{c} = \frac{\frac{2}{5}b}{10b} = \frac{\frac{2}{5}}{10} = \frac{2}{50} = \frac{1}{25} = .04$$

---

14. 48 Anytime a geometry question does not include a diagram, draw one. You are told that a triangle and a rectangle share the same base, and that the triangle has an area 6 times the area of the rectangle. Therefore, your diagram should look something like this:

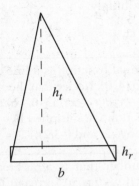

It should be pretty clear that the height of the triangle must be much greater than the height of the rectangle in order for the area of the triangle to be 6 times as great. To be more precise, set up an equation using the formulas for the area of a rectangle and the area of a triangle.

The triangle area is 6 times the rectangle area.

Translate:　　　　　$(bh_t)/2 = 6bh_r$
Multiply by 2:　　　$bh_t = 12bh_r$
Divide by b:　　　　$h_t = 12h_r$
Substitute $h_r = 4$:　$h_t = 12(4) = 48$

---

15. 106 The median of a set of numbers is the value of the "middle" number. If the median of a set of 5 integers is 10, and if the greatest number is 5 times the least number, then the set of integers, listed in increasing order, can be expressed as

$$n, p, 10, r, 5n$$

Since n and p are different integers, and since they must be less than 10, the greatest values they can have are 8 and 9, respectively. This means that the greatest integer in the set is $5(8) = 40$. So now the set is

$$8, 9, 10, r, 40$$

In order to maximize the sum, r must be chosen to be as large as possible, but since it must be an integer less than 40, its greatest possible value is 39. The greatest possible sum of these numbers, then, is $8 + 9 + 10 + 39 + 40 = 106$.

---

16. 108 Recall the relationships among the sides of a 30°–60°–90° triangle, which is always given in the

reference information at the beginning of each math section of the SAT. If you apply this relationship to the diagram, you can determine the length of each side. Write these values into the diagram as shown here:

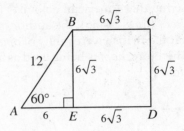

The area of the square is therefore $(6\sqrt{3})(6\sqrt{3}) = 36 \times 3 = 108$.

---

17. 16/3 or 5.33 Call the nth term of this sequence a_n. If each term after the first is equal to the previous term times k, then the first five terms can be expressed as

$$a_1, a_2 = ka_1, a_3 = k^2a_1, a_4 = k^3a_1, a_5 = k^4a_1$$

Since the 3rd term is 12 and the 5th term is 27, $k^2a_1 = 12$ and $k^4a_1 = 27$. You can divide these two equations to solve for k:

$$\frac{k^4a_1}{k^2a_1} = \frac{27}{12}$$

Simplify:　　　　　　　$k^2 = \frac{9}{4}$

Take the square root:　$k = \frac{3}{2}$

Substituting this value into the equation for the third term, you can solve for the first term:

$$k^2a_1 = \left(\frac{3}{2}\right)^2 a_1 = 12$$

Simplify:　　　　　$\frac{9}{4}a_1 = 12$

Multiply by 4/9:　$a_1 = 16/3 = 5.33$

---

18. 5/6 or .833 Since the question provides information about the areas of the rectangle and the triangle, and since the formulas for these areas involve the base and height of each, it is best to start by examining these lengths. Notice that the rectangle has base b and height c, and the triangle has base $b–a$ and height c. Write these into the diagram:

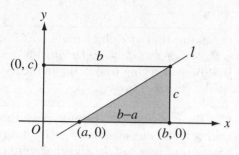

Recall the formulas for the area of a triangle and the area of a rectangle. Since the area of the shaded triangle is $\frac{2}{5}$ the area of the rectangle,

$$\frac{1}{2}(b-a)c = \frac{2}{5}bc$$

To simplify, multiply by 10:	$5(b-a)c = 4bc$
To simplify, divide by c:	$5(b-a) = 4b$
Distribute:	$5b - 5a = 4b$
Subtract $4b$:	$b - 5a = 0$
Add $5a$:	$b = 5a$
Recall that you are given the fact that	$2b = 3c$
Substitue $b = 5a$:	$2(5a) = 3c$
Simplify:	$10a = 3c$
Divide by 3:	$(10/3)a = c$

Now recall that you are trying to find the slope of the line, which is *rise/run* $= c/(b – a)$.

$$\frac{c}{b-a}$$

Substitute $c = (10/3)a$ and $b = 5a$:

$$\frac{\frac{10}{3}a}{(5a-a)} = \frac{\frac{10}{3}a}{4a} = \frac{10}{3} \times \frac{1}{4} = \frac{10}{12} = \frac{5}{6} = .833$$

Whew!
Obviously, a numerical approach would likely be easier here. Since you are told that $2b = 3c$, it is a good idea to start by choosing simple values for b and c that work in this equation, like $b = 6$ and $c = 4$. Of course, a is still an unknown, but one unknown is better than three! Write this information into the diagram:

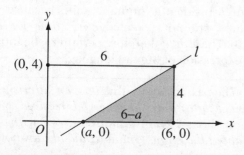

Since the area of the shaded triangle is $\frac{2}{5}$ the area of the rectangle,

$$\frac{1}{2}(6-a)4 = \frac{2}{5}(4)(6)$$

Simplify:	$12 - 2a = 9.6$
Subtract 9.6:	$2.4 - 2a = 0$
Add $2a$:	$2.4 = 2a$
Divide by 2:	$1.2 = a$

Therefore the base of the triangle is $6 – 1.2 = 4.8$, and the slope of the line is $4/4.8 = .833 = 5/6$.

Section 6

1. **D** A philosophy that *never achiev[es] a clear and consistent form* can be said to be *nebulous* (vague). *indisputable* = beyond question; *homogenous* = uniform

2. **B** This sentence is somewhat ambiguous. Either she was *disappointed* by the evidence because it did not *support* her theory, or she *was pleased with* the evidence because it did not *contradict* her theory. The only choice that fits either of these interpretations is (B). *refute* = disprove; *substantiate* = provide substantial evidence for; *chasten* = correct by punishment; *bolstered* = supported

3. **A** An animal that travels so far in a given year is certainly *itinerant* (wandering from place to place). *indigenous* = native to a particular region; *subdued* = calm; *nocturnal* = night-active; *arboreal* = pertaining to trees

4. **E** Since Carlos believes that politicians are motivated by *selfish impulses*, he is *cynical about* their motives. He is so cynical that he doubts the motivation of even the politicians' most seemingly *altruistic* (selfless) initiatives. *skeptical* = inclined to doubting; *contemptible* = worthy of scorn; *sanguine* = cheerfully optimistic; *magnanimous* = generous; *disparaging* = criticizing; *callous* = emotionally hardened; *immaterial* = irrelevant; *cynical* = inclined to believe the worst about human motives

5. **A** The first word is clearly an adjective describing a *good literary agent*. Without the quality that this describes, the agent would think that some writing was *original and competent* when in fact it was not. This quality, then, must be *discernment* (the ability to distinguish good from bad), and writing that is not *original* is *derivative* (deriving from clichéd sources or formulas). *gauche* = socially

awkward; *sublime* = majestic; *obstinate* = stubborn; *proficient* = skilled; *diligent* = hard-working; *servile* = acting like a servant; *pedestrian* = ordinary

6. **C** This passage describes how *radiological methods* are used to *deduce the age of mineral samples* (lines 1–2). Therefore it is explaining a scientific technique.

7. **D** The passage states that *one problematic aspect of this dating method is that some of the stable element may have already been present when the mineral was formed, and therefore was not the result of radioactive decay* (lines 11–15). In other words, the technique is less reliable when the rock originally contained samples of the element into which the radioactive element will decay.

8. **C** In saying that *his lot may be heart-rending,* the author is saying that his *fate* may inspire pity.

9. **B** The paragraph is making the point that human beings, even tragic heroes, as depicted by Shakespeare, are *not contemptible* (line 14). The passage suggests that *cynics* are those who think otherwise about humanity, but who would be dissuaded from this belief by reading Shakespeare's tragedies.

10. **A** The paragraph conveys a clear tone of *reflective anticipation* by describing the *breathless pause at the threshold of a long passage* (lines 9–10) and the *appointed task of both our existences to be carried out* (lines 12–13).

11. **E** The narrator states *that there must have been some glare* (line 16) because it took him a while to notice *something which did away with the solemnity of perfect solitude* (lines 21–22), which turned out to be a ship in the distance. Therefore, the *glare* is mentioned to highlight the fact that the narrator did not see the ship's masthead immediately.

12. **D** The passage states that *in consequence of certain events ... I had been appointed to the command only a fortnight before* (lines 54–57). In other words, these events led to his being chosen as captain.

13. **D** The narrator says that *if all the truth must be told, I was somewhat of a stranger to myself ... I wondered how far I should turn out faithful to that ideal conception of one's own personality every man sets up for himself secretly* (lines 64–74). In other words, he was unsure if he was up to the task ahead of him, and wondered if he should *remain faithful* to his *ideal*

conception that he is a capable leader. He is not apprehensive about the ship, but rather about his own abilities.

14. **C** In saying that the chief mate *was trying to evolve a theory of the anchored ship*, the narrator means that he was trying to *generate* a theory to explain why the ship was there.

15. **E** The final paragraph characterizes the chief mate as being *meticulously thoughtful* by stating that *his dominant trait was to take all things into earnest consideration* (lines 79–80). The paragraph does not suggest at all that the chief mate was *intimidating, erudite* (well-read), *emotionally sensitive* or *dull-witted*.

16. **A** In saying that the *why and wherefore* (lines 85–86) of a scorpion *had exercised [the chief mate] infinitely* (lines 91–92), the narrator is continuing his discussion of the chief mate's need to *account to himself for practically everything that came in his way* (lines 82–83). Clearly, the chief mate had a difficult time explaining the scorpion because the *[mysterious] ship ... was more easily accounted for*. Therefore, the words *exercised* is being used to mean *perplexed*.

17. **C** The passage as a whole is concerned with discussing the ability of human beings to acquire language. Although it does state that *the scientific study of language acquisition began around the same time as the birth of cognitive science, in the late 1950s*, and is therefore a relatively new discipline, the passage as a whole is not concerned with the *history* of that discipline. The passage does not spend much time comparing species except to make the brief and obvious comments that *all normal humans speak, no nonhuman animal does* (lines 6–7) and that *all humans talk but no house pets or house plants do, no matter how pampered* (lines 58–59). The passage also clearly does not provide any *biographical sketches* or *refutations of an experimental method*.

18. **E** The phrase *these data* refers to *the facts of language structure* (line 12) which indicate *a system of extraordinary complexity*. This cannot refer to the structures inside the human brain, because these structures are not revealed *every time we speak* (line 10). These *data* therefore pertain to the intricacy of the expression of human language.

19. **B** The passage states that *it is not surprising that children's acquisition of language has received so much attention* (lines 19–21) because *anyone with strong views about the human mind would like to show that*

children's first few steps are steps in the right direction (lines 22–24). In other words, language theorists focus on language acquisition more than later language development.

---

20. **B** The passage states that *babies can think before they can talk* (line 39) as a way of refuting the assertion that *language acquisition [is equivalent to] learning to think* (lines 35–36). Therefore, the point of this statement is that verbal skill is not necessary to cognition (thinking).

---

21. **B** The passage states that *language acquisition might be our best hope of finding out how heredity and environment interact* (lines 68–70) in the development of human cognitive abilities.

---

22. **C** In the context of this discussion, *a theory that posits too much innate structure* (line 79) refers to a theory of language development that suggests that the human brain is born with so much "hard-wiring" that it can only learn a particular language. Therefore, the *structure* that this sentence refers to is the innate structure of cognitive machinery of the human brain.

---

23. **A** The passage states that *natural science, social science, and philosophy had come to a virtual consensus* (lines 99–100) about whether language ability is learned or innate. In other words, they agreed on a single theory of language acquisition.

---

24. **C** The claim that *language must be learned; it cannot be a module; and thinking must be a form of verbal behavior* (lines 105–107) is attributed to those philosophers and other academics *in the late 1950s* (lines 94–95) who *had come to a virtual consensus* (line 100) about how language was acquired. Noam Chomsky, most modern cognitive scientists, and most modern linguists believe that the human brain is born with innate language-learning structures.

Section 7

1. **C** The simplest way to approach this question is to just approximate the value of the coordinates and add them, using your calculator if you need to. Point *J* seems to be around –1.8, and point *K* seems to be around 2.2. Their sum is –1.8 + 2.2 = .4, which is between 0 and 1.

---

2. **D** Notice that the expression that you are given and the expression you are asked to evaluate have a very simple relationship to one another: the first is 3 times the second.

Divide by 3:
$$6x + 9y = 8$$
$$2x + 3y = 8/3$$

---

3. **E** If Glenna gave one pencil each to 21 students and had 9 left over, she must have had 30 pencils to start with. Since she had three boxes of pencils, each one must have contained 30 ÷ 3 = 10 pencils.

---

4. **A** One efficient way to approach this question is just to find the least common multiple of 12 and 20. Since the greatest common factor of 12 and 20 is 4, the least common multiple is 12 × 20 ÷ 4 = 60. (Notice that 60 is 12 × 5 and also 20 × 3.) Notice that the only integer among the choices that is a factor of 60 is (A) 15.

---

5. **B** The container is only 3/4 filled when it contains 12 liters. Therefore 12 must be 3/4 of its total volume.

$$\frac{3}{4}x = 12$$

Multiply by 4/3:
$$\left(\frac{4}{3}\right)\frac{3}{4}x = \left(\frac{4}{3}\right)12$$

Simplify:
$$x = 16$$

---

6. **D** Profit, *P*, is equal to
$$R(x) - E(x) = (12x) - (3x + 12) = 12x - 3x - 12$$
$$= 9x - 12$$

---

7. **B** You can approach this question numerically or algebraically. To solve it numerically, pick simple values for *x*, *y*, and *m*. Since *m* must be the average of *x* and *y*, a good choice is *x* = 3, *y* = 5, and *m* = 4. Next find the average of *x*, *y*, and 2*m*: (3 + 5 + 2(4))/3 = 16/3. Now just plug these values into the choices and eliminate those that don't equal 16/3. Clearly, the only one that works is (B).

You can also take an algebraic approach. If the average of *x* and *y* is *m*, then

$$\frac{x+y}{2} = m$$

Multiply by 2:
$$x + y = 2m$$

Express the average of *x*, *y* and 2*m*
$$\frac{x+y+2m}{3}$$

Substitute: *x* + *y* = 2*m*:
$$\frac{2m+2m}{3}$$

Simplify:
$$\frac{4m}{3}$$

8. **D** The most efficient way to solve this is to use the external angle theorem, which states that the measure of an external angle in a triangle is equal to the sum of the two "remote interior" angles.

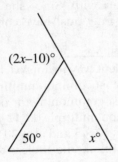

Therefore	$2x - 10 = x + 50$
Subtract x:	$x - 10 = 50$
Add 10:	$x = 60$

9. **E** Simply choose values for a and b that satisfy the given conditions, and evaluate $a \blacklozenge b$ from the given equation. Notice that $a = -1/2$ and $b = 1/2$ satisfy the conditions.

$$a \blacklozenge b = 2 - ab$$

Substitute $a = -1/2$ and $b = 1/2$:
$$(-1/2) \blacklozenge (1/2) = 2 - (-1/2)(1/2)$$

Simplify: $= 2 + 1/4 = 2.25$

Since this value is between 2 and 3, the answer is (E).

10. **D** Begin by drawing a diagonal of the rectangle. It should be clear that this is also a diameter of the circle.

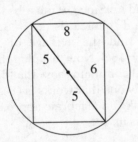

Since the area of the circle is 25π, $\pi r^2 = 25\pi$, and so $r = 5$. This means that the diameter $= 2r = 2(5) = 10$. The width of the rectangle now can be found with the Pythagorean Theorem, or simply by noticing that the rectangle consists of two 6–8–10 right triangles.

	$x^2 + 6^2 = 10^2$
Simplify:	$x^2 + 36 = 100$
Subtract 36:	$x^2 = 64$
Take the square root:	$x = 8$

Therefore the area of the rectangle is $(6)(8) = 48$.

11. **B**
$$2x + y = 8$$
Subtract $2x$: $y = -2x + 8$

Since this is in slope-intercept form, it should be clear that the slope of this line is –2. Recall that lines that are perpendicular in the x-y plane have slopes that are opposite reciprocals. The opposite reciprocal of –2 is 1/2. Therefore the line that goes through the origin and is perpendicular to the original line is $y = (1/2)x$. Notice that all of the coordinate pairs in the choices satisfy this equation with the exception of (B) (–1, 1).

12. **A** You can choose simple values for a and b and solve this problem numerically, or you can simply translate the expression a% of $5b$. Recall that % simply means *divided by 100* and *of* means *times*. Therefore a% of $5b$ is equivalent to $(a/100) = 5ab/100 = ab/20$.

13. **D**

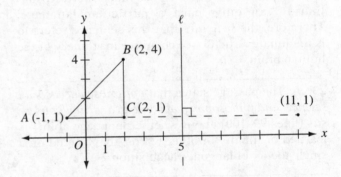

Since the question only asks about the reflection of point A, it is best to try to ignore the other points. Point A and its reflection over a line are an equal distance from the line but on the opposite side of the line. Also, the line is the perpendicular bisector of the segment joining the point and its reflection. Since point A is $5 - (-1) = 6$ units away from the line, so its reflection must also be 6 units away from the line, and therefore has an x-coordinate of $5 + 6 = 11$. Since the reflected point must have the same y-coordinate as the original point, it has coordinates (11, 1).

14. **C** Trying to list all of these integers is too cumbersome a task. The key to simplifying the problem is to notice that each of the three digits can be chosen randomly from a set of five digits: 1, 3, 5, 7, and 9. Since the three digits can be chosen independently, the total number of such three-digit integers is $5 \times 5 \times 5 = 125$.

15. **B** Like so many problems, this can be attacked either numerically or algebraically, or some combination of the two. As usual, the algebraic approach is simpler but requires more abstract thinking. To take the logical-algebraic approach, you must know the "parity" (odd-even) rules and how to factor polynomials. First notice that each quadratic in the choices is factorable:

(A) $k^2 - 4 = (k-2)(k+2)$
(B) $k^2 + 4k - 5 = (k-1)(k+5)$
(C) $k^2 + 5k + 6 = (k+2)(k+3)$
(D) $k^2 + 3k - 10 = (k-2)(k+5)$
(E) $k^2 + k - 20 = (k-4)(k+5)$

Next, recall the basic parity rules:

odd × odd = odd
odd × even = even
even × even = even
odd + odd = even
odd + even = odd
even + even = even

Applying these rules to the factors shows that (B) is the only choice that *always* produces the product of two even integers. If k is odd, then

(A) $(k-2)(k+2)$ = odd × odd
(B) $(k-1)(k+5)$ = even × even
(C) $(k+2)(k+3)$ = odd × even
(D) $(k-2)(k+5)$ = odd × even
(E) $(k-4)(k+5)$ = odd × even

Clearly, choice (B) represents the product of 2 even integers. Since choices (C), (D) and (E) also produce even integers, it is *possible* that these numbers can be expressed as the product of two even integers, but not *always*. For instance, if $k = 5$, then choice (C) gives (7)(8) = 56, which *can* be expressed as the product of two even integers: 2 × 28 = 56. However, if $k = 7$, then (C) gives (9)(10) = 90, which *cannot* be expressed as the product of two even integers. On the other hand, choice (B) can *always* be expressed as the product of two even integers.

16. **A** The graph of the function $f(x) = x^2 - k$ is symmetric to the y-axis. Therefore, points A and B are the same distance from the y-axis. Since $AB = 6$, each point must be 3 units from the y-axis. Since the area of rectangle $ABCD$ is 20, you can calculate the height

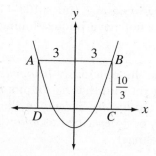

of the rectangle.

$$\text{Area} = 20 = base \times height = 6h$$
Divide by 6: $$10/3 = h$$

Be sure to write this information on the diagram. Point B, which has coordinates (3, 10/3), is on the parabola, so it must satisfy the equation $y = x^2 - k$

Substitute $y = 10/3$ and $x = 3$: $10/3 = 3^2 - k$
Subtract 9: $10/3 - 9 = -k$
Simplify: $-17/3 = -k$
Multiply by –1: $17/3 = k$

Section 8

1. **C** The sentence indicates that Gena believes that certain people *deserve the opportunity to return to society as productive citizens*. This suggests that these people were not part of society and are perhaps not always regarded as productive citizens. Such people were perhaps *incarcerated* (imprisoned) or *exiled*. One who believes that these people deserve the opportunity to return to society as productive citizens is an advocate of *rehabilitation* or *reform*. *revered* = held in high esteem; *perseverance* = steadfast in adhering to a course of action; *championed* = fought for.

2. **B** *Sweating and shivering* are examples of *physiological* (pertaining to the body) reactions. The contrasting conjunction *but* indicates a contrast between ideas; therefore, quinine must have had the opposite effect to *producing* those reactions; it must have *alleviated* them. *assuage* = to soothe; *ameliorate* = to make a bad situation better; *circumstantial* = incidental; *exacerbate* = make worse; *premeditated* = planned in advance; *rebuffed* = bluntly refused; *communicable* = contagious.

3. **C** His friends believe that Yuri was being too submissive; that is, they accused him of *complaisant* (cheerfully submissive) behavior. *headstrong* = adamant; *truculent* = disposed to fighting; *tactless* = lacking sensitivity.

4. **A** Efforts that *infuse the community with much–needed revenue* are clearly intended to *revive* (bring back to life) the economy, and the construction of the arts center would *facilitate* (help) such an effort. *debilitate* = to weaken; *expedite* = to help along, to make happen more quickly or easily; *reform* = improve; *initiate* = start; *table* = postpone consideration of; *preempt* = to take the place of; *subsidize* = to support financially.

5. **B** If Bennett *extoll[ed] the virtues of unencumbered* (free) *commerce*, then he is *a stalwart* (strong supporter) of free trade. *antagonist* = enemy; *caviler* = petty complainer; *diviner* = one who methodically foretells the future; *skeptic* = one inclined to doubting.

6. **A** *Altruism* is selflessness. If Federica *expressed doubt* about its existence, she must believe that people are basically selfish. Therefore she would believe that one would only make a sacrifice if he or she expects it to be *requited* (repaid). *repudiated* = rejected as invalid; *portended* = predicted; *rescinded* = made void; *expropriated* = stolen.

7. **B** Throughout the passage, the cultural phenomenon of Bohemianism is discussed. Although the first paragraph gives one definition of Bohemia as *a land-locked country in central Europe* (lines 1–2), the second paragraph makes it clear that Bohemia is more of a cultural phenomenon—a *country of the mind* (line 8). The passage then goes on to define the *basic elements* (line 41) of this phenomenon. Since one characterization of the phenomenon indicates that *every country has its Bohemians* (lines 81–82), it clearly is not discussing just one particular region.

8. **A** The *notion* referred to in line 17 is the idea that Bohemia was *the homeland of the gypsies* (line 17). The passage then states that this notion *ignored* (line 18) a critical fact, and is therefore mistaken. The passage does not suggest that this particular notion is bigoted, is a means of producing or inspiration for art, or is a celebration of a lifestyle.

9. **C** The author refers to *the "Egyptian" origin of "gypsy"* (lines 18–19) to make the point that since the word *gypsy* derives from the word *Egyptian*, gypsies likely originated in Egypt rather than Bohemia. Thus the word *Egyptian* is the source of the term *gypsy*.

10. **C** The passage states that, with the staging and publication of Murger's work, *the public's appetite had been whetted and a popular cult of the gypsy-artist was underway* (lines 35–37), that is, Murger's work inspired the popular fascination with the Bohemian lifestyle.

11. **C** Since this sentence concludes a paragraph discussing the origins of the public fascination with the Bohemian lifestyle, the statement that Murger's volume *became a textbook for the artistic life throughout the late nineteenth and early twentieth centuries* indicates that it sustained interest in that lifestyle for many decades.

12. **D** The passage states that Murger was a *Bohemian of the second generation* (line 74) because *he did not invent Bohemianism* (line 70) and indeed *most of [the] ingredients [of Bohemianism] had been in existence in Paris for at least two decades before he started writing* (lines 71–73). As a *malnourished Parisian poet* (line 26), Murger certainly participated in the Bohemian lifestyle as it is described throughout the passage.

13. **C** In saying that the artists were *the elect of the spirit, touched with the divine power of imagination* (lines 49–51), the author characterizes Bohemians as being *divinely selected*.

14. **E** *The people of no imagination* (lines 56–57) refers to the *commercial middle classes* (line 52).

15. **E** The Bohemians described by Jules Claretie *do not have the influence over the rest of the nation which they do in France—thanks to that poisonous element in the French character which is known as la blague—or cynicism* (lines 82–86). In other words, it is a *poisonous element* that allows the Bohemians to have influence in France, hence he believes that their influence is detrimental to French society. Henry Murger, on the other hand, equates Bohemianism with the *unconventional, outlandish behaviour of artists* (lines 68–69).

16. **B** Challamel's quotation does characterize the Bohemians' affectation (*affecting the most profound disdain*, lines 89–90), iconoclasm (*breaking with the customs of polite society*, lines 94–95), arrogance (*believing, in short, that everything is permissible to men of intelligence*, lines 95–97), and irresponsibility (*debauchery and immorality*, line 101), but it does not mention violence.

17. **C** The passage states that Houssaye *had generously befriended Bohemian poets* (lines 106–107) but *was far from blind: he was well aware that Bohemia included many impostors* (lines 108–110). In other words, he did not have unquestioning trust in all Bohemians.

18. **B** Because he *generously befriended* many Bohemians, and yet said that he did not *believe in the good faith of the literary Bohemian* (lines 110–111), his attitude is best described as *ambivalent* (having conflicting feelings).

19. **A** Houssaye says that *the real Bohemian is the one who has no communication with the public* (lines 116–117), and is therefore *aloof*.

Section 9

1. **C** The subject of this sentence is *way* and the verb is the linking verb *is*. What follows the verb, then, must be a predicate adjective describing the *way*, or a predicate noun that is equivalent to the *way*. The original sentence is grammatically incorrect because, rather than providing an adjective phrase or noun phrase, it provides a prepositional phrase that does not logically modify the subject. Choices (B) and (D) commit the same error. Choices (C) and (E) avoid this problem, because they both follow the verb with an infinitive, but only the infinitive in (C), *to provide*, is logically equivalent to *way*.

2. **E** The sentence describes a choice, and so should use parallelism in phrasing those choices. It must also use the standard idiomatic form *between A and B*. The first option is *currying favor*, a gerund phrase. To maintain parallel structure, the second option should also be a gerund phrase. The only option which uses a parallel phrase and correct idiom is (E).

3. **D** In the original sentence, the subjunctive verb *were* is illogical, because the subjunctive mood suggests that the order is hypothetical or counter to fact. The rest of the sentence, particularly the indicative main verb *are*, suggests that the sentence is describing a real situation. Choice (D) corrects this error, and leaves the rest of the phrasing, which is correct, intact. Choice (B) is also incorrectly subjunctive; choice (C) uses the unidiomatic phrase *for beginning*; and (E) omits the verb in the second clause.

4. **E** The underlined phrase in the original sentence does not logically modify either the subject or verb of the main clause: notice that it makes no sense to say either that *the advisor* is *with so many available* or that *the taking* is *with so many available*. Clearly the sentence is trying to suggest that *there are so many courses available*. Choices (C) and (D) are likewise illogical modifiers. Choice (B) uses the non-standard idiom *being that*. Choice (E) corrects the problem most effectively, using the conjunction *because* to indicate a reason.

5. **A** The sentence is correct as written.

6. **D** The verb *acknowledge* is a transitive verb, which means that it requires a logical object. The object in the original sentence, *controlled studies to be*, is not logical. What is being acknowledged? The fact *that controlled studies are most effective*. Therefore the best answer is (D).

7. **A** The sentence is correct as written. Notice that the definite pronoun *they* refers to the plural noun *chips*, and that choices (B) and (E) incorrectly use a singular pronoun. The original phrasing is preferable to choices (C) and (D) because it provides the most parallel structure. Notice that the adjectives *relatively large and expensive to manufacture* parallels the structure of *far smaller and more affordable*, and that the two clauses have the most similar structure overall in (A).

8. **C** The original sentence is not parallel. Since the sentence contrasts something to *attacking*, so it should be also phrased as a gerund: *ignoring*. Although choices (B) and (D) also use the gerund *ignoring*, they both insert extra words that violate the parallel structure.

9. **E** The sentence must be logical and use parallel form. The original sentence is redundant because the underlined phrase includes *let them*, which needlessly repeats the idea expressed in *will allow*. Choices (B) and (D) are not parallel, and (C) is not idiomatic. The only choice that is both logical and parallel is (E).

10. **B** Since the sentence discusses a possible situation about which the director is concerned, the subjunctive mood is required for the verb in the underlined clause. Choices (B), (C) and (E) use the subjunctive auxiliary *would*, but (C) is illogical and (E) is awkward and wordy.

11. **A** The original phrasing is the best.

12. **D** In the original phrasing, *him being* is an awkward and non-standard phrase. Likewise, choices (B), (C) and (E) include non-standard or illogical phrases. Clearly, the sentence is providing a reason for a situation, and so the word *because* is logically appropriate.

13. **E** A sentence must remain grammatically and logically sound when any interrupting phrase is removed. The original sentence is not grammatically sound because the phrase *as restrictive than* is not idiomatic. Choices (C) and (D) are likewise not idiomatic when the interrupter is removed, and choice (B) is not idiomatic because the comparative adjective *more* requires the word *than*.

14. **D** The subject of the sentence is the singular *revenue*, and so the verb *are* does not agree in number with its subject. Second, the comparison in the sentence is illogical because it compares the *revenue* generated by three drug therapies to the *newest drug*, rather than the revenue it generates. Third, the pronoun *their* does not agree in number with the singular antecedent *company*. The only choice that fixes all three problems is (D).

PRACTICE TEST 2

ANSWER SHEET

Last Name:_____   First Name:_____

Date:_____   Testing Location:_____

Directions for Test

- Remove these answer sheets from the book and use them to record your answers to this test.
- This test will require 3 hours and 20 minutes to complete. Take this test in one sitting.
- The time allotment for each section is written clearly at the beginning of each section. This test contains six 25-minute sections, two 20-minute sections, and one 10-minute section.
- This test is 25 minutes shorter than the actual SAT, which will include a 25-minute "experimental" section that does not count toward your score. That section has been omitted from this test.
- You may take one short break during the test, of no more than 10 minutes in length.
- You may only work on one section at any given time.
- You must stop ALL work on a section when time is called.
- If you finish a section before the time has elapsed, check your work on that section. You may NOT work on any other section.
- Do not waste time on questions that seem too difficult for you.
- Use the test book for scratchwork, but you will receive credit only for answers that are marked on the answer sheets.
- You will receive one point for every correct answer.
- You will receive no points for an omitted question.
- For each wrong answer on any multiple-choice question, your score will be reduced by ¼ point.
- For each wrong answer on any "numerical grid-in" question, you will receive no deduction.

When you take the real SAT, you will be asked to fill in your personal information in grids as shown below.

Start with number 1 for each new section. If a section has fewer questions than answer spaces, leave the extra answer spaces blank. Be sure to erase any errors or stray marks completely.

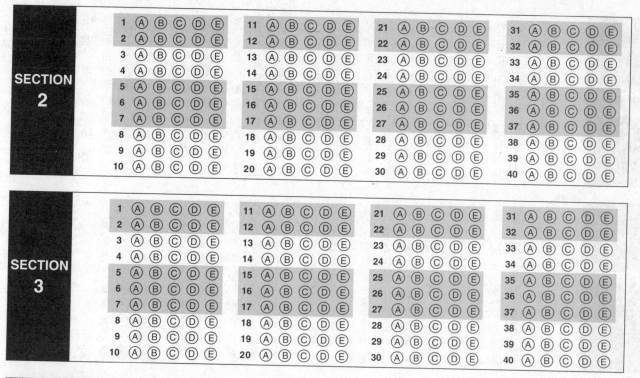

CAUTION Use the answer spaces in the grids below for Section 2 or Section 3 only if you are told to do so in your test book.

Student-Produced Responses

ONLY ANSWERS ENTERED IN THE CIRCLES IN EACH GRID WILL BE SCORED. YOU WILL NOT RECEIVE CREDIT FOR ANYTHING WRITTEN IN THE BOXES ABOVE THE CIRCLES.

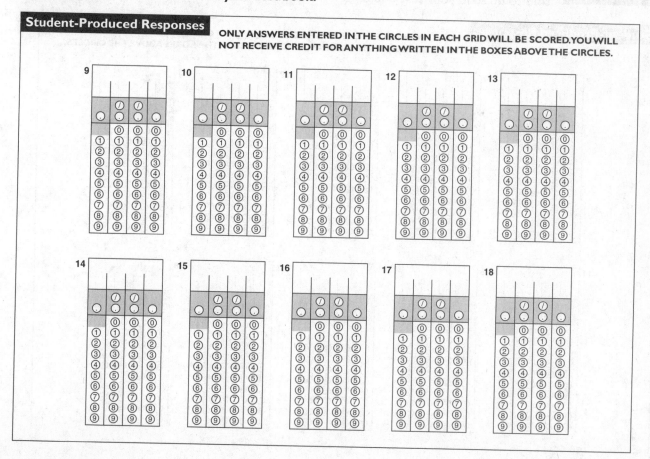

Start with number 1 for each new section. If a section has fewer questions than answer spaces, leave the extra answer spaces blank. Be sure to erase any errors or stray marks completely.

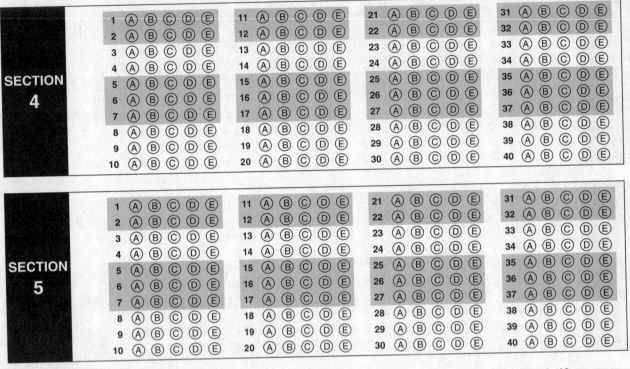

CAUTION Use the answer spaces in the grids below for Section 4 or Section 5 only if you are told to do so in your test book.

Student-Produced Responses ONLY ANSWERS ENTERED IN THE CIRCLES IN EACH GRID WILL BE SCORED. YOU WILL NOT RECEIVE CREDIT FOR ANYTHING WRITTEN IN THE BOXES ABOVE THE CIRCLES.

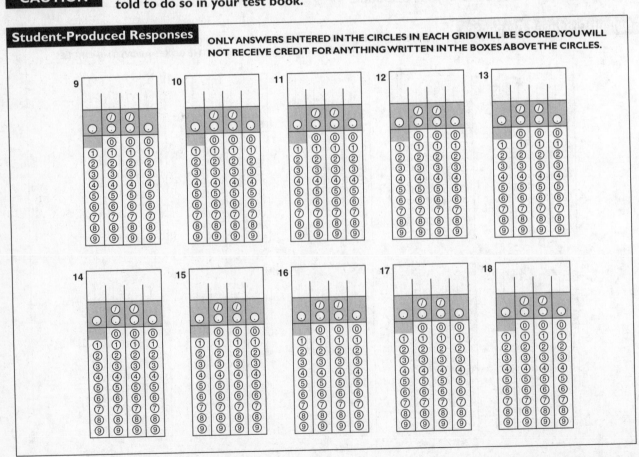

Start with number 1 for each new section. If a section has fewer questions than answer spaces, leave the extra answer spaces blank. Be sure to erase any errors or stray marks completely.

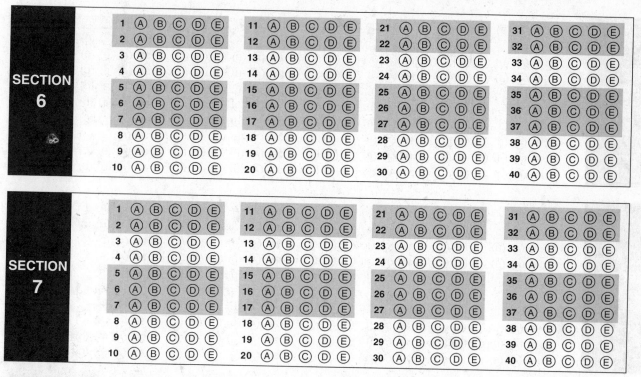

SECTION 6

SECTION 7

CAUTION Use the answer spaces in the grids below for Section 6 or Section 7 only if you are told to do so in your test book.

Student-Produced Responses

ONLY ANSWERS ENTERED IN THE CIRCLES IN EACH GRID WILL BE SCORED. YOU WILL NOT RECEIVE CREDIT FOR ANYTHING WRITTEN IN THE BOXES ABOVE THE CIRCLES.

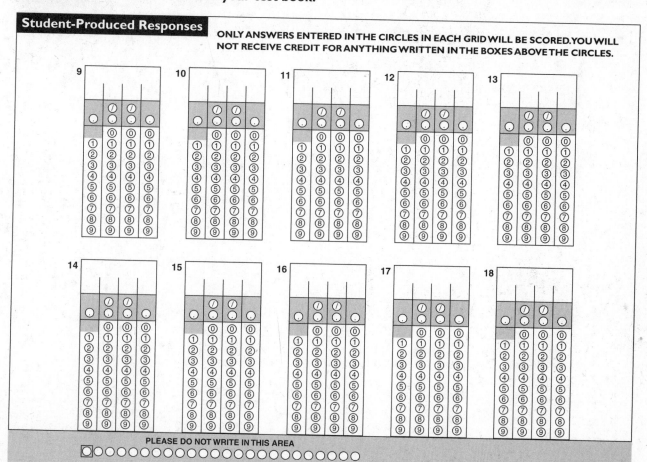

PLEASE DO NOT WRITE IN THIS AREA

Start with number 1 for each new section. If a section has fewer questions than answer spaces, leave the extra answer spaces blank. Be sure to erase any errors or stray marks completely.

SECTION 8

1 (A) (B) (C) (D) (E)	11 (A) (B) (C) (D) (E)	21 (A) (B) (C) (D) (E)	31 (A) (B) (C) (D) (E)
2 (A) (B) (C) (D) (E)	12 (A) (B) (C) (D) (E)	22 (A) (B) (C) (D) (E)	32 (A) (B) (C) (D) (E)
3 (A) (B) (C) (D) (E)	13 (A) (B) (C) (D) (E)	23 (A) (B) (C) (D) (E)	33 (A) (B) (C) (D) (E)
4 (A) (B) (C) (D) (E)	14 (A) (B) (C) (D) (E)	24 (A) (B) (C) (D) (E)	34 (A) (B) (C) (D) (E)
5 (A) (B) (C) (D) (E)	15 (A) (B) (C) (D) (E)	25 (A) (B) (C) (D) (E)	35 (A) (B) (C) (D) (E)
6 (A) (B) (C) (D) (E)	16 (A) (B) (C) (D) (E)	26 (A) (B) (C) (D) (E)	36 (A) (B) (C) (D) (E)
7 (A) (B) (C) (D) (E)	17 (A) (B) (C) (D) (E)	27 (A) (B) (C) (D) (E)	37 (A) (B) (C) (D) (E)
8 (A) (B) (C) (D) (E)	18 (A) (B) (C) (D) (E)	28 (A) (B) (C) (D) (E)	38 (A) (B) (C) (D) (E)
9 (A) (B) (C) (D) (E)	19 (A) (B) (C) (D) (E)	29 (A) (B) (C) (D) (E)	39 (A) (B) (C) (D) (E)
10 (A) (B) (C) (D) (E)	20 (A) (B) (C) (D) (E)	30 (A) (B) (C) (D) (E)	40 (A) (B) (C) (D) (E)

SECTION 9

1 (A) (B) (C) (D) (E)	11 (A) (B) (C) (D) (E)	21 (A) (B) (C) (D) (E)	31 (A) (B) (C) (D) (E)
2 (A) (B) (C) (D) (E)	12 (A) (B) (C) (D) (E)	22 (A) (B) (C) (D) (E)	32 (A) (B) (C) (D) (E)
3 (A) (B) (C) (D) (E)	13 (A) (B) (C) (D) (E)	23 (A) (B) (C) (D) (E)	33 (A) (B) (C) (D) (E)
4 (A) (B) (C) (D) (E)	14 (A) (B) (C) (D) (E)	24 (A) (B) (C) (D) (E)	34 (A) (B) (C) (D) (E)
5 (A) (B) (C) (D) (E)	15 (A) (B) (C) (D) (E)	25 (A) (B) (C) (D) (E)	35 (A) (B) (C) (D) (E)
6 (A) (B) (C) (D) (E)	16 (A) (B) (C) (D) (E)	26 (A) (B) (C) (D) (E)	36 (A) (B) (C) (D) (E)
7 (A) (B) (C) (D) (E)	17 (A) (B) (C) (D) (E)	27 (A) (B) (C) (D) (E)	37 (A) (B) (C) (D) (E)
8 (A) (B) (C) (D) (E)	18 (A) (B) (C) (D) (E)	28 (A) (B) (C) (D) (E)	38 (A) (B) (C) (D) (E)
9 (A) (B) (C) (D) (E)	19 (A) (B) (C) (D) (E)	29 (A) (B) (C) (D) (E)	39 (A) (B) (C) (D) (E)
10 (A) (B) (C) (D) (E)	20 (A) (B) (C) (D) (E)	30 (A) (B) (C) (D) (E)	40 (A) (B) (C) (D) (E)

ESSAY ESSAY

ESSAY
Time—25 minutes

Write your essay on separate sheets of standard lined paper.

The essay gives you an opportunity to show how effectively you can develop and express ideas. You should, therefore, take care to develop your point of view, present your ideas logically and clearly, and use language precisely.

Your essay must be written on the lines provided on your answer sheet—you will receive no other paper on which to write. You will have enough space if you write on every line, avoid wide margins, and keep your handwriting to a reasonable size. Remember that people who are not familiar with your handwriting will read what you write. Try to write or print so that what you are writing is legible to those readers.

Important Reminders:

- **A pencil is required for the essay.** An essay written in ink will receive a score of zero.
- **Do not write your essay in your test book.** You will receive credit only for what you write on your answer sheet.
- **An off-topic essay will receive a score of zero.**

You have twenty-five minutes to write an essay on the topic assigned below.

Consider carefully the issue discussed in the following passage, then write an essay that answers the question posed in the assignment.

> I have learned that success is to be measured not so much by the position that one has reached in life as by the obstacles which one has overcome while trying to succeed.
> —Booker T. Washington

Assignment: **Is the struggle endured to achieve success more important than the accomplishment itself?** Plan and write an essay in which you develop your point of view on this issue. Support your position with reasoning and examples taken from your reading, studies, experience, or observations.

If you finish before time is called, you may check your work on this section only.
Do not turn to any other section of the test.

2   2   2   2   2   2

SECTION 2
Time—25 minutes
20 questions

Turn to Section 2 of your answer sheet to answer the questions in this section.

Directions: For this section, solve each problem and decide which is the best of the choices given. Fill in the corresponding circle on the answer sheet. You may use any available space for scratchwork.

Notes

1. The use of a calculator is permitted.

2. All numbers used are real numbers.

3. Figures that accompany problems in this test are intended to provide information useful in solving the problems. They are drawn as accurately as possible EXCEPT when it is stated in a specific problem that the figure is not drawn to scale. All figures lie in a plane unless otherwise indicated.

4. Unless otherwise specified, the domain of any function f is assumed to be the set of all real numbers x for which $f(x)$ is a real number.

Reference Information

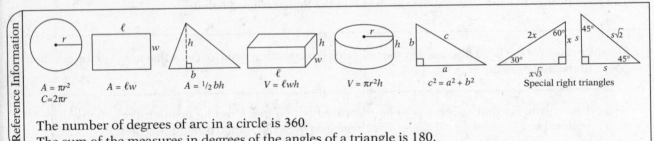

$A = \pi r^2$ $A = \ell w$ $A = \frac{1}{2}bh$ $V = \ell wh$ $V = \pi r^2 h$ $c^2 = a^2 + b^2$ Special right triangles
$C = 2\pi r$

The number of degrees of arc in a circle is 360.
The sum of the measures in degrees of the angles of a triangle is 180.

---

1. If $b = 4$ and $c = 7$, what is the value of $3b - 5c$?

   (A) -27
   (B) -23
   (C) 3
   (D) 6
   (E) 20

2. If the average (arithmetic mean) of 4 and w is equal to the average of 2, 8, and w, what is the value of w?

   (A)   2
   (B)   4
   (C)   6
   (D)   8
   (E) 10

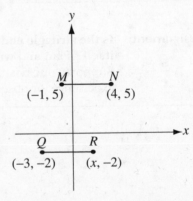

3. In the figure above, the length of MN is equal to the length of QR. What is the value of x?

   (A) -3
   (B) -1
   (C) 2
   (D) 5
   (E) 6

GO ON TO THE NEXT PAGE

2   2   2   2   2   2

4. The cost of a highway toll was \$0.75 in 2005. The following year the cost of the toll increased to \$1.00. By what percent did the toll increase?

(A) 10%
(B) 20%
(C) 25%
(D) 33⅓%
(E) 50%

5. The cost of four oranges is d dollars. At this rate, what is the cost of 40 oranges?

(A) $\dfrac{d}{40}$

(B) $\dfrac{40}{d}$

(C) $10d$
(D) $20d$
(E) $40d$

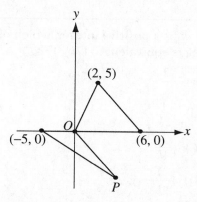

Note: Figure not drawn to scale.

6. If the areas of the two triangles in the figure above are equal, which of the following could be the coordinates of point P ?

(A) $(3, -4)$
(B) $(4, -6)$
(C) $(2, -4)$
(D) $(2, -5)$
(E) $(1, -7)$

7. If $a - b = -4$, what is the value of $a^2 - 2ab + b^2$?

(A) -32
(B) -16
(C) 0
(D) 16
(E) 32

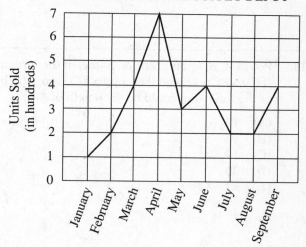

8. Between which two months did the Franklin Office Supply Depot experience the greatest change in the number of units sold?

(A) February to March
(B) March to April
(C) April to May
(D) June to July
(E) August to September

GO ON TO THE NEXT PAGE

2   2   2   2   2   2

9. The ratio of r to s is 3 to 4. The ratio of s to t is 2 to 9. What is the ratio of r to t?

(A) 1 to 3
(B) 1 to 6
(C) 2 to 9
(D) 3 to 10
(E) 4 to 5

10. Points A, B, C, and D lie on a line, in that order. If $CD > BC > AB$ and the length of CD is 6, which of the following could be the length of AD?

(A) 17
(B) 18
(C) 19
(D) 20
(E) 21

x	4	5	6	7
$f(x)$	10	12	14	16

11. The table above gives values of the linear function f for selected values of x. Which of the following functions defines f?

(A) $f(x) = \dfrac{3}{2}x + 4$

(B) $f(x) = -\dfrac{2}{3}x - 3$

(C) $f(x) = 2x + 2$

(D) $f(x) = 3x - 3$

(E) $f(x) = 4x - 6$

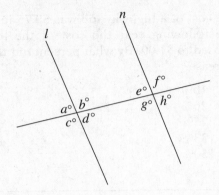

12. In the figure above, if $l \parallel n$, which of the following is NOT necessarily equal to e?

(A) a

(B) $\dfrac{(h+d)}{2}$

(C) $\dfrac{(a+d)}{2}$

(D) $\dfrac{(f+h)}{2}$

(E) d

13. If k is a positive integer, which of the following is equivalent to $(2k^{1/2})^{-2}$?

(A) $\dfrac{2}{k}$

(B) $\dfrac{1}{2k}$

(C) $\dfrac{1}{4k}$

(D) $\dfrac{1}{2k^2}$

(E) $\dfrac{4}{k}$

14. If t is 40 percent greater than p, and p is 40 percent less than 600, what is the value of $t - p$?

(A) 144
(B) 240
(C) 360
(D) 504
(E) 1008

GO ON TO THE NEXT PAGE

2   2   2   2   2   2

$$-2, 4, 8 \ldots$$

15. In the sequence above, each term after the second can be found by multiplying the two preceding terms together. For example, the third term is $-2 \times 4 = -8$. How many of the first 139 terms of this sequence are negative?

(A) 46
(B) 70
(C) 74
(D) 92
(E) 93

17. In a bag of marbles, $\frac{2}{5}$ of the marbles are red, $\frac{3}{10}$ of the marbles are white, and $\frac{1}{10}$ of the marbles are blue. If the remaining 10 marbles are green, how many marbles are in the bag?

(A) 15
(B) 20
(C) 35
(D) 45
(E) 50

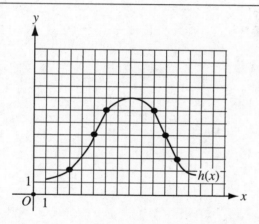

16. In the figure above, if the value of $h(5) = k$, then what is the value of $h(2k)$?

(A) 5
(B) 6
(C) 7
(D) 8
(E) 9

18. If x and y are positive numbers greater than 1, and $\dfrac{wx}{y+w} = 1$ then $w =$

(A) $\dfrac{x-1}{y-1}$

(B) $\dfrac{y}{x-1}$

(C) $\dfrac{x+1}{y}$

(D) $\dfrac{x-y}{x+y}$

(E) $\dfrac{y}{x+1}$

If you finish before time is called, you may check your work on this section only. Do not turn to any other section of the test.

GO ON TO THE NEXT PAGE ⟹

2   **2**   **2**   **2**   **2**   **2**

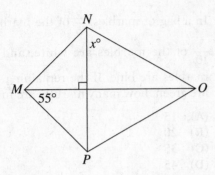

Note: Figure not drawn to scale.

19. In the quadrilateral above, $ON = OM = OP$.
     If $MN = MP$, then what is the value of x?

     (A)   15
     (B)   20
     (C)   25
     (D)   30
     (E)   35

20. There are five roads from Wilton to Norwalk
     and four roads from Norwalk to Darien. If
     Kristina drives from Wilton to Darien and
     back, passes through Norwalk in both direc-
     tions, and does not travel any road twice, how
     many different routes are possible for the
     round trip?

     (A)   16
     (B)   32
     (C)   160
     (D)   240
     (E)   360

◇ **STOP**   *If you finish before time is called, you may*
              check your work on this section only. Do not turn
              to any other section of the test.

SECTION 3
Time—25 minutes
35 questions

Turn to Section 3 of your answer sheet to answer the questions in this section.

Directions: For each question in this section, select the best answer from among the choices given and fill in the corresponding circle on the answer sheet.

The following sentences test correctness and effectiveness of expression. Part of each sentence or the entire sentence is underlined; beneath each sentence are five ways of phrasing the underlined material. Choice A repeats the original phrasing; the other four choices are different. Select the choice that completes the sentence most effectively.

In making your selection, follow the requirements of standard written English; that is, pay attention to grammar, choice of words, sentence construction, and punctuation. Your selection should result in the most effective sentence—clear and precise, without awkwardness or ambiguity.

EXAMPLE:

The children couldn't hardly believe their eyes.

(A) couldn't hardly believe their eyes
(B) could hardly believe their eyes
(C) would not hardly believe their eyes
(D) couldn't nearly believe their eyes
(E) couldn't hardly believe his or her eyes

1. The harmful effects of excessive alcohol intake on the hepatic system is extensively documented by medical studies.

   (A) is extensively documented by medical studies
   (B) is documented more extensively by medical studies
   (C) are extensively documented by medical studies
   (D) medical studies are extensively documenting
   (E) has documented extensively by medical studies

2. Harper's Conservative Party favors lowering taxes, a more decentralized government, and the spending of less money on imports.

   (A) favors lowering taxes, a more decentralized government, and the spending of less money
   (B) favor lower taxes, more decentralizing government, and spending less money
   (C) favors lower taxes, a more decentralized government, and a lesser expenditure
   (D) favoring lower taxes, a more decentralized government, and less money spent
   (E) favor lowering taxes, a more decentralized government, and spending less money

GO ON TO THE NEXT PAGE

3   **3**   **3**   **3**   **3**   **3**

3. Exhausted by consecutive years of tropical-cyclone mayhem, <u>many people are asking about future trends, notes Kerry Emanuel, an atmospheric scientist at the Massachusetts Institute of Technology</u>, who focuses on weather and climate in the tropics.

(A) many people are asking about future trends, notes Kerry Emanuel, an atmospheric scientist at the Massachusetts Institute of Technology

(B) an atmospheric scientist at the Massachusetts Institute of Technology, notes Kerry Emanuel, many people are asking about future trends

(C) many people are asking about future trends, an atmospheric scientist notes Kerry Emanuel, at the Massachusetts Institute of Technology

(D) the Massachusetts Institute of Technology, notes Kerry Emanuel, finds that many people are asking about future trends

(E) future trends are a topic that many people are asking about, notes Kerry Emanuel, an atmospheric scientist at the Massachusetts Institute of Technology

4. If asked to name a famous explorer, <u>Christopher Columbus would probably be the person most of us would choose</u>.

(A) Christopher Columbus would probably be the person most of us would choose

(B) most of us would probably choose Christopher Columbus

(C) our choice for the most of us would probably be Christopher Columbus

(D) Christopher Columbus would probably get most of our choices

(E) most of our choices would probably be for Christopher Columbus

5. Located in Manhattan, <u>many sightseers like to visit the Empire State building, a massive skyscraper constructed during the Great Depression</u>.

(A) many sightseers like to visit the Empire State building, a massive skyscraper constructed during the Great Depression

(B) the Empire state building, a massive skyscraper constructed during the Great Depression many sightseers like to visit

(C) and constructed during the Great Depression, many tourists like to visit the Empire State Building

(D) the Empire State Building is a massive skyscraper, constructed during the Great Depression, that many sightseers like to visit

(E) a massive skyscraper constructed during the Great Depression, the Empire State Building, is a place that sightseers like to visit

6. <u>The fact that the cancer, which was once thought to be untreatable, has gone into remission is still a mystery to the oncologists.</u>

(A) The fact that the cancer, which was once thought to be untreatable, has gone into remission is still a mystery to the oncologists.

(B) Originally thought to be untreatable, the remission of the cancer is still a mystery to the oncologists.

(C) The oncologists originally thought the cancer was untreatable and the remission still being a mystery.

(D) The remission of the cancer is still a mystery to the oncologists, which originally thought it to be untreatable.

(E) Still a mystery to the oncologists, originally thought to be untreatable was the remission of the cancer.

GO ON TO THE NEXT PAGE ⟶

7. <u>Being as he is a perfect gentleman</u>, Tommy is well known for his polite behavior even around strangers.

(A) Being as he is a perfect gentleman
(B) Although he is a perfect gentleman
(C) Being a gentleman perfectly
(D) A perfect gentleman
(E) In being a perfect gentleman

8. <u>Having poured down heavily throughout the night, Felisha observed that the rain had leaked into the cellar</u> through the cracked window.

(A) Having poured down heavily throughout the night, Felisha observed that the rain had leaked into the cellar
(B) Felisha observed that the rain, which had poured down heavily throughout the night, had leaked into the cellar
(C) Having poured down heavily throughout the night, the rain was observed by Felisha to have leaked into the cellar
(D) Felisha observed the rain, having poured down heavily throughout the night, had leaked into the cellar
(E) The rain, which poured down heavily throughout the night, leaked into the cellar as it was observed by Felisha

9. Sue Grafton, a mystery writer from Kentucky, is perhaps <u>best known for</u> the alphabet murder series she began writing in the 1980s.

(A) best known for
(B) best known by
(C) better known by
(D) well known by
(E) known in terms of

10. The validity of IQ tests as accurate measures of human intelligence <u>have been the subject of much debate</u>.

(A) have been the subject of much debate
(B) are often the subject of much debate
(C) has been the subject of much debate
(D) are a debate that is frequently held
(E) are something that many have been debating

11. <u>Bred in Portugal as a seafaring dog to carry messages between ships</u>, the Portuguese Water Dog is a strong and agile dog with enough stamina to do a full day's work.

(A) Bred in Portugal as a seafaring dog to carry messages between ships
(B) Breeding the seafaring dog that carried messages between ships in Portugal
(C) Although being bred in Portugal as a seafaring dog that carried messages between ships
(D) Since having been bred in Portugal as a seafaring dog that carried messages between ships
(E) Bred in Portugal carrying messages between ships as seafaring dogs

GO ON TO THE NEXT PAGE →

3   **3**   **3**   **3**   **3**   **3**

The following sentences test your ability to recognize grammar and usage errors. Each sentence contains either a single error or no error at all. No sentence contains more than one error. The error, if there is one, is underlined and lettered. If the sentence contains an error, select the one underlined part that must be changed to make the sentence correct. If the sentence is correct, select choice E. In choosing answers, follow the requirements of standard written English.

EXAMPLE:

By the time <u>they reached</u> the halfway point
             A
<u>in the race,</u> <u>most of the runners</u> <u>hadn't hardly</u>
   B   C   D
begun to hit their stride. <u>No error</u>
                      E

---

12. Bob Hope, <u>long</u> <u>considered</u> a hero by many
              A   B
members <u>of</u> the military, <u>were</u> very patriotic.
        C   D
<u>No error</u>
 E

13. <u>Between</u> the 32 NFL teams in 2005, the
   A
Indianapolis Colts <u>scored</u> the <u>most</u>
               B   C
first half points and <u>allowed</u> the fewest
              D
second half points. <u>No error</u>
               E

14. <u>On April</u> 30, 1789, George Washington,
   A
<u>standing on</u> the balcony of Federal Hall on
   B
Wall Street in New York, <u>took</u> his oath
                   C
of office <u>as the first President</u> of the
          D
United States. <u>No error</u>
           E

15. By virtue of <u>their</u> size and superior
          A
technological advances, the Russian army

<u>was able</u> to quell the <u>aggressive</u> rebellion
 B   C
<u>with</u> unmatched efficiency. <u>No error</u>
 D   E

16. <u>Too much</u> sugar <u>causes</u> a cake to sag
   A   B
<u>in the center,</u> to brown excessively, and
    C
<u>having sticky,</u> thick crust. <u>No error</u>
   D   E

17. After <u>much</u> debate, Julia and Patricia
      A
<u>agreed</u> that they would go to the movies
  B
together on Friday, but at the last minute

<u>she</u> <u>changed</u> her mind. <u>No error</u>
 C   D   E

GO ON TO THE NEXT PAGE →

18. It has long been believed that our solar
    A
    system came into existence when a
                B
    huge cloud of gas and dust collapsed
                                    C
    to form the sun and planets

    approximately 4.5 billion years ago.
                    D
    No error
    E

19. Some parents believe that a weekly
                    A
    allowance help children to appreciate
             B   C
    the importance of good money
                    D
    management skills. No error
                        E

20. Quick to take advantage of his mother's
    A   B
    preoccupation in proper nutrition,
    C
    Jules convinced her to cook a large
          D
    breakfast for him before he went to

    the beach for the day. No error
                            E

21. After being led through the museum
    A
    by a woman which they took to be the
              B   C
    curator, the patrons discovered that their
                    D
    tour guide was actually the owner of the

    museum. No error
            E

22. The surgical method of inserting the valve,
                    A
    which includes making a small incision
    B
    between the ribs, are intended to shorten
                    C
    recovery time and reduce complications

    associated with traditional open-heart
    D
    surgery. No error
            E

23. Scientists are amassing evidence that
             A
    the placebo affect is a physiological
                B
    reaction, and that the expectation of a

    benefit can trigger the same neurological
            C
    pathways as real medication does. No error
                    D   E

24. In the aftermath of the Cuban Missile
    A
    Crisis, the papers from all the national
                    B
    security agencies involved were scattered
                    C   D
    throughout the executive branch. No error
                                    E

25. After completing her examination of the
    A
    patient, the medical intern informed the
                                B
    chief resident that the patient was not only
                                C
    feeling sick, but dizzy, and therefore
                D
    might have an infection. No error
                            E

GO ON TO THE NEXT PAGE →

3   3   3   3   3   3

26. That Erica dedicated so much of her
    A   B
    time to charity work and she cared so little
                          C
    about those less fortunate than she is
                      D
    surprising. No error
                  E

27. When looking at satellite photographs
          A
    of the area affected by Hurricane Katrina,
                  B
    the effects of the massive storm are
                                      C
    clearly visible. No error
    D   E

28. The play director has announced that
                                      A
    if anyone wants to try out for the musical,
                B   C
    they should do so immediately. No error
    D   E

29. Neither Roger nor his sisters was able
                  A   B
    to understand what the conductor was
                                      C
    saying because they did not know how to
                      D
    speak French. No error
                  E

GO ON TO THE NEXT PAGE →

3   3   3   3   3   3

Directions: The following passage is an early draft of an essay. Some parts of the passage need to be rewritten.

Read the passage and select the best answers for the questions that follow. Some questions are about particular sentences or parts of sentences and ask you to improve sentence structure or word choice. Other questions ask you to consider organization and development. In choosing answers, follow the requirements of standard written English.

Questions 30–35 are based on the following passage.

(1) Crocodiles descended from creatures that walked on their hind legs, and lived during the late Triassic period. (2) The crocodiles having survived the still unknown factors wiping out most of the reptile class at the end of the Mesozoic period. (3) The skull and hind legs of the crocodile still resemble in many ways those structures of its primitive relatives. (4) Walking on four legs, their two legged ancestry is revealed by their hind legs, which are longer than their front legs, making them slant forward when they stand. (5) The crocodile has a rather long, pointed skull, especially in the fish eating species of crocodiles.

(6) The palate is the flat bony part at the roof of the mouth. (7) In its relatives, the nostril holes in the palate were located under the outer nostrils, which were shifted to the far back of their snout. (8) However, in crocodiles, the nostrils are located at the front of the snout. (9) A problem came from this in keeping the breathing passages from filling with water. (10) Millions of years of evolution have solved this problem. (11) A second palate was formed, channeling the air above the mouth and into the throat passageway, where it can be opened and closed by a special flap or valve of skin. (12) Crocodiles are actually classified on the basis of how far back their secondary palate extends, ranging from those that have no secondary palate to those with a fully formed palate separating the air they breathe from the water in their mouths.

---

30. In context, which is the best version of the underlined portion of sentence 2 (reproduced below)?

The crocodiles having survived the still unknown factors wiping out most of the reptile class at the end of the Mesozoic period.

(A) (As it is now)
(B) Crocodiles were somehow able to survive the unknown factors that wiped out most of the reptile class
(C) It is not clear how or why, but Crocodiles were able to survive the unknown factors wiping out most of the reptile class
(D) Having survived the unknown factors that wiped out most of the reptile class, it is not clear why crocodiles remained
(E) Most of the reptile class was wiped out by unknown factors but the crocodiles still have survived

31. In context, which is the best version of the underlined portion of sentence 4 (reproduced below)?

Walking on four legs, their two legged ancestry is revealed by their hind legs, which are longer than their front legs, making them slant forward when they stand.

(A) Though modern crocodiles walk on four legs,
(B) Four legged walkers,
(C) Modern crocodiles, despite walking on four legs,
(D) As four legged walkers, modern crocodiles,
(E) Having four legs,

GO ON TO THE NEXT PAGE ⟹

3   3   3   3   3   3

32. Which of the following should be done with sentence 5 (reproduced below)?

The crocodile has a rather long, pointed skull, especially in the fish eating species of crocodiles.

(A) Insert the phrase "In addition" at the beginning.
(B) Delete it; the sentence does not contain relevant information.
(C) Move it to the beginning of the essay as an introduction.
(D) Move it to the middle of paragraph 2 after sentence 10.
(E) Insert the word "Interestingly" at the beginning.

33. Which of the following is the best sentence to insert at the beginning of the second paragraph?

(A) Crocodiles are able to run at incredible speeds despite their small stature.
(B) There are 23 living species of crocodile found mostly in the southern hemisphere, a living throwback to the age of the dinosaurs.
(C) The first crocodilians were called Protosuchians, living during the late Triassic to early Jurassic times.
(D) The most prominent change in the crocodile since its early days has been the change in its palate.
(E) Beginning in the Jurassic period, crocodiles became large and fully aquatic reptiles

34. In context, which of the following is the best way to revise and combine sentences 8 and 9 (reproduced below)?

However, in crocodiles, the nostrils are located at the front of the snout. A problem came from this in keeping the breathing passages from filling with water.

(A) No change is necessary
(B) However, because a crocodile's nostrils are located at the front of the snout, its breathing passages often filled with water
(C) The nostrils of a crocodile are located at the front of the snout, however difficult it was to keep the breathing passages from filling with water.
(D) It was difficult keeping the breathing passages of the crocodile's nostrils from filling with water however, because they would be located at the front of the snout.
(E) Located at the front of the snout, water would get into the breathing passages of the crocodiles because of its nostrils.

35. In context, which is the best version of sentence 10 (reproduced below)?

Millions of years of evolution have solved this problem.

(A) (As it is now)
(B) This problem having been solved thanks to millions of years of evolution.
(C) It was after millions of years of evolution that the crocodile was able to solve this problem.
(D) This problem was no longer an issue after millions of years of evolution solving it.
(E) The solver of this problem, after millions of years, being evolution.

STOP   *If you finish before time is called, you may check your work on this section only. Do not turn to any other section of the test.*

4   4   4   4   4   4

SECTION 4
Time—25 minutes
24 questions

Turn to Section 4 of your answer sheet to answer the questions in this section.

Directions: For each question in this section, select the best answer from among the choices given and fill in the corresponding circle on the answer sheet.

Each sentence below has one or two blanks, each blank indicating that something has been omitted. Beneath the sentence are five words or sets of words labeled A through E. Choose the word or set of words that, when inserted in the sentence, best fits the meaning of the sentence as a whole.

EXAMPLE:

Rather than accepting the theory unquestioningly, Deborah regarded it with -----.

(A) mirth
(B) sadness
(C) responsibility
(D) ignorance
(E) skepticism

---

1. The earth minerals found within the thermal waters of the hot springs are known to ------- and revitalize the skin.

    (A) ingratiate
    (B) invigorate
    (C) exculpate
    (D) enervate
    (E) debilitate

2. Despite the ever-present curiosity about his life away from the presidency, Grover Cleveland enjoyed ------- that today's highly sought after public figures can only -------.

    (A) a candor . . remember
    (B) a popularity . . dissuade
    (C) an animosity . . crave
    (D) a privacy . . imagine
    (E) a frivolity . . imitate

3. With unanimous approval, the Senate ------- the new law that would prohibit companies from discriminating according to race in their hiring practices.

    (A) ratified   (B) nullified
    (C) refuted   (D) supplanted
    (E) pilfered

4. Her closest friends saw her confinement to a wheelchair as an -------, but LaToya instead saw it as an ------- that pushed her to achieve things that many thought were impossible.

    (A) atrocity . . irrelevance
    (B) omen . . elocution
    (C) invasion . . inspiration
    (D) idiosyncracy . . extinction
    (E) impediment . . impetus

5. During the struggle for Indian independence, Mahatma Gandhi was a ------- pacifist who may have steadfastly resisted authority but was never combative.

    (A) fickle   (B) recalcitrant
    (C) pugnacious   (D) lucrative
    (E) spurious

6. Several months after the devastating -------, all that remained of Jamjang village was a circle of burned huts, wood-and-mud walls reduced to a sad ring of blackened ashes, and ------- smell of smoke that still hung in the air.

    (A) wildfire . . a savory
    (B) cacophony . . a pungent
    (C) conflagration . . an acrid
    (D) abomination . . a lethargic
    (E) scourge . . an irascible

GO ON TO THE NEXT PAGE ⟶

4   4   4   4   4   4

7. My editor's meticulousness is revealed in his
    ------- red scribbles, which show that he thought
    about each word, eliminated all unnecessary
    ones, and considered the flow of each sentence
    to the next.

    (A) rapacious   (B) improvident
    (C) convoluted   (D) copious
    (E) ostentatious

8. In an effort to supplement his modest income,
    the ------- police officer would break the law
    for criminals who were willing to pay him ade-
    quately.

    (A) clairvoyant   (B) impassive
    (C) matriculated   (D) scrupulous
    (E) venal

The passages below are followed by questions
based on their content; questions following a
pair of related passages may also be based on
the relationship between the paired passages.
Answer the questions on the basis of what is
stated or implied in the passage and in any
introductory material that may be provided.

Questions 9–12 are based on the following passages.

PASSAGE 1

Many medical researchers now believe that
there is such a thing as being too clean.
Line   The "hygiene hypothesis" suggests that
excessively sanitary conditions can lower a
5   person's resistance to disease. One recent
study suggested that infection by the
hepatitis A virus actually prevented certain
individuals from developing allergies. But the
protection was not exclusively environmental:
10 only those infected patients who had also
inherited a particular gene saw the benefit.

PASSAGE 2

The triumph of antibiotics over disease-
causing bacteria is one of modern medicine's
greatest success stories. Since these drugs
15 first became widely used in the World War II
era, they have saved countless lives and
blunted serious complications of many feared
diseases and infections. After more than
50 years of widespread use, however, many
20 antibiotics don't pack the same punch they
once did. Over time, some bacteria have
developed ways to outwit the effects of
antibiotics. Widespread use of antibiotics is
thought to have spurred evolutionary changes
25 in bacteria that allow them to survive these
powerful drugs. While antibiotic resistance
benefits the microbes, it presents humans with
two big problems: it makes it more difficult
to purge infections from the body; and it
30 heightens the risk of acquiring infections
in a hospital.

9. Both passages indicate that

    (A) recently developed medications are
         ineffectual
    (B) doctors should prescribe antibiotics
         more liberally
    (C) environment plays a far greater role than
         genetics in human health
    (D) unsanitary conditions are a risk to
         human health
    (E) certain factors are decreasing the human
         body's ability to ward off disease

10. The "benefit" mentioned in line 11 is

    (A) resistance to allergies
    (B) the ability to ward off hepatitis A
    (C) cleanliness
    (D) more disease-resistant genes
    (E) popular awareness

First paragraph: © 2006 Christopher Black. Reprinted by permission of the author.
Second paragraph: http://www.niaid.nih.gov/factsheets/antimicro.htm

GO ON TO THE NEXT PAGE

4   4   4   4   4   4

11. Passage 2 discusses antibiotics primarily with a tone of

(A) strong optimism
(B) dismissiveness
(C) cynicism
(D) qualified enthusiasm
(E) jocularity

12. Unlike the "resistance" mentioned in line 5, the "resistance" in line 26 is a resistance to

(A) bacteria rather than viruses
(B) drugs rather than allergies
(C) genetic diseases rather than infectious diseases
(D) evolutionary changes rather than hepatitis A
(E) infection rather than antibiotics

Questions 13–24 are based on the following passages.

The following passages discuss the American farm subsidy program, which makes direct payments to farmers in order to control the supply of agricultural goods available for domestic sale or for export.

PASSAGE 1

Something is rotten down on the farm. The U.S. Department of Agriculture has for decades
Line managed the farm subsidy program, a multibillion-dollar system of direct payments
5 to American farmers. The General Accounting Office recently studied the management of this program, and the findings should horrify lawmakers. But they probably won't.

The GAO study revealed that government
10 administrators of these subsidies are too ill-trained and that federal laws are too vague to properly monitor the hundreds of thousands of farm subsidy payments granted each year. Many of the approved recipients were actually
15 ineligible for the program.

Such lack of USDA oversight is outrageous, given how much American taxpayers spend each year to support farmers. From 1995 to 2002, Congress doled out more than $114
20 billion to farmers. With so much money being freely handed out, the GAO report should inspire some tough questions for USDA officials on Capitol Hill. Yet, for all its detail, the 75-page report artfully avoids the
25 bigger question that no lawmaker wants to hear: why do we even have farm subsidies?

One popular misconception is that these subsidies produce lower food prices, and so
30 are a boon to consumers. This analysis ignores the fact that consumers are also paying for these subsidies through taxes. Because of the inefficiency of the program, the taxpayers—you and I—will probably pay

GO ON TO THE NEXT PAGE

4   4   4   4   4   4

35 more in excess taxes than we will ever get
back in lower corn or wheat prices.

In fact, farm subsidies are not intended to
reduce food prices significantly. When prices
are too low, farmers lose money. To prevent
40 such a situation, Congress also pays farmers
to leave their land fallow, resulting in lower
supply and thus higher prices. To obscure
this intended effect, and because eschewing
cultivation can improve the quality of soil,
45 these payments are called "environmental
conservation" subsidies.

Another myth is that farm subsidies
increase exports, and therefore benefit the
American economy, by lowering the price of
50 products and making them more attractive to
foreign consumers. This claim ignores at
least two realities. First, just as farm
subsidies transfer wealth from taxpayers to
domestic consumers, so they transfer tax
55 wealth to foreign consumers. Second, farm
subsidies are becoming a liability to
American exporters. In April 2004, the World
Trade Organization ruled that American
cotton subsidies violated global trade rules,
60 which could lead to billions of dollars in
retaliatory tariffs or fines. These realities are
doing more harm than good to our country's
economy.

Our most enduring and politically
65 appealing illusion about subsidies is that we
must maintain them in order to save the
small family farmer. Indeed, about 77 percent
of Americans said that they support giving
subsidies to small family farms, according to
70 a 2004 poll. However, small family farmers
are not, by a long shot, the primary recipients
of federal subsidies. According to the
Environmental Working Group, a watchdog
organization, 71 percent of farm subsidies go
75 to the top 10 percent of beneficiaries, almost
all of which are large wealthy farms.

The result of subsidizing the rich, more
landed farmers is that they can reduce the
prices of their goods, making it much harder
80 for small farmers to compete. Rather than
saving family farmers, subsidies work
against them.

Rich farmers are a powerful lobby in
American politics. In 2003, crop producers
85 gave $11.5 million in campaign contributions,
according to the Center for Responsive
Politics, and they are likely to give much
more in the future.

So don't be surprised that the GAO's report
90 won't be taken too seriously on Capitol Hill.
Farm subsidies are more than just payoffs to
wealthy, large landowners. They are subsidies
for elected officials, too.

PASSAGE 2

There has been much public outcry about the
95 farm subsidy system, but its critics fail to
recognize just how important these subsidies
really are. Farm subsidies protect farmers
from damaging fluctuations in commodity
prices that can result from wild fluctuations
100 in the market or crop failure due to weather.
At the same time, they protect consumers
from potential price spikes that can accompany
steep drops in crop inventories. Before price
supports became common in the 20th
105 century, crop failure was a fact of life driven
home with horrifying frequency.

Opponents of farm subsidies suggest that
the system creates the problem of inventory
oversupply. That is true, but this is only
110 because regular shortfalls would be even
more worrisome. The massive year-to-year
carryover of these inventories helps to
safeguard against excessive price fluctuations
that otherwise would follow natural or
115 market-driven setbacks. Subsidies protect
consumers from high prices and farmers
from low prices.

GO ON TO THE NEXT PAGE

Passage 1 © 2005 The Independent Institute. Adapted from an article by Nicolas Heidorn at *http://www.independent.org/newsroom/article.asp?id=1340*
Passage 2 © 2005 Mark Anestis. Reprinted with the permission of the author.

One of the major misconceptions associated with farm subsidies, particularly
120 among consumers, is that only the producers receive the benefits of this funding. This is untrue. Subsidies virtually guarantee that products are produced in large amounts. This does indeed benefit the producers, but it also
125 benefits others along the food processing, distribution and marketing chain. Farmers receive direct benefits, but others along the way receive indirect benefits thanks to cheaper production inputs, which, in turn,
130 contribute to lower production costs and thus lower prices for the consumers.

When assessing the costs and benefits of U.S. farm payments, it is important to compare these costs to those of other industrial nations.
135 American farmers receive a much lower percentage of their incomes—about 20%— from subsidies than do farmers from other countries. In some countries, more than 70 percent of farm revenue is derived from
140 government payments. The European Union spends more than twice as much annually as the United States does on farm supports, despite having a smaller farm economy. When used efficiently, farm subsidies can
145 be of great benefit. The farm subsidization system is not perfect, but its positive impacts far outweigh its negative ones.

13. The "rotten" (line 1) thing is the fact that

(A) the government is not doing enough to help small farmers
(B) many American farmers are violating the law
(C) a governmental program is ineffective and unfair
(D) farmers are not taking advantage of important new technologies
(E) American farmers are unable to compete in international markets

14. The statement that "they probably won't" (line 8) is intended to indicate that

(A) the subsidy program is not as bad as it seems
(B) lawmakers are unlikely to see the report
(C) legislators are not likely to be persuaded by reports of mismanagement
(D) the GAO report is not entirely accurate
(E) legislators do not care enough about the concerns of farmers

15. The purpose of the fourth paragraph of Passage 1 (lines 28–36) is to

(A) describe a problem that farmers face
(B) show how increased agricultural production lowers taxes
(C) describe an authoritative study that supports the author's claim
(D) dispel a belief about the effectiveness of subsidies
(E) reveal a hidden benefit to agricultural subsidies

16. The author of Passage 1 uses quotation marks around the phrase "environmental conservation" (lines 45–46) in order to show that it is

(A) a misleading term
(B) being used only in the context of this passage
(C) intended to be taken humorously
(D) beyond the understanding of most readers
(E) derived from an obscure foreign phrase

17. The "2004 poll" (line 79) was intended to determine

(A) the political affiliation of farmers
(B) the rate of consumption of certain agricultural products
(C) opinions on environmental issues
(D) instances of the misuse of farm subsidies
(E) public sentiment for a governmental program

GO ON TO THE NEXT PAGE

4   4   4   4   4   4

18. The statement that "They are subsidies for elected officials, too" (lines 92–93) means that legislators

   (A) receive indirect political benefits from the subsidy program
   (B) own the agricultural means of production
   (C) are permitted to receive direct subsidies under USDA guidelines
   (D) frequently compete with farmers for government funds
   (E) are working to reduce inefficiencies in the farm subsidies program

19. Passage 2 indicates that the "problem of inventory over supply" (lines 108–109) is

   (A) being alleviated by farm subsidy payments
   (B) not as problematic as it may seem
   (C) an unavoidable aspect of farming
   (D) the result of excessive price fluctuations
   (E) more dangerous to consumers than to farmers

20. The "chain" (line 126) is likely to include all of the following EXCEPT

   (A) produce truck drivers
   (B) fruit store owners
   (C) legislators who support subsidies
   (D) associations that promote agricultural products
   (E) vegetable canning factories

21. Both passages agree that the American farm subsidies program

   (A) is mismanaged
   (B) benefits small farmers
   (C) is not supported by most voters
   (D) is employed more for political than economic ends
   (E) can control the price of agricultural products

22. The author of Passage 1 would most likely respond to the claim that farm subsidies produce "lower prices for the consumers" (line 131) by claiming that

   (A) this is untrue because crop failures that lead to higher prices are unavoidable
   (B) the USDA pays too little in subsidies to provide such a benefit to consumers
   (C) owners of large farms do not benefit from these lower prices
   (D) higher prices can actually be beneficial to consumers
   (E) these lower prices are not worth the tax increases to consumers that are needed to pay for it

23. The attitudes toward farm subsidies of Passage 1 and Passage 2, respectively, can best be described as

   (A) cautiously optimistic and cynical
   (B) disdainful and supportive
   (C) critical and incredulous
   (D) objectively analytical and sarcastic
   (E) respectful and skeptical

24. Which of the following can be found in BOTH passages?

   I. a verifiable statistic
   II. a refutation of a misconception
   III. a reference to political corruption

   (A) I only
   (B) I and II only
   (C) I and III only
   (D) II and III only
   (E) I, II, and III

If you finish before time is called, you may check your work on this section only. Do not turn to any other section of the test.

5   5   5   5   5   5

SECTION 5
Time—25 minutes
18 questions

> **Turn to Section 5 of your answer sheet to answer the questions in this section.**

Directions: This section contains two types of questions. You have 25 minutes to complete both types. For questions 1–8, solve each problem and decide which is the best of the choices given. Fill in the corresponding circle on the answer sheet. You may use any available space for scratchwork.

Notes

1. The use of a calculator is permitted.
2. All numbers used are real numbers.
3. Figures that accompany problems in this test are intended to provide information useful in solving the problems. They are drawn as accurately as possible EXCEPT when it is stated in a specific problem that the figure is not drawn to scale. All figures lie in a plane unless otherwise indicated.
4. Unless otherwise specified, the domain of any function f is assumed to be the set of all real numbers x for which $f(x)$ is a real number.

Reference Information

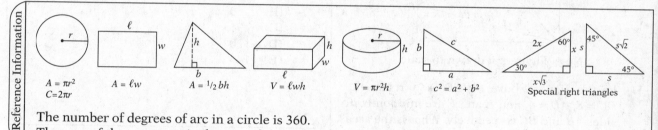

$A = \pi r^2$
$C = 2\pi r$

$A = \ell w$

$A = \frac{1}{2} bh$

$V = \ell w h$

$V = \pi r^2 h$

$c^2 = a^2 + b^2$

Special right triangles

The number of degrees of arc in a circle is 360.
The sum of the measures in degrees of the angles of a triangle is 180.

---

1. If pens cost \$3 each and binders cost \$2 each, which of the following represents the cost, in dollars, of p pens and b binders?

(A) $5(b + p)$
(B) $3bp$
(C) $3p + 2b$
(D) $2(p + b)$
(E) $6bp$

2. Which of the following integers is divisible by 4 and 6, but is not divisible by 8?

(A) 12
(B) 24
(C) 48
(D) 64
(E) 72

3. If $8{,}755 = 85(x + 2)$, then $x =$

(A) 12
(B) 14
(C) 100
(D) 101
(E) 102

GO ON TO THE NEXT PAGE

5   **5**   **5**   **5**   **5**   **5**

4. Let $x \Delta y \Delta z$ be defined by the equation

$$x \Delta y \Delta z = \left(\frac{x}{z}\right)y + xz$$

for all non-zero numbers x, y, and z. Which of the following is equal to an odd integer?

(A) $4 \Delta 8 \Delta 2$
(B) $3 \Delta 2 \Delta 1$
(C) $9 \Delta 3 \Delta 3$
(D) $8 \Delta 6 \Delta 4$
(E) $5 \Delta 7 \Delta 1$

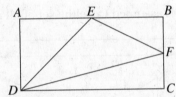

Note: Figure not drawn to scale.

5. In the figure above, $ABCD$ is a rectangle. $DC = 8$, $AD = 4$, and E and F are midpoints of sides AB and BC respectively. What is the area of $\triangle DEF$?

(A) 12
(B) 18
(C) 24
(D) 28
(E) 32

6. How many different four-digit integers can be formed using the digits 3, 4, 5, 6, 7, 8, 9 if the tens digit is 5 and no digit is repeated within an integer?

(A) 16
(B) 45
(C) 63
(D) 120
(E) 840

7. Zander drives to work at an average speed of 40 miles per hour and returns home along the same route at an average speed of 24 miles per hour. If his total travel time is 4 hours, what is the total number of miles in the roundtrip to and from work?

(A) 48
(B) 60
(C) 96
(D) 120
(E) 144

8. A swimming pool with a capacity of 20,000 gallons is one-quarter full. A pump can deliver g gallons of water every m minutes. If a company charges d dollars per minute for the use of the pump, then in terms of g, m, and d, how much will it cost, in dollars, to fill the pool?

(A) $\dfrac{15,000\,gd}{m}$

(B) $15,000gmd$

(C) $\dfrac{15,000md}{g}$

(D) $\dfrac{gd}{15,000m}$

(E) $\dfrac{gm}{15,000d}$

GO ON TO THE NEXT PAGE ⟹

5   5   5   5   5   5

Directions: For student-produced response questions 9–18, use the grids at the bottom of the answer sheet page on which you have answered questions 1–8.

Each of the remaining ten questions requires you to solve the problem and enter your answer by marking the circles in the special grid, as shown in the examples below. You may use any available space for scratchwork.

Answer: $\frac{7}{12}$

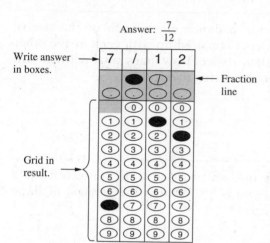

Write answer in boxes. — Fraction line

Grid in result.

Answer: 2.5

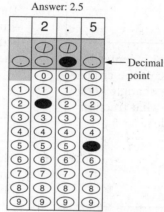

Decimal point

Answer: 201
Either position is correct.

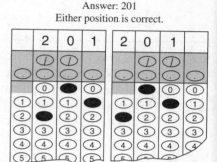

Note: You may start your answers in any column, space permitting. Columns not needed should be left blank.

- Mark no more than one circle in any column.

- Because the answer sheet will be machine-scored, **you will receive credit only if the circles are filled in correctly.**

- Although not required, it is suggested that you write your answer in the boxes at the top of the columns to help you fill in the circles accurately.

- Some problems may have more than one correct answer. In such cases, grid only one answer.

- No question has a negative answer.

- **Mixed numbers** such as $3\frac{1}{2}$ must be gridded as 3.5 or 7/2. (If [3 1 / 2] is gridded, it will be interpreted as, $\frac{31}{2}$ not $3\frac{1}{2}$.)

- **Decimal Answers:** If you obtain a decimal answer with more digits than the grid can accommodate, it may be either rounded or truncated, but it must fill the entire grid. For example, if you obtain an answer such as 0.6666..., you should record your result as .666 or .667. **A less accurate value such as .66 or .67 will be scored as incorrect.**

Acceptable ways to grid $2/3$ are:

$$\begin{array}{c} XYZ \\ + \quad ZYX \\ \hline 848 \end{array}$$

9. In the correctly solved addition problem above, the letters X, Y, and Z represent different digits. What is the value of $X + Y + Z$?

10. A rectangular shaped field has a perimeter of 300 feet and a width of 60 feet. What is the area of the field in square feet?

GO ON TO THE NEXT PAGE ⟩

5   5   5   5   5   5

$$f(x) = 8x - 4$$

$$g(x) = x^2 - 3$$

11. Given the functions above, what is the value of $f(g(3))$?

12. Points X and Y are on a circle with center O, and point Z is on the longer arc of the circle between X and Y. If the measure of angle XOY is $135°$, the length of arc XZY is what fraction of the circumference of the circle?

13. If $ab + \dfrac{1}{ab} = 4$, what is the value of $a^2 b^2 + \dfrac{1}{a^2 b^2}$?

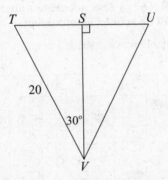

Note: Figure not drawn to scale.

14. In triangle TUV above, what is the length of TS?

15. If $|-3x + 5| < 6$, what is one possible value of x if x must be a positive odd integer?

16. During a dance class, each of the twelve students is paired up with each of the other students twice. How many total pairings will there be during the class?

17. The median of a set of 55 consecutive odd integers is 55. What is the greatest of these integers?

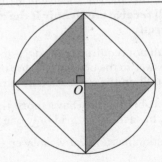

18. If the shaded region above has a perimeter of $24 + 12\sqrt{2}$ units, what is the area of the inscribed square?

If you finish before time is called, you may check your work on this section only. Do not turn to any other section of the test.

6   6   6   6   6   ·   **6**

SECTION 6
Time—25 minutes
24 questions

> **Turn to Section 6 of your answer sheet to answer the questions in this section.**

> **Directions:** For each question in this section, select the best answer from among the choices given and fill in the corresponding circle on the answer sheet.

Each sentence below has one or two blanks, each blank indicating that something has been omitted. Beneath the sentence are five words or sets of words labeled A through E. Choose the word or set of words that, when inserted in the sentence, <u>best</u> fits the meaning of the sentence as a whole.

EXAMPLE:

Rather than accepting the theory unquestioningly, Deborah regarded it with -----.

(A) mirth
(B) sadness
(C) responsibility
(D) ignorance
(E) skepticism

Ⓐ Ⓑ Ⓒ Ⓓ ●

---

1. The athlete committed such a ------- foul that the referee had no choice but to throw him out of the game and petition for a -------.

    (A) blatant . . suspension
    (B) miniscule . . fine
    (C) egregious . . celebration
    (D) obligatory . . decoration
    (E) nautical . . ceremony

2. During her first two years at the firm, Tracy worked with a ------- that helped her to become the youngest partner in company history; no associate before her had ever accomplished so much with such a consistent standard of excellence.

    (A) gratuity   (B) dormancy
    (C) lethargy   (D) capriciousness
    (E) diligence

3. Oprah Winfrey is one of her generation's most famous -------; she has a ------- for devoting her time and money to helping those who are less fortunate.

    (A) altruists . . dislike
    (B) charlatans . . prerequisite
    (C) philanthropists . . penchant
    (D) nihilists . . sympathy
    (E) despots . . culpability

4. Although many actual criminal confessions take several hundred sentences elicited over several hours, in *Crime and Punishment*, Dostoevsky stages Raskolnikov's confession with relentlessly ------- plainness by using fewer than 20 words.

    (A) laconic
    (B) verbose
    (C) lugubrious
    (D) sonorous
    (E) antiquated

5. Losing his championship title to a weaker opponent was such a humbling experience for the fighter that his swagger and ------- public demeanor were replaced by a more modest and self-effacing persona.

    (A) lofty
    (B) impecunious
    (C) obligatory
    (D) prescient
    (E) pusillanimous

GO ON TO THE NEXT PAGE ⟩

6   **6**   **6**   **6**   **6**   **6**

The passages below are followed by questions based on their content. Answer the questions on the basis of what is <u>stated</u> or <u>implied</u> in the passage and in any introductory material that may be provided.

Questions 6–7 are based on the following passage.

The kareze system of irrigation was invented three thousand years ago during the height of
Line the Persian Empire in what is now Iran. Persian engineers tapped water by first
5   sinking a well at the apex of an alluvial fan— the location where a mountain river deposits its sediment—until it reached the water table. These muqannis, as they were called, then calculated where a tunnel with a slight
10   downward slope would reach the surface near a village. From that point, a tunnel was built to the mother well, supplying the village with a steady supply of much-needed water. These systems were very time-consuming and
15   expensive to build. Typical tunnels were several kilometers in length, but some could run 50 kilometers and take many years to build. Once they were built, however, so dramatically did the kareze improve the conditions of life
20   for villagers that wholly new societal relations and systems were formed.

6.   The primary purpose of the passage is to describe

   (A)   an architectural disaster
   (B)   a historical era
   (C)   a technological advance
   (D)   a geographical feature
   (E)   a social system

7.   The "muqannis" (line 8) were

   (A)   common villagers
   (B)   Persian kings
   (C)   sedimentary deposits
   (D)   tunnels
   (E)   engineers

Questions 8–9 are based on the following passage.

The theory of evolution has been a boon not only to biologists, but also to anthropologists.
Line Many customs can be explained as means of expressing or exaggerating genetic traits that
5   we have inherited from our forebears through the process of natural selection. For instance, sports can be seen as a means of expressing our genetic endowment as hunters, even though most societies no longer require
10   hunting. Likewise, face painting and body adornments can be seen as exaggerated expressions of those genetic traits that reflect health and virility. Expressing and exercising these inherited traits once had quite definite
15   survival value to individuals and societies. More mysterious to evolutionary anthropologists, however, is music. To what genetic trait can we attribute the universal love of music, and what survival benefit causes it to merit
20   selection by the evolutionary process?

8.   The statement that "most societies no longer require hunting" (lines 9–10) is intended to emphasize the fact that

   (A)   technological progress has been very rapid in recent decades
   (B)   many political groups opposed the hunting of animals
   (C)   sports express vestigial genetic traits
   (D)   societies are becoming less violent over time
   (E)   hunting is not as competitive as most other sports

9.   According to the passage, music is "mysterious" (line 16) because

   (A)   musical skill varies greatly from person to person within a population
   (B)   it is not as aggressive an activity as hunting is
   (C)   it is found in some cultures but not others
   (D)   it does not to appear to convey an obvious survival benefit
   (E)   musical skill cannot be inherited

GO ON TO THE NEXT PAGE →

Both passages © 2006 Christopher Black and College Hill Coaching. All rights reserved. Reprinted by permission of the author.

6 6 6 6 6 6

The passages below are followed by questions based on their content. Answer the questions on the basis of what is <u>stated</u> or <u>implied</u> in the passage and in any introductory material that may be provided.

Questions 10–16 pertain to the following passage.

The following passage discusses the native Nepalese people, the Sherpa, who have long aided climbers of Mount Everest.

The cheerful smiles and legendary strength of the Sherpas have been an integral part of
Line Everest climbing expeditions from the very beginning. Indeed, very few significant
5 successes have been achieved without them.

When Western mountaineers first set their sights on the world's highest peak, they found in the Sherpas a people ideally suited to the rigors of high-altitude climbing, unfailingly
10 positive, stout at altitude, and seemingly resistant to cold.

Sherpas did not venture into the high peaks until European mountaineers began arriving to climb in the world's greatest
15 mountain range. Mount Everest, known as Chomolungma or "Goddess Mother of the Land" to Tibetan language speakers like the Sherpas, was long revered as an abode of the gods. Its slopes were considered off-limits
20 to humans.

Although Everest now sees many a human footprint, the Sherpas still regard the mountain as a holy place. All modern expeditions begin with a Puja ceremony in
25 which Sherpas and other team members leave offerings and pay homage to the gods of the mountain, hoping to remain in their good graces throughout the climb.

A Himalayan veteran in the early 1920s,
30 Alexander Kellas is generally regarded as the first person to recognize the natural aptitude of the Sherpa people for hard work and

climbing at high altitude. In his time, Kellas was perhaps the world's leading expert on
35 mountain sickness and the effects of high altitude. He recognized that Sherpas did not feel these effects in the same way as others, though it remains unclear what combination of genetics and an upbringing at high altitude
40 allows the Sherpas to deal physiologically with altitude better than others.

Sherpas were first employed as porters, tasked with carrying large amounts of equipment to supply the military-style
45 expeditions of the day. The British climbers were amazed at the strength of these people, from the fittest of mature men to the young and elderly. Arthur Wakefield described the team of porters on one early expedition as "a
50 motley throng of old men, women, boys and girls." Yet their accomplishments astonished him. At 18,000 feet, how the Sherpas carried their loads "completely puzzles me," he wrote. "Some were 80 pounds!" In addition
55 to their loads, some of the women carried along their babies. The whole troop slept outside, using only rocks for shelter, as temperatures dropped well below freezing.

Stronger Sherpas soon graduated from
60 porter status and began to undertake challenging climbing and work high on the mountain. Those who distinguished themselves high on the mountain were awarded the Tiger Medal, and many aspired to this honor
65 and the higher pay rate it afforded.

Unfortunately, Sherpas were also the first to suffer the consequences that can come from climbing high on Everest. A North Col avalanche killed seven Sherpa porters on the
70 1922 expedition, the first recorded climbing fatalities on the mountain. Even after the disaster, however, the Sherpa people remained enthusiastic about taking part in Everest expeditions, which even then were becoming
75 an important source of revenue for a poor mountain folk.

GO ON TO THE NEXT PAGE →

Excerpted from: http://www.news.nationalgeographic.com/news/2002/05/0507_020507_sherpas.html

10. According to the passage, Sherpas supply which of the following to the climbers of Mount Everest?

    I.   ability to work in harsh environments
    II. expertise in treating altitude sickness
    III. physical strength and climbing ability

  (A) I only
  (B) I and II only
  (C) I and III only
  (D) II and III only
  (E) I, II, and III

11. The passage indicates that, before Europeans arrived to climb Mount Everest, the Sherpas

  (A) were unaware of the mountain
  (B) regarded the mountain as evil
  (C) had been climbing the mountain for centuries
  (D) only climbed to the summit for religious purposes
  (E) had not explored the highest part of the mountain

12. Wakefield's description of the Sherpas in lines 49–51 emphasizes their

  (A) heterogeneity
  (B) intelligence
  (C) youth
  (D) wisdom
  (E) cheerfulness

13. Arthur Wakefield's attitude toward the Sherpas is best described as

  (A) awed
  (B) skeptical
  (C) condescending
  (D) antagonistic
  (E) detached

14. The passage contains information to answer all of the following questions EXCEPT

  (A) When were the first climbing fatalities on Mount Everest?
  (B) Who was the first European to climb Mount Everest?
  (C) What is the Tibetan name for Mount Everest?
  (D) What is the name of the Sherpa religious ceremony that begins an expedition?
  (E) Who was the first European to recognize the value of the Sherpas as climbing guides?

15. The reference to "rocks" in line 57 serves primarily to emphasize

  (A) the challenges endured by the European climbers
  (B) the barren landscape of Mount Everest
  (C) the sacredness of the mountain to the Sherpas
  (D) the ruggedness of the Sherpas
  (E) the aloofness of the Sherpas

16. The passage indicates that the Sherpas continue to assist in Everest expeditions despite the dangers because

    I.   it has been a social custom for many centuries
    II. the climbing prowess of the Sherpas often reflects their social status
    III. it sustains their economy
    IV. it is a religious duty

  (A) I and III only
  (B) II and III only
  (C) I, II, and III only
  (D) I, II, and IV only
  (E) II, III, and IV only

GO ON TO THE NEXT PAGE

Questions 17–24 are based on the following passage.

The following passage discusses recent research in the area of animal communication.

The fact that animals can communicate with each other is obvious to anyone who has ever
Line watched a pack of dogs or a group of farm cats interact. But just how complex is animal
5 communication? For instance, humans can communicate about concepts and about events in the past or in the future. Can animal communication come anywhere close to this level of complexity? Recent research
10 has shed a great deal of light on this subject. A scientific conference on animal communication held in 2000 drew together animal behaviorists studying species ranging from parrots to whales.
15   One of the more fascinating discoveries reported was that sperm whales, which have the largest brains on Earth, have a female-dominated, egalitarian society similar to that of the African elephant. Elephants
20 communicate with extremely low tones that can carry several kilometers. These tones, called infrasound because they are below the frequencies that humans can hear, can be as loud as a typical truck or tractor. Similarly,
25 whales generate very loud clicks that carry enormous distances—perhaps hundreds of miles—through the water. Whales can hear nearly all of the frequencies that humans can, as well as many far higher than the human
30 range. It appears whales are talking louder because of the increased noise in the oceans from ships—just as humans talk louder in a noisy bar than on a quiet beach.
To study dolphins, another highly evolved
35 mammal with a complex social life, scientists tow microphones behind boats to record the dolphins' conversations. It appears that each dolphin develops his or her own signature signal, which researcher Vincent Janik
40 compares to an Internet screen name. Janik studied wild bottlenose dolphins off Moray Firth, Scotland, recording 1,719 whistles in all. Each dolphin he studied made a distinctive whistle that other dolphins would

45 imitate in response, presumably to keep in touch. Janik employed human judges to determine if calls were identical, because computers are not yet up to the task.
The dolphins also use a distinctive sound
50 when they find food, a low-pitched noise that sounds very much like the braying of a donkey. When one dolphin utters this call, other dolphins rush in to feed. Janik doesn't like to call all this communication
55 "language," in deference to the complexity of human interaction, preferring to call it instead "a complex communication system," and says it resembles ancient humans' first steps toward language.
60   Dolphins are studied in this field because of their intelligence, as are chimpanzees, which some scientists consider to be our closest animal relatives. One study suggests that "food barks" uttered by chimpanzees
65 don't only announce the discovery of food, but also its type and quality. Similarly, studies of monkeys have found that they utter cries that don't just warn of the presence of predators, but tell what kind of
70 predator to look out for. Chimpanzees can even communicate silently. A researcher watched two chimpanzees cooperate with each other to catch and kill a small monkey without a sound, possibly because they were
75 within vocal range of other members of their tribe and preferred not to share their lunch.
Another study looked at chimpanzees' ability to read facial expressions. Chimpanzees were shown short videos
80 depicting positive and negative emotional events, and then were presented with images of two facial expressions, one of which conveyed an emotional meaning similar to that in the video. Without prompting, some
85 of the chimps associated negative facial expressions (such as screams and bared teeth) with scenes such as veterinary procedures and injection needles, and positive facial expressions with scenes of
90 favorite foods and objects, indicating that they can, indeed, inherently read facial expressions without being specifically trained to do so.

Excerpted from a column written by Edward Willett:
http://www.edwardwillett.com/Columns/animalcomm.htm

GO ON TO THE NEXT PAGE ➡

Other research presented at the conference
95 indicated that even sea lions can reason via
transitivity, that is, by logic analogous to "if A
equals B, and B equals C, then A equals C."
For instance, in the wild, male sea lions will
fight a male they have seen beaten by
100 another that they, in turn, have beaten.
Evolving research continues to show that
our animal cousins are more sophisticated
communicators, and have more sophisticated
societies, than we normally give them credit
105 for. So keep an eye on your pet: he may be
trying to tell you something.

17. The phrase "this level of complexity" (line 9)
refers to the process of

(A) studying the communication of a wide
range of animals
(B) maintaining animals in groups, such as
dog packs
(C) conveying abstract information through
language
(D) drawing together researchers from many
different fields
(E) remembering events from the distant
past

18. If the discovery mentioned in lines 15–19 ("One
of the...African elephant") was relevant to the
conference at which it was reported, then it can
be inferred that animal behaviorists

(A) believe that human societies should be as
egalitarian as other mammalian societies
(B) believe that sperm whales have more
sophisticated communication skills than
do African elephants
(C) have long assumed that language skill
increases in proportion to brain size
(D) consider females to be more communicative than males in most animal
societies
(E) regard systems of social organization
to be relevant to the study of animal
communication

19. The passage indicates that elephants are similar to sperm whales in terms of their

I. ability to hear lower frequencies
than those humans can perceive
II. complex social organization
III. ability to communicate over long
distances

(A) II only
(B) I and II only
(C) II and III only
(D) I and III only
(E) I, II, and III

20. The statement in lines 30–33 ("It appears
whales...on a quiet beach") suggests that
whales

(A) are often disoriented by the noise
coming from ships
(B) do not emit such powerful sounds when
they are far from shipping lanes
(C) are occasionally fooled into believing
that the sounds from ships are actually
coming from other whales
(D) emit high-frequency sounds in order to
avoid being perceived by humans and
other predators
(E) tend to spend more time near beaches
than they do in very deep waters

21. The words "appears" (line 37) and "presumably"
(line 45) serve primarily to

(A) indicate that some conjecture has been
applied to the results of Janik's research
(B) suggest that Janik's research method was
not very sophisticated
(C) refute the widely held assumption that
dolphins have an intricate system of
communication
(D) cast doubt on the scientific validity
of comparing dolphins to other
mammals
(E) imply that the number of distinct dolphin whistles that Janik distinguished
may not be as high as reported

GO ON TO THE NEXT PAGE

6   **6**   **6**   **6**   **6**   **6**

22. The "task" in line 48 refers to the process of

   (A) comparing underwater sounds
   (B) counting the number of whistles
   (C) determining why dolphins make certain noises
   (D) recording sounds in the ocean
   (E) communicating with dolphins

23. The study described in lines 77–93 was intended primarily to examine the ability of chimpanzees to

   (A) distinguish between human faces and chimpanzee faces
   (B) communicate effectively with other chimpanzees through emotional sounds
   (C) recognize relevant objects like their favorite foods
   (D) associate perceived facial expressions with emotions
   (E) convey emotions without sound

24. Which of the following, if true, would most effectively undermine the author's claim that a sea lion can reason "via transitivity" (lines 95–96)?

   (A) The sea lion sometimes fights members of his own family.
   (B) The sea lion fights other sea lions only to assert social dominance.
   (C) The sea lion only fights other sea lions that he has seen defeated by others.
   (D) The sea lion often fights others that he has seen defeat those sea lions that have also defeated him.
   (E) The sea lion refuses to fight any other sea lions.

 **STOP**

If you finish before time is called, you may check your work on this section only. Do not turn to any other section of the test.

7 **7** **7** **7** **7** **7**

SECTION 7
Time—20 minutes
16 questions

> **Turn to Section 7 of your answer sheet to answer the questions in this section.**

Directions: For this section, solve each problem and decide which is the best of the choices given. Fill in the corresponding circle on the answer sheet. You may use any available space for scratchwork.

Notes

1. The use of a calculator is permitted.

2. All numbers used are real numbers.

3. Figures that accompany problems in this test are intended to provide information useful in solving the problems. They are drawn as accurately as possible EXCEPT when it is stated in a specific problem that the figure is not drawn to scale. All figures lie in a plane unless otherwise indicated.

4. Unless otherwise specified, the domain of any function f is assumed to be the set of all real numbers x for which $f(x)$ is a real number.

Reference Information

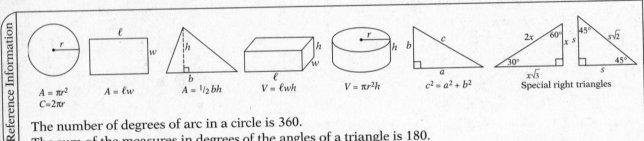

$A = \pi r^2$
$C = 2\pi r$

$A = \ell w$

$A = \frac{1}{2}bh$

$V = \ell w h$

$V = \pi r^2 h$

$c^2 = a^2 + b^2$

Special right triangles

The number of degrees of arc in a circle is 360.
The sum of the measures in degrees of the angles of a triangle is 180.

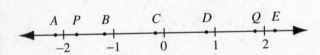

1. In the figure above, if the coordinates of points P and Q are multiplied together, the result will be closest to which of the following points?

(A) A
(B) B
(C) C
(D) D
(E) E

---

2. If $\frac{x}{8} = 5z$ and $\frac{1}{2z} = 5y$, then $xy =$

(A) 3
(B) 4
(C) 12
(D) 24
(E) 36

---

3. When a positive integer p is divided by 7, the remainder is 2. Which of the following expressions will yield a remainder of 4 when divided by 7?

(A) $p + 2$
(B) $p + 3$
(C) $p + 4$
(D) $p + 5$
(E) $p + 6$

GO ON TO THE NEXT PAGE ⟹

7   7   7   7   7   7

SALARY GROWTH AT ACME PLUS CO.

YEARS WITH COMPANY	1	2	3	4	5
SALARY (in thousands)	32	33	36	42	51

4. Which of the following graphs best represents the information in the table above?

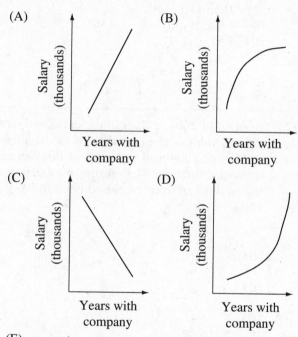

(A)

(B)

(C)

(D)

(E)

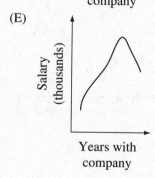

5. Four hundred dollars was invested at a yearly simple interest rate of x percent. If at the end of one year the investment had grown to 500 dollars, what is the value of x?

(A)   20
(B)   25
(C)   30
(D)   35
(E)   40

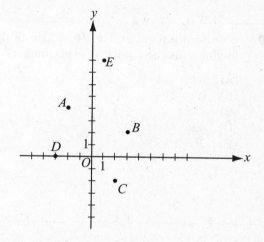

6. In the figure above, which of the following line segments (not shown) has a slope of −3?

(A) $\overline{AB}$

(B) $\overline{AC}$

(C) $\overline{AD}$

(D) $\overline{EB}$

(E) $\overline{DC}$

7. In a parking lot, ¾ of the vehicles are cars and ⅓ of the cars are more than 3 years old. If 20 cars in the lot are more than 3 years old, how many vehicles are there in total?

(A)   30
(B)   40
(C)   60
(D)   80
(E)   90

GO ON TO THE NEXT PAGE ⟩

8. What is the average (arithmetic mean) of 8 consecutive *odd* integers if the smallest of those integers is n?

(A) $n + 5$
(B) $n + 6$
(C) $n + 7$
(D) $n + 8$
(E) $n + 9$

9. If w is an integer and $w \neq 0$, which of the following must be a positive even integer?

(A) w^4
(B) $(w - 2)^3$
(C) $4w^2$
(D) $4w$
(E) $3(w^2)$

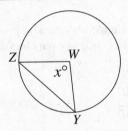

Note: Figure not drawn to scale.

10. In the circle above, W is the center of the circle and the length of ZY is 8. If the area of the circle is 64π, what is the value of x?

(A) 40
(B) 50
(C) 60
(D) 70
(E) 80

11. Which of the following expressions is equivalent to $16x^4$?

I. $(64x^6)^{2/3}$

II. $\left(\dfrac{1}{2x}\right)^{-4}$

III. $\dfrac{x^2}{16x^{-1}}$

(A) I only
(B) II only
(C) II and III only
(D) I and II only
(E) I, II, and III

12. In April of 2004, d dogs and c cats lived in an animal shelter. If 4 cats arrived at the shelter in May of 2004 and the ratio of dogs to cats remained unchanged, in terms of c and d, how many dogs arrived at the shelter in May of 2004?

(A) 4

(B) $\dfrac{4d}{c}$

(C) $\dfrac{d}{c}$

(D) $d^2 - 4d$

(E) $\dfrac{2cd + 4d}{c}$

13. If $2 < |a| < 6$ and $3 < |b| < 6$, which of the following must be true?

(A) $a > b$
(B) $b > a$
(C) $0 < ab$
(D) $|ab| > 6$
(E) $36 < |a + b|$

GO ON TO THE NEXT PAGE ⟹

14. When each side of a square is lengthened by 4 inches, the area of the square is increased by 112 square inches. What is the length, in inches, of one side of the original square?

    (A) 10
    (B) 11
    (C) 12
    (D) 13
    (E) 14

15. $(-4x^4y^{-3})^{-3} =$

    (A) $\dfrac{-4x}{y^6}$

    (B) $\dfrac{-64y^9}{x^{12}}$

    (C) $\dfrac{-64y^6}{x^7}$

    (D) $-4x^{12}y^9$

    (E) $\dfrac{y^9}{-64x^{12}}$

16. If the function h is defined by $h(x) = ax^2 + bx + c$, and both a and c are negative integers, which of the following could be the graph of the function h?

(A)

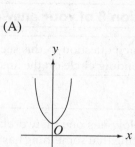

(B)

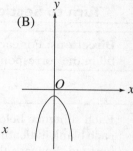

(C)

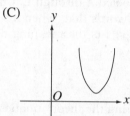

(D)

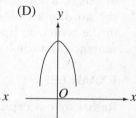

(E)

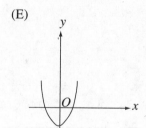

STOP

If you finish before time is called, you may check your work on this section only. Do not turn to any other section of the test.

8　　**8**　　**8**　　**8**　　**8**　　**8**

SECTION 8
Time—20 minutes
19 questions

Turn to Section 8 of your answer sheet to answer the questions in this section.

Directions: For each question in this section, select the best answer from among the choices given and fill in the corresponding circle on the answer sheet.

Each sentence below has one or two blanks, each blank indicating that something has been omitted. Beneath the sentence are five words or sets of words labeled A through E. Choose the word or set of words that, when inserted in the sentence, <u>best</u> fits the meaning of the sentence as a whole.

EXAMPLE:

Rather than accepting the theory unquestioningly, Deborah regarded it with-------.

(A) mirth
(B) sadness
(C) responsibility
(D) ignorance
(E) skepticism

Ⓐ Ⓑ Ⓒ Ⓓ ●

---

1. As one of the most ------- writers of the 20th century, Jack Kerouac authored several books that ------- to a wide variety of readers.

   (A) cryptic . . complained
   (B) prolific . . appealed
   (C) provocative . . attested
   (D) arrogant . . spoke
   (E) garish . . whispered

2. Since the downsizing, the company has shifted its focus from one that ------- many different points of view to one that ------- the voicing of different opinions.

   (A) amplifies . . condemns
   (B) eschews . . villifies
   (C) embraces . . denounces
   (D) seeks . . comprehends
   (E) anticipates . . incorporates

3. The calculus problem was so difficult that even the most ------- mathematicians in the class struggled to derive the answer.

   (A) agile　　　　(B) adept
   (C) abysmal　　 (D) insipid
   (E) eloquent

4. The student's ------- was something the principal was not going to -------, and she punished the sophomore harshly for undermining the teacher's authority.

   (A) insubordination . . condone
   (B) dissemination . . assuage
   (C) improvidence . . provoke
   (D) subterfuge . . expedite
   (E) impudence . . inundate

5. A good advertisement ------- potential customers to act, buy and consume; it persuades them that they must have the item on display.

   (A) perpetuates　(B) thwarts
   (C) consoles　　 (D) exhorts
   (E) reproaches

6. Bartlett Jere Whiting's articles, though written long ago, demonstrate such a ------- and clarity of thinking that they still are included in bibliographies relating to this discipline.

   (A) modicum　　 (B) respite
   (C) dearth　　　 (D) turpitude
   (E) perspicacity

GO ON TO THE NEXT PAGE

8   8   8   8   8   8

The passages below are followed by questions based on their content; questions following a pair of related passages may also be based on the relationship between the paired passages. Answer the questions on the basis of what is stated or implied in the passage and in any introductory material that may be provided.

Questions 7–19 pertain to the following passage.

The following essay discusses the development of mathematics throughout history.

Metaphysics and mathematics have crossed paths many times in history, and at various
Line angles and energies—often, but not exclusively, to their mutual benefit. In ancient
5 civilizations, both arts were remote to commoners, and were often practiced together in sacred temples. But today their spheres have become separate, one dedicated to persuading human subjects, the other to
10 revealing truths.

The Babylonians were among the first to learn the instrumental value of mathematics. They used it to calculate the quantities of bricks required to construct
15 edifices, and to predict the seasons and other astronomical occurrences. But because they regarded the celestial bodies as divine, mathematics came to be regarded also as an instrument of worship. Likewise,
20 the Egyptians employed geometrical methods to construct the pyramids and align them with the sacred heavens. Reciprocally, the gods could use mathematics to communicate with believers,
25 confounding them to set their minds properly, or so thought Plato in interpreting the oracle's demand that the Delians double the volume of their altar, a task beyond Greek mathematicians. The Neoplatonist
30 philosopher Proclus likely had this sacred instrumentality in mind when he wrote that mathematics "reminds one of the invisible form of the soul...[and] awakens the mind and purifies the intellect."

35 Even in the Middle Ages, numbers could represent mystical truths. The number 3 represented the Holy Trinity, and the infinitude of the counting numbers signified the infinitudes of God. Even as late as the
40 20th century, Christian mathematician Gregor Cantor believed that he could offer Christianity theology "the true theory of the infinite."

This metaphor, however, could reach
45 absurd levels when applied too literally, as when the number π, the ratio of the circumference of a circle to its diameter, was taken by Biblical literalists to be precisely 3, in affirmation of the Holy
50 Trinity. Ignorant of mathematical analysis, they took their evidence directly from the book of Kings, which stated that a circular cauldron in the temple of Solomon measured ten cubits across and thirty cubits
55 around. Yet not even an infinite power can construct a circle ten cubits across that can be encircled with fewer than 31.4 cubits, a fact proven centuries before the dawn of Christianity.

60 This power of deduction to prove truths beyond the whims of the gods has led some to posit that mathematics itself is a mystical power. The followers of Pythagoras, the *mathematekoi*, took this
65 manner of thinking to the extreme. Their creed was "all is number," and they regarded the pursuit of mathematical proof to be the pursuit of the divine. Mathematics acquired its own abstract
70 plane beyond the physical world. To the *mathematekoi*, the order of nature reflected the rules of mathematics, not divine caprice. The Pythagoreans were a conspicuously disciplined sect, eschewing
75 meat and animal skin clothing, and seeking purity in all things.

Yet even among the *mathematekoi*, as often happens when humans identify too closely with the divine, unreasoning
80 righteousness ascended. Every new proof was celebrated, with animal sacrifices, as a

GO ON TO THE NEXT PAGE

© 2006 Christopher Black and College Hill Coaching. All rights reserved. Reprinted by permission of the author.

confirmation of ideological purity. Yet
seeming transgressions were punished with
violence. When Hipposus dared to prove
85   that the length of the hypotenuse of a
unitary isosceles right triangle cannot be
expressed as the ratio of whole numbers, his
fellow cult members threw him from a ship
and drowned him. His proof refuted their
90   religious precept that all of reality can be
described with whole numbers and their
ratios.
      As Hipposus' hypotenuse revealed, either
mathematical logic or religious ideology
95   would have to yield, and history has favored
mathematics. Hipposus has been vindicated.
The power of mathematical deduction,
properly implemented, is absolute, unlike
the more human philosophies. Truth is not
100 revealed; it is deduced. Nature is not
controlled by the capricious and obscure
will of the gods, but rather by reliable and
knowable mathematical laws. Although the
explorers occasionally stumble in their quest
105 for understanding, their errors are due to
human weaknesses, not to the weakness of
logic. The inexorable march of reason
toward the true understanding of nature
cannot be denied.

7.   Which of the following is the best title for this
     passage?

     (A)   Number and Religion in the Pythagorean
           Cult
     (B)   The Religious Beliefs of Great
           Mathematicians
     (C)   The Contribution of Geometry to Ancient
           Astronomy
     (D)   The Historical Relationship between
           Mathematics and Metaphysics
     (E)   The Intellectual Legacy of the Babylonians

8.   In line 3, the phrase "angles and energies"
     refers to

     (A)   the motions of celestial bodies
     (B)   the rigidity of mathematical laws
     (C)   the manner in which disciplines have
           intersected
     (D)   the various interests of historians
     (E)   the mystical nature of some religions

9.   The phrase "but not exclusively" (lines 3–4)
     suggests that

     (A)   some historians do not focus only on
           the development of mathematical and
           scientific thought
     (B)   the relationship between mathematics
           and religion has not always been con-
           structive
     (C)   some people object to the application of
           mathematics to religious questions
     (D)   many mathematical facts can easily
           coexist with religious precepts
     (E)   some mathematical and religious ideas
           are beyond the understanding of the
           average person

10. The statement in lines 7–10 ("But today...
     revealing truths") suggests that, over time,
     religion and mathematics have become more

     (A)   independent
     (B)   mystical
     (C)   interrelated
     (D)   difficult to understand
     (E)   popular

11. In line 8, the word "spheres" most nearly
     means

     (A)   social groups
     (B)   perfect forms
     (C)   domains of influence
     (D)   worldly objects
     (E)   mathematical laws

12. The word "Reciprocally" (line 23) is intended
     to convey the fact that

     (A)   mathematics was thought to be a tool for
           both humans and the gods
     (B)   Plato was a mathematician as well as a
           moral philosopher
     (C)   the Egyptians contributed a great deal to
           Greek mathematics
     (D)   priests and mathematicians often posed
           problems to one another
     (E)   mathematicians were often employed in
           the building of temples

GO ON TO THE NEXT PAGE ➡

8   8   8   8   8   8

13. Plato is mentioned in line 26 because he

- (A) solved a mathematical problem that had confused the oracle
- (B) helped the Delians to construct an altar
- (C) presented the Delians with knowledge that helped them to interpret a prophecy
- (D) proclaimed that mathematical knowledge was independent of religious knowledge
- (E) suggested that the oracle's demand was intended to mystify the Delians

14. The statement in lines 55–59 ("Yet not even...dawn of Christianity") asserts the fact that

- (A) a proven mathematical fact cannot be contradicted
- (B) religious laws are similar to mathematical laws
- (C) ancient construction methods were inadequate
- (D) many mathematical discoveries were made after the dawn of Christianity
- (E) geometry was studied in great depth in the Christian era

15. The "manner of thinking" mentioned in lines 65 includes the belief that

- I. the primary purpose of mathematics is to solve worldly problems
- II. mathematical laws are not arbitrary
- III. mathematics has mystical power

- (A) III only
- (B) I and II only
- (C) I and III only
- (D) II and III only
- (E) I, II, and III

16. In line 70, "plane" most nearly means

- (A) geometric surface
- (B) method of conveyance
- (C) level of existence
- (D) lack of stability
- (E) angle of intersection

17. In line 80, the statement "righteousness ascended" means that

- (A) a mathematical theorem was proven
- (B) historians acquired a biased point of view
- (C) the Pythagoreans became ideologically intolerant
- (D) many people rejected the cult of Pythagoras for religious reasons
- (E) the cult of Pythagoras became politically divided

18. The final paragraph suggests that the "precept" mentioned in line 90 was

- (A) factually incorrect
- (B) proven only well after it was first declared
- (C) later rejected by the Pythagoreans
- (D) the foundation of many later discoveries
- (E) obvious to many other Greek thinkers

19. The "explorers" (line 104) are those who

- (A) seek mystical experiences
- (B) investigate historical claims
- (C) attempt to unify religion and mathematics
- (D) endeavor to explain nature through reason
- (E) adhere to the religious restrictions of the Pythagoreans

STOP

If you finish before time is called, you may check your work on this section only. Do not turn to any other section of the test.

9   9   9   9   9   9

SECTION 9
Time—10 minutes
14 questions

Turn to Section 9 of your answer sheet to answer the questions in this section.

Directions: For each question in this section, select the best answer from among the choices given and fill in the corresponding circle on the answer sheet.

The following sentences test correctness and effectiveness of expression. Part of each sentence or the entire sentence is underlined; beneath each sentence are five ways of phrasing the underlined material. Choice A repeats the original phrasing; the other four choices are different. Select the choice that completes the sentence most effectively.

In making your selection, follow the requirements of standard written English; that is, pay attention to grammar, choice of words, sentence construction, and punctuation. Your selection should result in the most effective sentence—clear and precise, without awkwardness or ambiguity.

EXAMPLE:

The children <u>couldn't hardly believe their eyes</u>.

(A) couldn't hardly believe their eyes
(B) could hardly believe their eyes
(C) would not hardly believe their eyes
(D) couldn't nearly believe their eyes
(E) couldn't hardly believe his or her eyes

1. Because the New York Yankees have spent the most money of any franchise in baseball over the past five seasons, the team has not met the expectations that such expenditures entail.

(A) Because the New York Yankees have spent the most money
(B) Although the New York Yankees have spent the most money
(C) Having spent the most money, the New York Yankees
(D) The New York Yankees, having spent the most money
(E) The most money spent by the New York Yankees

2. Like most foreign visitors, <u>the canal system of Venice mesmerized the recently married couple</u>.

(A) the canal system of Venice mesmerized the recently married couple
(B) there was a canal system in Venice that mesmerized the recently married couple
(C) the recently married couple, who was mesmerized by the canal system of Venice
(D) the recently married couple was mesmerized by the canal system of Venice
(E) the canal system of Venice having mesmerized the recently married couple

GO ON TO THE NEXT PAGE

9   9   9   9   9   9

3. The new state <u>zoo, built on a four-hundred acre plot of land, and was paid for entirely by the state government</u>.

(A) zoo, built on a four-hundred acre plot of land, and was paid for entirely by the state government
(B) zoo was paid for by the state government, it was built on a four-hundred acre plot of land
(C) zoo is paid for by the state government while being built on a four-hundred acre plot of land
(D) zoo, built on a four-hundred acre plot of land, was paid for entirely by the state government
(E) zoo, having been built on a four-hundred acre plot of land, and having been paid for entirely by the state government

4. Many universities are developing new financial aid <u>programs that offer economic advantages to both the students and</u> their families.

(A) programs that offer economic advantages to both the students and
(B) programs, which offer economic advantage to not only students but
(C) programs, which offers economic advantages to both the students and
(D) programs; the economic advantages of which are offered to both students and
(E) programs: economic advantages are being offered to both the students in addition to

5. No sooner had Elizabeth accepted the job to teach AP biology at her daughter's private school <u>but her former boss persuaded her to return</u> to work at the laboratory.

(A) but her former boss persuaded her to return
(B) however she was persuaded by her former boss that she should
(C) but her former boss had her persuaded into returning
(D) when she was persuaded to return by her former boss
(E) than her former boss persuaded her to return

6. <u>His renown as a pioneer in the field of fuel-cell technology, Geoffrey Ballard almost equals</u> that of William Grove, the inventor of the world's first fuel cell, is the founder of Ballard Power Systems.

(A) His renown as a pioneer in the field of fuel-cell technology, Geoffrey Ballard almost equals
(B) Geoffrey Ballard's renown as a pioneer is in the field of fuel-cell technology almost equaling
(C) Geoffrey Ballard almost equals the renown as a pioneer in the field of fuel-cell technology
(D) As a pioneer, Geoffrey Ballard's renown as a pioneer in the field of fuel-cell technology almost equals
(E) Geoffrey Ballard, whose renown as a pioneer in the field of fuel-cell technology almost equals

7. <u>To clean the entire garage, Eric</u> decided to lie down and take a nap to restore his energy.

(A) To clean the entire garage, Eric
(B) Having cleaned the entire garage, Eric
(C) Eric cleaned the entire garage,
(D) In cleaning the entire garage, Eric
(E) Eric, cleaning the entire garage,

8. A brilliant songwriter who is able to adjust her style as she ages, <u>Madonna's songs always seem to fit with the music of the time</u>.

(A) Madonna's songs always seem to fit with the music of the time
(B) the songs of Madonna always seem to fit with the music of the time
(C) Madonna always writes songs that fit with the music of the time
(D) the music of the time is always fit by Madonna's songs
(E) Madonna always fits the music of the time when writing her songs

GO ON TO THE NEXT PAGE ▷

9   9   9   9   9   9

9. When you bake sugar cookies, <u>it is important that one remembers to chill the dough</u> before cutting the shapes.

  (A) it is important that one remembers to chill the dough
  (B) remembering to chill the dough is important
  (C) it is important that you remember to chill the dough
  (D) chilling the dough is important for you to have remembered
  (E) to chill the dough is important for one to remember

10. When donating money to charity, <u>a nonprofit organization that will use your gift wisely should be your priority</u>.

  (A) a nonprofit organization that will use your gift wisely should be your priority
  (B) you should make it your priority to choose a nonprofit organization that will use your gift wisely
  (C) choose a nonprofit organization that will use your gift wisely as your priority
  (D) a nonprofit organization should be your priority that will use your gift wisely
  (E) using your gift wisely should be your priority when choosing a nonprofit organization

11. In 2005, online shoppers in the United States charged more money to their credit cards <u>than</u> 2004.

  (A) than
  (B) than online shoppers for
  (C) than in
  (D) than would online shoppers in
  (E) than they did in

12. <u>Written in the late 18th century, modern audiences have enjoyed the musical theater's rendition of the opera *Don Giovanni* by Mozart</u>.

  (A) Written in the late 18th century, modern audiences have enjoyed the musical theater's rendition of the opera *Don Giovanni* by Mozart
  (B) Modern audiences have enjoyed the musical theater's rendition of the opera *Don Giovanni*, written in the late 18th century by Mozart.
  (C) Mozart's late 18th century opera *Don Giovanni* was enjoyed by modern audiences seeing the musical theater's rendition.
  (D) *Don Giovanni*, written by Mozart in the 18th century, was a musical theater's rendition of an opera that modern audiences had enjoyed.
  (E) Having been written in the late 18th century by Mozart, the musical theater's rendition of the opera *Don Giovanni* was enjoyed by modern audiences.

13. Surfing the Internet for hours at a time, <u>Claudia stares at her computer screen until her eyes begin to hurt</u>.

  (A) Claudia stares at her computer screen until her eyes begin to hurt
  (B) Claudia's eyes begin to hurt as she stares at her computer screen
  (C) staring at her screen until her eyes begin to hurt was Claudia
  (D) Claudia was staring at her computer screen until her eyes would begin to hurt
  (E) until her eyes began to hurt, Claudia staring at her computer screen

14. Dr. Sosa's delightful sense of humor and friendly smile <u>puts her patients</u> at ease.

  (A) puts her patients
  (B) having put her patients
  (C) her patients have been put
  (D) put her patients
  (E) putting her patients

STOP

If you finish before time is called, you may check your work on this section only. Do not turn to any other section of the test.

ANSWER KEY

Critical Reading

	Section 3					Section 6					Section 8			
	COR. ANS.	DIFF. LEV.		COR. ANS.	DIFF. LEV.		COR. ANS.	DIFF. LEV.		COR. ANS.	DIFF. LEV.		COR. ANS.	DIFF. LEV.		COR. ANS.	DIFF. LEV.

Section 3						Section 6						Section 8				
1.	B	1	13.	C	2	1.	A	2	13.	A	3	1.	B	1	11.	C	4
2.	D	1	14.	C	3	2.	E	2	14.	B	4	2.	C	2	12.	A	2
3.	A	2	15.	D	3	3.	C	3	15.	D	3	3.	B	3	13.	E	2
4.	E	3	16.	A	4	4.	A	3	16.	B	4	4.	A	4	14.	A	4
5.	B	4	17.	E	4	5.	A	4	17.	C	4	5.	D	5	15.	D	4
6.	C	4	18.	A	3	6.	C	3	18.	E	5	6.	E	5	16.	C	3
7.	D	4	19.	B	3	7.	E	3	19.	C	3	7.	D	2	17.	C	3
8.	E	5	20.	C	4	8.	C	2	20.	B	3	8.	C	4	18.	A	3
9.	E	2	21.	E	3	9.	D	3	21.	A	4	9.	B	4	19.	D	4
10.	A	3	22.	E	2	10.	C	2	22.	A	3	10.	A	3			
11.	D	3	23.	B	3	11.	E	4	23.	D	4						
12.	B	4	24.	B	5	12.	A	5	24.	D	4						

Number correct _____

Number incorrect _____

Number correct _____

Number incorrect _____

Number correct _____

Number incorrect _____

Math

Section 2						Section 5						Section 7				

Section 2

	COR. ANS.	DIFF. LEV.		COR. ANS.	DIFF. LEV.
1.	B	1	11.	C	3
2.	D	1	12.	D	3
3.	C	3	13.	C	3
4.	D	2	14.	A	4
5.	C	2	15.	E	3
6.	B	2	16.	C	4
7.	D	3	17.	E	4
8.	C	2	18.	B	4
9.	B	3	19.	B	5
10.	A	3	20.	D	5

Number correct _____

Number incorrect _____

Section 5

Multiple-Choice Questions

	COR. ANS.	DIFF. LEV.
1.	C	1
2.	A	2
3.	D	3
4.	B	3
5.	A	3
6.	D	4
7.	D	4
8.	C	5

Student-produced Response questions

	COR. ANS.	DIFF. LEV.
9.	10	1
10.	5400	2
11.	44	3
12.	5/8 or .625	3
13.	14	3
14.	10	4
15.	1 or 3	3
16.	132	4
17.	109	5
18.	72	5

Number correct _____

Number incorrect _____

Number correct (9–18) _____

Section 7

	COR. ANS.	DIFF. LEV.		COR. ANS.	DIFF. LEV.
1.	A	2	9.	C	4
2.	B	2	10.	C	4
3.	A	2	11.	D	3
4.	D	3	12.	B	4
5.	B	3	13.	D	3
6.	D	3	14.	C	4
7.	D	3	15.	E	5
8.	C	3	16.	B	5

Number correct _____

Number incorrect _____

Writing

Section 4

	COR. ANS.	DIFF. LEV.		COR. ANS.	DIFF. LEV.		COR. ANS.	DIFF. LEV.		COR. ANS.	DIFF. LEV.
1.	C	1	11.	A	4	21.	B	3	31.	A	3
2.	C	1	12.	D	1	22.	C	4	32.	B	3
3.	A	2	13.	A	1	23.	B	3	33.	D	3
4.	B	3	14.	E	2	24.	E	4	34.	B	3
5.	D	4	15.	A	3	25.	D	3	35.	A	3
6.	A	2	16.	D	3	26.	C	3			
7.	D	3	17.	C	2	27.	A	4			
8.	B	4	18.	E	3	28.	D	4			
9.	A	4	19.	B	3	29.	B	5			
10.	C	3	20.	C	3	30.	B	3			

Number correct _____

Number incorrect _____

Section 9

	COR. ANS.	DIFF. LEV.		COR. ANS.	DIFF. LEV.
1.	B	1	11.	E	3
2.	D	2	12.	B	4
3.	D	2	13.	A	4
4.	A	2	14.	D	3
5.	E	2			
6.	E	2			
7.	B	3			
8.	C	3			
9.	C	3			
10.	B	3			

Number correct _____

Number incorrect _____

NOTE: Difficulty levels are estimates of question difficulty that range from 1 (easiest) to 5 (hardest).

SCORE CONVERSION TABLE

How to score your test

Use the answer key on the previous page to determine your raw score on each section. Your raw score on each section except Section 4 is simply the number of correct answers minus ¼ of the number of wrong answers. On Section 4, your raw score is the sum of the number of correct answers for questions 1–8 minus ¼ of the number of wrong answers for questions 1–8 plus the total number of correct answers for questions 9–18. Next, add the raw scores from Sections 3, 4, and 7 to get your Math raw score, add the raw scores from Sections 2, 5, and 8 to get your Critical Reading raw score and add the raw scores from Sections 6 and 9 to get your Writing raw score.

Write the three raw scores here:

Raw Critical Reading score: _____ Raw Math score: _____ Raw Writing score: _____

Use the table below to convert these to scaled scores.

Scaled scores: Critical Reading: _____ Math: _____ Writing: _____

Raw Score	Critical Reading Scaled Score	Math Scaled Score	Writing Scaled Score	Raw Score	Critical Reading Scaled Score	Math Scaled Score	Writing Scaled Score
67	800			32	520	570	610
66	800			31	510	560	600
65	790			30	510	550	580
64	780			29	500	540	570
63	770			28	490	530	560
62	750			27	490	520	550
61	740			26	480	510	540
60	730			25	480	500	530
59	720			24	470	490	520
58	700			23	460	480	510
57	690			22	460	480	500
56	680			21	450	470	490
55	670			20	440	460	480
54	660	800		19	440	450	470
53	650	800		18	430	450	460
52	650	780		17	420	440	450
51	640	760		16	420	430	440
50	630	740		15	410	420	440
49	620	730	800	14	400	410	430
48	620	710	800	13	400	410	420
47	610	710	800	12	390	400	410
46	600	700	790	11	380	390	400
45	600	690	780	10	370	380	390
44	590	680	760	9	360	370	380
43	590	670	740	8	350	360	380
42	580	660	730	7	340	350	370
41	570	650	710	6	330	340	360
40	570	640	700	5	320	330	350
39	560	630	690	4	310	320	340
38	550	620	670	3	300	310	320
37	550	620	660	2	280	290	310
36	540	610	650	1	270	280	300
35	540	600	640	0	250	260	280
34	530	590	630	−1	230	240	270
33	520	580	620	−2 or less	210	220	250

SCORE CONVERSION TABLE FOR ESSAY + MULTIPLE CHOICE WRITING COMPOSITE

Calculate your writing raw score as you did on the previous page and grade your essay from a 1 to a 6 according to the standards that follow in the detailed answer key.

Essay score: _____ Raw Writing score: _____

Use the table below to convert these to scaled scores.

Scaled score: Writing _____

Raw Score	Essay Score 0	Essay Score 1	Essay Score 2	Essay Score 3	Essay Score 4	Essay Score 5	Essay Score 6
−2 or less	200	230	250	280	310	340	370
−1	210	240	260	290	320	360	380
0	230	260	280	300	340	370	400
1	240	270	290	320	350	380	410
2	250	280	300	330	360	390	420
3	260	290	310	340	370	400	430
4	270	300	320	350	380	410	440
5	280	310	330	360	390	420	450
6	290	320	340	360	400	430	460
7	290	330	340	370	410	440	470
8	300	330	350	380	410	450	470
9	310	340	360	390	420	450	480
10	320	350	370	390	430	460	490
11	320	360	370	400	440	470	500
12	330	360	380	410	440	470	500
13	340	370	390	420	450	480	510
14	350	380	390	420	460	490	520
15	350	380	400	430	460	500	530
16	360	390	410	440	470	500	530
17	370	400	420	440	480	510	540
18	380	410	420	450	490	520	550
19	380	410	430	460	490	530	560
20	390	420	440	470	500	530	560
21	400	430	450	480	510	540	570
22	410	440	460	480	520	550	580
23	420	450	470	490	530	560	590
24	420	460	470	500	540	570	600
25	430	460	480	510	540	580	610
26	440	470	490	520	550	590	610
27	450	480	500	530	560	590	620
28	460	490	510	540	570	600	630
29	470	500	520	550	580	610	640
30	480	510	530	560	590	620	650
31	490	520	540	560	600	630	660
32	500	530	550	570	610	640	670
33	510	540	550	580	620	650	680
34	510	550	560	590	630	660	690
35	520	560	570	600	640	670	700
36	530	560	580	610	650	680	710
37	540	570	590	620	660	690	720
38	550	580	600	630	670	700	730
39	560	600	610	640	680	710	740
40	580	610	620	650	690	720	750
41	590	620	640	660	700	730	760
42	600	630	650	680	710	740	770
43	610	640	660	690	720	750	780
44	620	660	670	700	740	770	800
45	640	670	690	720	750	780	800
46	650	690	700	730	770	800	800
47	670	700	720	750	780	800	800
48	680	720	730	760	800	800	800
49	680	720	730	760	800	800	800

Detailed Answer Key

Section 1

The following essay received 12 points out of a possible 12. It demonstrates clear and consistent mastery in that it

- develops an insightful point of view on the topic
- demonstrates exemplary critical thinking
- uses very effective examples, reasons, and other evidence to support its thesis
- is consistently focused, coherent, and well-organized
- demonstrates skillful and effective use of language and sentence structure
- is largely (but not necessarily completely) free of grammatical and usage errors

SAMPLE STUDENT ESSAY

While overcoming obstacles can build character, I do not believe that such struggles are more important than the accomplishment itself. Struggles can help us learn and discover simpler paths toward success, but struggle is defined more by the pain it causes than by the lessons it teaches. We can see this in examining historic wars and modern heroes.

Many films and novels praise the nobility of battle and the lessons learned in war. But the price paid by soldiers and innocent people significantly outweighs these lessons. In international disputes, success without conflict is far better than the triumph of war. By avoiding war, nations avoid the tragedy of lost lives as well as the economic hardships involved in rebuilding infrastructure and paying off debt.

Many suggest that heroes like Lance Armstrong demonstrate the value of overcoming adversity. In the past seven years, Armstrong has overcome a battle with cancer to win an unprecedented seven straight championships at the Tour de France. His story has provided cancer patients with one of their most inspiring narratives. But as wonderful as those effects have been, Armstrong's story would have been better if he had *not* been forced to overcome cancer. Armstrong is an exceptional athlete, and accomplished an astonishing feat that his illness should not eclipse. In fact, he was stricken by a very treatable form of cancer. Are we truly helping cancer patients by making them believe that all cancer treatment can be easily scheduled between training runs? No. His story may help aspiring cyclists far more than it helps patients facing months of painful chemotherapy.

Another interesting example is Alice Sebold, a writer who has overcome a traumatic rape she suffered in college. It's difficult to overstate the magnitude of her struggles in overcoming this violation to write two beautifully crafted works, *The Lovely Bones* and *Lucky*. Although her battles undeniably helped to craft her work, her status as a writer is unrelated to her status as a victim. Without such pain in her life, I believe that she would have created different, but equally powerful stories. Artists suffer enough by being able to see so deeply into the human condition; literature is not served any better when its greatest writers are subjected to torture.

Stories of success despite adversity are well represented in books, films, and even daily newscasts. They inspire us by showing triumphs of the human spirit. The danger here, however, is in using these struggles as a crutch, depersonalizing adversity in an effort to feel less afraid of our own difficulties. There is nothing wrong with feeling inspired by a story of overcome obstacles and suggesting that struggle builds character. But it is the accomplishments themselves that represent success, not the struggle. Success without wounds leaves room for greater happiness, fewer losses, and better health.

Reader's Comments

This essay provides substantial, logical, and well-organized support for the thesis that "struggle is defined more by the pain it causes than by the lessons it teaches." The author's examination of global conflict, Lance Armstrong, and Alice Sebold exemplifies strong critical thinking, particularly because the latter two examples at first appear to support the author's antithesis, but are re-analyzed to support the author's point of view. The author maintains consistent focus on the thesis while providing insight into the nature of struggle and success. The essay is rarely wordy and its diction is effective without becoming pompous. Because of its masterful use of language and critical thinking, this essay merits the highest score of 12.

The following essay received 10 points out of a possible 12. It demonstrates reasonably consistent mastery in that it

- effectively develops a point of view on the topic
- demonstrates strong critical thinking
- uses good examples, reasons, and other evidence to support its thesis
- shows a good organization and consistent focus
- demonstrates consistent facility with language
- is mostly free of errors in grammar, usage, and mechanics

SAMPLE STUDENT ESSAY

When faced with adversity in some area of my life, I am often reminded of my mother's favorite saying that, "it is not about the ending—it is about the journey." Although it might seem like hackneyed advice to someone in the moment and frustrated by an obstacle that is difficult to overcome, the expression speaks the truth about success in life.

As I've gotten older, math class has become progressively more difficult for me. This year has been particularly difficult because I have worked my way into an advanced class. Each test seems like an obstacle or a hurdle that I have to get over and the tests seem to be getting progressively more difficult. So far this year, I have averaged a C+ in my math class, (which is not great) and my successes have been far and few between. When I have managed to succeed on a test, however, I know the good grade is the result of a lot of hard work and studying. In my opinion, the work I put into getting a good math grade is more a measure of my success as a person than the grade itself is. When I think back to the tests that I have done well on, what I remember clearly are the long nights of hard work and preparation that allowed me to achieve these rare successes and I feel very proud of the efforts.

Abraham Lincoln was a poor boy from a poor family, and the opportunity to become president was not handed to him as it might have been to someone with a higher social standing or with a greater disposable income. Lincoln made extraordinary efforts to gain knowledge while working on a farm, splitting rails for fences, and keeping store at New Salem, Illinois. He spent eight years in the Illinois legislature, and rode the circuit of courts for many years, as well. His colleagues said that his ambition was a little engine that knew no rest. In 1858 Lincoln ran against Stephen A. Douglas for Senator. He lost the election, but the famous Lincoln-Douglas debates helped him to gain a national reputation that won him the Republican nomination for President in 1860 and eventually the Presidency of the United States. When people think of Abraham Lincoln today, they think of "Honest Abe," one of the most influential and powerful Presidents in our history. The character he built by working hard to achieve his presidential position was more a measure of his success than it was an opportunity to call himself "President."

There are many examples of this belief that it is not about the ending—it is about the journey that can be found in other areas. The struggle to achieve a position teaches a person more about how to live than does the simple acquisition of the position. Using those valuable lessons throughout life will help make a person become more successful in the long run.

Reader's comments

This is a well-reasoned and well-organized essay supporting the thesis that "the struggle endured to achieve success is more important than the accomplishment itself." The author uses two well-organized examples to support her opinion. The essay does not get the highest possible score, however, because the author does not demonstrate strong enough facility with transition sentences. There is no flow from the second to the third paragraph—the author just jumps right into the Lincoln example without any sort of transition. In addition, her conclusion is not of the same quality and focus as the rest of the essay as it does not summarize the author's thoughts very clearly and strays a little from the main thesis. Nevertheless, the strong reasoning and effective examples in the essay merit a high score of 10.

The following essay received 4 points out of a possible 12, meaning that it demonstrates some incompetence in that it

- has a seriously limited point of view
- demonstrates weak critical thinking
- uses inappropriate or insufficient examples, reasons, and other evidence to support its thesis
- is poorly focused and organized, and has serious problems with coherence
- demonstrates frequent problems with language and sentence structure
- contains errors in grammar and usage that obscure the author's meaning seriously

SAMPLE STUDENT ESSAY

Success is not a measure of achievement but rather of heart. The novel *Huckleberry Finn* by Mark Twain shows how a black slave named Jim runs away from his masters' home in order to escape the threat of being sold to another slave owner. He joins Huck Finn, a ten year-old boy, and his ability to overcome obstacles and survive on the Mississippi River makes him successful. Similarly, as a tennis player, I always feel that I have succeeded if I have worked hard in practice and prepared the best that I could for tournaments. While winning means everything to me, I know that if I have come prepared to my tournament and executed my strategy, I have succeeded regardless of the result.

In *Huckleberry Finn*, Jim bravely runs away from his slave owner in order to be free. The fact that he and a ten year-old boy are able to survive as they travel down the river, both trying to escape the limitations of society, gives them ultimate success. Even though they had to disguise their identities and outsmart thieves, Huck and Jim were able to survive and continue their journey down the river until they were eventually found.

Similar to the experiences of Huck and Jim in *Huckleberry Finn*, I constantly struggle to achieve my goals. I have always been someone who has needed to work hard on my tennis game because I do not possess the natural talent that some of my adversaries

possess. Similarly, I have never been a fast kid so I have always had to work hard and improve my speed and agility in order to become faster and more nimble on the court. I have learned to realize that if I am training hard for my tournaments and spending a lot of attention on the aspects of my tennis game that I need to improve, I have already won. And often times, the result of my hard work is shown in my matches.

Reader's comments

The author attempts to answer the question posed in the prompt by discussing the struggle to achieve success. However, the author misses the mark and does not discuss the idea that the struggle is more important than the actual achievement. He instead defines success as a measure of an individual's "heart," an entirely different direction. The example in the second paragraph mentions a success achieved by Huck Finn that was not easy. This again strays from the question the prompt actually posed. Furthermore, the essay lacks a formal conclusion—it seems to end without warning. Lastly, the author demonstrates weak facility with language and structure, showing particular weakness in diction and transitions. This essay avoids a score of 0 (each reader giving it a 0) because it attempts to answer the question, and a score of 2 (each reader giving it a 1) because it attempts some reasoning and support for its claim.

Section 2

1. B

	$3b - 5c =$
Substitute for b and c:	$3(4) - 5(7) =$
Simplify:	$12 - 35 = -23$

2. D First write the equation to find the average of 4 and w. Then, write the equation to find the average of 2, 8, and w. Set those two equations equal to each other and solve.

$$\frac{4+w}{2} = \frac{2+8+w}{3}$$

Cross-multiply:	$3(4+w) = 2(10+w)$
Distribute:	$12 + 3w = 20 + 2w$
Subtract $2w$:	$12 + w = 20$
Subtract 12:	$w = 8$

3. C The length of MN can be determined by subtracting the x-coordinates of the two points M and N.

$$4 - (-1) = 5$$

The length of QR = the length of MN = 5.

The length of QR can be determined by subtracting the x-coordinates of the two points Q and R.

	$x - (-3) = 5$
	$x + 3 = 5$
Subtract 3:	$x = 2$

4. D To find the percent change use the formula:

$$\frac{final - original}{original} \times 100$$

The original (2005) was $0.75
The final (2006) was $1.00

$$\frac{\$1.00 - \$0.75}{\$0.75} \times 100 = \frac{\$0.25}{\$0.75} \times 100 = 33\frac{1}{3}\%$$

5. C Set up a proportion:

$$\frac{4\,oranges}{d\,dollars} = \frac{40\,oranges}{x\,dollars}$$

Cross multiply:	$4x = 40d$
Divide by 4:	$x = 10d$

6. B

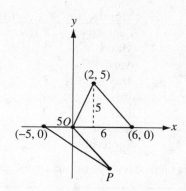

Area = ½(base)(height)

Start with the triangle on the right. The base rests along the x-axis and stretches from $x = 0$ to $x = 6$, so the base is 6 units. The height stretches from $y = 0$ to $y = 5$, so the height is 5 units. The area can now be calculated:

$$Area = \frac{1}{2}(6)(5) = 15$$

Because you are told the areas of the two triangles are equal, the area of the left triangle must also be 15. The base of this triangle stretches from $x = 0$ to $x = -5$ for a value of 5 units. We can use this to solve for its height:

	$Area = \frac{1}{2}(base)(height)$
Substitute:	$15 = \frac{1}{2}(5)(height)$
Simplify:	$15 = 2.5(height)$
Divide by 2.5:	$6 = height$

In order for the left triangle to have a height of 6 with a base on the x-axis, its height must equal 6 units, and answer choice (B) is the only point that is 6 units from the x-axis.

7. D Begin by factoring

$$a^2 - 2ab + b^2 = (a - b)(a - b)$$

Substitute for $(a - b)$: $a^2 - 2ab + b^2 = (-4)(-4) = 16$

8. C Remember that the greatest change can be either positive or negative.

Month	#	Change
February	2	–
March	4	+2
April	7	+3
May	3	–4
June	4	+1
July	2	–2
August	2	0
September	4	+2

The biggest change occurs from April to May.

9. B You could plug in simple values to solve this question. Let's say $r = 3$. If that is the case, then $s = 4$ because the ratio of r to s is 3 to 4. The ratio of s to t is 2 to 9.

$$\frac{s}{t} = \frac{2}{9} = \frac{4}{t}$$

Cross multiply: $2t = 36$
Divide by 2: $t = 18$

So, if $s = 4$, then $t = 18$.

Therefore the ratio of r to t is 3 to 18 or 1 to 6.

10. A You may wonder why 15 is not an answer choice since $4 + 5 + 6 = 15$. But, remember that you cannot assume that numbers on the SAT are integers. It *could* be 15 if $AB = 4$, $BC = 5$ and $CD = 6$, but that's not one of the choices. If $BC = 5.6$ and $AB = 5.4$, then AD would be $5.4 + 5.6 + 6.0 = 17$.

It is impossible for AD to be 18 or greater if $CD = 6$ because CD is larger than the other two segments and the only way to get 18 would be for AB and/or BC to be larger than or equal to CD, which is not possible. Therefore the answer is (A).

11. C To solve this problem, plug in a value of x from the table above and cross out any function that does not give the proper value for f(x). Often times if you start with the first value in the table, three or more answers will work, so it can work to your advantage to start with a middle value. If you start with $x = 5$, a few choices can be eliminated:

(A) $f(5) = \frac{3}{2}(5) + 4 = 7.5 + 4 = 11.5$

(B) $f(5) = -\frac{2}{3}(5) - 3 = -\frac{10}{3} - 3 = -6\frac{1}{3}$

(C) $f(5) = 2(5) + 2 = 12$

(D) $f(5) = 3(5) - 3 = 12$

(E) $f(5) = 4(5) - 6 = 14$

This leaves you with two choices: C and D. Try the next value of x.   (C) $f(6) = 2(6) + 2 = 14$
                                   (D) $f(6) = 3(6) - 3 = 15$

Only (C) remains and so must be the correct answer.

12. D Because the lines are parallel you know that:

$a = e$ because they are corresponding angles.
$h = e$ because they are vertical angles.
$d = e$ because they are alternate interior angles.
f is supplementary to e but not necessarily equal to it.
　　Look at each of the answer choices.
(A) a is necessarily equal to e.
(B) Because $h = e$ and $d = e$, you

can rewrite $\dfrac{(h + d)}{2}$ as $\dfrac{e + e}{2} = \dfrac{2e}{e} = e$

(C) Because $a = e$ and $d = e$, you

can rewrite $\dfrac{(a + d)}{2}$ as $\dfrac{e + e}{2} = \dfrac{2e}{e} = e$

(D) f is supplementary to e and therefore not necessarily equal to it. So $\dfrac{(f + h)}{2}$ is not necessarily equal to e.

(E) d is necessarily equal to e.

13. C Here is the algebraic solution:

$$(2k^{1/2})^{-2} = \frac{1}{(2k^{1/2})^2} = \frac{1}{2^2(k^{1/2})^2} = \frac{1}{4k}$$

If you prefer a numerical approach, just choose a convenient positive integer for k, such as 4, and evaluate the expression (with your calculator, if necessary). Since $(2(4)^{1/2})^{-2} = 1/16$, you should eliminate any choices that are not equal to 1/16 when $k = 4$, leaving only choice (C).

14. A p is 40% less than 600: $p = 0.60(600) = 360$
             t is 40% greater than p: $t = 1.40p$
             Substitute: $t = 1.40(360) = 504$
                                        $t - p = 504 - 360 = 144$

15. E Begin by writing out the first 6 to 8 terms of the sequence:

1st term $= -2$	–
2nd term $= 4$	+
3rd term $= -2(4) = -8$	–
4th term $= -8(4) = -32$	–
5th term $= -32(-8) = 256$	+
6th term $= 256(-32) = -8,192$	–

It does not matter what the value of each term is. What matters is the <u>sign</u> of each term. The first 6 terms are $- + - - + -$. The pattern is $- + -$ and repeats every 3 terms with two negative terms in each repetition of the pattern. To find out how many of the first 139 terms are negative, divide 139 by 3 and find the remainder. $139 \div 3 = 46$ remainder 1. This means that the pattern of three occurs 46 full times, which gives a total of $2 \times 46 = 92$ negative terms. The remainder of 1 means that the 139th term is the *first* term of the sequence, which is negative. This means there are a total of $92 + 1 = 93$ negative terms.

16. C You are told that the value of $h(5) = k$. To find the value of k, go to $x = 5$ on the x-axis and find the y-value of the function at that point. $h(5) = 5$.

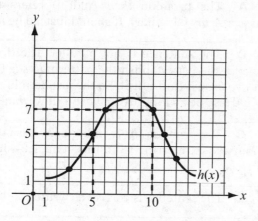

Therefore $k = 5$. The problem asks for the value of $h(2k)$ or $h(10)$. The value of $h(10)$ is 7.

17. E One challenging aspect of this problem is that some of the information is given as a fraction and some is given as an actual amount. Set up a table to help clarify the information:

	fraction	#
Red	$\frac{2}{5}$	?
White	$\frac{3}{10}$	?
Blue	$\frac{1}{10}$	?
Green	?	10
Total	1	?

The sum, of the fractional parts must be 1. This fact allows you to determine what fraction of the marbles are green. $\frac{2}{5} + \frac{3}{10} + \frac{1}{10} = \frac{8}{10}$ of the marbles are red, white or blue. Therefore $\frac{2}{10} = \frac{1}{5}$ = are green. Set up an equation and solve:

$$\frac{1}{5}x = 10$$

Multiply by 5: $\qquad x = 50$

18. B
$$\frac{wx}{y+w} = 1$$

Multiply by $(y + w)$: $\qquad wx = y + w$
Subtract w: $\qquad wx - w = y$
Factor out w: $\qquad w(x - 1) = y$

Divide by $(x - 1)$: $\qquad w = \dfrac{y}{x-1}$

19. B You are told that $ON = OM$.

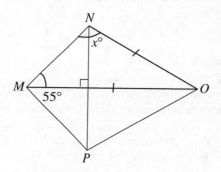

This means that $\angle ONM = \angle OMN$. You are also told that $ON = OP$.

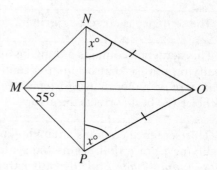

This means that $\angle ONP = \angle OPN = x$. Finally, you are told that $MN = MP$.

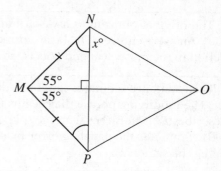

From this you can calculate the value of $\angle MNP$, which must be equal to $90° - 55° = 35°$. Because $\angle ONM = \angle OMN$, you know that $\angle ONM = 55°$. Therefore $x = 55° - 35° = 20°$.

20. D To solve this problem, determine how many roads can be taken each step of the way. To go from Wilton to Norwalk, Kristina can choose from five roads. To go from Norwalk to Darien, she can choose from four roads. Heading back from Darien to Norwalk, she can now only choose from *three* roads because she can't travel the same road twice. Heading back from Norwalk to Wilton, she can now only choose from *four* roads for the same reason. This means there are a total of $5 \times 4 \times 3 \times 4 = 240$ possible routes.

Section 3

1. C The subject *harmful effects* (plural) disagrees with the verb *is* (singular). The verb should be *are*.

2. C The sentence is not parallel. The first two items in the list establish the pattern: *lower taxes* (concrete noun phrase), *a more decentralized government* (concrete noun phrase). So the last item in the list should also be a concrete noun phrase: *a lesser expenditure*.

3. A The sentence is correct as written.

4. B This sentence contains a dangling modifier. The modifying phrase that begins the sentence describes *most of us* rather than *Christopher Columbus*. Answer choice (B) best corrects the error.

5. D This sentence contains a dangling modifier. The modifying phrase that begins the sentence describes *the Empire State Building* rather than *many sightseers*. Answer choice (D) best corrects the error.

6. A The sentence is correct as written.

7. D The original phrasing is awkward and nonidiomatic. Answer choice (D) best corrects the construction in the most clear and concise manner.

8. B This sentence contains another dangling modifier. The modifying phrase that begins the sentence describes *Felisha* rather than *the rain*. Answer choice (B) eliminates the dangling error by properly rearranging the sentence.

9. A The sentence is correct as written.

10. C The subject *validity* (singular) disagrees with the verb *have* (plural). The verb should be *has* (singular).

11. A The sentence is correct as written.

12. D The subject *Bob Hope* (singular) disagrees with the verb *were* (plural). The verb should be *was* (singular).

13. A Since the Colts are one of 32 NFL teams *between* should instead be *among*.

14. E The sentence is correct as written.

15. A The pronoun *their* (plural) refers to *the Russian Army* (singular). It should instead be *its*.

16. D The sentence is not parallel. The first two items in the list establish the pattern: *to sag* (infinitive), *to brown* (infinitive). So the last item in the list should also be an infinitive *to have a sticky thick crust.*

17. C The pronoun *she* is ambiguous. It is not clear whom *she* is referring to in this sentence—Julia or Patricia.

18. E The sentence is correct as written.

19. B The subject *allowance* (singular) disagrees with the verb *help* (plural). The verb should be *helps* (singular).

20. C This is an idiom error. The proper phrase is *preoccupation with*, not *in*.

21. B The pronoun *which* refers to the woman, and so should be replaced by the personal pronoun *whom*.

22. C The subject *technique* (singular) disagrees with the verb *are* (plural). The verb should be *is* (singular).

23. B This is a diction error. To *affect* means to influence. An *effect* is a result or consequence.

24. E The sentence is correct as written.

25. D The phrase *not only* A *but also* B indicates a parallel structure. To make the structure parallel, the phrase should instead be *but also feeling dizzy*.

26. C The word *and* connects the two thoughts as if they support each other. But they in fact contrast each other. The word *and* should be replaced with *even though, but* or *yet*.

27. A This contains a dangling modifier. Because *the effects*, the subject, is not underlined, it must be correct. *When looking* is a dangling participle because it suggests that the *effects* were *looking*, which is impossible. The sentence should begin with a phrase like *When one looks*.

28. **D** The pronoun *anyone* is singular. *They* should be replaced by *he* or *she*.

29. **B** When *neither .. nor ..* construction is used, the verb takes the same number as the noun that follows *nor*. In this case, *sisters* (plural) follows *nor*, so *was* should be changed to *were*.

30. **B** The original phrasing is not a complete sentence. Answer choice (B) provides the most logical, concise and clear phrasing.

31. **A** The original sentence contains a dangling modifier that needs to be corrected. The sentence suggests a bit of a contrast, so the *though* is an important addition to the correct selection.

32. **B** Sentence 5 does not contribute to the unity of the passage. The skull is not talked about in the rest of the passage.

33. **D** Answer choice (D) serves as a good introduction to the topic of the second paragraph since that paragraph focuses on the palate of the crocodile.

34. **B** Answer choice (B) provides the most logical and clear phrasing. Answer choice (C) creates an illogical contrast with its use of however. Answer choice (D) contains verb tense errors. Answer choice (E) creates a dangling modifier error.

35. **A** The sentence is best as written.

Section 4

1. **B** You are told that the minerals found in the waters do two things. They ___ and revitalize (bring new life to) the skin. The missing word should mean something similar to *revitalize*. *ingratiate* = to bring oneself into the good graces of another; *invigorate* = to impart vigor or strength; *exculpate* = to free of blame; *enervate* = to weaken; *debilitate* = to weaken.

2. **D** The word *despite* indicates a contrast. The sentence mentions an ever-present curiosity about Grover Cleveland, which suggests that his life was subject to much *scrutiny* (close examination). Despite this attention, though, he enjoyed *privacy*. This is something that other famous public figures would wish for or could only *imagine*. *candor* = honesty; *animosity* = bitter hostility; *frivolity* = inappropriate silliness.

3. **A** The senate unanimously *ratified* (formally approved) the law. *nullify* = to invalidate; *refute* = to argue against; *supplant* = to take the place of; *pilfer* = to steal.

4. **E** The *it* in the second half of the sentence refers to *her confinement to a wheelchair*. LaToya viewed it as something that *pushed* her to achieve. *Inspiration* and *impetus* are the two answer choices that would make sense in the second blank. The presence of the word *instead* indicates that LaToya's view was in opposition to the view of her friends, who must have seen it as a *problem*. *Impediment* (hurdle) is a good choice. *atrocity* = an appalling condition; *irrelevant* = unrelated to the subject; *omen* = a sign of something to come; *elocution* = a style of speaking; *idiosyncracy* = peculiar trait or habit; *impetus* = a driving force.

5. **B** Gandhi is described as *resistant to authority* without being *combative*. This takes *pugnacious* out of play and suggests that *recalcitrant* would be a good fit. *fickle* = known for unpredictable change; *recalcitrant* = hesitant to obey; *pugnacious* = combative; *lucrative* = profitable; *spurious* = fake.

6. **C** Whatever tragedy befell the Jamjang village resulted in *burned huts, blackened ashes*, and *a smell of smoke*. This suggests answer choices (A), *wildfire* and (C), *conflagration* (giant fire) are reasonable. The smell of smoke that hung in the air is probably not *savory* (appetizing) but instead *acrid* (unpleasantly sharp). *savory* = appetizing to the taste or smell; *cacophony* = harsh or discordant sounds; *pungent* = sharp taste or smell; *conflagration* = giant fire; *acrid* = unpleasantly sharp; *abomination* = disgust; *scourge* = a source of widespread suffering; *irascible* = easily angered.

7. **D** By looking at the editor's scribbles, the author could see how much thought he put into his work. The fact that he eliminates *all* unnecessary words suggests he makes a lot of marks on the page. *rapacious* = greedy; *improvident* = not providing for the future; *convoluted* = hard to follow; *copious* = abundant; *ostentatious* = showy.

8. **E** The officer is attempting to *supplement* (add to) his *modest income*. An individual who is willing to break the law for those who will pay enough money is one who *is able to be bribed (venal)*. *clairvoyant* = having the ability to see things that cannot be perceived by the normal senses; *impassive* = lacking emotion; *matriculated* = having been admitted into a group; *scrupulous* = moral; *venal* = able to be bribed.

9. **E** Both passages indicate that "certain factors are decreasing the human body's ability to ward off disease." In Passage 1, this factor is "excessively sanitary conditions" (line 4) and in Passage 2 it is the "widespread use of antibiotics" (lines 19–20). Choice (A) is incorrect because neither passage suggests that "recently developed medications are ineffectual," even though Passage 2 suggests that antibiotics are becoming *less* effectual. Choice (B) is incorrect because Passage 1 does not discuss antibiotics, and Passage 2 suggests that their overuse may be a problem. Choice (C) is incorrect because Passage 1 indicates that *both* genetics and environment are essential to developing resistance to allergies. Choice (D) is incorrect because Passage 1 suggests that excessively *sanitary*, not unsanitary, conditions are problematic.

10. **A** The benefit referred to in line 11 is the ability of infection to prevent "certain individuals from developing allergies" (lines 7–8).

11. **D** Although the first two sentences of Passage 2 tout the benefits of antibiotics, this enthusiasm is muted by the discussion of the ways in which bacteria have come to "outwit" (line 22) those antibiotics. The overall tone is best described as one of "qualified [muted] enthusiasm."

12. **B** The "resistance" in line 5 is "a person's resistance to disease," specifically allergies. The "resistance" in line 26 is a bacteria's ability to "outwit the effects of antibiotics" (lines 22–23), which are a type of drug.

13. **C** Overall, the purpose of this passage is to criticize the USDA farm subsidy program for its mismanagement (lines 9–15), its inefficiency (lines 28–36), its unfairness (lines 64–76) and its ineffectiveness (lines 47–63). Therefore the "something rotten" mentioned in line 1 must refer to the farm subsidy program itself.

14. **C** Passage 1 explains its claim that the GAO report documenting mismanagement in the farm subsidies program "probably won't" (line 8) horrify lawmakers in the last two paragraphs (lines 83–93), where it suggests that lawmakers are unlikely to change a program that benefits a "powerful lobby in American politics" (lines 83–84).

15. **D** The fourth paragraph describes a "misconception" (line 28) and explains why it is wrong. The misconception is that subsidies lead to reduced costs to consumers, and the fourth paragraph suggests that it is not beneficial to consumers at all.

16. **A** This sentence suggests that the name given to these payments serves to "obscure [the] intended effect" (lines 42–43) of increasing food prices, and therefore is somewhat misleading.

17. **E** This poll revealed that "77 percent of Americans said that they support giving subsidies to small family farms" (lines 67–69), therefore it was intended to determine the feelings that the public had toward the federal farm subsidies program.

18. **A** The last two paragraphs (lines 83–93) suggest that subsidies are "for elected officials, too" (line 93) because these subsidies benefit "a powerful lobby" (line 83) that in turn contributes large sums to political campaigns. Therefore, politicians receive indirect benefits from the subsidy program. The passage does not suggest that legislators own farms, receive direct subsidies, compete with farmers for government funds, or work to reduce inefficiencies in the subsidies program.

19. **B** This paragraph indicates that "regular shortfalls would be even more worrisome" (lines 110–111) than inventory oversupply, thereby suggesting that oversupply is not as troublesome as it may seem. Since this oversupply is the result of subsidies, it certainly is not "being alleviated" by those payments. The passage does not suggest that oversupply is "unavoidable," and in fact suggests otherwise since the government is taking measures to ensure it. This oversupply "helps to safeguard against excessive price fluctuations" (lines 112–113) and therefore cannot be a result of those fluctuations. Also, the paragraph does not compare the harm these fluctuations do to farmers with the harm done to consumers.

20. **C** All of these choices represent parts of the "food processing [canning factories], distribution [truck drivers] and marketing [fruit store owners and promotional associations] chain" (lines 125–126) except for legislators.

21. **E** Both passages agree that subsidies "can control the price of agricultural products." Passage 1 indicates this in lines 40–41, where it says that "Congress also pays farmers to leave their land fallow, resulting in lower supply and thus higher prices." Passage 2 indicates this in lines 122–131, where it shows how "Subsidies ... contribute to ... lower prices for consumers."

22. **E** The author of Passage 1 discusses the fact that subsidies lower prices for consumers in lines 32–36, which conclude that "the taxpayers ... will

probably pay more in excess taxes than [they] will ever get back in lower corn or wheat prices." Therefore, the benefit of subsidies is not worth the higher taxes to consumers.

---

23. **B**   Passage 1 is disdainful of the farm subsidies program, saying that it "should horrify lawmakers" (lines 7–9) because it is mismanaged, ineffective and unfair. Passage 2, however, generally supports the program by concluding that "its positive impacts far outweigh its negative ones" (lines 146–147).

---

24. **B**   Both passages contain verifiable statistics: (see lines 18–20 and lines 138–140) and refutations of misconceptions (see lines 28–30 and lines 118–121). Passage 2 does not mention any instance of political corruption, however.

Section 5

---

1. **C**   Each pen costs $3, so if you buy p pens, it costs $3p$ dollars. Each binder costs $2, so b binders cost $2b$ dollars. Together they cost $3p + 2b$ dollars.

---

2. **A**   The first number that is divisible by both 4 and 6 is 12, which is not divisible by 8. Therefore the answer is (A). 24, 48, 64 and 72 are all divisible by 4, 6, *and* 8.

---

3. **D**
	$8,755 = 85(x + 2)$
Divide by 85:	$103 = x + 2$
Subtract 2:	$x = 101$

---

4. **B**   To solve this problem, apply the definition to each of the answer choices and pick the one that gives you an odd number.

(A) $\dfrac{4}{2}(8) + 4(2) = 16 + 8 = 24$

(B) $\dfrac{3}{1}(2) + 3(1) = 6 + 3 = 9$

(C) $\dfrac{9}{3}(3) + 9(3) = 9 + 27 = 36$

(D) $\dfrac{8}{4}(6) + 8(4) = 12 + 32 = 44$

(E) $\dfrac{5}{1}(7) + 5(1) = 35 + 5 = 40$

Answer choice (B) is the only odd value.

---

5. **A**   Treat this like a shaded-area problem.

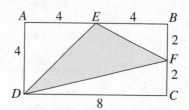

Because E and F are midpoints, you know that $AE = EB = 4$ and that $BF = FC = 2$. You can now find the area of the entire rectangle, and the area of the three unshaded triangles and subtract the area of the triangle from the area of the rectangle to get the area of triangle DEF.

Area of rectangle $ABCD = (8)(4) = 32$ units^2

Area of triangle $DCF = \frac{1}{2}(8)(2) = 8$ units^2

Area of triangle $EBF = \frac{1}{2}(4)(2) = 4$ units^2

Area of triangle $EAD = \frac{1}{2}(4)(4) = 8$ units^2

The area of triangle $DEF = 32 - 8 - 4 - 8 = 12$ units^2

---

6. **D**   Think about how many possible choices there are for each position and multiply those numbers together:

$$\underline{}, \; \underline{} \; \underline{} \; \underline{}$$
thousands hundreds tens units

You are told that the tens digit is 5. Therefore there is only one possible choice for that position.

$$\underline{}, \; \underline{} \; \underline{1} \; \underline{}$$
thousands hundreds tens units

There are no other restrictions so when filling the units place, you can choose among *six* possible digits.

$$\underline{}, \; \underline{} \; \underline{1} \; \underline{6}$$
thousands hundreds tens units

Now there are *five* digits left for the hundreds place.

$$\underline{}, \; \underline{5} \; \underline{1} \; \underline{6}$$
thousands hundreds tens units

Now there are *four* digits left for the thousands place.

$$\underline{4}, \; \underline{5} \; \underline{1} \; \underline{6}$$
thousands hundreds tens units

There are $4 \times 5 \times 1 \times 6 = 120$ possible integers.

---

7. **D**   This problem involves rates, so it helps to recall the rate equation: $d = rt$.

Because Zander returns home *along the same route*, you can use d for the distance both to and from work. Because he spends a total of 4 hours in the car, if he spends t hours on the way to work, he will spend $4 - t$ hours on the way home from work.

Set up rate equations for both legs of the trip:

To work:	$d = 40t$
From work:	$d = 24(4 - t)$
Set the expressions equal:	$40t = 24(4 - t)$
Distribute:	$40t = 96 - 24t$
Add 24t:	$64t = 96$
Divide by 64:	$t = 1.5$

Plug 1.5 in for t and solve for d: $d = 40(1.5) = 60$ miles to work. Therefore he travels $60 + 60 = 120$ miles to and from work that day.

---

8. **C** If a swimming pool that can hold 20,000 gallons is a quarter full, it holds $1/4(20,000) = 5,000$ gallons. It will take $20,000 - 5,000 = 15,000$ more gallons to fill the pool. The pump is delivering water at a rate of g gallons per m minutes or $\frac{g}{m}$.

Use amount = rate × time to determine how long it will take to fill the pool:

$$15,000 = \frac{g}{m} \cdot (t)$$

Divide by $\frac{g}{m}$: $\dfrac{15,000m}{g} = t$

If it costs d dollars per minute, then the total cost

is $\dfrac{15,000m}{g} \times d = \dfrac{15,000md}{g}$.

---

9. **10** The key to this problem is that the individual values of X and Z do not matter as much as their sum. Since the sum is a three digit number, there is no "carry" when X and Z are added. If you look at the far right column, you can see that $X + Z = 8$. The middle column tells you that $Y + Y = 4$, or $2Y = 4$. This means that $Y = 2$. The far left column confirms what you learned from the far right column: $Z + X = 8$. Therefore $Z + X + Y = 8 + 2 = 10$.

---

10. **5400**

| Perimeter $= 2L + 2W$ |
Substitute:	$300 = 2L + 2(60)$
Simplify:	$300 = 2L + 120$
Subtract 120:	$180 = 2L$
Divide by 2:	$90 = L$
Find the area:	Area $= LW = 90(60) = 5400$

---

11. **44**

	$g(x) = x^2 - 3$
Find $g(3)$:	$g(3) = 3^2 - 3$
Simplify:	$g(3) = 6$
	$f(g(3)) = ?$
Substitute for $g(3)$:	$f(6) =$
	$f(x) = 8x - 4$
Find $f(6)$:	$f(6) = 8(6) - 4$
Simplify:	$f(6) = 44$

---

12. **$\dfrac{5}{8}$** To solve this problem, it helps to draw a picture. Points X and Y are on the circle and Z can be found in between those two points on the longer arc of the circle as shown below:

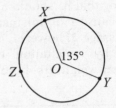

As shown, angle XOY is 135°. This means that the remainder of the circle makes up an angle of 360° − 135° = 225°. To find out what fraction of a circle this is, divide 225° by 360° $\dfrac{225}{360} = \dfrac{5}{8}$.

---

13. **14** Because you know that $ab + \dfrac{1}{ab} = 4$, it follows that if you square $ab + \dfrac{1}{ab}$, the result is $4^2 = 16$.

$$\left(ab + \frac{1}{ab}\right)\left(ab + \frac{1}{ab}\right) = a^2b^2 + \frac{ab}{ab} + \frac{ab}{ab} + \frac{1}{a^2b^2} = a^2b^2 + 2 + \frac{1}{a^2b^2}$$

$$16 = a^2b^2 + 2 + \frac{1}{a^2b^2}$$

Subtract 2: $14 = a^2b^2 + \dfrac{1}{a^2b^2}$

---

14. **10** This problem includes a 30°–60°–90° triangle.

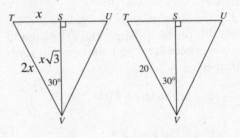

| | $20 = 2x$ |
| Divide by 2: | $10 = x$ |

---

15. **1 or 3** $|-3x + 5| < 6$

Write as two separate inequalities:

$$-3x + 5 < 6 \quad \text{and} \quad -3x + 5 > -6$$

| Subtract 5: | $-3x < 1$ and | $3x > -11$ |
| Divide by −3: | $x > -\dfrac{1}{3}$ and | $x < \dfrac{11}{3}$ |

The only odd integers between those two values are 1 and 3.

16. 132 Student A has 11 different partners: AB, AC, AD, AE, AF, AG, AH, AI, AJ, AK, AL

In fact, each student has 11 different partners, but you have to be careful to avoid counting the same pair more than once.

Student B has 11 different partners, but only 10 different partners that are not already counted: BC, BD, BE, BF, BG, BH, BI, BJ, BK, BL are new. BA was already counted.

Student C has 9 different partners not already counted: CD, CE, CF, CG, CH, CI, CJ, CK, and CL.

Student D has 8 different partners not already counted: DE, DF, DG, DH, DI, DJ, DK, and DL.

Student E has 7 different partners not already counted: EF, EG, EH, EI, EJ, EK, and EL

Student F has 6 different partners not already counted: FG, FH, FI, FJ, FK, and FL

Student G has 5 different partners not already counted: GH, GI, GJ, GK, and GL

Student H has 4 different partners not already counted: HI, HJ, HK, and HL

Student I has 3 different partners not already counted: IJ, IK, and IL

Student J has 2 different partners not already counted JK and JL

Student K has only 1 different partner not yet counted: KL

This yields a total of 11 + 10 + 9 + 8 + 7 + 6 + 5 + 4 + 3 + 2 + 1 = 66 total dance partnerships. Each student is paired up with each of the other students *twice*, so there are 66 × 2 = 132 different pairings.

17. 109 The median is the *middle* number. Aside from the median, there are 54 other numbers in the list. There are 27 numbers on each side of the median. The final term in the list can be found by adding 2 to the median twenty-seven times. 55 + 27(2) = 55 + 54 = 109

18. 72

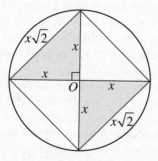

The shaded triangles are both 45°–45°–90° triangles as shown in the diagram above. To find the perimeter of the shaded region, add the 6 side lengths together:

$$x + x + x + x + x\sqrt{2} + x\sqrt{2} = 24 + 12\sqrt{2}$$

Combine terms: $4x + 2x\sqrt{2} = 24 + 12\sqrt{2}$

$4x = 24$, so x must be 6. If x is 6, then each side of the square is $x\sqrt{2}$ or $6\sqrt{2}$

The area of the square is $(6\sqrt{2})^2 = 72$.

Section 6

1. A The referee had no choice but to throw the athlete out of the game. This would indicate that the foul must have been pretty bad—*blatant* (obvious) and *egregious* (conspicuously bad or offensive) are two good choices. It is doubtful that the referee would petition for a *celebration* after the foul. A *suspension* would make sense for such an awful foul. *blatant* = obvious; *miniscule* = tiny; *egregious* = conspicuously bad or offensive; *nautical* = relating to shipping.

2. E Tracy became the youngest partner in firm history and no associate had ever performed with such a consistent *standard of excellence*. This would indicate she was a very *diligent* worker. *gratuity* = a gift given in return for service; *dormancy* = a period of inactivity; *lethargy* = fatigue; *capriciousness* = impulsiveness; *diligence* = hard work.

3. C Oprah is known for *helping those who are less fortunate*. This indicates that she is an *altruist* (selfless person) or a *philanthropist* (lover of mankind). Answer choice (A) does not make sense, however, because the second word, *dislike*, does not make sense in the context of the sentence. If she is an altruist, she won't have dislike for helping others. Answer choice (C) is a good fit because a *penchant* is an inclination to do something. *altruist* = selfless person; *charlatan* = a fraud; *prerequisite* = required as a prior condition; *philanthropist* = lover of mankind; *penchant* = inclination, a liking; *nihilist* = one who doubts the existence of knowable truths; *despot* = a tyrant; *culpability* = guilt.

4. A The word *although* establishes a contrast. Actual confessions take hours and several hundred sentences, whereas Dostoevsky's confession in his book takes a mere 20 words. You want to pick a word that suggests frugality with words. *laconic* = marked by the use of few words; *verbose* = wordy; *lugubrious* = exaggeratedly gloomy or mournful; *sonorous* = having a full deep sound; *antiquated* = outdated.

5. A The fighter was humbled by the experience of losing his title to a weaker opponent. His public demeanor changed to a *modest and self-effacing persona* from one that was previously not a modest one.

Lofty is a good fit for the missing word. *lofty* = exalted, arrogant; *impecunious* = penniless; *obligatory* = required; *prescient* = able to see the future; *pusillanimous* = cowardly.

---

6. **C**   The passage as a whole describes the technological advance of *the kareze system of irrigation*, and describes some technical details of its construction and its effects on the Persian villagers.

---

7. **E**   The phrase *these muqannis* (line 8) refers to the previous sentence, which describes how *Persian engineers* (line 4) constructed the kareze. Also, since these muqannis are said to have *calculated* the location of a tunnel, they must have been people, not inanimate things such as deposits or tunnels.

---

8. **C**   The passage states that *sports can be seen [by evolutionary anthropologists] as a means of expressing our genetic endowment as hunters, even though most societies no longer require hunting* (lines 7–10). This implies that we have acquired genes for a trait that is no longer essential. In other words, these traits are *vestiges* (remaining traces) we have inherited from our ancestors.

---

9. **D**   In saying that music is *more mysterious to evolutionary anthropologists* (lines 15–16), the author means that the cultural need for musical expression is not as easily explained as sports is, that is, as an expression of *inherited traits* that once *had definite survival value to individuals and societies* (lines 14–15).

---

10. **C**   The passages states that the Sherpas were *ideally suited to the rigors of high-altitude climbing ... stout at altitude, and seemingly resistant to cold* (lines 8–11). It also states that European climbers were *amazed at the strength of these people* (line 46). It does not, however, say that they had any *expertise in treating altitude sickness*.

---

11. **E**   The passage states that *Sherpas did not venture into the high peaks until European mountaineers began arriving to climb in the world's greatest mountain range* (lines 12–15).

---

12. **A**   In calling the team of porters a *motley* (miscellaneous) *throng of old men, women, boys and girls* (lines 50–51), Wakefield was clearly emphasizing their heterogeneity.

---

13. **A**   The passage states of Wakefield that the accomplishments of the Sherpa *astonished him* (lines 51–52), and his expression of amazement in describing their ability to carry 80 pound loads reinforces this sentiment.

---

14. **B**   The passage never answers the question *Who was the first European to climb Mount Everest?* It does, however, answer the questions regarding the first climbing fatalities on Everest (lines 68–71), the Tibetan name for Everest (line 16), the name of the Sherpa ceremony (line 24), and the first European to recognize the value of Sherpas (lines 31–33).

---

15. **D**   This paragraph is primarily concerned with describing the ruggedness of the Sherpas, which was made clear in particular by their ability to sleep *using only rocks for shelter* (line 57). Although these rocks could perhaps indicate the *barren landscape of Mount Everest*, their mention in this sentence is clearly for another purpose.

---

16. **B**   The passage states that *many [Sherpas] aspired to this honor [of the Tiger Medal] and the higher pay it afforded* (lines 64–65), and that assisting expeditions had become *an important source of revenue for a poor mountain folk* (lines 75–76). Since the Sherpa did not climb the mountain until the Europeans arrived, climbing could not have been a *social custom for many centuries*, and since the mountain was long considered *off-limits to humans* (lines 19–20) for religious reasons, climbing could not have been regarded as a *religious duty*.

---

17. **C**   In asking *can animal communication come anywhere close to this level of complexity?*, the author is asking whether animals can communicate about concepts and about events in the past or in the future. Therefore, the level of complexity this is referring to is the intricacy of language skill that allows animals to convey abstract information about concepts and events that cannot be directly perceived. Although choice (E) mentions events from the distant past, this question is not addressing the task of remembering, but the task of communication.

---

18. **E**   If the discovery that *sperm whales...have a female-dominated, egalitarian* (based on an equal distribution of power and rights) *society* was relevant to a *scientific conference on animal communication*, then the scientists at the conference must *regard systems of social organization to be relevant to the study of animal communication*. The conference did not discuss *human societies*, and this discovery did not compare whales and elephants in terms of the sophistication of their *communication skills*, discuss the relationship between *language skill* and *brain size*, or compare males to females in terms of their communicativeness.

---

19. **C**   Whales and elephants both have *a female-dominated, egalitarian society* (lines 17–18) and can both communicate over long distances, elephants

over *several kilometers* (line 21) and whales over *perhaps hundreds of miles* (lines 26–27). But while elephants use infrasound, which is below the frequencies that the human ear can detect, whales can hear *nearly all of the frequencies that humans can, as well as many higher than the human range* (lines 28–30), which suggests that elephants cannot hear frequencies lower than those that humans can.

20. B The statement that *it appears whales are talking louder because of the increased noise in the oceans from ships—just as humans talk louder in a noisy bar than on a quiet beach* implies that whales would not need to talk as loud if they were not in such a noisy environment, that is, away from the noisy ships. Nothing in this statement suggests that the whales are disoriented or fooled by this noise, nor does it give any indication of why whales may emit high-frequency sounds or whether they might occasionally go near beaches.

21. A These words appear in *conjectures* that are based on *the results of Janik's research* regarding dolphin whistles. Since this research did not produce data about the purpose of these whistles, the conclusion that the whistles were used to *keep in touch* must be a matter of conjecture, as the words *appears* and *presumably* indicate.

22. A The passage states that human judges were employed to *determine if [the dolphin] calls were identical*, that is, to compare the underwater whistles and try to distinguish them.

23. D The experiment described in lines 77–93 determined that *some of the chimps associated negative facial expressions* with scary scenes, and *positive facial expressions* with happy scenes, even without being trained to do so. This particular experiment did not examine the communication skills of the chimpanzees, but rather their ability to make associations.

24. D The passage suggests that sea lions reason by the law of transitivity when they conclude that "because sea lion A has defeated sea lion B, and sea lion B has defeated me, then I should not fight sea lion A because he is stronger than me." Therefore, if that sea lion fought sea lion A anyway, it would undermine the conclusion that the sea lion could reason "via transitivity."

Section 7

1. A First, assign values to points P and Q. Point P is about -1.75 and point Q is about 1.75. Now multiply those two values in that vicinity together: $-1.75 \times 1.75 = -3.0625$. The only point in that vicinity is point A.

2. B

$$\frac{x}{8} = 5z$$

Multiply by 8: $\qquad x = 40z$

$$\frac{1}{2z} = 5y$$

Divide by 5: $\qquad \dfrac{1}{10z} = y$

$$xy =$$

Substitute: $\qquad (40z)\dfrac{1}{10z} = 4$

3. A When p is divided by 7, it gives a remainder of 2. Think of a number for which this is a true statement and assign that number to be p. 9 divided by 7 is 1 with a remainder of 2. So, $p = 9$. Answer choice (A) becomes $9 + 2 = 11$. When 11 is divided by 7, the quotient is 1 with remainder 4.

4. D The best way to solve this problem is to plot the data points. As the x-values are increasing, the y values are increasing at a faster rate. So, the graph will be upward sloping with an increasing slope as it moves to the right. Answer choice D is a perfect fit.

5. B You can use the percent change formula to solve this problem. The original amount was $400 and the final amount was $500.

$$\frac{500 - 400}{400} \times 100 = \frac{100}{400} \times 100 = 25\%$$

6. D Begin by finding the coordinates of the 5 points:

A $\quad$ $(-2, 4)$
B $\quad$ $(3, 2)$
C $\quad$ $(2, -2)$
D $\quad$ $(-3, 0)$
E $\quad$ $(1, 8)$

The slope of AB is $\dfrac{4-2}{-2-3} = -\dfrac{2}{5}$

The slope of AC is $\dfrac{4-(-2)}{-2-2} = -\dfrac{6}{4}$

The slope of AD is $\dfrac{4-0}{-2-(-3)} = \dfrac{4}{1} = 4$

The slope of EB is $\dfrac{8-2}{1-3} = \dfrac{6}{-2} = -3$

The slope of DC is $\dfrac{0-(-2)}{-3-2} = -\dfrac{2}{5}$

7. D ¾ of the vehicles are cars and ⅓ of the cars are older than 3 years. Therefore ¾ × ⅓ = ¼ of the vehicles are cars older than 3 years. You are told that there are 20 cars older than 3 years in the lot, which means that 20 = ¼ (total)

Divide by ¼: total = 80 cars

---

8. C   The smallest integer is n. Remember they are consecutive *odd* integers. The set of integers would be: $n, n + 2, n + 4, n + 6, n + 8, n + 10, n + 12, n + 14$. To average the integers, add them together and divide by 8:

$$\frac{n+(n+2)+(n+4)+(n+6)+(n+8)+(n+10)+(n+12)+(n+14)}{8}$$

Combine terms: $\dfrac{8n+56}{8} = n+7$

---

9. C   You might solve this problem quickly with trial and error. Try $w = 1$.

(A) $w^4 = 1^4 = 1$
(B) $(w - 2)^3 = (1 - 2)^3 = -1^3 = -1$
(C) $4w^2 = 4(1)^2 = 4(1) = 4$
(D) $4w = 4(1) = 4$
(E) $3(w^2) = 3(1^2) = 3(1) = 3$

Answer choices A, B, and E are out. Now try $w = -2$

(C) $4w^2 = 4(-2)^2 = 4(4) = 16$
(D) $4w = 4(-2) = -8$

Only answer choice (C) remains.

---

10. C

$A = \pi r^2 = 64\pi$
Divide by π: $r^2 = 64$
Take square root: $r = 8$

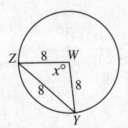

If the radius = 8 and $ZY = 8$, then triangle ZWY is an equilateral triangle and therefore $x = 60°$.

---

11. D   This question tests your understanding of exponent rules. Simplify each of the three expressions:

I. $(64x^6)^{\frac{2}{3}}$

Take the cube root and then square that result:

cube root: $4x^2$
square: $16x^4$ equivalent

II. $\left(\dfrac{1}{2x}\right)^{-4}$

Rewrite without negative exponents: $(2x)^4$
raise to the fourth: $16x^4$

III. $\dfrac{x^2}{16x^{-1}}$

Rewrite without negative exponents: $\dfrac{x^3}{16}$

So only I and II are the same, and the answer is D.

---

12. B   The original ratio of dogs to cats was $\dfrac{d}{c}$.

4 cats arrived, giving a total of $c + 4$ cats. You don't know how many dogs arrived, so call that number x, producing a total of $d + x$ dogs. The ratio remains unchanged, so set the new ratio of dogs to cats equal to the original ratio:

$$\frac{d+x}{c+4} = \frac{d}{c}$$

Cross multiply: $c(d + x) = d(c + 4)$
Distribute: $cd + cx = cd + 4d$
Subtract cd: $cx = 4d$
Divide by c: $x = \dfrac{4d}{c}$

---

13. D   To solve this problem, eliminate four of the five answer choices and you will be left with the one that *must* be true. Answer choice A says that $a > b$. If $b = 4$, and $a = 3$, this is not true.

Answer choice B says that $b > a$. If $b = 4$ and $a = 5$, this is not true.

Answer choice C says that $0 < ab$. If $a = -3$ and $b = 4$, then $ab = -12$ and this is not true.

Answer choice E says that $36 < |a + b|$. If $a = 3$ and $b = 4$, then $|a + b| = |3 + 4| = 7$. This leaves us with only answer choice D, which indeed must be true.

---

14. C   The original side length of the square is x. This means that the original area is x^2. The new side length is $x + 4$. The new area would be $(x + 4)^2$ and is 112 square inches larger than the original area, x^2.

$(x + 4)^2 = x^2 + 112$
FOIL: $x^2 + 8x + 16 = x^2 + 112$
Subtract x^2: $8x + 16 = 112$
Subtract 16: $8x = 96$
Divide by 8: $x = 12$

---

15. E $(-4x^4y^{-3})^{-3} =$

Rewrite as a fraction: $\dfrac{1}{(-4x^4y^{-3})^3}$

Raise everything in the denominator to the 3rd power:

$$\frac{1}{-64x^{12}y^{-9}}$$

Rewrite without negative exponents: $\dfrac{y^9}{-64x^{12}}$

16. **B**   A negative *a* coefficient makes the quadratic open downward, which eliminates A, C and E. A negative *c* coefficient means that the vertex of the graph intersects the *y*-axis at a negative value. This leaves answer choice B as the correct answer.

Section 8

1. **B**   If the first blank contains a positive word, then the second blank should contain a word such as *appeal*. If the first blank contains a negative word, the second blank should contain a word that means the opposite of *appeal*. The only word pairing of the bunch that makes sense is answer choice (B) *prolific* and *appealed*. *cryptic* = mysterious; *prolific* = producing abundant works; *provocative* = stimulating; *attest* = to affirm to be true; *garish* = excessively showy.

2. **C**   The downsizing of the company has brought about change. It's not certain from the context whether the change has been good or bad. What's important is that the words you choose establish a change in practice. Answer choice (C) does so as the company goes from one that embraces different points of view to one that *denounces* the voicing of different opinions.

3. **B**   The calculus problem was so extremely difficult that even the most *skilled* mathematicians struggled to derive the answer. *agile* = nimble; *adept* = skilled; *abysmal* = horrible; *insipid* = dull; *eloquent* = well-spoken.

4. **A**   The principal punished the student *harshly*, which suggests he or she must have misbehaved badly. The first word should be a word that relates to *misbehavior that undermines authority*. Two words fit that description well—*insubordination* (not submissive to authority) and *impudence* (rude boldness). The word *inundate* (to flood) does not make sense in the second blank, whereas *condone* (to excuse or overlook) does. Answer choice (A) is the best fit. *insubordination* = a failure to submit to authority; *condone* = to excuse or overlook; *disseminate* = to spread; *assuage* = to soothe; *improvident* = not providing for the future; *provoke* = to push into action; *subterfuge* = deceptiveness; *expedite* = to speed up; *impudence* = rude boldness; *inundate* = to flood.

5. **D**   A good advertisement is able to *persuade* consumers. *perpetuate* = to prolong the existence of; *thwart* = to prevent the occurrence of; *console* = to help ease the grief of another; *exhort* = to urge into action; *reproach* = criticism, disapproval.

6. **E**   Her articles are still used today, which suggests they must be of high quality. The missing word must be a positive word that relates to *clarity of thinking*. *modicum* = small amount; *respite* = a break; *dearth* = a lack; *turpitude* = depravity; *perspicacity* = acuteness of perception.

7. **D**   The central purpose of the passage is to discuss how *metaphysics and mathematics have crossed paths* (lines 1–2) throughout history. Although the passage does discuss the Babylonians and the Pythagoreans, they are not the focus of the passage as a whole.

8. **C**   These *angles and energies* describe the manner in which *metaphysics and mathematics have crossed paths* (lines 1–2) over the centuries, and therefore describe how two disciplines have intersected.

9. **B**   The phrase *but not exclusively* indicates that mathematics and religion have not always crossed paths to their mutual benefit, suggesting that the relationship between these two disciplines has not always been constructive.

10. **A**   The sentence previous to this one indicates that both disciplines *were practiced together* in ancient times, but today *their spheres have become separate* (lines 7–8), suggesting that the two disciplines have become more *independent* over time.

11. **C**   In saying that *their spheres have become separate* (lines 7–8), the author means that the two disciplines are largely independent in terms of what domains they influence.

12. **A**   This paragraph begins by describing the *instrumental* use of mathematics by humans to describe the motions of the heavens and to construct edifices. It then describes an incident in which the gods were thought to use mathematics to confound the believers. The word *Reciprocally* shows that the "instrumentality" of mathematics went both ways between humans and the gods.

13. **E**   Plato is said to have suggested that *the gods could use mathematics to communicate with believers, confounding them to set their minds properly* (lines 25–26), particularly in the instance in which the oracle demanded that the worshippers double the size of their altar, which was *a task beyond Greek mathematicians*. Therefore, Plato suggested that the oracle's demand was intended to mystify the Delians.

14. **A**   This sentence states that it was *proven centuries before the dawn of Christianity* that *not even an infinite power can construct a circle ten cubits across that can be encircled with fewer than 31.4 cubits*. This

states that a particular geometric fact cannot be contradicted, even by an infinite power.

15. D   The *manner of thinking* being discussed in this paragraph was inspired by the *power of deduction to prove truths beyond the whims of the gods* (lines 60–61) and includes the idea that *mathematics itself is a mystical power* (lines 62–63). The paragraph does not suggest that this *manner of thinking* included the belief that *the primary purpose of mathematics is to solve worldly problems*, and indeed it suggests, to the contrary, that it gave mathematics *its own abstract plane beyond the physical world* (lines 69–70). Therefore it includes beliefs II and III, but not I.

16. C   In saying that *mathematics acquired its own abstract plane beyond the physical world*, the author means that mathematics was considered to be on a *level of existence* beyond the level of worldly concerns.

17. C   This paragraph criticizes the Pythagoreans for punishing *transgressions* (violations of moral standards) with *violence* (lines 82–84) in drowning Hipposus for proving a mathematical fact that contradicted one of their religious precepts. The phrase *righteousness ascended*, then, means that the Pythagoreans became *ideologically intolerant*.

18. A   The *precept* in line 90 is the idea that *all of reality can be described with whole numbers and their ratios* (lines 90–92). The final paragraph shows that this precept is incorrect: *Hipposus has been vindicated* (cleared of suspicion) (line 96), that is, his proof is in fact correct, and the Pythagoreans' precept is incorrect.

19. D   This passage states that these *explorers* are on a *quest for understanding* (lines 103–105) and that their errors are *due to human weakness, not to the weakness of logic* (lines 105–107) and that they are on an *inexorable march...toward the true understanding of nature* (lines 107–109). In other words, they are trying to understand nature through logical reasoning.

Section 9

1. B   The error in this sentence is the use of the word *because*. The sentence shows contrast rather than a cause and effect relationship. The Yankees have spent more money than any other franchise, and yet they have only won once. A contrasting conjunction like *although* better conveys the correct relationship.

2. D   This sentence contains a dangling modifier. The modifying phrase that begins the sentence describes *the recently married couple rather than the canal system of Venice*. Answer choice (D) best corrects the error.

3. D   The word *and* is extraneous and creates an awkward sentence. Remove the word *and* to fix the error.

4. A   The sentence is correct as written.

5. E   The expression *no sooner ... but* is not a correct idiom. The correct idiom is *no sooner ... than*.

6. E   The sentence is awkwardly constructed. Answer choice (E) is clear, concise, and makes a logical comparison.

7. B   Eric would not decide to lie down in order to clean the garage—he would probably lie down *after* he has cleaned the garage. Answer choice (B) best corrects the error.

8. C   This contains a dangling modifier. The modifying phrase that begins the sentence describes *Madonna rather* than *Madonna's songs*. Answer choice (C) best corrects the error.

9. C   This sentence is inconsistent with its use of pronouns. It is not proper to say *you* and then switch to *one*.

10. B   This contains a dangling modifier. The original sentence implies that the nonprofit organization is donating money. It should instead be *you* that follows the comma because *you* are donating the money.

11. E   This is a comparison error. You need to compare the *amount of money* online shoppers charged in 2005 to the *amount of money* online shoppers charged in 2004. As it is originally written, it is illogically comparing the amount of money charged in 2005 to the year 2004.

12. B   Modern audiences were not written in the late 18th century. Answer choice (B) corrects the error in the most clear and concise manner.

13. A   The sentence is correct as written.

14. D   This is a subject-verb error. There are *two* things that put the patients at ease—her smile and her sense of humor. Therefore the subject is plural, which means that the verb should be *put*, the plural form.

PRACTICE TEST 3

ANSWER SHEET

Last Name:_____ First Name:_____

Date:_____ Testing Location:_____

Directions for Test

- Remove these answer sheets from the book and use them to record your answers to this test.
- This test will require 3 hours and 20 minutes to complete. Take this test in one sitting.
- The time allotment for each section is written clearly at the beginning of each section. This test contains six 25-minute sections, two 20-minute sections, and one 10-minute section.
- This test is 25 minutes shorter than the actual SAT, which will include a 25-minute "experimental" section that does not count toward your score. That section has been omitted from this test.
- You may take one short break during the test, of no more than 10 minutes in length.
- You may only work on one section at any given time.
- You must stop ALL work on a section when time is called.
- If you finish a section before the time has elapsed, check your work on that section. You may NOT work on any other section.
- Do not waste time on questions that seem too difficult for you.
- Use the test book for scratchwork, but you will receive credit only for answers that are marked on the answer sheets.
- You will receive one point for every correct answer.
- You will receive no points for an omitted question.
- For each wrong answer on any multiple-choice question, your score will be reduced by ¼ point.
- For each wrong answer on any "numerical grid-in" question, you will receive no deduction.

When you take the real SAT, you will be asked to fill in your personal information in grids as shown below.

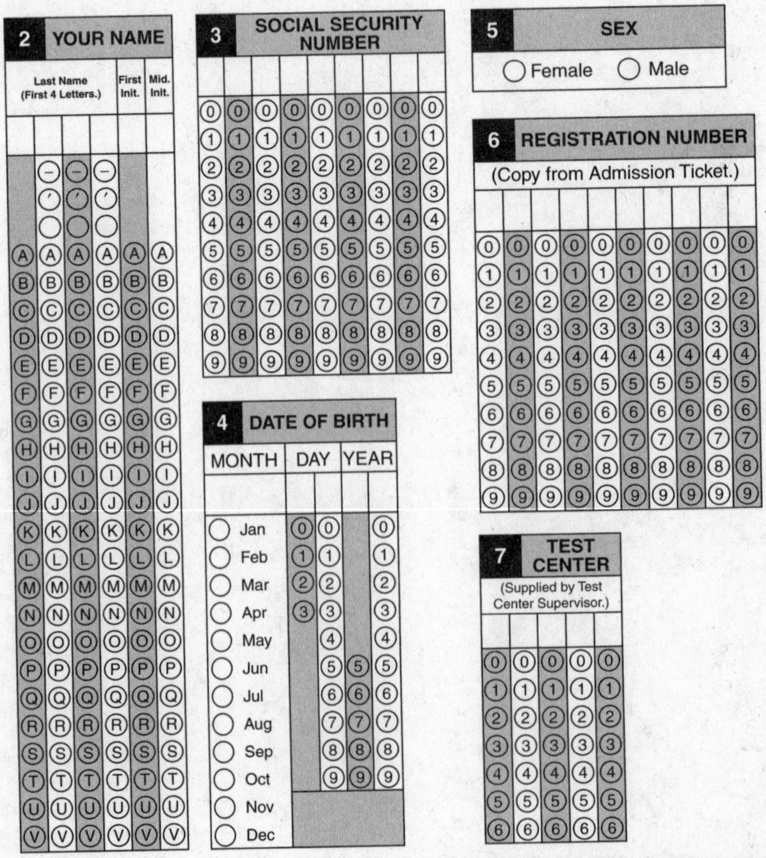

Start with number 1 for each new section. If a section has fewer questions than answer spaces, leave the extra answer spaces blank. Be sure to erase any errors or stray marks completely.

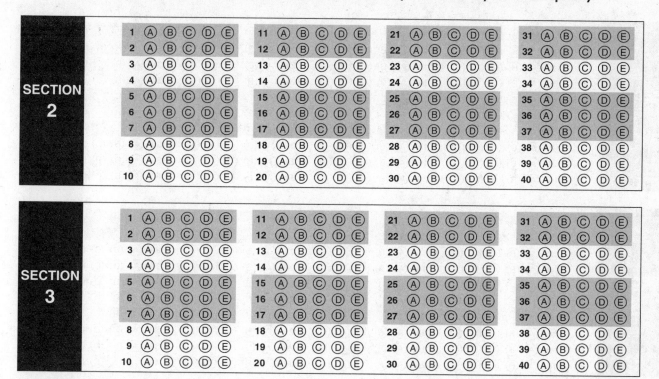

CAUTION Use the answer spaces in the grids below for Section 2 or Section 3 only if you are told to do so in your test book.

Student-Produced Responses

ONLY ANSWERS ENTERED IN THE CIRCLES IN EACH GRID WILL BE SCORED. YOU WILL NOT RECEIVE CREDIT FOR ANYTHING WRITTEN IN THE BOXES ABOVE THE CIRCLES.

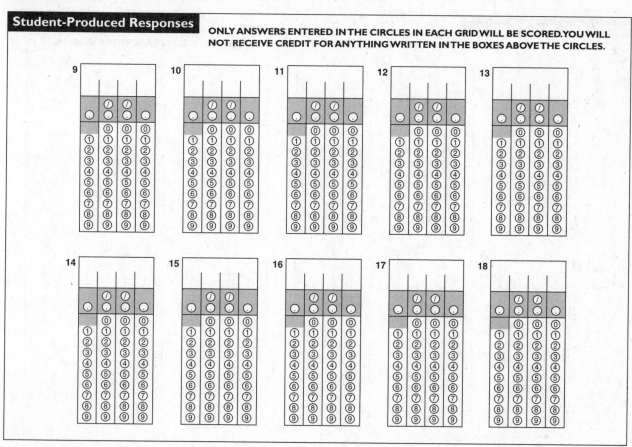

Start with number 1 for each new section. If a section has fewer questions than answer spaces, leave the extra answer spaces blank. Be sure to erase any errors or stray marks completely.

SECTION 4

SECTION 5

CAUTION   Use the answer spaces in the grids below for Section 4 or Section 5 only if you are told to do so in your test book.

Student-Produced Responses   ONLY ANSWERS ENTERED IN THE CIRCLES IN EACH GRID WILL BE SCORED. YOU WILL NOT RECEIVE CREDIT FOR ANYTHING WRITTEN IN THE BOXES ABOVE THE CIRCLES.

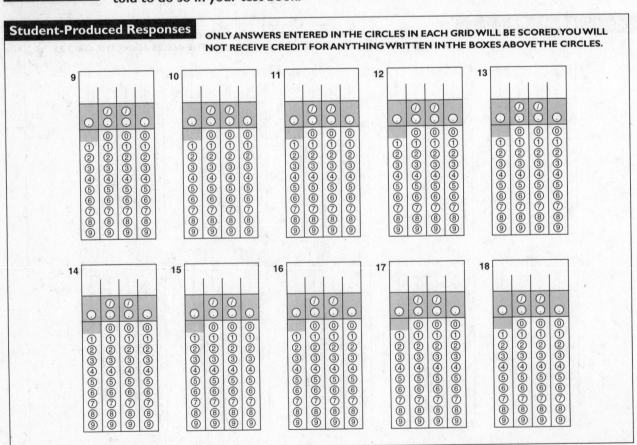

Start with number 1 for each new section. If a section has fewer questions than answer spaces, leave the extra answer spaces blank. Be sure to erase any errors or stray marks completely.

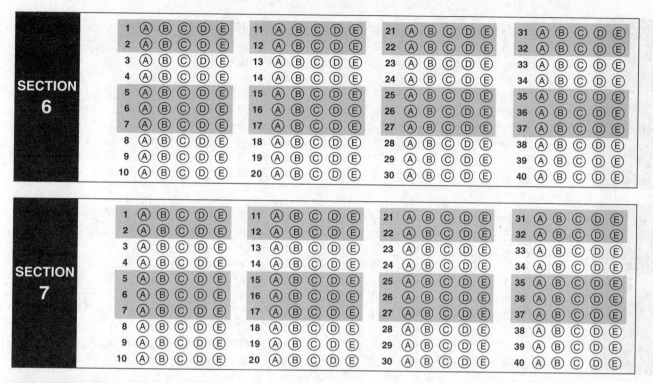

SECTION 6

SECTION 7

CAUTION Use the answer spaces in the grids below for Section 6 or Section 7 only if you are told to do so in your test book.

Student-Produced Responses ONLY ANSWERS ENTERED IN THE CIRCLES IN EACH GRID WILL BE SCORED. YOU WILL NOT RECEIVE CREDIT FOR ANYTHING WRITTEN IN THE BOXES ABOVE THE CIRCLES.

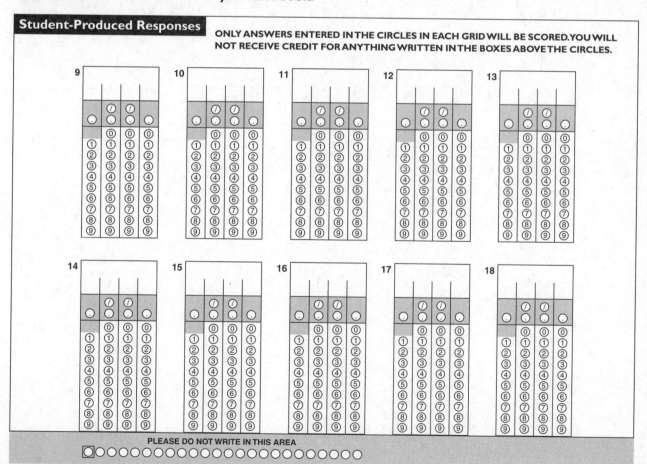

PLEASE DO NOT WRITE IN THIS AREA

Start with number 1 for each new section. If a section has fewer questions than answer spaces, leave the extra answer spaces blank. Be sure to erase any errors or stray marks completely.

SECTION 8

1 (A) (B) (C) (D) (E)	11 (A) (B) (C) (D) (E)	21 (A) (B) (C) (D) (E)	31 (A) (B) (C) (D) (E)
2 (A) (B) (C) (D) (E)	12 (A) (B) (C) (D) (E)	22 (A) (B) (C) (D) (E)	32 (A) (B) (C) (D) (E)
3 (A) (B) (C) (D) (E)	13 (A) (B) (C) (D) (E)	23 (A) (B) (C) (D) (E)	33 (A) (B) (C) (D) (E)
4 (A) (B) (C) (D) (E)	14 (A) (B) (C) (D) (E)	24 (A) (B) (C) (D) (E)	34 (A) (B) (C) (D) (E)
5 (A) (B) (C) (D) (E)	15 (A) (B) (C) (D) (E)	25 (A) (B) (C) (D) (E)	35 (A) (B) (C) (D) (E)
6 (A) (B) (C) (D) (E)	16 (A) (B) (C) (D) (E)	26 (A) (B) (C) (D) (E)	36 (A) (B) (C) (D) (E)
7 (A) (B) (C) (D) (E)	17 (A) (B) (C) (D) (E)	27 (A) (B) (C) (D) (E)	37 (A) (B) (C) (D) (E)
8 (A) (B) (C) (D) (E)	18 (A) (B) (C) (D) (E)	28 (A) (B) (C) (D) (E)	38 (A) (B) (C) (D) (E)
9 (A) (B) (C) (D) (E)	19 (A) (B) (C) (D) (E)	29 (A) (B) (C) (D) (E)	39 (A) (B) (C) (D) (E)
10 (A) (B) (C) (D) (E)	20 (A) (B) (C) (D) (E)	30 (A) (B) (C) (D) (E)	40 (A) (B) (C) (D) (E)

SECTION 9

1 (A) (B) (C) (D) (E)	11 (A) (B) (C) (D) (E)	21 (A) (B) (C) (D) (E)	31 (A) (B) (C) (D) (E)
2 (A) (B) (C) (D) (E)	12 (A) (B) (C) (D) (E)	22 (A) (B) (C) (D) (E)	32 (A) (B) (C) (D) (E)
3 (A) (B) (C) (D) (E)	13 (A) (B) (C) (D) (E)	23 (A) (B) (C) (D) (E)	33 (A) (B) (C) (D) (E)
4 (A) (B) (C) (D) (E)	14 (A) (B) (C) (D) (E)	24 (A) (B) (C) (D) (E)	34 (A) (B) (C) (D) (E)
5 (A) (B) (C) (D) (E)	15 (A) (B) (C) (D) (E)	25 (A) (B) (C) (D) (E)	35 (A) (B) (C) (D) (E)
6 (A) (B) (C) (D) (E)	16 (A) (B) (C) (D) (E)	26 (A) (B) (C) (D) (E)	36 (A) (B) (C) (D) (E)
7 (A) (B) (C) (D) (E)	17 (A) (B) (C) (D) (E)	27 (A) (B) (C) (D) (E)	37 (A) (B) (C) (D) (E)
8 (A) (B) (C) (D) (E)	18 (A) (B) (C) (D) (E)	28 (A) (B) (C) (D) (E)	38 (A) (B) (C) (D) (E)
9 (A) (B) (C) (D) (E)	19 (A) (B) (C) (D) (E)	29 (A) (B) (C) (D) (E)	39 (A) (B) (C) (D) (E)
10 (A) (B) (C) (D) (E)	20 (A) (B) (C) (D) (E)	30 (A) (B) (C) (D) (E)	40 (A) (B) (C) (D) (E)

ESSAY
ESSAY

ESSAY
Time—25 minutes

Write your essay on separate sheets of standard lined paper.

The essay gives you an opportunity to show how effectively you can develop and express ideas. You should, therefore, take care to develop your point of view, present your ideas logically and clearly, and use language precisely.

Your essay must be written on the lines provided on your answer sheet—you will receive no other paper on which to write. You will have enough space if you write on every line, avoid wide margins, and keep your handwriting to a reasonable size. Remember that people who are not familiar with your handwriting will read what you write. Try to write or print so that what you are writing is legible to those readers.

Important Reminders:

- **A pencil is required for the essay.** An essay written in ink will receive a score of zero.
- **Do not write your essay in your test book.** You will receive credit only for what you write on your answer sheet.
- **An off-topic essay will receive a score of zero.**

You have twenty-five minutes to write an essay on the topic assigned below.

Think carefully about the issue presented in the following excerpts and the assignment below.

> Very few important decisions, even deeply personal ones, are made in a vacuum. If we fail to realize how our personal decisions affect other people, then we run the risk of alienating those around us.
> As a member of a society of responsible individuals, you must take ownership of your own personal decisions. You alone bear the responsibility of a bad decision or can enjoy the satisfaction of a good one.

Assignment: **How important is it to seek the opinions of others when making significant personal decisions?** Plan and write an essay in which you develop your point of view on this issue. Support your position with reasoning and examples taken from your reading, studies, experience, or observations.

If you finish before time is called, you may check your work on this section only.
Do not turn to any other section of the test.

2   **2**   **2**   **2**   **2**   **2**

SECTION 2
Time—25 minutes
24 questions

Turn to Section 2 of your answer sheet to answer the questions in this section.

Directions: For each question in this section, select the best answer from among the choices given and fill in the corresponding circle on the answer sheet.

Each sentence below has one or two blanks, each blank indicating that something has been omitted. Beneath the sentence are five words or sets of words labeled A through E. Choose the word or set of words that, when inserted in the sentence, <u>best</u> fits the meaning of the sentence as a whole.

EXAMPLE:

Rather than accepting the theory unquestioningly, Deborah regarded it with------.

(A) mirth
(B) sadness
(C) responsibility
(D) ignorance
(E) skepticism

---

1. There is no consensus among doctors on the value of vitamin C supplements, and such ------- suggests that much further research on the subject is -------.

   (A) validity . . expected
   (B) controversy . . surprising
   (C) discovery . . resented
   (D) disagreement . . necessary
   (E) invariance . . irrelevant

2. Alana's ------- scary movies was not shared by her friends, who generally avoided the horror genre entirely.

   (A) disgust for
   (B) affinity for
   (C) indifference to
   (D) anticipation of
   (E) intolerance of

3. His sense of propriety was -------, and as such his behavior in social groups was often bizarrely inappropriate.

   (A) corollary
   (B) credible
   (C) distorted
   (D) routine
   (E) coherent

4. Many of the recent articles about the Balkan conflicts have provided only ------- and insubstantial anecdotal accounts; not surprisingly, many historians have criticized them for their lack of ------- .

   (A) sparse . . comprehensiveness
   (B) spontaneous . . economy
   (C) meager . . subjectivity
   (D) colloquial . . humor
   (E) abundant . . flexibility

GO ON TO THE NEXT PAGE ⟹

5. Modern philosophers who ------- Aristotle's contributions to the sciences nevertheless ------- his most significant assertions about the physical world, many of which could be easily disproved even by the simplest of experiments.

(A) admire . . laud
(B) acknowledge . . repudiate
(C) disdain . . dismiss
(D) contradict . . extol
(E) reassert . . anticipate

6. While the lips of most mammals play a significant role in eating, in horses they are actually -------, permitting them to grasp even very small foods such as grains.

(A) retracted
(B) therapeutic
(C) incongruous
(D) ameliorative
(E) prehensile

7. Eschewing the hierarchical structure of most large companies, Kenneth decided that his design firm should use a flexible collaborative system in order to ------- creativity and ------- the establishment of rigid practices.

(A) suppress . . release
(B) encourage . . entail
(C) resolve . . reiterate
(D) promote . . check
(E) prevent . . control

8. Some of Professor Davis' students feel that her demonstrations of erudition often go too far, almost to the point of -------.

(A) pedantry
(B) pragmatism
(C) exclusion
(D) evanescence
(E) deprecation

The passages below are followed by questions based on their content. Answer the questions on the basis of what is <u>stated</u> or <u>implied</u> in the passage and in any introductory material that may be provided.

Questions 9–12 are based on the following passages.

PASSAGE 1

    We dissect nature along lines laid down by our native languages. The sensory categories
Line that we isolate from the world of phenomena we do not find there because they stare every
5 observer in the face; on the contrary, the world is presented in a kaleidoscopic flux of impressions which has to be organized by our minds—and this means largely by the linguistic systems in our minds. We cut nature up,
10 organize it into concepts, and ascribe significances as we do, largely because we are parties to an agreement that is codified in the patterns of our language.

PASSAGE 2

    Physicists tell us that the spectrum of visi-
15 ble light is a continuum, a smooth flow of wavelengths from 400 nm to 700 nm. Then why is our experience of yellow so different from our experience of red? It is not because, as some linguists have suggested,
20 English speakers are forced by their limited vocabulary to divide the natural world into arbitrary discrete units of perception, like "yellow" and "red." Rather, it is because the three color-detecting cells in our retinas,
25 called cones, do not respond uniformly to all wavelengths of light. One type of cone prefers red wavelengths, another green, and a third blue. The combined responses of these cells give rise to our non-continuous
30 color perceptions. If our cones were tuned differently, we might detect more shades of green, or be able to perceive ultraviolet, as mosquitoes do, or infrared, as bees do.

GO ON TO THE NEXT PAGE →

2   2   2   2   2   2

9. In line 7, the word "impressions" most nearly means

(A) emotions
(B) imitations
(C) decisions
(D) stimuli
(E) indentations

10. The authors of both passages agree that

(A) language patterns greatly affect human perception
(B) the human mind divides stimuli from the natural world into discrete packets
(C) humans have keener senses than most other animals
(D) humans perceive light as a continuous spectrum
(E) all human societies have similar linguistic patterns

11. Which of the following would most likely agree with the central idea of Passage 1?

(A) the "linguists" in line 19
(B) the "physicists" in line 14
(C) the author of Passage 2
(D) the "observer" in line 5
(E) the "English speakers" of line 20

12. Which of the following in Passage 2 is the best example of one of the "sensory categories" discussed in Passage 1?

(A) "smooth flow" in line 15
(B) "experience" in line 17
(C) "red" in line 23
(D) "cells" in line 24
(E) "mosquitoes" in line 33

Questions 13–24 are based on the following passage.

The following passage is from a book about the appreciation of literature.

Reading literature is a common experience; it is by no means a simple experience. Literature
Line may seem a simple matter of fact when one thinks of it as being black marks on white
5 pages; but as soon as the reader recognizes the marks as words–and as phrases, and sentences, and paragraphs–he has begun to leave the realm of the simple experience of the "real" object, the printed page, and has begun to move in
10 the world of abstractions. The black marks are soon seen to be symbols of other things, to "stand for" objects, processes, and situations.

In spite of the abstract quality of language, there is a comforting familiarity about the
15 printed page, for the words can be appreciated as common sounds and meanings remembered from conversation. Even when the words are unfamiliar, the dictionary will tell the reader the correct sound and meaning. It all seems real
20 enough and simple enough, for language is second nature with the adult and he does not think much about it. Indeed, it is probably true that for most readers books are palliatives, something to fill the awkward pauses between periods of significant activity. Books pour from the
25 presses and are read without being remembered—but "when literature is not memorable it is nothing."

Readers who believe that literature provides a memorable experience, who take the printed
30 page seriously as an opportunity to enjoy a significant experience, are sometimes regarded with suspicion, as if they had lost their touch with reality and become escapists victimized by
35 the unrealities of the imagined world of fiction. Such suspicions are groundless, for the very world of reality in which we all live our daily lives is filled with imagined experience. We look out the window at the street and we say, "It is
40 wet out." This is an imagined experience, for wetness is a tactile sensation, not visual. We can judge weight of a stone without lifting it because our visual response to the stone stimulates through our imagination (recollections of
45 past experiences with stones) kinaesthetic sensations of muscular tensions. Much of thought

GO ON TO THE NEXT PAGE

proceeds by hypothesis–that is, by trial and error. Imagination, the representation of things not present, is essential to our lives.

50   Those who feel strongly the separation between literature and life, who are reluctant to suspend their disbelief, have in a great measure missed out on one of the most profoundly civilizing of processes–the education of the senses
55   and the pleasurable acquisition of that knowledge which is necessary for our understanding of human experience.

Yet life is not literature, nor is literature life; the two are distinct, but so much has been
60   made of the distinction that they are often seen as alien to one another. It is the alienation that does so much damage, that allows the writer to grow careless in his art and the reader to become casual and uncritical. It is when the real-
65   ity of life and the imagination of literature are brought together that the writer is honored for his skill and the reader is alerted to the importance of the art of reading.

A reader's experience with a book is no differ-
70   ent in its nature than his experience with other objects in life. All experience is interactive; it is a traffic between the object and the subject. Actuality, the sense of living through an event with its emotional quality of enjoyment or suffering,
75   characterizes the experience of reading as it does the experience of living.

In life, objects appear to us and we have sensations and impressions of them as they impinge on our sensory organs; we adjust to the
80   objects with every confidence that they are real. How often we are mistaken in our impression of the sensation, our judgment of the impression! Theseus, in *A Midsummer Night's Dream*, speaks of the errors we make in judging:
85   "in the night, imagining some fear, how easy is a bush supposed a bear!" The corrected impression may come in time or too late or it may never come at all.

In literature as in life the magic of the imagi-
90   nation creates vivid images that may develop in the reader a disposition to accept the images as physical reality, and what was at first imagined becomes at last directly sensed. John Keats went so far as to express a *preference* for the
95   imagined when he said, "Heard melodies are sweet, but those unheard are sweeter..."

Perhaps Keats was an uncommon reader, for most of us still cling to the notion that we enjoy direct, lively sensations in life, but only the pale,
100   reflected image of those sensations in literature. Generally, however, we underestimate the pow-er of literature to affect us directly. Indeed, we may not want it to move us deeply; in that case, when the images threaten to transcend their
105   mirrorlike flatness and to become solidly real, we seek refuge in further abstractness: we become more "educated," and a consciousness of words as words replaces the images evoked by the words, and consequently we are at a further
110   and safer remove from life.

13.   The statement that literature "is by no means a simple experience" (lines 1–2) means that

    (A)   it is very difficult to write good prose
    (B)   literary analysis requires a great deal of technical knowledge
    (C)   good literature elicits very powerful emotions
    (D)   the process of interpreting words is complex
    (E)   many of the best books are not widely available

14.   The word "move" in line 9 refers to the progress of

    (A)   a literary movement
    (B)   a social phenomenon
    (C)   a particular writer's work
    (D)   a reader's thought process
    (E)   literary criticism

15.   The quotation in (lines 22–28) is intended to contrast directly with the belief that

    (A)   books serve primarily to comfort readers
    (B)   a good story should be intellectually stimulating
    (C)   literature provides readers with vivid sensory experiences
    (D)   those who read a great deal are often poor conversationalists
    (E)   few people read great literature

Excerpted from *Literature as Experience*, Wallace Bacon and Robert Breen, © 1959 McGraw-Hill, pp. 3–6

GO ON TO THE NEXT PAGE ⟶

2   2   2   2   2   2

16. The "suspicions" mentioned in line 36 are held by those who believe that literature

(A) can be too difficult for many readers to interpret
(B) is a highly rewarding experience
(C) can alienate readers from reality
(D) is not taught well in schools
(E) contains too little moral instruction

17. The "damage" mentioned in line 62 is caused by

(A) bringing life experiences together with literary ones
(B) the failure to acknowledge the work history of an author
(C) writing that is dull and unimaginative
(D) writing that focuses on escapist fantasies
(E) the emphasis on distinguishing between literary experiences and life experiences

18. In line 72, the word "traffic" most nearly means

(A) congestion
(B) merchandise
(C) detour
(D) crowd
(E) communication

19. The passage mentions "confidence" in line 80 to make the point that

(A) we often cannot detect objects in our immediate environment
(B) writers must rely on their creative instincts
(C) we usually trust that our sensory perceptions are correct
(D) we should not allow the fantasy world of novels to influence our everyday decisions
(E) critics are often biased in their judgments of literature

20. In line 83, the word "impression" most nearly means

(A) interpretation
(B) imitation
(C) stamp
(D) questioning
(E) approval

21. According to the passage, the "stone" in line 43 is similar to the "bush" in line 86 in that both

(A) represent literary metaphors
(B) are easily confused with other objects
(C) convey a particular mood
(D) are incapable of emotion
(E) are apprehended through the imagination

22. In the final two paragraphs, John Keats is mentioned primarily as an example of

(A) a writer who used imagery in his work
(B) one who had a vivid imagination
(C) a poet who departed from tradition
(D) one who warned against overeducation
(E) one who preferred real experience to imagination

23. According to the author, those who "become more 'educated'" (lines 106–107) do so chiefly in order to

(A) learn the backgrounds of authors
(B) appreciate the nuances of a story they are reading
(C) become better writers
(D) avoid becoming too affected by literature
(E) change careers

24. Which of the following best summarizes the main idea of the passage?

(A) Schools should expose students to a wider range of literature.
(B) The power of literature is grasped through imagined experience.
(C) Escapist fiction is not true literature.
(D) Reading teachers should help students to translate words rather than to develop their imaginations.
(E) Good literature is comforting and familar.

If you finish before time is called, you may check your work on this section only. Do not turn to any other section of the test.

SECTION 3
Time—25 minutes
35 questions

Turn to Section 3 of your answer sheet to answer the questions in this section.

Directions: For each question in this section, select the best answer from among the choices given and fill in the corresponding circle on the answer sheet.

The following sentences test correctness and effectiveness of expression. Part of each sentence or the entire sentence is underlined; beneath each sentence are five ways of phrasing the underlined material. Choice A repeats the original phrasing; the other four choices are different. Select the choice that completes the sentence most effectively.

In making your selection, follow the requirements of standard written English; that is, pay attention to grammar, choice of words, sentence construction, and punctuation. Your selection should result in the most effective sentence—clear and precise, without awkwardness or ambiguity.

EXAMPLE:

The children <u>couldn't hardly believe their eyes</u>.

(A) couldn't hardly believe their eyes
(B) could hardly believe their eyes
(C) would not hardly believe their eyes
(D) couldn't nearly believe their eyes
(E) couldn't hardly believe his or her eyes

1. Winsor McCay, widely regarded as one of America's greatest graphic artists, not only created one of the most popular Sunday comic strips of the early 20th century, <u>and produced</u> one of the first animated cartoons.

   (A) and produced
   (B) but also produced
   (C) producing
   (D) but also producing
   (E) as well as producing

2. The festival began with a large parade <u>and thousands of people came to watch that</u>.

   (A) and thousands of people came to watch that
   (B) and thousands of people had watched it
   (C) and it was watched by thousands of people
   (D) which was seen by thousands who came to watch it
   (E) that thousands of people came to watch

3. The monument <u>stood</u> on that site for over eighty years when it was toppled by an earthquake.

   (A) stood
   (B) had stood
   (C) was standing
   (D) would be standing
   (E) stood there

GO ON TO THE NEXT PAGE

3   **3**   3   3   **3**   **3**

---

4. Not until well after the rain had subsided <u>the flood waters began to abate</u>.

   (A) the flood waters began to abate
   (B) the flood waters had begun to abate
   (C) did the flood waters begin to abate
   (D) was the flood waters beginning to abate
   (E) was it that the flood waters were beginning to abate

5. Popular magazines are not appropriate in school libraries, because <u>it is not benefiting students</u> educationally.

   (A) it is not benefiting students
   (B) it does not benefit students
   (C) they are not benefiting students
   (D) they do not benefit students
   (E) they are not providing students benefits

6. Movie critics <u>have had to alter their perspectives on what constitutes a "feature film"</u> in order to accommodate this new batch of documentaries.

   (A) have had to alter their perspectives on what constitutes a "feature film"
   (B) are having to alter one's perspective on what constitutes a "feature film"
   (C) have had to alter their perspectives on the "feature film" and what constitutes them
   (D) are having to alter their perspectives for the constitution of a "feature film"
   (E) having to alter their perspectives on what constitutes a "feature film"

7. Taking time off from her job as an attorney, <u>it was Courtney's intention to teach</u> math to middle school students in Boston.

   (A) it was Courtney's intention to teach
   (B) Courtney's intention was to teach
   (C) the intention of Courtney was to teach
   (D) Courtney had the intention for teaching
   (E) Courtney intended to teach

8. Printmakers can produce images using a wide range of surfaces, including stone for lithographs, metal for etchings, and <u>screen-printing, which employs fabric plates</u>.

   (A) screen-printing, which employs fabric plates
   (B) from fabric plates, for screen-printing
   (C) fabric plates for screen printing
   (D) screen-printing from fabric plates
   (E) using fabric plates for screen printing

9. Kaia <u>gave her presentation on Renaissance thinkers dressed as Copernicus</u>.

   (A) gave her presentation on Renaissance thinkers dressed as Copernicus
   (B) dressed as Copernicus to give her presentation on Renaissance thinkers
   (C) dressed as Copernicus and her presentation Renaissance thinkers was given
   (D) gave her presentation dressed as Copernicus on Renaissance thinkers
   (E) dressed as Copernicus giving her presentation on Renaissance thinkers

GO ON TO THE NEXT PAGE ⇒

3   3   3   3   3   3

10. In argumentation, the "straw man" device is <u>an easily refuted misrepresentation of an opponent's viewpoint</u>.

(A)   an easily refuted misrepresentation of an opponent's viewpoint

(B)   when someone misrepresents an opponent's viewpoint that is easy to refute

(C)   misrepresenting an opponent's viewpoint; so it is easy to refute

(D)   someone misrepresenting an opponent's viewpoint to make it easy to refute

(E)   an opponent's viewpoint being misrepresented therefore easily refutable

11. <u>Like what happened</u> in the industrial revolution that took place in Europe in the 19th century, the emergence of new industries in modern-day Asia is fraught with complications.

(A)   Like what happened in

(B)   In similar circumstances to

(C)   In comparison with

(D)   As

(E)   Like

GO ON TO THE NEXT PAGE ⟶

3   3   3   3   3   3

The following sentences test your ability to recognize grammar and usage errors. Each sentence contains either a single error or no error at all. No sentence contains more than one error. The error, if there is one, is underlined and lettered. If the sentence contains an error, select the one underlined part that must be changed to make the sentence correct. If the sentence is correct, select choice E. In choosing answers, follow the requirements of standard written English.

EXAMPLE:

By the time they reached the halfway point
               A
in the race, most of the runners hadn't hardly
      B   C   D
begun to hit their stride. No error
                            E

12. Only recently have the local citizens began
    A   B
    to realize that recycling is an important
               C
    economic as well as ecological issue.
                   D
    No error
    E

13. Khaled Hosseini's novel *The Kite Runner*,

    in which two friends are torn apart by culture
       A   B
    and by war, is a story about devotion, betrayal,
               C
    and, ultimately, how to redeem one's self.
                     D
    No error
    E

14. The hurricane would not have had such a
                   A
    devastating effect on the coastal village had
               B   C
    the storm surge not arrived during an

    abnormally high tide. No error
    D   E

15. Although Professor Mocan morally opposes
                                        A
    capital punishment, he has also discovered
                           B
    a great deal of evidence suggesting that
                           C
    they deter violent crimes. No error
    D   E

16. Despite having fared poorly
    A
    in each of the last five seasons, the cheerleaders
               B
    on the squad remained confident in their ability

    to defeat any team in their division. No error
              D   E

17. Neither the members of the audience

    or the reporters for the local press
       A
    were surprised by the lack of decorum
    B   C
    demonstrated by the debate participants.
    D
    No error
    E

18. The reluctance of the top ambassadors

    to initiate diplomatic exchanges with
       A   B
    neighboring countries were baffling to
                           C
    many observers. No error
    D   E

GO ON TO THE NEXT PAGE ⟹

19. <u>Because</u> the Raiders so dominated their
       A

opponents in the first seven games, many local

sports journalists predicted that they would go

undefeated, <u>and after</u> several key players
              B

<u>sustained</u> serious injuries, the press became
   C

<u>far less</u> optimistic. <u>No error</u>
   D   E

20. The agreement among the many warring

factions <u>were</u> temporary, <u>requiring</u> the parties
          A   B

<u>to meet again</u> in several months to resolve
   C

<u>other important issues</u> still in dispute.
                        D

<u>No error</u>
   E

21. The Constitutional Convention of 1787 <u>was</u> a
                                            A

contentious affair <u>for many reasons</u>, not the
                    B

least of which was the fact that <u>they</u> brought
                                  C

together <u>so many</u> disparate voices and
          D

concerns. <u>No error</u>
            E

22. Too many students have a tendency

<u>of memorizing</u> every formula and procedure
   A

<u>they</u> encounter in math class <u>while</u> ignoring
 B   C

the logic and purpose <u>of</u> each concept.
                        D

<u>No error</u>
   E

23. The same theory that allows linguists

<u>to explain</u> why certain verbs take only transitive
   A

or intransitive forms also <u>help</u> psychologists to
                            B

explain how the human mind <u>processes</u>
                            C

sensory information <u>from</u> the everyday world.
                    D

<u>No error</u>
   E

24. <u>Although</u> everyone on the debate team had
       A

received the same set of instructions,

<u>apparently</u> only <u>Ben and me</u> actually took the
   B   C

time <u>to prepare</u> our arguments and list our
      D

references. <u>No error</u>
              E

25. A careful reading of Galileo's written work and

correspondence, <u>which include</u> dozens of
                  A

letters to his daughter, <u>suggest</u> that his
                          B

experiment testing the theory of gravitation

<u>was</u> in fact <u>conducted</u> at the Leaning Tower of
 C   D
Pisa. <u>No error</u>
       E

26. Ever since <u>it was declared</u> a finalist for the
              A

National Book Award, Morgan's most recent

novel <u>has outsold</u> nearly all of her previous
      B

books, <u>with</u> the exception of <u>that of</u> her
        C   D

autobiography. <u>No error</u>
                E

GO ON TO THE NEXT PAGE

3   3   3   3   3   3

27. One reason that The International Astronomical

    Union <u>no longer considers</u> Pluto to be a planet
                  A

    is <u>that</u> Pluto's orbit <u>is</u> far more eccentric than
       B   C

    <u>other planets</u>. <u>No error</u>
         D   E

28. In the nineteenth century, a few respected

    thinkers <u>became convinced</u> that nations would
                    A

    not be able <u>to coexist</u> peacefully <u>until</u> all of the
                   B   C

    world's cultures <u>adopted</u> a single mutual
                         D

    language. <u>No error</u>
                  E

29. <u>Although</u> Ellen <u>had not danced</u> in decades, she
      A   B

    still felt comfortable <u>getting</u> back out onto the
                              C

    ballroom floor, and was <u>grateful to learn</u> to
                                  D

    waltz when she was a child. <u>No error</u>
                                    E

GO ON TO THE NEXT PAGE ▷

3   3   3   3   3   3

> **Directions:** The following passage is an early draft of an essay. Some parts of the passage need to be rewritten.
>
> Read the passage and select the best answers for the questions that follow. Some questions are about particular sentences or parts of sentences and ask you to improve sentence structure or word choice. Other questions ask you to consider organization and development. In choosing answers, follow the requirements of standard written English.

Questions 30–35 are based on the following passage.

(1) Even in today's modern society, many people still perform rituals on a daily basis; they knock on wood to ward off bad luck or throw salt over their shoulders to repel evil spirits. (2) Every culture has its own superstitions, and now anthropologists and psychologists think they know why.

(3) It is because our brains are always working to find the causes of the significant events that we perceive. (4) When something strange happens that we can't explain, our minds are uncomfortable with the uncertainty. (5) However, we fill this cognitive gap with whatever explanations are available to us, and superstitions provide a simple way to explain mysterious events. (6) They believe that spirits that live in wood have to be appeased, or that throwing salt blinds the devil. (7) Our minds are capable of great things, as anyone who has studied famous artists and inventors knows. (8) Superstitions may seem silly to nonbelievers not sharing them. (9) To believers those rituals on the other hand are providing a sense of control over situations otherwise which would be unsettling.

(10) But they can also sometimes cause great harm. (11) For instance, in Angola, some villagers still believe in witches. (12) If someone dies of a strange disease or a sudden misfortune befalls a family, the villagers might assume it is because someone in the family has secretly cast a spell. (13) Sometimes children will be taken by members of their own family and beaten, disowned or even killed.

(14) People should be careful not to let superstitions get in the way of their compassion for others. (15) They might also be better off using science to explain strange events whenever possible.

30. In context, which of the following is the best revision of the underlined portion of sentence 3 (reproduced below)?

    It is because our brains are always working to find the causes of the significant events that we perceive.

    (A) (As it is now)
    (B) They are saying that it is
    (C) For example, it is, these scientists say,
    (D) These scientists believe we adopt superstitions
    (E) Furthermore, the scientists say it is

31. In context, which is the best replacement for *However* in sentence 5?

    (A) Conversely
    (B) Therefore
    (C) As this demonstrates
    (D) As I personally believe
    (E) Otherwise

32. In context, which of the following changes best improves sentence 6?

    (A) replacing "They" with "For instance, we are inclined to"
    (B) replacing "that spirits" with "about spirits"
    (C) deleting "that live in wood"
    (D) replacing "have to be" with "would have been"
    (E) replacing "or" with "but"

GO ON TO THE NEXT PAGE

3   **3**   3   3   **3**   **3**

33. In context, which of the following is the best way to revise and combine sentences 8 and 9 (reproduced below)?

Superstitions may seem silly to nonbelievers not sharing them. To believers those rituals on the other hand are providing a sense of control over situations otherwise which would be unsettling.

(A) The superstitions seeming silly to nonbelievers who don't share them, however to believers those rituals provide a sense of control over otherwise unsettling situations.

(B) They seem silly to those nonbelievers who don't share the superstitions, but the rituals providing a sense of control over otherwise unsettling situations to believers.

(C) Although such superstitions may seem silly to nonbelievers, to believers those rituals provide a sense of control over otherwise unsettling situations.

(D) Instead of the superstitions seeming silly to those who don't believe in them, these rituals give believers a sense of control to situations otherwise unsettling.

(E) They may seem silly to nonbelievers who don't share the superstitions, hence those rituals provide a sense of control to believers over otherwise unsettling situations.

34. In context, which of the following is the most effective revision of the underlined portion of sentence 10 (reproduced below)?

But they can also sometimes cause great harm.

(A) On the other hand,
(B) Furthermore,
(C) Another issue is the fact that
(D) To my knowledge,
(E) Consequently,

35. Which of the following sentences should be omitted to improve the unity of the passage?

(A) Sentence 1
(B) Sentence 2
(C) Sentence 4
(D) Sentence 7
(E) Sentence 11

If you finish before time is called, you may check your work on this section only. Do not turn to any other section of the test.

SECTION 4
Time—25 minutes
20 questions

Turn to Section 4 of your answer sheet to answer the questions in this section.

Directions: For this section, solve each problem and decide which is the best of the choices given. Fill in the corresponding circle on the answer sheet. You may use any available space for scratchwork.

Notes

1. The use of a calculator is permitted.

2. All numbers used are real numbers.

3. Figures that accompany problems in this test are intended to provide information useful in solving the problems. They are drawn as accurately as possible EXCEPT when it is stated in a specific problem that the figure is not drawn to scale. All figures lie in a plane unless otherwise indicated.

4. Unless otherwise specified, the domain of any function f is assumed to be the set of all real numbers x for which $f(x)$ is a real number.

Reference Information

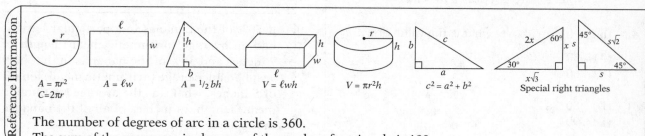

$A = \pi r^2$ $A = \ell w$ $A = \frac{1}{2}bh$ $V = \ell wh$ $V = \pi r^2 h$ $c^2 = a^2 + b^2$ Special right triangles
$C = 2\pi r$

The number of degrees of arc in a circle is 360.
The sum of the measures in degrees of the angles of a triangle is 180.

---

1. If $x = \frac{1}{4}$, then which of the following has the greatest value?

(A) x

(B) $\frac{1}{2}x$

(C) x^2

(D) $1 - x$

(E) x^3

2. If Alexa's car can typically travel 300 miles on a full tank of gasoline, and if her car's tank can hold 18 gallons, then at this rate how far should the car be able to travel on 12 gallons of gasoline?

(A)   120 miles
(B)   180 miles
(C)   200 miles
(D)   220 miles
(E)   240 miles

GO ON TO THE NEXT PAGE

4   **4**   **4**   **4**   **4**   **4**

3. If m and n are positive integers where $m > n$ and $6m + 2n = 22$, what is the value of n?

(A)   1
(B)   2
(C)   3
(D)   4
(E)   5

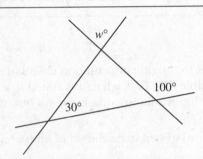

Note: Figure not drawn to scale.

4. In the figure above, what is the value of w?

(A)   50
(B)   60
(C)   70
(D)   80
(E)   90

5. If $\dfrac{n}{6}, \dfrac{n}{8}$, and $\dfrac{n}{9}$ are all integers, then n must be divisible by

(A)   54
(B)   64
(C)   65
(D)   68
(E)   72

6. A farmer has 10 baskets, numbered 1 through 10, each of which contains 10 apples. If he removes 1 apple from basket 1, 2 apples from basket 2, 3 apples from basket 3, and so on, until he removes 10 apples from basket 10, what percent of the original apples remain?

(A)   35%
(B)   40%
(C)   45%
(D)   50%
(E)   55%

7. Which of the following is equivalent to $4n^2 + 4n + 2$?

(A) $4\left(n^2 + n + \dfrac{1}{2}\right)$
(B) $2(2n + 1)^2$
(C) $2(2n^3 + 1)$
(D) $(2n + 1)(2n + 2)$
(E) $(2n - 1)(2n - 2)$

8. If a and b are positive integers, $(3^a)(3^b) = 243$, and $(3^a)^b = 729$, which of the following could be the value of a?

(A)   1
(B)   3
(C)   4
(D)   5
(E)   7

9. If 70% of the bananas in a particular harvest had an average (arithmetic mean) length of 7 inches and 30% of the bananas in that harvest had an average (arithmetic mean) length of 5 inches, what was the average (arithmetic mean) length, in inches, of all of the bananas in the harvest?

(A)   6.0
(B)   6.2
(C)   6.4
(D)   6.6
(E)   6.8

10. Point C lies in plane R. How many circles are there in plane R that have center C and an area of 16π square inches?

(A)   none
(B)   one
(C)   three
(D)   five
(E)   more than five

GO ON TO THE NEXT PAGE

4   4   4   4   4   4

11. Let the function h be defined by $h(x) = \left(\sqrt{5x} - 4\right)^2$.

If $h(m) = 36$, what is the value of m?

(A) 10
(B) 15
(C) 20
(D) 25
(E) 30

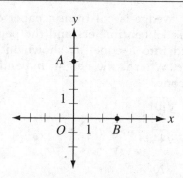

12. If line l (not shown) contains points A and B on the xy-plane above, which of the following could be the equation of a line perpendicular to line l?

(A) $y = \dfrac{4}{3}x + 2$

(B) $y = \dfrac{3}{4}x + 2$

(C) $y = -\dfrac{4}{3}x + 2$

(D) $y = -\dfrac{3}{4}x + 2$

(E) $y = x + 2$

13. If $x = 2^y$ and $y = z + 2$, then what is $\dfrac{x}{2}$ in terms of z?

(A) $z + 1$
(B) $z + 2$
(C) 2^z
(D) 2^{z+1}
(E) $2^z + 1$

$$2a = 3b, \quad \frac{b}{c} = \frac{5}{6}, \quad \text{and} \quad \frac{c}{d} = \frac{5}{2}$$

14. If a, b, c, and d in the equations above are all positive integers, which of the following is true?

(A) $d < b < c < a$
(B) $d < c < a < b$
(C) $c < d < b < a$
(D) $d < b < a < c$
(E) $c < b < d < a$

1, 2, 3, 1, 2, 3, 1, 2, ...

15. If the sequence above continues according to the pattern shown, what is the sum of the first 36 terms of the sequence?

(A) 36
(B) 42
(C) 48
(D) 64
(E) 72

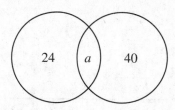

Lacrosse   Soccer

16. The Venn diagram above shows the distribution of students who play lacrosse, soccer, or both. If the ratio of the number of lacrosse players to the number of soccer players is 3:4, then what is the value of a?

(A) 6
(B) 8
(C) 12
(D) 16
(E) 24

GO ON TO THE NEXT PAGE

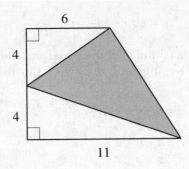

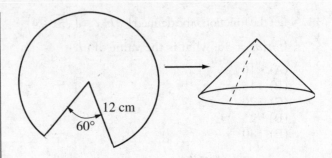

17. In the figure above, what is the area of the shaded triangle?

(A) 30
(B) 32
(C) 34
(D) 35
(E) 36

18. Let Ωp be defined as $\dfrac{p^2}{3} - p$ for all positive

integers, p. If $\Omega n = s$, and s is a positive integer, which of the following is a possible value for s?

(A) 1
(B) 3
(C) 5
(D) 6
(E) 8

19. The graph in the xy-plane of the quadratic function f contains the points $(0, 0)$, $(1, 5)$, and $(5, 5)$. What is the maximum value of $f(x)$?

(A) 12
(B) 11
(C) 10
(D) 9
(E) 8

20. A 60° wedge is cut from a paper circle with radius 12 centimeters and the paper is then folded into a cone, as shown in the figure above. What is the height, in centimeters, of this cone?

(A) $\sqrt{10\pi}$

(B) $\sqrt{44}$

(C) $\sqrt{70}$

(D) $\sqrt{90}$

(E) $\sqrt{108}$

STOP

If you finish before time is called, you may check your work on this section only. Do not turn to any other section of the test.

5   5   5   5   5   5

SECTION 5
Time—25 minutes
24 questions

Turn to Section 5 of your answer sheet to answer the questions in this section.

Directions: For each question in this section, select the best answer from among the choices given and fill in the corresponding circle on the answer sheet.

Each sentence below has one or two blanks, each blank indicating that something has been omitted. Beneath the sentence are five words or sets of words labeled A through E. Choose the word or set of words that, when inserted in the sentence, <u>best</u> fits the meaning of the sentence as a whole.

EXAMPLE:

Rather than accepting the theory unquestioningly, Deborah regarded it with ------.

(A) mirth
(B) sadness
(C) responsibility
(D) ignorance
(E) skepticism

---

1. Congresswoman Hyde preached ------- in order to counter the politics of ------- that she believed was destroying the nation.

   (A) conservation . . prudence
   (B) initiative . . diplomacy
   (C) activism . . responsibility
   (D) restraint . . isolation
   (E) inclusiveness . . division

2. Not surprisingly, whenever ------- song is ------- by an artist, it is always the most conservative music critics who complain the most vociferously.

   (A) a classic . . esteemed
   (B) an unconventional . . replaced
   (C) a popular . . disparaged
   (D) a familiar . . refashioned
   (E) a traditional . . replicated

3. Johanna ------- that attending college only two towns away from where she grew up would result in her developing too ------- an outlook.

   (A) resented . . resourceful
   (B) feared . . parochial
   (C) predicted . . cosmopolitan
   (D) hoped . . limited
   (E) assumed . . worldly

4. Because Ted behaved in such a docile manner at school, few of his teachers could believe that he was in fact ------- at home.

   (A) altruistic
   (B) intractable
   (C) taciturn
   (D) rational
   (E) diffident

GO ON TO THE NEXT PAGE

5   **5**   **5**   **5**   **5**   **5**

---

5. Regression therapy can be highly purgative, and the benefits that such ------- has for patients are acknowledged even by psychologists who question the intellectual foundations of the practice.

    (A) admiration
    (B) holism
    (C) replenishment
    (D) pretension
    (E) catharsis

> The passages below are followed by questions based on their content. Answer the questions on the basis of what is <u>stated</u> or <u>implied</u> in the passage and in any introductory material that may be provided.

Questions 6–7 are based on the following passage.

New York City is the most fatally fascinating thing in America. She sits like a great
Line witch at the gate of the country, showing her alluring white face and hiding her
5 crooked hands and feet under the folds of her wide garments—constantly enticing thousands from far within, and tempting those who come from across the seas to go no farther. And all these become the
10 victims of her caprice. Some she at once crushes beneath her cruel feet; others she condemns to a fate like that of galley slaves; a few she favors and fondles, riding them high on the bubbles of fortune; then
15 with a sudden breath she blows the bubbles out and laughs mockingly as she watches them fall.

6. This passage primarily characterizes New York City as

    (A) entertaining
    (B) treacherous
    (C) nurturing
    (D) providential
    (E) welcoming

7. The "bubbles" in lines 14 and 16 represent

    (A) enchanting decorations
    (B) effervescent conversation
    (C) promising statistics
    (D) flimsy explanations
    (E) deceptive lures

Questions 8–9 are based on the following passage.

As a music critic, I have long loathed the inclination of many in my profession to
Line rank their favorite works, but have remained silent on the matter, resigned to
5 the inane and inexplicable American passion for enumeration. That is, until the recent emergence of its even more insufferable cousin, the "worst" list. A critic should enhance the listening experience,
10 not sabotage it. It is one thing to attempt to objectify one's taste by arbitrarily assigning cardinal numbers to works of art, so long as one informs the public as to whether and why a new concert is (or is
15 not) worth attending or a new recording worth purchasing. It is another entirely to add insult to aesthetic injury by chiding listeners for having enjoyed a particular artist or recording for years. That is not
20 expository; it is petty.

8. The author's attitude toward "the 'worst' list" (line 8) is best described as

    (A) revulsion
    (B) reluctant acceptance
    (C) amusement
    (D) appreciation
    (E) bewilderment

GO ON TO THE NEXT PAGE ➡

Excerpted from *The Autobiography of An Ex-Colored Man* by James Weldon Johnson, copyright 1912. Public domain.
Printed with permission of Christopher Black, 2008

9. According to the author, the primary job of a critic is to

    (A) rank established works in terms of their quality
    (B) point out the flaws of long-established artists or works
    (C) identify historical antecedents to modern works
    (D) inform listeners about the merits of new works
    (E) summarize the most popular opinions of new works

Questions 10–18 are based on the following passage.

The following is a short story, excerpted from a collection of 20th century short stories, about an encounter in an American neighborhood.

He'd been in the area a long time, long enough to become background. When he
Line first emerged, a tall thin dark and silent presence on the local scene, everyone
5   talked about him, asking one another variations on the same question: Who is he? He never spoke and, without any answers, like children chasing their own shadows, people began to make up stories about
10   him. Maybe he'd been a Vietnam vet, some would venture. Others suggested that this seeming monastic stranger had come from some ashram in Tibet. Or perhaps he was a Somalian refugee, his African black skin
15   seemed so thin as to barely stretch around his bones. Eventually, the qualifying "maybes" and "perhaps" were dropped, and fiction was passed as fact.

Soundlessly he looked straight through
20   things, his eyes telling of unspeakable things. And I wondered. Had he run barefoot, like a crane skimming the surface of a lake, through the rice paddies of Vietnam? Had he seen a fatal flash? Were his saints
25   beheaded? Did a torch emblazon on his breast the mark, the scar of war? Had the earth become a molten sea, a hardened moonscape surface? Was there an immutable point at which he thought—he
30   knew—that every living thing had ended? And so he had stopped breathing, had

become shadow? Did he know what we would all come to know?

Too often to be mere coincidence, our
35   paths crossed and converged daily. It seemed as if he was everywhere I went, like a parallel life or a shadow I'd owned in another lifetime. Often he'd be in a crosswalk when I was in my car at a stoplight.
40   Before work in the morning, I usually stopped at a local diner for coffee and he would walk past the window, past the table where I sat, separated by only a pane of glass. As an assistant manager of a local
45   bookstore, I usually opened the place early in the morning. He would show up before any of the other employees did, gazing at the books on display in the front window, yet never looking directly at me.
50   I began to change my routine slightly. Sometimes I would go down to the beach to take an early walk before going into work. He would be walking at the edge of the shore, the sea a blue backdrop to this
55   moving shadow, this tree with legs. I began to take my walks at sunset instead, and there he'd be, at the edge of a cliff above the sea, at the edge of the world. He'd stand like a tall dark crane balanced on
60   one leg. Then poised and positioned on both legs, he'd begin a series of undulating, flowing movements. In Ina Coolbirth Park in San Francisco, I'd often see Chinese people exploring the air with fluid
65   movements, their bodies and the air in harmony. Though this was not Tai Chi, it seemed clearly ceremonial, religious, holy. His silhouette formed the character of a word in Japanese script; his movements
70   shaped haiku. What had seemed the figure of a black crow, a disquieting deathly form, through movement became a dark light, a black sun.

Then one day, I stopped at the diner for
75   a morning cup of coffee. I walked down the aisle toward my usual booth and noticed that the shadow man was sitting there. He was taking what looked like tea

GO ON TO THE NEXT PAGE →

leaves from a small leather bag that hung
80 around his neck and placing them in a cup
of hot water. As I came nearer, he looked
up, and for the first time he was seeing me,
not seeing through me. His look was clear,
not shrouded with darkness nor veiled
85 with otherness as I had come to expect. He
had seemed to journey momentarily out of
that dark place. I returned his look, nod-
ded my head. And for the first time since
I'd seen him, he smiled at me. He opened
90 his mouth, to speak, to speak to me. And I,
in awe, awaited the sound of his voice, the
words sure to shape around some thought
sprung from the well of a silence he occupied. A sound emerged, high and light as
95 air, full of jive and jazz, as he said, "What's
happenin', mama?"

10. The overall purpose of the passage is to

(A) describe the relationship between friends
(B) portray the nature of a small town
(C) recount an episode in the narrator's self-
    discovery
(D) chronicle an obsession with a mysterious
    individual
(E) analyze a general issue regarding per-
    sonal identity

11. The statement "fiction was passed as fact" in
line 18 means that the neighbors

(A) had learned more facts about the
    stranger's background
(B) gained more confidence in their assump-
    tions about the stranger
(C) grew more suspicious about the
    stranger's motives
(D) were not entirely honest with the
    stranger
(E) became less accepting of speculations
    about the stranger

12. The questions in lines 21–33 are primarily
intended as

(A) suspicions about the stranger's criminal
    past
(B) speculations about the stranger's war
    experience
(C) doubts about the stranger's sincerity
(D) assumptions about the stranger's piety
(E) guesses about the stranger's intentions

13. In line 28 the "moonscape surface" represents

(A) a desolate aftermath
(B) an idyllic location
(C) an imagined goal
(D) an unexplored vista
(E) a primordial stage

14. As it is used in line 68 the word "character"
most nearly means

(A) strange person
(B) abstract quality
(C) individuality
(D) visible symbol
(E) dance

15. The phrase "his look was clear" (line 83)
indicates that the stranger was

(A) uncharacteristically sober
(B) physically pale
(C) suddenly unmysterious
(D) lacking in arrogance
(E) focused on a particular goal

GO ON TO THE NEXT PAGE ⟶

Excerpted from *Earth, Song, Sky Spirit: Shadows and Sleepwalkers* by Cait Featherstone, copyright 1992, p. 333–337. Used by
permission of Random House, Inc.

Questions 16–24 are based on the following passage.

The following passage is from an article about recent developments in astrophysics written in 2007.

No self-respecting Civil War buff should
miss a visit to the breathtaking Gettysburg
Cyclorama, a 359-foot long, 29-foot high,
360-degree painting of the bloody 1863
5   Battle of Gettysburg. Visitors can turn in
every direction and feel that they have been
thrust into the past, into the midst of one
of the most important battles in American
history. Yet as marvelous as this exhibit is,
10 you are at this very moment in the midst
of an even more spectacular cyclorama of
an even more cataclysmic historical event
that took place about 13 billion years ago.
Unfortunately, to appreciate its full
15 splendor, you have to be able to see
microwaves, which are invisible to our
human eyes.

    This cyclorama is the cosmic microwave
background radiation, or CMB to its
20 friends in the astrophysics world, a
panoramic snapshot of the universe as it
appeared a mere 300,000 years after the
Big Bang. (Since the universe is between
12 and 14 billion years old, 300,000 years
25 is a virtual blink of an eye.) If you look in
any direction in the sky with the right
equipment, you can detect photons that
were among the first to be set free after the
universe began. We can't get much closer
30 to the Big Bang, because, for the first
300,000 years of its life, the universe was,
for all practical purposes, "invisible."

    In order to be "seen," an object or event
must emit or reflect light particles, or pho-
35 tons, that travel relatively unimpeded to a
detector, such as a telescope or your
retina. You see a candle flame because its
excited atoms produce photons that zip
into your eyeballs, and you see a painting
40 because myriad photons from a light
source reflect off of it. Sometimes, however, photons can be absorbed by atoms or
scattered by electrons, thwarting their
arrival at a detector and rendering their
45 source invisible.

    According to a theory published in 1948
by George Gamow, if the Big Bang theory
is correct, then when the universe was one
hundred millionth of its present size, and
50 before the CMB was emitted, atoms (electrons bound up with protons and neu-
trons) could not have existed. The cosmos
would have been so hot (273 million
degrees Kelvin, about 20 times hotter than
55 the center of the sun) that electrons would
have roamed free from protons in a super-
heated soup of charges called a plasma. In
this environment, uncharged photons
would scatter as if through a dense fog.
60 Then, 300,000 years after the Big Bang, the
universe would have cooled enough,
because of its expansion, to allow electrons
and protons to combine into atoms, and
the CMB photons, no longer scattered by
65 the free electrons, would have been set
free. Gamow's theory predicted that this
primordial scattering process would give
the CMB radiation distinctive spectrum,
known as a "blackbody" spectrum, and
70 that the microwaves would have cooled,
due to the further expanding universe, to
about 5 degrees Kelvin today.

    For nearly two decades, the CMB was
mere speculation. Then, in 1965, Arno
75 Penzias and Robert Wilson at Bell Laboratories in Murray Hill, New Jersey, became
troubled by persistent background noise
in a radio receiver that they had built.
(Their initial explanation was that it was
80 due to a "white dielectric substance,"
more commonly known as pigeon drop-
pings.) Remarkably, less than 40 miles
away, Princeton researchers Robert Dicke
and Dave Wilkinson had been searching
85 for evidence supporting Gamow's predictions, and instantly knew of a much better
explanation for the noise. Dicke and
Wilkinson published their cosmological
explanation of the phenomenon, but
90 Penzias and Wilson shared the 1978 Nobel
Prize in physics for its discovery.

Printed with the permission of Christopher Black, 2008.

GO ON TO THE NEXT PAGE

Much more careful observations of the CMB were made by the COBE (cosmic background explorer) satellite telescope in
95   1992. These observations confirmed Gamow's predictions, and hence the Big Bang theory itself, with astonishing accuracy. They determined that the temperature of the CMB was now 2.725° Kelvin,
100 barely more than 2 degrees from Gamow's guess. They also showed that the spectrum of the CMB was as a nearly perfect "blackbody" curve. Perhaps most remarkable, however, was the confirmation of the near-
105 uniformity, or "isotropism" of the CMB. Taken together, these observations unequivocally ruled out any other plausible explanation for the CMB then being considered.
110   Today, cosmologists are still reaping the benefits of Gamow's theory and the COBE data. Minor fluctuations in the CMB measurements have helped scientists explain the origin of galaxies and galaxy clusters,
115 calibrate the basic parameters of the Big Bang theory, and even gauge the speed at which our universe is expanding and the speed (about 600 kilometers per second) at which our galaxy is racing through the
120 universe.

16. This passage is primarily concerned with

(A) describing the merits of various cycloramas
(B) chronicling the invention of a radio receiver by Penzias and Wilson
(C) examining the controversies surrounding George Gamow's theory
(D) discussing the importance of the cosmic microwave background radiation
(E) deliberating questions raised by the Big Bang theory

17. This passage discusses the Gettysburg Cyclorama primarily as

(A) an illustrative analogy
(B) a historical antecedent
(C) a typical representation
(D) a misunderstood work
(E) an accidental success

18. According to the passage, scientists "can't get much closer to the Big Bang" (lines 29–30) because

(A) they lack a coherent theory for what happened prior to the CMB
(B) they lack powerful enough telescopes
(C) photons were too easily scattered prior to the CMB
(D) the data from COBE has not yet been thoroughly examined
(E) atoms were too densely packed prior to the CMB

19. The quotation marks around the words "invisible" (line 32) and "seen" (line 33) serve primarily to

(A) draw attention to recently coined terms
(B) suggest the author's disdain for such words
(C) imply that the author is speaking speculatively
(D) show irony
(E) indicate that common words are being used in a technical sense

20. The third paragraph (lines 33–45) serves primarily to

(A) describe a biological process
(B) provide historical background
(C) introduce experimental evidence
(D) explain a physical phenomenon
(E) refute a misconception

21. According to the passage, George Gamow's primary contribution to the discovery of the CMB was

(A) the invention of the COBE satellite
(B) the detection of the first cosmic microwaves
(C) the development of the first radio telescope
(D) the measurement of the rate at which the universe is expanding
(E) the prediction of the microwave background radiation

GO ON TO THE NEXT PAGE ⇒

5   5   5   5   5   5

22. The "much better explanation" (lines 86–87) is that the radio noise was in fact

    (A) the expansion of the universe
    (B) radiation released 300,000 years after the Big Bang
    (C) charged particles released by the Big Bang
    (D) a superheated plasma
    (E) a white dielectric substance

23. Which of the following can be inferred about the work that earned Penzias and Wilson the Nobel Prize?

    (A) It was the product of decades of research on the CMB.
    (B) It was the result of an accidental discovery.
    (C) It consisted mostly of a theoretical explanation of a known phenomenon.
    (D) It depended greatly on the data from the COBE satellite.
    (E) It provided a more plausible alternative to Gamow's theory.

24. The "minor fluctuations in the CMB measurements" (lines 112–113) had the primary effect of

    (A) calling into question the merits of the COBE data
    (B) thwarting an accurate quantification of the expansion of the universe
    (C) refuting the explanation Dicke and Wilkinson provided for the radio background noise
    (D) helping scientists to refine the Big Bang theory
    (E) inspiring alternatives to Gamow's theory

STOP

If you finish before time is called, you may check your work on this section only. Do not turn to any other section of the test.

6   6   6   6   6   6

SECTION 6
Time—25 minutes
18 questions

Turn to Section 6 of your answer sheet to answer the questions in this section.

Directions: This section contains two types of questions. You have 25 minutes to complete both types. For questions 1–8, solve each problem and decide which is the best of the choices given. Fill in the corresponding circle on the answer sheet. You may use any available space for scratchwork.

Notes

1. The use of a calculator is permitted.

2. All numbers used are real numbers.

3. Figures that accompany problems in this test are intended to provide information useful in solving the problems. They are drawn as accurately as possible EXCEPT when it is stated in a specific problem that the figure is not drawn to scale. All figures lie in a plane unless otherwise indicated.

4. Unless otherwise specified, the domain of any function f is assumed to be the set of all real numbers x for which $f(x)$ is a real number.

Reference Information

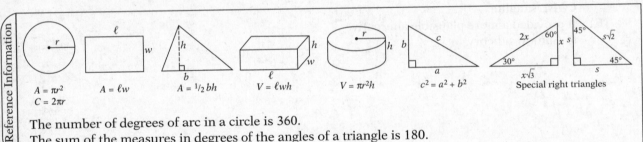

$A = \pi r^2$ $A = \ell w$ $A = 1/2\,bh$ $V = \ell wh$ $V = \pi r^2 h$ $c^2 = a^2 + b^2$ Special right triangles
$C = 2\pi r$

The number of degrees of arc in a circle is 360.
The sum of the measures in degrees of the angles of a triangle is 180.

---

1. The three interior angles of a triangle have measures of $a°$, $a°$, and $b°$. If $b = 80$, what is the value of a?

(A)   30
(B)   40
(C)   50
(D)   60
(E)   100

2. If x is a number greater than 0 and less than 1, which of the following is greatest?

(A) $1 - x$

(B) $\dfrac{1}{x}$

(C) $-\dfrac{1}{x}$

(D) x

(E) x^2

GO ON TO THE NEXT PAGE

3. Which of the following is a multiple of 3, 5, and 7?

(A)   35
(B)   70
(C)   75
(D)   105
(E)   112

4. A deluxe box of crayons contains 10 more crayons than a regular box of crayons. If a regular box contains m crayons, how many crayons do 5 deluxe boxes contain?

(A) $5m + 10$
(B) $5m + 50$
(C) $5(m + 50)$
(D) $10m + 50$
(E) $10(m + 50)$

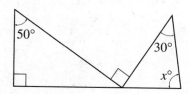

Note: Figure not drawn to scale.

5. In the figure above, what is the value of x?

(A)   100
(B)   90
(C)   80
(D)   70
(E)   60

x	y
2	$\dfrac{1}{2}$
4	$\dfrac{1}{8}$
6	$\dfrac{1}{18}$

6. Which of the following could be true about the relationship between x and y shown in the table above?

(A) y is directly proportional to x.
(B) y is inversely proportional to x.
(C) y is directly proportional to the square of x.
(D) x is inversely proportional to the square of y.
(E) y is inversely proportional to the square of x.

GO ON TO THE NEXT PAGE

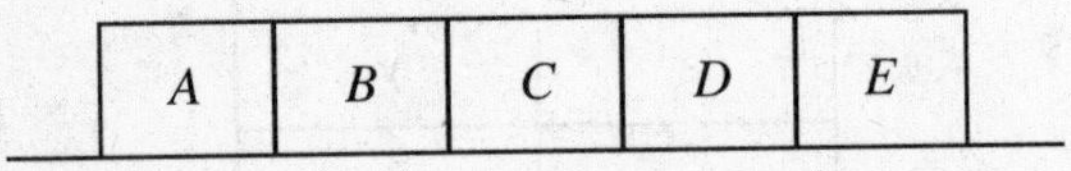

A	B	C	D	E

7. The figure above shows the arrangement of 5 cages in the primate house of a zoo. Each cage is to house one specimen from the following five species: capuchin, lemur, macaque, squirrel monkey, and tamarin. The lemur must be in a cage on one end, and the tamarin must be in the center cage. If the capuchin must be in a cage next to the macaque, and the tamarin must be in a cage next to the squirrel monkey, how many arrangements of these primates in these cages are possible?

(A) 2
(B) 3
(C) 4
(D) 6
(E) 8

$$(y + 4)(y - h) = y^2 - 2y + b$$

8. In the equation above, h and b are constants. If the equation is true for all values of y, what is the value of b?

(A)   −24
(B)   −8
(C)   6
(D)   8
(E)   24

GO ON TO THE NEXT PAGE

Directions: For Student-Produced Response questions 9–18, use the grids at the bottom of the answer sheet page on which you have answered questions 1–8.

Each of the remaining 10 questions requires you to solve the problem and enter your answer by marking the circles in the special grid, as shown in the examples below. You may use any available space for scratchwork.

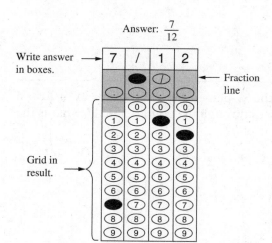

Answer: $\frac{7}{12}$

Write answer in boxes.

Fraction line

Grid in result.

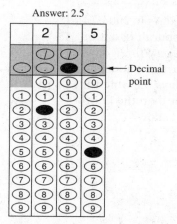

Answer: 2.5

Decimal point

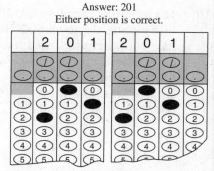

Answer: 201
Either position is correct.

Note: You may start your answers in any column, space permitting. Columns not needed should be left blank.

- Mark no more than one circle in any column.

- Because the answer sheet will be machine-scored, **you will receive credit only if the circles are filled in correctly.**

- Although not required, it is suggested that you write your answer in the boxes at the top of the columns to help you fill in the circles accurately.

- Some problems may have more than one correct answer. In such cases, grid only one answer.

- No question has a negative answer.

- **Mixed numbers** such as $3\frac{1}{2}$ must be gridded as

  3.5 or 7/2. (If $\boxed{3\ 1\ /\ 2}$ is gridded, it will be

  interpreted as $\frac{31}{2}$ not $3\frac{1}{2}$.)

- **Decimal Answers:** If you obtain a decimal answer with more digits than the grid can accommodate, it may be either rounded or truncated, but it must fill the entire grid. For example, if you obtain an answer such as 0.6666..., you should record your result as .666 or .667. **A less accurate value such as .66 or .67 will be scored as incorrect.**

Acceptable ways to grid $^2/_3$ are:

GO ON TO THE NEXT PAGE

9. If $\dfrac{(6-3)r+4}{2} = 13$, what is the value of r?

10. The month of February had 28 days in 2003. In that month, the town of Chillsburgh had four days on which it snowed for every three days on which it did not snow. For that month in Chillsburgh, the number of days on which it snowed was how much greater than the number of days on which it did not snow?

11. On a test worth a total of 200 points, Jenna lost 7% of those points because she forgot to answer one question, but she got 5 points added back to her score for answering the extra credit question correctly. If she answered all of the other questions on the test correctly, how many points did she earn on the test?

$$36, x, y, \dfrac{4}{3}, \ldots$$

12. In the sequence above, each term after the first is equal to the previous term times a positive constant k. What is the value of k?

13. In the xy-plane, the graph of $y = 2x^2 + hx - 6$ passes through the point $(-3, -21)$, what is the value of h?

GO ON TO THE NEXT PAGE

14. If $10 < |4b-8| < 15$ and b is a positive number, what is one possible value of b?

15. If $6w$ is an integer and $2\frac{1}{2} < 5w < 3\frac{1}{2}$, what is the value of w?

$$s = 3m + s$$
$$5t = 4m + 2s$$

16. In the system above, if $s > 0$, what is the value of $\frac{t}{s}$?

VOTING RESULTS OF REFERENDUM

	YES	NO
MONROE	600	900
BLACKSBURG	1400	m
TOTAL	2090	n

17. The table above shows the voting results in two towns for a certain referendum. If the percentage of Monroe voters who voted "no" is twice the percentage of Blacksburg voters who voted "no," what is the total number of voters in both towns who voted "no"?

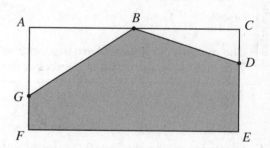

18. In the rectangle above, the ratio of AB to BC is 1:1, the ratio of CD to DE is 1:3, and the ratio of FG to GA is 1:3. What fraction of the area of the rectangle is shaded?

STOP

If you finish before time is called, you may check your work on this section only. Do not turn to any other section of the test.

7   **7**   **7**   **7**   **7**   **7**

SECTION 7
Time—20 minutes
16 questions

> ### Turn to Section 7 of your answer sheet to answer the questions in this section.

Directions: For this section, solve each problem and decide which is the best of the choices given. Fill in the corresponding circle on the answer sheet. You may use any available space for scratchwork.

Notes

1. The use of a calculator is permitted.

2. All numbers used are real numbers.

3. Figures that accompany problems in this test are intended to provide information useful in solving the problems. They are drawn as accurately as possible EXCEPT when it is stated in a specific problem that the figure is not drawn to scale. All figures lie in a plane unless otherwise indicated.

4. Unless otherwise specified, the domain of any function f is assumed to be the set of all real numbers x for which $f(x)$ is a real number.

Reference Information

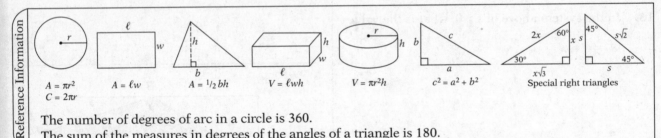

$A = \pi r^2$ $A = \ell w$ $A = \frac{1}{2}bh$ $V = \ell wh$ $V = \pi r^2 h$ $c^2 = a^2 + b^2$ Special right triangles
$C = 2\pi r$

The number of degrees of arc in a circle is 360.
The sum of the measures in degrees of the angles of a triangle is 180.

---

1. A cookie recipe requires $2\frac{1}{2}$ cups of flour and makes 36 cookies. At this rate, how many cups of flour are required to make 54 cookies?

   (A) $3\frac{1}{4}$

   (B) $3\frac{1}{2}$

   (C) $3\frac{3}{4}$

   (D) $4\frac{1}{4}$

   (E) $4\frac{1}{2}$

$$y = mx^2$$

2. In the equation above, m is a constant. If $y = 32$ when $x = 4$, then when $y = 18$, which of the following could be the value of x?

   (A)   1
   (B)   3
   (C)   9
   (D)   12
   (E)   18

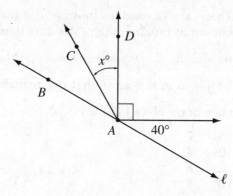

Note: Figure not drawn to scale.

3. In the figure above, points A and B lie on line ℓ, and ray AC bisects angle BAD. What is the value of x?

   (A) 25
   (B) 30
   (C) 35
   (D) 40
   (E) 45

4. Which of the following ratios is equivalent to the ratio of 2.4 to 5?

   (A) 6 : 15
   (B) 12 : 25
   (C) 1 : 2
   (D) 4 : 7
   (E) 24 : 25

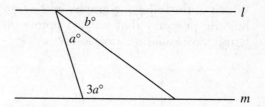

Note: Figure not drawn to scale.

5. In the figure above, line l is parallel to line m. If $b = 36$, what is the value of a?

   (A) 32
   (B) 33
   (C) 34
   (D) 35
   (E) 36

6. For all positive integers a and b, let $\langle a | b \rangle = \dfrac{a-b}{a+b}$.

   If m is a positive integer, what is $\langle m | 2m \rangle$?

   (A) $-\dfrac{1}{2}$

   (B) $-\dfrac{1}{3}$

   (C) $\dfrac{1}{3}$

   (D) $\dfrac{1}{2}$

   (E) 2

GO ON TO THE NEXT PAGE

7   **7**   **7**   **7**   **7**   **7**

7. Which of the following graphs in the xy-plane has the property that no two points on the graph have equal y-coordinates?

(A)

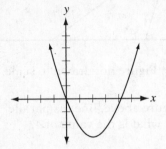

(B)

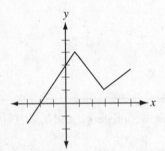

(C)

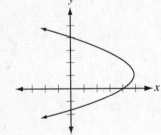

(D)

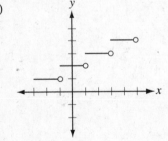

(E)

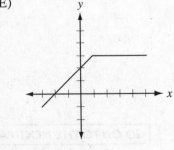

8. There are 72 marbles in a jar. If a marble is chosen at random, the probability that it will be black is $\frac{4}{9}$. How many black marbles must be added to the jar so that the probability of choosing a black marble is $\frac{1}{2}$?

(A) 2
(B) 4
(C) 6
(D) 8
(E) 10

9. Gregory must inspect 12 working devices, labeled alphabetically from A to L, that are arranged in a linear array. He must start with device A and proceed alphabetically, returning to the beginning and repeating the process after inspecting device L, stopping when he encounters a defective device. If the first defective device he encounters is device D, which of the following could be the total number of devices that Gregory inspects, including the defective one?

(A) 64
(B) 68
(C) 72
(D) 74
(E) 78

10. Kiara's goal is to sell at least $150 worth of cookies. If each box of cookies sells for $5, and she has already sold 16 boxes of cookies, which of the following inequalities could be used to determine x, where x is how many more boxes of cookies she must sell to make her goal?

(A) $(16) \cdot 5 - x \le 150$
(B) $(16) \cdot 5 + x \ge 150$
(C) $(16) \cdot 5 - x \ge 150$
(D) $(16) \cdot 5 + 5x \le 150$
(E) $(16) \cdot 5 + 5x \ge 150$

GO ON TO THE NEXT PAGE ⟶

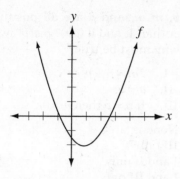

11. The figure above shows the graph of the function f in the xy-plane. If $g(x) = f(x - 2)$, which of the following is a true statement describing the graph of g in comparison with the graph of f?

(A) Its vertex is 2 units lower than the vertex of the graph of f.
(B) Its vertex is 2 units to the left of the vertex of the graph of f.
(C) Its vertex is 2 units to the right of the vertex of the graph of f.
(D) It is wider than the graph of f.
(E) It is narrower than the graph of f.

---

12. If $n^8 = 480$ and $n^7 = 12m$, what is the value of $3mn$?

(A) 30
(B) 60
(C) 90
(D) 120
(E) 480

13. In $\triangle PQR$, the length of side $\overline{PQ}$ is 24 and the length of side $\overline{QR}$ is 18. What is the least possible integer length of $\overline{PR}$?

(A) 6
(B) 7
(C) 18
(D) 30
(E) 41

---

14. A beaker contains 15 grams of a water and salt solution that is 20% salt. If x more grams of water are added to the solution, which of the following expresses the percentage of salt in the new solution?

(A) $\dfrac{3 \times 100}{15 + x}\%$

(B) $\dfrac{(3 + x) \times 100}{15 + x}\%$

(C) $\dfrac{3 \times (100 + x)}{15 + x}\%$

(D) $\dfrac{3}{15 + x}\%$

(E) $\dfrac{3 + x}{15 + x}\%$

GO ON TO THE NEXT PAGE

7   7   7   7   7   7

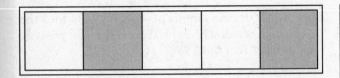

15. The figure above shows 5 cubbyholes in a day care center. Five different-colored jackets—one red, one blue, one green, one brown, and one white—are to be randomly placed in these cubby holes, one jacket per cubby hole. What is the probability that the red and brown jackets will each be assigned to one of the cubbyholes indicated by the shaded squares?

(A) $\dfrac{1}{4}$

(B) $\dfrac{1}{6}$

(C) $\dfrac{1}{10}$

(D) $\dfrac{1}{20}$

(E) $\dfrac{1}{40}$

16. If a, b, m, n, and p are all positive integers greater than 1, and if $(ab)^m = a^n b^p$, which of the following must be true?

    I. $2m = n + p$
   II. $a = b$
  III.   If $n = p$ then $n = m$.

(A)   None
(B)   III only
(C)   I and II only
(D)   I and III only
(E)   II and III only

STOP

If you finish before time is called, you may check your work on this section only. Do not turn to any other section of the test.

8   8   8   8   8   8

SECTION 8
Time—20 minutes
19 questions

Turn to Section 8 of your answer sheet to answer the questions in this section.

Directions: For each question in this section, select the best answer from among the choices given and fill in the corresponding circle on the answer sheet.

Each sentence below has one or two blanks, each blank indicating that something has been omitted. Beneath the sentence are five words or sets of words labeled A through E. Choose the word or set of words that, when inserted in the sentence, <u>best</u> fits the meaning of the sentence as a whole.

EXAMPLE:

Rather than accepting the theory unquestioningly, Deborah regarded it with -----.

(A) mirth
(B) sadness
(C) responsibility
(D) ignorance
(E) skepticism

1. This year's ------- in student population has forced the university to ------- temporary dormitories to accommodate the new students.

   (A) growth . . ignore
   (B) curtailment . . raze
   (C) reduction . . install
   (D) correlation . . permit
   (E) increase . . construct

2. The fact that feline images figure prominently in the tombs of pharaohs ------- the ------- role of the cat in ancient Egyptian culture.

   (A) repudiates . . daily
   (B) reveals . . irrelevant
   (C) demonstrates . . significant
   (D) refutes . . important
   (E) tolerates . . indispensable

3. The resounding success of his recent singing tour made Rob question whether he could ever be more popular; he seemed to be at the ------- of his career.

   (A) pinnacle
   (B) nadir
   (C) paradigm
   (D) inception
   (E) periphery

4. The Federal Reserve Board's decision to lower the prime lending rate had a ------- effect on the economy, for stock prices, consumer confidence, and corporate investment improved in very short order.

   (A) detrimental
   (B) dubious
   (C) conditional
   (D) salutary
   (E) perverse

GO ON TO THE NEXT PAGE ⇒

8   8   8   8   8   8

---

5. Helene was not so much a musical expert as she was -------; she enjoyed music and liked to be seen at concerts, but could not converse in great detail about the subject.

   (A) a polymath
   (B) a recluse
   (C) a dilettante
   (D) an ascetic
   (E) a pundit

6. The warring factions had ------- hopes for the peace conference: they did not expect any -------, but rather considered the conference as a launching point for more substantial agreements in the future.

   (A) poignant . . indifference
   (B) modest . . parsimony
   (C) adequate . . infirmity
   (D) qualified . . breakthroughs
   (E) exorbitant . . headway

The two passages below are followed by questions based on their content and on the relationship between the two passages. Answer the questions on the basis of what is <u>stated</u> or <u>implied</u> in the passages and in any introductory material that may be provided.

Questions 7–19 are based on the following passages.

The following passages discuss the topic of intuition. The first was written by an American essayist in 2007. The second is an excerpt from a book written by a research psychologist in 2002.

PASSAGE 1

According to a spate of recent popular books, your faculty of intuition is an untapped source
Line of boundless power. You can access the ageless wisdom of the universe, they claim, by simply
5   attuning yourself to the many non-rational frequencies of information that envelop you. To get an edge on your competition, learn to listen to your gut.

Recent scientific research, however,
10 sheds a less sanguine and more cautionary light on the power of irrationality. Studies from such diverse fields as neurobiology, evolutionary psychology, and economics suggest that what we call intuition is in fact
15 the encroachment upon awareness of many ancient systems of unconscious processing. The often inchoate thoughts from our unconscious are usually adorned by our rational minds with a veneer of reason and
20 meaning, but they emanate from neural systems better suited to our ancient ancestors than to modern humans. Trust them at your own peril, and only if you value the hunter-gatherer within you.

25   In order to survive and reproduce, our ancestors often needed to process stimuli quickly. When being chased by bears, they did not have the luxury of researching the behavior of omnivores in order to make the optimal
30 evasive maneuver. Mental systems evolved to help them process data instantaneously. Sensory input from their eyes, ears and skin linked directly to the sympathetic nervous system, so that sight of a saber-toothed tiger
35 would instantly speed up their heart rates and heighten their alertness. Quickly afterwards, their cerebral cortex would interpret this reaction as "fear" or "excitement," leading to a cascade of plans for attack or evasion.

40   These systems also seem to have encoded the rules for moral social behavior, such as identifying and protecting loved ones, respecting authority, and curbing selfishness. According to Jonathan Haight, a moral
45 psychologist at the University of Virginia, such moral behaviors are found in most every human culture, and likely emanate from innate psychological mechanisms that churn beneath the spotlight of our awareness.
50 Without such automatic processing, our societies could not be so cohesive.

But in a complex modern society in which decision-making requires more judiciousness than speed, these mechanisms often steer us
55 wrong. In the 1970s, Nobel Prize–winning psychologist Daniel Kahneman used the term

Passage 1: Printed with the permission of Christopher Black, 2008
Passage 2: Printed with the permission of Yale University Press.
Excerpted from *Intuition: Its Powers and Perils*, by Myers.
p. 145–146. © 2004

GO ON TO THE NEXT PAGE ⟩

"heuristics" to describe the innate quick-and-
dirty rules that humans use to process complex data in order to make rapid decisions.
60 By one such rule, the "availability heuristic,"
we predict the frequency, importance or
likelihood of an event on the basis of how
easily that event can be brought to mind.
Strong emotions tend to make events more
65 memorable and hence more available to recall,
so emotionally charged events tend to be
viewed as disproportionately likely or relevant.
For instance, Americans view preventing
terrorism as a more important issue than
70 cancer research, even though cancer is nearly
10,000 times more lethal to Americans than
terrorism is. Similarly, since lottery players
remember the elation of scratching a winning
ticket much more vividly than the mild
75 disappointment of their far more frequent
losses, they often persist in a self-defeating
habit until they are broke. When it comes to
making decisions to save or improve lives in
the modern world, intuition can be an
80 astonishingly poor guide.

PASSAGE 2

Unpredictability is a soil in which illusory
intuitions readily grow. In baseball, catching a
fly ball is reasonably routine. Because it has a
greater than 95 percent success rate, few
85 superstitious behaviors accompany fielding.
Batting is more fraught with uncertainties,
and uncertainty nurtures peculiar hunches
and habits. Batters therefore have a diverse
repertoire of approaches to hitting, each with
90 a peculiar sequence of warm-up swings, plate
tappings, leg lifts, and bat wiggles.
Another common sports intuition is that
points scored at the end of a game matter
more. In the laboratory and in life, we tend
95 to connect adjacent ("temporally contigu-
ous") events. In a close game, we associate
the last basket made with the game's outcome.
In reality, it counts no more than a basket
made at any other time. But cognitively the
100 game's final moments seem more
determinative of the outcome. Thus, most
fans, coaches, players, and announcers
concur that, at considerable cost, it's important
to have one's best players available for the

105 game's decisive moments. Use your best relief
pitcher as the closer. Sit Shaquille O'Neal, if
you must, to have him in at the end. "Have
your prime time player ready for prime time!
How many times have you seen a game come
110 down to the final basket?" (Never mind that
some games come down to the final basket
because prime time players have been sitting
on the bench.)
Social psychologists Dale Miller and Saku
115 Gunasegaram have asked people to imagine
that Jones and Cooper each flip a coin. If
they land the same, each gets $1,000; if they
land differently, each gets zero. Jones goes
first and gets heads. Cooper goes second and
120 gets tails. Who is to blame? Nearly everyone
blames Cooper, intuiting that he'd feel more
guilt. Likewise, Thomas Gilovich notes, if
Shaquille O'Neal makes 10 of 20 free throws
for the Lakers and teammate Kobe Bryant is
125 9 for 10—but his one miss is at the end of the
game and the Lakers lose by one—Kobe, not
Shaq, is considered to have lost the game.

7. Which of the following best characterizes the
individual perspectives presented in the two
passages?

(A) The first suggests that we should put for
faith in our intuition, while the second
cautions us against irrational thinking.

(B) The first examines the nature and origins
of intuition from a scientific perspective,
while the second analyzes dubious
notions in sports.

(C) The first is concerned with debunking a
theory about intuition, while the second
advocates intuitive thinking for improving sports performance.

(D) The first provides an objective account of
research on human intuition, while the
second presents a first-person account of
intuition at work.

(E) The first focuses on the fallible nature of
moral intuition, while the second argues
that intuitive thinking is more reliable
than many people think.

GO ON TO THE NEXT PAGE →

8   **8**   **8**   **8**   **8**   **8**

8. In line 15, the word "encroachment" refers to

(A) the popularity of some recent books
(B) the overlap in the areas of research of scientists from different fields
(C) the dominance of rational thought in our everyday lives
(D) the similarity between ancient humans and modern humans
(E) the intrusion of irrational thoughts into consciousness

9. Which of the following best describes the relationship between the statement in lines 7–8 ("To get an edge...your gut") and the statement in lines 22–24 (Trust them...within you")?

(A) The first represents a generalization about intuition, while the second represents a specific example of that general idea.
(B) They represent two contrasting recommendations about intuition.
(C) They reflect different stages of the author's evolving perspective on intuition.
(D) They are both recommendations from people who value the power of intuition.
(E) The first represents a medical opinion, while the second represents a popular misconception.

10. The sentence in lines 17–22 ("The often inchoate...modern humans") primarily describes

(A) how our minds rationalize rudimentary information
(B) why humans value intuitive thinking
(C) how scientists investigate psychological claims
(D) what parts of the brain are involved in rational thought
(E) the vast difference between our modern minds and the minds of our ancestors

11. Which of the following is the best example of a "heuristic" as it is described in Passage 1?

(A) the rules of debate in a formal legislature
(B) the system by which democratic societies choose leaders
(C) the process of deciding quickly whether or not an approaching person is friendly
(D) a procedure for solving complex algebraic equations
(E) a therapeutic method for resolving personal conflicts

12. The author of Passage 1 refers to the "hunter-gatherer" primarily to suggest that

(A) human history is more violent than we are inclined to acknowledge
(B) our human ancestors were more focused on acquiring food than on establishing social structures
(C) the human faculty of intuition has evolved considerably since the time of our ancient ancestors
(D) even our earliest ancestors were highly introspective
(E) human cognition developed to serve immediate survival needs

13. In line 66, the word "charged" most nearly means

(A) accused
(B) entrusted
(C) rushed
(D) probable
(E) energized

14. The author of Passage 2 indicates that, in baseball, "few superstitious behaviors accompany fielding" (lines 84–85) because

(A) fielding is a relatively predictable activity
(B) fielding requires more dexterity than many other athletic tasks
(C) baseball players appreciate the need for fielding practice more than fans do
(D) many athletes realize the dangers of superstition
(E) athletic endeavors are especially filled with uncertainty

GO ON TO THE NEXT PAGE

15. The parenthetical remark in lines 110–113 ("Never mind that...the bench") is intended to represent the opinion of

(A) a superstitious fan
(B) a skeptical analyst
(C) a typical coach
(D) a top athlete
(E) a popular sportscaster

16. Which of the following situations best illustrates the phenomenon described in the second paragraph of Passage 2 (lines 92–113)?

(A) A fan brings a stuffed animal to a football game because he believes that it will help his team's performance.
(B) A hockey team's best scorer flips a coin to decide which hockey stick he will use for that game.
(C) A sportswriter blames a team loss on a baseball player who struck out to end a game.
(D) A basketball team's best player feels more energized when she is on the court than when she is sitting on the bench.
(E) A rugby player feels more nervous playing in a championship game than he does playing in a regular-season game.

17. The author of Passage 2 would most likely regard the "spate of recent popular books" (line 1) mentioned in Passage 1 with

(A) righteous indignation
(B) informed skepticism
(C) eager anticipation
(D) sentimental regret
(E) bewilderment

18. The author of Passage 1 would most likely bolster the claim made in lines 99–101 of Passage 2 ("But cognitively...the outcome") by explaining that

(A) the final moments of a game are frequently more exciting than the other moments of the game, and hence seem more relevant
(B) the opinion of coaches is usually more informed, and hence more rational, than the opinion of sports fans
(C) superstitious thinking applies as much to the end of a game as it does to the beginning of a game
(D) the behavior in a basketball game is similar to the hunting behavior of our ancestors
(E) our intuitions regarding sporting events are surprisingly reliable

19. Unlike Passage 1, Passage 2 discusses

(A) the procedures of a specific experiment
(B) a mistaken assumption
(C) the work of professional researchers
(D) social behavior
(E) human emotions

STOP

If you finish before time is called, you may check your work on this section only. Do not turn to any other section of the test.

9   **9**   **9**   **9**   **9**   **9**

SECTION 9
Time—10 minutes
14 questions

Turn to Section 9 of your answer sheet to answer the questions in this section.

Directions: For each question in this section, select the best answer from among the choices given and fill in the corresponding circle on the answer sheet.

The following sentences test correctness and effectiveness of expression. Part of each sentence or the entire sentence is underlined; beneath each sentence are five ways of phrasing the underlined material. Choice A repeats the original phrasing; the other four choices are different. Select the choice that completes the sentence most effectively.

In making your selection, follow the requirements of standard written English; that is, pay attention to grammar, choice of words, sentence construction, and punctuation. Your selection should result in the most effective sentence—clear and precise, without awkwardness or ambiguity.

EXAMPLE:

The children <u>couldn't hardly believe their eyes</u>.

(A) couldn't hardly believe their eyes
(B) could hardly believe their eyes
(C) would not hardly believe their eyes
(D) couldn't nearly believe their eyes
(E) couldn't hardly believe his or her eyes

1. <u>It being</u> difficult to monitor the eating habits of adults, so doctors must trust their patients to follow dietary recommendations.

    (A) It being
    (B) Because it is
    (C) It is
    (D) Being that it is
    (E) Although it is

2. Playing a video basketball game is not nearly as demanding, either mentally or physically, as <u>a real</u> basketball game.

    (A) a real
    (B) that of a real
    (C) it is when playing a real
    (D) playing a real
    (E) when playing a real

3. The new recipe requires fewer exotic ingredients <u>and takes less time than it, but produces just as tasty a soufflé as the old recipe</u>.

    (A) and takes less time than it, but produces just as tasty a soufflé as the old recipe
    (B) that take less time than the old recipe, producing just as tasty a soufflé
    (C) and takes less time than the old recipe, but produces just as tasty a soufflé
    (D) also taking less time than the old recipe, but produces just as tasty a soufflé
    (E) but produces just as tasty a soufflé as the old recipe, but takes less time

GO ON TO THE NEXT PAGE

9 9 9 9 9 9

4. As Elena approached the finish line of her first cross-country race, <u>she had turned to myself and flashed</u> an exuberant grin.

(A) she had turned to myself and flashed
(B) she had turned to me and had flashed
(C) she turned to myself and flashed
(D) she turned to me and had flashed
(E) she turned to me and flashed

5. We had to submit our project without a bibliography, because listing our sources <u>would have took Jose and I</u> another day to complete.

(A) would have took Jose and I
(B) would have taken Jose and I
(C) would have taken Jose and me
(D) would have took Jose and me
(E) would be taking Jose and me

6. Oceanographers are studying how the increased atmospheric concentration of gases like carbon dioxide and sulfur dioxide <u>elevates the acidity of seawater and its affecting fish</u>.

(A) elevates the acidity of seawater and its affecting fish
(B) elevate the acidity of seawater and how they affect fish
(C) elevates the acidity of seawater and how that acidity affects fish
(D) elevate seawater acidity and its effect on fish
(E) elevates seawater acidity for its effect on fish

7. Renowned as an expert in linguistics, <u>modern intellectuals also acknowledge Pinker's many contributions to psychology</u>.

(A) modern intellectuals also acknowledge Pinker's many contributions to psychology
(B) Pinker's many contributions have been also acknowledged by modern intellectuals to psychology
(C) Pinker's many contributions to psychology are also acknowledged by modern intellectuals
(D) Pinker being also acknowledged for his many contributions to psychology and by modern intellectuals
(E) Pinker is also acknowledged by modern intellectuals for his many contributions to psychology

8. Many television commercials are <u>as well-produced, if not more so, than some of the most popular shows</u>.

(A) as well-produced, if not more so, than some of the most popular shows
(B) as well-produced as some of the most popular shows, if not more so
(C) if not more so, then as well-produced as some of the most popular shows
(D) well-produced, even if not more so, as some of the most popular shows
(E) like some of the most popular shows, in being well produced, if not more so

9. Among the chairman's many responsibilities <u>is the formulation of company policy</u>.

(A) is the formulation of company policy
(B) is company policy and how it is formulated
(C) is company policy being formulated
(D) are the formulation of company policy
(E) is how the formulation of company policy occurs

GO ON TO THE NEXT PAGE

9   9   9   9   9   9

10. Analysts could not reach consensus on whether the recession was <u>due primarily to the tightening of credit or because of the large national debt</u>.

(A) due primarily to the tightening of credit or because of the large national debt

(B) primarily due to the tightening of credit or to the large national debt

(C) due primarily to the tightening of credit or that of the large national debt

(D) because primarily of the tightening of credit or due to the large national debt

(E) due primarily to the tightening of credit or it was the large national debt

11. The modern Internet, first established in the mid-1980s, is based on the technology developed for the <u>ARPANET, it was created by the United States Department of Defense</u> in the 1960s.

(A) ARPANET, it was created by the United States Department of Defense

(B) ARPANET; it was created by the United States Department of Defense

(C) ARPANET, which was created by the United States Department of Defense

(D) ARPANET, being created by the United States Department of Defense

(E) ARPANET; the United States Department of Defense created it

12. The construction of the new pool <u>was to have been completed last month, but</u> the long spell of rainy weather has postponed the opening until October.

(A) was to have been completed last month, but

(B) will have been completed last month, but

(C) was to be completed last month, so

(D) has been completed last month, but

(E) were to be completed last month, nevertheless

13. In the fourth century BC, <u>the Greeks' emphasis on inquiry, art, and reason made it</u> one of the centers of world culture.

(A) the Greeks' emphasis on inquiry, art, and reason made it

(B) the emphasis in Greeks on inquiry, art, and reason made them

(C) the Greeks emphasizing inquiry, art, and reason made it

(D) the emphasis on inquiry, art, and reason made Greece

(E) the emphasis of the Greeks on inquiry, art, and reason made them

14. Beaming with pride, <u>the trophy was held aloft by Selene as the cheers reached a crescendo</u>.

(A) the trophy was held aloft by Selene as the cheers reached a crescendo

(B) the cheers reached a crescendo as Selene held the trophy aloft

(C) the trophy being held aloft by Selene as the cheers reached a crescendo

(D) Selene held the trophy aloft the cheers reaching a crescendo

(E) Selene held the trophy aloft as the cheers reached a crescendo

STOP

If you finish before time is called, you may check your work on this section only. Do not turn to any other section of the test.

ANSWER KEY

Critical Reading

Section 2

	COR. ANS.	DIFF. LEV.		COR. ANS.	DIFF. LEV.
1.	D	1	13.	D	2
2.	B	1	14.	D	3
3.	C	2	15.	A	3
4.	A	3	16.	C	4
5.	B	4	17.	E	4
6.	E	4	18.	E	3
7.	D	4	19.	C	3
8.	A	5	20.	A	4
9.	D	2	21.	E	3
10.	B	3	22.	B	2
11.	A	3	23.	D	3
12.	C	4	24.	B	5

Number correct

Number incorrect

Section 5

	COR. ANS.	DIFF. LEV.		COR. ANS.	DIFF. LEV.
1.	E	2	13.	A	3
2.	D	2	14.	D	4
3.	B	3	15.	C	3
4.	B	3	16.	D	4
5.	E	4	17.	A	4
6.	B	3	18.	C	5
7.	E	3	19.	E	3
8.	A	2	20.	D	3
9.	D	3	21.	E	3
10.	D	2	22.	B	3
11.	B	4	23.	B	4
12.	B	5	24.	D	4

Number correct

Number incorrect

Section 8

	COR. ANS.	DIFF. LEV.		COR. ANS.	DIFF. LEV.
1.	E	1	11.	C	4
2.	C	2	12.	E	2
3.	A	3	13.	E	2
4.	D	4	14.	A	4
5.	C	5	15.	B	4
6.	D	5	16.	C	3
7.	B	2	17.	B	3
8.	E	4	18.	A	3
9.	B	4	19.	A	4
10.	A	3			

Number correct

Number incorrect

Math

Section 4

	COR. ANS.	DIFF. LEV.		COR. ANS.	DIFF. LEV.
1.	D	1	11.	D	3
2.	C	1	12.	B	3
3.	A	3	13.	D	3
4.	C	2	14.	A	4
5.	E	2	15.	E	3
6.	C	2	16.	E	4
7.	A	3	17.	C	4
8.	B	2	18.	D	4
9.	C	3	19.	D	5
10.	B	3	20.	B	5

Number correct

Number incorrect

Section 6

Multiple-Choice Questions

	COR. ANS.	DIFF. LEV.
1.	C	1
2.	B	2
3.	D	3
4.	B	3
5.	A	3
6.	E	4
7.	C	4
8.	A	5

Number correct

Number incorrect

Student-produced Response questions

	COR. ANS.	DIFF. LEV.
9.	22/3 or 7.33	1
10.	4	2
11.	191	3
12.	1/3 or .333	3
13.	11	3
14.	$4.5 < b < 5.75$	4
15.	2/3 or .666 or .667	3
16.	2/5 or .4	4
17.	1500	5
18.	3/4 or .75	5

Number correct (9–18)

Section 7

	COR. ANS.	DIFF. LEV.		COR. ANS.	DIFF. LEV.
1.	C	2	9.	A	4
2.	B	2	10.	E	4
3.	A	2	11.	C	3
4.	B	3	12.	D	4
5.	E	3	13.	B	3
6.	B	3	14.	A	4
7.	C	3	15.	C	5
8.	D	3	16.	B	5

Number correct

Number incorrect

Writing

Section 3

	COR. ANS.	DIFF. LEV.		COR. ANS.	DIFF. LEV.		COR. ANS.	DIFF. LEV.		COR. ANS.	DIFF. LEV.
1.	B	1	11.	E	4	21.	C	3	31.	B	3
2.	E	1	12.	B	1	22.	A	4	32.	A	3
3.	B	2	13.	D	1	23.	B	3	33.	C	3
4.	C	3	14.	E	2	24.	C	4	34.	A	3
5.	D	4	15.	D	3	25.	B	3	35.	D	3
6.	A	2	16.	D	3	26.	D	3			
7.	E	3	17.	A	2	27.	D	4			
8.	C	4	18.	C	3	28.	E	4			
9.	B	4	19.	B	3	29.	D	5			
10.	A	3	20.	A	3	30.	D	3			

Number correct

Number incorrect

Section 9

	COR. ANS.	DIFF. LEV.		COR. ANS.	DIFF. LEV.
1.	C	1	11.	C	3
2.	D	2	12.	A	4
3.	C	2	13.	D	4
4.	E	2	14.	E	3
5.	C	2			
6.	C	2			
7.	E	3			
8.	B	3			
9.	A	3			
10.	B	3			

Number correct

Number incorrect

NOTE: Difficulty levels are estimates of question difficulty that range from 1 (easiest) to 5 (hardest).

SCORE CONVERSION TABLE

How to score your test

Use the answer key on the previous page to determine your raw score on each section. **Your raw score on each section except Section 5 is simply the number of correct answers minus ¼ of the number of wrong answers. On Section 5, your raw score is the sum of the number of correct answers for questions 1–8 minus ¼ of the number of wrong answers for questions 1–8 plus the total number of correct answers for questions 9–18.** Next, add the raw scores from Sections 3, 6, and 8 to get your Critical Reading raw score, add the raw scores from Sections 2, 5, and 7 to get your Math raw score, and the raw scores from Sections 4 and 9 to get your Writing raw score. Write the three raw scores here:

Raw Critical Reading score: _____   Raw Math score: _____   Raw Writing score: _____

Use the table below to convert these to scaled scores.

Scaled scores: Critical Reading: _____   Math: _____   Writing: _____

Raw Score	Critical Reading Scaled Score	Math Scaled Score	Writing Scaled Score	Raw Score	Critical Reading Scaled Score	Math Scaled Score	Writing Scaled Score
67	800			32	520	570	610
66	800			31	510	560	600
65	790			30	510	550	580
64	780			29	500	540	570
63	770			28	490	530	560
62	750			27	490	520	550
61	740			26	480	510	540
60	730			25	480	500	530
59	720			24	470	490	520
58	700			23	460	480	510
57	690			22	460	480	500
56	680			21	450	470	490
55	670			20	440	460	480
54	660	800		19	440	450	470
53	650	800		18	430	450	460
52	650	780		17	420	440	450
51	640	760		16	420	430	440
50	630	740		15	410	420	440
49	620	730	800	14	400	410	430
48	620	710	800	13	400	410	420
47	610	710	800	12	390	400	410
46	600	700	790	11	380	390	400
45	600	690	780	10	370	380	390
44	590	680	760	9	360	370	380
43	590	670	740	8	350	360	380
42	580	660	730	7	340	350	370
41	570	650	710	6	330	340	360
40	570	640	700	5	320	330	350
39	560	630	690	4	310	320	340
38	550	620	670	3	300	310	320
37	550	620	660	2	280	290	310
36	540	610	650	1	270	280	300
35	540	600	640	0	250	260	280
34	530	590	630	−1	230	240	270
33	520	580	620	−2 or less	210	220	250

SCORE CONVERSION TABLE FOR WRITING COMPOSITE
[ESSAY + MULTIPLE CHOICE]

Calculate your writing raw score as you did on the previous page, and grade your essay from a 1 to a 6 according to the standards that follow in the detailed answer key.

Essay score: _____   Raw Writing score: _____

Use the table below to convert these to scaled scores.

Scaled score: Writing: _____

Raw Score	Essay Score 0	Essay Score 1	Essay Score 2	Essay Score 3	Essay Score 4	Essay Score 5	Essay Score 6
−2 or less	200	230	250	280	310	340	370
−1	210	240	260	290	320	360	380
0	230	260	280	300	340	370	400
1	240	270	290	320	350	380	410
2	250	280	300	330	360	390	420
3	260	290	310	340	370	400	430
4	270	300	320	350	380	410	440
5	280	310	330	360	390	420	450
6	290	320	340	360	400	430	460
7	290	330	340	370	410	440	470
8	300	330	350	380	410	450	470
9	310	340	360	390	420	450	480
10	320	350	370	390	430	460	490
11	320	360	370	400	440	470	500
12	330	360	380	410	440	470	500
13	340	370	390	420	450	480	510
14	350	380	390	420	460	490	520
15	350	380	400	430	460	500	530
16	360	390	410	440	470	500	530
17	370	400	420	440	480	510	540
18	380	410	420	450	490	520	550
19	380	410	430	460	490	530	560
20	390	420	440	470	500	530	560
21	400	430	450	480	510	540	570
22	410	440	460	480	520	550	580
23	420	450	470	490	530	560	590
24	420	460	470	500	540	570	600
25	430	460	480	510	540	580	610
26	440	470	490	520	550	590	610
27	450	480	500	530	560	590	620
28	460	490	510	540	570	600	630
29	470	500	520	550	580	610	640
30	480	510	530	560	590	620	650
31	490	520	540	560	600	630	660
32	500	530	550	570	610	640	670
33	510	540	550	580	620	650	680
34	510	550	560	590	630	660	690
35	520	560	570	600	640	670	700
36	530	560	580	610	650	680	710
37	540	570	590	620	660	690	720
38	550	580	600	630	670	700	730
39	560	600	610	640	680	710	740
40	580	610	620	650	690	720	750
41	590	620	640	660	700	730	760
42	600	630	650	680	710	740	770
43	610	640	660	690	720	750	780
44	620	660	670	700	740	770	800
45	640	670	690	720	750	780	800
46	650	690	700	730	770	800	800
47	670	700	720	750	780	800	800
48	680	720	730	760	800	800	800
49	680	720	730	760	800	800	800

Detailed Answer Key

Section 1

The following essay received 12 points out of a possible 12. Although it is not a flawless essay, it demonstrates *clear and consistent mastery* in that it

- develops an insightful point of view on the topic
- demonstrates exemplary critical thinking
- uses very effective examples, reasons, and other evidence to support its thesis
- is consistently focused, coherent, and well-organized
- demonstrates skillful and effective use of language and sentence structure
- is largely (but not necessarily completely) free of grammatical and usage errors

> Very few important decisions, even deeply personal ones, are made in a vacuum. If we fail to realize how our personal decisions affect other people, then we run the risk of alienating people around us.
>
> As a member of society of responsible individuals, you must take ownership of your own personal decisions. You alone bear the responsibility of a bad decision or can enjoy the satisfaction of a good one.

Assignment: **How important is it to seek the opinions of others when making significant personal decisions?** Plan and write an essay in which you develop your point of view on this issue. Support your position with reasoning and examples taken from your reading, studies, experience, or observations.

SAMPLE STUDENT ESSAY

"Be true to yourself" is a commonly used saying, supporting individuals making decisions in accordance with their own beliefs. However, one should always take into consideration the thoughts and opinions of others, because an outsider can often see the situation from a different perspective, offering clarity and a different way of going about the problem. John F. Kennedy during the Cuban Missile Crisis sought the advice of others on how to handle the situation and ended up making the right decisions. Lily from Edith Wharton's "House of Mirth" was unable to listen to the advice of others and consequently made poor decisions. Asking for the opinion of others for personal or professional decisions can help one avoid making the wrong decision.

In 1962, the United States came to the brink of war with the Soviet Union. In the midst of the Cold War, the world was mainly divided into two entities, the allies of the U.S. and the allies of Soviet Russia. During the fall of 1962, when the Cubans received missiles from their Russian allies, the U.S. came close

to starting a preemptive, perhaps nuclear, war. However, JFK was unwilling to act irrationally. He convened all of his military advisors and cabinet members and listened to their opinions regarding the mindsets and capabilities of Nikita Kruschev and Fidel Castro. As a result, JFK, who was personally responsible for the ultimate decision, arrived at a strategy that allowed for the withdrawal of the missiles and avoided a disastrous war.

Unlike JFK, Lily, in "House of Mirth," is unwilling to listen to the opinions of others. She sees herself as a member of the upper class; however, slowly her reputation and position in society disintegrate due to a nasty and untrue rumor. Lily has all the proof to expose the rumor as false and the woman who started the rumor as a liar. However, she is unwilling to listen to her friends who advise her to reveal the truth. Lily is unable to be critical of her own opinions and is therefore unable to take the advice of others. Because Lily does not expose the rumor as a lie, she lives out a lonely and poor life, which ultimately ends in her suicide.

We are constantly inundated with the opinions of others. Some of these opinions are negative forces, such as the peer pressures on teenagers to drink. It is important in this overwhelming time to remain true to what each of us truly believes in. However, we must keep one ear open to listen to objective opinions. Without the thoughts of others, we will find it more difficult to see the flaws in our own arguments and without this self-reflection we can never grow. We must listen to others in order to grow as individuals.

Reader's Comments

This essay provides well-reasoned and well-written support to the thesis that "asking for the opinion of others for personal or professional decisions can help one avoid making the wrong decision." The author uses two examples to support this thesis, one demonstrating that "asking for the opinion of others" can be helpful, and another demonstrating that failing to do so can lead to trouble. The examples of John Kennedy during the Cuban Missile Crisis and Lily in *House of Mirth* are well-chosen. The conclusion provides an important qualification to the thesis without undermining it, demonstrating strong critical thinking: the author suggests that, although considering the opinions of others is a sign of wisdom, so is "remain[ing] true to what each of us truly believes in."

This essay shows solid mastery of vocabulary and syntax. The structure and length of sentences are varied eloquently. The author also demonstrates that good diction does not always require the use of obscure vocabulary; the author's words are effective without being unwieldy.

Section 2

1. D Since there is no *consensus* (general agreement) about vitamin C supplements among doctors, there must be a measure of *disagreement*. This implies that *much further research on the subject is necessary* in order to clear up the controversy. *resented* = felt bitterness; *invariance* = lack of change

2. B Since Alana's friends prefer *comedic films* (funny movies) to whatever Alana likes, Alana must like very different kinds of movies, so she must have an *affinity for* (attraction to) scary movies. *indifference* = lack of concern; *intolerance* = unwillingness to put up with something

3. C If *his behavior in social groups was often bizarrely inappropriate*, then his *sense of propriety* (knowledge of acceptable behavior) must have been *distorted* (twisted). *corollary* = forming a proposition that follows from one already proved; *credible* = believable; *routine* = performed as part of a regular procedure; *coherent* = logical and consistent

4. A This sentence gives the reason why historians have criticized recent articles. It is logical that historians would criticize the articles' lack of *comprehensiveness* (completeness) if they provided only *sparse* (thinly dispersed) *and insubstantial anecdotal accounts*. *spontaneous* = without premeditation; *economy* = conciseness; *meager* = lacking in quantity; *subjectivity* = bias; *colloquial* = characteristic of casual conversation

5. B If *Aristotle's assertions could be easily disproved even by the simplest of experiments*, then by modern standards they are not valid, and should be rejected by modern philosophers. *laud* = to praise highly; *repudiate* = to refuse to be associated with; *disdain* = to consider unworthy; *extol* = praise highly; *reassert* = to repeat a claim; *anticipate* = expect or predict

6. E Since horse lips can grasp, they are *prehensile* (capable of grasping). *retracted* = withdrawn; *therapeutic* = having a good effect on the body or mind; *infirm* = sickly; *ameliorative* = serving to improve a situation

7. D Since Kenneth's firm is *eschewing* (rejecting) *hierarchical* (rigid top-down) *structure* and using a *flexible collaborative system*, it is clearly trying to avoid *the establishment of rigid practices*, which would reasonably be expected to *promote* or *encourage* creativity. *suppress* = forcibly put an end to; *resolve* = settle an issue; *reiterate* = repeat a claim; *check* = stop the

progress of something; *entail* = involve as a necessary element

8. A *Demonstrations of erudition* are exhibitions of one's learning. If these *go too far*, then the professor must be acting like a know-it-all. She is being *pedantic*. *pedantry* = excessive display of learning; *pragmatism* = concern with reality rather than ideals; *evanescence* = the quality of vanishing quickly; *deprecation* = an expression of disapproval

9. D In saying that *the world is presented in a kaleidoscopic flux of impressions which has to be organized by our minds*, the author means that our minds must organize the *stimuli* (things that evoke a specific reaction in the brain) from the world around us.

10. B The authors of both passages agree that *the human mind divides stimuli from the natural world into discrete packets*. The author of Passage 1 states that we *cut nature up, organize it into concepts* (lines 9–10), and the author of Passage 2 states that *we divide the natural world into arbitary discrete units of perception* (lines 21–22).

11. A The author of Passage 1 believes that the mind organizes sensory *impressions largely by the linguistic systems in our minds* (lines 7–9), and the *linguists* in Passage 2 agree by suggesting that *English speakers are forced by their limited vocabulary to divide the natural world into arbitrary discrete units of perception* (lines 20–22).

12. C The *sensory categories* (line 2) in Passage 1 are what we *isolate from the world of phenomena* (line 3), how we *organize* [that world of phenomena] *into concepts* (lines 9–10). These sensory categories and concepts include things like "hot" and "cold," "rough" and "smooth," and so on. The only sensory category among the choices is (C) red. Although words like "cells" and "mosquitoes" represent categories of a sort from the natural world, they do not describe sensory impressions directly. The "smooth flow" (choice (A)) and the "experience" (choice (B)) are abstract concepts, rather than sensory concepts.

13. D The first parargaph explains how reading is a complex task in that the *simple experience of the...printed page* moves into the *world of abstractions* (lines 6–8).

14. D The word *move* here refers to the process in a reader's mind of translating words on a page into abstract thoughts.

15. A This quote presents a perspective that contrasts the idea in the previous sentence that *books are palliatives (objects of comfort)* (line 19).

16. C The *suspicions* are those of people who think that close readers have *lost their touch with reality* (lines 26–27).

17. E The passage states that it is the alienation that does so much damage (lines 48–49), and this alienation is described in the previous sentence as the distinction between life and literature.

18. E In saying that *experience...is a traffic between the object and the subject*, the author means that their is interaction or communication between them.

19. C This sentence states that we adjust to the objects with every confidence that they are real when we have sensations and impressions of objects (lines 61–64). In other words, we act under the belief that our perceptions are of real objects, and not illusions.

20. A The phrase *impression of the sensation* here means *interpretation of the experience*.

21. E The stone is said to *stimulate...our imagination* (lines 34–35) and the bush, likewise, is said to be an *impression of the sensation* (lines 64–65) which can be mistaken when *imagining some fear* (line 67).

22. B Keats is described as one who expressed *a preference for the imagined* (line 74), and as *an uncommon reader* (line 77). The passage does not discuss Keats' writing at all.

23. D The author suggests that *becoming more educated* is how some people *seek refuge in...abstractness* (line 84) in order to avoid the lively sensations (line 78) of literature.

24. B Each paragraph maintains a consistent focus on the importance of imagination in the interpretation and appreciation of literature.

Section 3

1. B The use of the idiomatic phrase *not only* requires the conjunction *but also*. Choice (D) includes the correct idiomatic phrase, but uses a verb form that is not parallel with the verb in the first clause.

2. E In the original sentence, the pronoun *that* is ambiguous: it could refer to the parade or to the festival. Choices (B) and (C) are likewise ambiguous. Choice (D) fixes that ambiguity, but it is redundant and wordy.

3. B Since the sentence clearly indicates a state of being lasting over an extended period prior to another fixed point in time, the past perfect tense, *had stood*, is more logical than the simple past tense, *stood*.

4. C The adverb *not* is part of the verb of this sentence, but modern standard English does not allow *began not* as the verb; the correct form is *did not begin*. The only choice that makes this correction is choice (C).

5. D The subject, *popular* magazines, is plural, and so the pronoun should be *they*, not *its*. In choice (C), the phrase *are not benefiting* is not idiomatic and is in the wrong tense: Since the sentence is expressing a general quality of popular magazines, the habitual present tense *do not benefit* is needed, rather than the present progressive *are not benefiting*.

6. A The sentence is correct as written.

7. E The original sentence contains a dangling participle. The participle *taking* should have *Courtney* as its subject, not the dummy subject *it*. (That is, *it* didn't take time off, *Courtney* did.) Therefore, the main clause must have *Courtney* as its subject. Choice (D) corrects the dangling participle, but is unidiomatic.

8. C The list should have parallel form: following *stone for lithographs* and *metal for etchings* should be the analogous phrase *fabric plates for screen printing*.

9. B   The original sentence contains a misplaced modifier: it implies that the *thinkers*, rather than *Kaia* herself, dressed as Copernicus. Choice (C) is disjointed and ambiguous because it uses the passive voice. Choice (D) misplaces a different modifying phrase: *on Renaissance thinkers* should follow *presentation* directly. Choice (E) commits yet another modifier error, implying that Copernicus actually gave Kaia's presentation.

10. A   The sentence is correct as written. The underlined phrase must be a definition of the *"straw man"* device, and hence must be a noun phrase. (B) is incorrect because *when* incorrectly suggests that the device is a time period or event. (C) is incorrect because it contains a dangling participle. (D) is incorrect because *someone* incorrectly suggests that the *"straw man"* is an actual person. (E) is incorrect because it is awkward and the pronoun *its* is ambiguous.

11. E   This sentence compares *the industrial revolution* with *the emergence of new industries*, and the standard phrasing for such a comparison requires us to say that one is *like* the other.

12. B   The present perfect form requires the past participle, and so the verb should be *have begun* rather than *have began*.

13. D   The list in the original sentence is not parallel. Since *devotion* and *betrayal* are abstract nouns, the final item in the list should also be an abstract noun: *redemption*.

14. E   The sentence is correct as written.

15. D   The pronoun *they* does not agree in number with its antecedent *capital punishment*, and should be changed to *it*.

16. D   The original sentence contains an illogical comparison. Since no team can defeat itself, the phrase in (D) must be changed to *any other team*.

17. A   The use of *neither* requires *nor*, not *or*.

18. C   The verb *were* does not agree in number with its subject, *reluctance*, and should be changed to *was*.

19. B   The sentence contains two clauses with contrasting ideas, so the conjunction between them should be *but*, not *and*. (If you chose (A), you should remember that it's not an error to start a sentence with *Because*, no matter what your grade school teachers may have told you!)

20. A   The verb *were* disagrees in number with its subject, *agreement*, and must be changed to *was*.

21. C   The pronoun *they* does not agree in number with its antecedent, *the Constitutional Convention*, and so should be changed to *it*.

22. A   The phrase *a tendency of memorizing* is an incorrect idiom, and should be changed to *a tendency to memorize*.

23. B   The verb *help* disagrees in number with its subject, *theory*, and must be changed to *helps*.

24. C   Since the phrase *Ben and me* serves as the subject of the verb *took*, it should be in the subjective case: *Ben and I*.

25. B   The verb *suggest* disagrees in number with its subject, *reading*, and must be changed to *suggests*.

26. D   As it is written, this sentence contains an illogical comparison between *Morgan's most recent novel* and *that of her autobiography*. Logically, a book can only be compared to another book, so the phrase *that of* must be deleted.

27. D   The sentence makes a comparison between *Pluto's orbit* and *the orbits of other planets*, so the phrase in (D) is incomplete, and should include *the orbits of*. (If you chose (B), remember that it would be incorrect to replace *that* with *because*, since the sentence requires a pronoun in that spot [to point to the *reason*] rather than a conjunction.)

28. E   The sentence is correct as written.

29. D   Since Ellen learned to dance long before she got back on the ballroom floor, the perfect form of the infinitive, *to have learned*, is required.

30. D   In context, the pronoun *it* has no clear antecedent. The second part of the sentence begins with *because*, and therefore is giving a reason for something mentioned in the first part of the sentence. Clearly, it is explaining why *we adopt superstitions*, according to the scientists mentioned in the previous sentence.

31. B   Since this sentence does not convey an idea that contrasts with the previous one, the transition *however* is illogical. It describes a consequence of the fact in the previous sentence, so *therefore* is more logical.

32. A   In context, the pronoun *They* has no clear antecedent. The sentence provides some examples of specific superstitions, so the transition *For example, we are inclined to* is much more effective.

33. C   The term *nonbelievers*, in this context, refers to people who do not share the superstitions. Therefore, phrases like *nonbelievers not sharing [the superstitions]* are redundant. Notice that choices (A), (B), and (E) contain similar redundancies. Choice (D) is illogical because it does not show an idea that is *instead of* (that is, replacing) the other.

34. A   This sentence represents a shift in the discussion from the benefits of superstitions to the pitfalls of superstitions. Therefore, the transition *On the other hand* is most logical.

35. D   Sentence 7 is in a paragraph discussing the process by which superstitions are formed, as silly as they may seem to others. Therefore, a sentence about *the great things our minds are capable of* is inappropriate.

Section 4

1. D   If $x = \dfrac{1}{4}$, then the choices give values of

(A) $\dfrac{1}{4}$

(B) $\dfrac{1}{2} \times \dfrac{1}{4} = \dfrac{1}{8}$

(C) $\left(\dfrac{1}{4}\right)^2 = \dfrac{1}{16}$

(D) $1 - \dfrac{1}{4} = \dfrac{3}{4}$

(E) $\left(\dfrac{1}{4}\right)^3 = \dfrac{1}{64}$

2. C   The phrase "at this rate" suggests that you can set up a proportion: $\dfrac{300 \text{ miles}}{18 \text{ gallons}} = \dfrac{x \text{ miles}}{12 \text{ gallons}}$

Cross-multiply: $3600 = 18x$
Divide by 18: $200 = x$

3. A   Since both m and n must be positive integers, and because $6m + 2n$ must add up to only 22, then m can't be more than 3, because $6m = 6(4) = 24$ would already be more than 22. Since m must also be greater than n, and n is a positive integer (and therefore at least 1), m must be at least 2. This only gives two possibilities for the value of m: 2 or 3, and only $m = 3$ and $n = 2$ works to satisfy all the conditions of the problem.

4. C   Remember that the sum of angles in a triangle is 180°. Mark the diagram to indicate those interior angles:

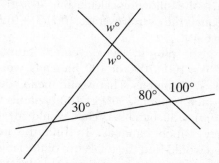

Since $30 + 80 + w = 180$, w must equal 70.

5. E   If $\dfrac{n}{6}$, $\dfrac{n}{8}$, and $\dfrac{n}{9}$ are all integers, then n must be a multiple of 6, 8, and 9. The least common multiple of these numbers is 72. (Since the prime factorization of the three numbers is $6 = 2 \times 3$, $8 = 2 \times 2 \times 2$, and $9 = 3 \times 3$, the least common multiple is $2 \times 2 \times 2 \times 3 \times 3 = 72$.) The number n can be larger than 72, but it must always be a multiple of 72, like 144, 216, and so on.

6. **C**   The total number of apples in the beginning is $10 \times 10 = 100$. The farmer then removes $1 + 2 + 3 + 4 + 5 + 6 + 7 + 8 + 9 + 10 = 55$ of them. (You can do this sum easily in your head by adding in pairs from the outside in: notice that $(1+10) + (2+9) + (3+8) + (4+7) + (5+6) = 11 \times 5 = 55$.) This leaves 45 of the original 100, or 45%.

---

7. **A**   You can distribute the multiplication in each choice to see which one is equivalent to $4n^2 + 4n + 2$.

(A) $4(n^2 + n + \frac{1}{2}) = 4n^2 + 4n + 2$

(B) $2(2n + 1)^2 = 2(4n^2 + 4n + 1) = 8n^2 + 8n + 2$

(C) $2(2n^3 + 1) = 4n^3 + 2$

(D) $(2n + 1)(2n + 2) = 4n^2 + 6n + 2$

(E) $(2n - 1)(2n - 2) = 4n^2 - 6n + 2$

---

8. **B**   It is easier to compare exponentials if they have the same base, so it helps to first represent 243 and 729 as powers of 3, like so: $243 = 3^5$ and $729 = 3^6$.

$$(3^a)(3^b) = 243$$

Substitute: $\qquad\qquad (3^a)(3^b) = 3^5$

Simplify the left side: $\qquad 3^{a+b} = 3^5$

Set exponents equal: $\qquad a + b = 5$

Now look at the second equation: $\quad (3^a)^b = 729$

Substitute: $\qquad\qquad (3^a)^b = 3^6$

Simplify the left side: $\qquad 3^{ab} = 3^6$

Set exponents equal: $\qquad ab = 6$

Because a and b are positive integers with a product of 6, they must each be one of the factors of 6, that is: 1, 2, 3, or 6. Because $a + b = 5$, either $a = 2$ and $b = 3$, or $a = 3$ and $b = 2$.

---

9. **C**   The simple mathematical way to do this problem is to use the following calculation: 70% of 7 plus 30% of 5 equals the overall average: $(0.7)(7) + (0.3)(5) = 4.9 + 1.5 = 6.4$

You can also "plug-in" a convenient number of bananas, like 100. 70% of 100 bananas would be $(0.7)(100) = 70$ bananas. That would mean you have seventy 7-inch bananas. 30% of 100 bananas would be $(0.3)(100) = 30$ bananas. That would mean you have thirty 5-inch bananas. To find the average length, you would find the total sum of the lengths of all the bananas together and divide that by the total number of bananas.

$$\frac{70(7) + 30(3)}{70 + 30} = \frac{490 + 150}{100} = \frac{640}{100} = 6.4$$

---

10. **B**   A circle that has an area of 16π must have a radius of 4, because Area $= 16\pi = \pi r^2$. Only one circle can exist in a plane with a fixed center and a fixed radius.

---

11. **D** $\qquad\qquad\qquad\qquad h(m) = \left(\sqrt{5m} - 4\right)^2$

To find $h(m)$, plug in m for x: $\quad h(m) = \left(\sqrt{5m} - 4\right)^2$

Substitute $h(m) = 36$: $\qquad\qquad 36 = \left(\sqrt{5m} - 4\right)^2$

Take the square root of both sides: $6 = \sqrt{5m} - 4$

add 4: $\qquad\qquad\qquad\qquad 10 = \sqrt{5m}$

Square both sides: $\qquad\qquad 100 = 5m$

Divide by 5: $\qquad\qquad\qquad m = 20$

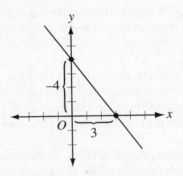

12. **B**   Line l, as shown above, has a slope of $\frac{-4}{3}$. (Recall that the slope of a line is its $\frac{\text{rise}}{\text{run}}$, given by the equation $\frac{y_2 - y_1}{x_2 - x_1}$.) Two lines that are perpendicular in the xy-plane must have slopes that are negative reciprocals of each other. So, any line perpendicular to l has a slope of $\frac{3}{4}$. The choices are all in the form $y = mx + b$, where m is the slope of the line. The only equation of a line with slope $\frac{3}{4}$ is choice (B).

---

13. **D**   Since the question asks for the value of $\frac{x}{2}$ in terms of z, the extra variable y is just getting in the way. You can get rid of it by substituting: since $y = z + 2$, we can say that $2^y = 2^{z+2}$. Therefore $x = 2^{z+2}$. Now to find the value of $\frac{x}{2}$, just divide both sides by 2: $\frac{x}{2} = \frac{2^{z+2}}{2}$. Remember when dividing two exponentials with the same base, you subtract the exponents: $\frac{2^{z+2}}{2^1} = 2^{z+2-1} = 2^{z+1}$.

If you prefer, though, you can solve this problem by just picking a value for z and working from there. For instance, what if z equals 1? Then $y = 1 + 2 = 3$, and so $x = 2^3 = 8$. Therefore, $\frac{x}{2} = \frac{8}{2} = 4$. So this is the value we are looking for in the choices. Plugging in $z = 1$ gives us (A) 2, (B) 3, (C) 2, (D) 4, and (E) 3. Since choice (D) is the only one that gives a value of 4, it must be the correct answer.

---

14. **A** If we apply the law of cross-multiplication to the second and third equations, we get $2a = 3b$, $6b = 5c$, and $2c = 5d$. To compare all four numbers, it might be helpful to "link" all of the equations. We can link the first two by multiplying both sides of the first equation by 2. This gives $4a = 6b$, and linking this with the second equation gives $4a = 6b = 5c$. To link this with the final equation, multiply all sides by 2, giving $8a = 12b = 10c$, and multiply both sides of the final equation by 5, giving $10c = 25d$. Now we have $8a = 12b = 10c = 25d$. What does this all mean? Since all of these products are equal, the unknown with the *smallest* coefficient must be the *biggest* positive number. (Test some possible solutions—like $a = 150$, $b = 100$, $c = 120$, $d = 48$—if you're not convinced.) Using this fact, we get $d < b < c < a$.

---

15. **E** The pattern 1, 2, 3 repeats indefinitely in this sequence. Each of these patterns has a sum of $1 + 2 + 3 = 6$. In the first 36 terms of this sequence, this pattern repeats $36 \div 3 = 12$ times. Therefore the sum of all 36 terms is $6 \times 12 = 72$.

---

16. **E** The diagram indicates that $24 + a$ students play lacrosse and $40 + a$ students play soccer, because a represents the number of students who play *both* lacrosse and soccer. If these numbers are in the ratio of 3:4, then you can set up a proportion:

$$\frac{24 + a}{40 + a} = \frac{3}{4}$$

Cross-multiply: $96 + 4a = 120 + 3a$
Subtract $96 + 3a$: $a = 24$

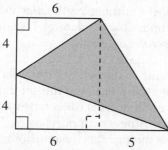

17. **C** You might have tried the "direct" method for finding the area of the triangle using the formula

$A = \frac{1}{2}bh$. But this gets messy fast, because it's tough the length of any base or height in this triangle. A much more straightforward approach is actually the "indirect" method, where you find the area of the whole figure and then just subtract the areas of the two right triangles. Notice, by drawing in the line shown in the figure above, that the area of the whole figure is the combined area of a rectangle and a right triangle. The rectangle has an area of $6 \times 8 = 48$, and the right triangle has area $\frac{1}{2}(5)(8) = 20$. So the whole figure has an area of $48 + 20 = 68$. The two "cutout" triangles have areas of $\frac{1}{2}(6)(4) = 12$ and $\frac{1}{2}(11)(4) = 22$, so the shaded triangle has an area of $68 - 12 - 22 = 34$.

---

18. **D** Using the definition of the function, $\Omega n = \frac{n^2}{3} - n = s$. Since both n and s must be integers, it helps to start thinking about how this fact restricts the possible values of n. Trying out a few positive integers for n should make it clear that s will only turn out to be an integer if n is a multiple of 3, because otherwise $\frac{n^2}{3}$ cannot be an integer. Now, let's try simple multiples of 3 for n and see what we get for s.

Let $n = 3$: $\frac{n^2}{3} - n = \frac{3^2}{3} - 3 = 3 - 3 = 0 = s$

But since $s = 0$ isn't one of the choices, we have to keep going.

Let $n = 6$: $\frac{n^2}{3} - n = \frac{6^2}{3} - 6 = 12 - 6 = 6 = s$

Bingo!

---

19. **D** Since f is a quadratic function, it has the form $f(x) = ax^2 + bx + c$ where a, b, and c are constants. If it contains the points $(0, 0)$, $(1, 5)$, and $(5, 5)$, then $f(0) = 0$, $f(1) = 5$, and $f(5) = 5$. Substituting these into the general quadratic equation gives three equations:

$$c = 0$$
$$a + b + c = 5$$
$$25a + 5b + c = 5$$

Substituting $c = 0$ into the second and third equations gives:

$$a + b = 5$$
$$25a + 5b = 5$$

Multiply both sides of "$a + b = 5$" by 5: $5a + 5b = 25$
Subtract other equation: $- (25a + 5b = 5)$
$$\overline{\qquad -20a \qquad = 20}$$

Divide by –20: $a = -1$
Substitute $a = -1$ into $a + b = 5$: $-1 + b = 5$
Add 1: $b = 6$

Therefore the equation is $f(x) = -x^2 + 6x$. But how do we find its greatest value? Notice that the points (1, 5) and (5, 5) have the same y-coordinate, so they must be reflections of each other over the axis of symmetry, which must be halfway between them at $x = 3$. Since the axis of symmetry must go through the vertex, we just substitute $x = 3$ into the equation: $f(3) = -(3)^2 + 6(3) = 9$.

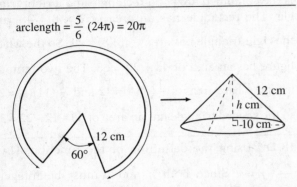

$$\text{arclength} = \frac{5}{6}(24\pi) = 20\pi$$

20. B   Notice that, as the sliced circle is folded into the cone, the radius of the circle, which is 12 cm, becomes the "slant height" of the cone, and the arc of the circle becomes the circumference of the base of the cone. Since 60° is removed from the circle, 360° − 60° = 300° remains, which is 5/6 of the circle. Therefore, the arc length is 5/6 of 2(12π) = 20π cm, which is also the circumference of the base of the cone. Now analyze the cone. Since the circumference of its base is 20π = 2πr, the radius of the circular base must be 10 cm. To find the height of the cone, notice the right triangle shown. Use the Pythagorean theorem:

$$h^2 + 10^2 = 12^2$$
Simplify: $\quad\quad\quad\quad\quad h^2 + 100 = 144$
Subtract 100: $\quad\quad\quad\quad h^2 = 44$
Take the square root: $\quad\quad h = \sqrt{44}$

Section 5

1. E   Since Congresswoman Hyde is trying to *counter* (work against) something, the two missing words must represent opposite ideas. The only pair of opposites among the choices is (E) inclusiveness . . division. *conservation* = the act of conserving a resource; *prudence* = wisdom; *initiative* = the ability to take charge before others do

2. D   What would *the most conservative music critics* complain about? To be *conservative* means to resist change, so they would complain about changes being made to traditional songs. The only choice that conveys that idea is (D): *conservative* critics would complain *vociferously* (loudly) about *familiar* songs being *refashioned* (changed). *esteemed* = held in high

regard; *unconventional* = not traditional; *disparaged* = regarded as being of low worth; *replicated* = made an exact copy of

3. B   The phrase *would result in* indicates that the sentence must show a logical cause and effect. Attending college very close to home would reasonably be expected to cause a student to develop too *parochial* (unsophisticated and narrow-minded) an outlook. *cosmopolitan* = sophisticated and worldly

4. B   Because Ted was *docile* (obedient) at school, his teachers would be surprised to know that he was *intractable* (hard to work with) at home. *altruistic* = unselfish; *taciturn* = quiet; *diffident* = lacking self-confidence

5. E   *Purgative* means *having the effect of getting rid of unwanted feelings or memories.* Such a therapy produces *catharsis* (the elimination of repressed emotions). *holism* = the theory that the parts of the whole are intimately connected; *replenishment* = the act of filling up again; *pretension* = the use of affectation to impress another

6. B   Although the first sentence describes New York City as *fascinating*, and the second sentence describes her as *alluring, enticing*, and *tempting*, all of which seem positive, the passage as a whole clearly portrays New York City as *treacherous*, that is, deceitful and hazardous. The phrase *hiding her crooked hands* clearly suggests the menace that she is concealing, as do the phrases *cruel feet, condemns to a fate like that of galley slaves,* and *laughs mockingly. nurturing* = providing care for the development of another; *providential* = occurring at a favorable time

7. E   The *bubbles of fortune* are the fates of those *few [that New York City] favors and fondles*, but soon after the city *blows the bubbles out and laughs mockingly as she watches them fall.* Therefore, they are deceptive lures that the city uses to entice and then torture.

8. A   Since the author says that *the "worst" list* is *insufferable* (impossible to tolerate), his attitude toward it is clearly *revulsion* (disgust).

9. D   The author states that a critic should enhance the listening experience, and inform the public as to whether a new concert is (or is not) worth attending or a new recording worth purchasing. Therefore he believes that the primary responsibility of a music critic is to inform listeners about the merits of new works.

10. D   Since the narrator and the subject of this portrayal do not meet until the very end of this passage, it cannot be said to be a story about friends. Its focus is also not on the narrator's identity, nor on the character of the town, although such things are mentioned throughout the passage. It is more properly a chronicle of the narrator's obsession with a mysterious stranger, whom she finally meets at the end of the story.

11. B   In saying that *fiction was passed as fact*, the narrator means that the "fictions," the stories passed around about the imagined background of the stranger, were eventually regarded as true. That is, the neighbors gained more confidence in their assumptions about the stranger.

12. B   The previous paragraph mentions three hypotheses about the stranger: that he had been a veteran of the Vietnam war, that he was a monk, and that he was a Somalian refugee. The questions here mention Vietnam, so it can be surmised that they are questions regarding his war experience.

13. A   This paragraph consists of the narrator's questions about the *unspeakable things* that she imagines the stranger has experienced. In the previous paragraph she mentions the hypothesis that the stranger had been *a Vietnam vet*, and these questions continue that line of thought, asking whether he had run through *the rice paddies of Vietnam* and had *seen a fatal flash*. The narrator is, therefore, clearly imagining scenes of war. The *moonscape surface* therefore represents the desolate aftermath of that war.

14. D   The author states that the stranger's *silhouette formed the character of a word in Japanese script*. Since a silhouette can be seen, this sentence indicates clearly that the narrator is describing something visible, not abstract. The *character*, in this case, is a Japanese word, which is a visible symbol.

15. C   The phrase *his look was clear* is explained in this sentence and the next, where the narrator says that the stranger was *not shrouded with darkness nor veiled in otherness. He seemed to journey momentarily out of that dark place.* That is, he seemed less mysterious than he had before.

16. D   Although the first paragraph seems to be discussing cycloramas, this particular topic goes no further, and the passage as a whole is focused on a discussion of the cosmic microwave background radiation. Penzias' and Wilson's discovery is discussed, but only insofar as it provided evidence for the CMB, and is not discussed beyond the fifth paragraph. Gamow's theory and the Big Bang theory are featured prominently, but the passage neither *examines controversies* about Gamow's theory nor *deliberates [engages in long and careful consideration about] questions* raised by the Big Bang theory.

17. A   The first paragraph discusses the Gettysburg Cyclorama only to provide an analogy for the cosmic microwave background radiation, which is likewise a panoramic snapshot of a cataclysmic historical event. It is not a *historical antecedent*, because it did not precede the CMB, and it is certainly not a *typical* representation, since cycloramas are very unusual.

18. C   The statement that scientists *can't get much closer to the Big Bang* is explained in the two paragraphs that follow, where it is explained that photon radiation, which must be emitted or reflected from objects or events in order for them to be seen, was scattered *as if through a dense fog* until 300,000 years after the Big Bang, thereby rendering the early universe invisible.

19. E   In this discussion, the terms *"invisible"* and *"seen,"* which are common (and not recently coined) terms, are given technical definitions in terms of the emission or reflection of photons and their unimpeded path to a detector. Since this is a technical discussion, the author is not expressing *disdain* (disgust) or *irony* (reversal of expectations), nor is he *speaking speculatively* (expressing predictions about the future).

20. D   The third paragraph explains what it means, in terms of physical processes, to be "seen" in order to show how the earliest stage of the universe cannot be directly examined. Although the human eye is mentioned as a detector, this discussion is by no means *biological*, nor is it *historical*. It also mentions no specific experimental results, nor does it *refute* (disprove) any misconceptions.

21. E   The fourth paragraph indicates that George Gamow published a theory that claimed that, if the Big Bang theory is correct, then photons (light particles) would have first been *set free* 300,000 years after the Big Bang, and called this earliest emission of unimpeded photons the cosmic microwave background radiation, or CMB.

22. B   The *much better explanation* that Dicke and Wilkinson provided was clearly the topic that they had been studying, the CMB radiation predicted by Gamow. This was of course *radiation released 300,000 years after the Big Bang*. This radiation consisted of photons, which the fourth paragraph indicates are *uncharged*, so choice (C) is not correct.

23. B The fifth paragraph indicates that Penzias and Wilson were not specifically looking for the CMB, and in fact were *troubled by* the background noise, and could not correctly explain it at first. Since the CMB had not previously been detected, it was not a *known phenomenon* and since this discovery preceded the COBE satellite, it could not have depended on data from COBE.

24. D The final paragraph indicates that the *minor fluctuations in the CMB measurements*, far from being troubling, in fact *helped scientists...calibrate [adjust precisely] the parameters [factors that set the conditions of a system] of the Big Bang theory.*

Section 6

1. C The interior angles of a triangle must have a sum of 180°, so $a + a + b = 180$. If $b = 80$, Then $2a + 80 = 180$. Subtracting 80 from both sides gives $2a = 100$, so $a = 50$.

2. B Just pick a simple value for x, such as 1/2, and evaluate each choice:
(A) $1 - 1/2 = 1/2$
(B) $\dfrac{1}{1/2} = 2$
(C) $-\dfrac{1}{1/2} = -2$
(D) $1/2$
(E) $(1/2)^2 = 1/4$

3. D Since 3, 5, and 7 are all prime numbers, their least common multiple is $3 \times 5 \times 7 = 105$. Therefore any number that is a multiple of all three numbers must also be a multiple of 105.

4. B If a regular box contains m crayons, then a deluxe box contains $m + 10$ crayons. Therefore 5 deluxe boxes contain $5(m + 10) = 5m + 50$ crayons.

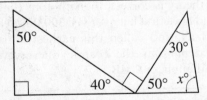

5. A First recall that the angles in a triangle must add up to 180°. Therefore, the other acute angle in the triangle at left must be $180° - 90° - 50° = 40°$, as shown

in the figure above. Since the three angles in the center form a straight angle, their sum must also be 180°, and therefore the third angle is $180° - 40° - 90° = 50°$. The three angles in the other triangle must also have a sum of 180°, so $x = 180 - 50 - 30 = 100$.

x	y
2	$\dfrac{1}{2}$
4	$\dfrac{1}{8}$
6	$\dfrac{1}{18}$

6. E First, notice that as x increases, y decreases. This means that the relation cannot be a *direct* variation, which leaves choices (B), (D), and (E). Let's look at each in turn:
(B) If y is inversely proportional to x, then $y = \dfrac{k}{x}$, where k is a constant, and so $k = xy$. Does xy equal a constant for all of the pairs in the table of values? No: $xy = 1$ for the first pair, but $xy = \dfrac{1}{2}$ for the second pair. Therefore, (B) is incorrect.
(D) If x is inversely proportional to the square of y, then $x = \dfrac{k}{y^2}$, where k is a constant, and so $k = xy^2$.

Does xy^2 equal a constant for all of the pairs in the table of values? No: $xy^2 = \dfrac{1}{2}$ for the first pair, but $xy^2 = \dfrac{1}{16}$ for the second pair. Therefore, (D) is incorrect.
(E) y is inversely proportional to the square of x, then $y = \dfrac{k}{x^2}$, where k is a constant, and so $k = x^2y$.

Does x^2y equal a constant for all of the pairs in the table of values? Yes: $x^2y = 2$ for all three pairs. Therefore, (E) is correct.

7. C If all conditions are met, there are only 4 possible arrangements:
　　L, SM, T, C, M
　　L, SM, T, M, C
　　M, C, T, SM, L
　　C, M, T, SM, L
(C = capuchin, L = lemur, M = macaque, SM = squirrel monkey, and T = tamarind)

8. A If the equation is true for all values of y, then the two quadratics on either side of the equal sign must be identical. Distribute the multiplication on the left side to get the two equations to look more alike:

Distribute:
Combine "y terms":

$$(y + 4)(y - h) = y^2 - 2y + b$$
$$y^2 - hy + 4y - 4h = y^2 - 2y + b$$
$$y^2 + (4 - h)y - 4h = y^2 - 2y + b$$

Equating the coefficients on both sides, you can see that $4 - h = -2$ and $-4h = b$.

Subtract 4:
Multiply by -1:

$$4 - h = -2$$
$$-h = -6$$
$$h = 6$$

To find b, we use $b = -4h = -4(6) = -24$.

---

9. **22/3 or 7.33**

$$\frac{(6 - 3)r + 4}{2} = 13$$

Multiply by 2: $(6 - 3)r + 4 = 26$
Subtract 4: $(6 - 3)r = 22$
Simplify: $3r = 22$
Divide by 3: $r = \dfrac{22}{3}$

---

10. **4**   For every four days it snowed, there were three days on which it did not snow. This means that it snowed on four out of every seven days. Since 4/7 of 28 is 16, it snowed on 16 days, and did not snow on $28 - 16 = 12$ days. Therefore, the number of days on which it snowed is $16 - 12 = 4$ greater than the number of days it did not snow.

---

11. **191**   7% of $200 = .07 \times 200 = 14$, so Jenna lost 14 points. But since she got 5 points back, she scored a total of $200 - 14 + 5 = 191$ points.

---

12. **1/3 or .333**   Since each term after the first is equal to the previous term times k, we can express the first four terms as $36, 36k, 36k^2, 36k^3$. Since we know that the fourth term is 4/3,

$$36k^3 = \frac{4}{3}$$

Divide by 36: $k^3 = \dfrac{4}{108} = \dfrac{1}{27}$

Take cube root of both sides: $k = \dfrac{1}{3}$

---

13. **11**   Begin by substituting $x = -3$ and $y = -21$ into the equation:
$$-21 = 2(-3)^2 + h(-3) - 6$$
Simplify: $-21 = 18 - 3h - 6$
Simplify: $-21 = 12 - 3h$
Subtract 12: $-33 = -3h$
Divide by -3: $11 = h$

---

14. **4.5 < b < 5.75**   If $10 < |4b - 8| < 15$, then either $10 < 4b - 8 < 15$ or $-15 < 4b - 8 < -10$. The first inequality should seem more likely to yield a positive b, which is what we're looking for.

Add 8:
Divide by 4:

$$10 < 4b - 8 < 15$$
$$18 < 4b < 23$$
$$4.5 < b < 5.75$$

Therefore any number greater than 4.5 and less than 5.75 will work.

---

15. **2/3 or .666 or .667**   Begin by solving the inequality for w:
$$2\frac{1}{2} < 5w < 3\frac{1}{2}$$

Express as improper fractions: $\dfrac{5}{2} < 5w < \dfrac{7}{2}$

Divide by 5: $\dfrac{5}{10} < w < \dfrac{7}{10}$

Therefore w must be a number between .5 and .7. But since $6w$ must be an integer, w must be a multiple of 1/6. The only multiple of 1/6 that is between .5 and .7 is $4/6 = .666$.

---

16. **2/5 or .4**   Start by examining the first equation:
$$s = 3m + s$$
Subtract s: $0 = 3m$
Divide by 3: $0 = m$
Since $m = 0$, the second equation becomes $5t = 2s$
Now, to find $\dfrac{t}{s}$, divide both sides by $5s$: $\dfrac{5t}{5s} = \dfrac{2s}{5s}$
Simplify: $\dfrac{t}{s} = \dfrac{2}{5}$

VOTING RESULTS OF REFERENDUM

	YES	NO
MONROE	600	900
BLACKSBURG	1400	m
TOTAL	2090	n

17. **1500**   Since we know that the percentage of Monroe voters who voted "no" is twice the percentage of Blacksburg voters who voted "no," it would be helpful to find what fraction of "no" voters from Monroe as a first step. Since 900 voted "no" from Monroe, out of a total of $600 + 900 = 1500$ voters, this fraction is $900/1500 = 3/5$. This is twice the fraction of "no" votes from Blacksburg, so that fraction must be 3/10. This means that

$$\frac{m}{m + 1400} = \frac{3}{10}$$

Cross-multiply: $10m = 3m + 4200$
Subtract $3m$: $7m = 4200$
Divide by 7: $m = 600$

Therefore the number of "no" votes from Blacksburg is 600, and the total number of "no" votes is 900 + 600 = 1500.

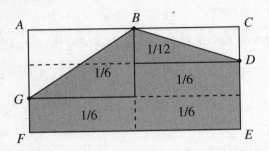

18. 3/4 or .75 The simplest way to analyze the diagram is perhaps to divide the rectangle into 6 congruent rectangles, as shown above. Notice that the shaded region then divides into 3 rectangles and 2 triangles (outlined in solid lines). Each of the smaller rectangles is 1/6 of the entire rectangle, and the smaller triangle is 1/12 of the entire rectangle, because it is 1/2 of one of these small rectangles. The larger triangle is 1/6 of the entire rectangle, because it is 1/2 of *two* of these smaller rectangles. Therefore, the total fraction that is shaded is 1/6 + 1/6 + 1/6 + 1/6 + 1/12 = 2/12 + 2/12 + 2/12 + 2/12 + 1/12 = 9/12 = 3/4 of the entire rectangle.

Section 7

1. C If one batch is 36 cookies, then to make 54 cookies we need to make 18 more, which is another 1/2 of a batch. Therefore, this would require $2\frac{1}{2} \times 1\frac{1}{2} = \frac{5}{2} \times \frac{3}{2} = \frac{15}{4} = 3\frac{3}{4}$ cups of flour.

2. B	$y = mx^2$
Plug in 32 for y and 4 for x:	$32 = m(4)^2$
Simplify:	$32 = 16m$
Divide by 16:	$2 = m$
Substitute into original equation:	$y = 2x^2$
Plug in 18 for y and solve for x:	$18 = 2x^2$
Divide by 2:	$9 = x^2$
Take the square root:	$3 = x$ or $-3 = x$

3. A Since the measure of any straight angle is 180°, angle *BAD* must have a measure of 180° − 40° − 90° = 50°. Since this angle is bisected, x must be half of 50, or 25.

4. B We can simplify any ratio by dividing the terms by the greatest common factor, but the two terms must be integers. Since 2.4 is not an integer, it would be helpful to multiply both terms by 10 first, in order to turn them both into integers. This gives us

24:50, but these terms have a common factor of 2. Dividing both terms by 2 gives us 12:25.

5. E Since line l is parallel to line m, the two angles indicated by the "Σ" (opposite interior angles) below must be equal. Therefore, the angle on the bottom left must measure $(a + b)°$.

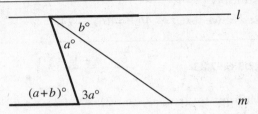

Since a straight angle measures 180°:	$3a + (a + b) = 180°$
Combine terms:	$4a + b = 180°$
Substitute 36 for b:	$4a + 36 = 180°$
Subtract 36:	$4a = 144°$
Divide by 4:	$a = 36°$

6. B Simply plug into the formula and simplify:

$$\langle m | 2m \rangle = \frac{m - 2m}{m + 2m} = \frac{-m}{3m} = -\frac{1}{3}.$$

7. C If a graph has the property that no two points on the graph have equal y-coordinates, then it "passes the horizontal line test." That is, any horizontal line that you draw through the graph will never touch more than one point. (Remember that a horizontal line in the xy-plane is just the set of all points that have a particular y-coordinate.) Notice that in each graph below, except that in (C), we can draw a horizontal line that touches more than one point.

(A)

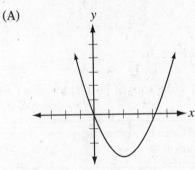

(B)

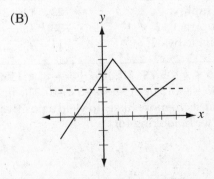

(C)

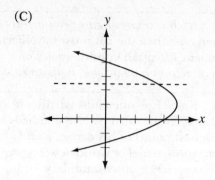

(D)

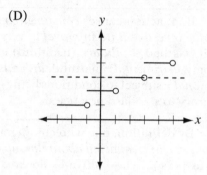

(E)

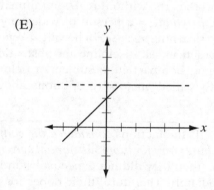

8. D If the probability that a randomly chosen marble will be black is $\frac{4}{9}$, then $\frac{4}{9}$ of the marbles are black so there are $\frac{4}{9} \times 72 = 32$ black marbles in a jar.

We want to add n black marbles to the jar so that $\frac{1}{2}$ of them are black. This means that $\frac{32+n}{72+n} = \frac{1}{2}$.

Cross-multiply:	$64 + 2n = 72 + n$
Subtract 64:	$2n = 8 + n$
Subtract n:	$n = 8$

9. A Since device D is the fourth device in the array, Gregory will inspect it as the 4th device, the 16th device, the 28th device, and so on. Notice that these numbers are all 4 greater than a multiple of 12. The only number among the choices that is 4 greater than a multiple of 12 is (A) 64, which is equivalent to $5(12) + 4$.

10. E The inequality should state what we know about this situation, which is that, after Kiara sells x boxes of cookies, she earns at least \$150. Therefore, we want to find an expression that represents how much money she has earned, and set that value greater than or equal to \$150. Since she has already sold 16 boxes, and each box sells for \$5, she has earned \$(16)(5). The additional x boxes she sells will earn her $5x$ more dollars. Therefore $(16) \cdot 5 + 5x \geq 150$.

11. C No matter what the graph of f looks like, the graph of $g(x) = f(x - 2)$ will always look like the graph of f shifted 2 units to the *right*. To see why, pick a number for x, like 4. According to the formula, $g(4) = f(4 - 2) = f(2)$. Think about what this means: $g(4)$ means the y-coordinate of the point on g that has an x-coordinate of 4, and $f(2)$ means the y-coordinate of the point on f that has an x-coordinate of 2. If these y-coordinates are the same, then the point on g is simply 2 units to the right of the point on f.

12. D Since you are given two equations, you might first think that, to find the value of $3mn$, you should solve the first equation for n, and then substitute and solve the next equation for m. If you try this and you are *very* careful, it will work, but (1) you will need a calculator to find the 8th root of 480 (which isn't super-easy), (2) this results in a very ugly-looking decimal value for n that you will need to round off, and (3) plugging in and solving for m also involves some ugly decimals. Remember, the SAT isn't about *calculation*, it's about *reasoning*.

Instead, first notice that $n^8 = (n^7)(n)$, which will help you to relate the two equations very elegantly.

	$n^8 = 480$
Substitute $n^8 = (n^7)(n)$:	$(n)(n^7) = 480$
Substitute $n^7 = 12m$:	$(n)(12m) = 480$
Simplify:	$12mn = 480$
Divide by 4 to find $3mn$:	$3mn = 120$

13. B According to the triangle inequality theorem, the length of any side of a triangle is always between the sum and the difference of the other sides. Therefore, $24 - 18 < PR < 24 + 18$. So PR is greater than 6 but less than 42. The least possible integer that fits is 7.

14. A If 15 grams of a solution is 20% salt, then it must contain $15 \times .20 = 3$ grams of salt. If x more grams of water are added to the solution, then there are $15 + x$ grams of solution, but still only 3 grams of salt (because we didn't add any more salt). Therefore the *fraction* of the solution, by weight, that is salt is $\frac{3}{15+x}$, but to express this as a percent we must multiply this fraction by 100% to get $\frac{3 \times 100}{15 + x}\%$.

15. **C** The probability of an event occurring

$$= \frac{\text{number of desired outcome}}{\text{total number of outcomes}}$$

Begin by finding out how many total arrangements of jackets are possible in these five cubbyholes. To make such an arrangement, you must make 5 decisions. First, you have 5 jackets to choose from to fill the first cubbyhole, then 4 left for the second, then 3 left for the third, and so on. This gives a total of $5 \times 4 \times 3 \times 2 \times 1 = 120$ possible arrangements of jackets.

In how many of these arrangements are the red and brown jackets each in one of the shaded cubby-holes? To count them, again notice that you must make 5 decisions. First fill the shaded cubbyholes. You have 2 options (red or brown) for the first shaded cubbyhole, and then 1 choice (the one that remains) for the other shaded cubbyhole. Then you can fill the others as before: there are 3 options for the next remaining cubbyhole, then 2 for the next, and 1 for the next. This gives a total of $3 \times 2 \times 2 \times 1 \times 1 = 12$ possible arrangements of jackets.

Of the 120 total possible arrangements, 12 of them give the desired outcome, so the probability of the event is $\frac{12}{120} = \frac{1}{10}$.

16. **B** It should not take much work to "guess and check" possible solutions: notice that $a = 2$, $b = 2$, $m = 2$, $n = 2$, and $p = 2$ works, because $(2 \times 2)^2 = (2)^2(2)^2$. Unfortunately, this solution is not helpful because all three statements are true *for this solution*, but this does not prove that the statements must *always* be true. Therefore, we should try to find *counterexamples* for these statements. For instance, can we find a solution in which a does *not* equal b? Sure: notice that $a = 2$, $b = 4$, $m = 3$, $n = 5$, and $p = 2$ could work, because $(2 \times 4)^3 = (2)^5(4)^2$. This proves that statement II is not necessarily true. Luckily, it is also a counterexample for statement I, because in this solution, $2m$ does not equal $n + p$. This eliminates choices (C), (D), and (E). What about statement III? We can check it logically: if $n = p$, then substituting in the equation $(ab)^m = a^n b^p$ gives us $(ab)^m = a^n b^n = (ab)^n$. If all of the unknowns are positive integers, this means that n must equal m.

Section 8

1. **E** The sentence states that the university must *accommodate the new students*, so the student population must have grown. This would logically force the university to *construct* temporary dormitories to accommodate them. *curtailment* = the act of imposing a restriction on something; *raze* = completely destroy; *correlation* = a mutual relationship between things

2. **C** If *feline images figure prominently in the tombs of pharaohs*, then the cat must have been *significant* to ancient Egyptian culture. *repudiates* = denies the truth of; *refutes* = disproves; *indispensable* = essential

3. **A** Since Rob questions whether *he could ever be more popular*, he must believe that he is at the *pinnacle* (highest point) of his career. *nadir* = lowest point; *paradigm* = a model or worldview; *inception* = starting point; *periphery* = outer boundary

4. **D** If an action causes *consumer confidence and corporate investment [to improve] in very short order*, then it has had a *salutary* (healthful) effect on the economy. *detrimental* = harmful; *dubious* = doubtful; *conditional* = subject to conditions being met; *perverse* = contrary to standard practice

5. **C** By definition, one who enjoys music yet cannot *converse in great detail about the subject* is a *dilettante* (a person who cultivates an area of interest, such as the arts, without real commitment or knowledge). *polymath* = a person of wide-ranging knowledge or learning; *recluse* = a hermit; *ascetic* = a person who practices self-discipline and abstention; *pundit* = an expert in a particular subject or field who is frequently called on to give opinions about it to the public

6. **D** If the factions *considered the conference as a launching point for more substantial agreements in the future*, then they did not expect substantial progress immediately. Therefore, their hopes for the conference were *qualified* (containing reservations) and they did not expect any *breakthroughs*. *poignant* = evoking keen emotions, usually sadness; *indifference* = lack of interest; *parsimony* = stinginess; *infirmity* = illness; *exorbitant* = unreasonably high; *headway* = significant progress

7. **B** Passage 1 focuses on the *scientific research [that] sheds a less sanguine and more cautionary light on the power of irrationality* (lines 10–11). Passage 2 focuses on intuitions about sports, particularly the dubious notion that *[a] game's final moments [are] more determinative of the outcome*.

8. **E** This sentence states that *what we call intuition is in fact the encroachment upon awareness of many ancient systems of unconscious processing*, that is, that our intuitive thoughts are actually *the intrusion of irrational thoughts into consciousness*.

9. **B** These two statements represent *contrasting recommendations about intuition*—the first suggests

that we should trust it, but the second suggests that we should not. The first comes from the authors of the *spate of recent popular books* by advocates of intuition, whereas the second derives from analysis of *scientific research* that *sheds a less sanguine (optimistic) and more cautionary light on the power of irrationality.*

---

10. A This sentence states that *often inchoate (rudimentary or unformed) thoughts from our unconscious are usually adorned by our rational minds with a veneer (an attractive decoration that disguises the true nature of something) of reason and meaning.* That is, *our minds rationalize (attempt to justify with plausible reasons, even if those reasons are not true) rudimentary information.*

---

11. C The passage defines *heuristics* as *the innate quick-and-dirty rules that humans use to process complex data in order to make rapid decisions* (lines 57–59). The best example of a heuristic among the choices, then, is *the process of deciding quickly whether or not an approaching person is friendly.*

---

12. E The author refers to the *hunter-gatherer* in his discussion of the claim that *in order to survive and reproduce, our ancestors often needed to process stimuli quickly* (lines 25–27) in order to, for instance, avoid getting eaten by tigers. Therefore, *human cognition developed to serve immediate survival needs.*

---

13. E In saying that *emotionally charged events tend to be viewed as disproportionately likely or relevant,* the author means that events that are *energized* with emotion tend to be more easily brought to mind.

---

14. A The author indicates that *few superstitious behaviors accompany fielding* because it is *reasonably routine* and *has a greater than 95 percent success rate* (lines 83–84). That is, *fielding is a relatively predictable activity.*

---

15. B This remark represents the author's own skeptical opinion of the practice of saving *one's best players...for the game's decisive moments.* Therefore it is the opinion of *a skeptical analyst.*

---

16. C In this paragraph, the author of Passage 2 is examining the *intuition* that *points scored at the end of a game matter more,* and, more generally, that any significant action by a team at the end of a game is more significant than the same action at the beginning or in the middle of the game. Therefore the best example of this phenomenon among the choices is (C) [*a*] *sportswriter* [*blaming*] *a team loss on a baseball player who struck out to end a game.*

---

17. B The author of Passage 2 demonstrates an *informed skepticism* toward the belief that intuitions are useful in his refutation of the belief that the *last basket made* (line 97) is the most important one in the game.

---

18. A The author of Passage 1 states that *(s)trong emotions tend to make events more memorable and hence more available to recall, so emotionally charged events tend to be viewed as disproportionately likely or relevant* (lines 64–67), so he would most likely bolster the claim that *cognitively the game's final moments seem more determinative of the outcome* (lines 99–101) by explaining that *the final moments of a game are frequently more exciting than the other moments of the game, and hence seem more relevant.*

---

19. A Passage 1 does discuss *a mistaken assumption* (in its refutation of the belief that *intuition is an untapped source of boundless power* (lines 2–3), *the work of professional researchers* (in its discussion of the work of Jonathan Haight and Daniel Kahneman), *social behavior* (lines 40–51), and *human emotions* (lines 36–39). However, it does not describe the procedures of a specific experiment as Passage 2 does in lines 114–120.

Section 9

1. C Phrases like *it being* and *being that* are nonstandard phrases that are often used to mean *because* in casual speech. To convey the relationship between a statement and its reason, we should use words like *since* or *because* (placed before the *reason*), or words like *therefore* or *so* (placed before the *statement*). Notice that this sentence already contains the conjunction *so* before the second clause, so there is no need to use *because* or *since* at the start of the sentence. Therefore the best choice is (C) *It is.*

---

2. D Since this sentence is making a comparison, it must follow the law of parallelism. Notice that the first task in the comparison is *playing a video basketball game,* so the second task should take a parallel form: *playing a real basketball game.*

---

3. C The original sentence is awkward and unclear because the pronoun *it* precedes its antecedent, *the old recipe.* Choice (C) most concisely fixes this problem by switching the places of the pronoun and antecedent.

---

4. E The original sentence contains two mistakes: *had turned* is in the wrong tense (it should be in the past tense, not the past perfect tense), and *myself* is in the wrong case (the context requires the objective case *me*, not the reflexive case *myself*). Choice (E) is the only one that makes both corrections.

---

5. **C**   The subjunctive verb in this sentence requires the past participle, *taken*, rather than the past tense verb *took*. Also, since the noun phrase *Jose and I* is the direct object of the verb, the pronoun should be in the objective case: *Jose and me*.

---

6. **C**   This sentence lists two things that oceanographers are studying, and therefore the two parts should have parallel phrasing. Since the first thing they are studying is *how the increased atmospheric concentration of gases…elevates the acidity*, the second should be phrased similarly: *how that acidity affects fish*. Choice (B) is close, but the verb *elevate* does not agree with its subject *concentration*.

7: **E**   The opening phrase, *Renowned as an expert in linguistics*, is an appositive modifying *Pinker*, so these two must be adjacent. Choices (A), (B), and (C) allow this appositive to dangle. Choice (D) is awkward and illogical, so choice (E) is best.

---

8. **B**   The original sentence contains a modifying phrase separated from the main clause by commas: *if not more so*. When such phrases are removed, the remaining sentence should still be grammatical and logical. However, removing this phrase leaves the unidiomatic phrase *as well-produced than*. Choices (C), (D), and (E) are unidiomatic.

---

9. **A**   The sentence is correct as written. This sentence is inverted, with the verb *is* taking the subject *formulation*. Choice (B) contains subject-verb disagreement, because the subject has been changed to

the plural *company policy and how it is formulated*. Choice (C) is illogical because *company policy being formulated* is not a *responsibility*. Choice (D) contains subject-verb disagreement, and choice (E) is illogical.

---

10. **B**   The original sentence violates the law of parallelism. Only choice (B) uses correct parallel structure, following the pattern *due to A or to B*, where the phrases in *A* and *B* take the same grammatical form.

---

11. **C**   The original sentence is a run-on, joining two independent clauses with only a comma. Choice (B) corrects the run-on problem, but it is illogical, since the law of parallelism suggests that the pronoun *it* refers to *the Internet*, thereby suggesting that it was invented both in the 1960s and the 1980s. Choice (E) also uses the ambiguous *it*. Choice (D) is illogical because the participle *being* takes *the internet* as its subject, which is nonsensical.

---

12. **A**   The sentence is correct as written.

---

13. **D**   In the original sentence, the pronoun *it* has no clear antecedent. Clearly it refers to Greece, but the sentence only refers to *the Greeks*, not Greece. Choice (C) makes a similar mistake. Semantically, only *Greece*, and not *the Greeks*, can be *one of the centers of world culture*, so we can also eliminate choices (B) and (E). Only choice (D) expresses a clear and grammatical idea.

---

14. **E**   This sentence begins with a participial phrase, so the subject of the main clause must be the subject of the participle. Since *the trophy* cannot be *beaming with pride*, the original sentence is incorrect, as are choices (B) and (C), for similar reasons. Choice (D) is awkward and illogical, so the best choice is (E).

PRACTICE TEST 4

ANSWER SHEET

Last Name:_____   First Name:_____

Date:_____   Testing Location:_____

Directions for Test

- Remove these answer sheets from the book and use them to record your answers to this test.
- This test will require 3 hours and 20 minutes to complete. Take this test in one sitting.
- The time allotment for each section is written clearly at the beginning of each section. This test contains six 25-minute sections, two 20-minute sections, and one 10-minute section.
- This test is 25 minutes shorter than the actual SAT, which will include a 25-minute "experimental" section that does not count toward your score. That section has been omitted from this test.
- You may take one short break during the test, of no more than 10 minutes in length.
- You may only work on one section at any given time.
- You must stop ALL work on a section when time is called.
- If you finish a section before the time has elapsed, check your work on that section. You may NOT work on any other section.
- Do not waste time on questions that seem too difficult for you.
- Use the test book for scratchwork, but you will receive credit only for answers that are marked on the answer sheets.
- You will receive one point for every correct answer.
- You will receive no points for an omitted question.
- For each wrong answer on any multiple-choice question, your score will be reduced by ¼ point.
- For each wrong answer on any "numerical grid-in" question, you will receive no deduction.

When you take the real SAT, you will be asked to fill in your personal information in grids as shown below.

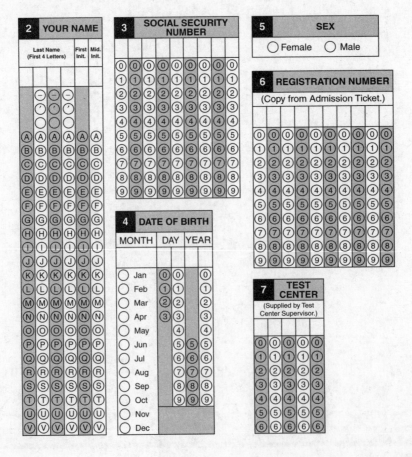

Start with number 1 for each new section. If a section has fewer questions than answer spaces, leave the extra answer spaces blank. Be sure to erase any errors or stray marks completely.

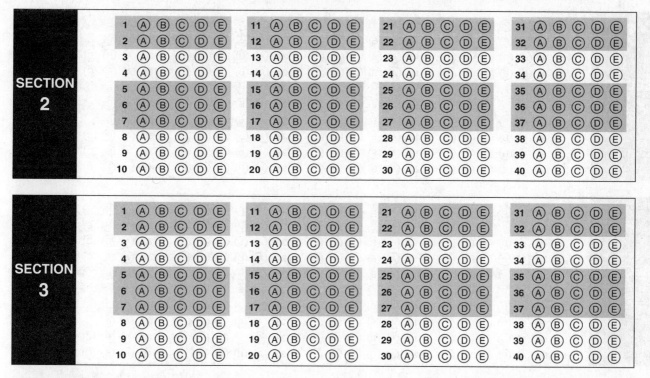

CAUTION Use the answer spaces in the grids below for Section 2 or Section 3 only if you are told to do so in your test book.

Student-Produced Responses ONLY ANSWERS ENTERED IN THE CIRCLES IN EACH GRID WILL BE SCORED. YOU WILL NOT RECEIVE CREDIT FOR ANYTHING WRITTEN IN THE BOXES ABOVE THE CIRCLES.

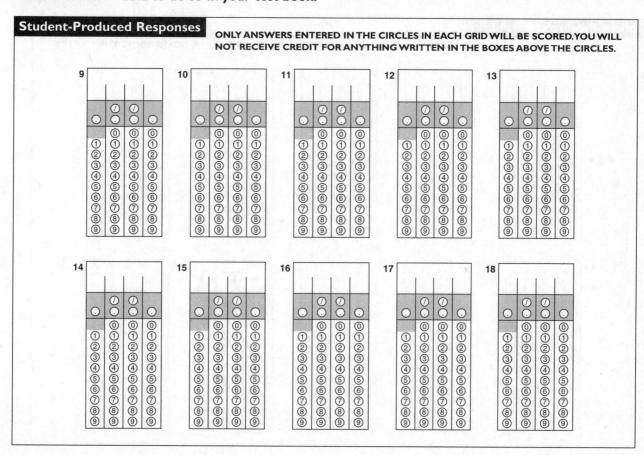

Start with number 1 for each new section. If a section has fewer questions than answer spaces, leave the extra answer spaces blank. Be sure to erase any errors or stray marks completely.

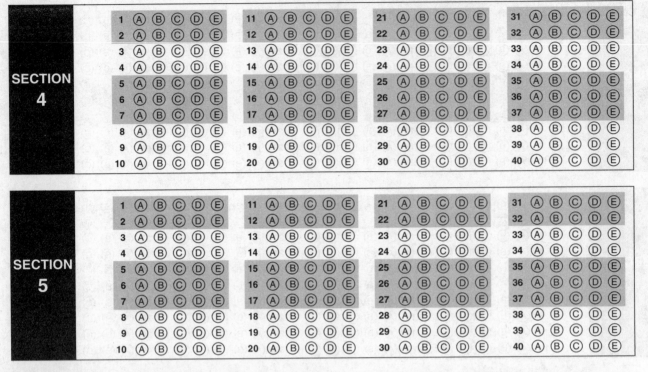

CAUTION   Use the answer spaces in the grids below for Section 4 or Section 5 only if you are told to do so in your test book.

Student-Produced Responses   ONLY ANSWERS ENTERED IN THE CIRCLES IN EACH GRID WILL BE SCORED. YOU WILL NOT RECEIVE CREDIT FOR ANYTHING WRITTEN IN THE BOXES ABOVE THE CIRCLES.

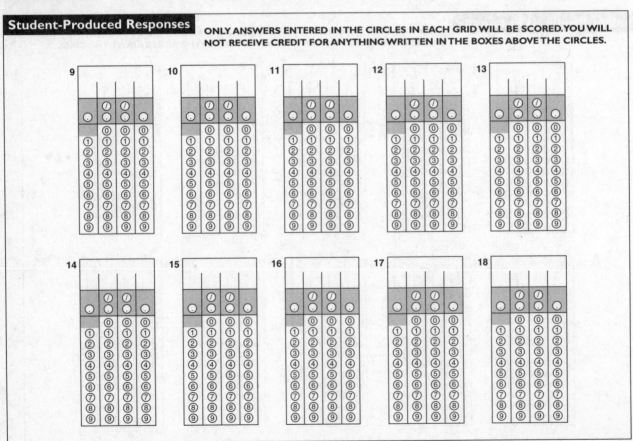

Start with number 1 for each new section. If a section has fewer questions than answer spaces,
leave the extra answer spaces blank. Be sure to erase any errors or stray marks completely.

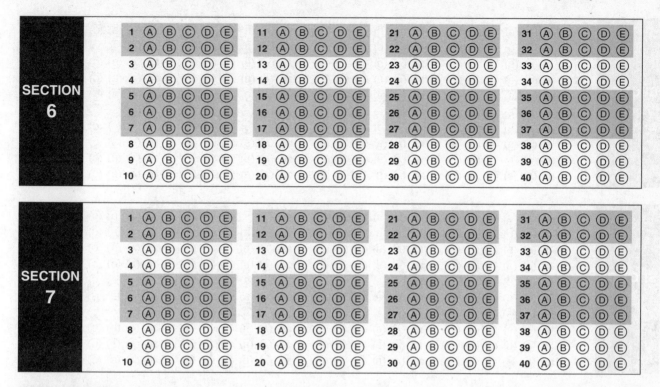

SECTION 6

SECTION 7

CAUTION   Use the answer spaces in the grids below for Section 6 or Section 7 only if you are
told to do so in your test book.

Student-Produced Responses   ONLY ANSWERS ENTERED IN THE CIRCLES IN EACH GRID WILL BE SCORED. YOU WILL
NOT RECEIVE CREDIT FOR ANYTHING WRITTEN IN THE BOXES ABOVE THE CIRCLES.

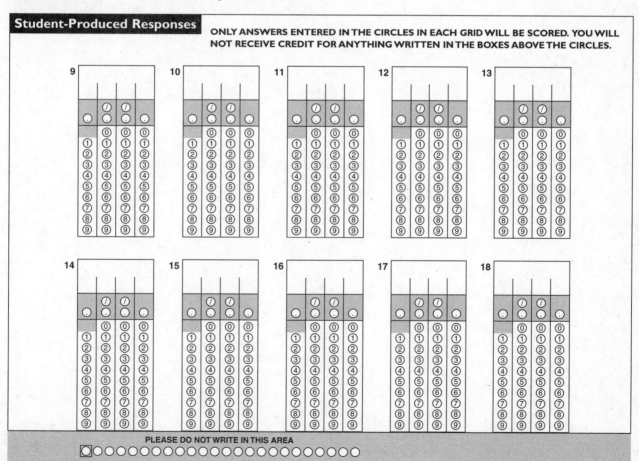

PLEASE DO NOT WRITE IN THIS AREA

Start with number 1 for each new section. If a section has fewer questions than answer spaces, leave the extra answer spaces blank. Be sure to erase any errors or stray marks completely.

SECTION 8

1 Ⓐ Ⓑ Ⓒ Ⓓ Ⓔ	11 Ⓐ Ⓑ Ⓒ Ⓓ Ⓔ	21 Ⓐ Ⓑ Ⓒ Ⓓ Ⓔ	31 Ⓐ Ⓑ Ⓒ Ⓓ Ⓔ
2 Ⓐ Ⓑ Ⓒ Ⓓ Ⓔ	12 Ⓐ Ⓑ Ⓒ Ⓓ Ⓔ	22 Ⓐ Ⓑ Ⓒ Ⓓ Ⓔ	32 Ⓐ Ⓑ Ⓒ Ⓓ Ⓔ
3 Ⓐ Ⓑ Ⓒ Ⓓ Ⓔ	13 Ⓐ Ⓑ Ⓒ Ⓓ Ⓔ	23 Ⓐ Ⓑ Ⓒ Ⓓ Ⓔ	33 Ⓐ Ⓑ Ⓒ Ⓓ Ⓔ
4 Ⓐ Ⓑ Ⓒ Ⓓ Ⓔ	14 Ⓐ Ⓑ Ⓒ Ⓓ Ⓔ	24 Ⓐ Ⓑ Ⓒ Ⓓ Ⓔ	34 Ⓐ Ⓑ Ⓒ Ⓓ Ⓔ
5 Ⓐ Ⓑ Ⓒ Ⓓ Ⓔ	15 Ⓐ Ⓑ Ⓒ Ⓓ Ⓔ	25 Ⓐ Ⓑ Ⓒ Ⓓ Ⓔ	35 Ⓐ Ⓑ Ⓒ Ⓓ Ⓔ
6 Ⓐ Ⓑ Ⓒ Ⓓ Ⓔ	16 Ⓐ Ⓑ Ⓒ Ⓓ Ⓔ	26 Ⓐ Ⓑ Ⓒ Ⓓ Ⓔ	36 Ⓐ Ⓑ Ⓒ Ⓓ Ⓔ
7 Ⓐ Ⓑ Ⓒ Ⓓ Ⓔ	17 Ⓐ Ⓑ Ⓒ Ⓓ Ⓔ	27 Ⓐ Ⓑ Ⓒ Ⓓ Ⓔ	37 Ⓐ Ⓑ Ⓒ Ⓓ Ⓔ
8 Ⓐ Ⓑ Ⓒ Ⓓ Ⓔ	18 Ⓐ Ⓑ Ⓒ Ⓓ Ⓔ	28 Ⓐ Ⓑ Ⓒ Ⓓ Ⓔ	38 Ⓐ Ⓑ Ⓒ Ⓓ Ⓔ
9 Ⓐ Ⓑ Ⓒ Ⓓ Ⓔ	19 Ⓐ Ⓑ Ⓒ Ⓓ Ⓔ	29 Ⓐ Ⓑ Ⓒ Ⓓ Ⓔ	39 Ⓐ Ⓑ Ⓒ Ⓓ Ⓔ
10 Ⓐ Ⓑ Ⓒ Ⓓ Ⓔ	20 Ⓐ Ⓑ Ⓒ Ⓓ Ⓔ	30 Ⓐ Ⓑ Ⓒ Ⓓ Ⓔ	40 Ⓐ Ⓑ Ⓒ Ⓓ Ⓔ

SECTION 9

1 Ⓐ Ⓑ Ⓒ Ⓓ Ⓔ	11 Ⓐ Ⓑ Ⓒ Ⓓ Ⓔ	21 Ⓐ Ⓑ Ⓒ Ⓓ Ⓔ	31 Ⓐ Ⓑ Ⓒ Ⓓ Ⓔ
2 Ⓐ Ⓑ Ⓒ Ⓓ Ⓔ	12 Ⓐ Ⓑ Ⓒ Ⓓ Ⓔ	22 Ⓐ Ⓑ Ⓒ Ⓓ Ⓔ	32 Ⓐ Ⓑ Ⓒ Ⓓ Ⓔ
3 Ⓐ Ⓑ Ⓒ Ⓓ Ⓔ	13 Ⓐ Ⓑ Ⓒ Ⓓ Ⓔ	23 Ⓐ Ⓑ Ⓒ Ⓓ Ⓔ	33 Ⓐ Ⓑ Ⓒ Ⓓ Ⓔ
4 Ⓐ Ⓑ Ⓒ Ⓓ Ⓔ	14 Ⓐ Ⓑ Ⓒ Ⓓ Ⓔ	24 Ⓐ Ⓑ Ⓒ Ⓓ Ⓔ	34 Ⓐ Ⓑ Ⓒ Ⓓ Ⓔ
5 Ⓐ Ⓑ Ⓒ Ⓓ Ⓔ	15 Ⓐ Ⓑ Ⓒ Ⓓ Ⓔ	25 Ⓐ Ⓑ Ⓒ Ⓓ Ⓔ	35 Ⓐ Ⓑ Ⓒ Ⓓ Ⓔ
6 Ⓐ Ⓑ Ⓒ Ⓓ Ⓔ	16 Ⓐ Ⓑ Ⓒ Ⓓ Ⓔ	26 Ⓐ Ⓑ Ⓒ Ⓓ Ⓔ	36 Ⓐ Ⓑ Ⓒ Ⓓ Ⓔ
7 Ⓐ Ⓑ Ⓒ Ⓓ Ⓔ	17 Ⓐ Ⓑ Ⓒ Ⓓ Ⓔ	27 Ⓐ Ⓑ Ⓒ Ⓓ Ⓔ	37 Ⓐ Ⓑ Ⓒ Ⓓ Ⓔ
8 Ⓐ Ⓑ Ⓒ Ⓓ Ⓔ	18 Ⓐ Ⓑ Ⓒ Ⓓ Ⓔ	28 Ⓐ Ⓑ Ⓒ Ⓓ Ⓔ	38 Ⓐ Ⓑ Ⓒ Ⓓ Ⓔ
9 Ⓐ Ⓑ Ⓒ Ⓓ Ⓔ	19 Ⓐ Ⓑ Ⓒ Ⓓ Ⓔ	29 Ⓐ Ⓑ Ⓒ Ⓓ Ⓔ	39 Ⓐ Ⓑ Ⓒ Ⓓ Ⓔ
10 Ⓐ Ⓑ Ⓒ Ⓓ Ⓔ	20 Ⓐ Ⓑ Ⓒ Ⓓ Ⓔ	30 Ⓐ Ⓑ Ⓒ Ⓓ Ⓔ	40 Ⓐ Ⓑ Ⓒ Ⓓ Ⓔ

ESSAY ESSAY

ESSAY
Time—25 minutes

Write your essay on separate sheets of standard lined paper.

The essay gives you an opportunity to show how effectively you can develop and express ideas. You should, therefore, take care to develop your point of view, present your ideas logically and clearly, and use language precisely.

Your essay must be written on the lines provided on your answer sheet—you will receive no other paper on which to write. You will have enough space if you write on every line, avoid wide margins, and keep your handwriting to a reasonable size. Remember that people who are not familiar with your handwriting will read what you write. Try to write or print so that what you are writing is legible to those readers.

Important Reminders:

- **A pencil is required for the essay.** An essay written in ink will receive a score of zero.
- **Do not write your essay in your test book.** You will receive credit only for what you write on your answer sheet.
- **An off-topic essay will receive a score of zero.**

You have twenty-five minutes to write an essay on the topic assigned below.

Think carefully about the quote and the assignment below.

Honesty is the cornerstone of all success, without which confidence and ability to perform shall cease to exist.

—Mary Kay Ash, founder of Mary Kay Cosmetics, Inc.

Assignment: **Are people bound to tell the truth at all times, or are there situations in which it is better to lie or tell only partial truths?** Plan and write an essay in which you develop your point of view on this issue. Support your position with reasoning and examples taken from your reading, studies, experience, or observations.

If you finish before time is called, you may check your work on this section only.
Do not turn to any other section of the test.

2   2   2   2   2   2

SECTION 2
Time—25 minutes
18 questions

> **Turn to Section 2 of your answer sheet to answer the questions in this section.**

Directions: This section contains two types of questions. You have 25 minutes to complete both types. For questions 1–8, solve each problem and decide which is the best of the choices given. Fill in the corresponding circle on the answer sheet. You may use any available space for scratchwork.

Notes

1. The use of a calculator is permitted.
2. All numbers used are real numbers.
3. Figures that accompany problems in this test are intended to provide information useful in solving the problems. They are drawn as accurately as possible EXCEPT when it is stated in a specific problem that the figure is not drawn to scale. All figures lie in a plane unless otherwise indicated.
4. Unless otherwise specified, the domain of any function f is assumed to be the set of all real numbers x for which $f(x)$ is a real number.

Reference Information

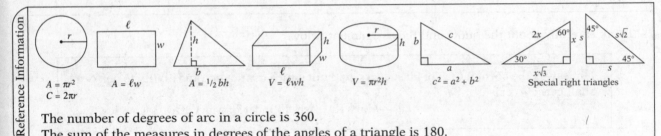

$A = \pi r^2$ $A = \ell w$ $A = \frac{1}{2}bh$ $V = \ell wh$ $V = \pi r^2 h$ $c^2 = a^2 + b^2$ Special right triangles
$C = 2\pi r$

The number of degrees of arc in a circle is 360.
The sum of the measures in degrees of the angles of a triangle is 180.

---

1.   If $x = 4$ and $3x + 2 = y$, what is the value of y?

   (A)   2
   (B)   4
   (C)   8
   (D)   14
   (E)   18

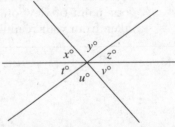

Note: Figure not drawn to scale.

2.   In the figure above, three lines intersect at a point. If $x = 71$ and $u = 64$, what is the value of z?

   (A)   40
   (B)   45
   (C)   50
   (D)   55
   (E)   60

GO ON TO THE NEXT PAGE ⟩

2   2   2   2   2   2

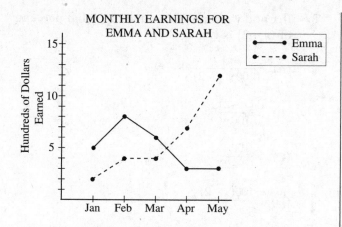

MONTHLY EARNINGS FOR
EMMA AND SARAH

3. According to the graph above, for which month did Sarah earn $400 more than Emma?

(A) January
(B) February
(C) March
(D) April
(E) May

4. If the average (arithmetic mean) of 3, 7, 10, and x is 7, then what is the median of 3, 7, 10, and x?

(A) 5.5
(B) 6
(C) 6.5
(D) 7
(E) 7.5

5. A home appliance salesperson makes a commission of p percent of the selling price of a dishwasher. Which of the following represents the commission, in dollars, on 4 dishwashers that sold for $650 each?

(A) $\dfrac{650p}{4}$

(B) $\dfrac{2{,}600}{p}$

(C) $26p$
(D) $650p$
(E) $2{,}600p$

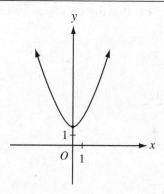

6. The graph of $y = x^2 + 2$ is shown above. If the graph were to be shifted up 2 and left 3, which of the following would be the equation of the transformed function?

(A) $y = (x - 3)^2 + 4$
(B) $y = (x + 3)^2 - 2$
(C) $y = (x + 3)^2 + 4$
(D) $y = (x - 3)^2 + 2$
(E) $y = (x + 3)^2 + 2$

GO ON TO THE NEXT PAGE

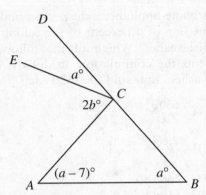

Note: Figure not drawn to scale.

7.   In the figure above, C lies on $\overline{DB}$. In terms of a, which of the following must be equivalent to b?

(A) $a - 15$

(B) $\dfrac{(a-7)}{2}$

(C) $\dfrac{(a+12)}{3}$

(D) $\dfrac{(a+7)}{2}$

(E) $\dfrac{(a-2)}{4}$

8.   If x and y are positive numbers, what percent of $(x - 2)$ is y?

(A) $\dfrac{1}{100y(x-2)}\%$

(B) $\dfrac{(x-2)}{100y}\%$

(C) $\dfrac{100y}{(x-2)}\%$

(D) $\dfrac{100(x-2)}{y}\%$

(E) $\left(\dfrac{100y}{x}-2\right)\%$

GO ON TO THE NEXT PAGE ⟹

$$2 \qquad 2 \qquad 2 \qquad 2 \qquad 2 \qquad 2$$

Directions: For Student-Produced Response questions 9–18, use the grids at the bottom of the answer sheet page on which you have answered questions 1–8.

Each of the remaining 10 questions requires you to solve the problem and enter your answer by marking the circles in the special grid, as shown in the examples below. You may use any available space for scratchwork.

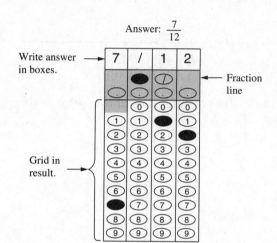

Answer: $\frac{7}{12}$

Write answer in boxes.

Fraction line

Grid in result.

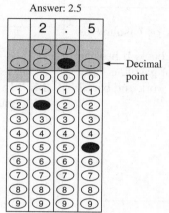

Answer: 2.5

Decimal point

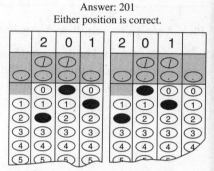

Answer: 201
Either position is correct.

Note: You may start your answers in any column, space permitting. Columns not needed should be left blank.

- Mark no more than one circle in any column.

- Because the answer sheet will be machine-scored, **you will receive credit only if the circles are filled in correctly.**

- Although not required, it is suggested that you write your answer in the boxes at the top of the columns to help you fill in the circles accurately.

- Some problems may have more than one correct answer. In such cases, grid only one answer.

- No question has a negative answer.

- **Mixed numbers** such as $3\frac{1}{2}$ must be gridded as 3.5 or 7/2. (If ⬚ is gridded, it will be interpreted as $\frac{31}{2}$ not $3\frac{1}{2}$.)

- **Decimal Answers:** If you obtain a decimal answer with more digits than the grid can accommodate, it may be either rounded or truncated, but it must fill the entire grid. For example, if you obtain an answer such as 0.6666..., you should record your result as .666 or .667. **A less accurate value such as .66 or .67 will be scored as incorrect.**

Acceptable ways to grid $^2/_3$ are:

GO ON TO THE NEXT PAGE ➡

2   2   2   2   2   2

9. If a circle has an area of 49π, what is the diameter of the circle?

10. Anna's car requires $5\frac{1}{2}$ gallons of gasoline to make 4 round-trips to work and back. If her car can travel 24 miles per gallon of gasoline, how far, in miles, is one round-trip to work and back?

11. If the function f is defined by $f(x) = \frac{2x-4}{3}$, for what value of x does $f(x) = 18$?

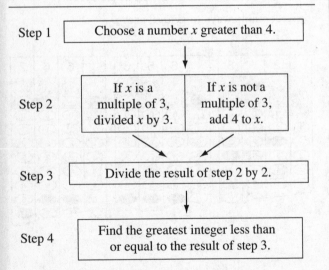

Step 1 | Choose a number x greater than 4.

Step 2 | If x is a multiple of 3, divided x by 3. | If x is not a multiple of 3, add 4 to x.

Step 3 | Divide the result of step 2 by 2.

Step 4 | Find the greatest integer less than or equal to the result of step 3.

12. In the chart above, if the number x chosen in step 1 is 17, what number will be the result in step 4?

13. One side of square A is $\frac{1}{2}$ the length of the <u>diagonal</u> of square B. If the area of square A is 16, what is the area of square B?

$$a + b - 4z = 500$$
$$a + b + 6z = 1200$$

14. In the system of equations above, what is the value of $a + b$?

$$-2, 1, 3, -1, 1 \ldots$$

15. A sequence is formed by repeating the five numbers above in the same order indefinitely. What is the sum of the first 37 terms of the sequence?

GO ON TO THE NEXT PAGE ⟩

16. Zander is a waiter at restaurant A and David is a waiter at restaurant B. Zander's weekly salary consists of $250 plus 15 percent of the total weekly tips received by all of the waiters at restaurant A. David's weekly salary consists of $50 plus 35 percent of the total weekly tips received by all of the waiters at restaurant B. If both restaurants received the same total amount in tips and Zander and David both had the same weekly salary for a particular week, what was that salary in dollars? (Disregard the dollar sign when giving your answer.)

17. The sphere above has a radius of 4 inches. What is the surface area, in square inches, of the smallest cube that can contain the entire sphere?

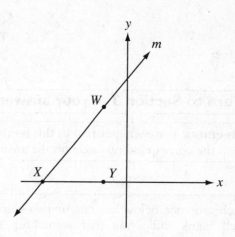

Note: Figure not drawn to scale

18. In the xy-coordinate plane above, $XY = 5$, $XW = 13$, and $\overline{YW}$ is perpendicular to $\overline{XY}$. If the coordinates of point Y are $(-4, 0)$, what is the y-intercept of line m?

STOP

If you finish before time is called, you may check your work on this section only. Do not turn to any other section of the test.

3   **3**   **3**   **3**   **3**   **3**

SECTION 3
Time—25 minutes
24 questions

Turn to Section 3 of your answer sheet to answer the questions in this section.

Directions: For each question in this section, select the best answer from among the choices given and fill in the corresponding circle on the answer sheet.

Each sentence below has one or two blanks, each blank indicating that something has been omitted. Beneath the sentence are five words or sets of words labeled A through E. Choose the word or set of words that, when inserted in the sentence, <u>best</u> fits the meaning of the sentence as a whole.

EXAMPLE:

Rather than accepting the theory unquestioningly, Deborah regarded it with -----.

(A) mirth
(B) sadness
(C) responsibility
(D) ignorance
(E) skepticism

1. Samantha sobbed uncontrollably and hid in the locker room, so ------- was she about having lost in the finals of the state championship.

   (A) pragmatic
   (B) querulous
   (C) dejected
   (D) jubilant
   (E) indifferent

2. Although her daughter's explanation for missing her curfew at first seemed -------, Rita was stunned, after further discussion, to find that it was -------.

   (A) dubious . . mistaken
   (B) illogical . . inconsistent
   (C) reasonable . . accurate
   (D) outlandish . . factual
   (E) histrionic . . awkward

3. Maya Lin was an undergraduate student at Yale when she was ------- to create the Vietnam Veterans Memorial in 1981; she was granted this honor when she won the public design competition for the memorial.

   (A) commissioned
   (B) conditioned
   (C) politicized
   (D) streamlined
   (E) aggregated

4. The tryptophan in the Thanksgiving turkey had ------- effect, inducing sleep in those who consumed it.

   (A) a mundane
   (B) a depreciatory
   (C) an invigorating
   (D) a lugubrious
   (E) a soporific

GO ON TO THE NEXT PAGE ⟹

3 3 3 3 3 3

5. Because Nevada receives only 7 inches of rainfall each year, the Nevada state government has put forth strong recommendations to its municipalities that urge them to practice ------- with water and to avoid ------- during the driest times of the year.

(A) latency . . dissemination
(B) complacency . . circumspection
(C) salvation . . discretion
(D) husbandry . . improvidence
(E) partisanship . . immoderation

6. Since the passage of the Endangered Species Act in the 1970s, the once dwindling Bald Eagle population in the continental United States has ------- to such an extent that it has been officially removed from the endangered species list.

(A) burgeoned
(B) waned
(C) attenuated
(D) dispersed
(E) conflated

7. After graduation, optimistic and energetic business school students frequently lose their -------; their enthusiasm ------- by their exposure to the harsh and often unpleasant realities of the business world.

(A) cynicism . . bedraggled
(B) ardor . . sullied
(C) mendacity . . dilapidated
(D) earnestness . . substantiated
(E) autonomy . . buttressed

8. Despite the ------- of published information about Clifford Longear's preadolescent years, Gilda was somehow able to put together ------- report that covered all aspects of his childhood in great detail.

(A) inadequacy . . a superficial
(B) complexity . . an unintelligible
(C) profusion . . an inclusive
(D) surfeit . . an obtuse
(E) dearth . . a comprehensive

The passages below are followed by questions based on their content. Answer the questions on the basis of what is <u>stated</u> or <u>implied</u> in the passage and in any introductory material that may be provided.

Questions 9–12 are based on the following passages.

PASSAGE 1

According to one theory of dinosaur extinction, a hypothetical dwarf star, dubbed
Line "Nemesis," approaches the earth every 26 million years and drags meteors that
5 collide with Earth and alter its climate. One of these extraterrestrial intruders likely struck the Yucatan Peninsula, lowered global temperatures, and killed off all of the dinosaurs 65 million years ago. This theory
10 accounts for the periodicity with which mass extinctions seemed to have occurred according to the fossil record. But geologists suggest that such dramatic cooling may have also resulted from a
15 massive volcanic eruption, called a "mantle plume, " from deep within the earth's mantle under the Indian Ocean that lasted over a million years.

PASSAGE 2

The dinosaurs could not have all gone
20 extinct 65 million years ago, because we see millions of them, or more properly millions of their ancestors, today. Most paleontologists believe that modern birds are the direct descendants of dinosaurs known as
25 maniraptorans, many of which evolved feathers not for flight but for warmth. The pressure to evolve feathers was a robust one, potentially affecting many different species, most likely because the climate was cooling
30 due to particulate debris from the impact of a meteor or volcanic eruptions. The climatic effect was so dramatic that all of the larger dinosaurs, like *Triceratops*, died out along with some of the feathered species, like
35 *Archaeopteryx.*

Passages 1 and 2: Printed with permission of Christopher Black, 2008.

GO ON TO THE NEXT PAGE ⟹

9. Unlike the "mantle plume" theory, the "Nemesis" theory helps to explain

  (A) the regularity with which mass extinctions have occurred
  (B) the evolution of maniraptorans into birds
  (C) the extinction of many dinosaur species
  (D) the dramatic drop in global temperatures
  (E) why certain species developed feathers

10. In line 27 the word "pressure" indicates

  (A) a physical weight
  (B) a deep-seated anxiety
  (C) an effective intimidation
  (D) a natural influence
  (E) a geological stress

11. All of the following phenomena are mentioned in both passages EXCEPT

  (A) global cooling
  (B) mass extinction
  (C) meteoric impact
  (D) volcanic activity
  (E) evolution

12. The authors of both passages would agree with all of the following statements about the mass extinction event of 65 million years ago EXCEPT

  (A) It involved a drop in global temperatures.
  (B) There is still debate among scientists about its cause.
  (C) No dinosaurs could adapt to the dramatic climate change.
  (D) It may have been influenced by volcanic activity.
  (E) The cause may have had extraterrestrial origins.

GO ON TO THE NEXT PAGE →

Questions 13–24 are based on the following passage.

The following is excerpted from a book that discusses the history of weather forecasting in the United States.

They usually save it for last or just about last—like dessert or like the announcement
Line of best picture at the Academy Awards. It's the part of the broadcast more people watch
5 than any other. It's the silliest and longest-running joke on air. What else could "it" be but our national lullabye—the nightly television weather forecast?

It's amazing how much history television
10 weather forecasting has generated in just half a century. Even more amazing is the impact of this brief history—how radically it has altered our relationship with the elements. If you're a weather buff of any
15 sort, you probably can't even conceive of weather without television. We might as well have video screens hanging from the sky.

Considering how wild and crazy it was to become, television weather got off to a sober
20 start. In the first few years after the war, military veterans, tweedy old professors of meteorology, and former Weather Bureau personnel barely cracked a smile as they stood in front of their wispy little maps and
25 droned on about fronts and pressure systems. But this crew got the ax pretty fast, and once they were gone, television weather reports turned to show biz. Weather was no longer just news: now it was also, and
30 sometimes primarily, entertainment—slapstick when the weather was calm and dull; high drama when major storms hit; tragedy when the elements destroyed human life and property. Uncle Wetherbee, a
35 cartoon character who sported a handlebar mustache, helped New York's Tex Antoine chuckle out his daily forecast. In Chicago paper cutouts of Susanna South Wind battled it out with Nanook North Wind. Rain or
40 shine, snowstorm or heat wave, the weather was relentlessly cute from coast to coast.

Why the glitz and shtick and antics? Tex Antoine said it laid a nice "sugarcoating on a rather dull subject," and there's something to

45 that. The puppets and doodles and smiling women brought weather "to life" as they say—and back in the old days before satellite loops, swirling maps, and zippy color graphics, there weren't very many lively
50 options. Gimmicks were a way for weather forecasters to "distinguish themselves from the crowd," according to Chicago forecaster Tom Skilling.

All true enough. But I also think that
55 television tapped into an essential absurdity at the heart of forecasting. There is the built-in risk factor that the forecast will be wrong and the forecaster will come off looking like a fool. There is the widespread
60 assumption, lingering from the age of superstition, that the weather is by nature perverse, vindictive, irascible, or downright cruel—and that anybody who gets up and claims to understand it must be touched
65 with these qualities as well. There is our unconscious, illogical, but nonetheless deep-seated tendency to blame the weatherman for whatever type of weather we don't want. Government forecasters can hide
70 behind their supercomputers and numerical models—but the television weathermen are right there in our faces night after night. The clowning is thus a kind of protective coloring, a disguise that turns our suspicion
75 into laughter. "Here is some nice guy who gets up and stick his neck out day after day," says Allan Eustis, who worked as a television meteorologist for twenty-three years. "The audience is sitting there just waiting for him
80 to be wrong. Maybe it's human nature to laugh at someone who's trying to be a shaman about the weather. There's the presumptuousness of announcing, 'Here's my forecast.' The bottom line is, it's humbling to
85 forecast." As journalist Jay Rosen wrote in a recent essay in Harper's magazine, "Alone among experts on television, the weatherman is constantly being humbled by events. His outstanding trait is usually a sense of
90 humor...In a sense, the weather on television is one long joke." And not always in the best taste either. Tom Skilling finds the

GO ON TO THE NEXT PAGE

Excerpted from *Braving the Elements: The Stormy History of American Weather* by David Laskin. © 1996, p 175–178. Used with permission of Random House, Inc.

3   **3**   **3**   **3**   **3**   **3**

comedy tradition rather strange given the severity of America's weather: "Isn't it odd
95 that fun and games got associated with tele-vision weather reporting and not with sports, which after all is about grown human beings playing games with balls? Sports is big busi-ness and taken very seriously, while
100 weather—which can actually kill people—has been presented as something of a joke on the air."

Shaman or fool, the television forecaster has become a fixture of our media-driven
105 global village. He or she has made weather not only amusing but intimate, taking highs and lows, jet streams and occluded fronts into our living rooms and bedrooms. Doing the weather can be a career path to
110 stardom—think David Letterman, who began his life on the air as the weathercaster for WLWI-TV in Indianapolis. These people become as familiar to us as our friends. We rely on them. We judge them. We jeer them.
115 And we just keep watching them. We really have put the weather in their hands.

13. In line 2, "dessert" is used as an example of something that is

(A) generally unhealthful
(B) occasionally trivial
(C) frequently avoided
(D) often expensive
(E) usually savored

14. The question in lines 6–8 serves primarily to

(A) inquire into a cultural mystery
(B) introduce the general topic of discussion
(C) inject humor into an otherwise sober analysis
(D) criticize a particular point of view
(E) summarize a controversy

15. In line 14, "elements" most nearly means

(A) essential components
(B) atmospheric conditions
(C) procedural steps
(D) philosophical principles
(E) cultural aspects

16. The "military veterans" (line 21) are charac-terized primarily as being

(A) intrepid
(B) monotonous
(C) comical
(D) senile
(E) untamed

17. Unlike the final sentence of the third para-graph ("Rain or shine...from coast to coast"), the sentence in lines 39–41 ("Weather was no longer...life and property") suggests that weather forecasts are sometimes

(A) grave
(B) cheerful
(C) tedious
(D) jocular
(E) inaccurate

18. The battle mentioned in lines 37–39 ("In Chicago...Nanook North Wind") is best described as

(A) a technical dispute between coworkers
(B) a bitter fight between former employees and new employees
(C) a playful exchange between characters
(D) a friendly rivalry between forecasters from different cities
(E) a disagreement about how best to present weather forecasts

GO ON TO THE NEXT PAGE

3   **3**   **3**   **3**   **3**   **3**

19. The "absurdity" mentioned in line 55 lies primarily in the combination of

(A) confidence and uncertainty
(B) the tragic and the humorous
(C) the public and the private
(D) the logical and the illogical
(E) acceptance and dismissal

20. In lines 64–65, "touched with" most nearly means

(A) tainted by
(B) annoyed by
(C) blessed with
(D) compassionate toward
(E) handled by

21. The passage indicates that "supercomputers and numerical models" (lines 70–71) are used to

(A) enliven the presentations of forecasters
(B) ensure highly accurate forecasts
(C) make television forecasters appear more professional
(D) provide cover for inaccurate predictions
(E) distract viewers of television forecasts

22. The comments by Allan Eustis in lines 75–85 suggest that he believes that viewers of television weather forecasts

(A) expect to be entertained by forecasters and their antics
(B) believe that forecasting is a very serious task
(C) are humbled by the technical aspects of meteorology
(D) are more interested in the accuracy of forecasts than they used to be
(E) are not sympathetic to television meteorologists

23. Tom Skilling's comments in lines 94–102 criticize weather forecasts as being

(A) all too frequently unreliable
(B) not always entertaining
(C) often inappropriately flippant
(D) sometimes excessively solemn
(E) subject to the whims of big business

24. In lines 106–107, "high and lows" refer to

(A) emotional vicissitudes
(B) stages of a professional career
(C) attitudes toward a performance
(D) weather phenomena
(E) aspects of a culture

STOP

If you finish before time is called, you may check your work on this section only. Do not turn to any other section of the test.

4 4 4 4 4 4

SECTION 4
Time—25 minutes
35 questions

Turn to Section 4 of your answer sheet to answer the questions in this section.

Directions: For each question in this section, select the best answer from among the choices given and fill in the corresponding circle on the answer sheet.

The following sentences test correctness and effectiveness of expression. Part of each sentence or the entire sentence is underlined; beneath each sentence are five ways of phrasing the underlined material. Choice A repeats the original phrasing; the other four choices are different. Select the choice that completes the sentence most effectively.

In making your selection, follow the requirements of standard written English; that is, pay attention to grammar, choice of words, sentence construction, and punctuation. Your selection should result in the most effective sentence—clear and precise, without awkwardness or ambiguity.

EXAMPLE:

The children <u>couldn't hardly believe their eyes</u>.

(A) couldn't hardly believe their eyes
(B) could hardly believe their eyes
(C) would not hardly believe their eyes
(D) couldn't nearly believe their eyes
(E) couldn't hardly believe his or her eyes

Ⓐ ● Ⓒ Ⓓ Ⓔ

---

1. The harmful effects that excessive drinking can have on the liver <u>is increasingly well publicized</u>.

    (A) is increasingly well publicized
    (B) are increasing in better publicity
    (C) are increasingly well publicized
    (D) is more and more well publicized
    (E) has increased in better publicity

2. Airplanes are able to climb and maintain altitude by utilizing a combination of the Bernoulli effect and momentum transfer to generate <u>lift, this is generated primarily by the wing of the aircraft</u>.

    (A) lift, this is generated primarily by the wing of the aircraft
    (B) lift, which is generated primarily by the wing of the aircraft
    (C) lift; this generated primarily by the wing of the aircraft
    (D) lift, the wing of the aircraft primarily having generated it
    (E) lift, which the wing of the aircraft primarily generated

GO ON TO THE NEXT PAGE ⟶

3. <u>Reading my shopping list aloud</u> usually helps me remember it better.

   (A) Reading my shopping list aloud
   (B) To read my shopping list aloud, this
   (C) I read my shopping list aloud, it
   (D) My shopping list, read aloud,
   (E) If one reads my shopping list aloud it

4. We wanted to hire a babysitter who was able to work flexible hours, display patience with a crying child, and, above all, <u>she must have</u> fun playing with children.

   (A) she must have
   (B) she should have
   (C) have
   (D) having
   (E) be able to have

5. <u>The ice-skating partners, who were never finishing higher than seventh place,</u> surprised their coaches by finally winning a competition.

   (A) The ice-skating partners, who were never finishing higher than seventh place,
   (B) The ice-skating partners, who had never finished higher than seventh place,
   (C) Having never finished higher than seventh place as ice-skating partners,
   (D) The ice-skating partners never finished higher than seventh place,
   (E) Never finishing higher than seventh place, the skating partners has

6. The oldest known civilization in the Western Hemisphere, the Norte Chico civilization <u>having comprised</u> many interconnected settlements leading to the Peruvian coast.

   (A) having comprised
   (B) comprising
   (C) comprised
   (D) was comprising of
   (E) had been comprised

7. Walking together in the park, <u>it surprised us to see an a capella group performing on the green</u>.

   (A) it surprised us to see an a capella group performing on the green
   (B) an a capella group performing on the green surprised us
   (C) we were surprised about our seeing an a capella group on the green performing
   (D) we were surprised in seeing an a capella group performing on the green
   (E) we were surprised to see an a capella group performing on the green

8. Mario Andretti's name is synonymous <u>to</u> auto-racing; he has won Race Car Driver of the Year in three different decades.

   (A) to
   (B) of
   (C) with
   (D) in
   (E) for

9. <u>The Treaty of Versailles, which formally ended the First World War, is blamed by some historians for the eventual outbreak of World War II.</u>

   (A) The Treaty of Versailles, which formally ended the First World War, is blamed by some historians for the eventual outbreak of World War II.
   (B) Blamed by some historians for the eventual outbreak of World War II was the Treaty of Versailles, having formally ended the First World War.
   (C) The Treaty of Versailles is blamed by some historians for the eventual outbreak of World War II, which formally ended the First World War.
   (D) The Treaty of Versailles, being as it formally ended the First World War, is blamed by some historians for the eventual outbreak of World War II.
   (E) Some historians blame the Treaty of Versailles, which formally ended the First World War, as the eventual outbreak of World War II.

GO ON TO THE NEXT PAGE ⟶

4   **4**   **4**   **4**   **4**   **4**

10. Cubism was a 20th century art movement that revolutionized European painting and sculpture, it inspired also related movements in music and literature.

(A) Cubism was a 20th century art movement that revolutionized European painting and sculpture, it inspired also

(B) Cubism, a 20th century art movement that revolutionized European painting and sculpture, also inspired

(C) Cubism, a 20th century art movement that revolutionized European painting and sculpture, having also inspired

(D) A 20th century art movement revolutionizing European painting and sculpture, therefore Cubism also inspired

(E) Cubism revolutionized European painting and sculpture, being a 20th century art movement also inspiring

11. Known for his slow, monotone delivery of deeply philosophical jokes, Steven Wright having been considered to be one of the most underrated comics of all time.

(A) Known for his slow, monotone delivery of deeply philosophical jokes, Steven Wright having been considered to be one of the most underrated comics of all time

(B) Considered to be one of the most underrated comics of all time, Steven Wright's slow, monotone delivery of deeply philosophical jokes is what he is known for

(C) Steven Wright, who is known for his slow, monotone delivery of deeply philosophical jokes, is considered to be one of the most underrated comics of all time

(D) One of the most underrated comics of all time, known for his slow, monotone delivery of deeply philosophical jokes is Steven Wright

(E) Steven Wright is considered to be one of the most underrated comics of all time, who is known for his slow, monotone delivery of deeply philosophical jokes

GO ON TO THE NEXT PAGE

4   4   4   4   4   4

The following sentences test your ability to recognize grammar and usage errors. Each sentence contains either a single error or no error at all. No sentence contains more than one error. The error, if there is one, is under-lined and lettered. If the sentence contains an error, select the one underlined part that must be changed to make the sentence correct. If the sentence is correct, select choice E. In choosing answers, follow the requirements of standard written English.

EXAMPLE:

By the time <u>they reached</u> the halfway point
           A
<u>in the race</u>, <u>most of the runners</u> <u>hadn't hardly</u>
   B   C   D
begun to hit their stride. <u>No error</u>
             E

Ⓐ Ⓑ Ⓒ ● Ⓔ

---

12. The forecasts for the company suggested that

not only was its client base <u>growing</u>
                  A
<u>more stronger</u>, but also <u>its</u> outlook for
   B   C
expansion <u>was improving</u>. <u>No error</u>
       D   E

13. Senator Fred Thompson, a <u>member of</u> the
                   A
Republican party, <u>has begun</u> his career
          B
<u>as a lawyer</u> but went on <u>to become</u> a politician.
   C   D
<u>No error</u>
  E

14. Because of its savory sauce <u>and its</u> elegant
                A
presentation, the chicken and broccoli at

Kudeta <u>received</u> a better review
      B
<u>in the Dining Guide</u> than
       C
<u>did Hunan Garden</u>. <u>No error</u>
    D   E

15. The driver of the tow-truck <u>informed us</u> that
                  A
to safely jump-start an engine, we <u>must not only</u>
                   B
avoid connecting the negative end of the cable

to the carburetor, <u>and also</u> avoid touching the
            C
positive end of the cable <u>to</u> anything metal.
              D
<u>No error</u>
  E

16. <u>Known for</u> <u>their</u> hunting skill, the heron
    A   B
<u>feeds on</u> fish, frogs, and crustaceans that it
  C
<u>grabs</u> with its spear-like beak. <u>No error</u>
  D   E

17. <u>While visiting</u> my grandparents in Amsterdam,
     A
I <u>saw</u> an impressive model of the Rotterdam
   B
library <u>roaming</u> through the <u>various exhibits</u>
       C   D
at the Madurodam. <u>No error</u>
           E

GO ON TO THE NEXT PAGE ⟩

4   4   4   4   4   4

18. Recent polls <u>have shown</u> that the mayor's
                        A
improper handling of the tax hike <u>angered</u> a
                                         B
<u>surprising</u> large <u>number of</u> voters. <u>No error</u>
     C   D   E

19. Because the hospital emergency room was

clearly <u>understaffed</u> and the entrance bay
             A

<u>overran</u> by arriving ambulances, the patients
   B

in the waiting room knew they <u>would not see</u>
                                      C

the doctors <u>for a long time</u>. <u>No error</u>
                  D   E

20. When Victoria Woodhull <u>was selected</u> by the
                                   A
Equal Rights Party to be <u>its</u> candidate in the
                              B
1872 election, <u>she became</u> the first woman
                     C
<u>to run</u> for President of the United States.
   D
<u>No error</u>
   E

21. When Jerry Lee Lewis recorded *Great Balls of*

Fire in 1957, <u>it</u> <u>instantly established</u> himself
                   A   B
as one of the <u>greatest musicians</u> of <u>his time</u>.
                     C   D
<u>No error</u>
   E

22. The magnet high school <u>differs from</u> other
                                   A
high schools, <u>such as</u> Joel Barlow High and
                   B
Staples High, <u>in that</u> its students are so <u>widely</u>
                   C   D
spread out geographically. <u>No error</u>
                                 E

23. Marisa's senior thesis argued that workers in

border nations <u>struggle</u> because <u>his or her</u>
                    A   B
wages barely <u>keep pace with</u> the <u>rising</u> cost of
                    C   D
living. <u>No error</u>
            E

24. When the office manager <u>announces</u> his weekly
                                   A
sales assignments, <u>there is</u> <u>rarely</u> any
                         B   C
opposition <u>against</u> these decisions. <u>No error</u>
                D   E

25. The math team, <u>which</u> included <u>Tom and me</u>,
                         A   B
<u>was</u> stuck at the airport overnight <u>because of</u>
   C   D
inclement weather. <u>No error</u>
                         E

GO ON TO THE NEXT PAGE →

26. At the concert, Julie <u>enjoyed listening to</u> Yo-Yo
                           A
    Ma's passionate cello music, <u>which she</u>
                                  B
    thought was <u>even more inspired</u>
                       C
    <u>than</u> Jacqueline du Pre. <u>No error</u>
       D   E

27. <u>After</u> nearly 70 years <u>at the bottom</u> of the
    A   B
    ocean, the lost storage containers from the

    Thorold, a Canadian merchant ship that was

    torpedoed during the Second World War,

    <u>is being</u> <u>brought to</u> the surface. <u>No error</u>
       C   D   E

28. A dance that <u>evolved</u> in Buenos Aires at the end
                    A
    of the 19th <u>century, the tango</u> probably <u>derives in</u>
                   B   C
    the milonga, a <u>lively</u> Argentinean dance.
                      D
    <u>No error</u>
       E

29. Michael Jordan, Wayne Gretzky, Jim Brown—

    each <u>of these athletes</u> <u>was</u> considered to be
            A   B
    the <u>best</u> at his sport at the time <u>they were</u>
            C   D
    playing. <u>No error</u>
                 E

GO ON TO THE NEXT PAGE

Directions: The following passage is an early draft of an essay. Some parts of the passage need to be rewritten.

Read the passage and select the best answers for the questions that follow. Some questions are about particular sentences or parts of sentences and ask you to improve sentence structure or word choice. Other questions ask you to consider organization and development. In choosing answers, follow the requirements of standard written English.

Questions 30–35 are based on the following passage.

(1) My parents used to put olives on everything. (2) Salads, pizza, pasta, chicken, even some desserts. (3) In those days we used to eat many black olives before they got the high fat content bad name. (4) I never ate green olives. (5) For some reason, the little pimentos that protrude out of them turned me off.

(6) But then, many years later, I actually visited Greece, where I was first introduced to the green olive I had always resisted. (7) At a market in Athens, I found a vendor selling dozens of different kinds of olives. (8) Each type having been made with a different type of vinegar, spices or mixed with different vegetables including small onions or even little pickled carrots. (9) How had I never tried green olives before? (10) I was hooked.

(11) Now I find it hard to believe that I ever had such bad thoughts about green olives. (12) They are even better than black olives. (13) I put them on everything! (14) I also put pepper on most of the food that I eat. (15) When I have children, I will definitely expose them to green olives at a young age so that they don't miss out on them for as long as I did.

30. Which of the following, if inserted before sentence 1, would make a good introduction to the essay?

(A) Growing up as part of a Greek American family that takes its cuisine very seriously, I was exposed heavily to many of the classic Greek foods: olives, feta cheese, and stuffed grape leaves to name a few.
(B) The olive tree is among the oldest known cultivated trees in the world.
(C) In the past several hundred years the olive has spread to North and South America, Japan, New Zealand and Australia.
(D) My experience with olives started when I was very young.
(E) People living in the Mediterranean area who use olive oil as their main source of fat have surprisingly low susceptibility to heart disease.

31. Which of the following is the best version of the ideas conveyed in sentences 1 and 2 (reproduced below)?

My parents used to put olives on everything. Salads, pizza, pasta, chicken, even some desserts.

(A) (As it is now)
(B) My parents used to put olives on everything; salads, pizza, pasta, chicken, even some desserts.
(C) My parents used to put olives on everything, salads, pizza, pasta, chicken, even some desserts.
(D) My parents used to put olives on everything: salads, pizza, pasta, chicken, and even some desserts.
(E) My parents used to put olives on everything; including salads, pizza, pasta, chicken, even some desserts.

GO ON TO THE NEXT PAGE

4   4   4   4   4   4

32. In context, which of the following is the best version of the underlined portion of sentence 3 (reproduced below)?

In those days we used to eat many black olives before they got the high fat content bad name.

(A) (As it is now)
(B) In those days, before having found the high fat content in black olives, we used to eat many of them.
(C) Before black olives were considered unhealthy due to high fat content, we ate lots of them.
(D) Until black olives had a high fat content we used to eat many of them.
(E) Black olives were consumed in high numbers before the high fat content bad name was given.

33. All of the following devices are used by the writer of the passage EXCEPT

(A) sentence length variation
(B) personal narration
(C) detailed description
(D) rhetorical question
(E) metaphor

34. In context, what is the best way to deal with sentence 8?

(A) Change "mixed" to "mixing."
(B) Insert "However" at the beginning.
(C) Change "having been" to "was."
(D) Delete "including small onions or even little pickled carrots."
(E) Change "made with" to "made for."

35. The final paragraph would be improved by the deletion of which sentence?

(A) Sentence 11
(B) Sentence 12
(C) Sentence 13
(D) Sentence 14
(E) Sentence 15

STOP

If you finish before time is called, you may check your work on this section only. Do not turn to any other section of the test.

5 5 5 5 5 5

SECTION 5
Time—25 minutes
24 questions

Turn to Section 5 of your answer sheet to answer the questions in this section.

Directions: For each question in this section, select the best answer from among the choices given and fill in the corresponding circle on the answer sheet.

Each sentence below has one or two blanks, each blank indicating that something has been omitted. Beneath the sentence are five words or sets of words labeled A through E. Choose the word or set of words that, when inserted in the sentence, <u>best</u> fits the meaning of the sentence as a whole.

EXAMPLE:

Rather than accepting the theory unquestioningly, Deborah regarded it with -----.

(A) mirth
(B) sadness
(C) responsibility
(D) ignorance
(E) skepticism

---

1. Marisa is a ------- director: she has directed thrillers, romances, comedies, and dramas.

(A) mediocre
(B) laconic
(C) versatile
(D) demonstrative
(E) lethargic

2. Improvements in the ------- of data transfer in the 21st century have ------- mobile communication for business travelers.

(A) proficiency . . transcended
(B) efficiency . . revolutionized
(C) aggregation . . degenerated
(D) aesthetics . . streamlined
(E) manifestation . . qualified

3. Unable to eat in the hours leading up to her operation, Silvia could only enjoy her sister's birthday feast -------, watching her family members consume the delicious food.

(A) sporadically
(B) gluttonously
(C) meticulously
(D) munificently
(E) vicariously

4. While accepting the Arthur Ashe Courage and Humanitarian award in March of 1993, Jim Valvano gave a ------- speech that moved the entire audience to tears.

(A) mundane
(B) hackneyed
(C) spare
(D) poignant
(E) bucolic

GO ON TO THE NEXT PAGE

5. The director complained that the song origi-
    nally written for the mournful funeral scene
    was too ------- and that it should be replaced
    by music that was a bit more -------.

    (A) melancholic . . lugubrious
    (B) buoyant . . doleful
    (C) upbeat . . sprightly
    (D) voluble . . inchoate
    (E) tedious . . bombastic

The passages below are followed by questions based on their content. Answer the
questions on the basis of what is <u>stated</u> or
<u>implied</u> in the passage and in any introduc-
tory material that may be provided.

Questions 6–7 are based on the following passage.

   If you stare at a checkerboard you can see it
   as black on red, or red on black, as series of
Line horizontal, vertical or diagonal steps that
   recede or protrude. The longer you look the
 5 more patterns you can trace, and the more
   certain it becomes that there is no single
   way of looking at the board. So it is with
   political issues. There is no obvious cleavage
   that everyone recognizes. Many patterns
10 appear in the national life. The Progressives
   say the issue is between "the privileged" and
   "the people"; the Socialists, that it is between
   the "working class" and the "master class."

6. The first two sentences serve primarily to
    present a

    (A) psychological controversy
    (B) theory of art
    (C) visual analogy
    (D) geometric theorem
    (E) political position

7. In line 8 "cleavage" most nearly means

    (A) social division
    (B) visual impression
    (C) optical illusion
    (D) moral value
    (E) emotional attachment

Questions 8–9 are based on the following passage.

   Social history sometimes suffers from the
   reproach that it is vague and general, unable
Line to compete with the attractions of political
   history either for the student or for the
 5 general reader, because of its lack of
   outstanding personalities. In point of fact
   there is often as much material for
   reconstructing the life of some quite
   ordinary person as there is for writing the
10 history of Robert of Normandy or Philippa
   of Hainhault; and the lives of ordinary
   people so reconstructed are, if less spectacular, certainly not less interesting. I believe
   that social history lends itself particularly to
15 what may be called a personal treatment,
   and that the past may be made to live again
   for the general reader more effectively by
   personifying it than by presenting it in the
   form of learned treatises on the
20 development of the manor or on medieval
   trade, essential as these are to the specialist.
   For history, after all, is valuable only in so
   far as it lives, and Maeterlinck's cry, "There
   are no dead," should always be the historian's
25 motto.

8. This passage is primarily concerned with the
    contrast between

    (A) accounts of modern times and accounts
        of ancient times
    (B) fictionalized historical accounts and
        objective historical analyses
    (C) the concerns of the affluent and the
        concerns of the poor
    (D) depictions of ordinary citizens and
        depictions of political leaders and
        institutions
    (E) analysis of economic activity and
        analysis of international conflicts

Printed with the permission of University Paperbacks: *Medieval People*, Eileen Power © 1963, p vii.

GO ON TO THE NEXT PAGE ⟩

9. In context, the quote from Maeterlinck that "There are no dead" (lines 23–24) means that historians

(A) focus inordinately on accounts of war
(B) should personify their subjects
(C) are overly concerned with appealing to the masses
(D) lack an appreciation of human mortality
(E) are superior scholars

Questions 10–18 are based on the following passage.

The following essay analyzes the character Holden Caulfield, the protagonist of J. D. Salinger's 1951 novel The Catcher in the Rye, *particularly in comparison to Huckleberry Finn, the protagonist of Mark Twain's 1884 novel* The Adventures of Huckleberry Finn, *and Hester Prynne, the protagonist of Nathaniel Hawthorne's 1850 romance* The Scarlet Letter.

Holden Caulfield, like Huck Finn and Hester Prynne, is one of the most evocative
Line characters in all of American literature. Seeking moral purity in a society filled with
5 deceit, corruption and prejudice, he personifies a struggle familiar to readers of classic American fiction. But as a twentieth century protagonist, his relationship with his social environment differs from those
10 depicted in *The Adventures of Huckleberry Finn* and *The Scarlet Letter* in that Holden is very much a part of his society. Even more, he is, as the critic Joyce Rowe has written, "the heir of all the ages, blessed with the
15 material splendors of the Promised Land." Finn and Prynne, on the other hand, are characters thrust to the periphery of a society in which prosperity finds purchase only in enclaves.
20   Despite his endowments, Holden does not feel privileged, but rather trapped and victimized by a world that is likewise in a state of brash young adulthood. In an effort to differentiate himself from his surround-
25 ings, he responds in the only way he can, by wasting his blessings. This commitment to

profligacy, rather than to improving his lot or to changing his environment, amounts to little more than what Rowe calls "self-
30 mutilation against that part of himself that is hostage to the society that has shaped him."
     But whereas Hester and Huck define themselves only in withdrawal from society,
35 Holden's differentiation cannot be so complete. He is drawn to defining a role for himself within his social world, as a "catcher in the rye," a protector of the weak and innocent. This ambivalence, this irony of the
40 modern world, can only find resolution in a strong individual will. Without such a will, the man-child Holden cannot tame his dual impulses—toward and from the people around him—and he is led inexorably to the
45 sanitarium.
     Yet so sympathetically does Salinger portray Caulfield that, to the reader, Holden is anything but crazy. We understand his world, his motivations, his ways of thinking.
50 Does our empathy suggest that we, too, are destined for an institution? This question, which Salinger places deliberately in our path, serves to replicate Caulfield's most trenchant conflict within us.
55   We resolve our own version of this conflict by also accepting the asylum, the therapeutic practices we fashion to manage the complex challenges of living in a modern society. Our asylums are not necessarily Holden's—
60 they include *Oprah*, self-help books, meditation classes, and spa retreats—but we cannot help but recognize ourselves today within the walls of Holden's sanitarium.

GO ON TO THE NEXT PAGE ⟶

5   5   5   5   5   5

10. According to the passage, Holden Caulfield differs from Huck Finn and Hester Prynne primarily in that he

(A) has a strong individual will
(B) is more integrated into his social environment
(C) tries to remediate social prejudice
(D) must cope with poverty
(E) is not a sympathetic character

11. The quotation from Joyce Rowe in lines 14–15 focuses primarily on Caulfield's

(A) moral disillusionment
(B) social struggles
(C) fortunate circumstances
(D) sense of ambivalence
(E) deceitfulness

12. Lines 16–19 ("Finn and Prynne...only in enclaves") indicate that both Huck Finn and Hester Prynne belong to societies in which

(A) most citizens are outcasts
(B) idiosyncrasies are rewarded
(C) affluence is not widespread
(D) laws are not uniformly enforced
(E) wastefulness is common

13. The "commitment" (line 26) consists of Holden's dedication to

(A) prodigal behavior
(B) changing the social order
(C) moral self-improvement
(D) becoming more productive
(E) accepting the standards of society

14. Holden's "ambivalence" (line 39) consists of his inclinations toward

(A) the past and the future
(B) actively confronting prejudice and becoming resigned to it
(C) wasting his resources and hoarding them
(D) helping others and punishing them
(E) withdrawing from society and becoming part of it

15. In line 51 the "institution" is

(A) a ceremonial practice
(B) an established law
(C) a hopeful prospect
(D) a corrective facility
(E) an unhealthy habit

16. As a whole, this passage characterizes Holden Caulfield primarily as being

(A) conflicted
(B) strong-willed
(C) sophisticated
(D) composed
(E) sadistic

17. Lines 51–54 ("This question...conflict within us") indicates that Salinger is trying to

(A) suggest a solution to a psychological problem
(B) distance himself from the character of Holden
(C) criticize the social order of his era
(D) employ a sophisticated literary device
(E) make the reader sympathize with Holden's angst

18. In context, "accepting the asylum" (line 56) most nearly means

(A) acknowledging our own need for emotional treatment
(B) understanding the techniques used by health-care professionals
(C) recognizing the need for stricter law enforcement
(D) facilitating the construction of sanitoriums
(E) taking responsibility for the well-being of others

GO ON TO THE NEXT PAGE →

Questions 19–24 are based on the following passage.

The following passage is excerpted from a book that discusses the social history of Modern Art.

People don't read the morning newspaper, Marshall McLuhan once said, they slip into
Line it like a warm bath. Too true, Marshall! Imagine being in New York City on the
5   morning of Sunday, April 28, 1974, like I was, slipping into that great public bath, that regional physiotherapy tank, that River Jordan for a million souls which is the Sunday *New York Times*. Soon after I sub-
10 merged, weightless, suspended in the tepid depths of the thing, in Arts & Leisure, Section 2, page 19, in a state of perfect sensory deprivation, when all at once an extraordinary thing happened:
15   I noticed something!
       Yet another clam-broth-colored current had begun to roll over me, as warm and predictable as the Gulf Stream—a review, it was, by the Times's dean of the arts, Hilton
20 Kramer, of an exhibition at Yale University of "Seven Realists," seven realist painters, when I was jerked alert by the following:
       "Realism does not lack its partisans, but it does rather conspicuously lack a persua-
25 sive theory. And given the nature of our intellectual commerce with works of art, to lack a persuasive theory is to lack something crucial—the means by which our experience of individual works is joined to our
30 understanding of the values they signify."
       Now, you may say, My God, man! You woke up over that? You forsook your blissful coma over a mere swell in the sea of words?
       But I knew what I was looking at. I real-
35 ized that without making the slightest effort I had come upon one of those utterances in search of which psychoanalysts and State Department monitors of the Moscow or Belgrade press are willing to endure a
40 lifetime of tedium: namely, the seemingly innocuous *obiter dicta*, the words in passing, that give the game away.
       What I saw before me was the critic-in-chief of *The New York Times* saying: In
45 looking at a painting today, "to lack a persuasive theory is to lack something

crucial." I read it again. It didn't say "something helpful" or "enriching" or even "extremely valuable." No, the word was
50 "crucial."
       In short: frankly, these days, without a theory to go with it, I can't see a painting.
       Then and there I experienced a flash known as the Aha! phenomenon, and the
55 buried life of contemporary art was revealed to me for the first time. The fogs lifted! The clouds passed!
       All these years I, like so many others, had stood in front of a thousand, two thousand,
60 who-knows-how-many thousand Pollocks, de Koonings, Newmans, Nolands, Rothkos, Rauschenbergs, Judds, Johnses, Olitskis, Louises, Stills, Franz, Klines, Frankehtlers, Kellys, and Frank Stellas, now squinting,
65 now popping the eye sockets open, now drawing back, now moving closer—waiting, waiting, forever waiting for it to come into focus, namely, the visual reward (for so much effort) which must be there, which
70 everyone knew to be there—waiting for something to radiate directly from the paintings on these invariably pure white walls, in this room, in this moment, into my own optic chiasma. All these years, in short,
75 I had assumed that in art, if nowhere else, seeing is believing.
       Well—how very shortsighted! Now, at last, on April 28, 1974, I could see. I had gotten it backward all along. Not "seeing is believing,"
80 you ninny, but "believing is seeing," for Modern Art has become completely literary: the paintings and other works exist only to illustrate the text.

Excerpt from *The Painted Word* by Tom Wolfe. Copyright © 1999. Reprinted by permission of Bantam, a division of Farrar, Straus and Giroux, LLC.

GO ON TO THE NEXT PAGE →

5 5 5 5 5 5

19. The quotation from Marshall McLuhan in lines 1–3 suggests that newspapers are

    (A) less popular than they used to be
    (B) soothing to the senses
    (C) not as objective as they should be
    (D) sometimes incomprehensible to their readers
    (E) intellectually stimulating

20. In lines 31–33 ("Now, you may say...sea of words?") the author assumes that the reader

    (A) disagrees with Kramer's review of the art exhibit
    (B) is a reader of *The New York Times*
    (C) does not share the author's enthusiasm for Kramer's statement
    (D) understands the theory behind the realist movement
    (E) finds art reviews to be particularly engaging

21. The author suggests that Kramer did not use a phrase like "extremely valuable" (line 49) in his review because Kramer

    (A) is not a strong advocate of realism
    (B) does not feel that the "Seven Realists" exhibit was worthwhile
    (C) is unable to articulate his idea with precise language
    (D) resists using terms that are too extreme
    (E) is adamant about the need to have a theory of art

22. The phrase "now squinting, now popping the eye sockets open" (lines 64–65) describes the experience of

    (A) reading bewildering art reviews
    (B) trying to understand a complex theory
    (C) attempting to find meaning in art through sight alone
    (D) preparing to write about the theory of art
    (E) waiting for a new art exhibit to open

23. The author uses the phrase "you ninny" (line 80) primarily in order to

    (A) chastise himself for his ignorance
    (B) impugn the reader's complacency
    (C) suggest that not all art is intended to be taken seriously
    (D) poke fun at artists who are too somber about their art
    (E) denounce critics who employ complex theories

24. The statement that "Modern Art has become completely literary" (line 81) means that

    (A) appreciating Modern Art requires the understanding of aesthetic principles
    (B) many modern literary works have been based on Modern Art paintings
    (C) critics of Modern Art are more accomplished writers than critics in the past
    (D) creating Modern Art paintings does not require as much skill as it seems
    (E) there are many parallels between the art of writing and the art of painting

STOP

If you finish before time is called, you may check your work on this section only. Do not turn to any other section of the test.

6   **6**   **6**   **6**   **6**   **6**

SECTION 6
Time—25 minutes
20 questions

Turn to Section 6 of your answer sheet to answer the questions in this section.

Directions: For this section, solve each problem and decide which is the best of the choices given. Fill in the corresponding circle on the answer sheet. You may use any available space for scratchwork.

Notes

1. The use of a calculator is permitted.
2. All numbers used are real numbers.
3. Figures that accompany problems in this test are intended to provide information useful in solving the problems. They are drawn as accurately as possible EXCEPT when it is stated in a specific problem that the figure is not drawn to scale. All figures lie in a plane unless otherwise indicated.
4. Unless otherwise specified, the domain of any function f is assumed to be the set of all real numbers x for which $f(x)$ is a real number.

Reference Information

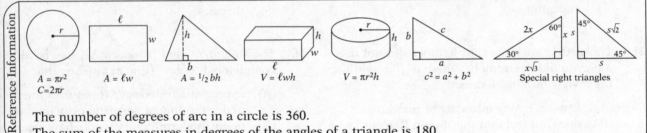

$A = \pi r^2$
$C = 2\pi r$

$A = \ell w$

$A = \frac{1}{2} bh$

$V = \ell wh$

$V = \pi r^2 h$

$c^2 = a^2 + b^2$

Special right triangles

The number of degrees of arc in a circle is 360.
The sum of the measures in degrees of the angles of a triangle is 180.

1. There are 5 CD racks in a room. Each rack contains at least 10 CDs but not more than 14 CDs. Which of the following could be the total number of CDs on all five racks?

   (A) 25
   (B) 35
   (C) 55
   (D) 75
   (E) 85

2. If x is 4 less than p and p is 2 more than m, then what is the value of x when $m = 2$?

   (A) −1
   (B) 0
   (C) 1
   (D) 2
   (E) 4

GO ON TO THE NEXT PAGE

6 6 6 6 6 6

3. The drawing above is to be rotated 90° about point X in the direction indicated. Which of the following shows the end result of this rotation?

(A)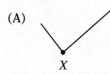

(B)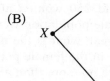

(C)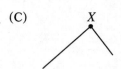

(D)

(E)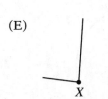

4. The price of admission to the New Haven Children's Museum is $6 more for adults than for children. If a group of 6 adults and 18 children pays a total of $108 to visit the museum, what is the cost, in dollars, of the ticket for one adult?

(A) $7.00
(B) $9.00
(C) $10.00
(D) $12.00
(E) $13.00

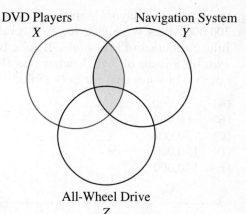

5. In the figure above, circular region X represents cars with DVD players, circular region Y represents cars with navigation systems, and circular region Z represents cars with all-wheel drive. What is represented by the shaded region?

(A) cars with DVD players, navigation systems, and all-wheel drive
(B) cars with DVD players and all-wheel drive, but without navigation systems
(C) cars with navigation systems and all-wheel drive (some possibly with DVD players)
(D) cars with DVD players and all-wheel drive (some possibly with navigation systems)
(E) cars with DVD players and navigation systems (some possibly with all-wheel drive)

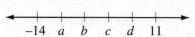

6. The tick marks on the number line above are equally spaced and their coordinates are shown. Of these coordinates, which has the smallest nonnegative value?

(A) a
(B) b
(C) c
(D) d
(E) It cannot be determined from the given information.

GO ON TO THE NEXT PAGE

6   **6**   **6**   **6**   **6**   **6**

7. In a recent mayoral election, a total of 200,000 votes were cast for two candidates, Julie Sanders and Bob Tanks. If Julie Sanders won by a ratio of 7 to 3, what was the total number of votes cast for Bob Tanks?

(A) 30,000
(B) 60,000
(C) 90,000
(D) 120,000
(E) 140,000

"All multiples of 3 are odd."

8. Which of the following numbers provides a counterexample to the statement above?

(A) 9
(B) 12
(C) 13
(D) 14
(E) 15

---

9. For how many integer values of x is $|x - 2.5| < 12$?

(A) 20
(B) 21
(C) 22
(D) 23
(E) 24

---

10. If the average of 8 and x is 10 and the average of 7 and y is 11, what is the average of x and y?

(A) 9.0
(B) 10.5
(C) 12.0
(D) 13.5
(E) 15.0

---

11. Of the 360 students at a private school, $\frac{4}{5}$ were from Connecticut. If $\frac{3}{8}$ of the students lived on campus, what was the least possible number of students who lived on campus and were from Connecticut?

(A) 55
(B) 63
(C) 72
(D) 135
(E) 155

---

12. This year, 200 men and 250 women attend State College. If the male population were to increase by 10% next year, what is the maximum possible increase in the female population that would produce no more than an 8% increase in the overall student population next year?

(A) 16
(B) 17
(C) 20
(D) 22
(E) 26

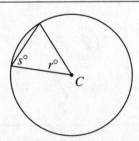

13. In the figure above, if C is the center of the circle and $20 < r < 40$, then which of the following expresses all possible values of s?

(A) $30 < s < 50$
(B) $50 < s < 70$
(C) $70 < s < 80$
(D) $75 < s < 90$
(E) $140 < s < 160$

GO ON TO THE NEXT PAGE ⟩

14. If a and b are positive integers such that $(a - 4)(b - 5) = 0$, what is the least possible value of $a + b$?

(A) 5
(B) 6
(C) 8
(D) 10
(E) 11

15. A meal that costs m dollars is to be split equally among a group of coworkers. In terms of m, how many dollars less will each person pay for the meal if there are 6 people in the group instead of 4?

(A) $\dfrac{m}{12}$

(B) $\dfrac{m}{6}$

(C) $\dfrac{m}{4}$

(D) $\dfrac{3m}{5}$

(E) $10m$

16. If the length of $\overline{RS}$ is 12 and the length of $\overline{ST}$ is 13, which of the following could be the length of $\overline{RT}$?

(A) 24
(B) 26
(C) 28
(D) 29
(E) 30

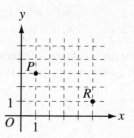

17. In the figure above, points P and R are to be consecutive vertices of square $PRST$ (not shown). What is the area of square $PRST$?

(A) 16
(B) 20
(C) 22
(D) 24
(E) 25

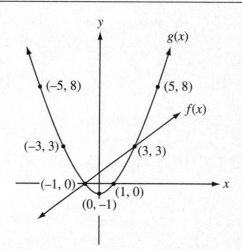

18. Based on the portions of the graphs of the functions f and g shown above, what are the values of x between -5 and 5 for which $g(x) < f(x)$?

(A) $-2 < x < -1$ only
(B) $-1 < x < 2$ only
(C) $-1 < x < 3$ only
(D) $2 < x < 5$ only
(E) $-5 < x < -1$ and $2 < x < 5$

GO ON TO THE NEXT PAGE

6   6   6   6   6   6

$$m^2 - n^2 < 12$$
$$m + n > 10$$

19. If m and n are positive integers in the inequalities above and $m > n$, what is the value of m?

(A) 5
(B) 6
(C) 7
(D) 8
(E) 9

20. A student is instructed to arrange four cards in a row on a table. She has six cards to choose from, each of which has a different color: *black, red, blue, green, yellow,* and *brown.* If the student follows these instructions but otherwise chooses her cards randomly, what is the probability that her arrangement will be *blue, red, yellow,* and *green,* in that order?

(A) $\dfrac{1}{90}$

(B) $\dfrac{1}{180}$

(C) $\dfrac{1}{360}$

(D) $\dfrac{1}{540}$

(E) $\dfrac{1}{720}$

STOP

If you finish before time is called, you may check your work on this section only. Do not turn to any other section of the test.

7   7   7   7   7   7

SECTION 7
Time—20 minutes
19 questions

Turn to Section 7 of your answer sheet to answer the questions in this section.

Directions: For each question in this section, select the best answer from among the choices given and fill in the corresponding circle on the answer sheet.

Each sentence below has one or two blanks, each blank indicating that something has been omitted. Beneath the sentence are five words or sets of words labeled A through E. Choose the word or set of words that, when inserted in the sentence, best fits the meaning of the sentence as a whole.

EXAMPLE:

Rather than accepting the theory unquestioningly, Deborah regarded it with -----.

(A) mirth
(B) sadness
(C) responsibility
(D) ignorance
(E) skepticism

---

1. The addictive nature of online gambling has forced many ------- gamers to seek treatment.

   (A) delectable
   (B) palliative
   (C) compulsive
   (D) fortified
   (E) provident

2. In Arthur Miller's *Death of a Salesman*, Willy Loman craves success to such a degree that this desire for ------- drives him to madness.

   (A) prosperity
   (B) scrutiny
   (C) infamy
   (D) spontaneity
   (E) negligence

3. In the sequel to her first novel, the author gave the protagonist more ------- in an effort to ------- critics who criticized her characters for being too shallow.

   (A) precision . . exacerbate
   (B) paucity . . compensate
   (C) profundity . . aggravate
   (D) brevity . . assuage
   (E) depth . . appease

4. Jim Leyland, typically one of the least ------- managers in Major League Baseball, surprised the crowd when he engaged in an explosive altercation with an umpire.

   (A) contentious
   (B) magnanimous
   (C) serene
   (D) solicitous
   (E) imperturbable

GO ON TO THE NEXT PAGE

7   **7**   **7**   **7**   **7**   **7**

5. Polio has been so effectively suppressed by vaccination programs that most doctors have never even encountered its symptoms; in fact, when the rare patient today is ------- with the polio virus, doctors are likely to ------- the illness.

   (A) infected . . reduce
   (B) exposed . . retract
   (C) transmuted . . capitulate
   (D) afflicted . . misdiagnose
   (E) engaged . . eradicate

6. The Chief Resident loathed the ------- behavior of some medical students who would ------- her excessively in an effort to win her favor.

   (A) sycophantic . . complement
   (B) recalcitrant . . castigate
   (C) obsequious . . commend
   (D) unwitting . . antagonize
   (E) gluttonous . . belabor

The two passages below are followed by questions based on their content and on the relationship between the two passages. Answer the questions on the basis of what is stated or implied in the passages and in any introductory material that may be provided.

Questions 7–19 are based on the following passages.

The following passages discuss the relationship between economics and environmentalism, particularly in regard to the phenomenon of global warming. The first was written in 2008 by a philosophy professor, and the second is an excerpt from a book published in 1999 by a professor of environmental economics.

PASSAGE 1

UPS delivered my hedge trimmer a few weeks ago. Actually, it is not just a hedge
Line trimmer but has interchangeable heads so that it can trim grass, mow down brush and
5 cut small tree limbs. As I powered it up, I felt pangs of guilt—the two-cycle contraption uses a mixture of oil and gas, which

makes it not just copiously smelly but also a behemoth when it comes to producing
10 carbon dioxide.

I could have bought a slightly more expensive four-cycle model that does not require mixing the oil and gas. I knew I was doing wrong. But my knowledge did not
15 translate into action. My weakness, what Aristotle called "akrasia," is something Ulysses understood when he instructed his crew to tie him to the mast when they passed the Sirens. I need to be tied up going
20 to Home Depot.

I have also suffered from akrasia when it comes to my car—a dirty, used diesel that gets 40 miles per gallon. I couldn't resist the initial low price and the promise of ongoing
25 savings.

On and on it goes. I spend most of my waking hours worrying about how to reduce my output of carbon dioxide and other greenhouse gases[1]. Yet my behavior seems to
30 march to a different drummer. I need to get the best deal, and my values don't get incorporated into the calculation. I am attuned only to price. And I don't think I am alone in this.
35 Fine, you say. The solution is obvious: let's adjust the price so that the "right thing" is priced right for people like me. But when it comes to pricing I am totally irrational. Offer me two washing machines, one of
40 which is more expensive now but more efficient and hence cheaper over its lifetime, and I'll choose the one that is cheaper now. I can do the calculation in my head using a formula of the discounted value of future
45 savings to see how much they are worth in present-day dollars. But behavioral economists would say my actual discounting is hyperbolic. In the end, all I care about is the deal today. The sad truth is that if you
50 want me to buy the more efficient machine, you will have to give me a subsidy up front.

---

[1]Greenhouse gases, such as carbon dioxide, are those gases that are known to contribute to global warming.

GO ON TO THE NEXT PAGE →

7   7   7   7   7   7

No problem, you might say. We don't need
to waste money on subsidies; we should just
create a tax to make the washing machines'
55 prices equivalent, the same for the prices of
the diesel and the Prius[2], and the two-cycle
trimmer and the four-cycle version, and so
on. Then you will step into line.

But there is another problem. I like
60 Hummers[3]. I like their boxy design and their
commanding presence on the road. Here I
am not irrational, just retrograde when it
comes to my preferences. And if my
preferences are strong enough and my wallet
65 is large enough, no tax is going to make me
give up my Hummer for a Prius. I am not
alone in loving Hummers. An effective tax
will have to take into account all variety of
Hummer lovers, the strength of their
70 preferences and the size of their wallets.

Better not to tempt me in the first place.
Don't clutter my world with things I should
not have. Don't dangle them in front of me,
creating desire, only to then try to have me
75 renounce them. Just ban the damn two-cycle
hedge trimmer and let me be done with the
matter.

PASSAGE 2

A near revolution has occurred over the past
decade in our understanding of the impacts
80 of climate change. Both the natural science
and the economics underlying predictions of
climate-change impacts have altered
dramatically. Climate scientists have reduced
the magnitude of predicted warming,
85 suggesting milder future climate scenarios.
Ecologists have shifted from predicting
ecosystem collapse to predicting that net
primary productivity will likely increase over
the long run. And economists are no longer
90 predicting large damages, but rather a
mixture of damages and benefits.

These changes are so dramatic that it is
not clear whether the net economic effects
from climate change over the next century

95 will be harmful or helpful. The new research
further suggests that effects are likely to
vary across the planet. We now expect temperate and polar countries to enjoy small
economic gains, whereas tropical countries
100 are more likely to suffer economic losses.

Of course, we have not banished all
uncertainty, which will always haunt future
projections of outcomes. The dynamics of
ecosystems are poorly understood; carbon
105 cycles may change over time; polar ice may
generate unwelcome surprises; and the
effects of change on tropical regions have
not yet had the thorough study they require.
Nonetheless, the recent scientific and
110 economic findings create a new perspective
on the greenhouse-gas problem, and this
new vision, in turn, calls for new strategies
and new political outcomes.

The reduction in damage-estimates
115 removes the urgency to engage in costly
crash abatement programs. Our initial
perspective on greenhouse gases suggested
that we were rapidly approaching the edge
of a cliff. Those fears now appear
120 unfounded, for the impacts from climate
warming seem to be relatively small for the
next century. There will be damages to be
sure, but they will be offset by benefits. The
net expected effect now is closer to zero
125 rather than to 2 percent of GDP. As a
consequence, new abatement policies should
be designed for the long run, and should be
inexpensive and cost-effective.

[2]The Prius is a fuel-efficient car that runs on both electricity and
gasoline and emits only very small amounts of greenhouse
gases.
[3]Hummers are very large vehicles that consume a great deal of
gasoline and emit large quantities of greenhouse gases.

Printed with the permission of the author, Dr. Martin Bunzi.
Excerpted from *Ulysses and the Hedge Trimmer*.

GO ON TO THE NEXT PAGE ⟶

7 7 7 7 7 7

7. Which of the following best characterizes the individual perspectives presented in the two passages?

(A) Passage 1 asserts scientific proof for global warming, while Passage 2 provides evidence to refute it.

(B) Passage 1 focuses on the causes of global warming, while Passage 1 focuses on its effects.

(C) Passage 1 questions the effectiveness of particular policies for reducing greenhouse emissions, while Passage 2 argues that those policies are working.

(D) Passage 1 suggests incentives that will reduce greenhouse emissions, while Passage 2 argues that efforts to reduce greenhouse emissions should be moderated.

(E) Passage 1 enumerates the dangers of global warming, while Passage 2 enumerates its benefits.

8. The "pangs of guilt" (line 6) are due primarily to the author's belief that

(A) he has overpaid for an item

(B) he is violating a tax law

(C) his hedge trimmer is not as durable as it should be

(D) he is contributing to the emission of greenhouse gases

(E) his hedge trimmer will require too much effort to operate

9. The author mentions Ulysses in line 17 primarily as an example of someone who

(A) has endured a lengthy journey

(B) is ignorant of the effects of his actions

(C) struggles with the technologies of his day

(D) is vilified by people around him

(E) lacks a strong moral will

10. Which of the following is the best example of "akrasia"?

(A) being unable to resist eating chocolate despite knowing its health risks

(B) planning and executing a complex and dangerous bank heist

(C) denying symptoms of an injury in order to play in a football game

(D) improving one's commitment to recycling plastic containers

(E) failing to understand a complicated tax code

11. In line 32 "attuned" most nearly means

(A) calibrated

(B) sensitive

(C) skeptical

(D) assimilated

(E) resistant

12. In lines 35–37 ("Fine, you say...like me") the author assumes that the reader

(A) is not an expert in the science behind global warming

(B) owns highly fuel-efficient appliances

(C) believes that financial incentives can effectively influence behavior

(D) does not believe that the author's problem is a common one

(E) considers more than price when making a purchase

GO ON TO THE NEXT PAGE

7   **7**   **7**   **7**   **7**   **7**

13. The overall purpose of Passage 2 is to

(A) point out flaws in current methods of climate analysis

(B) raise awareness of the potentially devastating impact of global warming

(C) propose a new method for studying the effects of global warming

(D) suggest policy changes in light of recent scientific findings

(E) refute the claim that human activity is responsible for global warming

14. The third paragraph of Passage 2 (lines 101–113) serves primarily to

(A) explore an implication of the author's thesis

(B) qualify claims that were presented earlier

(C) summarize a political controversy

(D) present the results of a scientific study

(E) disprove a theory that was stated earlier

15. Passage 2 suggests that the "new perspective" (line 110) is the result of a shift from

(A) scientific analysis to economic analysis

(B) dire predictions to moderate predictions

(C) a focus on the past to a focus on the future

(D) a focus on polar regions to a focus on tropical regions

(E) apathy to activism

16. Unlike the "economists" in line 89, the "economists" in line 47 are focused primarily on

(A) anticipating future outcomes of current economic policies

(B) examining the effects of modern industries on global warming

(C) analyzing how individuals make decisions

(D) estimating the cost of reducing greenhouse gas emissions

(E) establishing sound tax policies

17. With which of the following statements would the authors of BOTH passages most likely agree?

(A) Governments should act swiftly to curb greenhouse gas emissions.

(B) It is unclear whether carbon dioxide contributes to global warming.

(C) Consumers are usually inclined to consider the environmental impact of their purchases.

(D) The impacts from global warming will be very high in the coming century.

(E) Economic analysis should be considered when formulating a policy for dealing with global warming.

GO ON TO THE NEXT PAGE

7　　**7**　　**7**　　**7**　　**7**　　**7**

18. The author of Passage 2 would most likely respond to the suggestion in Passage 1 that "we should just create a tax to make the washing machines' prices equivalent" (lines 53–55) by pointing out that such a recommendation

(A) might be needlessly expensive and shortsighted

(B) will not work because it cannot be implemented quickly

(C) would work well because it would punish harmful behavior

(D) would not adequately curb greenhouse gas emissions

(E) is unnecessary because lowering energy consumption would not affect global warming

19. Unlike the author of Passage 1, the author of Passage 2 assumes that the reader

(A) is concerned more with the benefits of policies than their costs

(B) is concerned with curbing the emissions of greenhouse gases

(C) is willing to consider long-term economic effects

(D) has a weakness for inefficient cars and appliances

(E) believes that abatement programs are ineffective

STOP

If you finish before time is called, you may check your work on this section only. Do not turn to any other section of the test.

8   8   8   8   8   8

SECTION 8
Time—20 minutes
16 questions

Turn to Section 8 of your answer sheet to answer the questions in this section.

Directions: For this section, solve each problem and decide which is the best of the choices given. Fill in the corresponding circle on the answer sheet. You may use any available space for scratchwork.

Notes

1. The use of a calculator is permitted.

2. All numbers used are real numbers.

3. Figures that accompany problems in this test are intended to provide information useful in solving the problems. They are drawn as accurately as possible EXCEPT when it is stated in a specific problem that the figure is not drawn to scale. All figures lie in a plane unless otherwise indicated.

4. Unless otherwise specified, the domain of any function f is assumed to be the set of all real numbers x for which $f(x)$ is a real number.

Reference Information

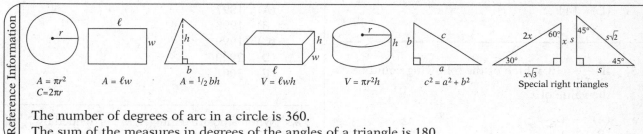

$A = \pi r^2$ $A = \ell w$ $A = 1/2\, bh$ $V = \ell wh$ $V = \pi r^2 h$ $c^2 = a^2 + b^2$ Special right triangles
$C = 2\pi r$

The number of degrees of arc in a circle is 360.
The sum of the measures in degrees of the angles of a triangle is 180.

---

1. If $\dfrac{5}{8}$ of a number is 20, what is $\dfrac{1}{8}$ of the number?

   (A) $\dfrac{1}{2}$

   (B) 4
   (C) 8
   (D) 16
   (E) 32

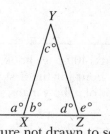

Note: Figure not drawn to scale.

2. In $\triangle XYZ$ above, $XY = ZY$. Which of the following must be true?

   (A) $a = c$
   (B) $a = e$
   (C) $a = d$
   (D) $b = e$
   (E) $c = d$

GO ON TO THE NEXT PAGE ⇨

8   8   8   8   8   8

All of Mark's former students go to college.

3. If the statement above is true, which of the following must also be true?

(A) If Ethan was not Mark's student, then he is not going to college.
(B) If Joyelle goes to college, then she was not Mark's student.
(C) If Ginger goes to college, then she was Mark's student.
(D) If Stephanie was Mark's student, then she is not going to college.
(E) If Steve does not go to college, then he was not Mark's student.

4. If 30 percent of n is 72, what is 15 percent of $2n$?

(A)   18
(B)   36
(C)   64
(D)   72
(E)   144

5. If $\dfrac{1}{x^{-2}} = 16$, which of the following could be the value of x?

(A) -4
(B) -2
(C)   2
(D)   3
(E)   5

6. While reading a 400-page book, Colin averages 50 pages per hour for the first p hours, where $p < 8$. In terms of p, how many pages remain to be read?

(A) $50p + 400$
(B) $400 - \dfrac{50}{p}$
(C) $400 - 50p$
(D) $50p - 400$
(E) $\dfrac{400}{50p}$

SALES REVENUE FOR BARTSWELL CORPORATION

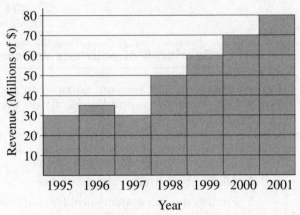

7. The bar graph above shows the annual sales revenue for the Bartswell Corporation for the years 1995 through 2001. For which of the following years was the percent increase in revenue from the previous year the same as it was in 1996?

(A)   1997
(B)   1998
(C)   1999
(D)   2000
(E)   2001

8. When a positive integer, m, is divided by 7, the remainder is 4. Which of the following expressions will yield a remainder of 3 when it is divided by 7?

(A) $m + 2$
(B) $m + 3$
(C) $m + 4$
(D) $m + 5$
(E) $m + 6$

GO ON TO THE NEXT PAGE ⟶

9. If $a^2 - b^2 = 12$, and $(a - b) = 4$, then what is the value of ab?

(A) $-1\frac{3}{4}$

(B) $-\frac{1}{2}$

(C) 0

(D) $3\frac{1}{2}$

(E) $4\frac{1}{4}$

10. For all numbers x and y, let $x \clubsuit y$ be defined as $x \clubsuit y = x^2 - 2xy + y^2$. What is the value of $(2 \clubsuit 4) \clubsuit 8$?

(A) 1
(B) 4
(C) 12
(D) 16
(E) 20

11. If each of the equations below is graphed on the xy-plane, which one will produce a line with a positive slope containing the point $(3, 2)$?

(A) $x + y = 5$
(B) $x - y = 1$
(C) $3x - 2y = 10$
(D) $x^2 - y = 5$
(E) $x + y^2 = 7$

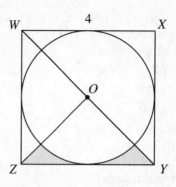

12. In the figure above, the circle with center O is inscribed in square $WXYZ$. What is the area of the shaded portion of the figure?

(A) $8 - 2\pi$
(B) $8 - \pi$
(C) $4 - 2\pi$
(D) $2 - \pi$
(E) $4 - \pi$

13. Muriel goes to a bead store to make a bracelet for her sister. She begins by putting on 3 yellow beads, 2 green beads, 1 black bead, and 3 orange beads in that order. She repeats this pattern until she completes the bracelet. If the final bead she puts on the bracelet is a black bead, which of the following could be the total number of beads on the bracelet?

(A) 85
(B) 87
(C) 89
(D) 91
(E) 93

GO ON TO THE NEXT PAGE

8   8   8   8   8   8

14. The integer 70 is to be expressed as a sum of m consecutive integers. The value of m could be which of the following?

    I. 3
    II. 5
    III. 7

    (A) II only
    (B) III only
    (C) II and III only
    (D) I and II only
    (E) I, II, and III

$$5a + 9b = 14$$
$$15a - tb = 38$$

15. For which of the following values of t will there be no solutions to the system of equations given above?

    (A) 27
    (B) 18
    (C)   0
    (D) -18
    (E) -27

16. The graph in the xy-plane of the function $f(x) = ax^2 + bx + c$ is a parabola with a vertex at $(3, -6)$. If $a > 0$, which of the following cannot be a value of c?

    (A) 6
    (B) 3
    (C) 0
    (D) -3
    (E) -6

STOP

If you finish before time is called, you may check your work on this section only. Do not turn to any other section of the test.

9   9   9   9   9   9

SECTION 9
Time—10 minutes
14 questions

Turn to Section 9 of your answer sheet to answer the questions in this section.

Directions: For each question in this section, select the best answer from among the choices given and fill in the corresponding circle on the answer sheet.

The following sentences test correctness and effectiveness of expression. Part of each sentence or the entire sentence is underlined; beneath each sentence are five ways of phrasing the underlined material. Choice A repeats the original phrasing; the other four choices are different. Select the choice that completes the sentence most effectively.

In making your selection, follow the requirements of standard written English; that is, pay attention to grammar, choice of words, sentence construction, and punctuation. Your selection should result in the most effective sentence—clear and precise, without awkwardness or ambiguity.

EXAMPLE:

The children <u>couldn't hardly believe their eyes</u>.

(A) couldn't hardly believe their eyes
(B) could hardly believe their eyes
(C) would not hardly believe their eyes
(D) couldn't nearly believe their eyes
(E) couldn't hardly believe his or her eyes

1. <u>A one-year old, the pre-school teachers were shocked to hear him speak in full sentences.</u>

    (A) A one-year old, the pre-school teachers were shocked to hear him speak in full sentences.
    (B) The pre-school teachers were shocked by the speaking in full sentences by the one-year old.
    (C) The pre-school teachers were shocked to hear a one-year old speaking in full sentences.
    (D) A one-year old speaking in full sentences, the pre-school teachers were shocked to hear him.
    (E) The pre-school teachers, who were shocked to hear a one-year old speaking in full sentences.

2. At the end of the physical exam, my doctor told me that I could lower my blood pressure <u>by exercising, improving my diet, and relaxing more</u>.

    (A) by exercising, improving my diet, and relaxing more
    (B) in my exercising, improving my diet, and more relaxation
    (C) because of exercising, improving my diet, and relaxing more
    (D) by exercising, improving my diet, and more relaxation
    (E) with exercising, improving my diet, and more relaxation

GO ON TO THE NEXT PAGE ⟩

9   9   9   9   9   9

3. The model of the city may not have moving cars on its roads, <u>but there are a functional set of streetlamps</u>.

   (A) but there are a functional set of streetlamps
   (B) but it does have a functional set of streetlamps
   (C) but there is a functional set of streetlamps
   (D) although a functional set of streetlamps are what it does have
   (E) and there is a functional set of streetlamps

4. Receiving no advice to the contrary from his brothers, <u>Timmy's decision was to take a year off from medical school</u>.

   (A) Timmy's decision was to take a year off from medical school
   (B) taking a year off from medical school was Timmy's decision
   (C) Timmy deciding to take a year off from medical school
   (D) a year off from medical school was what Timmy decided to take
   (E) Timmy decided to take a year off from medical school

5. One of the most important agricultural resources of the Phillipines, <u>the coconut tree faces the threat of extinction</u> within three years due to coconut leaf beetle infestation.

   (A) the coconut tree faces the threat of extinction
   (B) the coconut tree has been facing the threat of extinction
   (C) the threat of extinction faced by the coconut tree is
   (D) the coconut tree, facing the extinction threat,
   (E) facing the coconut tree with the threat of extinction

6. Before sending an angry email to someone, <u>you should wait several hours and then decide if it is still worth sending</u>.

   (A) you should wait several hours and then decide if it is still worth sending
   (B) they should wait several hours to be sure that the email is something that is still worth sending
   (C) they should wait several hours to decide if it is still worth sending
   (D) wait several hours to decide if sending the email was worth it
   (E) several hours of waiting should help you decide if it is still worth sending

7. An experimental accident in London led to the discovery of penicillin <u>in the 1920s, and Alexander Fleming learned</u> of the mold's curative properties.

   (A) in the 1920s, and Alexander Fleming learned
   (B) and Alexander Fleming learned, in the 1920s,
   (C) in the 1920s, when Alexander Fleming learned
   (D) from Alexander Fleming, who learned in the 1920s
   (E) since Alexander Fleming learned in the 1920s

8. Attracted by the movement of the red cape, <u>the matador starts the fight with a series of passes as the bull charges</u>.

   (A) the matador starts the fight with a series of passes as the bull charges
   (B) the fight with the bull is started by the matador with a series of passes
   (C) the series of passes by the matador starts the fight with the bull
   (D) the bull charges as the matador starts the fight with a series of passes
   (E) the bull charges in starting the fight with a couple of passes done by the matador

GO ON TO THE NEXT PAGE ▷

9   9   9   9   9   9

9. After carefully reviewing the two student essays, Professor Magil and Professor Thompson found that the only difference between <u>them were the size of their fonts</u>.

   (A) them were the size of their fonts
   (B) them was the size of their fonts
   (C) the essays were the size of their fonts
   (D) the essays was that of the size of their fonts
   (E) the essays was the size of their fonts

10. <u>As a child growing up in Upper St. Claire</u>, my brothers and I played in travel soccer leagues together.

    (A) As a child growing up in Upper St. Claire
    (B) In Upper St. Claire, as a child growing up,
    (C) A child who grew up in Upper St. Claire
    (D) Growing up in Upper St. Claire
    (E) Since growing up in Upper St. Claire

11. Running a successful bed and breakfast is challenging, because of both the seasonality of travel <u>but also the expensive maintenance</u>.

    (A) but also the expensive maintenance
    (B) and it is expensive to maintain
    (C) and the expense of maintenance
    (D) but the expense of maintenance
    (E) and because of the expensive maintenance

12. <u>St. Augustine was founded forty-two years before the English colony at Jamestown, Virginia, it is</u> the oldest permanent European settlement on the North American continent.

    (A) St. Augustine was founded forty-two years before the English colony at Jamestown, Virginia, it is
    (B) St. Augustine was founded forty-two years before the English colony at Jamestown, Virginia;
    (C) Founded forty-two years before the English colony at Jamestown, Virginia, St. Augustine is
    (D) St. Augustine was founded forty-two years before the English colony at Jamestown, Virginia,
    (E) Founded forty-two years before the English colony at Jamestown, Virginia, St. Augustine being

13. Hopelessly surrounded during the Battle of Little Bighorn, Custer and his men knew defeat <u>was inevitable, and would happen in the future</u>.

    (A) was inevitable, and would happen in the future
    (B) will be inevitable and happen in the future
    (C) is an inevitable thing
    (D) was inevitable
    (E) could happen in the future inevitably

14. <u>Prized as a delicacy, people will pay between $1,000 and $2,000 per pound for the renowned odorous white truffles.</u>

    (A) Prized as a delicacy, people will pay between $1,000 and $2,000 per pound for the renowned odorous white truffles.
    (B) Prizing the renowned odorous white truffles as a delicacy is what makes people pay between $1,000 and $2,000 per pound for them.
    (C) Prizing it as a delicacy, people will pay between $1,000 and $2,000 per pound for the renowned odorous white truffles.
    (D) Prized as a delicacy, $1,000 and $2,000 is paid per pound by people for the renowned odorous white truffle.
    (E) Prizing the renowned odorous white truffles as a delicacy, people will pay between $1,000 and $2,000 per pound for them.

STOP

If you finish before time is called, you may check your work on this section only. Do not turn to any other section of the test.

ANSWER KEY

Critical Reading

Section 3

	COR. ANS.	DIFF. LEV.		COR. ANS.	DIFF. LEV.
1.	C	1	13.	E	3
2.	D	2	14.	B	4
3.	A	2	15.	B	4
4.	E	3	16.	B	3
5.	D	4	17.	A	4
6.	A	3	18.	C	3
7.	B	4	19.	A	4
8.	E	5	20.	A	3
9.	A	2	21.	D	3
10.	D	2	22.	E	3
11.	E	3	23.	C	4
12.	C	4	24.	D	4

Number correct ____

Number incorrect ____

Section 5

	COR. ANS.	DIFF. LEV.		COR. ANS.	DIFF. LEV.
1.	C	1	13.	A	5
2.	B	3	14.	E	4
3.	E	3	15.	D	5
4.	D	4	16.	A	3
5.	B	5	17.	E	3
6.	C	4	18.	A	3
7.	A	4	19.	B	3
8.	D	4	20.	C	4
9.	B	3	21.	E	4
10.	B	3	22.	C	3
11.	C	3	23.	A	3
12.	C	4	24.	A	4

Number correct ____

Number incorrect ____

Section 7

	COR. ANS.	DIFF. LEV.		COR. ANS.	DIFF. LEV.
1.	C	1	11.	B	3
2.	A	2	12.	C	4
3.	E	3	13.	D	4
4.	A	3	14.	B	4
5.	D	5	15.	B	3
6.	C	5	16.	C	3
7.	D	3	17.	E	4
8.	D	2	18.	A	3
9.	E	4	19.	C	4
10.	A	3			

Number correct ____

Number incorrect ____

Math

Section 2

Multiple-Choice Questions			Student-produced Response questions		
	COR. ANS.	DIFF. LEV.		COR. ANS.	DIFF. LEV.
1.	D	1	9.	14	1
2.	B	1	10.	33	2
3.	D	2	11.	29	2
4.	E	3	12.	10	3
5.	C	3	13.	32	3
6.	C	4	14.	780	3
7.	B	4	15.	13	3
8.	C	5	16.	400	4
			17.	384	4
			18.	21.6	5

Number correct ____

Number incorrect ____

Number correct (9–18) ____

Section 6

	COR. ANS.	DIFF. LEV.		COR. ANS.	DIFF. LEV.
1.	C	1	11.	B	3
2.	B	1	12.	A	3
3.	C	2	13.	C	3
4.	B	2	14.	A	4
5.	E	2	15.	A	4
6.	C	3	16.	A	4
7.	B	2	17.	B	4
8.	B	3	18.	C	4
9.	E	3	19.	B	3
10.	D	3	20.	C	5

Number correct ____

Number incorrect ____

Section 8

	COR. ANS.	DIFF. LEV.		COR. ANS.	DIFF. LEV.
1.	B	1	9.	A	4
2.	B	2	10.	D	3
3.	E	2	11.	B	4
4.	D	2	12.	E	4
5.	A	3	13.	B	3
6.	C	3	14.	C	4
7.	D	3	15.	E	5
8.	E	3	16.	E	5

Number correct ____

Number incorrect ____

Writing

Section 4

	COR. ANS.	DIFF. LEV.		COR. ANS.	DIFF. LEV.		COR. ANS.	DIFF. LEV.		COR. ANS.	DIFF. LEV.
1.	C	1	11.	C	5	21.	A	4	31.	D	4
2.	B	1	12.	B	1	22.	E	3	32.	C	3
3.	A	2	13.	B	2	23.	B	3	33.	E	3
4.	C	2	14.	D	3	24.	D	4	34.	C	3
5.	B	2	15.	C	2	25.	E	4	35.	D	3
6.	C	3	16.	B	3	26.	D	3			
7.	E	3	17.	C	3	27.	C	3			
8.	C	3	18.	C	2	28.	C	3			
9.	A	4	19.	B	3	29.	D	5			
10.	B	4	20.	E	3	30.	D	3			

Number correct ____

Number incorrect ____

Section 9

	COR. ANS.	DIFF. LEV.		COR. ANS.	DIFF. LEV.
1.	C	2	11.	C	3
2.	A	2	12.	C	3
3.	B	2	13.	D	4
4.	E	4	14.	E	4
5.	A	4			
6.	A	3			
7.	C	3			
8.	D	4			
9.	E	3			
10.	D	3			

Number correct ____

Number incorrect ____

NOTE: Difficulty levels are estimates of question difficulty that range from 1 (easiest) to 5 (hardest).

SCORE CONVERSION TABLE

How to score your test

Use the answer key on the previous page to determine your raw score on each section. **Your raw score on each section except Section 5 is simply the number of correct answers minus ¼ of the number of wrong answers. On Section 5, your raw score is the sum of the number of correct answers for questions 1–8 minus ¼ of the number of wrong answers for questions 1–8 plus the total number of correct answers for questions 9–18.** Next, add the raw scores from Sections 3, 6, and 8 to get your Critical Reading raw score, add the raw scores from Sections 2, 5, and 7 to get your Math raw score, and the raw scores from Sections 4 and 9 to get your Writing raw score. Write the three raw scores here:

Raw Critical Reading score: _____ Raw Math score: _____ Raw Writing score: _____

Use the table below to convert these to scaled scores.

Scaled scores: Critical Reading: _____ Math: _____ Writing: _____

Raw Score	Critical Reading Scaled Score	Math Scaled Score	Writing Scaled Score	Raw Score	Critical Reading Scaled Score	Math Scaled Score	Writing Scaled Score
67	800			32	520	570	610
66	800			31	510	560	600
65	790			30	510	550	580
64	780			29	500	540	570
63	770			28	490	530	560
62	750			27	490	520	550
61	740			26	480	510	540
60	730			25	480	500	530
59	720			24	470	490	520
58	700			23	460	480	510
57	690			22	460	480	500
56	680			21	450	470	490
55	670			20	440	460	480
54	660	800		19	440	450	470
53	650	800		18	430	450	460
52	650	780		17	420	440	450
51	640	760		16	420	430	440
50	630	740		15	410	420	440
49	620	730	800	14	400	410	430
48	620	710	800	13	400	410	420
47	610	710	800	12	390	400	410
46	600	700	790	11	380	390	400
45	600	690	780	10	370	380	390
44	590	680	760	9	360	370	380
43	590	670	740	8	350	360	380
42	580	660	730	7	340	350	370
41	570	650	710	6	330	340	360
40	570	640	700	5	320	330	350
39	560	630	690	4	310	320	340
38	550	620	670	3	300	310	320
37	550	620	660	2	280	290	310
36	540	610	650	1	270	280	300
35	540	600	640	0	250	260	280
34	530	590	630	−1	230	240	270
33	520	580	620	−2 or less	210	220	250

SCORE CONVERSION TABLE FOR WRITING COMPOSITE
[ESSAY + MULTIPLE CHOICE]

Calculate your writing raw score as you did on the previous page, and grade your essay from a 1 to a 6 according to the standards that follow in the detailed answer key.

Essay score: _____   Raw Writing score: _____

Use the table below to convert these to scaled scores.

Scaled score: Writing: _____

Raw Score	Essay Score 0	Essay Score 1	Essay Score 2	Essay Score 3	Essay Score 4	Essay Score 5	Essay Score 6
−2 or less	200	230	250	280	310	340	370
−1	210	240	260	290	320	360	380
0	230	260	280	300	340	370	400
1	240	270	290	320	350	380	410
2	250	280	300	330	360	390	420
3	260	290	310	340	370	400	430
4	270	300	320	350	380	410	440
5	280	310	330	360	390	420	450
6	290	320	340	360	400	430	460
7	290	330	340	370	410	440	470
8	300	330	350	380	410	450	470
9	310	340	360	390	420	450	480
10	320	350	370	390	430	460	490
11	320	360	370	400	440	470	500
12	330	360	380	410	440	470	500
13	340	370	390	420	450	480	510
14	350	380	390	420	460	490	520
15	350	380	400	430	460	500	530
16	360	390	410	440	470	500	530
17	370	400	420	440	480	510	540
18	380	410	420	450	490	520	550
19	380	410	430	460	490	530	560
20	390	420	440	470	500	540	570
21	400	430	450	480	510	550	580
22	410	440	460	480	520	560	590
23	420	450	470	490	530	570	600
24	420	460	470	500	540	580	610
25	430	460	480	510	540	590	610
26	440	470	490	520	550	590	620
27	450	480	500	530	560	600	630
28	460	490	510	540	570	610	640
29	470	500	520	550	580	620	650
30	480	510	530	560	590	630	660
31	490	520	540	560	600	640	670
32	500	530	550	570	610	650	680
33	510	540	550	580	620	660	690
34	510	550	560	590	630	670	700
35	520	560	570	600	640	680	710
36	530	560	580	610	650	690	720
37	540	570	590	620	660	700	730
38	550	580	600	630	670	710	740
39	560	600	610	640	680	720	750
40	580	610	620	650	690	730	760
41	590	620	640	660	700	740	770
42	600	630	650	680	710	750	780
43	610	640	660	690	720	770	800
44	620	660	670	700	740	780	800
45	640	670	690	720	750	800	800
46	650	690	700	730	770	800	800
47	670	700	720	750	780	800	800
48	680	720	730	760	800	800	800
49	680	720	730	760	800	800	800

Detailed Answer Key

Section I

The following essay received 12 points out of a possible 12. Although it is not a flawless essay, it demonstrates *clear and consistent mastery* in that it

- develops an insightful point of view on the topic
- demonstrates exemplary critical thinking
- uses very effective examples, reasons, and other evidence to support its thesis
- is consistently focused, coherent, and well-organized
- demonstrates skillful and effective use of language and sentence structure
- is largely (but not necessarily completely) free of grammatical and usage errors

> Honesty is the cornerstone of all success, without which confidence and ability to perform shall cease to exist.
>
> —Mary Kay Ash, founder of Mary Kay Cosmetics, Inc.

Assignment: **Are people bound to tell the truth at all times, or are there situations in which it is better to lie or tell only partial truths?** Plan and write an essay in which you develop your point of view on this issue. Support your position with reasoning and examples taken from your reading, studies, experience, or observations.

SAMPLE STUDENT ESSAY

Countless examples of the inner battle between honesty and deception are found in literature and history. Although there are many situations in which it would be much easier to tell a lie than to tell the truth, a sense of personal integrity, which can only be maintained when we are scrupulously honest with ourselves, is the cornerstone of a life well-lived.

In the movie *School Ties*, David Greene is a rising senior at a prestigious prep school who becomes friends with the other students, and does well academically and athletically. However, realizing that he may not be accepted by his peers, he neglects to mention is that he is Jewish. When this fact is uncovered, he is ostracized and harassed and even his closest friends accuse him of lying to them. He objects by saying that merely neglecting to mention his faith is not a lie. Yet, on a deeper level, he realizes that he has in fact lied to himself by not showing the whole truth of who he is. He sees that being accepted by others, even at a prestigious prep school, is not as important as maintaining his integrity.

Likewise, in *The Crucible*, Arthur Miller demonstrates that a life without integrity is not worth living. In 17th century Massachusetts, accusations of witchcraft were cast recklessly among the inhabitants of Salem Village. Realizing that the only way to save their lives was to "confess" to being witches, many good Christians felt compelled to lie—to confirm false accusations against them—in order to live. But when John Proctor was asked to sign his name to a list of witches, he could not—not even to save his life. When asked why, he replied, "Because it is my name! Because in my life I cannot have another!...leave me my name!" He realized that his name—more than just his reputation, but also his deepest sense of himself—is more important than even his life.

Some think that we may lie to save the feelings of others or to create a sense of magic. These "white lies," like telling your friend her breath isn't so bad or telling a child that the Tooth Fairy brings him cash for his teeth, may avoid (temporarily) hurt feelings, or support some cultural traditions, but at what costs? Your friend is better served with a breath mint, and the child is better served by understanding that Tooth Fairy money is really her parent's hard-earned cash.

We encounter many opportunities every day to deceive, to lie, to withhold, and to tell half-truths. Yet each time we tell even a "white lie," perhaps out of the sincere wish to avoid harming another, we damage our own personal integrity. We can see everywhere the sad results of losing touch with our moral integrity: corrupt politicians, rapacious businessmen, tax cheats, insurance scammers, to name but a few. I cannot say that my honesty is beyond reproach, but I can say that John Proctor's words echo in my head whenever I want to lie.

Reader's Comments

This excellent essay supports the thesis that "a sense of personal integrity, which can only be maintained when we are scrupulously honest with ourselves, is the cornerstone of a life well-lived." The examples, from the movie *School Ties*, about a Jewish boy faced with being honest about himself, and from Miller's *The Crucible*, support the idea that honesty is essential to integrity, which is in turn essential to a good life,

and perhaps more important even than life itself. Both examples are explained well in the context of the thesis. Likewise, the discussion of hypothetical "white lies" is well-reasoned and addresses some of the strongest counterarguments to the author's thesis.

The essay is well-organized and provides logical transitions within and between paragraphs. The conclusion demonstrates good critical thinking by addressing the effects of neglecting personal integrity, rather than merely restating the thesis.

These qualities, together with its exemplary (though not perfect) use of diction and syntax, merits the highest possible score of 12.

Section 2

1. D
Plug in 4 for x:

$$3x + 2 = y$$
$$3(4) + 2 = y = 14$$

---

2. B Angles y and u are *vertical angles*, so they are equal. This means that $u = y = 64°$
There are 180° on one side of a line: $x + y + z = 180°$
Plug in 64 for y and 71 for x: $71° + 64° + z = 180°$
Simplify: $135° + z = 180°$
Subtract 135: $z = 45°$

---

3. D Go month by month until you find the answer they are looking for. In January, Emma earned $500 and Sarah earned $200—a difference of $500 − $200 = $300. In February, Emma earned $800 and Sarah earned $400—a difference of $800 − $400 = $400. Be careful though... the question wants to know when Sarah earned $400 more than Emma did. So, B is not the right answer—it is backwards. In March, Emma earned $600 and Sarah earned $400—a difference of $600 − $400 = $200. In April, Emma earned $300 and Sarah earned $700—a difference of $700 − $300 = $400. Answer choice D is the correct answer.

---

4. E If the average (arithmetic mean) of 3, 7, 10, and x is 7, then $\dfrac{3+7+10+x}{4} = 7$.

Simplify: $\dfrac{20+x}{4} = 7$

Multiply by 4: $20 + x = 28$
Subtract 20: $x = 8$

So the four numbers, in order, are 3, 7, 8, and 10. The *median* of a set of four numbers is the average of the two middle numbers, which in this case are 7 and 8. The average of 7 and 8 is 7.5.

---

5. C First find the commission the salesperson receives for selling one dishwasher, and then multiply that amount by 4. The commission for selling one dishwasher is p percent of the selling price, which is $650. To find p percent of something, multiply it by $\dfrac{p}{100}$.

Commission from the sale of one dishwasher:
$$\frac{p}{100}(650) = 6.5p$$

Commission from the sale of FOUR dishwashers:
$$(6.5p)(4) = 26p$$

---

6. C To transform a function $f(x)$ up two units, you add 2 to make it $f(x) + 2$.
To transform a function $f(x)$ left 3 units, you add 3 inside the parentheses to make it: $f(x + 3)$.
To transform a function $f(x)$ up 2 units *and* left 3 units, you would do both: $f(x + 3) + 2$.
You are told that $y = x^2 + 2$. This would become $y = (x + 3)^2 + 2 + 2$, or $y = (x + 3)^2 + 4$.

---

7. B You can begin by finding $\angle ACB$. There are 180° on one side of a line, so set up an equation to solve for $\angle ACB$: $a + 2b + \angle ACB = 180$
Subtract a: $2b + \angle ACB = 180 - a$
Subtract $2b$: $\angle ACB = 180 - a - 2b$

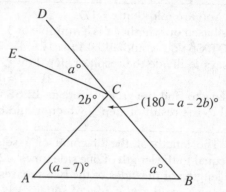

There are 180° in a triangle:
$$(a - 7) + (a) + (180 - a - 2b) = 180$$
Combine terms: $a + 173 - 2b = 180$
Add $2b$: $a + 173 = 180 + 2b$
Subtract 180: $a - 7 = 2b$
Divide by 2: $\dfrac{a-7}{2} = b$

---

8. C What percent of $(x - 2)$ is y? $\dfrac{is}{of} = \dfrac{\%}{100}$

"What percent"—so put the p where the percent is "of $(x - 2)$"—so put the $(x - 2)$ where the *of* is "is y"—so put the y where the *is* is

$$\frac{y}{(x-2)} = \frac{p}{100}$$

Multiply by 100: $\dfrac{100y}{(x-2)} = p$

---

9. 14

$$\text{Area} = \pi r^2$$
$$49\pi = \pi r^2$$
Divide by π: $49 = r^2$
Take square root: $7 = r$
Multiply by 2 to go from radius to diameter:
$$7(2) = 14$$

---

10. 33 Since Anna's car requires $5\dfrac{1}{2}\left(= \dfrac{11}{2}\right)$ gallons of gasoline to make 4 round-trips to work, it requires $\dfrac{1}{4} \times \dfrac{11}{2} = \dfrac{11}{8}$ gallons for each round-trip. Since her car gets 24 miles per gallon, the round-trip must be $\left(\dfrac{11}{8}\text{ gallons}\right) \times (24\text{ miles per gallon}) = 33$ miles per round-trip.

11. 29
Set the function equal to 18: $f(x) = \dfrac{2x-4}{3} = 18$

Multiply by 3: $2x - 4 = 54$
Add 4: $2x = 58$
Divide by 2: $x = 29$

---

12. 10   You are told that $x = 17$.
Step 2 is based on whether x is a multiple of 3, which 17 is NOT. So you would add 4 to x: $17 + 4 = 21$.
Step 3 says to divide the result of step 2 by 2:
$$21 \div 2 = 10.5.$$
Step 4 says to find the greatest integer LESS than or equal to the result of step 3, which would be 10.

---

13. 32   The length of the diagonal of a square is always equal to the length of one side times $\sqrt{2}$. Let's call the lengths of the sides of the two squares a and b, respectively, so that the area of square A is a^2 and the area of square B is b^2. If the length of one side of square A is $\dfrac{1}{2}$ the length of the <u>diagonal</u> of square B, then $a = \dfrac{1}{2}(b\sqrt{2})$

Square both sides: $a^2 = \dfrac{1}{4}(2b^2) = \dfrac{1}{2}b^2$

Since the area of square A is 16: $16 = \dfrac{1}{2}b^2$

Multiply by 2: $32 = b^2$

---

14. 780

$$a + b - 4z = 500$$
$$\underline{a + b + 6z = 1200}$$
Subtract straight down: $0 + 0 - 10z = -700$
Divide by -10: $z = 70$
                                               $a + b - 4z = 500$
Plug in 70 for z and solve: $a + b - 4(70) = 500$
Simplify: $a + b - 280 = 500$
Add 280: $a + b = 780$

---

15. 13   You are told that the sequence listed is a pattern that repeats every *five* terms. To find the sum of the first 37 terms, begin by finding out how many times the pattern of 5 terms occurs. Divide 37 by 5 and find the remainder:

$$5\overline{)37}\ \ ^{7 R2}$$

The pattern occurs 7 FULL times with a remainder of 2. That means that the 37th term is the SECOND term in the sequence.

Each repetition of the pattern has a sum of $-2 + 1 + 3 + -1 + 1 = 2$.
If that pattern occurs seven FULL times, that would give a sum of $7(2) = 14$.
But you have to include the 36th and 37th terms as well, which are -2 and 1, respectively.
As a result, the sum of the first 37 terms is $14 + -2 + 1 = 13$.

---

16. 400   This is another system of equations problem. Set up an equation for Zander's weekly salary and set up an equation for David's weekly salary. Let S = salary and T = tips:

Zander: $S = \$250 + .15T$
David: $S = \$50 + .35T$

Set the two equations equal to each other and solve for T: $\$250 + .15T = \$50 + .35T$
Subtract $.15T$: $\$250 = \$50 + .20T$
Subtract 50: $\$200 = .20T$
Divide by .20: $\$1,000 = T$

Be careful here. Do not bubble-in $1000 as tempting as that might be. The question wants to know what the SALARY was. So, plug that $1,000 in for T and solve for S.

                             $S = \$250 + .15T$
Plug in $1000 for T $S = \$250 + .15(1000)$
Simplify: $S = \$250 + \$150 = \$400$

---

17. 384   The smallest cube that would contain the sphere shown would stretch the length of the diameter of the sphere—the sphere would extend right up to the edge of each face of the cube.

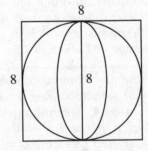

This means that the edge of the cube would be 8 inches (the radius of the sphere is 4, so the diameter of the sphere would be 8). The surface area of a cube is equal to the sum of the areas of the six faces. Each side has an area of $(8)^2 = 64$ square inches. There are 6 identical faces in a cube, which means that the area would be $6(64) = 384$ square inches.

18. 21.6 You are told that $\overline{YW}$ is perpendicular to $\overline{XY}$, which means that triangle XYW is a right triangle.

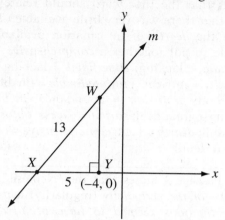

Because it is a right triangle, you can find the value of WY by using the Pythagorean theorem:

$$(XY)^2 + (WY)^2 = (XW)^2$$
$$(5)^2 + (WY)^2 = (13)^2$$

Simplify: $\quad\quad\quad 25 + (WY)^2 = 169$

Subtract 25: $\quad\quad\quad\quad (WY)^2 = 144$

Take square root: $\quad\quad\quad (WY) = 12$

You can find the coordinates of point X because you know it is 5 units to the left of Y, which has the coordinates $(-4, 0)$. So, the coordinates of point X are $(-9, 0)$.

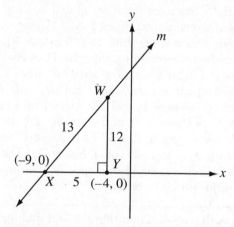

The question wants to know the y-intercept of line m. We can find the coordinate of point W because we know it is 12 units above point Y, which has the coordinates $(-4, 0)$. So, the coordinates of point W are $(-4, 12)$.

You can visually determine the slope of the line (rise over run) from point X to point W, as it goes

up 12 and right 5: $\quad\quad \dfrac{rise}{run} = \dfrac{12}{5} = m$

$$y = mx + b$$

Plug in the coordinates of X, $(-9, 0)$ to that equation:
$$0 = m(-9) + b$$

Plug in the slope for m: $\quad\quad 0 = \dfrac{12}{5}(-9) + b$

Simplify: $\quad\quad\quad\quad\quad 0 = \dfrac{-108}{5} + b$

Add $\dfrac{108}{5}$: $\quad\quad\quad\quad \dfrac{108}{5} = b = 21.6$

Section 3

1. C Because Samantha *sobbed* **uncontrollably,** she was clearly *quite upset (dejected)* about having lost in the finals. *pragmatic* = practical; *querulous* = full of complaints; *jubilant* = joyful; *indifferent* = without interest or concern

2. D The word *although* lets us know that a contrast is coming. Because she was stunned by what she found, the two missing words should have opposite meanings. If the explanation seemed *outlandish* (peculiar, freakishly odd) at first, it would likely stun her to find out it was *factual* (real). *dubious* = doubtful; *mistaken* = incorrect; *illogical* = senseless; *inconsistent* = lacking agreement; *reasonable* = logical; *accurate* = correct; *outlandish* = peculiar, freakishly odd; *factual* = real; *histrionic* = overly dramatic; *awkward* = clumsy

3. A Lin was *granted the honor* of creating the Vietnam Veterans Memorial in 1981. Therefore, the missing word should mean *selected* or *empowered*. *commissioned* = granted authority to carry out a task; *conditioned* = characterized by a consistent pattern of behavior; *politicized* = made political; *streamlined* = modernized; *aggregated* = combined

4. E The tryptophan had an effect that *induced sleep*, which is what the missing word should mean. *mundane* = common, everyday; *depreciatory* = diminishing in value; *invigorating* = filling with life and energy; *lugubrious* = gloomy; *soporific* = tending to induce sleep

5. D Nevada only gets 7 inches of rain in a year, so it is logical that the state government would urge its municipalities to avoid **waste** during the driest times of the year. Look at the second words and keep anything that suggests waste:

dissemination = spread; *circumspection* = caution, prudence; *discretion* = judgment; *improvidence* = wastefulness; *immoderation* = the quality of being excessive

Choices (D) and (E) are reasonable choices for the second blank.

Turn your attention to the first blank now. The government would urge them to avoid waste and to practice **care** *with the water.*

latency = inactivity; *complacency* = a feeling of self-satisfaction; *salvation* = the act of saving from harm; *husbandry* = controlled use of resources; *partisanship* = an inclination to favor one group over others

Given the small amount of rainfall, it makes good sense that the Nevada state government would *put forth strong recommendations to its municipalities that urge them to practice* **husbandry** *with water and to avoid* **improvidence** *during the driest times of the year.*

6. A Prior to the passage of the Endangered Species Act, the Bald Eagle population was *dwindling.* You are told that it has been removed from the Endangered Species List, which suggests that it must no longer be dwindling, and in fact must be *flourishing* or *burgeoning. wan* = to decrease in strength or intensity; *attenuate* = to weaken or reduce in force; *disperse* = to scatter in various directions; *conflate* = to merge, to fuse into one entity

7. B The first missing word should relate to the phrase following the semicolon: *their enthusiasm.*
cynicism = an outlook of scornful negativity; *ardor* = fervor, passion; *mendacity* = untruthfulness; *earnestness* = sincere zealousness; *autonomy* = freedom of will
Of the 5 choices, *ardor* and *earnestness* work for the first blank. The *exposure to the harsh and often unpleasant realities of the business world* has done something to the positive outlooks. Looking at the choices B and D: *sullied* = stained, tarnished; *substantiated* = established by proof. Choice B works best. *dilapidated* = allowed to fall into a state of disrepair; *bedraggled* = made limp and soiled; *buttressed* = supported, reinforced

8. E Despite the —— of published information about Longear's *preadolescent years*, Gilda was able to put together a report that *covered all aspects of his childhood in* **great detail** (This means that the report was *comprehensive*). The *despite* at the beginning of the sentence sets up a contrast, which suggests that the first word should relate to the notion that there was very little available (*dearth*). Despite the *dearth* of information available, she was able to put together a *comprehensive* report. *inadequate* = lacking; *superficial* = lacking depth; *complexity* = intricacy; *unintelligible* = unable to be understood; *profusion* = abundance; *inclusive* = including a great deal; *surfeit* = excess; *obtuse* = not sharp, dull; *dearth* = lack; *comprehensive* = containing great detail

9. A Passage 1 states that the "Nemesis" theory *accounts for the periodicity* (regularity) *with which mass extinctions seemed to have occurred* (lines 10–12), that is, it explains the fact that they have occurred every 26 million years or so.

10. D Passage 2 states that *the pressure to evolve feathers was a robust one...because the climate was cooling* (lines 26–31), that is the forces of natural selection made it advantageous for animals to have warm feathers. This "pressure," then, is a natural influence on the development of many species.

11. E Both passages mention global cooling (*lowered global temperatures*, lines 7–8 of Passage 1, and *the climate was cooling*, line 29 of Passage 2), mass extinction (*mass extinctions*, lines 10–11 of Passage 1, and *all of the larger dinosaurs...died out*, lines 32–33), meteoric impact (*meteors that collide with Earth*, lines 4–5 of Passage 1, and *the impact of a meteor*, lines 30–31 of Passage 2), and volcanic activity (*massive volcanic eruption*, line 15 of Passage 1, and *volcanic eruptions*, line 31 of Passage 2), but only Passage 2 discusses evolution, specifically the evolution of dinosaurs into birds.

12. C Both passages mention the fact that the mass extinction event of 65 million years ago involved global cooling, possibly with a terrestrial cause, like a massive volcano, or an extraterrestrial cause, like a meteor. They also both suggest that both of these explanations are plausible, and therefore that neither has been definitively proved, and therefore that there is debate among scientists on this issue. The passages disagree, however, on the question of whether the dinosaurs could have adapted to this dramatic climate change: Passage 1 states that it *killed off all of the dinosaurs* (lines 8–9), while Passage 2 states that *modern birds are the direct descendants of the dinosaurs* (lines 23–24).

13. E   The *dessert* in this sentence is something that is *save[d]...for last,* and compared to *the part of the broadcast more people watch than any other.* As such, it is described as something that is savored.

14. B   The question *What else could it be...* is rhetorical: the author is not really inquiring, but making a point that he expects the reader to agree with. In this case, the point is that weather forecasts are the most eagerly anticipated part of news programs. This introduces the central topic of the passage: television weather forecasting. This is certainly not a *cultural mystery,* nor is it part of a *controversy* or a *sober analysis,* since the passage as a whole is a fairly lighthearted examination of a well-known cultural phenomenon.

15. B   Our *relationship with the elements,* as is explained in the sentence that follows, is our relationship with the weather itself, which the passage suggests has been altered by television weather forecasts. Therefore *elements* in this context refers to atmospheric conditions.

16. B   The *military veterans* who gave old television weather forecasts are said to be people who *barely cracked a smile* and who *droned on about fronts and pressure systems.* Clearly, these phrases characterize these folks as being dull and monotonous.

17. A   The final sentence of the third paragraph says that *the weather [that is, television weather forecasts] was relentlessly cute from coast to coast,* but the sentence in lines 28–34 indicates that these forecasts could also be *high drama* or even *tragedy,* suggesting that they could also be occasionally *grave.*

18. C   The battle between *Susanna South Wind* and *Nanook North Wind* is a playful exchange between two characters in a particular local forecast in Chicago. It is cited as an example of how *the weather was relentlessly cute.*

19. A   The *absurdity* that the author discusses in this paragraph is the combination of two facts: the fact that there is *a built-in risk factor that the forecast will be wrong,* and the fact that the forecaster *claims to understand [the weather].* That is, it is a combination of *confidence and uncertainty.* Although the absurd juxtaposition of *the tragic and the humorous* is later mentioned in the quotation from Tom Skilling, this is not the absurdity that the author is discussing here. This absurdity is also not a combination of the *logical and the illogical,* because the passage does not suggest that weather or its forecasting is *illogical,* but merely that it is *unpredictable.*

20. A   The statement that *anybody who gets up and claims to understand [the weather] must be touched with [perversity, vindictiveness, irascibility, and cruelty] as well* is saying that weather forecasters are *tainted with* these negative qualities.

21. D   This sentence states that *government forecasters can hide behind their supercomputers and numerical models,* unlike television forecasters who are *right there in our faces,* and therefore unable to hide from their responsibility for their predictions. Therefore, these *supercomputers and numerical models* provide government forecasters with *cover for inaccurate predictions.*

22. E   Eustis' comments suggest that television viewers are not sympathetic to television meteorologists. He says that *the audience is just waiting for [the forecaster] to be wrong,* and that the audience expresses the natural instinct to *laugh at someone who's trying to be a shaman about the weather.* This suggests that the audience finds the mere *presumptuousness* of the forecaster's task to be funny, not the forecaster's antics per se.

23. C   Skilling's comments indicate that he believes that sometimes television forecasts are too *flippant* (not showing an appropriately respectful attitude). He suggests that it is inappropriate that *weather—which can actually kill people—has been presented as something of a joke on the air*

24. D   The *highs and lows* mentioned in this sentence, like *jet streams and occluded fronts,* are weather phenomena.

Section 4

1. C   The singular verb *is* should instead be the plural form *are* because it is describing a plural subject, *effects.* Choice (C) fixes that problem.

2. B   The original sentence is a run-on sentence. Choice (B) properly links the two clauses.

3. A   The sentence is correct as written.

4. C   This sentence lists three things they want their babysitter to be able to do, and therefore the three qualities should have parallel phrasing. Since the first thing they want the babysitter to be able to do is *work flexible hours,* and the second thing is *display patience* (both in the infinitive form), the third thing should be phrased similarly: *have fun.*

5. **B** The verb phrase *were never finishing* is in the wrong form and should instead be replaced by *who had never finished* (answer choice B). Answer choice (D) seems tempting, but when you read the entire sentence it is actually now a run-on. Answer choice (E) would be correct if the verb *has* were not there.

6. **C** The verb phrase *having comprised* should instead be *comprised*. Answer choices (C) makes that fix. Answer choice (B) is a sentence fragment.

7. **E** The original sentence contains a dangling participle. The participle *walking* should have *we* as its subject, not the dummy subject *it*. (That is, *it* wasn't walking, *we* were.) Therefore, the main clause must have *we* as its subject. Choices (C) and (D) correct the dangling participle, but are unidiomatic.

8. **C** This is an *idiom/preposition* error. The phrase *synonymous to* should instead be *synonymous with*—choice C.

9. **A** The sentence is correct as written.

10. **B** The original contains a comma splice joining two independent clauses, and is therefore a "run-on" sentence. Choice (C) is a sentence fragment, choice (D) contains a misplaced appositive phrase and an illogical coordinator (*therefore*), and choice (E) is unidiomatic and awkward.

11. **C** This verb phrase *having been* is not in the correct form. Choice (B) creates a dangling participle: Wright's *delivery* is considered to be a great comic. Choice (D) is excessively awkward and unidiomatic. Choice (C) correctly changes the verb phrase *having been* to the present form *is*.

12. **B** The phrase *more stronger* should just be *stronger*.

13. **B** The verb phrase *has begun* should be replaced by *began* (simple past), because it occurred in the past.

14. **D** The sentence makes a comparison between *the chicken and broccoli at Kudeta* and *Hunan Garden*, so the phrase in (D) is incomplete, and should include *the chicken and broccoli at*.

15. **C** The use of the idiomatic phrase *not only* requires the conjunction *but also*.

16. **B** The plural subject, *their*, is referring to a singular subject *the Heron*. It should instead be *its*.

17. **C** As the sentence is currently constructed, the *impressive model* is actually *roaming through the various exhibits*, which would be neat to see, but is highly unlikely. The *roaming* should be replaced with *as I roamed*.

18. **C** This is a modifier error. The adjective *surprising* should be replaced by the adverb form *surprisingly* because it modifies an adjective (large).

19. **B** The word *overran* is the past tense conjugation of the verb *to overrun*, but the sentence requires an adjective to describe the entrance bay, so the past participle *overrun* is required.

20. **E** The sentence is correct as written.

21. **A** The subject *it* should be replaced by *he*.

22. **E** The sentence is correct as written.

23. **B** The subject *his or her* disagrees in number with a prior reference to that same subject, *workers*. It should be changed to *their*.

24. **D** This is an *idiom/preposition* error. The phrase *opposition against* should instead be *opposition to*.

25. **E** The sentence is correct as written.

26. **D** As it is written, this sentence contains an illogical comparison between *Yo-Yo Ma's cello play* and *Jacqueline du Pre*. The phrase in (D) is incomplete, and should include *the cello play of*.

27. **C** The verb *is* does not agree with the plural subject *lost storage containers* and should be changed to *are*.

28. **C** This is an *idiom/preposition* error. The phrase *derives in* should be changed to *derives from*.

29. **D** The subject *each* is always singular, so the subject *they were* should be changed to *he was*.

30. **D** The passage focuses on an individual's personal experience with olives. So, the introductory sentence should give personal background information about that person that relates to her life history with olives.

31. **D** As currently written, the second sentence is a fragment. Because the second clause contains a list of examples to support the first clause, the two sentences should be connected by a colon.

32. C   The sentence is conveying the notion that they behaved a certain way until they learned something about olives. Choice (C) creates the proper temporal relationship.

33. E   The passage clearly contains sentence length variation as some sentences contain 3 words and others contain more than 10 words. The passage is most certainly being personally narrated by an individual who grew up in a Greek-American household. The passage contains detailed descriptions: *I found a vendor selling dozens of different kinds of olives* (sentence 7) and *the little pimentos that protrude out of them turned me off* (sentence 5). Sentence 9, *How had I never tried green olives before?*, contains a rhetorical question. The passage lacks metaphor.

34. C   The verb phrase *having been* should be changed to the simple past tense form *was*.

35. D   Sentence 14 tells us that she puts *pepper* on a lot of the food that she eats. The entire passage focuses on olives. This sentence is unrelated to the rest of the passage.

Section 5

1. C   Marisa has directed quite a variety of films—*she has directed thrillers, romances, comedies, and dramas.* So, you are looking for an adjective that would describe someone who is *versatile* (capable of doing many things). *mediocre* = moderate or inferior in quality; *laconic* = using few words; *demonstrative* = given to open expression of emotion; *lethargic* = lacking energy

2. B   The sentence is discussing *improvements in data transfer that have ------- mobile communication.* It is logical to conclude that these improvements would have a positive effect on communication, so the 2nd missing word should be a positive word. Choice (B) *revolutionized* = effected a radical change in, choice (D) *streamlined* = designed to give maximum efficiency, and choice (E) *qualified* = made capable, modified, or limited in some way, could all work. Choice (A) *transcended* = passed beyond the limits of, is a positive word, but it doesn't really fit in the context here. Choice (C), *degenerated* = diminished in quality should be eliminated.
For the first blank, you want an improvement that would make mobile communication easier for those on the move (*business travelers*). We are left with choices (B) *efficiency* = competency in performance, (D) *aesthetics* = pertaining to beauty, and (E) *manifestation* = outward or perceptible indication. Only choice (B), *efficiency*, makes sense in that blank.

proficiency = expertness; *aggregation* = collection into an unorganized whole

3. E   She was not able to actually eat the food and had to enjoy by watching others. This is a classic description of *vicarious* enjoyment (acting or serving as a substitute). *sporadic* = appearing or happening at irregular intervals; *gluttonous* = tending to eat or drink excessively; *meticulous* = attentive to details; *munificent* = generous

4. D   Jim Valvano gave a speech that *moved the entire audience to tears*, so it would need to be a speech that would affect or move emotions (*poignant*). *mundane* = common, everyday; *hackneyed* = overused, trite; *spare* = concise, not wasteful; *bucolic* = pertaining to a rural lifestyle

5. B   Music played during a *mournful funeral scene* ought to be appropriate for that mood—it should be *doleful* (sorrowful) or *lugubrious* (gloomy). It would not be *sprightly* (lively, animated), *bombastic* (pretentious), or *inchoate* (not yet fully developed). If the director complained about the music, that suggests that the music, was *not* appropriate for the mood and that it was instead *upbeat*. The director would not complain if the music was *melancholic* (gloomy). But the director *would* complain if it was *buoyant* (cheering). Choice B is the best match. *voluble* = talkative; *tedious* = long and tiresome

6. C   The first two sentences describe viewing a checkerboard as an analogy for viewing social divisions from a political viewpoint. The point of the analogy is that *there is no single way of looking* at either a checkerboard or the divisions in a society.

7. A   The *cleavage* in this sentence refers to a way that someone can divide society into distinct groups according to a political ideology like progressivism or socialism. The examples of these distinctions, those between *the privileged* and *the people* and then between *the working class* and *the master class*, make it clear that these are social divisions.

8. D   The passage contrasts *social history* (line 1) with *political history* (lines 3–4) and explains this contrast with the examples of *some quite ordinary person* versus *Robert of Normandy* (lines 8–10) and a *personal treatment* (line 15) versus *learned treatises on the development of the manor or on medieval trade* (lines 19–21). These exemplify the contrast between depictions of ordinary citizens on the one hand and depictions of political leaders and institutions on the other.

9. B The thesis of this passage is that *social history lends itself particularly to what may be called a personal treatment, and that the past may be made to live again for the general reader more effectively by personifying it* (lines 14–18). The quote from Maeterlinck, therefore, is used to mean that historians should bring their subjects back to life by personifying them.

10. B The passage states that Holden's *relationship with his social environment differs from those [of Huck Finn and Hester Prynne] in that Holden is very much a part of his society* (lines 11–12), whereas Finn and Prynne are *thrust to the periphery* (line 17) of their societies.

11. C The quotation from Joyce Rowe in lines 14–15 states that Holden was *blessed with the Materials of the Promised Land*, unlike Huck Finn and Hester Prynne. That is, he was a much more fortunate member of society than they were.

12. C In the statement *Finn and Prynne...are...thrust to the periphery of a society in which prosperity finds purchase only in enclaves*, the phrase *finds purchase in* (gains a foothold) and the noun *enclaves* (culturally isolated regions) may not be familiar to you. However, the phrase *on the other hand* should still enable you to make sense of this sentence. This phrase suggests that Finn and Prynne are in a very different situation than Caulfield's. The quotation from Joyce Rowe suggests that Caulfield is part of the *Promised Land*, which is a place where everyone can enjoy its *material splendors*. Therefore, this sentence suggests that Finn and Prynne are not part of any *Promised Land*, and in fact that, in their societies, affluence is not widespread.

13. A The passage states that Caulfield has a *commitment to profligacy*, which means a devotion to wasting his blessings, which is *prodigal* (wastefully extravagant) *behavior*.

14. E Caulfield's ambivalence is later referred to as *his dual impulses—toward and from the people around him*. Therefore his ambivalence consists of his inclinations toward *withdrawing from society* on the one hand and *becoming part of it* on the other.

15. D In asking whether *we, too, are destined for an institution*, the author is referring to the fact that Caulfield was *led inexorably to the sanitorium*, which is a mental hospital. The author is asking whether we, too, should enter such a *corrective facility*, because we empathize with Caulfield.

16. A Caulfield is clearly characterized as being *conflicted* at several points in this passage: Rowe's quotation refers to Caulfield's *self-mutilation*, and the passage later refers to his *ambivalence* and *his dual impulses*. The passage does not mention anything about whether Caulfield is *sophisticated, composed*, or *sadistic*, although it did mention that Caulfield actually <u>lacked</u> a strong will to *tame his dual impulses*.

17. E This sentence states that *Salinger places [the question of whether we, since we empathize with Caulfield, also belong in a sanitorium] deliberately in our path*, which means that Salinger has tried successfully to make the reader sympathize with Holden's angst.

18. A In saying that *we resolve our own version of this conflict by also accepting the asylum*, the author suggests that we do, in fact, require emotional treatment, as Caulfield does, although ours comes in the form of *Oprah, self-help books, meditation classes, and spa retreats*.

19. B McLuhan's quotation likens a newspaper to *a warm bath*, and the author likewise extends the metaphor by calling *The New York Times* a *great public bath* and *regional physiotherapy tank*, all of which suggest that newspapers are *soothing to the senses*.

20. C When the author says *Now, you may say, My God, man! You woke up over that? You forsook your blissful coma over a mere swell in the sea of words?* he is suggesting that the reader is surprised that such a seemingly innocuous comment had such a strong impact on the author. In other words, he suggests that the reader *does not share the author's enthusiasm for Kramer's statement*. This comment does not imply that the reader might disagree with the actual content of Kramer's review, but just that the reader would find it uninteresting.

21. E The author states that Kramer's review *didn't say "something helpful" or "enriching" or even "extremely valuable." No, the word was "crucial."* Here the author is emphasizing the weight that Kramer is giving to the need for a *persuasive theory of art*.

22. C Here the author describes his experience of standing in front of thousands of paintings, waiting for the *visual reward which must be there...waiting for something to radiate directly from the paintings*, that is, he was *attempting to find meaning in art through sight alone*, rather than from the perspective of some theory of art.

23. **A**   In this sentence, the author is talking to himself about the revelation that he has just had about the need for a theory of art. In saying *Not "seeing is believing," you ninny, but "believing is seeing,"* the author is affirming his realization that he can't appreciate art without first believing in some theory of art.

24. **A**   The author's concluding statement is a concise summary of his thesis that *the paintings and other works exist only to illustrate the text*, where the *text* is a theory of art, or a set of *aesthetic principles*.

Section 6

1. **C**   The easiest way to solve this problem is to find the fewest possible number of CDs on the racks and the greatest possible number of CDs on the racks. If each rack contains at least 10 CDs, and there are 5 racks, then there must be at least $5(10) = 50$ CDs. If each rack contains no more than 14 CDs and there are 5 racks, then there must be no more than $5(14) = 70$ CDs. This leaves us with only answer choice C as a possibility.

2. **B**   You are told that p is 2 more than m. You are also told that $m = 2$. Find p: $p = m + 2 = 2 + 2 = 4$. You are told that x is 4 less than p, which is 4. So, $x = p - 4 = 4 - 4 = 0$.

3. **C**   This question tests your ability to arrange shapes spatially. You might want to draw an *xy*-coordinate plane around the original figure you are given:

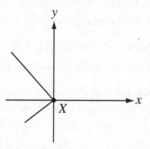

The shape is to be rotated 90 degrees counterclockwise. So, the longer side of the L-shape should end up in the bottom-left quadrant of the picture, about halfway between the x and y axes.

4. **B**   This is a system of equations question. Write two equations to represent the given information. The price of admission is $6 more for adults than for children: $A = C + 6$

A group of 6 adults and 18 children pay a total of $108:
$$6A + 18C = 108$$
Now, substitute $(C + 6)$ for A:
$$6(C + 6) + 18C = 108$$
Distribute: $6C + 36 + 18C = 108$
Combine terms: $24C + 36 = 108$
Subtract 36: $24C = 72$
Divide by 24: $C = 3$
Now plug in for C to solve for A: $A = C + 6 = 3 + 6 = 9$

5. **E**   The bottom portion of the shaded region includes a part of all three circles. This would represent cars with all three features. The top portion of the shaded region includes a part of two circles: DVD players and navigation systems. So, the shaded area would represent cars with DVD players and navigation systems (some possibly with all-wheel drive)—choice E.

6. **C**   To get from -14 to 11, you must take 5 "equally spaced" steps past the tick marks. The distance covered from -14 to 11 is equal to $11 - (-14) = 11 + 14 = 25$ units. If the five steps are equally spaced, then each step is equal to $25 \div 5 = 5$ units. Now you can label each tick mark with a number rather than a letter.

7. **B**   Ratios such as 7:3 can also be written as $7x : 3x$. So, the number of votes Julie received was $7x$ and the number of votes Bob received was $3x$. The total number of votes can be represented by the following equation: $7x + 3x = 200,000$
   Combine terms: $10x = 200,000$
   Divide by 10: $x = 20,000$
The question wants to know how many votes were cast for Bob Tanks, who received $3x$ votes. Plug in 20,000 for x and solve:
$$3x = 3(20,000) = 60,000$$

8. **B**   A counterexample is an example that demonstrates that a certain statement is false. In order to prove that the statement "All multiples of 3 are odd" is false, you need to show that at least one multiple of 3 is *not* odd. The only number among the choices that is a multiple of 3 and *not* odd is (B) 12.

9. **E**
$$|x - 2.5| < 12$$
Split the absolute value into two inequalities:
$$x - 2.5 < 12 \quad \text{and} \quad x - 2.5 > -12$$
Add 2.5: $x < 14.5$ and $x > -9.5$
Now find all the integer values within that range:
$-9, -8, -7, -6, -5, -4, -3, -2, -1, 0, 1, 2, 3, 4, 5, 6, 7, 8, 9, 10, 11, 12, 13, 14$
There are 24 integer values.

10. **D**   Begin by writing an equation for the average of 8 and x and set it equal to 10.

$$\frac{8+x}{2} = 10$$

Multiply by 2: $8 + x = 20$
Subtract 8: $x = 12$

Next, write an equation for the average of 7 and y and set it equal to 11.

$$\frac{7+y}{2} = 11$$

Multiply by 2: $7 + y = 22$
Subtract 7: $y = 15$

Finally, find the average of x and y:

$$\frac{x+y}{2} = \frac{12+15}{2} = \frac{27}{2} = 13.5$$

---

11. **B**   Turn *Of the 360 students at a private school, $\frac{4}{5}$ were from the state of Connecticut* into a mathematical equation: Let C = # of people from CT:

$$\frac{4}{5}(360) = C$$

Simplify: $288 = C$

Turn $\frac{3}{8}$ *of the students lived on campus* into a mathematical equation. Let X = # of students living on campus:

$$\frac{3}{8}(360) = X$$

Simplify: $135 = X$

If you want to find the least possible number of students that lived on campus who were from Connecticut, find the greatest possible number of students that lived on campus who were NOT from Connecticut.

Of the 360 students, 288 of them were from CT. This means that $360 - 288 = 72$ were NOT from CT. The greatest possible number of students that lived on campus that were NOT from CT would be 72 if every single student who was not from CT did not live on campus.

This would mean that the least possible number of students who lived on campus who were from CT would be $135 - 72 = 63$.

---

12. **A**   If the male population increases by 10% next year, then $200 \times .10 = 20$ more men will be enrolled next year. If the total student population is to increase by no more than 8%, then at most $(200 + 250) \times .08 = 36$ more students can be enrolled next year. This means that no more than $36 - 20 = 16$ additional women can be enrolled next year.

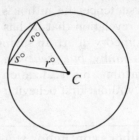

13. **C**   Notice that two of the sides of the triangle are radii of the circle, and since all radii of a circle are equal, the triangle is isosceles. In an isosceles triangle, the angles across from the equal sides are also equal, so the missing angle also has a measure of $s°$. Since all of the angles in triangle have a sum of 180°, $s + s + r = 180$. Now let's solve this equation for s, because that's what the question asks about.

Simplify: $2s + r = 180$
Subtract r: $2s = 180 - r$

Divide by 2: $s = \dfrac{180 - r}{2}$

Now since r is between 20 and 40, we can find the range of values for s by plugging in $r = 20$ and $r = 40$.

$$\frac{180-40}{2} < s < \frac{180-20}{2}$$

Simplify: $70 < s < 80$

---

14. **A**   If $(a-4)(b-5) = 0$, then *either* $(a-4)$ equals 0 *or* $(b-5)$ equals 0. This means that either $a = 4$ or $b = 5$. If we want to *minimize* the value of $a + b$, then we should let $a = 4$. If this is true, then b can be anything, because 0 times anything is 0. Since both numbers must be positive integers, the least value b could have is 1. So the least possible value of $a + b$ is $4 + 1 = 5$.

---

15. **A**   A meal that costs m dollars that is split equally among 4 individuals, would cost $\dfrac{m}{4}$ dollars per person.

A meal that costs m dollars that is split equally among 6 individuals, would cost $\dfrac{m}{6}$ dollars per person. The difference in cost when there are 4 people rather than 6 can be found by subtracting those two amounts:

$$\frac{m}{4} - \frac{m}{6}$$

Find a common denominator (12): $\dfrac{3m}{12} - \dfrac{2m}{12} = \dfrac{m}{12}$

16. A This question tests your understanding of the triangle inequality theorem, which states that the third side of a triangle must be larger than the difference of the other two sides and smaller than the sum of the other two sides. $(A - B) < C < (A + B)$ You are told that the length of $\overline{RS}$ is 12 and the length of $\overline{ST}$ is 13. Using the triangle inequality theorem, we can find all of the possible lengths of $\overline{RT}$.

$$13 - 12 < \overline{RT} < 13 + 12$$

Simplify: $1 < \overline{RT} < 25$

The only answer choice that falls within that range is choice A, 24 units.

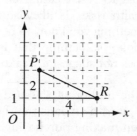

17. B If P and R are consecutive vertices of the square, then $\overline{PR}$ is one side of the square, and the area of this square is $(PR)^2$. Notice that if we apply the Pythagorean theorem to the diagram above, we get $2^2 + 4^2 = (PR)^2$. So the area of the square is $2^2 + 4^2 = 4 + 16 = 20$.

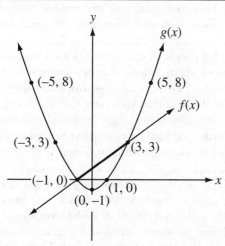

18. C To solve this question, you need to find the portions of the graph where the graph of $f(x)$ is ABOVE the graph of $g(x)$. This occurs from $x = -1$ to $x = 3$ (See bold line above).

19. B This question looks like pure algebra at first, but in fact it requires more *numerical reasoning* than algebra. However, there is *one* useful algebraic fact to

use here: $m^2 - n^2 = (m + n)(m - n)$ for any values of m and n. Now, since $m^2 - n^2 < 12$ and $m + n > 10$, the equation $m^2 - n^2 = (m + n)(m - n)$ tells us that some positive integer less than 12 equals some positive integer greater than 10 times another positive integer. (We know $m - n$ is positive because we are told that $m > n$.) How could that be? Just the tiniest bit of guessing and checking shows that the only way that could work is if $m^2 - n^2 = 11$, $m + n = 11$, and $m - n = 1$. So m and n are two integers that are 1 apart and add up to 11. The only solution is $m = 6$ and $n = 5$. Check it and see!

20. C   The probability of an event occurring =

$$\frac{\text{number of desired outcomes}}{\text{total number of outcomes}}$$

Begin by finding out how many total four-card arrangements are possible. To make such an arrangement, you must make 4 decisions. First, you have 6 card colors to choose from to fill the first spot, then 5 left for the second, then 4 left for the third, and then 3 left for last spot. This gives a total of $6 \times 5 \times 4 \times 3 = 360$ possible four-card arrangements.

Only ONE of those 360 four-card arrangements will have the exact arrangement of *blue, red, yellow,* and *green,* in that order. So, the probability is $\frac{1}{60}$.

Section 7

1. C The *addictive nature* of online gambling has forced many to *seek treatment. Compulsive* (governed by an irresistible impulse to perform certain actions) behavior is certainly something that would be displayed by *addicted* gamblers. *delectable* = delicious, delightful; *palliative* = soothing; *fortified* = strengthened; *provident* = providing for the future

2. A An individual who *craves success* would likely be governed by a desire for things that would come with success, such as *wealth, celebrity,* and *prosperity* (thriving condition, especially related to wealth). *scrutiny* = close examination; *infamy* = fame for bad reasons; *spontaneity* = the quality of acting without restraint; impulsiveness; *negligence* = carelessness

3. E The critics *criticized her characters for being too shallow.* So, it would make sense that she was attempting to *appease* (soothe) the critics. She would do so by adding *depth* to her characters—choice (E). *precision* = accuracy; *exacerbate* = to make worse; *paucity* = scarcity, a lack; *compensate* = to counterbalance, to make payment; *profundity* = deepness; *aggravate* = to make worse; *brevity* = briefness; *assuage* = to soothe

4. **A** Jim Leyland *surprised the crowd when he engaged in an explosive altercation with the umpire after he made a bad call*. This would suggest that he was generally not one who would engage in arguments. Answer choice (A), *contentious* (prone to argument) is a good fit. *magnanimous* = generous; *serene* = peaceful; *solicitous* = anxious; *imperturbable* = incapable of being upset

5. **D** The Polio vaccine has suppressed the number of worldwide cases to such a small number that doctors rarely encounter the illness. Because it is so rare, it's reasonable that a doctor might *misdiagnose* the virus if he or she saw a patient with polio (an *afflicted* individual) because it would be such an unusual thing to see. *infected* = contaminated with a pathogen; *disregard* = to pay no attention to; *exposed* = susceptible to attack; *retract* = to draw back; *transmuted* = changed; *capitulate* = to surrender; *engaged* = occupied; *eradicate* = to eliminate completely

6. **C** The Chief Resident *loathed* (hated) medical students who would ------- her *in an effort to win her favor*. The second word should be something along the lines of *praise highly*. Answer choice (C), *commend* = extol, praise, fits very well. *castigate* = criticize severely; *antagonize* = to provoke the hostility of; *belabor* = to assail persistently; *complement* = to complete Be very careful with choice (A) for this question. *Sycophant* (servile flatterer) fits very well in the first blank and *complement* **looks** like it fits perfectly in the second blank. But, notice the spelling. The word listed in choice (A) is *complement* (to complete) and not *compliment* (to say something that expresses praise).
If you know all the words, only choice C works for the second blank. The first missing word should be similar in meaning to the second word, and *obsequious* (overly submissive) fits well in that first blank. *recalcitrant* = hesitant to obey; *unwitting* = inadvertent; *gluttonous* = greedy, insatiable

7. **D** In Passage 1, the author discusses the challenges he faces in choosing "environmentally friendly" products. He confesses that he, like many other people, is shortsighted and selfish, and can best be persuaded to buy things that help the environment by either being provided financial incentives or having his choices reduced. Passage 2 focuses on scientific and economic findings that suggest, to the author, that global warming may not be universally harmful, and so efforts to curb it should be reasonable and cost-effective, rather than rash and expensive. Choice (D) best summarizes these two perspectives.

8. **D** The author feels *pangs of guilt* in buying the power-hungry and carbon dioxide-producing hedge trimmer because he *knew [he] was doing wrong* in that he also wants to *reduce [his] output of carbon dioxide and other greenhouse gases*.

9. **E** The author of Passage 1 mentions Ulysses because he understood "akrasia," [or moral weakness] when he instructed his crew to tie him to the mast when they passed the Sirens. That is, Ulysses is an example of someone who lacks a strong moral will.

10. **A** "Akrasia" is defined in this passage as "weakness," specifically a weakness to resist doing what you know to be wrong, which in the author's case is buying carbon-spewing products. Of the choices, only (A) being unable to resist eating chocolate despite knowing its health risks, is likewise a weakness to resist doing something you know to be wrong. Choice (B) describes doing something that is immoral and illegal, but it does not suggest a weakness of will.

11. **B** When the author of Passage 1 states *I am attuned only to price*, he means that he is only *sensitive to* cost when making purchasing decisions, and not to environmental needs.

12. **C** In saying *Fine, you say. The solution is obvious: let's adjust the price so that the "right thing" is priced right for people like me*, the author is presenting a solution that provides a financial incentive to the author, and suggesting that the reader might offer it. This assumes that the reader believes that *financial incentives can effectively influence behavior*.

13. **D** The thesis of Passage 2 is that recently both the natural science and the economics underlying predictions of climate-change impacts have altered dramatically, and that this new vision, in turn, calls for new strategies and new political outcomes. In other words, the author is suggesting policy changes in light of recent scientific findings.

14. **B** The third paragraph begins with the statement *Of course, we have not banished all uncertainty [about the predicted effects of global warming]* and so is qualifying, or moderating, the predictions made in the previous paragraph that global warming will be moderate and that productivity will likely increase over the long run. This qualification is certainly not disproving the claims made in the previous paragraph, so choice (E) is too extreme. It is also not exploring an implication of the author's thesis, as choice (A) suggests, because the claim that global warming may produce benefits does not imply that such predictions may be wrong.

15. **B**   The new perspective discussed in Passage 2 results from a *near revolution...in our understanding of the impacts of climate change.* This revolution has evidently led to a reduction in the magnitude of predicted warming and a situation in which economists are no longer predicting large damages, but rather a mixture of damages and benefits. In other words, it is a shift from dire predictions to moderate predictions.

16. **C**   The economists in line 47 are behavioral economists who have something to say about how the author does his discounting, that is, how he makes his decision about which washing machine to buy. On the other hand, the economists in line 89 are concerned with the net economic effects from climate change, and not on how individuals make decisions.

17. **E**   Both authors agree that *economic analysis should be considered when formulating a policy for dealing with global warming.* The author of Passage 1 suggests this in his lengthy discussion of how personal economics effect his decisions about purchasing environmentally friendly (or unfriendly) products. The author of Passage 2 suggests this when he states that *new abatement policies should be designed for the long run, and should be inexpensive and cost-effective.*

18. **A**   The conclusion of Passage 2 states that *new abatement policies* (that is, policies for trying to curb greenhouse gas emissions) *should be designed for the long run, and should be inexpensive and cost-effective;* therefore, he would likely question whether any such policy—for instance, manipulating the prices of washing machines to make the more carbon-efficient model more appealing—is *needlessly expensive and shortsighted.*

19. **C**   The author of Passage 1 states *all I care about is the deal today* (lines 48–49) and *I don't think I am alone in this* (lines 33–34), thereby demonstrating that he assumes that many readers are <u>not</u> *willing to consider long-term economic effects.* The author of Passage 2, however, suggests that readers <u>are</u> willing to consider the *net economic effects from climate change over the next century,* (lines 93–94), because he uses estimates of these effects as a basis for his policy recommendations.

Section 8

1. **B**   Write an equation for "$\frac{5}{8}$ of a number is 20":

$$\frac{5}{8}n = 20$$

| Multiply by 8: | $5n = 160$ |
| Divide by 5: | $n = 32$ |

Now find $\frac{1}{8}$ of that number: $\frac{1}{8}(32) = 4$

2. **B**   If $XY = ZY$, then $\triangle XYZ$ is an isosceles triangle, which means that $b = d$.

There are 180° on one side of a line: $a + b = 180°$
Subtract a: $b = 180° - a$
There are 180° on one side of a line: $d + e = 180°$
Subtract e: $d = 180° - e$
Because it is isosceles, $b = d$, so set the two equations equal: $180° - a = 180° - e$
Subtract 180°: $-a = -e$
Divide by -1: $a = e$

In general, if two angles are equal, then their complementary angles should be equal to each other as well.

3. **E**   This is a logic problem. The given statement says that all of Mark's former students go to college. If this is true, then answer choice E also has to be true because if Steve did NOT go to college, then he cannot be Mark's student because all of Mark's students went to college.

Choice A is wrong because the relationship does not say that all students who do NOT go to college must NOT have gone to Mark.

Choice B is wrong because the relationship does not generalize all students who went to college; it generalizes all students who went to Mark.

Choice C is wrong because it assumes that all students who go to college were Mark's students.

Choice D is the backwards relationship.

4. **D**   30 percent of n is $.30 \times n = .30n$, and 15 percent of $2n$ is $.15 \times 2n$, which also equals $.30n$, so 15 percent of $2n$ is also 72.

5. **A** $\frac{1}{x^{-2}} = 16$

$\frac{1}{x^{-2}}$ is the same thing as $\frac{x^2}{1}$ or x^2. $x^2 = 16$

Take square root: $x = 4$ or $x = -4$

6. **C**   If Colin averages 50 pages per hour for the first p hours, then over that span, he would read $50p$ pages. That would leave him with $400 - 50p$ pages to go.

You can also solve this problem by plugging in.

Let's say he reads 50 pages per hour for the first 3 hours ($p = 3$). This would mean he has read $50(3) = 150$ pages. If it was a 400-page book, he'd have $400 - 150 = 250$ pages left.

Now you plug in 3 for p in the answer choices and pick the one that gives you 250, which would be choice C.

SALES REVENUE FOR BARTSWELL CORPORATION

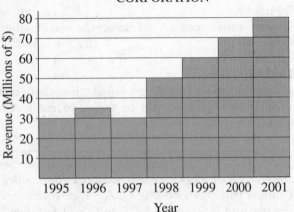

7. **D**   In 1996, the company's revenue was approximately $35 million, up from $30 million in 1995, an increase of $5 million. This $5 million is 1/6 of $30 million, so it is a 1/6 increase. The only other year in which there was a 1/6 increase from the previous year is 2000, where the previous year's revenue was $60 million, and the increase in revenue was $10 million.

---

8. **E**   Pick a value for m, like 11, that makes this statement true. (m must be 4 more than some multiple of 7.) If m is 11, then plug that into each of the answer choices and pick the answer choice that would yield a remainder of 3 when divided by 7:

(A) $m + 2 = 11 + 2 = 13$ (yields 1 remainder 6)
(B) $m + 3 = 11 + 3 = 14$ (yields 2 remainder 0)
(C) $m + 4 = 11 + 4 = 15$ (yields 2 remainder 1)
(D) $m + 5 = 11 + 5 = 16$ (yields 2 remainder 2)
(E) $m + 6 = 11 + 6 = 17$ (yields 2 remainder 3)

9. **A**   You are told that $a^2 - b^2 = 12$, and $(a - b) = 4$. When you encounter a difference of squares on the SAT ($a^2 - b^2$), it's a good idea to write down the difference of squares relationship:

$$a^2 - b^2 = (a + b)(a - b)$$

Plug in 12 for $a^2 - b^2$: $12 = (a + b)(a - b)$
Plug in 4 for $(a - b)$: $12 = (a + b)\,(4)$
Divide by 4: $3 = (a + b)$

Now we have a system of equations:

$$a + b = 3$$
$$\underline{a - b = 4}$$

Add straight down: $2a = 7$
Divide by 2: $a = 3.5$
Solve for b: $3 = a + b$
Plug in 3.5 for a: $3 = 3.5 + b$
Subtract 3.5: $-0.5 = b$
Find ab: $ab = (3.5)(-0.5) = -1.75$

---

10. **D**   You are told that $x \clubsuit y = x^2 - 2xy + y^2$ and asked to find the value of $(2 \clubsuit 4) \clubsuit 8$. First find the value of $(2 \clubsuit 4)$: $x \clubsuit y = x^2 - 2xy + y^2$
$$2 \clubsuit 4 = ?$$

Plug in 2 for each x and 4 for each y:
$$2 \clubsuit 4 = (2)^2 - 2(2)(4) + (4)^2$$
Simplify: $2 \clubsuit 4 = 4 - 16 + 16 = 4$

The question asks for the value of $(2 \clubsuit 4) \clubsuit 8$.
Substitute 4 for $2 \clubsuit 4$. $(2 \clubsuit 4) \clubsuit 8 = 4 \clubsuit 8$
Now do it again: $x \clubsuit y = x^2 - 2xy + y^2$
$$4 \clubsuit 8 = ?$$

Plug in 4 for each x and 8 for each y:
$$4 \clubsuit 8 = (4)^2 - 2(4)(8) + (8)^2$$
Simplify: $4 \clubsuit 8 = 16 - 64 + 64 = 16$

---

11. **B**   You might first recall that equations of lines cannot contain "squared" terms like x^2 or y^2, so the equations in (D) and (E) are not linear. Of the remaining choices, notice that $(3, 2)$ is a solution in (A) and (B) but not in (C), because $3(3) - 2(2)$ does not equal 10. This leaves only (A) and (B), but only (B) gives us a line with a *positive* slope. You can see this either by sketching a couple of solution points, or by putting the equation into "slope-intercept form:"

$$x - y = 1$$
Subtract x: $-y = -x + 1$
Multiply by -1: $y = x - 1$

Here, the coefficient of the "x" term is the slope of the line. Since this coefficient is 1, the slope of the line is positive.

12. **E**   As with most shaded area questions, in this question you will want to find the area of a larger shape and subtract the unshaded portion of that area to find the value of the shaded portion of that area. In this case, you need to find the area of the square and divide that by 4 because the triangle represents one-quarter of the entire figure. Contained within that triangle is one-quarter of the circle. So, to find the shaded area, you would subtract the one-quarter of the area of the circle from one-quarter of the area of the square.

First find the area of the square:

$$\text{area} = (\text{side})^2 = (4)^2 = 16$$

Second find the area of the circle:

$$\text{area} = \pi r^2$$

The diameter of the circle is 4 (it is equal to the side length of the square), which means that the radius of the circle is 2. $\text{area} = \pi(2)^2 = 4\pi$

The total area of the square is 16. One-quarter of that area would be 4.

The total area of the circle is 4π. One-quarter of that area would be π.

Therefore, the shaded area would be $4 - \pi$—choice E.

13. **B**   Each full repetition of the bead pattern consists of 3 yellow, 2 green, 1 black, and 3 orange, in that order. The pattern consists of a total of $3 + 2 + 1 + 3 = 9$ beads. If a bracelet were to be constructed that ended with a black bead, that would mean it was SIX beads into the pattern when the necklace was completed (3 yellow, 2 green, and that 1 black bead.) Look at the five answer choices and divide each of them by 9 (number of beads in a full pattern). This will tell you how many full repetitions of the pattern are in the necklace. The remainder from that quotient will tell you how many beads the necklace is into the repeating pattern. In the correct answer, the total number of beads must yield a remainder of 6 when it is divided by 9.

(A) $9\overline{)85}$ $\,^{9R4}$ —nope

(B) $9\overline{)87}$ $\,^{9R6}$ —there you go! The answer is 87

beads—choice B.

14. **C**   When you have a set that consists of an ODD number of consecutive integers, the *average* value of a member in that set is always the MIDDLE number. When you have a set that consists of an EVEN number of consecutive integers, the *average* value of a member in that set is always the average of the middle two numbers in the set. (So, the middle number of a set of consecutive integers either has to be an integer or end in .5 because the average of two consecutive integers will always be halfway between those two integers.)

I. If there were 3 integers in the set, then the average of the three integers would be

$$\frac{70}{3} = 23\,\frac{1}{3}$$

That is not possible.

II. If there were 5 integers in the set, then the average of the three integers would be

$$\frac{70}{5} = 214$$

So, the middle number would be 14:

12, 13, 14, 15, 16

$12 + 13 + 14 + 15 + 16 = 70$ This one works!

III. If there were 7 integers in the set, then the average of the three integers would be

$$\frac{70}{7} = 10$$

So, the middle number would be 10:

7, 8, 9, 10, 11, 12, 13

$7 + 8 + 9 + 10 + 11 + 12 + 13 = 70$ This one works!

It would be II and III—choice C.

15. **E** $5a + 9b = 14$
            $15a - tb = 38$

In a system of equations such as this, if you multiply the coefficient in front of a by 3, and you multiply the coefficient in front of b by 3, then in order for there to be solutions, the "answer" (in this case, 14), must also be multiplied by 3 ($14 \times 3 = 42$).

So, if t were -27, the system would look as follows:

$5a + 9b = 14$
$15a + 27b = 38$

The coefficients in front of a and b were both increased by a multiple of 3, while the answer was not, which means there would be no solutions for this system. It would be impossible to come up with a set of values (a, b) that holds true for BOTH equations.

16. **E**   If $a > 0$ in the quadratic $f(x) = ax^2 + bx + c$, then the graph is a parabola that "opens up," which means that the vertex $(3, -6)$ is at the "minimum" value of the function. Therefore -6 is the smallest possible y-coordinate on the graph. Since c represents the y-coordinate when $x = 0$ (plug it in if you are not convinced), c must be greater than -6.

Section 9

1. C The original sentence contains a dangling participle. As the sentence is currently constructed, the *pre-school teachers* are one year old. Answer choice (E) is not a complete sentence. Answer choice (D) contains another dangling participle. Answer choice (B) is awkward and unidiomatic.

2. A The sentence is correct as written.

3. B The plural verb *are* in the original sentence is improperly used to describe a singular subject *a full set of streetlamps*. Choice (B) corrects the error and maintains the proper parallel structure. Choice (C) corrects the error but fails to maintain proper parallel structure.

4. E The original sentence contains another dangling participle. As the sentence is currently constructed, *Timmy's decision* did not receive any *advice to the contrary*. But, it is *Timmy* who should be receiving no advice to the contrary. Answer choices (C) and (E) both correct the participle error, but choice (C) uses the wrong verb form *deciding*.

5. A The sentence is correct as written.

6. A The sentence is correct as written.

7. C This is a transition error, with the two improperly linked clauses. As written, the use of the word *and* makes it seem as if the discovery of penicillin and the learning about the curative properties were two separate events. The word *and* should be changed to *when*.

8. D The original sentence contains a misplaced modifier: it implies that the *matador*, rather than *bull* is attracted by the movement of the red cape. Only choices (D) and (E) properly tie that attraction to the bull, but choice (E) is awkward and unidiomatic.

9. E The original sentence contains two errors. The subject *them* is unclear and could refer to the *essays* or the *professors*. In addition, the plural verb *were* is used to refer to a singular subject *the only difference*.

10. D The singular subject *a child*, is improperly used to refer to a plural subject *my brothers and I*. If the sentence instead began with *As children growing up in Upper St. Claire*, it would be OK. But, that is not an answer choice. Choice (D) corrects the error by removing the incorrect subject from the first clause.

11. C Running a successful bed and breakfast is difficult because of two things, which must be described in parallel form. Since the first reason it is difficult is given in noun form: *the seasonality of travel*, the second thing should be phrased similarly: *the expense of maintenance*.

12. C The original sentence is a run-on sentence. Choice (B) shows improper use of a colon because the second clause is not a complete sentence. Choice (D) is another run-on sentence.

13. D The original sentence contains a redundancy error. If defeat was *inevitable*, then by definition, it *would happen in the future*, So, the phrase *would happen in the future* needs to be removed.

14. E The original sentence contains a misplaced modifier: it implies that the *people*, rather than *white truffles* are prized as a delicacy. Choice (C) improperly refers to the plural subject *truffles* with a singular subject *it*.

PRACTICE TEST 5

ANSWER SHEET

Last Name:_____   First Name:_____

Date:_____   Testing Location:_____

Directions for Test

- Remove these answer sheets from the book and use them to record your answers to this test.
- This test will require 3 hours and 20 minutes to complete. Take this test in one sitting.
- The time allotment for each section is written clearly at the beginning of each section. This test contains six 25-minute sections, two 20-minute sections, and one 10-minute section.
- This test is 25 minutes shorter than the actual SAT, which will include a 25-minute "experimental" section that does not count toward your score. That section has been omitted from this test.
- You may take one short break during the test, of no more than 10 minutes in length.
- You may only work on one section at any given time.
- You must stop ALL work on a section when time is called.
- If you finish a section before the time has elapsed, check your work on that section. You may NOT work on any other section.
- Do not waste time on questions that seem too difficult for you.
- Use the test book for scratchwork, but you will receive credit only for answers that are marked on the answer sheets.
- You will receive one point for every correct answer.
- You will receive no points for an omitted question.
- For each wrong answer on any multiple-choice question, your score will be reduced by ¼ point.
- For each wrong answer on any "numerical grid-in" question, you will receive no deduction.

When you take the real SAT, you will be asked to fill in your personal information in grids as shown below.

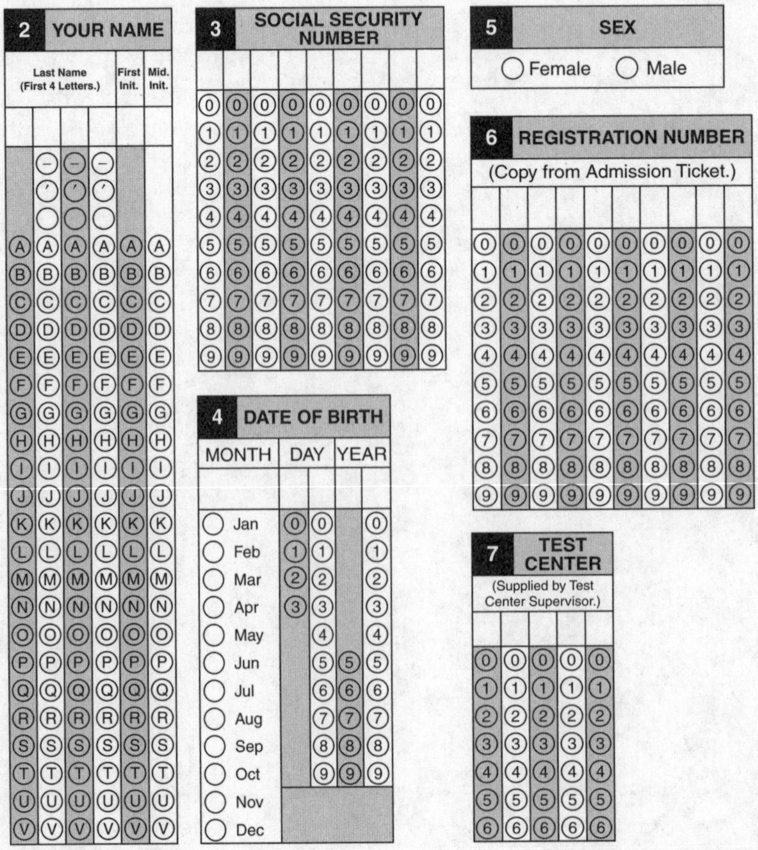

Start with number 1 for each new section. If a section has fewer questions than answer spaces, leave the extra answer spaces blank. Be sure to erase any errors or stray marks completely.

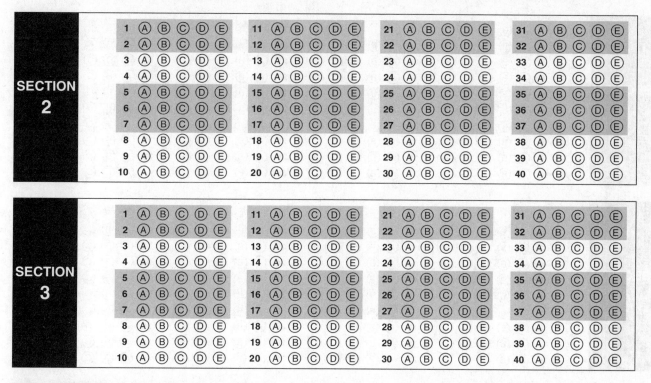

SECTION 2

SECTION 3

CAUTION Use the answer spaces in the grids below for Section 2 or Section 3 only if you are told to do so in your test book.

Student-Produced Responses

ONLY ANSWERS ENTERED IN THE CIRCLES IN EACH GRID WILL BE SCORED. YOU WILL NOT RECEIVE CREDIT FOR ANYTHING WRITTEN IN THE BOXES ABOVE THE CIRCLES.

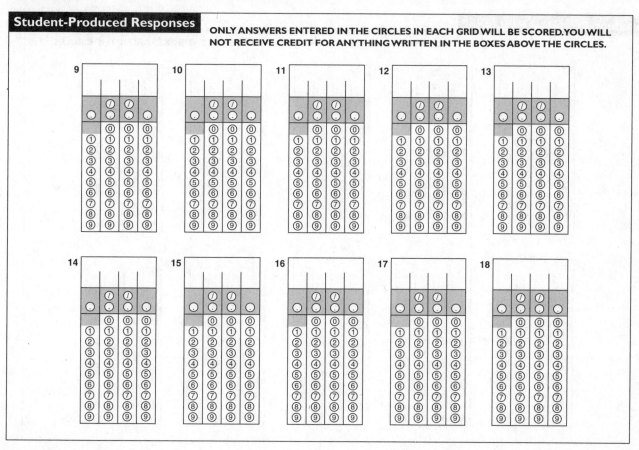

Start with number 1 for each new section. If a section has fewer questions than answer spaces, leave the extra answer spaces blank. Be sure to erase any errors or stray marks completely.

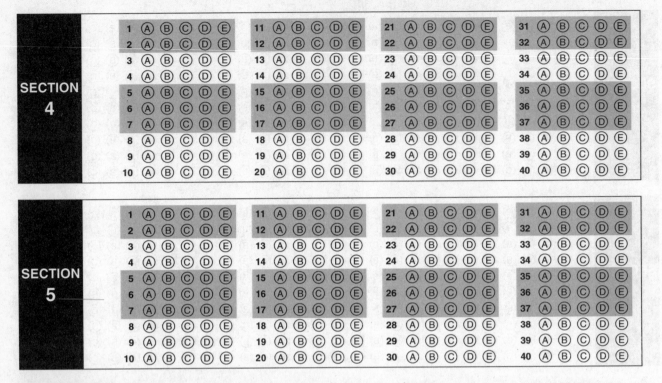

SECTION 4

SECTION 5

CAUTION   Use the answer spaces in the grids below for Section 4 or Section 5 only if you are told to do so in your test book.

Student-Produced Responses   ONLY ANSWERS ENTERED IN THE CIRCLES IN EACH GRID WILL BE SCORED. YOU WILL NOT RECEIVE CREDIT FOR ANYTHING WRITTEN IN THE BOXES ABOVE THE CIRCLES.

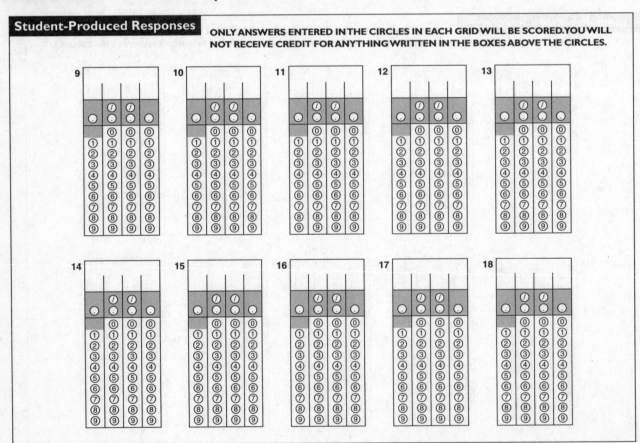

Start with number 1 for each new section. If a section has fewer questions than answer spaces, leave the extra answer spaces blank. Be sure to erase any errors or stray marks completely.

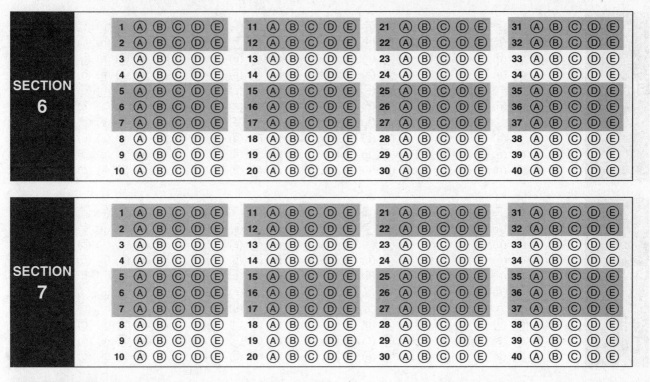

SECTION 6

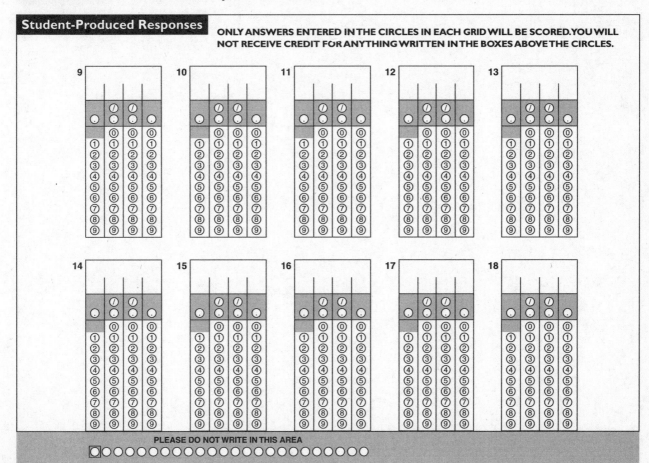

SECTION 7

CAUTION Use the answer spaces in the grids below for Section 6 or Section 7 only if you are told to do so in your test book.

Student-Produced Responses ONLY ANSWERS ENTERED IN THE CIRCLES IN EACH GRID WILL BE SCORED. YOU WILL NOT RECEIVE CREDIT FOR ANYTHING WRITTEN IN THE BOXES ABOVE THE CIRCLES.

PLEASE DO NOT WRITE IN THIS AREA

Start with number 1 for each new section. If a section has fewer questions than answer spaces, leave the extra answer spaces blank. Be sure to erase any errors or stray marks completely.

SECTION 8

1 Ⓐ Ⓑ Ⓒ Ⓓ Ⓔ
2 Ⓐ Ⓑ Ⓒ Ⓓ Ⓔ
3 Ⓐ Ⓑ Ⓒ Ⓓ Ⓔ
4 Ⓐ Ⓑ Ⓒ Ⓓ Ⓔ
5 Ⓐ Ⓑ Ⓒ Ⓓ Ⓔ
6 Ⓐ Ⓑ Ⓒ Ⓓ Ⓔ
7 Ⓐ Ⓑ Ⓒ Ⓓ Ⓔ
8 Ⓐ Ⓑ Ⓒ Ⓓ Ⓔ
9 Ⓐ Ⓑ Ⓒ Ⓓ Ⓔ
10 Ⓐ Ⓑ Ⓒ Ⓓ Ⓔ

11 Ⓐ Ⓑ Ⓒ Ⓓ Ⓔ
12 Ⓐ Ⓑ Ⓒ Ⓓ Ⓔ
13 Ⓐ Ⓑ Ⓒ Ⓓ Ⓔ
14 Ⓐ Ⓑ Ⓒ Ⓓ Ⓔ
15 Ⓐ Ⓑ Ⓒ Ⓓ Ⓔ
16 Ⓐ Ⓑ Ⓒ Ⓓ Ⓔ
17 Ⓐ Ⓑ Ⓒ Ⓓ Ⓔ
18 Ⓐ Ⓑ Ⓒ Ⓓ Ⓔ
19 Ⓐ Ⓑ Ⓒ Ⓓ Ⓔ
20 Ⓐ Ⓑ Ⓒ Ⓓ Ⓔ

21 Ⓐ Ⓑ Ⓒ Ⓓ Ⓔ
22 Ⓐ Ⓑ Ⓒ Ⓓ Ⓔ
23 Ⓐ Ⓑ Ⓒ Ⓓ Ⓔ
24 Ⓐ Ⓑ Ⓒ Ⓓ Ⓔ
25 Ⓐ Ⓑ Ⓒ Ⓓ Ⓔ
26 Ⓐ Ⓑ Ⓒ Ⓓ Ⓔ
27 Ⓐ Ⓑ Ⓒ Ⓓ Ⓔ
28 Ⓐ Ⓑ Ⓒ Ⓓ Ⓔ
29 Ⓐ Ⓑ Ⓒ Ⓓ Ⓔ
30 Ⓐ Ⓑ Ⓒ Ⓓ Ⓔ

31 Ⓐ Ⓑ Ⓒ Ⓓ Ⓔ
32 Ⓐ Ⓑ Ⓒ Ⓓ Ⓔ
33 Ⓐ Ⓑ Ⓒ Ⓓ Ⓔ
34 Ⓐ Ⓑ Ⓒ Ⓓ Ⓔ
35 Ⓐ Ⓑ Ⓒ Ⓓ Ⓔ
36 Ⓐ Ⓑ Ⓒ Ⓓ Ⓔ
37 Ⓐ Ⓑ Ⓒ Ⓓ Ⓔ
38 Ⓐ Ⓑ Ⓒ Ⓓ Ⓔ
39 Ⓐ Ⓑ Ⓒ Ⓓ Ⓔ
40 Ⓐ Ⓑ Ⓒ Ⓓ Ⓔ

SECTION 9

1 Ⓐ Ⓑ Ⓒ Ⓓ Ⓔ
2 Ⓐ Ⓑ Ⓒ Ⓓ Ⓔ
3 Ⓐ Ⓑ Ⓒ Ⓓ Ⓔ
4 Ⓐ Ⓑ Ⓒ Ⓓ Ⓔ
5 Ⓐ Ⓑ Ⓒ Ⓓ Ⓔ
6 Ⓐ Ⓑ Ⓒ Ⓓ Ⓔ
7 Ⓐ Ⓑ Ⓒ Ⓓ Ⓔ
8 Ⓐ Ⓑ Ⓒ Ⓓ Ⓔ
9 Ⓐ Ⓑ Ⓒ Ⓓ Ⓔ
10 Ⓐ Ⓑ Ⓒ Ⓓ Ⓔ

11 Ⓐ Ⓑ Ⓒ Ⓓ Ⓔ
12 Ⓐ Ⓑ Ⓒ Ⓓ Ⓔ
13 Ⓐ Ⓑ Ⓒ Ⓓ Ⓔ
14 Ⓐ Ⓑ Ⓒ Ⓓ Ⓔ
15 Ⓐ Ⓑ Ⓒ Ⓓ Ⓔ
16 Ⓐ Ⓑ Ⓒ Ⓓ Ⓔ
17 Ⓐ Ⓑ Ⓒ Ⓓ Ⓔ
18 Ⓐ Ⓑ Ⓒ Ⓓ Ⓔ
19 Ⓐ Ⓑ Ⓒ Ⓓ Ⓔ
20 Ⓐ Ⓑ Ⓒ Ⓓ Ⓔ

21 Ⓐ Ⓑ Ⓒ Ⓓ Ⓔ
22 Ⓐ Ⓑ Ⓒ Ⓓ Ⓔ
23 Ⓐ Ⓑ Ⓒ Ⓓ Ⓔ
24 Ⓐ Ⓑ Ⓒ Ⓓ Ⓔ
25 Ⓐ Ⓑ Ⓒ Ⓓ Ⓔ
26 Ⓐ Ⓑ Ⓒ Ⓓ Ⓔ
27 Ⓐ Ⓑ Ⓒ Ⓓ Ⓔ
28 Ⓐ Ⓑ Ⓒ Ⓓ Ⓔ
29 Ⓐ Ⓑ Ⓒ Ⓓ Ⓔ
30 Ⓐ Ⓑ Ⓒ Ⓓ Ⓔ

31 Ⓐ Ⓑ Ⓒ Ⓓ Ⓔ
32 Ⓐ Ⓑ Ⓒ Ⓓ Ⓔ
33 Ⓐ Ⓑ Ⓒ Ⓓ Ⓔ
34 Ⓐ Ⓑ Ⓒ Ⓓ Ⓔ
35 Ⓐ Ⓑ Ⓒ Ⓓ Ⓔ
36 Ⓐ Ⓑ Ⓒ Ⓓ Ⓔ
37 Ⓐ Ⓑ Ⓒ Ⓓ Ⓔ
38 Ⓐ Ⓑ Ⓒ Ⓓ Ⓔ
39 Ⓐ Ⓑ Ⓒ Ⓓ Ⓔ
40 Ⓐ Ⓑ Ⓒ Ⓓ Ⓔ

1 ESSAY   ESSAY 1

ESSAY
Time—25 minutes

> Write your essay on separate sheets of standard lined paper.

The essay gives you an opportunity to show how effectively you can develop and express ideas. You should, therefore, take care to develop your point of view, present your ideas logically and clearly, and use language precisely.

Your essay must be written on the lines provided on your answer sheet—you will receive no other paper on which to write. You will have enough space if you write on every line, avoid wide margins, and keep your handwriting to a reasonable size. Remember that people who are not familiar with your handwriting will read what you write. Try to write or print so that what you are writing is legible to those readers.

Important Reminders:

- **A pencil is required for the essay.** An essay written in ink will receive a score of zero.
- **Do not write your essay in your test book.** You will receive credit only for what you write on your answer sheet.
- **An off-topic essay will receive a score of zero.**

You have twenty-five minutes to write an essay on the topic assigned below.

Think carefully about the issue presented in the following excerpts and the assignment below.

> In any contest between power and patience, bet on patience.
>
> —W.B. Prescott

Assignment: **Which is a more powerful force of social change: power or patience?** Write an essay in which you answer this question and support your position logically with examples from literature, the arts, history, politics, science and technology, current events, or your experience or observation.

If you finish before time is called, you may check your work on this section only.
Do not turn to any other section of the test.

2   **2**   **2**   **2**   **2**   **2**

SECTION 2
Time—25 minutes
20 questions

Turn to Section 2 of your answer sheet to answer the questions in this section.

Directions: For this section, solve each problem and decide which is the best of the choices given. Fill in the corresponding circle on the answer sheet. You may use any available space for scratchwork.

Notes

1. The use of a calculator is permitted.
2. All numbers used are real numbers.
3. Figures that accompany problems in this test are intended to provide information useful in solving the problems. They are drawn as accurately as possible EXCEPT when it is stated in a specific problem that the figure is not drawn to scale. All figures lie in a plane unless otherwise indicated.
4. Unless otherwise specified, the domain of any function f is assumed to be the set of all real numbers x for which $f(x)$ is a real number.

Reference Information

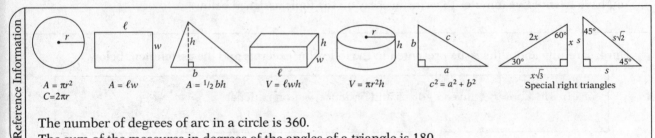

$A = \pi r^2$
$C = 2\pi r$

$A = \ell w$

$A = \frac{1}{2} bh$

$V = \ell w h$

$V = \pi r^2 h$

$c^2 = a^2 + b^2$

Special right triangles

The number of degrees of arc in a circle is 360.
The sum of the measures in degrees of the angles of a triangle is 180.

---

1. If $a = 3 + b$ and $a = 2b$, then $b =$

   (A) 1.5
   (B) 2
   (C) 3
   (D) 4
   (E) 6

2. If 1 pound of cheese costs $1.50 and 2 pounds of beef costs $4.00, then how much more expensive is 6 pounds of beef than 6 pounds of cheese?

   (A) $1.50
   (B) $2.00
   (C) $3.00
   (D) $4.00
   (E) $6.00

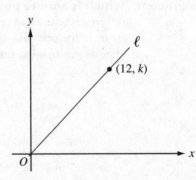

3. In the figure above, line ℓ passes through the origin and has a slope of 2. What is the value of k?

   (A) 2
   (B) 4
   (C) 6
   (D) 12
   (E) 24

GO ON TO THE NEXT PAGE ⟩

2   2   2   2   2   2

4. If x is 5 less than y, then what is the value of $5(x - y)$?

(A) −25
(B) −5
(C) 0
(D) 5
(E) 25

5. On a certain map that is drawn to scale, a distance of 50 miles is represented by 1 inch. How many inches on the map would represent a distance of 240 miles?

(A) 2.4
(B) 4.8
(C) 6.4
(D) 8.0
(E) 12.0

6. Three students have a total of 30 CDs among them. If one student has 40% of the CDs, and another has 33 ⅓% of the CDs, how many CDs does the third student have?

(A) 6
(B) 8
(C) 9
(D) 10
(E) 12

7. The average (arithmetic mean) of Marianne's scores on three tests is 85. If she scored 90 on both of the first two tests, what was her score on the third test?

(A) 70
(B) 75
(C) 80
(D) 85
(E) 90

−1, 0, 1, −1, 0, 1, . . .

8. The numbers −1, 0 and 1 repeat in a sequence, as shown above. If this pattern continues, what will be the sum of the first 100 terms of this sequence?

(A) −1
(B) 1
(C) 33
(D) 34
(E) 100

9. Fifty plastic balls numbered 1 to 50, inclusive, are placed in a bowl and one ball is to be selected at random. What is the probability that the ball selected will have a number that is a multiple of 3?

(A) $\dfrac{3}{50}$

(B) $\dfrac{3}{25}$

(C) $\dfrac{8}{25}$

(D) $\dfrac{1}{3}$

(E) $\dfrac{9}{25}$

10. If $a + b = 5$, $a - c = 15$, and $a = 10$, then $c - b =$

(A) −10
(B) −5
(C) 0
(D) 5
(E) 10

GO ON TO THE NEXT PAGE ⟩

$$\begin{array}{r} 3A \\ B7 \\ 4B \\ + 27 \\ \hline 178 \end{array}$$

11. In the correctly worked addition problem above, A and B represent digits. What is digit A?

(A) 5
(B) 6
(C) 7
(D) 8
(E) 9

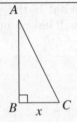

Note: Figure not drawn to scale.

12. In the figure above, point D (not shown) is drawn so that point C is the midpoint of $\overline{AD}$. If $CD = 4x$, then what is the length of AB in terms of x?

(A) $3x$
(B) $x\sqrt{15}$
(C) $4x$
(D) $x\sqrt{17}$
(E) $x\sqrt{63}$

13. The line that passes through $(-2, 4)$ and $(1, 6)$ also passes through which of the following points?

(A) $(4, 8)$
(B) $(4, 10)$
(C) $(5, 7)$
(D) $(5, 8)$
(E) $(5, 9)$

14. For which of the following sets of numbers is the first number equal to the sum of the second number and the square of the third number?

(A) 6, 4, 2
(B) 9, 6, 9
(C) 10, 9, 4
(D) 16, 7, 3
(E) 19, 16, 15

15. $3^x + 3^x + 3^x + 3^x + 3^x + 3^x + 3^x + 3^x + 3^x =$

(A) 3^{x+8}
(B) 3^{9x}
(C) 3^{x+2}
(D) 27^x
(E) $9(3^{9x})$

16. Which of the following graphs represents the set of all solutions of the statement $2 - |x + 1| < 0$?

(A) ←——○——+——+——+——○——→
　　　 −2　−1　0　1　2　3　4

(B) ←——+——○——+——○——+——→
　　　 −2　−1　0　1　2　3　4

(C) ←——+——○——+——+——+——○——→
　　　 −4　−3　−2　−1　0　1　2

(D) ←——+——○——+——○——+——→
　　　 −4　−3　−2　−1　0　1　2

(E) ←——+——+——○——+——○——+——→
　　　 −1　0　1　2　3　4　5

17. A publishing company wants to increase the price of one of its books by 10%. Research shows that this increase in price would decrease sales of the book by only 5%. By what percent would this change increase the money received through sales of this book?

(A) 4.0%
(B) 4.5%
(C) 5.0%
(D) 5.5%
(E) 6.0%

GO ON TO THE NEXT PAGE ⟹

2   2   2   2   2   2

18. A total of 32 teams play in a single-elimination tournament. In the first round, every team plays one game against another team, and the losing teams are eliminated from the tournament. No game ends in a tie. Every winning team procedes to the next round, in which they play another winning team. This single-elimination procedure continues until only one team remains. If each game takes precisely 2 hours to play, what is the total length of games played in the tournament, in hours?

(A) 30
(B) 32
(C) 48
(D) 62
(E) 64

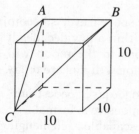

19. In the figure above, points *A*, *B*, and *C* are vertices of the cube shown. What is the area of triangle *ABC*?

(A) 50
(B) $50\sqrt{2}$
(C) $50\sqrt{3}$
(D) $100\sqrt{2}$
(E) $100\sqrt{3}$

20. A jar contains only red and black marbles. Originally, the ratio of black marbles to red marbles was 4:5. After 18 black marbles were added, the ratio of black marbles to red marbles became 5:4. How many marbles were in the jar originally?

(A) 45
(B) 54
(C) 63
(D) 72
(E) 81

STOP

If you finish before time is called, you may check your work on this section only. Do not turn to any other section of the test.

3   **3**   **3**   **3**   **3**   **3**

SECTION 3
Time—25 minutes
24 questions

Turn to Section 3 of your answer sheet to answer the questions in this section.

Directions: For each question in this section, select the best answer from among the choices given and fill in the corresponding circle on the answer sheet.

Each sentence below has one or two blanks, each blank indicating that something has been omitted. Beneath the sentence are five words or sets of words labeled A through E. Choose the word or set of words that, when inserted in the sentence, <u>best</u> fits the meaning of the sentence as a whole.

EXAMPLE:

Rather than accepting the theory unquestioningly, Deborah regarded it with -----.

(A) mirth
(B) sadness
(C) responsibility
(D) ignorance
(E) skepticism

Ⓐ Ⓑ Ⓒ Ⓓ ●

---

1. Journalists often have strong personal opinions about the political events they analyze, and so have great difficulty in remaining ------- in their writing.

   (A) eloquent
   (B) converted
   (C) neutral
   (D) biased
   (E) emotional

2. Although the topic of the lecture fascinated me, the speaker's presentation style was so ------- that I found it difficult to stay awake.

   (A) monotonous
   (B) rude
   (C) provocative
   (D) authoritative
   (E) trustworthy

3. Because space travel is becoming increasingly -------, within a few decades it is possible that excursions to the moon will be as ------- as international flights are today.

   (A) dangerous . . pedestrian
   (B) responsive . . formal
   (C) inescapable . . challenging
   (D) mundane . . exciting
   (E) inexpensive . . commonplace

4. The fact that viewers seem to ------- the stars of even the most vacuous popular television programs suggests that Americans value sheer ------- over talent or achievement.

   (A) exalt . . intelligence
   (B) lionize . . fame
   (C) criticize . . popularity
   (D) envy . . obscurity
   (E) tolerate . . aesthetics

GO ON TO THE NEXT PAGE ⇨

3   3   3   3   3   3

5. Anthropologists have discovered that many cultures employ only ------- strategies for resolving conflicts, in contradiction to those who suggest that warfare is -------.

   (A) ineffective . . dangerous
   (B) violent . . common
   (C) peaceful . . universal
   (D) restricted . . deleterious
   (E) idiosyncratic . . novel

6. Francisco Goya's cheerful ------- of social conditions in 18th century Spain was later ------- by a harshly critical view of its politics and society.

   (A) celebration . . supported
   (B) espousal . . returned
   (C) repression . . succeeded
   (D) acceptance . . supplanted
   (E) denunciation . . replaced

7. The pace with which the country's infrastructure was rebuilt after the war can best be described as -------; the government leaders reasoned that a hasty approach would likely create more problems later on.

   (A) accelerated
   (B) dexterous
   (C) indifferent
   (D) deliberate
   (E) dilapidated

8. Although racquetball was invented in 1949 in Greenwich, Connecticut, in fact many of its rules were ------- from older, well-established sports like handball and squash.

   (A) appropriated
   (B) discarded
   (C) advocated
   (D) elucidated
   (E) compensated

Each passage below is followed by one or two questions based on its content. Answer each question based on what is stated or implied in the preceding passage.

Questions 9–10 are based on the following passage.

The following passage is from an essay on American education and political values written in 2004.

American public schools teach capitalism not so much by directly instructing students in
Line the function and benefits of free markets as by embodying capitalistic qualities in their
5 very structure. For instance, they encourage students to compete for capital resources called grades, which teachers often keep arbitrarily scarce, thereby espousing the values of individual achievement and
10 competition. In socialist and communist countries, in contrast, we find schools in which cooperation is stressed far more than competition. Students in socialist systems regularly engage in practices that American
15 students would characterize as "cheating;" in such systems, knowledge is regarded as something that everyone should be willing to share. The American emphasis on knowledge as a source of competition contrasts starkly
20 with the American democratic ideal of universal education.

9. The passage indicates that the means by which capitalistic values are conveyed to American students is

   (A) socialistic
   (B) implicit
   (C) illegal
   (D) direct
   (E) challenging

GO ON TO THE NEXT PAGE ⟩

Passage 1: Excerpted from a piece found in public domain.
Passage 2: From *The Art of F. Scott Fitzgerald*, by Sergio Perosa, copyright © 1965. University of Michigan Press.

10. In line 12, the word "stressed" most nearly means

(A) anxious
(B) under pressure
(C) fragile
(D) evaluated
(E) emphasized

Questions 11–12 are based on the following passage.

The following passage discusses the life of F. Scott Fitzgerald, a famous American novelist of the early 20th century.

The life of F. Scott Fitzgerald was sharply divided in every sense. The years of youth, of
Line his first maturity and his early success in the 1910s and 1920s, contrast markedly with the
5 years full of personal and public happenings that led to his premature death in 1940. These later years, full of disillusionment and suffering, though identified with human and artistic growth, were cut off at the very
10 moment when Fitzgerald's career seemed about to bear its best fruits. But Fitzerald's life was divided above all in a personal and human sense. It was divided between the pursuit of the artistic ideal and the continual,
15 too frequent concessions to the taste of the moment or to the lure of easy success; it was divided between a rigorous application to the craft of fiction and the waste of precious energy in purely commercial literary activity.
20 Fitzgerald was a victim, in so many ways, of the myth of success and money, the false gods, as Hemingway was to call them in *Green Hills of Africa*, on whose altars so many promising young writers were sacrificed.

11. According to the author, Fitzgerald's pursuit of the "artistic ideal" (line 14) is best described as

(A) compromised
(B) premature
(C) effortless
(D) secretive
(E) uninterrupted

12. It can be inferred from the passage that, in *Green Hills of Africa*, Hemingway directly criticizes

(A) Fitzgerald's early writing
(B) those who depart from a stark literary style
(C) the pursuit of money
(D) Fitzgerald's public life
(E) those who adhere to strict artistic ideals

GO ON TO THE NEXT PAGE

The questions below are based on the content of the passage that precedes them. The questions are to be answered on the basis of what is stated or implied in the passage itself or the introductory material that precedes the passage.

Questions 13–24 are based on the following passage.

The following is an excerpt from a biography of Ayn Rand, a 20th century American philosopher and novelist.

The life of Ayn Rand was the material of fiction. But if one attempted to write it as a
Line novel, the result would be preposterously unbelievable. Everything about her life and
5 her person was of an epic scale. Her seventy-seven years encompassed the outer limits of triumph and defeat, of exaltation and tragedy, of passionate love and intransigent hatred, of dedicated effort and despairing
10 passivity. Her person encompassed the grandeur of the heroes of her novels, their iron determination, their vast powers of intellect and imagination, their impassioned pursuit of their goals, their worship of
15 achievement, their courage, their pride, and their love of life—as well as the terrors, the self-doubts, the lack of emotional balance, the private agonies that are so alien to an Ayn Rand hero. Her virtues were larger than
20 life—and so were her shortcomings.

Few figures in this century have been so admired and so savagely attacked. She is viewed as goddess and malefactor, as a seminal genius and an ominously dangerous
25 corrupter of the young, as the mightiest of voices for reason and the destroyer of traditional values, as the espouser of joy and the exponent of mindless greed, as the great defender of freedom and the introducer of
30 malevolent values into the mainstream of American thought. It is all but impossible to find a neutral voice among the millions who

have read her works; each reader takes an unequivocal stand for or against what she
35 represents. When her name is mentioned in any gathering, it is met with explosions of grateful, loving admiration or enraged disapproval.

Yet despite the furor her ideas have
40 generated, little is known about the human being who was Ayn Rand. Her public and professional activities took place on a lighted stage; her private life was lived backstage, curtained from view.
45 I first met Ayn Rand in 1950. At the age of forty-five, she had already achieved a singular renown as the author of *The Fountainhead*, and was writing her magnum opus, *Atlas Shrugged*—the work that was to
50 skyrocket her to international fame and place her in the center of a hurricane of controversy.

I shall not forget my first sight of Ayn Rand. When the door to her home opened
55 that spring evening in 1950, I found myself facing the most astonishing human being I had ever encountered. It was the eyes. The eyes were dark, too large for the face, fringed with dark lashes, alive with an intensity of
60 intelligence I had never imagined human eyes could hold. They seemed the eyes of a human being who was composed of the power of sight.

As the years passed, I was to observe all
65 the many changes of expression of those incredible eyes. I saw them ferocious with concentration on a new idea or question that had not occurred to her before. I saw them cold, so icily, inhumanly cold that they froze
70 one's heart and mind. I saw them radiant with the uninhibited delight of a child. I saw them menacing with anger at any hint of what she considered the irrational in human action. I saw them kind, touchingly kind,
75 tender with the desire to help and to protect. I saw the merciless, accusing eyes of the moralist, judging, condemning, unforgiving, the power of her reason becoming a whip to scourge the heretic. But I never saw those

GO ON TO THE NEXT PAGE

From *The Passion of Ayn Rand,* by Barbara Branden, copyright © 1986, by Barbara Branden. Used by permission of Doubleday, a division of Random House, Inc.

80   eyes without the light of a vast, consuming
     intelligence, the light of a ruthless intellect
     that was at once cold and passionate; this was
     the core of her life, the motor of her soul.
        There was something I never saw in Ayn
85   Rand's eyes. They never held an inward
     look—a look of turning inside to learn one's
     own spirit and consciousness. They gazed
     only and always outward. It was many years
     before I was to understand the absence of
90   that inward look, and what it revealed. It was
     to require all the knowledge of all the years
     to understand it.
        Those who worship Ayn Rand and those
     who damn her do her the same disservice; they
95   make her unreal and they deny her humanity.
     She was infinitely more fascinating and
     infinitely more valuable than either goddess or
     sinner. She was a human being. She lived, she
     loved, she fought her battles, and she knew
100 triumph and defeat. The scale was epic; the
     principle is inherent in human existence.

13.   The main purpose of this passage is to

(A)   refute some of Ayn Rand's theories
(B)   critique Ayn Rand's novels
(C)   bemoan Ayn Rand's obscurity
(D)   reveal how fame damaged
      Ayn Rand's life
(E)   humanize Ayn Rand

14.   The first paragraph (lines 1–20) characterizes
      Ayn Rand's life primarily as

(A)   impoverished
(B)   introspective
(C)   majestic
(D)   charitable
(E)   humble

15.   The sentence beginning on line 10 ("Her per-
      son encompassed ... an Ayn Rand hero") sug-
      gests that Rand

(A)   had difficulty depicting some of the char-
      acters in her novels
(B)   identified intellectually with the charac-
      ters in her novels
(C)   imbued the heroes of her novels with
      many emotional imperfections
(D)   was indifferent to the controversy her
      ideas generated
(E)   shared the fears that the heroes of her
      novels exhibited

16.   The first paragraph suggests that Rand shared
      which of the following with the heroes of her
      novels?

      I.   a passion for achievement
      II.   self-doubt
      III. equanimity

(A)   I only
(B)   I and II only
(C)   I and III only
(D)   II and III only
(E)   I, II, and III

17.   The second paragraph suggests that, as a group,
      those who have read Ayn Rand's works are

(A)   united in their admiration of her ideals
(B)   polarized
(C)   critical of her literary style
(D)   respectful of her life experiences
(E)   unaware of the breadth of her work

18.   The sixth paragraph (lines 64–83) contains all
      of the following EXCEPT

(A)   metaphor
(B)   stark contrast
(C)   parallel sentence structure
(D)   a definition of a term
(E)   characterization

GO ON TO THE NEXT PAGE ⇨

3   3   3   3   3   3

19. The author suggests that Ayn Rand lacked

    (A) childlike delight
    (B) logical rigor
    (C) introspection
    (D) tenderness
    (E) ruthlessness

20. The sentence beginning on line 90 ("It was to require...to understand it") suggests that the author of this passage

    (A) disagreed with an important tenet of Rand's philosophy
    (B) needed a great deal of time to appreciate an aspect of Rand's demeanor
    (C) lacked Rand's moral courage
    (D) shared Rand's judgmentalism
    (E) was unable to appreciate the literary inventiveness of Rand's writing style

21. The passage describes the contrast between which of the following?

    I.   Rand's private life and her public life
    II. Rand's philosophy and her literary style
    III. The author's philosophy and Rand's philosophy

    (A) I only
    (B) I and II only
    (C) I and III only
    (D) II and III only
    (E) I, II, and III

22. The author of this passage would most likely agree with which of the following statements?

    (A) Rand's works have long been unappreciated
    (B) Very few who read Rand's works closely have a negative opinion of her.
    (C) Rand's greatest works were published after her death
    (D) Rand's novels served to unify American thinkers
    (E) Although Rand lived an epic life, she is better appreciated as a flawed human being.

23. It can be inferred from the passage that the author

    (A) met Ayn Rand only once
    (B) met Ayn Rand before she became famous
    (C) knew Ayn Rand intimately over a long period of time
    (D) only saw Ayn Rand on social occasions
    (E) was Ayn Rand's literary editor

24. This passage contains enough information to answer all of the following questions EXCEPT

    (A) How were Rand's ideas received by the American public?
    (B) In what decade was Ayn Rand born?
    (C) What was considered to be Rand's greatest work?
    (D) In what country was Ayn Rand born?
    (E) How old was Rand when she died?

STOP

If you finish before time is called, you may check your work on this section only. Do not turn to any other section of the test.

4   **4**   **4**   **4**   **4**   **4**

SECTION 4
Time—25 minutes
35 questions

Turn to Section 4 of your answer sheet to answer the questions in this section.

Directions: For each question in this section, select the best answer from among the choices given and fill in the corresponding circle on the answer sheet.

The following sentences test correctness and effectiveness of expression. Part of each sentence or the entire sentence is underlined; beneath each sentence are five ways of phrasing the underlined material. Choice A repeats the original phrasing; the other four choices are different. Select the choice that completes the sentence most effectively.

In making your selection, follow the requirements of standard written English; that is, pay attention to grammar, choice of words, sentence construction, and punctuation. Your selection should result in the most effective sentence—clear and precise, without awkwardness or ambiguity.

EXAMPLE:

The children <u>couldn't hardly believe their eyes</u>.

(A) couldn't hardly believe their eyes
(B) could hardly believe their eyes
(C) would not hardly believe their eyes
(D) couldn't nearly believe their eyes
(E) couldn't hardly believe his or her eyes

---

1. Geothermal heat is not only an abundant and renewable energy source but also <u>clean as a fuel which emits</u> virtually no harmful gases.

   (A) clean as a fuel which emits
   (B) a clean fuel that emits
   (C) clean as a fuel which is emitting
   (D) the clean fuel emitting
   (E) a clean fuel for emitting

2. In the most recent election, voters were neither energized <u>about the importance of the campaign and they lacked awareness of the issues</u> that directed it.

   (A) about the importance of the campaign and they lacked awareness of the issues
   (B) to how important the campaign was nor to their lack of awareness of the issues
   (C) about how important the campaign was nor about their awareness of the issues
   (D) on the importance of the campaign nor the awareness of the issues
   (E) about the importance of the campaign nor aware of the issues

3. Many existentialistic works, such as Samuel Becket's *Malone Dies*, <u>which subordinates</u> the role of plot to the role of introspection.

   (A) which subordinates
   (B) which subordinate
   (C) subordinate
   (D) subordinates
   (E) that subordinate

GO ON TO THE NEXT PAGE ⟶

4   4   4   4   4   4

4. Although Allen popularized the use of angst-ridden monologue in film, <u>the device was not invented by him</u>.

(A) the device was not invented by him
(B) the device had not been invented by him
(C) he was not the inventor of the particular device
(D) he would not have invented the device
(E) he did not invent the device

5. Western culture has thrived because it values the open inquiry of science <u>more than the closed dogma</u> of state religion.

(A) more than the closed dogma
(B) to the closed dogma
(C) over the closed nature of the dogma of
(D) more than that of the closed dogma
(E) more than it values things like the closed dogma

6. Enormously creative yet focused on his own commercial success, <u>the film depicts Warhol as</u> a complex and enigmatic figure.

(A) the film depicts Warhol as
(B) the film is a depiction of Warhol as
(C) Warhol in the film has been the depiction of
(D) Warhol is depicted in the film as
(E) Warhol is depicted by the film for

7. The first African American to lead an Ivy League institution, Ruth Simmons, <u>who has not shrunk from controversial issues regarding</u> the role of the university in American society.

(A) who has not shrunk from controversial issues regarding
(B) has not shrunk from controversial issues regarding
(C) has not shrunken from controversial issues for
(D) who has not shrunk from controversial issues in
(E) has not shrank from controversial issues regarding

8. Most animals are able to produce vitamin C internally, but <u>there is no production by humans</u> and therefore they must incorporate it into their diets.

(A) there is no production by humans
(B) humans cannot be the producers of it
(C) there is no human production A
(D) humans cannot
(E) there is not by humans

9. The invention of the plow over 12,000 years ago enabled large populations to sustain themselves without <u>needing of migration in search of food</u>.

(A) needing of migration in search of food
(B) the need of migration for the search of food
(C) needing to be migratory for search of food
(D) the need to migrate in search of food
(E) the need for migration in the search for food

10. The interconnectivity of the thousands of electrical generators and relay stations <u>is able to magnify a small failure into</u> one of catastrophic proportions.

(A) is able to magnify a small failure into
(B) are able to magnify a small failure into
(C) is able to magnify a small failure for
(D) are able to magnify that of a small failure into
(E) is able to magnify that of a small failure into

GO ON TO THE NEXT PAGE

11. The film not only employs fine actors, <u>nevertheless it also gives them outstanding roles to play as well</u>.

   (A) nevertheless it also gives them outstanding roles to play as well

   (B) for it gives them also outstanding roles to play

   (C) but outstanding roles as well

   (D) but also the actors' roles are outstanding

   (E) but also gives them outstanding roles to play

The following sentences test your ability to recognize grammar and usage errors. Each sentence contains either a single error or no error at all. No sentence contains more than one error. The error, if there is one, is underlined and lettered. If the sentence contains an error, select the one underlined part that must be changed to make the sentence correct. If the sentence is correct, select choice E. In choosing answers, follow the requirements of standard written English.

EXAMPLE:

By the time <u>they reached</u> the halfway point
            A

<u>in the race,</u> <u>most of the runners</u> <u>hadn't hardly</u>
    B   C   D

begun to hit their stride. <u>No error</u>
                       E

---

12. The devastating failure <u>of the experiment</u>
                      A

<u>surprised</u> the scientists, who were expecting
    B

a <u>successive</u> outcome to <u>confirm</u> their
       C   D

theory. <u>No error</u>
        E

13. Once I finish <u>reading</u> this book, <u>I have read</u>
            A   B

every novel and essay that John Steinbeck

ever published, <u>including those</u> that were
                  C

released <u>posthumously</u>. <u>No error</u>
        D   E

GO ON TO THE NEXT PAGE ⟶

4   4   4   4   4   4

14.   Most linguists <u>are convinced</u> that the
                            A

      ability to speak, while uniquely human,

      <u>is simply</u> a combination of <u>cognitive skills</u>
         B   C
      that have been passed on <u>to our species</u>
                                        D

      through evolution. <u>No error</u>
                              E

15.   Our friends seemed <u>to think that</u> the movie
                                A

      was one of the best adventure films

      <u>of recent years</u>, but it <u>did not seem</u> that
         B   C
      way to <u>David and I</u>. <u>No error</u>
                  D   E

16.   The dispute <u>between the teachers' union</u>
                          A

      and the board of education <u>became</u> less
                                      B

      heated once <u>it agreed</u> to follow
                        C

      <u>the rules of arbitration</u>. <u>No error</u>
                  D   E

17.   Recent articles <u>have indicated</u> that
                              A

      individuals who <u>work on</u> professions that
                            B

      require a great deal of desk work have

      <u>a higher rate</u> of obesity <u>than those who</u>
            C   D
      work outdoors. <u>No error</u>
                          E

18.   Although <u>there is</u> a lot more than twenty
                      A

      copies of the book left <u>in the storeroom</u>,
                                    B

      they will sell out quickly, so I <u>recommend</u>
                                              C

      that <u>we order more</u> now. <u>No error</u>
              D   E

19.   The work involved <u>in doing research</u> on
                              A

      one's ancestors <u>has become</u> much less
                            B

      arduous because <u>you can now find</u> a great
                              C

      deal of genealogical information

      <u>on the internet</u>. <u>No error</u>
            D   E

20.   Many literary historians <u>regard</u> the novels
                                    A

      of Zora Neale Hurston, with their

      <u>rich characterizations</u>, as being among the
            B
      <u>most significant</u> works
            C
      <u>of the late Harlem Renaissance</u>. <u>No error</u>
                  D   E

21.   Health researchers <u>have accumulated</u>
                                A

      evidence <u>suggesting</u> that daily vitamin C
                    B
      supplements <u>can reduce</u> the risk of both
                        C
      heart disease <u>in addition to stroke</u>.
                            D

      <u>No error</u>
          E

GO ON TO THE NEXT PAGE ⇨

4   4   4   4   4   4

22. The multitude of similarities <u>between</u> the
                                        A
    dozens <u>of Europeans languages</u>
                    B
    <u>can be attributed</u> in large measure
           C
    <u>to the early development</u> of international
              D
    commerce. <u>No error</u>
                      E

23. There was <u>very little debate</u> among the
                        A
    conference participants <u>about the issue</u> of
                                    B
    whether the salaries of professional women

    <u>should be</u> comparable <u>to men</u>. <u>No error</u>.
        C   D   E

24. Being a <u>popular and well-respected</u>
                        A
    member of the community, <u>Andrea is</u>
                                    B
    clearly favored <u>to win</u> the nomination
                        C
    <u>for representative</u> to the city council.
              D
    <u>No error</u>
        E

25. The <u>entertaining and informative</u> lecture
                    A
    by the <u>eminent</u> cosmologist inspired Andre
                B
    <u>for reading</u> more about astronomy
        C
    <u>and to take</u> more science courses. <u>No error</u>
          D   E

26. Although they <u>would have preferred</u> to
                            A
    have several candidates

    <u>from which to choose,</u> the voters
              B
    nevertheless <u>excepted</u> the unopposed
                        C
    <u>candidacy of Senator Frumm</u>. <u>No error</u>
                  D   E

27. We walked for many hours through the

    thick forests and <u>over the rocky hills</u> until
                                A
    we <u>had reached</u> the clearing <u>in which</u> we
            B   C
    would pitch our tent <u>for the night</u>. <u>No error</u>
                                D   E

28. Over nearly four hundred acres in the

    valley <u>sprawl</u> the <u>majestic</u> Rancho Coronado,
              A   B
    <u>which</u> <u>has been owned</u> by the same family
        C   D
    for over two hundred years. <u>No error</u>
                                        E

29. Several writers who are <u>critics toward</u> the
                                    A
    president's environmental policy

    <u>have published</u> an anthology of essays and
            B
    research documents describing how

    <u>to improve</u> the country's
          C
    <u>commitment to ecology</u> without impeding
              D
    economic progress. <u>No error</u>
                                E

GO ON TO THE NEXT PAGE ⟶

Directions: The following passage is an early draft of an essay. Some parts of the passage need to be rewritten.

Read the passage and select the best answers for the questions that follow. Some questions are about particular sentences or parts of sentences and ask you to improve sentence structure or word choice. Other questions ask you to consider organization and development. In choosing answers, follow the requirements of standard written English.

Questions 30–35 pertain to the following passage.

(1) For most young people in America who are approaching voting age, choosing a president is very much like the process by which you choose a homecoming queen. (2) They simply select the candidate whose personality they like the most. (3) They don't realize that choosing a leader is a much more serious task than that. (4) The more informed the voters are, the more likely it is that they will pick a good and capable leader.

(6) The first step to making a reasonable choice for president is to read a good international newspaper every day. (7) This will give you a better perspective on both domestic and international issues. (8) The next step is to decide what issues are most important to you? (9) What are your interests that the president has some control over? (10) For instance, one candidate might want to eliminate environmental regulations so his industrial supporters can get richer. (11) But you have asthma that is affected by the pollution or you'd rather not swim in a lake that has become polluted because of it. (12) Or, you might be just the right age for a draft and one of the candidates wants to fight a new war that you don't approve of. (13) So many political commercials seem to focus on cutting the opponent down rather than discussing the important issues. (14) The fact is that the president can do a lot of things that influence your life and you may not be aware of it.

(15) Also, very few young adults really think about what kinds of qualifications and what skills the candidates might or might not have, they just pick the one whom their parents or their friends like. (16) They should be asking whether this person is going to solve the problems that are important to me because he or she is qualified to solve them?

(17) For instance, is someone who has been in Congress his whole adult life really prepared to represent people who run small businesses, or work in manual labor, or teach school? (18) Even if you may like someone's personality from an ad, they still might not be making very good decisions for you and your family. (19) It's important to look into a candidate's past for yourself rather than relying on political ads to tell you what the candidates are like. (20) Then, become an active participant in the politcal process rather than a passive observer.

30. Which of the following is the best revision of the underlined portion of sentence 1 (reproduced below)?

    For most young people in America who are approaching voting age, choosing a president is very much like the process by which you choose a homecoming queen.

    (A) (as it is now)
    (B) the process of choosing a homecoming queen
    (C) that of choosing a homecoming queen
    (D) the way you choose a homecoming queen
    (E) choosing a homecoming queen

31. Which of the following is the best way to combine sentences 2 and 3 (reproduced below)?

    They simply select the candidate by picking the one whose personality they like the most. They don't realize that choosing a leader is a much more serious task than that.

    (A) They don't realize that choosing a leader is more serious than that, selecting the one whose personality they like the most.
    (B) Selecting the one that has the personality they like most, they don't realize that it's more serious than that.
    (C) Not realizing how serious a task it is to choose a leader, they simply select the candidate whose personality they like most.
    (D) Because of not realizing how serious it is choosing a leader, they simply select the candidate whose personality they like most.
    (E) Because they simply select the candidate with the personality they like the most, they don't realize that choosing a leader is more serious than that.

GO ON TO THE NEXT PAGE

32. Which of the following is the best version of the underlined portions of sentences 10 and 11 (reproduced below)?

For instance, one candidate might want to eliminate environmental regulations <u>so his industrial supporters can get richer. But you have asthma that is affected by the pollution or you'd rather not swim in a lake that has become polluted because of it</u>.

(A)   (as it is now)
(B)   for the financial benefit of his industrial supporters, but to the detriment of your asthma and your favorite swimming lake, which are harmed by pollution.
(C)   for his industrial supporters' wealth, but you have asthma and your favorite swimming lake is getting worse because of pollution.
(D)   for his industrial supporters' wealth, but not for your asthma and your favorite swimming lake is harmed by pollution.
(E)   for the financial benefit of his industrial supporters, but to the detriment of your asthma and your favorite swimming lake are harmed by pollution.

33. Which of the following sentences contributes least to the unity of the second paragraph?

(A)   Sentence 10
(B)   Sentence 11
(C)   Sentence 12
(D)   Sentence 13
(E)   Sentence 14

34. Which of the following is the best version of the underlined portion of sentence 15 (reproduced below)?

Also, very few young adults really think about <u>what kinds of qualifications and skills the candidates might or might not have, they</u> just pick the one whom their parents or their friends like.

(A)   (as it is now)
(B)   the qualifications and skills of the candidates, but instead
(C)   what kinds of qualifications and skills the candidates might have, they instead
(D)   the qualifications and skills of the candidates, they
(E)   what are the qualifications and skills of the candidates, they instead

35. Which of the following is the best revision of the underlined portion of sentence 16 (reproduced below)?

They should be asking whether <u>this candidate is able to solve the problems that are important to me because he or she is qualified to solve them</u>?

(A)   the candidate is qualified to solve the problems that are important to them.
(B)   the candidate is qualified to solve the problems that are important to me?
(C)   is this candidate able to be qualified to solve the problems that are important to me?
(D)   the candidate is qualified to solve the problems that are important to him or her.
(E)   the candidate is or is not qualified to solve the problems that are important to him or her.

STOP

If you finish before time is called, you may check your work on this section only. Do not turn to any other section of the test.

5   **5**   **5**   **5**   **5**   **5**

SECTION 5
Time—25 minutes
18 questions

> **Turn to Section 5 of your answer sheet to answer the questions in this section.**

Directions: This section contains two types of questions. You have 25 minutes to complete both types. For questions 1–8, solve each problem and decide which is the best of the choices given. Fill in the corresponding circle on the answer sheet. You may use any available space for scratchwork.

Notes

1. The use of a calculator is permitted.

2. All numbers used are real numbers.

3. Figures that accompany problems in this test are intended to provide information useful in solving the problems. They are drawn as accurately as possible EXCEPT when it is stated in a specific problem that the figure is not drawn to scale. All figures lie in a plane unless otherwise indicated.

4. Unless otherwise specified, the domain of any function f is assumed to be the set of all real numbers x for which $f(x)$ is a real number.

Reference Information

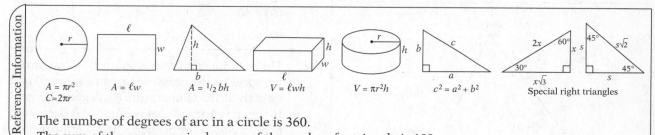

$A = \pi r^2$ $A = \ell w$ $A = \frac{1}{2} bh$ $V = \ell wh$ $V = \pi r^2 h$ $c^2 = a^2 + b^2$ Special right triangles
$C = 2\pi r$

The number of degrees of arc in a circle is 360.
The sum of the measures in degrees of the angles of a triangle is 180.

---

1. If $\dfrac{p}{9}$ and $\dfrac{p}{27}$ are both integers, then what is the least possible positive value of p?

(A) 3
(B) 6
(C) 9
(D) 18
(E) 27

---

2. If $4(x + 3) = 15$, then what is the value of $4x + 3$?

(A) $\dfrac{3}{4}$

(B) $\dfrac{3}{2}$

(C) 6
(D) 10
(E) 15

---

3. In a road race, a $4,000 prize is split among the first three finishers in the ratio of 5:2:1. What is the greatest amount, in dollars, that any of the three prize winners receives?

(A)   500
(B) 1000
(C) 1500
(D) 2000
(E) 2500

GO ON TO THE NEXT PAGE

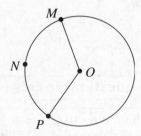

4. Point O is the center of the circle above, arc MNP has a length of 6π and MOP has a measure of $120°$. What is the length of PO?

(A) 6
(B) 9
(C) 12
(D) 15
(E) 18

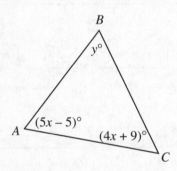

Note: Figure not drawn to scale.

5. In the figure above, $AB = BC$. What is the value of y?

(A) 40
(B) 50
(C) 65
(D) 70
(E) 75

6. The average (arithmetic mean) of f, g and h is one greater than their median, and $f < g < h$. If $f = 6$ and $h = 20$, then what is the value of g?

(A) 9
(B) 10.5
(C) 11.5
(D) 12
(E) 23

7. A jar contains marbles that are either red, white or blue. If the ratio of white marbles to red marbles is 3 to 5 and the ratio of red marbles to blue marbles is 6 to 5, then what is the least possible number of marbles in the jar?

(A) 18
(B) 25
(C) 63
(D) 73
(E) 80

8. The volume of a certain quantity of gas varies inversely as the pressure (in atmospheres) and directly as the temperature (in degrees Kelvin). If this quantity of gas occupies 10 liters at a pressure of 2 atmospheres and a temperature of 300 degrees Kelvin, what volume, in liters, will it occupy at 1 atmosphere and 450 degrees Kelvin?

(A) 15
(B) 30
(C) 90
(D) 300
(E) 450

GO ON TO THE NEXT PAGE ⇨

5   5   5   5   5   5

Directions: For student-produced response questions 9–18, use the grids at the bottom of the answer sheet page on which you have answered questions 1–8.

Each of the remaining ten questions requires you to solve the problem and enter your answer by marking the circles in the special grid, as shown in the examples below. You may use any available space for scratchwork.

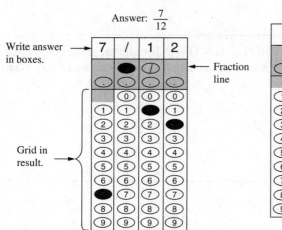

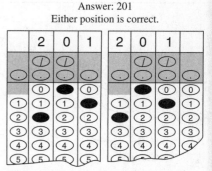

Note: You may start your answers in any column, space permitting. Columns not needed should be left blank.

- Mark no more than one circle in any column.

- Because the answer sheet will be machine-scored, **you will receive credit only if the circles are filled in correctly.**

- Although not required, it is suggested that you write your answer in the boxes at the top of the columns to help you fill in the circles accurately.

- Some problems may have more than one correct answer. In such cases, grid only one answer.

- No question has a negative answer.

- **Mixed numbers** such as $3\frac{1}{2}$ must be gridded as

  3.5 or 7/2. (If [3 1 / 2] is gridded, it will be

  interpreted as , $\frac{31}{2}$ not $3\frac{1}{2}$.)

- **Decimal Answers:** If you obtain a decimal answer with more digits than the grid can accommodate, it may be either rounded or truncated, but it must fill the entire grid. For example, if you obtain an answer such as 0.6666..., you should record your result as .666 or .667. **A less accurate value such as .66 or .67 will be scored as incorrect.**

  Acceptable ways to grid $^2/_3$ are:

9.   If 25% of 16 is x, then what is $x\%$ of 200?

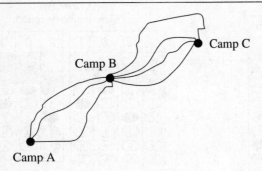

Camp C

Camp B

Camp A

10. The figure above represents all of the paths between Camp A and Camp B, and all of the possible paths from Camp B to Camp C. If you wish to travel from Camp A to Camp C using only these available paths and passing through Camp B only once, how many different routes can you chose from?

11. If $\dfrac{2}{x} = w$, then $(wx)^{-3} =$

12. Adding 2 to a number, x, then dividing this result by 4 is equivalent to multiplying x by $\dfrac{1}{4}$ and then adding what number?

13. If n and p are positive integers and $n^{-2p} = \dfrac{1}{16^p}$, what is the value of n?

14. If $f(x) = -(x-1)^2 + 2$ for all real values of x, then what is the greatest possible value of $f(x) + 3$?

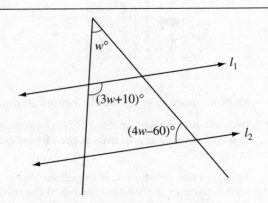

$w°$

$(3w+10)°$

$(4w-60)°$

l_1

l_2

15. In the figure above, if $l_1 \| l_2$, then what is the value of w?

16. If $x^2 - y^2 = 24$ and $x + y = 72$, then what is the value of $x - y$?

GO ON TO THE NEXT PAGE

17. If $f(x) = x - k$ where k is a constant, and the points (6, 1) and (8, 1) lie on the graph of $y = f(x)$, what is the value of $f(0)$?

Note: Figure not drawn to scale.

18. In the figure above, A, B and C are points on the number line with coordinates as shown. If $AC = 5AB$, then what is the value of x?

If you finish before time is called, you may check your work on this section only. Do not turn to any other section of the test.

6 **6** **6** **6** **6** **6**

SECTION 6
Time—25 minutes
24 questions

Turn to Section 6 of your answer sheet to answer the questions in this section.

Directions: For each question in this section, select the best answer from among the choices given and fill in the corresponding circle on the answer sheet.

Each sentence below has one or two blanks, each blank indicating that something has been omitted. Beneath the sentence are five words or sets of words labeled A through E. Choose the word or set of words that, when inserted in the sentence, best fits the meaning of the sentence as a whole.

EXAMPLE:

Rather than accepting the theory unquestioningly, Deborah regarded it with -----.

(A) mirth
(B) sadness
(C) responsibility
(D) ignorance
(E) skepticism

---

1. The fossil record suggests that new species do not arise -------, but instead develop gradually from other, existing species.

    (A) quietly
    (B) scientifically
    (C) instantaneously
    (D) permanently
    (E) falsely

2. Howard has a reputation for -------; although his self-serving claims always seem plausible, they are rarely true.

    (A) genius   (B) prevarication
    (C) fervency   (D) contemplation
    (E) forthrightness

3. Many psychoanalysts have claimed that great artists and composers constantly battle with derangement, theorizing that ------- and genius cannot -------.

    (A) equanimity .. conflict
    (B) sanity .. coexist
    (C) psychosis .. coincide
    (D) productivity .. differ
    (E) aesthetics .. interface

4. American oceanographers of the 1950s were relegated to using ------- maps of the ocean floor, because the highly detailed charts produced by the navy were ------- so that they did not fall into the hands of the Soviets.

    (A) counterfeit .. distributed
    (B) lucid .. apprehended
    (C) deficient .. classified
    (D) temporary .. disseminated
    (E) sketchy .. improved

5. Although he was a sincere Catholic, Galileo was considered by the Church to be ------- because his astronomic theories conflicted with its teachings.

    (A) an apostate
    (B) a conformist
    (C) a relic
    (D) an ascetic
    (E) a despot

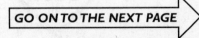

GO ON TO THE NEXT PAGE

6   6   6   6   6   6

Each passage below is followed by one or two questions based on its content. Answer each question based on what is stated or implied in the passage.

Questions 6–7 are based on the following passage.

The following is an excerpt from a book on the planet Mars by astronomer Percival Lowell.

Once in about every fifteen years a startling
visitant makes his appearance upon our
Line midnight skies—a great red star that rises at
sunset through the haze about the
5   eastern horizon, and then, mounting higher
with the deepening night, blazes forth against
the dark background of space with a
splendor that outshines Sirius and rivals the
giant Jupiter himself. Startling for its size,
10 the stranger looks the more fateful for being
a fiery red. Small wonder that by many folk it
is taken for a portent. Certainly, no one who
had not followed in their courses what the
Greeks so picturesquely called "the wanderers"
15 (hoi planetai) would recognize in the
apparition an orderly member of our own
solar family. Nevertheless, one of the
wanderers it is, for that star is the planet
Mars, large because for the moment near,
20 having in due course again been overtaken by
the Earth, in her swifter circling about the
Sun, at that point in space where his orbit
and hers make their closest approach.

6.   The passage suggests that, to many people, the redness of Mars indicates its

(A) ominousness
(B) ability to support life
(C) proximity to the sun
(D) enormous size
(E) swiftness

7.   In line 16, the word "apparition" most nearly means

(A) evil spirit
(B) figment of the imagination
(C) spectacle
(D) foreshadowing
(E) calculation

Questions 8–9 are based on the following passage.

Man is the only creature that consumes
without producing. He does not give milk, he
Line does not lay eggs, he is too weak to pull the
plough, he cannot run fast enough to catch
5   rabbits. Yet he is lord of all the animals. He
sets them to work, he gives back to them the
bare minimum that will prevent them from
starving, and the rest he keeps for himself.
Our labor tills the soil, our dung fertilizes it,
10 and yet there is not one of us who owns more
than his bare skin. You cows that I see before
me, how many thousands of gallons of milk
have you given during this last year? And
what has happened to that milk which should
15 have been breeding up sturdy calves? And
you hens, how many eggs have you laid in
this last year, and how many of those eggs
ever hatched into chickens? The rest have all
gone to market to bring in money for Jones
20 and his men. And you, Clover, where are
those four foals you bore, who should have
been the support and pleasure of your old
age? Each was sold at a year old; you will
never see one of them again. In return
25 for your confinements and all your labour in
the fields, what have you ever had except
your bare rations and a stall?

8.   This passage is written from the point of view of

(A) a man running for public office
(B) an underpaid farm worker
(C) a member of the clergy
(D) an owner of a large farm
(E) a farm animal

GO ON TO THE NEXT PAGE

First paragraph: "Mars," Percival Lowell, www.bibliomania.com, Public Domain, Chapter 1,"As a Star," p. 1
Second paragraph: George Orwell, *Animal Farm*, Public Domain

6   6   6   6   6   6

9. The questions posed in lines 11–23 indicate the speaker's dissatisfaction with

(A)   the low level of overall production of the farm animals
(B)   inefficient farming practices
(C)   the unfairness of the relationship between humans and animals
(D)   the excessive cost of maintaining a farm
(E)   the fact that some animals work harder than others

The questions below are based on the content of the passage that preceds them. The questions are to be answered on the basis of what is stated or implied in the passage itself or the introductory material that precedes the passage.

Questions 10–17 pertain to the following passage.

The following passage discusses medical advances in the fight against viruses.

Vaccination is one of medicine's cleverest tricks: making the body believe it is sick and
Line   thus causing it to marshal just the right forces to ward off that particular sickness.
5   The development of this practice stands as a twentieth-century accomplishment, but its roots reach far back into the past. Centuries ago, the Chinese and the Turks knew enough to produce a medicine against smallpox by
10   grinding up the scabs of people with mild cases of the disease. In 1796, Dr. Edward Jenner found he could induce resistance to smallpox by using the vaccinia virus (vacca is Latin for cow) to infect people with the
15   relatively mild cowpox. But it was Louis Pasteur, working a century later, who did the research that finally gave the field of immunology the creative boost that would propel it to the forefront of modern medicine.
20   In 1895, Pasteur produced a rabies vaccine without actually realizing that he was

enhancing the body's own immune system; he knew only that the vaccine worked.

But what was the infectious agent that
25   vaccines fought? Could it have been a bacterium? In Germany, in 1882, Robert Koch had shown that just such a germ caused tuberculosis. Microscopic parasites with similarities both to plants and animals,
30   bacteria were certainly the cause of much human misery. But they were not to play the starring role in the vaccine story.

The first tantalizing awareness of a virus—a microorganism even stranger than the
35   invisible bacteria and like nothing else ever known before—came in 1898 when Martinus Willem Beijerinick discovered a minuscule living thing he described with a name, "virus," derived from the Latin for poisonous
40   slime. A virus is really no more than a protein bag carrying its own set of genetic instructions. A virus cannot reproduce on its own. It must attach itself to a cell, impregnate the cell with the viral genes, and then,
45   parasite that it is, turn that cell into a reproductive machine for the virus's benefit. The body, for the most part, is able to recognize these viruses as foreign invaders by the signature proteins on their surface.
50   It then attacks them with antibodies and sends killer cells to destroy the cells that have already been infected. If the immune system is overwhelmed by the invasion, the body becomes sick and may die. If the body wins,
55   then its immune system keeps a record of this particular enemy and is better prepared to resist the next time. Sometimes the immunity is lifelong.

Thanks to advances in modern vaccines,
60   measles are nearly gone, and chicken pox, whooping cough, typhoid, and cholera are under control. From a purely psychological point of view, perhaps the biggest vaccine success of the century was the almost total
65   victory over polio, an effort that called upon everything scientists had learned in the new fields of immunology and virology. Polio was

GO ON TO THE NEXT PAGE

Excerpted from "Medicine's Great Journey", Schering Laboratories, Calloway Editions, Inc, © 1992, p 27-31.

thought to be a true childhood plague, a
crippler and a destroyer of young lives. It
70　seemed to come from nowhere in 1916 and
was virtually eradicated fifty years later.
　　　The advances against viruses continue.
There is now a vaccine for the vicious
hepatitis B virus, and vaccines for the
75　potentially deadly influenza viruses. But
herpes, another viral affliction, still
flourishes, and the most ubiquitous of all the
viral maladies—the common cold, caused by
well over a hundred different viruses—may
80　never be thwarted by a vaccine because the
viruses are too numerous. Scientists have
come a long way in the fight against viruses,
but further advances are necessary as it
seems new viruses appear as old viral foes
85　are eradicated. The fight will probably never
be completely won.

10. Which of the following is the best title for this
passage?

(A)　Medical Breakthroughs of the 19th
　　　Century
(B)　The Fight Against Bacterial Infections
(C)　The Power and Promise of Vaccines
(D)　How the Human Immune System Works
(E)　The Work of Edward Jenner

11. The passage mentions the "Chinese and the
Turks" (line 8) as examples of cultures that

(A)　identified viruses by name
(B)　employed early forms of vaccination
(C)　were nearly eradicated by viral diseases
(D)　mistook bacteria for viruses
(E)　used treatments that exacerbated rather
　　　than eliminated diseases

12. The passage indicates that viruses cause all of
the following EXCEPT

(A)　tuberculosis
(B)　cowpox
(C)　polio
(D)　herpes
(E)　hepatitis

13. Which of the following relationships is most
similar to the relationship between the virus
and the cell as it is described in the third paragraph (lines 33–58)?

(A)　the relationship between two birds of dif-
　　　ferent species, in which one bird lays its
　　　eggs in the nest of the other, which raises
　　　the young as its own
(B)　the relationship between a bear and a
　　　salmon, in which the bear captures and
　　　eats the salmon before it spawns
(C)　the relationship between a tickbird and a
　　　rhinoceros, in which the tickbird cleans
　　　parasites off the rhinoceros
(D)　the relationship between a bumblebee
　　　and a flower, in which the bumblebee
　　　carries pollen from the flower with
　　　which to fertilize other flowers
(E)　the relationship between two scavengers
　　　that fight over the same carcass

14. According to the passage, bacteria are like
viruses in that they

(A)　cannot reproduce on their own
(B)　have been virtually eradicated
(C)　played a major role in the discovery of
　　　vaccines
(D)　are parasitic
(E)　are largely beneficial

15. In line 49, the word "signature" most nearly
means

(A)　dangerous
(B)　official
(C)　identifying
(D)　invisible
(E)　beneficial

GO ON TO THE NEXT PAGE →

6   6   6   6   6   6

16. Which of the following best describes the relationship between the last two paragraphs?

    (A) The final paragraph makes a generalization based on the specific examples mentioned in the previous paragraph.
    (B) The final paragraph answers a question raised in the previous paragraph.
    (C) The final paragraph explains the time sequence of the events described in the previous paragraph.
    (D) The final paragraph gives an example of a concept defined in the previous paragraph.
    (E) The final paragraph qualifies the triumphant tone of the previous paragraph.

17. The passage cites which of the following as major impediments to eradicating viruses?

    I.   the abundance of viruses
    II. the inability of viruses to replicate on their own
    III. the ability of new viruses to replace old ones

    (A) I only
    (B) III only
    (C) I and II only
    (D) I and III only
    (E) I, II, and III

Questions 18–24 are based on the following passage.

The following is an excerpt taken from the memoirs of a Chinese woman born and raised in China during times of war.

My older brother, Ching-chung, six years older than I, was protective and vigilant; he was in
Line my eyes a man. He supervised my schooling and checked my home-work nightly; but most
5 of all I loved the stories he told me.

The Chinese language is a poetic one, and conversation—even among peasants—is often indirect and metaphorical, reflecting a philosophical turn of mind intrinsic to the
10 Chinese. Thus the teachings of Confucius or Buddha, codes of behavior, morality, and the like are often taught through the retelling, generation after generation, of the exploits of legendary heroes and heroines and stories
15 exemplifying the Chinese ideals.

Since both of my parents were so preoccupied—father with his business, and mother again pregnant—Ching-chung took it upon himself to be my teacher. Each day I
20 would wait impatiently for another story to begin. They always involved supreme sacrifice: the loyal servant ever ready to die for his master, the peasant equally willing to sacrifice himself for his emperor and country, the
25 good son eager to bring honor to his family.

As I was a girl, my brother would tell me of many heroines who sacrificed themselves for their fathers, brothers, or husbands, always practicing the virtues of humility,
30 modesty, and servitude. My favorite heroine was one Mu-lan, or "Wild Orchid." She was an only child when war broke out (the story

took place centuries earlier) and her father was obliged to fight. Being fifty years old, a
35 sanctified age at that time, he was far too old for battle. Because she loved her father and was imbued with the Chinese spirit of sacrifice, she dressed herself as a man and took her father's place in battle. Throughout
40 the fierce fighting no one realized she was female, and when the Emperor, in recognition of her achievements, offered her a distinguished wife, Mu-lan was forced to reveal her true sex.
45   These daily stories, exemplifying basic Chinese obligations and principles, made an enormous impression on me, and would affect my attitude and personal philosophy throughout my life.
50   But my brother had his tyrannical side as well. He went through a period during which he forced me to memorize the Four Chinese Classics—*The Analects of Confucius*, *The Great Learning*, *The Doctrine of the Mean*, and *The*
55 *Works of Mencius*—none of which I understood. He also made me memorize and copy out in careful calligraphy such maxims as: Render filial piety to parents, show respect to seniors by the generation age order, remain in
60 harmony with clan members and the community, teach and discipline sons and grandsons, attend to one's vocation properly, do not commit what the law forbids.
     From Ching-chung, I learned that sons
65 were to be filial to their fathers, wives dutiful to their husbands, and brothers affectionate to each other; and that laziness, extravagance, violence, and gambling were the most offensive conduct. He insisted that I copy out
70 each and every maxim. After holding the brush for hours on end, my fingers became cramped and useless. One day I simply burst into tears and, thoroughly exhausted, sat down on the floor and refused to get up.
75 Fortunately my father intervened, and my brother's tyranny came to an abrupt and permanent end.
     My reading was not confined exclusively to Chinese literature, however. Although my

80 father continued to make us all read and recite the tenets of certain Mandarin sages, by this time my adolescent, pre-teen tastes tended toward romantic European novels, many of them translated into Chinese. I
85 preferred to read the English translations of books like *The Three Musketeers* and *The Count of Monte Cristo*. It was this latter title that made the deepest impression on me. I knew whole passages by heart, and even took
90 the trouble to reread the book in Chinese, the title of which translates as *The Vengeance and the Gratitude of the Count of Monte Cristo*, reflecting a more Chinese concept in its translation.
95   In either version, I loved this strong and willful character who was so undeserving of all the misfortune that befell him. I suffered far more from his unhappiness than I delighted in his revenge; and like him, I felt I
100 should always be grateful to those people who had been kind to me.

18. The main purpose of this passage is to

(A) compare Asian literature to English literature

(B) explore one child's relationship with literature

(C) critique certain Chinese childrearing practices

(D) show the contrast between Chinese traditions and Western traditions

(E) reveal a painful episode between siblings

19. The passage mentions "peasants" in line 9 in order to make the point that

(A) some Chinese people tell stories because they are unable to read

(B) legends are retold mainly by people in the lower classes

(C) figurative and moralistic language is used by a wide range of Chinese people

(D) in China, the types of stories that are told differ widely from class to class

(E) most people in China are taught to write poetry

Excepted from *Journey in Tears*, Chow Ching-Li, McGraw-Hill.©1978 p25-27

GO ON TO THE NEXT PAGE

6   6   6   6   6   6

20. The passage suggests that, at first, the author's attitude towards her brother's stories was one of

(A) fear
(B) indignation
(C) ambivalence
(D) eagerness
(E) reluctant acceptance

21. The passage suggests that the author's brother expressed his "tyrannical side" (line 50) primarily through

(A) physical beatings
(B) stealing valued possessions
(C) cruel demands
(D) failing to acknowledge the author
(E) public humiliation

22. It can be inferred from the passage that the "more Chinese concept" mentioned in line 93 likely incudes an emphasis on

(A) brevity
(B) wealth
(C) Asian history
(D) thankfulness
(E) tyranny

23. According to the author, one significant difference between the story of *The Count of Monte Cristo* and *The Great Learning* was that

(A) one was about Chinese nobility and the other was about Chinese peasants
(B) she studied one book willingly and the other unwillingly
(C) one espoused violence as a virtue and the other condemned it
(D) one was widely popular, while the other was relatively obscure
(E) one was a comedy and the other a tragedy

24. As it is used in line 90, the word "trouble" most nearly means

(A) mental effort
(B) precarious situation
(C) emotional turmoil
(D) ethical difficulty
(E) reluctance

If you finish before time is called, you may check your work on this section only. Do not turn to any other section of the test.

7   7   7   7   7   7

SECTION 7
Time—20 minutes
16 questions

Turn to Section 7 of your answer sheet to answer the questions in this section.

Directions: For this section, solve each problem and decide which is the best of the choices given. Fill in the corresponding circle on the answer sheet. You may use any available space for scratchwork.

Notes

1. The use of a calculator is permitted.

2. All numbers used are real numbers.

3. Figures that accompany problems in this test are intended to provide information useful in solving the problems. They are drawn as accurately as possible EXCEPT when it is stated in a specific problem that the figure is not drawn to scale. All figures lie in a plane unless otherwise indicated.

4. Unless otherwise specified, the domain of any function f is assumed to be the set of all real numbers x for which $f(x)$ is a real number.

Reference Information

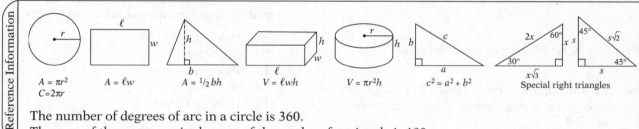

$A = \pi r^2$
$C = 2\pi r$

$A = \ell w$

$A = \frac{1}{2} bh$

$V = \ell w h$

$V = \pi r^2 h$

$c^2 = a^2 + b^2$

Special right triangles

The number of degrees of arc in a circle is 360.
The sum of the measures in degrees of the angles of a triangle is 180.

---

1. If one of the angles in a triangle is 100°, what is the average (arithmetic mean) of the measures, in degrees, of the other two angles?

   (A) 20°
   (B) 30°
   (C) 40°
   (D) 60°
   (E) 80°

2. If k is an integer that is 1 less than a multiple of 6, which of the following could be $k + 1$?

   (A) 16
   (B) 17
   (C) 18
   (D) 19
   (E) 20

GO ON TO THE NEXT PAGE

7   7   7   7   7   7

3. Which of the following expresses the number that is 15 more than the product of 3 and $m - 2$?

(A) $3m - 21$
(B) $3m - 13$
(C) $3m - 6$
(D) $3m + 9$
(E) $3m + 13$

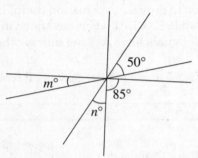

Note: Figure not drawn to scale

4. In the figure above, four line segments intersect at a single point. What is the value of $m + n$?

(A) 45
(B) 50
(C) 60
(D) 65
(E) 85

5. If $x\%$ of 30 is 12, what is $4x\%$ of 15?

(A) 6
(B) 12
(C) 18
(D) 24
(E) 48

6. If $0 < x < 1$ then which of the following must be true?

I. $\frac{1}{x} < x$

II. $x^2 > x$

III. $-x < -1$

(A) none
(B) I only
(C) II only
(D) III only
(E) I and III only

7. If every gadget costs p dollars to make, and each one sells for m dollars, then which of the following expressions represents the profit made if 10 gadgets are made but only 9 are sold?

(A) $10m - 9p$
(B) $9m - 10p$
(C) $10(m - p) - 9m$
(D) $9p + 10m$
(E) $10(m - p) + 9m$

8. If $y = f(x)$ such that y varies inversely as x, and the points $(4, 6)$ and $(2, m)$ lie on the graph of $y = f(x)$, what is the value of m?

(A) 4
(B) 6
(C) 8
(D) 10
(E) 12

GO ON TO THE NEXT PAGE ⟹

7   7   7   7   7   7

9. A machine can fill 200 boxes of cereal in 5 minutes. At this rate, how many <u>hours</u> will it take this machine to fill 24,000 boxes of cereal? (60 minutes = 1 hour)

(A)   10
(B)   24
(C)   100
(D)   210
(E)   600

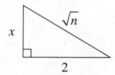

10. In the figure above, what is the value of x in terms of n ?

(A) $\sqrt{n-4}$
(B) $\sqrt{n-2}$
(C) $\sqrt{n+4}$
(D) $\sqrt{n+2}$
(D) $\sqrt{n+4}$

$$(r-5)^2 = (r+2)^2$$

11. Which of the following represents all possible solutions to the equation above?

(A)   −5 and 2 only
(B)   5 and −2 only
(C)   3.5 only
(D)   1.5 only
(E)   0 only

12. A certain class has 8 boys and 10 girls. How many different sets of four class officers—president, vice president, treasurer and secretary—can be formed from students in this class if the president and treasurer must be girls and the vice president and secretary must be boys?

(A)   25,600
(B)   6,400
(C)   5,040
(D)   3,200
(E)   2,520

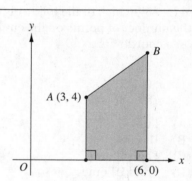

Note: Figure not drawn to scale.

13. In the figure above, if the shaded region has an area of 15, what is the slope of AB?

(A) $\dfrac{3}{5}$

(B) $\dfrac{2}{3}$

(C) $\dfrac{3}{4}$

(D) 1

(E) $\dfrac{3}{2}$

GO ON TO THE NEXT PAGE ⟹

7   7   7   7   7   7

14. If $m > 1$, then $\dfrac{m - \dfrac{1}{m}}{1 - \dfrac{1}{m}} =$

(A) $m + 1$
(B) m
(C) $m - 1$
(D) -1
(E) $\dfrac{m}{m-1}$

15. If a circle on the coordinate plane has a center at $(6, -6)$, which of the following could NOT be the number of points on the circle that also lie on a coordinate axis?

    I. 1
    II. 2
    III. 3

(A) I only
(B) II only
(C) I and II only
(D) I and III only
(E) II and III only

16. A certain car race consists of three legs of equal distance. On the first two legs of the race, a car travels an average of 50 miles per hour. On the last leg of the race, the car travels at an average of 75 miles per hour. What is the average speed, in miles per hour, for this car over the entire race?

(A) 52.00
(B) 56.25
(C) 58.33
(D) 62.50
(E) 66.67

STOP

If you finish before time is called, you may check your work on this section only. Do not turn to any other section of the test.

8   8   8   8   8   8

SECTION 8
Time—20 minutes
19 questions

Turn to Section 8 of your answer sheet to answer the questions in this section.

Directions: For each question in this section, select the best answer from among the choices given and fill in the corresponding circle on the answer sheet.

Each sentence below has one or two blanks, each blank indicating that something has been omitted. Beneath the sentence are five words or sets of words labeled A through E. Choose the word or set of words that, when inserted in the sentence, best fits the meaning of the sentence as a whole.

EXAMPLE:

Rather than accepting the theory unquestioningly, Deborah regarded it with -----.

(A) mirth
(B) sadness
(C) responsibility
(D) ignorance
(E) skepticism

Ⓐ Ⓑ Ⓒ Ⓓ ●

---

1. A clear model of the atom ------- physicists for decades; although they reasoned that the atom must exist, its ------- remained a mystery.

    (A) eluded .. structure
    (B) persuaded .. forces
    (C) inspired .. interest
    (D) mystified .. reality
    (E) investigated .. configuration

2. In contrast to the other interns who were exhausted by the drudgery of the 60-hour work week, Alynna seemed -------.

    (A) petrified
    (B) extensive
    (C) agitated
    (D) indefatigable
    (E) corrupted

3. Airborne germs are -------, yet surprisingly few are -------; despite the fact we inhale them with nearly every breath, the vast majority of them are innocuous and are neutralized easily by our immune systems.

    (A) omnipresent .. harmless
    (B) ubiquitous .. virulent
    (C) scarce .. malevolent
    (D) intolerable .. inconsequential
    (E) plentiful .. benign

4. Unlike *Vanity Fair*, which is occasionally didactic, *Middlemarch* is morally -------, challenging the reader to make his or her own ethical evaluations of the characters' actions.

    (A) resolute
    (B) corrupt
    (C) enervating
    (D) pedantic
    (E) ambiguous

5. The theory that humans have inhabited Australia for no more than 8,000 years was ------- when *Homo sapiens* bones that were discovered in the outback were ------- to be more than 50,000 years old.

    (A) refuted .. accustomed
    (B) invalidated .. established
    (C) introduced .. demonstrated
    (D) corroborated .. displayed
    (E) disproven .. deplored

GO ON TO THE NEXT PAGE ⟶

8   **8**   **8**   **8**   **8**   **8**

6. Judge Webster gave her instructions to the jury in such a ------- way that there was no doubt that they were to be obeyed strictly.

(A) loquacious
(B) desultory
(C) phlegmatic
(D) peremptory
(E) torpid

The questions below are based on the content of the passage that precedes them. The questions are to be answered on the basis of what is stated or implied in the passage itself or the introductory material that precedes the passage.

Questions 7–19 are based on the following passages.

The following are two recent essays on the economics of environmentalism.

PASSAGE 1

Many proponents of recycling regard it as a universal good. They assume that re-using
Line the remnants of any industrial or commercial process is better than putting them in a
5   landfill. Many opponents of recycling, on the other hand, scrutinize the economic costs of recycling. They suggest that recycling is often a bad idea because municipal recycling programs often waste more money than they
10   save, and companies can often produce new products more cheaply than they can recycle old ones. The debate rarely gets anywhere because it is too often politicized as a battle between a healthy economy and a healthy
15   environment. Of course, most of us want both. We must first stop the demonization; recycling proponents are not all economic ignoramuses, and recycling opponents are not all greedy troglodytes. We also must

20   learn to appreciate the real costs of recycling (or not recycling) to industry as well as the environment.

When discussing recycling, both environmentalists and industrialists must
25   examine the full life cycle of the commercial materials in question, and the effect that they have on the broader environment and economy throughout these life cycles. When debating the cost of a new road, for instance,
30   it is not enough to simply consider how much the contractors will charge or whether the materials are recycled. We must ask broader environmental questions like: what are the effects of things like the reduction of
35   natural water filtration, the leaching of dangerous elements from the road materials into the soil, the extra warming produced by the dark heat-absorbing materials, and the removal of flora and animal habitats in the
40   construction? Where will the road materials be in a thousand years? Will they be innocuous soil material, or environmental toxins? How will the extra traffic affect air quality?

We must also must consider broader
45   economic questions like: is the road made of local or imported materials? If they are imported, are they imported from countries with whom we have positive political and economic relations? Can the taxpayers afford
50   it? Is the money better spent elsewhere? Is the construction performed efficiently and by companies that were chosen through a fair and open bidding process? Will the road enhance commerce? How might the road
55   surface affect the life span or efficiency of the cars driving on it? How much will annual maintenance cost?

These are all responsible questions that the stewards of both our environment and
60   our economy should ask. They may lead us to interesting answers. Perhaps nature can do a more efficient and safer job of reusing waste matter in a landfill than a recycling plant can. Perhaps an economic system that
65   accounts for environmental costs and benefits will lead to a much better standard of living for the average citizen. Perhaps

GO ON TO THE NEXT PAGE

inserting some natural resources into a
responsible "industrial cycle" is better for
70 the environment than "conserving" those
resources. Perhaps some recycling practices
only delay environmental damage rather than
preventing it. Asking such questions openly,
respectfully and rigorously will help the
75 debaters to appreciate the attitudes of their
opponents, lead to a less rancorous debate
and a healthier economy and environment.

PASSAGE 2

The costs and benefits of preserving our
natural environment seem almost impossible
80 to quantify. One difficulty lies in the
diffuseness of the costs and benefits of
nature. Economists have a relatively easy
time with commerce, because money and
goods can be tracked through a series of
85 point-to-point exchanges. For instance, when
I give a store clerk a dollar, she gives me a
pack of gum. Part of the dollar I give her
goes to the gum company, some goes toward
the costs of running the store, some goes to
90 the government as tax, and some goes to her
as profit. It is all easily accounted for.

The benefits that ecosystems provide, like
biodiversity, the filtration of groundwater, the
maintenance of the oxygen and nitrogen
95 cycles, and climate stability, however, are not
simply bought-and-sold commodities.
They clearly benefit us, because without them
our lives would deteriorate dramatically, but
they are not part of a clear exchange, so they
100 fall into the class of benefits and costs that
economists call "externalities."

When you choose something, even if money
is not involved, the exchange is often clear.
When you pick an apple from a tree, the tree
105 loses an apple, and you gain one. If money is
involved—for instance, when an apple is
purchased—the exchange can be compared
with the billions of other monetary
transactions that occur in the economic
110 world every day. The diffuse, unchosen costs
and benefits that affect all of us daily—
annoying commercials or a beautiful sunset,
for instance—are much harder to valuate.

The "good feeling" that many people have
115 about recycling and maintaining
environmental quality is just such an
externality. Anti-environmentalists tend to
ridicule such feelings as unquantifiable and
hence irrelevant to economic decisions. But
120 its value is real: many investors will only
purchase the stock of companies with good
environmental records, and protests and
litigation against polluters can have steep
costs in terms of money and goodwill.

125 Some scientists have attempted to quantify
"external" ecological benefits rigorously.
Robert Costanza, formerly of the Center for
Environmental Science at the University of
Maryland, has estimated the value of nature
130 by tallying the cost to replace its services.
Imagine, for instance, that we paved over the
Florida Everglades and atop it somehow built
systems that maintained all of the functions
of the ecosystem we destroyed: gas
135 conversion and sequestering, food production,
water filtration, weather regulation, et cetera.
How much would it cost to keep these systems
running? Even though these systems almost
certainly would not account for some of the
140 most important externalities, like natural
beauty, the cost would be extraordinarily high.
Costanza places the cost "conservatively" at
$33 trillion dollars annually, far more than the
combined annual gross national products of
145 all of the countries in the world.

Some in the fields of both economics and
environmental science object to Costanza's
attempt to valuate nature. Environmentalists
argue that it simply cannot be done—how do
150 you put a price on the smell of heather and a
cool breeze? Industrialists argue that it
depends largely on speculation and renders
economic decision-making more cumbersome.
Nevertheless, Costanza's work is among the
155 most cited in the fields of environmental
science and economics. For any flaws it might
have, his work is giving a common
vocabulary to industrialists and
environmentalists alike, which we must do
160 if we are to coordinate intelligent
environmental policy with responsible
economic policy.

GO ON TO THE NEXT PAGE

8   8   8   8   8   8

7. The primary purpose of the first four sentences of Passage 1 is to

(A) introduce a discussion with a story
(B) establish the author's main thesis
(C) define several key concepts
(D) provide the historical background to a debate
(E) characterize two positions on an issue

8. The sentence beginning on line 16, "We must first stop … greedy troglodytes" suggests that those who debate the issue of recycling tend to

(A) mischaracterize their opponents
(B) ignore statistics
(C) use weak logical arguments
(D) employ misleading ad campaigns
(E) avoid personal confrontations

9. As they pertain to the "new road" mentioned in line 29, the "life cycles" mentioned in line 28 are those of

(A) the plants that are destroyed by road construction
(B) the animals that may be displaced by a new road
(C) economic and industrial trends
(D) the substances that constitute the road
(E) the companies involved in constructing the road

10. The questions listed in the second paragraph (lines 23–43) directly address all of the following possibilities EXCEPT

(A) the destruction of animals' natural homes
(B) the leakage of poisons into the soil
(C) the creation of landslides from soil displacement
(D) the emission of harmful car fumes
(E) the reduction of natural water purification

11. In line 69, the word "responsible" most nearly means

(A) guilty
(B) reactionary
(C) well-governed
(D) pleasant
(E) mature

12. The exchange with the "store clerk" (line 86) is used to represent

(A) an example of recycling
(B) an illustration of the value of human emotions
(C) a poorly understood and uncommon phenomenon
(D) a particular difficulty in economic analysis
(E) a transaction that is easily accounted for

13. Which of the following examples serves the same rhetorical purpose as that served by the "pack of gum" in line 87?

(A) the "apple" in line 104
(B) the "groundwater" in line 93
(C) the "climate stability" in line 95
(D) the "good feeling" in line 114
(E) the "beautiful sunset" in lines 112

14. In saying that the benefits of ecosystems are not "commodities" (line 96) Passage 2 suggests that they

(A) are less expensive to maintain than factories
(B) are difficult to track and evaluate
(C) are not as beneficial to consumers as purchased goods
(D) do not represent a financial burden if they are destroyed
(E) are found everywhere in abundance

GO ON TO THE NEXT PAGE ⇒

8 8 8 8 8 8

15. Which of the following would be an example of an "externality" as it is defined in Passage 2?

(A) the extra revenue produced by increasing the price of a service
(B) the annual cost of maintaining a municipal recycling program
(C) the value of a beaver pelt in the wholesale market
(D) the irritating noise caused by a neighbor's motorcycle
(E) the salaries paid to environmental workers

16. Passage 2 indicates that Costanza himself considers the true value of the world's ecosystems to be

(A) a subject more for psychologists than economists
(B) impossible to determine
(C) likely greater than his estimate
(D) independent of the value of human emotions
(E) roughly equal to the value of the gross national product of the United States

17. Which of the following is mentioned in Passage 2 as one of the potential "flaws" (line 156) in Costanza's work?

(A) contradictions with well-known theories of economics
(B) excessively technical language
(C) a failure to consider any externalities
(D) excessive reliance on guesswork
(E) incomplete mathematical models

18. The two passages differ in their perspectives on the debate between industrialists and environmentalists mainly in that Passage 1 emphasizes

(A) mathematics, while Passage 2 emphasizes psychology
(B) deficiencies in the debate, while Passage 2 emphasizes progress in the debate
(C) the irrelevance of externalities, while Passage 2 emphasizes their importance
(D) the impact on taxpayers, while Passage 2 emphasizes the views of politicians
(E) pollution, while Passage 2 emphasizes recycling

19. Both passages include which of the following elements?

   I. a discussion of the importance of human feelings in a debate
   II. a citation of an authoritative scientific study
   III. a reference to global warming

(A) I only
(B) II only
(C) I and II only
(D) II and III only
(E) I, II, and III

STOP

If you finish before time is called, you may check your work on this section only. Do not turn to any other section of the test.

9   9   9   9   9   9

SECTION 9
Time—10 minutes
14 questions

Turn to Section 9 of your answer sheet to answer the questions in this section.

Directions: For each question in this section, select the best answer from among the choices given and fill in the corresponding circle on the answer sheet.

The following sentences test correctness and effectiveness of expression. Part of each sentence or the entire sentence is underlined; beneath each sentence are five ways of phrasing the underlined material. Choice A repeats the original phrasing; the other four choices are different. Select the choice that completes the sentence most effectively.

In making your selection, follow the requirements of standard written English; that is, pay attention to grammar, choice of words, sentence construction, and punctuation. Your selection should result in the most effective sentence—clear and precise, without awkwardness or ambiguity.

EXAMPLE:

The children <u>couldn't hardly believe their eyes</u>.

(A) couldn't hardly believe their eyes
(B) could hardly believe their eyes
(C) would not hardly believe their eyes
(D) couldn't nearly believe their eyes
(E) couldn't hardly believe his or her eyes

1. Brian wanted to prepare well for the <u>exam; staying up</u> all night studying his textbook.

   (A) exam; staying up
   (B) exam; and staying up
   (C) exam in staying up
   (D) exam, so he stayed up
   (E) exam and staying up

2. Many athletes use yoga to enhance their flexibility <u>and so that they might improve their mind-body awareness</u>.

   (A) and so that they might improve their mind-body awareness
   (B) and to improve their mind-body awareness
   (C) as well as improving their mind-body awareness
   (D) and for improving their mind-body awareness
   (E) and improve their mind-body awareness also

GO ON TO THE NEXT PAGE ➡

9   **9**   **9**   **9**   **9**   **9**

3. Without speaking so much as a syllable, <u>Chaplin's emotions and intentions were clearly portrayed on the screen</u>.

  (A) Chaplin's emotions and intentions were clearly portrayed on the screen

  (B) Chaplin clearly on the screen portrayed his emotional intentions

  (C) Chaplin's emotions and intentions on the screen were clearly portrayed by him

  (D) Chaplin emotionally portrayed his intentions on the screen clearly

  (E) Chaplin clearly portrayed his emotions and intentions on the screen

4. The conversation between <u>Anna and me about her future plans was</u> frank and productive.

  (A) Anna and me about her future plans was

  (B) Anna and I about her future plans were

  (C) Anna and me about her future plans were

  (D) me and Anna about her future plans were

  (E) Anna and I about her future plans was

5. <u>The fact of the island's strong natural defenses made it a natural choice by the naval commander to station his ships there</u>

  (A) The fact of the island's strong natural defenses made it a natural choice by the naval commander to station his ships there.

  (B) The naval commander chose to station his ships on the island because it had strong natural defenses.

  (C) The island's strong natural defenses made the naval commander choose to station his ships on it.

  (D) Due to its strong natural defenses, the naval commander stationed his ships on the island by choice.

  (E) The island was the choice for the naval commander's stationing his ships because of its strong natural defenses.

6. Much of the night sky has never been examined carefully because <u>of the cumbersome nature of telescopes and the fact that they can only peer</u> into a tiny patch of the sky at one time.

  (A) of the cumbersome nature of telescopes and the fact that they can only peer

  (B) telescopes are cumbersome and can only peer

  (C) of the cumbersomeness of telescopes and the fact of their peering only

  (D) telescopes are cumbersome enough without peering

  (E) telescopes are too cumbersome yet unable to peer

7. Only recently have neural scientists come to realize that new nerve cells can, in certain situations, <u>be generated to assume</u> the function of dead or damaged ones.

  (A) be generated to assume

  (B) be generated for the assuming of

  (C) have been generated to assume

  (D) assume, being generated,

  (E) generate the assuming of

8. Prospective students should consider not only a school's curriculum and prestige, but also <u>what kind of student support programs it provides</u>.

  (A) what kind of student support programs it provides

  (B) how good are its student support programs

  (C) what its student support programs are

  (D) what student support programs they provide

  (E) its student support programs

GO ON TO THE NEXT PAGE →

9   9   9   9   9   9

9. William F. Buckley, <u>wrote his first book when he was 23</u>, also founded the *National Review*.

   (A) wrote his first book when he was 23
   (B) who wrote his first book when he was 23
   (C) who when he would have published his first book was 23
   (D) wrote, at 23, his first book
   (E) would write his first book at 23

10. <u>If they would not have been led astray by the faulty map</u>, the troop would have found camp by nightfall.

   (A) If they would not have been led astray by the faulty map
   (B) If the faulty map would not have led it astray
   (C) Had they not have been led astray by the faulty map
   (D) Had it not been led astray by the faulty map
   (E) Would they not have been led astray by the faulty map

11. Barely able to speak because of the cold, <u>the communication among the two explorers had to be done through gestures</u>.

   (A) the communication among the two explorers had to be done through gestures
   (B) the communication between the two explorers had to be done through gestures
   (C) the two explorers had to communicate through gestures
   (D) the two explorers had to communicate between themselves from gestures
   (E) gestures were used to communicate between the two explorers

12. The cost of crude oil is influenced dramatically not only by supply but also <u>by what the current geopolitical events are like</u>.

   (A) by what the current geopolitical events are like
   (B) because of current geopolitical events
   (C) by current geopolitical events
   (D) by what current geopolitical events are
   (E) because current geopolitical events influence it

13. The Ivy League was founded as a sports conference <u>and many think it was founded as an academic conference</u>.

   (A) and many think it was founded as an academic conference
   (B) and not, as many think, as an academic conference
   (C) but many people think instead that it was founded as an academic conference
   (D) yet many think mistakenly that it was founded as an academic conference instead
   (E) but not as an academic conference as many think

14. <u>They expended so much effort and money to be able to witness</u> the transit of Venus, the surveyors could not return to Europe without the valuable data they sought.

   (A) They expended so much effort and money to be able to witness
   (B) They had expended so much effort and money for witnessing
   (C) Having expended so much effort and money to be able to witness
   (D) The money and effort having been expended already to witness
   (E) To be able to witness, having expended so much effort and money

STOP

If you finish before time is called, you may check your work on this section only. Do not turn to any other section of the test.

ANSWER KEY

Critical Reading

Section 3

COR. ANS.	DIFF. LEV.		COR. ANS.	DIFF. LEV.
1. C	1	13.	E	2
2. A	1	14.	C	3
3. E	2	15.	B	3
4. B	3	16.	A	4
5. C	4	17.	B	4
6. D	4	18.	D	3
7. D	4	19.	C	3
8. A	5	20.	B	4
9. B	2	21.	A	3
10. E	3	22.	E	3
11. A	3	23.	C	3
12. C	4	24.	D	5

Number correct

Number incorrect

Section 6

COR. ANS.	DIFF. LEV.		COR. ANS.	DIFF. LEV.
1. C	2	13.	A	3
2. B	2	14.	D	4
3. B	3	15.	C	3
4. C	3	16.	E	4
5. A	4	17.	D	4
6. A	3	18.	B	5
7. C	3	19.	C	3
8. E	2	20.	D	3
9. C	3	21.	C	4
10. C	2	22.	D	3
11. B	4	23.	B	4
12. A	5	24.	A	4

Number correct

Number incorrect

Section 8

COR. ANS.	DIFF. LEV.		COR. ANS.	DIFF. LEV.
1. A	1	11.	C	4
2. D	2	12.	E	2
3. B	3	13.	A	2
4. E	4	14.	B	4
5. B	5	15.	D	4
6. D	5	16.	C	3
7. E	2	17.	D	3
8. A	4	18.	B	3
9. D	4	19.	A	4
10. C	3			

Number correct

Number incorrect

Math

Section 2

COR. ANS.	DIFF. LEV.		COR. ANS.	DIFF. LEV.
1. C	1	11.	D	3
2. C	1	12.	B	3
3. E	3	13.	A	3
4. A	2	14.	D	4
5. B	2	15.	C	3
6. B	2	16.	C	4
7. B	3	17.	B	4
8. A	2	18.	D	4
9. C	3	19.	B	5
10. C	3	20.	D	5

Number correct

Number incorrect

Section 5

Multiple-Choice Questions

COR. ANS.	DIFF. LEV.
1. E	1
2. C	2
3. E	3
4. B	3
5. B	3
6. C	4
7. D	4
8. B	5

Student-produced Response questions

	COR. ANS.	DIFF. LEV.
9.	8	1
10.	12	2
11.	1/8 or .125	3
12.	0.5 or 1/2	3
13.	4	3
14.	5	4
15.	35	3
16.	.333 or 1/3	4
17.	7	5
18.	7/6 or 1.16 or 1.17	5

Number correct

Number incorrect

Number correct (9–18)

Section 7

COR. ANS.	DIFF. LEV.		COR. ANS.	DIFF. LEV.
1. C	2	9.	A	4
2. C	2	10.	A	4
3. D	2	11.	D	3
4. A	3	12.	C	4
5. D	3	13.	B	3
6. A	3	14.	A	4
7. B	3	15.	A	5
8. E	3	16.	B	5

Number correct

Number incorrect

Writing

Section 4

COR. ANS.	DIFF. LEV.		COR. ANS.	DIFF. LEV.		COR. ANS.	DIFF. LEV.		COR. ANS.	DIFF. LEV.
1. B	1	11.	E	4	21.	D	3	31.	C	3
2. E	1	12.	C	1	22.	A	4	32.	B	3
3. C	2	13.	B	1	23.	D	3	33.	D	3
4. E	3	14.	E	2	24.	E	4	34.	B	3
5. A	4	15.	D	3	25.	C	3	35.	A	3
6. D	2	16.	C	3	26.	C	3			
7. B	3	17.	B	2	27.	B	4			
8. D	4	18.	A	3	28.	A	4			
9. D	4	19.	C	3	29.	A	5			
10. A	3	20.	E	3	30.	E	3			

Number correct

Number incorrect

Section 9

COR. ANS.	DIFF. LEV.		COR. ANS.	DIFF. LEV.
1. D	1	11.	C	3
2. B	2	12.	C	4
3. E	2	13.	B	4
4. A	2	14.	C	3
5. B	2			
6. B	2			
7. A	3			
8. E	3			
9. B	3			
10. D	3			

Number correct

Number incorrect

NOTE: Difficulty levels are estimates of question difficulty that range from 1 (easiest) to 5 (hardest).

SCORE CONVERSION TABLE

How to score your text

Use the answer key on the previous page to determine your raw score on each section. Your raw score on each section except Section 4 is simply the number of correct answers minus ¼ of the number of wrong answers. On Section 4, your raw score is the sum of the number of correct answers for questions 1–8 minus ¼ of the number of wrong answers for questions 1–8 plus the total number of correct answers for questions 9–18. Next, add the raw scores from Sections 3, 4, and 7 to get your Math raw score, add the raw scores from Sections 2, 5, and 8 to get your Critical Reading raw score and add the raw scores from Sections 6 and 9 to get your Writing raw score. Write the three raw scores here:

Raw Critical Reading score: _____ Raw Math score: _____ Raw Writing score: _____

Use the table below to convert these to scaled scores.

Scaled scores: Critical Reading: _____ Math: _____ Writing: _____

Raw Score	Critical Reading Scaled Score	Math Scaled Score	Writing Scaled Score	Raw Score	Critical Reading Scaled Score	Math Scaled Score	Writing Scaled Score
67	800			32	520	570	610
66	800			31	510	560	600
65	790			30	510	550	580
64	780			29	500	540	570
63	770			28	490	530	560
62	750			27	490	520	550
61	740			26	480	510	540
60	730			25	480	500	530
59	720			24	470	490	520
58	700			23	460	480	510
57	690			22	460	480	500
56	680			21	450	470	490
55	670			20	440	460	480
54	660	800		19	440	450	470
53	650	800		18	430	450	460
52	650	780		17	420	440	450
51	640	760		16	420	430	440
50	630	740		15	410	420	440
49	620	730	800	14	400	410	430
48	620	710	800	13	400	410	420
47	610	710	800	12	390	400	410
46	600	700	790	11	380	390	400
45	600	690	780	10	370	380	390
44	590	680	760	9	360	370	380
43	590	670	740	8	350	360	380
42	580	660	730	7	340	350	370
41	570	650	710	6	330	340	360
40	570	640	700	5	320	330	350
39	560	630	690	4	310	320	340
38	550	620	670	3	300	310	320
37	550	620	660	2	280	290	310
36	540	610	650	1	270	280	300
35	540	600	640	0	250	260	280
34	530	590	630	−1	230	240	270
33	520	580	620	−2 or less	210	220	250

SCORE CONVERSION TABLE FOR WRITING COMPOSITE
[ESSAY + MULTIPLE CHOICE]

Calculate your writing raw score as you did on the previous page and grade your essay from a 1 to a 6 according to the standards that follow in the detailed answer key.

Essay score: _____ Raw Writing score: _____

Use the table below to convert these to scaled scores.

Scaled score: Writing: _____

Raw Score	Essay Score 0	Essay Score 1	Essay Score 2	Essay Score 3	Essay Score 4	Essay Score 5	Essay Score 6
−2 or less	200	230	250	280	310	340	370
−1	210	240	260	290	320	360	380
0	230	260	280	300	340	370	400
1	240	270	290	320	350	380	410
2	250	280	300	330	360	390	420
3	260	290	310	340	370	400	430
4	270	300	320	350	380	410	440
5	280	310	330	360	390	420	450
6	290	320	340	360	400	430	460
7	290	330	340	370	410	440	470
8	300	330	350	380	410	450	470
9	310	340	360	390	420	450	480
10	320	350	370	390	430	460	490
11	320	360	370	400	440	470	500
12	330	360	380	410	440	470	500
13	340	370	390	420	450	480	510
14	350	380	390	420	460	490	520
15	350	380	400	430	460	500	530
16	360	390	410	440	470	500	530
17	370	400	420	440	480	510	540
18	380	410	420	450	490	520	550
19	380	410	430	460	490	530	560
20	390	420	440	470	500	530	560
21	400	430	450	480	510	540	570
22	410	440	460	480	520	550	580
23	420	450	470	490	530	560	590
24	420	460	470	500	540	570	600
25	430	460	480	510	540	580	610
26	440	470	490	520	550	590	610
27	450	480	500	530	560	590	620
28	460	490	510	540	570	600	630
29	470	500	520	550	580	610	640
30	480	510	530	560	590	620	650
31	490	520	540	560	600	630	660
32	500	530	550	570	610	640	670
33	510	540	550	580	620	650	680
34	510	550	560	590	630	660	690
35	520	560	570	600	640	670	700
36	530	560	580	610	650	680	710
37	540	570	590	620	660	690	720
38	550	580	600	630	670	700	730
39	560	600	610	640	680	710	740
40	580	610	620	650	690	720	750
41	590	620	640	660	700	730	760
42	600	630	650	680	710	740	770
43	610	640	660	690	720	750	780
44	620	660	670	700	740	770	800
45	640	670	690	720	750	780	800
46	650	690	700	730	770	800	800
47	670	700	720	750	780	800	800
48	680	720	730	760	800	800	800
49	680	720	730	760	800	800	800

Detailed Answer Key

Section 1

> The following essay received 12 points out of a possible 12, meaning that it demonstrates *clear and consistent mastery* in that it
>
> - develops an insightful point of view on the topic
> - demonstrates exemplary critical thinking
> - uses effective examples, reasons, and other evidence to support its thesis
> - is consistently focused, coherent, and well-organized
> - demonstrates skilful and effective use of language and sentence structure
> - is largely (but not necessarily completely) free of grammatical and usage errors
>
> Consider carefully the issue discussed in the following passage, then write an essay that answers the question posed in the assignment.
>
> > In any contest between power and patience, bet on patience.
> >
> > —W.B. Prescott
>
> **Assignment:** **Which is a more powerful force of social change: power or patience?** Write an essay in which you answer this question and support your position logically with examples from literature, the arts, history, politics, science and technology, current events, or your experience or observation.
>
> Write your essay on separate sheets of paper.

SAMPLE STUDENT ESSAY

Although the first two centuries of the American experiment have been characterized by the systematic disenfrachisement of African Americans, women, the destitute, and those from the "wrong" political party, democracy has slowly and patiently evolved and strengthened, not through military victories, but by patient commitment to an idea. Indeed, democracy is the antithesis of concentrated power. Yet, tragically, recent American leaders act as if it can be forced upon a people, in ignorance of the true history of their own democracy, and of the nature of democracy itself. They have come to believe that America, by dint of its relative success with democracy at home, has earned the right to exert its unbridled will throughout the world. They will fail because they do not understand the value of patience over power, of ideas over arms, of compassion over strategy. The patient commitment to true democracy will, in the long run, be more powerful than the strongest army on earth.

The current war in Iraq was first proclaimed as a "preemptive" strike against terrorists in order to protect our homeland. When it was revealed beyond doubt that Iraq in fact posed no threat to us, our leaders re-cast the war as one to "free Iraq" and "bring democracy to an oppressed people." But this could not possibly be so. Such proclamations express only the wishes of politicians, not human reality. Democracy is the patient triumph of ideas over might. It is a waging of words rather than a waging of war; it is a faith in humanity to choose what is right and good, not to force-feed a single-minded view down the throats of the masses.

But, the neoconservatives say, our own freedom, our own democracy, was earned only through wars like the Revolutionary War, the Civil War and the World Wars. We must exert our power and perhaps spill the blood of our brave soldiers so that freedom will reign! But this is true only for one's own freedom, not the freedom of others. Each people must earn its own freedom. No country on this earth will ever accept that it has been "given" democracy by an invading force. It's story must belong to its people, just as the story of our freedom is our own.

We have a long way to go before we understand democracy well enough to preach it to others, let alone force it down their throats. True leaders lead by example, not by force. When our leaders learn the true meaning of democracy well enough to live it, then they will have earned the right to speak it, and the world will follow their example. To reach that point, we need patient faith in an idea, not the powers of arms.

The following essay received 10 points out of a possible 12, meaning that it demonstrates *reasonably consistent* mastery in that it

- effectively develops a point of view on the topic
- demonstrates strong critical thinking
- uses good examples, reasons, and other evidence to support its thesis
- shows a good organization and consistent focus
- demonstrates consistent facility with language
- is mostly free of errors in grammar, usage, and mechanics

SAMPLE STUDENT ESSAY

Patience does bring about greater change than does power. We tend to see the world in terms of power. Our televisions are filled with scenes of powerful politicians and tycoons, of powerful bombs and natural disasters, but if our televisions could show us the world as it really is, we would see a lot more patient waiting than powerful expressions of force. Even though the universe may have been created in one huge big bang, life has only evolved to its current level patiently over millions and millions of years.

Our economy is supported more by the millions of workers who do their jobs faithfully and patiently day by day than by the mega-powerful CEOs with billion dollar salaries. In fact, the most successful CEOs become successful only by learning the patience of the common people. McDonald's is successful because it consistently gives the people the food they want, day in and day out. Dell has become a successful company because it patiently listens to its consumers and helps them with difficulties they may have with their computers.

Another good example of the strength of patience is a colony of ants. No one ant has any extraordinary ability, but when they patiently do their jobs as a group, they create and maintain an enormous ecosystem almost as complex as a city. There are no tycoons in an ant colony.

It is wise to remember that patience is more important than power. For instance, great athletes become great by patiently and consistently working on their skills, their strength and their agility. If they tried to do all of their training in one powerful burst, they would quickly burn themselves out or get injured. Even one who is merely trying to stay in shape, or to learn a subject, should remember that steady patient work is more important than natural power.

The following essay received 4 points out of a possible 12, meaning that it demonstrates *some incompetence* in that it

- has a seriously limited point of view
- demonstrates weak critical thinking
- uses inappropriate or insufficient examples, reasons, and other evidence to support its thesis
- is poorly focused and organized, and has serious problems with coherence
- demonstrates frequent problems with language and sentence structure
- contains errors in grammar and usage that obscure the author's meaning seriously

SAMPLE STUDENT ESSAY

If to bet on patience means that you should just wait for things to happen, I don't think you should do that. Sometimes the most important thing is to take some action and show that you have some power. If somebody is trying to attack you, then patience isn't going to help you much, but having a gun probably will. That's just the way things are.

A lot of times people will tell me that it's better if you just wait and good things will happen. But when you see people who have made their mark in the world you see people have just took charge and did things on their own terms. Power works. Everybody can tell when somebody walks into the room who has confidence in themselves. It's very appealing and people like that tend to have a lot of infuence over people and things.

I don't want to just sit around and wait for things to happen that's why I try to make things happen. That's a lot better for all different areas like sports, business and politics.

Section 2

1. C First substitute $2b$ for a: $a = 3 + b$
    Substitute: $2b = 3 + b$
    Subtract b: $b = 3$

2. C 6 pounds of cheese cost $6 \times \$1.50 = \$9.00$.
6 pounds of beef cost $3 \times \$4.00 = \$12.00$.
$\$12.00 - \$9.00 = \$3.00$

3. E The slope of a line is the "rise divided by the run" between any two points. Use the origin as one point and $(12, k)$ as the other. The "rise" between these points is $k - 0 = k$. The "run" is $12 - 0 = 12$. If the slope is 2, then $k/12 = 2$, and therefore $k = 24$.

4. A The statement "x is 5 less than y" translates into
$$x = y - 5$$
    Subtract y: $x - y = -5$
    therefore: $5(x - y) = 5(-5) = -25$
You may also choose simple values for x and y, where x is 5 less than y, like $x = 2$ and $y = 7$.

5. B On a map that is drawn to scale, all distances are proportional to their corresponding lengths in the real world. Therefore, we can set up a proportion:
$$\frac{50 \text{ miles}}{1 \text{ inch}} = \frac{240 \text{ miles}}{x \text{ inches}}$$
    Cross-multiply: $50x = 240$
    Divide by 50: $x = 4.8$

6. B One student has 40% of the CDs, and 40% of $30 = .40(30) = 12$ CDs. The other student has 33⅓%, or ⅓ of the CDs. ⅓ of 30 = 10. Therefore the third student has $30 - 12 - 10 = 8$ CDs.

7. B If the average score of Marianne's 3 tests is 85, then the sum of the three scores is $85 \times 3 = 255$. If she scored 90 on the first two tests, then she must have received $255 - 90 - 90 = 75$ on the third test.

8. A The sequence consists of the repetition of three numbers, −1, 0 and 1 which have a sum of 0. In the first 100 terms, this pattern is repeated 33⅓ times. The first 33 repetitions yield a sum of $33(0) = 0$, but this leaves one more term, which is −1. Therefore the overall sum is $0 + -1 = -1$.

9. C Since $50 \div 3 = 16 \frac{2}{3}$, there are 16 multiples of 3 between 1 and 50, the last one being $16 \times 3 = 48$. Therefore the probability of choosing a multiple of 3 is $16/50 = 8/25$.

10. C Substitute $a = 10$ into both of the other equations and solve for b and c: $10 + b = 5$
    Subtract 10: $b = -5$
                   $10 - c = 15$
    Subtract 10: $-c = 5$
    Divide by −1: $c = -5$
    So $c - b = -5 - (-5) = 0$

11. D Examine the "ones" column first. $A + 7 + B + 7$ must equal either 18 or 28 in order to produce an 8 in the ones column as a result. (Think about why it can't equal 8 or 38 or greater.) Therefore $A + B = 4$ or 14. If $A + B = 4$, then there is a "carry" of 1 into the tens column, and so $1 + 3 + B + 4 + 2 = 17$ and $B = 7$. But this is impossible, because we had assumed that $A + B$ is only 4. Therefore, $A + B$ must equal 14, and the "carry" is 2. This means that $2 + 3 + B + 4 + 2 = 17$, and so $B = 6$. therefore $A = 8$.

12. B Draw point D so that C is the midpoint of AD. If $CD = 4x$, then $AC = 4x$ also. Then you can find AB by the Pythagorean Theorem:

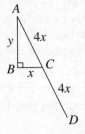

                           $y^2 + x^2 = (4x)^2$
    Simplify: $y^2 + x^2 = 16x^2$
    Subtract x^2: $y^2 = 15x^2$
Take the square root: $y = x\sqrt{15}$

13. **A**   A quick sketch of the two points may be helpful:

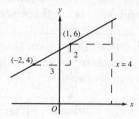

One approach is to determine the equation of the line joining the two points, but this is time consuming, then seeing which point "works" in the equation. (The equation is $y = (2/3)x + 16/3$.) A simpler method is to notice that, to get from the first point to the second, you need only move to the right 3 units and up 2 units. Repeating this again from the second point puts you at $(4, 8)$.

14. **D**   This is just a matter of checking each choice. Don't forget that *squaring* something is **not** the same as taking the *square root*. (If you made this mistake, you probably chose (B) as your answer.) The only choice that "works" is (D) because $16 = 7 + 3^2$.

15. **C** $3^y + 3^y + 3^y + 3^y + 3^y + 3^y + 3^y + 3^y + 3^y = 9(3^y)$
     Notice that 9 is a power of 3: $9(3^y) = 3^1(3^y)$
     Add exponents when multiplying exponentials with a common base: $3^2(3^y) = 3^{y+2}$

16. **C**   One approach is to "test" points and work by process of elimination. For instance, you might notice that 0 doesn't work (because $2 - |0 + 1|$ is not < 0), but 2 does work (because $2 - |2 + 1| < 0$. Therefore the solution set contains 2 but not 0. This eliminates choices (A) and (B). You can proceed like this until only one choice remains.

     Another approach is to simplify the inequality and "translate" it. $2 - |x + 1| < 0$
     Subtract 2: $- |x + 1| < -2$
     Divide by −1 and "flip": $|x + 1| > 2$
     Represent sum as a
     difference: $|x - (-1)| > 2$
     This means that the distance from x to −1 is greater than 2. The graph that shows all values more than 2 units away from −1 is choice (C).

17. **B**   Assume that the original price of the book is p and the total number of books sold at that price is n. At this price, the book would produce a revenue of np. The new price is 10% greater, or $1.1p$, and the new sales number is 5% less, or $.95n$. This would produce a revenue of $(1.1p)(.95n) = 1.045np$, which represents an increase in revenue of 4.5%.

18. **D**   In the first round, 16 games are played and 16 teams are eliminated. In the next round, 8 games are played and 8 are eliminated, and so on. Each round contains half as many games as the previous round. The total number of games played is $16 + 8 + 4 + 2 + 1 = 31$. (A simpler method of counting the games is simply to notice that 31 teams of the 32 must be eliminated in order to decide the one remaining champion!) Since each game takes 2 hours, the total number of hours is $31(2) = 62$ hours.

19. **B**   Sides AB and AC are perpendicular, so their lengths can be used as the base and height of the triangle. $AB = 10$, and since AC is the hypotenuse of an isosceles right triangle with legs of length 10, its length is $10\sqrt{2}$.

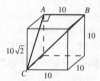

Therefore the area of the triangle is $(1/2)(10)(10\sqrt{2}) = 50\sqrt{2}$.

20. **D**   Let x represent the total of number of marbles in the jar to start. Since the ratio of black marbles to red marbles is 4:5, 4/9 of the marbles are black and 5/9 of the marbles are red. So there are $(4/9)x$ black marbles and $(5/9)x$ red marbles to start. After 18 black marbles are added, there are $(4/9)x + 18$ black marbles. Since the new ratio is 5:4,

$$\frac{\frac{4}{9}x + 18}{\frac{5}{9}x} = \frac{5}{4}$$

Cross-multiply: $\frac{16}{9}x + 72 = \frac{25}{9}x$

Multiply by 9: $16x + 648 = 25x$
Subtract $16x$: $648 = 9x$
Divide by 9: $72 = x$

Section 3

1. C If journalists have *strong personal opinion*, they must have a difficult time remaining *unbiased*. *eloquent* = well spoken; *converted* = changed into something else; *neutral* = unbiased; *biased* = partial.

2. A If the speaker found it *difficult to stay awake*, the lecture must have been very *dull*. *monotonous* = dull; *provocative* = inspiring a strong reaction; *authoritative* = characterized by authority.

3. E International flights today are very common, but few people can travel into space because of the enormous *expense*. If it is possible that space excursions will soon be like international flights, they must be getting *less expensive*. *pedestrian* = commonplace; *responsive* = reacting quickly to stimuli; *mundane* = ordinary.

4. B If audiences *value* stars of *vacuous* (empty-headed) programs, they must value *fame* over talent. *exalt* = praise highly; *lionize* = treat as a celebrity; *obscurity* = the quality of being hard to recognize; *aesthetics* = the philosophy of beauty.

5. C The two logical ways of completing this idea are to say that cultures use a variety of *war-like* strategies to resolve conflicts, contradicting those who think warfare is *rare*, or to say that cultures use a wide variety of *peaceful* strategies to resolve conflicts, contradicting those who think warfare is *dominant*. *universal* = found everywhere; *deleterious* = harmful; *idiosyncratic* = unique and odd.

6. D The terms *cheerful* and *harshly* suggest a change in attitude. Goya must have *tolerated* the social conditions early in life, but then *changed* this attitude. *espousal* = public embrace of an idea; *repression* = hiding of one's feelings; *succeeded* = followed; *supplanted* = replaced; *denunciation* = public criticism.

7. D If they believed that a *hasty* approach would cause problems, they must have preferred a *slow and careful* approach. *accelerated* = sped up; *dexterous* = nimble; *indifferent* = uncaring; *deliberate* = slow and careful; *delapidated* = run-down.

8. A The sentence suggests that although the game is relatively new, many aspects of it are old. The rules were *adapted from* or *taken from* older games. *appropriated* = taken and made one's own; *discarded* = thrown out; *advocated* = supported vocally; *elucidated* = explained in detail; *compensated* = made amends.

9. B The passage states that schools teach capitalism *not so much by directly instructing students* (lines 1–2) but by simply *embodying capitalistic qualities*. This suggests that capitalism is taught *implicitly*.

10. E By saying that *cooperation is stressed far more than competition*, the author means that *cooperation is emphasized over competition*.

11. A The passage states that Fitzgerald was guilty of *too frequent concessions to the taste of the moment* (lines 15–16) rather than steadfast pursuit of the *artistic ideal*. This means that he *compromised* that ideal.

12. C The passage states that Hemingway referred to *success and money as false gods* (line 21) in his work.

13. E The constant focus on the human qualities of Ayn Rand—*her life and her person* (lines 4–5), *astonishing human being* (line 56), *eyes of a human being* (line 62), *she was a human being* (line 98)—in relation to the *epic* (lines 5 and 100) scale of her life indicate the author's purpose to *humanize* Ayn Rand.

14. C The author states that Rand's life was *preposterously unbelievable* (line 4), that *she herself encompassed … grandeur* (lines 10–11) and that her *virtues were larger than life* (lines 19–20). These clearly characterize Rand's life as majestic.

15. B This sentence indicates that Ayn Rand shared a *vast powers of intellect* (lines 12–13) with her heroes.

16. A The first paragraph indicates that Rand shared an *impassioned pursuit of…goals* (lines 13–14) with her heroes, but that she possessed *self-doubt* (line 17) which they lacked, and they possessed *emotional balance* (line 17) which she lacked.

17. B This paragraph suggests that Rand's readers take one of two extreme positions on her philosophy: *grateful, loving admiration or enraged disapproval* (lines 37–38)

18. D This paragraph contains metaphor (*her reason becoming a whip* (line 78), stark contrast (*menacing with anger … touchingly kind* (lines 72–74), parallel sentence structure (*I saw them…*), and characterization of Rand herself, but no definitions.

19. C Although the author mentions that Rand possessed the *delight of a child* (line 71) and *the power of … reason* (line 78), and was *tender* (line 75) and *merciless* (line 76), it suggests that she lacked an *inward look* (lines 85–86).

20. **B** This sentence indicates that it would take *all the years* for the author to understand *the absence of* (Rand's) *inward look* (lines 89–90).

21. **A** The only one of these contrasts that is described in the passage is that between Rand's public life and private life: *Her public … activities took place on a lighted stage; her private life was lived backstage* (lines 41–43).

22. **E** The author clearly conveys the idea that Rand had both *epic virtues and epic shortcoming* (lines 19–20). The final sentence reinforces and summarizes this theme by emphasizing both the epic and the human qualities of her life.

23. **C** The author states that *as the years passsed,* (she) *was to observe all the many changes* of Rand's eyes, thereby suggesting that she knew Rand intimately over a long period of time.

24. **D** The passage contains information about how her ideas were received: *each reader takes an unequivocal stand for or against what she represents … and her name is met with explosions of grateful, loving admiration or enraged disapproval* (lines 36–38). It also indicates that she was born in the first decade of the 20th century, since she was *45 years old in 1950* (line 45), and that Rand was 77 years old when she died (line 5). It does not, however, indicate where Ayn Rand was born (but, if you're interested, it was St. Petersburg, Russia).

Section 4

1. **B** The phrase *not only … but also* indicates **parallel structure**. Choice B provides the most parallel structure.

2. **E** The sentence should have a *neither … nor* parallel structure. Choice E is most **parallel**.

3. **C** The sentence must be an **independent clause**, and the **verb must agree** with the plural subject *works*.

4. **E** The two clauses should be parallel, since they have the same subject. **The active** voice keeps the second clause parallel with the first.

5. **A** The original phrasing is best.

6. **D** The **modifying phrase** should be followed by the noun it modifies, which is *Warhol*. Choice D is also the most idiomatic.

7. **B** The original phrasing is a sentence **fragment**. Choice B is most idiomatic.

8. **D** The original phrasing is **wordy and awkward**. Choice D is most concise.

9. **D** the original phrasing is **wordy and awkward**. Choice D is most concise.

10. **A** The original phrasing is best.

11. **E** The phrase *not only* suggests a **parallel** phrasing in the form *not only A but also B*.

12. **C** This is a **diction error**. The correct word is *successful*. *Successive* means *following one after another*.

13. **B** This verb is the **wrong tense**. Since the book has not been finished yet, this verb should be in the **future** perfect tense: *will have read*.

14. **E** This sentence is correct.

15. **D** This pronoun is in the **wrong case**. Since it is the object of a preposition, it should have the **objective case**: *to David and me*.

16. **C** This pronoun has a **vague antecedent**. It could refer to the *union* or the *board*, so it should be made more specific.

17. **B** This is an **improper idiom**. The correct idiom is *work in*.

18. **A** This is a **subject-verb disagreement**. Since the subject of the verb is *copies*, the phrase should read *there are*.

19. **C** This is a **pronoun shift**. Since the pronoun *one's* has already been used, it should be maintained: *one can now find*.

20. **E** The sentence is correct.

21. **D** This phrase is **redundant** and non-idiomatic. It should read *and stroke*.

22. **A** The word *between* should only be used to refer to two things, not dozens. the correct word is *among*.

23. **D** This is an **illogical comparison**. The *salaries of professional women* should be compared to *the salaries of professional men*.

24. **E**   The sentence is correct.

25. **C**   This uses **incorrect idiom**. The correct phrase is to *read*.

26. **C**   This is a **diction error**. The correct word is *accepted*. *Excepted* means left out.

27. **B**   This is an improper use of the **perfect tense**. Since the *reaching* was not completed before the *walking*, it should take the simple past tense: *reached*.

28. **A**   This is a **subject-verb disagreement**. Since the subject of the verb is the singular *Rancho Coronado*, it should be *sprawls*.

29. **A**   This uses **incorrect idiom**. The correct idiom is *critics of*.

30. **E**   The **comparison** requires parallel form: *choosing … is like choosing*.

31. **C**   Choice C coordinates the ideas most **logically**, without the use of any **unclear pronoun antecedents**.

32. **B**   The ideas are **coordinated most logically** in choice B.

33. **D**   Sentence 13 is out of place because the main idea of the sentence is about how voters should inform themselves about political candidates and issues, not about the negativity of political ads.

34. **B**   The original phrasing is needlessly **wordy and awkward**. Choice B is preferable to D because D creates a run-on sentence.

35. **A**   Choice A is best because it is concise and avoids the **pronoun shift** of the others.

Section 5

1. **E**   27 is the least common multiple of 9 and 27.

2. **C**
$$4(x + 3) = 15$$
Distribute: $4x + 12 = 15$
Subtract 9: $4x + 3 = 6$

3. **E**   If the winnings are split in the ratio of 5:2:1, then each portion is 5/8, 2/8 and 1/8 of the total, respectively. The largest portion, then is (5/8)($4,000) = $2500.

4. **B**   Since 120° is 1/3 of 360°, arc *MNP* is 1/3 of the circumference. So the circumference is $3(6\pi) = 18\pi$. Since circumference $= 2\pi r = 18\pi$, $r = 9$.

5. **B**   If $AB = BC$, then the angles opposite those sides are equal, too: $5x - 5 = 4x + 9$
Subtract $4x$ $x - 5 = 9$
Add 5: $x = 14$
Substituting for x, this tells you that the base angles are both 65°. Since $65 + 65 + y = 180$, $y = 50$.

6. **C**   The median is the "middle number" in the set, which is g because $f < g < h$. If $f = 6$ and $h = 20$, then the average of the three numbers is

$$\frac{6 + g + 20}{3} = \frac{g + 26}{3}$$

If the average is 1 greater than the median, then

$$\frac{g + 26}{3} = g + 1$$

Multiply by 3: $g + 26 = 3g + 3$
Subtract g: $26 = 2g + 3$
Subtract 3: $23 = 2g$
Divide by 2: $11.5 = g$

7. **D**   If the ratio of white marbles to red marbles is 3 to 5, then the total number of red marbles must be a multiple of 5. If the ratio of red marbles to blue marbles is 6 to 5, then the number of red marbles must also be a multiple of 6. The least multiple of both 5 and 6 is 30, so the least number of red marbles is 30. Use the two ratios to find the number of white and blue marbles:
3/5 = (# white marbles)/30, so # white marbles = 18
6/5 = 30/(# blue marbles), so # blue marbles = 25
Therefore the total number of marbles is 30 + 18 + 25 = 73

8. **B**   If the volume varies inversely as the pressure and directly as the temperature, then $V = kT/P$ where k is a constant. You are given that $10 = k(300)/2$, therefore $k = 1/15$. So to find the volume at 1 atmosphere and 450 degrees, use the formula $V = (1/15)(450)/1 = 30$

9. **8**   Translate into an equation:
25% of 16 is x
$0.25(16) = x$
Simplify: $4 = x$
Substitute: 4% of 200
$.04(200) = 8$

10. **12**   Since, in choosing a route, you must first choose from 3 paths from A to B, then from 4 paths from B to C, the total number of routes is $3 \times 4 = 12$.

11. **1/8 or .125** $2/x = w$
Multiply by x: $2 = xw$
Raise to the −3 power: $1/8 = (wx)^{-3}$

12. 1/2 or 0.5   If we add 2 to x and then divide by 4, the result is $\frac{x+2}{4}$. Distributing, we can see that this is equivalent to $x/4 + 2/4 = x/4 + 1/2$.

13. 4

$$n^{-2p} = \frac{1}{16^p}$$

simplify: $\frac{1}{n^{2p}} = \frac{1}{16^p}$

Take the reciprocal: $n^{2p} = 16^p$
Take the pth root: $n^2 = 16$
Take the square root: $n = 4$

14. 5   The graph of the function $f(x) = -(x - 1)^2 + 2$ is a parabola with a vertex at $(1, 2)$, as shown here.

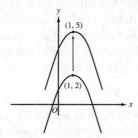

The graph of $y = f(x) + 3$ is simply the same graph shifted up 3 units. Its highest point is at $(1,5)$, so the greatest value of the function is 5. If you'd rather not graph, just notice that $f(x) = -(x - 1)^2 + 2$ can get no greater than 2 because the greatest $-(x - 1)^2$ can be is 0 (since "squares" cannot be negative). Therefore the greatest that $-(x - 1)^2 + 2 + 3$ can be is 5.

15. 35

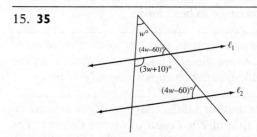

Focus on the "upper" triangle. Notice that one of its interior angles is equal to $(4w - 60)°$, because of the parallel lines theorem. By the exterior angle theorem

$$3w + 10 = (4w - 60) + w$$

Simplify: $3w + 10 = 5w - 60$
Subtract $3w$ $10 = 2w - 60$
Add 60: $70 = 2w$
Divide by 2: $35 = w$

16. 1/3 or .333   Recall the factoring formula
$$x^2 - y^2 = (x - y)(x + y)$$
Substitute: $24 = (x - y)(72)$
Divide by 72: $1/3 = (x - y)$
Don't worry about solving for x and y !

17. 7

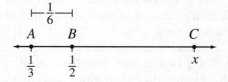

Substitute $(6, 1)$: $1 = |6 - k|$
Translate: $6 - k = 1$ or -1
Subtract 6: $-k = -5$ or -7
Multiply by -1: $k = 5$ or 7
Substitute $(8, 1)$: $1 = |8 - k|$
Translate: $8 - k = 1$ or -1
Subtract 8: $-k = -7$ or -9
Multiply by -1: $k = 7$ or 9
Therefore $k = 7$ and $f(x) = |x - 7|$ and $f(0) = |0 - 7| = 7$

18. 7/6 or 1.16 or 1.17

The distance from A to B is $1/2 - 1/3 = 1/6$. If $AC = 5AB$, then $AC = 5(1/6) = 5/6$. Therefore the coordinate of point C is $1/3 + 5/6 = 2/6 + 5/6 = 7/6$.

Section 6

1. C   If the species arise *gradually*, they must not arise *quickly*. *instantaneously* = in an instant.

2. B   If his claims are *rarely true*, then he must have a reputation for *lying*. *prevarication* = stretching or avoiding the truth; *fervency* = passion; *contemplation* = deep thought; *forthrightness* = honesty, candor.

3. B   A *tortured* life is one filled with severe emotional difficulties that can produce *insanity*. *equanimity* = level-headedness; *coexist* = live together; *psychosis* = severe mental disease; *coincide* = occur at the same time or place; *aesthetics* = the study of beauty; *interface* = a place where two things meet.

4. C   To keep the maps from falling into the hands of the Soviets, the maps would have to have been *kept secret*. Without these *detailed charts*, the oceanographers must have been relegated to using *incomplete* ones. *counterfeit* = fake; *lucid* = clear; *apprehended* = captured; *deficient* = lacking in important ways; *classified* = categorized as secret; *disseminated* = scattered or spread, as seed; *sketchy* = incomplete.

5. A   The word *although* indicates a contrast. One whose ideas conflict with those of his declared religion is a *heretic* or *apostate*. *apostate* = one who challenges a core tenet of his or her religion; *conformist* = one who does what is expected; *relic* = an object left over from ancient times; *ascetic* = one who lives a life of self-denial; *despot* = absolute ruler.

6. **A**   The passage states that *the stranger looks more fateful (ominous) for being a fiery red* (line 11).

7. **C**   The *apparition* refers to the spectacular appearance of Mars in the night sky.

8. **E**   The fact that the speaker speaks of *man* in the third person indicates that he or she is not a man. In saying that *our labor tills the soil, our dung fertilizes it* and so on, the speaker is indicating that he or she is a farm animal.

9. **C**   These questions reflect the perspective that animals do a great deal of work in a farm, but receive very little in return.

10. **C**   The passage does describe a medical breakthrough—vaccination—but does not focus exclusively on the 19th century or on the entire range of medical breakthroughs of the 19th century; therefore, (A) is a poor choice for a title. The passage focuses on viral infections, not bacterial ones, so (B) is also a poor choice. The passage does not focus on how the immune system works as a whole, but only on those aspects of the immune system that are affected by vaccines, so (D) is a weak choice for a title. Finally, Edward Jenner's work is described only briefly in the first paragraphs, so (E) is a poor choice. The best title is (C).

11. **B**   This reference is given as an example of the *roots* (line 7) of the practice of vaccination.

12. **A**   Lines 26–27 indicate that tuberculosis is caused by a bacterium.

13. **A**   The passage states that the virus attaches itself to the cell and inserts its genes so that the cell can become a reproductive machine (line 46) for the virus. This is analogous to a bird's laying its eggs in the nest of another bird who then becomes a reproductive machine for a line of genes that is not its own.

14. **D**   Line 28 refers to bacteria as *parasites* and line 45 uses the same term to describe a virus.

15. **C**   The *signature* proteins are those by which *the body…is able to recognize* viruses (lines 47–48), so they are able to *identify* the viruses.

16. **E**   The final paragraph states that *the common cold…may never be thwarted* (lines 78–80) and that the general fight against viruses *will probably never be completely won* (lines 85–86). This contrasts with the triumphant tones of the previous paragraph which describes the victory of vaccinations over polio, measles and many other diseases.

17. **D**   The final paragraph states that the common cold may never be thwarted because *the viruses are too numerous* and because *new viruses appear as old viral foes are eradicated*. The fact that viruses cannot reproduce on their own is not cited as an impediment to their eradication.

18. **B**   The idea that unifies all of the paragraphs is that of a child developing a relationship with literature. She does not compare English and Chinese literature in depth, and the painful episode between the author and her brother is only mentioned in two of the paragraphs.

19. **A**   This paragraph states that Chinese…conversation…is often indirect and metaphorical, reflecting a philosphical turn of mind, and that this conversation involves retelling codes of behavior and morality. It adds that this is true even among peasants, thereby suggesting that such language is not restricted to the upper classes.

20. **D**   The author states that she would *wait impatiently for another story to begin* (line 20), indicating that she was eager to hear more.

21. **C**   The author states that her brother *forced me to memorize* Chinese classics and *insisted that I copy* the maxims until *my fingers became cramped and useless*.

22. **D**   The author states that the Chinese translation of the title of *The Count of Monte Cristo* is *The Vengeance and Gratitude of the Count of Monte Cristo*. Since the author states that this *reflects a more Chinese concept*, it can be inferred that this includes an emphasis either on honor and vengeance or gratitude and thankfulness.

23. **B**   The author states that she was forced to memorize *The Great Learning*, which she did not understand, but that she *tended* (line 83) toward books like *The Count of Monte Cristo*, which *made the deepest impression* (line 87) on the author.

24. **A**   In saying that she *took the trouble to reread the book in Chinese*, she meant that it was an extra mental effort that she was willing to endure.

Section 7

1. C The sum of the angles in a triangle is 180°. If one has a measure of 100°, the other two must have a sum of 80°, so their average measure is 80°/2 = 40°.

2. C If k is one less than a multiple of 6, then $k + 1$ must be a multiple of 6. The only multiple of 6 among the choices is (C) 18.

3. D 15 more than the product of 3 and $m - 2$ means
$$15 + 3(m - 2)$$
Distribute: $15 + 3m - 6$
Combine like terms: $3m + 9$

4. A

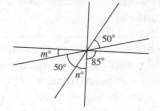

Draw in the measure of the angle that is "vertical" to the 50° angle and therefore equal. Notice that the four "bottom" angles have a sum of 180°.
$$m + 50 + n + 85 = 180$$
Simplify: $m + n + 135 = 180$
Subtract 135: $m + n = 45$

5. D $x\%$ of 30 is 12
Translate: $x\% \times 30 = 12$
Multiply by 4: $4x\% \times 30 = 48$
Divide by 2: $4x\% \times 15 = 24$

6. A Choosing $x = 0.5$ shows that none of the three statements is necessarily true. Plugging this in to statement I gives $1/0.5 < 0.5$, which simplifies to $2 < 0.5$ which is not true. (Notice that this eliminates choices (B) and (E).) Plugging in to statement II gives $(0.5)^2 > 0.5$ which simplifies to $0.25 > 0.5$ which is also not true. (Notice that this eliminates choice (C).) Finally, plugging in to statement III gives $-0.5 < -1$, which is also false, leaving only choice (A).

7. B If each gadget sells for m dollars, then selling 9 of them will generate $9m$ dollars in revenue. If it costs p dollars to make each one, then making 10 of them costs $10p$ dollars. So the profit would be $9m - 10p$

8. E If y varies inversely as x, then the product of x and y is always the same. Since (4, 6) is a point on the graph, then the product of x and y is always $4 \times 6 = 24$. Since (2, m) is also on the graph, $2m = 24$ also, so $m = 12$.

9. A The phrase "at this rate" suggests a proportion:
$$\frac{200 \text{ boxes}}{5 \text{ minutes}} = \frac{24,000 \text{ boxes}}{x \text{ minutes}}$$
Cross-multiply: $200x = 120,000$
Divide by 200: $x = 600$ minutes
Convert to hours:
600 minutes ÷ 60 minutes/hour = 10 hours

10. A Since the triangle is a right triangle, you can use the Pythagorean Theorem: $x^2 + 2^2 = \left(\sqrt{n}\right)^2$
Simplify: $x^2 + 4 = n$
Subtract 4: $x^2 = n - 4$
Take the square root: $x = \sqrt{n - 4}$

11. D $(r - 5)^2 = (r + 2)^2$
Distribute: $r^2 - 10r + 25 = r^2 + 4r + 4$
Subtract r^2: $-10r + 25 = 4r + 4$
Add $10r - 4$: $21 = 14r$
Divide by 14: $1.5 = r$

12. C Since the president must be a girl, there are 10 choices for president. Since the treasurer must also be a girl, there are 9 choices left for treasurer. Since the vice president must be a boy, there are 8 choices for vice president, and once he is chosen there are 7 choices left for secretary. This gives the total number of possibilities as $10 \times 9 \times 8 \times 7 = 5,040$.

13. B

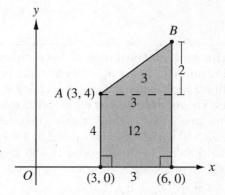

Mark up the diagram as shown. Notice that the shaded region consists of a right triangle and a rectangle. The area of the rectangle is $3 \times 4 = 12$, and since the total area is 15, the triangle must have an area of 3. Since the area of a triangle is one-half the base times the height, $(1/2)(3)(h) = 3$ and therefore $h = 2$. This means that the slope of AB is 2/3 (the "rise" over the "run").

14. A   One simple approach to this problem is simply to pick a value for *m* like 2. (Remember the condition that *m* > 1!) Plug this in to the expression and evaluate:

$$\frac{2-\frac{1}{2}}{1-\frac{1}{2}} = \frac{1.5}{0.5} = 3$$

Plugging in to the choices gives (A) 2+1 (B) 2 (C) 2–1 (D) –1 (E) 2/(2–1). The only choice that is equal to 3 is (A).
Alternately, you can simplify the expression by first multiplying by *m/m*, factoring, and canceling:

$$\frac{m-\frac{1}{m}}{1-\frac{1}{m}} = \frac{m^2-1}{m-1} = \frac{(m-1)(m+1)}{m-1} = m+1$$

15. A   Careful here: notice that the question asks which could NOT be the number of points on the circle that lie on a coordinate axis. These figures show how it is possible to have 2 or 3 such points, but it is impossible to have just 1.

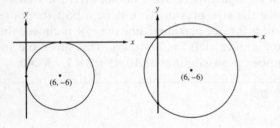

16. B   Imagine, for convenience, that each leg of the race is 150 miles. If the car averages 50 miles per hour for the first 2 legs, then the time for each leg is 150/50 = 3 hours. The time for the last leg is 150/75 = 2 hours. This means that the total distance of 150 + 150 + 150 = 450 miles is covered in 3 + 3 + 2 = 8 hours, so the car's average speed is 450 miles ÷ 8 hours = 56.25 miles per hour.

Section 8

1. A   Some aspect of the atom *remained a mystery*, so a clear model of the atom, which reveals its *structure*, must have *eluded* them. *eluded* = avoided capture; *configuration* = arrangement of parts.

2. D   If Alynna contrasted with the exhausted interns, she must have seemed *untiring*. *petrified* = turned to stone; *agitated* = riled up; *indefatigable* = untiring; *corrupted* = morally tainted.

3. B   If we *inhale them* (germs) *with nearly every breath* they must be quite common. The vast majority of them are *innocuous* (harmless) and our immune system is able to defeat them quite easily. This would suggest that few are *dangerous*. *omnipresent* = present at all times; *ubiquitous* = omnipresent; *virulent* = capable of causing disease; *scarce* = in short supply; *malevolent* = wishing harm on others; *benign* = harmless.

4. E   If it is not *didactic* (preachy), and leaves the reader *to make his or her own ethical evaluations*, it must be morally *ambiguous*. *resolute* = determined and steadfast; *corrupt* = morally tainted; *enervating* = weakening; *pedantic* = acting like a know-it-all; *ambiguous* = unclear.

5. B   If the bones were *determined* to be more than 50,000 years old, this fact would *disprove* the theory that humans had only been there for 8,000 years. *refuted* = disproved; *accustomed* = used to; *invalidated* = disproven or made unworthy; *established* = determined; *corroborated* = supported a claim with evidence; *deplored* = regretted.

6. D   The missing word must mean so *forceful as to leave no room for interpretation*. *loquacious* = talkative; *desultory* = aimless; *phlegmatic* = sluggish; *peremptory* = serving to end debate, expecting to be obeyed; *torpid* = lacking physical or mental energy.

7. E   The first four sentences characterize the positions of the proponents and opponents of recycling.

8. A   This sentence suggests that the debaters have "demonized" each other incorrectly.

9. D   The passage states that *we must examine the full life cycle of the commercial materials in question*. The *commercial materials* of the new road are the *substances that constitute the road*.

10. C   The questions do not address the problem of mudslides, but they do address (A) *the removal of… animal habitats* (line 39), (B) *the leaching of dangerous elements into the soil* (lines 35–37), (D) the *air quality* as it is effected by *extra traffic* (line 43), and (E) *the reduction of natural water filtration* (line 35).

11. C   The *responsible "industrial cycle"* refers to a means of processing resources that could be *better for the environment* than even "conserving" those resources. This suggests that the industrial cycle manages the resources well.

12. **E** This exchange is described as something where all of the value is *easily accounted for* (line 92).

13. **A** The *pack of gum* represents an item that is involved in a clear economic exchange. The *apple* in line 105 is part of a similar exchange.

14. **B** The passage suggests that *bought-and-sold commodities* are like the pack of gum in the first paragraph, which is *easily accounted for*. By saying that the benefits of ecosystems are not commodities, the passage suggests that they are more difficult to track and evaluate.

15. **D** The passage states that externalities are a *class of costs and benefits* that *are not part of a clear exchange*. The only choice that is not part of a clear economic exchange is the noise caused by a motorcycle.

16. **C** The passage states that *Costanza places the cost "conservatively" at $33 trillion dollars* (lines 142–143). This suggests that Costanza considers this to be a low estimate.

17. **D** One of the *potential flaws* mentioned in the last paragraph is that *industrialists argue that (Costanza's work) depends largely on speculation* (line 152). This means that it relies heavily on guesswork.

18. **B** Passage 1 focuses on the deficiencies in the debate about environmentalism, suggesting that there is little progress and too much *demonization* (line 16), and suggesting a broader range of analysis than is currently being used. Passage 2, however, suggests that Costanza's work *is giving a common vocabulary to industrialists and environmentalists alike* (lines 157–158), and so facilitating progress in the debate.

19. **A** Neither passage mentions global warming (even though Passage 1 mentions localized warming produced by road materials in line 37), and Passage 1 does not cite any scientific study. Both passages, however, discuss the importance of human feelings: Passage 1 mentions the harm done by *demonization* (line 16) of the debators, and their need to *appreciate the attitudes of their opponents* (lines 75–76), and Passage 2 emphasizes that the *"good feeling"* some people get from recycling has a real value.

Section 9

1. **D** Choice (D) is most logical, standard and clear.

2. **B** Choice B provides the most **parallel** phrasing.

3. **E** The **participial phrase dangles** in the original sentence. Choice E corrects this without **awkwardness**.

4. **A** The original phrasing is best. The pronoun *me* is properly in the **objective** case, and the subject of the verb *was* is the singular *conversation*.

5. **B** The original sentence is vague and awkward. Choice B is clearest and most concise.

6. **B** The original phrasing is awkward and wordy. Also, the phrasing *because of (noun phrase)* is almost always less clear than the phrasing *because (independent clause)*.

7. **A** The original phrasing is best.

8. **E** Choice E is the most concise and clear, and the phrasing is **parallel**.

9. **B** The underlined clause should be phrased as a dependent clause.

10. **D** The original phrase uses **incorrect subjunctive form**. Also, the antecedent *troop* is singular.

11. **C** The original phrasing produces a **misplaced modifying phrase**, which is corrected in choice C.

12. **C** The original phrasing is **awkward** and wordy.

13. **B** The original phrasing is **awkward** and wordy. Choice B is preferable to E because E contains a double negative *but not*.

14. **C** The original phrasing is a **run-on** or a **comma splice**. Choice C correctly subordinates the clause as a **participial phrase**.

PRACTICE TEST 6

ANSWER SHEET

Last Name:_____   First Name:_____

Date:_____   Testing Location:_____

Directions for Test

- Remove these answer sheets from the book and use them to record your answers to this test.
- This test will require 3 hours and 20 minutes to complete. Take this test in one sitting.
- The time allotment for each section is written clearly at the beginning of each section. This test contains six 25-minute sections, two 20-minute sections, and one 10-minute section.
- This test is 25 minutes shorter than the actual SAT, which will include a 25-minute "experimental" section that does not count toward your score. That section has been omitted from this test.
- You may take one short break during the test, of no more than 10 minutes in length.
- You may only work on one section at any given time.
- You must stop ALL work on a section when time is called.
- If you finish a section before the time has elapsed, check your work on that section. You may NOT work on any other section.
- Do not waste time on questions that seem too difficult for you.
- Use the test book for scratchwork, but you will receive credit only for answers that are marked on the answer sheets.
- You will receive one point for every correct answer.
- You will receive no points for an omitted question.
- For each wrong answer on any multiple-choice question, your score will be reduced by ¼ point.
- For each wrong answer on any "numerical grid-in" question, you will receive no deduction.

When you take the real SAT, you will be asked to fill in your personal information in grids as shown below.

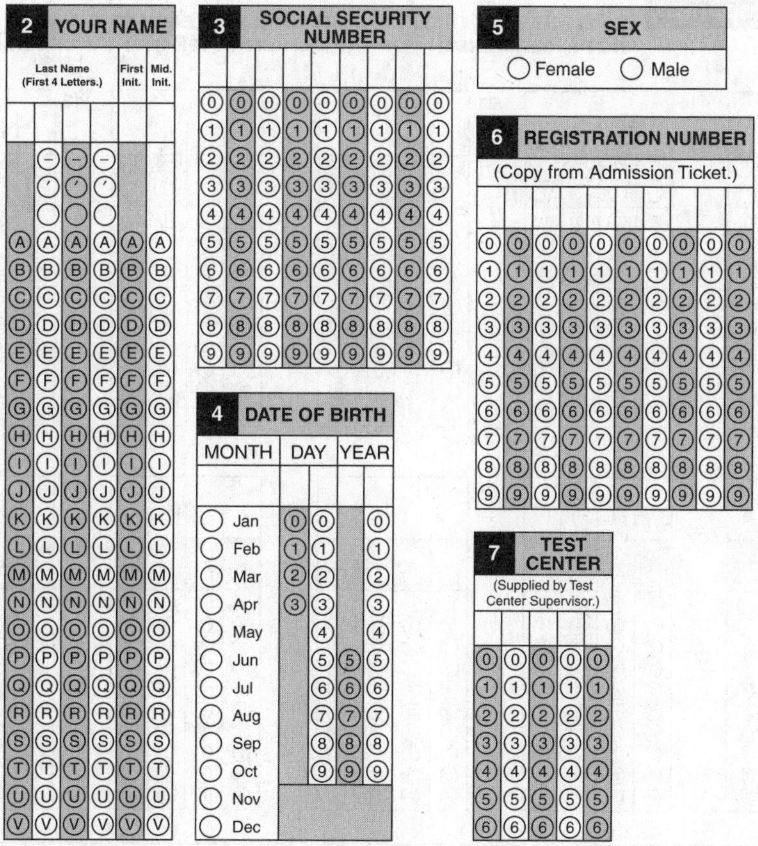

Start with number 1 for each new section. If a section has fewer questions than answer spaces, leave the extra answer spaces blank. Be sure to erase any errors or stray marks completely.

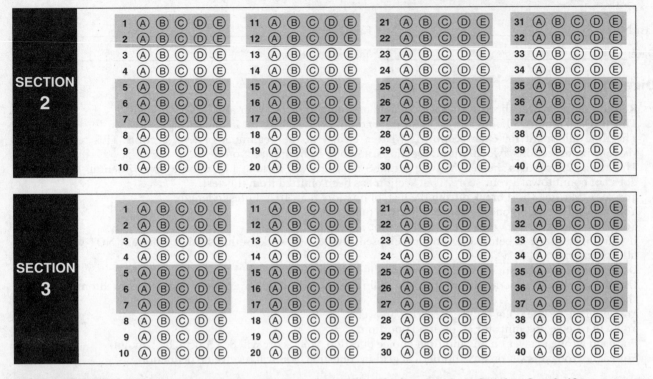

SECTION 2

SECTION 3

CAUTION Use the answer spaces in the grids below for Section 2 or Section 3 only if you are told to do so in your test book.

Student-Produced Responses ONLY ANSWERS ENTERED IN THE CIRCLES IN EACH GRID WILL BE SCORED. YOU WILL NOT RECEIVE CREDIT FOR ANYTHING WRITTEN IN THE BOXES ABOVE THE CIRCLES.

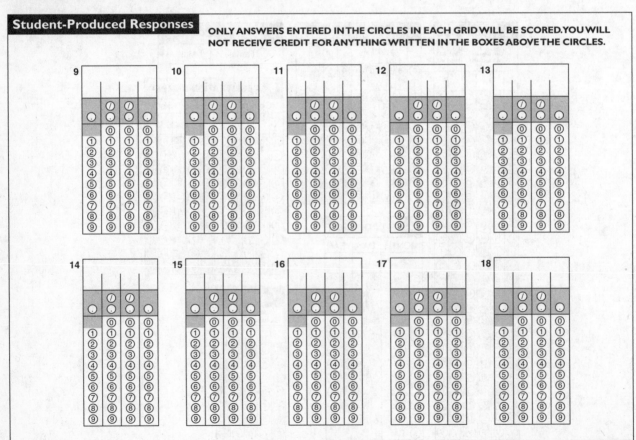

Start with number 1 for each new section. If a section has fewer questions than answer spaces, leave the extra answer spaces blank. Be sure to erase any errors or stray marks completely.

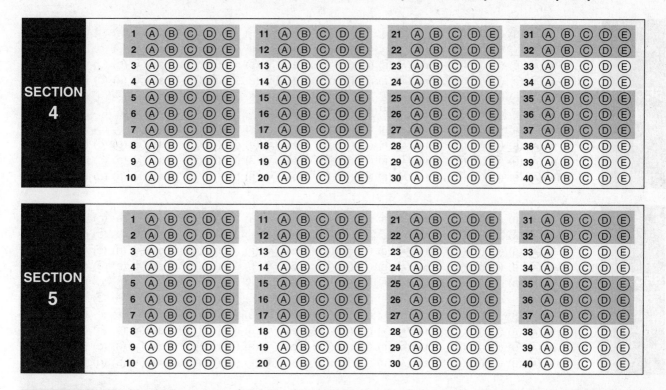

SECTION 4

SECTION 5

CAUTION   Use the answer spaces in the grids below for Section 4 or Section 5 only if you are told to do so in your test book.

Student-Produced Responses   ONLY ANSWERS ENTERED IN THE CIRCLES IN EACH GRID WILL BE SCORED. YOU WILL NOT RECEIVE CREDIT FOR ANYTHING WRITTEN IN THE BOXES ABOVE THE CIRCLES.

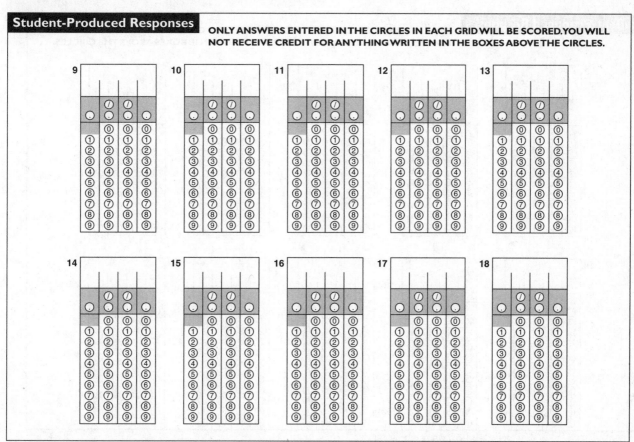

Start with number 1 for each new section. If a section has fewer questions than answer spaces, leave the extra answer spaces blank. Be sure to erase any errors or stray marks completely.

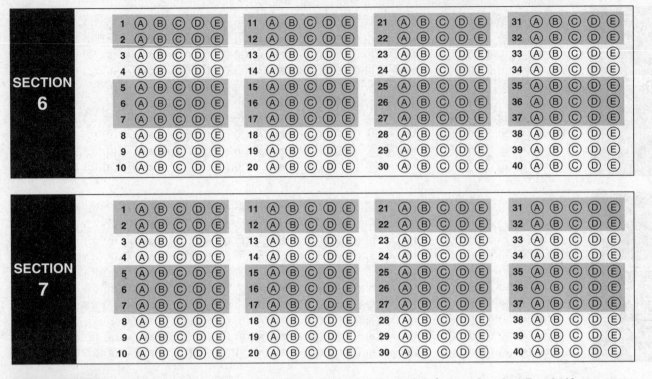

SECTION 6

SECTION 7

CAUTION   Use the answer spaces in the grids below for Section 6 or Section 7 only if you are told to do so in your test book.

Student-Produced Responses   ONLY ANSWERS ENTERED IN THE CIRCLES IN EACH GRID WILL BE SCORED. YOU WILL NOT RECEIVE CREDIT FOR ANYTHING WRITTEN IN THE BOXES ABOVE THE CIRCLES.

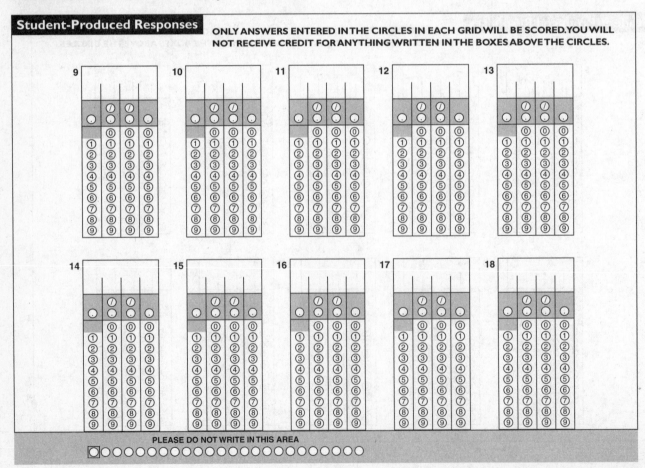

PLEASE DO NOT WRITE IN THIS AREA

Start with number 1 for each new section. If a section has fewer questions than answer spaces, leave the extra answer spaces blank. Be sure to erase any errors or stray marks completely.

SECTION 8

1 Ⓐ Ⓑ Ⓒ Ⓓ Ⓔ	11 Ⓐ Ⓑ Ⓒ Ⓓ Ⓔ	21 Ⓐ Ⓑ Ⓒ Ⓓ Ⓔ	31 Ⓐ Ⓑ Ⓒ Ⓓ Ⓔ
2 Ⓐ Ⓑ Ⓒ Ⓓ Ⓔ	12 Ⓐ Ⓑ Ⓒ Ⓓ Ⓔ	22 Ⓐ Ⓑ Ⓒ Ⓓ Ⓔ	32 Ⓐ Ⓑ Ⓒ Ⓓ Ⓔ
3 Ⓐ Ⓑ Ⓒ Ⓓ Ⓔ	13 Ⓐ Ⓑ Ⓒ Ⓓ Ⓔ	23 Ⓐ Ⓑ Ⓒ Ⓓ Ⓔ	33 Ⓐ Ⓑ Ⓒ Ⓓ Ⓔ
4 Ⓐ Ⓑ Ⓒ Ⓓ Ⓔ	14 Ⓐ Ⓑ Ⓒ Ⓓ Ⓔ	24 Ⓐ Ⓑ Ⓒ Ⓓ Ⓔ	34 Ⓐ Ⓑ Ⓒ Ⓓ Ⓔ
5 Ⓐ Ⓑ Ⓒ Ⓓ Ⓔ	15 Ⓐ Ⓑ Ⓒ Ⓓ Ⓔ	25 Ⓐ Ⓑ Ⓒ Ⓓ Ⓔ	35 Ⓐ Ⓑ Ⓒ Ⓓ Ⓔ
6 Ⓐ Ⓑ Ⓒ Ⓓ Ⓔ	16 Ⓐ Ⓑ Ⓒ Ⓓ Ⓔ	26 Ⓐ Ⓑ Ⓒ Ⓓ Ⓔ	36 Ⓐ Ⓑ Ⓒ Ⓓ Ⓔ
7 Ⓐ Ⓑ Ⓒ Ⓓ Ⓔ	17 Ⓐ Ⓑ Ⓒ Ⓓ Ⓔ	27 Ⓐ Ⓑ Ⓒ Ⓓ Ⓔ	37 Ⓐ Ⓑ Ⓒ Ⓓ Ⓔ
8 Ⓐ Ⓑ Ⓒ Ⓓ Ⓔ	18 Ⓐ Ⓑ Ⓒ Ⓓ Ⓔ	28 Ⓐ Ⓑ Ⓒ Ⓓ Ⓔ	38 Ⓐ Ⓑ Ⓒ Ⓓ Ⓔ
9 Ⓐ Ⓑ Ⓒ Ⓓ Ⓔ	19 Ⓐ Ⓑ Ⓒ Ⓓ Ⓔ	29 Ⓐ Ⓑ Ⓒ Ⓓ Ⓔ	39 Ⓐ Ⓑ Ⓒ Ⓓ Ⓔ
10 Ⓐ Ⓑ Ⓒ Ⓓ Ⓔ	20 Ⓐ Ⓑ Ⓒ Ⓓ Ⓔ	30 Ⓐ Ⓑ Ⓒ Ⓓ Ⓔ	40 Ⓐ Ⓑ Ⓒ Ⓓ Ⓔ

SECTION 9

1 Ⓐ Ⓑ Ⓒ Ⓓ Ⓔ	11 Ⓐ Ⓑ Ⓒ Ⓓ Ⓔ	21 Ⓐ Ⓑ Ⓒ Ⓓ Ⓔ	31 Ⓐ Ⓑ Ⓒ Ⓓ Ⓔ
2 Ⓐ Ⓑ Ⓒ Ⓓ Ⓔ	12 Ⓐ Ⓑ Ⓒ Ⓓ Ⓔ	22 Ⓐ Ⓑ Ⓒ Ⓓ Ⓔ	32 Ⓐ Ⓑ Ⓒ Ⓓ Ⓔ
3 Ⓐ Ⓑ Ⓒ Ⓓ Ⓔ	13 Ⓐ Ⓑ Ⓒ Ⓓ Ⓔ	23 Ⓐ Ⓑ Ⓒ Ⓓ Ⓔ	33 Ⓐ Ⓑ Ⓒ Ⓓ Ⓔ
4 Ⓐ Ⓑ Ⓒ Ⓓ Ⓔ	14 Ⓐ Ⓑ Ⓒ Ⓓ Ⓔ	24 Ⓐ Ⓑ Ⓒ Ⓓ Ⓔ	34 Ⓐ Ⓑ Ⓒ Ⓓ Ⓔ
5 Ⓐ Ⓑ Ⓒ Ⓓ Ⓔ	15 Ⓐ Ⓑ Ⓒ Ⓓ Ⓔ	25 Ⓐ Ⓑ Ⓒ Ⓓ Ⓔ	35 Ⓐ Ⓑ Ⓒ Ⓓ Ⓔ
6 Ⓐ Ⓑ Ⓒ Ⓓ Ⓔ	16 Ⓐ Ⓑ Ⓒ Ⓓ Ⓔ	26 Ⓐ Ⓑ Ⓒ Ⓓ Ⓔ	36 Ⓐ Ⓑ Ⓒ Ⓓ Ⓔ
7 Ⓐ Ⓑ Ⓒ Ⓓ Ⓔ	17 Ⓐ Ⓑ Ⓒ Ⓓ Ⓔ	27 Ⓐ Ⓑ Ⓒ Ⓓ Ⓔ	37 Ⓐ Ⓑ Ⓒ Ⓓ Ⓔ
8 Ⓐ Ⓑ Ⓒ Ⓓ Ⓔ	18 Ⓐ Ⓑ Ⓒ Ⓓ Ⓔ	28 Ⓐ Ⓑ Ⓒ Ⓓ Ⓔ	38 Ⓐ Ⓑ Ⓒ Ⓓ Ⓔ
9 Ⓐ Ⓑ Ⓒ Ⓓ Ⓔ	19 Ⓐ Ⓑ Ⓒ Ⓓ Ⓔ	29 Ⓐ Ⓑ Ⓒ Ⓓ Ⓔ	39 Ⓐ Ⓑ Ⓒ Ⓓ Ⓔ
10 Ⓐ Ⓑ Ⓒ Ⓓ Ⓔ	20 Ⓐ Ⓑ Ⓒ Ⓓ Ⓔ	30 Ⓐ Ⓑ Ⓒ Ⓓ Ⓔ	40 Ⓐ Ⓑ Ⓒ Ⓓ Ⓔ

1   ESSAY   ESSAY   1

ESSAY
Time—25 minutes

Write your essay on separate sheets of standard lined paper.

The essay gives you an opportunity to show how effectively you can develop and express ideas. You should, therefore, take care to develop your point of view, present your ideas logically and clearly, and use language precisely.

Your essay must be written on the lines provided on your answer sheet—you will receive no other paper on which to write. You will have enough space if you write on every line, avoid wide margins, and keep your handwriting to a reasonable size. Remember that people who are not familiar with your handwriting will read what you write. Try to write or print so that what you are writing is legible to those readers.

Important Reminders:

- **A pencil is required for the essay.** An essay written in ink will receive a score of zero.
- **Do not write your essay in your test book.** You will receive credit only for what you write on your answer sheet.
- **An off-topic essay will receive a score of zero.**

You have twenty-five minutes to write an essay on the topic assigned below.

Consider carefully the issue discussed in the following passage, then write an essay that answers the question posed in the assignment.

> All art is a lie, and all art is the truth. The beholder determines which.

Assignment: **Do artistic endeavors such as music, painting, literature, and drama enhance our understanding of reality or provide escape from reality?** Write an essay in which you agree or disagree with the statement above, using an example or examples from history, politics, literature, the arts, current events, or your experience or observation.

If you finish before time is called, you may check your work on this section only.
Do not turn to any other section of the test.

2   2   2   2   2   2

SECTION 2
Time—25 minutes
20 questions

Turn to Section 2 of your answer sheet to answer the questions in this section.

Directions: For this section, solve each problem and decide which is the best of the choices given. Fill in the corresponding circle on the answer sheet. You may use any available space for scratchwork.

Notes

1. The use of a calculator is permitted.
2. All numbers used are real numbers.
3. Figures that accompany problems in this test are intended to provide information useful in solving the problems. They are drawn as accurately as possible EXCEPT when it is stated in a specific problem that the figure is not drawn to scale. All figures lie in a plane unless otherwise indicated.
4. Unless otherwise specified, the domain of any function f is assumed to be the set of all real numbers x for which $f(x)$ is a real number.

Reference Information

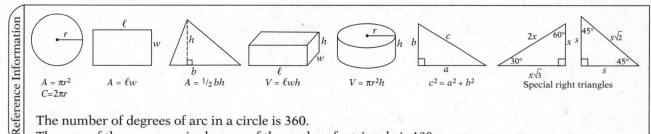

$A = \pi r^2$
$C = 2\pi r$ $A = \ell w$ $A = \frac{1}{2} bh$ $V = \ell wh$ $V = \pi r^2 h$ $c^2 = a^2 + b^2$ Special right triangles

The number of degrees of arc in a circle is 360.
The sum of the measures in degrees of the angles of a triangle is 180.

---

1. If $(x - y) = -2$, then $3(x - y)(x - y)(x - y) =$

(A) -24
(B) -12
(C) 0
(D) 12
(E) 24

---

2. If $w \neq 0$, then 40 percent of $20w$ is equal to

(A) $2w$
(B) $4w$
(C) $8w$
(D) $20w$
(E) $80w$

x	3	4	5	6
y	10	14	18	22

3. The table above shows a relationship between two variables, x and y. Which of the following equations could describe this relationship?

(A) $y = x + 7$
(B) $y = 4x - 2$
(C) $y = 3x + 1$
(D) $y = 5x - 5$
(E) $y = 2x + 4$

GO ON TO THE NEXT PAGE

2   2   2   2   2   2

4. The points W, X, Y, and Z lie on a line in that order. If $XY = 50$, WY is 30 more than XY, and $WX = YZ$, what is XZ?

(A)   30
(B)   50
(C)   70
(D)   80
(E)   100

6. If $3^{y+4} = 81$, what is the value of y?

(A)   −2
(B)   −1
(C)   0
(D)   1
(E)   2

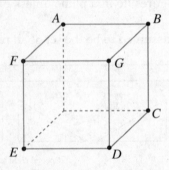

5. In the cube in the figure above, all of the following line segments are the same length EXCEPT

(A) AG
(B) BE
(C) BD
(D) EG
(E) AE

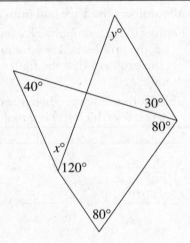

7. In the figure above, what is the value of $x + y$?

(A)   120
(B)   110
(C)   100
(D)   90
(E)   80

GO ON TO THE NEXT PAGE

2   2   2   2   2   2

8. If a and b are non-zero integers and $a > b$, which of the following must be true?

    I. $ab \neq 0$
    II. $a - b > 0$
    III. $a \div b > 1$

(A) I only
(B) II only
(C) I and II only
(D) I and III only
(E) I, II, and III

9. The distance from Appletown to Brickton is 6 miles and the distance from Brickton to Caper City is 9 miles. Which of the following could be the distance, in miles, from Appletown to Caper City?

(A) 14
(B) 16
(C) 17
(D) 18
(E) 19

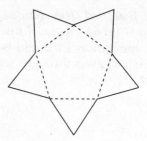

10. The figure above shows five triangles arranged around a regular pentagon. All of the solid line segments are equal in length. If the perimeter of the figure indicated by the solid segments is 100 and the perimeter of the pentagon indicated by the dotted lines is 60, what is the area of one of the triangles?

(A) 24
(B) 32
(C) 36
(D) 48
(E) 64

11. The sum of two numbers is 71. If one number is 2 greater than one-half of the other number, what is the value of the greater number?

(A) 23
(B) 25
(C) 42
(D) 43
(E) 46

GO ON TO THE NEXT PAGE

2   2   2   2   2   2

12. Points A, B, C, and D lie on line l and points D, E, F, and G lie on line m. If lines l and m are distinct, how many lines can be drawn such that each line passes through exactly 2 of these 7 points?

(A)   4
(B)   5
(C)   6
(D)   9
(E) 12

13. What fraction of the even integers between 2 and 16, inclusive, satisfy the statement $3w - 2 > 28$?

(A) $\dfrac{1}{8}$

(B) $\dfrac{1}{4}$

(C) $\dfrac{3}{8}$

(D) $\dfrac{1}{2}$

(E) $\dfrac{5}{8}$

14. If a is 20 percent less than b, and b is 20 percent greater than 400, then what is the value of $b - a$?

(A)   80
(B)   96
(C) 100
(D) 104
(E) 108

15. If $m = n(n - 3)$, what is the value of $-3m$ in terms of n?

(A) $3n + 3n^2$
(B) $9n + 3n^2$
(C) $3n + 9n^2$
(D) $3n - 3n^2$
(E) $9n - 3n^2$

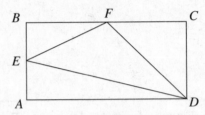

16. In the figure above, $ABCD$ is a rectangle and points E and F are midpoints of their respective sides. If $BC = 2AB = 8$, what is the area of $\triangle EFD$?

(A)   8
(B) 12
(C) 16
(D) 20
(E) 24

17. What is the average (arithmetic mean) of 8 consecutive odd integers if the least of these integers is x?

(A) $x + 5$
(B) $x + 6$
(C) $x + 7$
(D) $x + 8$
(E) $x + 9$

GO ON TO THE NEXT PAGE ⇨

2 2 2 2 2 2

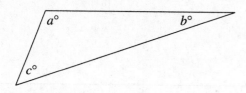

Note: Figure not drawn to scale.

18. In the figure above, $20 < b < 30$ and $a > c > b$. If a, b and c are integers, what is the largest possible value of a?

(A) 119
(B) 121
(C) 140
(D) 137
(E) 139

19. If $\dfrac{4}{v} + w = 6$ and $v \neq 0$, which of the following expresses v in terms of w?

(A) $\dfrac{4}{6 - w}$

(B) $\dfrac{w}{6 - w}$

(C) $\dfrac{w}{4 - w}$

(D) $\dfrac{w - 6}{w}$

(E) $\dfrac{w - 2}{4}$

20. The distance from the center of a clock to the tip of the minute hand is 4 inches. What is the length of the arc, in <u>feet,</u> that this tip traces between 2:45 pm and 7:15 pm? (1 foot = 12 inches)

(A) 3π
(B) 12π
(C) 16π
(D) 24π
(E) 36π

STOP

If you finish before time is called, you may check your work on this section only. Do not turn to any other section of the test.

3   **3**   **3**   **3**   **3**   **3**

SECTION 3
Time—25 minutes
24 questions

Turn to Section 3 of your answer sheet to answer the questions in this section.

Directions: For each question in this section, select the best answer from among the choices given and fill in the corresponding circle on the answer sheet.

Each sentence below has one or two blanks, each blank indicating that something has been omitted. Beneath the sentence are five words or sets of words labeled A through E. Choose the word or set of words that, when inserted in the sentence, best fits the meaning of the sentence as a whole.

EXAMPLE:

Rather than accepting the theory unquestioningly, Deborah regarded it with -----.

(A) mirth
(B) sadness
(C) responsibility
(D) ignorance
(E) skepticism

Ⓐ Ⓑ Ⓒ Ⓓ ●

---

1. Ptolemy's theory that the universe revolved around the sun was ------- by his contemporaries, but is ------- today for its naive assumptions.

   (A) believed .. supported
   (B) counteracted .. satirized
   (C) accepted .. ridiculed
   (D) mesmerized .. corroborated
   (E) affiliated .. mocked

2. Although the rebels attacked with great ferocity, the ------- and undisciplined manner in which they assaulted the fort left no doubt that they would be defeated.

   (A) haphazard
   (B) spartan
   (C) apathetic
   (D) civilized
   (E) strict

3. Only after the massive rains and winds produced by Hurricane Alysha had ------- were the volunteer crews able to come to the aid of those ------- by the storm.

   (A) commenced .. enthralled
   (B) ebbed .. encouraged
   (C) compounded .. masticated
   (D) intensified .. harmed
   (E) abated .. afflicted

4. Madonna's musical work over the past 20 years is more ------- than that of many popular singers; she has incorporated a wide variety of styles into her songs.

   (A) repugnant
   (B) negligent
   (C) banal
   (D) eclectic
   (E) incompetent

GO ON TO THE NEXT PAGE ▷

5. Early in his medical school career, Blake real-
    ized that his ------- personality was not ideally
    suited to a career in therapy; he could not pro-
    vide a stabilizing influence on his patients if he
    himself was so easily -------.

    (A) cantankerous .. placated
    (B) irascible .. riled
    (C) equanimous .. infuriated
    (D) euphoric .. provoked
    (E) choleric .. assuaged

6. The talk show host was taken aback by the -------
    demeanor of his guest, having never been so
    harshly accosted before.

    (A) jocular
    (B) congenial
    (C) impudent
    (D) urbane
    (E) erudite

7. Bicycle champion Lance Armstrong showed
    incredible ------- in overcoming cancer to
    become the first person to win six consecutive
    Tour de France victories.

    (A) perspicacity
    (B) magnanimity
    (C) delirium
    (D) vanity
    (E) pertinacity

8. The senator ------- the claims of the opposing
    party that he had lied about his health care
    policies, arguing that he had actually kept all
    of his campaign promises.

    (A) championed
    (B) impugned
    (C) emulated
    (D) lauded
    (E) concurred with

Each passage below is followed by questions based on its content. Answer each
question based on what is stated or implied
in the passage.

Questions 9–10 are based on the following passage.

*The following passage is an excerpt from a novel
set in modern-day Africa.*

Na-ne's absence now is a vertiginous[1] hollow
in my being, a dark hole that is my constant
Line companion. I did not know the gravity of
such holes, of the extra weight on
5   every organ, of the soul becoming an old
man. My son Semu runs about oblivious, like
a goat; he is not even two full years, and his
happiness is inaccessible to me. He calls
"Papa, papa, look," but I cannot look. He bats
10   at my hand and he climbs on my leg. He is
Na-ne as I remember him, and so he is a
shadow. My brother was this age when I was
nearly ten. I may tell Semu "Na-ne, mother
wants us to get more thatch," and he looks
15.   at me and smiles, and I do not know if he is
happy to be Na-ne, but he is happy.

[1]causing dizziness

9. It can be inferred from the passage that
    Na-ne is Semu's

    (A) father
    (B) son
    (C) uncle
    (D) nephew
    (E) grandfather

GO ON TO THE NEXT PAGE

First paragraph: Reprinted by permission of the author © 2004 Christopher F. Black

10. Unlike the quotation in line 9, the quotation in lines 13–14

(A) uses figurative language
(B) conveys a request
(C) addresses an absent person
(D) describes a happy scene
(E) is spoken with great urgency

Questions 11–12 are based on the following passage.

The following is from a book about American public policy written in 1982.

    For most of human history the plight of the poor has been easily excluded from the
Line consciousness of those with the power to act. Inaction was justified by elaborate theories
5 that the poor were by nature inferior or happy in their condition or both. But human society confronts a new reality: pressures of population and technology on the fragile balance of our planet's ecosystem are
10 compelling the rich not only to re-examine their own lifestyles, but also to take a greater interest in the lifestyles of the poor whose conditions leave them dependent for short-term survival on large families and the
15 destructive use of crop lands, forests, and watersheds—thus posing a threat to the affluent more certain in its occurrence and consequences than the threat of armed revolution. Poverty has become salient to
20 the powerful and the implications are far reaching.

11. According to the passage, before the "new reality"(line 7), some powerful people

(A) depended on large families for their survival
(B) destroyed crop land
(C) took a great interest in the poor
(D) were self-conscious about their lifestyles
(E) believed that the poor enjoyed their status

12. The passage suggests that the poor affect the lives of the affluent chiefly by

(A) draining money from the government
(B) damaging the natural environment
(C) making the wealthy feel guilty for their relative affluence
(D) making unrealistic political demands
(E) threatening armed revolution

Questions 13–17 are based on the following passage.

The following is a story taken from a collection of short stories written by Heinrich Böll.

    They have patched up my legs and given me a job I can do sitting down: I count the
Line people crossing the new bridge. They get such a kick out of it, documenting their
5 efficiency with figures; that senseless nothing made up of a few numbers goes to their heads, and all day long, all day long, my soundless mouth ticks away like clockwork, piling number on number, just so I can
10 present them each evening with the triumph of a figure.
    They beam delightedly when I hand over the result of my day's labors, the higher the figure the broader their smiles, and they have
15 every reason to hug themselves when they climb into bed, for many thousands of pedestrians cross their new bridge every day...

GO ON TO THE NEXT PAGE ⇨

Second paragraph: *Bureaucracy and the Poor: Closing the Gap*, Davud Korten and Felipe Alfonso, McGraw Hill 1982, p xi

3   3   3   3   3   3

But their statistics are wrong. I am sorry,
but they are wrong. I am an untrustworthy
soul, although I have no trouble giving an
impression of sterling integrity.

Secretly it gives me pleasure to do them
out of one pedestrian every so often, and
then again, when I feel sorry for them, to
throw in a few extra. I hold their happiness
in the palm of my hand. When I am mad at
the world, when I have smoked all my
cigarettes, I just give them the average,
sometimes less than the average; and when
my spirits soar, when I am in a good mood,
I pour out my generosity in a five-digit
number. It makes them so happy! They
positively snatch the sheet from my hand,
their eyes light up, and they pat me on
the back. How blissfully ignorant they are!
And then they start multiplying, dividing,
working out percentages, God knows what
all. They figure out how many people crossed
the bridge per minute today, and how many
will have crossed the bridge in ten years.
They are in love with the future-present
tense, the future-perfect is their specialty—
and yet I can't help being sorry that the
whole thing is a fallacy.

When my little sweetheart crosses the
bridge—which she does twice a day—my heart
simply stops beating. The tireless ticking of
my heart just comes to a halt until she has
turned into the avenue and disappeared.
And all the people who pass by during that
time don't get counted. Those two minutes
are mine, all mine, and nobody is going to
take them away from me. And when she
returns every evening from her ice-cream
parlor, when she walks along on the far side,
past my soundless mouth which must count,
count, then my heart stops beating again,
and I don't resume counting until she is out
of sight. And all those who are lucky enough
to file past my unseeing eyes during those
minutes will not be immortalized in
statistics: shadow-men and shadow-women,
creatures of no account, they are barred from
the parade of future-perfect statistics.

Needless to say, I love her. But she hasn't
the slightest idea, and I would rather she
didn't find out. I don't want her to suspect
what havoc she wreaks in all those
calculations, I want her to walk serenely off
to her ice-cream parlor, unsuspecting and
innocent with her long brown hair and
slender feet, and go get lots of tips. I love her.
It must surely be obvious that I love her.

Not long ago they checked up on me.
My partner, who sits across the street and has
to count the cars, gave me plenty of warning,
and that day, I was a lynx-eyed devil. I
counted like crazy, no speedometer could do
better. The chief statistician, no less, posted
himself across the street for an hour, and
then compared his tally with me. I was only
one short. My little sweetheart had walked
past, and as long as I live I won't allow that
adorable child to be whisked off into the
future-perfect tense; they're not going to take
my little sweetheart and multiply her and
divide her and turn her into a meaningless
percentage. It made my heart bleed to have
to go on counting without turning round to
watch her, and I am certainly grateful to my
partner across the street who has to count
the cars. It might have cost me my job, my
very existence.

The chief statistician clapped me on the
shoulder and said I was a good fellow,
trustworthy and loyal. "To be out one in one
hour," he said, "really makes no odds.
We allow for a certain margin of error
anyway. I'm going to apply for your transfer
to horse-drawn vehicles."

Horse-drawn vehicles are, of course,
a piece of cake. There's nothing to it. There
are never more than a couple of dozen
horse-drawn vehicles a day, and to tick over
the next number in your brain once every
half hour—what a cinch!

Horse-drawn vehicles would be terrific.
Between four and eight they are not allowed
across the bridge at all, and I could walk
to the ice-cream parlor, feast my eyes on her
or maybe walk her partway home, my little
uncounted sweetheart.

Excerpted from *The Stories of Heinrich Böll: At the Bridge*, Heinrich Böll, © 1986 Alfred
A Knopf. Used with the permission of the Jennifer Lyons Agency LLC on the behalf of
the estate of the proprietor.

GO ON TO THE NEXT PAGE ⟶

3   **3**   **3**   **3**   **3**   **3**

13. The first paragraph suggests that the narrator regards his task with

(A) disdain
(B) unreserved excitement
(C) subdued respect
(D) extreme fear
(E) mild trepidation

14. The second paragraph suggests that the narrator's superiors are primarily concerned with

(A) allowing the narrator to work in comfort
(B) ensuring the quality of the narrator's work
(C) determining the number of people who cross the bridge
(D) giving the narrator tedious tasks
(E) avoiding demanding work

15. In line 43, the reference to the "future perfect" suggests

(A) the narrator's anticipation of seeing his sweetheart
(B) the narrator's need to deceive his supervisors
(C) the narrator's hope to be finished with his task
(D) the supervisors' inhumane treatment of the narrator
(E) the supervisors' obsession with extrapolation

16. The passage suggests that a "lynx-eyed devil" (line 78) is one who

(A) can deceive without being caught
(B) can tally quickly and accurately
(C) walks across the bridge without being detected
(D) keeps a sharp eye on workers he is supervising
(E) is concerned with speed rather than accuracy

17. In line 98, the word "odds" most nearly means

(A) difference
(B) advantage
(C) probability
(D) ignorance
(E) idiosyncracy

Questions 18–24 are based on the following passage.

The following is an excerpt taken from a textbook on the interpretation of art.

Look around you. Do you see art in your immediate surroundings? What qualities
Line determine that certain things are art? Definitions of art vary widely, but most tend
5 to fall within general notions developed over the centuries. The technical ability of an ancient Egyptian potter to produce a well-made clay vessel defined his "art." By extension, the ceramic pot itself, the
10 product of such skillful execution, also qualified as art. In Europe 600 years ago, all the trade and professional associations, from shoemaking to banking, still held to this broad definition of art as skill or craft in a
15 particular field. The currently popular notion of the artist as the creator and definer of art—put simply, "Art is what artists create"— is a relatively recent concept. The social and professional role of the artist, and the
20 identification of his or her works as art, began to develop about six centuries ago in the ancient artisan tradition.

According to the ancient, encompassing definition of art as products and activities
25 skillfully done, the finely made clothes you are wearing, the well-crafted chair you are sitting on, and the masterful athletic performance you watched the other day are considered art. So are mass-media forms
30 such as compact disc covers, posters, magazine advertisements, music videos and Internet Web sites, because all of these show human skill and technical ability.

GO ON TO THE NEXT PAGE →

Excerpted from *Responding to Art*, Robert Bersson, McGraw-Hill. © 2004, p2–4.

3 3 3 3 3 3

Some items and activities in our environment, however, stand out from the rest. They are somehow more artistic, more "art" than other buildings, chairs, album covers, and athletic performances. Their appearance or form, that is, the way their line, color, shape, texture, and other visual elements combine to please the senses, is so satisfying or perfect that we call them beautiful. We apply this notion when we call a graceful bridge or majestic skyscraper "a beauty," a stellar basketball play "beautiful," and the stunning photograph of the player "a work of art".

Prior to the twentieth century, most aestheticians, or philosophers of art, believed that beauty was the central defining feature of art. Aesthetics, the philosophy of art, centered on the study of the nature of art and beauty. By the turn of the twentieth century, however, some aestheticians had begun to find this identification of beauty with art insufficient. Some called the expression of emotion art's defining characteristic; others argued that the effective communication of feelings and ideas to the viewer defined art. One group of influential aesthetic theorists, the formalists, emphasized the unique effect of artistic form on the viewer. They hypothesized that an object or activity qualifies as art if its visual form is sufficiently compelling or inspiring or beautiful to provoke an intensely felt, sensory-based response or aesthetic experience. This concept echoed the ancient Greek definition of aesthetic, meaning "of or pertaining to the senses" or "sensuous perception." You might think that aesthetic experiences are extremely rare. They are not. If you have ever felt yourself swept away in the sensuous experience of a sports event, a musical performance, a film, a sunset, or a painting of a sunset, you have had an aesthetic experience.

Look around again. How much of your surroundings do you consider visually captivating or beautiful, expressive or communicative? Do any objects in your field of vision provoke an aesthetic experience? Do you consider these things art? Is it skill, beauty, expression, communication, compelling form, aesthetic experience, or all of the above that make these art for you? Or is it some quality not mentioned here, such as originality or creativity, that makes these objects or activities stand out as art? Might a change in setting or context more fully establish you selections as art? If it were moved into the impressive surroundings of an art museum, would a sports photo or CD cover become more fully art in you eyes? According to aesthetician George Dickie's "institutional theory of art," major art institutions such as museums determine what is and is not art in a given culture.

As you can see, art has been defined in a variety of ways. Given this diversity of definitions, many contemporary aestheticians conclude that there can be no single, fixed definition of art. Instead, they subscribe to the notion of art as a concept that evolves as we and the artwork of our period change. Your own concept of art might build upon the definitions of the past, but it will also be influenced by those of the present and changed by the art and ideas of the future. From this array of possibilities you yourself will ultimately determine, like an aesthetician, your definition or concept of art.

18. The primary purpose of this passage is to

(A) explain the connection between art and craftsmanship

(B) trace the origins of the institutional theory of art

(C) explain the role of aestheticians in the broader field of philosophy

(D) refute an ancient theory of art

(E) discuss the variety of definitions of art through the ages

GO ON TO THE NEXT PAGE

3   3   3   3   3   3

---

19. In line 9, the "extension" refers to a connection between

    (A) Egyptian art and European art
    (B) a skill and a physical object
    (C) crafts and fine arts
    (D) ancient philosophy and modern philosophy
    (E) a potter's skill and a critic's evaluation of it

20. The first paragraph suggests that, over the centuries, conceptions of art have become focused more on

    (A) the skills of businessmen than on the skills of painters and sculptors
    (B) the monetary value of art than on the aesthetic value of art
    (C) the activities of individual artists than on the skills of artisans
    (D) the ideas of consumers than on the theories of philosophers
    (E) industrial values than on agricultural values

21. The author uses the word "somehow" in line 36 to make the point that

    (A) very few people who paint are true artists
    (B) most people do not regard commercial art as beautiful
    (C) our senses often deceive us
    (D) the criteria for beauty are often difficult to explain
    (E) we tend to believe that only works in museums are true art

22. Unlike the "ancient, encompassing definition of art" (line 23–24) the "ancient Greek definition of aesthetic" (lines 68–69) emphasized

    (A) the experiences of the viewer
    (B) the intent of the artist
    (C) popular opinion
    (D) skillful execution
    (E) historical value

23. According to the the "institutional theory of art" (line 96), a photograph can only be considered art if it

    (A) elicits a strong sensory response in viewers
    (B) is produced by a skillful and renowned photographer
    (C) attempts to convey a deep emotion of the photographer
    (D) is sanctioned by an official body
    (E) is purchased by an art connoisseur

24. In line 103, the word "fixed" most nearly means

    (A) repaired
    (B) subtle
    (C) undetermined
    (D) unchanging
    (E) focused

STOP

If you finish before time is called, you may check your work on this section only. Do not turn to any other section of the test.

4   4   4   4   4   4

SECTION 4
Time—25 minutes
35 questions

Turn to Section 4 of your answer sheet to answer the questions in this section.

Directions: For each question in this section, select the best answer from among the choices given and fill in the corresponding circle on the answer sheet.

The following sentences test correctness and effectiveness of expression. Part of each sentence or the entire sentence is underlined; beneath each sentence are five ways of phrasing the underlined material. Choice A repeats the original phrasing; the other four choices are different. Select the choice that completes the sentence most effectively.

In making your selection, follow the requirements of standard written English; that is, pay attention to grammar, choice of words, sentence construction, and punctuation. Your selection should result in the most effective sentence—clear and precise, without awkwardness or ambiguity.

EXAMPLE:

The children couldn't hardly believe their eyes.

(A) couldn't hardly believe their eyes
(B) could hardly believe their eyes
(C) would not hardly believe their eyes
(D) couldn't nearly believe their eyes
(E) couldn't hardly believe his or her eyes

Ⓐ ● Ⓒ Ⓓ Ⓔ

1. My favorite activity at this camp is you get to swim.

   (A) you get to swim
   (B) getting to go swimming
   (C) the swimming
   (D) to swim so much
   (E) the swimming you get to do

2. The newer video games for children are very engaging, but ones that don't have anything in the way of real educational value.

   (A) but ones that don't have anything in the way of real
   (B) but lack any real
   (C) and do not have any real
   (D) but no real
   (E) but not any real

3. We could not reach the clearing having a large tree that had fallen blocking our path.

   (A) having a large tree that had fallen blocking
   (B) because a large tree had fallen and blocked
   (C) for a large tree that fell blocking
   (D) due to a large tree that fell and had been blocking
   (E) because a large tree which fell blocking

4. Having run with little effort for over an hour, Jane was disheartened to feel a sudden pain in her knee.

   (A) Jane was disheartened to feel a sudden pain in her knee
   (B) it was disheartening for Jane to feel a sudden pain in her knee
   (C) the sudden pain in her knee disheartened Jane
   (D) Jane's sudden pain in her knee was disheartening to her
   (E) Jane's sudden pain in her knee disheartened her

GO ON TO THE NEXT PAGE ⟶

4   **4**   **4**   **4**   **4**   **4**

5. Americans like to hear stories of those who have amassed fortunes through their own hard work, <u>and so seem also happy to see</u> those same tycoons fall in disgrace.

(A) and so seem also happy to see
(B) but so seem also happy seeing
(C) but seem also happy in seeing
(D) yet also seem happy to see
(E) seeming also happy to see

6. Curators of modern museums understand that they must create exhibits that are not only informative <u>but also attract visitors.</u>

(A) but also attract visitors
(B) and also attractive to visitors
(C) as well as attractive to visitors
(D) but also attracting visitors
(E) but also attractive to visitors

7. Many absurdist writers, notably Eugene Ionesco, believed that novels and plays <u>need not</u> rely on plot.

(A) need not
(B) don't have to need to
(C) would not need to
(D) should not have to need to
(E) need not have to

8. Several of the protestors began to question their methods when they realized that, <u>perhaps because they were promoting confrontation rather than dialogue</u>, they were not changing the minds of their opponents.

(A) perhaps because they were promoting confrontation rather than dialogue
(B) perhaps because their promotion was of confrontation rather than of dialogue
(C) because they have been promoting confrontation rather than dialogue, perhaps
(D) maybe for promoting confrontation instead of dialogue
(E) because they would promote confrontation rather than dialogue

9. Einstein formulated nearly all of his most influential theories in the course of a single year, <u>1905, which have had</u> a profound effect on the whole world of physics, from consumer electronics to quantum theory and space travel.

(A) 1905, which have had
(B) 1905; having
(C) 1905, and these theories have had
(D) 1905; but these theories have had
(E) 1905, however, these have had

10. Sandra's coaching style <u>had been uncompromising and she was</u> more sensitive after many of her players broke down in tears.

(A) had been uncompromising and she was
(B) was uncompromising when she became
(C) had been uncompromising, but she became
(D) was uncompromising, but she had become
(E) was uncompromising, nevertheless she was

11. Although many universities embrace the responsibility of training students to get jobs, <u>there is more of a focus on learning for elevating the mind among other universities</u>.

(A) there is more of a focus on learning for elevating the mind among other universities
(B) there is more of a focus among other universities on learning as a way to elevate the mind
(C) others have a focus on learning as a way of elevating the mind
(D) other universities focus on having learning be a way of elevating the mind
(E) others focus on learning as a way to elevate the mind

GO ON TO THE NEXT PAGE ➡

4   4   4   4   4   4

The following sentences test your ability to recognize grammar and usage errors. Each sentence contains either a single error or no error at all. No sentence contains more than one error. The error, if there is one, is underlined and lettered. If the sentence contains an error, select the one underlined part that must be changed to make the sentence correct. If the sentence is correct, select choice E. In choosing answers, follow the requirements of standard written English.

EXAMPLE:

By the time <u>they reached</u> the halfway point
               A

<u>in the race,</u> <u>most of the runners</u> <u>hadn't hardly</u>
   B   C   D

begun to hit their stride. <u>No error</u>
                        E

---

12. Although our football team <u>does not win</u>
                     A

all of its games, Coach Palmer

<u>usually never</u> fails to put every one
   B

<u>of his players into the game,</u> because he
      C

feels that they <u>have earned</u> the right
           D

to play. <u>No error</u>
        E

13. The bombs <u>destroyed</u> much of the
           A

infrastructure of the city,

<u>but it did not disrupt</u> commerce
   B

<u>in the busy markets</u> for <u>more than</u>
    C   D

a few days. <u>No error</u>
           E

14. By the time <u>the first light of morning</u>
             A

showed <u>above the trees</u>, the circus workers
        B

<u>had took</u> all of the equipment out of the
   C

trucks and had <u>begun</u> to erect the tents.
            D

<u>No error</u>
  E

15. We <u>could not have hoped</u> for better
        A

conditions <u>in which to play</u> the game;
          B

not only was the weather perfect, <u>but also</u>
                C

the field <u>had never been</u> in better shape.
          D

<u>No error</u>
  E

16. As soon as the gun sounded, the racers

<u>had begun</u> to jostle one another for
   A

position <u>at the front</u> of the pack,
       B

<u>safely away from</u> the <u>peril</u> of flying knees
    C   D

and elbows. <u>No error</u>
        E

GO ON TO THE NEXT PAGE ⇨

4   4   4   4   4   4

17. The effort <u>required</u> to study
                        A
<u>for seven final exams</u> within the span of
            B
four days <u>are far more</u> than the typical
                    C
student <u>can manage</u>. <u>No error</u>
                D   E

18. After <u>having eaten</u> nothing <u>but nuts</u> and
                    A   B
berries for forty days <u>in the wilderness</u>,
                                    C
Jon had no desire <u>of eating</u> more fruit.
                            D
<u>No error</u>
    E

19. Appearing <u>like an apparition</u> in the distance
                        A
<u>was</u> the beautiful Blue Ridge Mountains,
    B
<u>where</u> we <u>were going to spend</u> the last
    C   D
week of our vacation. <u>No error</u>
                                E

20. Neither the president, <u>who was</u> on
                                    A
vacation, <u>or even</u> the vice-president,
                B
who was ill, <u>was</u> available <u>to give</u> the
                    C   D
keynote address. <u>No error</u>
                            E

21. Many <u>of the voters</u> who came to the
                A
meeting <u>voiced</u> their <u>concerns for</u> the
                B   C
mayor's new plan to create a new

municipal parking lot <u>next to</u> the
                                D
elementary school. <u>No error</u>
                            E

22. The ability of insects <u>to detect</u> members
                                    A
of their own species from

<u>hundreds of meters</u> away <u>is</u> actually quite
            B   C
different from <u>whales</u>. <u>No error</u>
                        D   E

23. The damage to the building

<u>would not have been</u> so great <u>if</u> the roof
            A   B
<u>had been constructed</u> according
            C
<u>to the recently adopted</u> specifications.
                    D
<u>No error</u>
    E

24. Without the expertise <u>of Alan and I</u> at their
                                    A
disposal, the researchers <u>struggled</u> to
                                    B
interpret the documents <u>they</u> had found
                                    C
<u>in the archives</u>. <u>No error</u>
            D   E

25. The investment required <u>to develop</u>
                                    A
new technologies <u>are</u> often so enormous
                        B
that very few energy companies <u>are able</u> to
                                        C
undertake <u>innovative</u> ventures. <u>No error</u>
                    D   E

26. The petition <u>requesting that</u> the president
                        A
reconsider his <u>stance on</u> stem-cell research
                    B
<u>included</u> the signatures of dozens of
    C
<u>imminent</u> scientists. <u>No error</u>
    D   E

GO ON TO THE NEXT PAGE →

4   4   4   4   4   4

27. For many students, the realization that

<u>his or her</u> academic success can be <u>affected</u>
   A   B

<u>by dietary habits</u> <u>comes</u> as a great surprise.
     C   D

<u>No error</u>
  E

28. The fingerprints that <u>were found</u> at the
                     A

scene of the crime <u>clearly did not</u> match
                  B

<u>the defendant</u>, so the prosecuting team
    C

<u>was forced</u> to alter its original theory.
    D

<u>No error</u>
  E

29. The athletes standing <u>on the podium</u> were
                  A

clearly affected <u>about</u> the warm <u>reception</u>
          B   C

that they received <u>from the audience.</u>
                  D

<u>No error</u>
  E

Directions: The following passage is an early draft of an essay. Some parts of the passage need to be rewritten.

Read the passage and select the best answers for the questions that follow. Some questions are about particular sentences or parts of sentences and ask you to improve sentence structure or word choice. Other questions ask you to consider organization and development. In choosing answers, follow the requirements of standard written English.

Questions 30–35 pertain to the following passage.

(1) Do we idolize sports heroes too much? (2) Since the beginning of recorded history, every major culture has had sports and sports heroes. (3) In the United States, the Hollywood movie industry is the only thing that outdoes professional sports in regards to attracting viewers and the money it makes in entertainment. (4) Some people think that sports are just a distraction from important things like how some guys spend more time thinking about who is the best quarterback than about who should be president. (5) Others say that it's worse than a waste of time, that it promotes violence and immaturity. (6) They cite all of the crime and drug abuse committed by athletes, some of whom can even get away with murder if they're famous enough. (7) Nevertheless, we will always look up to most good athletes, because sports perform important services for a society. (8) The Taleban tried to get rid of sports completely as being against their religion.

(9) Sports provide a civilization with a way for its warriors to hone the skills they need for fighting. (10) So in worshipping sports heroes we are kind of paying respect to our soldiers. (11) But many anthropologists claim that the instinct to play sports comes from an activity that is not war but something similar but much older which is hunting. (12) You can easily see that the skills used in sports are precisely the

GO ON TO THE NEXT PAGE

4   4   4   4   4   4

skills required for being a successful hunter: throwing things accurately, running quickly, tackling things, hitting things with sticks and acting deceptively. **(13)** This instinct is not something we can just get rid of; we may not need to hunt any more, so we need to play sports. **(14)** Our need to play sports is like a kitten playing with string: it is our brain's way of helping us learn the skills needed for hunting.

(15) It is true that we idolize sports figures far too much. **(16)** Since they are only doing what, essentially, their most basic instincts tell them to do, they are not nearly as worthy of admiration as those who actually use their minds and creativity to improve humanity.

30. Which of the following is the best revision of sentence 4 (reproduced below)?

Some people think that sports are just a distraction from important things like how some guys spend more time thinking about who is the best quarterback than about who should be president.

(A) Some people think that sports distract us from important things like thinking about who is the best quarterback rather than who should be president.

(B) Some people complain that sports distract us from important things, focusing us on questions like who is the best quarterback rather than who is the best presidential candidate.

(C) Who is the best quarterback, for instance, is one distraction from questions like who should be president that is caused by sports.

(D) Some people think that who should be president is much more important than who is the best quarterback, but also that sports distract us from that.

(E) Some people complain about the distraction of sports, focusing on questions like who is the best quarterback instead of who is the best presidential candidate.

31. Which of the following is the best version of the underlined portion of sentence 5 (reproduced below)?

In the United States, the Hollywood movie industry is the only *thing that outdoes professional sports in regards to attracting viewers and the money it makes in entertainment.*

(A) (as it is now)

(B) things that are more attractive and money-making than professional sports

(C) form of entertainment more attractive of viewers and making more money than professional sports

(D) thing attracting more viewers and making more money in the entertainment field than professional sports makes

(E) form of entertainment that attracts more viewers and makes more money than professional sports

32. Which sentence in the first paragraph contributes the least to the logical coherence of the paragraph?

(A) sentence 4

(B) sentence 5

(C) sentence 6

(D) sentence 7

(E) sentence 8

GO ON TO THE NEXT PAGE

4 4 4 4 4 4

33. Which of the following is the best version of the underlined portion of sentence 11 (reproduced below)?

But many anthropologists claim that the instinct to play sports comes <u>from an activity that is not war but something similar but much older which is hunting.</u>

(A) (as it is now)
(B) from hunting, which is not war but similar but much older
(C) not from war but from hunting, a similar but much older activity
(D) from hunting, which is similar to war and which is older
(E) not from war but instead it comes from hunting, which is an older activity than war but still similar

34. In context, which of the following revisions of the underlined portion of sentence 13 (reproduced below) provides the clearest logical transition?

<u>This instinct</u> is not something we can just get rid of; we may not need to hunt any more, so we need to play sports.

(A) Nevertheless, this instinct
(B) The instinct to use these skills
(C) Instead, this instinct
(D) All the while this instinct
(E) For example, this instinct

35. Which of the following is the best version of the underlined portion of sentence 14 (reproduced below)?

Our need to play sports is like a <u>kitten playing with string:</u> it is our brain's way of helping us learn the skills needed for hunting.

(A) a kitten when it is playing with a string
(B) the way that a kitten plays with a string
(C) the string that a kitten plays with
(D) a kitten when it needs to play with string
(E) a kitten's need to play with string

STOP

If you finish before time is called, you may check your work on this section only. Do not turn to any other section of the test.

5   **5**   **5**   **5**   **5**   **5**

SECTION 5
Time—25 minutes
18 questions

Turn to Section 5 of your answer sheet to answer the questions in this section.

Directions: This section contains two types of questions. You have 25 minutes to complete both types. For questions 1–8, solve each problem and decide which is the best of the choices given. Fill in the corresponding circle on the answer sheet. You may use any available space for scratchwork.

Notes

1. The use of a calculator is permitted.

2. All numbers used are real numbers.

3. Figures that accompany problems in this test are intended to provide information useful in solving the problems. They are drawn as accurately as possible EXCEPT when it is stated in a specific problem that the figure is not drawn to scale. All figures lie in a plane unless otherwise indicated.

4. Unless otherwise specified, the domain of any function f is assumed to be the set of all real numbers x for which $f(x)$ is a real number.

Reference Information

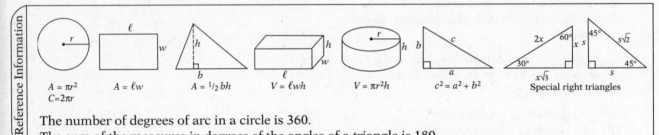

$A = \pi r^2$ $A = \ell w$ $A = \frac{1}{2} bh$ $V = \ell wh$ $V = \pi r^2 h$ $c^2 = a^2 + b^2$ Special right triangles
$C = 2\pi r$

The number of degrees of arc in a circle is 360.
The sum of the measures in degrees of the angles of a triangle is 180.

---

1. If $\dfrac{a}{3} = \dfrac{b}{2}$ and $a = 36$, then $b =$

(A) 12
(B) 24
(C) 28
(D) 32
(E) 54

2. If $2c + d = 9.25$, then $6c + 3d + 3 =$

(A) 22.75
(B) 24.75
(C) 27.75
(D) 30.75
(E) 32.75

If you finish before time is called, you may check your work on this section only. Do not turn to any other section of the test.

GO ON TO THE NEXT PAGE ⇨

5 5 5 5 5 5

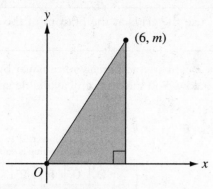

Note: Figure not drawn to scale.

3. If the shaded triangle in the figure above has an area of 12, what is the value of m?

   (A) 2
   (B) 4
   (C) 6
   (D) 8
   (E) 10

4. A pizzeria offers one or more of the following toppings on its pizzas: pepperoni, mushrooms, meatballs. How many different combinations of one or more toppings are possible? (Assume that the order of the toppings does not matter.)

   (A) 5
   (B) 6
   (C) 7
   (D) 8
   (E) 9

5. If the perimeter of a rectangle is 5 times the width of the rectangle, then the length of the rectangle is how many times longer than the width?

   (A) $\dfrac{2}{3}$

   (B) $\dfrac{3}{2}$

   (C) 2

   (D) $\dfrac{5}{2}$

   (E) 3

6. If $16^{w+2} = 2^{11}$, what is the value of w?

   (A) 0.75
   (B) 1.33
   (C) 2.00
   (D) 3.50
   (E) 4.75

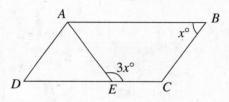

Note: Figure not drawn to scale.

7. In the figure above, $ABCD$ is a parallelogram and AE bisects $\angle DAB$. What is the value of x?

   (A) 24
   (B) 28
   (C) 32
   (D) 36
   (E) 40

8. The width of a rectangle is 75% the length of the rectangle. The perimeter of the rectangle is 84 centimeters. A circle is drawn that contains all four vertices of this rectangle. If the area of this circle is $k\pi$ square centimeters, what is the value of k?

   (A) 160
   (B) 175
   (C) 185
   (D) 210
   (E) 225

GO ON TO THE NEXT PAGE

5   **5**   **5**   **5**   **5**   **5**

Directions: For student-produced response questions 9–18, use the grids at the bottom of the answer sheet page on which you have answered questions 1–8.

Each of the remaining ten questions requires you to solve the problem and enter your answer by marking the circles in the special grid, as shown in the examples below. You may use any available space for scratchwork.

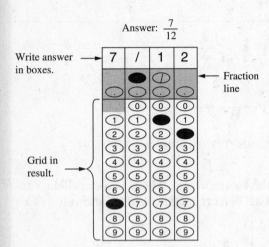

Answer: $\frac{7}{12}$

Write answer in boxes.

Fraction line

Grid in result.

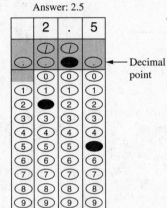

Answer: 2.5

Decimal point

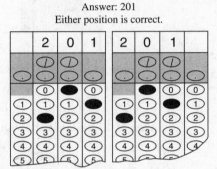

Answer: 201
Either position is correct.

Note: You may start your answers in any column, space permitting. Columns not needed should be left blank.

- Mark no more than one circle in any column.

- Because the answer sheet will be machine-scored, **you will receive credit only if the circles are filled in correctly.**

- Although not required, it is suggested that you write your answer in the boxes at the top of the columns to help you fill in the circles accurately.

- Some problems may have more than one correct answer. In such cases, grid only one answer.

- No question has a negative answer.

- **Mixed numbers** such as $3\frac{1}{2}$ must be gridded as 3.5 or 7/2. (If $\boxed{3\ 1\ /\ 2}$ is gridded, it will be interpreted as $\frac{31}{2}$ not $3\frac{1}{2}$.)

- **Decimal Answers:** If you obtain a decimal answer with more digits than the grid can accommodate, it may be either rounded or truncated, but it must fill the entire grid. For example, if you obtain an answer such as 0.6666..., you should record your result as .666 or .667. **A less accurate value such as .66 or .67 will be scored as incorrect.**

Acceptable ways to grid $^2/_3$ are:

5   **5**   **5**   **5**   **5**   **5**

9. If a car travels at a constant rate of 75 miles per hour, how many <u>minutes</u> will it take to travel 100 miles? (60 minutes = 1 hour)

10. What is the only integer that satisfies the statement $|3x - 53| < 1.2$?

11. The average (arithmetic mean) of five different integers is 30. If the least of these integers is 7, what is the greatest possible value of any of the numbers?

12. The ratio of girls to boys at a certain school is 8:5. If there are 520 students at the school altogether, how many boys are at the school?

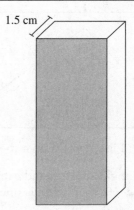

1.5 cm

13. The volume of the rectangular solid above is 27 cubic centimeters. What is the area, in square centimeters, of the shaded face?

GO ON TO THE NEXT PAGE

5   **5**   **5**   **5**   **5**   **5**

14. At the beginning of the year, the price of stock A was 35% greater than the price of stock B. Over the course of the year, the price of stock A doubled while the price of stock B decreased by 10%. At the end of the year, how many times greater was the price of stock A than the price of stock B?

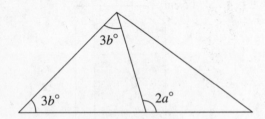

Note: Figure not drawn to scale.

15. In the triangle above, *a* and *b* are odd integers. If 50 > *a* > 60, then what is one possible value of *b*?

16. If *L* represents the sum of the first three terms of a geometric sequence in which the second and third terms are 1 and 3, respectively, and *M* represents the sum of the first three terms of a geometric sequence in which the second and third terms are 3 and 1, respectively, then what is *M* − *L*?

17. If the range of the function $y = f(x)$ is all real numbers between −1 and 12, inclusive, then what is the maximum value of $g(x)$ if $g(x) = 2f(x-1) + 3$?

18. Let #*x* represent the greatest even number less than *x*. If 20 < *x* < 30, then what is the maximum possible value of #5*x* − #4*x*?

STOP

If you finish before time is called, you may check your work on this section only. Do not turn to any other section of the test.

6   **6**   **6**   **6**   **6**   **6**

SECTION 6
Time—25 minutes
24 questions

Turn to Section 6 of your answer sheet to answer the questions in this section.

Directions: For each question in this section, select the best answer from among the choices given and fill in the corresponding circle on the answer sheet.

Each sentence below has one or two blanks, each blank indicating that something has been omitted. Beneath the sentence are five words or sets of words labeled A through E. Choose the word or set of words that, when inserted in the sentence, best fits the meaning of the sentence as a whole.

EXAMPLE:

Rather than accepting the theory unquestioningly, Deborah regarded it with -----.

(A) mirth
(B) sadness
(C) responsibility
(D) ignorance
(E) skepticism

---

1. Veteran coaches can often reflect on past experiences to draw lessons for the present; young players, however, rarely have the advantage of such -------.

   (A) vagueness
   (B) misconceptions
   (C) hindsight
   (D) antagonism
   (E) premonitions

2. The males of many bird species rely on ------- displays like elaborate plumage and energetic dances to attract females, yet such exhibitions are ------- for the many males who are not chosen as mates.

   (A) eternal . . tolerable
   (B) misleading . . successful
   (C) carnivorous . . irrelevant
   (D) ostentatious . . futile
   (E) passive . . inexplicable

3. The memoir was filled with entertaining ------- about the author's experiences as an army nurse, but many readers thought that the disjointed nature of these stories detracted from the ------- of the book.

   (A) pluralities . . consistency
   (B) themes . . implausibility
   (C) missives . . frivolity
   (D) treatises . . authenticity
   (E) vignettes . . cohesiveness

4. Fast horses often tend to be hard to control, so riders who are concerned about safety should look for steeds that are slower and more -------.

   (A) nimble
   (B) irascible
   (C) tractable
   (D) recalcitrant
   (E) erroneous

GO ON TO THE NEXT PAGE ⟶

6   **6**   **6**   **6**   **6**   **6**

5. One critical flaw of the new trade regulations is that they require much greater oversight of commerce, but do not ------- the necessary funds for such an increase in -------.

(A) appropriate . . vigilance
(B) provide . . taxation
(C) determine . . empathy
(D) embezzle . . organization
(E) sequester . . industry

Each passage below is followed by questions based on its content. Answer each question based on what is stated or implied in the passage.

Questions 6–7 are based on the following passage.

The following is an excerpt from a biography of Albert Einstein that discusses his relationship with the American silent film star Charlie Chaplin.

The essence of Einstein's profundity lay in his simplicity, and the essence of his science lay in
Line his artistry—his phenomenal sense of beauty. He is, of course, best known for his theory of
5   relativity, which brought him world fame. But with fame came a form of near idolatry that Einstein found incomprehensible. To his amazement, he became a living legend, a veritable folk hero, looked upon as an oracle,
10   entertained by royalty, statesmen, and other celebrities, and treated by public and press as if he were a movie star rather than a scientist. When, in Hollywood's glittering heyday, Chaplin took Einstein to the gala opening of
15   his film *City Lights*, the crowds surged around the limousine as much to gape at Einstein as at Chaplin. Turning in bewilderment to his host, Einstein asked, "What does it mean?" to which the worldly-
20   wise Chaplain bitterly replied, "Nothing."

6. The passage suggests that, unlike Einstein, Chaplin

(A) was widely adored by the public
(B) understood the nature of celebrity
(C) did not consider himself an artist
(D) knew people in powerful positions
(E) was annoyed by the press

7. Einstein's question in line 19 is inquiring about

(A) a piece of art
(B) a scientific puzzle
(C) a social phenomenon
(D) a polite gesture
(E) an invitation

Questions 8–9 are based on the following passage.

The following is an excerpt from a book about biomedical ethics.

Traditional codes of medical ethics, as well other traditional expositions, emphasize the
Line moral obligations of health-care professionals rather than the moral rights of patients.
5   Physicians are expected to perform those actions which will benefit their patients and to refrain from performing those that will harm them. Thus traditional medical ethics stresses two fundamental principles as governing the
10   physician-patient relationship—the principles of *beneficence* and *nonmaleficence*. Both of these are expressed in the dictum, "Benefit and do no harm to the patient." In contrast, recent discussions of medical ethics speak
15   more and more about the moral rights of patients, especially about the right to make their own medical decisions. These discussions emphasize the right of patients to act as autonomous decision makers, determining for
20   themselves what will be done to their bodies. This change of emphasis reflects a growing change in lay attitudes toward health-care professionals, especially physicians.

GO ON TO THE NEXT PAGE →

First paragraph: *Albert Einstein, Creator & Rebel*, Banesh Hoffman, © 1992, Penguin Books, p 3.
Second paragraph: *Biomedical Ethics*, Thomas Mappes, Jane Zempaty, McGraw Hill. © 1981, pp 44–45

6 6 6 6 6 6

8. The sentence beginning on line 5 ("Physicians are expected to ... harm them") represents the perspective of

(A) theorists with whom the author adamantly disagrees
(B) modern physicians
(C) patients with life-threatening illnesses
(D) long-established tenets
(E) recent treatises on medical ethics

9. The passage indicates that "lay attitudes" (line 22) are becoming increasingly focused on

(A) traditional codes
(B) the behavior of professionals
(C) emotional health
(D) the rights of physicians
(E) the rights of those receiving treatment

Questions 10–16 are based on the following passage.

The following excerpt is taken from a book devoted to the argumentation, particularly with regard to its merits, purposes and techniques.

Why do we argue? Why do we make trouble? Why are we obnoxious and disagreeable?
Line Why not just go along and not make waves? Because we are constantly faced with decisions.
5 In order to make good decisions we have to consider the issues and the relevant arguments and positions. It is necessary to decide what issues are the most important, what topics the most vital.
10 Arguing provides the opportunity to explore and probe the claims and positions offered. In arguing we have a chance to examine exactly what the position rests upon. The territorial limit should be extended to two hundred miles
15 off-shore: Why? What rights are involved? Who will suffer and who will gain? Are there alternatives to the move? What problem forced this solution? What will happen if it is not extended? In arguing we need not disagree
20 with a position in order to attack it. We need only want to test or explore it. One major reason for arguing, then, is to learn: to explore, probe, and test in order to examine a belief.

Very often when we engage in arguments
25 we already have a conviction but argue to persuade others. Sometimes we are being persuaded, at other times we are doing the persuading. This aspect of argument is around us at all times. When the daily newspaper
30 editorial supports compulsory seat-belt legislation and offers arguments, the aim is to convince us, the readers. The same holds for all arguments and positions presented on television and radio. In these situations we
35 do not have the opportunity to reply. The argument is stated and there it is, we can take it or leave it. We are presented with very polished and convincing arguments but cannot ourselves object.
40 Other forms of argument designed to persuade us are the advertising messages that reach us by way of commercials, posters, jingles, and so on. The reasons presented for trying a product can be good, such as
45 efficiency or low cost, or poor, such as prestige or an irrelevant endorsement. The errors in reasoning one finds in advertising are the same as elsewhere. When Polly Politician says, "Unemployment may be reduced as
50 much as 22 percent in the next six months," she relies on the same "hedge-words" as an advertisement saying, "Shine toothpaste may reduce cavities by as much as 36 percent." Both use the expression "as much as,"

GO ON TO THE NEXT PAGE

Excerpted from *How to Win an Argument*, Michael A. Gilbert, McGraw-Hill. © 1979, p 5–7.

55 indicating only an outside possibility, and
    both use the word "may" instead of "will."
        We often aim to convince someone of our
    view. When we suggest to a colleague that
    opening a new branch might not be a
60 good idea, we are arguing. He might, at the
    same time, be aiming to convince us that it is a
    good idea. In these situations we must be very
    quick. Someone presenting us with a position
    expects either assent or disagreement. If we
65 dissent, then there is a responsibility to explain
    why we disagree. If we cannot come up with
    a reason, then we are expected to agree.
        Arguments can also be fun, especially when
    they are not about something too vital. Arguing
70 is like playing, and to appreciate it on its own,
    without any desire to achieve some other end,
    is not only possible, but desirable. Arguing
    when nothing is at stake can be a valuable
    experience, like playing a friendly game of
75 tennis to prepare for a tournament. We are
    more at ease, and so can pay more attention to
    what we are saying and how we are saying it.
    We can take more risks on outrageous
    maneuvers, maybe try out a new shot.
80   A common old saying is that one should
    never argue about religion or politics. This is
    nonsense. One of our aims is to have true
    beliefs. In this sense we all seek the truth. Yet
    the adage warns us not to examine or test the
85 most important and basic of beliefs. Should
    these be left alone? No. These are just the
    beliefs that should be most carefully
    examined. By spotting weaknesses, mistakes,
    and falsehoods we stand a much better
90 chance of holding and acting on true beliefs.
    The advantage of this is success: making
    decisions on false beliefs can only lead to
    error and trouble.

10. In the first paragraph, (lines 1–9) the author
     assumes that the reader

     (A) understands the basic value of
         argumentation
     (B) lives in a democratic society
     (C) wants to act judiciously
     (D) reads newspapers
     (E) has had experience in dealing with
         obnoxious people

11. Unlike the questions in the first paragraph, the
     questions in the second paragraph

     (A) pertain to argumentation
     (B) are not questions that the author believes
         are appropriate
     (C) have answers that are already
         well-known
     (D) are not answered in this passage
     (E) are not related to any particular policy

12. The main purpose of the second and third
     paragraphs is to

     (A) describe different purposes of
         argumentation
     (B) illustrate different methods of
         arguing
     (C) present opposite perspectives on a
         political issue
     (D) describe some common misconceptions
         about argumentation
     (E) summarize the findings of researchers

13. The passage suggests that "Polly Politician"
     (line 48) is guilty of

     (A) corruption
     (B) inefficiency
     (C) ignorance
     (D) egotism
     (E) equivocation

GO ON TO THE NEXT PAGE →

6   6   6   6   6   6

14. The "arguments" mentioned in line 31 differ significantly from the argument described in the fifth paragraph (lines 57–67) chiefly in that they are

   (A) about petty topics
   (B) poorly reasoned
   (C) one-sided
   (D) for entertainment purposes
   (E) irrefutable

15. According to the analogy used in the sixth paragraph, the "outrageous maneuvers" (lines 78–79) are like

   (A) novel ways of making a point in casual conversation
   (B) tricks used by politicians in debates
   (C) the deceptive practices of journalists
   (D) unethical practices in business
   (E) unorthodox coaching practices

16. The purpose of the last paragraph (lines 80–93) is to

   (A) continue an analogy from the previous paragraph
   (B) refute a misconception
   (C) provide a specific example that supports a political theory
   (D) support the author's thesis by citing an authoritative opinion
   (E) present a personal reflection

Questions 17–24 are based on the following passage.

The following passage is from a memoir written in 1970 by Lady Mary Dolling Sanders O'Malley, who wrote under the pseudonym Ann Bridge.

In 1924 George Mallory set out with the third
expedition to attempt to reach the summit of
Line Mount Everest. My brother Jack and I had
first met George at Zermatt in 1909, and both
5 made friends with him. Till my marriage in
1913, George and I climbed a great deal
together in Wales; we met in the Alps; he
often stayed with us in London.
  Naturally, I took great interest in his
10 Everest expeditions. With George I pored
over the routes and studied the photographs;
when he was first asked to lecture about it I
went and stayed with them, and George tried
out his original lecture on Ruth (his wife) and
15 me, in his roomy study at The Holt—he was
rather nervous, but in fact the lectures were a
great success, delivered in his beautiful voice,
with an engaging hint of shyness. Both Ruth
and I noticed, though, before he left for the
20 third time, that some of the happy enthusiasm
that had been so evident before the two earlier
expeditions was lacking—he was what he
himself called "heavy," a frame of mind he
detested if it took him before or during a climb.
25   We read of course in the papers every
scrap of news that came from the expedition—
always with a time-lag of about a fortnight
while despatches were being brought down
through Tibet by runners to the nearest
30 telegraph office.
  One night at the end of the first week in
that June, at Bridge End, our house in Surrey,
I had a peculiarly vivid dream. In it Ruth and
I decided to go out and visit the Everest
35 expedition. With the absurd inconsequence
so frequent in dreams we took the train to
Chur, in eastern Switzerland, and then drove
in an open two-horse carriage through streets
of high gray stone-built houses, till we reached

GO ON TO THE NEXT PAGE ➔

Excerpted from *Moment of Knowing*, Ann Bridge, Mcgraw-Hill. © 1970, p 24–27.

40   the headquarters of the expedition. We went
in; the men were all out, and we decided to
get tea ready for them; there was no milk, so
we took a large jug to the *Meierei*, the dairy
along the street, and filled it—I clearly
45   remember explaining the word *Meierei* to
Ruth, who knew no German. Then the men
came in, hungry and cheerful, with snowy
boots, and we all had tea. And afterwards
George took me into what he called the
50   maproom, where there was a huge
enlargement of a photograph of the ridge of
Everest, running down to the North Col, on
the wall; he took a thing like a billiard-cue and
showed me the new camps, and explained
55   how certain it was that they would reach the
summit tomorrow. Then he put down the
cue, and we sat on the big table in the middle
of the room, swinging our legs, and talked—
George spoke, more fully and openly than he
60   had ever done before to me of what mountains
and his relationship to mountains meant to
him—he spoke with a strange mixture of
reverence and what I can only call rapture.
     This dream frightened me terribly. He had
65   been so alive, so near, in it—just as when a
beloved friend whom one has not seen for
some time comes to stay, and for days after
they have left the whole house is glowing and
warm from their recent presence—so Bridge
70   End, next morning, as I went about my daily
tasks, was full of the presence of George. I did
not want to worry Ruth, but I wrote to Marjorie
Turner, her sister, at Westbrook, saying I had
been worried by a dream, and asking what
75   the latest news was of George? In reply I got
a laconic post-card: "Last heard from R. three
days ago; he was all right then. M."
     I don't think I even tried to comfort myself
with the absurd setting of the dream, like the
80   Everest Expedition's headquarters being in a
stone-built house in a Swiss town—I was too
accustomed to the inconsequent dottiness of
dreams. And on a Saturday morning nearly a
fortnight later Owen came out to me where I
85   was sorting linen in the big workroom behind
the kitchen with the newspaper in his hand.
"I've got some bad news for you," he said.

"George and Irvine have been killed on
Everest."
90   Odell reported having his last sight of the
pair after noon on 8 June, above the last step,
on the open arête, "going strongly for the
top." Having climbed a lot with George, I
cannot believe, with only a perfectly straight-
95   forward snow ridge between him and the
summit, the last obstacle surmounted, that
he did not reach it. And when in 1933 a later
expedition found an ice-axe *below* the first
rock step, it confirmed my belief, and that of
100   many others, that Mallory and Irvine had
reached the top, and that disaster had
overtaken them on the way down. Descent is
always more difficult than ascent; and who
would leave an ice-axe behind, with that
105   snow arête still in front of him? Certainly not
George.
     In 1953 Everest was successfully climbed
by Hunt's party. I was in Ireland, but our
daughter Jane, George's godchild, who was in
110   London, telephoned me the news first thing.
I was especially glad to hear it from her.

17.   In line 24, the word "took" most nearly means

     (A)   acquired
     (B)   derived from
     (C)   overcame
     (D)   required
     (E)   endured

18.   The narrator uses the phrase "every scrap" in
lines 25–26 in order to convey

     (A)   the unreliable nature of the news
     (B)   the slow speed of the news
     (C)   her lack of interest in the
technicalities of climbing
     (D)   the awkward relationship between the
narrator and Ruth
     (E)   her eagerness to hear news of the
expedition

GO ON TO THE NEXT PAGE ⟶

19. The "absurd inconsequence" in the narrator's dream is the

    (A) absence of milk in the expedition headquarters
    (B) cheerfulness of the men
    (C) location of the expedition headquarters
    (D) speed of the train ride
    (E) photograph of Mount Everest

20. In the author's dream, Mallory's attitude toward the mountains can best be described as

    (A) awed
    (B) fearful
    (C) cavalier
    (D) objectively analytical
    (E) ambivalent

21. In saying that she was "too accustomed to the inconsequent dottiness of dreams" (line 83) the author suggests that she was unable to

    (A) warn Mallory of the dangers of his climb
    (B) appease the anxiety caused by her dream
    (C) allow herself to be affected by her dream
    (D) understand the symbolism of her dream
    (E) determine the location of the expedition's headquarters

22. The references to "a fortnight" in both lines 27 and line 84 are significant because, when considered together, they suggest that

    (A) communications technology had improved significantly
    (B) the ascent took far longer than Mallory had anticipated
    (C) the information that the author received about Mallory's expedition was unreliable
    (D) Mallory had insufficient time to prepare for his ascent
    (E) the author's dream roughly coincided with Mallory's death

23. In the sentence beginning on line 93, "Having climbed ... did not reach it" the author expresses her opinion that Mallory

    (A) lacked some important mountain climbing skills
    (B) was hindered by weather
    (C) was an exceptionally able climber
    (D) was not killed
    (E) was misled by his fellow climbers

24. It can be inferred from the passage that the narrator was "especially glad" (line 111) that the news of a successful climb came from her daughter because her daughter

    (A) had been away for a long time
    (B) was an adept climber
    (C) rarely communicated with other members of the family
    (D) had had a special relationship with George Mallory
    (E) was not accustomed to good news

If you finish before time is called, you may check your work on this section only. Do not turn to any other section of the test.

7   **7**   **7**   **7**   **7**   **7**

SECTION 7
Time—20 minutes
16 questions

Turn to Section 7 of your answer sheet to answer the questions in this section.

Directions: For this section, solve each problem and decide which is the best of the choices given. Fill in the corresponding circle on the answer sheet. You may use any available space for scratchwork.

Notes

1. The use of a calculator is permitted.

2. All numbers used are real numbers.

3. Figures that accompany problems in this test are intended to provide information useful in solving the problems. They are drawn as accurately as possible EXCEPT when it is stated in a specific problem that the figure is not drawn to scale. All figures lie in a plane unless otherwise indicated.

4. Unless otherwise specified, the domain of any function f is assumed to be the set of all real numbers x for which $f(x)$ is a real number.

Reference Information

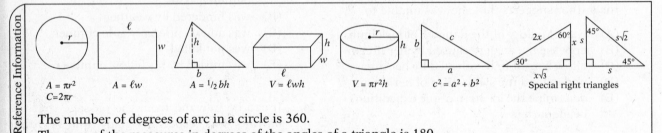

$A = \pi r^2$ $A = \ell w$ $A = \frac{1}{2} bh$ $V = \ell wh$ $V = \pi r^2 h$ $c^2 = a^2 + b^2$ Special right triangles
$C = 2\pi r$

The number of degrees of arc in a circle is 360.
The sum of the measures in degrees of the angles of a triangle is 180.

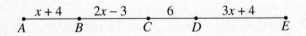

1. In the figure above, what is the length of line segment AE in terms of x?

    (A) $3x + 11$
    (B) $5x + 14$
    (C) $7x + 8$
    (D) $6x + 11$
    (E) $6x + 17$

2. A video store charges an annual account fee of $3.00 per customer and has a total of 5,400 members. If everyone pays the fee, what is the total amount collected from the members?

    (A) $16.20
    (B) $162.00
    (C) $1,620.00
    (D) $16,200.00
    (E) $162,000.00

GO ON TO THE NEXT PAGE

7   7   7   7   7   7

1 pint = 2 cups
1 cup = 16 tablespoons

3. A plastic container contains 2 pints of water. If 8 tablespoons of water are poured out, what fraction of the original amount remains?

(A) $\dfrac{1}{8}$

(B) $\dfrac{1}{4}$

(C) $\dfrac{1}{2}$

(D) $\dfrac{3}{4}$

(E) $\dfrac{7}{8}$

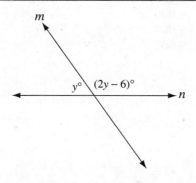

Note: Figure not drawn to scale.

4. Lines m and n intersect, as shown, in the figure above. What is the value of y?

(A) 52
(B) 58
(C) 62
(D) 68
(E) 72

5. Elysha uses air-conditioning year round and spends, on average, $125 per month to cool her apartment. A new energy-efficient air con- ditioning system would cost her $3,000 to in- stall and only $25 per month thereafter to cool the apartment. If she installs the new system, how many months will it take for her total sav- ings in cooling costs to equal the cost of the system?

(A) 30
(B) 35
(C) 40
(D) 45
(E) 50

$$\begin{array}{r} BA \\ +6B \\ \hline CAB \end{array}$$

6. In the correctly worked addition problem above, A, B, and C represent different digits. What is the value of B?

(A) 0
(B) 1
(C) 4
(D) 5
(E) 8

GO ON TO THE NEXT PAGE

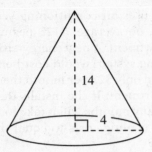

Note: Figure not drawn to scale.

7. The radius of the base of the right circular cone above is 4 inches and the height of the cone is 14 inches. A cut is made parallel to the circular base such that it produces a smaller cone with a radius of 3 inches. What is the height, in inches, of the smaller cone?

(A) 3.5
(B) 6.0
(C) 7.0
(D) 10.5
(E) 11.0

8. A right triangle has side lengths of $x - 1$, $x + 1$, and $x + 3$. What is its perimeter?

(A) 7
(B) 24
(C) 28
(D) 32
(E) 36

$0.\overline{24516} = 0.245162451624516 \ldots$

9. In the repeating decimal above, what is the 3,000th digit to the right of the decimal?

(A) 2
(B) 4
(C) 5
(D) 1
(E) 6

Housing Situation of Glenville Families

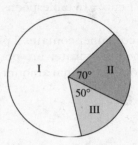

Region I: Families who own their own homes
Region II: Families who own condominiums
Region III: Families who rent apartments

10. The pie graph above shows the housing situation of families in Glenville. If there are 12,000 families in Glenville, then how many families own homes?

(A) 3,000
(B) 4,000
(C) 6,000
(D) 8,000
(E) 9,000

GO ON TO THE NEXT PAGE

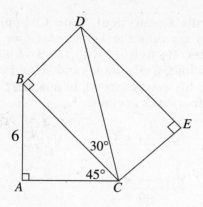

Note: Figure not drawn to scale.

11. In the figure above, $BD \parallel CE$. What is the length of DE?

(A) $6\sqrt{3}$

(B) $6\sqrt{2}$

(C) $2\sqrt{6}$

(D) $4\sqrt{6}$

(E) $3\sqrt{5}$

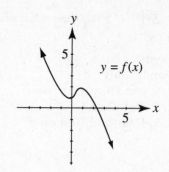

$y = f(x)$

12. Given the graph of $y = f(x)$ above, which of the following represents the graph of $y = f(x + 3) + 3$?

(A)

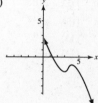

(B)

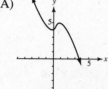

(C)

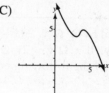

(D)

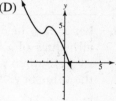

(E)

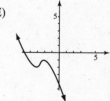

GO ON TO THE NEXT PAGE

7   **7**   **7**   **7**   **7**   **7**

13. If $n = 5^{2000} + 5^{2002}$, then what are the prime factors of n?

(A) 5 only
(B) 2 and 5 only
(C) 2, 5, and 10 only
(D) 2, 5, and 13 only
(E) 2, 5, 1000, and 1001 only

14. If $r = s^6 = t^4$ and r is positive, then $st =$

(A) $r^{1/24}$
(B) $r^{1/10}$
(C) $r^{5/12}$
(D) r^{10}
(E) r^{24}

15. Let $x \, \Omega \, y$ be defined by $x \, \Omega \, y = (x - y)^2$ for all values of x and y. If $x \, \Omega \, y = 2y \, \Omega \, 3$ and $x = y - 3$, then which of the following could be the value of y?

(A) -1
(B) 1
(C) 3
(D) 4
(E) 6

16. In the Connecticut State Championships, Rodrigo runs the 1-mile race four different times. He finishes with times of a minutes, b minutes, c minutes and d minutes. What was his average speed, in <u>miles per hour</u>, for all four races combined?

(A) $\dfrac{a + b + c + d}{4}$

(B) $\dfrac{a + b + c + d}{240}$

(C) $\dfrac{a + b + c + d}{15}$

(D) $\dfrac{4}{a + b + c + d}$

(E) $\dfrac{240}{a + b + c + d}$

STOP

If you finish before time is called, you may check your work on this section only. Do not turn to any other section of the test.

8 **8** **8** **8** **8** **8**

SECTION 8
Time—20 minutes
19 questions

Turn to Section 8 of your answer sheet to answer the questions in this section.

Directions: For each question in this section, select the best answer from among the choices given and fill in the corresponding circle on the answer sheet.

Each sentence below has one or two blanks, each blank indicating that something has been omitted. Beneath the sentence are five words or sets of words labeled A through E. Choose the word or set of words that, when inserted in the sentence, <u>best</u> fits the meaning of the sentence as a whole.

EXAMPLE:

Rather than accepting the theory unquestioningly, Deborah regarded it with -----.

(A) mirth
(B) sadness
(C) responsibility
(D) ignorance
(E) skepticism

1. Donna's aggressive style was a ------- when she was a young student, but it turned into an asset when she became a trial lawyer.

   (A) liability   (B) novelty
   (C) compliment   (D) symbol
   (E) protection

2. Although the report is -------, it would be ------- of the committee to accept it without revision; it discusses the topic thoroughly, but contains several significant errors that need to be corrected.

   (A) flawed . . foreign
   (B) inarticulate . . negligent
   (C) comprehensive . . remiss
   (D) complete . . acceptable
   (E) subtle . . irresponsible

3. Davis was confident in her ability to win the race, but not so ------- as to believe that she could do so without her greatest effort.

   (A) thorough
   (B) doubtful
   (C) complacent
   (D) coherent
   (E) latent

4. The diet and exercise regimen did not work to invigorate Dina as the doctors had hoped; indeed she felt ------- by the effort and more ------- than ever.

   (A) defeated . . sanguine
   (B) weakened . . lithe
   (C) energized . . torpid
   (D) conciliated . . despondent
   (E) enervated . . phlegmatic

5. The film contains a ------- of sophisticated symbols, far more than even a perspicacious critic can interpret in several viewings.

   (A) modicum
   (B) rectitude
   (C) surfeit
   (D) dearth
   (E) deficit

GO ON TO THE NEXT PAGE

6. Planning to divert their pursuers with a
------- lead, the conspirators knew they would
escape if no one unraveled their ------- plan.

(A) veritable . . venerable
(B) contrived . . decrepit
(C) specious . . forthright
(D) credible . . scheming
(E) spurious . . duplicitous

The passages below are followed by questions
based on its content and on the relationship between the passages. Answer each question based on
what is stated or implied in the passages or in any
introductory material that precedes the passages.

Questions 7–19 are based on the following passages.

*The following passages present two perspectives on
author Nathaniel Hawthorne and his works. The
first passage was written by an American author
and critic in 1872, and the second passage was
written as a response 8 years later.*

PASSAGE 1

Mr. Hawthorne is having a posthumous
productivity almost as active as that of his
Line   lifetime. Six volumes have been compounded
from his private journals, an unfinished
5   romance is doing duty as a "serial[1]," and a
number of his letters, with other personal
memorials, have been given to the world.
These liberal excisions from the privacy of so
reserved and shade-seeking a genius suggest
10   forcibly the general question of the proper
limits of curiosity as to that passive
personality of an artist of which the elements
are scattered in portfolios and table-drawers.
The question is really brought to an open
15   dispute between the instinct of self-
conservatism and the general fondness for

[1]A novel published in installments in a periodical

First passage: "*Nathaniel Hawthorne*", The Nation,
March 14, 1872. Henry James.

squeezing an orange dry. Artists, of course, as
time goes on, will be likely to take the alarm,
empty their table-drawers, and level the
20   approaches to their privacy. The critics,
psychologists, and gossip-mongers may then
glean amid the stubble.
Our remarks are not provoked by any
visible detriment conferred on Mr. Hawthorne's
25   fame by these recent publications. He has very
fairly withstood the ordeal; which, indeed, is
as little as possible an ordeal in his case,
owing to the superficial character of the
documents. His journals throw little light on
30   his personal feelings, and even less on his
genius *per se*. Their general effect is difficult
to express. They deepen our sense of that
genius, while they singularly diminish our
impression of his general intellectual power.
35   They represent him, judged with any real
critical rigor, as superficial, uninformed,
incurious, inappreciative; but from beginning
to end they cast no faintest shadow upon the
purity of his peculiar gift. The truth is that
40   Mr. Hawthorne belonged to the race of
magicians, and that his genius took its
nutriment as insensibly—to our vision—as the
flowers take the dew. He was the last man to
have attempted to explain himself, and these
45   pages offer no adequate explanation of him.
They show us one of the gentlest, lightest,
and most leisurely of observers, strolling at
his ease among foreign sights in blessed
intellectual irresponsibility, and weaving his
50   chance impressions into a tissue as smooth
as fireside gossip. Mr. Hawthorne had what
belongs to genius—a style individual and
delightful; he seems to have written as well
for himself as he did for others—to have
55   written from the impulse to keep up a sort of
literary tradition in a career singularly devoid
of the air of professional authorship; but as
regards substance, his narrative flows along
in a current as fitfully diffuse and shallow as
60   a regular correspondence with a distant
friend—a friend familiar but not intimate—
sensitive but not exacting. With all allowance

GO ON TO THE NEXT PAGE

for suppressions, his entries are never confidential; the author seems to have been
65 reserved even with himself. They are a record of things slight and usual. Some of the facts noted are incredibly minute; they imply a peculiar *leisure* of attention. How little his journal was the receptacle of Mr. Hawthorne's
70 deeper feelings is indicated by the fact that during a long and dangerous illness of his daughter in Rome, which he speaks of later as "a trouble that pierced into his very vitals," he never touched his pen.

Passage 2

75 Mr. James's book on Hawthorne, in Morley's *English Men of Letters* series, merits far closer examination and carefuller notice than we can give it here, alike for the interest of its subject, the peculiarity of its point of view,
80 and the charm and distinction of its literature. An American author writing of an American author for an English public incurs risks with his fellow-countrymen which Mr. James must have faced, and is much more
85 likely to possess the foreigner whom he addresses with a clear idea of our conditions than to please the civilization whose portrait is taken. Forty-six, fifty, sixty-four, are not dates so remote, nor are Salem and Concord
90 societies so extinct, that the people of those periods and places can be safely described as "provincial[2]," not once, but a dozen times; and we foresee, without any very powerful prophetic lens, that Mr. James will be in
95 some quarters accused of high treason. For ourselves, we will be content with saying that the provinciality strikes us as somewhat over-insisted upon, and that, speaking from the point of not being at all provincial ourselves,
100 we think the epithet is sometimes mistaken. If it is not provincial for an Englishman to be English, or a Frenchman French, then it is not so for an American to be American; and if Hawthorne was "exquisitely provincial," one

105 had better take one's chance of universality with him than with almost any Londoner or Parisian of his time. Provinciality, we understand it, is a thing of the mind or the soul; but if it is a thing of the experiences,
110 then that is another matter, and there is no quarrel. Hawthorne undoubtedly saw less of the world in New England than one sees in Europe, but he was no cockney[3], as Europeans are apt to be.
115 We think, too, that, in his conscience against bragging and chauvinism, Mr. James puts too slight a value upon some of Hawthorne's work. It is not enough to say of a book so wholly unrivaled as *The Scarlet Letter*
120 that it was "the finest piece of imaginative writing put forth in America," as if it had its parallel in any literature. No one better than Mr. James knows the radical difference between a romance and a novel, but he speaks
125 now of Hawthorne's novels, and now of his romances, throughout, as if the terms were convertible; whereas the romance and the novel are as distinct as the poem and the novel. Hawthorne's fictions being always and
130 essentially, in conception and performance, romances, and not novels, something of all Mr. James's special criticism is invalidated by the confusion which, for some reason not made clear, he permits himself.
135 What gives us entire satisfaction, however, is Mr. James's characterization, or illustrations of Hawthorne's own nature. He finds him an innocent, affectionate heart, extremely domestic, a life of definite, high purposes
140 singularly un-baffled, and an "unperplexed intellect." This strikes us as beautifully reasonable and true, and we will not cloud it with comment of ours. But satisfactorily as Mr. James declares Hawthorne's personality
145 in large, we do not find him sufficient as to minor details and facts. His defect, or his error, appears most often in his discussion of the notebooks, where he makes plain to himself the simple, domestic, democratic

[2]Unsophisticated and narrow-minded
[3]A resident of London's East End who is looked down upon by some Londoners as being unsophisticated.

Second passage: "*Review of Hawthorne, by Henry James*" William Dean Howells, 1880.

GO ON TO THE NEXT PAGE →

150 qualities in Hawthorne, and yet maintains
that he sets down slight and little aspects of
nature because his world is small and vacant.
Hawthorne noted these because he loved
them, and as a great painter, however full
155 and vast his world is, continues to jot down
whatever strikes him as picturesque and
characteristic. As a romance, the twelve years
of boyhood which he spent in the wild
solitudes of Maine were probably of greater
160 advantage to him than if they had been passed
at Eton and Oxford. At least, until some other
civilization has produced a romantic genius at
all comparable to his, we must believe this.

7. In the second sentence, (lines 3–7) the author of
Passage 1 lists several works of Hawthorne that

(A) were roundly criticized by other authors
(B) were published without his consent
(C) were not as popular as his other works
(D) were superior to most of his other works
(E) demonstrated Hawthorne's need for
adulation

8. The "orange" in line 17 is intended to represent

(A) the greed of certain publishers
(B) the creative work of an author or artist
(C) the conservative nature of writers
(D) the published musings of gossip-
mongers
(E) the respect for the privacy of artists

9. The first sentence of the second paragraph
(lines 23–25) makes the concession that

(A) Hawthorne became famous only after his
death
(B) few of Hawthorne's manuscripts
acquired after his death have actually
been published
(C) Hawthorne approved of most of the
publications under discussion
(D) Hawthorne's works are inferior to those
of his contemporaries
(E) Hawthorne's reputation has not been
damaged by the posthumous publication
of his works

10. The reference to Hawthorne as the "last man"
(line 43) serves to emphasize

(A) the lack of self-consciousness in his
writing
(B) the difficulty he had in articulating his
observations
(C) his lack of moral responsibility
(D) his inability to notice details
(E) the deep symbolism in his writing

11. In the second paragraph of Passage 1, (lines
23–74) the author indicates that Hawthorne's
journals are characterized by

  I.   repressed feelings
 II.   intellectual casualness
III.   an engaging style

(A) I only
(B) I and II only
(C) I and III only
(D) II and III only
(E) I, II and III

12. As it is used in line 95, the word "quarters"
most nearly means

(A) segments of society
(B) housing units
(C) postures
(D) criticisms
(E) mercies

13. The author of Passage 2 foresees that James
will be accused of "high treason" (line 95)
because he has

(A) suggested that Hawthorne is an
inferior author
(B) failed to acknowledge basic historical
facts
(C) criticized the American government
(D) mischaracterized certain Americans
(E) violated a federal law

GO ON TO THE NEXT PAGE →

8   8   8   8   8   8

14. The author of Passage 2 mentions the "Parisian" in line 107 primarily as an example of one who

(A) lacks sophistication
(B) would not appreciate The Scarlet Letter
(C) has not visited New England
(D) is widely regarded as being cosmopolitan
(E) is unfamiliar with Hawthorne's work

15. In the first two sentences of the second paragraph (lines 115–122), the author of Passage 2 criticizes James for

(A) showing bias toward American writers and against British writers
(B) maligning Hawthorne's writing style
(C) being insufficiently enthusiastic in his praise for Hawthorne
(D) focusing on Hawthorne's personal life rather than Hawthorne's work
(E) being too romantic

16. Which of the following best describes that attitude of the author of Passage 2 toward Nathaniel Hawthorne and his works?

(A) affectionate
(B) harshly critical
(C) mildly disapproving
(D) ambivalent
(E) incredulous

17. With which of the following statements about romance literature would the author of Passage 2 most likely agree?

(A) an international perspective enhances the quality of romances
(B) all romances are novels, but not all novels are romances
(C) the best romances reflect simple lifestyles, but not simple minds
(D) romance literature is inferior to poetry
(E) romance literature is intellectually challenging

18. The two authors differ in their evaluations of Hawthorne's journals primarily in that the author of Passage 1

(A) feels that they deserved to be published, while the author of Passage 2 does not
(B) feels that they have been unjustly criticized, while the author of Passage 2 feels that the criticisms are valid
(C) criticizes them for being too sophisticated, while the author of Passage 2 criticizes them for being too provincial
(D) praises them for their candidness, while the author of Passage 2 criticizes them for it
(E) suggests that they do not reflect Hawthorne's true genius, while the author of Passage 2 suggests that they do

19. How would the author of Passage 2 most likely respond to the statement in Passage 1 that Hawthorne's journals "show us one of the gentlest, lightest, and most leisurely of observers" (lines 46–47)?

(A) He would agree, and use this fact to criticize Hawthorne's style.
(B) He would disagree, and suggest that Hawthorne is in fact a very analytical observer.
(C) He would agree, and add that these are aspects of his genius.
(D) He would suggest that this fact is irrelevant to Hawthorne's work.
(E) He would suggest that this observation would apply to almost all American writing.

STOP

If you finish before time is called, you may check your work on this section only. Do not turn to any other section of the test.

9   9   9   9   9   9

SECTION 9
Time—10 minutes
14 questions

Turn to Section 9 of your answer sheet to answer the questions in this section.

Directions: For each question in this section, select the best answer from among the choices given and fill in the corresponding circle on the answer sheet.

The following sentences test correctness and effectiveness of expression. Part of each sentence or the entire sentence is underlined; beneath each sentence are five ways of phrasing the underlined material. Choice A repeats the original phrasing; the other four choices are different. Select the choice that completes the sentence most effectively.

In making your selection, follow the requirements of standard written English; that is, pay attention to grammar, choice of words, sentence construction, and punctuation. Your selection should result in the most effective sentence—clear and precise, without awkwardness or ambiguity.

EXAMPLE:

The children <u>couldn't hardly believe their eyes</u>.

(A) couldn't hardly believe their eyes
(B) could hardly believe their eyes
(C) would not hardly believe their eyes
(D) couldn't nearly believe their eyes
(E) couldn't hardly believe his or her eyes

1. Voters seem as interested in this <u>election, if not more so, than the last one.</u>

   (A) election, if not more so, than the last one
   (B) election as the last one, if not more so
   (C) election, if not more than, as the last one
   (D) election as it was for the last one, if not more so
   (E) election, if not more, than the last one

2. An indefatigable researcher as well as an engaging writer, <u>Tony Horwitz's book Blue Latitudes explores the journeys of James Cook.</u>

   (A) Tony Horwitz's book *Blue Latitudes* explores the journeys of James Cook
   (B) the book *Blue Latitudes* is where Tony Horwitz explores the journeys of James Cook
   (C) Tony Horwitz explores the journeys of James Cook in the book *Blue Latitudes*
   (D) Tony Horwitz explores the journeys, in the book *Blue Latitudes*, of James Cook
   (E) *Blue Latitudes*, a book by Tony Horwitz, explores the journeys of James Cook

3. His grade on the test <u>came as a surprise to Isaac, being since he had</u> studied so hard the previous night.

   (A) came as a surprise to Isaac, being since he had
   (B) came as a surprising fact for Isaac, being that he had
   (C) was surprising to Isaac for the fact that he had
   (D) surprised Isaac, especially because he had
   (E) surprised Isaac being that he had

GO ON TO THE NEXT PAGE

9 9 9 9 9 9

4. <u>As opposed to women during the industrial revolution</u>, the treatment of women in today's work force is close to being equitable, although there is still much progress to be made.

(A) As opposed to women during the industrial revolution
(B) Unlike the treatment of women during the industrial revolution
(C) Unlike women in the industrial revolution
(D) As compared to women and their treatment of the industrial revolution
(E) Unlike women's treatment of the industrial revolution

5. Finding a fulfilling second career is particularly important for former professional athletes, <u>most of them retire</u> from their first careers before they reach the age of forty.

(A) most of them retire
(B) although most of them retire
(C) most of whom retire
(D) while most of them retire
(E) but most of them retiring

6. Because the rules governing the behavior of electrons are so unlike any rules we commonly <u>experience is the reason why understanding</u> quantum physics is difficult.

(A) experience is the reason why understanding
(B) experience, understanding
(C) experience is why anyone's understanding
(D) experience, is why understanding
(E) experience, is the reason why to understand

7. Mark Twain's *Huckleberry Finn* is regarded not only as a classic of literature, <u>it is a scathing attack on</u> nineteenth century American society.

(A) it is a scathing attack on
(B) it attacks scathingly
(C) but it attacks scathingly
(D) but also as a scathing attack on
(E) but also it scathingly attacks

8. <u>Reading magazine advertisements carefully</u>, the writers seem more interested in impact than in correct grammatical form.

(A) Reading magazine advertisements carefully
(B) While we read magazine advertisements carefully
(C) Reading carefully the contents of magazine advertisements
(D) When you read magazine advertisements carefully
(E) As a careful reading of magazine advertisements demonstrates

9. The committee charged with finding a new chief executive wanted to find someone with a strong track record, a good reputation, and <u>someone with an ability to inspire the workers</u>.

(A) someone with an ability to inspire the workers
(B) they wanted someone to inspire the workers
(C) someone to inspire the workers
(D) an ability to be able to inspire the workers
(E) an ability to inspire the workers

GO ON TO THE NEXT PAGE ⟩

9   9   9   9   9   9

10. Nearly every summer afternoon, the park fills with the sounds of children who come to swim and play with their friends.

(A) Nearly every summer afternoon, the park fills with the sounds of children who come to swim and play with their friends.

(B) Coming to swim and play with their friends nearly every summer afternoon, the park fills with the sounds of children.

(C) The sounds of children fill the park nearly every summer afternoon, them coming to swim and play with their friends.

(D) Coming to swim and play with their friends, the park fills with the sounds of children nearly every summer afternoon.

(E) The park fills with the sounds of children nearly every summer afternoon, who come to swim and play with their friends.

11. The campaign was not as much fun as Eleanor had hoped, being pursued by the press and attacked by her opponent at almost every turn.

(A) had hoped, being
(B) hoped in the sense that she was
(C) had hoped: she was
(D) had hoped because of being
(E) hoped; she has been

12. The artificial reef, constructed to protect coral and other anemones, occupies a large portion of the inlet; but, therefore, obstructs the migration of larger fish and sea mammals.

(A) inlet; but, therefore, obstructs
(B) inlet and therefore obstructs
(C) inlet; thereby obstructing
(D) inlet but because of this obstructs
(E) inlet but therefore obstructing

13. Being accelerated by a rocket in space provides the same experience to an observer as if by gravity.

(A) if by gravity
(B) gravity
(C) by gravity
(D) being accelerated by gravity
(E) acceleration by gravity

14. When applying to graduate school, one should visit the schools in person, as the campus environment at one may differ vastly from another university.

(A) as the campus environment at one may differ vastly from another university

(B) since the campus environment may differ vastly from another university to this one

(C) because the campus environment may differ greatly from university to university

(D) because the campus environment is greatly different from one another

(E) as the campus environment at one may be vastly different from another university

STOP

If you finish before time is called, you may check your work on this section only. Do not turn to any other section of the test.

ANSWER KEY

Critical Reading

	Section 3					Section 6					Section 8			
	COR. ANS.	DIFF. LEV.		COR. ANS.	DIFF. LEV.	COR. ANS.	DIFF. LEV.		COR. ANS.	DIFF. LEV.	COR. ANS.	DIFF. LEV.		COR. ANS.	DIFF. LEV.

Section 3

	COR. ANS.	DIFF. LEV.		COR. ANS.	DIFF. LEV.
1.	C	1	13.	A	2
2.	A	1	14.	C	3
3.	E	2	15.	E	3
4.	D	3	16.	B	4
5.	B	4	17.	A	4
6.	C	4	18.	E	3
7.	E	4	19.	B	3
8.	B	5	20.	C	4
9.	C	2	21.	D	3
10.	C	3	22.	A	2
11.	E	3	23.	D	3
12.	B	4	24.	D	5

Number correct

Number incorrect

Section 6

	COR. ANS.	DIFF. LEV.		COR. ANS.	DIFF. LEV.
1.	C	2	13.	E	3
2.	D	2	14.	C	4
3.	E	3	15.	A	3
4.	C	3	16.	B	4
5.	A	4	17.	C	4
6.	B	3	18.	E	5
7.	C	3	19.	C	3
8.	D	2	20.	A	3
9.	E	3	21.	B	4
10.	C	2	22.	E	3
11.	D	4	23.	C	3
12.	A	5	24.	D	4

Number correct

Number incorrect

Section 8

	COR. ANS.	DIFF. LEV.		COR. ANS.	DIFF. LEV.
1.	A	1	11.	E	4
2.	C	2	12.	A	2
3.	C	3	13.	D	2
4.	E	4	14.	D	4
5.	C	5	15.	C	4
6.	E	5	16.	A	3
7.	B	2	17.	C	3
8.	B	4	18.	E	3
9.	E	4	19.	C	4
10.	A	3			

Number correct

Number incorrect

Math

Section 2

	COR. ANS.	DIFF. LEV.		COR. ANS.	DIFF. LEV.
1.	A	1	11.	E	3
2.	C	1	12.	D	3
3.	B	3	13.	C	3
4.	D	2	14.	B	4
5.	B	2	15.	E	3
6.	C	2	16.	B	4
7.	D	3	17.	C	4
8.	C	2	18.	D	4
9.	A	3	19.	A	5
10.	D	3	20.	A	5

Number correct

Number incorrect

Section 5

Multiple-Choice Questions

	COR. ANS.	DIFF. LEV.
1.	B	1
2.	D	2
3.	B	3
4.	C	3
5.	B	3
6.	A	4
7.	D	4
8.	E	5

Student-produced Response questions

	COR. ANS.	DIFF. LEV.
9.	80	1
10.	18	2
11.	116	3
12.	200	3
13.	18	3
14.	3	4
15.	17 or 19	3
16.	26/3 or 8.66 or 8.67	4
17.	27	5
18.	30	5

Number correct

Number incorrect

Number correct (9–18)

Section 7

	COR. ANS.	DIFF. LEV.		COR. ANS.	DIFF. LEV.
1.	D	2	9.	E	4
2.	D	2	10.	D	4
3.	E	2	11.	B	3
4.	C	3	12.	D	4
5.	A	3	13.	D	3
6.	C	3	14.	C	4
7.	D	3	15.	C	5
8.	B	3	16.	E	5

Number correct

Number incorrect

Writing

Section 4

	COR. ANS.	DIFF. LEV.		COR. ANS.	DIFF. LEV.		COR. ANS.	DIFF. LEV.		COR. ANS.	DIFF. LEV.
1.	C	1	11.	E	4	21.	C	3	31.	E	3
2.	B	1	12.	B	1	22.	D	4	32.	E	3
3.	B	2	13.	B	1	23.	E	3	33.	C	3
4.	A	3	14.	C	2	24.	A	4	34.	B	3
5.	D	4	15.	E	3	25.	B	3	35.	E	3
6.	E	2	16.	A	3	26.	D	3			
7.	A	3	17.	C	2	27.	A	4			
8.	A	4	18.	D	3	28.	C	4			
9.	C	4	19.	B	3	29.	B	5			
10.	C	3	20.	B	3	30.	B	3			

Number correct

Number incorrect

Section 9

	COR. ANS.	DIFF. LEV.		COR. ANS.	DIFF. LEV.
1.	B	1	11.	C	3
2.	C	2	12.	B	4
3.	D	2	13.	D	4
4.	B	2	14.	C	3
5.	C	2			
6.	B	2			
7.	D	3			
8.	E	3			
9.	E	3			
10.	A	3			

Number correct

Number incorrect

NOTE: Difficulty levels are estimates of question difficulty that range from 1 (easiest) to 5 (hardest).

SCORE CONVERSION TABLE

How to score your test

Use the answer key on the previous page to determine your raw score on each section. **Your raw score on each section except Section 4 is simply the number of correct answers minus ¼ of the number of wrong answers. On Section 4, your raw score is the sum of the number of correct answers for questions 1–8 minus ¼ of the number of wrong answers for questions 1–8 plus the total number of correct answers for questions 9–18.** Next, add the raw scores from Sections 3, 4, and 7 to get your Math raw score, add the raw scores from Sections 2, 5, and 8 to get your Critical Reading raw score and add the raw scores from Sections 6 and 9 to get your Writing raw score. Write the three raw scores here:

Raw Critical Reading score: _____ Raw Math score: _____ Raw Writing score: _____

Use the table below to convert these to scaled scores.

Scaled scores: Critical Reading: _____ Math: _____ Writing: _____

Raw Score	Critical Reading Scaled Score	Math Scaled Score	Writing Scaled Score	Raw Score	Critical Reading Scaled Score	Math Scaled Score	Writing Scaled Score
67	800			32	520	570	610
66	800			31	510	560	600
65	790			30	510	550	580
64	780			29	500	540	570
63	770			28	490	530	560
62	750			27	490	520	550
61	740			26	480	510	540
60	730			25	480	500	530
59	720			24	470	490	520
58	700			23	460	480	510
57	690			22	460	480	500
56	680			21	450	470	490
55	670			20	440	460	480
54	660	800		19	440	450	470
53	650	800		18	430	450	460
52	650	780		17	420	440	450
51	640	760		16	420	430	440
50	630	740		15	410	420	440
49	620	730	800	14	400	410	430
48	620	710	800	13	400	410	420
47	610	710	800	12	390	400	410
46	600	700	790	11	380	390	400
45	600	690	780	10	370	380	390
44	590	680	760	9	360	370	380
43	590	670	740	8	350	360	380
42	580	660	730	7	340	350	370
41	570	650	710	6	330	340	360
40	570	640	700	5	320	330	350
39	560	630	690	4	310	320	340
38	550	620	670	3	300	310	320
37	550	620	660	2	280	290	310
36	540	610	650	1	270	280	300
35	540	600	640	0	250	260	280
34	530	590	630	−1	230	240	270
33	520	580	620	−2 or less	210	220	250

CONVERSION TABLE FOR WRITING COMPOSITE
[ESSAY + MULTIPLE CHOICE]

Calculate your writing raw score as you did on the previous page and grade your essay from a 1 to a 6 according to the standards that follow in the detailed answer key. Essay score: _____ Raw Writing score: _____

Use the table below to convert these to scaled scores.

Scaled scores: Writing _____

Raw Score	Essay Score 0	Essay Score 1	Essay Score 2	Essay Score 3	Essay Score 4	Essay Score 5	Essay Score 6
−2 or less	200	230	250	280	310	340	370
−1	210	240	260	290	320	360	380
0	230	260	280	300	340	370	400
1	240	270	290	320	350	380	410
2	250	280	300	330	360	390	420
3	260	290	310	340	370	400	430
4	270	300	320	350	380	410	440
5	280	310	330	360	390	420	450
6	290	320	340	360	400	430	460
7	290	330	340	370	410	440	470
8	300	330	350	380	410	450	470
9	310	340	360	390	420	450	480
10	320	350	370	390	430	460	490
11	320	360	370	400	440	470	500
12	330	360	380	410	440	470	500
13	340	370	390	420	450	480	510
14	350	380	390	420	460	490	520
15	350	380	400	430	460	500	530
16	360	390	410	440	470	500	530
17	370	400	420	440	480	510	540
18	380	410	420	450	490	520	550
19	380	410	430	460	490	530	560
20	390	420	440	470	500	530	560
21	400	430	450	480	510	540	570
22	410	440	460	480	520	550	580
23	420	450	470	490	530	560	590
24	420	460	470	500	540	570	600
25	430	460	480	510	540	580	610
26	440	470	490	520	550	590	610
27	450	480	500	530	560	590	620
28	460	490	510	540	570	600	630
29	470	500	520	550	580	610	640
30	480	510	530	560	590	620	650
31	490	520	540	560	600	630	660
32	500	530	550	570	610	640	670
33	510	540	550	580	620	650	680
34	510	550	560	590	630	660	690
35	520	560	570	600	640	670	700
36	530	560	580	610	650	680	710
37	540	570	590	620	660	690	720
38	550	580	600	630	670	700	730
39	560	600	610	640	680	710	740
40	580	610	620	650	690	720	750
41	590	620	640	660	700	730	760
42	600	630	650	680	710	740	770
43	610	640	660	690	720	750	780
44	620	660	670	700	740	770	800
45	640	670	690	720	750	780	800
46	650	690	700	730	770	800	800
47	670	700	720	750	780	800	800
48	680	720	730	760	800	800	800
49	680	720	730	760	800	800	800

Detailed Answer Key

Section 1

The following essay received 12 points out of a possible 12, meaning that it demonstrates *clear and consistent competence* in that it

- develops an insightful point of view on the topic
- demonstrates exemplary critical thinking
- uses effective examples, reasons, and other evidence to support its thesis
- is consistently focused, coherent, and well-organized
- demonstrates skillful and effective use of language and sentence structure
- is largely (but not necessarily completely) free of grammatical and usage errors

Consider the following statement:

> *All art is a lie, and all art is the truth. The beholder determines which.*

Assignment: **Do artistic endeavours such as music, painting and drama enhance our understanding of reality or provide escape from reality?** Write an essay in which you agree or disagree with the statement above, using an example or examples from history, politics, literature, the arts, current events, or your experience or observation.

SAMPLE STUDENT ESSAY

For centuries, aestheticians and common people alike have wondered about the nature of art. Most of us haven't formulated a philosophical definition of art, but we "know it when we see it." Although this does not constitute a formal definition of art, it indicates an important aspect of art: it must have a significant impact on the viewer (or reader or listener). Of course, any particular painting, or book, or piece of music, no matter how well-crafted, is not likely to have the same impact on all who experience it. Thus, it may be art for some but not for others; it has meaning or "truth" for some, but not for others. In this regard, all art is a lie, and all art is the truth.

Art that is "a lie" is art that does not "ring true," that is, it does not resonate with our beings. I remember taking a trip into Manhattan to visit the Metropolitan Museum of Art with my parents when I was ten years old. My father wanted us to see the ancient artifacts of the Greek and Mesopotamian civilizations. We had to pass huge colorful paintings of gallant men on horses and vibrant depictions of battle to get to the musty motionless stone statues of heads. None of the heads, it seemed, smiled. They didn't welcome us, they didn't want us to be there. These may have been "true" depictions of ancient heads, but to me they were a lie; they did not resonate in my soul.

The oil paintings in the upstairs galleries were a different story, though. Although my sophisticated 10 year-old brain told me that knights almost certainly did not carry their armor so lightly, that the clouds did not gleam so brightly above them, and that their horses could not have been so spotless and majestic, somehow they were nevertheless "true." They communicated to me. They told me that the people of 18th century Europe valued gallantry and adventure and romance, even if they may not have experienced it as vividly as these paintings suggested. They put me in touch with a people, if only in terms of their ideals and not their reality. The motionless, lifeless heads and torsos in the basements communicated nothing to me.

As we were eating ten-dollar sandwiches in the museum cafeteria, my dad said "It gives me chills to see those ancient statues and think about the artisans who carved them three or four thousand years ago. I feel like I'm touching one of those ancient Mesopotamians himself when I touch those statues." I knew he wasn't just saying that for my sake or my brother's sake. He really felt that way. The statues were "the truth" to him. A few years later, when I studied Greek civilization with a great teacher, I began to appreciate my father's words. But when I was ten, those statues were a lie.

The following essay received 10 points out of a possible 12, meaning that it demonstrates *adequate competence* in that it

- develops a point of view on the topic
- demonstrates some critical thinking, but perhaps not consistently
- uses some examples, reasons, and other evidence to support its thesis, but perhaps not adequately
- shows a general organization and focus, but shows occasional lapses in this regard
- demonstrates adequate but occasionally inconsistent facility with language
- contains occasional errors in grammar, usage, and mechanics

SAMPLE STUDENT ESSAY

Every work of art reveals some degree of truth about the artist. The choice of subject matter, the arrangement of the parts, the use of color, and so on, tell us perhaps more about who created the art than what the art is about. On the other hand, it is true that no piece of art can capture the whole truth.

A good example of a great work of art is the Mona Lisa. It is considered great perhaps not only because it conveys a great truth about beauty, but because it also leaves so much unsaid for the viewer to interpret. Who is this woman? What is her relationship with the artist? What does her elusive smile mean?

Leonardo Da Vinci perhaps left such questions unanswered because he wanted to "hide" something, so perhaps in that sense the work is a "lie." But is that such a bad thing? The challenge of interpretation and discovering some answers to questions that may not be perfectly answerable is one of the great challenges of appreciating art. Also, perhaps that is one of its greatest pleasures.

What makes any piece of art—a painting, a sculpture, a building, a piece of music—truly great is not it's ability to "reveal" a great truth but to merely hint at a greater beauty beyond the surface. Great music, like Beethoven's Ninth Symphony, take the listener to new places. It almost doesn't matter whether these new places are "true" or not, but just that they take us there.

The following essay received 2 points out of a possible 12, meaning that it demonstrates *some incompetence* in that it

- has a seriously limited point of view
- demonstrates weak critical thinking
- uses inappropriate or insufficient examples, reasons, and other evidence to support its thesis
- is poorly focused and organized, and has serious problems with coherence
- demonstrates frequent problems with language and sentence structure
- contains errors in grammar and usage that obscure the author's meaning

SAMPLE STUDENT ESSAY

I don't know how you could say that all art is the truth and all art is a lie at the same time. It's saying two completely different things! What I think is that all art is fake basically. It doesn't really show the world like it is it only shows the way one guy sees it. People who are just artists don't always get out and see what is going on in the world, instead they spend a lot of time by themselves doing there art.

So maybe it isn't a lie but it isn't the truth because its just what one person thinks. A painting of someone sitting on a chair doesn't look exactly like her. Also, the amount of money people pay for some paintings is ridiculous. A lot of the paintings that sell for millions of dollars look like things that I could do easy. It makes me angry to think that some people can throw paint on a canvas in a couple of minutes and then have somebody pay them millions of dollars for it.

Section 2

1. A
$$(x - y) = -2.$$
$$3(x - y)(x - y)(x - y) =$$
Plug in: $3(-2)(-2)(-2) = -24$

---

2. C   What is 40% of $20w$?
Write equation: $x = 0.40(20w)$
Simplify: $x = 8w$

---

3. B Notice that whenever an x-value increases by 1, the corresponding y-value increases by 4. This means that the "slope" of the linear equation is 4. This suggests that choice (B) is best, but you should plug in to check:

(A) $y = x + 7$
Plug in 3 for x: $y = 3 + 7 = 10$ OK
Plug in 4 for x: $y = 4 + 7 = 11$ NO
(B) $y = 4x - 2$
Plug in 3 for x: $y = 12 - 2 = 10$ OK
Plug in 4 for x: $y = 16 - 2 = 14$ OK
Plug in 5 for x: $y = 20 - 2 = 18$ OK
Plug in 6 for x: $y = 24 - 2 = 22$ OK
So (B) is clearly best!

---

4. D

```
    30      50      30
●──────●──────●──────●
W      X      Y      Z
```

You are told that $XY = 50$ and that WY is 30 more than that. Therefore $WY = 80$, which means that $WX = 30 = YZ$. Therefore $XZ = 50 + 30 = 80$.

---

5. B Segments AG, BD, EG, and AE are each diagonals of a face of the cube, but BE goes through the center of the cube and is longer than the others.

---

6. C $3^{y+4} = 81$
$$3^4 = 81$$
$$3^4 = 3^{y+4}$$
Remove bases: $4 = y + 4$
Subtract 4: $y = 0$

---

7. D Starting with quadrilateral at the bottom of the figure, solve for one the unmarked angle using the fact that there are 360° in a quadrilateral:
$$80° + 80° + 120° + \omega = 360°$$
Combine like terms: $280° + \omega = 360°$
Subtract 280°: $\omega = 80°$

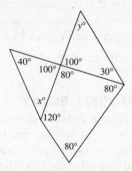

Since linear pairs have a sum of 180°, the two triangles contain angles of 100°.

There are 180° in a triangle: $x + 40 + 100 = 180$
Combine like terms: $x + 140 = 180$
Subtract 140°: $x = 40$

There are 180° in a triangle: $y + 30 + 100 = 180$
Combine like terms: $y + 130 = 180$
Subtract 130°: $y = 50$
                        $x + y = 40 + 50 = 90$

---

8. C If neither a not b is 0, then ab cannot possibly equal 0, hence statement I is true. This eliminates choice (B). Since $a > b$, then $a - b$ must be positive. (Try a few examples with positive and negative numbers to convince yourself that this is true.) Therefore, statement II is true. This eliminates choices (A) and (D). Notice that a could equal 3 and b could equal -1, and so $a \div b$ could equal -3. So, statement III is false, leaving choice (C).

---

9. A The closest the two towns can be to each other is $9 - 6 = 3$ miles. The farthest apart the two towns can be from each other is $9 + 6 = 15$ miles.

10. D If the perimeter of the solid-line figure is 100, then each side is $100 \div 10 = 10$ units long. If the pentagon has a perimeter of 60, then each of its sides is $60 \div 5 = 12$ units long. The altitude of one of the triangles, shown below, is one leg of a right triangle with a leg of 6 and hypotenuse of 10. You can find h, then, with the Pythagorean Theorem: $h^2 + 6^2 = 10^2$. This gives $h = 8$. So each triangle has a base of 12 and height of 8, so it has an area of $(1/2)(12)(8) = 48$.

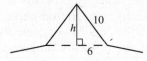

11. E The sum is 71:

The sum is 71:	$x + y = 71$
One is 2 + half the other:	$x = 2 + 0.5y$
Substitute for x:	$2 + 0.5y + y = 71$
Combine like terms:	$2 + 1.5y = 71$
Subtract 2:	$1.5y = 69$
Divide by 1.5:	$y = 46$

Since the sum is 71, the other number must be $71 - 46 = 25$, and the larger number is 46.

12. D A good diagram makes it clear:

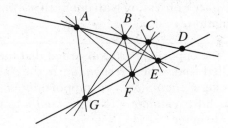

There are nine possible paths.

13. C There are 8 even integers between 2 and 16, inclusive: 2, 4, 6, 8, 10, 12, 14 and 16.

Solve:	$3w - 2 > 28$
Add 2:	$3w > 30$
Divide by 3:	$w > 10$

There are only three integers in the set greater than 10, so the fraction is 3/8.

14. B First solve for b: b is 20% greater than 400:
$$b = 1.20(400) = 480$$
Next solve for a: a is 20 percent less than b
$$a = 0.80(b) = 0.80(480) = 384$$
$$b - a = 480 - 384 = 96$$

15. E

	$m = n(n - 3)$
Multiply by -3:	$-3m = -3n(n - 3)$
Distribute:	$-3m = -3n^2 + 9n$
Rearrange:	$-3m = 9n - 3n^2$

16. B Don't try to find the area of the triangle directly (with $A = (1/2)bh$), because finding the base and height is too much work. Instead, find it *indirectly*: find the area of the rectangle and subtract the areas of the three "surrounding" triangles. The area of the rectangle $= (8)(4) = 32$. The area of $\triangle BEF = \frac{1}{2}(4)(2) = 4$. The area of $\triangle FCD = \frac{1}{2}(4)(4) = 8$. The area of $EAD = \frac{1}{2}(8)(2) = 8$. Therefore the area of $\triangle EFD = 32 - 4 - 8 - 8 = 12$.

17. C Eight consecutive odd integers can be represented as: $x, x + 2, x + 4, x + 6, x + 8, x + 10, x + 12$ and $x + 14$.
You can find their average with the formula:

$$\frac{x + (x + 2) + (x + 4) + (x + 6) + (x + 8) + (x + 10) + (x + 12) + (x + 14)}{8}$$

Combine like terms:	$\dfrac{8x + 56}{8}$
Simplify:	$x + 7$

18. D To get the largest possible value of a, you must make the other angles as *small* as possible. The smallest possible value of b is 21°, and, because $c > b$, the smallest possible value of c is 22°. There are 180° in a triangle, so set up an equation to find the largest possible value of a:

	$a + b + c = 180°$
Plug in for b and c:	$a + 21° + 22° = 180°$
Combine like terms:	$a + 43° = 180°$
Subtract 43°:	$a = 137°$

19. **A**   Set up and solve: $\dfrac{4}{v} + w = 6$

Subtract : w $\dfrac{4}{v} = 6 - w$

Divide by 4: $\dfrac{1}{v} = \dfrac{6 - w}{4}$

Take reciprocal of both sides: $v = \dfrac{4}{6 - w}$

20. **A**   The radius, r, of the arc that the tip traces is 4 inches. So in one full hour the minute hand traces an arc equal to the full circumference of the circle.

$$C = 2\pi r$$
Plug in for r: $C = 2\pi(4) = 8\pi$

Each hour, the tip of the minute hand moves 8π inches. From 2:40 to 7:10 is $5^1/_2$ hours, so in that time the tip traces an arc of $(5.5)8\pi = 36\pi$ inches. Since there are 12 inches in a foot, this distance is $36\pi \div 12 = 3\pi$ feet.

Section 3

1. **C**   The word *but* indicates a contrast. *Contemporaries* are individuals that live in the same time period. *Naive assumptions* are ignorant, and so may be *mocked*. The *acceptance* of his *contempraries* would contrast the *lack of acceptance* today. *ridicule* = to make fun of; *corroborate* = to support; *affiliate* = to associate with; *mock* = to make fun of.

2. **A**   The word *although* indicates contrast. The rebels' *ferocity* will help their cause, but they are also *undisciplined*, a fact which will lead to their defeat. the missing word must go with *undisciplined*. *haphazard* = random, without form; *spartan* = disciplined; *apathetic* = lacking concern

3. **E**   The crews would be better able to help others after the massive rains and winds had *stopped*. The storm's *wrath* (fury) would "hurt" those in its path. *subside* = to settle down; *enthrall* = to thrill, *ebb* = to weaken; *compound* = to make worse; *masticate* = to chew; *abate* = to reduce in amount; *afflicted* = harmed.

4. **D**   The *wide variety of styles* suggests that her collection is *diverse*. *repugnant* = disgusting; *negligent* = lacking care; *banal* = boring, common; *eclectic* = of a wide variety; *incompetent* = lacking skill.

5. **B**   Blake's personality is not an ideal fit for a therapist because he cannot *provide a stabilizing influence* on his patients. This suggests that he is *irritable* and easily *riled* up. *cantankerous* = cranky; *placate* = to calm; *irascible* = easily angered; *riled* = upset; *equanimous* = even tempered; *infuriated* = angered; *euphoric* = full of joy; *provoked* = riled up, bothered; *choleric* = easily angered; *assuaged* = soothed.

6. **C**   The host was *taken aback* (surprised) by the demeanor of his guest. It was unusual for him to be so *harshly accosted* (attacked). The missing word should mean something like *confrontational*. *jocular* = joking; *congenial* = polite, friendly; *impudent* = bold, rude; *urbane* = polite; *erudite* = learned.

7. **E**   *Overcoming cancer* to win championships requires a large amount of determination. *perspicacity* = the ability to sense what others are feeling. *magnanimity* = generosity; *delirium* = a state of mental confusion; *vanity* = obsession with one's self; *pertinacity* = determination.

8. **B**   The opposing party suggested that the senator had lied, and so he is *responding to* the claims by his attackers. *champion* = to support; *impugn* = to attack as false; *emulate* = to copy; *laud* = to praise; *concur* = to agree

9. **C**   The narrator refers to *my son Semu* (line 6) and the quote in lines 13–14 makes it clear that Na-ne is the narrator's dead brother. Therefore Na-ne is Semu's uncle.

10. **C**   The first line makes it clear that Na-ne is absent, and perhaps has died. Therefore the quote in lines 13-14 addresses an absent person.

11. **E**   The passage states that before the *new reality*, some with the *power to act* had *elaborate theories that the poor were ... happy in their condition* (lines 4–5).

12. **B**   The passage states that *pressures ... on the fragile balance of our planet's ecosystem are compelling the rich. To take greater interest* in the poor and their *destructive use of crop lands, forests and watersheds* (lines 8–17).

13. A The narrator describes his task as *senseless nothing* (line 5), indicating that he regards his task with scorn or disdain.

14. C The paragraph indicates that his superiors are interested only in the *number* that the narrator presents to them, and this number represents the number of people who have crossed the bridge.

15. E The narrator says of his superiors that *the future perfect is their specialty* (line 42) *after having stated that they figure out ... how many people will have crossed the bridge in ten years* (line 40). This last statement, which uses the future-perfect tense, refers to his superior's need to use the current Numbers to predict future numbers. This task is called *extrapolation*.

16. B In saying that he *was a lynx-eyed devil*, the narrator says that *no speedometer could do better*, meaning that he counted accurately and quickly.

17. A In saying that the difference between their two counts really makes no odds, the chief statistician is saying that it does not matter. That is it makes no real difference because they allow for a *certain margin of error* (line 83).

18. E The purpose of the passage is to discuss various definitions of art, like *technical ability* (line 6) of artisans, the *product of such skillful execution* (line 10), *what artists create* (line 17), the *expression of emotion* (lines 56–57), and so on.

19. B The *extension* refers to the fact that a ceramic pot (an object) can be considered art because it is the result of *skillful execution* (line 10). therefore this refers to a connection between a skill and an object.

20. C The first parargaph suggests that, while earlier definitions of art focused on *technical ability* (line 6), the *currently popular* notion of art is that art is *what artists create* (line 7).

21. D In saying that *some items and activities in our environment... are somehow more artistic than others*, the author is saying that it is often hard to explain why some things seem beautiful to our senses.

22. A The *ancient, encompassing definition of art* (lines 23–24) defines art *as products and activities skillfully done*. The *ancient Greek definition of aesthetic* (lines 68–70), however, focuses on *sensuous perception*, emphasizing the experiences of the viewer.

23. D According to this theory, *major art institutions ...determine what is and what is not art* (lines 97–98).

24. D In referring to a *fixed definition of art* (line 104), the author is contrasting a theory *that evolves* (line 105). Therefore, *fixed* means *not evolving*.

Section 4

1. C The phrase that follows *is* should be logically and grammatically equivalent to *activity*, like *the swimming*.

2. B Choice B provides the most concise, yet logically parallel, alternative.

3. B The original sentence does not show the logical relationship between the ideas. Choice B shows the most logical relationship and contains a logical sequence of tenses.

4. A The sentence is correct. The sentence begins with a **participial phrase**, which must be followed by the subject of the participle, which is *Jane*.

5. D The two ideas contrast each other, and so require a contrasting conjunction. Also, the correct **idiom** is *happy to see*, not *happy in seeing*.

6. E The original sentence is not **parallel**. The phrase *not only A but also B* requires that *A* and *B* be in the same grammatical form.

7. A The sentence is correct.

8. A The sentence is correct. It contains the clearest verb and the least awkward phrasing.

9. C The pronoun *which* in the original sentence has an unclear antecedent. Choices (B) and (D) misuse the semicolon, and choice (E) contains a **comma splice**.

10. C The ideas must be joined with a contrasting conjunction, and the tense sequence must be logical. Choice (C) shows correct temporal and logical sequencing.

11. E   The original phrasing is wordy, awkward, and vague. Choice (E) is the most concise and clear.

12. B   The phrase *usually never* is **illogical**, because *usually* and *never* are logically exclusive terms. The word *usually* should be eliminated.

13. B   The pronoun *it* is singular, but its **antecedent**, *bombs*, is plural. The pronoun should be *they*.

14. C   This verb tense, the past perfect, requires a **past participle**. The past participle of the verb *to take* is *taken*.

15. E   The sentence is correct.

16. A   This verb is in the **past perfect** tense, but it should not be, because it refers to an action that occurred at the same time as the *gun sounded*, and so should be in the **simple past** tense: *began*. (Chapter 18, Lesson 9)

17. C   The verb *are* is conjugated for a plural subject, but its subject is *effort*, which is singular. The verb should be changed to *is*.

18. D   This is an incorrect **idiom**. The correct idiom is *desire to eat*.

19. B   This is an **inverted sentence**, in which the subject comes after the verb. The subject of the verb *was* is *Blue Ridge Mountains*, which is a plural subject. Therefore the verb should be *were*.

20. B   This is an incorrect **parallel form**. The correct form is *neither A nor B*.

21. C   This is an incorrect **idiom**. The correct idiom is *voiced concerns **about***.

22. D   This is an **illogical comparison**. The *ability of insects* is not the same kinds of things as *whales*. this should be changed to *the ability of whales*.

23. E   The sentence is correct.

24. A   The word *I* is a pronoun in the **improper case**. Since it is the object of a preposition, *of*, it should be in the **objective case**, *me*.

25. B   The subject of this verb is *investment*, which is singular. Therefore, the verb should be *is*.

26. D   This is a **diction error**. *Imminent* means *likely to happen soon*, but *eminent* means *well-known and well-respected*.

27. A   The **antecedent** of these pronouns is *students*. The pronoun should therefore be plural: *them*.

28. C   This is an **illogical comparison**. The *fingerprints* cannot logically match the *defendant*, but rather the *defendant's fingerprints*.

29. B   This is an **improper idiom**. One is *affected **by*** things rather than *affected about* them.

30. B   Choice (B) provides the most logical, concise and clear phrasing.

31. E   Choice (E) provides the most logical, concise and clear phrasing.

32. E   Sentence 8 is not logically related to the topic of the paragraph, which is the meaning of sports and the idolization of sports figures in the United States.

33. C   Choice (C) provides the most logical, concise and clear phrasing.

34. B   Choice (B) provides the most logical transition from the previous sentence, which discusses particular *skills* related to both sports and hunting.

35. E   Choice (E) provides the most parallel and logical comparison with *our need to play sports*.

Section 5

1. B

	$a/3 = b/2$
Substitute $a = 36$:	$36/3 = b/2$
Simplify:	$12 = b/2$
Multiply by 2:	$24 = b$

2. D

	$2c + d = 9.25$
Multiply by 3:	$6c + 3d = 27.75$
Add 3:	$6c + 3d + 3 = 30.75$

3. B   The fact that the vertex of the triangle has coordinates $(6, m)$ means that the triangle has a base of 6 and a height of m. Use the formula *area* $= (1/2)bh$

Substitute:	$12 = (1/2)m(6)$
Simplify:	$12 = 3m$
Divide by 3	$4 = m$

4. C The seven possible combinations: 1) just pepperoni, 2) just mushrooms, 3) just meatballs, 4) pepperoni and mushroom, 5) pepperoni and meatballs, 6) meatballs and mushroom, 7) all 3.

5. B If the length of a rectangle is l and its width is w, then its perimeter is $2l + 2w$. If the perimeter is 5 times the width, then

$$2l + 2w = 5w$$

Subtract $2w$: $2l = 3w$

Divide by 2: $l = 1.5w$

6. A $16^{w+2} = 2^{11}$

Notice that 16 is equal to 2^4: $(2^4)^{w+2} = 2^{11}$

Simplify: $(2)^{4w+8} = 2^{11}$

Equate exponents: $4w + 8 = 11$

Subtract 8: $4w = 3$

Divide by 4: $w = 3/4$ or 0.75

7. D In a parallelogram, consecutive angles must be supplementary. Therefore, if the angle at B is $x°$, the angles at A and C are each $180–x°$. Since the angle at A is bisected, it is divided into two angles each with measure $90 – \frac{1}{2}x°$.

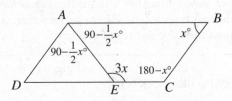

Now you can use the fact that the sum of the angles in a quadrilateral is 360°. In quadrilateral $ABCE$,

$$x + (180–x) + 3x + (90 – \tfrac{1}{2}x) = 360$$

Simplify: $2.5x + 270 = 360$

Subtract 270: $2.5x = 90$

Divide by 2.5: $x = 36$

8. E Since the width of the rectangle is 75% as long as the length, $w = .75l$. The perimeter, then, is $l + l + .75l + .75l = 3.5l$. $3.5l = 84$

Divide by 3.5: $l = 24$

Find the width: $w = (.75)(24) = 18$

Now you can find the diagonal of the rectangle with the Pythagorean Theorem: $d^2 = 18^2 + 24^2$

Simplify: $d^2 = 900$

Take the square root: $d = 30$

Therefore the diagonal of the circle is 30, and its radius is $30/2 = 15$. The area of the circle, then, is $\pi(15)^2 = 225\pi$.

9. 80 Recall the *formula distance = rate × time*.

Substitute: $100 \text{ miles} = 75 \text{ mph} \times time$

Divide by 75 mph: $4/3 \text{ hours} = time$

Convert: $4/3 \text{ hours} \times 60 \text{ min/hr} = 80 \text{ minutes}$

10. 18 $|3x – 53| < 1.2$

Translate: $-1.2 < 3x – 53 < 1.2$

Add 53: $51.8 < 3x < 54.2$

Divide by 3: $17.3 < x < 18.1$

The only integer in that range is 18.

11. 116 If the average of five numbers is 30, then their sum must be $5 \times 30 = 150$. To maximize one of these numbers, you must minimize the sum of the other four. If they are all *different integers*, and the least of them is 7, then the least possible sum of four of these numbers is $7 + 8 + 9 + 10$. To find the greatest value,

$$7 + 8 + 9 + 10 + x = 150$$

Simplify: $34 + x = 150$

Subtract 34: $x = 116$

12. 200 If the ratio of girls to boys is 8:5, then (since the "whole" is $8 + 5 = 13$) girls are 8/13 of the class and boys are 5/13 of the class. The total number of boys, then is 5/13 of $520 = 200$.

13. 18 The volume of a rectangular solid is given by the formula *volume* $= l \times w \times h$. Since the width of this box is 1.5 and its volume is 27, then $27 = (1.5)(l \times h)$

Divide by 1.5: $18 = l \times h$

This formula, $l \times h$, gives the area of the shaded face.

14. 3 Perhaps the simplest approach is to assume that the price of stock B is $100. If the price of stock B is 35% greater than the price of stock B to start, then stock A starts at $135. If the price of stock A doubles, then it ends up at $2 \times \$135 = \$270$. If the price of stock B decreases by 10%, it ends up at $(0.9)(\$100) = \$90$. $270/90 = 3$, so stock A ends up at 3 times the price of stock B.

15. 17 or 19 Here, the key is noticing that the $2a°$ angle is an "exterior" angle to the triangle on the left, and so is equal to the sum of the two "remote interior" angles.

Therefore	$2a = 3b + 3b$
Simplify:	$2a = 6b$
Divide by 2:	$a = 3b$

Since the problem states that a and b are integers, this means that a is a multiple of 3. Since the problem also states that a is odd and between 50 and 60, the only possibilities for a are 51 and 57.

16. 26/3 or 8.66 or 8.67 A geometric sequence is one in which each term is calculated by multiplying the previous term by some constant. The problem states that $L = a + 1 + 3$, and $M = b + 3 + 1$. If these are both geometric sequences, then in the first sequence, we are multiplying by 3, and in the second sequence, we are multiplying by 1/3. Therefore, you can calculate to find the missing terms: $L = 1/3 + 1 + 3$ and $M = 9 + 3 + 1$. So $M - L = 13 - 4\ 1/3 = 8\ 2/3$ which is 26/3 or 8.666 . . .

17. 27 If the range of $y = f(x)$ is all real numbers between –1 and 12, inclusive, then its greatest possible value is 12. The graph of the function $y = f(x–1)$ is simply the graph of $y = f(x)$ "shifted right" 1 unit. This means that the range of y values remains the same, and the maximum value is still 12. Finding the maximum value of $g(x) = 2f(x–1) + 3$ is a tiny bit trickier, but just involves substituting 12 as the maximum value for $f(x–1)$. This gives $2(12) + 3 = 27$.

18. 30 $20 < x < 30$
Choose x to be a number very close to 30, like 29.9. This means $5x = 149.5$ and $4x = 119.6$. Therefore #$5x = 148$ and #$4x = 118$, and $148 – 118 = 30$.

Section 6

1. C The ability to *reflect on past experiences* is called *hindsight* or *retrospection. vagueness* = lack of clarity; *misconceptions* = erroneous ideas; *hindsight* = ability to reflect on past experiences; *antagonism* = personal dislike; *premonitions* = predictions

2. D *Elaborate plumage and energetic dances* are examples of *showy* displays; but if they are used by males who are not chosen as mates, they are *pointless. carnivorous* = meat-eating; *ostentatious* = showy; *futile* = having no effect; *passive* = not active

3. E the passage states that these are *entertaining stories*, but the fact that they are *disjointed* would detract from the *cohesiveness* of the story. *pluralities* = multitudes; *implausibility* = incredibleness; *missives* = written letters; *frivolity* = lack of seriousness; *treatises* = formal written analyses; *vignettes* = humorous or telling stories; *cohesiveness* = focus, lack of digression

4. C If *fast* horses are *hard to control*, then *slower* horses would be relatively *easy to control. nimble* = quick and flexible; *irascible* = easily angered; *tractable* = easy to control; *recalcitrant* = stubborn

5. A A *greater oversight* is an *increase in vigilance*. If this requires funds, then not providing them would be a *critical flaw. appropriate* = to set aside for a specific purpose; *vigilance* = watchfulness; *empathy* = deep sympathy; *embezzle* = steal from one's employer; *sequester* = to place in isolation; *industry* = diligent, productive work

6. B The passage says that Einstein found fame *incomprehensible*, but that Chaplin was *worldly-wise*, and Chaplin's response to Einstein demonstrates that he understands the nature of celebrity.

7. C Einstein's question is asking why people are treating him like a celebrity.

8. D This sentence summarizes something that *traditional codes of medical ethics ... emphasize* (lines 1–2). therefore it comes from a long-established tenet.

9. E The passage states that these attitudes are reflected in discussions that *speak more and more about the moral rights of patients* (lines 14–15).

10. C The first paragraph states that we do such a disagreeable thing as arguing because we want to *make good decisions* (line 5), or act judiciously.

11. D The purpose of the passage as a whole is to answer the questions in the first paragraph, which pertain to the purpose of argumentation. The questions in the second paragraph, however, are examples of questions that might help someone to explore a particular issue, but which are not answered in this passage.

12. A The purpose of the passage as a whole is to discuss the different purposes of argumentation. The second paragraph describes arguing as *an opportunity to explore and probe ... claims*. The third paragraph describes the ability of an argument to *persuade others*.

13. E *Polly Politician* is described as using *"hedge Words"* which render her claims very vague. This is also called *equivocation*, which is a failure to make definitive statements.

14. C The *arguments* mentioned in the third paragraph are *situations (in which) we do not have the opportunity to reply*, unlike those in the fifth paragraph, in which *someone presenting us with a position expects either assent or disagreement*, and also expects us to *explain* our position. The latter Arguments are dialogues, while the former are one-sided.

15. A The analogy is used to liken an informal argument with *a friendly game of tennis*, and the *outrageous maneuvers* are intended to parallel novel methods of making a persuasive point.

16. B This paragraph refutes the misconception that one should never argue about religion or politics (lines 80–81) by explaining why doing so helps us to avoid problems.

17. C In saying that a frame of mind *took him before or during a climb* (line 24), the author means that it *overcame* him.

18. E The statement *we read … every scrap* conveys the idea that they eagerly awaited every bit of news that came to them about Mallory's expedition.

19. C The narrator mentions in the previous paragraph (line 29) that the expedition was in Tibet, which is where Mount Everest is located. In the dream, however, the expedition headquarters was in Switzerland. the narrator restates the absurdity of this aspect of her dream in line 79, where she refers to the absurd setting of the dream, and particularly that the headquarters was in a Swiss town. (An inconsequence is something that does not follow logically.)

20. A Mallory's attitude is said to be characterized by *a strange mixture of reverence and what I can only call rapture* (line 63). These clearly express a feeling of awe.

21. B When the author says that she is *too accustomed to the inconsequent dottiness of dreams* (lines 83–84), she is saying that she knows too well that dreams can have very silly elements in them, but this quality is *inconsequent* because she *could not comfort (herself)* (line 78) with the thought that it was a dream, and was still *frightened ... terribly* (line 64).

22. E The first reference to a *fortnight (two weeks)* mentions that it took about that long for information about the expedition to reach the author. The second reference mentions that she received notice of George's death one fortnight after her dream, suggesting that her dream and his death may have occurred at about the same time.

23. C This sentence states that the author *cannot believe* that George did not reach the summit, because she had climbed with him before and was confident of his skill.

24. D The passage as a whole focuses on the narrator's relationship with George Mallory, who was killed on Mount Everest. The narrator mentions that her daughter was George's godchild (line 109) and therefore had a special connection to Mallory.

Section 7

1. D Just combine like terms:
$(x + 4) + (2x - 3) + 6 + (3x + 4) = 6x + 11$

2. D To find the total amount, find the product of those two numbers: $\$3.00 \times 5,400 = \$16,200$

3. E The container contains 2 pints of water. Since there are 2 cups in 1 pint, it contains $2 \times 2 = 4$ cups. Since there are 16 tablespoons in 1 cup, it contains $4 \times 16 = 64$ tablespoons. If 8 tablespoons are poured out, there are $64 - 8 - 56$ remaining of the original 64. $56/64 = 7/8$.

4. C There are 180° on one side of a line.

$$y° + (2y - 6)° = 180°$$

Combine like terms:	$3y - 6° = 180°$
Add 6°:	$3y = 186°$
Divide by 3:	$y = 62°$

5. A The question asks, essentially, how long it will take her to make up the $3,000 she spends on her air-conditioning system. She saves $125 – $25 = $100 per month. It would therefore take her $3,000 ÷ $100 = 30 months to make up the cost.

6. **C**   Start in the "units" column at the far right: if there is no "carry," then $A + B = B$, and $A = 0$. Then look at the hundreds column and notice that C must equal 1 because the sum of two two-digit numbers cannot exceed 198. Now you can rewrite the problem as:

$$\begin{array}{r} B\,0 \\ +6\,B \\ \hline 10\,B \end{array}$$

From the tens column, $B + 6 = 10$, so $B = 4$.

7. **D**

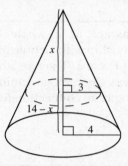

Dividing the cone with a parallel cross section forms similar triangles as shown in the diagram above. To solve for the height of the smaller cone set up a ratio:

$$\frac{14}{4} = \frac{x}{3}$$

Cross multiply: $42 = 4x$
Divide by 4: $10.5 = x$

8. **B**   The longest side of the triangle is the hypotenuse, which is $x + 3$. The legs are $x + 1$ and $x - 1$.

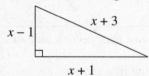

Now, solve for x using the Pythagorean Theorem:
$$(x + 1)^2 + (x - 1)^2 = (x + 3)^2$$
FOIL: $(x^2 + 2x + 1) + (x^2 - 2x + 1) = (x^2 + 6x + 9)$
Combine like terms: $2x^2 + 2 = x^2 + 6x + 9$
Subtract x^2: $x^2 + 2 = 6x + 9$
Subtract $6x$: $x^2 - 6x + 2 = 9$
Subtract 9: $x^2 - 6x - 7 = 0$
Factor: $(x - 7)(x + 1) = 0$
Find zeroes: $x = 7$ or $x = -1$
Of course, x cannot be -1 because the sides cannot have a negative length, so $x = 7$ and the sides are 6, 8, and 10. The perimeter therefore $= 6 + 8 + 10 = 24$

9. **E**   The pattern repeats every 5 terms, to find which digit is in the 3,000th place divide 3,000 by 5 and find the remainder: $3,000 \div 5 = 600.00$. Since there is no remainder, the term must be the last one in the pattern.

10. **D**   The portions of the pie graph dedicated to regions II and III constitute $70° + 50° = 120°$, which is 1/3 of the whole circle (1/3 of $360° = 240°$). Therefore, region I represents 2/3 of the whole, and 2/3 of 12,000 is 8000.

11. **B**

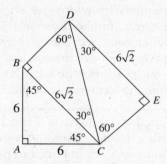

The figure consists of a 45–45–90 triangle and two identical 30–60–90 triangles. You know that they are identical because you are told that side BD and CE are parallel and thus hypotenuse CD creates alternate interior angles that are equal to each other. Because triangle *BAC* is a 45–45–90 triangle, the sides are $x - x - x\sqrt{2}$. Therefore the hypotenuse of the triangle is $6\sqrt{2}$. Because the two 30–60–90 triangles are identical, you do not need to do any further math as side *DE* will be the same as side *BC*.

12. **D**   The graph of the function $y = f(x + 3) + 3$ is equivalent to the function $y = f(x)$ shifted to the LEFT 3 and UP 3, as shown in answer choice D.

13. **D**   Don't calculate; the number is too big, so you will need to use your factoring skills and knowledge of exponents. $5^{2000} + 5^{2002} = 5^{2000}(1 + 5^2) = 5^{2000}(26) = 5^{2000}(13)(2)$. This is a complete prime factorization, so the prime factors are 2, 5, and 13.

14. **C**   If $r = s^6$, then it follows that $s = r^{1/6}$.
If $r = t^4$, then it follows that $t = r^{1/4}$.
$st = (r^{1/6})(r^{1/4})$
Add exponents: $st = r^{((1/6)+(1/4))}$
Simplify: $st = r^{5/12}$

15. **C** $x \,\Omega\, y = (x - y)^2$
                              $x \,\Omega\, y = 2x \,\Omega\, 3$
                              $(x - y)^2 = (2x - 3)^2$
Substitute $(y - 3)$ for x: $((y - 3) - y)^2 = (2x - 3)^2$
Combine like terms: $(-3)^2 = (2x - 3)^2$
FOIL: $9 = 4x^2 - 6x - 6x + 9$
Combine like terms: $0 = 4x^2 - 12x$
Factor: $0 = 4x(x - 3)$
Divide by x: $4x = 0$ or $x - 3 = 0$
Use the zero-product property: $x = 0$ or $x = 3$

16. **E** To find his average speed in miles per hour for the four races combined, divide the total distance traveled (in miles) by the total time of the races (in hours). Each race was 1 mile, so he ran a total distance of 4 miles. He finished the four races in a combined $(a + b + c + d)$ minutes, which is equivalent to $(a + b + c + d)/60$ <u>hours</u>.

$$\frac{4 \text{ miles}}{\dfrac{a + b + c + d}{60} \text{ hours}} = \frac{240}{a + b + c + d} \text{ mph}$$

Section 8

1. **A** The word *but* indicates a contrast; the opposite of an asset is a *liability*. *liability* = handicap; *novelty* = new experience; *compliment* = kind words.

2. **C** The *although* indicates an impending contrast. The fact that they would consider *accepting it without revision* suggests that it must be a quality report. After the semi-colon the sentence states that the report was *thorough* (complete), but contained errors. So, it would be inappropriate (*remiss*) to accept it without first correcting those errors. *inarticulate* = incomprehensible at speech; *negligent* = characterized by careless informality; *comprehensive* = complete; *remiss* = exhibiting carelessness.

3. **C** Davis was confident, but not *excessively confident. complacent* = overconfident; *coherent* = clear-headed; *latent* = present, but hidden.

4. **E** The doctors hoped the regimen would *energize* Dina, but it did not. The word *indeed* indicates that it in fact had the opposite effect, so she must have felt *weakened* and more *sluggish* than ever. *sanguine* = cheerfully optimistic; *lithe* = graceful and flexible; *torpid* = lethargic, lacking energy; *conciliated* = placated; *despondent* = depressed; *enervated* = weakened; *phlegmatic* = sluggish.

5. **C** If there are *far more (symbols) than even a perspicacious (keenly perceptive) critic can interpret*, it must have *tons* of them! *modicum* = small amount; *rectitude* = properness; *surfeit* = excessive amount; *dearth* = lack; *sequester* = to place in isolation.

6. **E** The criminals are planning to *divert* (distract) their pursuers; a *false* lead would do that. Such a plan is very *sneaky. venerable* = worthy of respect; *veritable* = genuine, real; *decrepit* = old, worn down; *contrived* = planned, calculated; *forthright* = honest; *specious* = false but plausible; *scheming* = sneaky; *credible* = legitimate; *duplicitous* = sneaky; *spurious* = false.

7. **B** These works are described as *liberal excisions from the privacy* (line 8) of Hawthorne. This means that they were taken from a man who wanted them kept private, so they were published without his permission.

8. **B** The *orange* being squeezed dry, in this case, is Hawthorne's genius, which is being exploited by those who wish to publish his posthumous (after-death) works.

9. **E** The sentence says that there is no *visible detriment conferred on Mr. Hawthorne's fame*, that is, that his reputation is not harmed, by the publication of these works.

10. **A** By saying that Hawthorne was *the last man to have attempted to explain himself*, the author is saying that Hawthorne was not concerned with his own emotions or motivations in his writings.

11. **E** The last paragraph states that Hawthorne's journals were characterized by repressed feelings (*the author seems to have been reserved even with himself*, lines 64–65), intellectual casualness (*strolling ... in blessed intellectual irresponsibility*, lines 47–49), and an engaging style (*a style individual and delightful*, lines 52–53).

12. **A** In saying that James will *in some quarters be attainted of high treason*, the author means that some people in American society will be very upset with James' characterizations of them.

13. **D** The *treason* is the description of the people of Salem and Concord as "*provincial*," when, according to the author, they are not.

14. **D** The *Parisian of his time* is intended to provide an ironic contrast to the "provincial" Hawthorne, whom, the author of Passage 2 claims, is actually more *universal* than most city-dwellers.

15. **C** The author complains that James *puts too slight a value upon Hawthorne's work*, or does not praise it highly enough.

16. **A** The author of Passage 2 expresses great affection for Hawthorne by calling him *a romantic genius* (line 162) and for his works by saying that they have no parallel in any literature (lines 118–122).

17. **C** The two central points in this passage are that Hawthorne is not a *provincial*, that is, simple-minded man, and that he is a singularly masterful writer of romances, which are characterized by *simple, domestic, democratic* qualities. Therefore, romances are the products of simple lifestyles, but not simple minds.

18. **E** The author of passage 1 states that Hawthorne's journals *singularly diminish our impression of his general intellectual power* (lines 33–34), while the author of Passage 2 says that they reflect his thoughts as a *great painter* (line 155).

19. **C** In the first three sentences of the final paragraph of Passage 2, the author summarizes these same qualities of Hawthorne in making the point that Hawthorne is a *romantic genius* (line 163).

Section 9

1. **B** The phrase *if not more so* is an interrupter. When an interrupter is removed, the remaining sentence should be logically and grammatically correct. Choice (B) provides a clear rephrasing.

2. **C** The sentence begins with an **appositive**, which is a noun phrase that is adjacent to another noun or noun phrase and which explains it. This appositive clearly refers to *Tony Horwitz* and not his book. Choice (C) corrects the dangling appositive, and places the other modifiers correctly.

3. **D** The phrase *being since* is not standard. Choice (D) is most logical, standard and clear.

4. **B** The original comparison is **illogical**. The *treatment of women* cannot logically oppose *women*. Choice (C) provides the most logical comparison.

5. **C** As it is phrased, the original sentence is a **run-on** or a **comma splice**. The clause that follows the commas must be a **dependent clause**, like the one in (C).

6. **B** The word *because* allows for a very concise phrasing to relate the two clauses. Choice (B) is the most concise.

7. **D** The phrase *not only A but also B* requires that A and B be parallel. Choice (D) is most parallel.

8. **E** The original sentence starts with a **dangling participial phrase**, that is a participial phrase without a noun to modify. Choice (E) provides a logical and complete phrasing.

9. **E** The original phrasing is **not parallel**. The three items in the list are most parallel with choice (E).

10. **A** The original sentence is best.

11. **C** In the original phrasing, the participle *being* is misplaced. The second clause explains the first, so the semicolon in (C) provides a logical conjunction.

12. **B** Phrases joined by a semicolon must be **independent clauses**, and so the original phrasing is incorrect. Choice (B) joins independent clauses with a conjunction, and the logical coordinator *therefore*.

13. **D** The comparison in the original sentence is **illogical**. Choice (D) provides a logical and parallel comparison.

14. **C** The comparison in the original sentence is **illogical**. Choice (C) provides a logical and parallel comparison.

PRACTICE TEST 7

ANSWER SHEET

Last Name:_____   First Name:_____

Date:_____   Testing Location:_____

Directions for Test

- Remove these answer sheets from the book and use them to record your answers to this test.
- This test will require 3 hours and 20 minutes to complete. Take this test in one sitting.
- The time allotment for each section is written clearly at the beginning of each section. This test contains six 25-minute sections, two 20-minute sections, and one 10-minute section.
- This test is 25 minutes shorter than the actual SAT, which will include a 25-minute "experimental" section that does not count toward your score. That section has been omitted from this test.
- You may take one short break during the test, of no more than 10 minutes in length.
- You may only work on one section at any given time.
- You must stop ALL work on a section when time is called.
- If you finish a section before the time has elapsed, check your work on that section. You may NOT work on any other section.
- Do not waste time on questions that seem too difficult for you.
- Use the test book for scratchwork, but you will receive credit only for answers that are marked on the answer sheets.
- You will receive one point for every correct answer.
- You will receive no points for an omitted question.
- For each wrong answer on any multiple-choice question, your score will be reduced by ¼ point.
- For each wrong answer on any "numerical grid-in" question, you will receive no deduction.

When you take the real SAT, you will be asked to fill in your personal information in grids as shown below.

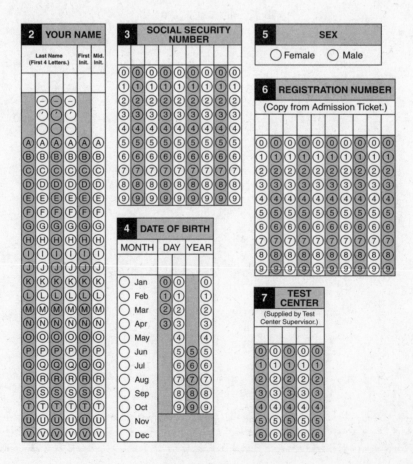

Start with number 1 for each new section. If a section has fewer questions than answer spaces, leave the extra answer spaces blank. Be sure to erase any errors or stray marks completely.

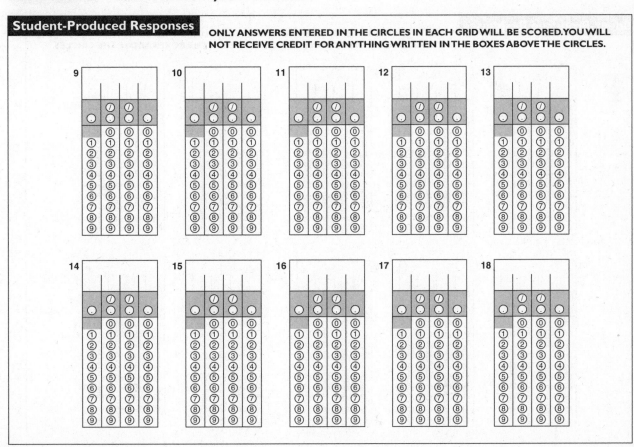

SECTION 2

SECTION 3

CAUTION Use the answer spaces in the grids below for Section 2 or Section 3 only if you are told to do so in your test book.

Student-Produced Responses ONLY ANSWERS ENTERED IN THE CIRCLES IN EACH GRID WILL BE SCORED. YOU WILL NOT RECEIVE CREDIT FOR ANYTHING WRITTEN IN THE BOXES ABOVE THE CIRCLES.

Start with number 1 for each new section. If a section has fewer questions than answer spaces, leave the extra answer spaces blank. Be sure to erase any errors or stray marks completely.

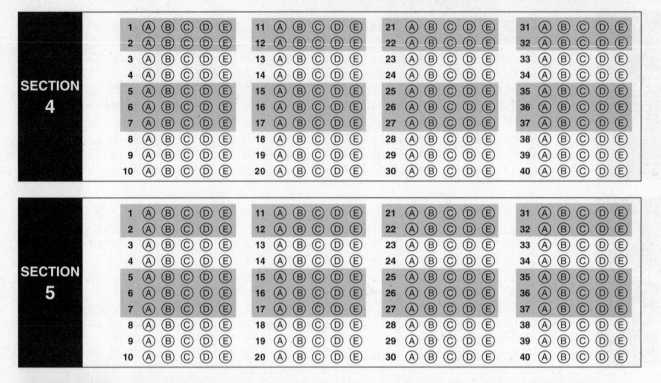

SECTION 4

SECTION 5

CAUTION Use the answer spaces in the grids below for Section 4 or Section 5 only if you are told to do so in your test book.

Student-Produced Responses ONLY ANSWERS ENTERED IN THE CIRCLES IN EACH GRID WILL BE SCORED. YOU WILL NOT RECEIVE CREDIT FOR ANYTHING WRITTEN IN THE BOXES ABOVE THE CIRCLES.

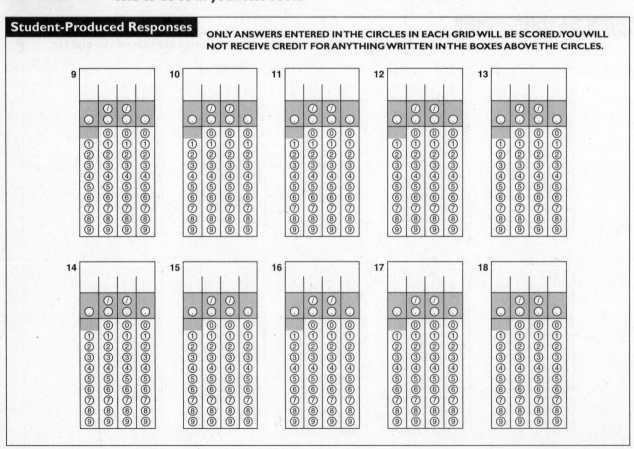

Start with number 1 for each new section. If a section has fewer questions than answer spaces, leave the extra answer spaces blank. Be sure to erase any errors or stray marks completely.

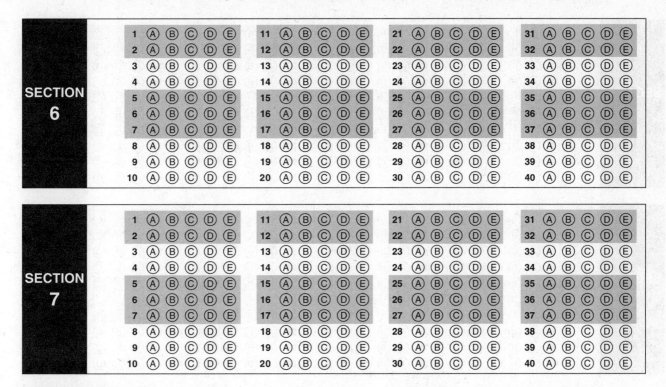

SECTION 6

SECTION 7

CAUTION **Use the answer spaces in the grids below for Section 6 or Section 7 only if you are told to do so in your test book.**

Student-Produced Responses ONLY ANSWERS ENTERED IN THE CIRCLES IN EACH GRID WILL BE SCORED. YOU WILL NOT RECEIVE CREDIT FOR ANYTHING WRITTEN IN THE BOXES ABOVE THE CIRCLES.

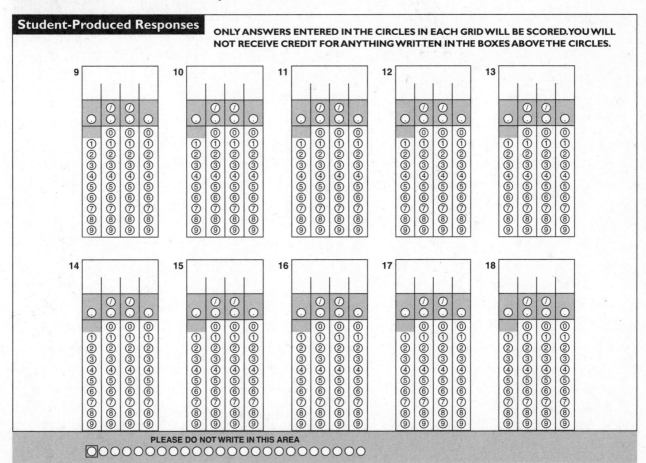

PLEASE DO NOT WRITE IN THIS AREA

Start with number 1 for each new section. If a section has fewer questions than answer spaces,
leave the extra answer spaces blank. Be sure to erase any errors or stray marks completely.

SECTION 8

1. Ⓐ Ⓑ Ⓒ Ⓓ Ⓔ
2. Ⓐ Ⓑ Ⓒ Ⓓ Ⓔ
3. Ⓐ Ⓑ Ⓒ Ⓓ Ⓔ
4. Ⓐ Ⓑ Ⓒ Ⓓ Ⓔ
5. Ⓐ Ⓑ Ⓒ Ⓓ Ⓔ
6. Ⓐ Ⓑ Ⓒ Ⓓ Ⓔ
7. Ⓐ Ⓑ Ⓒ Ⓓ Ⓔ
8. Ⓐ Ⓑ Ⓒ Ⓓ Ⓔ
9. Ⓐ Ⓑ Ⓒ Ⓓ Ⓔ
10. Ⓐ Ⓑ Ⓒ Ⓓ Ⓔ

11. Ⓐ Ⓑ Ⓒ Ⓓ Ⓔ
12. Ⓐ Ⓑ Ⓒ Ⓓ Ⓔ
13. Ⓐ Ⓑ Ⓒ Ⓓ Ⓔ
14. Ⓐ Ⓑ Ⓒ Ⓓ Ⓔ
15. Ⓐ Ⓑ Ⓒ Ⓓ Ⓔ
16. Ⓐ Ⓑ Ⓒ Ⓓ Ⓔ
17. Ⓐ Ⓑ Ⓒ Ⓓ Ⓔ
18. Ⓐ Ⓑ Ⓒ Ⓓ Ⓔ
19. Ⓐ Ⓑ Ⓒ Ⓓ Ⓔ
20. Ⓐ Ⓑ Ⓒ Ⓓ Ⓔ

21. Ⓐ Ⓑ Ⓒ Ⓓ Ⓔ
22. Ⓐ Ⓑ Ⓒ Ⓓ Ⓔ
23. Ⓐ Ⓑ Ⓒ Ⓓ Ⓔ
24. Ⓐ Ⓑ Ⓒ Ⓓ Ⓔ
25. Ⓐ Ⓑ Ⓒ Ⓓ Ⓔ
26. Ⓐ Ⓑ Ⓒ Ⓓ Ⓔ
27. Ⓐ Ⓑ Ⓒ Ⓓ Ⓔ
28. Ⓐ Ⓑ Ⓒ Ⓓ Ⓔ
29. Ⓐ Ⓑ Ⓒ Ⓓ Ⓔ
30. Ⓐ Ⓑ Ⓒ Ⓓ Ⓔ

31. Ⓐ Ⓑ Ⓒ Ⓓ Ⓔ
32. Ⓐ Ⓑ Ⓒ Ⓓ Ⓔ
33. Ⓐ Ⓑ Ⓒ Ⓓ Ⓔ
34. Ⓐ Ⓑ Ⓒ Ⓓ Ⓔ
35. Ⓐ Ⓑ Ⓒ Ⓓ Ⓔ
36. Ⓐ Ⓑ Ⓒ Ⓓ Ⓔ
37. Ⓐ Ⓑ Ⓒ Ⓓ Ⓔ
38. Ⓐ Ⓑ Ⓒ Ⓓ Ⓔ
39. Ⓐ Ⓑ Ⓒ Ⓓ Ⓔ
40. Ⓐ Ⓑ Ⓒ Ⓓ Ⓔ

SECTION 9

1. Ⓐ Ⓑ Ⓒ Ⓓ Ⓔ
2. Ⓐ Ⓑ Ⓒ Ⓓ Ⓔ
3. Ⓐ Ⓑ Ⓒ Ⓓ Ⓔ
4. Ⓐ Ⓑ Ⓒ Ⓓ Ⓔ
5. Ⓐ Ⓑ Ⓒ Ⓓ Ⓔ
6. Ⓐ Ⓑ Ⓒ Ⓓ Ⓔ
7. Ⓐ Ⓑ Ⓒ Ⓓ Ⓔ
8. Ⓐ Ⓑ Ⓒ Ⓓ Ⓔ
9. Ⓐ Ⓑ Ⓒ Ⓓ Ⓔ
10. Ⓐ Ⓑ Ⓒ Ⓓ Ⓔ

11. Ⓐ Ⓑ Ⓒ Ⓓ Ⓔ
12. Ⓐ Ⓑ Ⓒ Ⓓ Ⓔ
13. Ⓐ Ⓑ Ⓒ Ⓓ Ⓔ
14. Ⓐ Ⓑ Ⓒ Ⓓ Ⓔ
15. Ⓐ Ⓑ Ⓒ Ⓓ Ⓔ
16. Ⓐ Ⓑ Ⓒ Ⓓ Ⓔ
17. Ⓐ Ⓑ Ⓒ Ⓓ Ⓔ
18. Ⓐ Ⓑ Ⓒ Ⓓ Ⓔ
19. Ⓐ Ⓑ Ⓒ Ⓓ Ⓔ
20. Ⓐ Ⓑ Ⓒ Ⓓ Ⓔ

21. Ⓐ Ⓑ Ⓒ Ⓓ Ⓔ
22. Ⓐ Ⓑ Ⓒ Ⓓ Ⓔ
23. Ⓐ Ⓑ Ⓒ Ⓓ Ⓔ
24. Ⓐ Ⓑ Ⓒ Ⓓ Ⓔ
25. Ⓐ Ⓑ Ⓒ Ⓓ Ⓔ
26. Ⓐ Ⓑ Ⓒ Ⓓ Ⓔ
27. Ⓐ Ⓑ Ⓒ Ⓓ Ⓔ
28. Ⓐ Ⓑ Ⓒ Ⓓ Ⓔ
29. Ⓐ Ⓑ Ⓒ Ⓓ Ⓔ
30. Ⓐ Ⓑ Ⓒ Ⓓ Ⓔ

31. Ⓐ Ⓑ Ⓒ Ⓓ Ⓔ
32. Ⓐ Ⓑ Ⓒ Ⓓ Ⓔ
33. Ⓐ Ⓑ Ⓒ Ⓓ Ⓔ
34. Ⓐ Ⓑ Ⓒ Ⓓ Ⓔ
35. Ⓐ Ⓑ Ⓒ Ⓓ Ⓔ
36. Ⓐ Ⓑ Ⓒ Ⓓ Ⓔ
37. Ⓐ Ⓑ Ⓒ Ⓓ Ⓔ
38. Ⓐ Ⓑ Ⓒ Ⓓ Ⓔ
39. Ⓐ Ⓑ Ⓒ Ⓓ Ⓔ
40. Ⓐ Ⓑ Ⓒ Ⓓ Ⓔ

1 ESSAY   ESSAY 1

ESSAY
Time—25 minutes

Write your essay on separate sheets of standard lined paper.

The essay gives you an opportunity to show how effectively you can develop and express ideas. You should, therefore, take care to develop your point of view, present your ideas logically and clearly, and use language precisely.

Your essay must be written on the lines provided on your answer sheet—you will receive no other paper on which to write. You will have enough space if you write on every line, avoid wide margins, and keep your handwriting to a reasonable size. Remember that people who are not familiar with your handwriting will read what you write. Try to write or print so that what you are writing is legible to those readers.

Important Reminders:

- **A pencil is required for the essay.** An essay written in ink will receive a score of zero.
- **Do not write your essay in your test book.** You will receive credit only for what you write on your answer sheet.
- **An off-topic essay will receive a score of zero.**

You have twenty-five minutes to write an essay on the topic assigned below.

Consider carefully the issue discussed in the following passage, then write an essay that answers the question posed in the assignment.

> If you believe you will succeed, you are probably right. If you think you will fail, you are also probably right.

Assignment: **Which has a stronger effect on one's life: one's circumstances, or one's system of beliefs?** Write an essay in which you answer this question and support your position logically with examples from literature, the arts, history, politics, science and technology, current events, or your experience or observation.

If you finish before time is called, you may check your work on this section only.
Do not turn to any other section of the test.

SECTION 2
Time—25 minutes
24 questions

Turn to Section 3 of your answer sheet to answer the questions in this section.

Directions: For each question in this section, select the best answer from among the choices given and fill in the corresponding circle on the answer sheet.

Each sentence below has one or two blanks, each blank indicating that something has been omitted. Beneath the sentence are five words or sets of words labeled A through E. Choose the word or set of words that, when inserted in the sentence, <u>best</u> fits the meaning of the sentence as a whole.

EXAMPLE:

Rather than accepting the theory unquestioningly, Deborah regarded it with -----.

(A) mirth
(B) sadness
(C) responsibility
(D) ignorance
(E) skepticism

---

1. From the 1930's until the 1960s, T.S. Eliot's reputation grew to mythic proportions, making him the most ------- English-speaking poet in the world.

   (A) callous
   (B) infamous
   (C) aloof
   (D) renowned
   (E) obtuse

2. Because of the cold and rainy weather that has enveloped the resort areas this summer, the beaches have been ------- people.

   (A) devoid of
   (B) overpopulated by
   (C) overrun with
   (D) packed with
   (E) manipulated by

3. Amid the controversy surrounding her reign, the queen decided to ------- her throne and retire to the countryside.

   (A) commemorate   (B) abdicate
   (C) rectify   (D) replicate
   (E) disenfranchise

4. Although I expected ------- for raking my neighbor's lawn, I was surprised that she paid me so much because I had always been told that she was -------.

   (A) remuneration . . frugal
   (B) perquisite . . venal
   (C) beneficiary . . penniless
   (D) gratification . . arbitrary
   (E) provisions . . thrifty

5. Despite having been ------- for several years, the vegetable garden had great potential, and Mrs. Nelson was excited about ------- it.

   (A) fertile . . planting
   (B) fallow . . cultivating
   (C) aquatic . . fertilizing
   (D) praiseworthy . . culminating
   (E) painstaking . . sterilizing

6. Having never before been subjected to the rigors of a presidential campaign, Senator Thomas found the ------- pace of the primaries overwhelming and as a result he took his name off the ballot.

   (A) reticent   (B) mundane
   (C) pastoral   (D) frenetic
   (E) prosaic

GO ON TO THE NEXT PAGE

7. The literature of Gabriel García Márquez has defined the "magical realism" genre of fiction; he writes of seemingly impossible and ------- events that are woven flawlessly into the universal themes of love and war.

   (A) plausible   (B) chimerical
   (C) obsequious   (D) itinerant
   (E) perfunctory

8. The deliberation of the jury was ------- and even escalated to physical combat after two ------- jurors exchanged vicious invectives.

   (A) dignified . . temperate
   (B) decorous . . belligerent
   (C) sedate . . amiable
   (D) staid . . pugnacious
   (E) contentious . . truculent

The passages below are followed by questions based on their content. Answer the questions on the basis of what is stated or implied in the passages and in any introductory material that may be provided.

Questions 9–10 are based on the following passage.

Johannes Kepler, whose audience was more friendly than Galileo's when it came to his
Line theories concerning the universe, refined Galileo's telescope design. Kepler's refracting
5 telescope employed a convex-lens objective with a long focal length and a smaller convex-lens eyepiece with a short focal length. Unlike the galilean telescope, the keplerian refractor produces an inverted
10 image; it is upside-down and backwards. The distance between the objective and the eyepiece must be exactly equal to the sum of the focal lengths of the two lenses in order for the image to be clear.

9. The passage indicates that, unlike Kepler's theories, Galileo's theories were

   (A) not well researched
   (B) hindered by limited access to scientific instruments
   (C) not well received
   (D) rigorously tested
   (E) highly inventive

10. According to the passage, a Galilean telescope produces an image that is

   (A) precisely the distance from the objective to the eyepiece
   (B) clearer than that produced by the keplerian refractor
   (C) larger than that produced by the keplerian refractor
   (D) not inverted
   (E) larger than the distance from the objective to the eyepiece

Questions 11–12 are based on the following passage.

As the nineteenth century progressed, the Romanticists ferreted out every possible
Line subject of melodramatic or sentimental potentialities from history, literature, and the
5 strange portions of the globe. Whereupon the Impressionists turned the whole ingenious business on its ear as violently as possible in the name of progress, by insisting that the subject mattered not at all. Monet, high
10 priest of the Impressionist painters, said he would make great art from the simplest things he could think of, which were a couple of haystacks, and he did a whole series of canvases of them, at different times of the
15 day, under different atmospheric conditions, producing a wide variety of color effects according to the precise quality of changing light and shade.

GO ON TO THE NEXT PAGE ⟶

First paragraph: *Physics Demystified*, Stan Gibilisco, McGraw-Hill, 2002, p. 513
Second paragraph: *Sculpture Through the Ages*, Lincoln Rothschild, McGraw Hill, 1942, p. 238

11. The "ingenious business" mentioned in lines 6–7 is

   (A) the tendency of artists to choose emotionally suggestive subjects
   (B) Monet's artwork as a whole
   (C) the use of natural forms in painting
   (D) the inventive use of light and shade
   (E) the inclination of artists to invent new modes of expression

12. The passage suggests that Monet most likely chose haystacks as his subject because they

   (A) evoked the peaceful feelings of a pastoral scene
   (B) had subtle and complex textures
   (C) were subjects that appealed to the Romanticists
   (D) were devoid of emotional content
   (E) could be depicted with a narrow range of hues

The questions below are based on the content of the passage that precedes them. The questions are to be answered on the basis of what is stated or implied in the passage itself or the introductory material that precedes the passage.

Questions 13–18 are based on the following passage.

The following passage is an excerpt from a book written by a famous American composer, Aaron Copland, about what to listen for in music.

There is a tendency to exaggerate the difficulty of properly understanding music. We
Line musicians are constantly meeting some
      honest soul who says: "I love music very
5   much, but I don't understand anything about
      it." My playwright and novelist friends rarely
      hear any one say, "I don't understand any-
      thing about the theater or the novel." Yet I
      strongly suspect that those very same people,
10   so modest about music, have just as much

reason to be modest about the other arts. Or,
to put it more graciously, have just as little
reason to be modest about their understanding of music. If you have any feelings of
15 inferiority about your musical reactions, try
to rid yourself of them. They are often not
justified.

   At any rate, you have no reason to be
downcast about your musical capacities until
20 you have some idea of what it means to be
musical. There are many strange popular
notions about what "being musical" consists of.
One is always being told, as the unarguable
proof of a musical person, that he or she can
25 "go to a show and then come home and play
all the tunes on the piano." That fact alone
bespeaks a certain musicality in the person in
question, but it does not indicate the kind of
sensitivity to music that is under examina-
30 tion here. The entertainer who mimics well is
not yet an actor, and the musical mimic is not
necessarily a profoundly musical individual.
Another attribute which is trotted forth
whenever the question of being musical
35 arises is that of having absolute pitch. To be
able to recognize the note A when you hear it
may, at times, be helpful, but it certainly does
not prove, taken by itself, that you are a
musical person. It should not be taken to
40 indicate anything more than a glib musicality
which has only a limited significance in
relationship to the real understanding of
music which concerns us here.

   There is, however, one minimum require-
45 ment for the potentially intelligent listener. He
must be able to recognize a melody when he
hears it. If there is such a thing as being tone-
deaf, then it suggests the inability to recognize
a tune. Such a person has my sympathy, but
50 he cannot be helped; just as the color-blind are
a useless lot to the painter. But if you feel
confident that you can recognize a given
melody—not *sing* a melody, but recognize it
when played, even after an interval of a few
55 minutes and after other and different melodies
have been sounded—the key to a deeper
appreciation of music is in your hands.

Excerpted from *What to Listen for in Music*, Aaron Copland,
   © 1957 McGraw-Hill. Reprinted by permission of the Aaron
   Copland Fund for Music, Inc., copyright holder.

GO ON TO THE NEXT PAGE ⇨

It is insufficient merely to hear music in
terms of the separate moments at which it exists.
60 You must be able to relate what you hear at
any given moment to what just happened
before and what is about to come afterward.
In other words, music is an art that exists in
points of time. In that sense it is like a novel,
65 except that the events of a novel are easier to
keep in mind, partly because real happenings
are narrated and partly because one can turn
back and refresh one's memory of them. Musical "events" are more abstract by nature, so the
70 act of pulling them all together in the imagination is not so easy as in reading a novel.

13. Which of the following best describes the
overall structure of the passage?

(A) A historical phenomenon is described
and then evaluated.
(B) A problem is summarized and its effects on
a wide range of situations are discussed.
(C) A story is told to illustrate a moral, and
then this moral is discussed and
generalized.
(D) The contributions of several artists are
described and then evaluated.
(E) A common misconception is described
and then followed by authoritative
instruction.

14. The statement in lines 11–14 ("Or, to
put...understanding of music") is intended
primarily as

(A) a rephrasing of a definition
(B) a refutation of a common belief
(C) an expression of self-deprecation
(D) a moderation of an assessment
(E) a plea for action

15. According to the author, "being musical"
(line 22) necessarily includes which of the
following?

I.   the ability to distinguish good
music from bad music
II. the ability to play an instrument
III. the ability to detect a melody line

(A) I only
(B) III only
(C) I and III only
(D) II and III only
(E) I, II, and III

16. The "fact" in line 26 refers to

(A) the importance of practice to musical
proficiency
(B) the ability to discern great works of
music from mediocre ones
(C) the tendency of people to underestimate
their musical skills
(D) the challenge of appreciating great music
(E) the ability to replicate music from
memory

17. As used in line 51, "lot" most nearly means

(A) group
(B) large amount
(C) empty region
(D) fate
(E) foundation

18. The author suggests that the task of appreciating music is particularly challenging because,
unlike the task of appreciating literature, it
involves

(A) recalling events from the past
(B) having some knowledge of the
composer's life
(C) synthesizing abstract events
(D) recognizing the pitch of particular notes
(E) understanding theories of music

GO ON TO THE NEXT PAGE ⇒

The questions below are based on the content of the passage that precedes them. The questions are to be answered on the basis of what is stated or implied in the passage itself or the introductory material that precedes the passage.

Questions 19–24 are based on the following passage.

The following is an excerpt from an essay on the pragmatic method written by American psychologist William James in 1907.

The pragmatic method is primarily a method
of settling metaphysical disputes that other-
Line wise might be interminable. Is the world one
or many?—fated or free?—material or spiri-
5   tual? The pragmatic method attempts to evaluate a notion by tracing its practical
consequences. What difference would it practically make to anyone if this notion rather
than that notion were true? If no practical
10 difference whatever can be traced, then the
alternatives mean practically the same thing,
and all dispute is idle. Whenever a dispute is
serious, we ought to be able to show some
practical difference that must follow from
15 one side or the other's being right.
    A glance at the history of the idea will
show you still better what pragmatism
means. The term is derived from the Greek
word *pragma*, meaning action, from which
20 our words "practice" and "practical" come. It
was first introduced into philosophy by
Mr. Charles Peirce in 1878. In an article
entitled "How to Make Our Ideas Clear,"
Mr. Peirce, after pointing out that our beliefs
25 are really rules for action, said that to develop an idea's meaning, we need only determine what action it produces. No distinction
among ideas, however subtle, is so fine as to
consist in anything but a possible difference
30 of practice. To attain perfect clarity about
an idea, then, we need only consider what
practical effects that idea may involve—what
sensations we are to expect if it is true, and
what reactions we must prepare.

35 This principle of pragmatism lay entirely un-
noticed for twenty years, until I brought it
forward again in 1898 and made a special
application of it to religion. The word
"pragmatism" then spread, and at present it
40 fairly spots the pages of the philosophic
journals. Today we hear frequent mention of
the "pragmatic movement," sometimes with
respect, but seldom with clear understanding.
    To understand the importance of Peirce's
45 principle, one must apply it to concrete cases.
I found a few years ago that Ostwald, the
illustrious Leipzig chemist, had been making
perfectly distinct use of the principle of
pragmatism in his lectures on the philosophy
50 of science, though he had not called it by that
name.
    "All realities influence our practice," he
wrote me, "and that influence is their meaning
for us. I am accustomed to putting questions
55 to my classes in this way: In what respects
would the world be different if this alternative
or that were true? If I can find nothing that
would become different, then the alternative
has no sense."
60   That is, the rival views mean practically
the same thing, and practical meaning is the
only meaning that counts. For example,
chemists have long wrangled over the inner
constitution of certain bodies called
65 "tautomerous." Their properties seemed
equally consistent with the notion that an
unstable hydrogen atom oscillates inside of
them, or that they are unstable mixtures of
two bodies. Controversy raged, but was never
70 resolved. "It would never have begun," says
Ostwald, "if the combatants had asked
themselves what particular experimental fact
could have been made different by one or the
other view being correct. For it would then
75 have appeared that no difference of fact
could possibly ensue; and the quarrel was as
unreal as if, theorizing in primitive times
about the raising of dough by yeast, one
party should have invoked a 'sprite,' while
80 another insisted on an 'elf' as the true cause
of the phenomenon."

GO ON TO THE NEXT PAGE →

Excerpted from an essay on pragmatism by William James – Public Domain.

19. According to the passage, the pragmatic method holds that two claims are equivalent if they

(A) are based on the same premise
(B) have essentially the same effect
(C) follow from the same chain of logical reasoning
(D) can both be proven true by experimentation
(E) can be expressed using similar terminology

20. The author suggests that a "serious" (line 13) dispute is one that

(A) concerns scientists from different disciplines
(B) employs proper terminology when naming concepts
(C) affects the everyday lives of common citizens
(D) cannot be resolved except through negotiation
(E) involves alternatives with distinct outcomes

21. As used in line 28, "fine" most nearly means

(A) fragile
(B) healthy
(C) meaningful
(D) satisfactory
(E) discerning

22. The author discusses the work of Ostwald primarily in order to

(A) emphasize the importance of distinguishing the pragmatic method from the scientific method
(B) indicate a specific misunderstanding of the definition of pragmatism
(C) show how the pragmatic method extends to the study of religion
(D) examine a specific application of the pragmatic method to the sciences
(E) acknowledge that some scientists object to the pragmatic method

23. The passage suggests that the controversy surrounding "tautomerous" bodies could be resolved in favor of one of the two competing theories only if

(A) scientists determined the structure of an unstable hydrogen atom
(B) the theories predicted different outcomes to a feasible experiment
(C) at least one of the theories avoided superstitious claims
(D) the theories were analyzed by philosophical pragmatists
(E) the disputants opened the debate to a wider audience

24. The final sentence mentions invoking a "sprite" and an "elf" primarily to emphasize the fact that

(A) in earlier times, people were more concerned with supernatural debates than scientific ones
(B) modern scientists avoid making hypotheses that involve superstitious claims
(C) scientists have now determined what causes yeast to rise
(D) a pragmatic perspective renders certain kinds of claims irrelevant
(E) scientific understanding of chemical processes has advanced greatly in recent years

STOP

If you finish before time is called, you may check your work on this section only. Do not turn to any other section of the test.

3   **3**   **3**   **3**   **3**   **3**

SECTION 3
Time—25 minutes
20 questions

| **Turn to Section 3 of your answer sheet to answer the questions in this section.** |

Directions: For this section, solve each problem and decide which is the best of the choices given. Fill in the corresponding circle on the answer sheet. You may use any available space for scratchwork.

Notes

1. The use of a calculator is permitted.

2. All numbers used are real numbers.

3. Figures that accompany problems in this test are intended to provide information useful in solving the problems. They are drawn as accurately as possible EXCEPT when it is stated in a specific problem that the figure is not drawn to scale. All figures lie in a plane unless otherwise indicated.

4. Unless otherwise specified, the domain of any function f is assumed to be the set of all real numbers x for which $f(x)$ is a real number.

Reference Information

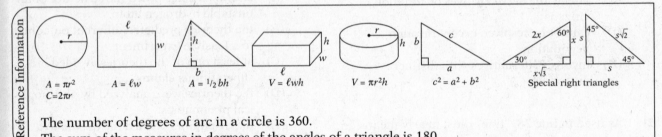

$A = \pi r^2$ $A = \ell w$ $A = \frac{1}{2} bh$ $V = \ell w h$ $V = \pi r^2 h$ $c^2 = a^2 + b^2$ Special right triangles
$C = 2\pi r$

The number of degrees of arc in a circle is 360.
The sum of the measures in degrees of the angles of a triangle is 180.

---

1. If $2x + 7 = 4x + 5$, what is the value of x?

   (A) 1
   (B) 2
   (C) 4
   (D) 5
   (E) 8

---

2. If n is any positive integer, which of the following must be even?

   (A) $n + 2$
   (B) $2n$
   (C) $3n$
   (D) n^2
   (E) n^3

---

3. The length of a nail rounded to the nearest inch is 5 inches. Which of the following could be the actual length of the nail, in inches?

   (A) 4.46
   (B) 4.48
   (C) 5.32
   (D) 5.51
   (E) 5.89

GO ON TO THE NEXT PAGE

3   **3**   **3**   **3**   **3**   **3**

4. The walls of Jane's living room have an area of 340 square feet. If she can paint 60 square feet per hour, how many minutes after she starts painting will there be only 100 square feet left to paint?

(A) 120
(B) 150
(C) 180
(D) 240
(E) 270

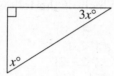

Note: Figure not drawn to scale.

5. In the right triangle above, what is the value of $3x$?

(A) 18.0
(B) 22.5
(C) 27.0
(D) 30.0
(E) 67.5

6. What is 50% of 60% of 180?

(A) 48
(B) 54
(C) 60
(D) 90
(E) 92

7. If $\dfrac{1}{c^2} = b^2 + 4b + 4$ then $c =$

(A) $\dfrac{1}{(b-2)}$

(B) $\dfrac{1}{\sqrt{(b-2)}}$

(C) $\dfrac{1}{\sqrt{(4b+2)}}$

(D) $\dfrac{1}{\sqrt{(b^2+2)}}$

(E) $\dfrac{1}{(b+2)}$

8. If the average of $3y$, $4y$, and $(y-5)$ is 9, what is the value of y?

(A) 1.50
(B) 1.75
(C) 2.00
(D) 3.25
(E) 4.00

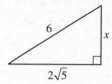

Note: Figure not drawn to scale.

9. In the figure above, right triangle ABC has side lengths as shown. What is the value of x?

(A) 2
(B) 3
(C) 4
(D) 5
(E) 6

10. Which of the following represents the set of all values of x for which is defined the function

$f(x) = \dfrac{\sqrt{x+4}}{(x-6)}$?

(A) $x \geq -4$
(B) $x > -4$
(C) $x \geq -4$ and $x \neq 6$
(D) $x > -4$ and $x \neq 6$
(E) $x \neq 6$

11. When the positive integer w is divided by 6, the remainder is 2. What is the remainder when $5w$ is divided by 6?

(A) 1
(B) 2
(C) 3
(D) 4
(E) 5

GO ON TO THE NEXT PAGE

COLOR OF VARIOUS PETS AT THE PET STORE

	White	Black	Brown	Total
Dogs	35	60	y	105
Cats	x	37	16	w
Pigs	15	5	8	28
Total	75	m	34	z

12. Given the information in the table above, what is the value of $x + y + z$?

   (A)   35
   (B)   113
   (C)   246
   (D)   299
   (E)   314

13. If a circle with center (3, 4) is tangent to the x-axis, what is the circumference of the circle?

   (A) 4π
   (B) 6π
   (C) 8π
   (D) 12π
   (E) 16π

14. If the length of line segment $\overline{DE}$ is 7 and the length of line segment $\overline{EF}$ is 9, which of the following could NOT be the length of line segment $\overline{DF}$?

   (A)   6
   (B)   8
   (C)   12
   (D)   16
   (E)   18

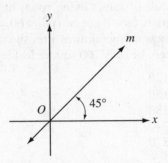

15. In the figure above, line m passes through the origin. Which of the following points lies on line m?

   I.   (−2, 1)
   II. (−2, −2)
   III. (1, 1)

   (A)   II only
   (B)   I and II only
   (C)   I and III only
   (D)   II and III only
   (E)   I, II, and III

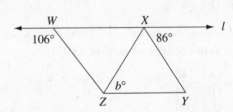

Note: Figure not drawn to scale.

16. In the figure above, $WX = XZ = ZY$. What is the value of b?

   (A)   56
   (B)   76
   (C)   78
   (D)   84
   (E)   128

GO ON TO THE NEXT PAGE ⟹

17. In one day, Mitchell spends 30% of the day sleeping, 35% of the day at work, 5% of the day at the gym, five additional hours at home, and the rest of the day in the car. How many minutes does he spend in the car each day? (1 hour = 60 minutes)

(A) 2.2
(B) 60
(C) 120
(D) 132
(E) 432

18. What is the slope of the line containing the point (2, 5) and the midpoint of the line segment with endpoints (8, 8) and (6, –2)?

(A) $\dfrac{1}{2}$

(B) $-\dfrac{2}{5}$

(C) $-\dfrac{7}{4}$

(D) $-\dfrac{5}{2}$

(E) $-\dfrac{4}{7}$

19. A square has a diagonal of length m. Which of the following represents the area of the square in terms of m?

(A) $\dfrac{m^2}{2}$

(B) $2m$
(C) m^2
(D) m^3
(E) $\dfrac{2}{m^2}$

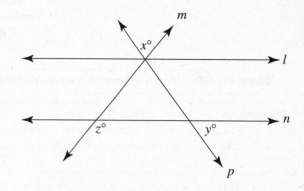

20. In the figure above, line l is parallel to line n. Which of the following represents the value of x in terms of y and z?

(A) $z - y$
(B) $z + y$
(C) $180 - z - y$
(D) $180 - z + y$
(E) $90 - y$

STOP   *If you finish before time is called, you may check your work on this section only. Do not turn to any other section of the test.*

4 **4** **4** **4** **4** **4**

SECTION 4
Time—25 minutes
18 questions

Turn to Section 4 of your answer sheet to answer the questions in this section.

Directions: This section contains two types of questions. You have 25 minutes to complete both types. For questions 1–8, solve each problem and decide which is the best of the choices given. Fill in the corresponding circle on the answer sheet. You may use any available space for scratchwork.

Notes

1. The use of a calculator is permitted.

2. All numbers used are real numbers.

3. Figures that accompany problems in this test are intended to provide information useful in solving the problems. They are drawn as accurately as possible EXCEPT when it is stated in a specific problem that the figure is not drawn to scale. All figures lie in a plane unless otherwise indicated.

4. Unless otherwise specified, the domain of any function f is assumed to be the set of all real numbers x for which $f(x)$ is a real number.

Reference Information

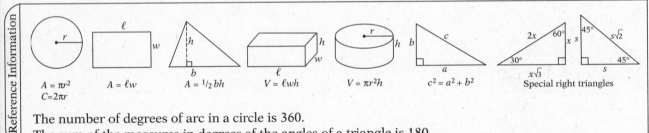

$A = \pi r^2$
$C = 2\pi r$

$A = \ell w$

$A = \frac{1}{2}bh$

$V = \ell w h$

$V = \pi r^2 h$

$c^2 = a^2 + b^2$

Special right triangles

The number of degrees of arc in a circle is 360.
The sum of the measures in degrees of the angles of a triangle is 180.

1. Let $x \$ y$ be defined by the equation $x \$ y = x^y + 3$. What is the value of $4 \$ 2$?

    (A) 9
    (B) 11
    (C) 19
    (D) 20
    (E) 25

2. If $m + n = 7$ and $2n - 3m = 6$, what is the value of $3n - 2m$?

    (A) 7
    (B) 13
    (C) 14
    (D) 17
    (E) 18

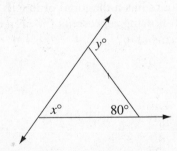

Note: Figure not drawn to scale.

3. In the triangle above, if x and y are integers and $x < 40$, what is the smallest possible value of y?

    (A) 39
    (B) 61
    (C) 84
    (D) 119
    (E) 141

GO ON TO THE NEXT PAGE

4   4   4   4   4   4

4. Triangle *ABC* has side lengths that are all integers. If two of the sides are 7 and 11, how many possible values are there for the third side length?

(A) 11
(B) 12
(C) 13
(D) 14
(E) 15

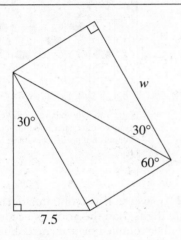

5. In the figure above, what is the value of *w*?

(A) 15
(B) 14
(C) 13
(D) 12
(E) 11

6. In 1995, the Jones family sold their home for $192,500. They spent $175,000 to buy the house in 1988. What percent profit did they make on the sale?

(A) 9%
(B) 10%
(C) 11%
(D) 12%
(E) 13%

7. How many different committees of four people can be assembled from a group of six people?

(A) 8
(B) 12
(C) 15
(D) 20
(E) 24

–3, 6, –2 …

8. After the second term in the sequence above, each term is equivalent to the ratio of the preceding term to the term before that. For example, the third term, –2, is equal to the ratio of 6 to –3. How many of the first 100 terms of this sequence are negative?

(A) 33
(B) 34
(C) 50
(D) 66
(E) 67

GO ON TO THE NEXT PAGE

4   4   4   4   4   4

Directions: For student-produced response questions 9–18, use the grids at the bottom of the answer sheet page on which you have answered questions 1–8.

Each of the remaining ten questions requires you to solve the problem and enter your answer by marking the circles in the special grid, as shown in the examples below. You may use any available space for scratchwork.

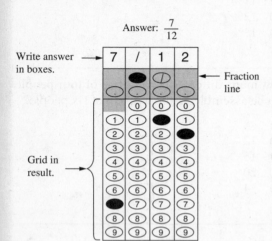

Answer: $\frac{7}{12}$

Write answer in boxes.

Fraction line

Grid in result.

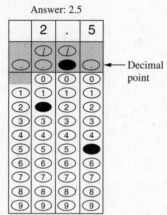

Answer: 2.5

Decimal point

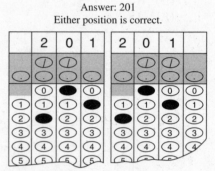

Answer: 201
Either position is correct.

<u>Note:</u> You may start your answers in any column, space permitting. Columns not needed should be left blank.

- Mark no more than one circle in any column.

- Because the answer sheet will be machine-scored, **you will receive credit only if the circles are filled in correctly.**

- Although not required, it is suggested that you write your answer in the boxes at the top of the columns to help you fill in the circles accurately.

- Some problems may have more than one correct answer. In such cases, grid only one answer.

- No question has a negative answer.

- **Mixed numbers** such as $3\frac{1}{2}$ must be gridded as 3.5 or 7/2. (If [3 1 / 2] is gridded, it will be interpreted as, $\frac{31}{2}$ not $3\frac{1}{2}$.)

- **Decimal Answers:** If you obtain a decimal answer with more digits than the grid can accommodate, it may be either rounded or truncated, but it must fill the entire grid. For example, if you obtain an answer such as 0.6666..., you should record your result as .666 or .667. **A less accurate value such as .66 or .67 will be scored as incorrect.**

Acceptable ways to grid $^2/_3$ are:

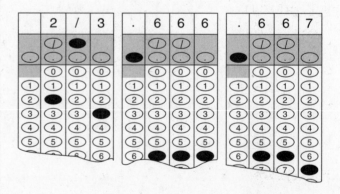

---

9. If Liz's car can travel 24 miles on one gallon of gasoline, then, at this rate, how many gallons will her car need to travel 96 miles?

10. If b is a positive number and $b^3 < b^2$, what is one possible value of b?

GO ON TO THE NEXT PAGE ⟹

4   **4**   **4**   **4**   **4**   **4**

11. Eric is 40 pounds heavier than Bill. If together they weigh 320 pounds, how much does Eric weigh?

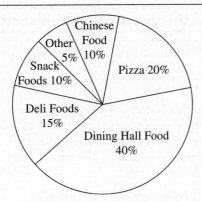

12. The circle graph above shows the results of a survey in which 3,000 college students indicated what they most often eat for dinner. How many fewer students eat snack food than dining hall food for dinner?

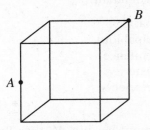

13. The cube shown above has edges of length 4. Point A is a midpoint on one of the edges. What is the length of AB (not shown)?

14. A cooler filled with cans of soda weighs 20 pounds. After three-quarters of the cans of soda have been consumed, the cooler, together with the remaining sodas, weighs 14 pounds. If each can of soda weighs the same, how much does the empty cooler weigh?

15. Jim rides his bike to work each morning at an average speed of 15 miles per hour. He rides home along the same route at 10 miles per hour. If the total time of his commute to and from work is 60 minutes each day, how far, in miles, is Jim's trip to work?

16. Of 1,000 people surveyed, each person owned a dog, a cat, or both. One-third of the 630 people who owned a cat also owned a dog. How many of the people surveyed owned a dog?

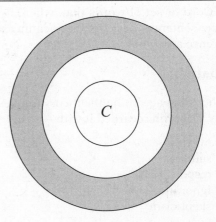

17. The dart board above consists of three concentric circles with center C. The innermost circle has a radius of 1, the middle circle a radius of 2, and the outermost circle has a radius of 3. What is the probability that a dart thrown at random lands in the shaded area?

18. Every marble in a jar is either red or black, and either striped or unstriped. There are three times as many red marbles as black marbles. Among the red marbles, there are twice as many striped marbles as unstriped marbles. If you were to randomly select a marble from this jar, what is the probability that it would be an unstriped red marble?

If you finish before time is called, you may
STOP *check your work on this section only. Do not turn*
to any other section of the test.

SECTION 5
Time—25 minutes
24 questions

Turn to Section 5 of your answer sheet to answer the questions in this section.

Directions: For each question in this section, select the best answer from among the choices given and fill in the corresponding circle on the answer sheet.

Each sentence below has one or two blanks, each blank indicating that something has been omitted. Beneath the sentence are five words or sets of words labeled A through E. Choose the word or set of words that, when inserted in the sentence, <u>best</u> fits the meaning of the sentence as a whole.

EXAMPLE:

Rather than accepting the theory unquestioningly, Deborah regarded it with -----.

(A) mirth
(B) sadness
(C) responsibility
(D) ignorance
(E) skepticism

---

1. The ------- odor was easily explained when Elmo found the bag of rotten garbage that he had forgotten to throw out three weeks earlier.

   (A) putrid
   (B) delectable
   (C) piquant
   (D) divine
   (E) savory

2. Unable to ------- his mother's ------- handwriting, Doug had to call her for clarification when attempting to use the recipe.

   (A) reconfigure .. illegible
   (B) recapitulate .. lucid
   (C) reiterate .. placid
   (D) recognize .. cogent
   (E) decipher .. unintelligible

3. The thousands of fragile artifacts that had been ------- by generations of archaeologists were stored without the requisite safeguards against ------- and so became utterly useless to students.

   (A) collected .. preservation
   (B) projected .. dissipation
   (C) assembled .. retrieval
   (D) amassed .. deterioration
   (E) disseminated .. desiccation

4. The incontrovertible evidence presented by the prosecution proved conclusively the ------- of the defendant.

   (A) apathy
   (B) culpability
   (C) penitence
   (D) dexterity
   (E) prescience

5. Throughout her life, Mother Teresa, the winner of the 1979 Nobel Peace Prize, was ------- with her time, devoting herself to providing medical care and nutrition to the dying poor of the world.

   (A) rhetorical
   (B) munificent
   (C) felicitous
   (D) austere
   (E) mellifluous

GO ON TO THE NEXT PAGE →

5   5   5   5   5   5

Each passage below is followed by questions based on its content. Answer each question based on what is stated or implied in the passage that precedes it.

Questions 6–7 are based on the following passage.

As hominid history has unfolded, social and cultural means of adaptation have
Line become increasingly important. In this process, humans have devised diverse ways
5 of coping with the range of environments and social systems they have occupied in time and space. The rate of cultural change has accelerated, particularly during the past 10,000 years. For millions of years, hunting
10 and gathering of nature's bounty—foraging— was the sole basis of hominid subsistence. However, it took only a few thousand years for food production (cultivation of plants and domestication of animals), which originated
15 in the Middle East 10,000 to 12,000 years ago, to replace foraging in most areas. People started producing their own food, planting crops and stockbreeding animals, rather than simply taking what nature had to offer.

6. The passage indicates that, unlike the practice of food gathering, the practice of food production among hominids

    (A) was not widely available
    (B) was introduced over one million years ago
    (C) developed rapidly
    (D) damaged the environment in which they lived
    (E) did not require great changes in behavior

7. According to the passage, which of the following is NOT an example of food production?

    (A) harvesting corn planted on a hillside
    (B) breeding fish in a protected lake
    (C) herding goats to gather their milk
    (D) organizing a group to hunt deer
    (E) transplanting wheat to a more hospitable location

Questions 8–9 are based on the following passage.

In Egypt in 450 B.C., religion was the function of the priesthood, a mystic practice
Line of elaborate ceremo nial performed in the depths of temple sanctuaries. In Greece
5 generally, and in the Panathenaea particularly, however, the temple served simply for the performance of the crucial rite of sacrifice. Various preliminaries were engaged in by all the citizens outside the
10 temple and in other parts of the city, which were of the very fabric of their lives. They witnessed or took part in games and activities that were familiar activities; the power of the Athenian state was expressed in the presence
15 of the tributaries, and her national prominence was implied in the six-day spectacle as a whole for it had consciously been elaborated to rival the time-honored Olympic games.

8. The passage indicates that Egyptian religious rites differed from Greek religious rites primarily in terms of

    (A) the clothing worn by the priests
    (B) the degree to which the public participated
    (C) the length of the ceremonies
    (D) the willingness of the priests to participate
    (E) the elaborateness of the temples in which they were held

9. In line 9, the word "engaged" most nearly means

    (A) betrothed
    (B) entertained
    (C) loved
    (D) revealed
    (E) participated

GO ON TO THE NEXT PAGE

First paragraph: *Anthropology: The Exploration of Human Diversity*, Conrad Phillip Kottak, McGraw-Hill, 1997
Second paragraph: *Sculpture Through the Ages*, Lincoln Rothschild, McGraw-Hill, 1942, p. 62

5   5   5   5   5   5

Questions 10–16 are based on the following passage.

The following passage is an excerpt from a modern textbook on psychology.

The cognitive strategies used to carry out the steps in problem-solving can be of three
Line general types: trial and error, algorithmic, or heuristic. Let's look at each of these cognitive
5 strategies one at a time. We humans often approach problems without any cognitive strategy at all, simply trying one possible solution after another. This is usually referred to as the trial-and-error approach. Although
10 common, this approach to problem solving can be very time consuming and certainly does not guarantee that a solution will be discovered.

In contrast, algorithms are systematic
15 patterns of reasoning that (if followed) guarantee a correct solution. Computers generally use algorithms. Indeed computers are especially suited for them, since they can quickly consider the many alternatives
20 required by complex algorithms. Computers do not always use algorithms, however. For extremely complex problems, computers are sometimes programmed to use shortcuts known as heuristics. Heuristics are strategies
25 that increase the probabilities of finding a correct solution. But since they do not systematically evaluate every possible solution, heuristics do not guarantee finding the correct one. Indeed, they often lead to
30 poor solutions.

The concept of heuristic reasoning is derived partially from research that attempts to simulate human intelligence using computers. Efforts to program computers to
35 play the game of chess, for example, were originally frustrated by the enormous number of possible solutions that would have to be considered before making each move. To avoid such extensive algorithmic
40 programs, heuristic programs were written. For example, the program is written to maximize protection of the queen or to control the center of the board. Moves that meet these goals are executed, but the long-

45 range consequences of each move are not considered by the artificial intelligence program. That is why excellent chess players can generally beat computers at chess.

The concept of heuristic reasoning is an
50 important one because there is reason to believe that humans operate using heuristics more than algorithms. This is so either because algorithms require so much cognitive capacity and effort or because we
55 simply do not possess algorithms for most of the problems we face in life.

Suppose you are presented with the following problem: What occupation should Steve pursue in college? You are told that
60 Steve is shy, helpful, good with figures, and has a passion for detail. You are also told that you can ask for and receive additional information to use in solving the problem. How would you solve this problem?
65 Amos Tversky has identified two heuristics that are frequently used in human problem solving: representativeness and availability. The representativeness heuristic makes predictions based on the similarity between the
70 information you have and the outcome you want to predict. For example, we might use this heuristic to predict Steve's best choice of an occupation on the basis of which occupation we believe his personality is most
75 representative of (accountant, pharmacist, etc.). This might be a good strategy, but it leads us not to seek and evaluate other information that might be helpful (such as Steve's preferences, his previous school
80 grades, or the employment opportunities in different occupations).

The availability heuristic bases decisions on the availability of relevant information in memory. Rather than seeking additional
85 information, we take another shortcut and use whatever information we can remember. In the case of predicting Steve's best occupation, we might recommend that he become an attorney based on our recollection
90 of an attorney to whom Steve bears a striking

Excerpted from *Psychology: An Introduction*, Benjamin B. Lahey, © 1998 McGraw-Hill

GO ON TO THE NEXT PAGE ⟶

resemblance in ability and temperament.
These cognitive shortcuts are obviously
efficient in terms of effort but certainly do
not always lead to effective problem solving.

95   However, humans frequently think heuristically.

10. This passage is primarily concerned with

(A)   the origins of human error
(B)   the computer as a model for human
      reasoning
(C)   how human beings make decisions
(D)   the development of algorithms
(E)   comparing heuristics with trial-
      and-error methods

11. It can be inferred from the passage that the
     "research" mentioned in line 32 led to the con-
     clusion that

(A)   computers cannot be programmed to use
      heuristics
(B)   computers are important aids to human
      reasoning
(C)   computers can be programmed to defeat
      chess masters
(D)   humans prefer using trial-and-error
      methods to using representativeness
      heuristics
(E)   heuristics simulate human reasoning
      better than algorithms

12. The passage mentions the strategy of control-
     ling the center of the board in a chess game as
     an example of

(A)   a means of reducing the number of options
      to be evaluated before making a decision
(B)   a thorough algorithmic approach that
      has been employed by most chess-
      playing programs
(C)   a trial-and-error method that is easier for
      a computer to employ than a human
(D)   an availability heuristic
(E)   a representativeness heuristic

13. In line 44, the word "executed" most nearly means

(A)   removed
(B)   destroyed
(C)   frustrated
(D)   empowered
(E)   carried out

14. The passage suggests that we humans tend to
     use heuristics more frequently than algorithms
     because heuristics

(A)   are less mentally taxing than algorithms
(B)   guarantee the correct answer
(C)   evaluate more possible solutions than
      algorithms do
(D)   are less systematic than trial-and-error
      approaches
(E)   lead us to seek more information about a
      problem

15. The author suggests that the representative-
     ness heuristic may be insufficient in helping
     Steve to choose an occupation because

(A)   it does not take Steve's personality
      characteristics into account
(B)   it does not take into account what Steve
      wants to do
(C)   it requires an infinite amount of
      information
(D)   it requires the use of an elaborate
      algorithm
(E)   it is similar to a trial-and-error approach

16. According to the passage, the availability
     heuristic differs from the representativeness
     heuristic in that the availability heuristic relies
     more on the ability to

(A)   compare current information about the
      problem to the desired outcome
(B)   recall information
(C)   follow a specified set of directions
(D)   consider every possible solution to a
      problem
(E)   test hypotheses

GO ON TO THE NEXT PAGE

5   **5**   **5**   **5**   **5**   **5**

Questions 17–24 are based on the following passage.

The following passage is an excerpt from an essay about the relationship between politics and art in nineteenth century Europe.

For two years after the fall of the Bastille, July 14, 1789, the vacillation of Louis XVI
Line   between liberal counselors like Mirabeau and Lafayette on the one hand, the blindly
5   reactionary queen Marie Antoinette and the conniving *émigré* nobles on the other, finally goaded the frantic forces of the Revolution to remove by violence the threat of a restoration of the *ancien régime*. However, it was many
10   years before France in the constitution of 1875 caught up politically with the grand trend toward parliamentary, constitutional rule, based upon wide popular suffrage with a stable and fairly high grade of civil
15   administration. Monarchists and clericals preached reaction and restoration on the Right; the new working class and socialist organizations, which arose with the mechanization of industry, called for
20   "completion" of the Revolution on the Left; and business sat solidly in the center trying to get a little order and stability without interference.

     Released politically and culturally as well
25   as economically from their anomalous subjection to an incapable and irresponsible nobility, the entrepreneurial groups in commerce and manufacture, the people who were working with astounding new methods of
30   making things, soon inaugurated an age of unparalleled growth. Technical advance of unbelievable speed and scope increased material production beyond measure and created services hitherto undreamed of.
35   Constructive as well as destructive influences of the development are reflected in the dynamic character and unprecedented activity of cultural expression.

     In the first place the individualistic
40   tendencies of the economy of opportunity reached their most extreme stage, producing an appearance of infinite variety in cultural expression. The various groups working for control represented forces with basically
45   distinct attitudes toward manners and art. But also, every factory owner, every large-scale merchant, after a brief period of stability and profit, felt himself a lord in his particular domain and proudly sought
50   appropriate distinction for his position. The number of people who might wish to own and could afford to buy some kinds of art became large in comparison with other periods. So that each might have the feeling
55   of making a personal choice expressive of his free, individual personality, "original" aspects of style achieved a special value. The artist exaggerated his every whim and impulse, which led inevitably to the development of
60   exotic and bizarre styles.

     It was an age of rapid and sometimes accidental accessions of wealth, tremendous profits in business often resulting from chance or from cutthroat competition as well
65   as from sagacity and service to the community, while great fortunes were rare or unattainable in the ranks of the professional and industrial employment. The wealthy, especially the parvenu,[1] wished to find means of indicating
70   that there was an intrinsic difference between themselves and others, partly because they believed it and partly because to justify the vast inequalities. This encouraged a debased intensification of artificiality in culture to a
75   point where it lost all direct contact with natural experience and might not readily be understood by those who had no special introduction. The more abstruse the forms of art, the more impenetrable to the uninitiated,
80   the greater their value as a distinction to the "connoisseur," which means precisely one who is "in the know." This is an important consideration in the extravagant forms of modern art, each of which starts out by being
85   notoriously "incomprehensible."

---

[1] One who has become suddenly wealthy and has risen to a higher social status

Excerpted from *Sculpture Through the Ages*, Lincoln Rothschild, © 1942 McGraw-Hill

GO ON TO THE NEXT PAGE

17. The first sentence characterizes Louis XVI primarily as

    (A) indecisive
    (B) tyrannical
    (C) reactionary
    (D) liberal
    (E) shrewd

18. It can be inferred from the passage that the French constitution of 1875 ensured which of the following?

    I. a powerful monarchy
    II. an expansion of the right to vote
    III. a well-organized system of government

    (A) II only
    (B) III only
    (C) I and II only
    (D) II and III only
    (E) I, II, and III

19. In line 26, the word "subjection" most nearly means

    (A) opinion
    (B) theme
    (C) state of submission
    (D) course of study
    (E) approval

20. The passage indicates that, in France in the late 18th century, entrepreneurs and business owners primarily sought

    (A) favorable economic policies from the government
    (B) freedom from political interference
    (C) the right to vote
    (D) a return to private ownership
    (E) investment capital from the ruling elite

21. The passage indicates that the "economy of opportunity" (line 40) influenced the world of art primarily by

    (A) allowing former merchants to become artists
    (B) imposing universal standards for art
    (C) eliminating distinctions between the wealthy and the poor
    (D) providing more investment in public museums
    (E) encouraging a wider range of individual expression

22. The description of the relationship between artists and merchants described in lines 46–60 assumes that many artists

    (A) were working actively toward the restoration of the monarchy
    (B) were largely able to ignore the political upheaval of the time
    (C) were better trained than artists in previous centuries
    (D) made aesthetic decisions based on the needs of patrons
    (E) had much to lose in abandoning traditional forms

23. In line 62, the word "accessions" most nearly means

    (A) wisdom
    (B) accidents
    (C) successions
    (D) accumulation
    (E) declines

24. The final paragraph suggests that, to the newly wealthy, the most valuable forms of art were those that were

    (A) imitative of the works of the ancient masters
    (B) produced with exotic materials
    (C) created by artists with foreign backgrounds
    (D) difficult to understand
    (E) reflective of the political and social struggles of the time

STOP

If you finish before time is called, you may check your work on this section only. Do not turn to any other section of the test.

6   **6**   **6**   **6**   **6**   **6**

SECTION 6
Time—25 minutes
35 questions

Turn to Section 6 of your answer sheet to answer the questions in this section.

Directions: For each question in this section, select the best answer from among the choices given and fill in the corresponding circle on the answer sheet.

The following sentences test correctness and effectiveness of expression. Part of each sentence or the entire sentence is underlined; beneath each sentence are five ways of phrasing the underlined material. Choice A repeats the original phrasing; the other four choices are different. Select the choice that completes the sentence most effectively.

In making your selection, follow the requirements of standard written English; that is, pay attention to grammar, choice of words, sentence construction, and punctuation. Your selection should result in the most effective sentence—clear and precise, without awkwardness or ambiguity.

EXAMPLE:

The children <u>couldn't hardly believe their eyes</u>.

(A) couldn't hardly believe their eyes
(B) could hardly believe their eyes
(C) would not hardly believe their eyes
(D) couldn't nearly believe their eyes
(E) couldn't hardly believe his or her eyes

1. She crouched <u>all quiet behind the couch, hoping that she would win</u> this round of hide and seek.

(A) all quiet behind the couch, hoping that she would win
(B) quietly behind the couch, and hoping that she would win
(C) quiet behind the couch, hoping that she would win
(D) quietly behind the couch, hoping to win
(E) quietly behind the couch, in the hope to win

2. The most knowledgeable member of the group, <u>David's answers to all of the questions were correct</u>.

(A) David's answers to all of the questions were correct
(B) David answered all of the questions correctly
(C) David's answers were all correct to the questions
(D) David answered all the questions with complete correctness
(E) David's answers to the questions were completely correct

3. Betsy founded the club, but <u>the meetings are not dominated by her</u>.

(A) the meetings are not dominated by her
(B) the meetings do not have her dominating them
(C) she would not be dominating the meetings
(D) she is not the one dominating over the meetings
(E) she does not dominate the meetings

4. Jon was thrilled that his scores on this test were so much better than <u>last time he took the test</u>.

(A) last time he took the test
(B) his previous test
(C) those on his previous test
(D) his scores on the previous test he took
(E) those on the previous test that he had taken before

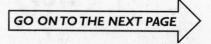
GO ON TO THE NEXT PAGE

6 6 6 6 6 6

5. Frustrated by the lack of jobs in his home town, <u>Tyler sought opportunity in the city</u>, leaving behind a myriad of dreamless peers and wasted lives.

(A) Tyler sought opportunity in the city
(B) Tyler sought the city for the opportunities in it
(C) Tyler's opportunity could be sought in the city
(D) opportunity in the city was what Tyler sought
(E) Tyler sought opportunity and he did it in the city

6. The tasks of <u>renting the van, packing the boxes, and the drive across town were</u> <u>much more time-consuming</u> than we had anticipated.

(A) renting the van, packing the boxes, and the drive across town were much more time-consuming
(B) renting the van, packing the boxes, and the drive across town were all things that took much more time
(C) the renting of the van, packing of boxes, and the drive across town were all much more time-consuming
(D) renting the van, packing the boxes, and driving across town were much more time-consuming
(E) renting the van and packing the boxes together with driving across town was more time-consuming

7. Many scholars believe that a biography <u>of the sort that delves into J. D. Salinger's reclusive life</u> would be even more fascinating than another of his works of fiction.

(A) of the sort that delves into J. D. Salinger's reclusive life
(B) that had delved into the reclusive life of J. D. Salinger
(C) of the type delving into J. D. Salinger's reclusive life
(D) delving into J. D. Salinger's reclusive life
(E) that would be delving into the reclusive life of J.D. Salinger

8. Although Alison was neither the most <u>experienced nor the best educated candidate</u>, she was clearly the most enthusiastic of those who interviewed for the job.

(A) experienced nor the best educated candidate
(B) experienced or a well-educated candidate
(C) experienced candidate and lacked the best education
(D) experienced, nor was she well-educated as a candidate
(E) experienced, nor a candidate who is best educated

9. Ralph Waldo <u>Emerson, who believed that the greatest obstacle in the way of</u> genius is the reliance on the ideas of previous generations.

(A) Emerson, who believed that the greatest obstacle in the way of
(B) Emerson believed that the greatest obstacle to
(C) Emerson, believing that the greatest obstacle to
(D) Emerson, in believing that the greatest obstacle to
(E) Emerson, whose belief that the greatest obstacle in the way of

10. The coach of the women's softball team made sure that <u>every team member had their turn at bat</u>.

(A) every team member had their turn at bat
(B) every member of the team had their turn at bat
(C) every team member had her turn at bat
(D) every team member having their turn at bat
(E) every member of the team having his turn at bat

11. <u>His French rusty after years of neglect</u>, Jeff stumbled through most of his conversations during his visit to Paris.

(A) His French rusty after years of neglect
(B) His French was rusty after years of neglect
(C) His French, rusty after years of neglect
(D) After years of neglect, his French was rusty
(E) Rusty after years of neglecting his French

GO ON TO THE NEXT PAGE >

6   **6**   **6**   **6**   **6**   **6**

The following sentences test your ability to recognize grammar and usage errors. Each sentence contains either a single error or no error at all. No sentence contains more than one error. The error, if there is one, is underlined and lettered. If the sentence contains an error, select the one underlined part that must be changed to make the sentence correct. If the sentence is correct, select choice E. In choosing answers, follow the requirements of standard written English.

EXAMPLE:

By the time <u>they reached</u> the halfway point
                A

<u>in the race</u>, <u>most of the runners</u> <u>hadn't hardly</u>
  B   C   D

begun to hit their stride. <u>No error</u>
                  E

Ⓐ Ⓑ Ⓒ ● Ⓔ

---

12. Although she was <u>an expert climber</u>,
                      A

Marcie <u>struggled</u> <u>for ascending</u> the steep
       B   C

and <u>slippery precipice</u>. <u>No error</u>
      D   E

13. The logs that <u>had been piled</u> in the
             A

backyard throughout the long winter

<u>finally fell</u> over <u>when</u> the dog <u>had jumped</u>
  B   C   D

on them. <u>No error</u>
       E

14. Audrey <u>thought</u> that her ideas were better
      A

than <u>the rest of the class</u> and <u>was outraged</u>
        B   C

when her classmates <u>selected</u> another plan
              D

for the project. <u>No error</u>
           E

15. The <u>abstract and subjective</u> nature of
        A

modern art often <u>leaves observers</u> confused
           B

and unable to grasp the <u>subtle</u> messages
              C

<u>embedded</u> in its form. <u>No error</u>
  D   E

16. By the time election day arrived, he <u>shifted</u>
                      A

his position <u>on the bond issue</u> several
          B

times, <u>leaving even</u> his staunchest
       C

supporters <u>confused</u>. <u>No error</u>
       D   E

17. Exhausted and <u>being tired</u> of the noise
          A

from the back seat, Pedro <u>threatened</u> to
              B

turn the car around and <u>end the vacation</u>
              C

before it could <u>even begin</u>. <u>No error</u>
        D   E

18. Lithe in <u>both body and mind</u>, Horatio was
        A

<u>well-suited</u> to Greco-Roman <u>wrestling: he</u>
  B   C

was <u>often able</u> to out-smart as well as
    D

out-maneuver his opponents. <u>No error</u>
                E

GO ON TO THE NEXT PAGE ⟶

6   6   6   6   6   6

19. The design of the new car is <u>vastly superior</u> to
                                         A

     those of prior models, <u>but</u> a few inadequacies
                              B

     <u>are expectant</u>, as perfection is not
          C

     <u>an attainable goal</u>. <u>No error</u>
               D   E

20. <u>A vocal opponent</u> of the war, Veronica was
          A

     <u>nevertheless</u> strongly in favor of giving the
          B

     troops <u>his or her</u> proper compensation
               C

     <u>upon returning</u> home. <u>No error</u>
          D   E

21. Noam Chomsky has long argued that the

     media <u>plays</u> a large role in skewing
               A

     <u>our perception</u> of reality, presenting images
          B

     and <u>framing stories</u> in such a manner <u>as to</u>
              C   D

     misrepresent the truth. <u>No error</u>
                                   E

22. The family of the victim <u>has reserved</u> its
                                    A

     right to <u>sue</u> the defendant for civil
                 B

     damages, stating publicly that his prison

     sentence <u>wasn't hardly</u> sufficient
                  C

     punishment <u>for the crime</u>. <u>No error</u>
                      D   E

23. Each of the stories <u>end</u> with a moral,
                              A

     but some of these lessons are

     <u>more obvious than others</u>, spelled out
               B

     so as to <u>make</u> them impossible
                  C

     <u>to overlook</u>. <u>No error</u>
          D   E

24. The head of the used car dealership

     <u>assured</u> the woman that <u>their</u> integrity
          A   B

     was unshakable and that the

     <u>odometer readings</u> were entirely
               C

     <u>accurate</u>. <u>No error</u>
          D   E

25. The <u>rapid</u> growth in the <u>rate of construction</u>
              A   B

     of private homes and apartment

     buildings <u>have been</u> stimulated
                    C

     <u>by low interest rates</u>. <u>No error</u>
               D   E

26. The work that Michael <u>did</u> at summer
                                A

     camp <u>to improve his soccer skills</u> <u>helped</u>
              B   C

     him to become more <u>adapt</u> at passing and
                              D

     shooting. <u>No error</u>
                    E

27. The voters <u>in this state</u> should be concerned
                    A

     about the outcome of this election, and

     cast <u>his or her ballot</u> in November
              B

     <u>to re-elect</u> the <u>incumbent</u>. <u>No error</u>
          C   D   E

GO ON TO THE NEXT PAGE →

28. Orlando did not want to <u>miss out on</u> the
                                    A
opportunity to try out <u>for the debate team</u>,
                            B
so he <u>rescheduled</u> his music lesson <u>so that</u>
        C   D
he could stay after school. <u>No error</u>
                              E

29. Justine practiced <u>her dance routine</u> for
                            A
several hours on Sunday, trying

<u>to make sure</u> that it would be
    B
<u>as graceful</u> as <u>the other dancers</u> when
    C   D
she performed it on Wednesday. <u>No error</u>
                                  E

GO ON TO THE NEXT PAGE ⟶

6   6   6   6   6   6

Directions: The following passage is an early draft of an essay. Some parts of the passage need to be rewritten.

Read the passage and select the best answers for the questions that follow. Some questions are about particular sentences or parts of sentences and ask you to improve sentence structure or word choice. Other questions ask you to consider organization and development. In choosing answers, follow the requirements of standard written English.

Questions 30–35 are based on the following passage.

(1) One of the best-studied and most fascinating of the great apes is the chimpanzee. (2) This species, that is homo sapiens' closest living relative, is known for their intelligence and social complexity. (3) One of the ways in which chimpanzees are similar to humans is their degree of bonding with other members of the group.

(4) Chimpanzees live in complex and large groups of which include adults, adolescents, juveniles and infants and can include as many as 100 members. (5) Their social system is called 'fission-fusion' because they do not spend all of their time with their whole group, they often split into smaller parties to forage for food. (6) Female chimpanzees move to new groups when they mature and form new relationships there.

(7) An important aspect of chimpanzee society is the dominance hierarchy. (8) One individual will fight to become the alpha male, which means that he can have the best foods and the respect of the other individuals in the group. (9) However, being alpha male is not guaranteed for life, since other males also want the position of top dog, and the alpha has to defend his position against his rivals. (10) Dominance displays like chest-thumping are common in many other animal species. (11) This is where friendships and alliances become important.

(12) Female chimpanzees also compete with each other, but do not achieve alpha status because males are physically bigger and stronger. (13) Nevertheless, females can and do form complex relationships with each other and with their offspring, and also form bonds with adult males. (14) These are some of the reasons why chimpanzees are so fascinating, and that make them so much like humans.

30. Which of the following is the best revision of the underlined section of sentence 2 (reproduced below)?

This species, that is homo sapiens' closest living relative, is known for their intelligence and social complexity.

(A) that is the closest relative to *homo sapiens*, is known for its intelligence and also its social complexity

(B) of which *homo sapiens'* is its closest relative, is known for their intelligence and social complexity

(C) the most closely related to *homo sapiens*, is known for how intelligent they are and for their social complexity

(D) the closest relative of *homo sapiens*, is known for its intelligence and social complexity

(E) of which it is *homo sapiens'* closest living relative, is known for its intelligence and its social complexity

31. Which of the following is the best revision of the underlined portion of sentence 4 (reproduced below)?

Chimpanzees live in complex and large groups of which include adults, adolescents, juveniles, and infants and can include as many as 100 members.

(A) large, complex groups of adults, adolescents, juveniles, and infants and can include as many as 100 members

(B) complex and large groups which include adults, adolescents, juveniles, and infants and as many as 100 members

(C) large, complex groups which would include adults, adolescents, juveniles, and infants and as many as 100 members

(D) complex, large groups, which includes adults, adolescents, juveniles, and infants and can include as many as 100 members

(E) large, complex groups containing as many as 100 members, including adults, adolescents, juveniles, and infants

GO ON TO THE NEXT PAGE ▷

6   6   6   6   6   6

---

32. Which of the following is the best version of the underlined portion of sentence 5 (reproduced below)?

    Their social system is called 'fission-fusion' because they do not spend all of their time with their whole group, they often split into smaller parties to forage for food.

    (A) (as it is now)
    (B) group; rather, they often split
    (C) group instead often split
    (D) group and also often split
    (E) group, but instead often splitting

33. Which is the best sentence to insert after sentence 6 to maintain the logic and unity of the second paragraph?

    (A) Male chimpanzees are skilled hunters that prefer to prey on monkeys and small mammals.
    (B) Female chimpanzees spend much of their time foraging for fruit.
    (C) They are known for their use of tools, such as leaves as sponges.
    (D) Male chimpanzees, on the other hand, stay in their natal group for life, and often form friendships with other males.
    (E) Males, in contrast to females, are known for their loud dominance displays.

34. Which sentence contributes the least to the unity of the third paragraph?

    (A) sentence 7
    (B) sentence 8
    (C) sentence 9
    (D) sentence 10
    (E) sentence 11

35. Where is the best place to insert the following sentence?

    For instance, male chimpanzees often maintain strong bonds with allies who can support their challenge to the alpha male.

    (A) after sentence 4
    (B) after sentence 6
    (C) after sentence 11
    (D) after sentence 12
    (E) There is no appropriate place for this sentence.

STOP

If you finish before time is called, you may check your work on this section only. Do not turn to any other section of the test.

7　　7　　7　　7　　7　　7

SECTION 7
Time—20 minutes
16 questions

Turn to Section 7 of your answer sheet to answer the questions in this section.

Directions: For this section, solve each problem and decide which is the best of the choices given. Fill in the corresponding circle on the answer sheet. You may use any available space for scratchwork.

Notes

1. The use of a calculator is permitted.
2. All numbers used are real numbers.
3. Figures that accompany problems in this test are intended to provide information useful in solving the problems. They are drawn as accurately as possible EXCEPT when it is stated in a specific problem that the figure is not drawn to scale. All figures lie in a plane unless otherwise indicated.
4. Unless otherwise specified, the domain of any function f is assumed to be the set of all real numbers x for which $f(x)$ is a real number.

Reference Information

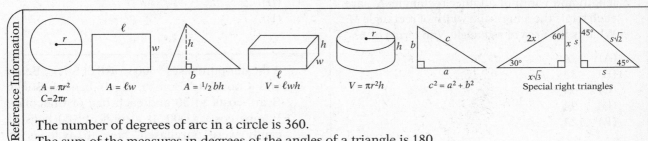

$A = \pi r^2$ $A = \ell w$ $A = \frac{1}{2}bh$ $V = \ell wh$ $V = \pi r^2 h$ $c^2 = a^2 + b^2$ Special right triangles
$C = 2\pi r$

The number of degrees of arc in a circle is 360.
The sum of the measures in degrees of the angles of a triangle is 180.

---

1. If $x^{3y} = x^9$ and $x > 1$, then $y =$

(A) 2
(B) 3
(C) 4
(D) 5
(E) 6

2. The ratio of 1 to 1.4 is equal to the ratio of

(A) 1 to 4
(B) 3 to 4
(C) 5 to 7
(D) 7 to 5
(E) 4 to 3

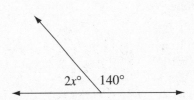

Note: Figure not drawn to scale.

3. A line and a ray intersect as shown above. What is the value of $2x + 5$?

(A) 20
(B) 25
(C) 40
(D) 45
(E) 50

GO ON TO THE NEXT PAGE

7   7   7   7   7   7

4. When three times a number is divided by two, the result is 39. What is that number?

(A) 20
(B) 21
(C) 24
(D) 26
(E) 30

5. How much greater is $x + 5$ than $x - 5$?

(A) 2
(B) 5
(C) 7
(D) 10
(E) 12

6. Rectangle M has an area of A square feet. The length and width of another rectangle, N, are each triple the length and width of rectangle M. What is the area of rectangle N in terms of A?

(A) $2A$
(B) $3A$
(C) $6A$
(D) $9A$
(E) $12A$

7. If a circle has a circumference of 10, what is the ratio of the circumference of the circle to its diameter?

(A) $1 : 2\pi$
(B) $1 : \pi$
(C) $\pi : 1$
(D) $2\pi : 1$
(E) $\pi : 2$

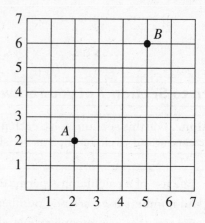

8. What is the distance from point A to point B in the figure above?

(A) 1
(B) 3
(C) 4
(D) 5
(E) 7

9. A theater purchases $500 worth of Sticky Bears and Chocolate Bombs. Each bag of Sticky Bears costs $1.50 and each bag of Chocolate Bombs costs $1.00. If a total of 400 bags of candy were purchased, how many bags of Chocolate Bombs did the theater buy?

(A) 100
(B) 150
(C) 200
(D) 250
(E) 300

10. The median of a set of seven consecutive even integers is 10. What is the average (arithmetic mean) of this set?

(A) 8
(B) 10
(C) 12
(D) 14
(E) 16

GO ON TO THE NEXT PAGE ⇨

Questions 11 and 12 refer to the following tables.

NUMBER OF MOVIE TICKETS SOLD

	Adult	Child	Matinee (Adult or Child)
Village Theater	100	20	70
Bijou	120	30	20
Community Cinema	220	40	90
Triplex	x	30	0

PRICE OF MOVIE TICKETS AT ALL THEATERS

Adult	$9.00
Child	$6.00
Matinee (Adult or Child)	$6.00

11. The total revenue collected for movie tickets at the Bijou is what percent of the total revenue collected for movie tickets at the Community Cinema?

(A) 25%
(B) 50%
(C) 75%
(D) 100%
(E) 200%

12. If the ticket revenue at the Triplex is greater than the ticket revenue at the Village Theater, what is the least possible value of x ?

(A) 137
(B) 138
(C) 139
(D) 140
(E) 141

13. How many integers between 100 and 1000 contain only the digits 3, 4 or 5, if any digit may be repeated?

(A) 16
(B) 18
(C) 20
(D) 24
(E) 27

14. If $\dfrac{1}{4y+6} = x^2$, which of the following represents the value of y in terms of x?

(A) $\dfrac{1}{4x^2} - \dfrac{3}{2}$

(B) $\dfrac{1}{4x^2} - \dfrac{3}{4}$

(C) $\dfrac{1}{x^2} - \dfrac{3}{2}$

(D) $\dfrac{1}{\sqrt{x}} + \dfrac{3}{2}$

(E) $\dfrac{1}{4x^2} - 24$

GO ON TO THE NEXT PAGE

7   7   7   7   7   7

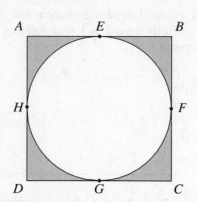

16. A chef spends c hours each day at her restaurant, $\frac{c}{3}$ hours of which she spends preparing desserts. At this rate, after how many days will the chef have spent 24 hours preparing desserts?

    (A) $\frac{c}{72}$

    (B) $\frac{24}{c}$

    (C) $\frac{c}{24}$

    (D) $24c$

    (E) $\frac{72}{c}$

15. The inscribed circle touches square $ABCD$ at points E, F, G, and H, which are all midpoints of their respective sides. If the length of one side of the square is 6, what is the area of the shaded region?

    (A) $36 - 9\pi$
    (B) $36 - 36\pi$
    (C) $24 - 9\pi$
    (D) $36\pi - 36$
    (E) $24 - 9\pi$

STOP

If you finish before time is called, you may check your work on this section only. Do not turn to any other section of the test.

8   8   8   8   8   8

SECTION 8
Time—20 minutes
19 questions

Turn to Section 8 of your answer sheet to answer the questions in this section.

Directions: For each question in this section, select the best answer from among the choices given and fill in the corresponding circle on the answer sheet.

Each sentence below has one or two blanks, each blank indicating that something has been omitted. Beneath the sentence are five words or sets of words labeled A through E. Choose the word or set of words that, when inserted in the sentence, best fits the meaning of the sentence as a whole.

EXAMPLE:

Rather than accepting the theory unquestioningly, Deborah regarded it with -----.

(A) mirth
(B) sadness
(C) responsibility
(D) ignorance
(E) skepticism

Ⓐ Ⓑ Ⓒ Ⓓ ●

---

1. As the lunar cycle progresses in the coming days, the moon will continue to ------- in apparent size until it is not even visible next week.

   (A) progress
   (B) wane
   (C) debunk
   (D) convoke
   (E) coalesce

2. Because General Randolph's stratagem had been ------- by the opposing forces, his army was ------- by a well-coordinated and lethal counterattack.

   (A) foreseen . . defoliated
   (B) contradicted . . disavowed
   (C) predicted . . decimated
   (D) resolved . . destroyed
   (E) established . . demarcated

3. During the presidential debate, the candidates practiced the art of -------; they used roundabout expressions and evasive tactics to avoid the questions they were asked.

   (A) matriculation
   (B) circumlocution
   (C) contemplation
   (D) homogeneity
   (E) serendipity

4. It was George's propensity to ------- that caused his peers to view him as a ------- and grandiose individual.

   (A) vacillate . . phlegmatic
   (B) eulogize . . loquacious
   (C) prophecy . . mercurial
   (D) pilfer . . colloquial
   (E) pontificate . . bombastic

5. Napoleon Bonaparte's ------- frame ------- his ability to dominate a room; in fact, people often remembered him as being much taller than he actually was.

   (A) gargantuan . . disproved
   (B) voluminous . . showed
   (C) scanty . . exemplified
   (D) diminutive . . belied
   (E) meager . . propagated

GO ON TO THE NEXT PAGE ⇨

8   **8**   **8**   **8**   **8**   **8**

6. The journalist's reputation for ------- has led many of his readers to doubt the ------- of his articles.

(A) candor . . legitimacy
(B) perfidiousness . . ingenuity
(C) fabrication . . veracity
(D) virtuosity . . aptitude
(E) perspicacity . . autonomy

> The passages below are followed by questions based on their content and on the relationship between the passages. Answer the questions on the basis of what is stated or implied in the passages and in any introductory material that may be provided.

Questions 7–19 are based on the following passage.

The following passages present two perspectives on the works and impact of twentieth century author Ernest Hemingway.

PASSAGE 1

For members of my generation, the young
men born between 1918, roughly, and 1924,
Line there was a special charm about Hemingway.
By the time most of us were old enough to
5 read him he had become a legendary figure,
a kind of twentieth-century Lord Byron; and
like Byron, he had learned to play himself,
his own best hero, with superb conviction.
He was Hemingway of the rugged outdoor
10 grin and the hairy chest posing beside a
marlin he had just landed or a lion he had
just shot. He was Tarzan Hemingway,
crouching in the African bush with elephant
gun at ready, Bwana Hemingway
15 commanding his native bearers in terse
Swahili; he was War Correspondent
Hemingway writing a play in the Hotel
Florida in Madrid while thirty fascist shells
crashed through the roof; later on he was

20 Task Force Hemingway swathed in
ammunition belts and defending his post
singlehanded against fierce German attacks.
But even without the legend he created
around himself, the chest-beating,
25 wisecracking pose that was later to seem so
incredibly absurd, his impact upon us was
tremendous. The feeling he gave us was one
of immense expansiveness and freedom and
at the same time, of absolute stability and
30 control. We could put our whole faith in him
and he would not fail us. We could follow
him, ape his manner, his cold detachment,
through all the doubts and fears of
adolescence and come out pure and
35 untouched. The words he put down seemed
to us to have been carved from the living
stone of life. They were absolutely, nakedly
true because the man behind them had
reduced himself to the bare tissue of his soul
40 to write them and because he was a
dedicated man. The words of Hemingway
conveyed so exactly the taste, smell and feel
of experience as it was, as it might possibly
be, that we began unconsciously to translate
45 our own sensations into their terms and to
impose on everything we did and felt the
particular emotions they aroused in us.
The Hemingway time was a good time to
be young. It seems to me that we had much
50 then which the war later forced out of us and
that in the end what many of us lost was
something far greater than Hemingway and
his strong formative influence. There are
young writers today who, in losing or getting
55 rid of Hemingway, have been able to find
nothing to put in his place, who have rejected
his time as untrue for them only to fail at
finding themselves in their own time. There
are others, who, in their embarrassment at
60 the hold he once had over them, have not
profited by the lessons he had to teach, and
still others who were never touched by him at
all. These last are perhaps the real
unfortunates, for they have been denied
65 access to a powerful tradition, one that is as
important and true as any my generation can
ever have.

Printed with the permission of the alter John Aldridge

GO ON TO THE NEXT PAGE ➤

PASSAGE 2

One wonders why *The Sun Also Rises* (1926) and A *Farewell to Arms* (1929) now seem
70 unable to evoke the same awesome sense of a tottering world, captured poignantly and precisely in language, which in the nineteen twenties established Ernest Hemingway's reputation. These novels should be speaking
75 to us. Our social structure is as shaken, our philosophical despair as great, our everyday experience as unsatisfying. We have had more war than Hemingway ever saw or dreamed of. Our violence—physical,
80 emotional and intellectual—is not inferior to that of the nineteen twenties. Yet, though Hemingway's books still offer great moments, they no longer seem to penetrate too deeply and steadily below the surface of existence;
85 one begins to doubt that they ever did so significantly in the nineteen twenties,
It is not merely that our times are worse, which they are. Life in the nineteen twenties, after all, tended on the whole to be more
90 excruciating than life in the two previous decades. In retrospect, however, Hemingway's novels cajoled the dominant genteel tradition in American culture while seeming to repudiate it. They yielded to the functionalist,
95 technological aesthetic of the culture instead of resisting in the manner of Frank Lloyd Wright. Hemingway, in effect, became a dupe of his culture rather than its moral-aesthetic conscience. As a consequence, the import of
100 his work has diminished.
There is some evidence from his stylistic evolution that Hemingway himself must have felt as much, for Hemingway's famous stylistic economy frequently seems to conceal
105 another kind of writer, with much richer rhetorical resources to hand. So, *Death in the Afternoon* (1932), Hemingway's bullfighting opus and his first book after *A Farewell to Arms* reveals great uneasiness over his earlier
110 accomplishment. One of the more important of the aggressive defenses of his literary method that appear in the work incorporates a doctrine of ambiguity which justifies confusion and encourages ambivalence:

Excerpted from *The American Novel and the Nineteen Twenties*:
"Ernest Hemingway's Genteel Bullfight," Brom Weber. © 1971.
Printed with the permission of Hodder Education

115   *If a writer of prose knows enough about
       what he is writing about he may omit
       things that he knows and the reader, if the
       writer is writing truly enough, will have a
       feeling of those things as strongly as though
120   the writer had stated them.*
Hemingway made much the same theoretical point in another way in *Death in the Afternoon* apparently believing that a formal reduction of aesthetic complexity was
125 the only kind of design that had value.
But in fact, Hemingway's famous economy of prose was by no means as omnipresent as he himself suggests; he had his own baroque inclinations. His work is really a mixture of
130 stylistic forces. Thus a still greater irony of *Death in the Afternoon* was its unmistakably baroque prose, which he at one point embarrassedly admitted was 'flowery'. Reviewers, unable to challenge Hemingway's
135 expertise in the art of bullfighting and confused by the eccentricities of the book, noted that its style was 'awkward, tortuous, [and] belligerently clumsy'.
Hemingway had written an extraordinarily
140 personal, self-indulgent, garrulous, capricious, playful, bellicose and satiric book, even more unruly and clownish than *The Torrents of Spring*. There is no need here for a schema of the book, beyond noting that it
145 contains scrambled chronology and thematic arrangement, willful digressions, mock-scholarly apparatus (for example, a 'bibliographical note' refers readers to a Spanish bibliography—undated—for the
150 '2077 books and pamphlets in Spanish dealing with or touching on tauromaquia[1]' which he mock-modestly claimed to have read), fictional interludes, scathing allusions and references to contemporary writers and critics.

[1] bullfighting

7. Which of the following is the best title for Passage 1?

(A) How Hemingway Influenced a Generation
(B) Fiction and the Art of War
(C) Humor in Hemingway's Prose
(D) The Literary Giants of the 1920s
(E) Growing up in the 1920s

GO ON TO THE NEXT PAGE →

8. The sentence beginning on line 41 ("The words of Hemingway ... they aroused in us") indicates that Hemingway's readers were inclined to

  (A) emulate his style of writing
  (B) look skeptically at his writing in light of the horrors of war
  (C) empathize deeply with his narratives
  (D) view his writing more as poetry than prose
  (E) doubt the veracity of some of his writing

9. Unlike the wars that Hemingway witnessed as described in the first paragraph of Passage 1, "the war" referred to in line 50 had the effect of

  (A) discouraging young people from pursuing careers in writing
  (B) encouraging the portrayal of soldiers as heroes
  (C) inspiring many new authors to write about conflict
  (D) disillusioning a generation
  (E) elevating the status of Hemingway among literary critics

10. In line 57, "untrue" most nearly means

  (A) not meaningful
  (B) treacherous
  (C) indecisive
  (D) historically inaccurate
  (E) intolerable

11. The author of Passage 1 indicates that writers of his generation differ from some young writers today in which of the following regards?

  I. their reverence for Hemingway
  II. their willingness to write about war
  III. their ability to find meaning in the period of history in which they live

  (A) I only
  (B) I and II only
  (C) I and III only
  (D) II and III only
  (E) I, II and III

12. The last paragraph of Passage 1 suggests that the least fortunate of modern writers are those who

  (A) have not experienced war first hand
  (B) criticize Hemingway for his literary inadequacies
  (C) have attempted to deviate from Hemingway's style
  (D) have not been exposed to Hemingway's writing
  (E) do not investigate the historical background of the 1920s before reading Hemingway

13. In saying that Hemingway's novels "should be speaking to us" (lines 74–75), the author of Passage 2 suggests that

  (A) modern readers should be more educated
  (B) literary critics are not doing their jobs properly
  (C) educators should emphasize Hemingway's works
  (D) readers prefer simplistic prose
  (E) the modern world is similar to the world of Hemingway's time

14. The quotation from *Death in the Afternoon* in lines 115–120 suggests that Hemingway assumes that his readers

  (A) prefer an ornate style of prose to an unadorned style
  (B) can read beyond what is directly stated
  (C) can empathize with the violence of his narratives
  (D) are familiar with the European countryside he describes
  (E) have read the works of writers who are contemporaries of Hemingway

GO ON TO THE NEXT PAGE

15. Passage 2 indicates that Hemingway implied in his own prose that good writers must

   (A) draw upon their own experiences
   (B) imitate the great masters of the novel
   (C) use a florid literary style
   (D) continually endeavor to simplify their prose
   (E) employ their knowledge of history in their writing

16. Passage 2 indicates that, over his entire literary career, Hemingway's literary style was in fact

   (A) always sparse and simple
   (B) persistently embellished
   (C) inconsistent
   (D) better suited to describing human relationships than the horrors of war
   (E) consistently allegorical

17. The final paragraph of Passage 2 indicates that *Death in the Afternoon* contains which of the following?

   I. descriptions of events that are ordered improperly
   II. egocentric prose
   III. recollections of Hemingway's wartime experiences

   (A) I only
   (B) II only
   (C) I and II only
   (D) I and III only
   (E) I, II, and III

18. Which of the following best describes how each passage characterizes Hemingway's relationship to the dominant culture of his time?

   (A) Passage 1 portrays him as a hero to his generation, while Passage 2 suggests that he was a conformist.
   (B) Passage 1 suggests that he felt out of place in his generation, while Passage 2 suggests that he was comfortable in the dominant culture.
   (C) Passage 1 suggests that he was persistently skeptical about the society in which he lived, while Passage 2 indicates that he always avoided social commentary.
   (D) Passage 1 suggests that he was only a marginal figure in his generation, while Passage 2 portrays him as the dominant writer of his time.
   (E) Both passages portray him as a rebel against the dominant culture.

19. Which of the following best describes the contrast in focus of the two passages?

   (A) Passage 1 focuses on Hemingway's wartime writing, while Passage 2 focuses on his writing about sports.
   (B) Passage 1 analyzes Hemingway's prose, while Passage 2 focuses on his cultural background.
   (C) Passage 1 examines the views of several literary critics, while Passage 2 objectively examines the inconsistencies in Hemingway's writings.
   (D) Passage 1 describes Hemingway's scholarly work, while Passage 2 describes the effect of his prose on a generation.
   (E) Passage 1 focuses on Hemingway as a man, while Passage 2 focuses on his literary style.

 STOP

If you finish before time is called, you may check your work on this section only. Do not turn to any other section of the test.

9   9   9   9   9   9

SECTION 9
Time—10 minutes
14 questions

Turn to Section 9 of your answer sheet to answer the questions in this section.

Directions: For each question in this section, select the best answer from among the choices given and fill in the corresponding circle on the answer sheet.

The following sentences test correctness and effectiveness of expression. Part of each sentence or the entire sentence is underlined; beneath each sentence are five ways of phrasing the underlined material. Choice A repeats the original phrasing; the other four choices are different. Select the choice that completes the sentence most effectively.

In making your selection, follow the requirements of standard written English; that is, pay attention to grammar, choice of words, sentence construction, and punctuation. Your selection should result in the most effective sentence—clear and precise, without awkwardness or ambiguity.

EXAMPLE:

The children <u>couldn't hardly believe their eyes</u>.

(A) couldn't hardly believe their eyes
(B) could hardly believe their eyes
(C) would not hardly believe their eyes
(D) couldn't nearly believe their eyes
(E) couldn't hardly believe his or her eyes

1. Having no more food in her backpack, <u>it was necessary for Maria</u> to begin foraging for edible berries.

   (A) it was necessary for Maria
   (B) made it necessary for Maria
   (C) Maria had
   (D) was why Maria had
   (E) required Maria

2. Anna Warren, an accomplished painter whose art has been shown in museums and galleries throughout America and Europe, <u>becoming as well known for her landscapes as for</u> her still lifes.

   (A) becoming as well known for her landscapes as for
   (B) in order to become as well known for her landscapes as
   (C) has become equally well known for her landscapes and still-lifes
   (D) has become as well known for her landscapes as
   (E) has become as well known for her landscapes as for

3. Some psychologists continue to believe that the mind is largely independent <u>of the body; most, however, believe</u> that human behavior can be explained solely in terms of the functions of the brain.

   (A) of the body; most, however, believe
   (B) from the body, but most however believe
   (C) of the body, most believe however
   (D) from the body; most though believe
   (E) from the body and most believe, however

4. The reason that television networks air such trashy programs is <u>because it is what the</u> viewers want to see.

   (A) because it is what the
   (B) that these are what
   (C) that this is what
   (D) because they are the things that
   (E) that is it these that

GO ON TO THE NEXT PAGE ➡

9   9   9   9   9   9

5. The greatest feature of this audio system is <u>it is able to play</u> music in almost any format.

   (A) it is able to play
   (B) it can play
   (C) the fact of its being able to play
   (D) its ability to play
   (E) it being able to play

6. <u>If I wouldn't have been</u> in such a hurry to get to the reception, I would not have left my wallet at the hotel.

   (A) If I wouldn't have been
   (B) I had not been
   (C) If I had not been
   (D) Having been
   (E) If not for being I was

7. The vacation cottage was tiny, dirty, and <u>it was lit with very dim lighting</u>.

   (A) it was lit with very dim lighting
   (B) it was dimly lit
   (C) lit with very dim lighting
   (D) the lighting was dim
   (E) dimly lit

8. Although most people shudder when they recall analyzing sentences in school, <u>nevertheless a recent book about grammar has become a best seller</u>.

   (A) nevertheless a recent book about grammar has become a best seller
   (B) a recent book about grammar has become a best seller
   (C) a recent book about grammar becoming a best seller
   (D) a book has become a best seller recently about grammar
   (E) yet a recent book about grammar became a best seller

9. As a writer, <u>it is surprising to me that so few</u> high school graduates can write a coherent sentence.

   (A) it is surprising to me that so few
   (B) it is surprising that hardly any
   (C) I am surprised that so few
   (D) it surprises me that so few
   (E) I am surprised of the fact that so few

10. The coach gave Fernando a few words of encouragement before the <u>game, this was in order</u> to boost the pitcher's confidence.

   (A) game, this was in order
   (B) game
   (C) game, this was
   (D) game; in order
   (E) game and this was

11. Although John Dewey profoundly influenced American philosophy of the 20th century, <u>modern philosophers do not find his ideas to be as resonant in the regard that they find his writings</u> almost incomprehensible.

   (A) modern philosophers do not find his ideas to be as resonant in the regard that they find his writings
   (B) modern philsophers are not so much influenced by the resonance of his ideas in that they find that his writings are
   (C) his ideas are not as resonant with modern philosophers so that to them his writings are
   (D) his ideas are not as well resonant with modern philosophers in the sense that they find his writings to be
   (E) his ideas are not as well resonant with modern philosophers, who find his writings

GO ON TO THE NEXT PAGE ⟶

12. A hierarchical power structure is not <u>a necessity of modern society, and actually that is antithetical to</u> true democracy.

   (A) a necessity of modern society, and actually that is antithetical to

   (B) necessarily needed by modern society, and is antithetical of

   (C) necessary to modern society; in fact, it is antithetical to

   (D) needed for modern society and so is antithetical to

   (E) necessary to modern society; in fact is antithetical of

13. When one of my seizures <u>strikes, I feel as if I were</u> paralyzed, if only for a moment.

   (A) strikes, I feel as if I were
   (B) strikes, I feel as if I was
   (C) strike, I feel like I was
   (D) strikes, it is a feeling like being
   (E) strikes, I feel like being

14. Completely devoid of artistic merit, the film used shock tactics in an effort to gain publicity <u>and increasing their ticket sales</u>.

   (A) and increasing their ticket sales
   (B) and increase ticket sales
   (C) and increasing the sales of their tickets
   (D) and tickets
   (E) and, as such, their increasing ticket sales

STOP

If you finish before time is called, you may check your work on this section only. Do not turn to any other section of the test.

ANSWER KEY

Critical Reading

Section 2

	COR. ANS.	DIFF. LEV.		COR. ANS.	DIFF. LEV.
1.	D	1	13.	E	2
2.	A	1	14.	D	3
3.	B	2	15.	B	3
4.	A	3	16.	E	4
5.	B	4	17.	A	4
6.	D	4	18.	C	3
7.	B	4	19.	B	3
8.	E	5	20.	E	4
9.	C	2	21.	E	3
10.	D	3	22.	D	2
11.	A	3	23.	B	3
12.	D	4	24.	D	5

Number correct

Number incorrect

Section 5

	COR. ANS.	DIFF. LEV.		COR. ANS.	DIFF. LEV.
1.	A	2	13.	E	3
2.	E	2	14.	A	4
3.	D	3	15.	B	3
4.	B	3	16.	B	4
5.	B	4	17.	A	4
6.	C	3	18.	D	5
7.	D	3	19.	C	3
8.	B	2	20.	B	3
9.	E	3	21.	E	4
10.	C	2	22.	D	3
11.	E	4	23.	D	4
12.	A	5	24.	D	4

Number correct

Number incorrect

Section 8

	COR. ANS.	DIFF. LEV.		COR. ANS.	DIFF. LEV.
1.	B	1	11.	C	4
2.	C	2	12.	D	2
3.	B	3	13.	E	2
4.	E	4	14.	B	4
5.	D	3	15.	D	4
6.	C	5	16.	C	3
7.	A	2	17.	C	3
8.	C	4	18.	A	3
9.	D	4	19.	E	4
10.	A	3			

Number correct

Number incorrect

Math

Section 3

	COR. ANS.	DIFF. LEV.		COR. ANS.	DIFF. LEV.
1.	A	1	11.	D	3
2.	B	1	12.	C	3
3.	C	3	13.	B	3
4.	D	2	14.	E	4
5.	E	2	15.	D	3
6.	B	2	16.	A	4
7.	E	3	17.	D	4
8.	E	2	18.	B	4
9.	C	3	19.	A	5
10.	C	3	20.	A	5

Number correct

Number incorrect

Section 4

Multiple-Choice Questions

	COR. ANS.	DIFF. LEV.
1.	C	1
2.	B	2
3.	D	3
4.	C	3
5.	A	3
6.	B	4
7.	C	4
8.	E	5

Student-produced Response questions

	COR. ANS.	DIFF. LEV.
9.	4	1
10.	$0 < b < 1$	2
11.	180	3
12.	900	3
13.	6	3
14.	12	4
15.	6	3
16.	580	4
17.	5/9 or .555 or .556	5
18.	1/4 or .25	

Number correct

Number incorrect

Number correct (9–18)

Section 7

	COR. ANS.	DIFF. LEV.		COR. ANS.	DIFF. LEV.
1.	B	2	9.	C	4
2.	C	2	10.	B	4
3.	D	2	11.	B	3
4.	D	3	12.	E	4
5.	D	3	13.	E	3
6.	D	3	14.	A	4
7.	C	3	15.	A	5
8.	D	3	16.	E	5

Number correct

Number incorrect

Writing

Section 6

	COR. ANS.	DIFF. LEV.		COR. ANS.	DIFF. LEV.		COR. ANS.	DIFF. LEV.		COR. ANS.	DIFF. LEV.
1.	D	1	11.	A	4	21.	A	3	31.	E	3
2.	B	1	12.	C	1	22.	C	4	32.	B	3
3.	E	2	13.	D	1	23.	A	3	33.	D	3
4.	C	3	14.	B	2	24.	B	4	34.	D	3
5.	A	4	15.	E	3	25.	C	3	35.	C	3
6.	D	2	16.	A	3	26.	D	3			
7.	D	3	17.	A	2	27.	B	4			
8.	A	4	18.	E	3	28.	A	4			
9.	B	4	19.	C	3	29.	D	5			
10.	C	3	20.	C	3	30.	D	3			

Number correct

Number incorrect

Section 9

	COR. ANS.	DIFF. LEV.		COR. ANS.	DIFF. LEV.
1.	C	1	11.	E	3
2.	E	2	12.	C	4
3.	A	2	13.	A	4
4.	B	2	14.	B	3
5.	D	2			
6.	C	2			
7.	E	3			
8.	B	3			
9.	C	3			
10.	B	3			

Number correct

Number incorrect

NOTE: Difficulty levels are estimates of question difficulty that range from 1 (easiest) to 5 (hardest).

SCORE CONVERSION TABLE

How to score your test

Use the answer key on the previous page to determine your raw score on each section. **Your raw score on each section except Section 4 is simply the number of correct answers minus ¼ of the number of wrong answers. On Section 4, your raw score is the sum of the number of correct answers for questions 1–8 minus ¼ of the number of wrong answers for questions 1–8 plus the total number of correct answers for questions 9–18.** Next, add the raw scores from Sections 3, 4, and 7 to get your Math raw score, add the raw scores from Sections 2, 5, and 8 to get your Critical Reading raw score and add the raw scores from Sections 6 and 9 to get your Writing raw score. Write the three raw scores here:

Raw Critical Reading score: _____   Raw Math score: _____   Raw Writing score: _____

Use the table below to convert these to scaled scores.

Scaled scores: Critical Reading: _____   Math: _____   Writing: _____

Raw Score	Critical Reading Scaled Score	Math Scaled Score	Writing Scaled Score	Raw Score	Critical Reading Scaled Score	Math Scaled Score	Writing Scaled Score
67	800			32	520	570	610
66	800			31	510	560	600
65	790			30	510	550	580
64	780			29	500	540	570
63	770			28	490	530	560
62	750			27	490	520	550
61	740			26	480	510	540
60	730			25	480	500	530
59	720			24	470	490	520
58	700			23	460	480	510
57	690			22	460	480	500
56	680			21	450	470	490
55	670			20	440	460	480
54	660	800		19	440	450	470
53	650	800		18	430	450	460
52	650	780		17	420	440	450
51	640	760		16	420	430	440
50	630	740		15	410	420	440
49	620	730	800	14	400	410	430
48	620	710	800	13	400	410	420
47	610	710	800	12	390	400	410
46	600	700	790	11	380	390	400
45	600	690	780	10	370	380	390
44	590	680	760	9	360	370	380
43	590	670	740	8	350	360	380
42	580	660	730	7	340	350	370
41	570	650	710	6	330	340	360
40	570	640	700	5	320	330	350
39	560	630	690	4	310	320	340
38	550	620	670	3	300	310	320
37	550	620	660	2	280	290	310
36	540	610	650	1	270	280	300
35	540	600	640	0	250	260	280
34	530	590	630	−1	230	240	270
33	520	580	620	−2 or less	210	220	250

SCORE CONVERSION TABLE FOR WRITING COMPOSITE
[ESSAY + MULTIPLE CHOICE]

Calculate your writing raw score as you did on the previous page and grade your essay from a 1 to a 6 according to the standards that follow in the detailed answer key.

Essay score: _____ Raw Writing score: _____

Use the table below to convert these to scaled scores.

Scaled score: Writing: _____

Raw Score	Essay Score 0	Essay Score 1	Essay Score 2	Essay Score 3	Essay Score 4	Essay Score 5	Essay Score 6
−2 or less	200	230	250	280	310	340	370
−1	210	240	260	290	320	360	380
0	230	260	280	300	340	370	400
1	240	270	290	320	350	380	410
2	250	280	300	330	360	390	420
3	260	290	310	340	370	400	430
4	270	300	320	350	380	410	440
5	280	310	330	360	390	420	450
6	290	320	340	360	400	430	460
7	290	330	340	370	410	440	470
8	300	330	350	380	410	450	470
9	310	340	360	390	420	450	480
10	320	350	370	390	430	460	490
11	320	360	370	400	440	470	500
12	330	360	380	410	440	470	500
13	340	370	390	420	450	480	510
14	350	380	390	420	460	490	520
15	350	380	400	430	460	500	530
16	360	390	410	440	470	500	530
17	370	400	420	440	480	510	540
18	380	410	420	450	490	520	550
19	380	410	430	460	490	530	560
20	390	420	440	470	500	530	560
21	400	430	450	480	510	540	570
22	410	440	460	480	520	550	580
23	420	450	470	490	530	560	590
24	420	460	470	500	540	570	600
25	430	460	480	510	540	580	610
26	440	470	490	520	550	590	610
27	450	480	500	530	560	590	620
28	460	490	510	540	570	600	630
29	470	500	520	550	580	610	640
30	480	510	530	560	590	620	650
31	490	520	540	560	600	630	660
32	500	530	550	570	610	640	670
33	510	540	550	580	620	650	680
34	510	550	560	590	630	660	690
35	520	560	570	600	640	670	700
36	530	560	580	610	650	680	710
37	540	570	590	620	660	690	720
38	550	580	600	630	670	700	730
39	560	600	610	640	680	710	740
40	580	610	620	650	690	720	750
41	590	620	640	660	700	730	760
42	600	630	650	680	710	740	770
43	610	640	660	690	720	750	780
44	620	660	670	700	740	770	800
45	640	670	690	720	750	780	800
46	650	690	700	730	770	800	800
47	670	700	720	750	780	800	800
48	680	720	730	760	800	800	800
49	680	720	730	760	800	800	800

Detailed Answer Key

Section 1

The following essay received 12 points out of a possible 12, meaning that it demonstrates *clear and consistent competence* in that it

- develops an insightful point of view on the topic
- demonstrates exemplary critical thinking
- uses effective examples, reasons, and other evidence to support its thesis
- is consistently focused, coherent and well-organized
- demonstrates skilful and effective use of language and sentence structure
- is largely (but not necessarily completely) free of grammatical and usage errors

Consider carefully the issue discussed in the following passage, then write an essay that answers the question posed in the assignment.

> *If you believe you will succeed, you are probably right. If you think you will fail, you are also probably right.*

Assignment: **Which has a stronger effect on one's life: one's circumstances, or one's system of beliefs?** Write an essay in which you answer this question and support your position logically with examples from literature, the arts, history, politics, science and technology, current events, or your experience or observation.

SAMPLE STUDENT ESSAY

Our success is based, to a large degree, on our self confidence. Very self confident people generally succeed because they are comfortable with themselves, and they are assertive, aggressive, and enthusiastic. Since they believe that they will succeed, confident people make more opportunities for themselves. Yet, many confident and idealistic people struggle nevertheless, because success so often requires luck and the help of others.

During the early twentieth century, masses of immigrants from eastern and southern Europe and China flooded into the United States. They all came in search of opportunity and success, confident that America's "streets paved with gold" would deliver them to riches and power. These immigrants, though, no matter how deeply they believed that they would succeed, struggled. Americans who had lived in the Unites States for generations saw these immigrants as impostors who would accept lower wages and dilapidated working conditions, thereby thrusting the American union workers out of jobs. These indigent immigrants were stuck in tenement apartments that were so small they could not fit entire families at one time. "Nativist" American families regarded each

immigrant group as having unique and appalling traits. In Jacob Riis's "How the Other Half Lives," a progressive documentation of immigrant communities, black, Italian, and Chinese neighborhoods are all described as filled with dirty, ignorant, unwelcoming and lazy people. The dreams of success in America that were illustrated by exceptional men like Andrew Carnegie, who emigrated to America from Scotland and worked his way to world renown and economic success, pervaded immigrant communities, even though it was often futile for most immigrants to try to gain decent lives in America.

There are, as well, many people who believe that they will not succeed at their endeavors, and yet attain them because they are lucky, or because the belief that one might fail pushes that person to work harder to attain success. In the novel "Into Thin Air," a team of hikers and climbers, all from different walks of life and of different ages, attempts to climb Mount Everest. The voyage up the Greta mountain goes smoothly until, when the team has almost reached the summit, a huge storm blows in and overtakes the team, killing a majority of the climbers. A few men, however, survived the storm and the fury of Everest. These people did not believe that they would survive but, miraculously, and through the aid of rescue teams that combed the mountain after the storm, were saved, hospitalized, and nursed back to health.

Success, as it is experienced in the real world, is made in part of ambition, in part confidence and belief, and in large part opportunity, without which belief and ambition are irrelevant. It has been said that "luck is when preparation meets opportunity,"

and so, if furnished with the opportunity, ambitious and confident people are predisposed to succeed in their endeavors. There are situations, though, that occur randomly and unexpectedly, that no one can prepare for or avoid. It is, therefore, important and healthy to believe in one's self, with the knowledge that belief and confidence are but two of the many factors that contribute to attaining success.

The following essay received 8 points out of a possible 12, meaning that it demonstrates *adequate competence* in that it

- develops a point of view on the topic
- demonstrates some critical thinking, but perhaps not consistently
- uses some examples, reasons, and other evidence to support its thesis, but perhaps not adequately
- shows a general organization and focus, but shows occasional lapses in this regard
- demonstrates adequate but occasionally inconsistent facility with language
- contains occasional errors in grammar, usage, and mechanics

---

SAMPLE STUDENT ESSAY

Failure and success are often dependent on your attitude. If one thinks that one is going to fail, that means that you are not setting goals for yourself. If you don't have high goals, then it is impossible to achieve incredible things.

For instance last year, I tried out for the golf team. I thought I wasn't good enough to get on the team, and I ended up playing way over my handicap. I wasn't confident and it effected how I played. I was instead worrying about what excuse I would give for why I missed a shot so badly. I was missing some putts by 10 feet or more. I was cut after the first tryout. Over the summer I played a lot of golf by myself and that gives a person a lot of time to ponder. I reflected on my experiences about how badly I played at the tryouts, and how well I was playing during the summer. Then I was playing like a completely different person. I realized that this was because I was not worried about what others thought. I knew what I was capable of and did not feel the need to prove it to other people. I knew right then that I needed to play with others the way I played by myself—with mental toughness and confidence.

I was able to try and correct this problem when I was partnered up with someone I had never played with before but who was the defending club champion which made me nervous. This guy shoots barely over par every round. He's a formidable opponent. The "old" me would have crumpled under the pressure and thought before each shot how nervous I was that he'd say my swing was horrible looking or that he had never seen someone slice a golf ball so horribly before. But, instead the new me visualized the perfect shot before each swing and I played one of the best rounds of my life. He even said I should join the club championship later that month, which was an enormous compliment coming from him. (I actually was not able to play in that tournament because I was out of town.) The only difference between my round that day and my rounds during the tryouts the previous year was my attitude.

I think if you try hard you can do anything. When I tried out for the team again I knew I had improved over the summer. I decided to focus on the game and not worry or think about what would happen if I failed. I am happy to say that as I write this essay, I am the third ranked player on our high school golf team.

> The following essay received 4 points out of a possible 12, meaning that it demonstrates *some incompetence* in that it
>
> - has a seriously limited point of view
> - demonstrates weak critical thinking
> - uses inappropriate or insufficient examples, reasons, and other evidence to support its thesis
> - is poorly focused and organized, and has serious problems with coherence
> - demonstrates frequent problems with language and sentence structure
> - contains errors in grammar and usage that obscure the author's meaning

SAMPLE STUDENT ESSAY

It's hard to say really whether just because you believe something it will happen. I think that's sometimes true, but not always. Like I think most basketball teams think they can win the championship, or they believe it, but they don't because only one team can and there are twenty in the league. But the winner of the bicycle race the Tour de France shows that you can do great things if you believe in yourself and you give it 110%. He had cancer and people accused him of taking steroids when he was racing in a foreign country, but he won anyways three times in a row.

More people should be like Lance Armstrong because he didn't let anything get in his way. Sometimes when you feel that things are too much or things are getting in your way or you feel depressed you should think about a guy who rode his bike up steep mountains with competitors trying to kick his bike and people yelling things at him but winning never the less. All this in addition to overcoming the disease of cancer and the chemotherapy that goes along with it and saps your energy. My uncle had to go through chemotherapy and, thank god it worked and he's better now, but it really took a lot of his energy out. So its even more remarkable that he could overcome that.

Also, many characters in books and movies prove that when you think positively you can accomplish great things. Macbeth for instance became the king of Scotland because it was his dream and he did everything he could to do it. He was tenacious in his endeavors, therfore proving that great things come to those who work hard and believe in himself or herself.

Section 2

1. D If his reputation grew to *mythic proportions*, he has achieved great fame. *callous* = hardened, insensitive; *infamous* = famous for bad things; *aloof* = distant physically or emotionally; *renowned* = famous; *obtuse* = unintelligent, dense.

2. A When the weather is *cold and rainy* people do not tend to go to the beach, so it would be empty. *devoid of* = lacking; *overpopulated by* = overcrowded; *overrun with* = overflowing.

3. B A *controversy* would encourage the queen to *step down from* her throne and *retire to the countryside*. *commemorate* = to honor; *abdicate* = to give up power; *rectify* = to set right; *replicate* = to copy; *disenfranchise* = to deprive the rights of.

4. A *Although* indicates contrast. Someone would expect to receive *payment* for raking the neighbor's lawn. The *surprise* suggests that the woman is not very generous with her money. *remuneration* = payment; *frugal* = economical; *perquisite* = a tip, gratuity; *venal* = able to be bribed; *beneficiary* = one that receives benefit; *gratification* = pleasure; *arbitrary* = whimsical; *provisions* = supplies; *thrifty* = economical.

5. B *Although* suggests that this garden with *great potential* must have been less than great in the past. Given the potential for greatness, it would make sense for Mrs. Nelson to be excited to *plant or grow* things. *fertile* = capable of growth; *fallow* = left unseeded; inactive; *cultivate* = to prepare to grow on; *culminate* = to climax, to come to a conclusion; *painstaking* = diligent.

6. D If the senator was not used to the *rigors* (demands) of the campaign, he would be overwhelmed by a *frantic* pace *reticent* = reluctant to share feelings; *mundane* = common; *pastoral* = relating to country life; *frenetic* = frantic; *prosaic* = dull.

7. B If his writing defines *magical realism*, he must write about *fantastical* events. *plausible* = conceivable; *chimerical* = fantastical; *obsequious* = overly submissive; *itinerant* = traveling from place to place; *perfunctory* = performed in a mechanical fashion.

8. E The deliberation escalated to physical violence which would indicate it was definitely a heated discussion. Jurors exchanging vicious *invectives* (abusive language) would be understandably agitated. *dignified* = full of dignity; *temperate* = self-restrained; *decorous* = proper; *belligerent* = war-like; *sedate* = calm; *amiable* = friendly; *staid* = calm and dignified; *pugnacious* = ready to fight; *contentious* = quarrelsome; *truculent* = ready to fight.

9. C The passage says that Kepler's *audience was more friendly than Galileo's* (lines 1–2) regarding their theories.

10. D The keplerian refractor produces an *inverted image* (lines 9–10), *unlike the Galilean telescope*.

11. A The Impressionists *turned the whole ingenious business on its ear* (lines 6–7), meaning they rebelled against the Romanticist tendency to use *every possible subject of melodramatic or sentimental potentialities* (lines 2–4)

12. D Because Monet was the *high priest* (lines 9–10) of the Impressionists, who believed that *subject mattered not at all* (line 9), and rebelled against the sentimentality of the Romanticists, must have chosen haystacks because they are not sentimental.

13. E This passage does not discuss any *historical phenomenon or the contributions of artists*. The first two paragraphs discuss the misconception that it is difficult to properly understand music. The last two paragraphs describe what is required to properly understand music, according to the author who is a famous composer, and so this portion of the passage can be considered *authoritative instruction*.

14. D This statement moderates the assessment made in the previous sentence. Whereas the previous sentence appears to criticize those who are modest about music as having *just as much reason to be modest about the other arts*, this sentence is more complimentary, suggesting that those same people have *just as little reason to be modest about their understanding of music*.

15. B The author states in lines 43–47 that the *minimum* skill required to appreciate music is *the ability to recognize a melody*.

16. **E** The *fact* mentioned in line 26 is the fact that some people can *"go to a show and then come home and play all the tunes on the piano,"* that is, that they can replicate music from memory.

17. **A** In saying *the color-blind are a useless lot to the painter*, the author is saying that those who cannot distinguish colors are a *useless group of people* to the painter.

18. **C** The passage states that *musical "events" are more abstract [than events in a novel]...so the act of pulling them all together in the imagination is not so easy as in reading a novel* (lines 68–71), which means that appreciating music is more challenging than appreciating literature because it involves synthesizing abstract events.

19. **B** The passage states that *if no practical difference whatever can be traced [in their effects], then the alternatives mean practically the same thing, and all dispute is idle* (lines 9–12). In other words, two claims are equivalent if the have essentially the same effect.

20. **E** The passage states that *(w)henever a dispute is serious, we ought to be able to show some practical difference that must follow from one side or the other's being right* (lines 12–15). In other words, a "serious" dispute, as opposed to an "idle" one, must involve alternatives with distinct outcomes.

21. **E** In saying that *(n)o distinction among ideas, however subtle, is so fine as to consist in anything but a possible difference of practice*, the author means that no distinction is more *discerning* (representing a fine distinction or judgment) than the distinction produced by different practical outcomes.

22. **D** The author discusses Ostwald's work because he *had been making perfectly distinct use of the principle of pragmatism in his lectures on the philosophy of science* (lines 47–51), that is, he had applied the pragmatic method to the sciences.

23. **B** Ostwald is quoted as saying that the dispute regarding the composition of "tautomerous" bodies *would never have begun...if the combatants had asked themselves what particular experimental fact could have been made different by one or the other view being correct* (lines 70–74), in other words, that the dispute was not resolvable because the two theories did not suggest any difference in experimental results. The passage makes clear, however, that such conflicts can only be resolved via the pragmatic method when the theories predict *different outcomes to a feasible experiment*.

24. **D** The point of the final sentence is that, from a pragmatic point of view, the theory that a "sprite" causes dough to rise is no different from the theory that an "elf" causes the dough to rise, because both are "unreal," that is, neither theory can be tested by examining the outcome of any experiment. Therefore, the pragmatic perspective renders both claims irrelevant.

Section 3

1. **A**

$$2x + 7 = 4x + 5$$

Subtract 5: $\quad 2x + 2 = 4x$

Subtract $2x$: $\quad 2 = 2x$

Divide by 2 $\quad 1 = x$

2. **B** Pick any postive integer for n and plug it into the equation and eliminate anything that is odd. Try $n = 3$. (A) $= n + 2 = 3 + 2 = 5$. (B) $= 2(n) = 2(3) = 6$. (C) $= 3n = 3(3) = 9$. (D) $= n^2 = 3^2 = 9$. (E) $= n^3 = 3^3 = 27$. Only answer choice B is even.

3. **C** When rounding to the nearest inch, answer choices A and B become 4. ($4.00 < x < 4.50$ is rounded down to 4). Answer choices D and E become 6. ($5.50 < x < 6.00$ is rounded up to 6.00)

4. **D** When there are 100 ft² left to paint, Jane has already painted 340 – 100 = 240 ft². You can construct a rate pyramid for this problem:

If a problem gives you two of the quantities, just put them in their places in the pyramid and do the operation between them to find the missing quantity:

$$240 \div 60 = 4 \text{ hrs.}$$

There are 60 minutes in an hour. $4 \times 60 = 240$ minutes.

5. **E** There are 180° in a triangle:

$$90° + 3x + x = 180°$$

Subtract 90: $\quad 4x = 90°$

Divide by 4: $\quad x = 22.5°$

Multiply by 3: $\quad 3x = 67.5°$

6. **B** 50% of 60% of 180 = (.5)(.6)(180) = 54

7. **E**

$$\frac{1}{c^2} = b^2 + 4b + 4$$

Factor: $\quad \dfrac{1}{c^2} = (b + 2)^2$

Take reciprocals: $\quad c^2 = \dfrac{1}{(b + 2)^2}$

Take the square root: $\quad c = \dfrac{1}{\sqrt{(b + 2)^2}} = \dfrac{1}{b + 2}$

8. **E** Set up an equation to find the average.

$$\frac{3y + 4y + (y-5)}{3} = 9$$

Multiply by 3: $3y + 4y + (y-5) = 27$
Combine like terms: $8y - 5 = 27$
Add 5: $8y = 32$
Divide by 8: $y = 4$

9. **C** Use the Pythagorean Theorem to solve for x.

$$(x)^2 + (2\sqrt{5})^2 = (6)^2$$

Square each part: $x^2 + 20 = 36$
Subtract 20: $x^2 = 16$
Take the square root: $x = 4$

10. **C** Both "domain rules" apply.

$(x - 6) \neq 0$ $(x + 4) \geq 0$
Add 6: $x \neq 6$
Subtract 4: $x \geq -4$

11. **D** Pick a value for w that satisfies the condition. It must be 2 more than a multiple of 6, like $6 + 2 = 8$. If $w = 8$, then $5w = 40$. When 40 is divided by 6, the remainder is 4.

12. **C** In the "dogs" row: $35 + 60 + y = 105$
Combine: $95 + y = 105$
Subtract 95: $y = 10$
In the "white" column: $35 + x + 15 = 75$
Combine: $50 + x = 75$
Subtract 50: $x = 25$
In the "cats" row: $x + 37 + 16 = w$
Substitute 25 for x: $25 + 37 + 16 = w$
Solve for w: $78 = w$
In the "total" column: $105 + w + 28 = z$
Substitute 78 for w: $105 + 78 + 28 = z$
Solve for z: $246 = z$

13. **B** If the circle is tangent to the x-axis, it only touches the axis at one point. The x-intercept will share the same x-value as the center point. The center of the circle is (3, 4) and the circle must touch the x-axis at the point (3, 0) and thus the radius = $4 - 0 = 4$.

$$\text{Circumference} = 2\pi r = 2(\pi)(4) = 8\pi$$

14. **E** The triangle inequality theorem states that $EF - DE < DF < EF + DE$
Substitute 9 for EF and 7 for DE: $9 - 7 < DF < 9 + 7$
$2 < DF < 16$

15. **D** If the line creates an angle of 45° with the x-axis and passes through the origin, then its equation is $y = x$ and therefore any point where the x and y coordinates are the same is on the line.

16. **A** Mark the information on the diagram, and use the facts that (1) "linear" angles have a sum of 180°, (2) angles in a triangle have a sum of 180°, and (3) in a triangle, angles across from equal sides are equal. Your diagram should look like this:

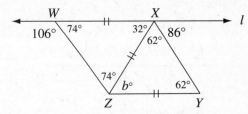

Therefore $62 + 62 + b = 180$ and so $b = 56$

17. **D** A chart may help you organize the information.

	%	Hours	(%) (24) = hours
sleep	30	7.2	(.30)(24) = 7.2
work	35	8.4	(.35)(24) = 8.4
gym	5	1.2	(.05)(24) = 1.2
home		5.0	
car		x	
total	100	24.0	

Hours in car = $24 - 7.2 - 8.4 - 1.2 - 5.0 = 2.2$ hours
2.2 hours × 60 minutes/hour = 132 minutes.

18. **B** First find the midpoint of (8, 8) and (6, –2).

$$\text{midpoint} = \left(\frac{X_1 + X_2}{2}, \frac{Y_1 + Y_2}{2}\right)$$

$$\text{midpoint} = \left(\frac{8+6}{2}, \frac{8 + -2}{2}\right)$$

$$\text{midpoint} = (7, 3)$$

Next find the slope of the line connecting the two points (7, 3) and (2, 5).

$$\text{slope} = \frac{(Y_2 - Y_1)}{(X_2 - X_1)} = \frac{(3-5)}{(7-2)} = -\frac{2}{5}$$

19. **A** The diagonal of a square splits it into two 45°–45°–90° triangles. The sides of a 45°–45°–90° triangle are x, x, and $x\sqrt{2}$. So if the sides of the square have length x, the diagonal has length $x\sqrt{2}$.

Therefore $x\sqrt{2} = m$

Divide by $\sqrt{2}$: $x = m/\sqrt{2}$

The area of a square is x^2 or $\dfrac{m^2}{2}$

20. **A**   Since vertical angles are equal, label the two interior angles x and y. The quickest method is to notice that z is the measure of an "exterior angle" to the triangle, and so it equals the sum of the two "remote interior" angles. Therefore $z = x + y$ and so $x = z - y$.

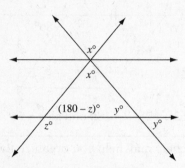

Or you can "plug in:"
        Let's say $x = 40°$ and $y = 70°$
There are 180° in a triangle:
$$40° + 70° + (180 - z) = 180°$$
        Subtract 290: $-z = -110°$
        Divide by –1: $z = 110°$
Next, plug the values for z and y into the answer choices and pick the one that equals 40°: $z - y = 110° - 70° = 40°$.

Section 4

1. **C** $x \ \$ \ y = x^y + 3$
        Plug in for x and y: $4 \ \$ \ 2 = 4^2 + 3 = 19$

---

2. **B**   When given a system of equations and asked to evaluate another expression, begin by writing the two expressions on top of each other and see if adding or subtracting yields the answer.
$$n + m = 7$$
$$\underline{2n - 3m = 6}$$
        Add the two together: $3n - 2m = 13$ Done!

---

3. **D**   In order to find the smallest value of y, you must make x as large as possible. Since you know that $x < 40$, and x and y are both positive integers, it follows that the largest possible value of x is 39. Since y is the measure of an exterior angle to the triangle, $y = 39 + 80 = 119$

---

4. **C**   The triangle inequality theorem states that:
$$11 - 7 < x < 11 + 7$$
$$4 < x < 18$$
Therefore x can be any integer from 5 to 17, which includes $17 - 5 + 1 = 13$ possible integers.

---

5. **A**
All three of the triangles in the figure are 30° – 60° – 90°.

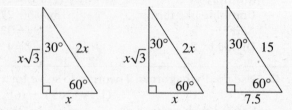

The side across from the 30° in the triangle on the far left is 7.5. The hypotenuse is double that or $2(7.5) = 15$.
That hypotenuse is the $x\sqrt{3}$ side of the middle triangle.

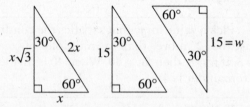

Both are 30 – 60 – 90 triangles and they share the same hypotenuse. This means that they are exactly the same and since w is also across from the 60°, it too is equal to 15.

---

6. **B**   Use the percent change formula:
$$\text{percent change} = \frac{\text{final} - \text{original}}{\text{original}} \times 100\%$$

$$= \frac{192,500 - 175,000}{175,000} \times 100\%$$

$$= \frac{17,500}{175,000} \times 100\% = 10\%$$

---

7. **C**   To simplify the problem, notice that for every group of four people chosen, another group of two people is "left out," so the number of two-person groups is equal to the number of four-person groups. To count the number of two-person groups, Think of the people as A, B, C, D, E and F. How many two-person groups contain A? Five: AB, AC, AD, AE and AF. Once these are counted, ask: how many more two-person groups contain B? Four: BC, BD, BE, and BF. Continuing in this manner, you can see that the total number of two-person groups is $5 + 4 + 3 + 2 + 1 = 15$. Therefore, the number of four-person groups is also 15.

8. **E** Just focus on the sign of each term. The signs of the first three terms are −, +, − respectively. The sign of the fourth term is $(+) \div (−) = +$. The sign of the fifth term is $(−) \div (−) = +$. The sign of the sixth term is $(−) \div (+) = −$. The signs of first 6 terms of the sequence are: −, +, −, −, +, −.

The pattern of three terms. −,+,−, repeats indefinitely. This pattern repeats $100 \div 3 = 33\ 1/3⅓$ times. Each repetition contains 2 negative numbers. The 33 full repetitions (which account for the first 99 terms) contain $33 \times 2 = 66$ negative numbers. The 100th term is also negative, giving a total of $66 + 1 = 67$ negative terms.

9. **4** Set up a ratio and solve:

$$\frac{24}{1}\frac{miles}{gallon} = \frac{96}{x}\frac{miles}{gallons}$$

Cross Multiply: $\quad 24x = 96$
Divide by 24: $\quad\quad x = 4$ gallons

10. **0 < b < 1** In order for b^3 to be less than b^2, b must be a fraction between 0 and 1. When a fraction between zero and one is multiplied by itself, its value decreases.

11. **180** Begin by writing equations that represent what you are told in the problem: $E = $ Eric, $B = $ Bill.

$$E = 40 + B$$
$$E + B = 320$$

Plug $(40 + B)$ in for E: $\quad (40 + B) + B = 320$
Subtract 40: $\quad\quad 2B = 280$
Divide by 2: $\quad\quad B = 140$
Solve for E: $\quad\quad E = 40 + 140 = 180$

12. **900** Using the pie chart, first calculate how many students eat dining hall food and how many students eat snack food.

Snack: 10% of 3,000 = (.10)(3,000) = 300 Students
Dining Hall: $\quad$ 40% of 3,000 = (.40)
$\quad\quad$ (3,000) = 1,200 students
$\quad$ 1,200 − 300 = 900 students

13. **6**

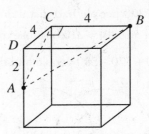

Each side of the cube is 4 units long. $AD = 2$ because point A is the midpoint of that side. To find the distance from A to B set up a right triangle ($\triangle ABC$) where the length you're trying to find is a side. You know that the value of BC is 4 because it is an edge of the cube. To find AB, you need to first find the value of AC, which can be found by solving right triangle ADC using the Pythagorean Theorem:

$$2^2 + 4^2 = AC^2$$
Combine: $\quad\quad 20 = AC^2$
Take the square root: $\quad \sqrt{20} = AC$

Next, solve right triangle ABC to find the value of AB.

$$AC^2 + BC^2 = AB^2$$
Substitute: $\quad (\sqrt{20})^2 + 4^2 = AB^2$
Combine: $\quad\quad 36 = AB^2$
Take the square root: $\quad\quad 6 = AB$

14. **12** Begin by writing a system of equations: $S = $ weight of soda cans; $C = $ weight of cooler

$$C + S = 20$$
$$C + ¼S = 14$$

Subtract two equations : $\quad ¾S = 6$
Divide by ¾: $\quad\quad S = 8$
Plug in 8 for S and solve: $\quad C + 8 = 20$
Subtract 8: $\quad\quad C = 12$

15. **6** First set up a distance = (rate)(time) equation for the trips to and from work.

to work: $\quad\quad d = 15(t)$
from work: $\quad\quad d = 10(1 − t)$
Set 2 equations equal: $\quad 15t = 10(1 − t)$
Distribute: $\quad\quad 15t = 10 − 10t$
Add 10t: $\quad\quad 25t = 10$

Divide by 25: $\quad\quad t = \frac{2}{5}$

Plug in for t: $\quad d = 15(t) = 15\left(\frac{2}{5}\right) = 6$ miles

16. **580**   Set up a Venn diagram to solve this problem:

$1{,}000 - 630 = 370$ people had just a dog. 630 people had a cat, and $\frac{1}{3}(630) = 210$ of those also had a dog.

Therefore $210 + 370 - 580$ people had dogs.

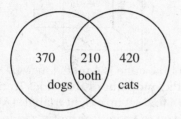

17. **5/9 or .555 or .556**

Find area of middle circle: $\pi r^2 = \pi(2)^2 = 4\pi$
Find area of outermost circle: $\pi r^2 = \pi(3)^2 = 9\pi$
The area of the shaded region = $9\pi - 4\pi = 5\pi$
The probability that the dart will land in the shaded area is $5\pi/9\pi = 5/9$.

18. **0.25 or ¼**

If there are three times as many red marbles as black marbles, then if there are x black marbles, there are $3x$ red marbles. This means there are a total of $x + 3x = 4x$ marbles, $3x$ of which are black. Therefore the probability of choosing a red marble is $3x/4x = ¾$. Of these red marbles, twice as many are striped as unstriped, so if there are y unstriped red marbles, there are $2y$ striped red marbles, for a total of $3y$ red marbles, y of which are unstriped. Therefore $y/3y = ⅓$ of the red marbles are unstriped. $¾ \times ⅓ = ¼$, so the probability of choosing an unstriped red marble at random is ¼.

Section 5

1. **A**   A bag of rotten garbage that had been sitting there for three weeks would probably be disgusting. *putrid* = rotten; *delectable* = delightful; *piquant* = pleasant tasting; *savory* = tasty

2. **E**   Doug had to call his mother for *clarification*, which would indicate that he was confused when attempting to use the handwritten recipe. *reconfigure* = to rearrange; *illegible* = unable to be read; *recapitulate* = to summarize; *lucid* = clear; *reiterate* = to recap; *placid* = calm; *cogent* = convincing; *decipher* = to figure out; *unintelligible* = incapable of being understood.

3. **D**   Fragile artifacts that archaeologists *collect* require safeguards against *deterioration*. *projected* = extended forward into space or time; *dissipation* = wasteful expenditure; *amassed* = collected; *disseminated* = scattered as seed; *desiccation* = drying out.

4. **B**   *Incontrovertible* (indisputable) evidence presented by a prosecutor would be bad news for a defendant and would probably prove his or her guilt. *apathy* = lack of feeling; *culpable* = guilty; *penitence* = regret; *dexterity* = grace and skill; *prescience* = foresight.

5. **B**   Mother Teresa was *selfless or generous* with her time. *rhetorical* = used to persuade; *munificent* = generous; *felicitous* = apt, well suited; *austere* = severe; *mellifluous* = smooth flowing.

6. **C**   The passage says that the *rate of cultural change has accelerated* (lines 7–8) in recent history, and uses the development of food production as an example.

7. **D**   Food production, according to the passage, involves any kind of *cultivation of plants* or *domestication of animals* (line 13–14).

8. **B**   The first sentence describes Egyptian rites as *mystic* practices *performed in the depths of temple sanctuaries* exclusively by priests. The Greek rituals, however, were *engaged in by all citizens* (line 9).

9. **E**   Saying that *preliminaries were engaged in by citizens* is the same as saying that *preliminaries were participated in by citizens*.

10. **C**   The passage as a whole discusses the different ways that humans make decisions: trial and error, algorithms and heuristics.

11. **E**   The *research* is described as what led to the derivation of *the concept of heuristic reasoning* (line 31). Furthermore, this research was designed to *simulate human intelligence using computers* (lines 33–34). Therefore, the attempt to simulate human intelligence must have led researchers to believe that heuristics simulate human thinking.

12. **A**   This strategy is described as a response to frustration over the *enormous number of possible solutions* (lines 36–37) involved in making a chess move.

13. **E**   In saying that *moves that meet these goals are executed*, the author means that helpful moves are carried out. Since moves are not people, they *cannot* be *empowered* or *frustrated*.

14. **A**   The passage suggests that one reason why we use heuristics is *because algorithms require so much cognitive capacity and effort* (lines 53–54).

15. **B**   The author states that the representativeness heuristic *leads us not to seek and evaluate other information that might be helpful ... such as Steve's preferences* (lines 77–79). Such a heuristic does take personality characteristics into account. Also, it does not require an infinite amount of information or an elaborate algorithm and it is quite distinct from the trial-and-error approach described earlier in the passage.

16. **B**   Unlike the representativeness heuristic, the availability heuristic *bases decisions on the availability of relevant information in memory* (lines 82–84).

17. **A**   Louis is said to *vacillate* (waver) between liberal and reactionary counselors. Thus he was indecisive.

18. **D**   The constitution ended the monarchy and safeguarded *wide popular suffrage* (voting rights) ... *and fairly high grade of civil administration* (lines 13–15).

19. **C**   In saying that the entrepreneurial groups were *released politically and culturally as well as economically from their anomalous subjection to an incapable and irresponsibly nobility* (lines 24–27), the author is saying that entrepreneurs became free of the nobility, to whom they previously had to submit politically and economically. Therefore, the word *subjection* most nearly means *state of submission*.

20. **B**   The passage says that *business sat solidly in the center trying to get a little order and stability without interference* (lines 21–23).

21. **E**   The economy of opportunity is said to produce *an appearance of infinite variety in cultural expression* (lines 42–43) and encouraged art that was *expressive of ... free, individual personality* (lines 55–56).

22. **D**   The paragraph says that merchants sought *distinction for (their) position* (line 50) and used art to that end. The merchant bought art *expressive of his free, individual personality* and as a result the *artist exaggerated his every whim and impulse* (lines 55–58). Therefore the needs of the patrons influenced the aesthetic decisions of the artists.

23. **D**   In saying that *it was an age of rapid and sometimes accidental accessions of wealth*, the author is saying that many merchants of this time acquired sudden wealth. Therefore *accessions* most nearly means *accumulation*.

24. **D**   The passage says *the more abstruse the forms of art, the more impenetrable to the uninitiated, the greater their value as a distinction to the "connoisseur"* (lines 78–81).

Section 6

1. **D**   *All quiet* is slang and *hoping that she would win* is nonstandard form. Choice D is clear, concise and standard.

2. **B**   The non-underlined phrase is an **appositive**, and should be followed by its equivalent *David*.

3. **E**   The first clause is in the active voice, so the second clause should maintain the active voice.

4. **C**   This is a comparison error. Jon's *scores* can only be compared to other *scores*.

5. **A**   The original phrasing is best.

6. **D**   This is a violation of parallelism. The items in the list should have similar grammatical forms. Choice D creates a concise phrasing in which all of the items are **gerunds**.

7. **D**   The phrase *of the sort that delves* is wordy and nonstandard.

8. **A**   The original phrasing is best.

9. **B**   The original phrasing produces a sentence fragment. Choice B creates a complete thought concisely.

10. **C**   The phrase *every member* is singular, but the pronoun *their* is plural. Choice C provides pronoun-antecedent agreement.

11. **A**   The original phrasing is best.

12. **C**   The phrase *for ascending* contains an idiom error. The idiom is *struggle to*, so the phrase in C should be *to ascend*.

13. **D**   The past perfect tense is incorrect because the *jumping* occurred at the same time as the *falling*. This should be the simple past tense *jumped*.

14. **B**   This is a comparison error. Audrey's *ideas* should not be compared to a *class*. The correction is *those of the rest of the class*.

15. **E**   The sentence is correct.

16. **A**   This is a tense error. Since the shifting had occurred many times before election day *arrived* (simple past tense), it should take the past perfect tense, *had shifted*.

17. **A**   This is a violation of parallelism. Omit the word *being*.

18. **E**   This sentence is correct.

19. **C**   This is a diction error. *Expectant* means *eagerly awaiting*, and inadequacies can't await things. The proper word is *expected*.

20. **C**   This is a pronoun-antecedent disagreement. The antecedent is *troops* which is plural, so the proper pronoun is *their*.

21. **A**   The word *media* is plural. (The singular form is *medium*.) Therefore the proper verb conjugation is *play*.

22. **C**   The phrase *wasn't hardly* is a double negative, and should be changed to *wasn't* or *was hardly*.

23. **A**   The subject of the verb is *each*, which is singular. The correct conjugation, then, is *ends*.

24. **B**   Ambiguous pronoun antecedent. The pronoun *their* indicates a plural antecedent, but none is available in the sentence. Since the salesman is most logically talking about his own integrity, the pronoun should be *his* or *her*.

25. **C**   The subject of the verb *have been stimulated* is the singular subject *growth*, and so it does not agree. It should be changed to *has been*.

26. **D**   The word *adapt* is a verb meaning *change for a specific purpose*, and so is used improperly here. The correct word is the adjective *adept*.

27. **B**   The pronouns *his* or *her* have a plural antecedent, *the voters*. Therefore, this phrase should be changed to *their ballots*.

28. **A**   The phrase *miss out on* is a nonstandard idiom because it is needlessly wordy. It should be re-phrased to simply *miss*.

29. **D**   This is an illogical comparison. Since the comparison is being made to *her dance routine*, this should be rephrased as *the routines of the other dancers*.

30. **D**   The phrase *closest living relative* pertains to a specific living person rather than a species. Also, *species* is a singular noun.

31. **E**   The original phrasing is very awkward and unclear. The several ideas in the sentence do not coordinate logically.

32. **B**   The original phrasing contains a comma splice. Choice B separates the independent clauses with a semicolon and coordinates the ideas logically.

33. **D**   This sentence logically follows the sentence about female social habits.

34. **D**   Sentence 10 contributes the least to the unity because it is the only sentence that deviates from the topic of the chimpanzee society.

35. **C**   This sentence expands upon sentence 11 and provides a solid conclusion to the paragraph.

Section 7

1. **B**   Since the exponentials have the same base, you can disregard the base and set the exponents equal to each other: $3y = 9$
Divide by 3: $y = 3$

2. **C** $\dfrac{1}{1.4} = .7143$

"Divide out" the fractions and look for the same quotient.
Answer choice C: $5 \div 7 = .7143$

3. **D**   Angles that form a line have a sum of 180°.
Write an equation: $2x + 140° = 180°$
Subtract 140°: $2x = 40°$
Add 5 to both sides: $2x + 5 = 40° + 5°$
Combine like terms: $2x + 5 = 45°$

4. **D**   Write an equation: $\dfrac{3x}{2} = 39$

Multiply by 2: $3x = 78$
Divide by 3: $x = 26$

5. **D**
To find out how much greater $x + 5$ is than $x - 5$, subtract them from each other:
                $(x + 5) - (x - 5)$
Distribute: $x + 5 - x + 5$
Combine like terms: 10

6. **D**

Find Area of Rectangle M: $(L)(W) = LW = A$
Find Area of Rectangle P: $(3L)(3W) = 9LW$
Substitute A for LW: $9LW = 9A$.

---

7. **C** There is no need to actually calculate the length of the diameter. You should know that, by definition, the number π is the ratio of the circumference to the diameter of *any* circle. (Just remember the formula $c = \pi d$ so $\pi = c/d$.) The actual length of the circumference doesn't matter. Therefore, the ratio is $\pi:1$.

---

8. **D** Draw $\overline{AB}$ and construct a right triangle:

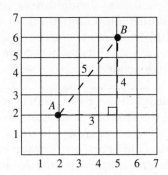

You should notice that this forms a "special" 3–4–5 right triangle, so calculating the distance algebraically is unnecessary. If you don't notice this, however, you can use the Pythagorean Theorem:

$$3^2 + 4^2 = (AB)^2$$

Simplify: $25 = (AB)^2$
Take the square root: $5 = AB$

---

9. **C** Begin by writing a system of equations:
s = # of bags of sticky bears
c = # of bags of chocolate bombs
Total cost is $500: $1.50s + 1.00c = 500$
400 bags were bought: $s + c = 400$
Solve for s: $s = 400 - c$
Subst. into first eq.: $1.50(400 - c) + c = 500$
Distribute: $600 - 1.50c + c = 500$
Subtract 600: $-0.50c = -100$
Divide by -0.50: $c = 200$

---

10. **B** The simplest way to solve this is to remember that, in a set of "evenly spaced" numbers, the median and the mean are always equal. Since consecutive even integers are certainly "evenly spaced," the average (arithmetic mean) must also be 10.
Alternately, you can construct a set of 7 consecutive even integers that has 10 as its middle number:
4, 6, 8, 10, 12, 14, 16

$$\text{mean} = \frac{(4+6+8+10+12+14+16)}{7} = 10$$

---

11. **B** First calculate the revenue for each theater.
Bijou = $120(9) + 30(6) + 20(6) = \$1380$
Community = $220(9) + 40(6) + 90(6) = \$2760$
1380 is what percent of $2760?

$$1380 = \frac{x}{100}(2760)$$

Simplify: $1380 = 27.6x$
Divide by 27.6: $50 = x$

So the total revenue the Bijou receives is 50% of the revenue the Community Cinema receives.

---

12. **E** The total revenue at the Triplex is $9x + 30(6) = 9x + 180$ dollars. The total revenue at Village Theater is $100(9) + 20(6) + 70(6) = 1440$ dollars. If the revenue at the Triplex is greater, then $9x + 180 > 1440$
Subtract 180: $9x > 1260$
Divide by 9: $x > 140$

Since x is an integer greater than 140, the least value it could have is 141.

---

13. **E** Remember that any digit may be repeated. Because the number has three digits, you can regard this as a "counting" problem with three choices. There are three choices for each digit, so the total number of distinct integers is $3 \times 3 \times 3 = 27$.

---

14. **A** Take reciprocal of both sides: $\dfrac{1}{x^2} = 4y + 6$

Subtract 6: $\dfrac{1}{x^2} - 6 = 4y$

Divide by 4: $\dfrac{1}{4x^2} - \dfrac{6}{4} = \dfrac{1}{4x^2} - \dfrac{3}{2} = y$

---

15. **A** To find the area of the shaded region, subtract the area of the circle from the area of the square.
Area of the square = $(\text{side})^2 = 6^2 = 36$
Area of the circle = $\pi(r)^2 = \pi(3)^2 = 9\pi$
Shaded area = $36 - 9\pi$

---

16. **E** Try plugging in values. If $c = 12$, for instance, then she spends $12 \div 3 = 4$ hours each day preparing desserts. Desserts that require 24 hours of preparation would take $24 \div 4 = 6$ days to make. Plug $c = 12$ into the answer choices and eliminate those that do NOT equal 6.

(A) $\dfrac{c}{72} = \dfrac{12}{72} = \dfrac{1}{6}$

(B) $\dfrac{24}{c} = \dfrac{24}{12} = 2$

(C) $\dfrac{c}{24} = \dfrac{12}{24} = \dfrac{1}{2}$

(D) $24c = 24(12) = 288$

(E) $\dfrac{72}{c} = \dfrac{72}{12} = 6$

Alternatively, you can solve this problem using your algebra skills. This is a "rate" problem, so use the formula

$$\text{Amount of work} = \text{rate} \times \text{time}$$

The amount of work is 24 "dessert hours." The rate at which she prepares desserts is c/3 "dessert hours per day,"

so $\qquad\qquad\qquad 24 = \dfrac{c}{3} \times \text{time (in days)}$

Multiply by 3: $\qquad 72 = c \times \text{time (in days)}$

Divide by c: $\qquad \dfrac{72}{c} = \text{time (in days)}$

Section 8

1. **B** The size of the moon is changing such that it will soon no longer be visible. It must be getting smaller. *desiccate* = to dry out; *wane* = to shrink in size; *debunk* = to expose something as false; *convoke* = to call together; *coalesce* = to fuse together.

2. **C** The *opposing forces* saw the attack coming, so they could prepare themselves for the attacking army and defeat them badly. *foreseen* = predicted; *defoliate* = to lose leaves; *disavowed* = sworn off; *decimate* = to destroy; *resolved* = brought to a resolution; *demarcate* = to set boundaries.

3. **B** The candidates used *roundabout expressions* and *evasive tactics* to *avoid* the questions. They were speaking *around the subject*. This makes *circumlocution* a perfect fit. *matriculation* = the admission to a group, usually a university; *circumlocution* = evasive speech; *contemplation* = thoughtfulness; *homogeneity* = the state of being similar; *serendipity* = good luck in making a fortunate discovery.

4. **E** A *propensity* is a tendency to do something. George does something that causes his peers to look at him as a *grandiose*, or pompous person. *vacillate* = to go back and forth; *phlegmatic* = sluggish; *eulogize* = to praise; *loquacious* = very talkative; *prophesy* = to tell the future; *mercurial* = changing, volatile; *pilfer* = to steal; *colloquial* = using everyday language, conversational; *pontificate* = to speak in an arrogant way; *bombastic* = grandiloquent, pompous.

5. **D** If he was remembered as being *taller than she actually was*, he is actually small. Despite being small, he is able to *dominate a room*. *gargantuan* = gigantic; *voluminous* = of large capacity; *scanty* = insufficient; *exemplify* = to serve as an example; *diminutive* = tiny; *belied* = misrepresented; *meager* = lacking in quantity; *propagate* = to grow or multiply.

6. **C** The journalist has an *infamous* (notorious) history, which indicates he has not behaved properly in the past. A reputation for *fabrication* (making things up) would lead his readers to doubt the authenticity or truth of his articles. *candor* = honesty; *perfidiousness* = unfaithfulness; *ingenuity* = cleverness; *fabrication* = something invented, a lie; *veracity* = truth; *virtuosity* = great skill; *aptitude* = talent; *perspicacity* = ability to discern or understand; *autonomy* = independence.

7. **A** Passage 1 discusses the impact of Hemingway on writers of the author's generation, *the young men born between 1918, roughly, and 1924* (lines 1–2). The author is consistent on this topic, discussing Hemingway's *impact upon us* (line 26) in the second paragraph, and comparing Hemingway's impact on his generation to his impact on today's generation in the final paragraph.

8. **C** The author states that the impact of Hemingway's words on his generation was so great that *we began unconsciously to translate our own sensations into their term*. This kind of translation is *empathy*.

9. **D** The *war* mentioned in line 50 is said to have *forced (much) out of us* ... and the author says that this loss *was something far greater than Hemingway and his formative influence* ... In other words, this war disillusioned them on the images of war presented in Hemingway's writing.

10. **A** In saying that *many young writers ... have rejected (Hemingway's) time as untrue*, the author is saying that those writers have decided that Hemingway's depiction of his times have little meaning for them.

11. **C** Statement I is supported in line 5, *he had become a legendary figure (to my generation)* and in the final paragraph, in which the author states that today's writers *have not profited (from Hemingway) or were never touched by him at all*. Statement III is supported by lines 57–58, in which the author says that modern writers have failed *at finding themselves in their own time*, while his own generation, as he says in lines 48–49, felt that the *Hemingway time was a good time to be young*.

12. **D** The author states that *perhaps the real unfortunates* are those who *have been denied access to a powerful tradition* (in Hemingway's writings) (lines 63–65).

13. **E** In this first paragraph of Passage 2, the author describes the similarities between Hemingway's world and the modern world, to suggest that Hemingway's writing should have meaning for us because of those similarities.

14. **B** This excerpt in lines 115–120 says that a reader *will have a feeling of those things* which are not directly mentioned by the author. This would require the ability to read beyond what an author has explicitly stated.

15. **D** The author of Passage 2 says that *Hemingway's famous economy of prose was by no means as omnipresent as he himself suggests* in *Death of the Afternoon* which discusses his literary method. In other words, he claimed that writers should write *economically* but did not always do so himself.

16. **C** Passage 2 mentions that Hemingway's writing seems to be influenced by *a mixture of stylistic forces* (lines 129–130).

17. **C** Choice I is supported in line 145, which says that Hemingway's writing *contains scrambled chronology*. Choice II is supported by line 140, which says that the book is *self-indulgent*. There is no mention that the book contains recollections of his wartime experiences.

18. **A** Passage 1 clearly states that Hemingway *had become a legendary figure* (line 5) to his generation. Passage states that Hemingway *became a dupe of his culture* (lines 97–98) who *yielded to the functionalist, technological aesthetic of the culture instead of resisting* (lines 94–96).

19. **E** The first passage is concerned with the influence of Hemingway as a hero to his generation, but does not delve into his literary style. The second passage, however, is concerned almost exclusively with Hemingway's writing style.

Section 9

1. **C** Since the sentence begins with a participial phrase modifying *Maria*, the clause that follows should begin with *Maria*.

2. **E** As it is originally phrased, the sentence has no verb, and so isn't even a sentence! Choices (C), (D), and (E) correct that problem, but only (E) contains a clear and idiomatic phrasing of the comparison.

3. **A** The original phrasing is best. It is parallel and idiomatic and uses the semicolon correctly.

4. **B** The clause *the reason is because* is illogical, because the word *because* is neither a noun nor a pronoun and so cannot be equated with a noun. Since *programs* is plural, (B) is the best choice.

5. **D** The word *feature* can only be equated with a noun phrase that represents a feature. Choice (D) does this in the most concise way.

6. **C** Choice (C) is the only one that contains a standard phrasing in the subjunctive mood.

7. **E** Choice (E) is the most concise and parallel.

8. **B** The use of *nevertheless* in the original phrasing is redundant, since the sentence starts with *although*.

9. **C** The opening participial phrase *as a writer*, should be followed by the noun or pronoun that it modifies, which is *I*. Choice (C) does this most clearly.

10. **B** The original sentence contains a comma splice and a pronoun, *this*, with an unclear antecedent. Choice (B) corrects both of these problems.

11. **E** The original phrasing is wordy and nonstandard. Choice (E) is the most concise and clear.

12. **C** The phrase *a necessity of* uses wordy and nonstandard diction. Also, the two ideas are not strongly coordinated in the original phrasing. Choice (C) uses parallel phrasing to strengthen the coordination between the ideas, provides a more logical coordinator, *in fact*, and uses more concise and standard diction.

13. **A** The original phrasing is best. Since the *feeling* in the second clause is in the subjunctive mood, because it is counter to fact, the correct verb form is *were*.

14. **B** The sentence must maintain a parallel structure: the film used shock tactics *to gain publicity and increase ticket sales*.

PRACTICE TEST 8

ANSWER SHEET

Last Name:_____ First Name:_____

Date:_____ Testing Location:_____

Directions for Test

- Remove these answer sheets from the book and use them to record your answers to this test.
- This test will require 3 hours and 20 minutes to complete. Take this test in one sitting.
- The time allotment for each section is written clearly at the beginning of each section. This test contains six 25-minute sections, two 20-minute sections, and one 10-minute section.
- This test is 25 minutes shorter than the actual SAT, which will include a 25-minute "experimental" section that does not count toward your score. That section has been omitted from this test.
- You may take one short break during the test, of no more than 10 minutes in length.
- You may only work on one section at any given time.
- You must stop ALL work on a section when time is called.
- If you finish a section before the time has elapsed, check your work on that section. You may NOT work on any other section.
- Do not waste time on questions that seem too difficult for you.
- Use the test book for scratchwork, but you will receive credit only for answers that are marked on the answer sheets.
- You will receive one point for every correct answer.
- You will receive no points for an omitted question.
- For each wrong answer on any multiple-choice question, your score will be reduced by ¼ point.
- For each wrong answer on any "numerical grid-in" question, you will receive no deduction.

When you take the real SAT, you will be asked to fill in your personal information in grids as shown below.

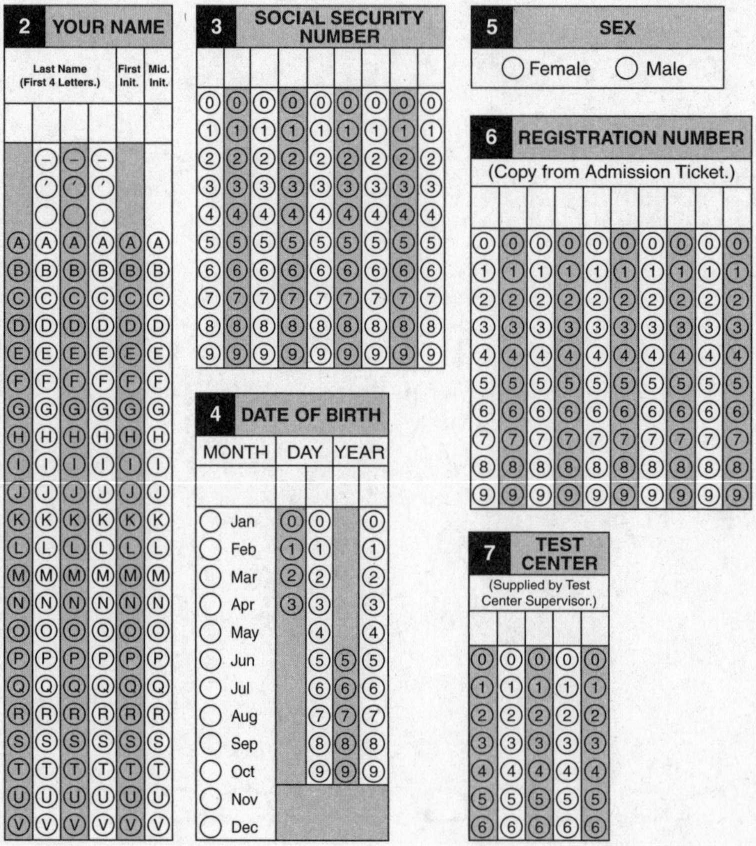

Start with number 1 for each new section. If a section has fewer questions than answer spaces, leave the extra answer spaces blank. Be sure to erase any errors or stray marks completely.

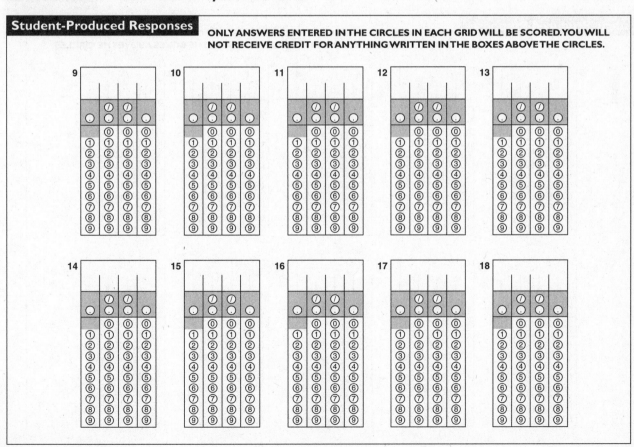

CAUTION   **Use the answer spaces in the grids below for Section 2 or Section 3 only if you are told to do so in your test book.**

Student-Produced Responses   ONLY ANSWERS ENTERED IN THE CIRCLES IN EACH GRID WILL BE SCORED. YOU WILL NOT RECEIVE CREDIT FOR ANYTHING WRITTEN IN THE BOXES ABOVE THE CIRCLES.

Start with number 1 for each new section. If a section has fewer questions than answer spaces, leave the extra answer spaces blank. Be sure to erase any errors or stray marks completely.

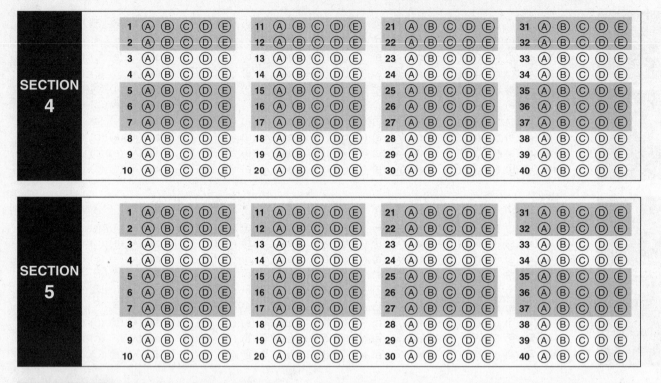

SECTION 4

SECTION 5

CAUTION   Use the answer spaces in the grids below for Section 4 or Section 5 only if you are told to do so in your test book.

Student-Produced Responses   ONLY ANSWERS ENTERED IN THE CIRCLES IN EACH GRID WILL BE SCORED. YOU WILL NOT RECEIVE CREDIT FOR ANYTHING WRITTEN IN THE BOXES ABOVE THE CIRCLES.

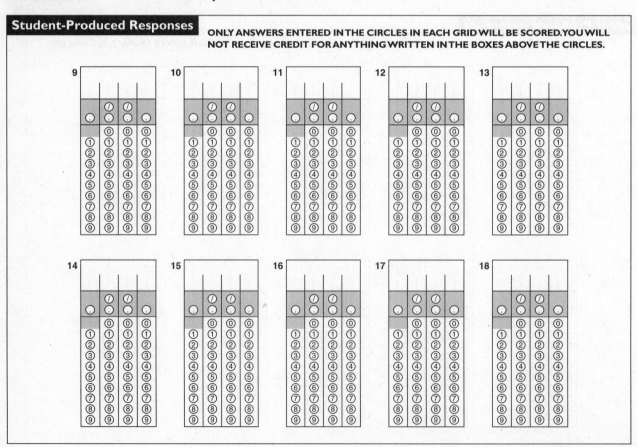

Start with number 1 for each new section. If a section has fewer questions than answer spaces, leave the extra answer spaces blank. Be sure to erase any errors or stray marks completely.

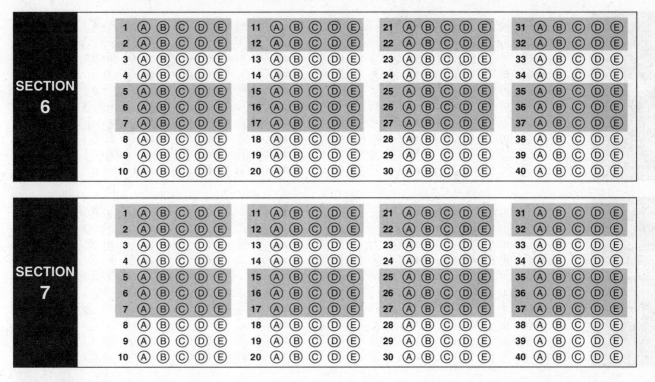

SECTION 6

SECTION 7

CAUTION Use the answer spaces in the grids below for Section 6 or Section 7 only if you are told to do so in your test book.

Student-Produced Responses ONLY ANSWERS ENTERED IN THE CIRCLES IN EACH GRID WILL BE SCORED. YOU WILL NOT RECEIVE CREDIT FOR ANYTHING WRITTEN IN THE BOXES ABOVE THE CIRCLES.

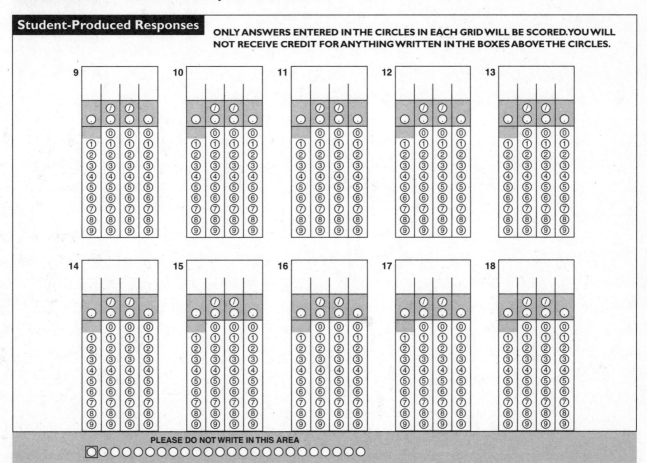

PLEASE DO NOT WRITE IN THIS AREA

Start with number 1 for each new section. If a section has fewer questions than answer spaces, leave the extra answer spaces blank. Be sure to erase any errors or stray marks completely.

SECTION 8

1 Ⓐ Ⓑ Ⓒ Ⓓ Ⓔ	11 Ⓐ Ⓑ Ⓒ Ⓓ Ⓔ	21 Ⓐ Ⓑ Ⓒ Ⓓ Ⓔ	31 Ⓐ Ⓑ Ⓒ Ⓓ Ⓔ
2 Ⓐ Ⓑ Ⓒ Ⓓ Ⓔ	12 Ⓐ Ⓑ Ⓒ Ⓓ Ⓔ	22 Ⓐ Ⓑ Ⓒ Ⓓ Ⓔ	32 Ⓐ Ⓑ Ⓒ Ⓓ Ⓔ
3 Ⓐ Ⓑ Ⓒ Ⓓ Ⓔ	13 Ⓐ Ⓑ Ⓒ Ⓓ Ⓔ	23 Ⓐ Ⓑ Ⓒ Ⓓ Ⓔ	33 Ⓐ Ⓑ Ⓒ Ⓓ Ⓔ
4 Ⓐ Ⓑ Ⓒ Ⓓ Ⓔ	14 Ⓐ Ⓑ Ⓒ Ⓓ Ⓔ	24 Ⓐ Ⓑ Ⓒ Ⓓ Ⓔ	34 Ⓐ Ⓑ Ⓒ Ⓓ Ⓔ
5 Ⓐ Ⓑ Ⓒ Ⓓ Ⓔ	15 Ⓐ Ⓑ Ⓒ Ⓓ Ⓔ	25 Ⓐ Ⓑ Ⓒ Ⓓ Ⓔ	35 Ⓐ Ⓑ Ⓒ Ⓓ Ⓔ
6 Ⓐ Ⓑ Ⓒ Ⓓ Ⓔ	16 Ⓐ Ⓑ Ⓒ Ⓓ Ⓔ	26 Ⓐ Ⓑ Ⓒ Ⓓ Ⓔ	36 Ⓐ Ⓑ Ⓒ Ⓓ Ⓔ
7 Ⓐ Ⓑ Ⓒ Ⓓ Ⓔ	17 Ⓐ Ⓑ Ⓒ Ⓓ Ⓔ	27 Ⓐ Ⓑ Ⓒ Ⓓ Ⓔ	37 Ⓐ Ⓑ Ⓒ Ⓓ Ⓔ
8 Ⓐ Ⓑ Ⓒ Ⓓ Ⓔ	18 Ⓐ Ⓑ Ⓒ Ⓓ Ⓔ	28 Ⓐ Ⓑ Ⓒ Ⓓ Ⓔ	38 Ⓐ Ⓑ Ⓒ Ⓓ Ⓔ
9 Ⓐ Ⓑ Ⓒ Ⓓ Ⓔ	19 Ⓐ Ⓑ Ⓒ Ⓓ Ⓔ	29 Ⓐ Ⓑ Ⓒ Ⓓ Ⓔ	39 Ⓐ Ⓑ Ⓒ Ⓓ Ⓔ
10 Ⓐ Ⓑ Ⓒ Ⓓ Ⓔ	20 Ⓐ Ⓑ Ⓒ Ⓓ Ⓔ	30 Ⓐ Ⓑ Ⓒ Ⓓ Ⓔ	40 Ⓐ Ⓑ Ⓒ Ⓓ Ⓔ

SECTION 9

1 Ⓐ Ⓑ Ⓒ Ⓓ Ⓔ	11 Ⓐ Ⓑ Ⓒ Ⓓ Ⓔ	21 Ⓐ Ⓑ Ⓒ Ⓓ Ⓔ	31 Ⓐ Ⓑ Ⓒ Ⓓ Ⓔ
2 Ⓐ Ⓑ Ⓒ Ⓓ Ⓔ	12 Ⓐ Ⓑ Ⓒ Ⓓ Ⓔ	22 Ⓐ Ⓑ Ⓒ Ⓓ Ⓔ	32 Ⓐ Ⓑ Ⓒ Ⓓ Ⓔ
3 Ⓐ Ⓑ Ⓒ Ⓓ Ⓔ	13 Ⓐ Ⓑ Ⓒ Ⓓ Ⓔ	23 Ⓐ Ⓑ Ⓒ Ⓓ Ⓔ	33 Ⓐ Ⓑ Ⓒ Ⓓ Ⓔ
4 Ⓐ Ⓑ Ⓒ Ⓓ Ⓔ	14 Ⓐ Ⓑ Ⓒ Ⓓ Ⓔ	24 Ⓐ Ⓑ Ⓒ Ⓓ Ⓔ	34 Ⓐ Ⓑ Ⓒ Ⓓ Ⓔ
5 Ⓐ Ⓑ Ⓒ Ⓓ Ⓔ	15 Ⓐ Ⓑ Ⓒ Ⓓ Ⓔ	25 Ⓐ Ⓑ Ⓒ Ⓓ Ⓔ	35 Ⓐ Ⓑ Ⓒ Ⓓ Ⓔ
6 Ⓐ Ⓑ Ⓒ Ⓓ Ⓔ	16 Ⓐ Ⓑ Ⓒ Ⓓ Ⓔ	26 Ⓐ Ⓑ Ⓒ Ⓓ Ⓔ	36 Ⓐ Ⓑ Ⓒ Ⓓ Ⓔ
7 Ⓐ Ⓑ Ⓒ Ⓓ Ⓔ	17 Ⓐ Ⓑ Ⓒ Ⓓ Ⓔ	27 Ⓐ Ⓑ Ⓒ Ⓓ Ⓔ	37 Ⓐ Ⓑ Ⓒ Ⓓ Ⓔ
8 Ⓐ Ⓑ Ⓒ Ⓓ Ⓔ	18 Ⓐ Ⓑ Ⓒ Ⓓ Ⓔ	28 Ⓐ Ⓑ Ⓒ Ⓓ Ⓔ	38 Ⓐ Ⓑ Ⓒ Ⓓ Ⓔ
9 Ⓐ Ⓑ Ⓒ Ⓓ Ⓔ	19 Ⓐ Ⓑ Ⓒ Ⓓ Ⓔ	29 Ⓐ Ⓑ Ⓒ Ⓓ Ⓔ	39 Ⓐ Ⓑ Ⓒ Ⓓ Ⓔ
10 Ⓐ Ⓑ Ⓒ Ⓓ Ⓔ	20 Ⓐ Ⓑ Ⓒ Ⓓ Ⓔ	30 Ⓐ Ⓑ Ⓒ Ⓓ Ⓔ	40 Ⓐ Ⓑ Ⓒ Ⓓ Ⓔ

ESSAY — ESSAY

ESSAY
Time—25 minutes

Write your essay on separate sheets of standard lined paper.

The essay gives you an opportunity to show how effectively you can develop and express ideas. You should, therefore, take care to develop your point of view, present your ideas logically and clearly, and use language precisely.

Your essay must be written on the lines provided on your answer sheet—you will receive no other paper on which to write. You will have enough space if you write on every line, avoid wide margins, and keep your handwriting to a reasonable size. Remember that people who are not familiar with your handwriting will read what you write. Try to write or print so that what you are writing is legible to those readers.

Important Reminders:

- **A pencil is required for the essay.** An essay written in ink will receive a score of zero.
- **Do not write your essay in your test book.** You will receive credit only for what you write on your answer sheet.
- **An off-topic essay will receive a score of zero.**

You have twenty-five minutes to write an essay on the topic assigned below.

Consider carefully the issue discussed in the following passage, then write an essay that answers the question posed in the assignment.

> *None know the unfortunate and the fortunate do not know themselves.*
> —Benjamin Franklin

Assignment: **Are people today generally too unaware of their good fortune?** Write an essay in which you answer this question and support your position logically with examples from literature, the arts, history, politics, science and technology, current events, or your experience or observation.

If you finish before time is called, you may check your work on this section only.
Do not turn to any other section of the test.

2   2   2   2   2   2

SECTION 2
Time—25 minutes
24 questions

Turn to Section 2 of your answer sheet to answer the questions in this section.

Directions: For each question in this section, select the best answer from among the choices given and fill in the corresponding circle on the answer sheet.

Each sentence below has one or two blanks, each blank indicating that something has been omitted. Beneath the sentence are five words or sets of words labeled A through E. Choose the word or set of words that, when inserted in the sentence, <u>best</u> fits the meaning of the sentence as a whole.

EXAMPLE:

Rather than accepting the theory unquestioningly, Deborah regarded it with -----.

(A) mirth
(B) sadness
(C) responsibility
(D) ignorance
(E) skepticism

Ⓐ Ⓑ Ⓒ Ⓓ ●

---

1. After the doctor administered the -------, Ingrid could no longer feel the left side of her face, allowing the doctor to stitch the wound without causing any further pain.

    (A) emollient
    (B) antibody
    (C) antidote
    (D) correction
    (E) anesthetic

2. This particular strain of the flu is extremely ------- and leaves its victims -------, often unable even to get out of bed.

    (A) benign . . exhausted
    (B) mild . . incapacitated
    (C) harmless . . energized
    (D) debilitating . . lethargic
    (E) popular . . revitalized

3. The earthquake ------- the entire village; not a single building survived the disaster.

    (A) preserved
    (B) reiterated
    (C) debunked
    (D) razed
    (E) salvaged

4. The newly released version of Shakespeare's *Othello* was condemned by critics for being just another ------- remake that fails to bring anything new to the movie screen.

    (A) innovative
    (B) hackneyed
    (C) novel
    (D) quixotic
    (E) profound

GO ON TO THE NEXT PAGE ⟹

2   2   2   2   2   2

5. During the economic downturn, the airline industry was on the verge of collapse, and many companies survived only because a large government ------- provided a vital ------- of cash.

    (A) subsidy . . infusion
    (B) censure . . influx
    (C) endowment . . emission
    (D) endorsement . . alimony
    (E) allowance . . emanation

6. Having been ------- himself in college, Mr. Davis found it difficult to ------- his daughter for her inability to stay away from parties while at school.

    (A) an ascetic . . castigate
    (B) an altruist . . extol
    (C) a sybarite . . censure
    (D) a philanthropist . . accommodate
    (E) a hedonist . . rebuke

7. While writing *Walden*, Henry David Thoreau lived alone in a one room shack, but did not live the life of -------; he made many trips to the nearby village and entertained frequently at his house.

    (A) a miscreant
    (B) an exhibitionist
    (C) a recluse
    (D) a curator
    (E) a polemicist

8. The saleswoman has a ------- that helps her sell more cars than anyone else at the dealership; she is ------- in her efforts to close a deal.

    (A) doggedness . . inexorable
    (B) pertinacity . . lackadaisical
    (C) diffidence . . submissive
    (D) temerity . . munificent
    (E) tenacity . . indolent

Each passage below is followed by questions based on its content. Answer each question based on what is stated or implied in the passage.

Questions 9–10 are based on the following passage.

Strategy is the employment of the battle to gain the end of the war; it must therefore
Line give an aim to the whole military action, which must be in accordance with the object
5   of the war; in other words, strategy forms the plan of the war; and to this end it links together the series of acts which are to lead to the final decision; that is to say it makes the plans for the separate campaigns and
10 regulates the combats to be fought in each. As these are all things which to a great extent can only be determined on conjectures some of which turn out incorrect, while a number of other arrangements pertaining to details
15 cannot be made at all beforehand, it follows, as a matter of course, that strategy must go with the army to the field in order to arrange the particulars on the spot, and to make the modifications to the general plan which
20 incessantly become necessary in war,

9. In line 4, "object" most nearly means

    (A) weapon
    (B) opposition
    (C) observation
    (D) goal
    (E) link

10. The reference to "modifications" in line 19 serves primarily to emphasize the observation that war is

    (A) dangerous
    (B) inspirational
    (C) unpredictable
    (D) easily controlled
    (E) an ancient art

First passage: *On War*, Clausewitz; Bibliomania.com

GO ON TO THE NEXT PAGE ⇨

Questions 11–12 are based on the following passage.

It was a strange figure—like a child: yet not
so like a child as like an old man, viewed
Line through some supernatural medium, which
gave him the appearance of having receded
5   from the view, and being diminished to a
child's proportions. Its hair, which hung
about its neck and down its back, was white
as if with age; and yet the face had not a
wrinkle in it, and the tenderest bloom was on
10   the skin. The arms were very long and
muscular; the hands the same, as if its hold
were of uncommon strength. Its legs and
feet, most delicately formed, were, like those
upper members, bare.

11. In line 3, the word "medium" most nearly
means

(A) average
(B) clairvoyant
(C) substance
(D) artistic work
(E) impossibility

12. The reference to the "bloom" (line 9) serves
primarily to emphasize the figure's

(A) old age
(B) long hair
(C) eeriness
(D) strength
(E) youthful appearance

Questions 13–17 are based on the following passage.

*The following passage is excerpted from a recent
book written by Dr. Patricia McConnell, an applied
animal behaviorist and dog trainer, that discusses
the relationship between dogs and humans.*

All dogs are brilliant at perceiving the
slightest movement that we make, and they
Line assume that each tiny motion has meaning.
So do we humans, if you think about it.
5   Remember that minuscule turn of the head
that caught your attention when you were
dating? Think about how little someone's lips
have to move to change a sweet smile into a
smirk. How far does an eyebrow have to rise
10   to change the message we read from the face
it's on–a tenth of an inch? You'd think that
we would automatically generalize this
common knowledge to our interactions with
our dogs. But we don't. We are often
15   oblivious to how we're moving around our
dogs. It seems to be very human not to know
what we're doing with our body, unconscious
of where our hands are or that we just tilted
our head. We radiate random signals like
20   some crazed semaphore flag, while our dogs
watch in confusion, their eyes rolling around
in circles like cartoon dogs.
These visual signals, like all the rest of our
actions, have a profound influence on what
25   our dogs do. Who dogs are and how they
behave are partly defined by who we humans
are and how we ourselves behave. Domestic
dogs, by definition, share their lives with
another species: us.
30   Our species shares so much with dogs. If
you look across the vast range of all animal
life, from beetles to bears, humans and dogs
are more alike than we are different. Like
dogs, we make milk for our young and raise

GO ON TO THE NEXT PAGE ⟹

Second passage: *A Christmas Carol*, Charles Dickens, 1893
From *The Other End of the Leash*, by Patricia B. McConnell, Ph. D., copyright © 2002, by Patricia B. McConnell, Ph. D. Used by
permission of Ballantine Books, a division of Random House, Inc.

35   them in a pack. Our babies have lots to learn while growing up; we hunt cooperatively; we play silly games even as adults; we snore; we scratch and blink and yawn on sunny afternoons. Look at what Pam Brown, a New
40   Zealand poet, had to say about people and dogs in the book *Bond for Life*:

> "Humankind is drawn to dogs because they are so like ourselves—bumbling, affectionate, confused, easily disappointed,
45   eager to be amused, grateful for kindness and the least attention."

These similarities allow the members of two different species to live together intimately, sharing food, recreation, and even
50   bearing young together. Lots of animals live closely linked to others, but our level of connection with our dogs is profound.

Most of us exercise with our dogs, play with our dogs, eat at the same time as our dogs
55   (and sometimes the same food), and sleep with our dogs. Some of us still depend on our dogs for our work. Sheep ranchers in Wyoming and dairy farmers in Wisconsin need their dogs as much as or more than
60   they do machinery or high-tech feeding systems. We know that dogs enrich the lives of many of us, providing comfort and joy to millions around the world. Studies even show that they decrease the probability of a second
65   heart attack. We don't put up with shedding and barking and carrying pooper scoopers on walks for nothing.

13.   Which of the following is the best title for this passage?

(A)   Visual Acuity in Dogs
(B)   The Ties That Bind Dogs and Humans
(C)   The Utility of Animals in the Workplace
(D)   Close Relationships in the Animal Kingdom
(E)   How to Communicate with your Dog

14.   The passage mentions the "minuscule turn of the head" (line 5) primarily as an example of

(A)   a common gesture that dogs perform
(B)   a small action that has meaning to humans
(C)   something that dogs often detect but humans don't
(D)   something that is difficult to measure
(E)   an action that binds dogs and humans

15.   The reference to the "semaphore flag" in line 20 serves primarily to emphasize the author's observation that dogs

(A)   are more confused than they seem
(B)   are in constant motion
(C)   cannot detect many of the signals that are intended for them
(D)   are capable of conveying sophisticated information
(E)   can detect unintended signals

16.   The passage indicates that humans and dogs are alike in all the following aspects EXCEPT

(A)   eating habits
(B)   the ability to detect small movements
(C)   child rearing practices
(D)   the need for attention
(E)   acute hearing

17.   The author mentions "high-tech feeding systems" (lines 60–61) as examples of

(A)   technologies that can benefit dogs
(B)   resources for all pet owners
(C)   advances that have yet to be developed
(D)   equipment that some farmers find necessary
(E)   systems that require further study

GO ON TO THE NEXT PAGE ⟶

Questions 18–24 are based on the following passage.

The following is adapted from an essay written by Ralph Waldo Emerson in 1841.

What right have I to write on Prudence, of
which I have little, and that of the negative
Line sort? My prudence consists in avoiding and
going without, not in the inventing of means
5   and methods, not in adroit steering, not in
gentle repairing. I have no skill to make
money spend well, no genius in my economy,
and whoever sees my garden discovers that
I must have some other garden. Yet I love
10   facts, and hate deceitfulness and people
without perception. Then I have the same title
to write on prudence that I have to write on
poetry or holiness. We write from aspiration
and antagonism, as well as from experience.
15   We paint those qualities which we do not
possess. The poet admires the man of energy
and tactics; the merchant breeds his son for
the church or the bar; and where a man is
not vain and egotistic you shall find what he
20   has not by his praise.

Prudence is the virtue of the senses. It is
the science of appearances. It is the outmost
action of the inward life. It is content to seek
health of body by complying with physical
25   conditions, and health of mind by the laws of
the intellect.

The world of the senses is a world of
shows; it does not exist for itself, but has a
symbolic character; and a true prudence or
30   law of shows recognizes the existence of much
deeper laws. Prudence is false when detached.
It is legitimate when it is the Natural History
of the soul incarnate, when it unfolds the beauty
of laws within the narrow scope of the senses.

35   There are all degrees of proficiency in
knowledge of the world. It is sufficient to our
present purpose to indicate three. One class
live to the utility of the symbol, esteeming
health and wealth a final good. Another class
40   live above this mark to the beauty of the
symbol, as the poet and artist and the
naturalist and man of science. A third class

live above the beauty of the symbol to the
beauty of the thing signified; these are wise
45   men. The first class have common sense; the
second, taste; and the third, spiritual
perception. Once in a long time, a man
traverses the whole scale, and sees and enjoys
the symbol solidly, then also has a clear eye
50   for its beauty, and lastly, whilst he pitches his
tent on this sacred volcanic isle of nature,
does not offer to build houses and barns
thereon, reverencing the splendor of the God
which he sees bursting through each chink
55   and cranny.

The world is filled with the proverbs and
acts of a base prudence, which is a devotion
to matter, as if we possessed no other faculties
than the palate, the nose, the touch, the eye
60   and ear; a prudence which never subscribes,
which never gives, which seldom lends, and
asks but one question of any project: will it
bake bread? But culture, revealing the high
origin of the apparent world and aiming at
65   the perfection of the man as the end,
degrades every thing else, as health and
bodily life, into means. It sees prudence not
as a distinct faculty, but a name for
wisdom and virtue conversing with the body
70   and its wants. Cultivated men always feel and
speak so, as if a great fortune, the achievement
of a civil or social measure, great personal
influence, a graceful and commanding
address, had their value as proofs of the
75   energy of the spirit. If a man lose his balance
and immerse himself in any trades or
pleasures for their own sake, he may be a good
wheel or pin, but he is not a cultivated man.

GO ON TO THE NEXT PAGE ⟶

2   2   2   2   2   2

18. In saying that others discover that the author "must have some other garden" (line 9), he suggests that he

    (A) owns a great deal of land
    (B) is not adept at growing things
    (C) enjoys gardening a great deal
    (D) is frequently disoriented
    (E) wants to acquire more land

19. In line 11, the word "title" most nearly means

    (A) ownership
    (B) name
    (C) literary work
    (D) right
    (E) opposition

20. In the first paragraph, the author argues that he is justified in writing about prudence because he

    (A) exercises prudence in many different areas
    (B) has written many stories with prudent characters
    (C) understands the topic from studying classic philosophy
    (D) admires prudence more than he possesses it
    (E) is an expert gardener

21. According to the passage, members of the "third class" (line 42) are superior to the members of the other classes primarily in their ability to

    (A) create art
    (B) solve practical problems
    (C) perceive supernatural qualities
    (D) establish facts scientifically
    (E) reason logically

22. The reference to "houses and barns" (line 52) serves primarily to emphasize the fact that one who "traverses the whole scale" (line 48) appreciates

    (A) the relative insignificance of worldly things
    (B) the importance of sturdy construction
    (C) the necessity of capturing the beauty of nature through art
    (D) the nobility of farm life
    (E) the dangers of religious fervor

23. The sentence "The world is filled with... will it bake bread?" (lines 56–63) suggests that the "base prudence" of proverbs is

    (A) too preachy
    (B) not taught with enough care
    (C) too concerned with practical things
    (D) insufficiently sensual
    (E) difficult to understand

24. In the final paragraph, the author's attitude toward culture is best characterized as

    (A) reverential
    (B) jocular
    (C) objective
    (D) indifferent
    (E) critical

STOP

If you finish before time is called, you may check your work on this section only. Do not turn to any other section of the test.

3   3   3   3   3   3

SECTION 3
Time—25 minutes
20 questions

Turn to Section 3 of your answer sheet to answer the questions in this section.

Directions: For this section, solve each problem and decide which is the best of the choices given. Fill in the corresponding circle on the answer sheet. You may use any available space for scratchwork.

Notes

1. The use of a calculator is permitted.

2. All numbers used are real numbers.

3. Figures that accompany problems in this test are intended to provide information useful in solving the problems. They are drawn as accurately as possible EXCEPT when it is stated in a specific problem that the figure is not drawn to scale. All figures lie in a plane unless otherwise indicated.

4. Unless otherwise specified, the domain of any function f is assumed to be the set of all real numbers x for which $f(x)$ is a real number.

Reference Information

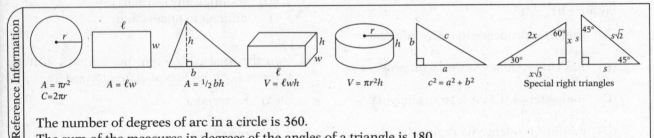

$A = \pi r^2$
$C = 2\pi r$

$A = \ell w$

$A = \frac{1}{2}bh$

$V = \ell wh$

$V = \pi r^2 h$

$c^2 = a^2 + b^2$

Special right triangles

The number of degrees of arc in a circle is 360.
The sum of the measures in degrees of the angles of a triangle is 180.

---

1. How many CD cases, each holding 120 CDs, are needed to hold 20 dozen CDs? (1 dozen = 12 CDs)

(A) 1
(B) 2
(C) 3
(D) 4
(E) 5

2. Which of the following has the digit 4 in both the units place and the thousandths place?

(A) 4,004.040
(B) 4,000.400
(C) 3,004.004
(D) 3,040.444
(E) 4,040.004

3. If $f(x) = 2x^2 + 8$, what is the value of $f(8)$?

(A) 116
(B) 133
(C) 136
(D) 256
(E) 264

GO ON TO THE NEXT PAGE ⟹

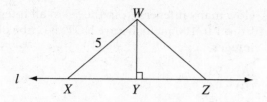

4. In the figure above, points X, Y, and Z lie on line l, and $\overline{WY}$ bisects $\overline{XZ}$. If $XZ = 8$, what is the length of $\overline{WY}$?

(A) 2
(B) 3
(C) 4

(D) $4\sqrt{3}$ (approximately 6.93)

(E) $5\sqrt{3}$ (approximately 8.66)

5. At a science fair, the prize money of $3,000 is to be split in the ratio 3:2:1 by the first, second, and third place finishers, respectively. What is the amount of the third prize?

(A) $500
(B) $1,000
(C) $1,500
(D) $2,000
(E) $2,500

6. If $(x - y) = -2$, then $(x - y)^2 =$

(A) −4
(B) −2
(C) 0
(D) 2
(E) 4

11	B	7	3
A	1	10	9
4	12	2	16
5	8	C	D

7. In the table above, all of the columns and rows have the same sum. What is the value of $A + B + C + D$?

(A) 48
(B) 56
(C) 62
(D) 74
(E) 90

8. If $a < b < -1$, which of the following has the greatest value?

(A) $-3a + b$
(B) $-(a-b)$
(C) $-(3a + b)$
(D) $3a$
(E) $a-b$

GO ON TO THE NEXT PAGE ⇒

3   **3**   **3**   **3**   **3**   **3**

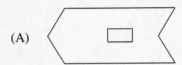

9. A piece of paper is folded in half about side *AB*. Cuts are then made along the dotted lines. Which of the following best represents the result when unfolded?

(A)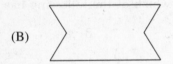

(B)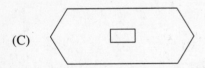

(C)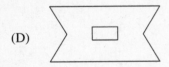

(D)

(E)

10. How many integers from the set of all integers from 1 to 100 inclusive are NOT the cube of an integer?

(A) 93
(B) 94
(C) 95
(D) 96
(E) 97

11. In a pet store, there are three times as many goldfish as there are tropical fish. There are twice as many orange goldfish as there are black goldfish. What is the probability that a randomly selected fish from the store is a black goldfish?

(A) $\dfrac{1}{12}$

(B) $\dfrac{1}{6}$

(C) $\dfrac{1}{4}$

(D) $\dfrac{1}{2}$

(E) $\dfrac{3}{4}$

12. The ideal gas law states that pressure, *P*, varies inversely as volume, *V*, and directly as the temperature, *T*. If $P = 700$ and $V = 10$, then $T = 350$. What is the value of *T* when $P = 500$ and $V = 20$?

(A) 20
(B) 120
(C) 200
(D) 350
(E) 500

GO ON TO THE NEXT PAGE

3   3   3   3   3   3

$$x - 2y > 13$$
$$y + x < 13$$

13. Which of the following ordered pairs (x, y) is a solution of both of the inequalities above?

(A) (3, –1)
(B) (12, 3)
(C) (8, 3)
(D) (10, 2)
(E) (1, 5)

14. After Andrea gives Chris $10 and Liz $3, Chris gives $4 to Liz. At this point, Andrea has $10 more than Chris and $16 more than Liz. How much more money did Andrea have than Chris originally?

(A) $10
(B) $20
(C) $24
(D) $29
(E) $36

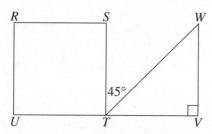

Note: Figure not drawn to scale.

15. In the figure above, points U, T, and V lie on the same line and point T is the midpoint of $\overline{UV}$. What is the ratio of the perimeter of square $RSTU$ to the perimeter of triangle TVW?

(A) $2 + \sqrt{2} : 4$

(B) $4 : 2 + \sqrt{2}$

(C) $2 : 1$

(D) $4 : 2 + \sqrt{3}$

(E) $2 + \sqrt{3} : 6$

16. A parking lot has 5 spots remaining and 5 different cars in line waiting to be parked. If one of the cars is too big to fit in the two outermost spots, in how many different ways can the five cars be arranged?

(A) 15
(B) 54
(C) 72
(D) 96
(E) 120

17. Seven students took a quiz and their average (arithmetic mean) score was 83. If the average score for three of the students was 79, what was the average score for the other four students?

(A) 85
(B) 86
(C) 87
(D) 88
(E) 89

HISTORY OF THE FEDERAL
HOURLY MINIMUM WAGE

1974	$2.00
1976	$2.30
1978	$2.65
1980	$3.10
1982	$3.35

18. According to the data listed in the table above, the minimum wage in 1980 was what percent larger than the minimum wage in 1974?

(A   30%
(B) 55%
(C) 64.5%
(D) 110%
(E) 155%

GO ON TO THE NEXT PAGE ⇨

3   3   3   3   3   3

8, 13, 21...

19. After the first two terms in the sequence above, each subsequent term is the sum of the two immediately preceding numbers. For example, $21 = 13 + 8$. How many of the first 60 terms of this sequence are odd?

(A) 20
(B) 30
(C) 33
(D) 40
(E) 44

20. A snow-removal company charges a business d dollars for removing any amount of snow from their parking lot up to 6 inches, and f dollars for each additional inch of snow. Which of the following represents the cost of hiring the company to shovel p inches of snow from the parking lot, if $p > 6$?

(A) $pd + pf$
(B) $fd + p$
(C) $f + d - p$
(D) $fp - 6f + 6d$
(E) $f(p - 6) + d$

If you finish before time is called, you may check your work on this section only. Do not turn to any other section of the test.

4   4   4   4   4   4

SECTION 4
Time—25 minutes
24 questions

Turn to Section 4 of your answer sheet to answer the questions in this section.

Directions: For each question in this section, select the best answer from among the choices given and fill in the corresponding circle on the answer sheet.

Each sentence below has one or two blanks, each blank indicating that something has been omitted. Beneath the sentence are five words or sets of words labeled A through E. Choose the word or set of words that, when inserted in the sentence, <u>best</u> fits the meaning of the sentence as a whole.

EXAMPLE:

Rather than accepting the theory unquestioningly, Deborah regarded it with -----.

(A) mirth
(B) sadness
(C) responsibility
(D) ignorance
(E) skepticism

Ⓐ Ⓑ Ⓒ Ⓓ ●

---

1. Rita was understandably consumed by ------- when she was forced to put her beloved seventeen year-old cat to sleep.

   (A) inversion
   (B) anguish
   (C) frivolity
   (D) hilarity
   (E) sluggishness

2. The epidemiologists were astonished by the incredible rate at which the virus was ------; few had ever seen anything replicate at such a remarkable speed.

   (A) pontificating   (B) diverging
   (C) saturating   (D) proliferating
   (E) dissipating

3. Despite being from the wealthiest family in Australia, Leah was ------- and sometimes even ------- with her money, refusing to waste even a few dollars.

   (A) prudent . . munificent
   (B) thrifty . . stingy
   (C) frugal . . outspoken
   (D) extravagant . . improvident
   (E) reckless . . miserly

4. After two consecutive weeks of grueling practice Tony got a much needed ------- from his workout with the arrival of spring break.

   (A) continuance
   (B) encore
   (C) respite
   (D) commencement
   (E) conviction

5. Throughout his time in school, Emil has always been a -------; his ------- antics may have won favor with some of the teachers, but most could see through his superficial flattery.

   (A) toady . . irreverent
   (B) sycophant . . fawning
   (C) lackey . . insubordinate
   (D) mercenary . . intractable
   (E) clairvoyant . . altruistic

GO ON TO THE NEXT PAGE ⟹

4   **4**   **4**   **4**   **4**   **4**

Each passage below is followed by questions based on its content. Answer each question based on what is stated or implied in the passage.

Questions 6–7 are based on the following passage.

Suppose that a mass attached to the end of a string is set in motion. The mass comes to
Line rest at the top of its swing, then falls back in the other direction, gains speed, reaches
5   maximum speed at the bottom of its swing, rises on the other side, and again comes to rest at the top of its swing. Then the process repeats. If there were no friction and no outside disturbance, the pendulum would
10 keep swinging forever.
    If we make the string very light, the pendulum bob is essentially the only mass in the system. Since the bob changes height during its swing, its gravitational energy
15 changes. The pendulum has zero speed and therefore zero kinetic energy at the top of its swing, at maximum height, when its gravitational energy is largest; it has maximum speed and therefore maximum
20 kinetic energy at the bottom of its swing, when its gravitational energy is smallest. Total energy will be conserved if the gain of kinetic energy exactly equals the loss of gravitational energy.

6. The passage suggests that the gravitational energy of the bob depends on

(A) its distance from the ground
(B) the length of its string
(C) the force applied to it
(D) its speed
(E) the time it takes for one full swing

7. Which of the following best describes the relationship between gravitational energy and kinetic energy of the bob as it is explained in the passage?

(A) As kinetic energy increases, gravitational energy increases.
(B) As kinetic energy increases, gravitational energy decreases.
(C) Gravitational energy remains constant, even as kinetic energy changes.
(D) Kinetic energy remains constant, even as gravitational energy changes.
(E) Kinetic energy and gravitational energy are exactly equal when the bob is at the bottom of its swing.

First passage: *Great Ideas in Physics*, Alan Lightman; McGraw Hill, July 2000

GO ON TO THE NEXT PAGE

Questions 8–9 are based on the following passage.

The old woman was a gnarled and leathery
personage who could don, at will, an
Line expression of great virtue. She possessed a
small music-box capable of one tune, and a
5 collection of "God bless yehs" pitched in
assorted keys of fervency. Each day she took
a position upon the stones of Fifth Avenue,
where she crooked her legs under her and
crouched immovable and hideous, like an
10 idol. She received daily a small sum in
pennies. It was contributed, for the most part,
by persons who did not make their homes in
that vicinity.

8. It can be inferred from the passage that the old
    woman is most likely a

    (A) shop owner
    (B) beggar
    (C) recluse
    (D) musician
    (E) mother

9. In line 6, the word "keys" most nearly means

    (A) tones of voice
    (B) principles
    (C) necessities
    (D) tools
    (E) sponsors

Questions 10–16 are based on the following passage.

The following passage is adapted from a debate
about government surveillance and the phenomenon
known as "Big Brother."

The first video surveillance systems were
installed in the early 1970s to assist in road
Line traffic management and deter bank robbers.
During the 1980s their use spread rapidly to
5 public transport, shops, the workplace,
leisure venues and the approaches to public
buildings. A further step in this direction was
taken at the beginning of the 1990s, when
cameras were installed on public highways,
10 in sports stadiums and on the streets of
certain cities.
   This new form of surveillance aroused
misgivings from the onset. In France, the
CNIL (National Committee on Computer
15 Data and Individual Freedom) proposed the
first legal safeguards at the end of the 1980s.
But the general public accepted the new
technology as a means of crime prevention.
However, a survey carried out in 1996
20 showed that social acceptability varied
according to the type of application. Only 9%
of respondents considered the presence of
cameras in car parks and shops as an
invasion of privacy. On the other hand, 51%
25 thought that showing pictures of a person
taken in a public place without that person's
consent was a serious violation.
   The cameras involved are becoming more
and more powerful. There are even "smart"
30 cameras equipped with sensors that trigger
alarm systems when incidents occur. The
transmission of images over public telephone
networks means that people can be kept
under surveillance worldwide without regard
35 to national frontiers.
   Once installed, video surveillance systems
can be used for purposes other than those for
which they were originally intended. The use
of the cameras of Beijing's Tiananmen Square

Second passage: *Maggie, A Girl of the Streets*, Stephen Crane.
Public Domain

GO ON TO THE NEXT PAGE ⇨

40 to identify and arrest demonstrators in June
    1989 is a notorious example.

    It is becoming apparent that the closed
    circuit systems installed in large department
    stores in order to counter shoplifting are
45 now being used for staff surveillance. They
    have become an instrument for monitoring
    work and productivity. Video systems can
    also be used to monitor specific aspects of
    consumer behavior. Detailed analysis of tiny
50 movements and gestures enables stores to
    optimize the positioning of goods and
    devise the most effective shopping
    itineraries.

    Video surveillance is a new form of
55 control. An abstract, remote, impersonal,
    automatic, bureaucratic, largely invisible and
    inherently mysterious device enables a
    machine to create information and, if need
    be, initiate action. Here, the essence of
60 control is manipulation rather than coercion,
    as if a distant hand were pulling invisible
    strings. The person under surveillance is
    reduced to an object of information. His
    records are contained in countless files, and
65 everywhere he goes he leaves electronic
    traces of his passage. As if this were not
    enough, his activities are rendered even more
    transparent by video cameras that track
    his image. The subject himself remains
70 ignorant of the processes and manipulation
    of data going on behind his back.

    In democracies, where freedoms are
    guaranteed by law, the loss of privacy
    entailed in the taking of pictures must not be
75 disproportionate to the end in view. It may be
    justified in certain places where security is at
    risk, but it is not justified in all cases. In a
    Belgian secondary school, smokers were
    pursued right into the toilets, where cameras
80 were installed to catch them in the act. It has
    also been established that cameras installed
    on the public highway, or set up outside
    department stores to keep watch on the
    entrances, can see into adjacent houses and

85 apartment blocks. Safeguarding the rights of
    persons subjected to video surveillance is
    absolutely essential if a proper balance is to
    be struck between security and freedom.

10. The primary purpose of the first paragraph
    is to

    (A) evaluate a new technology
    (B) provide a brief history of a
         phenomenon
    (C) describe a characteristic quality of an era
    (D) summarize a misconception
    (E) present an individual's point of view

11. It can be inferred from the passage that, at the
    end of the 1980s, the CNIL was concerned with

    (A) making video surveillance less expensive
    (B) improving road traffic management
    (C) preventing misuses of electronic
         surveillance
    (D) encouraging wider use of electronic
         surveillance
    (E) deterring bank theft

12. The statistics cited in the second paragraph
    suggest that people's concerns about electronic
    surveillance of their activities depend on

    (A) whether the surveillance is indoors or
         outdoors
    (B) what kinds of crimes are prevented with
         its use
    (C) how expensive the equipment is to install
         and maintain
    (D) how accurate the equipment is
    (E) what control they have over the distribu-
         tion of the gathered information

GO ON TO THE NEXT PAGE ⟶

Excerpted from: http://mondediplo.com/1998/03/11video, Big Brother is Watching you on Video; March, 1998

Available on subscription,
email: lmdsubs@granta.com
or visit our website: www.mondediplo.com>

13. The "aspects of consumer behavior" mentioned in lines 48–49 can be inferred to most directly include

(A) shoplifting of small items
(B) purchasing habits
(C) misgivings about surveillance
(D) concerns about safety
(E) rude behavior toward store workers

14. In line 66, the word "passage" most nearly means

(A) death
(B) writing
(C) entryway
(D) travels
(E) objection

15. The list of adjectives in lines 55–57 serve primarily to characterize electronic surveillance as

(A) effective
(B) expensive
(C) detached
(D) useless
(E) coercive

16. The author objects to the use of cameras "installed on the public highway" (lines 81–82) chiefly because

(A) they can be used to invade the privacy of non-drivers
(B) the use of cameras in a public place is never justified
(C) they can be easily damaged
(D) they have not been proven to prevent traffic accidents
(E) they are insufficiently powerful

Questions 17–24 are based on the following passage.

The following passage is an excerpt from an essay written in 1896 on women in the northeastern United States.

The exodus of women, for one reason or another, to the cities in the last ten years
Line parallels that of men. They have come from the West in regiments, and from the South in
5 brigades. Each year they come younger and younger. They have ameliorated the customs and diversified the streets.
New York and perhaps city women in general, when they are suddenly called upon
10 to earn their livings, are much more independent about it, and more original in their methods than women in smaller places, where womanly pursuits, as they are called, follow more closely prescribed lines. The
15 New York woman has more knowledge of the world, and she knows that one can do pretty much what one pleases, if it is done with a certain dash, *élan*, carrying-all-before-it air. When she comes to work for her living
20 she profits by this knowledge. Instead of becoming a governess or a teacher of music, she tries to get hold of something original that will excite interest. When she has found it she holds it up, as it were, on a blazoned
25 banner, inscribed with this legend, "I have not a penny to my name, and I'm going to work." She accepts the situation with the greatest good-humor and makes herself more acceptable to the old set by relating her
30 discouragements, trials, and mistakes so comically that she is better company than before. If her story is not bad enough she embroiders it to the proper point of attractiveness.
35 In the measure that women are determining their own lives, they want their own homes. The desire is entirely reasonable.

GO ON TO THE NEXT PAGE →

from "Women Bachelors" by Mary Gay Humphreys, 1896, in *Early American Women* © 1992 by Nancy Woloch, Wadsworth Publishing Company, pp. 550–552

The woman who is occupied with daily work
needs greater freedom of movement, more
40 isolation, more personal comforts, and the
exemption, moreover, from being agreeable
at all times and places. She wants to be able
to shut her doors against all the world, and
not to be confined within four walls herself;
45 and she wants to open her doors when it
pleases her, and to exercise the rites
of hospitality unquestioned. In fact, she
wants many things that cannot be had except
in her own home. It is an interesting fact in
50 natural history that women in their first
breathing-spell should revert to constructing
homes as their natural background, to which
is added the male realization that the home is
the proper stimulus to achievement.
55   To be the mistress of a home, to extend
hospitalities, briefly to be within the
circumference of a social circle, instead of
gliding with uneasy foot on the periphery, is
the reasonable desire of every woman. When
60 this is achieved many temptations, so freely
recognized that nobody disputes them, are
eliminated. It is a noticeable fact that in all
women-bachelor households, no matter how
humble, that the rugs are scarcely down and
65 the curtains up, until the kettle is lighted and
the reign of hospitality has begun. It is
interesting to observe how soon the shyest
novice over the tea-cup loses her timidity,
and assumes that air of confidence that once
70 was the enviable property of only married
women.

17. The passage suggests that, compared to city
women, women who live in "smaller places"
(line 12) are

(A) better educated
(B) more aggressive
(C) less attractive
(D) more traditional
(E) wealthier

18. In line 18, the word "dash" most nearly means

(A) carelessness
(B) properness
(C) quickness
(D) danger
(E) flair

19. The "knowledge" referred to in line 20 is
knowledge of how to

(A) teach music
(B) make one's self interesting to others
(C) assert the superiority of women
over men
(D) sustain a traditional profession
(E) maintain a home

20. The "attractiveness" referred to in line 34
refers to

(A) a woman's outward appearance
(B) the pitifulness of a woman's situation
(C) a woman's wealth
(D) the formal education a woman has
achieved
(E) a woman's desire to help others become
beautiful

21. The third paragraph (lines 35–54) indicates
that women who work outside of the home
need which of the following?

      I.   the ability to entertain when
           they wish
      II. the freedom to abstain from
           propriety
      III. free access to higher education

(A) I only
(B) II only
(C) I and II only
(D) II and III only
(E) I, II, and III

GO ON TO THE NEXT PAGE ⟩

4   4   4   4   4   4

22. The phrase "uneasy foot on the periphery" (line 58) refers to some women's

(A) exclusion from certain social groups
(B) inability to maintain a home
(C) lack of success in acquiring employment
(D) superior skills at public speaking
(E) warm hospitality

23. In line 68, the phrase "over the tea-cup" most nearly means

(A) when purchasing dinner
(B) when cleaning dishes
(C) when hosting guests
(D) when looking for a job
(E) when moving to the city

24. The last paragraph suggests most directly that owning and maintaining her own home makes a woman more

(A) confident
(B) affluent
(C) emotionally stable
(D) adept at making household repairs
(E) attractive to men

STOP   *If you finish before time is called, you may check your work on this section only. Do not turn to any other section of the test.*

5   **5**   **5**   **5**   **5**   **5**

SECTION 5
Time—25 minutes
18 questions

Turn to Section 5 of your answer sheet to answer the questions in this section.

Directions: This section contains two types of questions. You have 25 minutes to complete both types. For questions 1–8, solve each problem and decide which is the best of the choices given. Fill in the corresponding circle on the answer sheet. You may use any available space for scratchwork.

Notes

1. The use of a calculator is permitted.

2. All numbers used are real numbers.

3. Figures that accompany problems in this test are intended to provide information useful in solving the problems. They are drawn as accurately as possible EXCEPT when it is stated in a specific problem that the figure is not drawn to scale. All figures lie in a plane unless otherwise indicated.

4. Unless otherwise specified, the domain of any function f is assumed to be the set of all real numbers x for which $f(x)$ is a real number.

Reference Information

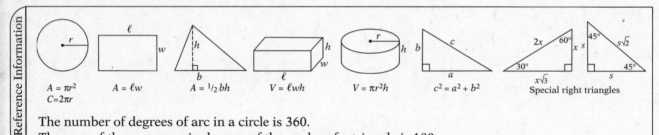

$A = \pi r^2$
$C = 2\pi r$ $A = \ell w$ $A = \frac{1}{2}bh$ $V = \ell w h$ $V = \pi r^2 h$ $c^2 = a^2 + b^2$ Special right triangles

The number of degrees of arc in a circle is 360.
The sum of the measures in degrees of the angles of a triangle is 180.

---

1. If $3 - x = 2x - 6$, what is the value of x?

   (A) 1
   (B) 2
   (C) 3
   (D) 6
   (E) 9

$$\begin{array}{r} RP \\ + \ 7T \\ \hline 15P \end{array}$$

2. In the correctly worked addition problem above, R, P, and T, represent different digits. What is the value of R?

   (A) 0
   (B) 2
   (C) 5
   (D) 8
   (E) 9

GO ON TO THE NEXT PAGE ⟶

5   5   5   5   5   5

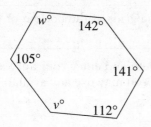

3. In the figure above, what is the value of $w + v$?

   (A)   40
   (B)   125
   (C)   140
   (D)   220
   (E)   300

4. One number is twice as large as another positive number, and their difference is 4. What is the greater of the two numbers?

   (A)   4
   (B)   6
   (C)   8
   (D)   10
   (E)   12

5. In a movie theater, $\frac{1}{3}$ of the seats were filled when the previews started. After 50 more people came in, $\frac{3}{4}$ of the seats were filled. How many seats are in the movie theater?

   (A)   90
   (B)   120
   (C)   150
   (D)   170
   (E)   190

6. How many of the first fifty positive integers contain the digit 4?

   (A)   12
   (B)   13
   (C)   14
   (D)   15
   (E)   16

7. If $3x = y + z$, $y = 6 - z$, and $z + x = 8$, what is the value of $\frac{y}{z}$?

   (A)   0
   (B)   2
   (C)   4
   (D)   5
   (E)   7

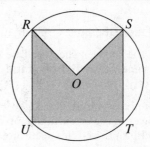

8. In the figure above, the four vertices of square *RSTU* lie on circle *O*, which has a radius of 8. What is the area of the shaded region?

   (A)   32
   (B)   96
   (C)   128
   (D)   150
   (E)   166

GO ON TO THE NEXT PAGE ⟩

5   5   5   5   5   5

Directions: For student-produced response questions 9–18, use the grids at the bottom of the answer sheet page on which you have answered questions 1–8.

Each of the remaining 10 questions requires you to solve the problem and enter your answer by marking the circles in the special grid, as shown in the examples below. You may use any available space for scratchwork.

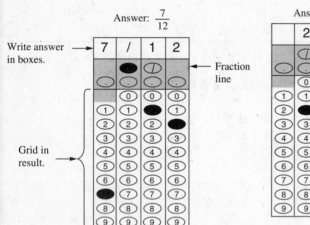

Answer: $\frac{7}{12}$

Write answer in boxes.

Fraction line

Grid in result.

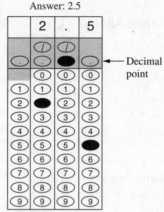

Answer: 2.5

Decimal point

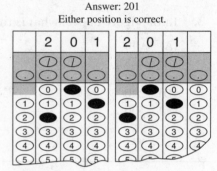

Answer: 201
Either position is correct.

Note: You may start your answers in any column, space permitting. Columns not needed should be left blank.

- Mark no more than one circle in any column.

- Because the answer sheet will be machine-scored, **you will receive credit only if the circles are filled in correctly.**

- Although not required, it is suggested that you write your answer in the boxes at the top of the columns to help you fill in the circles accurately.

- Some problems may have more than one correct answer. In such cases, grid only one answer.

- No question has a negative answer.

- **Mixed numbers** such as $3\frac{1}{2}$ must be gridded as 3.5 or 7/2. (If ⎡3 1 / 2⎤ is gridded, it will be interpreted as $\frac{31}{2}$ not $3\frac{1}{2}$.)

- **Decimal Answers:** If you obtain a decimal answer with more digits than the grid can accommodate, it may be either rounded or truncated, but it must fill the entire grid. For example, if you obtain an answer such as 0.6666..., you should record your result as .666 or .667. **A less accurate value such as .66 or .67 will be scored as incorrect.**

Acceptable ways to grid $^2/_3$ are:

GO ON TO THE NEXT PAGE

5   5   5   5   5   5

9. If $f(x) = 3x + 7$ and $g(x) = x^2 - 1$, what is the value of $g(f(2))$?

10. At Streams Elementary School, the four home-room classes have 14, 18, 21, and 23 students. What is the fewest number of students that would have to change homerooms for each class to contain the same number of students?

TIME ALLOCATION FOR ACTIVITIES FOR AN AVERAGE COLLEGE STUDENT

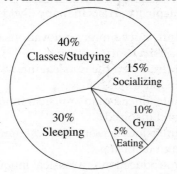

11. According to the data in the circle graph above, how many combined hours does an average college student spend at the gym and socializing during an average seven-day week?

12. Two sides of a triangle have lengths of 6 and 8. The length of the third side is unknown. What is the largest possible area of this triangle?

13. If x is a positive integer and $|2x + 6| > 10$, what is the least possible value of x?

14. A pile of five coins consists of one penny (1 cent), one nickel (5 cents), one dime (10 cents), one quarter (25 cents) and one 50-cent piece. If two different coins are selected at random, what is the probability that the sum of these coins will be less than 35 cents?

15. If one can of paint costs $15.00 and contains enough paint to cover an area of 300 square feet, what is the cost, in dollars, of the paint needed to cover a large rectangular ballroom that measures 150 feet by 100 feet? (Disregard the dollar sign when gridding your answer.)

16. If a rectangular solid has edge lengths of 6, 4, and 3. If its surface area is m square units, and its volume is n cubic units, what is the value of $\dfrac{m}{n}$?

Set X is the set of positive integers between 1 and 50 (inclusive)

Set Y is the set of positive integers between 1 and 100 (inclusive)

17. If x is a member of set X and y is a member of set Y, what is the greatest value of $x + y$ such that both $x + y$ and xy are members of set Y?

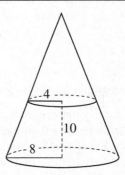

18. The radius of the base of a right circular cone is 8. A parallel cross section is made through the cone and has a radius of 4. If the distance between the cross section and the base of the cone is 10, what is the height of the cone?

If you finish before time is called, you may check your work on this section only. Do not turn to any other section of the test.

6   6   6   6   6   6

SECTION 6
Time—25 minutes
35 questions

Turn to Section 6 of your answer sheet to answer the questions in this section.

Directions: For each question in this section, select the best answer from among the choices given and fill in the corresponding circle on the answer sheet.

The following sentences test correctness and effectiveness of expression. Part of each sentence or the entire sentence is underlined; beneath each sentence are five ways of phrasing the underlined material. Choice A repeats the original phrasing; the other four choices are different. Select the choice that completes the sentence most effectively.

In making your selection, follow the requirements of standard written English; that is, pay attention to grammar, choice of words, sentence construction, and punctuation. Your selection should result in the most effective sentence— clear and precise, without awkwardness or ambiguity.

EXAMPLE:

The children <u>couldn't hardly believe their eyes</u>.

(A) couldn't hardly believe their eyes
(B) could hardly believe their eyes
(C) would not hardly believe their eyes
(D) couldn't nearly believe their eyes
(E) couldn't hardly believe his or her eyes

1. Although it is often dismissed as a vulgar popular phenomenon, hip hop culture has actually <u>introduced many innovations of the musical sort, inspiring</u> artists in many divergent genres.

    (A) introduced many innovations of the musical sort, inspiring
    (B) introduced the musical innovations and inspirations for
    (C) introduced many musical innovations and inspired
    (D) introducing many musical innovations and inspiring
    (E) introduced many musical innovations, inspired

2. Jeremy had not realized that newspaper internships could lead to editorial jobs until he spoke with his uncle <u>who had also, at another point in time in the past, followed such a route</u>.

    (A) who had also, at another point in time in the past, followed such a route
    (B) who had also, therefore, followed such a route
    (C) who had once followed that very route
    (D) who, at one point, had followed that very exact same route
    (E) who had also, henceforth, followed such a route

GO ON TO THE NEXT PAGE ⟹

3. Charles denied any wrongdoing, claiming <u>there was no way he could of known</u> that his friend had lied.

   (A) there was no way he could of known
   (B) there wasn't any way he could of known
   (C) there was no way he could have known
   (D) there wasn't no way he could have known
   (E) how he could not have known

4. Although many children dream of owning a pet, <u>the responsibility of taking care of them is something few of them consider</u>.

   (A) the responsibility of taking care of them is something few of them consider
   (B) it is the responsibility of taking care of them that so many children do not consider
   (C) taking care of one is the responsibility that so few consider
   (D) it is rarely considered, the responsibility of taking care of one
   (E) few consider the responsibility that comes with taking care of one

5. Ronald's daily workout regimen is intense: <u>he runs, swims, and he likes to lift weights</u>.

   (A) he runs, swims, and he likes to lift weights
   (B) he runs, swims, and lifts weights
   (C) he is a runner, a swimmer, and lifts weights
   (D) he runs, swims and lifts weights
   (E) running, swimming, and lifting weights

6. <u>It is the debate of historians whether</u> the New Deal of World War II actually provided the economic stimulus that ended the Great Depression.

   (A) It is the debate of historians whether
   (B) Historians have their debate of whether
   (C) Whether or not historians debate over
   (D) Historians debate whether
   (E) Of the debate, historians think

7. <u>The tragedy of unrequited love</u> often serves as inspiration to artists and musicians.

   (A) The tragedy of unrequited love
   (B) Unrequited love is tragic, so
   (C) It is a tragic phenomenon, unrequited love, which
   (D) Unrequited love being tragic
   (E) For the tragedy of unrequited love

8. James Joyce's novel *Finnegans Wake* is not easily accessible, <u>being that it often is requiring of hours of research to interpret a single sentence</u>.

   (A) being that it often is requiring of hours of research to interpret a single sentence
   (B) and often requiring hours of research to interpret a single sentence
   (C) often requiring hours of research to interpret a single sentence
   (D) with its requirement of hours of research for a single sentence to be interpreted
   (E) the interpretation of which often requires hours of research to interpret a single sentence

9. Many critics believe that film can never do justice to literature, <u>a failure to consider the depth added by visual representation</u>.

   (A) a failure to consider the depth added by visual representation
   (B) a failing in consideration of the depth added by visual representation
   (C) failing, considering the depth added by visual representation
   (D) failing to consider the depth added by visual representation
   (E) a failure, considering the depth added by visual representation

GO ON TO THE NEXT PAGE ⇨

10. Harry <u>Truman, facing the onerous decision of</u> whether or not to use the atomic bomb and usher in the age of nuclear warfare.

(A) Truman, facing the onerous decision of
(B) Truman faced the onerous decision of
(C) Truman had faced the onerous decision, debating
(D) Truman, as he faced the onerous decision of
(E) Truman faced the onerous decision which was debating

11. In a symbol of unity, the students gathered in the court yard, <u>their lighting candles to express hope</u> that the labor dispute would be resolved.

(A) their lighting candles to express hope
(B) in the hope of lighting candles for
(C) expressing hope and lighting candles so
(D) which lit candles to express hope
(E) lighting candles to express hope

GO ON TO THE NEXT PAGE ⟹

6   6   6   6   6   6

The following sentences test your ability to recognize grammar and usage errors. Each sentence contains either a single error or no error at all. No sentence contains more than one error. The error, if there is one, is underlined and lettered. If the sentence contains an error, select the one underlined part that must be changed to make the sentence correct. If the sentence is correct, select choice E. In choosing answers, follow the requirements of standard written English.

EXAMPLE:

By the time <u>they reached</u> the halfway point
                        A

<u>in the race</u>, <u>most of the runners</u> <u>hadn't hardly</u>
    B   C   D

begun to hit their stride. <u>No error</u>
                                    E

---

12. After Tara was <u>aroused</u> from sleep by a sharp
                              A

noise, she <u>raced</u> for the front <u>door; fearing</u>
              B   C

the <u>presence</u> of an intruder. <u>No error</u>
        D   E

13. <u>Asked what he wanted</u> for his birthday,
            A

Virgil <u>turned around</u> and quickly <u>replied</u>
            B   C

that he would like a bike, a new computer,

and <u>staying up</u> past nine o'clock. <u>No error</u>
        D   E

14. Every day, John sits in his garage <u>admiring</u>
                                              A

his vintage cars, each of which <u>runs</u> as
                                    B

though <u>it was</u> brand new, <u>never driven</u> out
            C   D

of the show room. <u>No error</u>
                        E

15. <u>When placed</u> in new surroundings, even the
            A

<u>most lively</u> cats <u>sink</u> to the floor,
    B   C

<u>seeming to be suspicious</u> of all they see.
                D

<u>No error</u>
    E

16. The new governor, <u>who was more radical</u> than
                                A

his <u>predecessor, came</u> to power <u>on a platform</u>
        B   C

of reform, equality, and <u>being honest</u>. <u>No error</u>
                              D   E

17. <u>Unable to find</u> her <u>driver's license</u>, Mary
            A   B

asked the agent whether a credit card

would be <u>sufficient enough</u> evidence
                C

<u>to prove</u> her identity. <u>No error</u>
    D   E

18. The new movie was <u>disliked</u> by critics who
                              A

<u>expected</u> it to be <u>as well-written</u> and as
    B   C

tightly acted as <u>those of the director's</u>
                        D

previous films, which included several

award winners. <u>No error</u>
                    E

GO ON TO THE NEXT PAGE ⟹

19. Each of the boys wanted to hear their name
                                    A
    called as the coach announced the final
    B   C
    roster for the upcoming season. No error
                    D   E

20. Although he has matured in many ways,
                            A
    Gordon still occasionally resorted to childish
                             B
    habits when he feels sad, using memories
          C
    from youth to help him through tough times.
                    D
    No error
    E

21. Overwhelmed by the speed of the city,
    A
    Catherine often hid in her hotel room, only
             B
    occasionally braving the streets and the
    C
    swarming crowds of holiday shoppers.
    D
    No error
    E

22. Peter, the store manager, assured the
           A
    customer that their prices were comparable
                  B
    to those in other stores on all items,
       C
    even the most expensive ones. No error
    D   E

23. Admired by his peers, adored by his family,
    A
    and a man respected even by his enemies,
        B
    Chadwick was confident that he had lived a
             C
    good life, completely devoid of selfish
               D
    motives. No error
             E

24. Erica was irritated by her husband's
                A
    impulsive shopping because she knew that
    B   C
    the price he paid at Joe's Appliances

    was higher than Acme Video.
                D
    No error
    E

25. Only after David had wrote the first two
                        A
    paragraphs of his essay did he realize that
                B   C
    he was not entirely convinced of the
                         D
    validity of his own argument. No error
                                  E

26. Renee's responsibilities at the aquarium
                A
    were not only to train and perform with
                  B
    the seals, but also in feeding them
                      C
    according to a very strict dietary regimen.
    D
    No error
    E

27. The festival was more a celebration of jazz

    culture than simply like a series of concerts;
                          A
    it included many exhibits and lectures
       B
    on the various movements and eras
    C
    that influenced the art form. No error
    D   E

GO ON TO THE NEXT PAGE ⇒

6 6 6 6 6 6

28. The four hurricanes <u>that struck</u> Florida
$\qquad\qquad$ A
<u>in the summer of 2004</u> were unprecedented
$\qquad$ B
in their effects; <u>it was something</u> that the
$\qquad\qquad\qquad$ C
citizens <u>had never experienced</u> before.
$\qquad\qquad$ D
<u>No error</u>
$\quad$ E

29. The concerns that consumers

<u>have recently voiced</u> about the safety
$\qquad$ A
of sport utility vehicles

<u>have been addressed</u> <u>by manufacturers</u>,
$\qquad$ B $\qquad\qquad$ C
although many critics still claim that the

designs of these trucks can

be <u>dramatically improved</u>. <u>No error</u>
$\qquad$ D $\qquad\qquad$ E

GO ON TO THE NEXT PAGE ⟶

Directions: The following passage is an early draft of an essay. Some parts of the passage need to be rewritten.

Read the passage and select the best answers for the questions that follow. Some questions are about particular sentences or parts of sentences and ask you to improve sentence structure or word choice. Other questions ask you to consider organization and development. In choosing answers, follow the requirements of standard written English.

Questions 30–35 are based on the following passage.

(1) The structure of television news has undergone dramatic changes and many of those changes have occurred during the past fifty years. (2) In the industry's early years, networks were required by law to provide "public service" programming. (3) News shows fell under the category of public service. (4) As such, news was originally viewed not as a profit-making venture, but rather as a way to fulfill a requirement. (5) Because they felt little financial pressure, producers were able to create expansive intellectual documentaries, and in them, they put long excerpts from political speeches and worldwide visually stunning imagery. (6) However, the airwaves were devoid of much in the way of investigative journalism.

(7) In 1969, 60 Minutes debuted on CBS. (8) The first television "news magazine," the show provided short sound bites, a dramatic narrative structure, and a promise to uncover hidden truths. (9) Suddenly, a new perspective was born: journalists became the public watchdog, perpetually seeking the unjust and corrupt lurking behind the closed doors of government and corporate offices.

(10) Amid all these changes, many ethical issues were raised. (11) Does sensationalizing the news make the information less valuable? (12) Is public opinion being skewed to fit a particular network's political leanings or are people still able to sift through balanced information on their own?

(13) Without question, the new television news shows have attracted wide audiences and are profitable to the networks. (14) Their ratings often compete with those of the most popular sitcoms. (15) Television journalists regularly achieve celebrity status unknown to journalists in the 1950s. (16) 60 Minutes remains at the top of the ratings, continuing to generate enormous revenues for CBS. (17) The world as we see it today is born in a studio and crafted by intelligent professionals with the talent of Hollywood producers.

30. Which of the following is the best version of the underlined portion of sentence 1 (reproduced below)?

The structure of television news has undergone dramatic changes <u>and all of those changes have occurred over the past fifty years</u>.

(A) (As it is now)
(B) and those changes have all occurred over the past fifty years
(C) all of which have occurred over the past fifty years
(D) over the past fifty years
(E) and it has happened over fifty years

31. In context, which of the following is the best way to combine sentences 2 and 3 (reproduced below)?

(A) In the industry's early years, networks were required by law to provide "public service" programming, and news shows being under that category.
(B) In the industry's early years, networks were required by law to provide "public service" programming, which included news shows.
(C) News shows had been under a category of "public service" programming, which would have been required of the industry in its early years by law.
(D) The category of "public service" programming included news shows and was a requirement of the industry in the early years by law.
(E) In the industry's early years, networks were required by law to provide "public service" programming, as such, news shows fell under that category.

GO ON TO THE NEXT PAGE ⟶

6 6 6 6 6 6

32. Which of the following is the best version of the underlined portion of sentence 5 (reproduced below)?

Because they felt little financial pressure, producers could create expansive intellectual documentaries, <u>and in them, they put long excerpts from political speeches and worldwide visually stunning imagery</u>.

(A) (As it is now)

(B) often including long excerpts from political speeches and visually stunning imagery from around the world

(C) often including excerpts from political speeches that were long and imagery from around the world that were stunning

(D) and in them, they included long excerpts from political speeches and visually stunning imagery from around the world

(E) often including long excerpts and visually stunning imagery from political speeches and around the world

33. Which of the following revisions of sentence 7 (reproduced below) provides the most effective transition from the first paragraph to the second paragraph?

(A) All this changed in 1969, when *60 Minutes* debuted on CBS.

(B) And so it was not surprising when *60 Minutes* debuted on CBS in 1969.

(C) Another example of this phenomenon was *60 Minutes,* which debuted on CBS in 1969.

(D) Therefore it was in 1969 that *60 Minutes* debuted on CBS.

(E) The debut of *60 Minutes* on CBS in 1969 signaled the end of an era.

34. Where is the best place to insert the following sentence?

Such questions still concern media observers, but the harshness of their critiques is mitigated by the great popularity of such news magazines.

(A) after sentence 6, to end the first paragraph

(B) after sentence 9, to end the second paragraph

(C) after sentence 10

(D) after sentence 12, to end the third paragraph

(E) after sentence 13

35. In context, which of the following is the most effective version of sentence 14 (reproduced below)?

Their ratings often compete with those of the most popular sitcoms.

(A) (As it is now)

(B) Ratings of theirs compete with the most popular sitcoms.

(C) Ratings of sitcoms compete with the ones of news programs.

(D) Their ratings compete against sitcoms, even the most popular ones.

(E) Their ratings are competitive with sitcoms.

If you finish before time is called, you may check your work on this section only. Do not turn to any other section of the test.

SECTION 7
Time—20 minutes
16 questions

Turn to Section 7 of your answer sheet to answer the questions in this section.

Directions: For this section, solve each problem and decide which is the best of the choices given. Fill in the corresponding circle on the answer sheet. You may use any available space for scratchwork.

Notes

1. The use of a calculator is permitted.

2. All numbers used are real numbers.

3. Figures that accompany problems in this test are intended to provide information useful in solving the problems. They are drawn as accurately as possible EXCEPT when it is stated in a specific problem that the figure is not drawn to scale. All figures lie in a plane unless otherwise indicated.

4. Unless otherwise specified, the domain of any function f is assumed to be the set of all real numbers x for which $f(x)$ is a real number.

Reference Information

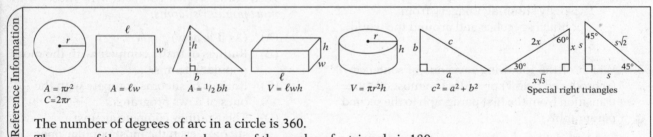

$A = \pi r^2$
$C = 2\pi r$

$A = \ell w$

$A = \frac{1}{2} bh$

$V = \ell wh$

$V = \pi r^2 h$

$c^2 = a^2 + b^2$

Special right triangles

The number of degrees of arc in a circle is 360.
The sum of the measures in degrees of the angles of a triangle is 180.

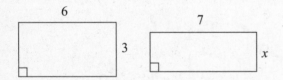

1. If the rectangles shown above have the same perimeter, what is the value of x?

(A) 2
(B) 3
(C) 4
(D) 5
(E) 6

2. If b represents a positive integer, which of the following expressions necessarily represents an even integer?

(A) $2b$
(B) $b + 2$
(C) $2b + 1$
(D) $3b$
(E) $2b - 1$

GO ON TO THE NEXT PAGE

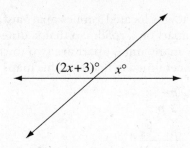

Note: Figure not drawn to scale.

3. Two lines intersect as shown in the figure above, what is the value of x?

(A) 54
(B) 56
(C) 57
(D) 59
(E) 62

---

4. If x and y are both positive, which of the following is equivalent to $\left(x^6 y^4\right)^{-\frac{1}{2}}$?

(A) $x^3 y^2$

(B) $x^{12} y^8$

(C) $\dfrac{1}{x^3 y^2}$

(D) $\dfrac{1}{x^6 y^4}$

(E) $\dfrac{1}{x^{12} y^8}$

FINAL EXAM GRADES FOR MR. PRICE'S CLASS

Grade	Number of Students
95	4
90	3
85	4
80	3
75	1
60	2

5. Based on the information in the table above, what is the median final exam grade for Mr. Price's class?

(A) 75
(B) 80
(C) 85
(D) 90
(E) 95

---

6. If $a = b^3$, and b is positive, then by what factor does a increase if b is tripled?

(A) 3
(B) 8
(C) 9
(D) 27
(E) 81

---

7. If $f(x) = (x - 2)^2 + 4$, what is the least possible value of $f(x)$?

(A) 0
(B) 1
(C) 2
(D) 3
(E) 4

GO ON TO THE NEXT PAGE

8. If $20^w = 5^3 \times 4^3$, what is the value of w?

(A) 1
(B) 3
(C) 6
(D) 8
(E) 10

Step 1: Subtract 5 from x
Step 2: Multiply this difference by 2
Step 3: Add 6 to this product

9. Which of the following represents the result if the three operations above are performed in sequence?

(A) $x - 4$
(B) $2x + 1$
(C) $2x - 4$
(D) $2x - 6$
(E) $2x + 2$

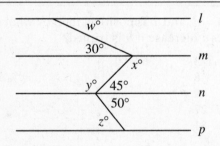

10. In the figure above, $l \parallel m \parallel n \parallel p$. What is the value of $w + x + y + z$?

(A) $100°$
(B) $160°$
(C) $280°$
(D) $310°$
(E) $350°$

11. Two towns located x miles apart are p centimeters apart on a roadmap that is drawn to scale. How many miles apart are two towns that are $p + 5$ centimeters apart on this map?

(A) $\dfrac{p + 5x}{p}$

(B) $\dfrac{px + 5x}{p}$

(C) $\dfrac{p - 5x}{x}$

(D) $\dfrac{p}{px + 5}$

(E) $\dfrac{x}{p + 5x}$

Digit in n	Digit in $\lceil n$
0	2
1	3
2	4
3	5
4	6
5	7
6	8
7	9
8	0
9	1

12. For any positive integer, n, let $\lceil n$ be defined as the integer obtained when each digit in n has been replaced with the corresponding digit in the table above, ignoring any leading zeroes.

For example, $\lceil 326 = 548$ and $\lceil 86 = 08 = 8$. Which of the following is equivalent to $\lceil 820 + \lceil 104$?

(A) $\lceil 146$
(B) $\lceil 368$
(C) $\lceil 580$
(D) $\lceil 621$
(E) $\lceil 746$

GO ON TO THE NEXT PAGE

7 7 7 7 7 7

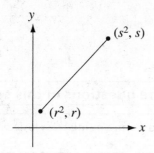

13. In the figure above, if $r \neq s$, what is the slope of the line segment?

(A) $r + s$

(B) $r - s$

(C) $\dfrac{s^2 - s}{r^2 - r}$

(D) $\dfrac{1}{(s+r)}$

(E) $\dfrac{1}{(s-r)}$

14. If the point (3, 4) is on a circle with center at (0, 0), which of the following points is outside of the circle?

(A) (2, 4)
(B) (5, 0)
(C) (−3, −4)
(D) (−2, −5)
(E) (−4, −3)

15. Both m and x are positive integers and $m + x = 8$. If $16m^2 + 56m + 49 = (mx + 7)^2$, what is the value of $m - x$?

(A) −8
(B) −4
(C) 0
(D) 4
(E) 8

$$\frac{b-a}{a} = x$$

$$\frac{b+a}{a} = y$$

16. In the equations above, if $a \neq 0$, which of the following is equal to $(x - y)(x + y)$?

(A) $-4a$

(B) $-4b$

(C) $\dfrac{-4b}{a}$

(D) $\dfrac{(b^2 - a^2)}{a}$

(E) $\dfrac{(b^2 - a^2)}{a^2}$

 STOP

If you finish before time is called, you may check your work on this section only. Do not turn to any other section of the test.

8   8   8   8   8   8

SECTION 8
Time—20 minutes
19 questions

Turn to Section 8 of your answer sheet to answer the questions in this section.

Directions: For each question in this section, select the best answer from among the choices given and fill in the corresponding circle on the answer sheet.

Each sentence below has one or two blanks, each blank indicating that something has been omitted. Beneath the sentence are five words or sets of words labeled A through E. Choose the word or set of words that, when inserted in the sentence, <u>best</u> fits the meaning of the sentence as a whole.

EXAMPLE:

Rather than accepting the theory unquestioningly, Deborah regarded it with -----.

(A) mirth
(B) sadness
(C) responsibility
(D) ignorance
(E) skepticism

Ⓐ Ⓑ Ⓒ Ⓓ ●

---

1. The decade following the Great Depression was one of -------, in which the United States began the slow return to economic stability.

   (A) inflammation
   (B) acrimony
   (C) mirth
   (D) aggregation
   (E) recovery

2. As a gourmet, Jorge bemoaned the ------- of good restaurants in his new home city.

   (A) paucity
   (B) quality
   (C) surfeit
   (D) conglomeration
   (E) consumption

3. Before Dr. Shutkin's experiments demonstrated that the new fuel was harmless to the environment, ecologists regarded its benefits as merely ------- rather than proven.

   (A) speculative
   (B) lucid
   (C) dynamic
   (D) fastidious
   (E) monotonous

4. Although the ------- despot had spent much of the previous thirty years persecuting his citizens, his recent near-death experience has turned him into a much less ------- ruler.

   (A) repugnant . . beneficent
   (B) liberal . . abominable
   (C) nefarious . . odious
   (D) patriarchal . . vile
   (E) malevolent . . mellifluous

GO ON TO THE NEXT PAGE ⟹

8   8   8   8   8   8

5. Several of Huffman's characters are -------,
    and so resist any impulse to ------- the social
    standards of their times.

    (A) heretical . . denounce
    (B) obsequious . . assimilate to
    (C) recalcitrant . . migrate to
    (D) itinerant . . habituate to
    (E) iconoclastic . . conform to

6. Lacking the natural ------- of so many other
    dancers, Helene nevertheless manages ------- on
    stage that belies the toil she has endured to
    achieve the appearance of grace.

    (A) nimbleness . . an ineptitude
    (B) agility . . a deftness
    (C) poise . . a treachery
    (D) cunning . . an aptitude
    (E) dexterity . . an idiosyncrasy

The passages below are followed by questions
based on their content and on the relationship
between the passages. Answer each question
on the basis of what is stated or implied in the
passages and in any introductory material that
may be provided.

Questions 7–19 are based on the following passages.

*The following passages debate the ethics of the use
of animals for the advancement of scientific
knowledge.*

PASSAGE 1

To deny science the use of animals in research
is, it might be said, to bring scientific and
Line allied medical progress to a halt, and that is
reason enough to oppose it. This claim is an
5   exaggeration. It is not an exaggeration,
however, to claim that the protection of
animal rights requires massive redirection of
scientific research. Current practice involves
routinely harming animals, so it should come
10 as no surprise that the "rights view" has
principled objections to its continuation.

    If we are seriously to challenge the use of
animals in research, we must challenge the
practice itself, not only individual instances of
15 it or merely the liabilities in its present
methodology. The rights view issues such a
challenge. Routine use of animals in research
assumes that the value of animals is
reducible to their possible utility relative to
20 the interests of humans. The rights view
rejects this view of animals and their value,
as it rejects the justice of institutions that
treat them as renewable resources. They, like
us, have a value of their own, logically
25 independent of their utility for others and of
their being the object of anyone else's
interests. Therefore, we must not sanction

First passage: Tom Regan, *"The Case Against Animal Research"*, *Contemporary Issues in Bioethics*, Wadsworth Publishing Company, 1999

practices that institutionalize their value as
mere instruments. It is not enough first
30 conscientiously to look for nominal
alternatives and then, having failed to find
any, to resort to using animals.

Though that approach is laudable as far
as it goes, and though taking it would mark
35 significant progress, it does not go far
enough. *The best we can do in terms of
not using animals is not to use them.*

The rights view does not oppose using what
is learned from conscientious efforts to treat a
40 sick animal (or human) to facilitate and
improve the treatment tendered other animals
(or humans). In *this* respect, the rights view
raises no objection to the "many human
and humane benefits" that flow from medical
45 science and the research with which it is allied.
What the rights view opposes are practices
that cause intentional harm to laboratory
animals preparatory to "looking for something
that just might yield some human or humane
50 benefit." Whatever benefits happen to accrue
from such a practice are irrelevant to assessing
its tragic injustice. Lab animals are not our
tasters; we are not their kings.

Passage 2

Whether animals have rights is a question of
55 great importance because if they do, those
rights must be respected, even at the cost of
great burdens for human beings. A right
(unlike an interest) is a valid claim, or potential
claim, made by a moral agent, under
60 principles that govern both the claimant and
the target of the claim. Rights are precious;
they are dispositive; they count.

You have the right to the return of money
you lent me; we both understand that. It may
65 be very convenient for me to keep the money,
and you may have no need of it whatever; but
my convenience and your needs are not to
the point. You have a *right* to it, and we have
courts of law partly to ensure that such rights
70 will be respected.

Some persons believe that animals have
rights and they therefore look on the uses of

animals in medical investigations with moral
loathing. If animals have rights they certainly
75 have the right not to be killed, even to
advance our important interests.

Some may say, "Well, they have rights, but
we have rights too, and our rights override
theirs." That may be true in some cases, but it
80 will not solve the problem because, although
we may have a weighty *interest* in learning,
say, how to vaccinate against polio or other
diseases, we do not have a *right* to learn such
things. Nor could we honestly claim that we
85 kill research animals in self-defense; they did
not attack us. If animals have rights, they
certainly have the right not to be killed to
advance the interests of others, whatever rights
those others may have.

90 In 1952 there were about 58,000 cases of
polio reported in the United States and 3,000
polio deaths; my parents, parents everywhere,
trembled in fear for their children at camp or
away from home. Polio vaccination became
95 routine in 1955, and cases dropped to about
a dozen a year; today polio has been
eradicated completely from the Western
Hemisphere. The vaccine that achieved this
could have been developed *only* with the
100 substantial use of animals.

Many obligations are owed by humans to
animals; few will deny that. But it certainly
does not follow from this that animals have
rights because it is certainly not true that
105 every obligation of ours arises from the rights
of another. Not at all. We need to be clear
and careful here. Rights entail obligations. If
you have a right to the return of the money
I borrowed, I have an obligation to repay it.
110 No issue. But the proposition *all rights entail
obligations* does not convert simply, as the
logicians say. From the true proposition that
all trees are plants, it does not follow that all
plants are trees. Similarly, not all obligations
115 are entailed by rights. Some obligations, like
mine to repay the money I borrowed from you,
do arise out of rights. But many obligations
are owed to persons or other beings who
have no rights whatever in the matter.

GO ON TO THE NEXT PAGE →

Second passage: Carl Cohen, *"Do Animals Have Rights?"*, *Contemporary Issues in Bioethics*, Wadsworth Publishing Company, 1999

8   8   8   8   8   8

120   I emphasize this because, although animals
       have no rights, it surely does not follow from
       this that one is free to treat them
       with callous disregard. Animals are not stones;
       they feel. A rat may suffer; surely we have the
125   obligation not to torture it gratuitously, even
       though it be true that the concept of a right
       could not possibly apply to it.
           Animals cannot be the bearers of rights
       because the concept of rights is essentially
130   *human*; it is rooted in, and has force within,
       a human moral world. Humans must deal
       with rats and must be moral in their dealing
       with them; but a rat can no more be said to
       have rights than a table can be said to have
135   ambition.

7. The author of Passage 1 indicates that those who
   subscribe to the "rights view" necessarily

   (A) deny that animals can feel pain
   (B) value medical progress over animal
        rights
   (C) oppose medical research that harms
        animals
   (D) believe that the rights of the sick
        supersede the rights of the healthy
   (E) believe that only human beings have
        rights

8. The passage indicates that the "institutions"
   mentioned in line 22 often assume that
   animals used for medical research

   (A) should be set free
   (B) do not suffer during testing
   (C) have a biochemical makeup that is
        similar to that of humans
   (D) will remain in abundance
   (E) are capable of distinguishing between
        right and wrong

9. In line 27, the word "sanction" most nearly
   means

   (A) penalize
   (B) approve
   (C) destroy
   (D) formally decree
   (E) control

10. According to the passage, the "approach"
   mentioned in line 33 is one that

   (A) acknowledges the impracticality of
        animal research
   (B) tries to eliminate animal research on
        moral grounds
   (C) utilizes animal research only as a last
        resort
   (D) attempts to minimize the expense of
        medical research
   (E) represents the mainstream of established
        medical practice

11. In line 41, the word "tendered" most nearly
   means

   (A) administered to
   (B) denied to
   (C) relinquished to
   (D) inspired by
   (E) reduced to

12. In line 56, the statement that the rights of animals
   "must be respected" is made because this claim

   (A) summarizes the author's main thesis
   (B) represents the dominant view of medical
        researchers
   (C) is part of a proposition that the author
        refutes
   (D) is a quotation from a respected authority
   (E) represents a principle that the author
        believes should be upheld by the courts

13. Passage 2 indicates that, unlike an interest,
   a right is necessarily

   (A) representative of an individual need
   (B) a factor in social decisions
   (C) something that animals can have
   (D) beyond ethical analysis
   (E) binding to more than one party

GO ON TO THE NEXT PAGE ⇒

8   **8**   **8**   **8**   **8**   **8**

14. The statistics cited in the discussion of polio in the fifth paragraph of Passage 2 (lines 90–100) are intended primarily to support the author's claim that animals

(A) can contract diseases as easily as humans can
(B) often carry dangerous diseases
(C) are invaluable in the campaign to eradicate disease
(D) do not have the same rights as humans have
(E) share our concern for the well-being of children

15. The sixth paragraph of Passage 2 (lines 101–127) serves primarily to

(A) discuss a logical fallacy
(B) cite an authority on an issue
(C) provide historical background to a debate
(D) illustrate the suffering of animals under certain conditions
(E) present a moral objection to medical research performed on animals

16. In saying that a certain statement "does not convert simply" (line 111), the author of Passage 2 means that such a statement

(A) cannot be easily translated into another language
(B) is not based on factual evidence
(C) is logically impossible
(D) does not logically imply another statement
(E) does not easily change the minds of skeptics

17. The author of Passage 2 would likely characterize the concept of "animal rights" described in Passage 1 as

(A) a misnomer
(B) an anachronism
(C) a moral necessity
(D) a clever application
(E) inconsistent with the "rights view" discussed in Passage 1

18. With which of the following statements would the authors of both passages most likely agree?

(A) Animals do not have rights that bind human beings.
(B) Medical research cannot proceed if the use of animals in such research is prohibited.
(C) Animals are renewable resources.
(D) Gratuitous violence to animals is never morally justified.
(E) Humans have a right to learn how to prevent disease.

19. The two passages differ in their perspectives on animal experimentation in medical research in that Passage 1

(A) considers it a moral obligation, while Passage 2 does not
(B) devalues it, while Passage 2 values it highly
(C) claims that it harms animals, while Passage 2 claims that it does not
(D) claims that it requires harming the animals, while Passage 2 states that it does not
(E) states that the researchers who engage in it are moral agents, while Passage 2 states that they are not

If you finish before time is called, you may check your work on this section only. Do not turn to any other section of the test.

9   9   9   9   9   9

SECTION 9
Time—10 minutes
14 questions

Turn to Section 9 of your answer sheet to answer the questions in this section.

Directions: For each question in this section, select the best answer from among the choices given and fill in the corresponding circle on the answer sheet.

The following sentences test correctness and effectiveness of expression. Part of each sentence or the entire sentence is underlined; beneath each sentence are five ways of phrasing the underlined material. Choice A repeats the original phrasing; the other four choices are different. Select the choice that completes the sentence most effectively.

In making your selection, follow the requirements of standard written English; that is, pay attention to grammar, choice of words, sentence construction, and punctuation. Your selection should result in the most effective sentence—clear and precise, without awkwardness or ambiguity.

EXAMPLE:

The children couldn't hardly believe their eyes.

(A) couldn't hardly believe their eyes
(B) could hardly believe their eyes
(C) would not hardly believe their eyes
(D) couldn't nearly believe their eyes
(E) couldn't hardly believe his or her eyes

1. Richard Avedon has created photographic portraits and these capture unique and often bizarre aspects of their subjects' personalities.

(A) and these capture unique
(B) which are capturing unique
(C) that uniquely capture
(D) that capture unique
(E) in capturing unique

2. Generally, election years especially, viewers should be careful to seek information on political issues from many different sources.

(A) election years especially
(B) and especially in election years
(C) election year's especially
(D) especially election year's
(E) and election years

3. The change in seasons, while beautiful, often cause people to fall ill.

(A) often cause
(B) often causing
(C) often causes
(D) therefore causes
(E) however, causes

GO ON TO THE NEXT PAGE

9   9   9   9   9   9

4. Suddenly faced with an opportunity to earn large incomes, recent college graduates often forsake personal happiness for the pursuit of material wealth.

(A) incomes, recent
(B) incomes; recent
(C) incomes recent
(D) incomes, recently
(E) incomes of recent

5. The patient, unable to tolerate the seemingly interminable wait, angrily leaving the doctor's office.

(A) angrily leaving the doctor's office
(B) left the doctor's office with anger
(C) left the doctor's office in a state of anger
(D) angrily left the doctor's office
(E) left angrily from the doctor's office

6. Bill was ecstatic about the new accounting software, which allowed organization of his current finances and to construct a detailed financial plan.

(A) organization of his current finances and to construct a detailed financial plan
(B) organization of his current finances and let him construct a detailed financial plan
(C) him to organize his current finances and for a detailed financial plan to be constructed
(D) him to organize his current finances and construct a detailed financial plan
(E) him to organize his current finances and for the construction of a detailed financial plan

7. During the meeting, the board created a plan where teachers would receive pay raises according to their students' performance on standardized examinations.

(A) created a plan where teachers would receive
(B) creates a plan in which teachers are receiving
(C) created a plan where teachers receive
(D) creates a plan for teachers receiving
(E) created a plan in which teachers would receive

8. The beleaguered fans left the game silently, unable to envision a time when their team would once again stand tall in victory.

(A) The beleaguered fans left the game silently
(B) The beleaguered fans, in silence, had left the game
(C) They left the game silently, the beleaguered fans
(D) The beleaguered fans leaving the game silently
(E) Leaving the game silently, the beleaguered fans can be

9. When he lost his internet connection, Rufus punched his computer monitor and this clearly demonstrates his dire need for anger management therapy.

(A) monitor and this clearly demonstrates
(B) monitor, clearly demonstrating
(C) monitor, clearly to demonstrate
(D) monitor; clearly demonstrating
(E) monitor, clearly by demonstrating

GO ON TO THE NEXT PAGE ⟹

10. The mentor program requires that its members <u>provide guidance, act respectfully, and act patiently</u> even when things are not going well.

(A) provide guidance, act respectfully, and act patience
(B) provide guidance, respectful action, and to show patience
(C) provide guidance, respectful action, and to show patience
(D) provide guidance, act respectfully, and show patience
(E) guidance, respectful action, and patience

11. The <u>country, once on the brink of financial collapse, now</u> boasts a thriving economy.

(A) country, once on the brink of financial collapse, now
(B) country, being on the brink of financial collapse, now
(C) country, being once on the brink of financial collapse and now
(D) country once on the brink of financial collapse and now
(E) country, that was once on the brink of financial collapse, but now

12. The claim that a nation's strength depends on its military capabilities is belied by the fact that many of the world's economic <u>powers, like Japan, has almost no</u> soldiers beyond their own borders.

(A) powers, like Japan, has almost no
(B) powers, Japan being one, have just about no
(C) powers, like Japan, have almost no
(D) powers like Japan, has almost no
(E) powers have almost, like Japan, no

13. <u>Being an affluent metropolitan area with a large fan base, the baseball commissioner decided that Washington, DC</u> would be a fine city to host a new franchise.

(A) Being an affluent metropolitan area with a large fan base, the baseball commissioner decided that Washington, DC
(B) The fact that it is an affluent metropolitan area with a large fan base was why the baseball commissioner decided that Washington, DC
(C) The baseball commissioner decided that Washington, DC, an affluent metropolitan area with a large fan base,
(D) Because of it being an affluent metropolitan area with a large fan base, the baseball commissioner decided that Washington, DC
(E) An affluent metropolitan area with a large fan base, the baseball commissioner decided that Washington, DC

14. The new health insurance plan is not only more expensive than the old one, <u>but it is less comprehensive in addition</u>.

(A) but it is less comprehensive in addition
(B) it is less comprehensive also
(C) it is also less comprehensive, however
(D) but also less comprehensive
(E) but additionally not as comprehensive

STOP

If you finish before time is called, you may check your work on this section only. Do not turn to any other section of the test.

ANSWER KEY

Critical Reading

Section 2

	COR. ANS.	DIFF. LEV.		COR. ANS.	DIFF. LEV.
1.	E	1	13.	B	2
2.	D	1	14.	B	3
3.	D	2	15.	E	3
4.	B	3	16.	E	4
5.	A	4	17.	D	4
6.	E	4	18.	B	3
7.	C	4	19.	D	3
8.	A	5	20.	D	4
9.	D	2	21.	C	3
10.	C	3	22.	A	2
11.	C	3	23.	C	3
12.	E	4	24.	E	5

Number correct

Number incorrect

Section 4

	COR. ANS.	DIFF. LEV.		COR. ANS.	DIFF. LEV.
1.	B	2	13.	B	3
2.	D	2	14.	D	4
3.	B	3	15.	C	3
4.	C	3	16.	A	4
5.	B	4	17.	D	4
6.	A	3	18.	E	5
7.	B	3	19.	B	3
8.	B	2	20.	B	3
9.	A	3	21.	C	4
10.	B	2	22.	A	3
11.	C	4	23.	C	4
12.	E	5	24.	A	4

Number correct

Number incorrect

Section 8

	COR. ANS.	DIFF. LEV.		COR. ANS.	DIFF. LEV.
1.	E	1	11.	A	4
2.	A	2	12.	C	2
3.	A	3	13.	E	2
4.	C	4	14.	C	4
5.	E	5	15.	A	4
6.	B	5	16.	D	3
7.	C	2	17.	A	3
8.	D	4	18.	D	3
9.	B	4	19.	B	4
10.	C	3			

Number correct

Number incorrect

Math

Section 3

	COR. ANS.	DIFF. LEV.		COR. ANS.	DIFF. LEV.
1.	B	1	11.	C	3
2.	C	1	12.	E	3
3.	C	3	13.	D	3
4.	B	2	14.	D	4
5.	A	2	15.	B	3
6.	E	2	16.	C	4
7.	A	3	17.	B	4
8.	C	2	18.	B	4
9.	D	3	19.	D	5
10.	D	3	20.	E	5

Number correct

Number incorrect

Section 5

Multiple-Choice Questions

	COR. ANS.	DIFF. LEV.
1.	C	1
2.	D	2
3.	D	3
4.	C	3
5.	B	3
6.	C	4
7.	A	4
8.	B	5

Student-produced Response questions

	COR. ANS.	DIFF. LEV.
9.	168	1
10.	6	2
11.	42	3
12.	24	3
13.	3	3
14.	1/2 or 0.5	4
15.	750	3
16.	1.5 or 3/2	4
17.	100	5
18.	20	5

Number correct

Number incorrect

Number correct (9–18)

Section 7

	COR. ANS.	DIFF. LEV.		COR. ANS.	DIFF. LEV.
1.	A	2	9.	C	4
2.	A	2	10.	E	4
3.	D	2	11.	B	3
4.	C	3	12.	A	4
5.	C	3	13.	D	3
6.	D	3	14.	D	4
7.	E	3	15.	C	5
8.	B	3	16.	C	5

Number correct

Number incorrect

Writing

Section 6

	COR. ANS.	DIFF. LEV.		COR. ANS.	DIFF. LEV.		COR. ANS.	DIFF. LEV.		COR. ANS.	DIFF. LEV.
1.	C	1	11.	E	4	21.	E	3	31.	B	3
2.	C	1	12.	C	1	22.	B	4	32.	B	3
3.	C	2	13.	D	1	23.	B	3	33.	A	3
4.	E	3	14.	C	2	24.	D	4	34.	D	3
5.	B	4	15.	E	3	25.	A	3	35.	A	3
6.	D	2	16.	D	3	26.	C	3			
7.	A	3	17.	C	2	27.	A	4			
8.	C	4	18.	D	3	28.	C	4			
9.	D	4	19.	A	3	29.	E	5			
10.	B	3	20.	B	3	30.	D	3			

Number correct

Number incorrect

Section 9

	COR. ANS.	DIFF. LEV.		COR. ANS.	DIFF. LEV.
1.	D	1	11.	A	3
2.	B	2	12.	C	4
3.	C	2	13.	C	4
4.	A	2	14.	D	3
5.	D	2			
6.	D	2			
7.	E	3			
8.	A	3			
9.	B	3			
10.	D	3			

Number correct

Number incorrect

NOTE: Difficulty levels are estimates of question difficulty that range from 1 (easiest) to 5 (hardest).

SCORE CONVERSION TABLE

How to score your test

Use the answer key on the previous page to determine your raw score on each section. **Your raw score on each section except Section 4 is simply the number of correct answers minus ¼ of the number of wrong answers. On Section 4, your raw score is the sum of the number of correct answers for questions 1–8 minus ¼ of the number of wrong answers for questions 1–8 plus the total number of correct answers for questions 9–18.** Next, add the raw scores from Sections 3, 4, and 7 to get your Math raw score, add the raw scores from Sections 2, 5, and 8 to get your Critical Reading raw score and add the raw scores from sections 6 and 9 to get your Writing raw score. Write the three raw scores here:

Raw Critical Reading score: _____ Raw Math score: _____ Raw Writing score: _____

Use the table below to convert these to scaled scores.

Scaled scores: Critical Reading: _____ Math: _____ Writing: _____

Raw Score	Critical Reading Scaled Score	Math Scaled Score	Writing Scaled Score	Raw Score	Critical Reading Scaled Score	Math Scaled Score	Writing Scaled Score
67	800			32	520	570	610
66	800			31	510	560	600
65	790			30	510	550	580
64	780			29	500	540	570
63	770			28	490	530	560
62	750			27	490	520	550
61	740			26	480	510	540
60	730			25	480	500	530
59	720			24	470	490	520
58	700			23	460	480	510
57	690			22	460	480	500
56	680			21	450	470	490
55	670			20	440	460	480
54	660	800		19	440	450	470
53	650	800		18	430	450	460
52	650	780		17	420	440	450
51	640	760		16	420	430	440
50	630	740		15	410	420	440
49	620	730	800	14	400	410	430
48	620	710	800	13	400	410	420
47	610	710	800	12	390	400	410
46	600	700	790	11	380	390	400
45	600	690	780	10	370	380	390
44	590	680	760	9	360	370	380
43	590	670	740	8	350	360	380
42	580	660	730	7	340	350	370
41	570	650	710	6	330	340	360
40	570	640	700	5	320	330	350
39	560	630	690	4	310	320	340
38	550	620	670	3	300	310	320
37	550	620	660	2	280	290	310
36	540	610	650	1	270	280	300
35	540	600	640	0	250	260	280
34	530	590	630	−1	230	240	270
33	520	580	620	−2 or less	210	220	250

SCORE CONVERSION TABLE FOR WRITING COMPOSITE
[ESSAY + MULTIPLE CHOICE]

Calculate your writing raw score as you did on the previous page and grade your essay from a 1 to a 6 according to the standards that follow in the detailed answer key.

Essay score: _____ Raw Writing score: _____

Use the table below to convert these to scaled scores.

Scaled score: Writing: _____

Raw Score	Essay Score 0	Essay Score 1	Essay Score 2	Essay Score 3	Essay Score 4	Essay Score 5	Essay Score 6
−2 or less	200	230	250	280	310	340	370
−1	210	240	260	290	320	360	380
0	230	260	280	300	340	370	400
1	240	270	290	320	350	380	410
2	250	280	300	330	360	390	420
3	260	290	310	340	370	400	430
4	270	300	320	350	380	410	440
5	280	310	330	360	390	420	450
6	290	320	340	360	400	430	460
7	290	330	340	370	410	440	470
8	300	330	350	380	410	450	470
9	310	340	360	390	420	450	480
10	320	350	370	390	430	460	490
11	320	360	370	400	440	470	500
12	330	360	380	410	440	470	500
13	340	370	390	420	450	480	510
14	350	380	390	420	460	490	520
15	350	380	400	430	460	500	530
16	360	390	410	440	470	500	530
17	370	400	420	440	480	510	540
18	380	410	420	450	490	520	550
19	380	410	430	460	490	530	560
20	390	420	440	470	500	530	560
21	400	430	450	480	510	540	570
22	410	440	460	480	520	550	580
23	420	450	470	490	530	560	590
24	420	460	470	500	540	570	600
25	430	460	480	510	540	580	610
26	440	470	490	520	550	590	610
27	450	480	500	530	560	590	620
28	460	490	510	540	570	600	630
29	470	500	520	550	580	610	640
30	480	510	530	560	590	620	650
31	490	520	540	560	600	630	660
32	500	530	550	570	610	640	670
33	510	540	550	580	620	650	680
34	510	550	560	590	630	660	690
35	520	560	570	600	640	670	700
36	530	560	580	610	650	680	710
37	540	570	590	620	660	690	720
38	550	580	600	630	670	700	730
39	560	600	610	640	680	710	740
40	580	610	620	650	690	720	750
41	590	620	640	660	700	730	760
42	600	630	650	680	710	740	770
43	610	640	660	690	720	750	780
44	620	660	670	700	740	770	800
45	640	670	690	720	750	780	800
46	650	690	700	730	770	800	800
47	670	700	720	750	780	800	800
48	680	720	730	760	800	800	800
49	680	720	730	760	800	800	800

Detailed Answer Key

Section I

The following essay received 12 points out of a possible 12, meaning that it demonstrates *clear and consistent competence* in that it

- develops an insightful point of view on the topic
- demonstrates exemplary critical thinking
- uses effective examples, reasons, and other evidence to support its thesis
- is consistently focused, coherent, and well-organized
- demonstrates skilful and effective use of language and sentence structure
- is largely (but not necessarily completely) free of grammatical and usage errors

Consider carefully the issue discussed in the following passage, then write an essay that answers the question posed in the assignment.

> *None know the unfortunate and the fortunate do not know themselves.*
> —Benjamin Franklin

Assignment: **Are people today generally too unaware of their good fortune?** Write an essay in which you answer this question and support your position logically with examples from literature, the arts, history, politics, science and technology, current events, or your experience or observation.

SAMPLE STUDENT ESSAY

When running against George Bush for governor of Texas, Ann Richards said that the future president "was born on third base but thinks he hit a triple," and was born "with a silver foot in his mouth." Not only do these turns of phrase belong in the political humor hall of fame, but they also reveal an important truth. Governor Richard's comments could as easily apply to millions of us Americans as it did to George Bush, which is, in part, why we elected him as president in 2000. We have no real sense of our privilege as nation, and mistakenly think that it is simply the product of our hard work and worthiness.

In fact, the origin of our privilege as a nation is not hard to determine, and it has very little to do with our moral or intellectual superiority as a people. This is not to say that America is not filled with good, smart, honest and hard-working people, but that it is a profoundly dangerous mistake to imagine, as so many of us do, that our status of superpower is simply a natural product of our superiority as a people.

So often, modern neo-conservatives claim that we are so productive and powerful as a nation because our "American values" of hard work and freedom are superior to those of other cultures. What they rarely acknowledge, however, yet what is painfully obvious, is that the history of "American values" has included such beliefs as that Africans are not human, that women should not have the right to vote, that money and possessions are virtues, and that violence solves every problem. Furthermore, we have succeeded economically not because of these "American values" but despite them. Our country is uniquely endowed with rich natural resources, free access to water on two oceans, friendly neighbors, and geographical barriers from our enemies. These were not achieved through hard work or a dedication to high moral standards, but a willingness to conquer the native people and appropriate their lands.

What is perhaps even more dangerous than assuming that we have earned our prosperity by hard work and virtue alone is assuming that poorer countries fail to prosper merely because they aren't "democratic" or "free" enough. Our country has been run long enough by those with this privileged mindset, who believe that they have not only the right but the duty to impose their values on others.

This kind of thinking is precisely what the rest of the world hates about America. So many of our citizens seem genuinely befuddled by the fact that the world consumes our music, our films and our technology, yet so many people in the world hate us. It is not so hard to understand when one realizes that the vast majority of the world's people are not born into countries so isolated from their enemies and so abundant in natural resources. Most are born in the third world, not on third base.

The following essay received 8 points out of a possible 12, meaning that it demonstrates *adequate competence* in that it
- develops a point of view on the topic
- demonstrates some critical thinking, but perhaps not consistently
- uses some examples, reasons, and other evidence to support its thesis, but perhaps not adequately
- shows a general organization and focus, but shows occasional lapses in this regard
- demonstrates adequate but occasionally inconsistent facility with language
- contains occasional errors in grammar, usage, and mechanics

SAMPLE STUDENT ESSAY

While Franklin's quotation serves as a valid consideration for much of the world's population, it is not a totally universal fact. Most people in the world are quite lucky to be where they are. Most people in this fortunate position are unaware of the scope of their luck. Even worse, a large percentage of these people are ignorant to the difficulties faced by those who do not share in their blessings. But to accept this situation as a truth without exception, would be an error in judgment, for many people are quite aware how lucky they are and many of those people are more than willing to face and fight for the pain of those less fortunate.

Perhaps no moment in history was more indicative of the flaws in Ben Franklin's quote than the summer of 1964, Freedom Summer. With a presidential election on the horizon, America was in the midst of unprecedented social upheaval. Racial tension had reached a boiling point and conservatives unwilling to accept social change in the South were excluding African-Americans from voting, threatening them with violence in order to maintain the status quo. To

battle this situation, northern white college students, many of them privileged upper class Ivy Leaguers, drove down to Mississippi in an effort to help African-Americans register to vote. Facing the threat of violent repercussions, these intrepid youths took it upon themselves to bridge a racial and economic gap and push for a cause far removed from their own sheltered lives.

History is littered with such instances of selflessness. Whether demonstrated through a course of action as difficult and substantial as Freedom Summer or through a simple charitable contribution, the virtue remains the same. Their good deeds, however, often remain unseen simply because they are not newsworthy. Most of what we hear about today has to deal with crime and hate. What we miss are the optimistic stories where people step outside of their own lives to make a difference. Altruism, it seems, does not sell newspapers. While there are many people ignorant of their own good luck and blind to the pain of others, there are also many who understand their position in life and do what they can to improve the fortunes of others.

The following essay received 4 points out of a possible 12, meaning that it demonstrates *some incompetence* in that it
- has a seriously limited point of view
- demonstrates weak critical thinking
- uses inappropriate or insufficient examples, reasons, and other evidence to support its thesis
- is poorly focused and organized, and has serious problems with coherence
- demonstrates frequent problems with language and sentence structure
- contains errors in grammar and usage that obscure the author's meaning

SAMPLE STUDENT ESSAY

This quote by Ben Franklin says that people who are lucky do not realize they are fortunate. But this is not always true. There are many examples in life of people being very thankful for the things that they have. The most obvious example of this is the very existence of the annual holiday called Thanksgiving, where families come together and name the things they are most thankful for. This is one of the only holidays that the entire country celebrates, regardless of religion or background, and it shows how important people believe it is to be aware of one's good fortune.

People also often talk about having a streak of good luck, for example saying that good things come in threes, or that their good luck charm must be working. When I have a streak of good luck, I always notice it, and hope that it will last, and am thankful for it.

I know that I am fortunate when this happens. Also, there are many examples of people being aware of poor and starving people. People give to charities and give money to beggars on the street. They know that misfortune exists and wish that it were not the case and they do every little thing that they can to help out those in need. I have spent three years volunteering for the Key Club at my school, which is an organization that helps out with community projects, often helping those less fortunate. This has been a great experience for me, because it has opened my eyes to those who need help.

Sometimes you are lucky and you don't even know why. To you, it may be just your everyday life but when you compare it with what some other people go through, you can realize that you are actually very fortunate. This is a very important quality in life, one that we should all strive to achieve.

Section 2

1. **E**   Doctors often *administer* medication, and this medication left Ingrid without feeling on the left side of her face and removed the pain. *emollient* = something that softens; *antibody* = body substance that fights infection; *antidote* = a remedy to a poison; *cathartic* = something that assists in removing substances from the body; *anesthetic* = something that causes a loss of sensation.

2. **D**   This strain of the flu leaves its victims _____. Because she is unable to get out of bed, this strain must be particularly *harsh* or *harmful*. *benign* = harmless; *incapacitated* = disabled; *debilitating* = removing the strength from someone; *lethargic* = sluggish, lacking energy; *revitalized* = restored with life and energy.

3. **D**   A *gigantic earthquake* would cause serious damage. The fact that not a single building survived and so many were injured supports the idea. Look for a word that means *destroyed*. *preserve* = to maintain; *reiterate* = to state again; *debunk* = to disprove; *raze* = to destroy completely, to demolish; *salvage* = to save from destruction.

4. **B**   The newly released version of *Othello* was *condemned* (criticized) because it was just like the other remakes and did not bring anything new to the screen. *innovative* = new, fresh; *hackneyed* = overused, trite; *novel* = new; *quixotic* = idealistic, lacking realism; *profound* = deep, insightful.

5. **A**   The *airline industry was on the verge of collapse* and some businesses somehow survived because of government intervention. The intervention must have given the airlines money and such an intervention is known as a *subsidy*. *subsidy* = financial assistance; *infusion* = a flowing inward; *censure* = harsh criticism; *influx* = a flowing in; *endowment* = donated funds; *emission* = a substance that is discharged; *endorsement* = support; *alimony* = an allowance; *emanation* = something that comes off a source.

6. **E**   The father behaved in a manner similar to his daughter. Therefore, he would find it hard to *punish* his daughter for her excessive partying. He must also be a *hedonist* or pleasure-seeker. *ascetic* = one who leads a life of self denial; *castigate* = to criticize harshly; *altruist* = a selfless individual; *extol* = to praise; *sybarite* = one who seeks luxury; *censure* = to

publicly criticize; *philanthropist* = one who loves mankind; *hedonist* = pleasure seeker; *rebuke* = to scold harshly.

7. **C**   While writing his famous book, the author lived alone in a shack, much as a *hermit* would. But, the sentence explains that he did not lead the life of a hermit and that he instead actually did many social things such as go to the village and entertain at his house. *miscreant* = villain; *recluse* = a hermit; *curator* = a manager; *arborist* = a tree specialist.

8. **A**   The saleswoman *sells more cars than anyone else*, so she must be good at what she does. She would most likely be *unrelenting* in her efforts to close a deal. *inexorable* = relentless; *doggedness* = unwillingness to surrender; *lackadaisical* = uninterested; *pertinacity* = stubborn persistence; *submissive* = willing to yield; *diffident* = lacking confidence; *munificent* = generous; *temerity* = recklessness; *indolent* = lazy; *tenacity* = persistent.

9. **D**   The statement *the whole military action... must be in accordance with the object of the war* is saying that the strategy should fit with the *goal*.

10. **C**   The passage states that *modifications to the general plan... incessantly become necessary in war*, thereby suggesting that war is unpredictable.

11. **C**   The figure is viewed *through some supernatural medium*, which is perhaps a substance like a fog.

12. **E**   The face, which *had not a wrinkle in it*, must have therefore looked youthful. The phrase *tenderest bloom* reinforces this image.

13. **B**   Each paragraph, and hence the passage as a whole, explains how *our species shares so much with dogs* (line 30).

14. **B**   This action, in the context of a date between two human beings, is meant to describe a small but meaningful gesture.

15. **E**   The term *crazed semaphore flag* is a simile to describe what humans seem like to dogs, that is, we constantly send unintended signals that dogs pick up.

16. E The passage specifically indicates that dogs and humans are alike in all these ways except in sharpness of hearing.

17. D The passage says that farmers *need their dogs as much as or more than they do machinery or high-tech feeding systems,* thereby implying that these feeding systems are necessary to some farmers.

18. B The author is describing some of his inadequacies: *My prudence consists … not in the inventing of mans and methods … I have no skill to make money well …* he therefore is suggesting in line 9 that he is no good at gardening, either.

19. D By saying *I have the same title to write on prudence as I have to write on poetry or holiness …* the author is saying that he has the right, and indeed he is exercising that right throughout the passage.

20. D The author states in the first line that he has little prudence and that what he has is *of the negative sort* (lines 2–3). He later states that *we write from aspiration and antagonism* (lines 13–14) and that *we paint those qualities which we do not possess* (lines 15–16). Therefore, he is claiming the right to write about prudence because he admires it more than he possesses it.

21. C The *third class* is described as those who *live above* those of the second class, who are the artists and scientists. This third class is the *wise men* who have *spiritual perception.*

22. A By saying that the wise person *does not offer to build houses and barns* on the *sacred volcanic isle of nature,* the author is saying metaphorically that a wise person can see beyond nature to the *Splendor of the God* and does not see earthly life as his or her permanent status.

23. C This *base prudence* was described as a *devotion to matter* which concerns the five senses, rather than what lies beyond. This is a clear reference to the *first class* described in the previous paragraph, which lives *to the utility of the symbol,* or is concerned primarily with practical matters.

24. E In this paragraph, the author says that *culture … degrades every thing else, as health and bodily life, into means,* and then goes on to say that *cultivated men* in this sense of *culture* are not truly cultivated. Therefore, he is criticizing culture for the way it defines human activity.

Section 3

1. B $20 \text{ dozen CDs} \times \dfrac{12 \text{ CDs}}{1 \text{ dozen}} = 240 \text{ CDs}.$

$240 \text{ CDs} \times \dfrac{1 \text{ case}}{120 \text{ CDs}} = 2 \text{ cases}.$

2. C

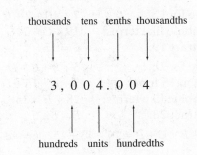

3. C This question can be read as: "What is the value of y when $x = 8$?"
Plug 8 in for x and solve for y:
$$f(x) = 2x^2 + 8$$
$$y = 2(8)^2 + 8$$
$$y = 2(64) + 8 = 136$$

4. B

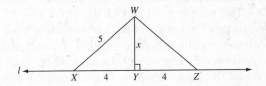

Line segment $\overline{WY}$ bisects $\overline{XZ}$. Therefore if $XZ = 8$, $XY = YZ = 4$.
Solve for x using the Pythagorean Theorem:
$$4^2 + x^2 = 5^2$$
$$16 + x^2 = 25$$
Subtract 16: $\qquad x^2 = 9$
Take square root: $\qquad x = 3$

5. A

They split the money in the ratio $3x:2x:1x$.
Write an equation: $\qquad 3x + 2x + x = \$3,000$
Combine like terms: $\qquad 6x = \$3,000$
Divide by 6: $\qquad x = \$500$

6. E Don't do more work than you have to here. The question asks for the value of $(x - y)^2$ and it tells you that $(x - y) = -2$.

$(x - y)^2$
Plug in −2 for $(x - y)$: $\qquad (-2)^2$
Simplify: $\qquad 4$

7. A   Use the third row to find the common sum:
$$4 + 12 + 2 + 16 = 34$$

Solve for B:	$11 + B + 7 + 3 = 34$
Combine like terms:	$21 + B = 34$
Subtract 21:	$B = 13$
Solve for A:	$A + 1 + 10 + 9 = 34$
Combine like terms:	$20 + A = 34$
Subtract 20:	$A = 14$
Solve for C:	$7 + 10 + 2 + C = 34$
Combine like terms:	$19 + C = 34$
Subtract 19:	$C = 15$
Solve for D:	$5 + 8 + C + D = 34$
Plug in 15 for C:	$5 + 8 + 15 + D = 34$
Combine like terms:	$28 + D = 34$
Subtract 28:	$B = 6$

$$A + B + C + D = 14 + 13 + 15 + 6 = 48$$

---

8. C   Pick values for a and b and see which is greatest.
Plug in -3 for a and -2 for b:
(A) $-3a + b = -3(-3) + (-2) = 9 + -2 = 7$
(B) $-(a + b) = -((-3) + (-2)) = -(-5) = 5$
(C) $-(3a + b) = -(3(-3) + (-2)) = -(-9 + -2) = 11$
(D) $3a = 3(-3) = -9$
(E) $a - b = (-3) - (-2) = -3 + 2 = -1$

---

9. D   The triangle cut out of the right side of the folded piece of paper will take a triangular chunk out of both sides of the unfolded product. This eliminates answer choice E. The loss of the triangle on each end will make the paper smaller. This eliminates answer choices A and C. The rectangular piece cut off of side AB will leave a hole in the middle, which eliminates choice B.

---

10. D   One simple way is to find out how many integers between 1 and 100 **are** the cube of an integer.
$$1^3 = 1; \ 2^3 = 8; \ 3^3 = 27; \ 4^3 = 64$$
Four integers **are**, therefore $100 - 4 = 96$ are not.

---

11. C   If there are three times as many goldfish as there are tropical fish, then 3 out of every 4 fish are goldfish.

The probability of selecting a goldfish at random is $\frac{3}{4}$.

There are twice as many orange as black goldfish, so 1/3 of the goldfish are black, and the probability

of selecting a black goldfish is $\frac{1}{3} \times \frac{3}{4} = \frac{3}{12} = \frac{1}{4}$.

---

12. E

Set up an equation:	$P = \dfrac{kT}{V}$
Plug in given values:	$700 = \dfrac{k(350)}{(10)} = 35k$
Divide by 35:	$k = 20$
Write new equation:	$P = \dfrac{20T}{V}$
Plug in new values:	$500 = \dfrac{20T}{20}; 500 = T$

---

13. D   Plug in the ordered pairs listed and see which one works:
$$x - 2y > 5$$
$$y + x < 13$$

(A)	$3 - 2(-1) > 5; 5 > 5$	NO
	$3 + -1 < 13, 2 < 13$	works
(B)	$12 - 2(3) > 5; 6 > 5$	works
	$3 + 12 < 13; 15 < 13$	NO
(C)	$8 - 2(3) > 5; 2 > 5$	NO
	$8 + 3 < 13; 11 < 13$	works
(D)	$10 - 2(2) > 5; 6 > 5$	works
	$2 + 10 < 13; 12 < 13$	works
(E)	$1 - 2(5) > 5; -9 > 5$	NO
	$1 + 5 < 13$	works

---

14. D   Let a be the number of dollars Andrea had to start, let c be the number of dollars Chris had to start, and let l be the number of dollars Liz had to start. The question asks for the value of c. After Andrea gives $10 to Chris she has $a - 10$ dollars and Chris has $c + 10$ dollars. Andrea then gives $3 to Liz leaving her with $a - 13$ dollars and Liz with $l + 3$ dollars. Chris then gives $4 to Liz leaving him with $c + 6$ dollars and Liz now has $l + 7$ dollars. If Andrea still has $10 more than Chris, then:

$$(a - 13) = (c + 6) + 10$$

Simplify:	$a - 13 = c + 16$
Add 13:	$a = c + 29$

Therefore, Andrea has $29 more than Chris.
Alternatively, you could plug in numbers to solve this problem: Let's say Andrea finished with $30. She had $10 more than Chris and $16 more than Liz.
Final Totals: Andrea = $30; Chris = $20; Liz = $14
Before Andrea gave $10 to Chris, she had $30 + $10 = $40 and Chris had $20 - $10 = $10.
Before Andrea gave $3 to Liz, she had $40 + $3 = $43
Before Chris gave $4 to Liz, he had $10 + $4 = $14, and $43 - $14 = $29.

15. B

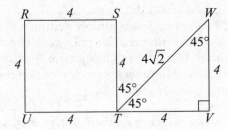

Because we know that T is a midpoint of line segment $\overline{UV}$ we know that $UT = TV$. Let's say that the length of a side of the square is 4. That would make the perimeter of the square $4 + 4 + 4 + 4 = 16$. The two legs of right triangle TVW would also be 4 and the hypotenuse can be found using the Pythagorean theorem: $4^2 + 4^2 = (TW)^2$

Simplify: $32 = (TW)^2$

Take square root: $\sqrt{32} = TW = 4\sqrt{2}$

The perimeter of the triangle is $4 + 4 + 4\sqrt{2} = 8 + 4\sqrt{2}$

Set up ratio: $\dfrac{\text{perimeter of square}}{\text{perimeter of triangle}} = \dfrac{16}{8 + 4\sqrt{2}}$

Divide numerator and denominator by 4: $\dfrac{4}{2 + \sqrt{2}}$

16. C "Park" the cars to solve this problem. You have 5 parking spaces to fill. Deal with the restrictions first. One of the cars is too big to fit in the two spots closest to the street so you only have 4 choices for the spot closest to the street. Once you have parked one of those four cars in that spot, you have 3 choices for the spot that is the second closest to the street. Now the restrictions are lifted and you have 3 choices for the third spot, then 2 choices for the fourth spot, and 1 choice for the last spot. $4 \times 3 \times 3 \times 2 \times 1 = 72$

17. B A total of 7 students took the quiz and had an average score of 83, so the sum of their scores is $(83)(7) = 581$ points. Three of the students had an average score of 79, so the sum of their scores is $(79)(3) = 237$ points. Therefore the four remaining students scored $581 - 237 = 344$ points.
Find the average: $344 \div 4 = 86$ points

18. B First look at the table to find the minimum wage in each of those two years:

$$1980: \$3.10$$
$$1974: \$2.00$$

$$\text{Percent change} = \frac{\text{final} - \text{original}}{\text{original}} \times 100\%$$

Plug in values: $\dfrac{3.10 - 2.00}{2.00}(100\%) = \dfrac{1.10}{2.00}(100\%) = 55\%$

19. D Write out the first nine terms: $t_3 = 13 + 8 = 21$; $t_4 = 21 + 13 = 34$; $t_5 = 34 + 21 = 55$; $t_6 = 55 + 34 = 89$; $t_7 = 89 + 55 = 144$; $t_8 = 144 + 89 = 233$; $t_9 = 233 + 144 = 377$. So the sequence is:

8, 13, 21, 34, 55, 89, 144, 233, 377…
E, O, O, E, O, O, E, O, O

The repeating pattern is {even, odd, odd} which repeats every three terms. In 60 terms, the pattern repeats $60 \div 3 = 20$ times. In each repetition there are 2 odd numbers, so in 20 full repetitions there are $20 \cdot 2 = 40$ odd numbers.

20. E Break this problem into two parts: the cost of the first 6 inches, and the cost of the additional inches. They charge d dollars total for the first 6 inches and f dollars for *each* additional inch. Be careful to remember to remove the first 6 inches from the calculation of the "additional" inches to be shoveled.

Cost of first 6 inches: d
Cost of additional: $(p - 6)f$
Total cost: $\text{Cost} = d + (p - 6)f$

Section 4

1. B Rita's cat was *beloved*, so putting it to sleep would be a sad experience. You would expect her to be consumed by grief. *inversion* = the act of turning upside-down; *anguish* = agonizing emotional pain; *frivolity* = silliness; *hilarity* = extreme humor.

2. D If the virus was replicating *at a remarkable speed*, then it was *proliferating*. *pontificate* = to speak pompously; *diverge* = to move apart; *saturate* = to fill completely; *proliferate* = to grow; *dissipate* = to disperse.

3. B Leah came from a wealthy family. The word *Despite* indicates that we should expect an irony, so she must be behaving differently from how you would expect a rich woman to behave. If she won't waste *even a few dollars* she must be relatively *stingy*. The phrase *sometimes even* indicates a greater degree. *prudent* = wise; *munificent* = generous; *thrifty* = conservative with money; *stingy* = unwilling to part with money; *frugal* = good with your money; *outspoken* = inclined to speak one's mind; *improvident* = wasteful; *miserly* = stingy.

4. C If his midterms were *grueling*, they tired him out. He must be in need of a rest. *encore* = an additional performance; *respite* = a break, a rest; *commencement* = a beginning; *conviction* = strong belief.

5. B Emil has *always been* a particular way throughout medical school. He is prone to *superficial flattery*, so he is a flatterer. *toady* = one who flatters; *irreverent* = disrespectful; *sycophant* = one who flatters; *fawning* = giving excessive praise; *lackey* = a servant; *insubordinate* = resistant to authority; *mercenary* = one who is paid to fight; *intractable* = stubborn; *clairvoyant* = able to see the future; *altruistic* = selfless.

6. A The passage says that *since the bob changes height ... its gravitational energy changes*, thereby suggesting that gravitational energy depends on height.

7. B Lines 15–21 indicate the inverse relationship between gravitational and kinetic energy.

8. B The fact that she *took a position on the stones* in the street and *received daily a small sum in pennies* which were *contributed* by others implies that she is a beggar.

9. A The *keys* describe the way she says "God bless yeh," so it indicates her tones of voice.

10. B This paragraph is simply stating a brief history of video surveillance. This paragraph contains no central thesis. It is preventing objective facts, and so it is also not describing a *misconception* or presenting an *individual's point of view*.

11. C Since CNIL *proposed safeguards* against electronic surveillance, they must be concerned with potential misuses.

12. E The statistics suggest that people do not disapprove widely of the use of video surveillance, but are widely disapproving of *showing pictures of a person taken in a public place without that person's consent*.

13. B The stores *monitor specific aspects of consumer behavior* like *movements and gestures* in order to *optimize the position of goods*.

14. D In saying that *everywhere he goes he leaves electronic traces of his passage*, the author means that the person's activities are being surveilled by electronic detectors everywhere he goes.

15. C Adjectives like *remote, impersonal* and *largely invisible* indicate that electronic surveillance is *detached*.

16. A The central topic of the passage is the invasion of privacy. The author states that the *loss of privacy entailed in the taking of pictures ... may be justified in certain places where security is at risk, but it is not justified in all cases* (lines 73–77). The examples that are then cited represent examples where the taking of pictures has stepped over the line of prudent security. The author's objection to the cameras on the highway is that they *can see into adjacent houses and apartment blocks* (lines 84–85), thereby invading the privacy of non-drivers.

17. D The passage says that *city women* are *more original ... than women in smaller places* (lines 11–12). Therefore, women in smaller places are more traditional.

18. E This *dash* is *something original that will excite interest* (lines 22–23).

19. B This *knowledge* is the *knowledge of the world* that allows one to *excite interest*.

20. **B** The *attractiveness* of her story is enhanced by *relating her discouragements, trials and mistakes* (lines 29–30) to make her *better company*.

21. **C** The paragraph says that such women need to *exercise the rites of hospitality unquestioned* (lines 46–47), which supports statement I. It also says that they need *the exemption … from being agreeable at all times and places* (lines 39–42), which supports statement II. The paragraph says nothing about education.

22. **A** The sentence conveys the idea that women want to *be within the circumference of a social circle* rather than *on the periphery*.

23. **C** This paragraph discusses the value of a woman bachelor extending *hospitalities* (line 56), and in saying that *the shyest novice over the tea cup loses her timidity*, the author is saying that women become more bold when they are hosting guests.

24. **A** The passage states that a woman with her own home *loses her timidity* (line 68).

Section 5

1. **C** $3 - x = 2x - 6$

    Add x: $3 = 3x - 6$

    Add 6: $9 = 3x$

    Divide by 3: $3 = x$

2. **D** The rightmost (units) column seems to indicate that $P + T = P$ and so $T = 0$. There can be no "carry" as long as T is less than 10, which it must be. According to the tens column, $R + 7 = 15$, so $R = 8$.

3. **D** The sum of the angles in an n-sided polygon is $(n - 2)\,180° =$ degrees because any n-sided polygon can be divided into $n-2$ triangles. The sum of the angles in a 6-sided polygon, then, is $(6 - 2)180° = 4(180°) = 720°$

So, $142° + 141° + 112° + 105° + w° + v° = 720°$

Simplify: $500° + w° + v° = 720°$

Subtract $500°$: $w° + v° = 220°$

4. **C** Write equations to represent the information:

                         $x = 2y$

                         $x - y = 4$

Substitute $2y$ for x: $2y - y = 4$

Combine like terms: $y = 4$

Solve for x: $x = 2y = 2(4) = 8$

The greater of these two numbers is 8.

5. **B** Let $n =$ the number of seats in the theater

$$\frac{1}{3}n + 50 = \frac{3}{4}n$$

Subtract $\frac{1}{3}n$: $50 = \frac{5}{12}n$

Divide by $\frac{5}{12}$: $n = 120$

6. **C** Just write them out, keeping in mind that the 4 can be in the ones or tens place:

4, 14, 24, 34, 40, 41, 42, 43, 44, 45, 46, 47, 48, 49

(A common mistake here is to count 44 twice because it contains two 4s)

7. **A**   You must combine the equations to solve:

         (a) $3x = y + z$
         (b) $y = 6 - z$
         (c) $z + x = 8$

Substitute $(6 - z)$ for y: $3x = (6 - z) + z$
Combine like terms: $3x = 6$
Divide by 3: $x = 2$
Plug in 2 for x: $z + 2 = 8$
Subtract 2: $z = 6$
Plug in 6 for z: $y = 6 - 6 = 0$
Divide y by z: $\dfrac{y}{z} = \dfrac{0}{6} = 0$

8. **B**   The diagonal of the square is the diameter of the circle.

$$d = 2r = 2(8) = 16$$

The diagonal of a square divides it into two 45°– 45°–90° triangles as shown here:

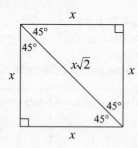

The diagonal $= 16 = x\sqrt{2}$

Divide by $\sqrt{2}$: $\dfrac{16}{\sqrt{2}} = \dfrac{16\sqrt{2}}{2} = 8\sqrt{2} = x$

$$\text{Area}_{\text{square}} = \text{side}^2 = \left(8\sqrt{2}\right)^2 = 128$$

Now you might notice that the shaded region is ¾ of the whole square, so its area is ¾(128) = 96. Or, you might notice that the shaded region is the square minus the area of triangles *ROS:*

$$\text{Area}_{\triangle ROS} = \tfrac{1}{2}(\text{base})(\text{height}) = \tfrac{1}{2}(8)(8) = 32$$

Shaded Area $= \text{Area}_{\text{square}} - \text{Area}_{\text{triangle}} = 128 - 32 = 96$

9. **168**   If two things are equal, you can substitute either one for the other. $f(x) = 3x + 7$
Substitute: $g(f(x)) = g(3x + 7)$
Use the definition of $g(x)$: $g(3x + 7) = (3x + 7)^2 - 1$
Plug in 2 for x: $y = (3(2) + 7)^2 - 1$
Simplify: $y = 13^2 - 1 = 168$

10. **6**   First find out how many students would be in each homeroom if they were all the same size. You can do this by finding the average size of the classes:

$$\text{Average} = \frac{14 + 18 + 21 + 23}{4} = 19$$

This means each class must have 19 students when you are done moving children around. Start with the largest class, 23 students, and move 4 of those students into the class with 14. This leaves us with classes with

        18   18   21   19

Next move one from the class with 21 students into each of the 18-student classes to move those three classes to 19 students as well. This means a total of 6 must be moved.

11. **42**   The pie chart shows that 15 + 10 = 25% of an average day is spent either socializing or at the gym: (0.25)(24 hours) = 6 hours per day. So in a seven-day week, the student would spend 6 × 7 = 42 hours.

12. **24**   You are given only two sides of a triangle, with the third as an unknown. To find the maximum area, first set it up as if it were a *right* triangle:

$$\text{Area} = \tfrac{1}{2}(\text{base})(\text{height})$$

$$\text{Area} = \tfrac{1}{2}(6)(8) = 24$$

It doesn't have to be a right triangle though, it could look like these:

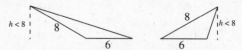

But these have smaller heights, and therefore smaller areas. Therefore the right triangle has maximum area.

13. **3** $|2x + 6| > 10$
Translate without the absolute value:
           $2x + 6 > 10$ or $2x + 6 < -10$
Subtract 6: $2x > 4$ $2x < -16$
Divide by 2: $x > 2$ $x < -8$
Since x is a positive integer, it must be greater than 2. The least integer greater than 2 is 3.

14. $\frac{1}{2}$ or **.5**

There are ten possible combinations of two coins: $1 + 5 = 6$; $1 + 10 = 11$; $1 + 25 = 26$; $1 + 50 = 51$; $5 + 10 = 15$; $5 + 25 = 30$; $5 + 50 = 55$; $10 + 25 = 35$; $10 + 50 = 60$; $25 + 50 = 75$

Five of these have a sum that is less than 35 cents, so the probability is $\frac{1}{2}$ or 0.5.

15. 750

Area of ballroom = $150 \times 100 = 15,000$ ft^2

Set up ratio: $\dfrac{1 \text{ can}}{300 \text{ ft}^2} = \dfrac{x \text{ cans}}{15,000 \text{ ft}^2}$

Cross multiply: $300x = 15,000$

Divide by 300: $x = 50$ cans of paint

Set up ratio: $\dfrac{1 \text{ can}}{\$15.00} = \dfrac{50 \text{ cans}}{y}$

Cross multiply: $y = \$750.00$

16. 1.5 or $\dfrac{3}{2}$

Volume = $n = lwh$
Plug in values: $n = (6)(4)(3) = 72$
Surface Area = $m = 2lw + 2hw + 2lh$
Plug in: $m = 2(6)(4) + 2(3)(4) + 2(6)(3)$
Simplify: $m = 48 + 24 + 36 = 108$
$m/n = 108/72 = 1.5$

17. 100 First remember that "inclusive" means including the smallest and largest numbers listed. In order for xy to be a member of set Y, it must be a positive integer between 1 and 100. To maximize the sum, find the largest numbers possible. 99 from set Y and 1 from set X will give you a sum of 100 and a product of 99, both of which are in set Y.

18. 20 This problem can be solved using similar triangles. Draw two right triangles, one with a base of 4, and the other with a base of 8. The first triangle has a height of x, and the other has a height of $x + 10$.

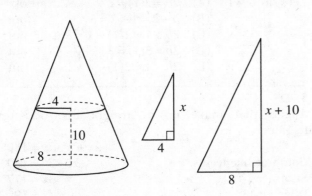

Set up a ratio and solve for x: $\dfrac{x}{4} = \dfrac{x+10}{8}$

Cross multiply: $8x = 4(x + 10)$
Distribute: $8x = 4x + 40$
Subtract $4x$: $4x = 40$
Divide by 4: $x = 10$

Therefore the height of the cone is $10 + 10 = 20$
(Chapter 13, Lesson 6: Similar Figures)

Section 6

1. C Choice C is the most concise and grammatically appropriate choice.

2. C The phrase *at another point in time in the past* is unnecessarily wordy and redundant, because the tense conveys the time.

3. C The phrase *could of* is a common diction error that stems from mispronunciation of the contraction *could've*. *Could have* is the correct phrase.

4. E Choice E is most parallel with the preceding clause.

5. B This choice follows the rules of parallel structure, keeping the entire list in the same format.

6. D The original phrase is unclear because it uses a weak verb and the "dummy" subject *It*. Choice D is most clear and concise.

7. A The sentence is best as written.

8. C The phrase *being that* is a non-standard form of *because*. The use of the participial phrase *often requiring … to describe the novel* is most concise and clear.

9. D The original phrase is an **appositive**, which should only be used next to a noun that describes the same thing as the appositive. Since this phrase does not describe *literature*, it is inappropriate. The participial phrase in D is most appropriate and effective.

10. B The original choice produces a sentence fragment: it contains no verb. Choice B conveys the idea most directly and completely.

11. E The phrase *their lighting candles to express hope* is a noun phrase in the place where a participial phrase belongs.

12. C   A comma is better suited for joining the two phrases. The second phrase is not an independent clause, so the semi-colon is inappropriate.

13. D   Answer choice (D) is incorrect because it does not follow the rules of parallel structure. One good alternative is *permission to stay up*.

14. C   The cars are not brand new, so the statement *it was brand new* is counter to fact, and is therefore in the subjunctive mood. The proper form is *it were*.

15. E   The sentence is correct.

16. D   Choice (D) does not follow the rules of parallel structure. The correct word is *honesty*.

17. C   The phrase *sufficient enough* is redundant.

18. D   The comparison is illogical. The sentence is comparing one *movie* to other *movies*, so the phrase *those of* should be eliminated.

19. A   The pronoun does not agree in number with its antecedent, *each*, which is singular. The correct pronoun is *his*.

20. B   The use of the present perfect *has matured* and the present tense *feels* implies the present tense for the verb in choice (B). Therefore, the correct word is *resorts*.

21. E   The sentence is correct.

22. B   The pronoun *their* has no clear antecedent. It logically refers to the store, so it should be replaced with *the store's prices* or *the prices the store offered*.

23. B   Answer choice (B) violates the rules of parallel structure. The correction is *respected*.

24. D   This is a comparison error. It is not logical to suggest that the *price of video equipment at Joe's Appliances* is more than *Acme Video*. A better phrasing would be *those at Acme Video*.

25. A   The past perfect tense requires the use of the past participle. The past participle of *to write* is *written*, not *wrote*.

26. C   The parallel construction of the list requires that the phrase in (C) be changed to *to feed*.

27. A   The parallel construction *more A than B* requires that the phrases A and B be parallel. Therefore, the word *like* should be omitted.

28. C   The antecedent of the pronoun *it* is the plural noun *storms*; the two do not agree in number, so the phrase should be changed to *they were something*.

29. E   The sentence is correct as written.

30. D   This choice conveys the right idea in the fewest words.

31. B   Choice (B) is most concise and clear.

32. B   This option is more concise than the others and maintains a logical structure.

33. A   Choice (A) most effectively conveys the idea that *60 Minutes* changed the nature of television journalism.

34. D   This sentence serves as a transition from the ideas of paragraph 3 into those of paragraph 4.

35. A   The sentence is most effective as it is.

Section 7

1. A
Perimeter = length + length + width + width
The perimeter of the 1st rectangle is $6 + 6 + 3 + 3 = 18$
The perimeter of the 2nd rectangle is $7 + 7 + x + x = 18$
Combine like terms: $14 + 2x = 18$
Subtract 14: $2x = 4$
Divide by 2: $x = 2$

2. A
To solve this problem, pick an odd number for b:
Let's say $b = 1$.   (A) $2b = 2(1) = 2$ ok
                         (B) $b + 2 = 1 + 2 = 3$ out
                         (C) $2b + 1 = 2(1) + 1 = 3$ out
                         (D) $3b = 3(1) = 3$ out
                         (E) $2b - 1 = 2(1) - 1 = 1$ out

3. D
Angles that make up a straight line add up to 180°.

$$2x + 3° + x = 180°$$
Combine like terms: $3x + 3° = 180°$
Subtract 3°: $3x = 177°$
Divide by 3: $x = 59°$

4. C

$$\left(x^6y^4\right)^{-\frac{1}{2}} = \left(x^{-3}y^{-2}\right) = \frac{1}{\left(x^3y^2\right)}$$

5. C

The median is the middle value. Write out the final exam grades from smallest to largest, then cross off the "outer" terms two at a time:

~~60~~, ~~60~~, ~~75~~, ~~80~~, ~~80~~, ~~80~~, ~~85~~, ~~85~~, 85, ~~85~~, ~~90~~, ~~90~~, ~~90~~, ~~95~~, ~~95~~, ~~95~~, ~~95~~

This leaves 85 as the median.

6. D

Choose a simple value like 1 for b: $a = 1^3 = 1$
Now triple b and find a: $a = 3^3 = 27$
Therefore, the value of a is multiplied by 27.

> $a = b^3$

7. E

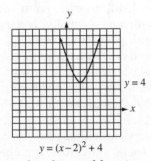

$y = (x-2)^2 + 4$

A quick way to solve this problem is to graph it on your calculator:

As you can see on the graph, $y = 4$ at its minimum value. Alternately, you may simply notice that the smallest the square of a real number can be is 0. This means that the smallest $(x - 2)^2$ can be is 0, so the smallest that y can be is 4. Be careful not to pick 2 as your answer. This is the value of x that *yields* the minimum value of the function, but is not actually the minimum value. Sometimes they will ask which value of x gives the minimum value of y, so you will sometimes look for that as an answer.

8. B $(5^3)(4^3) = (5 \times 4)^3 = 20^3 = 20^w$ so $w = 3$

9. C

Subtract 5 from x:	$x - 5$
Multiply by 2:	$2(x - 5)$
Add 6:	$2(x - 5) + 6$
Distribute:	$2x - 10 + 6$
Combine like terms:	$2x - 4$

10. E

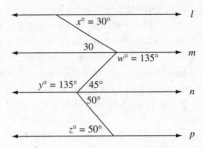

Remember, with parallel lines, angles that make a "Z" are equal. Mark up the diagram as shown.
$w + x + y + z = 135 + 30 + 135 + 50 = 350$

11. B   Set up a ratio: $\dfrac{x \text{ miles}}{p \text{ cms}} = \dfrac{y \text{ miles}}{p + 5 \text{ cms}}$

Cross multiply: $x(p + 5) = yp$
Distribute: $xp + 5x = yp$

Divide by p: $\dfrac{xp + 5x}{p} = y$

12. A   The question asks the value of $\sqrt{820} + \sqrt{104}$
$\sqrt{820} = 042$
$\sqrt{104} = 326$
$\sqrt{820} + \sqrt{104} = 042 + 326 = 368$
Careful! Don't pick answer B, $\sqrt{368}$, which equals 580.
Answer choice A, $\sqrt{146} = 368$

13. D

Slope $= m = \dfrac{y_2 - y_1}{x_2 - x_1} = \dfrac{s - r}{s^2 - r^2}$

Factor: $\dfrac{s - r}{(s - r)(s + r)} = \dfrac{1}{(s + r)}$

14. D

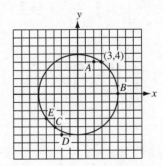

Using the distance formula to find the distance from $(0, 0)$ to $(3, 4)$ you can find that the radius = 5. Sketch a circle centered at the origin with a radius of 5, and plot the 5 answer choices. Answer choice D would be outside the circle. The others are either inside the circle or on it.

15. C

$$16m^2 + 56m + 49 = (mx + 7)^2$$

Since $m + x = 8$, substitute $8 - m$ for x:

$$16m^2 + 56m + 49 = (m(8 - m) + 7)^2$$

Simplify:

$$16m^2 + 56m + 49 = (-m^2 + 8m + 7)^2$$

Factor:

$$(4m + 7)^2 = (-m^2 + 8m + 7)^2$$

Take the square root: $|4m + 7| = |-m^2 + 8m + 7|$

Since m is positive but less than 8, both $4m + 7$ and $-m^2 + 8m + 7$ are positive, so $4m + 7 = -m^2 + 8m + 7$

Add $m^2 - 8m - 7$: $m^2 - 4m = 0$

Divide by m: $m - 4 = 0$

Add 4: $m = 4$

Substitute into $m + x = 8$: $4 + x = 8$

Subtract 4: $x = 4$

So $m - x = 4 - 4 = 0$

16. C

$(x - y)(x + y) = x^2 - y^2$. Plug in and simplify:

$$x^2 - y^2 = \left(\frac{b-a}{a}\right)^2 - \left(\frac{b+a}{a}\right)^2$$

Square both expressions:

$$\left(\frac{b^2 - 2ab + a^2}{a^2}\right) - \left(\frac{b^2 + 2ab + a^2}{a^2}\right)$$

Combine the fractions:

$$\frac{\left(b^2 - 2ab + a^2\right) - \left(b^2 + 2ab + a^2\right)}{a^2}$$

Combine like terms:

$$\left(\frac{-4ab}{a^2}\right) = \frac{-4b}{a}$$

Alternatively, if you wish to avoid the algebra, pick a value for b and a and see which answer choice works. Let's say $a = 2$ and $b = 4$:

$$\left(\frac{b-a}{a}\right)^2 - \left(\frac{b+a}{a}\right)^2 = \left(\frac{4-2}{2}\right)^2 - \left(\frac{4+2}{2}\right)^2 = 1 - 9 = -8$$

Answer choice C: $\dfrac{-4b}{a} = \dfrac{-4(4)}{2} = -8$

Section 8

1. E The decade witnessed a *slow return to economic stability*, which is a recovery. *inflammation* = swelling due to injury or infection; *acrimony* = harsh words; *mirth* = laughter; *aggregation* = making up a whole of something.

2. A If Jorge is a *gourmet*, he enjoys fine food. A gourmet would logically *bemoan* (complain about) a *lack* of good restaurants. *paucity* = a lack; *surfeit* = an excess; *conglomeration* = a combination

3. A Since the fuel had not yet been proven effective through experiment, its benefits were merely *speculative* (based on inconclusive evidence). *lucid* = clear; *dynamic* = full of energy; *fastidious* = difficult to please, meticulously attentive to detail; *monotonous* = boring

4. C The sentence clearly indicates the despot's transformation from an evil tyrant to less malevolent leader. *repugnant* = causing feelings of disgust; *beneficent* = kind, generous; *liberal* = favoring openness, freedom and new ideas; *abominable* = abhorrent; *nefarious* = wicked; *odious* = worthy of hatred; *patriarchal* = ruled by males; *vile* = disgusting; *malevolent* = evil-wishing; *mellifluous* = sweet sounding

5. E A character can either *conform to* social standards or *resist* social standards. If a character *resists any impulse to conform* to social standards, he or she must be an *iconoclast. heretic* = an individual with controversial opinions; *denounce* = to condemn; *obsequious* = overly submissive; *assimilate* = to make similar; *recalcitrant* = hesitant to obey; *itinerant* = wandering; *habituate* = become accustomed to; *iconoclast* = one who attacks tradition; *conform* = to do what is expected.

6. B Helene had to endure a great deal of toil in order to achieve the appearance of grace, so she must not have been naturally graceful. *nimbleness* = quickness and grace; *ineptitude* = lack of skill; *agility* = ability to move quickly and easily; *deftness* = skill in movement; *poise* = graceful bearing; *treachery* = betrayal; *cunning* = skillful deceitfulness; *aptitude* = ability; *dexterity* = skill; *idiosyncrasy* = an unusual mannerism.

7. C Passage 1 states that *the rights view has principled objections* (lines 10–11) to the continuation of animal research because it harms animals.

8. D The passage states that these institutions *treat (animals) as renewable resources* (line 23).

9. B The passage states that treating animals well requires *that we not sanction practices* that deny them their rights. This means that we should not *approve* such practices.

10. C This approach is one that looks *for nominal alternatives (to research on animals) and then, having failed to find any, (resorts) to using animals* (lines 30–32).

11. A The phrase *treatment tendered other animals* the author means *treatment administered to other animals.*

12. C The assumption made in this statement—*if they do (have rights), those rights must be respected*—is the claim that the passage attempts to refute.

13. E The passage explains that *a right (unlike an interest) is a valid claim, or potential claim, made by a moral agent, under principles that govern both the claimant and the target of the claim* (lines 57–61). This suggests that they bind more than one party.

14. C These statistics illustrate the fact that important medical breakthroughs, like the elimination of polio, depended on the use of animal experimentation.

15. A This paragraph discusses the logical fallacy which is "Since rights entail obligations, obligations imply rights."

16. D The point of this paragraph is that the converse of the statement "All rights entail obligations" is not true, so this statement does not logically imply another.

17. A Since the author of Passage 2 argues that animals cannot have rights because the concepts of rights is *essentially human*, then the author would regard this use of the term as incorrect.

18. D Both passages suggest that the statement in choice D is true. Passage 1 argues that harming animals is wrong even if such harms brings benefits to humans. Passage 2 states that *surely we have the obligation not to torture [a rat] gratuitously* (lines 124–125).

19. B Passage 1 devalues animal experimentation by saying that stopping it would not bring medical research *to a halt* (line 3) and that only research performed in treating animals that are sick is morally justified. Passage 2 states that polio could not have been cured without such animal experimentation.

Section 9

1. D The phrasing in (D) is most concise and clear.

2. B The underlined phrase must be parallel with the opening modifier, *generally*, which is an adverb. Choice (B) is the only one that provides the correct adverbial form.

3. C Since the subject of the sentence is *change*, which is singular, the correct verb form is *causes*. Choices (D) and (E) include illogical coordinators.

4. A The modifying phrase that opens the sentence should be set apart from the main clause by a comma.

5. D The original phrasing is not a complete sentence. The phrases *with anger* and *in a state of anger* are not idiomatic. Choice (D) is preferable to choice (E) because the object *the doctor's office* should not be separated from its verb *left*.

6. D The original phrasing is not parallel. Choice (D) provides the most concise and parallel phrasing.

7. E Since a plan is not a place, the use of *where* in the original phrasing is incorrect. Choice (B) is incorrect because the verb *are receiving* is in the wrong tense. Choice (D) is incorrect because the verb *causes* is in the wrong tense. Choice (E) uses the correct tense and pronouns.

8. A The original phrasing is the most logical and concise. The verb in choice (B) is in the wrong tense. Choice (C) contains a misplaced appositive. Choices (D) and (E) produce sentence fragments.

9. **B** Choice (B) is the only phrasing that logically coordinates the two clauses in the sentence.

10. **D** Choice (D) is the only phrasing that includes logical and parallel phrasing

11. **A** The original phrasing is clear, concise and logical.

12. **C** In the original phrasing, the verb *has* does not agree with its subject *powers*. Choice (C) corrects this problem and uses thie modifying phrase correctly.

13. **C** The original phrasing contains a dangling participle, *being*. Choice (B) is awkward and contains a pronoun, *it*, with an unclear antecedent. Choice (D) begins with a non-standard phrasing, *because of it being*. Choice (E) contains a misplaced appositive.

14. **D** This choice best follows the law of parallelism.

PRACTICE TEST 9

ANSWER SHEET

Last Name:_____   First Name:_____

Date:_____   Testing Location:_____

Directions for Test

- Remove these answer sheets from the book and use them to record your answers to this test.
- This test will require 3 hours and 20 minutes to complete. Take this test in one sitting.
- The time allotment for each section is written clearly at the beginning of each section. This test contains six 25-minute sections, two 20-minute sections, and one 10-minute section.
- This test is 25 minutes shorter than the actual SAT, which will include a 25-minute "experimental" section that does not count toward your score. That section has been omitted from this test.
- You may take one short break during the test, of no more than 10 minutes in length.
- You may only work on one section at any given time.
- You must stop ALL work on a section when time is called.
- If you finish a section before the time has elapsed, check your work on that section. You may NOT work on any other section.
- Do not waste time on questions that seem too difficult for you.
- Use the test book for scratchwork, but you will receive credit only for answers that are marked on the answer sheets.
- You will receive one point for every correct answer.
- You will receive no points for an omitted question.
- For each wrong answer on any multiple-choice question, your score will be reduced by ¼ point.
- For each wrong answer on any "numerical grid-in" question, you will receive no deduction.

When you take the real SAT, you will be asked to fill in your personal information in grids as shown below.

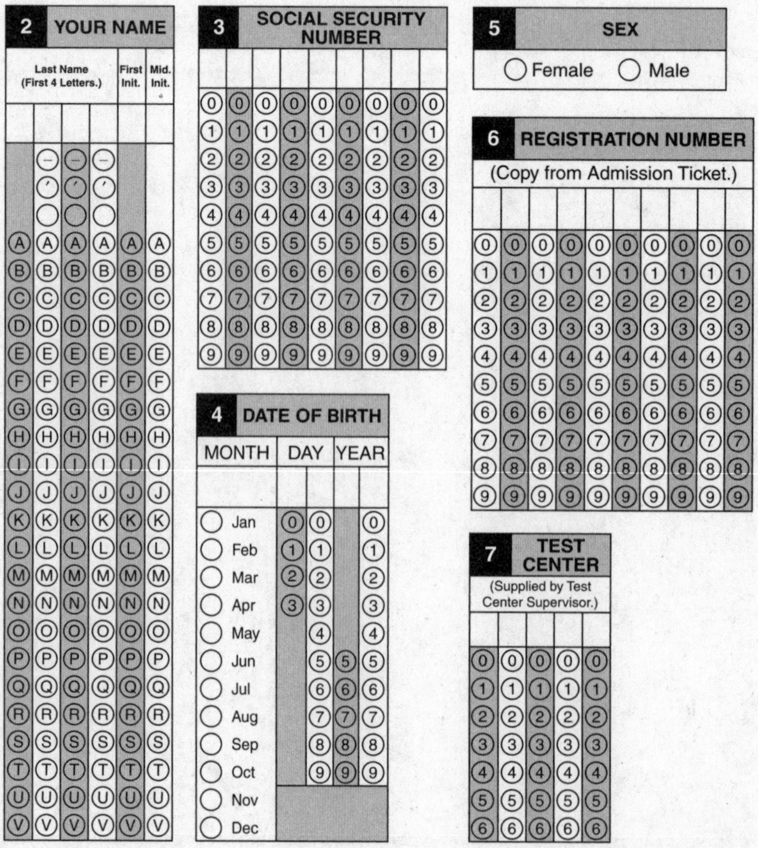

Start with number 1 for each new section. If a section has fewer questions than answer spaces, leave the extra answer spaces blank. Be sure to erase any errors or stray marks completely.

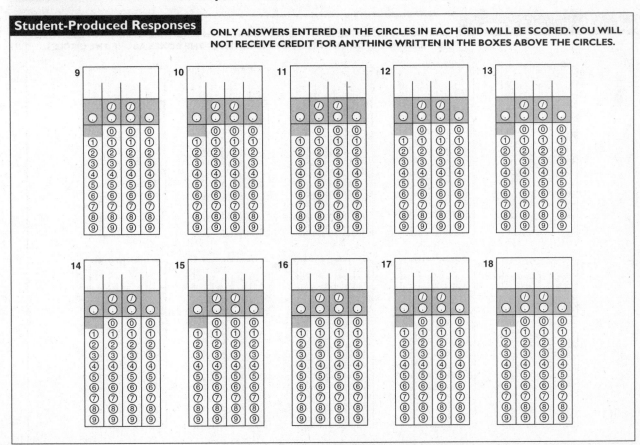

CAUTION Use the answer spaces in the grids below for Section 2 or Section 3 only if you are told to do so in your test book.

Student-Produced Responses ONLY ANSWERS ENTERED IN THE CIRCLES IN EACH GRID WILL BE SCORED. YOU WILL NOT RECEIVE CREDIT FOR ANYTHING WRITTEN IN THE BOXES ABOVE THE CIRCLES.

Start with number 1 for each new section. If a section has fewer questions than answer spaces, leave the extra answer spaces blank. Be sure to erase any errors or stray marks completely.

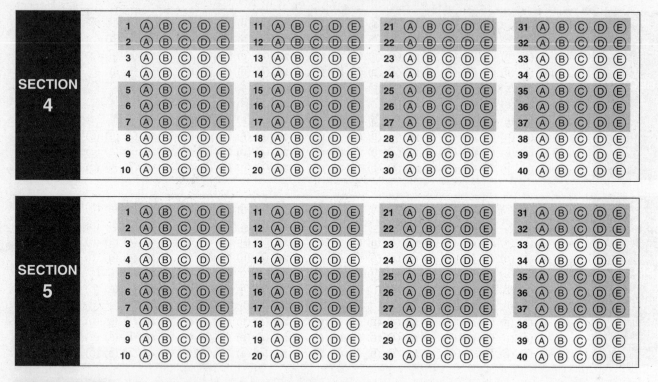

SECTION 4

SECTION 5

CAUTION — Use the answer spaces in the grids below for Section 4 or Section 5 only if you are told to do so in your test book.

Student-Produced Responses — ONLY ANSWERS ENTERED IN THE CIRCLES IN EACH GRID WILL BE SCORED. YOU WILL NOT RECEIVE CREDIT FOR ANYTHING WRITTEN IN THE BOXES ABOVE THE CIRCLES.

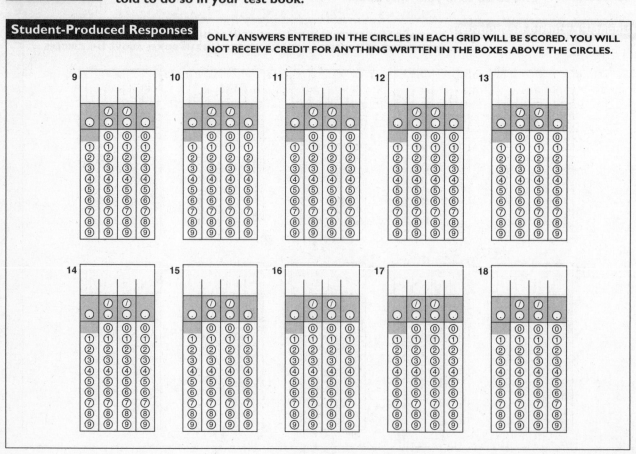

Start with number 1 for each new section. If a section has fewer questions than answer spaces, leave the extra answer spaces blank. Be sure to erase any errors or stray marks completely.

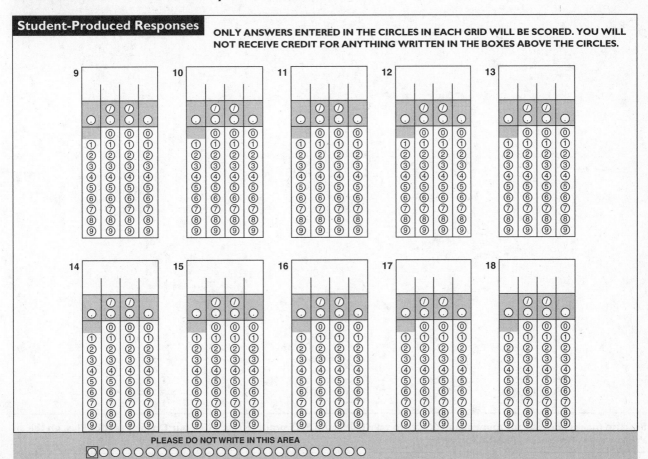

CAUTION   **Use the answer spaces in the grids below for Section 6 or Section 7 only if you are told to do so in your test book.**

Student-Produced Responses   ONLY ANSWERS ENTERED IN THE CIRCLES IN EACH GRID WILL BE SCORED. YOU WILL NOT RECEIVE CREDIT FOR ANYTHING WRITTEN IN THE BOXES ABOVE THE CIRCLES.

PLEASE DO NOT WRITE IN THIS AREA

Start with number 1 for each new section. If a section has fewer questions than answer spaces, leave the extra answer spaces blank. Be sure to erase any errors or stray marks completely.

SECTION 8

1 (A) (B) (C) (D) (E)
2 (A) (B) (C) (D) (E)
3 (A) (B) (C) (D) (E)
4 (A) (B) (C) (D) (E)
5 (A) (B) (C) (D) (E)
6 (A) (B) (C) (D) (E)
7 (A) (B) (C) (D) (E)
8 (A) (B) (C) (D) (E)
9 (A) (B) (C) (D) (E)
10 (A) (B) (C) (D) (E)

11 (A) (B) (C) (D) (E)
12 (A) (B) (C) (D) (E)
13 (A) (B) (C) (D) (E)
14 (A) (B) (C) (D) (E)
15 (A) (B) (C) (D) (E)
16 (A) (B) (C) (D) (E)
17 (A) (B) (C) (D) (E)
18 (A) (B) (C) (D) (E)
19 (A) (B) (C) (D) (E)
20 (A) (B) (C) (D) (E)

21 (A) (B) (C) (D) (E)
22 (A) (B) (C) (D) (E)
23 (A) (B) (C) (D) (E)
24 (A) (B) (C) (D) (E)
25 (A) (B) (C) (D) (E)
26 (A) (B) (C) (D) (E)
27 (A) (B) (C) (D) (E)
28 (A) (B) (C) (D) (E)
29 (A) (B) (C) (D) (E)
30 (A) (B) (C) (D) (E)

31 (A) (B) (C) (D) (E)
32 (A) (B) (C) (D) (E)
33 (A) (B) (C) (D) (E)
34 (A) (B) (C) (D) (E)
35 (A) (B) (C) (D) (E)
36 (A) (B) (C) (D) (E)
37 (A) (B) (C) (D) (E)
38 (A) (B) (C) (D) (E)
39 (A) (B) (C) (D) (E)
40 (A) (B) (C) (D) (E)

SECTION 9

1 (A) (B) (C) (D) (E)
2 (A) (B) (C) (D) (E)
3 (A) (B) (C) (D) (E)
4 (A) (B) (C) (D) (E)
5 (A) (B) (C) (D) (E)
6 (A) (B) (C) (D) (E)
7 (A) (B) (C) (D) (E)
8 (A) (B) (C) (D) (E)
9 (A) (B) (C) (D) (E)
10 (A) (B) (C) (D) (E)

11 (A) (B) (C) (D) (E)
12 (A) (B) (C) (D) (E)
13 (A) (B) (C) (D) (E)
14 (A) (B) (C) (D) (E)
15 (A) (B) (C) (D) (E)
16 (A) (B) (C) (D) (E)
17 (A) (B) (C) (D) (E)
18 (A) (B) (C) (D) (E)
19 (A) (B) (C) (D) (E)
20 (A) (B) (C) (D) (E)

21 (A) (B) (C) (D) (E)
22 (A) (B) (C) (D) (E)
23 (A) (B) (C) (D) (E)
24 (A) (B) (C) (D) (E)
25 (A) (B) (C) (D) (E)
26 (A) (B) (C) (D) (E)
27 (A) (B) (C) (D) (E)
28 (A) (B) (C) (D) (E)
29 (A) (B) (C) (D) (E)
30 (A) (B) (C) (D) (E)

31 (A) (B) (C) (D) (E)
32 (A) (B) (C) (D) (E)
33 (A) (B) (C) (D) (E)
34 (A) (B) (C) (D) (E)
35 (A) (B) (C) (D) (E)
36 (A) (B) (C) (D) (E)
37 (A) (B) (C) (D) (E)
38 (A) (B) (C) (D) (E)
39 (A) (B) (C) (D) (E)
40 (A) (B) (C) (D) (E)

Practice makes perfect—for more opportunities to take full-length SAT practice tests, visit our Online Practice Plus, on the Web at www.MHPracticePlus/SATpractice.

| 1 | ESSAY | ESSAY | 1 |

ESSAY
Time—25 minutes

Write your essay on separate sheets of standard lined paper.

The essay gives you an opportunity to show how effectively you can develop and express ideas. You should therefore take care to develop your point of view, present your ideas logically and clearly, and use language precisely.

Your essay must be written on the lines provided on your answer sheet—you will receive no other paper on which to write. You will have enough space if you write on every line, avoid wide margins, and keep your handwriting to a reasonable size. Remember that people who are not familiar with your handwriting will read what you write. Try to write or print so that what you are writing is legible to those readers.

Important reminders:

- **A pencil is required for the essay.** An essay written in ink will receive a score of zero.
- **Do not write your essay in your test book.** You will receive credit only for what you write on your answer sheet.
- **An off-topic essay will receive a score of zero.**

You have twenty-five minutes to write an essay on the topic assigned below.

Think carefully about the issue presented in the following excerpt and the assignment below.

> An entertainment-driven culture runs the risk of encouraging passivity among its citizens. If they can experience something vicariously through a movie, television show, or video game, why should they get involved with the activity itself? It's safer, after all, to watch someone scale a mountain than to do it yourself. The effect of this passivity, of course, is an apathetic frame of mind. We cease to care deeply about so many things because they are experienced, at best, second-hand.

Assignment: **Is apathy a problem in today's society?** Write an essay in which you answer this question and discuss your point of view on this issue. Support your position logically with examples from literature, the arts, history, politics, science and technology, current events, or your experience or observation.

If you finish before time is called, you may check your work on this section only.
Do not turn to any other section of the test.

2   **2**   **2**   **2**   **2**   **2**

SECTION 2
Time—25 minutes
20 questions

Turn to Section 2 of your answer sheet to answer the questions in this section.

Directions: For this section, solve each problem and decide which is the best of the choices given. Fill in the corresponding circle on the answer sheet. You may use any available space for scratchwork.

Notes

1. The use of a calculator is permitted.

2. All numbers used are real numbers.

3. Figures that accompany problems in this test are intended to provide information useful in solving the problems. They are drawn as accurately as possible EXCEPT when it is stated in a specific problem that the figure is not drawn to scale. All figures lie in a plane unless otherwise indicated.

4. Unless otherwise specified, the domain of any function f is assumed to be the set of all real numbers x for which $f(x)$ is a real number.

Reference Information

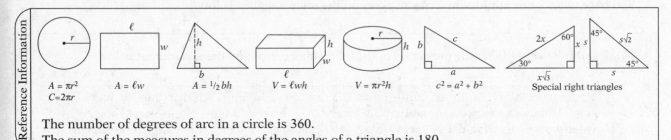

$A = \pi r^2$ $A = \ell w$ $A = \frac{1}{2} bh$ $V = \ell wh$ $V = \pi r^2 h$ $c^2 = a^2 + b^2$ Special right triangles
$C = 2\pi r$

The number of degrees of arc in a circle is 360.
The sum of the measures in degrees of the angles of a triangle is 180.

---

1. If $x = 3$ and $5x = 3x + y$, then $y =$

  (A)   1.5
  (B)   2
  (C)   3
  (D)   4
  (E)   6

2. A store sells a package of 6 batteries for $4 and a package of 24 of the same batteries for $12. If you need to buy 48 of these batteries, how much money will you save by buying them in packages of 24 rather than packages of 6?

  (A) $4
  (B) $8
  (C) $12
  (D) $16
  (E) $20

GO ON TO THE NEXT PAGE

2   2   2   2   2   2

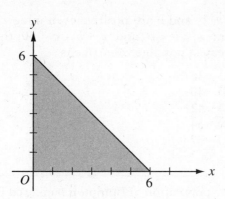

3. Which of the following points does NOT lie in the shaded region above?

    (A) (1, 1)
    (B) (1, 4)
    (C) (2, 3)
    (D) (4, 1)
    (E) (5, 5)

---

4. If $\frac{1}{3}$ of $2x$ is 5, what is $\frac{2}{3}$ of $4x$?

    (A)   5
    (B) 10
    (C) 15
    (D) 20
    (E) 25

---

5. If n is a positive integer that is divisible by 12 and 16, then n must also be divisible by

    (A)   28
    (B)   32
    (C)   48
    (D)   96
    (E) 192

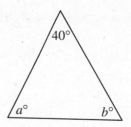

Note: Figure not drawn to scale.

6. In the figure above, if $a - b = 10$, then $a =$

    (A) 60
    (B) 65
    (C) 70
    (D) 75
    (E) 80

---

7. If n is an integer, which of the following must be an even integer?

    (A) $\dfrac{n}{2}$
    (B) $n + 2$
    (C) $2n + 1$
    (D) n^2
    (E) $n^2 + n$

---

8. Mike sold a total of 48 sodas at a snack stand. The stand sells only cola and root beer. If he sold twice as many colas as root beers, how many root beers did he sell?

    (A) 32
    (B) 24
    (C) 18
    (D) 16
    (E)   8

---

9. If m and n are both squares of integers, which of the following is NOT necessarily the square of an integer?

    (A) $9m$
    (B) mn
    (C) m^2
    (D) $9mn$
    (E) $9m - 9n$

GO ON TO THE NEXT PAGE

2   **2**   **2**   **2**   **2**   **2**

10. If $a + b = 9$, $a - c = 14$, and $a = 10$, then $c - b =$

    (A) −5
    (B) −3
    (C)   3
    (D)   5
    (E) 23

11. If the average (arithmetic mean) of $a, b, 4$, and 10 is 8, what is the value of $a + b$?

    (A)   4
    (B)   6
    (C)   9
    (D) 15
    (E) 18

0	1	2	3	4	5
1	2	4			
2					
3		x			
4					
5					

12. With the exception of the shaded squares, every square in the figure above contains the sum of the number in the square directly above it and the number in the square directly to its left. For example, the number 4 in the unshaded square above is the sum of the 2 in the square above it and the 2 in the square directly to its left. What is the value of x?

    (A)   6
    (B)   7
    (C)   8
    (D) 15
    (E) 30

13. If a, b, and c are positive even integers such that $a < b < c$ and $a + b + c = 60$, then the greatest possible value of c is

    (A) 36
    (B) 40
    (C) 42
    (D) 54
    (E) 57

14. The population of Bumpton increased by 10% from 1980 to 1990 and decreased by 10% from 1990 to 2000. What is the net percent change in the population of Bumpton from 1980 to 2000?

    (A) −9%
    (B) −1%
    (C) +0%
    (D) +1%
    (E) +9%

x	$f(x)$
−2	−29
−1	−21
0	−13
1	−5
2	3
3	11
4	19

15. Several values of the function f are shown above. The function g is defined by $g(x) = 2f(x) - 1$. What is the value of $g(3)$?

    (A) −21
    (B) −13
    (C)   3
    (D)   11
    (E)   21

GO ON TO THE NEXT PAGE

$$2 \qquad 2 \qquad 2 \qquad 2 \qquad 2 \qquad 2$$

16. If $x > 0$ and $x = 5y$, then $\sqrt{x^2 - 2xy + y^2} =$

(A) $2y$
(B) $y\sqrt{6}$
(C) $4y$
(D) $16y$
(E) $24y$

---

17. If $x > x^2$, which of the following must be true?

    I. $x < 1$
    II. $x > 0$
    III. $x^2 > 1$

(A) I only
(B) II only
(C) I and II only
(D) I and III only
(E) I, II, and III

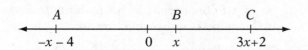

18. Which of the following represents the distance from the midpoint of $\overline{AB}$ to the midpoint of $\overline{BC}$ on the number line above?

(A) $\dfrac{3x+2}{2}$

(B) $2x - 1$

(C) $2x + 3$

(D) $3x + 1$

(E) $4x$

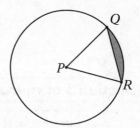

19. P is the center of the circle above and $PQ = QR$. If $\triangle PQR$ has an area of $9\sqrt{3}$, what is the area of the shaded region?

(A) $36\pi - 9\sqrt{3}$

(B) $24\pi - 9\sqrt{3}$

(C) $18\pi - 9\sqrt{3}$

(D) $9\pi - 9\sqrt{3}$

(E) $6\pi - 9\sqrt{3}$

---

20. In a class of 160 seniors, the ratio of boys to girls is 3 to 5. In the junior class, the ratio of boys to girls is 3 to 2. When the two classes are combined, the ratio of boys to girls is 1 to 1. How many students are in the junior class?

(A) 400
(B) 360
(C) 200
(D) 180
(E) 160

STOP

If you finish before time is called, you may check your work on this section only. Do not turn to any other section of the test.

SECTION 3
Time—25 minutes
24 questions

Turn to Section 3 of your answer sheet to answer the questions in this section.

Directions: For each question in this section, select the best answer from among the choices given and fill in the corresponding circle on the answer sheet.

Each sentence below has one or two blanks, each blank indicating that something has been omitted. Beneath the sentence are five words or sets of words labeled A through E. Choose the word or set of words that, when inserted in the sentence, best fits the meaning of the sentence as a whole.

EXAMPLE:

Rather than accepting the theory unquestioningly, Deborah regarded it with -----.

(A) mirth
(B) sadness
(C) responsibility
(D) ignorance
(E) skepticism

---

1. Julia feared that her 6-month hiatus from playing the piano would cause her musical skills to -------.

   (A) atrophy
   (B) align
   (C) develop
   (D) reconcile
   (E) disseminate

2. Senator Harris is widely viewed as a ------- orator; his speeches are full of ------- commentary and domineering opinions.

   (A) vindictive . . pedantic
   (B) conciliatory . . treacherous
   (C) didactic . . moralizing
   (D) dogmatic . . meek
   (E) simplistic . . prosaic

3. Walter's ------- was beginning to annoy his co-workers; although they appreciated the thought he gave to his decisions, his inability to make up his mind was growing tiresome.

   (A) vacillation
   (B) solicitation
   (C) rejuvenation
   (D) admonishment
   (E) professionalism

4. To succeed as a writer, one needs a great deal of -------; successful writers are ------- even in the face of countless rejections.

   (A) affluence . . haughty
   (B) pertinacity . . apologetic
   (C) intimidation . . resilient
   (D) tenacity . . relentless
   (E) stoutness . . craven

GO ON TO THE NEXT PAGE

5. Although direct, forceful stances usually appeal to voters on the campaign trail, candidates usually resort to ------- during debates to avoid alienating any potential supporters.

   (A) pontification
   (B) circumlocution
   (C) logic
   (D) exaggeration
   (E) brevity

6. Counselors in the prison rehabilitation program must have faith in the ------- of those who have committed felonies, yet be wary of -------; they must believe that criminals can change, but know that they can often return to their old habits.

   (A) mutability . . astuteness
   (B) variability . . consistency
   (C) coarseness . . responsibility
   (D) persuasion . . transcendence
   (E) malleability . . relapse

7. Marullus' reference to "chimney-tops" during his monologue in *Julius Caesar* is considered by some historians -------, since such things are unlikely to have existed in Rome in the first century B.C.

   (A) a miscalculation
   (B) an anachronism
   (C) an idiom
   (D) an interlocutor
   (E) a mirage

8. The letter "h" at the end of Pittsburgh is ------- of American sentiments soon after World War I; it was added as part of a movement during that time to make the names of American cities sound less German.

   (A) an inference
   (B) an analogy
   (C) a vestige
   (D) an anomaly
   (E) a quandary

The passages below are followed by questions based on their content. Answer the questions on the basis of what is stated or implied in the passage and in any introductory material that may be provided.

Questions 9–10 are based on the following passage.

Although countries can construct redoubtable stone barriers to separate "us" from "others,"
Line no barrier is stronger than language. We infer volumes from the language of another,
5 whether he is erudite or philistine, whether she is noble or mean. Our labels, too, can be impenetrable walls: we are "freedom fighters," they are "terrorists"; we are the "faithful," they are the "infidels." Those people who use such
10 wall-language are the Manichaeans,[1] those who refuse to see, or cannot see, shades of gray, the subtle truths of humanity. Their "truths" are the most dangerous weapons, wielded by the blind and the ignorant.

9. In this paragraph, language is characterized primarily as

   (A) biased
   (B) enlightening
   (C) difficult to understand
   (D) unifying
   (E) changeable

10. In line 4, the word "volumes" most nearly means

   (A) spaces
   (B) editions
   (C) measurements
   (D) an abundance
   (E) capacities

[1]Those who believe in absolute good and evil

GO ON TO THE NEXT PAGE ⟶

3   **3**   3   3   **3**   **3**

Questions 11 and 12 are based on the following passage.

It may be difficult for adults to learn not to interfere but rather to support the child's desire
Line for freedom and autonomy. For example, if
you watch a boy of three trying to tie his
5 shoes, you may see him work with extraordinary motivation even though the loops aren't
matched, and well over half the time as he
tries for the final knot, he ends up with two
separate laces, one in each hand. Then watch
10 his parents as they watch their children attempt a task like this. Too often the parent
will step in and take over, tie the shoes the
"right way" and defeat the child's growing
attempt at self-mastery. The same goes for
15 putting on boots, coats, and even playing with
toys. It is exceedingly easy to fall into the trap
of almost always responding negatively to a
child at this age. Commonly, a parent might
say no up to 200 times a day at this stage.
20 Such nagging not only is aversive in the
extreme, but also a constant reminder to the
child of his or her lack of self-control.

11. The passage suggests that helping a boy to tie
his shoes the "right way" (line 13) can be

(A) necessary to his self-esteem
(B) important to his personal hygiene
(C) appropriate only if the boy has the neces-
sary fine motor skills
(D) essential to teaching him patience
(E) harmful to his autonomous development

12. The passage indicates that negative responses to
a child can lead to the child's

(A) rebellion
(B) feeling of helplessness
(C) persistence in the task
(D) mimicking of the negative behavior
(E) anger

Second passage: *Educational Psychology: A Developmental Approach*, Norman A. Sprinthall et al., McGraw-Hill, 1994, p. 149

Questions 13–18 are based on the following passage.

The following is an essay about T. S. Eliot, an American poet of the early 20th century, and the Modernist movement, of which he was a part.

Modernism is the most peculiar of all artistic
movements of the twentieth century and the
Line most difficult to pin down since people started
coming up with "movements" in the first
5 place. Modernism is the only thing that strikes
more fear into the heart of an English undergraduate than the idea of going to a lecture.
Critics and academics, not unwisely, prefer
their artistic movements to be readily compre-
10 hensible and clearly enough defined to make
some logical sense. Modernism, however, will
not be tamed. It is straggly, begins nowhere
and with no one in particular, and ends only
when its writers have started to baffle even
15 themselves. One treads carefully through its
key texts: James Joyce's *Ulysses*, T. S. Eliot's
The Waste Land (both 1922), and Virginia
Woolf's *Mrs. Dalloway* (1925). The authors of
these aberrations, these posturing, egotistical,
20 lunatic, kaleidoscopic works of blatant and
self-conscious genius, have laid literary landmines throughout their works. Joyce said of
Ulysses that "I've put in so many enigmas and
puzzles that it will keep the professors busy
25 for centuries arguing over what I meant, and
that's the only way of insuring one's immortal-
ity." This statement sums up the enigma of
modernism (if one can be said to sum up an
enigma) in that it contains arrogance min-
30 gling with modesty, cleverness tied up in self-
effacing humour, and above all absurdity with
a purpose. Plots, such as they exist at all in
modernist writing, are submerged beneath
wave upon wave of classical allusions,
35 archaisms, neologisms, foreign languages,
quotations, swear words and other hyper-
literary and meta-literary indulgences. If I
haven't made it clear already, it is hard not to
love modernism. It is hard to work out what
40 exactly it is.

GO ON TO THE NEXT PAGE →

3　　　3　　　3　　　3　　　3　　　3

Recently, while browsing in an Oxford bookshop, a friend of mine picked up a copy of *Finnegans Wake*—James Joyce's final book—and read the first page. Between tears

45　of laughter, he managed to indicate to me that he couldn't understand a word of it. It is hard not to sympathise with the outsider's attitude so amply demonstrated by my friend's outburst of shock and wonder. To find one of

50　our most famous authors writing gibberish is rather heartening. Yet we remain outsiders to the work. *Finnegans Wake*, you see, is emblematic of all that is right and wrong with modernism. It took a spectacularly long time

55　to write and was finally published in 1939, seventeen years after its predecessor, *Ulysses*. That probably had something to do with the fact that over 40 different languages crept into its catalogue of portmanteau words

60　(ersatz words consisting of two or more real words or word elements, like those of Lewis Carroll in his poem "Jabberwocky"). The resulting book is uniquely inventive and at the same time uniquely confusing. In that sense,

65　it is the perfect example of a modernist text. It alienates its readers just as it tries to mimic how they think. The English modernist novel is a sociopath and a cad: dangerous and reprehensible but somehow roguishly

70　likeable.

13. In the first paragraph, the author characterizes Modernism as which of the following?

　　I. self-centered
　　II. ill-defined
　　III. politically oriented

(A) I only
(B) II only
(C) I and II only
(D) II and III only
(E) I, II, and III

14. The passage suggests that critics and academics dislike artistic movements that are

(A) enigmatic
(B) comprehensible
(C) wide-ranging
(D) inventive
(E) socially conscious

15. The "landmines" in lines 21–22 are

(A) episodes in novels that refer to violence
(B) criticisms of the works of other novelists
(C) new methods of analyzing literature
(D) literary devices intended to baffle academics
(E) limitations that publishers place on an author's work

16. The reference to "wave upon wave" (line 34) suggests that, in Modernist fiction, plot is

(A) a powerfully moving element
(B) secondary to other considerations
(C) dominant over diction
(D) characterized by redundancy
(E) dangerous

17. The author's overall attitude toward Modernism can best be described as

(A) ambivalent
(B) reverential
(C) cynical
(D) indignant
(E) jocular

18. The final sentence of the passage employs each of the following EXCEPT

(A) simile
(B) juxtaposition
(C) personification
(D) contrast
(E) metaphor

Excerpted from *T. S. Eliot and the Elitism of Modernism*, by David Pinching, on http://www.bibliomania.com

GO ON TO THE NEXT PAGE ▷

Questions 19–24 are based on the following passage.

The following is an excerpt from a book on ge-
nomics, the new science of gathering and using
the information encoded in the genes of an
organism.

Biology is being reborn as an information science, a progeny of the Information Age. As in-
Line formation scientists, biologists concern
themselves with the messages that sustain life,
5   such as the intricate series of signals that tell a
fertilized egg to develop into a full-grown organism, or the orchestrated response the immune system makes to an invading pathogen.
Molecules convey information, and it is their
10 messages that are of paramount importance.
Each molecule interacts with a set of other
molecules and each set communicates with another set, such that all are interconnected. Networks of molecules give rise to cells; networks
15 of cells produce multicellular organisms; networks of people bring about cultures and societies; and networks of species encompass
ecosystems. Life is a web and the web is life.
Ironically, it was the euphoria for molecules
20 that touched off this scientific revolution. In
the 1980s only a tiny percentage of the millions of different molecular components of living beings was known. In order to gain access
to these molecules, a new science and even a
25 new industry had to be created. Genomics is
the development and application of research
tools that uncover and analyze thousands of
different molecules at a time. This new approach to biology has been so successful that
30 universities have created entire departments
devoted to it, and all major pharmaceutical
companies now have large genomics divisions. Genomics has granted biologists unprecedented access to the molecules of life,
35 but this is more than just a technological revolution. Through genomics massive amounts of
biological information can be converted into
an electronic format. This directly links the
life sciences to the information sciences,
40 thereby facilitating a dramatically new framework for understanding life.
Information is a message, a bit of news.
It may be encoded or decoded. It may be

conveyed by smoke signals, pictures, sound
45 waves, electromagnetic waves, or innumer-
ous other media, but the information itself is
not made of anything. It has no mass. Furthermore, information always has a sender
and an intended receiver. This implies an un-
50 derlying intent, meaning, or purpose. Information theory thus may seem unfit for the
cold objectivism of science. The focus of the
information sciences, however, is not so
much on information content, but rather on
55 how messages are conveyed, processed, and
stored.
Advances in this area have been great and
have helped to propel the remarkable development of the computer and telecommunication
60 industries. Could these forces be harnessed to
better understand the human body and to improve human health?

19. The primary purpose of this passage is to

(A) refute a theory
(B) describe the origins of a misconception
(C) analyze different perspectives on a
        phenomenon
(D) describe a new trend in a field of study
(E) suggest a new method of teaching

20. The passage mentions each of the following as
an example of elements interrelating to form a
larger whole EXCEPT

(A) molecules forming a cell
(B) organisms forming an ecosystem
(C) pathogens forming the immune system
(D) individuals forming a society
(E) cells forming an organism

21. The passage mentions the "orchestrated
response" (line 7) primarily as an example of

(A) the coordinated efforts of scientists
(B) molecules conveying information
(C) the work being done to promote
        genomics
(D) the similarity between cells and
        computers
(E) an unrealized potential of the cell

Excerpted from *Transducing the Genome*, Gary Zweiger,
McGraw-Hill, pp. xi–xii

GO ON TO THE NEXT PAGE

3   3   3   3   3   3

22. According to the passage, the "dramatically new framework" (lines 40–41) is one in which

(A) new university buildings are being built
(B) the immune system attacks a pathogen
(C) networks of molecules give rise to cells
(D) genomics research receives more federal funding
(E) biological data is translated into a new form

23. According to the passage, information theory "may seem unfit for the cold objectivism of science" (line 51–52) because

(A) it is better suited to commercial industry than to academic study
(B) it can be conveyed by sound waves
(C) it suggests that messages may have meaning or purpose
(D) it is not rigorously studied
(E) it analyzes biological information

24. Which of the following best describes the function of the final paragraph in relation to the rest of the passage?

(A) It modifies a theory presented earlier.
(B) It provides a solution to a problem mentioned earlier.
(C) It raises doubts about the value of genomics.
(D) It indicates actual and potential consequences of genomics.
(E) It mentions a viable alternative to genomics.

STOP

If you finish before time is called, you may check your work on this section only. Do not turn to any other section of the test.

4   4   4   4   4   4

SECTION 4
Time—25 minutes
35 questions

Turn to Section 4 of your answer sheet to answer the questions in this section.

Directions: For each question in this section, select the best answer from among the choices given and fill in the corresponding circle on the answer sheet.

The following sentences test correctness and effectiveness of expression. Part of each sentence or the entire sentence is underlined; beneath each sentence are five ways of phrasing the underlined material. Choice A repeats the original phrasing; the other four choices are different. Select the choice that completes the sentence most effectively.

In making your selection, follow the requirements of standard written English; that is, pay attention to grammar, choice of words, sentence construction, and punctuation. Your selection should result in the most effective sentence—clear and precise, without awkwardness or ambiguity.

EXAMPLE:

The children <u>couldn't hardly believe their eyes</u>.

(A) couldn't hardly believe their eyes
(B) could hardly believe their eyes
(C) would not hardly believe their eyes
(D) couldn't nearly believe their eyes
(E) couldn't hardly believe his or her eyes

1. The controversial themes, which resonate with recent political events, <u>explain why the book is selling at such a feverish pace</u>.

    (A) explain why the book is selling at such a feverish pace
    (B) explains the feverish pace of the book
    (C) explain the reason for the pace of the book's feverish sales
    (D) explains why the book's selling pace is so feverish
    (E) is why the book is selling well

2. One of the best features of the journalist's lifestyle is <u>you never know what's next</u>.

    (A) you never know what's next
    (B) it's so unpredictable
    (C) that you never know what's next
    (D) one can never predict what's next
    (E) its unpredictability

3. Despite having an engaging personality and an outstanding education, <u>Greg's search for a satisfying job was fruitless</u>.

    (A) Greg's search for a satisfying job was fruitless
    (B) Greg searched fruitlessly for a satisfying job
    (C) Greg's job search was fruitless because he insisted on a satisfying job
    (D) the satisfying job that Greg sought was nowhere to be found
    (E) Greg searched for a satisfying job, but it was fruitless

GO ON TO THE NEXT PAGE

4   **4**   **4**   **4**   **4**   **4**

4. The plot of the movie was neither plausible <u>and it was not even faithful to the novel</u>.

   (A)   and it was not even faithful to the novel
   (B)   nor was it faithful to the novel
   (C)   nor faithful to the novel
   (D)   and certainly not faithful to the novel
   (E)   yet hardly faithful to the novel

5. We were astonished that the package <u>had took so long to get</u> to its destination.

   (A)   had took so long to get
   (B)   had took so long getting
   (C)   had taken so long in its getting
   (D)   had taken so long to get
   (E)   had been so long getting

6. The committee agreed that the new principal should be able to inspire teachers, uphold tradition, and, above all, <u>he or she must maintain a scholarly atmosphere</u>.

   (A)   he or she must maintain a scholarly atmosphere
   (B)   they should maintain a scholarly atmosphere
   (C)   maintain a scholarly atmosphere
   (D)   keep things scholarly
   (E)   he or she should keep things scholarly

7. Although critics say that many have portrayed Othello with more passion than <u>he, they can't help but admire his acting</u>.

   (A)   he, they can't help but admire his acting
   (B)   him, they can't help but admire his acting
   (C)   he, they can't help but admire him acting
   (D)   him, they can't help but admire him acting
   (E)   him, they must only admire his acting

8. Neither <u>of the battling rams appeared to feel the pain of their wounds</u>.

   (A)   of the battling rams appeared to feel the pain of their wounds
   (B)   of the battling rams appeared to feel the pain of its wounds
   (C)   ram, that was battling, appeared to feel the pain of their wounds
   (D)   ram who were battling appeared to feel the pain of its wounds
   (E)   battling ram appeared as if to feel the pain of their wounds

9. Walking into her house after a hard day's work, <u>Liz's family surprised her with a warm, delicious meal and a clean house</u>.

   (A)   Liz's family surprised her with a warm, delicious meal and a clean house
   (B)   Liz was surprised to find a warm, delicious meal and a clean house, courtesy of her family
   (C)   Liz's family made her a warm, delicious meal and cleaned the house, surprising her
   (D)   Liz found a warm, delicious meal and a clean house surprising her from her family
   (E)   a warm, delicious meal and a clean house surprised Liz, courtesy of her family

10. An increasing number of students are coming to realize that an education at a public university can be <u>as good, if not better, than an elite private college</u>.

   (A)   as good, if not better, than an elite private college
   (B)   as good, if not better, as one at an elite private college
   (C)   as good as, if not better, than an elite private college education
   (D)   as good an education as, if not better, than one at an elite private college
   (E)   as good as, if not better than, one at an elite private college

GO ON TO THE NEXT PAGE ▷

4　　**4**　　　**4**　　　　**4**　　　　**4**　　　　**4**

11. S. J. Perelman, whose hallmark of a grandilo-
    quent writing style is widely regarded as one of
    the finest American wits of all time.

    (A) S. J. Perelman, whose hallmark of a
        grandiloquent writing style is
    (B) Being that his hallmark is a grandilo-
        quent writing style, S. J. Perelman is
    (C) S. J. Perelman's grandiloquent writing
        style is his hallmark and is
    (D) S. J. Perelman and his hallmark of a
        grandiloquent writing style are
    (E) S. J. Perelman, whose hallmark is a
        grandiloquent writing style, is

The following sentences test your ability to recognize grammar and usage errors. Each sentence contains either a single error or no error
at all. No sentence contains more than one
error. The error, if there is one, is underlined
and lettered. If the sentence contains an error,
select the one underlined part that must be
changed to make the sentence correct. If the
sentence is correct, select choice E. In choosing answers, follow the requirements of standard written English.

EXAMPLE:

By the time they reached the halfway point
                  A
in the race, most of the runners hadn't hardly
     B   C   D
begun to hit their stride.   No error
                               E

Ⓐ Ⓑ Ⓒ ● Ⓔ

---

12. The lack of progress

    in international relations reveals that
              A   B
    governments must study the art of
                     C
    diplomacy much closer.   No error
                  D   E

13. Because Deborah has been a representative
                        A
    for over 20 years and also her popularity
                            B
    among her constituents, few are willing
              C
    to challenge her in an election.   No error
        D   E

14. Caravaggio demonstrated the great range
                  A
    of his artistic talent in such paintings as
           B   C
    "Bacchus" and "Basket of Fruit," painted in

    1593 and 1596, respectfully.   No error
                     D   E

15. Grizzly bears rarely show aggression toward
                  A
    humans, but they will protect their territory
       B
    from anyone whom they
       C
    would have considered to be a threat.
              D
    No error
       E

GO ON TO THE NEXT PAGE ⟹

4   4   4   4   4   4

16. The choir's rendition of "America the

Beautiful" was stirring, particularly after the
               A

children had finished their presentation on
          B   C

the meaning of freedom.   No error
      D   E

17. Andre suggested to the board that both the
                        A

fund deficit and the disillusionment of the
                          B

investors were a problem that
                  C

had to be addressed immediately.
        D

No error
    E

18. Because Phillips reasoned that either

accepting or rejecting the proposal were
    A   B

going to upset some political faction,
                          C

he decided to delay the vote until

after his reelection.   No error
        D   E

19. The Attorney General spoke at length about
                            A

the detrimental effects of having less
                  B   C

defense attorneys to serve indigent
                      D

defendants.   No error
                    E

20. The service at Centro is much better than
                A

the other restaurants we frequent, so
          B

we prefer to go there when
      C

we are entertaining guests.   No error
        D   E

21. Before the curtain rose, Anthony wished
                      A

that he were back in bed, only dreaming
        B   C

about performing in front of

hundreds of strangers rather than actually
          D

doing it.   No error
                  E

22. James, like many parents, believes that if a
                            A

child can read at a very young age, they will
                  B   C

grow to have exceptional literary talent.
                  D

No error
    E

23. The decline of the Enlightenment
        A

was hastened not only by tyrants but also
    B

because of intellectual opposition.   No error
    C   D   E

GO ON TO THE NEXT PAGE ⟶

4   4   4   4   4   4

24. Although he pitched <u>professionally</u> for 3
                        A
    decades, Nolan Ryan <u>never lost</u> any velocity
                        B
    on his fastball, and few <u>maintained</u> such
                            C
    <u>control over</u> so many pitches as he.
    D
    <u>No error</u>
    E

25. The Senator and his <u>opponent</u>, Thomas
                        A
    Cowher, were running a very tight race until

    <u>he</u> made a <u>racially insensitive</u> comment that
    B   C
    <u>offended</u> many voters.   <u>No error</u>
    D   E

26. Just when <u>those who</u> were observing
                A
    the heart transplant procedure assumed

    <u>the worst</u>, the surgeons themselves <u>are</u> <u>most</u>
    B   C   D
    confident.   <u>No error</u>
                 E

27. <u>Although</u> testing <u>for unsafe</u> levels of
    A   B
    asbestos particles is widely <u>advocated for</u>
                                 C
    houses <u>built before</u> 1950, many home
           D
    owners ignore this suggestion.   <u>No error</u>
                                     E

28. Between my brother <u>and I</u> <u>existed</u> a strong
                       A   B
    bond that did not weaken even <u>when</u> he
                                  C
    chose to live <u>thousands of miles</u> away on a
                  D
    different continent.   <u>No error</u>
                           E

29. <u>Writing about</u> the folk duo, *The Indigo Girls*,
    A
    one critic <u>has suggested</u> that <u>their</u> longevity
               B   C
    is <u>due to</u> its ability to remain faithful to an
       D
    honest musical style while stretching the

    boundaries of convention.   <u>No error</u>
                                 E

GO ON TO THE NEXT PAGE ⟹

4   4   4   4   4   4

Directions: The following passage is an early draft of an essay. Some parts of the passage need to be rewritten.

Read the passage and select the best answers for the questions that follow. Some questions are about particular sentences or parts of sentences and ask you to improve sentence structure or word choice. Other questions ask you to consider organization and development. In choosing answers, follow the requirements of standard written English.

Questions 30–35 refer to the following passage.

(1) For thousands of years, philosophers have debated whether humans discover mathematics or it is something that has been invented. (2) Plato believed that perceived mathematical objects like lines were only vague shadows of abstract "ideals" that exist outside of human experience. (3) Circular objects or circles drawn on paper aren't "really" circles. (4) Rather, they are just a flawed approximation of the perfect circular form. (5) So, in this sense, Plato believed that mathematics was something revealed imperfectly to humans, not invented by them. (6) Many students surely wish that mathematics had not been invented at all. (7) A position that opposes Plato's idealism is called mathematical intuitionism, which is the belief that all mathematics is the product of human minds.

(8) There is one good way to understand the difference between idealism and intuitionism. (9) Look at big numbers. (10) An idealist would say that all numbers, no matter how large, truly exist, even if no one has ever actually calculated them. (11) An intuitionist, on the other hand, might say that some numbers may be so big that they are physically impossible to calculate or express in a meaningful way, and so do not truly "exist."

(12) Another point of view that is different from these ones is one that says that it is a pointless thing to ask the question as to whether mathematical objects "really exist" or not. (13) This view simply regards mathematics as a tool for interpreting information from the world around us. (14) This view is essentially a compromise between idealism and intuitionism. (15) Although it acknowledges that mathematics reaches beyond the mind of a mathematician, it also denies that it has any meaning outside of the mind. (16) The concept of a circle is not a reflection of an abstract "ideal," and also it is not completely a human invention. (17) Instead it is a concept that we form in our minds after perceiving and thinking about many circular objects in the world around us.

30. Which of the following is the best revision of the underlined portion of sentence 1 (reproduced below)?

For thousands of years, philosophers have debated whether humans discover mathematics or it is something that has been invented.

(A) humans discover mathematics or invent it
(B) humans so much discover mathematics as they do invent it
(C) the discovery of mathematics is what humans do or the invention
(D) humans discover mathematics or if it is invented
(E) mathematics is something discovered or if humans invent it

31. In context, which of the following is the most logical revision of the underlined portion of sentence 3 (reproduced below)?

Circular objects or circles drawn on paper aren't "really" circles.

(A) Nevertheless, circular objects
(B) According to his reasoning, circular objects
(C) Furthermore, circular objects
(D) Secondly, circular objects
(E) All the while, circular objects

GO ON TO THE NEXT PAGE ▷

4   **4**   **4**   **4**   **4**   **4**

32. Which of the following is the best revision of sentence 4 (reproduced below)?

    Rather, they are just a flawed approximation of the perfect circular form.

    (A) But instead they are only a flawed approximation of the perfect circular form.
    (B) Rather, they are only flawed approximations of the perfect circular form.
    (C) Rather, their forms are merely an approximation of circular perfection alone.
    (D) Instead, their approximation of the perfect circular form mentioned above is imperfect.
    (E) Rather, their perfection as circular forms is only an approximation of it.

33. Which of the following sentences contributes least to the unity of the first paragraph?

    (A) Sentence 3
    (B) Sentence 4
    (C) Sentence 5
    (D) Sentence 6
    (E) Sentence 7

34. Which of the following is the best way to combine sentences 8 and 9 (reproduced below)?

    There is one good way to understand the difference between idealism and intuitionism. Look at big numbers.

    (A) One good way to understand the difference between idealism and intuitionism is the following: look at large numbers.
    (B) It is a good way to understand the difference between idealism and intuitionism in considering large numbers.
    (C) The consideration of large numbers provides one good way toward the understanding of the difference between idealism and intuitionism.
    (D) To consider large numbers is to have one good way of understanding the difference between idealism and intuitionism.
    (E) One good way to understand the difference between idealism and intuitionism is to consider large numbers.

35. In context, which of the following is the best revision of sentence 12 (reproduced below)?

    Another point of view that is different from these ones is one that says that it is a pointless thing to ask the question as to whether mathematical objects "really exist" or not.

    (A) A third point of view regards it as pointless to ask whether mathematical objects "really exist."
    (B) Another, completely different, point of view is the one that regards asking whether or not mathematical objects "really exist" as pointless.
    (C) Asking whether mathematical objects "really exist" is pointless, according to another, third, different point of view.
    (D) The asking of whether mathematical objects "really exist" is a pointless thing, says a third point of view.
    (E) Another different point of view says it is pointless to ask about whether mathematical objects "really exist" or not.

STOP

If you finish before time is called, you may check your work on this section only. Do not turn to any other section of the test.

5 5 5 5 5 5

SECTION 5
Time—25 minutes
18 questions

| Turn to Section 5 of your answer sheet to answer the questions in this section. |

Directions: This section contains two types of questions. You have 25 minutes to complete both types. For questions 1–8, solve each problem and decide which is the best of the choices given. Fill in the corresponding circle on the answer sheet. You may use any available space for scratchwork.

Notes

1. The use of a calculator is permitted.

2. All numbers used are real numbers.

3. Figures that accompany problems in this test are intended to provide information useful in solving the problems. They are drawn as accurately as possible EXCEPT when it is stated in a specific problem that the figure is not drawn to scale. All figures lie in a plane unless otherwise indicated.

4. Unless otherwise specified, the domain of any function f is assumed to be the set of all real numbers x for which $f(x)$ is a real number.

Reference Information

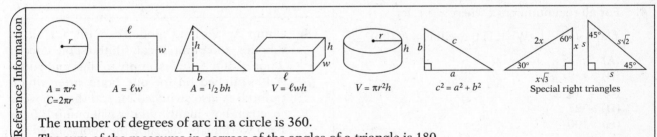

$A = \pi r^2$ $A = \ell w$ $A = \frac{1}{2}bh$ $V = \ell wh$ $V = \pi r^2 h$ $c^2 = a^2 + b^2$ Special right triangles
$C = 2\pi r$

The number of degrees of arc in a circle is 360.
The sum of the measures in degrees of the angles of a triangle is 180.

---

1. If $2x = 10$ and $3y = 12$, then $4x + 6y =$

(A) 10
(B) 12
(C) 22
(D) 32
(E) 44

2. The average (arithmetic mean) of three numbers is 5. If one of the numbers is 4, what is the sum of the other two numbers?

(A) 8
(B) 9
(C) 10
(D) 11
(E) 12

GO ON TO THE NEXT PAGE

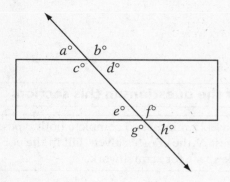

3. The figure above shows a rectangle intersected by a line. If $b = 2a$, then $d + e + g + h =$

(A)   120
(B)   240
(C)   300
(D)   320
(E)   360

4. For all real numbers x where $x \geq 1$, let $f(x) = \sqrt{\sqrt{x} - 1}$. What is the value of $f(100)$?

(A)   3
(B)   9
(C)   10
(D)   27
(E)   100

5. If $3^{k+m} = 243$ and $2^m = 8$, then what is the value of 2^k?

(A)   2
(B)   4
(C)   6
(D)   8
(E)   10

6. If b varies inversely as the square of c, and if $b = 8$ when $c = 3$, then what could be the value of c when $b = 2$?

(A)   2
(B)   5
(C)   6
(D)   25
(E)   36

7. In a certain soccer league, each of the five teams plays every other team in the league exactly three times each season. How many games are played in total in one season?

(A)   15
(B)   24
(C)   30
(D)   60
(E)   120

8. Pump A, working alone, can fill a tank in 3 hours, and pump B can fill the same tank in 2 hours. If the tank is empty to start and pump A is switched on for one hour, after which pump B is also switched on and the two work together, how many *minutes* will pump B have been working by the time the pool is filled?

(A)   48
(B)   50
(C)   54
(D)   60
(E)   64

GO ON TO THE NEXT PAGE

5 5 5 5 5 **5**

Directions: For student-produced response questions 9–18, use the grids at the bottom of the answer sheet page on which you have answered questions 1–8.

Each of the remaining ten questions requires you to solve the problem and enter your answer by marking the circles in the special grid, as shown in the examples below. You may use any available space for scratchwork.

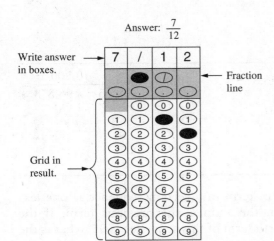

Answer: $\frac{7}{12}$

Write answer in boxes. → Fraction line

Grid in result. →

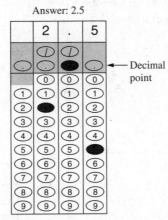

Answer: 2.5

Decimal point

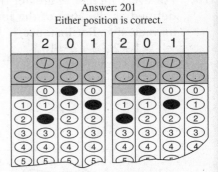

Answer: 201
Either position is correct.

<u>Note:</u> You may start your answers in any column, space permitting. Columns not needed should be left blank.

- Mark no more than one circle in any column.

- Because the answer sheet will be machine-scored, **you will receive credit only if the circles are filled in correctly.**

- Although not required, it is suggested that you write your answer in the boxes at the top of the columns to help you fill in the circles accurately.

- Some problems may have more than one correct answer. In such cases, grid only one answer.

- No question has a negative answer.

- **Mixed numbers** such as $3\frac{1}{2}$ must be gridded as

  3.5 or 7/2. (If ⒊① / ② is gridded, it will be

  interpreted as $\frac{31}{2}$ not $3\frac{1}{2}$.)

- **Decimal Answers:** If you obtain a decimal answer with more digits than the grid can accommodate, it may be either rounded or truncated, but it must fill the entire grid. For example, if you obtain an answer such as 0.6666..., you should record your result as .666 or .667. **A less accurate value such as .66 or .67 will be scored as incorrect.**

Acceptable ways to grid $^2/_3$ are:

GO ON TO THE NEXT PAGE ▷

5   5   5   5   5   5

9. If four times a certain number is decreased by 5, the result is 25. What is the number?

10. For every integer m greater than 1, let «m» be defined as the sum of the integers from 1 to m, inclusive. For instance,
«4» = 1 + 2 + 3 + 4 = 10.
What is the value of «7» − «5»?

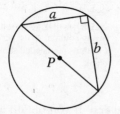

11. If the circumference of the circle above is 10π, then what is the value of $a^2 + b^2$?

A, B, C, D

12. How many different three-letter arrangements of the letters above are possible if no letter may be repeated? (An arrangement like *ABC* is distinct from an arrangement like *BCA*.)

13. If $96{,}878 \times x^2 = 10{,}200$, then $\dfrac{10{,}200}{5x^2 \times 96{,}878} =$

14. Every term in a certain sequence is one less than three times the previous term. If the fourth term of this sequence is 95, what is the first term of the sequence?

GO ON TO THE NEXT PAGE

15. If $4 + \sqrt{b} = 7.2$, what is the value of $4 - \sqrt{b}$?

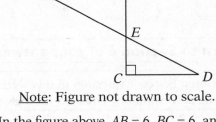

Note: Figure not drawn to scale.

16. Admission to a museum is $10 for each adult and $5 for each child. If a group of 30 people pays a total of $175 in admission, how many adults are in the group?

18. In the figure above, $AB = 6$, $BC = 6$, and $CD = 2$. What is AD?

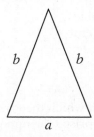

17. The perimeter of the isosceles triangle above is 24. If the ratio of a to b is 2 to 3, what is the value of b?

STOP

If you finish before time is called, you may check your work on this section only. Do not turn to any other section of the test.

6   **6**   **6**   **6**   **6**   **6**

SECTION 6
Time—25 minutes
24 questions

Turn to Section 6 of your answer sheet to answer the questions in this section.

Directions: For each question in this section, select the best answer from among the choices given and fill in the corresponding circle on the answer sheet.

Each sentence below has one or two blanks, each blank indicating that something has been omitted. Beneath the sentence are five words or sets of words labeled A through E. Choose the word or set of words that, when inserted in the sentence, best fits the meaning of the sentence as a whole.

EXAMPLE:

Rather than accepting the theory unquestioningly, Deborah regarded it with -----.

(A) mirth
(B) sadness
(C) responsibility
(D) ignorance
(E) skepticism

2. The long-standing divisions among the indigenous ethnic groups in the region have created an ------- problem that may never be solved without international intervention.

(A) impotent
(B) intractable
(C) evanescent
(D) irate
(E) insipid

3. The ease with which the army's defenses were breached surprised the opposing general, who expected resistance to be far more ------- than it was.

(A) ephemeral
(B) compatible
(C) egregious
(D) tolerable
(E) imposing

1. The strange signal detected by the radio telescope, rather than being taken as evidence of a new cosmological phenomenon, was instead treated as merely ------- of the equipment itself.

(A) a malfunction
(B) a bulwark
(C) an anthology
(D) a mutation
(E) a transfer

4. Although dependence on electronic devices has ------- in recent years, the increased efficiency of common appliances has ------- the demand on the power grid.

(A) abated . . decreased
(B) surged . . attenuated
(C) increased . . compromised
(D) diminished . . reduced
(E) flourished . . elevated

GO ON TO THE NEXT PAGE

5. Although persecution at the hands of ------- landowners vanquished the will of many, it ------- the dreams of revolution among the hardier insurgents.

(A) despotic . . squandered
(B) cruel . . destroyed
(C) amenable . . bore
(D) celebrated . . initiated
(E) ruthless . . forged

The passages below are followed by questions based on their content; questions following a pair of related passages may also be based on the relationship between the paired passages. Answer the questions on the basis of what is <u>stated</u> or <u>implied</u> in the passage and in any introductory material that may be provided.

Questions 6–9 are based on the following passages.

PASSAGE 1

The following is from a recent commentary on Jean-Jacques Rousseau (1712–1778), a French philosopher during the Enlightenment.

Taken as a whole, Rousseau's writings attacked the Age of Reason, gave impetus to the
Line Romantic movement by emphasizing feeling (leading Goethe to say that "feeling is all"),
5 revived religion even though he had doubts about some traditional teachings, provided a new direction for education (his book *Émile* was considered by some the best work on education since Plato's *Republic*), inspired the
10 French Revolution, made a unique impact on political philosophy, and, more than the writing of any of his contemporaries, influenced several subsequent philosophers, especially Immanuel Kant. On one occasion, Kant was
15 so absorbed in reading Rousseau's *Émile* that he forgot to take his celebrated daily walk. While Kant admitted that it was David Hume who awakened him from his dogmatic slumbers regarding the theory of knowledge, it was
20 Rousseau who showed him the way to a new

First passage: from "Rousseau: A Romantic in the Age of Reason," from *Socrates to Sartre*, McGraw-Hill, 1999, p. 278
Second passage: Copyright 2005 Christopher Black. All rights reserved.

theory of morality. So impressed was Kant by the insights of Rousseau that he hung a picture of him on the wall of his study, convinced that Rousseau was the Newton of the moral world.

PASSAGE 2

25 The roses we lay at Rousseau's feet for this theory of Natural Rights tend to overwhelm the less fragrant of his ideas. He persisted in believing in the nobility of the primitive state of nature, and that women's nature was to serve
30 men. His assertions about Natural Rights of Man laid the philosophical foundation of American independence, but his worship of emotion over reason and of "negative education" gave generations of parents permission to
35 ignore the need to discipline and teach their children.

6. Passage 1 suggests that Goethe

(A) was at the forefront of the Age of Reason
(B) was a traditionalist
(C) was influenced by Rousseau
(D) opposed the Romantic movement
(E) inspired much of Rousseau's work

7. Passage 1 mentions Kant's "daily walk" (line 16) in order to emphasize

(A) Kant's forgetfulness
(B) Kant's commitment to healthful practices
(C) the dogmatic nature of Rousseau's writings
(D) the effect of Rousseau's philosophy on Kant
(E) Kant's close friendship with Rousseau

8. Unlike Passage 1, Passage 2 characterizes Rousseau's emphasis on emotion as

(A) insincere
(B) innovative
(C) harmful
(D) temporary
(E) necessary

GO ON TO THE NEXT PAGE →

6   6   6   6   6   6

9. Both passages credit Rousseau with

    (A) attacking the Age of Reason
    (B) inspiring revolutionary thought
    (C) encouraging discipline
    (D) praising the primitive state of nature
    (E) establishing the Romantic movement

Questions 10–16 are based on the following passage.

The following passage was written by an American essayist in 2003 about the status of capitalism.

In response to a journalist's question, "What do you think about Western civilization?"
Line Mahatma Gandhi is said to have replied, "It would be a good idea." Any honest person
5 who values the concept of the free market, who believes in the promise of open economic competition, would say the same thing about capitalism. We hear our politicians, and of course the corporate news and entertainment
10 media, speaking as if the United States were a model of free-market capitalism, as if anyone could start a business to create and sell a product or service without the obstruction of the government. The truth is quite different.
15 Those we hear saying such things are quite often voices that are bankrolled by large corporations, which themselves are often protected from competition by mutual agreement with the federal government.
20   The concept of free trade is simple: if Company A can produce and distribute a product more efficiently and at a higher quality than Company B, it should be allowed to do so, and to charge any price for it that free consumers
25 are willing to pay. Although Company B would likely suffer as a result, humanity would benefit from freer and cheaper access to high-quality goods. Sometimes free trade works nicely, as when Company A is in the United States and
30 Company B is in India. Then, agreements are signed to "open up" India to the cheaper goods made by Company A, even if doing so crushes Company B because, we say, consumers have a right to cheap, high-quality goods. But if Com-
35 pany A were in India and Company B were in the United States, the story would likely be very different.

This isn't an idle example. India developed a pharmaceutical industry many years ago
40 that could produce drugs very cheaply that would have saved tens of thousands of lives each year. In a free-market economy, the Indian pharmaceutical industry would have been allowed to make drugs and get them to the
45 people who needed them. But that would mean that western pharmaceutical companies would make less profit. Of course, it's not that the American pharmaceutical companies don't care about Indian children dying be-
50 cause they can't get drugs; it's just that their responsibility is to their stockholders. They must maximize profits. But the "free market" was getting in the way, so they simply changed the rules.
55   Thus, in 1994 India "agreed" (that is, gave in to Western pressure) to "liberalize" its pharmaceutical industry by allowing its largest drug companies to be sold to Western interests, thereby reducing competition.
60 Drug prices predictably shot up, putting them out of reach of people who needed them, but the Western corporations made more money. It was a big triumph for the "liberalization" of markets, but a great blow
65 to free markets.
       In a free economy, businesses are also expected to wager their own capital on success in the marketplace. The adventurous entrepreneur is a moral icon in the United States.
70 The American pharmaceutical industry, however, receives over half a billion dollars annually in federal tax dollars in the form of research grants to develop medications and vaccines that they can then patent and sell
75 back to consumers at monopolistic prices. The legislators who sponsor these grants know that their campaigns will likely receive reciprocal monetary benefit as a result. What is worse, most American voters accept this sys-
80 tem happily because they believe that they are simply helping to find cures for diseases. The reality, however, is very different: by discouraging the competition that leads to real progress, this system of protectionism is actually a huge
85 impediment to the elimination of disease.

GO ON TO THE NEXT PAGE ▷

6 6 6 6 6 6

10. The quotation from Mahatma Gandhi (lines 3–4) suggests that Gandhi believed that Western civilization was

(A) on the decline
(B) the beneficiary of unfair economic practices
(C) antithetical to progress in Asia
(D) a great triumph
(E) an unrealized concept

11. The "voices" mentioned in line 16 can be inferred to include all of the following EXCEPT

(A) American politicians
(B) leaders like Mahatma Gandhi
(C) television journalists
(D) some leaders of large corporations
(E) those who believe that the United States is faithful to the capitalist ideal

12. The primary function of the second paragraph (lines 20–37) is to

(A) illustrate a debate
(B) provide a statistical analysis
(C) explain a concept
(D) give historical background
(E) describe a popular viewpoint

13. By saying that "the story would likely be very different" (lines 36–37), the passage suggests that

(A) the rules of a free market are selectively applied
(B) trade laws favor smaller countries
(C) American companies produce the best products
(D) Asian countries are moving away from the free market
(E) American companies share the same interests as Indian companies

14. The quotation marks around particular words in the fourth paragraph (lines 55–65) serve primarily to indicate that those words are

(A) being used ironically
(B) technical economic terms
(C) adaptations of foreign words
(D) recently coined
(E) direct quotations from a document described earlier

15. The "triumph" described in line 63 is characterized as

(A) a rare success for free markets
(B) a legislative victory
(C) a breakthrough in the development of inexpensive drugs
(D) a tragic violation of the principle of free trade
(E) a success that was based on luck

16. The passage suggests that the "entrepreneur" (lines 68–69) differs from executives in the pharmaceutical industry in that the entrepreneur

(A) does not abide by free-market ideals
(B) risks his or her own money
(C) does not hire employees from overseas
(D) works more closely with representatives in Washington
(E) needs less money to start a typical business

GO ON TO THE NEXT PAGE ⟹

6   **6**   6   6   6   **6**

Questions 17–24 are based on the following passage.

The following passage is an excerpt from Mary Shelley's Frankenstein, *written in 1831.*

Natural philosophy, and particularly chemistry, became nearly my sole occupation.
Line I read with ardor those works, so full of genius
and discrimination, that modern inquirers
5   have written on these subjects. I attended the
lectures and cultivated the acquaintance of
the men of science of the university. In
M. Waldman I found a true friend. His gentle-
ness was never tinged by dogmatism, and his
10   instructions were given with an air of frank-
ness and good nature that banished every idea
of pedantry. In a thousand ways he smoothed
for me the path of knowledge and made the
most abstruse inquiries clear and facile to my
15   apprehension.
    As I applied so closely, it may be easily
conceived that my progress was rapid. My
ardor was indeed the astonishment of the
students, and my proficiency that of the mas-
20   ters. None but those who have experienced
them can conceive of the enticements of science. A mind of moderate capacity which
closely pursues one study must infallibly arrive at great proficiency in that study; and I,
25   who continually sought the attainment of
one object of pursuit and was solely wrapped
up in this, improved so rapidly that at the
end of two years I made some discoveries in
the improvement of some chemical instru-
30   ments, which procured me great esteem and
admiration at the university. When I had
arrived at this point and had become as well
acquainted with the theory and practice of
natural philosophy as depended on the
35   lessons of any of the professors at Ingolstadt,
my residence there being no longer con-
ducive to my improvements, I thought of
returning to my friends and my native town,
when an incident happened that protracted
40   my stay.
    Whence, I often asked myself, did the prin-
ciple of life proceed? It was a bold question,
and one which has never been considered as a
mystery; yet with how many things are we
45   upon the brink of becoming acquainted, if

cowardice or carelessness did not restrain our
inquiries. I revolved these circumstances in
my mind and determined thenceforth to apply
myself more particularly to those branches of
50   natural philosophy which relate to physiology.
Unless I had been animated by an almost supernatural enthusiasm, my application to this
study would have been irksome and almost intolerable. To examine the causes of life, we
55   must first have recourse to death. I became acquainted with the science of anatomy, but this
was not sufficient; I must also observe the natural decay and corruption of the human body.
In my education my father had taken the
60   greatest precautions that my mind should be
impressed with no supernatural horrors. I do
not ever remember to have trembled at a tale
of superstition or to have feared the apparition of a spirit. Darkness had no effect upon
65   my fancy, and a churchyard was to me merely
the receptacle of bodies deprived of life,
which, from being the seat of beauty and
strength, had become food for the worm. I
saw how the fine form of man was degraded
70   and wasted; I beheld the corruption of death
succeed to the blooming cheek of life; I saw
how the worm inherited the wonders of the
eye and brain. I paused, examining and analyzing all the minutiae of causation, as exem-
75   plified in the change from life to death, and
death to life, until from the midst of this darkness a sudden light broke in upon me—a light
so brilliant and wondrous, yet so simple, that
while I became dizzy with the immensity of
80   the prospect which it illustrated, I was surprised that among so many men of genius
who had directed their inquiries towards the
same science, that I alone should be reserved
to discover so astonishing a secret.

Excerpted from *Frankenstein* by Mary Shelley. Public domain.
  Edited for length

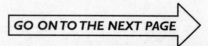

GO ON TO THE NEXT PAGE

6   6   6   6   6   6

---

17. In the first paragraph, the narrator indicates that the instruction given to him by M. Waldman was

    (A) haughty
    (B) challenging
    (C) easily understood
    (D) obscure
    (E) expensive

18. In line 15, the word "apprehension" most nearly means

    (A) fear
    (B) reservation
    (C) imprisonment
    (D) understanding
    (E) arrest

19. The narrator indicates that proficiency in an academic study requires which of the following?

    I.   genius
    II. diligence
    III. financial resources

    (A) I only
    (B) II only
    (C) I and II only
    (D) II and III only
    (E) I, II, and III

20. The narrator indicates that he considered leaving Ingolstadt because he

    (A) had learned all he could from its instructors
    (B) was acutely homesick
    (C) was offered another job
    (D) had a negative experience with a professor there
    (E) had become ill

21. In saying that he was "animated by an almost supernatural enthusiasm" (lines 51–52), the narrator suggests that he

    (A) was easily influenced by superstition
    (B) loved lecturing at Ingolstadt
    (C) was passionate about studying the physiology of life and death
    (D) was excited about the prospect of returning home
    (E) wanted to learn more about the origin of certain superstitions

22. The "seat of beauty and strength" (lines 67–68) is a reference to

    (A) the churchyard
    (B) the human body
    (C) the worm
    (D) the university at Ingolstadt
    (E) the narrator's studies

23. In line 71, the phrase "succeed to" most nearly means

    (A) inspire
    (B) thrive
    (C) replace
    (D) proceed to
    (E) promote

24. The final sentence of the passage suggests that the narrator feels

    (A) intimidated by the enormous task before him
    (B) grateful to those who instructed him
    (C) anxious about the moral dilemma posed by his work
    (D) baffled by particular scientific principles
    (E) privileged to be on the verge of a momentous discovery

STOP

If you finish before time is called, you may check your work on this section only. Do not turn to any other section of the test.

SECTION 7
Time—20 minutes
16 questions

Turn to Section 7 of your answer sheet to answer the questions in this section.

Directions: For this section, solve each problem and decide which is the best of the choices given. Fill in the corresponding circle on the answer sheet. You may use any available space for scratchwork.

Notes

1. The use of a calculator is permitted.

2. All numbers used are real numbers.

3. Figures that accompany problems in this test are intended to provide information useful in solving the problems. They are drawn as accurately as possible EXCEPT when it is stated in a specific problem that the figure is not drawn to scale. All figures lie in a plane unless otherwise indicated.

4. Unless otherwise specified, the domain of any function f is assumed to be the set of all real numbers x for which $f(x)$ is a real number.

Reference Information

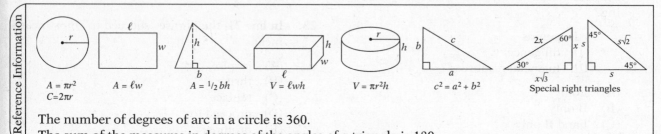

$A = \pi r^2$ $A = \ell w$ $A = \frac{1}{2}bh$ $V = \ell wh$ $V = \pi r^2 h$ $c^2 = a^2 + b^2$ Special right triangles
$C = 2\pi r$

The number of degrees of arc in a circle is 360.
The sum of the measures in degrees of the angles of a triangle is 180.

---

1. Which of the following integers is 2 greater than a multiple of 7?

   (A) 14
   (B) 15
   (C) 16
   (D) 17
   (E) 18

2. A store sells oranges for 20 cents each, but for every four oranges you buy, you may buy a fifth for only 5 cents. How many oranges can you buy from this store for $3.40?

   (A) 14
   (B) 17
   (C) 18
   (D) 19
   (E) 20

3. If r is a positive number and s is a negative number, all of the following must represent positive numbers EXCEPT

   (A) $-r + s$

   (B) $r - s$

   (C) $\dfrac{r}{s^2}$

   (D) rs^2

   (E) $(rs)^2$

---

4. Which of the following expresses the number that is 12 less than the product of 3 and $x + 1$?

(A) $x - 8$
(B) $x + 37$
(C) $3x - 11$
(D) $3x - 9$
(E) $3x + 15$

5. One bag of grass seed covers 5,000 square feet. If each bag costs $25, how much will it cost to buy enough grass seed to cover a square area that is 200 feet by 200 feet?

(A) $25
(B) $100
(C) $200
(D) $1,000
(E) $2,000

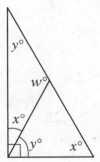

Note: Figure not drawn to scale.

6. In the right triangle above, what is the value of w?

(A) 30
(B) 60
(C) 90
(D) 120
(E) 150

7. Three integers have a sum of 7 and a product of 0. If the difference of the greatest number and the least number is 11, then the least of these numbers is

(A) −18
(B) −11
(C) −9
(D) −2
(E) 0

8. Four points lie on a circle. How many different triangles can be drawn with three of these points as vertices?

(A) 4
(B) 5
(C) 6
(D) 7
(E) 8

9. If a, b, and c are consecutive positive integers such that $a < b < c$ and abc is NOT a multiple of 4, then which of the following must be true?

(A) a is even
(B) b is even
(C) c is even
(D) $a + b + c$ is odd
(E) abc is odd

GO ON TO THE NEXT PAGE

7   **7**   **7**   **7**   **7**   **7**

Questions 10–12 refer to the following graph.

PARTICIPATION IN FUND-RAISER
FOR 5 CLASSES

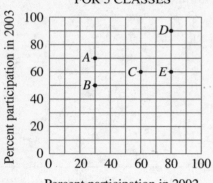

Percent participation in 2002

10. For which class was the change in percent participation the greatest from 2002 to 2003?

(A) A   (B) B   (C) C
(D) D   (E) E

11. If class *B* and class *E* each had 100 students in 2002 and 2003, then, in total, how many more students participated in the fund-raiser from class *E* than from class *B* over the 2 years?

(A) 10   (B) 20   (C) 30
(D) 40   (E) 60

12. In 2002, the same number of students participated in the fund-raiser from class *C* as from class *D*. If class *D* contained 120 students in 2002, how many students were there in class *C* in 2002?

(A) 90   (B) 100   (C) 120
(D) 140   (E) 160

13. If $x = -1$ is a solution of the equation $x^2 = 4x + c$ where c is a constant, what is another value of x that satisfies the equation?

(A) −5   (B) −2   (C) 1
(D) 2   (E) 5

$$1, 2, 6, 7, 9$$

14. A three-digit integer is to be formed from the digits listed above. If the first digit must be odd, either the second or the third digit must be 2, and no digit may be repeated, how many such integers are possible?

(A) 6   (B) 9   (C) 18
(D) 24   (E) 30

15. If one pound of grain can feed five chickens or two pigs, then ten pounds of grain can feed 20 chickens and how many pigs?

(A) 8   (B) 10   (C) 12
(D) 24   (E) 40

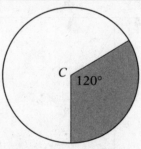

16. Point *C* is the center of the circle on the figure above. The shaded region has an area of 3π square centimeters. What is the *perimeter* of the shaded region in centimeters?

(A) $2\pi + 6$
(B) $2\pi + 9$
(C) $2\pi + 12$
(D) $3\pi + 6$
(E) $3\pi + 12$

*If you finish before time is called, you may
check your work on this section only. Do not
turn to any other section of the test.*

SECTION 8
Time—20 minutes
19 questions

Turn to Section 8 of your answer sheet to answer the questions in this section.

Directions: For each question in this section, select the best answer from among the choices given and fill in the corresponding circle on the answer sheet.

Each sentence below has one or two blanks, each blank indicating that something has been omitted. Beneath the sentence are five words or sets of words labeled A through E. Choose the word or set of words that, when inserted in the sentence, <u>best</u> fits the meaning of the sentence as a whole.

EXAMPLE:

Rather than accepting the theory unquestioningly, Deborah regarded it with ------.

(A) mirth
(B) sadness
(C) responsibility
(D) ignorance
(E) skepticism

1. The studio's most recent movies reflect a ------- of many different artistic visions rather than the ------- of a single director.

    (A) conglomeration . . insubordination
    (B) prudence . . unity
    (C) bastion . . despair
    (D) synthesis . . dominance
    (E) conspiracy . . retreat

2. Rather than endeavoring to write timeless fiction with lasting value, many novelists cater to the ------- tastes of those modern readers who read a book once and then discard it.

    (A) immoral
    (B) fleeting
    (C) valuable
    (D) solid
    (E) intellectual

3. Although many investors may tolerate short-term declines in the value of their securities, few will accept a ------- downturn in the stock market.

    (A) protracted
    (B) contemporaneous
    (C) transient
    (D) surreptitious
    (E) fickle

4. In most modern societies, athletes are ------- in the same way that successful warriors were celebrated by civilizations in years past.

    (A) invoked
    (B) repudiated
    (C) lionized
    (D) vilified
    (E) beguiled

GO ON TO THE NEXT PAGE

5. Dobson's overconfident and arrogant manner during press conferences was beginning to irritate his associates; there was no need to be ------- about the success of an endeavor that had yet to be launched.

(A) superficial
(B) capricious
(C) pious
(D) deferential
(E) supercilious

6. Although few literary critics approved of her criticism of the ------- society in which she lived, Virginia Woolf remained a ------- opponent of the male hegemony that hindered women's pursuit of professional and artistic success.

(A) matriarchal . . pugnacious
(B) patriarchal . . vociferous
(C) avuncular . . belligerent
(D) prejudiced . . rudimentary
(E) liberal . . negligent

The passages below are followed by questions based on their content. Answer the questions on the basis of what is <u>stated</u> or <u>implied</u> in the passage and in any introductory material that may be provided.

Questions 7–19 are based on the following passage.

The following are two essays on the American English spelling reform movement. Passage 1 was written in 1906 by the humorist Ellis Parker Butler. Passage 2 was written by a modern American writer in 2003.

Passage 1

My own opinion of the spelling profession is that it has nothing to do with genius, except to
Line　kill it. I know that Shakespeare was a promiscuous sort of speller, even as to his own name,
5　and no one can deny that he was a greater genius than Noah Webster. The reason America so long lagged behind Europe in the production of genius is that America, for many decades, was the slave of the spelling-book. No
10　man who devotes the fiery days of his youth to learning to spell has time to be a genius.

Serena says, and I agree with her, that it is the jealousy of a few college professors who are trying to undermine the younger writers.
15　They know that it is excusable to spell incorrectly now, but they want this new phonetic spelling brought into use so that there shall be no excuse for bad spelling, and that then, Serena says, self-made authors like me, who
20　never can spell but who simply blaze with genius, will be hooted out of the magazines to make room for a stupid sort of literature that is spelled correctly. Serena looks upon the whole thing as a direct, personal stab at me. I
25　look at it more philosophically.

To me it seems that the spelling reformers are entirely on the wrong track. Their proposed changes are almost a revolution, and we Americans do not like sudden changes. We
30　like our revolutions to come about gradually. Think how gradually automobiles have come to pass. If, in our horse age, the streets had suddenly been covered with sixty horsepower snorters going thirty miles an hour and
35　smelling like an eighteenth-century literary debate, and killing people right and left, we Americans would have arisen and destroyed every vestige of the automobile. But the automobile came gradually—first the bicycle, then
40　the motorcycle, and so, by stages, to the present monsters. So slowly and progressively did the automobile increase in size and number that it seemed a matter of course. We take to being killed by the automobile quite naturally
45　now.

Of course, the silent letters in our words are objectionable. They are lazy letters. We want no idle class in America, whether tramp, aristocrat, or silent letter, but we do not kill
50　the tramp and the aristocrat. We set them to work, or we would like to. My theory of spelling reform is to set the idle letters to work.

Take that prime offender, *although*. *Altho*
55　does all the work, and *ugh* sits on the fence and whittles. I would put *ugh* to work. *Ugh* is a syllable in itself. I would have the *ugh* follow

GO ON TO THE NEXT PAGE

the pronounced *altho* as a third syllable.
Doubtless the asthmatic islanders who con-
60 cocted our English language actually pronounced it so.

I propose to have some millionaire endow
my plan, and Serena and I will then form a society for the reforming of English pronuncia-
65 tion. I will not punch out the *i* of any chief,
nor shall any one drag *me* from any programme, however dull. I will pronounce
programme as it should be pronounced—
programmy—and, as for *chief*, he shall be
70 pronounced *chy-ef.*

The advantage of this plan is manifest. It is
so manifest that I am afraid it will never be
adopted.

Serena's plan is, perhaps, less intellectual,
75 but more American. Serena's plan is to ignore
all words that contain superfluous letters. She
would simply boycott them. Serena would
have people get along with such words as are
already phonetically spelled. Why should peo-
80 ple write *although,* when they can write
notwithstanding that, and not have a silent letter in it? I have myself often written a phrase
twelve words long to stand instead of a single
word I did not know how to spell. In fact, I
85 abandoned my Platonic friendship for Serena,
and replaced it with ardent love, because I did
know how to spell *sweetheart,* but could not
remember whether she was my *friend* or
freind.

PASSAGE 2
90 For centuries, thinkers as notable as Benjamin Franklin have registered the same complaint about English spelling: it is needlessly
complicated and inconsistent in pronunciation. Silent letters abound, and *ough* is pro-
95 nounced six different ways in the words
tough, bough, through, bought, although, and
cough. Franklin wanted to change the alphabet and institute new spelling rules to make
English more sensible, more usable, and eas-
100 ier to learn. Such good ideas have been
around a long time, and we should put them
to rest for three good reasons.

First, English, like most languages, has
dialects. In Boston, *Korea* and *career* are

105 homophones. In San Francisco, they are not.
To spell them the same way would be to impose a "preferred" dialect on all Americans,
forcing us all to talk like South Enders and violating our precious value of democracy over
110 elitism. Failure to do so would result in chaos.
Would a novelist from Alabama who was educated at Brown write in her native drawl, her
adopted New England dialect, or the homoge-
nized English of the educated elite? In a de-
115 mocratic society, isn't one of the great benefits
of a language-wide spelling system that it obscures those spoken dialects that are so often
used to stratify and separate us?

Second, languages evolve, adopting words
120 from other languages, coining new ones, and
changing pronunciations over time. The silent
letters in the word *eight,* a bane of the "rational" speller, are the echoes of the German
acht, the Latin *octo,* the Greek *okto* and even
125 (faintly) the Sanskrit *asta.* The spelling may be
vexing to some, but it is a historical treasure
trove to others. Furthermore, this example
shows the folly of trying to standardize
spelling by linking it with pronunciation. The
130 words won't stand still.

Third, languages are not influenced very
much by plan or reason; they develop by
evolving conventions of usage. They are cultural artifacts, not legislated standards.
135 Spelling is like football: there may be lots of
silly and illogical things in it, but that doesn't
mean you have a snowball's chance in hell of
replacing the rules.

GO ON TO THE NEXT PAGE ⟹

7. In the first paragraph of Passage 1, Noah Webster is mentioned as an example of

(A) a genius who was a poor speller
(B) one of the first spelling reformers
(C) a man devoted to proper spelling
(D) a famous playwright
(E) one who shares the author's opinion

8. Serena regards phonetic spelling as a "personal stab" (line 24) at the author of Passage 1 because its proponents

(A) have a history of vindictiveness
(B) do not like hard work
(C) are well educated
(D) are wealthy
(E) want to eliminate the author's excuse for poor spelling

9. The success of "Serena's plan" (line 74) depends on the ability of people to

(A) change their habits of pronunciation
(B) spell correctly
(C) perfect their handwriting skills
(D) learn an entirely new alphabet
(E) change their writing habits

10. By saying that Serena's plan is "more American" (line 75), the author of Passage 1 implies that Americans

(A) are good spellers
(B) regard writers with disdain
(C) are inclined to protest
(D) do not read enough
(E) can't take a joke

11. In Passage 1, the author's theory of spelling reform differs from that of Serena in that the author

(A) wants to alter the pronunciation of words that Serena wants to ignore
(B) regards Shakespeare as a genius but Serena does not
(C) wants to change the alphabet but Serena does not
(D) seeks to simplify spelling, while Serena does not
(E) understands how to alter American habits but Serena does not

12. The author of Passage 1 claims to have fallen in love with Serena because

(A) his spelling skills were weak
(B) they agreed on a plan for phonetic spelling
(C) she helped him to understand philosophy
(D) they shared a distaste for automobiles
(E) they were both writers

13. The "chaos" mentioned in line 110 refers to

(A) the difficulty of spelling words with silent letters
(B) the challenge of getting scholars to agree
(C) the many ways of pronouncing *ough*
(D) the possibility of many sets of spelling rules for different dialects
(E) the disagreement among linguists regarding spelling reform

GO ON TO THE NEXT PAGE ⟶

8   8   8   8   8   8

14. According to Passage 2, "one of the great benefits of a language-wide spelling system" (lines 115–116) is that it

   (A) simplifies commonly misspelled words
   (B) discourages social distinctions implied by pronunciation
   (C) eliminates silent letters
   (D) makes it easier to translate words from English to other languages
   (E) imposes a preferred dialect

15. Passage 2 mentions the word "eight" (line 122) as an example of

   (A) a word with a spelling that is edifying to some
   (B) a commonly mispronounced word
   (C) a word with a spelling that the author believes should be simplified
   (D) a recently coined term
   (E) a word that has remained unchanged for centuries

16. The tone of the two passages differs in that Passage 1 is

   (A) jocular, whereas Passage 2 is logical
   (B) cynical, whereas Passage 2 is whimsical
   (C) analytical, whereas Passage 2 is lighthearted
   (D) scientific, whereas Passage 2 is satirical
   (E) strident, whereas Passage 2 is reflective

17. With which of the following statements would the authors of both passages most likely agree?

   (A) The rules of English spelling need to be changed.
   (B) Modern conventions of grammar are illogical.
   (C) Americans are lazy.
   (D) Conventions of language are not easily changed.
   (E) Writers should read widely to perfect their craft.

18. If the author of Passage 1 were serious about his plan for reforming English pronunciation, the author of Passage 2 would likely regard that plan as

   (A) a necessary addition to phonetic spelling
   (B) a logical alternative to the current system
   (C) inferior to the plan for phonetic spelling
   (D) unworkable because it disregards the way that conventions of language develop
   (E) a more plausible plan than Serena's

19. In both passages, the word "although" is regarded as

   (A) a word that is commonly mispronounced
   (B) a word that is difficult to spell
   (C) an example of an idiosyncracy of English that some consider problematic
   (D) a word that reveals much about the development of the English language
   (E) a word that can easily be eliminated from the English language

STOP

If you finish before time is called, you may check your work on this section only. Do not turn to any other section of the test.

9   9   9   9   9   9

SECTION 9
Time—10 minutes
14 questions

Turn to Section 9 of your answer sheet to answer the questions in this section.

Directions: For each question in this section, select the best answer from among the choices given and fill in the corresponding circle on the answer sheet.

The following sentences test correctness and effectiveness of expression. Part of each sentence or the entire sentence is underlined; beneath each sentence are five ways of phrasing the underlined material. Choice A repeats the original phrasing; the other four choices are different. Select the choice that completes the sentence most effectively.

In making your selection, follow the requirements of standard written English; that is, pay attention to grammar, choice of words, sentence construction, and punctuation. Your selection should result in the most effective sentence—clear and precise, without awkwardness or ambiguity.

EXAMPLE:

The children couldn't hardly believe their eyes.

(A) couldn't hardly believe their eyes
(B) could hardly believe their eyes
(C) would not hardly believe their eyes
(D) couldn't nearly believe their eyes
(E) couldn't hardly believe his or her eyes

1. The chef's assistant cut the vegetables and laid them on the table, he then started to prepare the meat.

(A) The chef's assistant cut the vegetables and laid them on the table, he
(B) The vegetables were cut and laid on the table by the chef's assistant when he
(C) After cutting the vegetables and laying them on the table, the chef's assistant
(D) The chef's assistant, having cut the vegetables and laying them on the table,
(E) Laying on the table, the chef's assistant who cut the vegetables

2. Practicing their rebuttals ahead of time helps the forensics team members to become a better debater.

(A) helps the forensics team member to become a better debater
(B) helps forensic team members to become better debaters
(C) helping the forensics team members to become better debaters
(D) is helpful to the forensics team members who become better debaters
(E) the forensics team member becomes a better debater

GO ON TO THE NEXT PAGE ⟶

9 9 9 9 9 9

3. *Billy the Bobcat,* like other children's stories, have elements that can only be fully appreciated by adults.

(A) like other children's stories have
(B) like other children's stories, has
(C) a children's story, like others, has
(D) is like other stories for children in that they have
(E) like that of other children's stories, has also

4. Ernest Rutherford, a New Zealand scientist when measuring the charge and mass of alpha particles, discovered that they are virtually identical to the nuclei of helium atoms.

(A) a New Zealand scientist when measuring the charge and mass of alpha particles
(B) a New Zealand scientist who measured the charge and mass of alpha particles
(C) a New Zealand scientist which measured the charge and mass of alpha particles
(D) measuring the charge and mass of alpha particles, was a scientist when he
(E) being the one who measured the mass and charge of alpha particles as a scientist

5. Oxytocin is the hormone that triggers uterine contractions during labor, as well as the preliminary contractions known as Braxton Hicks.

(A) labor, as well as
(B) labor, as well as being the hormone that triggers
(C) labor, causing as well
(D) labor; and also causes
(E) labor; also causing

6. During the Clinton presidency, the U.S. enjoyed more than any time in its history peace and economic well being.

(A) the U.S. enjoyed more than any time in its history peace and economic well being
(B) the U.S. enjoying more than any other time in its history peace and economic well being
(C) more peace and economic well being was enjoyed by the U.S. than any other time
(D) economic peace and well being was enjoyed by the U.S. more so than any other time in the country's history
(E) the U.S. enjoyed more peace and economic well being than at any other time in its history

7. The final three months of the year tend to be profitable for technology companies because of increased consumer demand being around the holidays.

(A) because of increased consumer demand being around the holidays
(B) because of increasing consumer demand occurs around the holidays
(C) an increased consumer demand around the holidays makes it so
(D) because consumer demand increases around the holidays
(E) because the increased consumer demand is what occurs around the holidays

8. As his moviemaking career began to wane, Jerry Lewis remained in the public eye by hosting a variety show and on an annual telethon with benefits for the Muscular Dystrophy Association.

(A) on an annual telethon with benefits for the Muscular Dystrophy Association
(B) an annual telethon with benefits to the Muscular Dystrophy Association
(C) benefiting the Muscular Dystrophy Association with his annual telethon
(D) an annual telethon benefiting the Muscular Dystrophy Association
(E) the Muscular Dystrophy Association with an annual telethon

9. The development of bebop is attributed in large part to Dizzy Gillespie and also saxophonist Charlie Parker; and their unique styles helped to contribute to and typified the bebop sound.

(A) and their unique styles helped to contribute to and typified the bebop sound
(B) their unique styles contributed to and typified the bebop sound
(C) it was their unique styles that contributed to and were typifying the bebop sound
(D) but their unique styles helped contribute to the typical bebop sound
(E) the bebop sound was helped by the contributions of their unique styles and typified it

GO ON TO THE NEXT PAGE ⟹

9   9   9   9   9   9

10. Many critics believe that video games <u>are harmful to children that contain violent imagery</u>.

(A) are harmful to children that contain violent imagery

(B) containing violent imagery are harmful to children

(C) that contain violent imagery that harms children

(D) containing violent imagery that are harmful to children

(E) harmful to children containing violent imagery

11. Walking hand-in-hand along the boardwalk, <u>a vendor stopped the couple to try to sell them lemonade</u>.

(A) a vendor stopped the couple to try to sell them lemonade

(B) the couple was stopped by a vendor who tried to sell them lemonade

(C) trying to sell them lemonade, a vendor stopped the couple

(D) a vendor stopped the couple to try and sell them lemonade

(E) the couple having been stopped by the vendor who tried to sell them lemonade

12. Professor Peterson had just stepped into the classroom <u>and that was when he discovered</u> that several lab manuals were missing.

(A) and that was when he found out

(B) and then he discovered

(C) when he discovered

(D) after which he discovered

(E) discovering soon thereafter

13. Parents today spend more time working <u>than</u> 30 years ago.

(A) than

(B) than have

(C) than of the parents of

(D) than did parents

(E) than of the parents

14. The anthropologists would have considered their research a success <u>if they would have found a language that shares lexical elements with the Borneans they were studying</u>.

(A) if they would have found a language that shares lexical elements with the Borneans they were studying

(B) had they found a language that shares lexical elements with that of the Borneans they were studying

(C) if they found a language that shares lexical elements with the Borneans they were studying

(D) if they had found a language that shares lexical elements with the Borneans they were studying

(E) if they would have found a language that shares lexical elements with that of the Borneans they were studying

STOP

If you finish before time is called, you may check your work on this section only. Do not turn to any other section of the test.

ANSWER KEY

Critical Reading

	Section 3						Section 6						Section 8				
	COR. ANS.	DIFF. LEV.		COR. ANS.	DIFF. LEV.		COR. ANS.	DIFF. LEV.		COR. ANS.	DIFF. LEV.		COR. ANS.	DIFF. LEV.		COR. ANS.	DIFF. LEV.
1.	A	2	13.	C	4	1.	A	1	13.	A	3	1.	D	2	11.	A	4
2.	C	2	14.	A	3	2.	B	3	14.	A	4	2.	B	2	12.	A	3
3.	A	3	15.	D	3	3.	E	2	15.	D	3	3.	A	2	13.	D	2
4.	D	3	16.	B	4	4.	B	3	16.	B	4	4.	C	3	14.	B	3
5.	B	3	17.	A	4	5.	E	4	17.	C	3	5.	E	4	15.	A	4
6.	E	3	18.	A	5	6.	C	3	18.	D	5	6.	B	5	16.	A	3
7.	B	4	19.	D	3	7.	D	3	19.	B	4	7.	C	2	17.	D	3
8.	C	5	20.	C	3	8.	C	4	20.	A	3	8.	E	4	18.	D	3
9.	A	5	21.	B	3	9.	B	3	21.	C	2	9.	E	4	19.	C	4
10.	D	3	22.	E	3	10.	E	2	22.	B	3	10.	C	3			
11.	E	3	23.	C	4	11.	B	4	23.	C	4						
12.	B	4	24.	D	4	12.	C	3	24.	E	4						

Number correct   Number correct   Number correct

Number incorrect   Number incorrect   Number incorrect

Math

	Section 2						Section 5						Section 7				
	COR. ANS.	DIFF. LEV.		COR. ANS.	DIFF. LEV.	Multiple-Choice Questions			Student-produced Response questions				COR. ANS.	DIFF. LEV.		COR. ANS.	DIFF. LEV.
							COR. ANS.	DIFF. LEV.		COR. ANS.	DIFF. LEV.						
1.	E	1	11.	E	3	1.	E	1	9.	7.5	1	1.	C	1	9.	B	4
2.	B	2	12.	E	3	2.	D	2	10.	13	2	2.	E	2	10.	A	3
3.	E	2	13.	D	3	3.	C	3	11.	100	3	3.	A	2	11.	E	3
4.	D	2	14.	B	3	4.	A	4	12.	24	3	4.	D	2	12.	E	4
5.	C	3	15.	E	4	5.	B	3	13.	0.2 or	3	5.	C	2	13.	E	4
6.	D	2	16.	C	3	6.	C	3		1/5		6.	C	3	14.	C	4
7.	E	3	17.	C	4	7.	C	4	14.	4	4	7.	D	4	15.	C	4
8.	D	3	18.	C	4	8.	A	5	15.	0.8	3	8.	A	3	16.	A	5
9.	E	3	19.	E	5				16.	5	4						
10.	B	3	20.	C	5				17.	9	4						
									18.	10	5						

Number correct   Number correct   Number correct

Number incorrect   Number incorrect   Number correct   Number incorrect
                                          (9–18)

Writing

	Section 4										Section 9				
	COR. ANS.	DIFF. LEV.		COR. ANS.	DIFF. LEV.		COR. ANS.	DIFF. LEV.		COR. ANS.	DIFF. LEV.			COR. ANS.	DIFF. LEV.
1.	A	1	11.	E	4	21.	E	4				1.	C	1		
2.	E	1	12.	D	2	22.	C	3	31.	B	3	2.	B	2	11.	B	3
3.	B	2	13.	B	1	23.	C	3	32.	B	4	3.	B	2	12.	C	3
4.	C	3	14.	D	4	24.	E	3	33.	D	3	4.	B	2	13.	D	4
5.	D	2	15.	D	3	25.	B	3	34.	E	3	5.	A	3	14.	B	4
6.	C	2	16.	E	3	26.	C	3	35.	A	3	6.	E	2			
7.	A	4	17.	C	2	27.	E	4				7.	D	3			
8.	B	5	18.	B	3	28.	A	3				8.	D	3			
9.	B	4	19.	C	3	29.	C	4				9.	B	3			
10.	E	4	20.	B	4	30.	A	3				10.	B	3			

Number correct   Number correct

Number incorrect   Number incorrect

NOTE: Difficulty levels are estimates of question difficulty that range from 1 (easiest) to 5 (hardest).

SCORE CONVERSION TABLE

How to score your test

Use the answer key on the previous page to determine your raw score on each section. **Your raw score on each section except Section 5 is simply the number of correct answers minus ¼ of the number of wrong answers. On Section 5, your raw score is the sum of the number of correct answers for questions 1–18 minus ¼ of the number of wrong answers for questions 1–8.** Next, add the raw scores from Sections 3, 6, and 8 to get your Critical Reading raw score, add the raw scores from Sections 2, 5, and 7 to get your Math raw score, and add the raw scores from Sections 4 and 9 to get your Writing raw score.

Raw Critical Reading score: _____   Raw Math score: _____   Raw Writing score: _____

Use the table below to convert these to scaled scores.

Scaled scores: Critical Reading: _____   Math: _____   Writing: _____

Raw Score	Critical Reading Scaled Score	Math Scaled Score	Writing Scaled Score	Raw Score	Critical Reading Scaled Score	Math Scaled Score	Writing Scaled Score
67	800			32	520	570	610
66	800			31	510	560	600
65	790			30	510	550	580
64	780			29	500	540	570
63	770			28	490	530	560
62	750			27	490	520	550
61	740			26	480	510	540
60	730			25	480	500	530
59	720			24	470	490	520
58	700			23	460	480	510
57	690			22	460	480	500
56	680			21	450	470	490
55	670			20	440	460	480
54	660	800		19	440	450	470
53	650	800		18	430	450	460
52	650	780		17	420	440	450
51	640	760		16	420	430	440
50	630	740		15	410	420	440
49	620	730	800	14	400	410	430
48	620	710	800	13	400	410	420
47	610	710	800	12	390	400	410
46	600	700	790	11	380	390	400
45	600	690	780	10	370	380	390
44	590	680	760	9	360	370	380
43	590	670	740	8	350	360	380
42	580	660	730	7	340	350	370
41	570	650	710	6	330	340	360
40	570	640	700	5	320	330	350
39	560	630	690	4	310	320	340
38	550	620	670	3	300	310	320
37	550	620	660	2	280	290	310
36	540	610	650	1	270	280	300
35	540	600	640	0	250	260	280
34	530	590	630	−1	230	240	270
33	520	580	620	−2 or less	210	220	250

SCORE CONVERSION TABLE FOR WRITING COMPOSITE
[ESSAY + MULTIPLE CHOICE]

Calculate your Writing raw score as you did on the previous page and grade your essay from a 1 to a 6 according to the standards that follow in the detailed answer key.

Essay score: _____   Raw Writing score: _____

Use the table below to convert these to scaled scores.

Scaled score: Writing: _____

Raw Score	Essay Score 0	Essay Score 1	Essay Score 2	Essay Score 3	Essay Score 4	Essay Score 5	Essay Score 6
−2 or less	200	230	250	280	310	340	370
−1	210	240	260	290	320	360	380
0	230	260	280	300	340	370	400
1	240	270	290	320	350	380	410
2	250	280	300	330	360	390	420
3	260	290	310	340	370	400	430
4	270	300	320	350	380	410	440
5	280	310	330	360	390	420	450
6	290	320	340	360	400	430	460
7	290	330	340	370	410	440	470
8	300	330	350	380	410	450	470
9	310	340	360	390	420	450	480
10	320	350	370	390	430	460	490
11	320	360	370	400	440	470	500
12	330	360	380	410	440	470	500
13	340	370	390	420	450	480	510
14	350	380	390	420	460	490	520
15	350	380	400	430	460	500	530
16	360	390	410	440	470	500	530
17	370	400	420	440	480	510	540
18	380	410	420	450	490	520	550
19	380	410	430	460	490	530	560
20	390	420	440	470	500	530	560
21	400	430	450	480	510	540	570
22	410	440	460	480	520	550	580
23	420	450	470	490	530	560	590
24	420	460	470	500	540	570	600
25	430	460	480	510	540	580	610
26	440	470	490	520	550	590	610
27	450	480	500	530	560	590	620
28	460	490	510	540	570	600	630
29	470	500	520	550	580	610	640
30	480	510	530	560	590	620	650
31	490	520	540	560	600	630	660
32	500	530	550	570	610	640	670
33	510	540	550	580	620	650	680
34	510	550	560	590	630	660	690
35	520	560	570	600	640	670	700
36	530	560	580	610	650	680	710
37	540	570	590	620	660	690	720
38	550	580	600	630	670	700	730
39	560	600	610	640	680	710	740
40	580	610	620	650	690	720	750
41	590	620	640	660	700	730	760
42	600	630	650	680	710	740	770
43	610	640	660	690	720	750	780
44	620	660	670	700	740	770	800
45	640	670	690	720	750	780	800
46	650	690	700	730	770	800	800
47	670	700	720	750	780	800	800
48	680	720	730	760	800	800	800
49	680	720	730	760	800	800	800

Detailed Answer Key

Section 1

> Consider carefully the issue discussed in the following passage, then write an essay that answers the question posed in the assignment.
>
> > An entertainment-driven culture runs the risk of encouraging passivity among its citizens. If they can experience something vicariously through a movie, television show, or video game, why should they get involved with the activity itself? It's safer, after all, to watch someone scale a mountain than to do it yourself. The effect of this passivity, of course, is an apathetic frame of mind. We cease to care deeply about so many things because they are experienced, at best, second-hand.
>
> **Assignment:** **Is apathy a problem in today's society?** Write an essay in which you answer this question and discuss your point of view on this issue. Support your position logically with examples from literature, the arts, history, politics, science and technology, current events, or your experience or observation.

> The following essay received 12 points out of a possible 12, meaning that it demonstrates *clear and consistent competence* in that it
>
> - develops an insightful point of view on the topic
> - demonstrates exemplary critical thinking
> - uses effective examples, reasons, and other evidence to support its thesis
> - is consistently focused, coherent, and well organized
> - demonstrates skillful and effective use of language and sentence structure
> - is largely (but not necessarily completely) free of grammatical and usage errors

Every society seems to have platitudes about laziness, like "idle hands are the devil's workshop." This is because, to a society, the value of an individual is little more than his or her productivity. For many people, the worst kind of laziness is apathy, being too lazy to even care. But the fact is that we couldn't survive if we cared about everything that was worth caring about. We would go insane. Furthermore, those who complain about apathy are usually the great manipulators of the world, trying to blame others for their own failures.

Holden Caulfield seemed to be apathetic to his teachers at Pencey Prep. But he was far from apathetic; indeed, he probably cared too much. His brother's death and the suicide of a classmate affected him deeply, although he had trouble articulating his grief. He saw what the adults in his world seemed unable to see: the hypocrisy and meanness in the world. If he didn't get away from the things that the teachers and other adults wanted him to care about, he probably would have gone crazy. Indeed, those adults thought he was crazy, but to Holden, it was the hypocritical world that was mad. His desperation to protect himself

from the unbearable "phoniness" in the world led him, ironically, to often be phony himself. He hated his own hypocrisy, but he had to experience it to understand it. What others saw as apathy and cynicism was just his way of making it in the world.

Holden was quick to see that those who complained about his laziness and apathy were just the ones who wanted to control him because they couldn't control their own lives. Teachers too often assume that, if their students aren't "performing," they must be lazy and apathetic. "You're so smart. You would do well if you would just apply yourself." Teachers see this kind of comment as supporting, but it is supremely degrading, and it covers up the teachers' inability to inspire or even understand their students.

Some people even go so far as to assume that entire societies are lazy or apathetic, simply because they do not share their same sensibilities or "productivity," failing to see that productivity is often the product, not just of hard work, but of material and logistical advantage. I don't have to work as hard, for instance, to be "productive" as a teenager in rural China, because I have free access to a computer, the internet, a local library, and helpful adult professionals. The Chinese teenager might be far more intelligent, diligent and resourceful than I, but far less "productive."

Perhaps a sign of maturity and virtue in a society is the degree to which it values its citizens independently of their "productivity." Every human being desires to build a better world in his or her own way. Sometimes that way does not involve making more money, getting better grades, or doing what society has established as "productive."

The following essay received 8 points out of a possible 12, meaning that it demonstrates *adequate competence* in that it

- develops a point of view on the topic
- demonstrates some critical thinking, but perhaps not consistently
- uses some examples, reasons, and other evidence to support its thesis, but perhaps not adequately
- shows a general organization and focus but shows occasional lapses in this regard
- demonstrates adequate but occasionally inconsistent facility with language
- contains occasional errors in grammar, usage, and mechanics

---

The greatest danger to the modern world is not terrorists who have been indoctrinated into a twisted world view, but the masses of people who are indifferent to them, or even sympathize with them. "Live and let live," so many people say. "They have a right to their point of view that women are animals and that someone who speaks against their religion should have his tongue cut out. That is just their way of thinking." This apathy to the dangers of the world is even more dangerous than the terrorists themselves.

In Madrid, a band of Al Qaeda terrorists decided that it was a good idea, in March of 2004, to blow up 200 innocent commuters on a train so that they could influence the upcoming elections in Spain. They proclaimed that they love death more than westerners love life. They were hoping that the Spanish people would then be so frightened that they would elect a leader who would take Spain's troops out of Iraq, as Al Qaeda wished. And that is exactly what happened.

The people of Spain didn't care enough to realize that they were doing exactly what the terrorists were hoping they would do. The voters of Spain probably believed that they were making it less likely that the terrorists would strike again, but it was probably the exact opposite. The terrorists love to know that their violence scares people, and the Spanish people gave them what they wanted. Contrast this with the American response to terrorism: zero tolerance.

The worst evil occurs when good people do nothing. Millions of supposedly "good" German people sat on their hands as millions of "unwanted" Jews, gays and foreigners were slaughtered. Now, millions of people sit on their hands as religious fanatics look at the slaughter of innocent people as their ticket to paradise. It is unreasonable to believe that those with warped hatred of western cultures will stop their hatred and their evil deeds merely because they are appeased by weak governments.

The following essay received 4 points out of a possible 12, meaning that it demonstrates *some incompetence* in that it

- has a seriously limited point of view
- demonstrates weak critical thinking
- uses inappropriate or insufficient examples, reasons, and other evidence to support its thesis
- is poorly focused and organized and has serious problems with coherence
- demonstrates frequent problems with language and sentence structure
- contains errors in grammar and usage that seriously obscure the author's meaning

When people don't care about something, it's hard to get anything done. If a team has players that don't really want to play, for instance, it's almost impossible to get them to win a game, even if you're a master motivator. That's why it's so important to care about things and not have apathy.

If you don't care about something, also, it's just really difficult to be happy. You don't have anything to look forward to in life. Some people don't really care about school, and they just listen to their iPods and can't wait to hang out with their friends or play their XBoxes when they get home. College doesn't mean anything to them, and you can tell that they are miserable people. It's one thing to question your teachers and wonder whether the things you learn in school are relevant for your life, but it's entirely different to not even care about what you do in school even a little bit.

Research has shown that you can't really get anywhere without an education, so if you don't care about school you might as well not care about having any kind of successful life. If they would just find something important that they could care about, like a sport or a musical instrument or a job or something like that, then they might have something they could focus there life for, and have some positive purpose in life. Criminals probably come about because early on they didn't really learn to care about anything important, and that is the real tragedy. and foreigners were slaughtered. Now, millions of people sit on their hands as religious fanatics look at the slaughter of innocent people as their ticket to paradise. It is unreasonable to believe that those with warped hatred of western cultures will stop their hatred and their evil deeds merely because they are appeased by weak governments.

Section 2

1. **E** Just substitute 3 for x: $5x = 3x + y$
Substitute: $5(3) = 3(3) + y$
Simplify: $15 = 9 + y$
Subtract 9: $6 = y$

2. **B** To buy 48 batteries in packages of 24, you will need two packages, which will cost 2($12) = $24. To buy them in packages of 6, you will need eight packages, which will cost 8($4) = $32. Buying in packages of 24 will save $32 – $24 = $8.

3. **E** You can probably solve this one best by quickly graphing each point and just inspecting. Clearly, (5, 5) lies outside the region.

4. **D** Interpret the statement as an equation:
                              $(⅓)(2x) = 5$
Multiply by 2: $(⅔)(2x) = 10$
Multiply by 2: $(⅔)(4x) = 20$

5. **C** The smallest positive integer that is divisible by 12 and 16 is 48. If n is 48, the only factor among the choices is (C) 48.

6. **D** The sum of the angles in a triangle is 180°, so
                      $a + b + 40 = 180$
Subtract 40: $a + b = 140$
Add the given equation: $+ (a - b) = 10$
                               $2a = 150$
Divide by 2: $a = 75$

7. **E** Choose n = 1 as an example. Plugging this into the choices gives answers of (A) ½ (B) 3 (C) 3 (D) 1 (E) 2. The only even number here is (E) 2.

8. **D** Let c be the number of colas that Mike sold and r be the number of root beers. Since the total sold is 48, $c + r = 48$. Since he sold twice as many colas as root beers, $c = 2r$. Substituting this into the first equation gives
                      $2r + r = 48$
Simplify: $3r = 48$
Divide by 3: $r = 16$

9. **E** Pick two perfect squares for m and n, like 4 and 9. Plugging these in to the examples gives (A) 36 (B) 36 (C) 16 (D) 324 (E) −45. The only choice that is not a perfect square is (E) −45.

10. **B** One option is to solve each equation by plugging in 10 for a: $a + b = 10 + b = 9$
Subtract 10: $b = -1$
Second equation: $10 - c = 14$
Subtract 10: $- c = 4$
Divide by −1: $c = -4$
So $c - b = -4 - (-1) = -4 + 1 = -3$

11. **E** Since the average of four numbers is 8, the sum of those four numbers must be $8 \times 4 = 32$. Therefore $a + b + 10 + 4 = 32$. Subtracting 14 from both sides gives $a + b = 18$.

12. **E** Fill in the table above and to the left of the x by following the rule, like this:

0	1	2	3	4	5
1	2	4	7		
2	4	8	15		
3	7	15	x		
4					
5					

This shows that $x = 15 + 15 = 30$.

13. **D** To maximize c you must minimize the value of $a + b$. Since the numbers must be positive and even, the least values that a and b can have are 2 and 4:
                      $a + b + c = 60$
Plug in: $2 + 4 + c = 60$
Simplify: $6 + c = 60$
Subtract 6: $c = 54$

14. **B** It is easier to pick a simple value for the "starting" population in 1980, like 100. Since the population increased by 10% from 1980 to 1990, the 1990 population must have been (100)(1.10) = 110. Since it decreased by 10% from 1990 to 2000, the 2000 population must have been (110)(0.90) = 99. From 1980 to 2000, then, the percent change was (99 − 100)/100 = −1/100 = −1%.

15. **E** According to the definition of g, $g(3) = 2f(3) - 1$. According to the table, $f(3) = 11$, so $g(3) = 2f(3) - 1 = 2(11) - 1 = 22 - 1 = 21$.

16. C Although you may substitute $5y$ for x as a first step, it's probably easier to simplify the expression first:

$$\sqrt{(x^2 - 2xy + y^2)}$$

Factor: $\sqrt{(x-y)^2}$

Simplify: $|x - y|$

Substitute: $|5y - y|$

Simplify: $|4y| = 4y$

---

17. C Think of numbers that are larger than their squares. This excludes negatives, because the squares of negatives are always positive. It also excludes numbers greater than 1, because the squares of these are bigger than the original numbers. Therefore, $0 < x < 1$. This means I and II are true, but not III.

---

18. C Believe it or not, you don't need to find the two midpoints in order to answer this question. You need to know only that the distance between the two mid-points is half of the distance between the two endpoints. The distance between the endpoints is $(3x + 2) - (-x - 4) = 3x + 2 + x + 4 = 4x + 6$. Half of this is $2x + 3$.

---

19. E Since all radii of a triangle are equal, $PQ = PR$. Since $PQ = QR$ too, the triangle must be equilateral. Since its area is $9\sqrt{3}$, the lengths have the measures shown in the diagram. The circle has a radius of 6. The shaded region is equal to the area of the sector minus the area of the triangle. Since the central angle is 60°, the sector has an area that is ⅙ of the whole circle, or $(⅙)(\pi(6)^2) = 6\pi$. Subtracting the area of the triangle gives $6\pi - 9\sqrt{3}$.

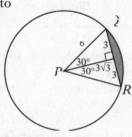

---

20. C If the ratio of boys to girls in a class is 3 to 5, then $3/(3 + 5) = ⅜$ of the class is boys and $5/(3 + 5) = ⅝$ of the class is girls. This means there are $(⅜)(160) = 60$ boys and $(⅝)(160) = 100$ girls in the senior class. Similarly, the fraction of boys in the junior class is ⅗ and the fraction of girls is ⅖. If there are x students in the junior class, then there are $(⅗)x$ boys and $(⅖)x$ girls in the junior class. If the ratio of boys to girls is 1:1 when the classes are combined, then

$$60 + (⅗)x = 100 + (⅖)x$$

Subtract 60 and $(⅖)x$: $(⅕)x = 40$

Multiply by 5: $x = 200$

Section 3

1. A A *six-month hiatus* (break) would cause her skills to *weaken*, something she might fear. *atrophy* = weaken from disuse; *align* = line up; *disseminate* = spread like seed

---

2. C *Domineering* opinions are overbearing and preachy. *vindictive* = inspired by revenge; *pedantic* = acting like a know-it-all; *conciliatory* = acting to bring people together; *treacherous* = betraying someone's confidence; *didactic* = preachy; *dogmatic* = condescendingly preachy; *prosaic* = ordinary

---

3. A The missing word must refer to Walter's *inability to make up his mind*. *vacillation* = inability to make up one's mind; *solicitation* = request for help; *rejuvenation* = restoration of one's youth; *admonishment* = mild reproof

---

4. D If a writer is *successful . . . even in the face of . . . rejections*, he or she must be very *persistent*. *affluence* = wealth; *haughty* = arrogant; *pertinacity* = strong persistence; *resilient* = able to endure hardship; *tenacity* = ability to hold fast; *relentless* = unwilling to give up; *stoutness* = courage or sturdiness; *craven* = cowardly

---

5. B The missing word must be in contrast to *direct, forceful stances*. *pontification* = haughty, self-important speech; *circumlocution* = indirect, evasive speech; *brevity* = conciseness

---

6. E The parallelism of the two clauses helps you to complete the sentence. If counselors *believe that criminals can change*, then they must *have faith in their changeability*. If they realize *that they can often return to their old habits*, they must by wary of *recidivism* (tendency to fall into old habits). *mutability* = changeability; *astuteness* = keen ability; *transcendence* = the quality of exceeding; *malleability* = ability to be bent; *relapse* = falling back into old ways

---

7. B If something is out of place in time, it is an *anachronism*. *anachronism* = something out of place in time; *idiom* = phrase with a meaning that is different from its literal meaning; *interlocutor* = someone who takes part in a conversation

---

8. C The sentence indicates that the "h" was evidence of an earlier time. *inference* = conclusion based on evidence; *analogy* = useful comparison; *vestige* = remaining trace; *anomaly* = unusual event; *quandary* = perplexing situation

9. **A** The passage states that language is used as *impenetrable walls* (line 7) between people, having biased connotations favoring one group over another.

10. **D** By saying that *we infer volumes* (lines 3–4), the author means that *we draw a lot of conclusions*.

11. **E** The passage states that instructing a child to tie shoes *the right way will defeat the child's growing attempt at self-mastery* (lines 12–14).

12. **B** The last sentence states that *nagging* is a *constant reminder to the child of his or her lack of self-control* (lines 21–22).

13. **C** The author states that Modernism is *egotistical* (line 19) and *self-conscious* (line 21) and also that it *begins nowhere and with no one in particular* (lines 12–13), suggesting that it is both *self-centered* and *ill-defined*, but the paragraph does not mention Modernism being *politically oriented*.

14. **A** The passage states that *Critics and academics . . . prefer their artistic movements to be readily comprehensible* (lines 8–10), so they do *not* like those that are hard to understand.

15. **D** The quotation from James Joyce in the next sentence describes these *landmines as enigmas and puzzles that . . . will keep the professors busy for centuries arguing over what I meant* (lines 21–25). In other words, they are literary devices placed in his novels to baffle professors.

16. **B** The passage states that *plots . . . are submerged beneath wave after wave of . . . hyper-literary and meta-literary indulgences* (lines 32–37), so it suggests that plot is not as important as other things.

17. **A** The author states that it is *hard not to love modernism* (lines 38–39) but also uses critical terms like *posturing aberrations* (line 19) to describe it. In the last two lines, he refers to modernism as *reprehensive but somehow roguishly likeable*. This is a very *ambivalent* characterization of modernism.

18. **A** The comparison is a *metaphor* but not a *simile* because it states that the *modernist novel* is *a sociopath*. *Juxtaposition* is the placement of two images one on top of the another, as in *a sociopath and a cad*. *Personification* is giving human qualities to something that is not human.

19. **D** The purpose of the passage is to introduce the reader to the new science of genomics.

20. **C** A *pathogen* (line 8) is not part of the *immune system* (lines 7–8) but rather what the immune system responds to.

21. **B** The *orchestrated response* of *the immune system* (lines 7–8) is mentioned as an example of how *molecules convey information* (line 9).

22. **E** The fact that *through genomics massive amounts of information can be converted into an electronic format* (lines 36–38) is what *facilitates a dramatically new framework for understanding life* (lines 40–41).

23. **C** The passage suggests that *information theory . . . may seem unfit for . . . science* (lines 50–52) because *information . . . implies an underlying intent* (lines 48–50).

24. **D** The final paragraph indicates that genomic advances *have helped to propel the remarkable development of the computer and telecommunication industries* (lines 58–60) and suggests that they may help to *improve human health* (lines 61–62). This discusses actual and potential consequences.

Section 4

1. **A** The sentence is correct.

2. **E** The underlined phrase should be a noun phrase that represents *one of the best features of the journalist's lifestyle*. Only (C) and (E) are noun phrases, and (E) is much clearer.

3. **B** The opening participial phrase modifies *Greg* and not *Greg's search*.

4. **C** Idiom requires *neither* to be followed by *nor*, and parallelism requires the *nor* to be followed by an adjective.

5. **D** The past participle of *to take* is *taken*, not *took*.

6. **C** Although choice (D) is parallel in structure, its phrasing is nonstandard. The phrasing in (C) is both parallel and clear.

7. **A** The pronoun *he* is the subject of an implied verb, *he (did)*, so it is used correctly in the subjective form. Also, the phrase *admire his acting* is correct, because the object of the verb is *acting*, not *him*.

8. **B** *Neither* is the singular subject of the verb, so the verb should be *was*, not *were*. Also, the pronoun should be *its* because the subject is singular and a ram can only feel its own pain, not the pain of them both.

9. **B** The participle *walking* modifies *Liz*, not *Liz's family*. Choice (D) makes this correction, but the modifiers are awkward and unclear.

10. **E** The phrase *if not better* is an interrupter, so the sentence should read well even if it is omitted. The only phrasing that meets this criterion is (E).

11. **E** The original is not a sentence but a fragment.

12. **D** The phrase *much closer* modifies the verb *study* and so should be in adverbial form: *much more closely*.

13. **B** The two clauses must be parallel: *has been so popular* would make this clause parallel to the first.

14. **D** This is a diction error. *Respectfully* means full of respect, which makes no sense here. The word should be *respectively*.

15. **D** The verb *would have considered* is in the wrong tense and mood. It should be *consider*.

16. **E** The sentence is correct.

17. **C** The *fund deficit and the disillusionment* are not a single problem, but two *problems*.

18. **B** The subject of the verb is *either accepting or rejecting*. If the subject of a verb is an *either . . . or* construction, the verb must agree with the noun after the *or*, which in this case is *rejecting*. Since this is a singular noun, the verb should be *was*.

19. **C** Since *defense attorneys* can be counted, the correct comparative word is *fewer*, not *less*.

20. **B** It is illogical to compare *service* to *other restaurants*. The phrase should be *the service at the other restaurants*.

21. **E** The sentence is correct.

22. **C** This pronoun refers to *a child*, so it must be the singular *he or she*.

23. **C** The phrase *not only A but also B* indicates a parallel structure. To make the structure parallel, the phrase should be replaced with *by*.

24. **E** The sentence is correct.

25. **B** The pronoun *he* is ambiguous. We are not certain which individual it is referring to. To correct the error, *he* should be changed to either Thomas Cowher or the Senator.

26. **C** The sentence indicates that this occurred in the past by saying those who *were observing*. Therefore *are* should instead be *were*.

27. **E** The sentence is correct.

28. **A** Between my brother and *I* should instead be between my brother and *me*. Subjective pronouns, such as *I*, should only be used as subjects. Objective pronouns, including *me*, can be used as objects of verbs or as objects of prepositions.

29. **C** The critic is writing about a *duo*, which is a singular subject. The *their* should therefore be replaced by *its*.

30. **A** Choice (A) is the most concise and clear, and the phrasing is parallel.

31. **B** Sentence 3 presents an example of Plato's reasoning as described in sentence 2. Choice (C) may be tempting, but since the sentence does not extend the idea from sentence 2 but only provides an example, the word *furthermore* is inappropriate.

32. **B** The pronoun *they* and the noun *approximations* should agree in number. Choice (B) provides the most straightforward phrasing.

33. **D** Sentence 6 does not fit because it shifts the discussion to what students dislike, rather than the nature of mathematical objects.

34. **E** Choice (E) provides the most logical, concise, and clear phrasing.

35. **A** Choice (A) provides the most logical, concise, and clear phrasing.

Section 5

1. E If $2x = 10$, then $4x = 20$, and if $3y = 12$, then $6y = 24$, so $4x + 6y = 20 + 24 = 44$.

2. D Set up the equation: $(a + b + 4)/3 = 5$
Multiply by 3: $a + b + 4 = 15$
Subtract 4: $a + b = 11$

3. C If $b = 2a$, then $a + 2a = 180$, because the two angles form a linear pair. So $3a = 180$ and $a = 60$. Your diagram should now look like this:

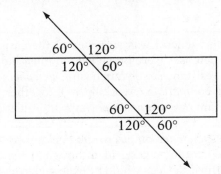

So $d + e + g + h = 60 + 60 + 120 + 60 = 300$.

4. A Substitute $x = 100$ into the function:

$$\sqrt{\sqrt{100} - 1} = \sqrt{10 - 1} = \sqrt{9} = 3$$

5. B If $2^m = 8$, then $m = 3$. So $3^{k+3} = 243$. Checking the powers of 3 shows that $k + 3 = 5$. Therefore, $k = 2$, so $2^k = 2^2 = 4$.

6. C If b varies inversely as the square of c, then the equation that relates them is $b = k/c^2$ where k is some constant. To find the value of k, just plug in the given values for b and c:

$$8 = k/3^2$$

Multiply by 9: $72 = k$
Therefore, the specific equation relating b and c is $b = 72/c^2$. To find the value of c when $b = 2$, just substitute and solve:

$$2 = 72/c^2$$

Cross-multiply: $2c^2 = 72$
Divide by 2: $c^2 = 36$
Take the square root: $c = \pm 6$

7. C Each of the five teams must play four other teams three times apiece. In other words, each team must play in $4 \times 3 = 12$ games. Since there are five teams, it might seem at first that there are a total of $5 \times 12 = 60$ games, but since each game needs two teams, the total number of games is $60/2 = 30$.

8. A If pump A can fill the tank in 3 hours, then it will fill ⅓ of the tank in 1 hour, leaving ⅔ of the tank to fill. Pump B can fill ½ of the tank in an hour, so working together, the two pumps can fill $½ + ⅓ = ⅚$ of the tank per hour. To fill ⅔ of the tank working together, then, takes $(⅔) \div (⅚) = ⅘$ hour, which equals $(⅘)(60) = 48$ minutes.

9. 7.5 Translate into an equation: $4x - 5 = 25$
Add 5: $4x = 30$
Divide by 4: $x = 7.5$

10. 13 «7» = $7 + 6 + 5 + 4 + 3 + 2 + 1$
«5» = $5 + 4 + 3 + 2 + 1$
So «7» − «5» = $7 + 6 = 13$

11. 100 Circumference = πd, so you can find the diameter:

$$\pi d = 10\pi$$
Divide by π: $d = 10$

This diameter is also the hypotenuse of a right triangle, so by the Pythagorean theorem, $a^2 + b^2 = d^2 = 10^2 = 100$.

12. 24 This is a "counting" problem, so it helps to know the fundamental counting principle from Chapter 9, Lesson 5. Since you are making a three-letter arrangement, there are three decisions to be made. The number of choices for the first letter is four; then there are three letters left for the second spot, then two left for the third spot. This gives a total of $4 \times 3 \times 2 = 24$ possible arrangements.

13. 0.2 or 1/5 This is a simple substitution. You can substitute 10,200 for $96,878 \times x^2$ because they are equal. So $10,200/(5 \times 96,878 \times x^2) = 10,200/(5 \times 10,200) = ⅕$. Notice that the 10,200s "cancel."

14. 4 If each term is 1 less than 3 times the *previous* term, then each term is also $1/3$ of the number that is 1 greater than the *successive* term. Since the fourth term is 95, the third term must be $1/3$ of 96, which is 32. Repeating this shows that the second term is 11 and the first term is 4. Check your work by confirming that the sequence satisfies the formula.

15. **0.8**   If $4 + \sqrt{b} = 7.2$ then $\sqrt{b} = 3.2$.

So $4 - \sqrt{b} = 4 - 3.2 = 0.8$.
(Notice that you don't really have to deal with the root!)

16. **5**   If their are a adults, there must be $30 - a$ children, because the total number of people is 30.

Therefore $\qquad 10a + 5(30 - a) = 175$
Distribute: $\qquad 10a + 150 - 5a = 175$
Simplify: $\qquad\qquad 5a + 150 = 175$
Subtract 150: $\qquad\qquad 5a = 25$
Divide by 5: $\qquad\qquad\quad a = 5$

Now check: if there are 5 adults, there must be 25 children, and the tickets would cost $5(10) + 25(5) = 50 + 125 = 175$ (yes!).

17. **9**   Since $a = (2/3)b$, the perimeter of the triangle is $b + b + (2/3)b = (8/3)b$. The perimeter is 24, so

$$(8/3)b = 24$$
Multiply by 3/8: $\qquad\qquad b = 9$

18. **10**

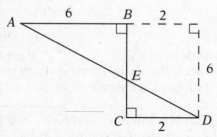

Mark the diagram with the given information. The dotted lines show that AD is the hypotenuse of a right triangle with legs of length 8 and 6. So to find it, just use the Pythagorean theorem: $\qquad 6^2 + 8^2 = (AD)^2$
Simplify: $\qquad\qquad\qquad 100 = (AD)^2$
Take the square root: $\qquad\quad 10 = AD$

Section 6

1. **A**   Because the signal was *strange*, it was clearly not an expected result, but it was also not from outside of the telescope, so it was a *strange happening* from the telescope itself. *malfunction* = disruption of the normal workings; *bulwark* = defensive fortification; *anthology* = collection of literary works; *mutation* = change in form

2. **B**   The problem is one that may never be solved, so it is *difficult* or *stubborn*. *impotent* = weak and ineffective; *intractable* = hard to manage, stubborn; *evanescent* = likely to vanish; *irate* = angry; *insipid* = dull, tasteless

3. **E**   If the general was *surprised* at the ease with which the defenses were breached, he must have expected the resistance to be much *stronger*. *ephemeral* = short-lived; *compatible* = working well together; *egregious* = blatant or extreme; *imposing* = intimidating

4. **B**   A *dependence on electronic devices* would be expected to *tax* the power grid, although *increased efficiency* of those devices would be expected to ease the burden. *abated* = decreased in intensity; *attenuated* = caused to be less intense; *compromised* = rendered vulnerable; *flourished* = thrived

5. **E**   The word *although* indicates a contrast. Although the persecution *vanquished* (conquered) the will of some, it must have *strengthened* the will of others. *despotic* = tyrannical; *squandered* = wasted; *amenable* = obedient; *celebrated* = eminent; *ruthless* = merciless; *forged* = established

6. **C**   The passage says that *Rousseau's writings* (line 1) were what led *Goethe to say that "feeling is all"* (line 4). Therefore, Goethe was influenced by Rousseau.

7. **D** The passage says that Kant *forgot to take his . . . daily walk* because he *was so absorbed in reading Rousseau's Émile* (lines 14–16).

8. **C** Passage 1 states that *"by emphasizing feeling"* (line 3) Rousseau inspired the Romantic movement and Goethe in particular, while Passage 2 criticizes Rousseau's *"worship of emotion"* (line 33) as encouraging poor parenting.

9. **B** Passage 1 states that Rousseau *"inspired the French Revolution"* (lines 9–10) and Passage 2 gives Rousseau credit for laying the *"philosophical foundation of American independence"* (lines 31–32).

10. **E** By saying *"It would be a good idea,"* Gandhi indicated that civilization in the West had not really been realized.

11. **B** The *voices* are those who are *bankrolled by large corporations* (lines 16–17) and who are *saying such things* (line 15) as that America is a *model of free-market capitalism* (line 11). This would certainly not include Mahatma Gandhi, but the passage indicates that it would include *politicians* and those in *corporate news and entertainment media* (lines 8–10).

12. **C** The second paragraph explains how *the concept of free trade* (line 20) works, so it is explaining a concept.

13. **A** The statement suggests that the rules of free trade would work differently if the parties involved were different, suggesting that the rules are selectively applied.

14. **A** This paragraph indicates that these words are being used ironically. It states that the Indians *(gave in to Western pressure)* (lines 55–56), so the agreement was not a completely free one. Also, the words "liberalize" and "liberalization" are used ironically because they refer to actions that in fact reduced competition and were *(a great blow to free markets)* (lines 64–65).

15. **D** The *triumph* was also described as *a great blow to free markets* (lines 63–65).

16. **B** The paragraph indicates that *businesses are . . . expected to wager their own capital on success in the marketplace* (lines 66–68) but that some pharmaceutical companies don't need to.

17. **C** In lines 14–15, the narrator describes the instruction as being "clear and facile to my apprehension," which means he found it easy to understand.

18. **D** The phrase *clear and facile to my apprehension* means *easy to understand.*

19. **B** The narrator says that *a mind of moderate capacity which closely pursues one study must infallibly arrive at great proficiency* (lines 22–24), thereby suggesting that only *diligence* is required for proficiency.

20. **A** The narrator was *as well acquainted with the theory and practice of natural philosophy as depended on the lessons of any of the professors at Ingolstadt* (lines 32–35), which means he had learned all he could from them.

21. **C** This *supernatural enthusiasm* describes the narrator's passion for his studies.

22. **B** The human bodies are described as changing from *the seat of beauty and strength* in life to *food for the worm* (line 68) in death.

23. **C** The rest of the sentence describes how the processes of death change a formerly living body. In saying that he *beheld the corruption of death succeed to the blooming cheek of life*, he is saying that death and decay have replaced or defeated life.

24. **E** The narrator reveals his sense of privilege in this discovery by stating that he is *alone* (line 83) among the *many men of genius* (line 81) who had studied this topic before.

Section 7

1. C 16 is equal to $2(7) + 2$, so it is two more than a multiple of 7.

2. E Five oranges can be bought for 5¢ more than the price of four, which is $4(20¢) + 5¢ = 85¢$. $3.40 is equivalent to $4(.85)$, so it will buy $4(5) = 20$ oranges.

3. A If r is positive, then $-r$ is negative. If you add another negative, then the result will be even more negative.

4. D Twelve less than the product of 3 and $x + 1$ can be represented as

$$3(x + 1) - 12$$

Distribute: $\quad\quad\quad 3x + 3 - 12$

Simplify: $\quad\quad\quad 3x - 9$

5. C The square has an area of $200 \times 200 = 40,000$ square feet. $40,000 \div 5,000 = 8$, so this will require eight bags of seed at $25 apiece. $8 \times \$25 = \$200$.

6. C Analyzing the right angle shows that $x + y = 90$. Since the sum of the angles in a triangle is always 180°,

$$x + y + w = 180$$

Substitute $x + y = 90$: $\quad 90 + w = 180$

Subtract 90: $\quad\quad\quad\quad w = 90$

7. D If the numbers have a product of 0, then at least one must equal 0. Call the numbers x, y, and 0. The problem also says that $x + y = 7$ and $x - y = 11$.

Add the equations:
$$x + y = 7$$
$$+ (x - y = 11)$$
$$2x = 18$$

Divide by 2: $\quad\quad\quad\quad\quad x = 9$

Plug back in, solve for y: $\quad 9 + y = 7$

Subtract 9: $\quad\quad\quad\quad\quad\quad y = -2$

So the least of the numbers is -2.

8. A You can draw a diagram and see that there are only four possible triangles:

If you prefer to look at it as a "combination" problem, the number of triangles is the number of ways of choosing three things from a set of four, or $_4C_3 = 4$.

9. B The only way that abc would not be a multiple of 4 is if none of the three numbers is a multiple of 4 *and* no two of them are even (because the product of two evens is always a multiple of 4). One simple example is $a = 1$, $b = 2$, and $c = 3$. This example rules out choices (A), (C), (D), and (E).

10. A A large percent change from 2002 to 2003 is represented by a point in which the y-coordinate is much greater than the x-coordinate. Point A represents a change from 30 in 2002 to 70 in 2003, which is a percent change of $(70 - 30)/30 \times 100\% = 133\%$.

11. E If both classes have 100 students, then class B had 30 students participate in 2002 and 50 in 2003, for a total of 80. Class E had 80 in 2002 and 60 in 2003, for a total of 140. The difference, then, is $140 - 80 = 60$.

12. E If class D has 120 students, then 80% of 120, or 96 students participated in 2002. If the same number participated from class C, then 96 is 60% of the number of students in class C. If the number of students in class C is x, then $.60x = 96$. Divide by .6: $x = 160$.

13. E Substitute $x = -1$ into the equation to find c.

Simplify: $\quad\quad\quad\quad\quad\quad 1 = -4 + c$

Add 4: $\quad\quad\quad\quad\quad\quad\quad 5 = c$

So the equation is $\quad\quad\quad x^2 = 4x + 5$

Subtract $(4x + 5)$: $\quad x^2 - 4x - 5 = 0$

Factor the quadratic (remember that since $x = -1$ is a solution, $(x + 1)$ must be a factor): $x^2 - 4x - 5 = (x + 1)(x - 5)$

Therefore $\quad\quad (x + 1)(x - 5) = 0$

So the solutions are $x = 1$ and $x = 5$

14. C To create a three-digit number, three decisions must be made: you must choose the first digit, then choose where to put the two, then choose the final digit. Since the first digit must be odd, there are three options for the first digit. Since the two may be placed in either the second or the third slot, there are two options. Then there are three digits left to choose for the final slot. This means there are $3 \times 2 \times 3 = 18$ possibilities.

15. C Since one pound feeds five chickens, four pounds are needed to feed 20 chickens. This leaves $10 - 4 = 6$ pounds of feed. Since each pound can feed two pigs, six pounds can feed $2 \times 6 = 12$ pigs.

16. A Since 120° is 1/3 of 360°, the shaded region has 1/3 the area of the circle. Therefore, the circle has an area of $3(3\pi) = 9\pi$. Since $A = \pi r^2$, the radius is 3 centimeters. The circumference of the circle, then, is $2\pi r = 2\pi(3) = 6\pi$, and the arc of the shaded region has length $(1/3)(6\pi) = 2\pi$. The perimeter of the shaded region, then, is $3 + 3 + 2\pi = 2\pi + 6$.

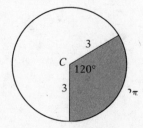

Section 8

1. **D** The word *rather* indicates the important contrast between the two ideas. The second word indicates something specific to a *single director* rather than *many visions*. *conglomeration* = collection; *insubordination* = disobedience; *prudence* = careful management; *bastion* = a well-fortified area; *synthesis* = a fusion of different elements; *conspiracy* = secret agreement to commit a crime

2. **B** The fact that modern readers *read a book once and then discard it* suggests that their interest in it is only *temporary*, rather than *timeless*. *immoral* = unethical; *fleeting* = short-lived

3. **A** *Although* indicates a contrast in ideas, so the missing word must mean *prolonged* rather than *short-term*. *protracted* = prolonged; *contemporaneous* = living or existing at the same time; *transient* = short-lived; *surreptitious* = secretive; *fickle* = tending to change one's mind often

4. **C** Since the sentence says that athletes are treated like successful warriors, you should look for a word like *celebrated*. *invoked* = called on or cited; *repudiated* = having to validity rejected its; *lionized* = treated like a celebrity; *vilified* = defamed; *beguiled* = deceived by charm

5. **E** The word *although* indicates a contrast. Although the persecution *vanquished* (conquered) the will of some, it must have *strengthened* the will of others. *despotic* = tyrannical; *squandered* = wasted; *amenable* = obedient; *celebrated* = eminent; *ruthless* = merciless; *forged* = established

6. **B** If she was an *opponent of the male hegemony* (dominance of one group over another), she must have been an *outspoken* critic of the *male-dominated* society. *matriarchal* = female-dominated; *pugnacious* = belligerent; *patriarchal* = male-dominated; *vociferous* = outspoken; *avuncular* = like a good-natured uncle; *belligerent* = inclined to picking fights; *rudimentary* = basic; *liberal* = free-thinking

7. **C** The author begins by making the point that *the spelling profession* (line 1) kills genius. By saying that Shakespeare was not a good speller but was more of a genius than Noah Webster, he is reinforcing the point, thereby suggesting that Webster is someone in the "spelling profession."

8. **E** The previous two sentences discuss the fact that any attempt to make spelling easier would undermine the author's *excuse for bad spelling* (line 18).

9. **E** Serena's plan is to have people avoid spelling words with silent letters, but not change the way they pronounce words. This would require a change in writing habits.

10. **C** Serena's plan is to *boycott* (line 77) words with superfluous letters. Boycotting is a form of protest. By saying that her plan is more American than his, the author suggests that Americans are inclined to protest things.

11. **A** The author says he wants to *set the idle letters to work* (lines 50–51) by pronouncing them, while Serena plans to *ignore all words that contain superfluous letters* (lines 75–76).

12. **A** In the final paragraph of Passage 1, the author says that he *replaced* the *Platonic friendship* he had with Serena with *ardent love* (lines 85–86) because he didn't know how to spell the word *friend*.

13. **D** The *chaos* is mentioned as the result of failing to impose standards for spelling particular words and instead spelling a word in many different ways according to how it is pronounced in different dialects.

14. **B** Passage 2 says that standardized spelling *obscures those spoken dialects that are so often used to stratify and separate us* (lines 116–118).

15. **A** Passage 2 says that the silent letters in the word "eight" are *a treasure trove* (lines 126–127) to those who study the history of language.

16. **A** Passage 1 is clearly intended to be humorous, while Passage 2 is very systematic in discussing the problems with the spelling reform movement.

17. **D** Passage 1 says that *Americans do not like sudden changes* (line 29) to suggest the difficulty in enacting spelling reform. Similarly, Passage 2 says that *languages are not influenced very much by plan or reason* (lines 131–132).

18. **D** Because the final paragraph of Passage 2 discusses the problem of enacting a *plan* to change the conventions of language, the author of Passage 2 would likely regard such a plan as unworkable.

19. **C** The first passage discusses *although* as a word with too many silent letters, while Passage 2 discusses it because it contains a letter sequence that can be pronounced in many different ways.

Section 9

1. **C** The original sentence is a run-on sentence. Answer choice (C) properly coordinates the two ideas.

2. **B** In the original sentence, *a better debater* should instead be *better debaters,* the plural form. Answer choice (B) corrects this error.

3. **B** *Billy the Bobcat* is a singular subject and the verb *have* is plural. It should instead be *has.*

4. **B** The pronoun *when* should be used only to refer to a time. It should be replaced by *who.*

5. **A** This sentence is correct as written.

6. **E** The original sentence is phrased awkwardly. As constructed it suggests that the U.S. enjoyed *peace and economic well being* more than *any time* did, which makes no sense. Answer choice (E) corrects this comparison error.

7. **D** The phrase *because of* is awkward. Answer choice (D) corrects the error in the most concise and logical fashion.

8. **D** The sentence requires parallel structure. Jerry Lewis hosted *a variety show* and *an annual telethon.* Answer choice (D) corrects the error.

9. **B** You should not begin the clause after a semicolon with *and* because it is supposed to be an *independent* clause. Answer choice (B) properly coordinates the two ideas.

10. **B** As originally constructed, the sentence suggests that the children themselves contain violent imagery, rather than the video games contain violent imagery. Answer choice (B) corrects this error.

11. **B** The opening participial phrase, *walking hand-in-hand* improperly modifies the *vendor* rather than *the couple.* Answer choice (B) corrects this error.

12. **C** The original sentence is awkward and wordy. The phrasing in answer choice (C) is the most concise and logical of the choices.

13. **D** This question presents an illogical comparison. As written, the parents today spend more time working than 30 years ago did. The sentence is *trying* to say that parents today spend more time working than *parents did* 30 years ago. Answer choice (D) corrects the error.

14. **B** The phrase *if they would have* in (E) is incorrect subjunctive form, and the comparison between the *language* and the *Borneans* is illogical.

PRACTICE TEST 10

ANSWER SHEET

Last Name:_____　First Name:_____

Date:_____　Testing Location:_____

Directions for Test

- Remove these answer sheets from the book and use them to record your answers to this test.
- This test will require 3 hours and 20 minutes to complete. Take this test in one sitting.
- The time allotment for each section is written clearly at the beginning of each section. This test contains six 25-minute sections, two 20-minute sections, and one 10-minute section.
- This test is 25 minutes shorter than the actual SAT, which will include a 25-minute "experimental" section that does not count toward your score. That section has been omitted from this test.
- You may take one short break during the test, of no more than 10 minutes in length.
- You may only work on one section at any given time.
- You must stop ALL work on a section when time is called.
- If you finish a section before the time has elapsed, check your work on that section. You may NOT work on any other section.
- Do not waste time on questions that seem too difficult for you.
- Use the test book for scratchwork, but you will receive credit only for answers that are marked on the answer sheets.
- You will receive one point for every correct answer.
- You will receive no points for an omitted question.
- For each wrong answer on any multiple-choice question, your score will be reduced by ¼ point.
- For each wrong answer on any "numerical grid-in" question, you will receive no deduction.

When you take the real SAT, you will be asked to fill in your personal information in grids as shown below.

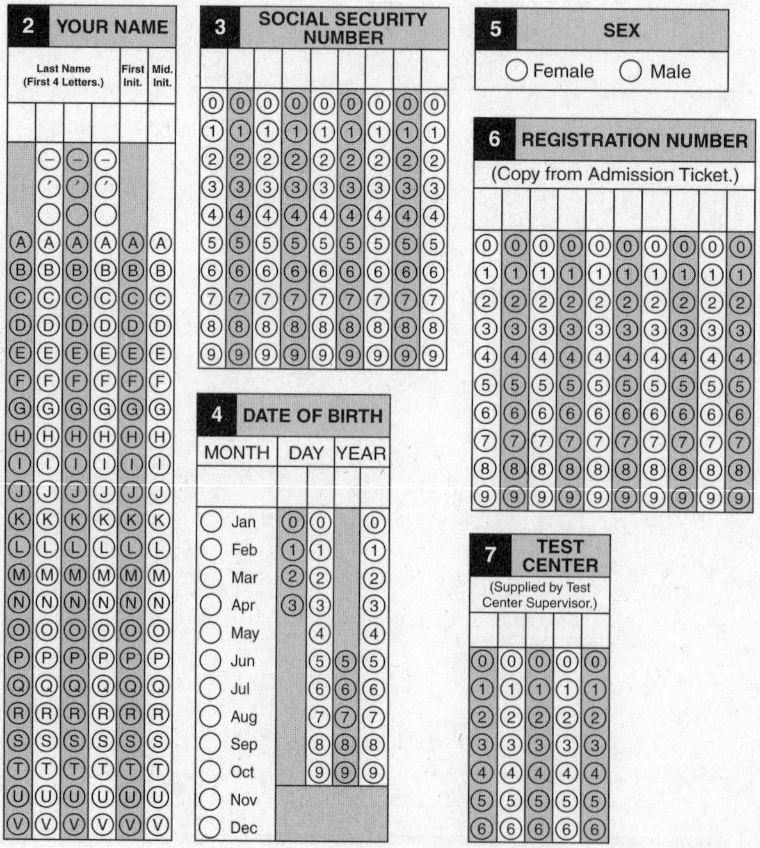

Start with number 1 for each new section. If a section has fewer questions than answer spaces, leave the extra answer spaces blank. Be sure to erase any errors or stray marks completely.

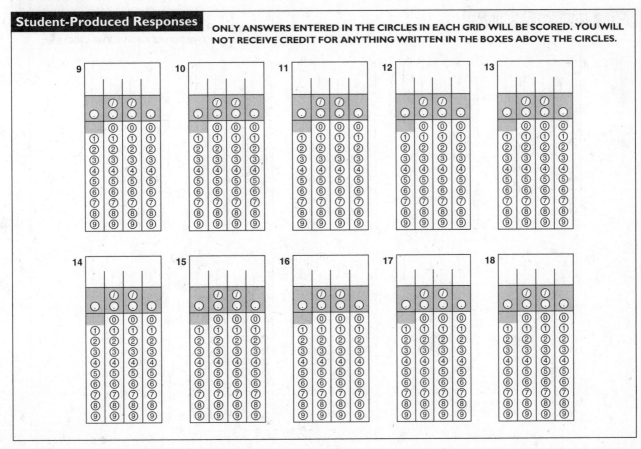

SECTION 2

1 A B C D E	11 A B C D E	21 A B C D E	31 A B C D E
2 A B C D E	12 A B C D E	22 A B C D E	32 A B C D E
3 A B C D E	13 A B C D E	23 A B C D E	33 A B C D E
4 A B C D E	14 A B C D E	24 A B C D E	34 A B C D E
5 A B C D E	15 A B C D E	25 A B C D E	35 A B C D E
6 A B C D E	16 A B C D E	26 A B C D E	36 A B C D E
7 A B C D E	17 A B C D E	27 A B C D E	37 A B C D E
8 A B C D E	18 A B C D E	28 A B C D E	38 A B C D E
9 A B C D E	19 A B C D E	29 A B C D E	39 A B C D E
10 A B C D E	20 A B C D E	30 A B C D E	40 A B C D E

SECTION 3

1 A B C D E	11 A B C D E	21 A B C D E	31 A B C D E
2 A B C D E	12 A B C D E	22 A B C D E	32 A B C D E
3 A B C D E	13 A B C D E	23 A B C D E	33 A B C D E
4 A B C D E	14 A B C D E	24 A B C D E	34 A B C D E
5 A B C D E	15 A B C D E	25 A B C D E	35 A B C D E
6 A B C D E	16 A B C D E	26 A B C D E	36 A B C D E
7 A B C D E	17 A B C D E	27 A B C D E	37 A B C D E
8 A B C D E	18 A B C D E	28 A B C D E	38 A B C D E
9 A B C D E	19 A B C D E	29 A B C D E	39 A B C D E
10 A B C D E	20 A B C D E	30 A B C D E	40 A B C D E

CAUTION Use the answer spaces in the grids below for Section 2 or Section 3 only if you are told to do so in your test book.

Student-Produced Responses ONLY ANSWERS ENTERED IN THE CIRCLES IN EACH GRID WILL BE SCORED. YOU WILL NOT RECEIVE CREDIT FOR ANYTHING WRITTEN IN THE BOXES ABOVE THE CIRCLES.

Start with number 1 for each new section. If a section has fewer questions than answer spaces, leave the extra answer spaces blank. Be sure to erase any errors or stray marks completely.

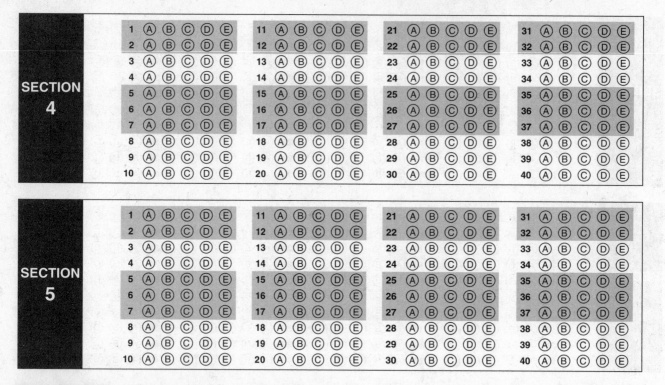

CAUTION Use the answer spaces in the grids below for Section 4 or Section 5 only if you are told to do so in your test book.

Student-Produced Responses   ONLY ANSWERS ENTERED IN THE CIRCLES IN EACH GRID WILL BE SCORED. YOU WILL NOT RECEIVE CREDIT FOR ANYTHING WRITTEN IN THE BOXES ABOVE THE CIRCLES.

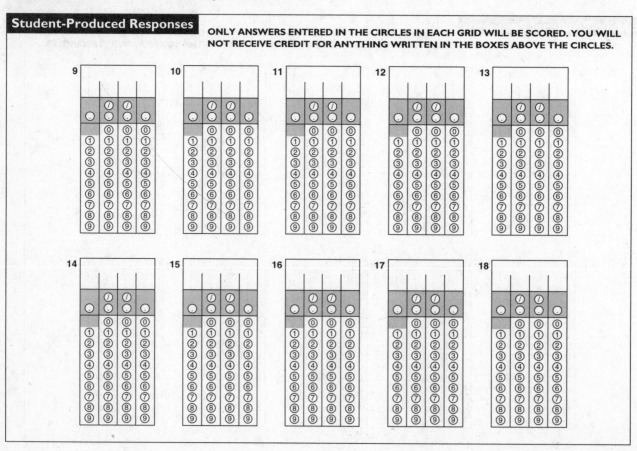

Start with number 1 for each new section. If a section has fewer questions than answer spaces, leave the extra answer spaces blank. Be sure to erase any errors or stray marks completely.

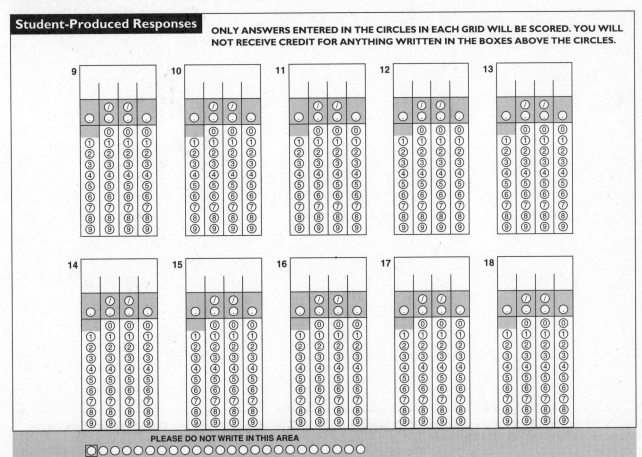

SECTION 6

SECTION 7

CAUTION Use the answer spaces in the grids below for Section 6 or Section 7 only if you are told to do so in your test book.

Student-Produced Responses ONLY ANSWERS ENTERED IN THE CIRCLES IN EACH GRID WILL BE SCORED. YOU WILL NOT RECEIVE CREDIT FOR ANYTHING WRITTEN IN THE BOXES ABOVE THE CIRCLES.

PLEASE DO NOT WRITE IN THIS AREA

Start with number 1 for each new section. If a section has fewer questions than answer spaces, leave the extra answer spaces blank. Be sure to erase any errors or stray marks completely.

SECTION 8

1. Ⓐ Ⓑ Ⓒ Ⓓ Ⓔ
2. Ⓐ Ⓑ Ⓒ Ⓓ Ⓔ
3. Ⓐ Ⓑ Ⓒ Ⓓ Ⓔ
4. Ⓐ Ⓑ Ⓒ Ⓓ Ⓔ
5. Ⓐ Ⓑ Ⓒ Ⓓ Ⓔ
6. Ⓐ Ⓑ Ⓒ Ⓓ Ⓔ
7. Ⓐ Ⓑ Ⓒ Ⓓ Ⓔ
8. Ⓐ Ⓑ Ⓒ Ⓓ Ⓔ
9. Ⓐ Ⓑ Ⓒ Ⓓ Ⓔ
10. Ⓐ Ⓑ Ⓒ Ⓓ Ⓔ

11. Ⓐ Ⓑ Ⓒ Ⓓ Ⓔ
12. Ⓐ Ⓑ Ⓒ Ⓓ Ⓔ
13. Ⓐ Ⓑ Ⓒ Ⓓ Ⓔ
14. Ⓐ Ⓑ Ⓒ Ⓓ Ⓔ
15. Ⓐ Ⓑ Ⓒ Ⓓ Ⓔ
16. Ⓐ Ⓑ Ⓒ Ⓓ Ⓔ
17. Ⓐ Ⓑ Ⓒ Ⓓ Ⓔ
18. Ⓐ Ⓑ Ⓒ Ⓓ Ⓔ
19. Ⓐ Ⓑ Ⓒ Ⓓ Ⓔ
20. Ⓐ Ⓑ Ⓒ Ⓓ Ⓔ

21. Ⓐ Ⓑ Ⓒ Ⓓ Ⓔ
22. Ⓐ Ⓑ Ⓒ Ⓓ Ⓔ
23. Ⓐ Ⓑ Ⓒ Ⓓ Ⓔ
24. Ⓐ Ⓑ Ⓒ Ⓓ Ⓔ
25. Ⓐ Ⓑ Ⓒ Ⓓ Ⓔ
26. Ⓐ Ⓑ Ⓒ Ⓓ Ⓔ
27. Ⓐ Ⓑ Ⓒ Ⓓ Ⓔ
28. Ⓐ Ⓑ Ⓒ Ⓓ Ⓔ
29. Ⓐ Ⓑ Ⓒ Ⓓ Ⓔ
30. Ⓐ Ⓑ Ⓒ Ⓓ Ⓔ

31. Ⓐ Ⓑ Ⓒ Ⓓ Ⓔ
32. Ⓐ Ⓑ Ⓒ Ⓓ Ⓔ
33. Ⓐ Ⓑ Ⓒ Ⓓ Ⓔ
34. Ⓐ Ⓑ Ⓒ Ⓓ Ⓔ
35. Ⓐ Ⓑ Ⓒ Ⓓ Ⓔ
36. Ⓐ Ⓑ Ⓒ Ⓓ Ⓔ
37. Ⓐ Ⓑ Ⓒ Ⓓ Ⓔ
38. Ⓐ Ⓑ Ⓒ Ⓓ Ⓔ
39. Ⓐ Ⓑ Ⓒ Ⓓ Ⓔ
40. Ⓐ Ⓑ Ⓒ Ⓓ Ⓔ

SECTION 9

1. Ⓐ Ⓑ Ⓒ Ⓓ Ⓔ
2. Ⓐ Ⓑ Ⓒ Ⓓ Ⓔ
3. Ⓐ Ⓑ Ⓒ Ⓓ Ⓔ
4. Ⓐ Ⓑ Ⓒ Ⓓ Ⓔ
5. Ⓐ Ⓑ Ⓒ Ⓓ Ⓔ
6. Ⓐ Ⓑ Ⓒ Ⓓ Ⓔ
7. Ⓐ Ⓑ Ⓒ Ⓓ Ⓔ
8. Ⓐ Ⓑ Ⓒ Ⓓ Ⓔ
9. Ⓐ Ⓑ Ⓒ Ⓓ Ⓔ
10. Ⓐ Ⓑ Ⓒ Ⓓ Ⓔ

11. Ⓐ Ⓑ Ⓒ Ⓓ Ⓔ
12. Ⓐ Ⓑ Ⓒ Ⓓ Ⓔ
13. Ⓐ Ⓑ Ⓒ Ⓓ Ⓔ
14. Ⓐ Ⓑ Ⓒ Ⓓ Ⓔ
15. Ⓐ Ⓑ Ⓒ Ⓓ Ⓔ
16. Ⓐ Ⓑ Ⓒ Ⓓ Ⓔ
17. Ⓐ Ⓑ Ⓒ Ⓓ Ⓔ
18. Ⓐ Ⓑ Ⓒ Ⓓ Ⓔ
19. Ⓐ Ⓑ Ⓒ Ⓓ Ⓔ
20. Ⓐ Ⓑ Ⓒ Ⓓ Ⓔ

21. Ⓐ Ⓑ Ⓒ Ⓓ Ⓔ
22. Ⓐ Ⓑ Ⓒ Ⓓ Ⓔ
23. Ⓐ Ⓑ Ⓒ Ⓓ Ⓔ
24. Ⓐ Ⓑ Ⓒ Ⓓ Ⓔ
25. Ⓐ Ⓑ Ⓒ Ⓓ Ⓔ
26. Ⓐ Ⓑ Ⓒ Ⓓ Ⓔ
27. Ⓐ Ⓑ Ⓒ Ⓓ Ⓔ
28. Ⓐ Ⓑ Ⓒ Ⓓ Ⓔ
29. Ⓐ Ⓑ Ⓒ Ⓓ Ⓔ
30. Ⓐ Ⓑ Ⓒ Ⓓ Ⓔ

31. Ⓐ Ⓑ Ⓒ Ⓓ Ⓔ
32. Ⓐ Ⓑ Ⓒ Ⓓ Ⓔ
33. Ⓐ Ⓑ Ⓒ Ⓓ Ⓔ
34. Ⓐ Ⓑ Ⓒ Ⓓ Ⓔ
35. Ⓐ Ⓑ Ⓒ Ⓓ Ⓔ
36. Ⓐ Ⓑ Ⓒ Ⓓ Ⓔ
37. Ⓐ Ⓑ Ⓒ Ⓓ Ⓔ
38. Ⓐ Ⓑ Ⓒ Ⓓ Ⓔ
39. Ⓐ Ⓑ Ⓒ Ⓓ Ⓔ
40. Ⓐ Ⓑ Ⓒ Ⓓ Ⓔ

▌ ▌ **ESSAY** ▪ **ESSAY** ▌ ▌

ESSAY
Time—25 minutes

Write your essay on separate sheets of standard lined paper.

The essay gives you an opportunity to show how effectively you can develop and express ideas. You should therefore take care to develop your point of view, present your ideas logically and clearly, and use language precisely.

Your essay must be written on the lines provided on your answer sheet—you will receive no other paper on which to write. You will have enough space if you write on every line, avoid wide margins, and keep your handwriting to a reasonable size. Remember that people who are not familiar with your handwriting will read what you write. Try to write or print so that what you are writing is legible to those readers.

Important reminders:

- **A pencil is required for the essay.** An essay written in ink will receive a score of zero.
- **Do not write your essay in your test book.** You will receive credit only for what you write on your answer sheet.
- **An off-topic essay will receive a score of zero.**

You have twenty-five minutes to write an essay on the topic assigned below.

Consider carefully the issue discussed in the following passage, then write an essay that answers the question posed in the assignment.

> The best leaders are not those who seek power or have great political skill. Great leaders—and these are exceptionally rare, especially today—represent the best selves of the people they represent.

Assignment: **What are the most important qualities of a leader?** Write an essay in which you answer this question and discuss your point of view on this issue. Support your position logically with examples from literature, the arts, history, politics, science and technology, current events, or your experience or observation.

If you finish before time is called, you may check your work on this section only.
Do not turn to any other section of the test.

2   **2**   **2**   **2**   **2**   **2**

SECTION 2
Time—25 minutes
24 questions

> ### Turn to Section 2 of your answer sheet to answer the questions in this section.

> **Directions:** For each question in this section, select the best answer from among the choices given and fill in the corresponding circle on the answer sheet.

Each sentence below has one or two blanks, each blank indicating that something has been omitted. Beneath the sentence are five words or sets of words labeled A through E. Choose the word or set of words that, when inserted in the sentence, <u>best</u> fits the meaning of the sentence as a whole.

EXAMPLE:

Rather than accepting the theory unquestioningly, Deborah regarded it with -----.

(A) mirth
(B) sadness
(C) responsibility
(D) ignorance
(E) skepticism

---

1. Even though Alisha had every reason to hold a grudge, she felt that ------- was not a healthful emotion.

   (A) resentment
   (B) fortitude
   (C) sarcasm
   (D) elation
   (E) fondness

2. Those who expected the governor to be inarticulate were surprised by his -------.

   (A) intolerance
   (B) fatigue
   (C) eloquence
   (D) endurance
   (E) violence

3. Before the Realist movement, novelists rarely utilized the ------- language of commoners, preferring the more ------- parlance of the upper classes.

   (A) normal . . ordinary
   (B) elite . . fancy
   (C) sympathetic . . wasteful
   (D) colloquial . . refined
   (E) effective . . utilitarian

4. Many college students are attracted to the ------- life of a journalist; the prospect of exploring the world is very appealing, even if the pay is not.

   (A) peripatetic
   (B) conventional
   (C) tolerant
   (D) coordinated
   (E) remunerative

5. A position that requires public speaking would be very difficult for one as ------- as he.

   (A) vivacious
   (B) garrulous
   (C) amiable
   (D) decent
   (E) reticent

GO ON TO THE NEXT PAGE

6. One example of a ------- relationship is provided by the tickbird, which gets protection and a free meal of ticks from the hippopotamus and in turn supplies free pest removal services.

(A) competitive
(B) deteriorating
(C) symbiotic
(D) regressive
(E) vacillating

7. Early philosophers used ------- alone to reach their conclusions; unlike modern scientists, they did not value the ------- information that comes only from close observation and experimentation.

(A) reason . . empirical
(B) coercion . . mathematical
(C) deduction . . clerical
(D) computation . . intuitive
(E) compassion . . numerical

8. The ------- of many media companies under a single owner is troublesome to those who believe that ------- is essential to the fair and balanced presentation of the news.

(A) retraction . . differentiation
(B) consolidation . . independence
(C) collaboration . . sharing
(D) unification . . dissemination
(E) disintegration . . variety

The following passages are followed by questions based on their content. Answer the questions on the basis of what is <u>stated</u> or <u>implied</u> in the passage and in any introductory material that may be provided.

Questions 9–12 are based on the following passages.

PASSAGE 1

Education, then, beyond all other devices of human origin, is the great equalizer of the con-
Line ditions of men—the balance-wheel of the social machinery. It gives each man the independence
5 and the means by which he can resist the self-ishness of other men. It does better than to dis-arm the poor of their hostility toward the rich; it prevents being poor. The spread of education, by enlarging the cultivated class or caste, will
10 open a wider area over which the social feelings will expand, and, if this education should be universal and complete, it would do more than all things else to obliterate factitious distinc-tions in society.

PASSAGE 2

15   For most students, the main product of schooling is not education but the acceptance of one's place in society and of the power of that society to mete out the symbols of status. Education is the acquisition of competence,
20 power, wisdom and discernment. These come only from the unadulterated struggle for sense in the world, and it is this struggle that is de-nied by schooling, which dictates experience and then evaluates that experience as it
25 chooses. But only the experiencer can really evaluate an experience.

9. Unlike Passage 1, Passage 2 focuses on the dis-tinction between

(A) educating the poor and educating the wealthy
(B) power and knowledge
(C) teachers and students
(D) educated people and uneducated people
(E) schooling and education

First passage: Horace Mann, *The Case for Public Schools*, a report to the Massachusetts Board of Education in 1848.
Second passage: Printed with the permission of its author, Christopher Black, and College Hill Coaching. © 2005

GO ON TO THE NEXT PAGE

2   **2**   **2**   **2**   **2**   **2**

10. Passage 1 mentions each of the following as benefits of public education to the poor EXCEPT

    (A) the diminishment of social distinctions
    (B) the improvement of living standards
    (C) better ability to counteract greed
    (D) increased self-sufficiency
    (E) the reduction of crime

11. Passage 1 suggests that the obliteration of "factitious distinctions" (lines 13–14) requires

    (A) unlimited access to education
    (B) a rigorous curriculum in civics
    (C) hostility toward the rich
    (D) dedicated teachers
    (E) aggressive legislation

12. The author of Passage 2 characterizes the "struggle" (line 21) as

    (A) regretful
    (B) empowering
    (C) illusionary
    (D) unwinnable
    (E) foreign

Questions 13–18 are based on the following passage.

The following is an essay from a textbook on the history of philosophy published in 1999.

The scientists of the Renaissance brought
about the most fundamental alterations in the
Line world of thought, and they accomplished this
feat by devising a new method for discovering
5 knowledge. Unlike the medieval thinkers, who
proceeded for the most part by reading traditional texts, the early modern scientists laid
greatest stress upon observation and the

formation of temporary hypotheses. The
10 method of observation implied two things:
namely, that traditional explanations of the
behavior of nature should be empirically
demonstrated, the new assumption being that
such explanations could very well be wrong,
15 and that new information might be available
to scientists if they could penetrate beyond the
superficial appearances of things. People now
began to look at the heavenly bodies with a
new attitude, hoping not solely to find the
20 confirmation of Biblical statements about the
firmament but, further, to discover the principles and laws that describe the movements of
bodies. Observation was directed not only
upon the stars but also in the opposite direc-
25 tion, toward the minutest constituents of
physical substance.

To enhance the exactness of their observations, they invented various scientific instruments. Tippershey, a Dutchman, invented the
30 telescope in 1608, although Galileo was the
first to make dramatic use of it. In 1590 the
first compound microscope was created. The
principle of the barometer was discovered by
Galileo's pupil Torricelli. The air pump, which
35 was so important in creating a vacuum for the
experiment that proved that all bodies regardless of their weight or size fall at the same rate
when there is no air resistance, was invented
by Otto von Guericke (1602–1686). With the
40 use of instruments and imaginative hypotheses, fresh knowledge began to unfold. Galileo
discovered the moons around Jupiter, and
Anton Leeuwenhoek (1632–1723) discovered
spermatozoa, protozoa, and bacteria.
45 Whereas Nicolaus Copernicus (1473–1543)
formed a new hypothesis of the revolution of
the earth around the sun, Harvey (1578–1657)
discovered the circulation of the blood.
William Gilbert (1540–1603) wrote a major
50 work on the magnet, and Robert Boyle
(1627–1691), the father of chemistry, formulated his famous law concerning the relation
of temperature, volume, and pressure of

Excerpted from "The Renaissance Interlude," in *Socrates to Sartre*, by Samuel Enoch Stumpf, McGraw-Hill, New York, 1999. Reproduced with permission of The McGraw-Hill Companies.

GO ON TO THE NEXT PAGE →

2   2   2   2   2   2

gases. Added to these inventions and discover-
55 ies was the decisive advance made in mathematics, especially by Sir Isaac Newton and
Leibniz, who independently invented differen-
tial and integral calculus. The method of
observation and mathematical calculation
60 now became the hallmarks of modern science.
    The new scientific mode of thought in time
influenced philosophic thought in two important ways. First, the assumption that the basic
processes of nature are observable and capa-
65 ble of mathematical calculation and description had the effect of engendering another
assumption, namely, that everything consists
of bodies in motion, that everything conforms
to a mechanical model. The heavens above
70 and the smallest particles below all exhibit the
same laws of motion. Even human thought
was soon explained in mechanical terms, not
to mention the realm of human behavior,
which the earlier moralists described as the
75 product of free will.

13. Which of the following is the best title for this
passage?

(A) The Beginnings of the Scientific Method
(B) Scientific Instruments of the Renaissance
(C) The Art and Science of the Renaissance
(D) Biblical Influence on the Scientific Mode
     of Thought
(E) The Importance of Hypotheses in
     Scientific Thinking

14. As it is used in line 8, "stress" most nearly
means

(A) anxiety
(B) pressure
(C) emphasis
(D) desperation
(E) contortion

15. It can be inferred from the passage that if pre-
Renaissance scientists observed the motions of
heavenly bodies, they did so most likely in
order to

(A) confirm the formulas that describe the
     motions of the planets and stars
(B) distinguish the motions of various
     planets
(C) validate what the Bible says about those
     bodies
(D) demonstrate the utility of their newly
     invented instruments
(E) refute the hypotheses of their rival
     scientists

16. The passage indicates that Galileo did which
of the following?

    I.   invented an important optical
         instrument
    II. instructed another famous scientist
    III. made an important astronomical
         discovery

(A) II only
(B) III only
(C) I and II only
(D) II and III only
(E) I, II, and III

17. The passage indicates that, unlike the "earlier
moralists" (line 74), Renaissance scientists
began to perceive human behavior as

(A) a matter of free choice
(B) influenced by heavenly bodies
(C) controlled by a metaphysical spirit
(D) affected by animalistic impulses
(E) subject to the laws of physical motion

18. The primary function of the last paragraph
is to

(A) propose a solution to a problem
(B) identify those responsible for a discovery
(C) discuss the effects of a change
(D) refute a misconception
(E) address an objection to the author's thesis

GO ON TO THE NEXT PAGE

2   2   2   2   2   2

Questions 19–24 are based on the following passage.

The following passage is from a recent book on the history of warfare.

Line

One of the high points of any production of Shakespeare's *Henry V* is the Saint Crispin's Day speech at the Battle of Agincourt, in which the English king rhapsodizes over the glorious

5   plight of his vastly outnumbered army with the words "We few, we happy few, we band of brothers." What prompts this outpouring of fraternal emotion is the Earl of Westmore-land's complaint that if only they had "ten

10 thousand of those men in England that do no work today," they would at least have a fight-ing chance. But Henry will have none of that, and delivers his justly famous rejoinder:

If we are marked to die, we are enow

15 *To do our country loss; and if to live,*
    The fewer men, the greater share of honor.
    God's will! I pray thee wish not one man more.
    This is usually assumed to be a show of stoic bravado that harks back to the prebattle

20 speeches recorded by ancient historians (no-tably Thucydides and Xenophon), speeches in which an outnumbered force cement their sol-idarity by reveling in their numerical disad-vantage. "The fewer men, the greater the

25 honor" was by Shakespeare's time a well-known proverb, trotted out in many instances of the glorious, fighting few. In Froissart's ac-count of the Battle of Poitiers in 1356, for ex-ample, the Prince of Wales harangues his men

30 prior to the battle in a speech that closely par-allels Henry's. Shakespeare was undoubtedly familiar with it.

Now, my gallant fellows, what though we be
a small body when compared to the army of our

35 *enemies; do not let us be cast down on that ac-*
    count, for victory does not always follow
    numbers, but where the Almighty God wishes
    to bestow it. If, through good fortune, the day
    shall be ours, we shall gain the greatest honor

40 *and glory in this world; if the contrary should*
    happen, and we be slain, I have a father and
    beloved brethren alive, and you all have some
    relations, or good friends, who will be sure to
    revenge our deaths. I therefore entreat of you

45 *to exert yourselves, and combat manfully; for,*
    if it please God and St. George, you shall see
    me this day act like a true knight.

Of course the race does not always go to the swift nor the battle to the stronger in number.

50 Despite being outmanned, both King Henry and Prince Edward managed to prevail quite handily due to the incompetence of their op-ponents. In each instance, the French squan-dered their numerical advantage by charging

55 before they were ready, by bunching up, and by underestimating the range and accuracy of the English longbow. The numbers not only fail to tell the whole story, but they actually obscure it. Ten thousand more men might ac-

60 tually have hindered the English, whereas fewer men (and less overconfidence) might have saved the French. It seems that in fact, as these and many other examples show, strength is not always proportional to size.

19. The passage suggests that Henry V requests "not one man more" (line 17) because

(A) his strategy can work only with a small band of fighters
(B) he considers it more honorable to fight while outnumbered
(C) the opposing soldiers are unreliable
(D) no other fighters have the skills of the ones he has assembled
(E) he does not wish to be victorious

20. In line 26, the phrase "trotted out" most nearly means

(A) abused
(B) removed
(C) employed for rhetorical effect
(D) spared an indignity
(E) used flippantly

Excerpted from *Damn the Torpedoes*, Brian Burrell, McGraw-Hill, New York, 1999. Reproduced with permission of The McGraw-Hill Companies.

GO ON TO THE NEXT PAGE

2   2   2   2   2   2

21. In line 34, the word "body" most nearly means

    (A) stature
    (B) strength
    (C) corpse
    (D) group
    (E) anthology

22. In line 54, the word "charging" most nearly means

    (A) accusing
    (B) inspiring
    (C) resting
    (D) attacking
    (E) prevailing

23. The passage indicates that the Battle of Agincourt and the Battle of Poitiers were similar in that in each case

    I.   the victorious army was the smaller
    II. the French army was defeated
    III. one side committed tactical errors

    (A) I only
    (B) I and II only
    (C) I and III only
    (D) II and III only
    (E) I, II, and III

24. The passage suggests that the "whole story" (line 58) should include the possibility that

    (A) numerical supremacy would not have been an advantage to the British
    (B) King Henry had more soldiers available than was previously believed
    (C) the English longbow was not as accurate as the French soldiers believed it to be
    (D) confidence aided the French more than the British
    (E) the French did not really outman the British

STOP

If you finish before time is called, you may check your work on this section only. Do not turn to any other section of the test.

3   **3**   **3**   **3**   **3**   **3**

SECTION 3
Time—25 minutes
20 questions

Turn to Section 3 of your answer sheet to answer the questions in this section.

Directions: For this section, solve each problem and decide which is the best of the choices given. Fill in the corresponding circle on the answer sheet. You may use any available space for scratchwork.

Notes

1. The use of a calculator is permitted.
2. All numbers used are real numbers.
3. Figures that accompany problems in this test are intended to provide information useful in solving the problems. They are drawn as accurately as possible EXCEPT when it is stated in a specific problem that the figure is not drawn to scale. All figures lie in a plane unless otherwise indicated.
4. Unless otherwise specified, the domain of any function f is assumed to be the set of all real numbers x for which $f(x)$ is a real number.

Reference Information

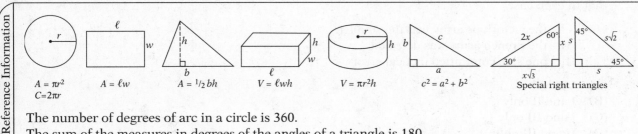

$A = \pi r^2$
$C = 2\pi r$

$A = \ell w$

$A = \frac{1}{2} bh$

$V = \ell wh$

$V = \pi r^2 h$

$c^2 = a^2 + b^2$

Special right triangles

The number of degrees of arc in a circle is 360.
The sum of the measures in degrees of the angles of a triangle is 180.

---

1. If n is 3 times an even number, then which of the following could be n?

   (A) 14
   (B) 15
   (C) 16
   (D) 17
   (E) 18

---

2. A machine can produce 50 computer chips in 2 hours. At this rate, how many computer chips can the machine produce in 7 hours?

   (A) 175
   (B) 200
   (C) 225
   (D) 250
   (E) 275

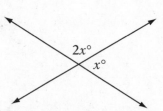

3. In the figure above, what is the value of x?

   (A) 40
   (B) 45
   (C) 60
   (D) 75
   (E) 90

GO ON TO THE NEXT PAGE

3 3 3 3 3 3

4. Any positive integer that is divisible by 6 and 15 must also be divisible by

(A) 12
(B) 21
(C) 30
(D) 72
(E) 90

5. If n percent of 20 is 4, what is n?

(A) $\dfrac{1}{5}$
(B) 2
(C) 5
(D) 20
(E) 500

6. If $f(x) = 3x + n$, where n is a constant, and $f(2) = 0$, then $f(0) =$

(A) −6
(B) −2
(C) 0
(D) 2
(E) 6

7. A square has the same area as a right triangle with sides of lengths 6, 8, and 10. What is the length of one side of the square?

(A) 4
(B) $2\sqrt{3}$
(C) $\sqrt{15}$
(D) $2\sqrt{6}$
(E) 12

8. If $12v = 3w$ and $v \neq 0$, then which of the following is equivalent to $2w - 8v$?

(A) 0
(B) $4w$
(C) $-6w$
(D) $2v$
(E) $-2v$

9. If x is a negative number and $2|x| + 1 > 5$, then which of the following must be true?

(A) $x < -3$
(B) $x < -2.5$
(C) $x < -2$
(D) $x > -2$
(E) $x > -5$

10. If $x = -2$, then $-x^2 - 8x - 5 =$

(A) 3
(B) 7
(C) 15
(D) 23
(E) 25

11. If $\dfrac{5}{m} \leq \dfrac{2}{3}$, then what is the smallest possible positive value of m?

(A) 6
(B) 6.5
(C) 7
(D) 7.5
(E) 8

12. Theo wants to buy a sweater that is priced at $60.00 before tax. The store charges a 6% sales tax on all purchases. If he gives the cashier $70.00 for the sweater, how much should he receive in change?

(A) $3.60
(B) $6.40
(C) $7.40
(D) $9.40
(E) $66.40

GO ON TO THE NEXT PAGE

3   **3**   **3**   **3**   **3**   **3**

13. When m is subtracted from n, the result is r. Which of the following expresses the result when $2m$ is added to s?

(A) $s + 2n - 2r$
(B) $s + 2n + 2r$
(C) $2s + 2n - 2r$
(D) $2s + 2n + 2r$
(E) $s - 2n + 2r$

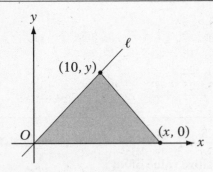

Note: Figure not drawn to scale.

14. In the figure above, the slope of line l is $\dfrac{3}{5}$ and the area of the triangle is 48 square units. What is the value of $x + y$?

(A) 13
(B) 14
(C) 19
(D) 22
(E) 96

15. Ellen takes a trip that is y miles long in total, where $y > 20$. She travels the first 15 miles at an average speed of 30 miles per hour and the rest of the trip at an average speed of 40 miles per hour. Which of the following represents the total time of the trip, in hours?

(A) $\dfrac{1}{2} + \dfrac{y - 15}{40}$

(B) $2 + \dfrac{y - 15}{40}$

(C) $\dfrac{1}{2} + 40y - 15$

(D) $2 + 40(y - 15)$

(E) $\dfrac{1}{2} + 40(y - 15)$

16. If y varies directly as m and inversely as the square of n, and if $y = 8$ when $m = 16$ and $n = 1$, then what is the value of y when $m = 8$ and $n = 4$?

(A) 0.125
(B) 0.25
(C) 0.5
(D) 1
(E) 2

17. If $a + b = s$ and $a - b = t$, then which of the following expresses the value of ab in terms of s and t?

(A) st

(B) $\dfrac{(s - t)}{2}$

(C) $\dfrac{(s + t)}{2}$

(D) $\dfrac{(s^2 - t^2)}{4}$

(E) $\dfrac{(s^2 - t^2)}{2}$

18. If $y = m^4 = n^3$ and y is greater than 1, then $mn =$

(A) $y^{\frac{1}{12}}$

(B) $y^{\frac{1}{7}}$

(C) $y^{\frac{7}{12}}$

(D) y^7

(E) y^{12}

GO ON TO THE NEXT PAGE

3   3   3   3   3   3

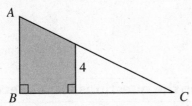

Note: Figure not drawn to scale.

19. In the figure above, if $AB = 6$ and $BC = 12$, what is the area of the shaded region?

(A) 20
(B) 22
(C) 24
(D) 26
(E) 28

20. Every car at a certain dealership is either a convertible, a sedan, or both. If one-fifth of the convertibles are also sedans and one-third of the sedans are also convertibles, which of the following could be the total number of cars at the dealership?

(A) 28
(B) 29
(C) 30
(D) 31
(E) 32

STOP

If you finish before time is called, you may check your work on this section only. Do not turn to any other section of the test.

4   **4**   **4**   **4**   **4**   **4**

SECTION 4
Time—25 minutes
18 questions

Turn to Section 4 of your answer sheet to answer the questions in this section.

Directions: This section contains two types of questions. You have 25 minutes to complete both types. For questions 1–8, solve each problem and decide which is the best of the choices given. Fill in the corresponding circle on the answer sheet. You may use any available space for scratchwork.

Notes

1. The use of a calculator is permitted.
2. All numbers used are real numbers.
3. Figures that accompany problems in this test are intended to provide information useful in solving the problems. They are drawn as accurately as possible EXCEPT when it is stated in a specific problem that the figure is not drawn to scale. All figures lie in a plane unless otherwise indicated.
4. Unless otherwise specified, the domain of any function f is assumed to be the set of all real numbers x for which $f(x)$ is a real number.

Reference Information

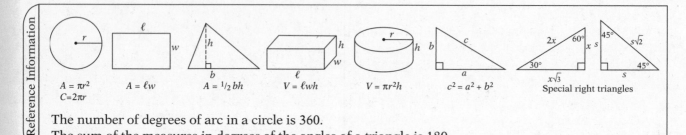

$A = \pi r^2$
$C = 2\pi r$

$A = \ell w$

$A = \frac{1}{2} bh$

$V = \ell wh$

$V = \pi r^2 h$

$c^2 = a^2 + b^2$

Special right triangles

The number of degrees of arc in a circle is 360.
The sum of the measures in degrees of the angles of a triangle is 180.

---

1. A square has a perimeter of 36 centimeters. What is its area in square centimeters?

    (A) 24
    (B) 36
    (C) 49
    (D) 64
    (E) 81

2. If b is a positive integer less than 100, then how many integer pairs (a, b) satisfy the equation $\dfrac{a}{b} = \dfrac{1}{10}$?

    (A)   7
    (B)   8
    (C)   9
    (D) 10
    (E) 11

GO ON TO THE NEXT PAGE

4   4   4   4   4   4

CLEANING COSTS IN THE McKENZIE OFFICE
BUILDING

Room Type	Number of Rooms in the Building	Cost per Room to Clean
Bathrooms	10	$20
Offices	30	$15

3. According to the table above, how much will it cost, in dollars, to clean each bathroom twice and each office once in the McKenzie Office Building?

(A) 200
(B) 400
(C) 450
(D) 600
(E) 850

4. If $a^2 - b^2 = 10$ and $a - b = 2$, what is the value of $a + b$?

(A) 5
(B) 6
(C) 7
(D) 8
(E) 9

5. For all integers n greater than 1, let $f(n) = k$, where k is the sum of all the prime factors of n. What is the value of $f(14) - f(6)$?

(A) 4
(B) 5
(C) 6
(D) 9
(E) 14

6. The average (arithmetic mean) of four different positive integers is 20. What is the greatest possible value of any of these integers?

(A) 68
(B) 70
(C) 73
(D) 74
(E) 77

7. The radius of circle A is twice the radius of circle B. If the sum of their circumferences is 36π, then what is the radius of circle A?

(A) 9
(B) 12
(C) 14
(D) 16
(E) 18

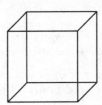

8. The figure above shows a cube. How many different planes can be drawn such that each contains *exactly* two edges of the cube?

(A) 4
(B) 5
(C) 6
(D) 7
(E) 8

GO ON TO THE NEXT PAGE ▷

4   **4**   **4**   **4**   **4**   **4**

Directions: For student-produced response questions 9–18, use the grids at the bottom of the answer sheet page on which you have answered questions 1–8.

Each of the remaining ten questions requires you to solve the problem and enter your answer by marking the circles in the special grid, as shown in the examples below. You may use any available space for scratchwork.

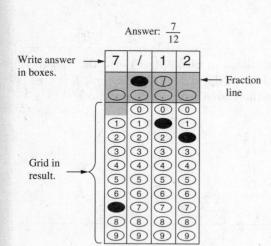

Answer: $\frac{7}{12}$

Write answer in boxes.

Fraction line

Grid in result.

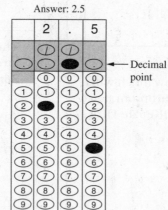

Answer: 2.5

Decimal point

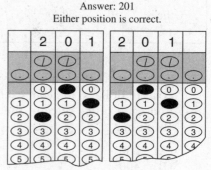

Answer: 201
Either position is correct.

<u>Note:</u> You may start your answers in any column, space permitting. Columns not needed should be left blank.

- Mark no more than one circle in any column.

- Because the answer sheet will be machine-scored, **you will receive credit only if the circles are filled in correctly.**

- Although not required, it is suggested that you write your answer in the boxes at the top of the columns to help you fill in the circles accurately.

- Some problems may have more than one correct answer. In such cases, grid only one answer.

- No question has a negative answer.

- **Mixed numbers** such as $3\frac{1}{2}$ must be gridded as 3.5 or 7/2. (If [3 1 / 2] is gridded, it will be interpreted as $\frac{31}{2}$ not $3\frac{1}{2}$.)

- **Decimal Answers:** If you obtain a decimal answer with more digits than the grid can accommodate, it may be either rounded or truncated, but it must fill the entire grid. For example, if you obtain an answer such as 0.6666..., you should record your result as .666 or .667. **A less accurate value such as .66 or .67 will be scored as incorrect.**

Acceptable ways to grid $2/3$ are:

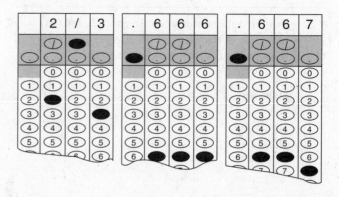

GO ON TO THE NEXT PAGE →

4   4   4   4   4   4

9. If 10 less than $2x$ is 22, then what is the value of x?

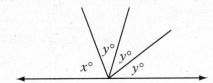

10. In the figure above, if $x = 2y$, then what is the value of y?

11. If $8x + 4y = 20$, then what is the value of $2x + y$?

12. In the xy-plane, the line $mx - 3y = 21$ passes through the point (3, 5). What is the value of m?

13. The ratio of men to women in a room is 4:5. If the room contains three more women than men, how many women are in the room?

14. If, for some constant value b, the equation $y = |2x - b|$ is satisfied by the point (5, 2), then what is one possible value of b?

GO ON TO THE NEXT PAGE

4   **4**   **4**   **4**   **4**   **4**

15. A mixture of water and sucrose is 10% sucrose by weight. How many grams of pure sucrose must be added to a 200-gram sample of this mixture to produce a mixture that is 20% sucrose?

16. A runner runs a 16-mile race at an average speed of 8 miles per hour. By how many <u>minutes</u> can she improve her time in this race if she trains and increases her average speed by 25%?

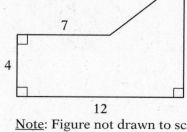

Note: Figure not drawn to scale.

17. The area of the figure above is 78. What is its perimeter?

18. Every sophomore at Hillside High School is required to study at least one language among Spanish, French, and Latin, but no one may study more than two. If 120 sophomores study Spanish, 80 study French, 75 study Latin, and 50 study two of the three languages, how many sophomores are there at Hillside High School?

STOP

If you finish before time is called, you may check your work on this section only. Do not turn to any other section of the test.

SECTION 5
Time—25 minutes
24 questions

Turn to Section 5 of your answer sheet to answer the questions in this section.

Directions: For each question in this section, select the best answer from among the choices given and fill in the corresponding circle on the answer sheet.

Each sentence below has one or two blanks, each blank indicating that something has been omitted. Beneath the sentence are five words or sets of words labeled A through E. Choose the word or set of words that, when inserted in the sentence, <u>best</u> fits the meaning of the sentence as a whole.

EXAMPLE:

Rather than accepting the theory unquestioningly, Deborah regarded it with -----.

(A) mirth
(B) sadness
(C) responsibility
(D) ignorance
(E) skepticism

---

1. The ------- with which the advisor managed the funds forced his clients to seek more reliable advice regarding investment.

(A) skill
(B) caution
(C) ineptitude
(D) recognition
(E) bitterness

2. As an Armenian born in Iran and educated in Lebanon, Vartan Gregorian brought ------- flavor to the presidency of Brown University that was unprecedented in the Ivy League.

(A) a perpetual
(B) an authoritative
(C) a structured
(D) an artificial
(E) a cosmopolitan

3. The lawyers did not have time to consider the contract in great detail; rather, they were able to give it only a ------- reading before they had to make their presentation on its merits.

(A) verbatim
(B) meandering
(C) tormented
(D) cursory
(E) substantial

4. The ------- in many parts of the city has made the ------- of infectious diseases more rapid, because pathogens spread quickly in close quarters.

(A) overcrowding . . propagation
(B) squalor . . circulation
(C) poverty . . deterioration
(D) congestion . . elimination
(E) proximity . . resilience

GO ON TO THE NEXT PAGE →

5. Much research in neuroscience today endeavors to ------- the mechanisms by which our brains turn the ------- data from our sense organs into coherent and understandable information.

(A) enhance . . quality of
(B) restore . . absence of
(C) enlighten . . source of
(D) attenuate . . dearth of
(E) elucidate . . deluge of

The passages below are followed by questions based on their content. Answer the questions on the basis of what is <u>stated</u> or <u>implied</u> in the passage and in any introductory material that may be provided.

Questions 6–7 are based on the following passage.

Towards the middle and the end of the sixteenth century there were many students and
Line scholars possessing a great deal of erudition, but very little means of subsistence. Nor were
5   their prospects very encouraging. They first went through that bitter experience, which, since then, so many have made after them— that whoever seeks a home in the realm of intellect runs the risk of losing the solid ground
10   on which the fruits for maintaining human life grow. The eye directed towards the Parnassus is not the most apt to spy out the small tortuous paths of daily gain. To get quick returns of interest, even though it be small, from the capi-
15   tal of knowledge and learning has always been, and still is, a question of difficult solution.

6. The "fruits" mentioned in line 10 represent

(A) spiritual growth
(B) artistic skill
(C) technological progress
(D) the means of acquiring food and shelter
(E) scientific knowledge

7. The "question" in line 16 is whether

(A) money can buy happiness
(B) intellectuals can earn a good living
(C) society can construct effective schools
(D) old ideas are relevant to modern society
(E) scholars are happier than merchants

Questions 8–9 are based on the following passage.

When there exists an inherited or instinctive tendency to the performance of an action, or
Line an inherited taste for certain kinds of food, some degree of habit in the individual is often
5   or generally requisite. We find this in the paces of the horse, and to a certain extent in the pointing of dogs; although some young dogs point excellently the first time they are taken out, yet they often associate the proper
10   inherited attitude with a wrong odour, and even with eyesight. I have heard it asserted that if a calf be allowed to suck its mother only once, it is much more difficult afterwards to rear it by hand. Caterpillars which have
15   been fed on the leaves of one kind of tree, have been known to perish from hunger rather than to eat the leaves of another tree, although this afforded them their proper food, under a state of nature.

8. The "pointing of dogs" (line 7) is mentioned primarily as an example of

(A) an innate habit
(B) a behavior that humans find useful
(C) a skill that is hard to learn
(D) an ability that many other animals also have
(E) a skill that helps animals to find food

First passage: Jacob Feis. *Shakespeare and Montaigne*, © 1890. Public domain
Second passage: Charles Darwin. *The Expression of the Emotions in Man and Animals.* © 1872. Public domain

GO ON TO THE NEXT PAGE ⇒

5   5   5   5   5   5

---

9. Which of the following best summarizes the main point of the paragraph?

   (A) People will eat only what they are genetically determined to eat.
   (B) All animal behavior is instinctive.
   (C) Cows and other animals should not be fed by humans.
   (D) Habits in animals are impossible to break.
   (E) Inherited tendencies manifest themselves in behavioral habits.

Questions 10–16 are based on the following passage.

The following is an excerpt from an essay entitled Political Ideals, *written in 1917 by Bertrand Russell.*

It is not one ideal for all men, but a separate ideal for each separate man, that has to be real-
Line ized if possible. Every man has it in his being to develop into something good or bad: there is a
5   best possible for him, and a worst possible. His circumstances will determine whether his capacities for good are developed or crushed, and whether his bad impulses are strengthened or gradually diverted into better channels.
10   But although we cannot set up in any detail an ideal of character which is to be universally applicable—although we cannot say, for instance, that all men ought to be industrious, or self-sacrificing, or fond of music—there are
15   some broad principles which can be used to guide our estimates as to what is possible or desirable.
     We may distinguish two sorts of goods, and two corresponding sorts of impulses.
20   There are goods in regard to which individual possession is possible, and there are goods in which all can share alike. The food and clothing of one man is not the food and clothing of another; if the supply is insufficient, what one
25   man has is obtained at the expense of some other man. This applies to material goods generally, and therefore to the greater part of the present economic life of the world. On the other hand, mental and spiritual goods do not
30   belong to one man to the exclusion of another. If one man knows a science, that does not prevent others from knowing it; on the contrary, it helps them to acquire the knowledge. If one man is a great artist or poet, that
35   does not prevent others from painting pictures or writing poems, but helps to create the atmosphere in which such things are possible. If one man is full of good-will toward others, that does not mean that there is less goodwill
40   to be shared among the rest; the more good-will one man has, the more he is likely to create among others.
     In such matters there is no possession, because there is not a definite amount to be
45   shared; any increase anywhere tends to produce an increase everywhere.
     There are two kinds of impulses, corresponding to the two kinds of goods. There are possessive impulses, which aim at acquiring or
50   retaining private goods that cannot be shared; these center in the impulse of property. And there are creative or constructive impulses, which aim at bringing into the world or making available for use the kind of goods in which
55   there is no privacy and no possession.
     The best life is the one in which the creative impulses play the largest part and the possessive impulses the smallest. This is no new discovery. The Gospel says: "Take no
60   thought, saying, What shall we eat? or What shall we drink? Or Wherewithal shall we be clothed?" The thought we give to these things is taken away from matters of more importance. And what is worse, the habit of mind
65   engendered by thinking of these things is a bad one; it leads to competition, envy, domination, cruelty, and almost all the moral evils that infest the world. In particular, it leads to the predatory use of force. Material posses-
70   sions can be taken by force and enjoyed by the robber. Spiritual possessions cannot be taken in this way. You may kill an artist or a thinker, but you cannot acquire his art or his thought. You may put a man to death because
75   he loves his fellow-men, but you will not by so doing acquire the love which made his happiness. Force is impotent in such matters; it is only as regards material goods that it is effective. For this reason the men who believe in
80   force are the men whose thoughts and desires are preoccupied with material goods.

GO ON TO THE NEXT PAGE

Reproduced with the permission of the McGraw-Hill companies. *Western Europe in the Middle Ages*, B Tierney and S Painter, © 1992 McGraw-Hill

5   5   5   5   5   5

10. Which of the following best summarizes the main point of the passage?

    (A) People should strive harder to appreciate the arts.

    (B) Nothing can be possessed exclusively by one person.

    (C) Societies need strong laws against stealing.

    (D) Creativity is of higher value than possessiveness.

    (E) Scarce resources should be shared equally in a society.

11. The passage mentions "food and clothing" (lines 22–23) primarily as examples of things that

    (A) everyone needs to survive

    (B) create a positive atmosphere of sharing

    (C) many underdeveloped countries lack

    (D) cannot be shared as freely as other things

    (E) are hard to find

12. As it is used in line 43, "such matters" can be inferred to refer to situations in which

    (A) people must compete for ownership of goods

    (B) artists struggle to sell their works

    (C) people strive to be industrious

    (D) philosophers endeavor to define human ideals

    (E) possessing a good does not deny it to someone else

13. In line 51, the phrase "impulse of" most nearly means

    (A) reaction against

    (B) restriction of

    (C) sharing of

    (D) fear of

    (E) desire for

14. According to the author, "force is impotent in such matters" (line 77) because

    (A) violence cannot influence another person's thoughts

    (B) moral people do not engage in violence

    (C) spiritual things cannot be acquired coercively

    (D) a good person will always be protected by friends

    (E) reason is more powerful than physical force

15. In the last paragraph, the author indicates that his thesis is not

    (A) ancient

    (B) a matter of logic

    (C) relevant to those who are already happy

    (D) original

    (E) universal

16. Which of the following examples, if it existed, would most directly refute the main point of the author?

    (A) a person who finds a large sum of money and gives it to charity

    (B) an invention that benefits all of humankind even though it was created only to make money for its inventor

    (C) a tyrant who murders intellectuals in order to maintain his authority

    (D) a thief who steals in order to feed his starving family

    (E) an army that invades another country and plunders its wealth

GO ON TO THE NEXT PAGE ⟶

5   **5**   **5**   **5**   **5**   **5**

Questions 17–24 are based on the following passage.

The following passage was written for The Atlantic Monthly *in 1902 by Native American writer Zitkala-Sa, also known as Gertrude Simmons Bonnin.*

The racial lines, which once were bitterly real, now serve nothing more than marking
Line out a living mosaic of human beings. And even here men of the same color are like the ivory
5 keys of one instrument where each represents all the rest, yet varies from them in pitch and quality of voice. Thus with a compassion for all echoes in human guise, I greet the solemn-faced "native preacher" whom I find awaiting
10 me. I listen with respect for God's creature, though he mouth most strangely the jangling phrases of a bigoted creed.

As our tribe is one large family, where every person is related to all the others, he ad-
15 dressed me:

"Cousin, I came from the morning church service to talk with you."

"Yes," I said interrogatively, as he paused for some word from me.

20   Shifting uneasily about in the straight-backed chair he sat upon, he began: "Every holy day (Sunday) I look about our little God's house, and not seeing you there, I am disappointed. This is why I come today. Cousin, as
25 I watch you from afar, I see no unbecoming behavior and hear only good reports of you, which all the more burns me with the wish that you were a church member. Cousin, I was taught long years ago by kind missionar-
30 ies to read the holy book. These godly men taught me also the folly of our old beliefs.

"There is one God who gives reward or punishment to the race of dead men. In the upper region the Christian dead are gathered in un-
35 ceasing song and prayer. In the deep pit below, the sinful ones dance in torturing flames.

"Think upon these things, my cousin, and choose now to avoid the after-doom of hell fire!" Then followed a long silence in which he
40 clasped tighter and unclasped again his inter-locked fingers.

Like instantaneous lightning flashes came pictures of my own mother's making, for she, too, is now a follower of the new superstition.

45 "Knocking out the chinking of our log cabin, some evil hand thrust in a burning taper of braided dry grass, but failed of his intent, for the fire died out and the half burned brand fell inward to the floor. Directly above
50 it, on a shelf, lay the holy book. This is what we found after our return from a several days' visit. Surely some great power is hid in the sacred book!"

Brushing away from my eyes many like pic-
55 tures, I offered midday meal to the converted Indian sitting wordless and with downcast face. No sooner had he risen from the table with "Cousin, I have relished it," than the church bell rang.

60   Thither he hurried forth with his afternoon sermon. I watched him as he hastened along, his eyes bent fast upon the dusty road till he disappeared at the end of a quarter of a mile.

The little incident recalled to mind the copy
65 of a missionary paper brought to my notice a few days ago, in which a "Christian" pugilist[1] commented upon a recent article of mine, grossly perverting the spirit of my pen. Still I would not forget that the pale-faced mission-
70 ary and the aborigine are both God's creatures, though small indeed their own conceptions of Infinite Love. A wee child toddling in a wonder world, I prefer to their dogma my excursions into the natural gardens where the voice of the
75 Great Spirit is heard in the twittering of birds, the rippling of mighty waters, and the sweet breathing of flowers. If this is Paganism, then at present, at least, I am a Pagan.

17. The main purpose of the passage as a whole is to

(A)   describe one person's perspective on an attempt at religious conversion

(B)   compare Native American religious tradition to European religious tradition

(C)   analyze the rise of Christianity in Native American tribes

(D)   refute a misconception about the nature of Paganism

(E)   describe a conflict between the author and her mother

[1]One who fights for a cause; also, a prize fighter

GO ON TO THE NEXT PAGE ⟶

5   5   5   5   5   5

18. The reference to "pitch and quality of voice" (lines 6–7) serves to emphasize

(A) the variety in vocal quality of religious singers
(B) the harshness with which many preachers rebuke their congregations
(C) the sounds that the author hears in nature
(D) the author's inability to understand what the native preacher is saying
(E) the differences among members of the same race

19. In the first paragraph, the author characterizes the preacher primarily as

(A) respectful
(B) articulate
(C) uneducated
(D) intolerant
(E) compassionate

20. According to the passage, the preacher addressed the author as "cousin" because

(A) it is customary for preachers to refer to church members with that term
(B) the tribe members are all related
(C) the preacher's mother and the author's mother are sisters
(D) the preacher had forgotten the author's name
(E) the author refused to answer to her given name

21. According to the passage, the native preacher and the author's mother are alike in that they both

(A) have experienced attempted arson
(B) must travel a great deal
(C) have similar religious beliefs
(D) relish the midday meal
(E) enjoy excursions into the natural gardens

22. In line 68, the word "spirit" most nearly means

(A) apparition
(B) lively nature
(C) intent
(D) fear
(E) presence

23. In the final paragraph, the author characterizes herself primarily as

(A) mature
(B) creative
(C) vengeful
(D) repressed
(E) awed

24. The author mentions "conceptions of Infinite Love" (lines 71–72) in order to emphasize which of the following characteristics of the "pale-faced missionary" (lines 69–70)?

(A) small-mindedness
(B) reluctance to persist in the attempt to convert the author to Christianity
(C) generosity toward aborigines
(D) sympathy for animals
(E) high intelligence

 **STOP**

If you finish before time is called, you may check your work on this section only. Do not turn to any other section of the test.

6 6 6 6 6 6

SECTION 6
Time—25 minutes
35 questions

Turn to Section 6 of your answer sheet to answer the questions in this section.

Directions: For each question in this section, select the best answer from among the choices given and fill in the corresponding circle on the answer sheet.

The following sentences test correctness and effectiveness of expression. Part of each sentence or the entire sentence is underlined; beneath each sentence are five ways of phrasing the underlined material. Choice A repeats the original phrasing; the other four choices are different. If you think the original phrasing produces a better sentence than any of the alternatives, select choice A; if not, select one of the other choices.

In making your selection, follow the requirements of standard written English; that is, pay attention to grammar, choice of words, sentence construction, and punctuation. Your selection should result in the most effective sentence—clear and precise, without awkwardness or ambiguity.

EXAMPLE:

The children couldn't hardly believe their eyes.

(A) couldn't hardly believe their eyes
(B) could hardly believe their eyes
(C) would not hardly believe their eyes
(D) couldn't nearly believe their eyes
(E) couldn't hardly believe his or her eyes

1. Claims about harmful effects of the genetic alteration of vegetables is more speculation than documented fact.

(A) is more speculation than documented fact
(B) are more with speculation than of a documented fact
(C) is more of a speculation than a documented fact
(D) are more speculation than documented fact
(E) are a matter of more speculation than documented fact

2. Having passed the test for certification, Mackenzie was looking forward to finding a challenging teaching position in her home town.

(A) Having passed
(B) Passing
(C) Being that she passed
(D) If she had passed
(E) For her passing

3. Having once been a provincial schoolmaster, Jean-Paul Sartre's writing was always oriented more towards clear instruction than pontification.

(A) Jean-Paul Sartre's writing was always oriented more towards clear instruction than pontification
(B) Jean-Paul Sartre always wrote more to instruct than to pontificate
(C) the writings of Jean-Paul Sartre were always oriented more toward instruction than pontification
(D) Jean-Paul Sartre was oriented in his writing more toward instruction than pontification
(E) Jean-Paul Sartre's writing was more to instruct than to pontificate

GO ON TO THE NEXT PAGE ⟶

6   **6**   6   6   **6**   **6**

4. Adam Smith was a professor of philosophy, <u>a commissioner of customs, and founded the field of modern economics</u>.

   (A) a commissioner of customs, and founded the field of modern economics
   (B) worked as commissioner of customs, and founded the field of modern economics
   (C) a commissioner of customs, and the founder of the field of modern economics
   (D) commissioned customs, and was the founder of the field of modern economics
   (E) a commissioner of customs, and was the founder of the field of modern economics

5. John Locke was one of the first philosophers to attack the principle of <u>primogeniture, the practice of handing the monarchy down</u> to the king's first-born son.

   (A) primogeniture, the practice of handing the monarchy down
   (B) primogeniture; the practice of handing the monarchy down
   (C) primogeniture being the practice of handing the monarchy down
   (D) primogeniture that which handed down the monarchy
   (E) primogeniture this was the practice of handing the monarchy down

6. The nation's fledgling economy struggled <u>because the investment from other countries into its major industries was lacking from most of them</u>.

   (A) because the investment from other countries into its major industries was lacking from most of them
   (B) because few other countries were willing to invest in its major industries
   (C) due to the fact that few other countries would have invested in its major industries
   (D) because of the lack of investment from few other countries in its major industries
   (E) for the lack of investment in its major industries from other countries

7. The corporation began construction on the new building in January, but <u>there is still no completion</u>.

   (A) there is still no completion
   (B) they have yet to complete it
   (C) it has yet to complete the project
   (D) they have not still completed it yet
   (E) it isn't hardly done yet

8. Having spread more quickly than antibiotics could be distributed, <u>doctors were prevented from effectively treating the virulent disease</u>.

   (A) doctors were prevented from effectively treating the virulent disease
   (B) doctors could not effectively treat the virulent disease because it thwarted them
   (C) the doctors who were trying to treat it effectively were prevented by the virulent disease
   (D) the virulent disease prevented itself from its being treated effectively by the doctors
   (E) the virulent disease prevented the doctors from treating it effectively

9. Although psychologist B. F. <u>Skinner, who is best known as the man who popularized behaviorism, he</u> also wrote a utopian novel entitled *Walden Two*.

   (A) Skinner, who is best known as the man who popularized behaviorism, he
   (B) Skinner, who is best known as the man who popularized behaviorism,
   (C) Skinner is best known as the man who popularized behaviorism, he
   (D) Skinner popularized behaviorism, for which he is well known, nevertheless he
   (E) Skinner, who is best known as the man who popularized behaviorism, is the one who

GO ON TO THE NEXT PAGE ⟶

6 6 6 6 6 6

10. Singing for over 2 hours, Anita's hoarseness prevented her hitting the high notes.

 (A) Singing for over 2 hours, Anita's hoarseness prevented her hitting the high notes.
 (B) Singing for over 2 hours, Anita was unable to hit the high notes because of her hoarseness.
 (C) Having sung for over 2 hours, Anita's hoarseness prevented her from hitting the high notes.
 (D) Having sung for over 2 hours, Anita was no longer able to hit the high notes because of her hoarseness.
 (E) Having sung for over 2 hours, Anita's ability to hit the high notes was prevented by her hoarseness.

11. Some philosophers maintain that language is essential to formulating certain thoughts; others, that even the most complex thoughts are independent of words.

 (A) thoughts; others, that
 (B) thoughts, however, that others maintain that
 (C) thoughts others suggest that
 (D) thoughts and that others believe
 (E) thoughts but others, however, that

The following sentences test your ability to recognize grammar and usage errors. Each sentence contains either a single error or no error at all. No sentence contains more than one error. The error, if there is one, is underlined and lettered. If the sentence contains an error, select the one underlined part that must be changed to make the sentence correct. If the sentence is correct, select choice E. In choosing answers, follow the requirements of standard written English.

EXAMPLE:

By the time they reached the halfway point
           A
in the race, most of the runners hadn't hardly
   B   C   D
begun to hit their stride.   No error
                      E

Ⓐ Ⓑ Ⓒ ● Ⓔ

---

12. Ellen turned around quick and noticed
                   A
 that the dog that had been following her was
     B   C
 now gone.   No error
      D   E

13. Marlena was honored not only for her

 initiative in establishing the fund for war
   A
 refugees but also in devoting so much
              B
 of her own time and money
     C
 to its success.   No error
    D   E

14. The Medieval era in music is considered
                     A
 by most scholars to begin during the reign
   B   C
 of Pope Gregory and to have ended

 around the middle of the 15th century.
             D
 No error
   E

15. Neither the artists who were at the vanguard
               A
 of the Expressionist movement or even the
                B
 critics of the era could have foreseen
     C
 the impact of this new mode on the general
    D
 public.   No error
        E

GO ON TO THE NEXT PAGE

6　　**6**　　**6**　　**6**　　**6**　　**6**

16. Several members <u>of the safety commission</u>
                                    A
    <u>suggested</u> that lowering the speed limit
        B
    <u>on the road</u> would not necessarily result in
        C
    <u>less</u> accidents.   <u>No error</u>
        D   E

17. By the time the operation <u>was completed</u>,
                                        A
    five surgeons <u>spent</u> over 20 hours <u>performing</u>
                      B   C
    more than a dozen <u>procedures</u>.   <u>No error</u>
                            D   E

18. Not until the recent scandal <u>has</u> the
                                    A
    newspapers published <u>anything</u> even
                            B
    vaguely <u>negative</u> about the company or
                C
    <u>its executives</u>.   <u>No error</u>
        D   E

19. <u>After falling asleep</u> on a horse-drawn bus in
        A
    Belgium in 1865, Friedrick Kekule had a

    <u>dream, it led</u> to <u>his discovery</u> of the structure
        B   C
    <u>of the benzene molecule</u>.   <u>No error</u>
        D   E

20. The movement <u>to establish</u> women's issues
                        A
    as important <u>subjects of study</u> <u>have had</u>
                        B   C
    a profound impact on the curricula

    <u>offered in colleges</u> today.   <u>No error</u>
        D   E

21. Legends and folk stories inevitably become

    transformed and <u>exaggerated</u> as they are
                        A
    <u>passed down</u> through the generations, often
        B
    in order <u>to conform</u> to changing political
                C
    and <u>social standards</u>.   <u>No error</u>
            D   E

22. Although the remarks <u>were made</u> to the
                            A
    entire group, <u>everyone</u> at the meeting could
                    B
    tell <u>that they were</u> particularly intended
            C
    <u>for Maria and I</u>.   <u>No error</u>
        D   E

23. By all accounts, the restructuring of the

    federal department was <u>successive</u>,
                                A
    <u>eliminating</u> unnecessary layers
        B
    <u>of bureaucracy</u> and dozens of
        C
    <u>wasteful procedures</u>.   <u>No error</u>
        D   E

24. The professor <u>suggested</u> that
                        A
    <u>those who wished</u> to attend the lecture next
        B
    week <u>be in the classroom</u> 10 minutes
                C
    <u>earlier than usual</u>.   <u>No error</u>
        D   E

GO ON TO THE NEXT PAGE ⟶

6   6   6   6   6   6

25. While in office a President can usually
                               A
    pass more legislation, and with fewer
                         B
    procedural obstacles, when the Congress

    and the administration are underneath the
                              C
    control of the same political party.
      D
    No error
      E

26. A quick inspection of Kurt's art collection
                A
    would show clearly that he has a discerning
         B   C
    eye for exemplary works of art.   No error
              D   E

27. Surprisingly absent from the debate were
       A   B
    the vice president's arrogance that he
                                    C
    typically displays in such forums.   No error
                        D   E

28. Of the numerous strains of *Streptococcus*

    bacteria that are known to cause
             A
    infections, type B is the more dangerous
                             B
    for pregnant women about to give
      C   D
    birth.   No error
              E

29. Since 2001, the company has spent
                             A
    more time on employee training than
             B
    they did in the previous 10 years combined.
      C   D
    No error
      E

GO ON TO THE NEXT PAGE

6   **6**   **6**   **6**   **6**   **6**

Directions: The following passage is an early draft of an essay. Some parts of the passage need to be rewritten.

Read the passage and select the best answers for the questions that follow. Some questions are about particular sentences or parts of sentences and ask you to improve sentence structure or word choice. Other questions ask you to consider organization and development. In choosing answers, follow the requirements of standard written English.

Questions 30–35 refer to the following passage.

(1) Most great scientists and artists are familiar with the so-called "eureka phenomenon." (2) This is the experience that a thinker has when, after they thought about a problem long and hard, they suddenly come upon a solution in a flash when they are no longer thinking about it. (3) The name of the phenomenon comes from the legend of Archimedes. (4) He had been thinking for days about a hard problem that had come from the king, King Hieron II. (5) The problem was how to determine whether the king's crown was pure gold without destroying it. (6) As he was bathing, the solution to the problem came to Archimedes in a flash and he ran naked through the streets of Syracuse shouting "Eureka!" meaning "I have found it!"

(7) Students should understand this also. (8) You have probably had the experience of thinking about a paper or a math problem for so long that it's like one's brain gets frozen. (9) When this happens, it is best to get away from the problem for a while rather than obsess about it. (10) Isaac Asimov, one of the most prolific writers of all time, used to go to the movies every time he got writer's block. (11) He claimed that he always came out of the movie knowing exactly how to get his story back on track.

(12) Unfortunately, many students today don't have time for that. (13) They feel so much pressure to get everything done—their homework, their jobs, their sports, their extracurricular activities—that they think that taking "time out" to relax their brains is just a costly waste of time. (14) This is really too bad because very often relaxation is more valuable to a student than just more hard work.

30. Which of the following is the best revision of the underlined portion of sentence 2 (reproduced below)?

This is the experience that a thinker has when, after they thought about a problem long and hard, they suddenly come upon a solution in a flash when they are no longer thinking about it.

(A) that a thinker has when, after they thought long and hard about a problem, their solution suddenly arises like a flash

(B) that thinkers have when a solution suddenly had arisen like a flash after they were thinking long and hard about a problem

(C) that a thinker has when, after having thought long and hard about a problem, they suddenly come upon a solution

(D) that thinkers have when, after having thought long and hard about a problem, they suddenly come upon a solution

(E) that thinkers have when, thinking long and hard about a problem, they suddenly come upon a solution in a flash

GO ON TO THE NEXT PAGE ⇒

6   6   6   6   6   6

31. Which of the following is the best way to combine sentences 3, 4, and 5?

(A) The name of the phenomenon comes from the legend of Archimedes, who had been thinking for days about how to determine whether King Hieron II's crown was pure gold without destroying it.

(B) Archimedes had been thinking for days about how to determine whether King Hieron II's crown was pure gold without destroying it, and this is where the name of the phenomenon comes from.

(C) The legend of Archimedes thinking about how to determine whether King Hieron II's crown was pure gold without destroying it is the origin of the name of the phenomenon.

(D) The phenomenon is named for Archimedes and his thinking for days about how to determine whether King Hieron II's crown was pure gold without destroying it.

(E) The name of the phenomenon was from Archimedes, and his thinking for days about how to determine without destroying it whether King Hieron II's crown was pure gold.

32. Which of the following revisions of sentence 7 most clearly and logically introduces the second paragraph?

(A) This historical episode is something that all students should learn about in school.

(B) Understanding this phenomenon may help students to improve their studies.

(C) Nevertheless, this episode is something that all students should know.

(D) Understanding this episode requires a more thorough understanding of its historical setting.

(E) Many have tried to understand this phenomenon, but few have succeeded.

33. Which of the following is the best revision of the underlined portion of sentence 8 (reproduced below)?

You have probably had the experience of thinking about a paper or a math problem for so long that it's like one's brain gets frozen.

(A) it seems that your brain gets frozen
(B) one's brain gets frozen
(C) your brain seems to freeze
(D) your brains seem to freeze
(E) one's brain seems to freeze

34. Where is the best place to insert the following sentence?

Perhaps if students could work such little excursions into their busy study schedules, they would have similar "eureka" experiences.

(A) after sentence 7
(B) after sentence 8
(C) after sentence 9
(D) after sentence 10
(E) after sentence 11 (as the last sentence of the second paragraph)

35. In context, which of the following revisions of the underlined portion of sentence 12 (reproduced below) is most effective at making it clearer and more specific?

Unfortunately, many students today don't have time for that.

(A) today have hardly even 1 hour for such things
(B) today, unlike those in Archimedes' time, don't have time to go to the movies
(C) today don't have time for such excursions
(D) of modern times lack sufficient time for the kinds of things explained above
(E) today lack sufficient time for things like this

STOP

If you finish before time is called, you may check your work on this section only. Do not turn to any other section of the test.

7   7   7   7   7   7

SECTION 7
Time—20 minutes
16 questions

Turn to Section 7 of your answer sheet to answer the questions in this section.

Directions: For this section, solve each problem and decide which is the best of the choices given. Fill in the corresponding circle on the answer sheet. You may use any available space for scratchwork.

Notes

1. The use of a calculator is permitted.

2. All numbers used are real numbers.

3. Figures that accompany problems in this test are intended to provide information useful in solving the problems. They are drawn as accurately as possible EXCEPT when it is stated in a specific problem that the figure is not drawn to scale. All figures lie in a plane unless otherwise indicated.

4. Unless otherwise specified, the domain of any function f is assumed to be the set of all real numbers x for which $f(x)$ is a real number.

Reference Information

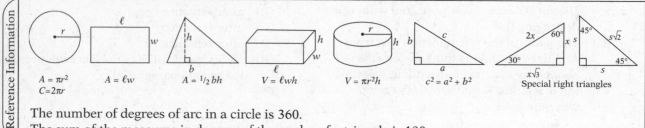

$A = \pi r^2$ $A = \ell w$ $A = \frac{1}{2}bh$ $V = \ell wh$ $V = \pi r^2 h$ $c^2 = a^2 + b^2$ Special right triangles
$C = 2\pi r$

The number of degrees of arc in a circle is 360.
The sum of the measures in degrees of the angles of a triangle is 180.

---

1. If four apples cost 20 cents, then, at this rate, how much would ten apples cost?

(A) $.40
(B) $.50
(C) $.60
(D) $.70
(E) $.80

2. If $2^b = 8$, then $3^b =$

(A) 6
(B) 9
(C) 27
(D) 64
(E) 81

3. How much greater is the average (arithmetic mean) of a, b, and 18 than the average of a, b, and 12?

(A) 2
(B) 3
(C) 4
(D) 5
(E) 6

GO ON TO THE NEXT PAGE ⟹

4. The first day of a particular month is a Tuesday. What day of the week will it be on the 31st day of the month?

(A) Wednesday
(B) Thursday
(C) Friday
(D) Saturday
(E) Sunday

5. How many integer pairs (m, n) satisfy the statements $0 < m + n < 50$ and $\dfrac{m}{n} = 8$?

(A) 5
(B) 6
(C) 7
(D) 8
(E) more than 8

6. If $y\%$ of 50 is 32, then what is 200% of y?

(A) 16
(B) 32
(C) 64
(D) 128
(E) 256

7. For $x > 0$, the function $g(x)$ is defined by the equation $g(x) = x + x^{1/2}$. What is the value of $g(16)$?

(A) 16
(B) 20
(C) 24
(D) 64
(E) 272

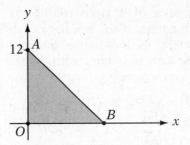

Note: Figure not drawn to scale.

8. In the figure above, if the slope of $\overline{AB}$ is $-\frac{3}{4}$, what is the area of $\triangle ABO$?

(A) 54
(B) 72
(C) 96
(D) 108
(E) 192

$$-1, 1, 2, -1, 1, 2, -1, 1, 2, \ldots$$

9. The sequence above continues according to the pattern shown. What is the sum of the first 25 terms of this sequence?

(A) 15
(B) 16
(C) 18
(D) 19
(E) 21

10. A jar contains only white and blue marbles of identical size and weight. The ratio of the number of white marbles to the number of blue marbles is 4 to b. If the probability of choosing a white marble from the jar at random is $\frac{1}{4}$, then what is the value of b?

(A) 1
(B) 2
(C) 6
(D) 12
(E) 16

GO ON TO THE NEXT PAGE

7   7   7   7   7   7

11. The area of a right triangle is 10 square centimeters. If the length of each leg, in centimeters, is a positive integer, then what is the *least* possible length, in centimeters, of the hypotenuse?

   (A) $\sqrt{29}$
   (B) $\sqrt{41}$
   (C) $\sqrt{101}$
   (D) $\sqrt{104}$
   (E) $\sqrt{401}$

12. If y is a number less than 0 but greater than –1, which of the following expressions has the greatest value?

   (A) $100y$
   (B) y^2
   (C) y^3
   (D) y^4
   (E) y^5

If at least one wuzzle is grumpy, then some fuzzles are lumpy.

13. If the statement above is true, then which of the following must also be true?

   (A) If all wuzzles are grumpy, then all fuzzles are lumpy.
   (B) If no wuzzle is grumpy, then all fuzzles are lumpy.
   (C) If all fuzzles are lumpy, then all wuzzles are grumpy.
   (D) If no wuzzle is grumpy, then no fuzzle is lumpy.
   (E) If no fuzzle is lumpy, then no wuzzle is grumpy.

14. Six buses are to carry 200 students on a field trip. If each bus must have no more than 40 students and no fewer than 30 students, then what is the greatest number of buses that can have 40 students?

   (A) 6
   (B) 5
   (C) 4
   (D) 3
   (E) 2

15. The volume of right cylinder A is twice the volume of right cylinder B. If the height of cylinder B is twice the height of cylinder A, then what is the ratio of the radius of cylinder A to the radius of cylinder B?

   (A) 1 to 2
   (B) 1 to 1
   (C) $\sqrt{2}$ to 1
   (D) 2 to 1
   (E) 4 to 1

16. In a garden that is divided into x rows of x squares each, w of the squares lie along the boundary of the garden. Which of the following is a possible value for w?

   (A) 29
   (B) 34
   (C) 40
   (D) 46
   (E) 55

STOP

If you finish before time is called, you may check your work on this section only. Do not turn to any other section of the test.

8   8   8   8   8   8

SECTION 8
Time—20 minutes
19 questions

Turn to Section 8 of your answer sheet to answer the questions in this section.

Directions: For each question in this section, select the best answer from among the choices given and fill in the corresponding circle on the answer sheet.

Each sentence below has one or two blanks, each blank indicating that something has been omitted. Beneath the sentence are five words or sets of words labeled A through E. Choose the word or set of words that, when inserted in the sentence, best fits the meaning of the sentence as a whole.

EXAMPLE:

Rather than accepting the theory unquestioningly, Deborah regarded it with -----.

(A) mirth
(B) sadness
(C) responsibility
(D) ignorance
(E) skepticism

---

1. The evidence for ESP is ------- at best, so very few reputable scientists are willing to even ------- that the phenomenon exists.

    (A) meager . . regret
    (B) unconvincing . . suggest
    (C) plentiful . . admit
    (D) paltry . . deny
    (E) strong . . assume

2. The concept that the Earth is round was once ------- theory, but is now accepted as an inarguable truth.

    (A) an incontrovertible
    (B) a mellifluous
    (C) an admirable
    (D) a dubious
    (E) an accurate

3. The controversy within the party produced a ------- that broke it into several factions even before the matter could be fully discussed among the members.

    (A) unanimity
    (B) schism
    (C) caucus
    (D) commemoration
    (E) prognostication

4. Horace Mann, widely acknowledged as the father of American public schooling, ------- the Massachusetts legislature to institute a system for ------- universal access to education.

    (A) petitioned . . restricting
    (B) established . . denying
    (C) persuaded . . ensuring
    (D) tolerated . . requiring
    (E) discouraged . . vouchsafing

GO ON TO THE NEXT PAGE ⟶

5. The light from most stars takes millions of years to reach us, so not only is the present existence of these stars -------, but so are the very concepts of "the present" and "existence."

    (A) debatable
    (B) methodical
    (C) indecorous
    (D) imperious
    (E) profuse

6. Although many parents prefer to be ------- when their children broach sensitive personal subjects, others resort instead to ------- so as to make any potentially offensive matters seem less objectionable.

    (A) honest . . anachronism
    (B) intolerant . . laudation
    (C) clandestine . . obligation
    (D) candid . . euphemism
    (E) forthright . . coercion

The passages below are followed by questions based on their content; questions following a pair of related passages may also be based on the relationship between the paired passages. Answer the questions on the basis of what is <u>stated</u> or <u>implied</u> in the passage and in any introductory material that may be provided.

Questions 7–19 are based on the following passages.

The following two passages concern the use of "reinforcers," which are rewards or punishments used to encourage desired behaviors, and "contingencies," which are the arrangements of those reinforcers to shape behavior.

PASSAGE 1

    "Avoid compulsion," said Plato in *The Republic*, "and let your children's lessons take the form
Line of play." Horace, among others, recommended rewarding a child with cakes. Eras-
5 mus tells of an English gentleman who tried to teach his son Greek and Latin without punishment. He taught the boy to use a bow and arrow and set up targets in the shape of Greek and Latin letters, rewarding each hit with a
10 cherry. He also fed the boy letters cut from

delicious biscuits. Privileges and favors are often suggested, and the teacher may be personally reinforcing as friend or entertainer. In industrial education students are paid for learning.
15 Certain explicit contrived reinforcers, such as marks, grades, and diplomas, are characteristic of education as an institution. (These suggest progress, but like progress they must be made reinforcing for other reasons.) Prizes
20 are intrinsically reinforcing. Honors and medals derive their power from prestige or esteem. This varies between cultures and epochs. In 1876 Oscar Wilde, then 22 years old and halfway toward his B.A. at Oxford, got
25 a "first in Mods." He wrote to a friend: ". . . I did not know what I had got till the next morning at 12 o'clock, breakfasting at the Mitre, I read it in the *Times*. Altogether I swaggered horribly but am really pleased with
30 myself. My poor mother is in great delight, and I was overwhelmed with telegrams on Thursday from everyone I knew." The contemporary student graduating *summa cum laude* is less widely acclaimed.
35   Although free of some of the by-products of aversive control, positive reinforcers of this sort are not without their problems. Many are effective only in certain states of deprivation which are not always easily arranged. Making
40 a student hungry in order to reinforce him with food would raise personal issues which are not entirely avoided with other kinds of reinforcers. We cannot all get prizes, and if some students get high grades, others must
45 get low.
    But the main problem again is the contingencies. Much of what the child is to do in school does not have the form of play, with its naturally reinforcing consequences, nor is
50 there any natural connection with food or a passing grade or a medal. Such contingencies must be arranged by the teacher, and the arrangement is often defective. The boy mentioned by Erasmus may have salivated slightly

First passage: B. F. Skinner, *The Technology of Teaching*, © 1968 Prentice-Hall. Courtesy of the B. F. Skinner Foundation.
Second passage: © 2004 Christopher Black. All rights reserved. Reprinted by permission of the author.

GO ON TO THE NEXT PAGE ⟶

8   8   8   8   8   8

55 upon seeing a Greek or Latin text, and he was
    probably a better archer, but his knowledge of
    Greek and Latin could not have been appre-
    ciably improved. Grades are almost always
    given long after the student has stopped be-
60 having as a student. We must know that such
    contingencies are weak because we would
    never use them to shape skilled behavior. In
    industrial education pay is usually by the
    hour—in other words, contingent mainly on
65 being present. Scholarships are contingent on
    a general level of performance. All these con-
    tingencies could no doubt be improved, but
    there is probably good reason why they re-
    main defective.

PASSAGE 2

70   Even if they don't study it as a philosophi-
    cal matter, all teachers must at some point
    confront the issue of whether, when, and how
    to punish or reward student behavior. Unless
    a teacher is blessed with a class full of highly
75 motivated adult-pleasers, it is nearly impossi-
    ble to avoid the need to nudge students in one
    direction or another. Simple suggestion works
    occasionally, but not frequently enough. Rea-
    soning sometimes works, too, but explaining
80 the logical nuances of behavioral standards is
    often time-consuming and too often falls on
    deaf ears. So the practical question becomes:
    the carrot or the stick?
        Most educators and psychologists agree
85 that reward is always better than punishment,
    but a small yet vocal group of psychologists
    have maintained since the 1960s that reward
    is often just as harmful as punishment, if not
    more so. Their arguments are subtle but very
90 persuasive. Educators like Alfie Kohn and psy-
    chologists like Edward Deci claim that careful
    study has shown that the introduction of a re-
    ward system, like gold stars on an attendance
    sheet or extra recess time for good behavior,
95 changes the nature of the desired behavior
    completely, and not for the better. For in-
    stance, Deci conducted a study in which peo-
    ple were given a puzzle to solve. Some were
    given money as a "reward" for solving the
100 puzzle and others were simply asked to solve
    the puzzle. Afterwards, both groups were left

alone but watched carefully. Those who had
been paid stopped playing, but those who had
not been paid continued. Deci concluded that
105 the subjects who were paid probably construed the task as being manipulative: the experimenter was trying to get them to do
something through bribery. The unpaid subjects, however, were more likely to see the
110 task as fun and worth doing for its own sake.
    This study and many like it have profound
implications for the classroom. Several experiments have demonstrated that "pay-to-read"
programs, where students are given money or
115 certificates to read books, have surprisingly
negative effects on literacy. Such programs
usually get kids to "read" a lot more books,
but their reading skills and, far more importantly, their love of reading decline. Such pro-
120 grams, research suggests, turn reading into a
performance rather than a fulfilling personal
experience. They encourage students to read
books only superficially and only to get the
reward. What is worse, like Deci's puzzle-
125 solvers, the students don't want to continue
reading after the payments stop. Books have
become only enrichment for the pocket, not
enrichment for the mind.
    Of course, the human mind is an enor-
130 mously complex machine, and it would be a
mistake to use these few experiments to generalize that all rewards are bad. Certainly,
honest and mindful praise from a respected
teacher can do a great deal to encourage not
135 only good behavior but rigorous intellectual
curiosity. Parents and teachers, however, need
to be very aware of children's need to feel in
control of themselves.

7. It can be inferred that the "English gentleman"
    (line 5) believed that good teaching utilized

    (A) punishment
    (B) well-written books
    (C) reward
    (D) humor
    (E) careful grading

GO ON TO THE NEXT PAGE ⇒

8. The parenthetical remark in lines 17–19 is intended to caution educators against

(A) failing to make grades and diplomas meaningful to students
(B) punishing students unnecessarily
(C) employing dull lessons
(D) emphasizing entertainment over rigor
(E) using rewards as reinforcers

9. Passage 1 indicates that "cultures and epochs" (lines 22–23) vary in the ways that

(A) universities choose from among their applicants
(B) academic awards are effective as motivators
(C) universities teach literature
(D) students are paid money for learning
(E) the media portray educational crises

10. The Wilde story in lines 23–32, "In 1876 . . . everyone I knew,'" is intended to illustrate

(A) how the modern cultural perception of academic honors differs from that of a previous era
(B) a particularly effective teaching strategy
(C) how a famous author used rewards to teach his students
(D) the dangerous effects of using academic rewards
(E) the point that Plato makes in the first sentence

11. Passage 1 mentions which of the following as "problems" (line 37) inherent in the use of positive reinforcers in education?

    I. difficulties in scheduling the reinforcers
    II. limitations in the supply of reinforcers
    III. the fact that rewards encourage only superficial learning

(A) I only
(B) II only
(C) I and II only
(D) I and III only
(E) I, II, and III

12. In the final paragraph of Passage 1, the author suggests that grades are problematic as reinforcers because they

(A) cannot be given to every student
(B) do not provide sensual gratification, as food does
(C) are not publicized enough
(D) are not given immediately after the desired behavior is exhibited
(E) are not as useful to the student as money

13. The sentence that begins on line 78, "Reasoning sometimes works . . . on deaf ears" is intended to describe the interaction between

(A) those who promote the use of punishments and those who oppose it
(B) educators and philosophers
(C) parents and teachers
(D) teachers and administrators
(E) teachers and students

14. In Passage 2, Alfie Kohn and Edward Deci (lines 90–91) are mentioned as examples of

(A) teachers who use rewards as reinforcers
(B) experts who question the effectiveness of rewards as reinforcers
(C) scientists on opposite sides of a debate
(D) educators who prefer negative reinforcers to positive reinforcers
(E) educators who advocate a careful schedule of contingencies for students

GO ON TO THE NEXT PAGE

8   8   8   8   8   8

15. In saying that "the introduction of a reward system . . . changes the nature of the desired behavior" (lines 92–95), the author of Passage 2 indicates that

   (A) many people object to the use of punishments in school

   (B) teachers find it difficult to find the right kinds of rewards for student performance

   (C) experts disagree about the effects of rewards on human behavior

   (D) such systems tend to decrease student interest in the activity for its own sake

   (E) not enough study has been done on the effectiveness of rewards in education

16. Deci's conclusion about the experiment described in Passage 2 (lines 96–110) assumes that the subjects in the study

   (A) are well educated

   (B) are highly proficient at solving puzzles

   (C) have not participated in reward systems before

   (D) can make inferences about the motives of the experimenter

   (E) have some teaching experience

17. The author of Passage 2 mentions that "the human mind is an enormously complex machine" (lines 129–130) in order to suggest that

   (A) a simplistic theory about the effectiveness of rewards is unwise

   (B) people cannot be easily fooled

   (C) many learning disabilities require special attention

   (D) teachers often find it hard to teach certain subjects

   (E) Deci's experiment was poorly constructed

18. The description of the "problems" (line 37) with positive reinforcers in Passage 1 would most likely be regarded by Edward Deci as

   (A) thorough and fair

   (B) presumptuous and incomplete

   (C) unfair to educators

   (D) erroneous in concluding that the methods of the "gentleman" were ineffective

   (E) likely correct, but worthy of further study

19. Which of the following assumptions is shared by the authors of both passages?

   (A) Rewards are ineffective as reinforcers of behavior.

   (B) Honors and grades are necessary elements of institutional education.

   (C) Good teaching is always focused on play.

   (D) Negative feedback is not an effective teaching tool.

   (E) If prizes are to be used in a classroom, there must be enough for all students.

STOP

If you finish before time is called, you may check your work on this section only. Do not turn to any other section of the test.

9   9   9   9   9   9

SECTION 9
Time—10 minutes
14 questions

Turn to Section 9 of your answer sheet to answer the questions in this section.

Directions: For each question in this section, select the best answer from among the choices given and fill in the corresponding circle on the answer sheet.

The following sentences test correctness and effectiveness of expression. Part of each sentence or the entire sentence is underlined; beneath each sentence are five ways of phrasing the underlined material. Choice A repeats the original phrasing; the other four choices are different. If you think the original phrasing produces a better sentence than any of the alternatives, select choice A; if not, select one of the other choices.

In making your selection, follow the requirements of standard written English; that is, pay attention to grammar, choice of words, sentence construction, and punctuation. Your selection should result in the most effective sentence—clear and precise, without awkwardness or ambiguity.

EXAMPLE:

The children <u>couldn't hardly believe their eyes</u>.

(A) couldn't hardly believe their eyes
(B) could hardly believe their eyes
(C) would not hardly believe their eyes
(D) couldn't nearly believe their eyes
(E) couldn't hardly believe his or her eyes

1. <u>Choreographer Alvin Ailey's works, whose style is rooted in the techniques of modern dance, jazz dance and ballet, draw upon African American themes.</u>

(A) Choreographer Alvin Ailey's works, whose style is rooted in the techniques of modern dance, jazz dance and ballet, draw upon African American themes.
(B) Alvin Ailey has a style of a choreographer that is rooted in the techniques of modern dance, jazz dance and ballet of which also draws upon African American themes.
(C) The works of choreographer Alvin Ailey, which draw upon African American themes, have a style that is rooted in the techniques of modern dance, jazz dance, and ballet.
(D) Choreographer Alvin Ailey's works, which have a style that is rooted in the techniques of modern dance, jazz dance, and ballet, drawing upon African American themes.
(E) Alvin Ailey's style, a choreographer, is rooted in the techniques of modern dance and jazz dance and ballet which also draws upon African American themes.

GO ON TO THE NEXT PAGE ⟹

9 9 9 9 9 9

2. <u>The mountain climbers getting this far, they</u> did not want to return without having reached the peak.

(A) The mountain climbers getting this far, they

(B) Having gotten this far, the mountain climbers

(C) To have gotten this far, the mountain climbers

(D) The mountain climbers having gotten so far that they

(E) Mountain climbers getting this far

3. Although usually even-tempered, <u>Rachel's irritation with her supervisor caused her to become</u> uncharacteristically cantankerous.

(A) Rachel's irritation with her supervisor caused her to become

(B) Rachel being irritated by her supervisor caused her to become

(C) Rachel was irritated by her supervisor, and so became

(D) her supervisor caused Rachel through irritation to become

(E) Rachel, due to her supervisor's irritation, caused her to become

4. Because Alberta worked harder than her associates, she assumed that her salary <u>would be higher than the</u> other workers in the firm.

(A) would be higher than the

(B) was higher than that of the

(C) had been higher than the

(D) being higher than the salary of

(E) was highest of the

5. The police chief was hoping that, by assigning an extra officer to the patrol, he <u>would decrease the amount of elicit</u> behavior in the neighborhood.

(A) would decrease the amount of elicit

(B) would be able to decrease the elicit

(C) would decrease the amount of illicit

(D) might be able to lessen that of the illicit

(E) decreases the amount of illicit

6. <u>Watching from the balcony</u>, the paraders marched triumphantly through the streets below us.

(A) Watching from the balcony

(B) While watching from the balcony

(C) As we had been watching from the balcony

(D) As we watched from the balcony

(E) From the balcony, while watching

7. By the time we arrived at the campsite where the troop would be staying, <u>the counselors set up all the tents</u>.

(A) the counselors set up all the tents

(B) setting up all the tents were the counselors

(C) set up by the counselors are the tents

(D) the tents are set up by the counselors

(E) the counselors had set up all the tents

8. By the time the movie had finished, <u>neither Eric nor his daughters was able to stay awake because of the boredom caused by the film's inferior plot</u>.

(A) neither Eric nor his daughters was able to stay awake because of the boredom caused by the film's inferior plot

(B) staying awake was an impossibility for Eric and his daughters because of the boredom caused by the inferiority of the plot

(C) neither Eric nor his daughters were able to stay awake because of the boredom caused by the film's inferior plot

(D) Eric and his daughters was unable to stay awake because of the boredom caused by the film's inferior plot

(E) the film's inferior plot had made it impossible for neither Eric nor his daughters to stay awake

GO ON TO THE NEXT PAGE ⟶

9   9   9   9   9   9

9. An outstanding tennis player, Erica was concerned not only with working her way to the top of the national rankings, but <u>also wanted to compete with class and dignity</u>.

(A) also wanted to compete with class and dignity
(B) also with competing with class and dignity
(C) also with wanting to have competed with class and dignity
(D) she also wanted to compete with class and dignity
(E) she was also wanting to compete with class and dignity

10. Roberto volunteered to be an usher, not wanting to be the one <u>that had to clean up the petals after the ceremony</u>.

(A) that had to clean up the petals after the ceremony
(B) which had to clean up the petals after the ceremony
(C) who had to clean up the petals after the ceremony
(D) that was cleaning the petals up after the ceremony
(E) who was to be cleaning the petals after the ceremony

11. Rebecca liked to read <u>books, of which she found autobiographies being the most interesting</u>.

(A) books, of which she found autobiographies being the most interesting
(B) books, the most fascinating of which to her she found the autobiographies
(C) books, autobiographies being the most interesting she found
(D) books; she found autobiographies to be the most interesting
(E) books, to which autobiographies were the most interesting

12. Forced to live apart from his family and to move from place to place to avoid detection by the government's ubiquitous informers, <u>St. Pierre adopting a number of disguises</u>.

(A) St. Pierre adopting a number of disguises
(B) St. Pierre having adopted a number of disguises
(C) had adopted for St. Pierre a number of disguises
(D) a number of disguises by St. Pierre had adopted
(E) St. Pierre had to adopt a number of disguises

13. The Santa Catalina <u>Mountains, forming 12 million years ago during a period when the Western North American Continent was stretching</u>, cracking into blocks bordered by steep faults.

(A) Mountains, forming 12 million years ago during a period when the Western North American Continent was stretching
(B) Mountains were formed 12 million years ago during a period when the Western North American Continent was being stretched
(C) Mountains, having been formed 12 million years ago during a period when the Western North American Continent was stretching
(D) Mountains was formed 12 million years ago during a period when the Western North American Continent was being stretched
(E) Mountains had been formed during a period 12 million years ago when the Western North American Continent was stretching

14. The most challenging aspect of the project is <u>we have to coordinate our work carefully</u>.

(A) we have to coordinate our work carefully
(B) we must coordinate our work carefully
(C) our coordination of our work carefully
(D) coordinating our work carefully
(E) in careful coordination of our work

If you finish before time is called, you may check your work on this section only. Do not turn to any other section of the test.

ANSWER KEY

Critical Reading

Section 2

	COR. ANS.	DIFF. LEV.		COR. ANS.	DIFF. LEV.
1.	A	1	13.	A	4
2.	C	2	14.	C	3
3.	D	3	15.	C	4
4.	A	4	16.	D	4
5.	E	4	17.	E	4
6.	C	3	18.	C	3
7.	A	4	19.	B	3
8.	B	3	20.	C	4
9.	E	3	21.	D	4
10.	E	2	22.	D	3
11.	A	3	23.	E	4
12.	B	4	24.	A	4

Number correct

Number incorrect

Section 5

	COR. ANS.	DIFF. LEV.		COR. ANS.	DIFF. LEV.
1.	C	2	13.	E	3
2.	E	3	14.	C	4
3.	D	3	15.	D	3
4.	A	4	16.	B	4
5.	E	4	17.	A	3
6.	D	3	18.	E	4
7.	B	4	19.	D	4
8.	A	3	20.	B	1
9.	E	4	21.	C	3
10.	D	4	22.	C	5
11.	D	5	23.	E	5
12.	E	4	24.	A	4

Number correct

Number incorrect

Section 8

	COR. ANS.	DIFF. LEV.		COR. ANS.	DIFF. LEV.
1.	B	2			
2.	D	3	11.	C	4
3.	B	2	12.	D	2
4.	C	3	13.	E	2
5.	A	4	14.	B	3
6.	D	5	15.	D	4
7.	C	1	16.	D	4
8.	A	3	17.	A	3
9.	B	4	18.	B	4
10.	A	3	19.	D	3

Number correct

Number incorrect

Math

Section 3

	COR. ANS.	DIFF. LEV.		COR. ANS.	DIFF. LEV.
1.	E	1	11.	D	3
2.	A	2	12.	B	3
3.	C	2	13.	A	3
4.	C	2	14.	D	3
5.	D	2	15.	A	4
6.	A	3	16.	B	3
7.	D	3	17.	D	4
8.	A	3	18.	C	4
9.	C	3	19.	A	4
10.	B	2	20.	A	5

Number correct

Number incorrect

Section 4

Multiple-Choice Questions

	COR. ANS.	DIFF. LEV.
1.	E	1
2.	C	3
3.	E	2
4.	A	3
5.	A	3
6.	D	3
7.	B	4
8.	C	4

Number correct

Number incorrect

Student-produced Response questions

	COR. ANS.	DIFF. LEV.
9.	16	1
10.	36	2
11.	5	2
12.	12	3
13.	15	3
14.	8 or 12	4
15.	25	4
16.	24	3
17.	52	4
18.	225	5

Number correct (9–18)

Section 7

	COR. ANS.	DIFF. LEV.		COR. ANS.	DIFF. LEV.
1.	B	2	9.	A	4
2.	C	2	10.	D	4
3.	A	3	11.	B	3
4.	B	3	12.	B	4
5.	A	3	13.	E	4
6.	D	3	14.	E	4
7.	B	4	15.	D	5
8.	C	3	16.	C	5

Number correct

Number incorrect

Writing

Section 6

	COR. ANS.	DIFF. LEV.		COR. ANS.	DIFF. LEV.		COR. ANS.	DIFF. LEV.		COR. ANS.	DIFF. LEV.
1.	D	1	11.	A	5	21.	E	4	31.	A	4
2.	A	1	12.	A	1	22.	D	3	32.	B	3
3.	B	2	13.	B	2	23.	A	3	33.	C	3
4.	C	2	14.	C	3	24.	E	4	34.	E	3
5.	A	2	15.	B	2	25.	C	4	35.	C	3
6.	B	3	16.	D	3	26.	E	3			
7.	C	3	17.	B	3	27.	B	3			
8.	E	3	18.	A	2	28.	B	3			
9.	C	4	19.	B	3	29.	C	5			
10.	D	4	20.	C	3	30.	D	3			

Number correct

Number incorrect

Section 9

	COR. ANS.	DIFF. LEV.		COR. ANS.	DIFF. LEV.
1.	C	2	11.	D	3
2.	B	2	12.	E	3
3.	C	2	13.	B	4
4.	B	4	14.	D	4
5.	C	4			
6.	D	3			
7.	E	3			
8.	C	4			
9.	B	3			
10.	C	3			

Number correct

Number incorrect

NOTE: Difficulty levels are estimates of question difficulty that range from 1 (easiest) to 5 (hardest).

SCORE CONVERSION TABLE

How to score your test

Use the answer key on the previous page to determine your raw score on each section. **Your raw score on each section except Section 4 is simply the number of correct answers minus ¼ of the number of wrong answers. On Section 4, your raw score is the sum of the number of correct answers for questions 1–18 minus ¼ of the number of wrong answers for questions 1–8.** Next, add the raw scores from Sections 2, 5, and 8 to get your Critical Reading raw score, add the raw scores from Sections 3, 4, and 7 to get your Math raw score, and add the raw scores from Sections 6 and 9 to get your Writing raw score. Write the three raw scores here:

Raw Critical Reading score: _____   Raw Math score: _____   Raw Writing score: _____

Use the table below to convert these to scaled scores.

Scaled scores: Critical Reading: _____   Math: _____   Writing: _____

Raw Score	Critical Reading Scaled Score	Math Scaled Score	Writing Scaled Score	Raw Score	Critical Reading Scaled Score	Math Scaled Score	Writing Scaled Score
67	800			32	520	570	610
66	800			31	510	560	600
65	790			30	510	550	580
64	780			29	500	540	570
63	770			28	490	530	560
62	750			27	490	520	550
61	740			26	480	510	540
60	730			25	480	500	530
59	720			24	470	490	520
58	700			23	460	480	510
57	690			22	460	480	500
56	680			21	450	470	490
55	670			20	440	460	480
54	660	800		19	440	450	470
53	650	800		18	430	450	460
52	650	780		17	420	440	450
51	640	760		16	420	430	440
50	630	740		15	410	420	440
49	620	730	800	14	400	410	430
48	620	710	800	13	400	410	420
47	610	710	800	12	390	400	410
46	600	700	790	11	380	390	400
45	600	690	780	10	370	380	390
44	590	680	760	9	360	370	380
43	590	670	740	8	350	360	380
42	580	660	730	7	340	350	370
41	570	650	710	6	330	340	360
40	570	640	700	5	320	330	350
39	560	630	690	4	310	320	340
38	550	620	670	3	300	310	320
37	550	620	660	2	280	290	310
36	540	610	650	1	270	280	300
35	540	600	640	0	250	260	280
34	530	590	630	−1	230	240	270
33	520	580	620	−2 or less	210	220	250

SCORE CONVERSION TABLE FOR WRITING COMPOSITE
[ESSAY + MULTIPLE CHOICE]

Calculate your Writing raw score as you did on the previous page and grade your essay from a 1 to a 6 according to the standards that follow in the detailed answer key.

Essay score: _____   Raw Writing score: _____

Use the table below to convert these to scaled scores.

Scaled score: Writing: _____

Raw Score	Essay Score 0	Essay Score 1	Essay Score 2	Essay Score 3	Essay Score 4	Essay Score 5	Essay Score 6
−2 or less	200	230	250	280	310	340	370
−1	210	240	260	290	320	360	380
0	230	260	280	300	340	370	400
1	240	270	290	320	350	380	410
2	250	280	300	330	360	390	420
3	260	290	310	340	370	400	430
4	270	300	320	350	380	410	440
5	280	310	330	360	390	420	450
6	290	320	340	360	400	430	460
7	290	330	340	370	410	440	470
8	300	330	350	380	410	450	470
9	310	340	360	390	420	450	480
10	320	350	370	390	430	460	490
11	320	360	370	400	440	470	500
12	330	360	380	410	440	470	500
13	340	370	390	420	450	480	510
14	350	380	390	420	460	490	520
15	350	380	400	430	460	500	530
16	360	390	410	440	470	500	530
17	370	400	420	440	480	510	540
18	380	410	420	450	490	520	550
19	380	410	430	460	490	530	560
20	390	420	440	470	500	530	560
21	400	430	450	480	510	540	570
22	410	440	460	480	520	550	580
23	420	450	470	490	530	560	590
24	420	460	470	500	540	570	600
25	430	460	480	510	540	580	610
26	440	470	490	520	550	590	610
27	450	480	500	530	560	590	620
28	460	490	510	540	570	600	630
29	470	500	520	550	580	610	640
30	480	510	530	560	590	620	650
31	490	520	540	560	600	630	660
32	500	530	550	570	610	640	670
33	510	540	550	580	620	650	680
34	510	550	560	590	630	660	690
35	520	560	570	600	640	670	700
36	530	560	580	610	650	680	710
37	540	570	590	620	660	690	720
38	550	580	600	630	670	700	730
39	560	600	610	640	680	710	740
40	580	610	620	650	690	720	750
41	590	620	640	660	700	730	760
42	600	630	650	680	710	740	770
43	610	640	660	690	720	750	780
44	620	660	670	700	740	770	800
45	640	670	690	720	750	780	800
46	650	690	700	730	770	800	800
47	670	700	720	750	780	800	800
48	680	720	730	760	800	800	800
49	680	720	730	760	800	800	800

Detailed Answer Key

Section 1

Consider carefully the issue discussed in the following passage, then write an essay that answers the question posed in the assignment.

> The best leaders are not those who seek power or have great political skill. Great leaders—and these are exceptionally rare, especially today—represent the best selves of the people they represent.

Assignment: **What are the most important qualities of a leader?** Write an essay in which you answer this question and discuss your point of view on this issue. Support your position logically with examples from literature, the arts, history, politics, science and technology, current events, or your experience or observation.

The following essay received 12 points out of a possible 12. This means that, according to the graders, it

- develops an insightful point of view on the topic
- demonstrates exemplary critical thinking
- uses effective examples, reasons, and other evidence to support its thesis
- is consistently focused, coherent, and well organized
- demonstrates skillful and effective use of language and sentence structure
- is largely (but not necessarily completely) free of grammatical and usage errors

There is no more important decision that a citizen can make than one's choice of a leader. I am inclined to agree with Thomas Hobbes, who believed that humans are hardly better than other mammals without a social contract that binds us to work together as a society. Artists could not survive in a society that does not provide a means of trading art for food. Great teachers cannot survive in a society without a means of trading wisdom for shelter. This requires a social order, a division of labor, and a group we call leaders. Yet we know that power corrupts, and absolute power corrupts absolutely. So how do we maintain a just society when we must bestow corrupting powers upon members of that society?

Those who seek power are too often not our best leaders, but rather our best politicians. George Bush, John F. Kennedy and Ronald Reagan came to power not so much because of their visionary leadership but because of their appeal to a television-viewing audience. The problems with democracy are well known. In order to become elected, most politicians must appeal to a broad range of citizens. To gain this appeal, they must pander to their constituents, and often take conflicting or equivocal stances on issues. Of course, the politicians claim that they are taking "forceful

stances" to "bring the people together." But it is far more likely that they are simply doing their best to make everyone happy without putting their feet in their mouths.

So why is democracy the best way of electing a leader? Because the alternatives are much worse. To gain power, one must either use force or pander to those who do. Which is a better alternative? A country is weak if its people do not support it, and, at the very least, a democracy can claim a good degree of public support. Even more importantly, only a democracy allows for the possibility of finding a reluctant leader with genuine leadership skills. It doesn't happen often enough, but when it does, it is breathtaking. Witness the phenomenon of Howard Dean's campaign for the 2004 Democratic nomination for president, or Ross Perot's run in 1992. Neither was ultimately successful, but both demonstrated the potential of motivated citizens to change their country.

Without democracy, there is no hope for an ordinary citizen to change his or her country. What makes America great is not that its policies are always correct. Indeed, they are often deeply flawed. What makes America great is that it is run by those who are not even seeking power: the citizens.

The following essay received 8 points out of a possible 12, meaning that it demonstrates *adequate competence* in that it

- develops a point of view on the topic
- demonstrates some critical thinking, but perhaps not consistently
- uses some examples, reasons, and other evidence to support its thesis, but perhaps not adequately
- shows a general organization and focus, but shows occasional lapses in this regard
- demonstrates adequate but occasionally inconsistent facility with language
- contains occasional errors in grammar, usage, and mechanics

Someone once said that great men don't seek greatness but have it thrust upon them. I think this is true, because those who have really changed the world were not slick politicians but rather people who had such great leadership skill and charisma that others forced them into leadership roles. Good examples of this are Jesus, Mahatma Gandhi, Mother Theresa and George Washington.

After his great victories in the American Revolutionary War against Great Britain, George Washington wanted to retire to his farm in Virginia and live out the rest of his days as a humble farmer. He did not want to become the political leader of a brand new country. But the Continental Congress looked to him for leadership, and sought him out to be the first President of the United States. Washington saw that his country needed him and answered the call.

Similarly, Mahatma Gandhi did not seek personal power, but only justice for his people. His humility and selflessness are what made him one of the great leaders of the twentieth century, and a model for the cause of nonviolent activism.

It is unfortunate that today only millionaires with big political connections seem to have any chance at being elected to national office. Maybe they have a shot at a local race, but the congress and the presidency seem to be off limits. The answer is to get more involved in politics yourself, as a voter, and avoid voting for candidates just because they are popular but instead because they have good souls.

The following essay received 4 points out of a possible 12, meaning that it demonstrates *some incompetence* in that it

- has a seriously limited point of view
- demonstrates weak critical thinking
- uses inappropriate or insufficient examples, reasons, and other evidence to support its thesis
- is poorly focused and organized and has serious problems with coherence
- demonstrates frequent problems with language and sentence structure
- contains errors in grammar and usage that seriously obscure the author's meaning

I'm not sure how it can be that you can be the best person to be in power if you don't want to be. In this country, at least, running for president or something like that takes a lot of effort, and I think you have to be a really hard worker in order to become president or senator.

An example of somebody who is a hard worker who got into office is former president Bill Clinton. Although many people think he had indiscretions in office, he came from a very poor family where he was only raised by his mother because his father left the family when he was young. He worked really hard and became a Rhodes scholar and was elected as governor at a very young age. He knew even when he was a very young kid that he wanted to become a great leader like John F. Kennedy.

Clinton was a good leader because he understood where a lot of people were coming from. He wasn't just a rich guy who got into office because he had rich relatives who got him there. I don't think you can say that the best leaders are the ones who don't want to be in office. If you didn't want to be in office, then you shouldn't run.

Section 2

1. A   Alisha was holding a *grudge,* which is a feeling of resentment.
resentment = ill will; *fortitude* = strength of mind to endure; *sarcasm* = wit used to ridicule; *elation* = extreme joy

2. C   There were people who expected the governor to be *inarticulate* (unable to speak clearly), so they would be surprised if he were *articulate. intolerance* = inability to put up with something; *fatigue* = tiredness; *eloquence* = persuasiveness in speech; *endurance* = ability to last, often through hard times

3. D   The *language of commoners* would be logically described as *common.* But the novelists preferred another kind of *parlance* (speech): that of the *upper* classes. A word such as *elegant* would work nicely. *elite* = superior; *sympathetic* = compassionate; *colloquial* = characteristic of everyday language; *refined* = precise, elegant; *utilitarian* = practical, stressing utility

4. A   The second half of this sentence presents a definition. The word in the blank should mean *"exploring the world." peripatetic* = walking from place to place; *conventional* = customary; *tolerant* = willing to put up with something; *coordinated* = well-matched; *remunerative* = profitable

5. E   A position that requires public speaking would be *difficult* for a person who does not like to speak or is afraid of crowds. *vivacious* = full of life; *garrulous* = talkative; *amiable* = friendly; *reticent* = hesitant to share one's feelings or opinions with others

6. C   The tickbird gets something from the hippopotamus, and the hippopotamus gets something from the tickbird; it's a *give-and-receive* relationship. *deteriorating* = diminishing in quality; *symbiotic* = of mutual benefit; *regressive* = going backwards; *vacillating* = going back and forth

7. A   This sentence establishes a contrast between how *modern scientists* think and how *early philosophers* thought. The contrast shows that the early philosophers were not using experiments as much as their own minds to draw conclusions and that the modern scientists rely more on experimental data to draw their conclusions. *empirical* = relying on the observations made from experiments; *coercion* = pressure on someone to act; *deduction* = reaching a conclusion through the use of logic; *clerical* = relating to office work; *intuitive* = known innately

8. B   The first blank should be a word like *merging* or *unification,* because many companies are under a *single owner.* This would be *troublesome* to those who value independence. *retraction* = taking something back; *differentiation* = finding a difference between two things; *consolidation* = combining of multiple things into one common entity; *collaboration* = working together on something; *dissemination* = the spread of something

9. E   Passage 2 distinguishes between education and schooling. It states that the *main product of schooling is not education* (lines 15–16) and that the struggle that defines education *is denied by schooling* (lines 22–23). Passage 1 makes no such distinction, and speaks of education as if it is inseparable from the idea of schooling.

10. E   The passage mentions that education would diminish social distinctions ("obliterate factitious distinctions in society" (lines 13–14)), improve living standards ("prevents being poor" (line 8)), provide the means to counteract greed ("resist the selfishness of other men" (lines 5–6)), and increase self-sufficiency ("gives each man the independence" (line 4)). It does not, however, mention anything about reducing crime.

11. A   The passage suggests that education *is the great equalizer* and that *the spread of education will open a wider area over which the social feelings will expand.* It concludes by commenting that *if this education should be universal and complete* it would *obliterate factitious distinctions in society.*

12. B   Passage 2 states that education, which is *the acquisition of competence, power, wisdom and discernment* (lines 19–20), is achieved only through the *struggle for sense in the world* (lines 21–22). Therefore, this struggle is empowering.

13. A   "The Beginnings of the Scientific Method" is the best title, because this passage begins by discussing the scientists of the Renaissance and how they *brought about the most fundamental alterations in the world of thought . . . by devising a new method for discovering knowledge* (lines 1–5). This new method was the scientific method.

14. C   Saying that *the early modern scientists laid greatest stress upon observation and the formation of temporary hypotheses* (lines 7–9) is like saying they *emphasized* observation and hypotheses.

15. C   In lines 19–21 the passage suggests that earlier scientists were simply trying *to find the confirmation of Biblical statements about the firmament.*

16. D Choice II is confirmed in lines 32–34: *The principle of the barometer was discovered by Galileo's **pupil*** (student) *Torricelli.* Choice III is confirmed in lines 41–42: *Galileo discovered the moons around Jupiter.*

17. E The final paragraph states that Renaissance scientists believed *that everything consists of bodies in motion, that everything conforms to a mechanical model. The heavens above and the smallest particles below all exhibit the same laws of motion*—even, as it says in the next sentence, *human thought* (lines 67–71).

18. C The final paragraph discusses how the scientific method changed the way science was done.

19. B The passage mentions in lines 22–24 that many military leaders *cement their solidarity by reveling* (taking delight) *in their numerical disadvantage.* They considered it more honorable to fight with fewer men and beat a larger opponent.

20. C Stating that *a well-known proverb was **trotted out** in many instances of the glorious, fighting few* (lines 25–27), in this context, is like saying that the proverb was *used for rhetorical effect* because it was used to persuade and inspire the troops.

21. D When the prince says that *we be a small **body** when compared to the army of our enemies,* he is saying that they are a small army or group of men.

22. D This sentence is discussing the tactical errors of the French in two different battles. The phrase *charging before they were ready* simply means *attacking before they were ready.*

23. E All three of these facts are true and are mentioned in the passage.

24. A The passage states in the final paragraph that *ten thousand more men might actually have hindered the English* (lines 59–60) and that *it seems that in fact . . . strength is not always proportional to size* (lines 62–64).

Section 3

1. E Since n is equal to 3 times an even number, you can eliminate any answer choice that is not a multiple of 3 (A, C, and D). Answer choice (B): $15 = 3 \times 5$; 5 is an odd number, so this answer choice is out. Answer choice (E): $18 = 3 \times 6$; 6 is an even number.

2. A Set up a ratio: $\dfrac{50 \text{ chips}}{2 \text{ hours}} = \dfrac{x \text{ chips}}{7 \text{ hours}}$

Cross-multiply: $350 = 2x$

Divide by 2: $175 = x$

3. C Angles that form a straight angle have a sum of 180°:

$$x + 2x = 180°$$

Combine like terms: $3x = 180°$

Divide by 3: $x = 60°$

4. C Find the smallest number that is divisible by both 15 and 6 and see which answer choice works.

Multiples of 15: 15, **30**, 45, . . .

Multiples of 6: 6, 12, 18, 24, **30**, . . .

5. D $n\%$ of 20 is 4

$$\frac{n}{100} \times 20 = 4$$

Simplify: $.20n = 4$

Divide by .20: $n = 20$

6. A $f(x) = 3x + n$

Plug in 2 for x: $f(2) = 3(2) + n = 0$

Simplify: $6 + n = 0$

Subtract 6: $n = -6$

Substitute for n: $f(x) = 3x - 6$

Plug in 0 for x: $f(0) = 3(0) - 6 = -6$

7. D First find the area of the right triangle:

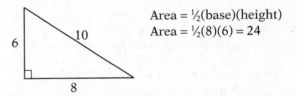

Area = ½(base)(height)

Area = ½(8)(6) = 24

Next, set up an equation for the area of a square.

Area = (side)²

Substitute 24 for area: $24 = (\text{side})^2$

Take the square root: $\sqrt{24} = \text{side}$

Simplify the radical: $2\sqrt{6} = \text{side}$

8. A   You are told that: $12v = 3w$
Divide by 3: $4v = w$
Multiply by 2: $8v = 2w$
The question asks for the value of: $2w - 8v$
Substitute for $2w$: $8v - 8v = 0$
Alternatively, you can try finding values for v and w that work, like 1 and 4, and plug them into $2w - 8v$ and into the choices and find the match.

9. C $2|x| + 1 > 5$
Subtract 1: $2|x| > 4$
Divide by 2: $|x| > 2$
Interpret the absolute value: $x > 2$ OR $x < -2$
You are told that x is negative, so $x < -2$ is the answer.

10. B $-x^2 - 8x - 5$
Substitute -2 for x: $-(-2)^2 - 8(-2) - 5$
Square -2: $-(4) - 8(-2) - 5$
Simplify: $-4 + 16 - 5 = 7$
When evaluating $-x^2$, don't forget to square the value *before* taking its opposite!

11. D $\dfrac{5}{m} \le \dfrac{2}{3}$
Cross-multiply: $15 \le 2m$
Divide by 2: $7.5 \le m$
Since m is greater than *or equal to* 7.5, (D) is the answer.

12. B   First find the price after the 6% sales tax:
$\$60.00 \times .06 = \$3.60$ tax
$\$60.00 + \$3.60 = \$63.60$ price with tax
(A simpler way is just to multiply 60 by 1.06.)
Now find how much change Theo received:
$\$70.00 - \$63.60 = \$6.40$ change

13. A   Write an equation for the first sentence.
$n - m = r$
Because none of the answer choices contain m, solve for m in terms of r and n: $n - m = r$
Add m: $n = r + m$
Subtract r: $n - r = m$
Now write an expression for what the question asks for:
$s + 2m$
Substitute for m: $s + 2(n - r)$
Distribute: $s + 2n - 2r$
Alternatively, you can substitute numbers for n, m, and r, making sure they "work," and get a numerical answer to the question.

14. D   Two points on line l are $(0, 0)$ and $(10, y)$.
Find the slope of the line:
$$m = \frac{y_2 - y_1}{x_2 - x_1} = \frac{y - 0}{10 - 0} = \frac{y}{10} = \frac{3}{5}$$
Cross-multiply: $5y = 30$
Divide by 5: $y = 6$
Since $y = 6$, the height of the triangle is 6. Find the area:
$A = \frac{1}{2}(\text{base})(\text{height})$
Substitute 48 for A: $48 = \frac{1}{2}(\text{base})(6)$
Simplify: $48 = 3(\text{base})$
Divide by 3: $16 = \text{base} = x$
Now find $x + y = 16 + 6 = 22$.

15. A   Ellen travels the first 15 miles at 30 miles per hour. Find out how much time that takes:
$d = (\text{rate})(\text{time})$
Plug in known values: $15 = 30t$
Divide by 30: $\frac{1}{2}$ hour $= t$
The rest of the trip, which is $(y - 15)$ miles long, she travels at an average speed of 40 miles per hour:
$d = (\text{rate})(\text{time})$
Plug in known values: $(y - 15) = 40t$
Divide by 40: $\dfrac{y - 15}{40} = t$
Add the two values together to find the total time:
$$\frac{1}{2} + \frac{y - 15}{40}$$

16. B   Set up the relationship in equation form:
$$y = \frac{km}{n^2}$$
Plug in what you're given: $8 = \dfrac{k(16)}{(1)^2}$
Simplify: $8 = 16k$
Divide by 16: $\frac{1}{2} = k$
Write the new equation: $y = \dfrac{\frac{1}{2}(m)}{(n)^2}$
Plug in new values: $y = \dfrac{\frac{1}{2}(8)}{(4)^2} = \dfrac{4}{16} = \dfrac{1}{4}$

17. D

$$a + b = s$$
$$a - b = t$$

Add straight down: $2a = s + t$

Divide by 2: $a = \dfrac{s+t}{2}$

$$a + b = s$$
$$a - b = t$$

Subtract straight down: $2b = s - t$

Divide by 2: $b = \dfrac{s-t}{2}$

Find the product: $(a)(b) = \left(\dfrac{s+t}{2}\right)\left(\dfrac{s-t}{2}\right) = \left(\dfrac{s^2 - t^2}{4}\right)$

---

18. C $\quad y = m^4 = n^3$

The answer is in terms of y alone, so find m and n in terms of y:

$$y = m^4$$

Take the 4th root: $\quad y^{1/4} = m$

$$y = n^3$$

Take the cube root: $\quad y^{1/3} = n$

Find the product mn: $\quad mn = (y^{1/4})(y^{1/3}) = y^{1/3 + 1/4}$

Add exponents: $\quad mn = y^{7/12}$

---

19. A This question deals with similar triangles:

Set up ratio: $\dfrac{6}{12} = \dfrac{4}{x}$

Cross-multiply: $6x = 48$

Divide by 6: $\quad x = 8$

Area of big triangle = ½(base)(height) = ½(12)(6) = 36
Area of small triangle = ½(base)(height) = ½(8)(4) = 16
Shaded area = area of big triangle − area of small triangle = 36 − 16 = 20

---

20. A Set up a Venn diagram to visualize the information.

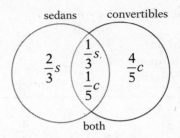

Notice that ⅓ the number of sedans must equal ⅕ the number of convertibles. Say the number of convertible sedans is x. If this is ⅓ the number of sedans, then there must be $3x$ sedans in total, and $3x − x = 2x$ of these are *not* convertibles. Similarly, if x is ⅕ the number of convertibles, then there must be $5x$ convertibles altogether, and $5x − x = 4x$ of these are *not* sedans. So now your diagram can look like this:

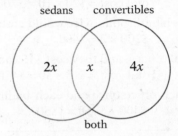

So there must be a total of $2x + x + 4x = 7x$ cars at the dealership. The only choice that is a multiple of 7 is (A): 28.

Section 4

1. E

Perimeter of a square $= 4s$

$36 = 4s$

Divide by 4: $\quad 9 = s$

Area of a square $= (s)^2$

Area $= (9)^2 = 81$

2. C

$$\frac{a}{b} = \frac{1}{10}$$

Cross-multiply: $\qquad b = 10a$

Try positive integer values of a to see how many work:

a	1	2	3	4	5	6	7	8	9
b	10	20	30	40	50	60	70	80	90

There are nine integer pairs that satisfy the equation.

3. E The ten bathrooms cost $20 each to clean:

Total cost $= \$20 \times 10 = \$200$

To clean each bathroom twice would cost:

$\$200 \times 2 = \$400$

There are 30 offices, and they cost $15 each to clean:

Total cost $= \$15 \times 30 = \$450$

To clean each office once and each bathroom twice will cost: $\qquad \$400 + \$450 = \$850$

4. A Remember the "difference of squares" factoring formula: $\qquad a^2 - b^2 = (a-b)(a+b)$

Substitute: $\qquad 10 = (2)(a+b)$

Divide by 2: $\qquad 5 = a + b$

5. A

To find the value of $f(14)$, find all the factors of 14:

$1, \underline{2}, \underline{7}, 14$

There are two prime factors, 2 and 7.

$2 + 7 = 9$

$f(14) = 9$

To find the value of $f(6)$, find all the factors of 6:

$1, \underline{2}, \underline{3}, 6$

There are two prime factors, 2 and 3.

$2 + 3 = 5$

$f(6) = 5$

$f(14) - f(6) = 9 - 5 = 4$

6. D First write an equation to find the average.

$$\frac{a+b+c+d}{4} = 20$$

Multiply by 4: $\qquad a + b + c + d = 80$

If you want a to be as large as possible, make b, c, and d as small as possible. You are told that they are all *different* positive integers: $\qquad a + b + c + d = 80$

Let $b = 1, c = 2, d = 3$: $\quad a + 1 + 2 + 3 = 80$

Combine like terms: $\qquad a + 6 = 80$

Subtract 6: $\qquad a = 74$

7. B Let the radius of circle A $= a$ and the radius of circle B $= b$. It is given that $a = 2b$. The circumference of a circle can be found with the equation $C = 2\pi r$. The sum of their circumferences is 36π:

$$36\pi = 2\pi a + 2\pi b$$

Divide by π: $\qquad 36 = 2a + 2b$

Substitute for a: $\qquad 36 = 2(2b) + 2b$

Simplify: $\qquad 36 = 4b + 2b$

Combine like terms: $\quad 36 = 6b$

Divide by 6: $\qquad 6 = b$

Solve for a: $\qquad a = 2(b) = 2(6) = 12$

8. C This is a visualization problem. The six possible planes are illustrated below. Notice that the six faces of the cube "don't count," because each of those contains four edges of the cube.

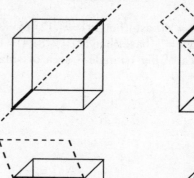

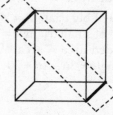

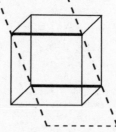

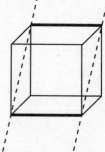

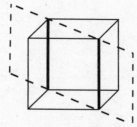

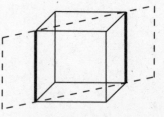

9. **16** Set up an equation: $2x - 10 = 22$
   Add 10: $2x = 32$
   Divide by 2: $x = 16$

10. **36**

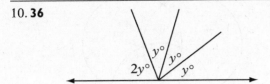

There are 180° on one side of a line:
$$2y + y + y + y = 180°$$
Combine like terms: $5y = 180°$
Divide by 5: $y = 36°$

11. **5** Think simple: What's the simplest way to turn $8x + 4y$ into $2x + y$? Just divide by 4!
$$8x + 4y = 20$$
Divide by 4: $2x + y = 5$

12. **12** Just substitute $x = 3$ and $y = 5$ into the equation and solve for m:
$$3m - 15 = 21$$
Add 15: $3m = 36$
Divide by 3: $m = 12$

13. **15** Ratios such as 4:5 can also be written as $4x:5x$. So the number of men m is $4x$ and the number of women w is $5x$.

Plug those values into the equation $w = m + 3$
$$5x = 4x + 3$$
Subtract 4x: $x = 3$
Plug 3 in to 5x: $w = 5x = 5(3) = 15$

14. **8 or 12**
$$y = |2x - b|$$
Plug in (5, 2): $2 = |2(5) - b|$
Simplify: $2 = |10 - b|$
$$(10 - b) = 2 \text{ or } (10 - b) = -2$$
Subtract 10: $-b = -8 \text{ or } -b = -12$
Multiply by −1: $b = 8 \text{ or } b = 12$

15. **25** First calculate how many grams of sucrose there are in 200 grams of a 10% mixture.
$$(200 \text{ grams})(.10) = 20 \text{ grams of sucrose}$$

Since you will be adding x grams of sucrose, the total weight of sucrose will be $20 + x$ grams, and the total weight of the mixture will be $200 + x$ grams. Since the fraction that will be sucrose is 20%,
$$\frac{20 + x}{200 + x} = \frac{20}{100}$$
Cross-multiply: $(20 + x)(100) = 20(200 + x)$
Distribute: $2,000 + 100x = 4,000 + 20x$
Subtract 2,000: $100x = 2,000 + 20x$
Subtract 20x: $80x = 2,000$
Divide by 80: $x = 25$

16. **24** First calculate how long the race took.
$$distance = rate \times time$$
$$16 = (8)(time)$$
Divide by 8: 2 hours $= time = 120$ minutes

Next, find the new rate that is 25% faster:
$$new\ rate = (8)(1.25) = 10 \text{ mph}$$

Calculate how long the new race would take:
$$distance = rate \times time$$
$$16 = (10)(time)$$
Divide by 10: 1.6 hours $= time = 96$ minutes
So she can improve her time by $(120 - 96) = 24$ minutes.

17. 52

Break a shape like this into recognizable four-sided figures and triangles that are easier to deal with.

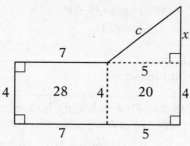

The area of the rectangle on the left is 7 × 4 = 28.

The area of the rectangle on the right is 5 × 4 = 20. The sum of those two areas is 28 + 20 = 48. The area remaining for the triangle is the difference 78 − 48 = 30. Set up an equation for the area of a triangle to solve for *x*:

$$\text{Area} = \frac{1}{2}(\text{base})(\text{height})$$
$$30 = \frac{1}{2}(5)(\text{height})$$

Divide by ½: $60 = 5(\text{height})$
Divide by 5: $12 = \text{height}$

To find the hypotenuse of the right triangle, set up the Pythagorean theorem and solve:

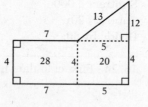

$$5^2 + 12^2 = c^2$$
$$25 + 144 = c^2$$
$$169 = c^2$$
$$c = 13$$

(Or just notice that it's a 5-12-13 triangle!)

To find the perimeter of the figure, add up all of the sides:

$$13 + 12 + 4 + 5 + 7 + 4 + 7 = 52$$

18. 225   Set up a three-circle Venn diagram to visualize this information.

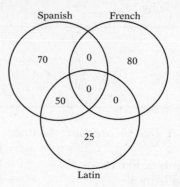

Fifty students study two of the three languages, so let's say that 50 students study both Spanish and Latin. (It doesn't matter *which* two languages those 50 students take; the result turns out the same.) This means that zero students study both Spanish and French, zero students study both French and Latin, and zero students study all three languages.

There are 120 Spanish students in all. There are therefore 120 − 50 = 70 students who study Spanish alone. There are 80 French students in all, all of whom study just French, and there are 75 total Latin students including 75 − 50 = 25 students who study only Latin.

This means that there are 70 + 50 + 80 + 25 = 225 sophomores at Hillside High School.

Section 5

1. C The clients were forced to seek more *reliable* investment advice, so the manager must have managed their funds badly. *ineptitude* = lack of skill

2. E Vartan is Armenian; he was born in Iran and educated in Lebanon and is now president of the American Brown University. He has a lot of *worldly* experience. *perpetual* = lasting forever; *authoritative* = showing authority; *cosmopolitan* = worldly

3. D They didn't consider it in great detail, so the reading must have been *without great care*. *verbatim* = word for word; *meandering* = wandering; *tormented* = feeling anguish or pain; *cursory* = quick and without care; *substantial* = of substance, quite large

4. A If the *pathogens* (infectious agents) spread more quickly in close quarters, the *crowding* would be a problem. This would cause the disease to *spread*. *propagation* = reproduction, increase in number; *squalor* = horrible or dirty conditions; *circulation* = moving of something around from place to place; *poverty* = state of being poor; *deterioration* = wearing down; *congestion* = crowdedness; *proximity* = closeness; *resilience* = ability to recover from a challenge

5. E The purpose of research is to find answers to questions of interest. Therefore, the research *endeavors* (attempts) to *determine* or *understand* the mechanisms by which our brains do things. If the data must be turned into *coherent and understandable information*, it must not have been coherent to begin with, but rather just a big rush of information. *enhance* = make better; *attenuate* = reduce in amount; *dearth* = scarcity, lack; *elucidate* = make clear; *deluge* = huge flood

6. D The *fruits* mentioned in line 10 refer to the means of acquiring food and shelter, because they are described as the *fruits for maintaining human life*.

7. B The question is whether one can *get quick returns of interest* (make money) *from the capital of knowledge and learning* (from one's education) (lines 13–15).

8. A The pointing of dogs is mentioned as an *instinctive tendency to the performance of an action* (lines 1–2).

9. E Inherited tendencies tend to show themselves in the behavior of an organism. The paragraph mentions the calf and the caterpillar as examples of organisms with instincts that show themselves in later behavior.

10. D The final paragraph begins with *The best life is the one in which the creative impulses play the largest part and the possessive impulses the smallest* (lines 56–58).

11. D Lines 22–26 say that *the food and clothing of one man is not the food and clothing of another; if the supply is insufficient, what one man has is obtained at the expense of some other man*. Therefore, food and clothing exist in finite amounts and can be used up.

12. E This section of the passage discusses matters such as *good-will* (line 38), *science* (line 31), and *painting pictures or writing poems* (lines 35–36) as things that are not denied to someone else when one person possesses them.

13. E This sentence discusses the *possessive impulses* (line 49) as distinct from the *creative impulses* discussed in the next sentence. The *impulse of property* in lines 51–52 is the *desire to possess property*.

14. C This statement echoes the point made in lines 71–72 that *spiritual possessions cannot be taken in this way*, that is, by force.

15. D Lines 58–59 say *This is no new discovery* and go on to cite the Gospel as a prior source expressing the same opinions as Russell's.

16. B The author's main point is that creativity is of higher value than possessiveness. The invention mentioned in answer choice (B) was created to make money for its inventor (a possessive and materialistic motive) but has the side effect of benefitting all of humankind.

17. A The passage discusses the perspective one Native American has on the appearance of the *new superstition* (line 44). It discusses how some villagers have taken to the new religion and also mentions one fellow tribe member's attempting to convert the main character.

18. E In saying that *men of the same color are like the ivory keys of one instrument where each represents all the rest, yet varies from them in pitch and quality of voice* (lines 4–7), the author is saying that people of the same race possess important differences.

19. D The author describes the preacher as *mouth[ing] most strangely the jangling phrases of a bigoted creed* (lines 11–12), indicating that she considers him to be an intolerant person. She describes herself as having *compassion* (line 7) and *respect* (line 10), but does not attribute these qualities to the preacher.

20. B Lines 13–14 say that *our tribe is one large family, where every person is related to all the others.*

21. C Both the preacher and the author's mother have become followers of *the new superstition* (line 44).

22. C In saying that a *pugilist commented upon a recent article of mine, grossly perverting the spirit of my pen* (lines 66–68), the author is saying that the pugilist distorted the author's words in a grotesque way.

23. E The author characterizes herself as *a wee child toddling in a wonder world* (lines 72–73), indicating that she is in awe of the world around her. Although one might expect her to be vengeful in response to the *pugilist* (line 66) who *grossly pervert[ed] the spirit of [her] pen* (line 68), there is no indication in the paragraph that she is vengeful.

24. A The author says in lines 68–72 that *still I would not forget that the pale-faced missionary and the aborigine are both God's creatures, though* **small indeed in their own conceptions of Infinite Love.** In other words, the author respects the missionary but believes he is small-minded.

Section 6

1. D The verb must agree with the plural subject *claims*. Choice (D) is most concise and correct.

2. A The original sentence is best.

3. B The participial phrase opening the sentence modifies Sartre himself, not his *writing*. This being the case, the phrase dangles.

4. C Choice (C) best follows the law of parallelism.

5. A The original sentence is best.

6. B Choice (B) is the most concise, logical, and complete.

7. C The original phrasing contains an incomplete thought. Choice (C) is by far the most concise and direct.

8. E The participle *having spread* modifies the *disease*, not the *doctors*.

9. C The original phrasing contains an incomplete thought. Choice (C) is by far the most concise and direct.

10. D The participle *singing* modifies *Anita*, not her hoarseness. Furthermore, the participle is in the wrong form; it should be in the perfect form *having sung*, because only the *previous* singing could have contributed to her hoarseness.

11. A The original sentence is best.

12. A The word *quick* is an adjective and can thus modify only a noun. But since it modifies the verb *turned*, the adverb *quickly* is needed here.

13. B This sentence violates the law of parallelism. If she is known *for her initiative*, she should also be known *for devoting her own time*.

14. C Since the Medieval era is long past, its *beginning* is "completed" or, in grammar terms, "perfect." So this phrase should be the "perfect" form of the infinitive: *to have begun.*

15. B The word *neither* is almost always part of the phrase *neither of . . .* or *neither A nor B*. So choice (B) should read *nor even.*

16. D The word *less* is used to compare only quantities that can't be counted. If the quantities are countable, as accidents are, the word should be *fewer.*

17. B To convey the proper sequence of events, the perfect tense is required: *had spent.*

18. A The subject of the verb *has* is the plural noun *newspapers*. (The sentence is "inverted," because the subject follows the verb.) The proper form of the verb, then, is *have.*

19. B The original sentence has a "comma splice" that incorrectly joins two sentences with only a comma. A better phrasing is *dream that led.*

20. C The subject of the verb is the singular noun *movement*, so the proper verb form is *has led.*

21. E The sentence is correct as written.

22. D This is a prepositional phrase, so the pronoun is the object of the preposition and should be in the objective case. The correct phrasing is *for Maria and me.*

23. A The word *successive* means *consecutive*, so it does not make sense in this context. The right word is *successful.*

24. **E**   The sentence is correct as written.

25. **C**   The word *underneath* means that it is physically *below* something else. It should be changed to *under*.

26. **E**   The sentence is correct as written.

27. **B**   The subject of the verb *were* is *arrogance*, which is singular. It should instead be *was*.

28. **B**   The sentence mentions there are *numerous* strains of the bacteria, which means that *more* should instead be *most*.

29. **C**   The subject *company* is singular. Therefore, *they* should instead be *it*.

30. **D**   Choice (D) is most consistent, logical, and concise.

31. **A**   Choice (A) is most logical.

32. **B**   The first paragraph ends with the description of an idea. The second paragraph begins with an illustration of how students experience this idea in their daily lives and then goes on to explain how it can help them get through their *brain freezes*. Choice (B) is the best introduction to the paragraph, because it explains that a student using the phenomenon can improve his or her studies.

33. **C**   The sentence begins using the pronoun *you*, so that usage should be maintained throughout the sentence. Choice (D) is incorrect because a person has only one brain.

34. **E**   Sentence 11 concludes a discussion of Isaac Asimov's "eureka" experience. The additional sentence expands upon that idea, relating it back to the lives of students.

35. **C**   Choice (C) is the most concise and logical revision.

Section 7

1. **B**   Set up a ratio to solve this problem:

$$\frac{4 \text{ apples}}{20 \text{ cents}} = \frac{10 \text{ apples}}{x \text{ cents}}$$

Cross-multiply: $4x = 200$
Divide by 4: $x = 50 \text{ cents}$

2. **C**   Solve for *b*: $2^b = 8$
                       $b = 3$
Plug in 3: $3^b = 3^3 = 27$

3. **A**   The sum of *a*, *b*, and 18 is 6 greater than the sum of *a*, *b*, and 12. Since there are three terms in the group, it follows that the average of *a*, *b*, and 18 would be $6 \div 3 = 2$ greater than the average of *a*, *b*, and 12.

4. **B**   If you have the patience, you can write out a quick calendar for yourself to track the days:

Su	M	T	W	**Th**	F	Sa
		1	2	3	4	5
6	7	8	9	10	11	12
13	14	15	16	17	18	19
20	21	22	23	24	25	26
27	28	29	30	**31**		

Or you can use the simple fact that successive Tuesdays (like any other days) are always 7 days apart. Therefore, if the 1st of the month is a Tuesday, so are the 8th, the 15th, the 22nd, and the 29th. Therefore, the 30th is a Wednesday and the 31st is a Thursday.

5. **A**   From the given information: $m = 8n$
                               $0 < m + n < 50$
Substitute for *m*: $0 < 8n + n < 50$
Combine like terms: $0 < 9n < 50$
Divide by 9: $0 < n < 5\frac{5}{9}$
Since *n* must be an integer, *n* can be 1, 2, 3, 4, or 5.

6. **D**   First find the value of *y*:   *y*% of 50 is 32.

Simplify: $\dfrac{y}{100} \times 50 = 32$

Cross-multiply: $50y = 3{,}200$
Divide by 50: $y = 64$

What is 200% of 64?
Interpret: $2.00 \times 64 = 128$

7. **B** $g(x) = x + x^{1/2}$
Plug in 16 for *x*: $g(16) = 16 + 16^{1/2}$
Take square root of 16: $g(16) = 16 + 4$
Combine like terms: $g(16) = 20$

8. C The slope of the line is $-\frac{3}{4}$, so use the slope equation and the coordinates of point A $(0, 12)$ to find the coordinates of point B $(x, 0)$:

$$m = \frac{y_2 - y_1}{x_2 - x_1} = \frac{0 - 12}{x - 0} = \frac{-12}{x} = -\frac{3}{4}$$

Cross-multiply:　　　　$4(-12) = -3(x)$
Simplify:　　　　　　　$-48 = -3x$
Divide by -3:　　　　　$16 = x$

The base of the triangle is 16, and its height is 12.

　　　　　　　　　　　　Area = ½(base)(height)
Substitute:　　　　　　Area = ½(16)(12)
Simplify:　　　　　　　Area = 96

9. A Find the sum of each repetition of the pattern:
$$-1 + 1 + 2 = 2$$

Next, determine how many times the pattern repeats in the first 25 terms: $25 \div 3 = 8$ with a remainder of 1.

Multiply the sum of the pattern by 8 to obtain the sum of the first 24 terms:　$2 \times 8 = 16$

The 25th term is -1, which makes the sum $16 + -1 = 15$.

10. D The ratio of white marbles to blue marbles is 4 to b. The probability of randomly selecting a white marble from the jar is $\frac{1}{4}$. This means that one out of every four marbles in the jar is white and three out of every four marbles are blue. If there are four white marbles, then there are $4 \times 3 = 12$ blue marbles.

11. B　　Area = ½(base)(height)
　　Substitute:　　　　$10 = ½(base)(height)$
　　Divide by ½:　　　 $20 = (base)(height)$

The base and the height are both integers. Find all the "factor pairs" of 20:　　1, 20; 2, 10; and 4, 5

Plug each pair into the Pythagorean theorem to find the least possible length of the hypotenuse:

$$a^2 + b^2 = c^2$$
$$4^2 + 5^2 = c^2$$

Combine like terms:　　$41 = c^2$
Take square root:　　　$\sqrt{41} = c$

$$a^2 + b^2 = c^2$$
$$2^2 + 10^2 = c^2$$

Combine like terms:　　$104 = c^2$
Take square root:　　　$\sqrt{104} = c$

$$a^2 + b^2 = c^2$$
$$1^2 + 20^2 = c^2$$

Combine like terms:　　$401 = c^2$
Take square root:　　　$\sqrt{401} = c$

$\sqrt{41}$ is the shortest possible hypotenuse.

12. B　$-1 < y < 0$
This means that y is a negative decimal fraction. Answer choices (A), (C), and (E) will all be negative numbers. Answer choices (B) and (D) are positive numbers. When you raise a simple fraction to a positive number larger than 1, it gets smaller. $y^4 < y^2$, which makes (B) the greatest value. Pick a value like $y = -\frac{1}{2}$ and see.

13. E　Any statement of the form *"If A is true, then B is true"* is logically equivalent to *"If B is not true, then A is not true."* Try this with some common-sense examples of such statements. For instance, saying *"If I am under 16 years old, then I am not allowed to drive"* is the same as saying *"If I am allowed to drive, then I must not be under 16 years old."* The statement in (E) is logically equivalent to the original.

14. E　If each bus contained only the minimum number of students, the buses would accommodate $6 \times 30 = 180$ students. But since you have 200 students to accommodate, you have 20 more students to place. To maximize the number of 40-student buses, place 10 more students in two of the buses. Therefore, a maximum of two buses can have 40 students.

15. D　The volume of a cylinder is equal to $\pi r^2 h$. Let's say that the radius of cylinder A is a and the radius of cylinder B is b. Since the height of cylinder B is twice the height of cylinder A, if the height of cylinder A is h, then the height of cylinder B is $2h$. The volume of A is twice that of B:　　　　$\pi a^2 h = 2\pi b^2 (2h)$
Simplify:　　　　　　　　　　　　$\pi a^2 h = 4\pi b^2 h$
Divide by π:　　　　　　　　　　$a^2 h = 4b^2 h$
Divide by h:　　　　　　　　　　$a^2 = 4b^2$
Take the square root of both sides:　$a = 2b$
Divide by b:

$$\frac{a}{b} = \frac{2}{1}$$

16. C   The key is to find a pattern among the many possible solutions. Pick some values for x to see if you can see a pattern. For instance, if $x = 3$, then the garden looks like this:

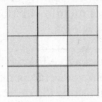

In this case $w = 8$. But if $x = 4$, the garden looks like this:

And here, $w = 12$. You might notice that the value of w has increased by 4. Does this pattern continue? Let's try $x = 5$ to check:

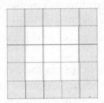

Sure enough, $w = 16$, and it seems that the pattern continues and w is always a multiple of 4. Only choice (C), 40, is a multiple of 4, so that must be the correct answer.

Section 8

1. B   A *reputable* scientist is well known and well respected. Saying *the evidence is ------- at best* indicates that there is not much evidence at all. It must be *flimsy*. Reputable scientists would not likely *admit* that a phenomenon exists if the evidence is weak. *meager* = scanty, deficient; *regret* = feel bad about an action, wish it hadn't happened; *paltry* = lacking worth

2. D   The concept that the Earth is round is *now accepted as an inarguable truth*. It can be inferred that it was at some point a fact that was thought to be wrong. *incontrovertible* = cannot be questioned; *mellifluous* = smooth flowing; *dubious* = doubtful

3. B   A profound break of a political party or religion into factions is a *schism*. (The Latin word *schisma* = split.) *unanimity* = full agreement; *schism* = division into factions; *caucus* = meeting of party members; *commemoration* = event that honors something or someone; *prognostication* = prediction

4. C   As the father of the American public school system, Horace Mann would *pressure* or *push* the Massachusetts legislature to institute a system for *ensuring* or *guaranteeing* universal access to eduction. *petitioned* = requested, lobbied for; *vouchsafing* = conceding, granting

5. A   Since the light from most stars takes millions of years to reach us, it is plausible to imagine that by the time we see the light the star might actually no longer be there. This would make the present existence of these stars *questionable*. *debatable* = disputable; *methodical* = systematic; *indecorous* = not proper; *imperious* = acting as if one is superior to another; *profuse* = abundant

6. D   The *although* establishes a contrast. Something that makes *any potentially offensive matters seem less objectionable* is, by definition, a *euphemism*. The first blank should therefore be a word that contrasts with euphemism, like *straightforward*. *anachronism* = something out of place in time; *intolerant* = unable to put up with something; *laudation* = extreme praise; *clandestine* = secret, hidden; *candid* = honest, straightforward; *euphemism* = the substitution of an inoffensive term for an offensive one; *forthright* = honest; *coercion* = pressure on someone to act

7. C   The English gentleman *tried to teach his son Greek and Latin without punishment, . . . rewarding his son with cherries and biscuits* (lines 5–11).

8. A   In saying that *marks, grades, and diplomas . . . must be made reinforcing for other reasons* (lines 16–19), the author is saying that such things will not reinforce behavior by themselves but must be made to represent something more meaningful.

9. B The passage says that how *honors and medals derive their power from prestige or esteem* is what *varies between cultures and epochs* (lines 20–23). When Oscar Wilde got a *"first in Mods"* in 1876, he was the talk of the town. But the contemporary student graduating *summa cum laude* is *less widely acclaimed* (lines 33–34).

10. A The story follows the statement that how *honors and medals derive their power from prestige or esteem* is what *varies between cultures and epochs*. Therefore, the story is intended to illustrate that fact.

11. C Statement I is supported by lines 37–39, which say that certain kinds of reinforcements (like food) *are not always easily arranged*. Statement II is supported by line 43: *We cannot all get prizes*. The selection does not mention anything about rewards' encouraging only superficial learning.

12. D In lines 58–60, the passage says that *grades are almost always given long after the student has stopped behaving as a student*. It then goes on to discuss how *such contingencies are weak* (lines 60–61).

13. E The paragraph as a whole discusses the need for teachers to address the issues of whether, when, and how to punish or reward student behavior, so it is about teacher-student interactions.

14. B Kohn and Deci are mentioned as examples of experts who believe *that reward is often just as harmful as punishment, if not more so* (lines 87–89).

15. D The second paragraph of Passage 2 goes on to argue that those who are doing a task without a reward continue to perform the task because they see it as being "fun," whereas those who do it for a reward stop playing because they are no longer being paid to continue. The activity's sole value comes from the payment they get for it, not from the enjoyment they get from participating.

16. D We are told that Deci concluded that the *subjects who were paid probably construed* (interpreted) *the task as being manipulative* (lines 105–106). In order to draw such conclusions, the subjects would have to make inferences about the motivations of the experimenter.

17. A The author follows that statement with *it would be a mistake to use these few experiments to generalize that all rewards are bad* (lines 130–132). These statements caution against an overly simplistic theory about the effectiveness of rewards.

18. B Deci's opinion is that the introduction of a reward system changes things for the worse. He would see the description of the *problems* mentioned in line 37 as presumptuous because they presume that the rewards actually have a positive effect and incomplete because they do not mention all of the problems that he sees in reward systems.

19. D Both authors agree that positive feedback is a more effective teaching mechanism than negative feedback. Passage 1 mentions the need of good educators to *teach . . . without punishment* (lines 6–7) and mentions the negative *by-products of aversive control* (control by punishment) (lines 35–36). Passage 2 mentions that *most educators and psychologists agree that reward is always better than punishment* (lines 84–85), and since the writer goes on to criticize even reward systems, he implies that punishment is most certainly a bad teaching technique.

Section 9

1. C The word *whose* should refer to Alvin Ailey, but the way the sentence is constructed, it is referring to Alvin Ailey's *works*. Answer choice (C) corrects this error in the most concise and logical fashion.

2. B When a participle is used to indicate an action that is completed before another action, it should be *perfect. Getting* this far should instead be *Having gotten*.

3. C The sentence is improperly describing Rachel's irritation as being even-tempered. In reality, it should be *Rachel* who is even-tempered. Answer choice (C) corrects this error.

4. B This is a comparisons error. The literal translation of the sentence as written suggests that Alberta's salary is higher in the air than her co-workers are. It needs to be changed so that the sentence is comparing Alberta's salary to the *salary of her coworkers*.

5. C The word *elicit* means to call forth or draw out. The word should be *illicit*, which means unlawful.

6. D The paraders were not watching from the balcony. The sentence needs to be changed so that the subjects represented by the final pronoun *us* are the ones watching from the balcony.

7. E The sentence contains two past tense verbs, and one event was completed before the other. The tents were set up before they arrived. So *set up* needs to be in the past perfect tense—*had set up*.

8. **C**   When using neither . . . nor . . . phrasing, the verb should match in number the subject that follows the *nor.* Because daughters is plural, *was* should instead be *were.*

9. **B**   When using not only A but also B, the words or phrases that replace A and B must be parallel. It should be replaced by not only *with working* but also *with wanting.*

10. **C**   To correct this sentence, the word *that* should be replaced with *who,* since Roberto is a *person.*

11. **D**   Answer choice (D) connects the two clauses most effectively.

12. **E**   When reading this sentence you should ask yourself: "who was forced to live apart from his family?" The answer to that question, St. Pierre, is what should immediately follow the comma after *informers.*

13. **B**   The gerund form, *forming,* is not correct and needs to be changed to past tense *formed.* Choice (B) works best.

14. **D**   What follows the linking verb *is* must be a noun phrase representing *the most challenging aspect,* not an independent clause, as in the original. Choice (D) works best.

PRACTICE TEST II

ANSWER SHEET

Last Name:_____   First Name:_____

Date:_____   Testing Location:_____

Directions for Test

- Remove these answer sheets from the book and use them to record your answers to this test.
- This test will require 3 hours and 20 minutes to complete. Take this test in one sitting.
- The time allotment for each section is written clearly at the beginning of each section. This test contains six 25-minute sections, two 20-minute sections, and one 10-minute section.
- This test is 25 minutes shorter than the actual SAT, which will include a 25-minute "experimental" section that does not count toward your score. That section has been omitted from this test.
- You may take one short break during the test, of no more than 10 minutes in length.
- You may only work on one section at any given time.
- You must stop ALL work on a section when time is called.
- If you finish a section before the time has elapsed, check your work on that section. You may NOT work on any other section.
- Do not waste time on questions that seem too difficult for you.
- Use the test book for scratchwork, but you will receive credit only for answers that are marked on the answer sheets.
- You will receive one point for every correct answer.
- You will receive no points for an omitted question.
- For each wrong answer on any multiple-choice question, your score will be reduced by ¼ point.
- For each wrong answer on any "numerical grid-in" question, you will receive no deduction.

When you take the real SAT, you will be asked to fill in your personal information in grids as shown below.

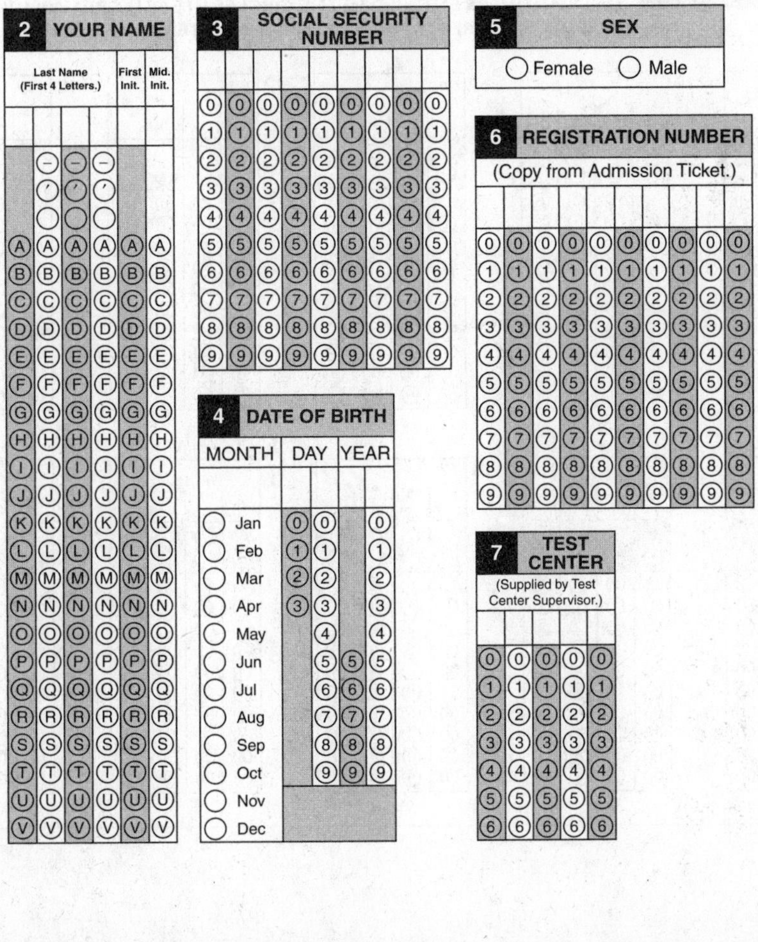

Start with number 1 for each new section. If a section has fewer questions than answer spaces, leave the extra answer spaces blank. Be sure to erase any errors or stray marks completely.

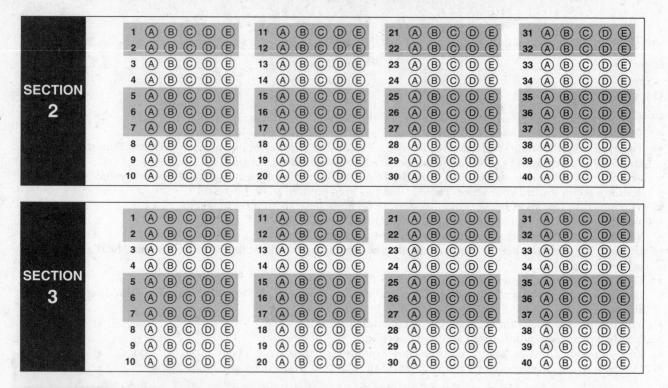

CAUTION   Use the answer spaces in the grids below for Section 2 or Section 3 only if you are told to do so in your test book.

Student-Produced Responses   ONLY ANSWERS ENTERED IN THE CIRCLES IN EACH GRID WILL BE SCORED. YOU WILL NOT RECEIVE CREDIT FOR ANYTHING WRITTEN IN THE BOXES ABOVE THE CIRCLES.

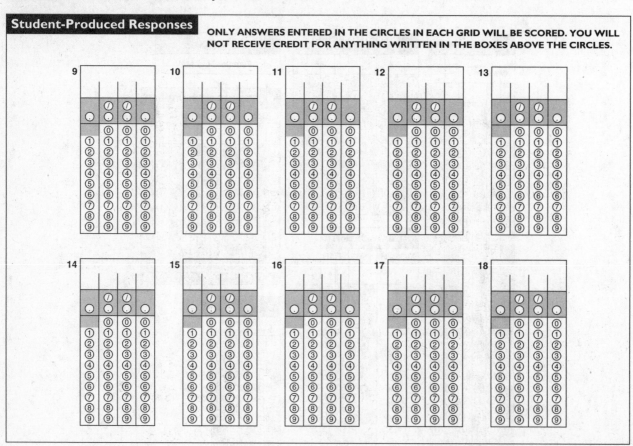

Start with number 1 for each new section. If a section has fewer questions than answer spaces,
leave the extra answer spaces blank. Be sure to erase any errors or stray marks completely.

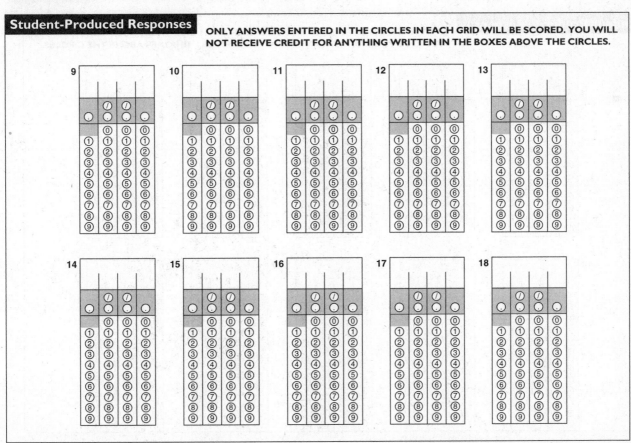

SECTION 4

1 Ⓐ Ⓑ Ⓒ Ⓓ Ⓔ   11 Ⓐ Ⓑ Ⓒ Ⓓ Ⓔ   21 Ⓐ Ⓑ Ⓒ Ⓓ Ⓔ   31 Ⓐ Ⓑ Ⓒ Ⓓ Ⓔ
2 Ⓐ Ⓑ Ⓒ Ⓓ Ⓔ   12 Ⓐ Ⓑ Ⓒ Ⓓ Ⓔ   22 Ⓐ Ⓑ Ⓒ Ⓓ Ⓔ   32 Ⓐ Ⓑ Ⓒ Ⓓ Ⓔ
3 Ⓐ Ⓑ Ⓒ Ⓓ Ⓔ   13 Ⓐ Ⓑ Ⓒ Ⓓ Ⓔ   23 Ⓐ Ⓑ Ⓒ Ⓓ Ⓔ   33 Ⓐ Ⓑ Ⓒ Ⓓ Ⓔ
4 Ⓐ Ⓑ Ⓒ Ⓓ Ⓔ   14 Ⓐ Ⓑ Ⓒ Ⓓ Ⓔ   24 Ⓐ Ⓑ Ⓒ Ⓓ Ⓔ   34 Ⓐ Ⓑ Ⓒ Ⓓ Ⓔ
5 Ⓐ Ⓑ Ⓒ Ⓓ Ⓔ   15 Ⓐ Ⓑ Ⓒ Ⓓ Ⓔ   25 Ⓐ Ⓑ Ⓒ Ⓓ Ⓔ   35 Ⓐ Ⓑ Ⓒ Ⓓ Ⓔ
6 Ⓐ Ⓑ Ⓒ Ⓓ Ⓔ   16 Ⓐ Ⓑ Ⓒ Ⓓ Ⓔ   26 Ⓐ Ⓑ Ⓒ Ⓓ Ⓔ   36 Ⓐ Ⓑ Ⓒ Ⓓ Ⓔ
7 Ⓐ Ⓑ Ⓒ Ⓓ Ⓔ   17 Ⓐ Ⓑ Ⓒ Ⓓ Ⓔ   27 Ⓐ Ⓑ Ⓒ Ⓓ Ⓔ   37 Ⓐ Ⓑ Ⓒ Ⓓ Ⓔ
8 Ⓐ Ⓑ Ⓒ Ⓓ Ⓔ   18 Ⓐ Ⓑ Ⓒ Ⓓ Ⓔ   28 Ⓐ Ⓑ Ⓒ Ⓓ Ⓔ   38 Ⓐ Ⓑ Ⓒ Ⓓ Ⓔ
9 Ⓐ Ⓑ Ⓒ Ⓓ Ⓔ   19 Ⓐ Ⓑ Ⓒ Ⓓ Ⓔ   29 Ⓐ Ⓑ Ⓒ Ⓓ Ⓔ   39 Ⓐ Ⓑ Ⓒ Ⓓ Ⓔ
10 Ⓐ Ⓑ Ⓒ Ⓓ Ⓔ   20 Ⓐ Ⓑ Ⓒ Ⓓ Ⓔ   30 Ⓐ Ⓑ Ⓒ Ⓓ Ⓔ   40 Ⓐ Ⓑ Ⓒ Ⓓ Ⓔ

SECTION 5

1 Ⓐ Ⓑ Ⓒ Ⓓ Ⓔ   11 Ⓐ Ⓑ Ⓒ Ⓓ Ⓔ   21 Ⓐ Ⓑ Ⓒ Ⓓ Ⓔ   31 Ⓐ Ⓑ Ⓒ Ⓓ Ⓔ
2 Ⓐ Ⓑ Ⓒ Ⓓ Ⓔ   12 Ⓐ Ⓑ Ⓒ Ⓓ Ⓔ   22 Ⓐ Ⓑ Ⓒ Ⓓ Ⓔ   32 Ⓐ Ⓑ Ⓒ Ⓓ Ⓔ
3 Ⓐ Ⓑ Ⓒ Ⓓ Ⓔ   13 Ⓐ Ⓑ Ⓒ Ⓓ Ⓔ   23 Ⓐ Ⓑ Ⓒ Ⓓ Ⓔ   33 Ⓐ Ⓑ Ⓒ Ⓓ Ⓔ
4 Ⓐ Ⓑ Ⓒ Ⓓ Ⓔ   14 Ⓐ Ⓑ Ⓒ Ⓓ Ⓔ   24 Ⓐ Ⓑ Ⓒ Ⓓ Ⓔ   34 Ⓐ Ⓑ Ⓒ Ⓓ Ⓔ
5 Ⓐ Ⓑ Ⓒ Ⓓ Ⓔ   15 Ⓐ Ⓑ Ⓒ Ⓓ Ⓔ   25 Ⓐ Ⓑ Ⓒ Ⓓ Ⓔ   35 Ⓐ Ⓑ Ⓒ Ⓓ Ⓔ
6 Ⓐ Ⓑ Ⓒ Ⓓ Ⓔ   16 Ⓐ Ⓑ Ⓒ Ⓓ Ⓔ   26 Ⓐ Ⓑ Ⓒ Ⓓ Ⓔ   36 Ⓐ Ⓑ Ⓒ Ⓓ Ⓔ
7 Ⓐ Ⓑ Ⓒ Ⓓ Ⓔ   17 Ⓐ Ⓑ Ⓒ Ⓓ Ⓔ   27 Ⓐ Ⓑ Ⓒ Ⓓ Ⓔ   37 Ⓐ Ⓑ Ⓒ Ⓓ Ⓔ
8 Ⓐ Ⓑ Ⓒ Ⓓ Ⓔ   18 Ⓐ Ⓑ Ⓒ Ⓓ Ⓔ   28 Ⓐ Ⓑ Ⓒ Ⓓ Ⓔ   38 Ⓐ Ⓑ Ⓒ Ⓓ Ⓔ
9 Ⓐ Ⓑ Ⓒ Ⓓ Ⓔ   19 Ⓐ Ⓑ Ⓒ Ⓓ Ⓔ   29 Ⓐ Ⓑ Ⓒ Ⓓ Ⓔ   39 Ⓐ Ⓑ Ⓒ Ⓓ Ⓔ
10 Ⓐ Ⓑ Ⓒ Ⓓ Ⓔ   20 Ⓐ Ⓑ Ⓒ Ⓓ Ⓔ   30 Ⓐ Ⓑ Ⓒ Ⓓ Ⓔ   40 Ⓐ Ⓑ Ⓒ Ⓓ Ⓔ

CAUTION Use the answer spaces in the grids below for Section 4 or Section 5 only if you are told to do so in your test book.

Student-Produced Responses ONLY ANSWERS ENTERED IN THE CIRCLES IN EACH GRID WILL BE SCORED. YOU WILL NOT RECEIVE CREDIT FOR ANYTHING WRITTEN IN THE BOXES ABOVE THE CIRCLES.

Start with number 1 for each new section. If a section has fewer questions than answer spaces, leave the extra answer spaces blank. Be sure to erase any errors or stray marks completely.

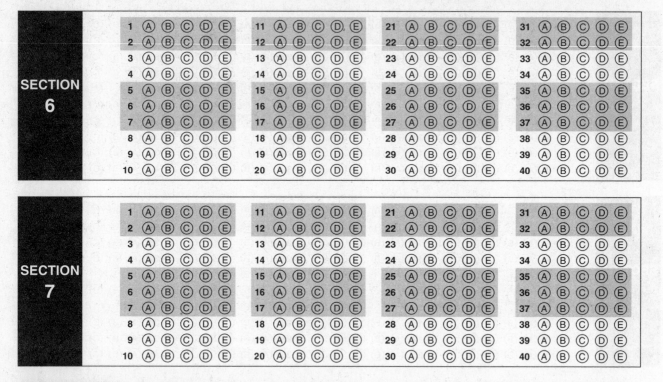

SECTION 6

SECTION 7

CAUTION Use the answer spaces in the grids below for Section 6 or Section 7 only if you are told to do so in your test book.

Student-Produced Responses

ONLY ANSWERS ENTERED IN THE CIRCLES IN EACH GRID WILL BE SCORED. YOU WILL NOT RECEIVE CREDIT FOR ANYTHING WRITTEN IN THE BOXES ABOVE THE CIRCLES.

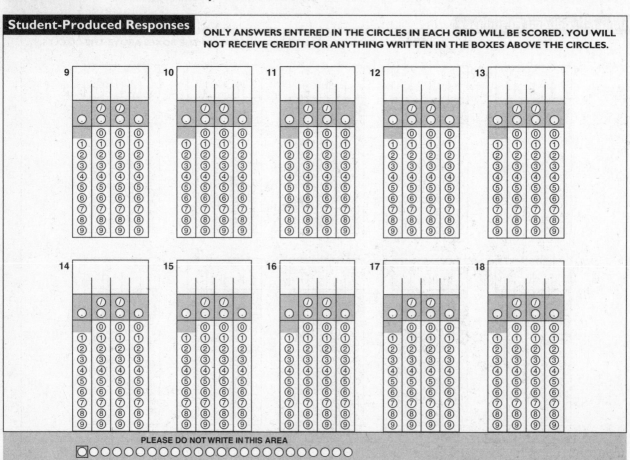

PLEASE DO NOT WRITE IN THIS AREA

Start with number 1 for each new section. If a section has fewer questions than answer spaces, leave the extra answer spaces blank. Be sure to erase any errors or stray marks completely.

SECTION 8

1 (A) (B) (C) (D) (E)   11 (A) (B) (C) (D) (E)   21 (A) (B) (C) (D) (E)   31 (A) (B) (C) (D) (E)
2 (A) (B) (C) (D) (E)   12 (A) (B) (C) (D) (E)   22 (A) (B) (C) (D) (E)   32 (A) (B) (C) (D) (E)
3 (A) (B) (C) (D) (E)   13 (A) (B) (C) (D) (E)   23 (A) (B) (C) (D) (E)   33 (A) (B) (C) (D) (E)
4 (A) (B) (C) (D) (E)   14 (A) (B) (C) (D) (E)   24 (A) (B) (C) (D) (E)   34 (A) (B) (C) (D) (E)
5 (A) (B) (C) (D) (E)   15 (A) (B) (C) (D) (E)   25 (A) (B) (C) (D) (E)   35 (A) (B) (C) (D) (E)
6 (A) (B) (C) (D) (E)   16 (A) (B) (C) (D) (E)   26 (A) (B) (C) (D) (E)   36 (A) (B) (C) (D) (E)
7 (A) (B) (C) (D) (E)   17 (A) (B) (C) (D) (E)   27 (A) (B) (C) (D) (E)   37 (A) (B) (C) (D) (E)
8 (A) (B) (C) (D) (E)   18 (A) (B) (C) (D) (E)   28 (A) (B) (C) (D) (E)   38 (A) (B) (C) (D) (E)
9 (A) (B) (C) (D) (E)   19 (A) (B) (C) (D) (E)   29 (A) (B) (C) (D) (E)   39 (A) (B) (C) (D) (E)
10 (A) (B) (C) (D) (E)   20 (A) (B) (C) (D) (E)   30 (A) (B) (C) (D) (E)   40 (A) (B) (C) (D) (E)

SECTION 9

1 (A) (B) (C) (D) (E)   11 (A) (B) (C) (D) (E)   21 (A) (B) (C) (D) (E)   31 (A) (B) (C) (D) (E)
2 (A) (B) (C) (D) (E)   12 (A) (B) (C) (D) (E)   22 (A) (B) (C) (D) (E)   32 (A) (B) (C) (D) (E)
3 (A) (B) (C) (D) (E)   13 (A) (B) (C) (D) (E)   23 (A) (B) (C) (D) (E)   33 (A) (B) (C) (D) (E)
4 (A) (B) (C) (D) (E)   14 (A) (B) (C) (D) (E)   24 (A) (B) (C) (D) (E)   34 (A) (B) (C) (D) (E)
5 (A) (B) (C) (D) (E)   15 (A) (B) (C) (D) (E)   25 (A) (B) (C) (D) (E)   35 (A) (B) (C) (D) (E)
6 (A) (B) (C) (D) (E)   16 (A) (B) (C) (D) (E)   26 (A) (B) (C) (D) (E)   36 (A) (B) (C) (D) (E)
7 (A) (B) (C) (D) (E)   17 (A) (B) (C) (D) (E)   27 (A) (B) (C) (D) (E)   37 (A) (B) (C) (D) (E)
8 (A) (B) (C) (D) (E)   18 (A) (B) (C) (D) (E)   28 (A) (B) (C) (D) (E)   38 (A) (B) (C) (D) (E)
9 (A) (B) (C) (D) (E)   19 (A) (B) (C) (D) (E)   29 (A) (B) (C) (D) (E)   39 (A) (B) (C) (D) (E)
10 (A) (B) (C) (D) (E)   20 (A) (B) (C) (D) (E)   30 (A) (B) (C) (D) (E)   40 (A) (B) (C) (D) (E)

Practice makes perfect—for more opportunities to take full-length SAT practice tests, visit our Online Practice Plus, on the Web at www.MHPracticePlus/SATpractice.

1   ESSAY   ESSAY   1

ESSAY
Time—25 minutes

Write your essay on separate sheets of standard lined paper.

The essay gives you an opportunity to show how effectively you can develop and express ideas. You should therefore take care to develop your point of view, present your ideas logically and clearly, and use language precisely.

Your essay must be written on the lines provided on your answer sheet—you will receive no other paper on which to write. You will have enough space if you write on every line, avoid wide margins, and keep your handwriting to a reasonable size. Remember that people who are not familiar with your handwriting will read what you write. Try to write or print so that what you are writing is legible to those readers.

Important reminders:

- **A pencil is required for the essay.** An essay written in ink will receive a score of zero.
- **Do not write your essay in your test book.** You will receive credit only for what you write on your answer sheet.
- **An off-topic essay will receive a score of zero.**

You have twenty-five minutes to write an essay on the topic assigned below.

Consider carefully the issue discussed in the following passage, then write an essay that answers the question posed in the assignment.

> Many among us like to blame violence and immorality in the media for a "decline in morals" in society. Yet these people seem to have lost touch with logic. Any objective examination shows that our society is far less violent or exploitative than virtually any society in the past. Early humans murdered and enslaved each other with astonishing regularity, without the help of gangsta rap or Jerry Bruckheimer films.

Assignment: **Do violence and immorality in the media make our society more dangerous and immoral?** Write an essay in which you answer this question and discuss your point of view on this issue. Support your position logically with examples from literature, the arts, history, politics, science and technology, current events, or your experience or observation.

If you finish before time is called, you may check your work on this section only.
Do not turn to any other section of the test.

2   2   2   2   2   2

SECTION 2
Time—25 minutes
20 questions

> **Turn to Section 2 of your answer sheet to answer the questions in this section.**

Directions: For this section, solve each problem and decide which is the best of the choices given. Fill in the corresponding circle on the answer sheet. You may use any available space for scratchwork.

Notes

1. The use of a calculator is permitted.
2. All numbers used are real numbers.
3. Figures that accompany problems in this test are intended to provide information useful in solving the problems. They are drawn as accurately as possible EXCEPT when it is stated in a specific problem that the figure is not drawn to scale. All figures lie in a plane unless otherwise indicated.
4. Unless otherwise specified, the domain of any function f is assumed to be the set of all real numbers x for which $f(x)$ is a real number.

Reference Information

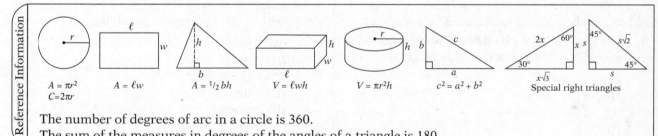

$A = \pi r^2$ $A = \ell w$ $A = \frac{1}{2} bh$ $V = \ell wh$ $V = \pi r^2 h$ $c^2 = a^2 + b^2$ Special right triangles
$C = 2\pi r$

The number of degrees of arc in a circle is 360.
The sum of the measures in degrees of the angles of a triangle is 180.

---

1. If $(x + 4) + 7 = 14$, what is the value of x?

(A) 3
(B) 7
(C) 11
(D) 17
(E) 25

2. Erica spends $.95 each day for her newspaper subscriptions. She would like to determine the approximate amount she spends during the month of July, which has 31 days. Which of the following would provide her with the best estimate?

(A) $.50 × 30
(B) $1.00 × 30
(C) $1.50 × 30
(D) $.50 × 35
(E) $1.00 × 35

GO ON TO THE NEXT PAGE ⟹

2   **2**   **2**   **2**   **2**   **2**

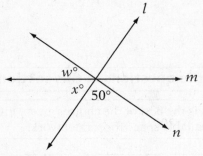

Note: Figure not drawn to scale.

3. In the figure above, lines *l*, *m*, and *n* intersect in a single point. What is the value of *w* + *x*?

(A)   40
(B)   70
(C)   90
(D)   130
(E)   140

---

4. Let the function *g* be defined by the equation $g(x) = 3x + 4$. What is the value of $g(5)$?

(A)   8
(B)   11
(C)   15
(D)   19
(E)   23

---

5. If $x > y$, which of the following equations expresses the fact that when the difference between x and y is multiplied by their sum, the product is 18?

(A) $(x - y)^2 = 18$
(B) $(x + y)^2 = 18$
(C) $(x - y) \div (x + y) = 18$
(D) $x^2 - y^2 = 18$
(E) $x^2 + y^2 = 18$

---

6. If $3\sqrt{x} - 7 = 20$, what is the value of *x*?

(A)   3
(B)   9
(C)   27
(D)   36
(E)   81

---

7. Chris buys a chocolate bar and a pack of gum for $1.75. If the chocolate bar costs $.25 more than the pack of gum, how much does the pack of gum cost?

(A) $0.25
(B) $0.50
(C) $0.75
(D) $1.00
(E) $1.50

---

8. 40% of 80 is what percent of 96?

(A)   20%
(B)   30%
(C)   33⅓%
(D)   50%
(E)   66⅔%

---

9. If *l*, *m*, and *n* are positive integers greater than 1, *lm* = 21, and *mn* = 39, then which of the following must be true?

(A) $n > l > m$
(B) $m > n > l$
(C) $m > l > n$
(D) $l > n > m$
(E) $n > m > l$

GO ON TO THE NEXT PAGE

2   2   2   2   2   2

ANNUAL PROFITS FOR ABC COMPANY
(IN THOUSANDS OF DOLLARS)

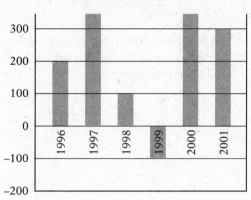

10. According to the graph above, ABC Company showed the greatest change in profits between which 2 years?

(A) 1996 and 1997
(B) 1997 and 1998
(C) 1998 and 1999
(D) 1999 and 2000
(E) 2000 and 2001

11. In a 9th-grade class, 12 students play soccer, 7 students play tennis, and 9 students play lacrosse. If 4 students play exactly two of the three sports and all other students play only one, how many students are in the class?

(A) 28
(B) 24
(C) 20
(D) 18
(E) 16

12. The point (14, 14) is the center of a circle, and (2, 9) is a point on the circle. What is the length of the diameter of the circle?

(A) 24
(B) 26
(C) 50
(D) 144π
(E) 169π

13. The population of Boomtown doubles every 18 months. In January of 2000, its population was exactly 12,000. At this rate, approximately when should the population reach 96,000?

(A) January 2003
(B) July 2004
(C) January 2006
(D) July 2007
(E) January 2012

14. In how many different ways can five students of different heights be arranged in a line if the tallest student cannot be on either end?

(A) 24
(B) 25
(C) 72
(D) 96
(E) 120

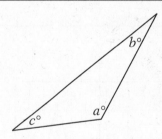

Note: Figure not drawn to scale.

15. In the figure above, $a > 90$ and $b = c + 3$. If a, b, and c are all integers, what is the greatest possible value of b?

(A) 43
(B) 46
(C) 60
(D) 86
(E) 89

GO ON TO THE NEXT PAGE

2   **2**   **2**   **2**   **2**   **2**

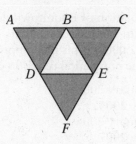

16. In the figure above, $\triangle ACF$ is equilateral, with sides of length 4. If B, D, and E are the midpoints of their respective sides, what is the sum of the areas of the shaded regions?

(A) $3\sqrt{2}$

(B) $3\sqrt{3}$

(C) $4\sqrt{2}$

(D) $4\sqrt{3}$

(E) $6\sqrt{3}$

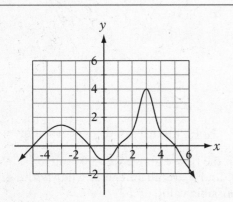

17. Given the graph of $y = f(x)$ above, which of the following sets represents all values of x for which $f(x) \geq 1$?

(A)   all real numbers
(B) $x \geq 1$
(C) $-5 \leq x \leq -1; 1 \leq x \leq 5$
(D) $-4 \leq x \leq -2; 2 \leq x \leq 4$
(E) $x \leq -4; x \geq 4$

X: {2, 4, 6, 8, 10}

Y: {1, 3, 5, 7, 9}

18. If a is a number chosen randomly from set X and b is a number chosen randomly from set Y, what is the probability that ab is greater than 20 but less than 50?

(A) $\dfrac{1}{5}$

(B) $\dfrac{6}{5}$

(C) $\dfrac{7}{25}$

(D) $\dfrac{3}{5}$

(E) $\dfrac{18}{25}$

19. If $w^a \times w^5 = w^{15}$ and $(w^4)^b = w^{12}$, what is the value of $a + b$?

(A)   6
(B)   7
(C)   11
(D)   12
(E)   13

GO ON TO THE NEXT PAGE ⟹

2   2   2   2   2   2

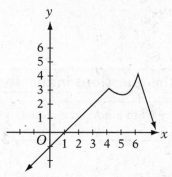

20. Given the graph of $y = f(x)$ above, which of the following represents the graph of $y = f(x - 2)$?

(A)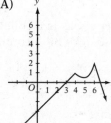

(B)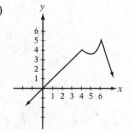

(C)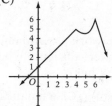

(D)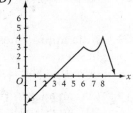

(E)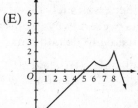

 STOP

If you finish before time is called, you may check your work on this section only. Do not turn to any other section of the test.

3   3   3   3   3   3

SECTION 3
Time—25 minutes
24 questions

> **Turn to Section 3 of your answer sheet to answer the questions in this section.**

> **Directions:** For each question in this section, select the best answer from among the choices given and fill in the corresponding circle on the answer sheet.

Each sentence below has one or two blanks, each blank indicating that something has been omitted. Beneath the sentence are five words or sets of words labeled A through E. Choose the word or set of words that, when inserted in the sentence, best fits the meaning of the sentence as a whole.

EXAMPLE:

Rather than accepting the theory unquestioningly, Deborah regarded it with -----.

(A) mirth
(B) sadness
(C) responsibility
(D) ignorance
(E) skepticism

Ⓐ Ⓑ Ⓒ Ⓓ ●

---

1. Although he purchased his computer only 10 months ago, rapid improvements in technology have left Raúl with ------- machine.

   (A) an obsolete   (B) an adjunct
   (C) a novel   (D) an automated
   (E) an elusive

2. Only if the number of applicants continues to -------- can the admissions committee justify offering more scholarships in order to increase the number of applications.

   (A) mushroom   (B) expand   (C) plummet
   (D) satiate   (E) burgeon

3. My father is so ------- that he will never even consider another person's viewpoint to be valid if it is different from his own.

   (A) pragmatic   (B) dogmatic   (C) phlegmatic
   (D) cordial   (E) curt

4. J. K. Rowling's *Harry Potter* series is a collection of works that are ------- for children but are still ------- to adults.

   (A) penned . . prosaic
   (B) employed . . morose
   (C) censored . . incongruous
   (D) designed . . tedious
   (E) authored . . engaging

5. Julia approaches her homework assignments in such ------- way that it is very difficult to believe that she is at the top of her class.

   (A) an adept   (B) a diligent   (C) a fanatical
   (D) an extroverted   (E) a laggardly

6. The President was such a ------- orator that his opponents were always supremely cautious about agreeing to debate him.

   (A) redoubtable   (B) staid   (C) magnanimous
   (D) weak   (E) stoic

7. The newest clothing line revealed at the show was an eclectic mix that ranged from the modest and unadorned to the ------- and garish.

   (A) austere   (B) prophetic   (C) cordial
   (D) ostentatious   (E) solitary

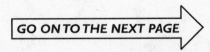
GO ON TO THE NEXT PAGE

3   3   3   3   3   3

8. Neil Campbell's textbook *Biology* is ------- and yet -------; it includes all of the essential information without ever being verbose.

    (A) compendious . . circumlocutory
    (B) reprehensible . . terse
    (C) comprehensive . . concise
    (D) praiseworthy . . grandiloquent
    (E) painstaking . . redundant

The passages below are followed by questions based on their content; questions following a pair of related passages may also be based on the relationship between the paired passages. Answer the questions on the basis of what is stated or implied in the passage and in any introductory material that may be provided.

Questions 9–12 are based on the following passages.

PASSAGE 1

The following is from President Bill Clinton's first inaugural address.

Today, a generation raised in the shadows of the Cold War assumes new responsibilities in a
Line world warmed by the sunshine of freedom, but threatened still by ancient hatreds and new
5   plagues. Raised in unrivaled prosperity, we inherit an economy that is still the world's strongest, but is weakened by business failures, stagnant wages, increasing inequality, and deep divisions among our own people. When
10   George Washington first took the oath I have just sworn to uphold, news traveled slowly across the land by horseback, and across the ocean by boat. Now the sights and sounds of this ceremony are broadcast instantaneously to
15   billions around the world. Communications and commerce are global. Investment is mobile. Technology is almost magical, and ambition for a better life is now universal.

PASSAGE 2

The following is a commentary on America written in 2005 by an American writer.

The people of the world, save the majority
20 of our own citizens, are growing to appreciate the difference between America and the United States. America is the heart and mind of the world. It is an ideal to which all free-
25 thinking men and women aspire. It is the spirit of hope, freedom, vision and creativity. But the United States, at least since the turn of the century, has become something different. It constantly grasps at the cloak of America,
30 but this cloak fits our current leaders quite poorly. Our leaders have become dominated by fear and its value as a political tool. They speak incessantly of freedom but revel in repression. They speak of a "culture of life"
35 but revel in the culture of siege and war. The hope, freedom, vision and creativity of America have slipped through their fingers, and they have little hope of recapturing it. In America, that task is left to the people.

9. The word "unrivaled" in line 5 most nearly means

    (A) without enemies
    (B) supremely abundant
    (C) militarily superior
    (D) unimaginable
    (E) highly intelligent

10. Which of the following best describes the contrast between the "people" (line 9) as characterized in Passage 1 and the "citizens" (line 20) as characterized in Passage 2?

    (A) the "people" are ignorant, while the "citizens" are well educated
    (B) the "people" lack fortitude, while the "citizens" are courageous
    (C) the "people" are worldly, while the "citizens" are parochial
    (D) the "people" are proud of their leaders, while the "citizens" are not
    (E) the "people" lack unity, while the "citizens" lack awareness

GO ON TO THE NEXT PAGE →

11. Passage 1 makes all of the following claims about the state of society EXCEPT that

(A) an increasing number of people are happy with their lives
(B) information is disseminated more rapidly than in the past
(C) the current economy is strong
(D) social inequities are deepening
(E) workers' incomes are not increasing

12. Unlike the author of Passage 1, the author of Passage 2 does which of the following?

(A) contrasts an ideal with a reality
(B) explains a study
(C) compares the past with the present
(D) describes an injustice
(E) acknowledges a responsibility

Questions 13–19 are based on the following passage.

The following passage is adapted from a short story published by a Russian author in the late 1970s.

What is all this? he thought, terrified. And yet . . . do I love her, or don't I? That is the
Line question!
But she, now that the most important and
5　difficult thing had at last been said, breathed lightly and freely. She, too, stood up and, looking straight into Ognev Alexeyich's face, began to talk quickly, irrepressibly and ardently.
Just as a man who is suddenly overwhelmed
10　by terror cannot afterwards remember the exact order of sounds accompanying the catastrophe which stuns him, Ognev could not remember Vera's words and phrases. His memory retained only the substance of her speech
15　itself and the sensation her speech produced in him. He remembered her voice, as though it were choked and slightly hoarse from excitement,
and the extraordinary music and passion of her intonation. Crying, laughing, the tears
20　glittering on her eyelashes, she was telling him that even from the first days of their acquaintance she had been struck by his originality, his intellect, his kind intelligent eyes, with the aims and objects of his life; that she had fallen pas-
25　sionately, madly and deeply in love with him; that whenever she had happened to come into the house from the garden that summer and had seen his coat in the vestibule or heard his voice in the distance, her heart had felt a cold
30　thrill of delight, a foretaste of happiness; that even the silliest jokes made her laugh helplessly, and in each figure of his copybook she could see something extraordinarily clever and grandiose; that his knotted walking stick
35　seemed to her more beautiful than the trees.
The forest and the wisps of fog and the black ditches alongside the road seemed to fall silent, listening to her, but something bad and strange was taking place in Ognev's
40　heart. . . . Vera was enchantingly beautiful as she told him of her love, she spoke with eloquence and passion, but much as he wanted to, he could feel no joy, no fundamental happiness, but only compassion for Vera, and
45　pain and regret that a good human being should be suffering because of him. The Lord only knows whether it was his bookish mind that now began to speak, or whether he was affected by that irresistible habit of objectivity
50　which so often prevents people from living, but Vera's raptures and suffering seemed to him only cloying and trivial. At the same time he was outraged with himself and something whispered to him that what he was now see-
55　ing and hearing was, from the point of view of human nature and his personal happiness, more important than any statistics, books or philosophical truths . . . And he was annoyed and blamed himself even though he himself
60　did not understand why he was to blame.

GO ON TO THE NEXT PAGE →

13. Which of the following best describes the characterization of the man and the woman in the first two paragraphs?

(A) He is confused, while she is passionate.
(B) He is angry, while she is jocular.
(C) He is stoic, while she is serene.
(D) He is ambivalent, while she is anxious.
(E) He is disdainful, while she is whimsical.

14. The author suggests that one "who is suddenly overwhelmed by terror" (lines 9–10) is temporarily

(A) vindictive
(B) defensive
(C) cautious
(D) disoriented
(E) resentful

15. The description of "the catastrophe" (lines 11–12) serves primarily to suggest that

(A) the couple has endured a terrible accident
(B) Ognev is devastated by Vera's harsh words
(C) Ognev is deeply troubled by Vera's passionate expression of love
(D) Ognev holds Vera responsible for a crime
(E) Vera has told Ognev a horrible secret

16. In line 24, "objects" most nearly means

(A) possessions
(B) facts
(C) decorations
(D) goals
(E) complaints

17. The passage suggests that the "bad and strange" (line 39) thing that was taking place in Ognev's heart was his

(A) eagerness
(B) sadism
(C) jealousy
(D) hatred
(E) disaffection

18. In lines 57–58, "statistics, books or philosophical truths" are mentioned as examples of things that

(A) Vera does not understand
(B) Ognev and Vera share reluctantly
(C) Ognev abandoned long ago
(D) Vera loves passionately
(E) Ognev inexplicably values more highly than passion

19. The primary function of the final paragraph is to show Ognev's

(A) struggle to understand his own feelings
(B) anger about Vera's misrepresentation of her feelings
(C) frustration with the voices in his head
(D) outrage with his inability to understand a philosophical concept
(E) appreciation of Vera's beauty

GO ON TO THE NEXT PAGE

Questions 20–24 are based on the following passage.

The following is part of an introduction to the publication of a speech delivered by President Lyndon B. Johnson in the 1960s.

"Somehow you never forget what poverty
and hatred can do when you see its scars on
Line   the hopeful face of a young child." So spoke
President Lyndon B. Johnson in the course of
5   one of the most deeply felt, and deeply moving, addresses ever delivered by an American
president. The date was March 15th, 1965; the
occasion was an extraordinary joint session at
night of the Senate and the House of Repre-
10   sentatives, televised across the nation. It was
the "time of Selma"—only a few days after the
historic mass demonstration in support of
voter registration in Alabama, in which many
of the peaceful marchers were physically at-
15   tacked and one of them, a white clergyman
from the north, was killed. The nation itself
was a shocked witness, via television, of much
of that unforgettable scene: the long rows of
marchers, a cross section of African Americans
20   and whites, Californians and New Yorkers,
resolutely striding, smiling, singing to hide
their exhaustion, trying not to see the hate-
twisted faces and shouting menace of the side-
walk crowd, trying not to fear the armored
25   troopers and police with their notorious supporting artillery of dogs, clubs, and cattle
prods.

This was the moment chosen by the President, himself a Southerner with a reputation
30   for compromise, to bear witness before the
nation, and to call upon his former associates
of Congress to stand up and be counted with
him—more specifically, to take action on a
bill which would correct the conspicuous
35   weakness of the 1964 Civil Rights Bill, its failure to protect the right of African Americans
to vote "when local officials are determined to
deny it." In forthright terms, President Johnson spelled out the full cruelty and ingenuity

40   of that discrimination, and crisply defined the
central issue involved: "There is no Constitutional issue here. The command of the Constitution is plain. There is no moral issue. It is
wrong—deadly wrong—to deny any of your
45   fellow Americans the right to vote in this
country. There is no issue of state's rights or
national rights. There is only the struggle for
human rights."

The President spoke slowly, solemnly, with
50   unmistakable determination. His words and
his manner were perfectly synchronized; indeed he made the nationwide audience aware
of how deeply personal the issue of African
American rights was to him. He recalled his
55   own southern origins, and his shattering encounter with Mexican-American children as a
young schoolteacher ("They never seemed to
know why people disliked them, but they
knew it was so because I saw it in their eyes.")
60   He spoke more directly, more explicitly, and
more warmly of the human experience of
prejudice than any president before him. But
he also placed the problem of African American rights in a broader frame of reference—
65   that of poverty and ignorance, bigotry and
fear. "Their cause must be our cause too.
Because it is not just African Americans, but
really it's all of us, who must overcome the
crippling legacy of bigotry and injustice. And
70   we shall overcome."

GO ON TO THE NEXT PAGE ⟹

---

20. In the first paragraph, the marchers are characterized as

(A) ruthless
(B) gleeful
(C) intellectual
(D) stoic
(E) shocked

21. The passage indicates that the 1964 Civil Rights Act was deficient in that it did not

(A) sufficiently pressure local officials to extend voting privileges to all citizens
(B) provide enough funds to promote voter registration drives
(C) punish felons who committed hate crimes
(D) provide military protection for the Selma marchers
(E) invest in minority-owned businesses

22. In line 55, *shattering* most nearly means

(A) exploding
(B) disturbing
(C) fragmenting
(D) violent
(E) loud

23. The quotation in lines 57–59 ("They never seemed . . . in their eyes") indicates that Johnson

(A) understood the political process at a young age
(B) was unfamiliar with Mexican-American customs
(C) empathized strongly with his students
(D) was a victim of bigotry
(E) was unaware of the difficulties his students faced

24. The passage indicates that Johnson, unlike previous presidents, handled the issue of civil rights by

(A) successfully integrating the issue into his reelection campaign
(B) approaching the cause with objectivity and impartiality
(C) speaking clearly to reporters using terms they wanted to hear
(D) focusing primarily on the Mexican-American population
(E) directly addressing the public on the issue and describing it in personal terms

If you finish before time is called, you may check your work on this section only. Do not turn to any other section of the test.

4   **4**   4   4   4   **4**

SECTION 4
Time—25 minutes
35 questions

Turn to Section 4 of your answer sheet to answer the questions in this section.

Directions: For each question in this section, select the best answer from among the choices given and fill in the corresponding circle on the answer sheet.

The following sentences test correctness and effectiveness of expression. Part of each sentence or the entire sentence is underlined; beneath each sentence are five ways of phrasing the underlined material. Choice A repeats the original phrasing; the other four choices are different. If you think the original phrasing produces a better sentence than any of the alternatives, select choice A; if not, select one of the other choices.

In making your selection, follow the requirements of standard written English; that is, pay attention to grammar, choice of words, sentence construction, and punctuation. Your selection should result in the most effective sentence—clear and precise, without awkwardness or ambiguity.

EXAMPLE:

The children <u>couldn't hardly believe their eyes</u>.

(A) couldn't hardly believe their eyes
(B) could hardly believe their eyes
(C) would not hardly believe their eyes
(D) couldn't nearly believe their eyes
(E) couldn't hardly believe his or her eyes

 Ⓐ ● Ⓒ Ⓓ Ⓔ

1. Exhausted from a day of hiking across steep, rain-soaked paths, the <u>group of campers were relieved upon the final reaching of the car</u>.

   (A) group of campers were relieved upon the final reaching of the car
   (B) camping group became relieved after they got to the car
   (C) group of campers was relieved to finally reach the car
   (D) campers were relieved after the car was finally reached
   (E) group was relieved after the campers finally reached the car

2. Theodore Roosevelt's first term as President <u>was marked by a ferocious battle between labor and management</u> in Pennsylvania's coal-mining industry.

   (A) was marked by a ferocious battle between labor and management
   (B) was marked by a ferocious battle of labor's and management's
   (C) saw a ferocious battle: between labor and management
   (D) was marked ferociously by labor and management's battle
   (E) was marking a ferocious battle between labor and management

GO ON TO THE NEXT PAGE ⟹

3. Many great scientists and inventors of the past, notably Nikola Tesla, <u>has possessed the ability of extraordinary visualization skills</u> that enabled them to analyze the most minute details of complex machines before the devices were even constructed.

   (A) has posessed the ability of extraordinary visualization skills

   (B) have been able to possess extraordinary visualization skills

   (C) possessed skills in visualization that was extraordinary

   (D) possessed extraordinary visualization skills

   (E) possessed skills of visualizing that was extraordinary

4. The Thracians, originally divided into numerous tribes, came together politically under King Teres in 500 BC, and <u>it enabled their resistance against</u> the many Roman invasions that would follow in the centuries to come.

   (A) it enabled their resistance against

   (B) this unity enabled them to resist

   (C) enabling the ability to resist

   (D) that enabled them to resist

   (E) this unity gave them the ability of resisting

5. Disillusioned by American politics and culture, Ernest Hemingway <u>led an exodus of expatriate authors on an overseas journey</u> across the Atlantic following the First World War.

   (A) led an exodus of expatriate authors on an overseas journey

   (B) took an overseas journey leading an exodus of expatriate authors

   (C) led an exodus of expatriate authors

   (D) has led an exodus of expatriate authors

   (E) leading an exodus of expatriate authors

6. Walter Cronkite was known for his honest presentation of the <u>news, plus the ability to be reassuring with his tone</u>.

   (A) news, plus the ability to be reassuring with his tone

   (B) news, plus his reassuring tone

   (C) news plus the reassuring nature of his tone

   (D) news and his tone that was reassuring

   (E) news and his reassuring tone

7. Only half as many students study computer science <u>than they did</u> just a decade ago.

   (A) than they did

   (B) than was true

   (C) as did

   (D) when compared to

   (E) than

8. Auto racing, often thought of as a regional phenomenon, <u>therefore is quite popular</u> throughout the nation.

   (A) therefore is quite popular

   (B) henceforth is quite popular

   (C) is thus quite popular

   (D) is actually quite popular

   (E) in retrospect, is quite popular

GO ON TO THE NEXT PAGE ⟩

9. The band decided to allow <u>downloading their songs for their fans free of charge</u>, in the hopes of increasing its popularity.

   (A) downloading their songs for their fans free of charge

   (B) their fans downloading their songs free of charge

   (C) its fans to download its songs free of charge

   (D) free downloading of their songs to its fans

   (E) downloading of its songs to its fans, which were free of charge

10. The most likely reasons for the recent surge in legislation <u>is the fact that the voters agree on the issues and the political parties stopping</u> bickering.

   (A) is the fact that the voters agree on the issues and the political parties stopping

   (B) are because the voters agree on the issues and the political parties have stopped

   (C) are that the voters agree on the issues and that the political parties have stopped

   (D) is the voters agreeing on the issues and the political parties stopping

   (E) are the voters agreeing on the issues and the political parties have stopped

11. An untiring defender of the downtrodden, <u>Clarence Darrow's oratory could mesmerize his audiences and devastate his opponents.</u>

   (A) Clarence Darrow's oratory could mesmerize his audiences and devastate his opponents

   (B) Clarence Darrow could mesmerize his audiences and devastate his opponents with his oratory

   (C) the oratory of Clarence Darrow could mesmerize his audiences and devastate his opponents

   (D) Clarence Darrow's audiences could be mesmerized by his oratory and his opponents devastated by it

   (E) Clarence Darrow could mesmerize his audiences with his oratory, and his opponents could be devastated by it

---

The following sentences test your ability to recognize grammar and usage errors. Each sentence contains either a single error or no error at all. No sentence contains more than one error. The error, if there is one, is underlined and lettered. If the sentence contains an error, select the one underlined part that must be changed to make the sentence correct. If the sentence is correct, select choice E. In choosing answers, follow the requirements of standard written English.

EXAMPLE:

By the time <u>they reached</u> the halfway point
          A

<u>in the race,</u> <u>most of the runners</u> <u>hadn't hardly</u>
    B   C   D

begun to hit their stride.   <u>No error</u>
                    E

12. The local dairy company is <u>one of the most</u>
                       A

<u>efficient</u> in the state, <u>so</u> it is surprising that
  B   C

the delivery of our milk products over the last

few days <u>have been</u> late.   <u>No error</u>
        D   E

13. Sea turtle hatchlings can find their way

<u>to the ocean</u> by sight alone, even at night, <u>because</u>
   A   B

they are capable <u>to distinguish</u> visually between
             C

the bright reflections from the ocean surface <u>and</u>
                       D

the dark silhouettes of sand dunes and

vegetation.   <u>No error</u>
          E

GO ON TO THE NEXT PAGE ⟶

4   4   4   4   4   4

14. This holiday season, several members of the
           A
     committee are sponsoring a dinner to raise
               B
     money for their efforts to encourage
                    C
     responsible driving.   No error
           D   E

15. The lavish photographs and fascinating

     diagrams in the biology textbook was so
                A   B
     engaging that I seriously considered
                              C
     becoming a zoologist.   No error
               D   E

16. Behavioral scientists believe that the way
                          A
     chimpanzees form friendships and alliances
                 B
     is very similar to humans.   No error
        C   D   E

17. When the window was opened, the affects of
                       A   B
     the cool spring breeze were felt immediately
                                   C
     by the uncomfortable workers.   No error
            D   E

18. The probability of getting hit by lightning
                     A
     are fewer than the probability of winning
         B   C
     the lottery, although both are minuscule.
                  D

     No error
        E

19. According to the new editorial guidelines for
     A
     publication, before an author submits a
                                  B
     manuscript to the publisher, they must first
                                  C
     have the text reviewed by a qualified content
           D
     expert.   No error
                   E

20. In his book Night, Elie Wiesel employs a
     A
     disjointed style, frequently shifting point of
                       B
     view in order to capture the fragmented nature
                    C
     of ghetto life in Germany in the time during
                               D
     the Second World War.   No error
                                   E

21. Although we had expected poor service at
     A
     the resort, we were more than satisfied at the
                 B   C
     attention we received throughout our stay.
                D
     No error
        E

22. After we had ate a leisurely meal, we walked
               A
     down the street and discovered a jazz club
          B   C
     where a talented young trio was playing.
                                  D
     No error
        E

GO ON TO THE NEXT PAGE

4   4   4   4   4   4

23. Ancient Babylonian physicians <u>were</u> among
                                   A
    the first <u>to investigate</u> the character and
              B
    course of diseases scientifically, <u>although</u>
                                        C
    they frequently attributed the causes of those

    ailments <u>to the anger</u> of gods or demons.
             D
    <u>No error</u>
    E

24. When <u>the filaments</u> of the angler fish
              A
    <u>are stimulated</u>, its jaws, <u>armed</u> with bands
         B   C
    of sharp inward-pointing teeth, <u>is</u> triggered
                                    D
    to snap shut. <u>No error</u>
                   E

25. Some doctors <u>believe that</u> taking vitamins
                    A
    <u>on a daily basis</u> <u>help</u> decrease a patient's
         B   C
    susceptibility <u>to infection</u>. <u>No error</u>
                   D   E

26. When my parents <u>went</u> out to dinner, they
                     A
    left me <u>underneath</u> the <u>control of</u> our
            B   C
    babysitter, <u>who lived</u> next door to us.
                D
    <u>No error</u>
    E

27. Since 2001, the company <u>has spent</u> <u>more on</u>
                              A   B
    employee training than <u>they did</u> in the
                           C
    previous 10 years <u>combined</u>.   <u>No error</u>
                      D   E

28. If teachers want <u>to be successful</u> in large
                        A
    public high schools, they <u>must learn</u> not
                              B
    only to command respect from their students,

    but also <u>they should develop</u> rapport with
             C
    those students in order <u>to create</u> a
                            D
    productive work environment.   <u>No error</u>
                                   E

29. After several trials, the chemists <u>discovered</u>
                                       A
    that the precipitates <u>could be</u> more
                          B
    effectively separated <u>by</u> a high-speed
                          C
    centrifuge <u>and not</u> by a filtration system.
               D
    <u>No error</u>
    E

GO ON TO THE NEXT PAGE ⇒

Directions: The following passage is an early draft of an essay. Some parts of the passage need to be rewritten.

Read the passage and select the best answers for the questions that follow. Some questions are about particular sentences or parts of sentences and ask you to improve sentence structure or word choice. Other questions ask you to consider organization and development. In choosing answers, follow the requirements of standard written English.

Questions 30–35 refer to the following passage.

(1) While known when he was the President for his abundant energy and muscular build as an adult, Theodore Roosevelt's build as a child was actually quite puny. **(2)** Stricken with asthma, he was taught early that strenuous physical activity might be dangerous to his health and that, in fact, it might even be fatal. **(3)** Determined to overcome this obstacle, Roosevelt trained his body relentlessly and built his impressive girth through sheer grit and determination. **(4)** That these childhood passions stayed with him throughout his adult life should not be surprising. **(5)** Physical activities, though, were not the only childhood fascination to play a prominent role later in his life.

(6) A skilled hunter, Roosevelt spent much of his leisure time hunting various forms of game. **(7)** Beginning during his undergraduate days at Harvard, he spent significant time in snow-covered Maine forests as well as the arid deserts of the Dakota territory. **(8)** As a child, Theodore was so enraptured by birds, he would spend hours observing and writing about them, even phonetically spelling out their various calls and songs. **(9)** Upon reaching government office, Roosevelt became the first true conservationist, pushing for laws to protect wildlife and resources. **(10)** He cherished nature in all its forms, seeking to understand its variety through research and experience.

(11) By openly maintaining these passions while in political office, Roosevelt redefined the role of the American politician. **(12)** While his predecessors had often been aloof with regard to their own personal feelings, Roosevelt advertised his sense of morality by talking openly about it repeatedly with citizens and reporters in speeches and newspapers. **(13)** In the dawning of a new, industrialized age, Roosevelt chose to take on controversial issues, battling through the spoils system, disputes between management and labor, and the question of imperialism.

30.   In context, which of the following is the best revision of sentence 1 (reproduced below)?

While known when he was the President for his abundant energy and muscular build as an adult, Theodore Roosevelt's build as a child was actually quite puny.

(A)   While Theodore Roosevelt was known for his energy and muscular build, but the President was actually a quite puny child.

(B)   Although known for his abundant energy and muscular build as an adult, President Theodore Roosevelt was actually quite puny as a child.

(C)   While puny as a child, Theodore Roosevelt was known for his abundant energy and muscular build while being President.

(D)   As President, Theodore Roosevelt was known for his abundant energy and muscular build, not for being puny as a child.

(E)   Theodore Roosevelt was puny as a child and was known for his abundant energy and muscular build as President.

31.   In context, which of the following is the best revision of the underlined portion of sentence 3 (reproduced below)?

Determined <u>to overcome this obstacle</u>, Roosevelt trained his body relentlessly and built his impressive girth through sheer grit and determination.

(A)   (no revision needed)
(B)   that this obstacle should be overcome
(C)   to overcome such ideas that became obstacles
(D)   not to allow this to become an obstacle standing in his way
(E)   to take obstacles out of his way

GO ON TO THE NEXT PAGE ⟩

32. Where is the most appropriate place to move sentence 4?

   (A) Before sentence 1
   (B) Before sentence 2
   (C) Before sentence 6, to start the second paragraph
   (D) After sentence 10, to end the second paragraph
   (E) After sentence 13

33. Which of the following provides the most logical ordering of the sentences in paragraph 2?

   (A) 7, 9, 10, 6, 8
   (B) 8, 10, 7, 6, 9
   (C) 8, 10, 9, 6, 7
   (D) 9, 7, 8, 10, 6
   (E) 7, 10, 8, 6, 9

34. If the author wanted to make sentence 7 more specific, which of the following details would fit best in the context of the second paragraph?

   (A) Roosevelt's age
   (B) information about Roosevelt's course of study
   (C) details of Roosevelt's activities in the deserts and forests
   (D) an explanation of why the climate of Maine is so different from the climate of the Dakota territory
   (E) information about Roosevelt's political affiliation prior to these excursions

35. Where is the best place to insert the following sentence?

   His brazen moves were often criticized, but Theodore Roosevelt will go down in the annals of history as a man who was always true to himself, whether as a private citizen or as President of the United States.

   (A) Before sentence 1
   (B) After sentence 1
   (C) After sentence 5
   (D) Before sentence 11
   (E) After sentence 13

STOP

If you finish before time is called, you may check your work on this section only. Do not turn to any other section of the test.

5   5   5   5   5   5

SECTION 5
Time—25 minutes
18 questions

Turn to Section 5 of your answer sheet to answer the questions in this section.

Directions: This section contains two types of questions. You have 25 minutes to complete both types. For questions 1–8, solve each problem and decide which is the best of the choices given. Fill in the corresponding circle on the answer sheet. You may use any available space for scratchwork.

Notes

1. The use of a calculator is permitted.
2. All numbers used are real numbers.
3. Figures that accompany problems in this test are intended to provide information useful in solving the problems. They are drawn as accurately as possible EXCEPT when it is stated in a specific problem that the figure is not drawn to scale. All figures lie in a plane unless otherwise indicated.
4. Unless otherwise specified, the domain of any function f is assumed to be the set of all real numbers x for which $f(x)$ is a real number.

Reference Information

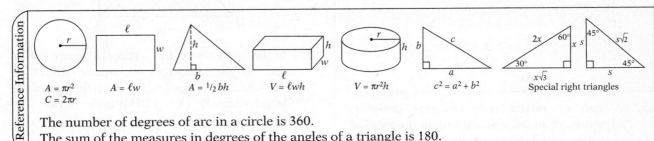

$A = \pi r^2$
$C = 2\pi r$
$A = \ell w$
$A = \frac{1}{2} bh$
$V = \ell wh$
$V = \pi r^2 h$
$c^2 = a^2 + b^2$
Special right triangles

The number of degrees of arc in a circle is 360.
The sum of the measures in degrees of the angles of a triangle is 180.

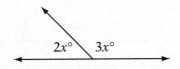

Note: Figure not drawn to scale.

1. In the figure above, what is the value of $2x$?

(A) 36
(B) 72
(C) 90
(D) 108
(E) 132

2. If $(x - 4)^2 = 36$, then x could be

(A) −6
(B) −2
(C) 0
(D) 4
(E) 6

GO ON TO THE NEXT PAGE

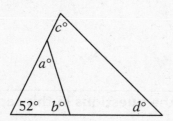

3.   In the figure above, what is the value of
$a + b + c + d$?

   (A)   56
   (B)   128
   (C)   256
   (D)   264
   (E)   322

---

4.   If $f(x) = x^2 - 4$, for what positive value of x does
$f(x) = 32$?

   (A)   5
   (B)   6
   (C)   7
   (D)   8
   (E)   9

---

5.   A can of mixed nuts contains cashews,
almonds, peanuts, and walnuts in the ratio of
2 to 4 to 5 to 7, respectively, by weight. What
fraction of the mixture by weight is almonds?

   (A) $\dfrac{1}{18}$

   (B) $\dfrac{1}{9}$

   (C) $\dfrac{2}{9}$

   (D) $\dfrac{1}{4}$

   (E) $\dfrac{5}{18}$

6.   Twenty students in a chemistry class took a
test on which the overall average score was 75.
If the average score for 12 of those students
was 83, what was the average score for the remaining members of the class?

   (A)   60
   (B)   61
   (C)   62
   (D)   63
   (E)   64

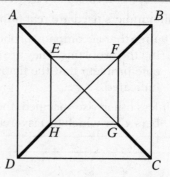

7.   In the figure above, the vertices of square *EFGH*
are on the diagonals of square *ABCD*. If
$EF = 8\sqrt{2}$ and $AB = 14\sqrt{2}$, what is the sum of the
lengths $AE + BF + CG + DH$ (heavier lines)?

   (A)   24
   (B)   28
   (C)   32
   (D)   36
   (E)   38

$$\begin{array}{r} RS \\ +\,\underline{SR} \\ TR4 \end{array}$$

8.   In the correctly worked addition problem
above, each letter represents a different non-
zero digit. What is the value of $2R + T$?

   (A)   4
   (B)   5
   (C)   10
   (D)   11
   (E)   13

GO ON TO THE NEXT PAGE ⟹

5   5   5   5   5   5

Directions: For student-produced response questions 9–18, use the grids at the bottom of the answer sheet page on which you have answered questions 1–8.

Each of the remaining ten questions requires you to solve the problem and enter your answer by marking the circles in the special grid, as shown in the examples below. You may use any available space for scratchwork.

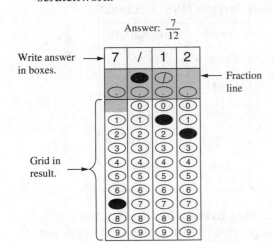

Write answer in boxes.

Grid in result.

Answer: $\frac{7}{12}$

Fraction line

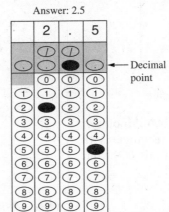

Answer: 2.5

Decimal point

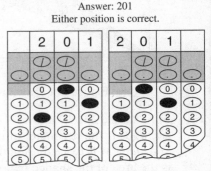

Answer: 201
Either position is correct.

Note: You may start your answers in any column, space permitting. Columns not needed should be left blank.

- Mark no more than one circle in any column.

- Because the answer sheet will be machine-scored, **you will receive credit only if the circles are filled in correctly.**

- Although not required, it is suggested that you write your answer in the boxes at the top of the columns to help you fill in the circles accurately.

- Some problems may have more than one correct answer. In such cases, grid only one answer.

- No question has a negative answer.

- **Mixed numbers** such as $3\frac{1}{2}$ must be gridded as

    3.5 or 7/2. (If ⬚ is gridded, it will be

    interpreted as $\frac{31}{2}$ not $3\frac{1}{2}$.)

- **Decimal Answers:** If you obtain a decimal answer with more digits than the grid can accommodate, it may be either rounded or truncated, but it must fill the entire grid. For example, if you obtain an answer such as 0.6666..., you should record your result as .666 or .667. **A less accurate value such as .66 or .67 will be scored as incorrect.**

Acceptable ways to grid $\frac{2}{3}$ are:

9. For all real numbers n, let $\boxed{n}$ be defined by $\boxed{n} = \dfrac{n^2}{16}$. What is the value of $\boxed{4}^2$?

10. The Civics Club earned 25% more at its bake sale in 2007 than it did in 2006. If it earned $600 at its bake sale in 2006, how much did it earn at its bake sale in 2007?

GO ON TO THE NEXT PAGE

11. If the sum of two numbers is 4 and their difference is 2, what is their product?

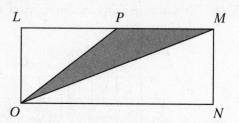

Note: Figure not drawn to scale.

12. In rectangle $LMNO$ above, P is the midpoint of side $\overline{LM}$. If the perimeter of the rectangle is 48 and side $\overline{LM}$ is twice the length of side $\overline{LO}$, what is the area of the shaded region?

13. If $64^3 = 4^x$, what is the value of x?

14. Points P, Q, R, and S lie on a line in that order. If $\overline{PS}$ is twice as long as $\overline{PR}$ and four times as long as $\overline{PQ}$, what is the value of $\dfrac{QS}{PQ}$?

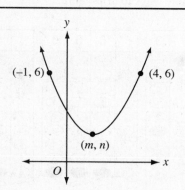

15. The figure above shows the graph in the xy-plane of a quadratic function with a vertex at (m, n). What is the value of m?

16. If the sum of five consecutive even integers is 110, what is the least of these integers?

NUMBER OF APPLICANTS TO COLLINS COLLEGE	
YEAR	APPLICANTS
1980	15,000
1985	18,000
1990	20,000
1995	24,000
2000	25,000

17. According to the data in the table above, by what percent did the number of applicants to Collins College increase from 1990 to 1995? (Disregard the % symbol when entering your answer into the grid. For instance, grid 50% as 50.)

18. A jar contains only black, white, and red marbles. If randomly choosing a black marble is four times as likely as randomly choosing a white marble, and randomly choosing a red marble is five times as likely as randomly choosing a black marble, then what is the smallest possible number of marbles in the jar?

If you finish before time is called, you may check your work on this section only. Do not turn to any other section of the test.

6 6 6 6 6 6

SECTION 6
Time—25 minutes
24 questions

Turn to Section 6 of your answer sheet to answer the questions in this section.

Directions: For each question in this section, select the best answer from among the choices given and fill in the corresponding circle on the answer sheet.

Each sentence below has one or two blanks, each blank indicating that something has been omitted. Beneath the sentence are five words or sets of words labeled A through E. Choose the word or set of words that, when inserted in the sentence, <u>best</u> fits the meaning of the sentence as a whole.

EXAMPLE:

Rather than accepting the theory unquestioningly, Deborah regarded it with -----.

(A) mirth
(B) sadness
(C) responsibility
(D) ignorance
(E) skepticism

---

1. If John had not been there to ------- when tensions began to rise at the meeting, a fight would surely have ensued.

    (A) intervene
    (B) coalesce
    (C) harass
    (D) intermingle
    (E) exacerbate

2. The defendant hoped that the testimony of the surprise witness would corroborate his alibi and ------- him of the crime of which he had been accused.

    (A) convoke
    (B) synthesize
    (C) impeach
    (D) absolve
    (E) magnify

3. Rachel's ------- driving is not surprising, given that she spends ------- hours each day ensnarled in traffic delays.

    (A) antipathy for . . delightful
    (B) penchant for . . uncountable
    (C) predilection for . . dreary
    (D) proclivity for . . desperate
    (E) aversion to . . insufferable

4. Many medical practices once considered "state of the art" are now thought to be ------- by physicians who are often incredulous that such barbaric acts were once -------.

    (A) primitive . . sanctioned
    (B) ingenious . . approved
    (C) boorish . . censured
    (D) innovative . . endorsed
    (E) foolhardy . . condemned

5. The Prime Minister had vetoed the proposal several times in the past; thus, it came as a great surprise to the public when he ------- the same law in his most recent speech.

    (A) articulated
    (B) sanctioned
    (C) denounced
    (D) initiated
    (E) abbreviated

GO ON TO THE NEXT PAGE ▷

6   6   6   6   6   6

The passages below are followed by questions based on the content. Answer the questions on the basis of what is <u>stated</u> or <u>implied</u> in the passage and in any introductory material that may be provided.

Questions 6–7 are based on the following passage.

> The reverence for their goddess of protection accounts for the respect Navajos show to the
> *Line* women of their tribe. The tradition is that a
> man never lifts his hand against a woman,
> 5 although it is not an unusual thing for a
> squaw to administer a sound thrashing to a
> warrior husband who has offended her. All of
> the sheep, which constitute the great wealth
> of the tribe, are owned by the women, and in
> 10 the various families the line of descent is al-
> ways on the side of the women. The Navajos
> have little or no idea of a future existence but
> are firm believers in the transmigration of
> souls. For this reason they have great rever-
> 15 ence for different animals and birds, which
> are supposed to be the re-embodiment of
> departed spirits of Navajos.

6. Based on the information in the passage, with which of the following statements would the author most likely agree?

(A) Navajo warriors obey their wives obsequiously.
(B) Birds are a particularly vital food source for the Navajo.
(C) A Navajo man who disrespects a woman would likely face censure.
(D) The Navajo do not believe in reincarnation.
(E) In the winter, the Navajo migrate to warmer climates.

7. The word "administer" in line 6 most nearly means

(A) manage
(B) maintain
(C) govern
(D) rehearse
(E) dispense

Questions 8–9 are based on the following passage.

> "Dying with dignity" is a topic that has inspired deep debate among the members of
> *Line* the medical community. Should an individual
> be allowed to determine when he or she wants
> 5 to die? Should a person who is merely receiv-
> ing palliative care that provides no hope of a
> cure be allowed to tell a doctor to stop all
> treatment so she can die in peace? How can a
> doctor know if a patient has the mental capac-
> 10 ity to decide for herself that the time has come
> to stop fighting the disease? It is a challenging
> and persistent debate.

8. As used in line 6, "palliative" most nearly means

(A) punitive
(B) remedial
(C) analgesic
(D) curative
(E) altruistic

9. The passage suggests that in cases of extreme illness, doctors may have difficulty in determining their patients'

(A) state of mind
(B) prognosis
(C) quality of life
(D) tolerance of pain
(E) ability to remember facts

First passage: "The Navajo Indians," William M. Edwardy, *Harper's Weekly*, July 1890
Second passage: Copyright 2004 Mark Anestis. All rights reserved.

GO ON TO THE NEXT PAGE →

Questions 10–16 are based on the following passage.

The following passage is excerpted from a recent book about seismology, the study of earthquakes.

In the 1970s, there was great optimism about earthquake prediction. A few so-called earth-
Line quake precursors had come to light, and there
    was even a theory (known as dilatancy) put
5   forth to explain many of the phenomena that
    come before a large earthquake. A series of
    foreshocks is an example of a precursor. How-
    ever, since foreshocks look just like any other
    earthquakes, they are not in themselves very
10 useful in prediction. From all points around
    the globe, there are numerous anecdotal re-
    ports about other precursors, earthquake folk-
    lore, if you will.
        Many widely reported earthquake precur-
15 sors are related to groundwater. A few hours
    before a large earthquake, marked changes
    have been reported in the level or flow of wells
    and springs. Groundwater has also reportedly
    changed temperature, become cloudy, or ac-
20 quired a bad taste. Occasionally, electrostatic
    phenomena such as earthquake lights (similar
    to St. Elmo's fire that appears on ships during
    electrical storms) and changes in the local
    magnetic field have been reported. Anecdotal
25 reports also persistently include the strange
    behavior of animals, which might be linked to
    electrostatic phenomena or foreshocks.
    Changes in strain and creep (silent tectonic
    motion, without accompanying earthquake)
30 along a fault normally locked by friction could
    also be considered precursors.
        In China in the 1970s, it became popular for
    people to predict earthquakes using "back-
    yard" measurements such as the monitoring
35 of well levels and observation of farm animals.
    At least one earthquake, the Haicheng quake
    in 1975, was successfully predicted and a

town evacuated, proving that, at least in some
cases, earthquake prediction is possible. The
40 Haicheng earthquake had hundreds of foreshocks, making it an easier-than-average
earthquake to predict. Groundwater changes
and anomalous animal behavior were also reported (for example, hibernating snakes sup-
45 posedly awoke and froze to death). In China,
"evacuation" meant that compulsory outdoor
movies were shown, so that when the quake
did happen and the town was severely damaged, no one was killed. But Chinese seismol-
50 ogists missed predicting the catastrophic
Tangshan earthquake, in which at least
250,000 reportedly perished.

10. Which of the following is the best title for this passage?

(A) The Effects of Earthquakes on Groundwater
(B) The Search for Earthquake Precursors
(C) A Novel Theory of the Origin of Earthquakes
(D) A History of Chinese Earthquakes
(E) How Animals Anticipate Earthquakes

11. The passage indicates that foreshocks are "not . . . very useful" (lines 9–10) in predicting earthquakes because they

(A) are exceptionally difficult to detect
(B) occur simultaneously with changes in groundwater
(C) are not part of the theory of dilatancy
(D) interfere with electrostatic phenomena
(E) are impossible to distinguish from earthquakes themselves

Excerpted from *Furious Earth*, by Ellen J. Prager, McGraw-Hill, New York, 2000. Reproduced with permission of The McGraw-Hill Companies.

GO ON TO THE NEXT PAGE

12. According to the passage, which of the following features of groundwater have been reported to change immediately prior to an earthquake (lines 16–20)?

    I. density
    II. clarity
    III. flow

(A) II only
(B) III only
(C) I and II only
(D) II and III only
(E) I, II, and III

13. Which of the following could be considered a logical inconsistency in the passage?

(A) The passage states that foreshocks are not useful predictors of earthquakes but then cites foreshocks as instrumental to predicting an earthquake.
(B) The passage says that the Chinese are interested in predicting earthquakes but then says that they were devastated by the Tangshan earthquake.
(C) The passage reports that animals behaved strangely before an earthquake but then attributes this behavior to electrostatic phenomena.
(D) The passage states that the town of Haicheng was safely evacuated but then says that its citizens were forced to watch outdoor movies.
(E) The passage suggests that both strain and creep could be considered earthquake precursors.

14. Which of the following best describes the function of the third paragraph?

(A) to describe an application of a theory
(B) to provide an alternative perspective
(C) to recount a scientific experiment
(D) to summarize the ancient origins of a theory
(E) to demonstrate the difficulties of employing a technique

15. The passage suggests that the Tangshan earthquake

(A) was caused by strain and creep
(B) was preceded by changes in the groundwater
(C) caused more damage than the Haicheng earthquake did
(D) was preceded by several foreshocks
(E) was anticipated by the theory of dilatancy

16. In line 46, the word "evacuation" is placed in quotations in order to

(A) imply that an action was ineffective
(B) indicate that it is an archaic term
(C) emphasize the primitiveness of Chinese scientific methods
(D) suggest that a certain practice was unconventional
(E) underscore that an action was intended, but not implemented

GO ON TO THE NEXT PAGE

6   6   6   6   6   6

Questions 17–24 are based on the following passage.

*The following passage contains an excerpt taken
from an anthology of autobiographies of American women.*

    On landing in America, a grievous dis-
appointment awaited us; my father did not
Line meet us. He was in New Bedford, Massachusetts, nursing his grief and preparing to return
5   to England, for he had been told that the *John
Jacob Westervelt* had been lost at sea with every
soul on board. One of the missionaries who met
the ship took us under his wing and conducted
us to a little hotel, where we remained until
10   father had received his incredible news and
rushed to New York. He could hardly believe
that we were really restored to him; and even
now, through the mists of more than half a century, I can still see the expression in his wet eyes
15   as he picked me up and tossed me into the air.
    I can see, too, the toys he brought me—
a little saw and a hatchet, which became the
dearest treasures of my childish days. They
were fatidical[1] gifts, that saw and hatchet; in
20   the years ahead of me I was to use tools as
well as my brothers did, as I proved when
I helped to build our frontier home.
    We went to New Bedford with father, who
had found work there at his old trade; and
25   here I laid the foundations of my first childhood friendship, not with another child, but
with my next-door neighbor, a ship-builder.
Morning after morning, this man swung me
on his big shoulder and took me to his ship-
30   yard, where my hatchet and saw had violent
exercise as I imitated the workers around me.
Discovering that my tiny petticoats were in
my way, my new friends had a little boy's suit
made for me; and thus emancipated, at this
35   tender age, I worked unwearyingly at his side
all day long and day after day.
    The move to Michigan meant a complete
upheaval in our lives. In Lawrence we had
around us the fine flower of New England

40   civilization. We children went to school; our
parents, though they were in very humble circumstances, were associated with the leading
spirits and the big movements of the day.
When we went to Michigan, we went to the
45   wilderness, to the wild pioneer life of those
times, and we were all old enough to keenly
feel the change.
    Every detail of our journey through the
wilderness is clear in my mind. My brother
50   James met us at Grand Rapids with what, in
those days, was called a lumber-wagon, but
which had a horrible resemblance to a vehicle
from the health department. My sisters and I
gave it one cold look and turned from it; we
55   were so pained by its appearance that we refused to ride in it through the town. Instead,
we started off on foot, trying to look as if we
had no association with it, and we climbed
into the unwieldy vehicle only when the city
60   streets were far behind us.

17. Immediately upon arriving in America, the
     author was cared for by

    (A) John Jacob Westervelt
    (B) her father
    (C) a missionary
    (D) a childhood friend
    (E) a shipbuilder neighbor

18. In line 12, the word "restored" most nearly means

    (A) updated
    (B) refurbished
    (C) put into storage
    (D) deposited
    (E) returned

[1]Prophetic

Excerpted from "The Story of a Pioneer" by Anna Howard Shaw,
   in *Autobiographies of American Women: An Anthology*
   © 1992 by Jill Ker Conway, ed., pp. 475–477

GO ON TO THE NEXT PAGE ▷

19. Which of the following best describes the relationship between the narrator and the men in her life?

(A) She gladly provides for their needs.
(B) She considers herself their equal.
(C) She feels overly dependent on them.
(D) She wishes to avoid them.
(E) She believes that they suppress her wishes.

20. The author was "emancipated" (line 34) so that she might more easily

(A) spend time with her father
(B) play with her young friends
(C) travel throughout New Bedford
(D) work with tools
(E) move to Michigan

21. In line 43, the word "movements" most nearly means

(A) travels
(B) cosmetic alterations
(C) cultural changes
(D) physical actions
(E) mechanical workings

22. The author indicates that she regarded New England as superior to Michigan in that New England

   I. had humbler citizens
   II. was more culturally developed
   III. had finer gardens

(A) II only
(B) III only
(C) I and II only
(D) II and III only
(E) I, II, and III

23. The author's attitude toward her move to Michigan is best described as

(A) eager
(B) awed
(C) fearful
(D) resentful
(E) bewildered

24. The sisters refused to ride in the lumber wagon mainly because

(A) they were embarrassed by its appearance
(B) they felt it was unsafe
(C) they had bad memories of it
(D) it was cold
(E) it lacked sufficient room for both of them

STOP

If you finish before time is called, you may check your work on this section only. Do not turn to any other section of the test.

7 7 7 7 7 7

SECTION 7
Time—20 minutes
16 questions

Turn to Section 7 of your answer sheet to answer the questions in this section.

Directions: For this section, solve each problem and decide which is the best of the choices given. Fill in the corresponding circle on the answer sheet. You may use any available space for scratchwork.

Notes

1. The use of a calculator is permitted.
2. All numbers used are real numbers.
3. Figures that accompany problems in this test are intended to provide information useful in solving the problems. They are drawn as accurately as possible EXCEPT when it is stated in a specific problem that the figure is not drawn to scale. All figures lie in a plane unless otherwise indicated.
4. Unless otherwise specified, the domain of any function f is assumed to be the set of all real numbers x for which $f(x)$ is a real number.

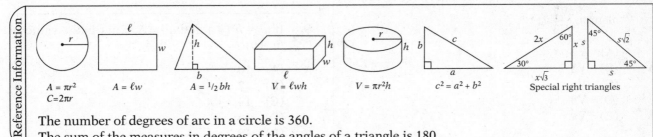

$A = \pi r^2$ $A = \ell w$ $A = \frac{1}{2}bh$ $V = \ell wh$ $V = \pi r^2 h$ $c^2 = a^2 + b^2$ Special right triangles
$C = 2\pi r$

The number of degrees of arc in a circle is 360.
The sum of the measures in degrees of the angles of a triangle is 180.

---

1. If $4x + 5 = 20$, what is the value of $4x + 8$?

   (A)   3
   (B)   7
   (C) 16
   (D) 23
   (E) 30

2. If one serving of cereal is $\frac{1}{3}$ cup, how many servings are in 3 pints of cereal? (1 pint = 2 cups)

   (A)   3
   (B)   9
   (C) 18
   (D) 27
   (E) 36

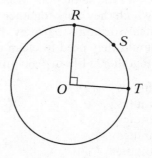

3. If the radius of the circle with center O above is 4, what is the length of arc RST?

   (A) 2π
   (B) 4π
   (C) 8π
   (D) 12π
   (E) 16π

GO ON TO THE NEXT PAGE

7   7   7   7   7   7

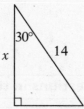

Note: Figure not drawn to scale.

4. In the triangle above, what is the value of x?

    (A) 7
    (B) $7\sqrt{2}$
    (C) $7\sqrt{3}$
    (D) $14\sqrt{3}$
    (E) $28\sqrt{3}$

5. For $x > 0$, let ∇x be defined by the equation $\nabla x = 3x - 3$. Which of the following is equivalent to $\dfrac{\nabla 7}{\nabla 3}$?

    (A) $\nabla 2$
    (B) $\nabla 3$
    (C) $\nabla 6$
    (D) $\nabla 8$
    (E) $\nabla 9$

6. Stephanie can clean a pool in 1 hour, and Mark can clean the same pool in 1.5 hours. If the rate at which they work together is the sum of their rates working separately, how many minutes should they need to clean the pool if they work together? (1 hour = 60 minutes)

    (A) 24 minutes
    (B) 36 minutes
    (C) 60 minutes
    (D) 72 minutes
    (E) 100 minutes

7. Which of the following has the greatest value?

    (A) $(100^3)^4$
    (B) $(100^5)(100^6)$
    (C) $(10,000)^4$
    (D) $(100^2 \times 100^2)^2$
    (E) $(1,000,000)^3$

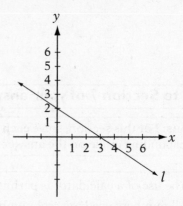

8. Line m (not shown) is the reflection of line l over the x-axis. What is the slope of line m?

    (A) 3/2
    (B) 2/3
    (C) 0
    (D) −2/3
    (E) −3/2

9. If $a^2 + b^2 = 4$ and $ab = 5$, what is the value of $(a + b)^2$?

    (A) 10
    (B) 12
    (C) 14
    (D) 16
    (E) 18

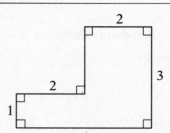

10. The figure above shows the dimensions, in feet, of a stone slab. How many of these slabs are required to construct a rectangular patio 24 feet long and 12 feet wide?

    (A) 18
    (B) 20
    (C) 24
    (D) 36
    (E) 48

GO ON TO THE NEXT PAGE

7 7 7 7 7 7

11. $12,000 in winnings for a golf tournament were distributed in the ratio of 7:2:1 to the first, second, and third-place finishers, respectively. How much money did the first-place finisher receive?

(A) $1,200
(B) $1,700
(C) $2,400
(D) $8,400
(E) $10,000

12. If $2x + 3y = 7$ and $4x - 5y = 12$, what is the value of $6x - 2y$?

(A) 5
(B) 8
(C) 15
(D) 17
(E) 19

13. If r and s are positive integers and $s + 1 = 2r$, which of the following must be true?

  I. s is odd
  II. r is even
  III. $\dfrac{s}{r} + \dfrac{1}{r}$ is an integer

(A) I only
(B) III only
(C) I and II only
(D) I and III only
(E) I, II, and III

14. A bag contains six chips, numbered 1 through 6. If two chips are chosen at random without replacement and the values on those two chips are multiplied, what is the probability that this product will be greater than 20?

(A) $\dfrac{1}{30}$ (B) $\dfrac{1}{15}$ (C) $\dfrac{2}{15}$

(D) $\dfrac{1}{5}$ (E) $\dfrac{13}{15}$

$$2, -4, -8, \ldots$$

15. In the sequence above, each term after the second is equal to the product of the two preceding terms. For example, the third term, −8, is the product of 2 and −4. How many of the first 100 terms of this sequence are negative?

(A) 33
(B) 34
(C) 50
(D) 66
(E) 67

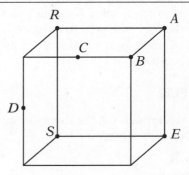

16. In the figure above, points C and D are midpoints of edges of a cube. A triangle is to be drawn with R and S as two of the vertices. Which of the following points should be the third vertex of the triangle if it is to have the largest possible perimeter?

(A) A
(B) B
(C) C
(D) D
(E) E

If you finish before time is called, you may check your work on this section only. Do not turn to any other section of the test.

8   8   8   8   8   8

SECTION 8
Time—20 minutes
19 questions

Turn to Section 8 of your answer sheet to answer the questions in this section.

Directions: For each question in this section, select the best answer from among the choices given and fill in the corresponding circle on the answer sheet.

Each sentence below has one or two blanks, each blank indicating that something has been omitted. Beneath the sentence are five words or sets of words labeled A through E. Choose the word or set of words that, when inserted in the sentence, <u>best</u> fits the meaning of the sentence as a whole.

EXAMPLE:

Rather than accepting the theory unquestioningly, Deborah regarded it with -----.

(A) mirth
(B) sadness
(C) responsibility
(D) ignorance
(E) skepticism

---

1. The latest review for the restaurant was -------, suggesting that the ------- cuisine came close to compensating for the insipid decor.

    (A) glowing . . indefatigable
    (B) banal . . mediocre
    (C) ambivalent . . sublime
    (D) severe . . piquant
    (E) antiquated . . tepid

2. As unexpected as the results of the experiment were, Dr. Thompson refused to characterize them as -------.

    (A) meticulous
    (B) belligerent
    (C) anomalous
    (D) convergent
    (E) warranted

3. The executives could only hope that the company's poor first-quarter performance was not ------- of the year to come.

    (A) an amalgam
    (B) a harbinger
    (C) an arbiter
    (D) a deception
    (E) a talisman

4. Around 1850, abolitionist and author Frederick Douglass sought to ------- those oppressed by slavery by facilitating the underground railroad, a widespread network of individuals and organizations that worked to transport former slaves out of bondage.

    (A) evaluate   (B) encumber   (C) unfetter
    (D) disorient   (E) forgo

5. Known for her ------- and decorative poetry, the author demonstrated her ------- by scribing a keenly analytical mystery novel.

    (A) flamboyant . . immutability
    (B) austere . . elegance
    (C) unadorned . . flexibility
    (D) florid . . versatility
    (E) grandiloquent . . insurgence

6. Because the mechanisms by which cancers attack the body are so -------, scientists have been ------- in their efforts to find a universal cure.

    (A) efficacious . . bilked
    (B) multifarious . . stymied
    (C) conspicuous . . thwarted
    (D) consistent . . hampered
    (E) lucid . . proscribed

GO ON TO THE NEXT PAGE ➡

8   8   8   8   8   8

The passages below are followed by questions based on their content; questions following a pair of related passages may also be based on the relationship between the paired passages. Answer the questions on the basis of what is <u>stated</u> or <u>implied</u> in the passage and in any introductory material that may be provided.

Questions 7–19 are based on the following passages.

The following passages are excerpts from a recent debate between two well-known astronomers. The author of Passage 1 is a professor of geological sciences and the author of Passage 2 is a principal scientist in the Department of Space Studies in Boulder, Colorado.

PASSAGE 1

There is a cultural assumption that there are many alien civilizations. This stems in no
Line small way from the famous estimate by Frank Drake—known as the "Drake Equation"—that
5   was later amended by Drake and Carl Sagan. They arrived at an estimate that there are perhaps a million intelligent civilizations in the Milky Way Galaxy alone.

The Drake and Sagan estimate was based
10   on their best guess about the number of planets in the galaxy, the percentage of those that might harbor life, and the percentage of planets on which life not only could exist but could have advanced to culture. Since our
15   galaxy is but one of hundreds of billions of galaxies in the universe, the number of intelligent alien species would be numbered in the billions. Surely, if there are so many intelligent aliens out there, then the number of

20   planets with life must be truly astronomical. But what if the Drake and Sagan estimates are way off? If, as could be the reality, our civilization is unique in the galaxy, does that mean that there might be much less life in
25   general as well?

In my view, life in the form of microbes or their equivalents is very common in the universe, perhaps more common than even Drake and Sagan envisioned. However, complex life
30   is likely to be far more rare than commonly assumed. Life on earth evolved from single celled organisms to multi-cellular creatures with tissues and organs, climaxing in animals and higher plants. But is Earth's particular
35   history of life—one of increasing complexity to an animal grade of evolution—an inevitable result of evolution, or even a common one? Perhaps life is common, but complex life— anything that is multicellular—is not.
40   On Earth, evolution has undergone a progressive development of ever more complex and sophisticated forms leading ultimately to human intelligence. Complex life—and even intelligence—could conceivably arise faster
45   than it did on Earth. A planet could go from an abiotic state to a civilization in 100 million years, as compared to the nearly 4 billion years it took on Earth. Evolution on Earth has been affected by chance events, such as the
50   configuration of the continents produced by continental drift. Furthermore, I believe that the way the solar system was produced, with its characteristic number and planetary positions, may have had a great impact on the
55   history of life here.

It has always been assumed that attaining the evolutionary grade we call animals would be the final and decisive step. Once we are at this level of evolution, a long and continuous
60   progression toward intelligence should occur. However, recent research shows that while attaining the stage of animal life is one thing, maintaining that level is quite another. The geologic record has shown that once evolved,
65   complex life is subject to an unending succession of planetary disasters, creating what are known as "mass extinction" events. These rare

First passage: Peter Ward, "Great Debates Part I," *Astrobiology Magazine*, 2003
Second passage: David Grinspoon, "Great Debates Part III," *Astrobiology Magazine*, 2003

GO ON TO THE NEXT PAGE ⟶

but devastating events can reset the evolutionary timetable and destroy complex life while
70 sparing simpler life forms. Such discoveries suggest that the conditions allowing the rise and existence of complex life are far more rigorous that are those for life's formation. On some planets, then, life might arise and ani-
75 mals eventually evolve—only to be soon destroyed by a global catastrophe.

PASSAGE 2

It is always shaky when we generalize from experiments with a sample size of one. So we have to be a bit cautious when we fill the cos-
80 mos with creatures based on the time scales of Earth history (it happened so fast here, therefore it must be easy) and the resourcefulness of Earth life (they are everywhere where there is water). This is one history, and one
85 example of life.

I am not convinced that the Earth's carbon-in-water example is the only way for the universe to solve the life riddle. I am not talking about silicon, which is a bad idea, but
90 systems of chemical complexity that we have not thought of, which may not manifest themselves at room temperature in our oxygen atmosphere. The universe is constantly more clever than we are, and we learn about com-
95 plex phenomena, like life, more through exploration than by theorizing and modeling. I think there are probably forms of life out there which use different chemical bases than we, and which we will know about only when
100 we find them, or when they find us.

An obvious rejoinder to this is, "But no one has invented another system that works as well as carbon-in-water." That is true. But to this I would answer, "We did not invent
105 carbon-in-water!" We discovered it. I don't believe that we are clever enough to have thought of life based on nucleic acids and proteins if we hadn't had this example handed to us. This makes me wonder what else the uni-
110 verse might be using for its refined, evolving complexity elsewhere, in other conditions that seem hostile to life as we know it.

I think it is a mistake to look at the many specific peculiarities of Earth's biosphere and
115 how unlikely such a combination of characteristics seems, and to then conclude that

complex life is rare. This argument can only be used to justify the conclusion that planets exactly like Earth, with life exactly like Earth-
120 life, are rare.

My cat, "Wookie" survived life as a near starving alley cat and wound up as a beloved house cat through an unlikely series of biographical accidents, which I won't take up
125 space describing but, trust me, given all of the incredible things that had to happen in just the right way, it is much more likely that there would be no Wookie than Wookie. From this I do not conclude that there are no other cats
130 (The Rare Cat Hypothesis), only that there are no other cats exactly like Wookie.

Life has evolved together with the Earth. Life is opportunistic. The biosphere has taken advantage of the myriad of strange idiosyncrasies
135 that our planet has to offer. So it is easy to look at our biosphere and conclude that this is the best of all possible worlds; that only on such a world could complex life evolve. My bet is that
140 many other worlds, with their own peculiar characteristics and histories, co-evolve their own biospheres. The complex creatures on those worlds, upon first developing intelligence and science, would observe how incredibly well
145 adapted life is to the many unique features of their home world. They might naively assume that these qualities, very different from Earth's, are the only ones that can breed complexity.

7. The discussion of the Drake equation in the first paragraph indicates that the author holds which of the following assumptions?

(A) The Drake equations are too complicated for most people to understand.
(B) Mathematical formulas can influence public opinion.
(C) Sagan did not substantially alter the Drake equation.
(D) Mathematics tend to obscure scientific exploration.
(E) Drake was not as reputable a scientist as Sagan was.

GO ON TO THE NEXT PAGE ⟶

8   8   8   8   8   8

8. Which of the following best describes the function of the third paragraph?

(A) It asks more questions similar to those posed in the second paragraph.
(B) It provides more background information on the debate discussed in the passage.
(C) It explains a comment made in the second paragraph.
(D) It defines an important term mentioned in the second paragraph.
(E) It presents an opinion contrary to one presented in the second paragraph.

9. In line 46, the word "abiotic" most nearly means

(A) resistant to bacteria
(B) devoid of life
(C) highly populated
(D) extremely advanced
(E) quick growing

10. Which of the following best summarizes the main idea of Passage 1?

(A) The conditions that support complex life may be much more difficult to maintain than is widely assumed.
(B) The Drake equation is not a valid predictor of life in the universe.
(C) Evolution on Earth has made it very unlikely that there would be complex life on other planets.
(D) The number of planets in the universe with complex life is astronomical.
(E) Conditions allowing for the existence of microbes are rare.

11. In line 57, "grade" most nearly means

(A) level
(B) slope
(C) evaluation
(D) life
(E) quantity

12. The author of Passage 1 makes all of the following claims in support of his argument EXCEPT

(A) Complex life on Earth was due in part to haphazard events.
(B) Higher life forms sometimes face the likelihood of extinction due to catastrophic events.
(C) The Earth's carbon-in-water example is probably not the only way for life to come into existence.
(D) Simple forms of life are far more common than highly evolved life forms.
(E) The evolution of life can be affected by the positions of planets around a star.

13. The "sample size of one" (line 78) refers to

(A) the Milky Way galaxy
(B) Drake and Sagan's data
(C) the planet Earth
(D) the Sun of our solar system
(E) mass extinction events

14. The quotations in lines 101–105 serve to

(A) show how the author would respond to someone who disagrees with him
(B) illustrate an argument for why there is no life on neighboring planets
(C) explain a theory the author has disagreed with his entire career
(D) describe a conversation the author had with a colleague
(E) illustrate the author's confusion about the origin of alternate life forms

15. The author includes the anecdote in lines 121–131 in order to

(A) compare his cat to the complex life forms in nearby galaxies
(B) give supporting evidence to the claim that life in the universe is unique to the Earth
(C) caution scientists about drawing premature conclusions from one specific occurrence
(D) mock scientists who believe that animals such as cats can live on other planets
(E) show the result of an evolutionary process

GO ON TO THE NEXT PAGE ⟶

16. In saying that "Life is opportunistic" (lines 132–133), the author of Passage 2 suggests that

  (A) only the most cunning animals survive

  (B) evolution takes advantage of the unique features of many different environments

  (C) humans will likely always be the dominant species on Earth

  (D) the theory of evolution is probably wrong

  (E) all life forms seek to dominate others

17. The author of Passage 2 suggests that the "complex creatures" discussed in lines 142–148 are likely to believe that

  (A) technological advancements are critical to their survival

  (B) life is unique to planet Earth

  (C) there is no life on other planets

  (D) life on all planets originates in the same manner

  (E) carbon is essential to the creation of life

18. The author of Passage 1 would most likely respond to the statement in Passage 2 that "The biosphere . . . offer" (lines 133–135) by saying that

  (A) our planet also offers many dangers to the biosphere

  (B) the biosphere is filled with far more complex life forms

  (C) life on Earth has not evolved to such a high level

  (D) our planet does not offer so many idiosyncrasies

  (E) carbon is one of the most complex elements in the universe

19. The authors of both passages would most likely agree with which of the following statements?

  (A) The estimates made by the Drake Equation are surprisingly accurate.

  (B) Mass extinction events are not a factor in predicting the existence of extraterrestrial life.

  (C) Mathematical models are the most helpful means of learning about the development of life in the universe.

  (D) There is likely an abundance of life in the universe that has yet to be discovered.

  (E) Complex life is very common in the universe.

STOP

If you finish before time is called, you may check your work on this section only. Do not turn to any other section of the test.

9   9   9   9   9   9

SECTION 9
Time—10 minutes
14 questions

Turn to Section 9 of your answer sheet to answer the questions in this section.

Directions: For each question in this section, select the best answer from among the choices given and fill in the corresponding circle on the answer sheet.

The following sentences test correctness and effectiveness of expression. Part of each sentence or the entire sentence is underlined; beneath each sentence are five ways of phrasing the underlined material. Choice A repeats the original phrasing; the other four choices are different. If you think the original phrasing produces a better sentence than any of the alternatives, select choice A; if not, select one of the other choices.

In making your selection, follow the requirements of standard written English; that is, pay attention to grammar, choice of words, sentence construction, and punctuation. Your selection should result in the most effective sentence—clear and precise, without awkwardness or ambiguity.

EXAMPLE:

The children couldn't hardly believe their eyes.

(A) couldn't hardly believe their eyes
(B) could hardly believe their eyes
(C) would not hardly believe their eyes
(D) couldn't nearly believe their eyes
(E) couldn't hardly believe his or her eyes

Ⓐ ● Ⓒ Ⓓ Ⓔ

1. His morning routine included eating an English muffin with grape jelly, <u>then to drink coffee from a styrofoam cup</u>, and sitting down to draw his daily comic strip.

   (A) then to drink coffee from a styrofoam cup
   (B) drinking coffee from a styrofoam cup
   (C) then drink coffee from a styrofoam cup
   (D) from a styrofoam cup he would drink coffee
   (E) he would drink coffee from a styrofoam cup

2. Pretending to have hurt his knee, <u>Mark's attempt to convince his coach to let him out of practice was a failure</u>.

   (A) Mark's attempt to convince his coach to let him out of practice was a failure
   (B) Mark's attempt to convince his coach failed to let him out of practice
   (C) Mark attempted to convince his coach to let him out of practice, but it was a failure
   (D) Mark attempted to convince his coach to let him out of practice, but failed
   (E) Mark attempted to convince his coach in letting him out of practice, but failed

3. The flier describing the details of the blood drive requested that we <u>are in the hospital lobby</u> promptly at 10 A.M.

   (A) are in the hospital lobby
   (B) should get at the hospital lobby
   (C) be in the hospital lobby
   (D) would be to the hospital lobby
   (E) should have been at the lobby of the hospital

4. <u>Known for his temper, impatience, and how easily he can be irritated</u>, Dr. McGee was not well liked by his patients.

   (A) Known for his temper, impatience, and how easily he can be irritated
   (B) Knowing his temper, impatience, and irritability
   (C) Known for his temper, impatience, and irritability
   (D) Known for his temper, impatience, and irritation
   (E) Known for his temper, for his impatience, and his irritability

GO ON TO THE NEXT PAGE

9   9   9   9   9   9

5. <u>Winning</u> the final match, Courtney gave a gracious speech thanking her competitor, the sponsors, and the spectators.

(A) Winning
(B) Having won
(C) Being that she won
(D) If she had won
(E) For her winning

6. Generally regarded as the most influential social science treatise of the 20th century, <u>John Maynard Keynes wrote a book, *The General Theory of Employment Interest and Money* that</u> forever changed the way scientists looked at the economy.

(A) John Maynard Keynes wrote a book, *The General Theory of Employment Interest and Money* that
(B) a book by John Maynard Keynes, *The General Theory of Employment Interest and Money,* that
(C) John Maynard Keynes' book *The General Theory of Employment Interest and Money* had already
(D) John Maynard Keynes wrote a book *The General Theory of Employment Interest and Money* having
(E) John Maynard Keynes' book *The General Theory of Employment Interest and Money*

7. <u>Neither of the proposals remained in their original form</u> by the time the legislature finished its deliberations.

(A) Neither of the proposals remained in their original form
(B) Neither proposal remained in its original form
(C) Both of the proposals did not remain in its original form
(D) With neither proposal remaining in its original form
(E) Neither proposal remained in their original forms

8. The Chief of Staff worked through the night <u>to prepare</u> the President's speech for the following day.

(A) to prepare
(B) in preparing
(C) in the preparation of
(D) for preparing
(E) in order for preparing

9. The storm waves crashed into the shore, inundating the stores along the <u>boardwalk and many cars in the parking lots were swept away by them.</u>

(A) boardwalk and many cars in the parking lots were swept away by them
(B) boardwalk with many cars in the parking lot being swept away
(C) boardwalk and sweeping away many cars in the parking lot
(D) boardwalk, and it swept away many cars in the parking lot
(E) boardwalk; sweeping away many cars in the parking lot

10. <u>The life of the ShinZanu, a tribe of the Australian Outback, have been realistically depicted in the books of Ronald Skinner.</u>

(A) The life of the ShinZanu, a tribe of the Australian Outback, have been realistically depicted in the books of Ronald Skinner.
(B) The life of the ShinZanu tribe of the Australian Outback has been realistically depicted in the books of Ronald Skinner.
(C) The ShinZanu, a tribe of the Australian Outback, has had its life realistically depicted with the books of Ronald Skinner.
(D) Ronald Skinner has depicted the life of the ShinZanu realistically in his books; they are of the Australian Outback.
(E) Depicting the lives of the ShinZanu tribe of the Australian Outback realistically, Ronald Skinner has done that in his books.

GO ON TO THE NEXT PAGE ▷

9   9   9   9   9   9

11. <u>At the age of seven, my father took me to see</u> my first baseball game.

   (A) At the age of seven, my father took me to see

   (B) My father took me, at the age of seven, to see

   (C) Being seven years old, my father took me to see

   (D) When I was seven years old, my father took me to see

   (E) I was taken by my father at seven years old, seeing

12. The President worked hard to implement legislation <u>that would stimulate growth, curb inflation, and increase employment</u>.

   (A) that would stimulate growth, curb inflation, and increase employment

   (B) stimulating growth, curbing inflation, and to increase employment

   (C) that stimulated growth, curbed inflation, and increasing employment

   (D) to stimulate growth, the curbing of inflation, and increasing employment

   (E) in order to stimulate growth, and for the purpose of curbing inflation and increasing employment

13. <u>If anyone asks for a doctor, send them</u> directly to the nurses' station for immediate assistance.

   (A) If anyone asks for a doctor, send them

   (B) Having asked for a doctor, send them

   (C) When anyone asks for a doctor, they should be sent

   (D) Had anyone asked for a doctor, send them

   (E) Send anyone who asks for a doctor

14. <u>Even if they have been declawed as kittens,</u> adult cats often run their paws along tall objects as if to sharpen their claws.

   (A) Even if they have been declawed as kittens

   (B) Even though they should have been declawed when being kittens

   (C) Even when being declawed as kittens

   (D) Declawed when kittens nevertheless

   (E) Declawed as kittens

STOP   *If you finish before time is called, you may check your work on this section only. Do not turn to any other section of the test.*

ANSWER KEY

Critical Reading

	Section 3				Section 6				Section 8		

Section 3

	COR. ANS.	DIFF. LEV.		COR. ANS.	DIFF. LEV.
1.	A	1	13.	A	1
2.	C	2	14.	D	2
3.	B	3	15.	C	3
4.	E	3	16.	D	3
5.	E	3	17.	E	4
6.	A	4	18.	E	3
7.	D	4	19.	A	3
8.	C	4	20.	D	5
9.	B	3	21.	A	3
10.	E	1	22.	B	3
11.	A	4	23.	C	4
12.	A	3	24.	E	4

Number correct

Number incorrect

Section 6

	COR. ANS.	DIFF. LEV.		COR. ANS.	DIFF. LEV.
1.	A	1	13.	A	3
2.	D	3	14.	A	4
3.	E	3	15.	C	3
4.	A	4	16.	D	5
5.	B	5	17.	C	2
6.	C	3	18.	E	2
7.	E	4	19.	B	4
8.	C	3	20.	D	2
9.	A	1	21.	C	2
10.	B	2	22.	A	3
11.	E	3	23.	D	4
12.	D	4	24.	A	4

Number correct

Number incorrect

Section 8

	COR. ANS.	DIFF. LEV.		COR. ANS.	DIFF. LEV.
1.	C	3	11.	A	4
2.	C	2	12.	C	2
3.	B	3	13.	C	1
4.	C	4	14.	A	3
5.	D	4	15.	C	2
6.	B	5	16.	B	3
7.	B	4	17.	D	3
8.	E	3	18.	A	4
9.	B	2	19.	D	3
10.	A	3			

Number correct

Number incorrect

Math

Section 2

	COR. ANS.	DIFF. LEV.		COR. ANS.	DIFF. LEV.
1.	A	1	11.	B	4
2.	B	2	12.	B	3
3.	D	2	13.	B	3
4.	D	3	14.	C	4
5.	D	2	15.	B	3
6.	E	2	16.	B	3
7.	C	3	17.	D	5
8.	C	3	18.	C	4
9.	A	3	19.	E	4
10.	D	3	20.	D	5

Number correct

Number incorrect

Section 5

Multiple-Choice Questions

	COR. ANS.	DIFF. LEV.
1.	B	1
2.	B	3
3.	C	3
4.	B	3
5.	C	3
6.	D	4
7.	A	5
8.	D	5

Student-produced Response questions

	COR. ANS.	DIFF. LEV.
9.	1	2
10.	750	2
11.	3	2
12.	32	3
13.	9	3
14.	3	4
15.	1.5 or 3/2	4
16.	18	4
17.	20	4
18.	25	5

Number correct

Number incorrect

Number correct (9–18)

Section 7

	COR. ANS.	DIFF. LEV.		COR. ANS.	DIFF. LEV.
1.	D	2	9.	C	4
2.	C	2	10.	D	3
3.	A	2	11.	D	3
4.	C	3	12.	E	4
5.	A	3	13.	D	4
6.	B	3	14.	C	4
7.	A	3	15.	D	5
8.	B	4	16.	B	5

Number correct

Number incorrect

Writing

Section 4

	COR. ANS.	DIFF. LEV.		COR. ANS.	DIFF. LEV.		COR. ANS.	DIFF. LEV.		COR. ANS.	DIFF. LEV.
1.	C	1	10.	C	3	19.	C	3	28.	C	4
2.	A	1	11.	B	3	20.	D	3	29.	D	5
3.	D	2	12.	D	1	21.	C	3	30.	B	3
4.	B	2	13.	C	3	22.	A	3	31.	A	3
5.	C	3	14.	E	3	23.	E	4	32.	D	3
6.	E	2	15.	B	3	24.	D	4	33.	B	4
7.	C	3	16.	D	4	25.	C	4	34.	C	3
8.	D	3	17.	B	3	26.	B	3	35.	E	3
9.	C	4	18.	B	2	27.	C	4			

Number correct

Number incorrect

Section 9

	COR. ANS.	DIFF. LEV.		COR. ANS.	DIFF. LEV.
1.	B	1	8.	A	4
2.	D	2	9.	C	3
3.	C	2	10.	B	4
4.	C	3	11.	D	4
5.	B	4	12.	A	4
6.	C	3	13.	E	3
7.	B	5	14.	A	4

Number correct

Number incorrect

NOTE: Difficulty levels are estimates of question difficulty that range from 1 (easiest) to 5 (hardest).

SCORE CONVERSION TABLE

How to score your test

Use the answer key on the previous page to determine your raw score on each section. **Your raw score on each section except Section 4 is simply the number of correct answers minus ¼ of the number of wrong answers. On Section 4, your raw score is the sum of the number of correct answers for questions 1–18 minus ¼ of the number of wrong answers for questions 1–8.** Next, add the raw scores from Sections 2, 5, and 8 to get your Critical Reading raw score, add the raw scores from Sections 3, 4, and 7 to get your Math raw score, and add the raw scores from Sections 6 and 9 to get your Writing raw score. Write the three raw scores here:

Raw Critical Reading score: _____ Raw Math score: _____ Raw Writing score: _____

Use the table below to convert these to scaled scores.

Scaled scores: Critical Reading: _____ Math: _____ Writing: _____

Raw Score	Critical Reading Scaled Score	Math Scaled Score	Writing Scaled Score	Raw Score	Critical Reading Scaled Score	Math Scaled Score	Writing Scaled Score
67	800			32	520	570	610
66	800			31	510	560	600
65	790			30	510	550	580
64	780			29	500	540	570
63	770			28	490	530	560
62	750			27	490	520	550
61	740			26	480	510	540
60	730			25	480	500	530
59	720			24	470	490	520
58	700			23	460	480	510
57	690			22	460	480	500
56	680			21	450	470	490
55	670			20	440	460	480
54	660	800		19	440	450	470
53	650	800		18	430	450	460
52	650	780		17	420	440	450
51	640	760		16	420	430	440
50	630	740		15	410	420	440
49	620	730	800	14	400	410	430
48	620	710	800	13	400	410	420
47	610	710	800	12	390	400	410
46	600	700	790	11	380	390	400
45	600	690	780	10	370	380	390
44	590	680	760	9	360	370	380
43	590	670	740	8	350	360	380
42	580	660	730	7	340	350	370
41	570	650	710	6	330	340	360
40	570	640	700	5	320	330	350
39	560	630	690	4	310	320	340
38	550	620	670	3	300	310	320
37	550	620	660	2	280	290	310
36	540	610	650	1	270	280	300
35	540	600	640	0	250	260	280
34	530	590	630	−1	230	240	270
33	520	580	620	−2 or less	210	220	250

SCORE CONVERSION TABLE FOR WRITING COMPOSITE
[ESSAY + MULTIPLE CHOICE]

Calculate your Writing raw score as you did on the previous page and grade your essay from a 1 to a 6 according to the standards that follow in the detailed answer key.

Essay score: _____   Raw Writing score: _____

Use the table below to convert these to scaled scores.

Scaled score: Writing: _____

Raw Score	Essay Score 0	Essay Score 1	Essay Score 2	Essay Score 3	Essay Score 4	Essay Score 5	Essay Score 6
−2 or less	200	230	250	280	310	340	370
−1	210	240	260	290	320	360	380
0	230	260	280	300	340	370	400
1	240	270	290	320	350	380	410
2	250	280	300	330	360	390	420
3	260	290	310	340	370	400	430
4	270	300	320	350	380	410	440
5	280	310	330	360	390	420	450
6	290	320	340	360	400	430	460
7	290	330	340	370	410	440	470
8	300	330	350	380	410	450	470
9	310	340	360	390	420	450	480
10	320	350	370	390	430	460	490
11	320	360	370	400	440	470	500
12	330	360	380	410	440	470	500
13	340	370	390	420	450	480	510
14	350	380	390	420	460	490	520
15	350	380	400	430	460	500	530
16	360	390	410	440	470	500	530
17	370	400	420	440	480	510	540
18	380	410	420	450	490	520	550
19	380	410	430	460	490	530	560
20	390	420	440	470	500	530	560
21	400	430	450	480	510	540	570
22	410	440	460	480	520	550	580
23	420	450	470	490	530	560	590
24	420	460	470	500	540	570	600
25	430	460	480	510	540	580	610
26	440	470	490	520	550	590	610
27	450	480	500	530	560	590	620
28	460	490	510	540	570	600	630
29	470	500	520	550	580	610	640
30	480	510	530	560	590	620	650
31	490	520	540	560	600	630	660
32	500	530	550	570	610	640	670
33	510	540	550	580	620	650	680
34	510	550	560	590	630	660	690
35	520	560	570	600	640	670	700
36	530	560	580	610	650	680	710
37	540	570	590	620	660	690	720
38	550	580	600	630	670	700	730
39	560	600	610	640	680	710	740
40	580	610	620	650	690	720	750
41	590	620	640	660	700	730	760
42	600	630	650	680	710	740	770
43	610	640	660	690	720	750	780
44	620	660	670	700	740	770	800
45	640	670	690	720	750	780	800
46	650	690	700	730	770	800	800
47	670	700	720	750	780	800	800
48	680	720	730	760	800	800	800
49	680	720	730	760	800	800	800

Detailed Answer Key

Section 1

Consider carefully the issue discussed in the following passage, then write an essay that answers the question posed in the assignment.

> Many among us like to blame violence and immorality in the media for a "decline in morals" in society. Yet these people seem to have lost touch with logic. Any objective examination shows that our society is far less violent or exploitative than virtually any society in the past. Early humans murdered and enslaved each other with astonishing regularity, without the help of gangsta rap or Jerry Bruckheimer films.

Assignment: **Do violence and immorality in the media make our society more dangerous and immoral?** Write an essay in which you answer this question and discuss your point of view on this issue. Support your position logically with examples from literature, the arts, history, politics, science and technology, current events, or your experience or observation.

The following essay received 12 points out of a possible 12. This means that, according to the graders, it

- develops an insightful point of view on the topic
- demonstrates exemplary critical thinking
- uses effective examples, reasons, and other evidence to support its thesis
- is consistently focused, coherent, and well organized
- demonstrates skillful and effective use of language and sentence structure
- is largely (but not necessarily completely) free of grammatical and usage errors

One of the most misguided notions of conventional wisdom is that depicting violence in the media makes our society more violent. A close examination shows that this claim is baseless. Societies with severe restrictions on violence in the media tend to be more, not less, violent than those with no such restrictions. Indeed, despite the popular myth of a more peaceful past, societies were far more violent before the advent of movies, television, and video games. Societies that restrict access to "immoral" western movies are the same ones that call their citizens to violent and irrational holy war.

As Michael Moore pointed out poignantly in the movie "Bowling for Columbine," Americans kill each other with firearms at a far greater rate than almost any other first-world nation. But he is quick to point out that our media is not more violent than those in Japan or Germany or even Canada, which have rates of violence that are a full order of magnitude lower than ours. Indeed, the killers among us are not likely to spend a lot of time listening to Marilyn Manson or playing Mortal Kombat on their Playstations, despite what our more nearsighted and sanctimonious politicians and preachers would like us to believe. Ted Kaczynski, the Unabomber, lived in a one-room shack without electricity or running water, let alone cable. But even if murderers like Kaczynski were video game addicts, attributing their motives to media violence would be missing the point entirely.

People who are habitually violent have adopted a "war mentality." They tend to see the world in black-and-white, us-against-them terms. Tragically, our leaders tend to have this very same mentality, but they couch it in "patriotism." Lobbing cruise missiles and landing marines in another country is not considered a horrible last resort, but a patriotic duty. If we wish to understand why Americans are more violent than the Japanese, violence in the media will hold no answers; Japanese kids watch just as much violence. Foreign policy is far more telling: which country has leaders who engage in violence against other countries at every opportunity, and constantly try to convince us that it's right?

If our pundits and politicians were truly concerned about making a safer world—and there are many reasons to believe they are not, since they profit the most from a fearful citizenry—they would begin by acknowledging that violence is almost a desperate grab for control from a person or people who believe they are being repressed. If we want a more peaceful and noble society, then we will stop coercing other countries with violence and economic oppression. As Franklin Roosevelt said, "We have nothing to fear but fear itself." We are the most fearful nation on the planet, and we are paying for it.

The following essay received 8 points out of a possible 12, meaning that it demonstrates *adequate competence* in that it

- develops a point of view on the topic
- demonstrates some critical thinking, but perhaps not consistently
- uses some examples, reasons, and other evidence to support its thesis, but perhaps not adequately
- shows a general organization and focus, but shows occasional lapses in this regard
- demonstrates adequate but occasionally inconsistent facility with language
- contains occasional errors in grammar, usage, and mechanics

People say that society today is much more violent due to all of the media portrayal of violence we see on a daily basis. The nightly news is often made up entirely of stories about murders, muggings, arson, and other gruesome crimes. The most successful shows on television are the investigative crime shows in which they solve disturbing murder mysteries. Movies like the Lord of the Rings contain gory fight scenes that show the death of hundreds of characters. It's hard even to find a video game anymore that doesn't somehow relate back to fighting.

Those who don't believe that violence breeds violence would argue that the United States murder rate had declined to its lowest level in 30 years and that this is proof that the violence in the media has not in fact made for a more violent society. But what they conveniently leave out is the fact that at the same time, youth gun killings were on the rise. This is who is being affected by the increased exposure to violence—the children. It is perhaps the video game violence and television/movie violence that can be held responsible.

Kids today are growing up in a society where violence is everywhere. It is difficult for a child to go through the day without witnessing some violent act on TV or hearing about a gruesome murder on the radio. A recent study we learned about in class concluded that because of what they see on television, children become immune to violence, accept it as something that is part of a "normal" life, and they often times will attempt to imitate what they see on television because it "looks fun."

Something needs to be done to reverse this trend of growing violence in our country and tighter regulation of the amount of violence on television, in music, and in the movies would be a great place to start. The youth of this country need to be reminded that violence is not an acceptable part of daily existence and that it should be avoided at all costs.

The following essay received 4 points out of a possible 12, meaning that it demonstrates *some incompetence* in that it

- has a seriously limited point of view
- demonstrates weak critical thinking
- uses inappropriate or insufficient examples, reasons, and other evidence to support its thesis
- is poorly focused and organized and has serious problems with coherence
- demonstrates frequent problems with language and sentence structure
- contains errors in grammar and usage that seriously obscure the author's meaning

Believing that the violence in the media has made the members of our society like violent murderers is an absurd notion. Sure, there are lots video games on the market that involve fighting ninjas and battling army troops. Yes, nightly television shows on the public television networks show many a violent episode. Sure, the nightly news is covered with violent crimes and such. For instance, the popular music of this era is full of violent references and foul language. But, no experiment or statistics that I have seen proves the above statement to be true. Just because a teenager kills over 500 fake people on his ninja fighting video-game, it does not mean that after he turns off the game console that he will run outside in his ninja costume and start attacking the people in his neighborhood.

It is absurd to say that violence is because of all the violence on video games television. Actually I think that video games make you better at eye-hand coordination which is a valuable skill. Hundreds of years before video games and movies and television, there were murder and violence. Human beings are violent people and the exposure to violence does not make us more violent than we already were. If we did not have all of these impressive technological advances such as radio, television and film, we would still be committing acts of violence. There will always be violent humans that are ready to hurt others to get what they want and eliminating violent references from our music and television shows might even make people madder.

Section 2

1. A

$$(x + 4) + 7 = 14$$

Subtract 7: $\quad x + 4 = 7$

Subtract 4: $\quad x = 3$

2. B Write out a mathematical equation for how you would actually find the cost for the month: $.95 × 31. Answer choice B, $1.00 × 30, is closest to that amount.

3. D A linear angle measures 180°. Write an equation:

$$w + x + 50 = 180°$$

Subtract 50°: $\quad w + x = 130°$

4. D

$$g(x) = 3x + 4$$

Substitute 5 for x: $\quad g(5) = 3(5) + 4$

Simplify: $\quad g(5) = 15 + 4 = 19$

5. D The difference between x and y is $(x - y)$. The sum of x and y is $(x + y)$. The product of those two is equal to 18:

$$(x - y)(x + y) = 18$$

FOIL: $\quad x^2 - xy + xy - y^2 = 18$

Combine like terms: $\quad x^2 - y^2 = 18$

6. E

$$3\sqrt{x} - 7 = 20$$

Add 7: $\quad 3\sqrt{x} = 27$

Divide by 3: $\quad \sqrt{x} = 9$

Square both sides: $\quad x = 81$

7. C Let b = cost of chocolate bar and g = cost of gum.

$$b + g = \$1.75$$

Chocolate bar is $.25 more: $\quad b = \$.25 + g$

Substitute for b: $\quad \$.25 + g + g = \$1.75$

Combine like terms: $\quad \$.25 + 2g = \$1.75$

Subtract $.25: $\quad 2g = \$1.50$

Divide by 2: $\quad g = \$.75$

8. C First find 40% of 80: $.40 \times 80 = 32$

Now find what percent of 96 is 32.

Translate: $\quad \dfrac{x}{100} \times 96 = 32$

Multiply by 100: $\quad 96x = 3,200$

Divide by 96: $\quad x = 33\frac{1}{3}$

9. A If $lm = 21$ and both l and m are integers, then m must be either 1, 3, 7, or 21. If $mn = 39$, however, then m must also be a factor of 39, so it must be 3. Therefore, $l = 21/3 = 7$ and $n = 39/3 = 13$, so $n > l > m$.

10. D There's no need to do a lot of calculation here. Look for the two adjacent bars with the greatest positive difference between them. Since 1999 shows the least profits of all the years on the graph and 2000 shows the greatest profits of any year on the graph, 1999–2000 must have the greatest change in profit.

11. B A Venn diagram can help you with this problem: Imagine that the 4 students who play two sports play soccer and tennis. (It doesn't matter which specific pair of sports they play.) This means that $12 - 4 = 8$ students play just soccer, $7 - 4 = 3$ students play just tennis, and 9 students play just lacrosse. This shows that there is a total of $9 + 8 + 4 + 3 = 24$ students.

12. B To solve this problem, you need to find the distance between the center of the circle (14, 14) and the point on the circle (2, 9). To do this, you can use the distance formula.

You can also draw a right triangle connecting the two points. It gives you a triangle with one leg of 5 and one leg of 12. Set up the Pythagorean theorem and solve for r.

$$5^2 + 12^2 = r^2$$

Simplify: $\quad 25 + 144 = r^2$

Combine like terms: $\quad 169 = r^2$

Take square root: $\quad 13 = r$

The diameter is twice the radius $= 2(r) = 2(13) = 26$.

13. B The population doubles every 18 months. Start with January of 2000 and start doubling.

	January 2000	12,000
18 months later:	July 2001	24,000
18 months later:	January 2003	48,000
18 months later:	July 2004	96,000

14. C Use the Fundamental Counting Principle from Chapter 9, Lesson 5. To arrange these students, five choices must be made. First select the students for each end. Since one of the five (the tallest) cannot go on either end, you have four students to choose from for one end, and then, once that choice has been made, three students to choose from for the other end:

$$\underset{*}{\underline{4}} \; \underline{} \; \underline{} \; \underline{} \; \underset{*}{\underline{3}}$$

Now fill the remaining spots. There are three students left to choose from for the second spot:

$$\underset{*}{\underline{4}} \; \underline{3} \; \underline{} \; \underline{} \; \underset{*}{\underline{3}}$$

Then, once that selection has been made, there are two for the next spot, then one for the remaining spot:

$$\underline{4} \; \underline{3} \; \underline{2} \; \underline{1} \; \underline{3}$$

To find the total number of possible arrangements, simply multiply: $4 \times 3 \times 2 \times 1 \times 3 = 72$.

15. B From the diagram, we know that $a + b + c = 180$, and we know that $b = c + 3$.

If you want b to be as large as possible, then you need to make the sum of a and c as small as possible. The smallest integer value of a possible is 91. So let's say that $a = 91$.

Substitute 91 for a:	$91 + b + c = 180$
Substitute $c + 3$ for b:	$91 + c + 3 + c = 180$
Combine like terms:	$94 + 2c = 180$
Subtract 94:	$2c = 86$
Divide by 2:	$c = 43$

So 43 is the largest possible value of c; this means that $43 + 3 = 46$ is the largest possible value of b.

16. B Begin by finding the area of the big equilateral triangle. An equilateral triangle with sides of length 4 has a height of $2\sqrt{3}$, because the height divides the triangle into two 30°-60°-90° triangles.

Area = ½(base)(height) = $\frac{1}{2}(4)(2\sqrt{3}) = 4\sqrt{3}$

The big triangle is divided into four equal parts, three of which are shaded, so the shaded area is ¾ of the total area.

Shaded area = $\frac{3}{4}(4\sqrt{3}) = 3\sqrt{3}$

17. D Just look at the graph and draw a line at $y = 1$.

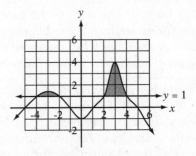

The y-values of the graph are at or above that line from $x = -4$ to $x = -2$ and from $x = 2$ to $x = 4$.

18. C This table shows all of the $5 \times 5 = 25$ possible values of ab:

x	2	4	6	8	10
1	2	4	6	8	10
3	6	12	18	24	30
5	10	20	30	40	50
7	14	28	42	56	70
9	18	36	54	72	90

Of those, only the seven shaded values are greater than 20 and less than 50, so the probability is 7/25.

19. E

	$(w^a)(w^5) = w^{15}$
Simplify:	$w^{5+a} = w^{15}$
Equate the exponents:	$5 + a = 15$
Subtract 5:	$a = 10$
	$(w^4)^b = w^{12}$
Simplify:	$w^{4b} = w^{12}$
Equate the exponents:	$4b = 12$
Divide by 4:	$b = 3$

So $a + b = 10 + 3 = 13$.

20. D The graph of $y = f(x - 2)$ is the graph of $y = f(x)$ shifted to the right two units without changing its shape. Therefore, the "peak" at point (6, 4) should shift to (8, 4).

Section 3

1. A   The word *although* indicates a contrast. Raúl purchased his computer only 10 months ago, but technology has been improving so fast that it is already *outdated*. *obsolete* = outdated; *adjunct* = auxiliary, or additional; *novel* = new, innovative; *elusive* = hard to catch

2. C   The admissions committee is looking to justify offering more scholarships to increase the number of applications, so the number of applicants must be *decreasing*. *mushroom* = expand rapidly; *plummet* = decrease rapidly; *satiate* = satisfy; *burgeon* = grow

3. B   If the father will not consider another person's viewpoint to be valid if it differs from his own, he must be pretty *stubborn* or *arrogant*. *pragmatic* = practical; *dogmatic* = arrogantly authoritative; *phlegmatic* = sluggish; *cordial* = polite; *curt* = abrupt and rude

4. E   The books are written for children but are still *enjoyable* to adults. *penned* = written; *prosaic* = dull; *morose* = gloomy; *censored* = cleansed of profanity; *incongruous* = not compatible; *tedious* = boring, dull; *authored* = written; *engaging* = captivating, interesting

5. E   Julia is at the top of her class, but if this is hard to believe, she must approach her work in a *lazy* or *irresponsible* way. *adept* = skilled; *diligent* = hardworking; *fanatical* = obsessive and crazy; *extroverted* = outgoing; *laggardly* = slow-moving, lagging behind

6. A   The President's opponents were always cautious about debating him, so the President must be *highly skilled* or *intimidating* or *mean*. *redoubtable* = formidable, imposing; *staid* = calm, not outwardly emotional; *magnanimous* = generous; *stoic* = indifferent to pain or pleasure

7. D   The new clothing line was described as being *eclectic* (containing much variety). It ranged from *modest* (not showy) and *unadorned* (undecorated) to -------- and *garish* (flashy). By parallelism, the missing word should be in opposition to the word *modest*. *austere* = severe, stern; *prophetic* = able to tell the future; *cordial* = polite; *ostentatious* = showy; *solitary* = alone

8. C   The textbook *includes all of the essential information* but it is not *verbose* (wordy); the two missing words should be parallel to *containing lots of information* and *not verbose*. *compendious* = succinct; *circumlocutory* = talking around the subject, indirect; *reprehensible* = blameworthy; *terse* = concise; *comprehensive* = including a large amount of information; *concise* = brief and to the point; *grandiloquent* = speaking in a pompous manner; *painstaking* = done with great care; *redundant* = repetitive

9. B   Saying that we were *raised in unrivaled prosperity* is like saying that the economy has been very strong and *abundant*.

10. E   The "people" are plagued by *deep divisions* (line 9), and the *citizens* are the only ones who are not *growing to appreciate the difference between America and the United States* (lines 20–22). Therefore, the *people* lack unity, while the *citizens* lack awareness.

11. A   Don't miss the word *EXCEPT* in the question. Choice (B) is supported in line 14, choice (C) in line 7, choice (D) in line 8, and choice (E) in line 8. The last lines say that *ambition for a better life is now universal*, implying that *not* everyone is happy with the status of their lives.

12. A   Unlike Passage 1, Passage 2 discusses the difference between the ideal of America and the reality of the United States.

13. A   The questions in the opening lines show the man's *confusion*, and the woman is said to talk *ardently* (passionately).

14. D   The author says that one *who is suddenly overwhelmed by terror cannot afterwards remember the exact order of sounds accompanying the catastrophe which stuns him*—that is, he becomes disoriented.

15. C   Line 11 suggests that Ognev is stunned by a *catastrophe*. The context of the passage makes it clear that this catastrophe is the expression of love from Vera, which Ognev has difficulty understanding.

16. D   In saying that *she had been struck by . . . the aims and objects of his life* (lines 22–24), the author is saying that she was impressed with Ognev's *life goals*.

17. E   In lines 42–44, the passage states that *much as he wanted to, he could feel no joy; no fundamental happiness*. In other words, the *bad and strange* thing was *disaffection*.

18. E   In lines 51–52, the passage states that *Vera's raptures and suffering seemed to him* (Ognev) *to be only cloying* (excessively sweet) *and trivial* (of little significance). He felt her passion to be unimportant and was *outraged at himself* for feeling this way. To him, his *statistics, books or philosophical truths* were more important than this passion.

19. A   The final sentence of the passage states that *he was annoyed and blamed himself even though he himself did not understand why he was to blame*. Ognev is confused and uncertain about how he *should* feel about Vera's passion. He feels indifference but thinks he should feel something different.

20. D In lines 21–22 the marchers are described as *singing to hide their exhaustion* and then as *trying not to fear. . . .* This commitment to hiding emotion is *stoicism*.

21. A Lines 35–38 criticize the bill's *failure to protect the right of African Americans to vote "when local officials are determined to deny it."* In other words, it did not sufficiently pressure local officials to extend voting rights to all citizens.

22. B In context, saying that *his . . . encounter with Mexican-American children* was *shattering* is like saying that the encounter bothered the President and had a major impact on the way he approached civil rights issues later in his career.

23. C Johnson indicates that he inferred, by looking into his students' eyes, that they knew that others disliked them. This indicates a strong empathy with his students, because he inferred it not from their words but from their expressions.

24. E Lines 52–54 say that Johnson *made the nationwide audience aware of how deeply personal the issue of African American rights was to him* and lines 60–62 say that *he spoke more directly, more explicitly, and more warmly of the human experience of prejudice than any president before him.* In other words, he addressed it directly and in personal terms.

Section 4

1. C The word *group* is the singular subject, so the verb should be *was*.

2. A The original sentence is best. Choice (B) is incorrect because the phrase *of labor's and management's* is redundant and unidiomatic. In choice (C), the use of the verb *saw* is nonstandard, although idiomatic, and the colon is misused because it is not followed by a list or an explanatory independent clause. In choice (D), the phrase *marked ferociously* is illogical. In choice (E), both the tense and voice of the verb, *was marking*, are illogical.

3. D The original sentence is awkward, and the verb *has possessed* does not agree with the plural subject, *scientists and inventors*. Choice (B) is incorrect because the verb *have been able to possess* is not logical. Choices (C) and (E) are incorrect because the verb *was* does not agree with the plural subject *skills*.

4. B In the original sentence, the pronoun *it* lacks a clear antecedent, as does the pronoun *that* in choice (D). Choice (C) is incorrect because it implies that the Thracians *enabled the ability*, which is illogical. In choice (E), the phrase *ability of resisting* is unidiomatic.

5. C The phrase *on an overseas journey* is redundant because the sentence also states that this journey was *across the Atlantic*. This redundancy is repeated in choice (B). Choice (D) uses an incorrect verb tense, and choice (E) produces a sentence fragment.

6. E In the original sentence, the use of *plus* instead of *and* is nonstandard, and the phrasing is not parallel. Only choice (E) avoids both problems.

7. C The phrase *half as many . . . than* is unidiomatic. The correct idiom is *half as many as*. Only choice (C) is phrased idiomatically.

8. D The use of *therefore* in the original phrasing is illogical, because the ideas in the sentence are related not as a cause and effect but rather as a contrast. The use of *actually* in choice (D) conveys the appropriate irony.

9. C In the original sentence, the prepositional phrase *for their fans* is unidiomatic and awkward, and the pronoun *their* does not agree in number with its antecedent, *the band*. Choices (B) and (D) repeat the pronoun problem. Choice (E) is incorrect because it implies that the *fans* are free of charge, rather than the downloading.

10. C The plural subject *reasons* requires the plural verb *are*, so choices (A) and (D) are incorrect. Choice (B) is incorrect because the phrase *the reasons are because* is nonstandard and illogical. Choice (E) is incorrect because the phrasing is not parallel.

11. B The appositive phrase *An untiring defender of the downtrodden* must be placed adjacent to the noun it modifies, which in this case is *Clarence Darrow*. Only choices (B) and (E) do this, but choice (E) is incorrect because it lacks parallel phrasing.

12. D The subject of this verb is *delivery*, which is singular, so the verb should be *has been*.

13. C The phrase *capable to distinguish* is unidiomatic. The correct phrasing is *capable of distinguishing*.

14. E   The sentence is correct.

15. B   The subject of this verb is *photographs . . . and diagrams*, which is plural, so the verb should be *were*.

16. D   This is a comparison error. The *way in which chimpanzees form friendships* cannot logically be compared to *humans*. Instead, the phrase should be *to the way humans form friendships*.

17. B   As a noun, *affects* means *feelings or emotions*, so its use here is a diction error. The proper word is *effects*.

18. B   There are two errors in this phrase. First, the subject *probability* is singular, so the verb should be *is*. Second, a probability can be *lower* than another, but not *fewer* than another.

19. C   The pronoun *they* does not agree in number with its antecedent *an author*, and should be replaced with the phrase *he or she*.

20. D   The phrase *in the time* is redundant because the word *during* conveys the same information. The entire phrase should be deleted.

21. C   People are satisfied *with* things, not *at* them.

22. A   The phrase *had ate* is an incorrect past perfect form. The correct form is *had eaten*. In this case, however, the word *after* conveys the time sequence, so the past perfect form isn't strictly necessary: *ate* (but not *had ate*) is an acceptable alternative.

23. E   The sentence is correct as written.

24. D   The verb *is* does not agree in number with its plural subject, *jaws*, and should be changed to *are*.

25. C   The subject of the verb *help* is *taking*, which is singular. Think of the subject as *it*. The word *help* should instead be *helps*.

26. B   The word *underneath* means physically below something. The word should instead be *under*.

27. C   The subject *they* is referring to *the company*, which is singular. *They* should instead be *it*.

28. C   The phrase *not only A, but also B* requires parallel phrasing for the phrases at *A* and *B*. The phrase following *not only* is an infinitive, *to command*, so the phrase following *but also* should likewise be an infinitive, *to develop*.

29. D   The comparison is unidiomatic. The proper idiom is *more effectively separated by A than by B*. Therefore, choice (D) should be replaced by *than*.

30. B   This phrasing is the most concise and logical of the choices.

31. A   The original phrasing is best.

32. D   Because the sentence refers to *these passions*, it is most logically placed after those passions are described. It also provides a logical transition to the third paragraph.

33. B   This order places the sentences in proper logical and chronological order: (8) identifies his childhood passion, (10) identifies his goals for this passion, (7) proceeds to his college years, (6) mentions where he pursued his passions, and (9) describes the connection between these passions and his later career.

34. C   The paragraph as a whole discusses Roosevelt's passion for nature, so details about his activities in these natural settings would be relevant.

35. E   This sentence would be a good conclusion to the passage because it gives historical perspective to the specific ideas in the passage.

Section 5

1. B   There are 180° on the side of a line.

$$2x + 3x = 180°$$

Combine like terms: $5x = 180°$
Divide by 5: $x = 36°$
Multiply by 2: $2x = 72°$

2. B   The equation states that some number, when squared, equals 36. That number can be either 6 or –6. Taking the square root of both sides of the equation gives:

$$x - 4 = \pm 6$$

Add 4: $x = 10 \text{ or } -2$

Therefore, the answer is (B) –2.

3. C   There are 180° in a triangle. Set up equations for the two triangles in the figure.

$$a + b + 52 = 180$$

Subtract 52: $a + b = 128$
    $c + d + 52 = 180$
Subtract 52: $c + d = 128$
    $a + b + c + d =$
Substitute: $128 + 128 = 256$

4. B
$$f(x) = x^2 - 4$$
Set $f(x)$ equal to 32: $x^2 - 4 = 32$
Add 4: $x^2 = 36$
Take positive square root: $x = 6$

---

5. C The ratio of the nuts is a part-to-part-to-part-to-part ratio. Adding these numbers gives the total number of parts: $2 + 4 + 5 + 7 = 18$. Since four of these parts are almonds, the fraction of the mixture that is almonds is 4/18, or 2/9.

---

6. D If 20 students scored an average of 75 points, then the sum of their scores is $20 \times 75 = 1,500$ total points.

If 12 of those students scored an average of 83 points, then the sum of their scores is $12 \times 83 = 996$ points.

Therefore, the remaining 8 students scored $1,500 - 996 = 504$ points altogether, so their average score is $504 \div 8 = 63$ points.

---

7. A The sides of square *EFGH* all have length $8\sqrt{2}$. A diagonal of this square can be found with the Pythagorean theorem: $(8\sqrt{2})^2 + (8\sqrt{2})^2 = \overline{EG}^2$.

Simplify: $128 + 128 = \overline{EG}^2$
                         $256 = \overline{EG}^2$
Take square root: $16 = \overline{EG}$

(Or, more simply, you can remember that the length of the diagonal of a 45°-45°-90° triangle is the length of the side times $\sqrt{2}$. So the diagonal is $8\sqrt{2} \times \sqrt{2} = 16$.) By the same reasoning, since the sides of square *ABCD* all have length $14\sqrt{2}$: $\overline{AD} = 14\sqrt{2} \times \sqrt{2} = 28$.

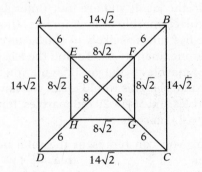

Notice that $\overline{AC} = \overline{AE} + \overline{EG} + \overline{CG}$; therefore, $28 = \overline{AE} + 16 + \overline{CG}$, so $\overline{AE} + \overline{CG} = 12$. By the same reasoning, $\overline{BF} + \overline{DH} = 12$, so $\overline{AE} + \overline{BF} + \overline{CG} + \overline{DH} = 24$.

---

8. D Although you were probably taught to add the "rightmost" digits first, here the "leftmost" digits provide more information about the number, so it's best to start there.

$$\begin{array}{r} RS \\ +SR \\ \hline TR4 \end{array}$$

The largest possible 3-digit number that can be formed by adding two 2-digit numbers is $99 + 99 = 198$. Therefore, T must be 1.

$$\begin{array}{r} RS \\ +SR \\ \hline 1R4 \end{array}$$

Therefore, there must be a "carry" of 1 from the addition of $R + S$ in the 10s column. Looking at the units column tells us that $S + R$ yields a units digit of 4, so $S + R = 14$. The addition in the 10s column tells us that $R + S + 1 = R + 10$. (The "+10" is needed for the carry into the 100s column.)

                                      $R + S + 1 = R + 10$
Substitute $R + S = 14$: $14 + 1 = R + 10$
Subtract 10: $5 = R$

So $2R + T = 2(5) + 1 = 11$.

---

9. 1
$$\boxed{n} = \frac{n^2}{16}$$

If it helps, you can think of this as $f(n) = \dfrac{n^2}{16}$.

Find the value of $(f(4))^2$

Plug in 4 for n: $f(4) = \dfrac{4^2}{16} = \dfrac{16}{16} = 1$

Plug in 1 for $f(4)$: $((f(4))^2 = (1)^2 = 1$

---

10. 750 25% of $600 is $150. Therefore, the club earned $150 more in 2007 than it did in 2006, or $600 + $150 = $750. Remember, also, that increasing any quantity by 25% is the same as multiplying that quantity by 1.25.

---

11. 3   Set up equations: $x + y = 4$
                                            $x - y = 2$
            Add straight down: $2x = 6$
            Divide by 2: $x = 3$
            Plug in 3 for x: $3 + y = 4$
            Subtract 3: $y = 1$
            Final product: $(x)(y) = (3)(1) = 3$

12. 32   Let $LM = x$, and let $LO = y$. Since x is twice the length of y, $x = 2y$.

$$x + x + y + y = P$$

Substitute for x: $2y + 2y + y + y = P$

Combine terms: $6y = P$

Plug in 48 for P: $6y = 48$

Divide by 6: $y = 8$

Solve for x: $x = 2y = 2(8) = 16$

To find the area of the shaded region, you might notice that if PM is the base of the shaded triangle, then LO is the height, so area = ½(base)(height) = ½(8)(8) = 32.

If you don't notice this, you can find the shaded area by finding the area of the rectangle and subtracting the areas of the two unshaded triangles.

Area of rectangle = (length)(width)
Area of rectangle = $(x)(y) = (16)(8) = 128$

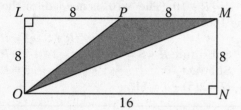

Area of triangle PLO = ½(base)(height)
Area of triangle PLO = ½(8)(8) = 32

Area of triangle MNO = ½(base)(height)
Area of triangle MNO = ½(16)(8) = 64

Area of triangle OPM = 128 − 64 − 32 = 32

---

13. 9 $64^3 = 4^x$

Substitute 4^3 for 64: $(4^3)^3 = 4^x$

Simplify: $4^9 = 4^x$

Equate the exponents: $x = 9$

---

14. 3   Draw a line with points P, Q, R, and S on the line in that order. You are given that $\overline{PS} = 2\overline{PR}$ and that $\overline{PS} = 4\overline{PQ}$, so choose values for those lengths, like $\overline{PS} = 12$, $\overline{PR} = 6$, and $\overline{PQ} = 3$.

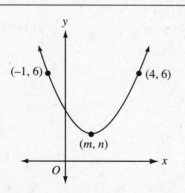

This means that $\overline{QS} = 9$, so $\overline{QS}/\overline{PQ} = 9/3 = 3$.

---

15. 1.5 or 3/2   Since the graph is a parabola, it has a vertical axis of symmetry through the vertex. The points $(-1, 6)$ and $(4, 6)$ have the same y-coordinate, so each one is the reflection of the other over the axis of symmetry. This axis, therefore, must be halfway between the two points. Since the average of −1 and 4 is $(-1 + 4)/2 = 1.5$, the axis of symmetry must be the line $x = 1.5$, and therefore $m = 1.5$.

16. 18   Since these numbers are "evenly spaced," their mean (average) is equal to their median (middle number). The average is easy to calculate: 110/5 = 22. Therefore, the middle number is 22, so the numbers are 18, 20, 22, 24, and 26.

Alternatively, you can set up an equation to find the sum of five consecutive unknown even integers, where x is the least of these:

$$x + (x + 2) + (x + 4) + (x + 6) + (x + 8) = 110$$

Combine like terms: $5x + 20 = 110$

Subtract 20: $5x = 90$

Divide by 5: $x = 18$

So the five integers are 18, 20, 22, 24, and 26.

17. 20   Use the percent change formula:

$$\frac{\text{Final} - \text{Original}}{\text{Original}} \times (100\%)$$

$$\frac{24{,}000 - 20{,}000}{20{,}000} \times (100\%) = 20\%$$

---

18. 25   Let b = the number of black marbles, w = the number of white marbles, and r = the number of red marbles in the jar. If you are four times as likely to choose a black marble as a white one, then $b = 4w$. If you are five times as likely to choose a red marble as a black one, then $r = 5b$. To find the least possible number of marbles in the jar, imagine you have only one white marble. This would mean you have $4(1) = 4$ black marbles and $5(4) = 20$ red marbles, for a total of $1 + 4 + 20 = 25$ marbles.

In general, you can represent the total number of marbles as   total $= b + w + r$

Since $r = 5b$:   total $= b + w + 5b$

Since $b = 4w$:   total $= 4w + w + 5(4w)$

Simplify: total $= 4w + w + 20w$

Simplify: total $= 25w$

In other words, the number of marbles in the jar must be a multiple of 25. The smallest positive multiple of 25 is, of course, 25.

Section 6

1. **A** If the fight did not ensue, John must have *intervened* to stop it. *intervene* = get in the way of something; *coalesce* = fuse together; *intermingle* = mix together; *exacerbate* = make worse

2. **D** The defendant hoped the testimony would *corroborate* (support) his alibi, which would *clear him of blame*. *convoke* = call together; *synthesize* = generate; *absolve* = free of blame; *impeach* = accuse

3. **E** Being *ensnarled* (tied up) in traffic is an unpleasant experience that Rachel would have an *aversion to* or *dislike for*. *antipathy* = feeling against; *penchant* = liking; *predilection* = liking; *proclivity* = tendency to do something; *aversion* = feeling of dislike; *insufferable* = intolerable

4. **A** If the practices are no longer considered *state of the art*, they must now be considered *outdated* or *unsophisticated*. The physicians are *incredulous* (not able to believe) that such barbaric acts were once *supported* or *condoned*. *primitive* = old, unsophisticated; *sanctioned* = approved; *ingenious* = incredible, brilliant; *boorish* = rude, *censured* = publicly condemned; *innovative* = new; *endorsed* = supported; *foolhardy* = recklessly bold; *condemned* = criticized

5. **B** The Prime Minister had vetoed the law in the past many times, so he didn't want it to pass. What would come *as a great surprise*? The Prime Minister's suddenly *supporting* the law. *articulated* = expressed clearly; *championed* = defended; *denounced* = spoke out against; *initiated* = began; *abbreviated* = shortened

6. **C** Lines 3–4 state that the *tradition is that a man never lifts his hand against a woman*. Furthermore, if a man offends a woman, she is entitled to give him *a sound thrashing* (line 6). Therefore, a man who disrespected a woman would face *censure*.

7. **E** Saying that *it is not an unusual thing for a squaw to administer a sound thrashing to a warrior husband* (lines 5–7) is like saying that it is not unusual for her to *give* him a beating, or *dispense* it.

8. **C** Lines 5–6 say that *merely receiving palliative care . . . provides no hope of a cure*. Therefore, palliative care only reduces the discomfort of the symptoms, without curing the disease, as something *analgesic* does.

9. **A** Lines 8–11 ask, *How can a doctor know if a patient has the mental capacity to decide for herself that the time has come to stop fighting the disease?* This question indicates that there may be some difficulty in determining a patient's *state of mind*.

10. **B** The first sentence of the passage says *there was great optimism about earthquake prediction*. Each paragraph discusses potential *precursors*, or predictors, of earthquakes.

11. **E** Lines 8–10 say that because *foreshocks look just like any other earthquake, they are not in themselves very useful in prediction*.

12. **D** Support for choice II can be found in line 19, which says that groundwater has *become cloudy* prior to an earthquake. Choice III is supported in lines 16–18, which say that *before a large earthquake, marked changes have been reported in the level or flow of wells and springs*. Nothing is said about density changes in the groundwater.

13. **A** The passage says (lines 8–10) that *since foreshocks look just like any other earthquakes, they are not in themselves very useful in prediction* but later (lines 39–42) mentions that because *the Haicheng earthquake had hundreds of foreshocks*, it was *easier than average . . . to predict*, thereby suggesting that foreshocks are, in fact, useful in predicting earthquakes.

14. **A** This paragraph describes a particular application of the theory of earthquake prediction, described in the previous paragraphs, which led to scientists' predicting a large earthquake and saving many lives. Although this is said to have *prov[ed] that . . . earthquake prediction is possible* (lines 38–39), it was not a scientific experiment, as there was no control group.

15. **C** Lines 49–50 mention that *seismologists missed predicting* the Tangshan earthquake and that over 250,000 people died. This was far worse than the Haicheng earthquake, which was *successfully predicted*, so that many lives were saved.

16. **D** The word "evacuation" in line 46 is placed in quotations to indicate that it is not being used in the traditional sense. The task of evacuating a population from a natural disaster does not typically involve showing movies, so doing so is unconventional.

17. **C** Lines 7–8 say that *one of the missionaries who met the ship took us under his wing*.

18. **E** Saying that *he could hardly believe that we were really restored to him* is like saying he couldn't believe that we were returned to him.

19. B The narrator states that she could *use tools as well as [her] brothers did* (lines 20–21), that her first childhood friendship was with a male ship-builder next door, and that she was eager and able to work with the ship-builders around her. Thus, she conveys a clear sense that she considers herself the equal of the males in her life.

20. D The author was emancipated from her confining clothing so that she could work with tools, such as her hatchet, in the shipyard.

21. C The *big movements of the day* refer to the changes in culture and *civilization* (line 43).

22. A Choice II is supported by lines 38–40, which say that *we had around us the fine flower of New England civilization*, as opposed to Michigan, which the author characterizes as *the wilderness* (line 45). The passage does not suggest that New England had finer gardens or humbler citizens than Michigan had.

23. D The author describes the move to Michigan as *a complete upheaval* (lines 37–38), and an unwelcome move from *the fine flower of New England civilization* (lines 39–40), thereby suggesting that she resents the move. She conveys no sign of bewilderment, fear, or awe in this passage, since she describes the move with insight and equanimity.

24. A The passage says that the sisters *were so pained by* (the lumber wagon's) *appearance that we refused to ride in it* (lines 55–56) and that they wanted to *look as if we had no association with it* (lines 57–58).

Section 7

1. D
$$4x + 5 = 20$$
Add 3: $4x + 8 = 23$

2. C First find out how many cups are in 3 pints.

Set up a ratio: $\dfrac{1 \text{ pint}}{2 \text{ cups}} = \dfrac{3 \text{ pints}}{x \text{ cups}}$

Cross-multiply: $x = 6$ cups

Set up a ratio to solve for servings:

$$\dfrac{1 \text{ serving}}{\frac{1}{3} \text{ cups}} = \dfrac{x \text{ servings}}{6 \text{ cups}}$$

Cross-multiply: $\frac{1}{3}x = 6$
Divide by $\frac{1}{3}$: $x = 18$

3. A Since the angle shown is a right angle, the arc represents ¼ of the circumference.

          length of arc $= \frac{1}{4}(2\pi r)$
Substitute 4 for r: length of arc $= \frac{1}{4}(2\pi(4))$
Simplify: length of arc $= 2\pi$

4. C This question tests your understanding of 30°-60°-90° triangles. The hypotenuse, which corresponds to $2x$, is 14. This means that the base is $x = 7$. The height is therefore $x\sqrt{3} = 7\sqrt{3}$.

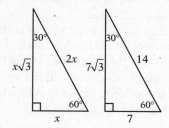

5. A Given that $\nabla x = 3x - 3$, find $\nabla 7$.

            $\nabla 7 = 3x - 3$
Plug in 7 for x: $3(7) - 3 = 18$
Find $\nabla 3$: $\nabla 3 = 3x - 3$
Plug in 3 for x: $3(3) - 3 = 6$

$$\dfrac{\nabla 7}{\nabla 3} = \dfrac{18}{6} = 3$$

Be careful not to pick answer choice (B) $\nabla 3$, because $\nabla 3 = 3(3) - 3 = 6$, not 3. Answer choice (A) $\nabla 2$ is correct, because $\nabla 2 = 3(2) - 3 = 3$.

6. B A little common sense should tell you that they will not need a full hour to clean the pool, because Stephanie can clean it in an hour all by herself, but Mark is helping. Therefore, you should eliminate choices (C), (D), and (E) right away. You might also notice that it can't take less than 30 minutes, because that is how long it would take if they both cleaned one pool per hour (so that the two working together could clean it in half the time), but Mark is slower, so they can't clean it quite that fast. This eliminates choice (A) and leaves (B) as the only possibility.

But you should know how to solve this problem if it were not a multiple-choice question, as well:

Stephanie's rate for cleaning the pool is one pool per hour. Mark's rate for cleaning the pool is one pool ÷ 1.5 hours $= \frac{2}{3}$ pools per hour. Combined, they can clean $1 + \frac{2}{3} = \frac{5}{3}$ pools per hour. Set up a rate equation using this rate to determine how much time it would take to clean one pool:

     1 pool $= (\frac{5}{3}$ pools per hour)(time)
Divide by $\frac{5}{3}$: $\frac{3}{5}$ hours to clean the pool
Multiply by 60: $\frac{3}{5}(60) = 36$ minutes

7. A Change each expression to a base-10 exponential:
(A) $= ((10^2)^3)^4 = 10^{24}$
(B) $= ((10^2)^5)((10^2)^6) = (10^{10})(10^{12}) = 10^{22}$
(C) $= ((10^4)^4) = 10^{16}$
(D) $= (((10^2)^2)((10^2)^2))^2 = ((10^4)(10^4))^2 = (10^8)^2 = 10^{16}$
(E) $= (10^6)^3 = 10^{18}$

8. B Consider the points $(0, 2)$ and $(3, 0)$ on line l. When these points are reflected over the x-axis, $(0, 2)$ transforms to $(0, -2)$ and $(3, 0)$ stays at $(3, 0)$ because it is on the x-axis. You can then use the slope formula to find the slope of line m:

$$\frac{y_2 - y_1}{x_2 - x_1} = \frac{0 - (-2)}{3 - 0} = \frac{2}{3}$$

It's helpful to notice that whenever a line is reflected over the x-axis (or the y-axis, for that matter—try it), its slope becomes the opposite of the original slope.

9. C

	$(a + b)^2 = (a + b)(a + b)$
FOIL:	$a^2 + ab + ab + b^2$
Combine like terms:	$a^2 + 2ab + b^2$
Plug in 5 for ab:	$a^2 + 2(5) + b^2$
Simplify:	$a^2 + b^2 + 10$
Plug in 4 for $a^2 + b^2$:	$4 + 10 = 14$

10. D The total area of the patio to be constructed is $24 \times 12 = 288$ ft². The slab shown in the figure has an area of 8 ft². Therefore, to fill the patio you will need $288 \div 8 = 36$ slabs.

11. D The prize money ratio can also be written as $7x:2x:1x$. Because the total prize money is $12,000,

$$7x + 2x + 1x = 12,000$$

Combine like terms: $\qquad 10x = 12,000$
Divide by 10: $\qquad x = 1,200$
The first place prize is $7x = 7(1,200) = \$8,400$.

12. E Always read the problem carefully and notice what it's asking for. Don't assume that you must solve for x and y here. Finding the value of $6x - 2y$ is much simpler than solving the entire system:

$$2x + 3y = 7$$
$$4x - 5y = 12$$

Add straight down: $\qquad 6x - 2y = 19$

13. D Think carefully about the given information and what it implies, then try to find counterexamples to disprove the given statements. For instance, try to disprove statement I by showing that s can be even. Imagine $s = 2$:

$$s + 1 = 2r$$
Substitute 6 for s: $\qquad 6 + 1 = 2r$
Combine like terms: $\qquad 7 = 2r$
Divide by 2: $\qquad 3.5 = r$ (nope)

This doesn't work because r must be an integer. Why didn't it work? Because $2r$ must be even, but if s is even, then $s + 1$ must be odd and cannot equal an even number, so s must always be odd and statement I is true. (Eliminate choice (B).)

Statement II can be disproven with $r = 1$:

$$s + 1 = 2r$$
Substitute 1 for r: $\qquad s + 1 = 2(1)$
Subtract 1: $\qquad s = 1$ (okay)

Since 1 is an integer, we've proven that r is not necessarily even, so II is false. (Eliminate choices (C) and (E).)

Since we still have two choices remaining, we have to check ugly old statement III. Try the values we used before. If $r = 1$ and $s = 1$, then $\frac{s}{r} + \frac{1}{r} = \frac{1}{1} + \frac{1}{1} = 2$, which is an integer. But is it always an integer? Plugging in more examples can't prove that it will **ALWAYS** be an integer, because we can never test all possible solutions. We can prove it easily with algebra, though. Since $s + 1 = 2r$:

Divide by r: $\qquad \dfrac{s + 1}{r} = 2$

Distribute: $\qquad \dfrac{s}{r} + \dfrac{1}{r} = 2$

Since 2 is an integer, statement III is necessarily true.

14. C Find all the possible products of the values on two chips: $(1)(2) = 2$; $(1)(3) = 3$; $(1)(4) = 4$; $(1)(5) = 5$; $(1)(6) = 6$; $(2)(3) = 6$; $(2)(4) = 8$; $(2)(5) = 10$; $(2)(6) = 12$; $(3)(4) = 12$; $(3)(5) = 15$; $(3)(6) = 18$; $(4)(5) = 20$; $(4)(6) = 24$; $(5)(6) = 30$. There are 15 different combinations of chips. Of these, only the last 2 yield products that are greater than 20. So the probability is 2/15.

15. D In this problem, only the signs of the terms matter. By following the rule of the sequence, you should see that the first six terms of the sequence are $+, -, -, +, -, -, \ldots$ The pattern $\{+, -, -\}$ repeats forever. In the first 100 terms, the pattern repeats $100 \div 3 = 33\frac{1}{3}$ times. Because each repetition contains two negative numbers, in 33 full repetitions there are $33 \times 2 = 66$ negative numbers. The 100th term is the first term of the next pattern, which is positive, so the total number of negative terms is 66.

16. B Draw the five triangles. The simplest way to solve this problem is to compare the choices one pair at a time. For instance, it should be clear just by inspection that $RB > RA$ and $SB > SA$, so we can eliminate A. Similarly, it should be clear that $RB > RC$ and $SB > SC$, so we can eliminate C. Likewise, since $RB > RD$ and $SB > SD$, we can eliminate D. Finally, we compare B with E. Since RB and RE are each a diagonal of one of the square faces, they must be equal. But SB is clearly longer than SE, because SB is the hypotenuse of triangle SEB, while SE is one of the legs.

Section 8

1. C If the review suggested that the décor of the restaurant was insipid (tasteless), but that the cuisine came close to *compensating* for it, the review must have been part positive and part negative, that is, *ambivalent*. *indefatigable* = untiring; *banal* = lacking originality; *ambivalent* = characterized by conflicting feelings; *sublime* = supreme, impressive; *piquant* = spicy; *tepid* = lukewarm

2. C The sentence suggests that Dr. Thompson should have characterized the results as unusual, but didn't. *meticulous* = concerned with detail; *belligerent* = prone to fighting; *anomalous* = deviating from the norm; *convergent* = coming together; *warranted* = appropriate to the situation

3. B They would hope that bad news did not predict further bad news. *amalgam* = a combination of diverse elements; *harbinge* = omen; *arbiter* = judge; *talisman* = an object with magical power

4. C To bring slaves *out of bondage* is to *free* or *unfetter* them. *encumber* = burden; *forgo* = relinquish

5. D A writer who can produce both *decorative poetry* and a *keenly analytical mystery novel* is a *versatile* writer; that is, she is able to write in divergent styles. *flamboyant* = ornate; *immutability* = permanence, unchangeability; *austere* = plain; *florid* = ornate; *grandiloquent* = characterized by pompous language

6. B The word *because* indicates that the sentence shows a cause-and-effect relationship. There are several ways to complete this sentence logically, but the only one among the choices is (B), because *multifarious* (widely varied) mechanisms would logically "stymie" (impede) scientists who are trying to investigate them. *efficacious* = capable of producing a desired effect; *bilked* = cheated; *conspicuous* = obvious; *thwarted* = prevented; *hampered* = hindered; *lucid* = clear; *proscribed* = forbidden

7. B If the *cultural assumption that there are many alien civilizations . . . stems in no small way from . . . the "Drake Equation,"* then this equation has had quite an influence on public opinion.

8. E The first two paragraphs discuss how the Drake Equation has led to the belief that there are many alien civilizations in the universe. The third paragraph discusses the author's contrasting view that there is indeed probably much simple life in the universe but very little if any other complex life.

9. B The sentence states that *a planet could go from an abiotic state to a civilization in 100 million years* thereby implying that a *civilization* must, by definition, not be *abiotic*. Choice (B) is the only choice that necessarily cannot apply to a civilization.

10. A The author states his thesis in lines 38–39: *perhaps life is common, but complex life is not,* and goes on to explain this thesis, stating in lines 61–67 that *research shows that while attaining the stage of animal life is one thing, maintaining that level is quite another. . . . Complex life is subject to an unending succession of planetary disasters, creating what are known as mass-extinction events.*

11. A The phrase *the evolutionary grade we call animals* refers to the *level* of life form produced by evolution.

12. C Statement (A) is supported in lines 48–50, statement (B) is supported in lines 74–76, statement (D) is supported in lines 38–39, and statement (E) is supported in lines 51–55.

13. C The *sample size of one* refers to the uniqueness of *Earth history* (line 78).

14. A The first quotation in lines 101–103 is described as a *rejoinder,* or an opposing response, to the author's thoughts. The author then responds with his own quotation.

15. C The author says that he does not *conclude that there are no other cats (Rare Cat Hypothesis), only that there are no other cats exactly like Wookie* in order to convey the idea that one should not draw conclusions based on one occurrence.

16. B The author says that *life is opportunistic* to summarize the next statement that *the biosphere has taken advantage of the myriad of strange idiosyncrasies that our planet has to offer.*

17. D The passage says that these creatures *might naively assume that these qualities, very different from Earth's, are the only ones that can breed complexity,* that is, that all life evolved the same way.

18. A The author of Passage 1 believes that complex life, once evolved, faces numerous dangers that push it toward extinction. The author would point this fact out in response to the statement in lines 134–135 of Passage 2.

19. D The author of Passage 1 says in line 26, *In my view, life in the form of microbes or their equivalents is very common in the universe, perhaps more common than even Drake and Sagan envisioned.* The author of Passage 2 says in line 139, *My bet is that many other worlds, with their own peculiar characteristics and histories, co-evolve their own biospheres.* Both authors seem to agree that there is a lot of undiscovered life out there in the universe.

Section 9

1. B When you list items in a sentence, the items should have the same grammatical form. If the first item is in the gerund, they should all be in the gerund. Because the sentence says *Eating* an english muffin and *sitting* down, *drink coffee* should instead be *drinking coffee*.

2. D The sentence begins with a participial phrase, so the subject of the participle, *pretending*, must also be the subject of the main clause. Since Mark is the one pretending, the subject of the main clause should be *Mark*. Choice (C) is incorrect because the pronoun *it* lacks a proper antecedent and appears to refer, illogically, to the *practice*. Choice (E) is incorrect because it uses an unidiomatic phrase, *convince in letting*, rather than the proper idiom, *convince to let*.

3. C The verb *are* is the improper tense. It should be *be* as in answer choice (C).

4. C When you list items in a sentence, the items should have the same grammatical form. If the first term is in the noun form, then they all should be in the noun form. Because the sentence says *his temper, impatience, how easily he can be irritated* should instead be *irritability*.

5. B Before she gave the *gracious speech,* she won the match. The verb *winning* should instead be in the past perfect form, *having won*.

6. C The sentence begins by describing something that was the most influential science treatise of the 20th century. The pronoun to follow the comma should describe this treatise. Choice (C) corrects the error in the most logical and concise fashion.

7. B The pronoun *their* does not agree in number with it singular antecedent, *neither*. Choice (B) corrects this error concisely. Choices (C) and (E) are also guilty of pronoun-antecedent disagreement, and choice (D) produces a sentence fragment.

8. A The original sentence is best. All other choices are unidiomatic.

9. C The sentence requires parallel phrasing of the two things that the storm waves did: *inundating* and *sweeping*. Choice (A) is not parallel and is needlessly wordy. Choice (B) is vague, since it does not explain what *swept away* the cars. In choice (D), the pronoun *it* does not agree in number with *storm waves*. Choice (E) misuses the semicolon, because the phrase that follows the semicolon is not an independent clause.

10. B In the original sentence, the verb *have been depicted* does not agree with its singular subject, *life*. In choice (C), the phrase *depicted with* is unidiomatic, and the verb *has had depicted* is illogical. In choice (D), the pronoun *they* lacks a clear and logical antecedent. The logic and phrasing in choice (E) are awkward.

11. D In the original sentence, the modifying phrase *at the age of seven* is misplaced and incorrectly implies that the speaker's father was seven rather than the speaker himself. Choices (B), (C), and (E) commit the same error, but in slightly different ways.

12. A The original sentence is best, since it uses concise and logical parallel phrasing.

13. E The pronoun *them* refers to a plural subject. However, anyone is singular. Answer choice (E) clears up this pronoun-antecedent disagreement in the most concise and logical way.

14. A Although the original phrasing is not the most concise option, it is the only one that logically coordinates the ideas in the sentence.

PRACTICE TEST 12

ANSWER SHEET

Last Name:_____   First Name:_____

Date:_____   Testing Location:_____

Directions for Test

- Remove these answer sheets from the book and use them to record your answers to this test.
- This test will require 3 hours and 20 minutes to complete. Take this test in one sitting.
- The time allotment for each section is written clearly at the beginning of each section. This test contains six 25-minute sections, two 20-minute sections, and one 10-minute section.
- This test is 25 minutes shorter than the actual SAT, which will include a 25-minute "experimental" section that does not count toward your score. That section has been omitted from this test.
- You may take one short break during the test, of no more than 10 minutes in length.
- You may only work on one section at any given time.
- You must stop ALL work on a section when time is called.
- If you finish a section before the time has elapsed, check your work on that section. You may NOT work on any other section.
- Do not waste time on questions that seem too difficult for you.
- Use the test book for scratchwork, but you will receive credit only for answers that are marked on the answer sheets.
- You will receive one point for every correct answer.
- You will receive no points for an omitted question.
- For each wrong answer on any multiple-choice question, your score will be reduced by ¼ point.
- For each wrong answer on any "numerical grid-in" question, you will receive no deduction.

When you take the real SAT, you will be asked to fill in your personal information in grids as shown below.

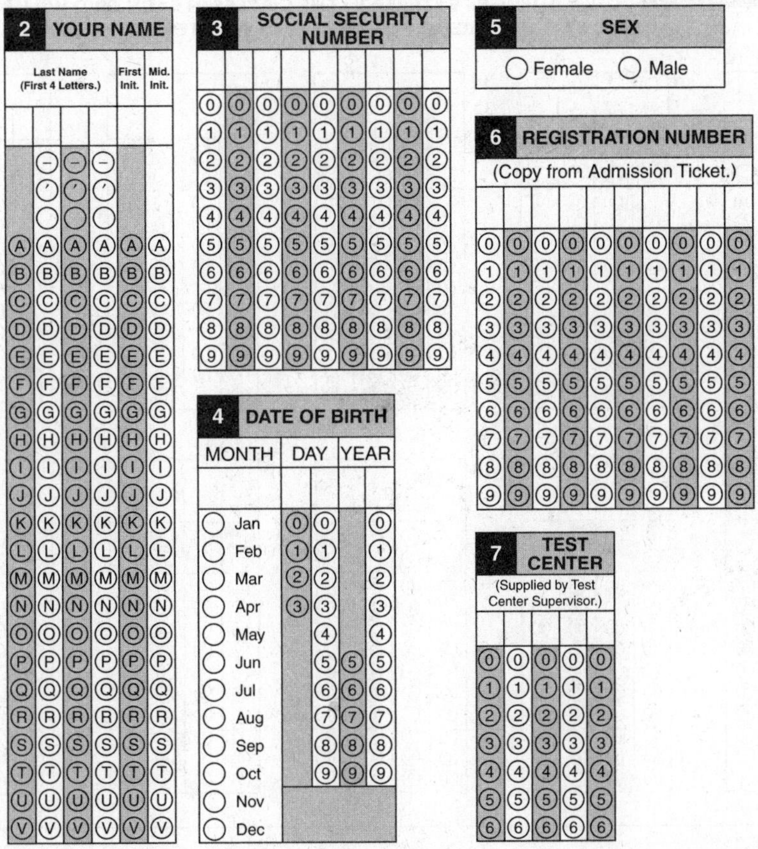

Start with number 1 for each new section. If a section has fewer questions than answer spaces, leave the extra answer spaces blank. Be sure to erase any errors or stray marks completely.

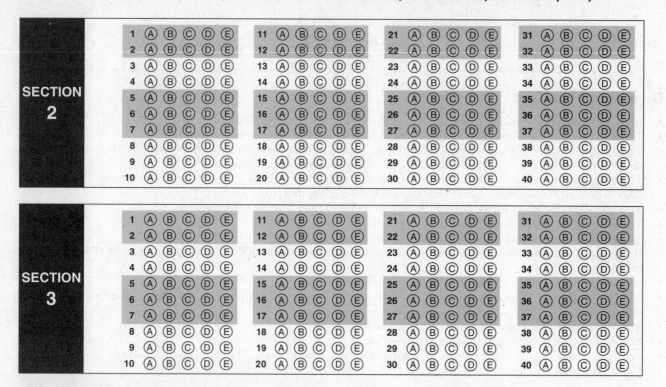

CAUTION   Use the answer spaces in the grids below for Section 2 or Section 3 only if you are told to do so in your test book.

Student-Produced Responses   ONLY ANSWERS ENTERED IN THE CIRCLES IN EACH GRID WILL BE SCORED. YOU WILL NOT RECEIVE CREDIT FOR ANYTHING WRITTEN IN THE BOXES ABOVE THE CIRCLES.

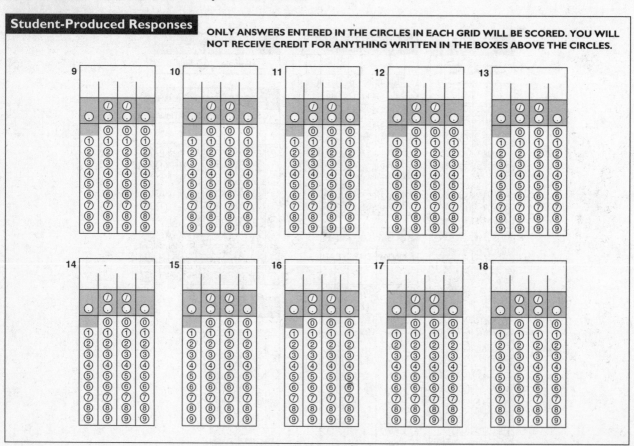

Start with number 1 for each new section. If a section has fewer questions than answer spaces, leave the extra answer spaces blank. Be sure to erase any errors or stray marks completely.

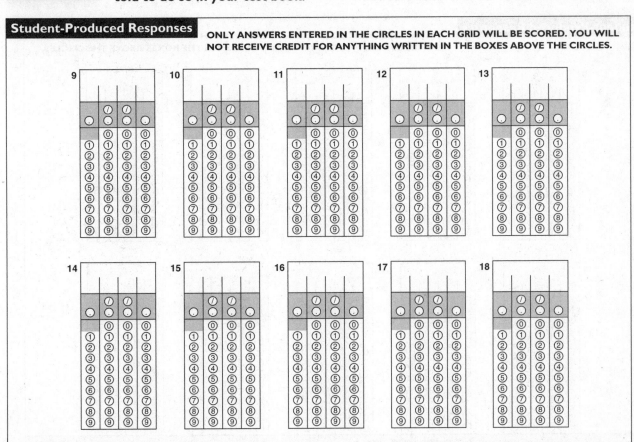

SECTION 4

SECTION 5

CAUTION   Use the answer spaces in the grids below for Section 4 or Section 5 only if you are told to do so in your test book.

Student-Produced Responses   ONLY ANSWERS ENTERED IN THE CIRCLES IN EACH GRID WILL BE SCORED. YOU WILL NOT RECEIVE CREDIT FOR ANYTHING WRITTEN IN THE BOXES ABOVE THE CIRCLES.

Start with number 1 for each new section. If a section has fewer questions than answer spaces, leave the extra answer spaces blank. Be sure to erase any errors or stray marks completely.

SECTION 6

1 Ⓐ Ⓑ Ⓒ Ⓓ Ⓔ	11 Ⓐ Ⓑ Ⓒ Ⓓ Ⓔ	21 Ⓐ Ⓑ Ⓒ Ⓓ Ⓔ	31 Ⓐ Ⓑ Ⓒ Ⓓ Ⓔ
2 Ⓐ Ⓑ Ⓒ Ⓓ Ⓔ	12 Ⓐ Ⓑ Ⓒ Ⓓ Ⓔ	22 Ⓐ Ⓑ Ⓒ Ⓓ Ⓔ	32 Ⓐ Ⓑ Ⓒ Ⓓ Ⓔ
3 Ⓐ Ⓑ Ⓒ Ⓓ Ⓔ	13 Ⓐ Ⓑ Ⓒ Ⓓ Ⓔ	23 Ⓐ Ⓑ Ⓒ Ⓓ Ⓔ	33 Ⓐ Ⓑ Ⓒ Ⓓ Ⓔ
4 Ⓐ Ⓑ Ⓒ Ⓓ Ⓔ	14 Ⓐ Ⓑ Ⓒ Ⓓ Ⓔ	24 Ⓐ Ⓑ Ⓒ Ⓓ Ⓔ	34 Ⓐ Ⓑ Ⓒ Ⓓ Ⓔ
5 Ⓐ Ⓑ Ⓒ Ⓓ Ⓔ	15 Ⓐ Ⓑ Ⓒ Ⓓ Ⓔ	25 Ⓐ Ⓑ Ⓒ Ⓓ Ⓔ	35 Ⓐ Ⓑ Ⓒ Ⓓ Ⓔ
6 Ⓐ Ⓑ Ⓒ Ⓓ Ⓔ	16 Ⓐ Ⓑ Ⓒ Ⓓ Ⓔ	26 Ⓐ Ⓑ Ⓒ Ⓓ Ⓔ	36 Ⓐ Ⓑ Ⓒ Ⓓ Ⓔ
7 Ⓐ Ⓑ Ⓒ Ⓓ Ⓔ	17 Ⓐ Ⓑ Ⓒ Ⓓ Ⓔ	27 Ⓐ Ⓑ Ⓒ Ⓓ Ⓔ	37 Ⓐ Ⓑ Ⓒ Ⓓ Ⓔ
8 Ⓐ Ⓑ Ⓒ Ⓓ Ⓔ	18 Ⓐ Ⓑ Ⓒ Ⓓ Ⓔ	28 Ⓐ Ⓑ Ⓒ Ⓓ Ⓔ	38 Ⓐ Ⓑ Ⓒ Ⓓ Ⓔ
9 Ⓐ Ⓑ Ⓒ Ⓓ Ⓔ	19 Ⓐ Ⓑ Ⓒ Ⓓ Ⓔ	29 Ⓐ Ⓑ Ⓒ Ⓓ Ⓔ	39 Ⓐ Ⓑ Ⓒ Ⓓ Ⓔ
10 Ⓐ Ⓑ Ⓒ Ⓓ Ⓔ	20 Ⓐ Ⓑ Ⓒ Ⓓ Ⓔ	30 Ⓐ Ⓑ Ⓒ Ⓓ Ⓔ	40 Ⓐ Ⓑ Ⓒ Ⓓ Ⓔ

SECTION 7

1 Ⓐ Ⓑ Ⓒ Ⓓ Ⓔ	11 Ⓐ Ⓑ Ⓒ Ⓓ Ⓔ	21 Ⓐ Ⓑ Ⓒ Ⓓ Ⓔ	31 Ⓐ Ⓑ Ⓒ Ⓓ Ⓔ
2 Ⓐ Ⓑ Ⓒ Ⓓ Ⓔ	12 Ⓐ Ⓑ Ⓒ Ⓓ Ⓔ	22 Ⓐ Ⓑ Ⓒ Ⓓ Ⓔ	32 Ⓐ Ⓑ Ⓒ Ⓓ Ⓔ
3 Ⓐ Ⓑ Ⓒ Ⓓ Ⓔ	13 Ⓐ Ⓑ Ⓒ Ⓓ Ⓔ	23 Ⓐ Ⓑ Ⓒ Ⓓ Ⓔ	33 Ⓐ Ⓑ Ⓒ Ⓓ Ⓔ
4 Ⓐ Ⓑ Ⓒ Ⓓ Ⓔ	14 Ⓐ Ⓑ Ⓒ Ⓓ Ⓔ	24 Ⓐ Ⓑ Ⓒ Ⓓ Ⓔ	34 Ⓐ Ⓑ Ⓒ Ⓓ Ⓔ
5 Ⓐ Ⓑ Ⓒ Ⓓ Ⓔ	15 Ⓐ Ⓑ Ⓒ Ⓓ Ⓔ	25 Ⓐ Ⓑ Ⓒ Ⓓ Ⓔ	35 Ⓐ Ⓑ Ⓒ Ⓓ Ⓔ
6 Ⓐ Ⓑ Ⓒ Ⓓ Ⓔ	16 Ⓐ Ⓑ Ⓒ Ⓓ Ⓔ	26 Ⓐ Ⓑ Ⓒ Ⓓ Ⓔ	36 Ⓐ Ⓑ Ⓒ Ⓓ Ⓔ
7 Ⓐ Ⓑ Ⓒ Ⓓ Ⓔ	17 Ⓐ Ⓑ Ⓒ Ⓓ Ⓔ	27 Ⓐ Ⓑ Ⓒ Ⓓ Ⓔ	37 Ⓐ Ⓑ Ⓒ Ⓓ Ⓔ
8 Ⓐ Ⓑ Ⓒ Ⓓ Ⓔ	18 Ⓐ Ⓑ Ⓒ Ⓓ Ⓔ	28 Ⓐ Ⓑ Ⓒ Ⓓ Ⓔ	38 Ⓐ Ⓑ Ⓒ Ⓓ Ⓔ
9 Ⓐ Ⓑ Ⓒ Ⓓ Ⓔ	19 Ⓐ Ⓑ Ⓒ Ⓓ Ⓔ	29 Ⓐ Ⓑ Ⓒ Ⓓ Ⓔ	39 Ⓐ Ⓑ Ⓒ Ⓓ Ⓔ
10 Ⓐ Ⓑ Ⓒ Ⓓ Ⓔ	20 Ⓐ Ⓑ Ⓒ Ⓓ Ⓔ	30 Ⓐ Ⓑ Ⓒ Ⓓ Ⓔ	40 Ⓐ Ⓑ Ⓒ Ⓓ Ⓔ

CAUTION Use the answer spaces in the grids below for Section 6 or Section 7 only if you are told to do so in your test book.

Student-Produced Responses   ONLY ANSWERS ENTERED IN THE CIRCLES IN EACH GRID WILL BE SCORED. YOU WILL NOT RECEIVE CREDIT FOR ANYTHING WRITTEN IN THE BOXES ABOVE THE CIRCLES.

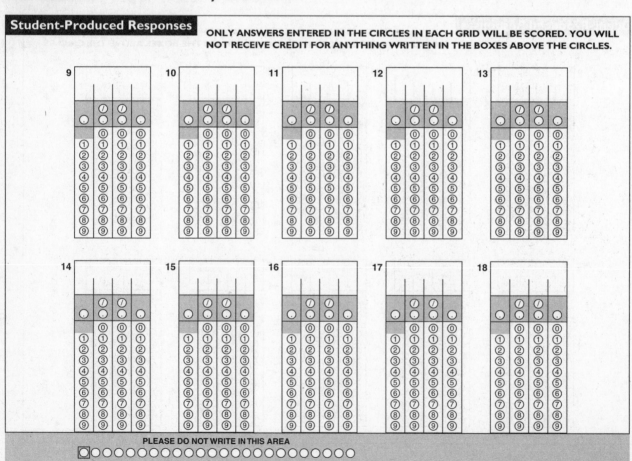

Start with number 1 for each new section. If a section has fewer questions than answer spaces, leave the extra answer spaces blank. Be sure to erase any errors or stray marks completely.

SECTION 8

1 Ⓐ Ⓑ Ⓒ Ⓓ Ⓔ	11 Ⓐ Ⓑ Ⓒ Ⓓ Ⓔ	21 Ⓐ Ⓑ Ⓒ Ⓓ Ⓔ	31 Ⓐ Ⓑ Ⓒ Ⓓ Ⓔ
2 Ⓐ Ⓑ Ⓒ Ⓓ Ⓔ	12 Ⓐ Ⓑ Ⓒ Ⓓ Ⓔ	22 Ⓐ Ⓑ Ⓒ Ⓓ Ⓔ	32 Ⓐ Ⓑ Ⓒ Ⓓ Ⓔ
3 Ⓐ Ⓑ Ⓒ Ⓓ Ⓔ	13 Ⓐ Ⓑ Ⓒ Ⓓ Ⓔ	23 Ⓐ Ⓑ Ⓒ Ⓓ Ⓔ	33 Ⓐ Ⓑ Ⓒ Ⓓ Ⓔ
4 Ⓐ Ⓑ Ⓒ Ⓓ Ⓔ	14 Ⓐ Ⓑ Ⓒ Ⓓ Ⓔ	24 Ⓐ Ⓑ Ⓒ Ⓓ Ⓔ	34 Ⓐ Ⓑ Ⓒ Ⓓ Ⓔ
5 Ⓐ Ⓑ Ⓒ Ⓓ Ⓔ	15 Ⓐ Ⓑ Ⓒ Ⓓ Ⓔ	25 Ⓐ Ⓑ Ⓒ Ⓓ Ⓔ	35 Ⓐ Ⓑ Ⓒ Ⓓ Ⓔ
6 Ⓐ Ⓑ Ⓒ Ⓓ Ⓔ	16 Ⓐ Ⓑ Ⓒ Ⓓ Ⓔ	26 Ⓐ Ⓑ Ⓒ Ⓓ Ⓔ	36 Ⓐ Ⓑ Ⓒ Ⓓ Ⓔ
7 Ⓐ Ⓑ Ⓒ Ⓓ Ⓔ	17 Ⓐ Ⓑ Ⓒ Ⓓ Ⓔ	27 Ⓐ Ⓑ Ⓒ Ⓓ Ⓔ	37 Ⓐ Ⓑ Ⓒ Ⓓ Ⓔ
8 Ⓐ Ⓑ Ⓒ Ⓓ Ⓔ	18 Ⓐ Ⓑ Ⓒ Ⓓ Ⓔ	28 Ⓐ Ⓑ Ⓒ Ⓓ Ⓔ	38 Ⓐ Ⓑ Ⓒ Ⓓ Ⓔ
9 Ⓐ Ⓑ Ⓒ Ⓓ Ⓔ	19 Ⓐ Ⓑ Ⓒ Ⓓ Ⓔ	29 Ⓐ Ⓑ Ⓒ Ⓓ Ⓔ	39 Ⓐ Ⓑ Ⓒ Ⓓ Ⓔ
10 Ⓐ Ⓑ Ⓒ Ⓓ Ⓔ	20 Ⓐ Ⓑ Ⓒ Ⓓ Ⓔ	30 Ⓐ Ⓑ Ⓒ Ⓓ Ⓔ	40 Ⓐ Ⓑ Ⓒ Ⓓ Ⓔ

SECTION 9

1 Ⓐ Ⓑ Ⓒ Ⓓ Ⓔ	11 Ⓐ Ⓑ Ⓒ Ⓓ Ⓔ	21 Ⓐ Ⓑ Ⓒ Ⓓ Ⓔ	31 Ⓐ Ⓑ Ⓒ Ⓓ Ⓔ
2 Ⓐ Ⓑ Ⓒ Ⓓ Ⓔ	12 Ⓐ Ⓑ Ⓒ Ⓓ Ⓔ	22 Ⓐ Ⓑ Ⓒ Ⓓ Ⓔ	32 Ⓐ Ⓑ Ⓒ Ⓓ Ⓔ
3 Ⓐ Ⓑ Ⓒ Ⓓ Ⓔ	13 Ⓐ Ⓑ Ⓒ Ⓓ Ⓔ	23 Ⓐ Ⓑ Ⓒ Ⓓ Ⓔ	33 Ⓐ Ⓑ Ⓒ Ⓓ Ⓔ
4 Ⓐ Ⓑ Ⓒ Ⓓ Ⓔ	14 Ⓐ Ⓑ Ⓒ Ⓓ Ⓔ	24 Ⓐ Ⓑ Ⓒ Ⓓ Ⓔ	34 Ⓐ Ⓑ Ⓒ Ⓓ Ⓔ
5 Ⓐ Ⓑ Ⓒ Ⓓ Ⓔ	15 Ⓐ Ⓑ Ⓒ Ⓓ Ⓔ	25 Ⓐ Ⓑ Ⓒ Ⓓ Ⓔ	35 Ⓐ Ⓑ Ⓒ Ⓓ Ⓔ
6 Ⓐ Ⓑ Ⓒ Ⓓ Ⓔ	16 Ⓐ Ⓑ Ⓒ Ⓓ Ⓔ	26 Ⓐ Ⓑ Ⓒ Ⓓ Ⓔ	36 Ⓐ Ⓑ Ⓒ Ⓓ Ⓔ
7 Ⓐ Ⓑ Ⓒ Ⓓ Ⓔ	17 Ⓐ Ⓑ Ⓒ Ⓓ Ⓔ	27 Ⓐ Ⓑ Ⓒ Ⓓ Ⓔ	37 Ⓐ Ⓑ Ⓒ Ⓓ Ⓔ
8 Ⓐ Ⓑ Ⓒ Ⓓ Ⓔ	18 Ⓐ Ⓑ Ⓒ Ⓓ Ⓔ	28 Ⓐ Ⓑ Ⓒ Ⓓ Ⓔ	38 Ⓐ Ⓑ Ⓒ Ⓓ Ⓔ
9 Ⓐ Ⓑ Ⓒ Ⓓ Ⓔ	19 Ⓐ Ⓑ Ⓒ Ⓓ Ⓔ	29 Ⓐ Ⓑ Ⓒ Ⓓ Ⓔ	39 Ⓐ Ⓑ Ⓒ Ⓓ Ⓔ
10 Ⓐ Ⓑ Ⓒ Ⓓ Ⓔ	20 Ⓐ Ⓑ Ⓒ Ⓓ Ⓔ	30 Ⓐ Ⓑ Ⓒ Ⓓ Ⓔ	40 Ⓐ Ⓑ Ⓒ Ⓓ Ⓔ

1 ESSAY   ESSAY 1

ESSAY
Time—25 minutes

Write your essay on separate sheets of standard lined paper.

The essay gives you an opportunity to show how effectively you can develop and express ideas. You should therefore take care to develop your point of view, present your ideas logically and clearly, and use language precisely.

Your essay must be written on the lines provided on your answer sheet—you will receive no other paper on which to write. You will have enough space if you write on every line, avoid wide margins, and keep your handwriting to a reasonable size. Remember that people who are not familiar with your handwriting will read what you write. Try to write or print so that what you are writing is legible to those readers.

Important reminders:

- **A pencil is required for the essay.** An essay written in ink will receive a score of zero.
- **Do not write your essay in your test book.** You will receive credit only for what you write on your answer sheet.
- **An off-topic essay will receive a score of zero.**

You have twenty-five minutes to write an essay on the topic assigned below.

Consider carefully the issue discussed in the following passage, then write an essay that answers the question posed in the assignment.

> We like to believe that physical phenomena, animals, people, and societies obey predictable rules, but such rules, even when carefully ascertained, have their limits. Every rule has its exceptions.

Assignment: **What is one particularly interesting "exception" to a rule?** Write an essay in which you answer this question and discuss your point of view on this issue. Support your position logically with examples from literature, the arts, history, politics, science and technology, current events, or your experience or observation.

If you finish before time is called, you may check your work on this section only.
Do not turn to any other section of the test.

2 2 2 2 2 2

SECTION 2
Time—25 minutes
20 questions

Turn to Section 2 of your answer sheet to answer the questions in this section.

Directions: For this section, solve each problem and decide which is the best of the choices given. Fill in the corresponding circle on the answer sheet. You may use any available space for scratchwork.

Notes

1. The use of a calculator is permitted.
2. All numbers used are real numbers.
3. Figures that accompany problems in this test are intended to provide information useful in solving the problems. They are drawn as accurately as possible EXCEPT when it is stated in a specific problem that the figure is not drawn to scale. All figures lie in a plane unless otherwise indicated.
4. Unless otherwise specified, the domain of any function f is assumed to be the set of all real numbers x for which $f(x)$ is a real number.

Reference Information

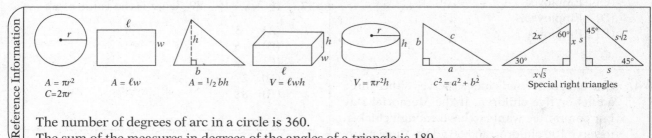

$A = \pi r^2$ $A = \ell w$ $A = \frac{1}{2}bh$ $V = \ell wh$ $V = \pi r^2 h$ $c^2 = a^2 + b^2$ Special right triangles
$C = 2\pi r$

The number of degrees of arc in a circle is 360.
The sum of the measures in degrees of the angles of a triangle is 180.

1. A playground with an area of 3,600 square feet is to be divided into six different play stations. What is the average (arithmetic mean) area, in square feet, of the six stations?

(A) 400
(B) 500
(C) 600
(D) 700
(E) 800

2. If $3a = 15$ and $4b = 10$, what is the value of $\frac{a}{b}$?

(A) $\frac{1}{2}$

(B) $\frac{2}{3}$

(C) $\frac{3}{2}$

(D) 2

(E) $\frac{5}{2}$

GO ON TO THE NEXT PAGE

2   2   2   2   2   2

SALARIES AT ULTRACORP

3. The graph above shows the salaries of five employees at UltraCorp over an eight-year period. Which employee's salary has risen at the fastest rate over this period?

(A) Employee 1
(B) Employee 2
(C) Employee 3
(D) Employee 4
(E) Employee 5

4. One bucket of fried chicken serves either three adults or five children. If the Memorial Day fair committee wants to have enough chicken to serve 100 children and 60 adults, how many buckets of chicken are needed?

(A) 29
(B) 32
(C) 35
(D) 40
(E) 45

5. $(5x - 3x + 4)(3x + 6x - 2) =$

(A) $9x^2 + 16x - 4$
(B) $18x^2 + 32x - 8$
(C) $18x^2 - 40x + 8$
(D) $72x^2 + 20x - 8$
(E) $72x^2 - 20x + 8$

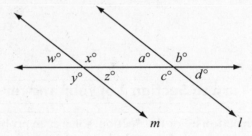

Note: Figure not drawn to scale.

6. In the figure above, $l \parallel m$ and $z = 55$. What is the value of $a + b + c$?

(A) 235
(B) 265
(C) 275
(D) 305
(E) 315

7. If $7\sqrt{x} + 16 = 79$, what is the value of x?

(A) 3
(B) 6
(C) 9
(D) 27
(E) 81

8. Each term in a sequence of numbers, except for the first term, is 2 less than the square root of the previous term. If the third term of this sequence is 1, what is the first term?

(A) 1
(B) 9
(C) 11
(D) 121
(E) 123

GO ON TO THE NEXT PAGE

2   2   2   2   2   2

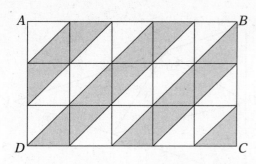

9. In the figure above, rectangle *ABCD* has an area of 90 and is divided into 15 smaller squares. What is the sum of the areas of the shaded regions?

(A) 39
(B) 42
(C) 45
(D) 48
(E) 51

---

10. For all x greater than 2, let $\boxed{\star x}$ be defined as the sum of the positive integers less than x.

What is the value of $\boxed{\star 16} - \boxed{\star 13}$?

(A) 27
(B) 29
(C) 42
(D) 45
(E) 54

$$\begin{array}{r} X3Y \\ + 5YX \\ \hline 1,33X \end{array}$$

11. In the correctly worked addition problem above, X and Y represent two different digits. What digit does X represent?

(A) 0
(B) 1
(C) 4
(D) 8
(E) 9

$x, y, 3y$

12. If the average (arithmetic mean) of the three numbers above is $3x$ and $x \neq 0$, what is y in terms of x?

(A) $\dfrac{x}{2}$
(B) $2x$
(C) $3x$
(D) $x + 7$
(E) $3x - 3$

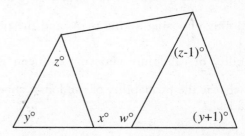

Note: Figure not drawn to scale.

13. In the figure above, what is the value of x in terms of w?

(A) $w - 2$
(B) $w - 1$
(C) w
(D) $w + 1$
(E) $w + 2$

---

14. When r is divided by 10, the remainder is 9. What is the remainder when $r + 2$ is divided by 5?

(A) 0
(B) 1
(C) 3
(D) 4
(E) 14

GO ON TO THE NEXT PAGE ⇨

15. If five distinct lines lie in a plane, then at most how many distinct points can lie on two or more of these lines?

(A)   6
(B)   7
(C)   8
(D)   9
(E)   10

16. A pile of playing cards consists of only kings, jacks, and queens. If the probability of randomly choosing a king is $\dfrac{1}{4}$ and the probability of randomly choosing a queen is $\dfrac{2}{7}$, what is the probability of randomly choosing a jack?

(A) $\dfrac{3}{7}$

(B) $\dfrac{13}{28}$

(C) $\dfrac{15}{28}$

(D) $\dfrac{4}{7}$

(E) $\dfrac{9}{14}$

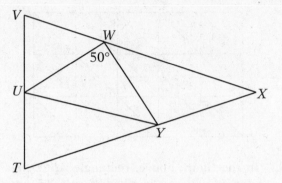

Note: Figure not drawn to scale.

17. In the figure above, $\triangle VXT$ is equilateral and $WU = WY$. If the measure of $\angle VWU$ is twice the measure of $\angle VUW$, what is the measure of $\angle TUY$?

(A)   55°
(B)   60°
(C)   65°
(D)   70°
(E)   75°

18. If m and n are positive numbers, what percent of $m - 4$ is $n + 2$?

(A) $\dfrac{100(n+2)}{(m-4)}\%$

(B) $\dfrac{m-4}{n+2}(100)\%$

(C) $\dfrac{100n+2}{(m-4)}\%$

(D) $\dfrac{m-4}{100n}\%$

(E) $\dfrac{n+2}{m-4}\%$

GO ON TO THE NEXT PAGE

2   **2**   **2**   **2**   **2**   **2**

$$h(t) = -5t^2 + 120t + m$$

19. At time $t = 0$, a rocket was launched from a platform m meters above the ground. Until the rocket hit the ground, its height, in meters, after t seconds was given by the function h above. For which of the following values of t did the rocket have the same height as it did when $t = 10$?

(A)   8
(B)   12
(C)   14
(D)   16
(E)   18

20. The price of a certain stock was d dollars on January 1, 2003. The price decreased by 20% in January, increased by 40% in February, decreased by 25% in March, and increased by 25% in April. In terms of d, what was the price of the stock at the end of April?

(A)   0.80d
(B)   0.84d
(C)   1.05d
(D)   1.12d
(E)   1.20d

STOP

If you finish before time is called, you may check your work on this section only. Do not turn to any other section of the test.

3   **3**   **3**   **3**   **3**   **3**

SECTION 3
Time—25 minutes
24 questions

Turn to Section 3 of your answer sheet to answer the questions in this section.

Directions: For each question in this section, select the best answer from among the choices given and fill in the corresponding circle on the answer sheet.

Each sentence below has one or two blanks, each blank indicating that something has been omitted. Beneath the sentence are five words or sets of words labeled A through E. Choose the word or set of words that, when inserted in the sentence, <u>best</u> fits the meaning of the sentence as a whole.

EXAMPLE:

Rather than accepting the theory unquestioningly, Deborah regarded it with -----.

(A) mirth
(B) sadness
(C) responsibility
(D) ignorance
(E) skepticism

Ⓐ Ⓑ Ⓒ Ⓓ ●

---

1. Jacques Lugard's world-renowned 34th-Street bistro is known best for its ------- main courses, but many go there simply to enjoy the restaurant's ------- desserts.

   (A) delectable . . scrumptious
   (B) unpalatable . . tantalizing
   (C) divine . . bland
   (D) debilitating . . uninspired
   (E) savory . . mediocre

2. Decades of political ------- have left the region on the brink of war; the slightest ------- could cause it to explode into destructive conflict.

   (A) dissension . . construct
   (B) tension . . communication
   (C) harmony . . instigation
   (D) strife . . provocation
   (E) unanimity . . agitation

3. For over 500 years, the smile on the *Mona Lisa* has been the source of much ------- among art historians, who continue to interpret her enigmatic expression in many different ways.

   (A) assent
   (B) deliberation
   (C) concurrence
   (D) remuneration
   (E) reconciliation

4. Even after his death, Elvis Presley continues to be one of the most ------- singers of all time; every year hundreds of thousands of fans travel to his hometown to pay tribute to his memory.

   (A) satirized
   (B) unexalted
   (C) revered
   (D) despised
   (E) shunned

GO ON TO THE NEXT PAGE ➔

5. Professional poker player Howard Lederer is known as "the professor" because of the ------- tactics he uses to outthink his opponents.

    (A) entertaining
    (B) obscure
    (C) cerebral
    (D) transparent
    (E) outlandish

6. Detractors of the new building say that it is ------- aesthetically and furthermore that, far from being the financial ------- that its developers claimed it would be, the project has cost the city dearly in lost revenue.

    (A) an eyesore . . adversary
    (B) an enhancement . . gratuity
    (C) an embellishment . . windfall
    (D) a defacement . . calamity
    (E) an atrocity . . boon

7. Nineteenth-century author Edgar Allen Poe was acclaimed for his ------- inventiveness; he had an unmatched ability to write ------- tales of cruelty and torture that mesmerized his readers.

    (A) tenuous . . spellbinding
    (B) grotesque . . enthralling
    (C) interminable . . sacrilegious
    (D) eclectic . . sadistic
    (E) chimerical . . mundane

8. DNA evidence taken from the scene of the crime was used to ------- the defendant; the genomic "fingerprint" taken from the blood sample was not a match for the accused, thus proving his innocence.

    (A) perambulate
    (B) expedite
    (C) incriminate
    (D) exculpate
    (E) equivocate

The passages below are followed by questions based on their content. Answer the questions on the basis of what is <u>stated</u> or <u>implied</u> in the passage and in any introductory material that may be provided.

Questions 9 and 10 are based on the following passage.

    Debussy, though less radical harmonically than Schoenberg, preceded him in starting
Line the breakdown of the old system. Debussy, one of the most instinctive musicians who
5 ever lived, was the first composer of our time who dared to make his ear the sole judge of what was good harmonically. With Debussy, analysts found chords that could no longer be explained according to the old harmony. If
10 one had asked Debussy why he used such chords, I am sure he would have given the only possible answer: "I like it that way!" It was as if one composer finally had confidence in his ear. I exaggerate a little, for, after all,
15 composers have never had to wait for theoreticians to tell them what or what not to do. On the contrary, it has always been the other way about—theoreticians have explained the logic of the composer's thought after he has
20 instinctively put it down.

9. It can be inferred from the passage that the "old system" (line 3) most likely involved

    (A) a way of developing musical intuition
    (B) a rigid method for writing musical harmonies
    (C) a means by which musicians could incorporate the ideas of theoreticians into their music
    (D) a method of transcribing music that arose spontaneously from a musician's imagination
    (E) methods that theoreticians used for distinguishing the harmonies of different composers

First passage: *What to Listen for in Music*, Aaron Copland, McGraw-Hill, 1957. Reprinted with permission of the Aaron Copland Fund for Music, Inc., Copyright owner.
Second passage: *The Oceans*, Ellen J. Prager; McGraw-Hill, 2000. Reprinted with permission of The McGraw-Hill Companies.

GO ON TO THE NEXT PAGE ➡

3   **3**   **3**   **3**   **3**   **3**

---

10. The passage characterizes Debussy primarily as being

   (A) less self-assured than other composers of his time

   (B) reverential of traditional musical forms

   (C) preoccupied more with musical theory than with practice

   (D) harmonically inventive

   (E) derisive of musical theoreticians

Questions 11 and 12 are based on the following passage.

     Imagine flying in a hot-air balloon over the lush, green canopy of a rainforest. Through
Line the clouds and mist you can barely make out the treetops and a few of the birds flying
5 among them. What lies hidden in the undergrowth? How many organisms are there, what do they look like, and how do they behave? Using a rope and bucket you blindly drag the rainforest from above hoping to ensnare some
10 of its inhabitants or the materials that make up its infrastructure. But alas, with such feeble and limited means you can learn little about the environment and life below. For years this is essentially how we have studied
15 the ocean—blindly sampling the sea with limited and relatively ineffective methods. Even today, with technology as advanced as it is, study of the ocean remains a difficult and expensive task. Whether through large-scale
20 satellite imagery, small-scale chemical and biological measures, or even the collecting of fossil impressions of ancient sea creatures, all aspects of oceanographic study require some type of observation or sample collection, and
25 herein lies the problem.

11. The passage describes a trip in a hot-air balloon primarily in order to

   (A) describe the variety of life forms in the rainforest

   (B) make an analogy to ocean exploration

   (C) exemplify the advanced equipment that land-based biologists have at their disposal

   (D) show the difficulties that most biologists encounter in extracting samples from the rainforest

   (E) demonstrate how methods of biological exploration have evolved over time

12. The "small-scale chemical and biological measures" (lines 20–21) are mentioned primarily as examples of

   (A) methods that are not as cost-effective or simple as the author would like

   (B) challenges for the explorer of the rainforest

   (C) technologies that hold great promise for revealing the nature of oceanic life

   (D) techniques that require little or no training to employ

   (E) inexpensive means of exploring the deepest parts of the ocean

Questions 13–17 are based on the following passage.

The following is an excerpt from a book about the history of primitive art.

     Pictures from the earliest artistic periods are the traces of a primal concept of the
Line world. In spite of the thematic treatment of real creatures we can still recognize, paintings
5 of animals or men from the early Stone Age are charged with magical strength, exaggerated and concentrated as they are into forms of existential experience. They fulfilled still other functions beyond the mere representa-
10 tion of the visible.
     The degree of naïveté in archaic primitive art varies. A certain naïveté is always present when observation of nature is not overlaid with rational thought. Art first had to discover
15 the world and to invent ways of making it perceivable. Along with visible things, invisible forces too were given form and substance and began to make their appearance. And as they achieved form they took on permanence.
20   The early hunters attempted to influence the chance fortunes of the hunt through magical practices. The power of magic was as real to them as the power of the stone ax they had invented. Art ensnared the form of the animal.

GO ON TO THE NEXT PAGE ⇒

25 Whenever the figure of woman appears it is a
sign of fertility; representations of men are
rarer, and when they occur they show him in
his role as hunter. Man does not yet look beyond the borders of existence that mark his
30 practical life. Magic precedes the fall of man
into knowledge.

It must have meant a considerable revolution in prehistoric times when man discovered that he did not have to live solely from
35 hunting, that not only the animals but indeed
all of nature round about him was full of life.
Stars and seasons take their rhythms from unknown forces; a mysterious power functioning
beyond human understanding, propitious or
40 forbidding, helpful or threatening; forces of
ancestors, spirits, and demons, and forces of
the departed and the coming gods.

With the transition from the early to the
late Stone Age there appears the first stylistic
45 change in art. The original naturalism based
on observation and experience gives way to a
geometrically stylized world of forms discoverable only through thought and speculation.

Prehistoric man, leaving behind him the
50 life of the hunter and gatherer, invents abbre-
viations and pictographic signs which are no
longer pictures proper but rather thought
models, reflections of his more settled existence as a beginning herdsman and farmer.

55 Following the late Stone Age, the art of the
Bronze Age—which in Asia dates from the middle of the third millennium B.C. and which
began in Europe around 2100 B.C.—contains,
as does the art of the Iron Age as well, elements
60 of naïveté and inventive immediacy side by side
with highly developed, formalized compositions. The bronze sculptures of the Celts and
the Illyrians are ample witnesses to them.

With the substitution of conceptual ratio-
65 nalization for more primitive, mythical explanations of the world, a kind of art arises in
which objective criteria of reality and the natural laws of optics come into play. The simplicity and vividness of the naïve become
70 more rare.

The art of the period of the catacombs was
informed with the naturalistic naïveté of late
antiquity. In medieval Christian art, which

was averse to any spatial illusions, a "moral"
75 perspective dominated; all action was pressed
onto the holy, two-dimensional surface.

While the primitive and instinctual accom-
panies the course of art until the Renaissance, it
recedes in the face of the humanistic concept of
80 the world and the discovery of linear and aerial
perspective. High art forsakes the realm of instinct in exchange for the province of reason.

But parallel with it, in folk art and among
so-called primitive peoples, naïve representa-
85 tion lives on.

13. The first paragraph suggests that the "primal
concept of the world" (lines 2–3) involved

(A) a belief that art was more important
even than hunting
(B) a need to preserve a record of events for
the future
(C) a focus on the realistic depiction of
animals
(D) a sense that paintings can have powers
beyond what can be seen
(E) a desire to communicate with animals

14. In line 6, the word "charged" most nearly means

(A) exchanged
(B) approached violently
(C) accused
(D) trampled
(E) filled

15. The "stylistic change" (lines 44–45) is a transition from

(A) representations of real things to representations of ideas
(B) magical applications of art to representations of hunting scenes
(C) depictions of gods to depictions of
herdsmen
(D) art used to depict the natural environment to art used for magical rituals
(E) a focus on the theme of hunting to a
focus on the theme of fertility

Masters of Naïve Art, Oto Bihalji-Merin. Reprinted with
permission of The McGraw-Hill Companies.

GO ON TO THE NEXT PAGE →

16. The "bronze sculptures of the Celts and the Illyrians" (lines 62–63) are mentioned primarily as examples of

   (A) a new appreciation of three-dimensional art
   (B) art with both primitive and formal characteristics
   (C) a revival of the art of the Stone Age
   (D) illustrations of the herding life
   (E) art with moralistic themes

17. The passage indicates that, unlike the "art of the period of the catacombs" (line 71), Renaissance art is characterized by

   (A) an appreciation of three-dimensional forms
   (B) an emphasis on religious themes
   (C) representations of magical creatures
   (D) a primitive view of the world
   (E) a focus on the realm of instinct

Questions 18–24 are based on the following passage.

The following passage, from a modern textbook on anthropology, discusses a debate among biologists and anthropologists about how humans evolved.

Does evolution occur gradually or in "punctuated equilibria"? Charles Darwin, a gradual-
Line ist, maintained that life forms arise from others in a gradual and orderly fashion. Small
5 modifications that accumulate over the generations add up to major changes after millions of years. Gradualists cite intermediate fossils as evidence for their position, contending that there would be even more transitional forms
10 if it weren't for gaps in the fossil record.

   The advocates of the punctuated equilibrium model believe that long periods of equilibrium, during which species change little, are interrupted (punctuated) by sudden
15 changes—evolutionary leaps. One reason for such jumps in the fossil record may be extinction followed by invasion by a closely related species. For example, a sea species may die out when a shallow body of water dries up, while a
20 closely related species will survive in deeper waters. Then, later, when the sea reinvades the first locale, the protected species will extend its range to the first area. Another possibility is that when barriers are removed, a group may
25 replace, rather than succeed, a related one because it has a trait that makes it adaptively superior in the environment they now share.

When a major environmental change occurs suddenly, one possibility is for the pace of evo-
30 lution to increase. Another possibility is extinction. The earth has witnessed several mass extinctions—worldwide ecosystem catastrophes that affect multiple species. The biggest one divided the era of "ancient life" (the
35 Paleozoic) from the era of "middle life" (the Mesozoic). This mass extinction occurred 245 million years ago, when 4.5 million of the earth's estimated 5 million species (mostly invertebrates) were wiped out. The second
40 biggest extinction, which occurred 65 million years ago, destroyed the dinosaurs and many other Mesozoic species. One explanation for the extinction of the dinosaurs is that a massive, long-lasting cloud of gas and dust arose
45 from the impact of a huge meteorite. The cloud blocked solar radiation and therefore photosynthesis, ultimately destroying most plants and the chain of animals that fed on them.

   The hominid fossil record exemplifies both
50 gradual and rapid change, confirming that evolution can be faster or slower depending on the rate of environmental change, the speed with which geographic barriers rise or fall, and the value of the group's adaptive re-
55 sponse. Australopithecine teeth and skulls show some gradual transitions. For example, some of the fossils that are intermediate between *Australopithecus* and early *Homo* combine a larger brain (characteristic of *Homo*)
60 with huge back teeth and supportive structures (characteristic of the australopithecines). However, there is no doubt that the pace of hominid evolution sped up around 18 million years ago. This spurt resulted in the emergence (in just
65 200,000 years) of *Homo erectus*. This was followed by a long period of relative stability. The probable key to the rapid emergence of *Homo erectus* was a dramatic change in adaptive strategy: greater reliance on hunting through
70 improved tools and other cultural means of adaptation. The new economy, tools, and phenotype arose and spread rapidly, then remained fairly stable for about 1 million years.

Anthropology: The Exploration of Human Diversity, Conrad Phillip Kottak, McGraw-Hill. Reprinted with permission of The McGraw-Hill Companies.

GO ON TO THE NEXT PAGE ⟹

3   3   3   3   3   3

18. The passage suggests that the existence of "transitional forms" (line 9) would demonstrate

    (A) how some species have come to dominate others

    (B) how life first arose on earth

    (C) the gradual nature of evolution

    (D) the divisions in the scientific community over the manner in which evolution occurs

    (E) how barriers arise between species

19. The example of the two "sea species" (line 18) described in the second paragraph is intended to demonstrate

    (A) the differences between the demands of an aquatic environment and the demands of a terrestrial environment

    (B) how the fossil record can misrepresent the history of a species

    (C) the manner in which one species gradually evolves into a more advanced one

    (D) a current theory of how mass extinctions occur

    (E) how punctuated evolution can occur

20. According to the passage, the dinosaurs most likely became extinct because

    (A) they were struck by a large meteorite

    (B) their food supply was eliminated

    (C) a more dominant species invaded their environment and destroyed them

    (D) the earth's temperature increased dramatically after the impact of a meteorite

    (E) a sudden ice age destroyed their environment

21. In line 60, "supportive" most nearly means

    (A) providing evidence

    (B) secondary

    (C) emotionally sustaining

    (D) weight-bearing

    (E) scientific

22. According to the passage, the early Mesozoic era differed from the late Paleozoic era chiefly in that the early Mesozoic era

    (A) was no longer dominated by the dinosaurs

    (B) was characterized by the rise of *Homo erectus*

    (C) was characterized by a greater diversity of life than that in the late Paleozoic era

    (D) was far colder than the late Paleozoic era

    (E) contained far fewer species than the late Paleozoic era did

23. According to the passage, "the pace of hominid evolution sped up around 18 million years ago" (lines 62–63) most likely because

    (A) *Australopithecus* developed a larger brain

    (B) *Homo erectus* developed better means of hunting and social interaction

    (C) *Homo erectus* invaded and took over the environment of *Australopithecus*

    (D) *Australopithecus* developed large teeth, which enabled it to eat a wider variety of foods

    (E) a natural catastrophe, perhaps a meteor, destroyed many species that were competing with the hominids

24. Given the information in the passage as a whole, how would the author most likely answer the opening question of the passage?

    (A) The gaps in the fossil record indicate clearly that all organisms evolve in punctuated equilibrium.

    (B) The example of *Homo erectus* demonstrates that no species can remain stable for very long.

    (C) The rapidity with which species evolve depends on many factors, so evolution can occur gradually or in a punctuated manner.

    (D) Only occasional mass extinctions interrupt the gradual evolution of species.

    (E) The father of evolution, Charles Darwin, was correct in believing that all species evolve gradually over long periods of time.

STOP

If you finish before time is called, you may check your work on this section only. Do not turn to any other section of the test.

4   4   4   4   4   4

SECTION 4
Time—25 minutes
35 questions

> ### Turn to Section 4 of your answer sheet to answer the questions in this section.

> **Directions:** For each question in this section, select the best answer from among the choices given and fill in the corresponding circle on the answer sheet.

The following sentences test correctness and effectiveness of expression. Part of each sentence or the entire sentence is underlined; beneath each sentence are five ways of phrasing the underlined material. Choice A repeats the original phrasing; the other four choices are different. If you think the original phrasing produces a better sentence than any of the alternatives, select choice A; if not, select one of the other choices.

In making your selection, follow the requirements of standard written English; that is, pay attention to grammar, choice of words, sentence construction, and punctuation. Your selection should result in the most effective sentence—clear and precise, without awkwardness or ambiguity.

EXAMPLE:

The children <u>couldn't hardly believe their eyes</u>.

(A) couldn't hardly believe their eyes
(B) could hardly believe their eyes
(C) would not hardly believe their eyes
(D) couldn't nearly believe their eyes
(E) couldn't hardly believe his or her eyes

Ⓐ ● Ⓒ Ⓓ Ⓔ

---

1. Renowned for his skills on the trumpet, Louis Armstrong also <u>thrilling listeners with his remarkable and unique singing voice</u>.

   (A) thrilling listeners with his remarkable and unique singing voice
   (B) thrilled listeners with his remarkable and unique singing voice
   (C) with his remarkable and unique singing voice thrilled listeners
   (D) thrilled listeners remarkably with his singing voice that was unique
   (E) thrilling listeners, his remarkable and unique singing voice

2. Like children, cats often develop a love for certain <u>toys, creating games and diversions</u> that can occupy them for hours.

   (A) toys, creating games and diversions
   (B) toys and creating games and diverting
   (C) toys and in creating games and diversions
   (D) toys; and these create games and diversions
   (E) toys, the creation of games and diversions

GO ON TO THE NEXT PAGE ⟹

4 · 4 · 4 · 4 · 4 · 4

3. Marcus Garvey argued that assimilation into mainstream culture, far from being a panacea for African Americans, <u>would be a distracting factor from their ultimate goals</u>.

(A) would be a distracting factor from their ultimate goals
(B) would factor to distract them from their ultimate goals
(C) would, for their ultimate goals, be a distraction
(D) distracting them from their ultimate goals
(E) would distract them from their ultimate goals

4. Ecology, biotechnology, and chemistry <u>are an example of sciences that</u> will be central to solving the problems of the 21st century.

(A) are an example of sciences that
(B) exemplify sciences where they
(C) are examples where sciences
(D) are examples of sciences that
(E) exemplify a science that

5. <u>Believing his speech to be superior to the other candidates</u>, Walter walked confidently into the assembly hall.

(A) Believing his speech to be superior to the other candidates
(B) Believing his speech superior to the other candidates
(C) Of the belief that his speech was superior to the other candidates
(D) Believing his speech to be superior to those of the other candidates
(E) Of the belief that his speech was superior over the other candidates

6. <u>Undeterred by her parents' opposition</u>, Rachel changed her major from economics to French literature.

(A) Undeterred by her parents' opposition
(B) Undeterred with the opposition of her parents
(C) Undeterred in that her parents opposed her
(D) Her parents' opposition, which did not deter her
(E) Being undeterred that her parents opposed her

7. The field commanders felt that they were losing control of their troops, who were becoming scattered, <u>as well as lacking discipline and becoming demoralized</u>.

(A) as well as lacking discipline and becoming demoralized
(B) lacking discipline, and becoming demoralized
(C) undisciplined, and demoralized
(D) being undisciplined and demoralized
(E) were undisciplined, and were demoralized

8. Standardized tests, some argue, do not indicate a student's academic skill but <u>rather their ability to memorize and use a set of test-taking tricks</u>.

(A) rather their ability to memorize and use a set of test-taking tricks
(B) instead it tests your ability to memorize and use test-taking tricks
(C) also the ability to memorize and use a set of test-taking tricks
(D) rather the ability to memorize and use a set of test-taking tricks
(E) instead the ability of memorizing and using a set of test-taking tricks

9. Muhammad Ali, known almost as much for his controversies outside the ring as for his glory within <u>it, becoming a great American icon</u>.

(A) it, becoming a great American icon
(B) it, has become a great American icon
(C) it; has thereby become a great American icon
(D) it; he has become a great American icon
(E) it, and so has become a great American icon

10. The brochure describing the camp requested that we <u>are at the registration center</u> promptly at noon.

(A) are at the registration center
(B) should be getting to the registration center
(C) should get at the registration center
(D) would be to the registration center
(E) be at the registration center

GO ON TO THE NEXT PAGE ⟩

4　　　**4**　　　　**4**　　　　**4**　　　　**4**　　　**4**

---

11. Without detailed information about the disaster, the relief agency could not <u>have allocated the proper resources to distribute</u> the necessary food, medicine, and clothing.

　(A) have allocated the proper resources to distribute
　(B) have been allocating the proper resources in order for the distribution of
　(C) have distributed by allocating the proper resources
　(D) have done the allocation of resources properly for distributing
　(E) be allocating the proper resources to distribute

The following sentences test your ability to recognize grammar and usage errors. Each sentence contains either a single error or no error at all. No sentence contains more than one error. The error, if there is one, is underlined and lettered. If the sentence contains an error, select the one underlined part that must be changed to make the sentence correct. If the sentence is correct, select choice E. In choosing answers, follow the requirements of standard written English.

EXAMPLE:

By the time <u>they reached</u> the halfway point
　　　　　　　　A
in the race, <u>most of the runners</u> <u>hadn't hardly</u>
　　B　　　　　　　C　　　　　　　　　D
begun to hit their stride. <u>No error</u>
　　　　　　　　　　　　　　E

Ⓐ Ⓑ Ⓒ ● Ⓔ

---

12. After the children <u>in</u> the chorus <u>had sang</u> their
　　　　　　　　　　　A　　　　　　B
final song, they were <u>led</u> from the stage by the
　　　　　　　　　　　　C
director, <u>who was holding</u> a bouquet of red
　　　　　　　　D
roses.　<u>No error</u>
　　　　　　E

---

13. Because <u>nearly</u> a dozen designs
　　　　　　　A
<u>have been submitted</u> for the new arts
　　　　B
center, the commission will need several

more weeks <u>to select</u> the best
　　　　　　C
<u>from those to choose from</u>.　<u>No error</u>
　　　D　　　　　　　　　　E

---

14. The film was <u>a watershed</u> in art <u>history: its</u>
　　　　　　　A　　　　　　　　　B
stylistic innovations <u>catalyzed</u> a revolution
　　　　　　　　　　C
<u>in American movies</u>.　<u>No error</u>
　　D　　　　　　　E

---

15. An <u>astute tactician</u>, an experienced player,
　　　　A
and <u>charismatic as a leader</u>, Terrence was
　　　　　B
<u>an obvious choice</u> to be the next captain
　　　C
<u>of the soccer team</u>.　<u>No error</u>
　　D　　　　　　　E

---

16. Without his notes <u>to help him</u> with his
　　　　　　　　　A
presentation, Claudio thought it wise <u>focusing</u>
　　　　　　　　　　　　　　　　B
on just those aspects of the project that he

<u>best understood</u> and then answer questions
　　　C
<u>from</u> the audience.　<u>No error</u>
　　D　　　　　　　E

GO ON TO THE NEXT PAGE ➡

4   4   4   4   4   4

17. Harland always <u>preferred</u> watching base-
              A
    ball games on television <u>to seeing</u> them in
                                B
    person, <u>because</u> he could not tolerate either
              C
    the high ticket prices <u>nor</u> the rowdy crowds.
                             D
    <u>No error</u>
      E

18. The <u>subtle oration</u> left Perry <u>confused; he</u>
           A   B
    was not confident that he <u>truly understood</u>
                                    C
    the message <u>eluded</u> to by the speaker.
                   D
    <u>No error</u>
      E

19. After registering online and

    <u>receiving confirmation</u> by e-mail, members
              A
    can upload <u>his or her</u> videos and photographs
                   B
    <u>to</u> the site, visit the pages that others have
    C
    created, and even <u>communicate</u> instantly with
                           D
    other members.   <u>No error</u>
                         E

20. <u>When</u> the package arrived from Tanzania,
      A
    Jerome could not <u>have been more excited</u>, his
                         B
    mind <u>filling</u> with images of the
           C
    wonderful things his grandfather

    <u>might</u> send him from Africa.   <u>No error</u>
      D   E

21. Although many great physicists developed

    their passion for physics <u>early in life</u>,
                                  A
    Murray Gell-Mann, who won the 1969

    Nobel Prize and <u>whose</u> theoretical work
                        B
    rivals <u>the greatest scientists</u> of the
              C
    20th century, <u>preferred</u> to study linguistics
                      D
    and archaeology as a youth.   <u>No error</u>
                                      E

22. The <u>emissary for</u> the committee stated that
           A
    <u>their</u> position <u>on the matter</u> remained
      B   C
    neutral and that no amount of <u>cajolery</u>
                                      D
    would cause a shift in either direction.

    <u>No error</u>
      E

23. <u>Feeling ambitious</u>, Tabitha has decided
           A
    <u>to bake</u> three different <u>kinds of</u> soufflé, each
      B   C
    of which <u>require</u> about two hours of
                 D
    preparation.   <u>No error</u>
                       D

GO ON TO THE NEXT PAGE

4   4   4   4   4   4

24. The magician's skill and showmanship <u>inspired</u>
                                              A
    all of the children at the party; <u>many</u> were
                                         B
    even convinced that, <u>if</u> they tried hard
                          C
    enough, they <u>could also learn</u> to make a
                   D
    coin disappear.   <u>No error</u>
                         E

25. The genre of romance literature, now

    <u>primarily associated</u> with love stories,
           A
    actually <u>encompass</u> a much broader range
              B
    of themes <u>including</u> chivalry, heroism,
               C
    <u>and travel</u> to foreign lands.   <u>No error</u>
      D   E

26. The settlers <u>experimented</u> for months
                      A
    <u>to find</u> the best method <u>to channel</u> water
      B   C
    from the river to <u>their</u> fields and homes.
                        D
    <u>No error</u>
      E

27. Ms. Parker <u>read</u> the account with <u>so much</u>
                   A   B
    emotion and urgency <u>as</u> we could clearly
                          C
    envision ourselves <u>embroiled</u> in the battle
                         D
    ourselves.   <u>No error</u>
                    E

28. Several college coaches came to the

    tournament hoping to find <u>perspective</u>
                                 A
    players <u>who</u> demonstrated <u>not only</u>
             B   C
    strong basketball skills but also the ability

    <u>to work</u> as members of a team.   <u>No error</u>
      D   E

29. In the school's new camp <u>for the performing</u>
                                 A
    <u>arts</u>, students choreograph <u>their own</u> dances,
                                        B
    develop <u>their acting skills</u>, and <u>will write</u>
             C   D
    and perform their own plays.   <u>No error</u>
                                      E

GO ON TO THE NEXT PAGE ⟹

4 4 4 4 4 4

Directions: The following passage is an early draft of an essay. Some parts of the passage need to be rewritten.

Read the passage and select the best answers for the questions that follow. Some questions are about particular sentences or parts of sentences and ask you to improve sentence structure or word choice. Other questions ask you to consider organization and development. In choosing answers, follow the requirements of standard written English.

Questions 30–35 refer to the following passage.

(1) Few people have had as strong an impact on an industry as the impact that Charlie Chaplin had on the world of film. (2) Born into an impoverished London family, Chaplin crossed the Atlantic and became a pioneer in silent comedic movies. (3) Charlie's mother suffered from severe mental illness, which forced her to spend time institutionalized. (4) Early in his film career, Chaplin developed his signature character, the "Little Tramp," who amused audiences repeatedly with his clever physical comedy and endearing sensitivity. (5) Modest yet clearly intelligent, shy yet always at the center of action, the Tramp's embodiment was of the genius of Chaplin's artistry.

(6) Being writer, director, and editing his own work, Chaplin faced a daunting challenge with the rise of "talkie" films, which dried up the market for the Tramp. (7) His response was to take on the additional role of composer, writing beautiful scores to accompany his work and thus allowing the Tramp to remain speechless. (8) Whether it was the mastery of his work or the audience's tendency, during the Great Depression, to identify with his character, Chaplin managed to defy the odds and maintain a tremendous level of popularity and success in the face of technological advancement.

(9) A vocal liberal in a time of conservative rule, he became a target for men like Senator Joseph McCarthy and his House Un-American Activities Committee. (10) While he managed to avoid being named to McCarthy's Hollywood Ten, a list of blacklisted entertainment industry figures suspected of Communist connections, he drew the ire of J. Edgar Hoover with the messages imbedded within his films. (11) The fascination with Chaplin went beyond his artistic genius, however.

(12) Chaplin saw the dangers in Hitler's rise to power before most of the world had heard of the dictator. (13) He saw industry becoming mechanized and impersonal and believed in a connection between the atomic bomb and murder. (14) Outraged at what they viewed as subversive propaganda created by an immoral man, the United States government revoked Chaplin's re-entry visa during a trip to London in 1952. (15) Sixty-three years old and tired of fighting against a force unwilling to hear his message, Chaplin agreed to exile rather than to going back to America and facing interrogation and lived the rest of his years in Europe. (16) He returned twenty years later to receive an Academy Award for lifetime achievement.

30. Which of the following is the best revision of the underlined portion of sentence 1 (reproduced below)?

    Few people have had as strong an impact on an industry as the impact that Charlie Chaplin had on the world of film.

    (A) the impact that Charlie Chaplin had on the world of film
    (B) Charlie Chaplin had on the world of film
    (C) the impact upon the world of film by Charlie Chaplin
    (D) Charlie Chaplin's impact on the world of film
    (E) Charlie Chaplin and his impact on the world of film

31. Which sentence contributes least to the unity of the first paragraph?

    (A) sentence 1
    (B) sentence 2
    (C) sentence 3
    (D) sentence 4
    (E) sentence 5

GO ON TO THE NEXT PAGE ▷

4   **4**   4   **4**   **4**   **4**

32. Which of the following is the best version of the underlined portion of sentence 5 (reproduced below)?

    Modest yet clearly intelligent, shy yet always at the center of action, the <u>Tramp's embodiment was of the genius of Chaplin's artistry</u>.

    (A) (no revision needed)
    (B) Tramp was embodied for the genius of Chaplin's artistry
    (C) Tramp and his embodiment of the genius of Chaplin's artistry
    (D) Tramp embodied the genius of Chaplin's artistry
    (E) Tramp's embodiment and the genius of Chaplin's artistry

33. Which of the following is the best version of the underlined portion of sentence 6 (reproduced below)?

    <u>Being writer, director, and editing his own work</u>, Chaplin faced a daunting challenge with the rise of "talkie" films, which dried up the market for the Tramp.

    (A) (no revision needed)
    (B) Writing, directing, and being editor of his own work
    (C) Being writer of his own work, directing and editing too
    (D) Writing his own work, directing, and editing also
    (E) As the writer, director, and editor of his own work

34. What is the most logical way to rearrange the sentences in paragraph 3?

    (A) 11, 9, 10
    (B) 10, 11, 9
    (C) 11, 10, 9
    (D) 9, 11, 10
    (E) 10, 9, 11

35. In context, which of the following sentences best precedes sentence 12 as an introduction to the fourth paragraph?

    (A) But Chaplin did not let his politics overwhelm his art.
    (B) Chaplin's films allowed audiences to escape from hard political and economic times.
    (C) Chaplin's fame and power came to dominate Hollywood.
    (D) These messages addressed political and moral issues both inside and outside of the United States.
    (E) Chaplin would never again be the same actor he once was.

STOP

If you finish before time is called, you may check your work on this section only. Do not turn to any other section of the test.

5   5   5   5   5   5

SECTION 5
Time—25 minutes
18 questions

Turn to Section 5 of your answer sheet to answer the questions in this section.

Directions: This section contains two types of questions. You have 25 minutes to complete both types. For questions 1–8, solve each problem and decide which is the best of the choices given. Fill in the corresponding circle on the answer sheet. You may use any available space for scratchwork.

Notes

1. The use of a calculator is permitted.

2. All numbers used are real numbers.

3. Figures that accompany problems in this test are intended to provide information useful in solving the problems. They are drawn as accurately as possible EXCEPT when it is stated in a specific problem that the figure is not drawn to scale. All figures lie in a plane unless otherwise indicated.

4. Unless otherwise specified, the domain of any function f is assumed to be the set of all real numbers x for which $f(x)$ is a real number.

Reference Information

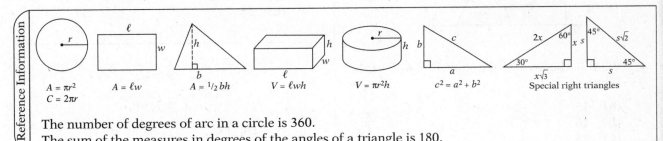

$A = \pi r^2$ $A = \ell w$ $A = \frac{1}{2} bh$ $V = \ell wh$ $V = \pi r^2 h$ $c^2 = a^2 + b^2$ Special right triangles
$C = 2\pi r$

The number of degrees of arc in a circle is 360.
The sum of the measures in degrees of the angles of a triangle is 180.

---

1. Eric earns a 5% commission on each $200 stereo that he sells. How many stereos must he sell to earn $100?

   (A)   5
   (B)   10
   (C)   15
   (D)   20
   (E)   25

JANE'S DISCOUNT MUSIC SUPERSTORE HOLIDAY SALES

	CDs	DVDs	Total
New		4,500	7,500
Used			
Total	7,000		14,000

2. Jane's Discount Music Superstore sells both new and used CDs and DVDs. On the basis of the information listed above, how many used DVDs were sold during the holiday season?

   (A)   2,500   (B)   3,000   (C)   4,000
   (D)   6,500   (E)   7,000

GO ON TO THE NEXT PAGE ⟹

5   5   5   5   5   5

3. One bag of potatoes of a certain brand weighs 40 ounces. Five pounds of these potatoes cost $4.00. If Larry has exactly $20.00 to spend on potatoes, what is the maximum number of bags he can buy? (1 pound = 16 ounces)

(A) 7
(B) 8
(C) 9
(D) 10
(E) 11

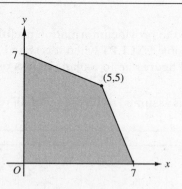

4. What is the area of the shaded region in the figure above?

(A) 15
(B) 20
(C) 25
(D) 30
(E) 35

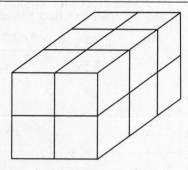

5. The rectangular solid above is constructed of 12 cubes that each have a volume of 8 cubic inches. What is the surface area of the solid?

(A) 32
(B) 48
(C) 96
(D) 128
(E) 144

6. Set M consists of the consecutive integers from -15 to y, inclusive. If the sum of all of the integers in set M is 70, how many numbers are in the set?

(A) 33
(B) 34
(C) 35
(D) 36
(E) 37

7. In a round robin tennis tournament involving seven players, each player will play every other player twice. How many total matches will be played in the tournament?

(A) 21
(B) 28
(C) 42
(D) 48
(E) 56

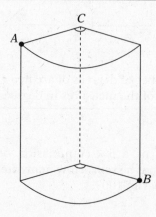

8. The figure above shows a right prism, the base of which is a quarter of a circle with center C. If the area of each base of the prism is 12.5π and the volume of the solid is 300π, what is the distance from point A to point B?

(A) 24
(B) 26
(C) 28
(D) 30
(E) 32

GO ON TO THE NEXT PAGE ⟩

5   5   5   5   5   5

Directions: For student-produced response questions 9–18, use the grids at the bottom of the answer sheet page on which you have answered questions 1–8.

Each of the remaining ten questions requires you to solve the problem and enter your answer by marking the circles in the special grid, as shown in the examples below. You may use any available space for scratchwork.

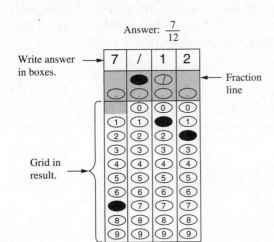

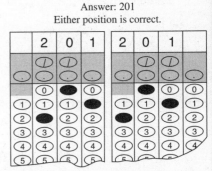

- Mark no more than one circle in any column.

- Because the answer sheet will be machine-scored, **you will receive credit only if the circles are filled in correctly.**

- Although not required, it is suggested that you write your answer in the boxes at the top of the columns to help you fill in the circles accurately.

- Some problems may have more than one correct answer. In such cases, grid only one answer.

- No question has a negative answer.

- **Mixed numbers** such as $3\frac{1}{2}$ must be gridded as

  3.5 or 7/2. (If $\boxed{3\ 1\ /\ 2}$ is gridded, it will be

  interpreted as $\frac{31}{2}$, not $3\frac{1}{2}$.)

- **Decimal answers:** If you obtain a decimal answer with more digits than the grid can accommodate, it may be either rounded or truncated, but it must fill the entire grid. For example, if you obtain an answer such as 0.6666..., you should record your result as .666 or .667. **A less accurate value such as .66 or .67 will be scored as incorrect.**

  Acceptable ways to grid ²/₃ are:

GO ON TO THE NEXT PAGE ▷

5   **5**   5   **5**   **5**   **5**

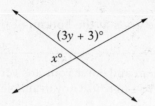

9. In the figure above, if $x = y + 1$, what is the value of $3y + 3$?

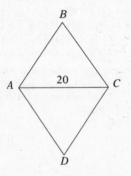

Note: Figure not drawn to scale.

10. In the figure above, $AB = BC = CD = AD$ and quadrilateral $ABCD$ has an area of 480 square inches. What is the perimeter, in inches, of quadrilateral $ABCD$?

$$f(x) = 7x + 2$$
$$g(x) = x^2 - 5$$

11. Given the functions above, what is the value of $f(g(3))$?

12. How much less than x is $\dfrac{6x - 9}{5} - \dfrac{x + 6}{5}$?

13. If a and b are positive integers, $a + b < 20$, and the product ab is an even number, what is the largest possible value of a?

U	V
W	X
Y	Z

Note: Figure not drawn to scale.

14. In the figure above, a large rectangle is divided into six smaller rectangles that each have integer lengths and widths. The areas of rectangles U, V, and W are 18, 21, and 12, respectively. If the area of the entire figure is 117, what is the area of rectangle Z?

GO ON TO THE NEXT PAGE

5   5   5   5   5   5

15. An elementary school class of 55 students is planning a field trip to a nearby aquarium. The price of admission is $15 per person. However, for groups of 60 or more people, the price is reduced to $13 per person. How much money would the class save by buying 60 tickets at the discounted price and using only 55 of them, instead of buying 55 individual tickets?

16. Points W, X, Y, and Z lie on a line in that order. If $WY = 15$, X is the midpoint of $\overline{WY}$, and $YZ = 2WX$, what is the length of $\overline{XZ}$?

17. For all numbers r and s, let $r \,\square\, s$ be defined by $r \,\square\, s = \dfrac{rs^2}{r - s}$. If $3 \,\square\, 2 = x$, what is the value of $x \,\square\, 3$?

Note: Figure not drawn to scale.

18. In $\triangle ABC$ above, $\overline{DC}$ is perpendicular to $\overline{AB}$, $BC = 5\sqrt{2}$, and $AD = 2DB$. What is the area of $\triangle ABC$?

STOP

If you finish before time is called, you may check your work on this section only. Do not turn to any other section of the test.

6   **6**   6   6   6   **6**

SECTION 6
Time—25 minutes
24 questions

Turn to Section 6 of your answer sheet to answer the questions in this section.

Directions: For each question in this section, select the best answer from among the choices given and fill in the corresponding circle on the answer sheet.

Each sentence below has one or two blanks, each blank indicating that something has been omitted. Beneath the sentence are five words or sets of words labeled A through E. Choose the word or set of words that, when inserted in the sentence, <u>best</u> fits the meaning of the sentence as a whole.

EXAMPLE:

Rather than accepting the theory unquestioningly, Deborah regarded it with -----.

(A) mirth
(B) sadness
(C) responsibility
(D) ignorance
(E) skepticism

Ⓐ Ⓑ Ⓒ Ⓓ ●

---

1. The knee-jerk reflex is nearly ------- because it produces an immediate muscular response without sending information to the brain.

    (A) transient
    (B) instantaneous
    (C) stagnant
    (D) revitalized
    (E) consecutive

2. Although starved and emaciated, the two stray cats nevertheless summoned the energy to fight ------- for the scraps of food.

    (A) humanely
    (B) vigilantly
    (C) fluently
    (D) ferociously
    (E) dispassionately

3. Jennifer's ------- demeanor irritated her peers, who hated listening to her supercilious and pretentious remarks.

    (A) reticent
    (B) belligerent
    (C) lofty
    (D) self-effacing
    (E) discomfited

4. The art of the sushi master takes years to grasp; only after years of ------- will a chef in training have the ------- to create his or her own work.

    (A) apprenticeship . . autonomy
    (B) tutelage . . ineptitude
    (C) dormancy . . sovereignty
    (D) cultivation . . boorishness
    (E) quiescence . . authority

5. The journalist had been called ------- by her editors because of her ability to get news stories before anyone else, but she later admitted that she had received early information from privileged sources, rather than through -------, as many thought.

    (A) prophetic . . prescience
    (B) premeditated . . predilection
    (C) dismissive . . omniscience
    (D) preeminent . . reluctance
    (E) insolvent . . foresight

GO ON TO THE NEXT PAGE ➡

6   6   6   6   6   6

The passages below are followed by questions based on their content; questions following a pair of related passages may also be based on the relationship between the paired passages. Answer the questions on the basis of what is <u>stated</u> or <u>implied</u> in the passage and in any introductory material that may be provided.

Questions 6–9 are based on the following passages.

PASSAGE 1

The very differentness of the medieval universe from our own invites our study of it, for
Line we cannot fully appreciate the world we live in until we contrast it with a different *weltan-*
5   *schauung,* or "world picture," and the older cosmology is indeed very unlike our own. For example, C. S. Lewis has pointed out that where our universe is thought to be dark, the other one was presumed to be illuminated;
10 and while Pascal could be disturbed by the silence of the vast spaces between the stars, the universe was formerly thought to produce the "music of the spheres" that only the wise man could hear. Furthermore, the often-heard
15 charge that the earth-centered universe of former times was the product of man's sense of self-importance is questionable, for we may observe in a medieval poet and philosopher like Dante that although the spheres are first
20 described as surrounding the earth, they are then more properly seen in an inverted order surrounding God, so that God, not man, is at the center.

PASSAGE 2

The mystical works of Hildegard of Bingen,
25 a 12th-century German nun and daughter of a knight, reveal a great deal about the medieval mind. One of the earliest known composers of hymns, she also wrote plays and other works based on her migraine-inspired visions. She
30 also composed treatises, like *Physica,* that analyzed the physical world from a religious perspective. Hildegard's science was based on the Aristotelian categories of earth, water, air and

fire, and on the then-common view of the rela-
35 tionship between mankind and nature: "All the elements served mankind and, sensing that man was alive, they busied themselves in aiding his life in every way."

6. Both passages are primarily concerned with

(A) describing the discoveries of great medieval scientists
(B) providing examples of how medieval thinkers perceived the world
(C) disproving modern assumptions about medieval history
(D) questioning medieval scientific theories
(E) showing the influence of religion on everyday life in medieval Europe

7. In Passage 1, the "other one" (line 9) refers to

(A) the far side of the galaxy
(B) the earth in contrast with outer space
(C) the sun
(D) the medieval universe
(E) an alternative cosmological theory

8. Pascal is mentioned in the passage primarily as an example of someone

(A) who could hear the "music of the spheres"
(B) who was among the first scientists to explore the medieval universe
(C) whose "world picture" was different from that of medieval times
(D) whose cosmology is very similar to that of poets like Dante
(E) who assumed that the universe was illuminated

9. Hildegard's view of the world as described in Passage 2 differs from Dante's view of the world as described in Passage 1 primarily in terms of its

(A) focus on religion
(B) assumption that the universe is ordered
(C) application of scientific methods
(D) public acceptance
(E) anthropocentrism

Passage 1: *The Literature of Medieval England,*
   D. W. Robertson, Jr., McGraw-Hill, 1970. Reprinted with permission of The McGraw-Hill Companies.
Passage 2: Christopher Black 2005. All Rights reserved.

GO ON TO THE NEXT PAGE ⟶

Questions 10–16 are based on the following passage.

The following passage was written by a naturalist about his studies of the wildlife in the African plains, particularly Serengeti National Park in Tanzania.

How can so many wild animals manage to
survive in the Serengeti? Their migrations of
Line   course tell part of the story. By moving from
place to place with the changing seasons, they
5   do not overuse and damage the grass in any
one area. But other, less obvious factors also
are involved.

Here on the eastern plains in January, it is
clear that most of the animals are eating the
10   abundant grass that springs up like a well-
mown lawn between low clumps of Sodom
apple and indigo plants. Nearly all of them,
from 1,500-pound eland bulls to tiny 10-pound
Thomson's gazelle calves, are grazers, rather
15   than browsers, which feed on shrubs or the
leaves of trees. Singly or in pairs, long lines,
or little groups, they move over the green
pastures, never remaining long in one place.
Where the grass is all short, as it will be when
20   it has been heavily grazed, all the animals apparently eat much the same sort of grass. But
where the grass is of varied lengths and toughness, we can see that each animal copes differently with the available fodder.
25   The herds of zebras tend to roam in areas
separate from the rest of the grazing multitude. Unlike all the other grazers on the plain,
they have teeth in both jaws. This enables
them to deal with taller, coarser grass than can
30   the other herbivores. All the rest are various
species of antelope, which nip off the grass between their lower incisors and toothless upper
palates. Thus, the zebras eat down the longer
grasses to a certain level and then move on.
35   Following the zebras come the wildebeests
and, in better-wooded areas, hartebeests.
These animals eat the grass down a stage further, until it is really short. (They also eat new
growth before it has had a chance to grow
40   tall.) Then the Thomson's gazelles take over.
With their tails flicking constantly, they nibble
at the individual leaves of the tussocks and on
the tiny plants that grow between them. By the

time all of them have finished, the plain resem-
45   bles a closely but rather unevenly mown lawn.

Thus, one species or another of animal
often predominates over a great expanse of the
plain, depending on the height to which the
grass has grown or has been grazed. Finally,
50   when all has been eaten down rather short,
most of the grazers leave the area altogether.

Two or three weeks later, when more rain
has brought on fresh growth, the herds may
return to feed over the area again. Perhaps
55   they move about in response to the intensity
of local showers, which can vary a good deal
over a distance of only a mile or two. In any
case, the result of their returning again and
again to the same areas is to keep the grass
60   green and short, just as the repeated mowing
of a lawn in summer does.

If, as a result of badly drawn park boundaries or some other cause, the migrant herds
of Serengeti were confined to either the west-
65   ern woodlands or the eastern short-grass
plains, they would be forced to return to the
same areas too often and would eventually so
weaken the grass that it would die out. But as
they eat it down, they move away and the
70   grass recovers.

10.   As a whole, this passage is primarily concerned with

(A)   criticizing human intervention in a
natural habitat
(B)   describing the life cycle of particular plants
(C)   suggesting a way to avert a natural
disaster
(D)   showing how to distinguish grazers from
browsers
(E)   describing how a particular ecosystem
works

Excerpted from *The Life of the African Plains*, Leslie Brown, McGraw-Hill, 1972. Reprinted with permission of The McGraw-Hill Companies.

GO ON TO THE NEXT PAGE ⟶

6   6   6   6   6   6

11. Lines 22–24 ("Where the grass . . . the available fodder") discuss the relationship between

(A) what they eat
(B) the seasons and relative animal populations
(C) plant size and dietary variety
(D) zebras and antelopes
(E) climate and plant health

12. According to the passage, browsers differ from grazers primarily in terms of

(A) what they eat
(B) how quickly they eat
(C) their weight
(D) how they digest their food
(E) the season in which they migrate

13. The passage indicates that the various species of antelope that graze on the Serengeti

(A) feed on shrubs and leaves of trees
(B) lack upper teeth
(C) can easily eat tall and coarse grass
(D) usually graze with zebras
(E) tend to consume all of the vegetation in an area before moving on

14. The passage suggests that the sequence of grazers described in lines 25–45— zebras followed by wildebeests followed by Thomson's gazelles— is generally maintained UNLESS

(A) the grazers arrive at a new pasture
(B) the grass is of various lengths and textures
(C) there are browsers among them
(D) fresh rains have fallen
(E) all of the available grass is short

15. According to the passage, rain affects the feeding habits of Serengeti grazers primarily by

(A) flooding and destroying some of the pastures
(B) forcing the browsers to take shelter under trees
(C) rendering the plants edible again
(D) weakening the grass
(E) confining the herds to high plateaus

16. The final paragraph suggests that maintaining the grasslands of the Serengeti requires

(A) freedom of the grazers to move as they wish
(B) frequent rainless periods
(C) frequent removal of dead plants
(D) the restriction of grazers to the woodlands
(E) a separation of grazers and browsers

Questions 17–24 are based on the following passage.

The following is an excerpt from an essay by George Bernard Shaw, written in 1889, on the economic basis of socialism.

All economic analyses begin with the cultivation of the earth. To the mind's eye of the
Line   astronomer the earth is a ball spinning in space without ulterior motives. To the bodily
5   eye of the primitive cultivator it is a vast green plain, from which, by sticking a spade into it, wheat and other edible matters can be made to spring. To the eye of the sophisticated city man this vast green plain appears rather as a
10   great gaming table, your chances in the game depending chiefly on the place where you deposit your stakes. To the economist, again, the green plain is a sort of burial place of hidden treasure, where all the forethought and indus-
15   try of man are set at naught by the caprice of the power which hid the treasure. The wise and patient workman strikes his spade in here, and with heavy toil can discover nothing but a poor quality of barley, some potatoes,
20   and plentiful nettles, with a few dock leaves to cure his stings. The foolish spendthrift on the other side of the hedge, gazing idly at the sand glittering in the sun, suddenly realizes that the earth is offering him gold—is dancing it be-
25   fore his listless eyes lest it should escape him. Another man, searching for some more of this tempting gold, comes upon a great hoard of coal, or taps a jet of petroleum. Thus is Man mocked by Earth his stepmother, and never
30   knows as he tugs at her closed hand whether

GO ON TO THE NEXT PAGE

6   6   6   6   6   6

it contains diamonds or flints, good red wheat
or a few clayey and blighted cabbages. Thus
too he becomes a gambler, and scoffs at the
theorists who prate of industry and honesty
35 and equality. Yet against this fate he eternally
rebels. For since in gambling the many must
lose in order that the few may win; since dis-
honesty is mere shadow-grasping where
everyone is dishonest; and since inequality is
40 bitter to all except the highest, and miserably
lonely for him, men come greatly to desire
that these capricious gifts of Nature might be
intercepted by some agency having the power
and the goodwill to distribute them justly
45 according to the labor done by each in the
collective search for them. This desire is
Socialism; and, as a means to its fulfillment,
Socialists have devised communes, kingdoms,
principalities, churches, manors, and finally,
50 when all these had succumbed to the old
gambling spirit, the Social Democratic State,
which yet remains to be tried. As against
Socialism, the gambling spirit urges man to
allow no rival to come between his private in-
55 dividual powers and Stepmother Earth, but
rather to secure some acres of her and take
his chance of getting diamonds instead of cabbages. This is private property or Unsocialism.
Our own choice is shown by our continual
60 aspiration to possess property, our common
hailing of it as sacred, our setting apart of the
word Respectable for those who have attained
it, our ascription of pre-eminent religiousness
to commandments forbidding its violation,
65 and our identification of law and order among
men with its protection. Therefore is it vital to
a living knowledge of our society that Private
Property should be known in every step of its
progress from its source in cupidity to its end
70 in confusion.

George Bernard Shaw, and H. G. Wilshire. Various authors. See
Contents. *Fabian Essays in Socialism.* New York: Humboldt
Publishing Co., ed. George Bernard Shaw, H. G. Wilshire,
and W. D. P. Bliss, 1891. Available at www.econlib.org/library/

17. Which of the following best summarizes the
main idea of this passage?

(A) Socialism provides the best means for
humanity to manage the capriciousness
of nature.
(B) Astronomers, farmers, and economists
have much to learn from each other.
(C) Patient and diligent farmers will always
be rewarded.
(D) Foolish people are often just as lucky as
industrious workers.
(E) All people properly aspire to own property and earn respectability.

18. The "primitive cultivator" (line 5) is

(A) a supernatural creator
(B) an astronomer
(C) a farmer
(D) a machine
(E) a philosopher

19. According to the passage, the perspective of the
"astronomer" (line 3) differs primarily from the
perspective of the "foolish spendthrift" (line 21)
in that the astronomer views the earth as

(A) generous, while the spendthrift views the
earth as stingy
(B) a beautiful gem, while the spendthrift
views the earth as a dull, sandy expanse
(C) dangerously capricious, while the spendthrift views the earth as a source of
unlimited riches
(D) lacking regard for humankind, while the
spendthrift views the earth as generous
(E) moving in an orderly fashion, while the
spendthrift views the earth's movements
as dangerously random

GO ON TO THE NEXT PAGE

20. The "closed hand" in line 30 refers to

   (A) the strength of the farmer
   (B) the tendency of the earth to hide its treasures
   (C) the abundance of resources that spring from the earth
   (D) the laziness of the foolish spendthrift
   (E) the fact that the earth is inanimate and lacking will

21. The author mentions "industry and honesty and equality" (lines 34–35) in order to make the point that

   (A) some moral habits are not as valuable as many claim
   (B) fate tends to favor those who are virtuous
   (C) too many people disdain ethical behavior
   (D) the natural order reflects a moral order
   (E) hard work and morality are their own reward

22. The "fate" mentioned in line 35 is the fate of

   (A) the hard-working farmer
   (B) the theorist who preaches honesty and equality
   (C) the gambler
   (D) the owner of private property
   (E) the socialist

23. The author qualifies his view of the "Social Democratic State" by indicating that it

   (A) appeals to the gambling instinct
   (B) will discourage workers from being industrious
   (C) places a high value on selfishness
   (D) encourages people to be wasteful
   (E) has not yet been attempted

24. The sentence "Our own choice . . . its protection" (lines 59–66) suggests that most people of the author's era

   (A) are deeply religious
   (B) are becoming skeptical of the concept of respectability
   (C) place a high value on the concept of private property
   (D) desire a socialist democratic state
   (E) are not as industrious as they believe themselves to be

STOP

If you finish before time is called, you may check your work on this section only. Do not turn to any other section of the test.

7   **7**   **7**   **7**   **7**   **7**

SECTION 7
Time—20 minutes
16 questions

> **Turn to Section 7 of your answer sheet to answer the questions in this section.**

Directions: For this section, solve each problem and decide which is the best of the choices given. Fill in the corresponding circle on the answer sheet. You may use any available space for scratchwork.

Notes

1. The use of a calculator is permitted.

2. All numbers used are real numbers.

3. Figures that accompany problems in this test are intended to provide information useful in solving the problems. They are drawn as accurately as possible EXCEPT when it is stated in a specific problem that the figure is not drawn to scale. All figures lie in a plane unless otherwise indicated.

4. Unless otherwise specified, the domain of any function f is assumed to be the set of all real numbers x for which $f(x)$ is a real number.

Reference Information

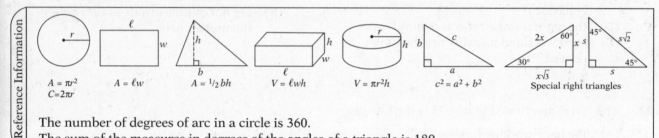

$A = \pi r^2$ $A = \ell w$ $A = \frac{1}{2}bh$ $V = \ell wh$ $V = \pi r^2 h$ $c^2 = a^2 + b^2$ Special right triangles
$C = 2\pi r$

The number of degrees of arc in a circle is 360.
The sum of the measures in degrees of the angles of a triangle is 180.

---

1. If $3x + 5x + 8x = 32$, what is the value of x?

   (A) 1
   (B) 2
   (C) 3
   (D) 4
   (E) 5

2. If $\left(\dfrac{1}{x}\right)\left(\dfrac{x}{3}\right)(6x) = 8$, then $x =$

   (A) 1
   (B) 2
   (C) 3
   (D) 4
   (E) 5

3. If $5b - 10 \geq 15$, which of the following expresses all of the possible values of b?

   (A) $b \geq 5$
   (B) $b \geq 1$
   (C) $b \geq 9$
   (D) $b \leq 1$
   (E) $b \leq 5$

4. If $t\%$ of 60 is equal to 30% of 50, what is the value of t?

   (A) 12
   (B) 15
   (C) 25
   (D) 30
   (E) 35

GO ON TO THE NEXT PAGE

7   7   7   7   7   7

5. If it takes 40 minutes to write h holiday cards, then in terms of h, how many holiday cards can be written at that rate in 8 hours?

(A) $\dfrac{5}{h}$

(B) $8h$

(C) $12h$

(D) $\dfrac{5}{h}$

(E) $\dfrac{12}{h}$

6. Which of the labeled points on the number line above could represent the product -1.5×1.25?

(A) A
(B) B
(C) C
(D) D
(E) E

7. If four people share 100 baseball cards and each person must receive a different positive whole number of cards, what is the <u>greatest</u> possible number of cards any one person may have?

(A) 28
(B) 29
(C) 94
(D) 95
(E) 97

FUEL EFFICIENCY OVER TIME

Age of car (in years)	1	2	3	4	5
Miles per gallon	36	35	31	26	20

8. Which of the following graphs best represents the data presented in the table above?

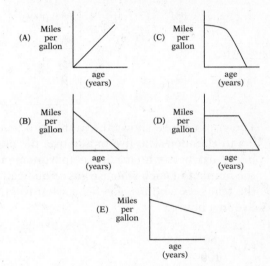

9. If the sum of seven integers is even, at most how many of these integers could be odd?

(A) 3
(B) 4
(C) 5
(D) 6
(E) 7

GO ON TO THE NEXT PAGE ⇒

7   **7**   **7**   **7**   **7**   **7**

10. In a particular year, if January 22 is the fourth Wednesday of the month, what is the date of the fourth Monday in January?

   (A)   January 20
   (B)   January 21
   (C)   January 26
   (D)   January 27
   (E)   January 28

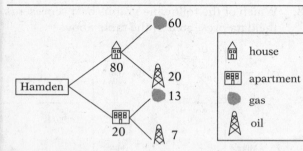

11. The graph above shows the number of teachers in Hamden who live in a house, the number of teachers who live in an apartment, and the number of each who use gas or oil heat. Of the teachers who use gas heat, what fraction live in a house?

   (A) $\dfrac{60}{100}$

   (B) $\dfrac{73}{100}$

   (C) $\dfrac{60}{80}$

   (D) $\dfrac{60}{73}$

   (E) $\dfrac{73}{80}$

12. If $5x + 7y = 18$ and $2x - 4y = 6$, what is the value of $7x + 3y$?

   (A)   7
   (B)   12
   (C)   19
   (D)   24
   (E)   31

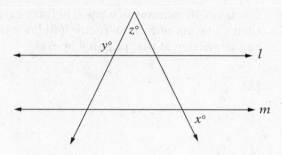

13. In the figure above, if $l \parallel m$, what is the value of x in terms of y and z?

   (A) $y - z$
   (B) $z - y$
   (C) $z + y$
   (D) $180 - y - z$
   (E) $90 - z - y$

14. Julie Ann commutes to work one morning at an average speed of 40 mph. She returns home along the same route at an average speed of 24 mph. If she spends a total of 2 hours traveling to and from work that day, how many miles is her commute to work?

   (A)   24
   (B)   30
   (C)   32
   (D)   34
   (E)   40

GO ON TO THE NEXT PAGE

7   7   7   7   7   7

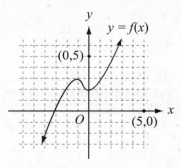

15. Given the graph of $y = f(x)$ above, which of the following represents the graph of $y = f(x-2) + 4$?

(A)
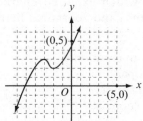

(B)
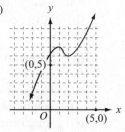

(C)
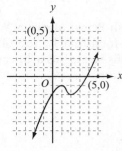

(D)
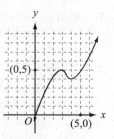

(E)
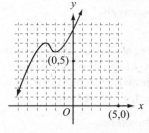

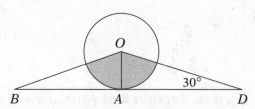

Note: Figure not drawn to scale.

16. Line segment $\overline{BD}$ is tangent to the circle with center O at point A. If $DO = BO = 12$, what is the area of the <u>unshaded</u> region of $\triangle BOD$?

(A) $36\sqrt{3} - 12\pi$

(B) $36\sqrt{2} - 12\pi$

(C) $36 - 12\pi$

(D) $72\sqrt{2} - 36\pi$

(E) $72\sqrt{3} - 36\pi$

STOP

If you finish before time is called, you may check your work on this section only. Do not turn to any other section of the test.

8   **8**   **8**   **8**   **8**   **8**

SECTION 8
Time—20 minutes
19 questions

> ## Turn to Section 8 of your answer sheet to answer the questions in this section.

> **Directions:** For each question in this section, select the best answer from among the choices given and fill in the corresponding circle on the answer sheet.

Each sentence below has one or two blanks, each blank indicating that something has been omitted. Beneath the sentence are five words or sets of words labeled A through E. Choose the word or set of words that, when inserted in the sentence, best fits the meaning of the sentence as a whole.

EXAMPLE:

Rather than accepting the theory unquestioningly, Deborah regarded it with -----.

(A) mirth
(B) sadness
(C) responsibility
(D) ignorance
(E) skepticism

---

1. The ------- with which technology is advancing makes it difficult for businesses to stay current, and as a result, they often find themselves using ------- equipment.

   (A) urgency . . progressive
   (B) swiftness . . conventional
   (C) torpidity . . antiquated
   (D) lassitude . . innovative
   (E) rapidity . . outdated

2. The ------- of James Joyce's early works, which used clear prose to reveal the inner dimensions of his characters, gave way to ------- and arcane style of writing in such books as *Ulysses* and *Finnegan's, Wake*, which explored character through neologisms and obscure literary tricks.

   (A) inspiration . . an emotional
   (B) lucidity . . an opaque
   (C) vagueness . . a simple
   (D) popularity . . a concise
   (E) anachronism . . a derivative

3. Critics of former British Prime Minister Winston Churchill complained that he too often acted -------, choosing his strategies arbitrarily without much explanation.

   (A) diligently
   (B) impulsively
   (C) viciously
   (D) malevolently
   (E) savagely

4. Sixteenth-century British monarch Henry VIII was a king who demanded ------- from his courtiers; he did not hesitate to execute anyone who acted irreverently.

   (A) insolence
   (B) impudence
   (C) truculence
   (D) deference
   (E) ignominy

GO ON TO THE NEXT PAGE ⟶

5. In the 1600s, Italian scientist Galileo Galilei was ------- and sentenced to life in prison for being a ------- when, contrary to church teachings, he proposed that the sun, rather than the earth, was the center of the universe.

   (A) ostracized . . hermit
   (B) venerated . . demagogue
   (C) hallowed . . revisionist
   (D) denounced . . heretic
   (E) reviled . . luminary

6. Known for her ------- and iconoclastic stance on most political matters, the Senator had a hard time securing the votes of the more ------- party members during her presidential campaign.

   (A) contentious . . orthodox
   (B) controversial . . litigious
   (C) disingenuous . . vituperative
   (D) dissident . . idolatrous
   (E) heretical . . polemical

The passages below are followed by questions based on their content; questions following a pair of related passages may also be based on the relationship between the paired passages. Answer the questions on the basis of what is <u>stated</u> or <u>implied</u> in the passage and in any introductory material that may be provided.

Questions 7–19 are based on the following passages.

The following passages present two viewpoints on the assimilation of ex-slaves into American culture in the late 19th century. Passage 1 is from a speech given by Booker T. Washington, an African American ex-slave and prominent educator, at the Atlanta Exposition in 1895. Passage 2 is an excerpt from a paper entitled The Conservation of Races *written by W. E. B. Du Bois in 1897.*

PASSAGE 1

A ship lost at sea for many days suddenly sighted a friendly vessel. From the mast of the
Line unfortunate vessel was seen a signal, "Water, water; we die of thirst!" The answer from the
5 friendly vessel at once came back, "Cast down your bucket where you are." And a second, third and fourth signal for water were answered, "Cast down your bucket where you are." The captain of the distressed vessel, at last

10 heeding the injunction, cast down his bucket, and it came up full of fresh, sparkling water from the mouth of the Amazon River. To those of my race who depend upon bettering their condition in a foreign land or who underesti-
15 mate the importance of cultivating friendly relations with the Southern white man, who is their next-door neighbor, I would say: "Cast down your bucket where you are"—cast it down in making friends in every manly way of the peo-
20 ple of all races by whom we are surrounded.

Cast it down in agriculture, in mechanics, in commerce, in domestic service, and in the professions. And in this connection it is well to bear, when it comes to business, pure and
25 simple, it is in the South that the Negro[1] is given a man's chance in the commercial world, and in nothing is this Exposition more eloquent than in emphasizing this chance. Our greatest danger is that in the great leap
30 from slavery to freedom we may overlook the fact that the masses of us are to live by the production of our hands, and fail to keep in mind that we shall prosper in proportion as we learn to dignify and glorify common labor
35 and put brains and skill into the common occupations of life; shall prosper in proportion as we learn to draw the line between the superficial and the substantial, the ornamental gew-gaws of life and the useful. No race can
40 prosper till it learns that there is as much dignity in tilling a field as in writing a poem. It is at the bottom of life we must begin, and not at the top. Nor should we permit our grievances to overshadow our opportunities.

45 To those of the white race who look to the incoming of those of foreign birth and strange tongue and habits for the prosperity of the South, were I permitted I would repeat what I say to my own race, "Cast down your bucket
50 where you are." Cast it down among the eight millions of Negroes whose habits you know, whose fidelity and love you have tested in days when to have proved treacherous meant the ruin of your firesides. Cast down your bucket among
55 these people who have, without strikes and labor wars, tilled your fields, cleared your

[1]African American

GO ON TO THE NEXT PAGE ➡

forests, built your railroads and cities, and
brought forth treasures from the bowels of the
earth, and helped make possible this magnifi-
60 cent representation of the progress of the South.
Casting down your bucket among my people,
helping and encouraging them as you are doing
on these grounds, and to education of head,
hand and heart, you will find that they will buy
65 your surplus land, make blossom the waste
places in your fields, and run your factories.

PASSAGE 2

Here, then, is the dilemma, and it is a puz-
zling one, I admit. No Negro who has given
earnest thought to the situation of his people in
70 America has failed, at some time in life, to find
himself at these cross-roads; has failed to ask
himself at some time: What, after all, am I? Am
I an American or am I a Negro? Can I be both?
Or is it my duty to cease to be a Negro as soon
75 as possible and be an American? If I strive as a
Negro, am I not perpetuating the very cleft that
threatens and separates Black and White
America? Is not my only possible practical aim
the subduction of all that is Negro in me to the
80 American? Does my black blood place upon me
any more obligation to assert my nationality
than German, or Irish or Italian blood would?

It is such incessant self-questioning and the
hesitation that arises from it, that is making the
85 present period a time of vacillation and contradiction for the American Negro; combined race
action is stifled, race responsibility is shirked,
race enterprises languish, and the best blood, the
best talent, the best energy of the Negro people
90 cannot be marshalled to do the bidding of the
race. They stand back to make room for every
rascal and demagogue who chooses to cloak his
selfish deviltry under the veil of race pride.

Is this right? Is it rational? Is it good policy?
95 Have we in America a distinct mission as a
race—a distinct sphere of action and an opportunity for race development, or is self-
obliteration the highest end to which Negro
blood dare aspire?

100 If we carefully consider what race prejudice
really is, we find it, historically, to be nothing
but the friction between different groups of
people; it is the difference in aim, in feeling, in
ideals of two different races; if, now, this dif-
105 ference exists touching territory, laws,

language, or even religion, it is manifest that
these people cannot live in the same territory
without fatal collision; but if, on the other
hand, there is substantial agreement in laws,
110 language and religion; if there is a satisfactory
adjustment of economic life, then there is no
reason why, in the same country and on the
same street, two or three great national ideals
might not thrive and develop, that men of dif-
115 ferent races might not strive together for their
race ideals as well, perhaps even better, than
in isolation. Here, it seems to me, is the reading of the riddle that puzzles so many of us.
We are Americans, not only by birth and by
120 citizenship, but by our political ideals, our
language, our religion. Farther than that, our
Americanism does not go. At that point, we
are Negroes, members of a vast historic race
that from the very dawn of creation has slept,
125 but half awakening in the dark forests of its
African fatherland. We are the first fruits of
this new nation, the harbinger of that black
tomorrow which is yet destined to soften the
whiteness of the Teutonic today. We are that
130 people whose subtle sense of song has given
America its only American music, its only
American fairy tales, its only touch of pathos
and humor amid its mad money-getting plu-
tocracy. As such, it is our duty to conserve our
135 physical powers, our intellectual endowments,
our spiritual ideals; as a race we must strive
by race organization, by race solidarity, by
race unity to the realization of that broader
humanity which freely recognizes differences
140 in men, but sternly deprecates inequality in
their opportunities of development.

7. Passage 1 is primarily concerned with

(A) educating former slave owners about the
social plight of African Americans
(B) describing the many cultural contribu-
tions of African Americans
(C) presenting an argument for creating
schools to educate former slaves
(D) convincing African Americans and white
Americans to work together to build a
vibrant Southern economy
(E) preventing future labor strikes

GO ON TO THE NEXT PAGE

8   8   8   8   8   8

8. The author of Passage 1 specifically addresses each of the following audiences EXCEPT

(A) Southern whites who were active in the movement to end slavery
(B) Southern whites who are considering hiring foreign laborers
(C) African Americans who seek to improve their social conditions
(D) Southern whites who have employed African Americans in the past
(E) African Americans who do not consider it necessary to build friendly relationships with Southern whites

9. Passage 1 suggests that, upon hearing the first response from the friendly vessel, the captain of the distressed vessel was

(A) elated
(B) arrogant
(C) incredulous
(D) indifferent
(E) angry

10. In lines 23–28 ("And in this connection . . . emphasizing this chance,") the author of Passage 1 suggests that the Exposition at which he is speaking

(A) is overly concerned with superficial things
(B) does not represent the full spectrum of the American population
(C) provides excellent economic opportunities for African Americans
(D) is in distress, much like the ship in his story
(E) will encourage African Americans to seek employment in the North

11. The author of Passage 1 mentions "writing a poem" in line 41 in order to suggest that

(A) manual labor is a worthy activity
(B) poetry can convey emotions more effectively than prose
(C) expanding literacy should be a major focus of the Exposition
(D) African Americans should consider careers in writing
(E) political leaders should be more articulate

12. The questions in lines 72–82 are intended to represent the thoughts of

(A) a former slave owner
(B) one who is doubtful about the morality of slavery
(C) an African American who is seeking a new life in a foreign country
(D) an African American who is concerned with the issue of race identity
(E) any political leader who represents a substantial population of African Americans

13. In line 90, the word "marshalled" most nearly means

(A) arrested
(B) discovered
(C) organized for a purpose
(D) interrogated
(E) determined

14. Lines 91–93 ("They stand back . . . the veil of race pride,") suggest that those who incessantly question themselves run the risk of

(A) violating the law
(B) alienating friends
(C) losing gainful employment
(D) falling under the influence of disreputable people
(E) squandering their education

15. The phrase "that point" (line 122) refers to the boundary between

(A) the needs of the dominant class of society and the needs of the minority classes
(B) the past and the future
(C) white Americans and African Americans
(D) the qualities that bind all Americans and the qualities that make one race unique
(E) those who support racial discrimination and those who oppose it

GO ON TO THE NEXT PAGE ⟶

8   8   8   8   8   8

---

16. The term "broader humanity" (lines 138–139) refers to people who

(A) hinder the progress of African Americans

(B) acknowledge the substantial cultural contributions African Americans have made to American culture

(C) believe that all races deserve equal opportunity in society

(D) seek a better life outside of their home countries

(E) have little understanding of cultures beyond their own

17. The two passages differ in their characterizations of the contributions of African Americans to American culture in that Passage 1 emphasizes

(A) agricultural contributions, while Passage 2 emphasizes scientific innovations

(B) religious heritage, while Passage 2 emphasizes political contributions

(C) musical innovations, while Passage 2 emphasizes social contributions

(D) contributions of the past, while Passage 2 focuses only on potential contributions in the future

(E) economic contributions, while Passage 2 emphasizes artistic contributions

18. Unlike the "black tomorrow" (lines 127–128) described in Passage 2, the vision of the future of African Americans described in Passage 1 involves

(A) the incorporation of African Americans into the dominant system rather than a change in dominant American cultural values

(B) the restructuring of political institutions rather than maintenance of the status quo

(C) the reeducation of all Americans rather than the submission of one race to another

(D) a strong reliance on the lessons of the past rather than a complete rejection of the past

(E) travel to foreign lands rather than the commitment to stay in America

19. Which of the following best characterizes the tone each author takes toward the dominant American culture of his time?

(A) The author of Passage 1 is sarcastic, while the author of Passage 2 is respectful.

(B) The author of Passage 1 is tongue-in-cheek, while the author of Passage 2 is didactic.

(C) The author of Passage 1 is aggressive, while the author of Passage 2 is nonchalant.

(D) The author of Passage 1 is pontifical, while the author of Passage 2 is colloquial.

(E) The author of Passage 1 is deferential, while the author of Passage 2 is assertive.

If you finish before time is called, you may
check your work on this section only. Do not
turn to any other section of the test.

9   9   9   9   9   9

SECTION 9
Time—10 minutes
14 questions

Turn to Section 9 of your answer sheet to answer the questions in this section.

Directions: For each question in this section, select the best answer from among the choices given and fill in the corresponding circle on the answer sheet.

The following sentences test correctness and effectiveness of expression. Part of each sentence or the entire sentence is underlined; beneath each sentence are five ways of phrasing the underlined material. Choice A repeats the original phrasing; the other four choices are different. If you think the original phrasing produces a better sentence than any of the alternatives, select choice A; if not, select one of the other choices.

In making your selection, follow the requirements of standard written English; that is, pay attention to grammar, choice of words, sentence construction, and punctuation. Your selection should result in the most effective sentence— clear and precise, without awkwardness or ambiguity.

EXAMPLE:

The children couldn't hardly believe their eyes.

(A) couldn't hardly believe their eyes
(B) could hardly believe their eyes
(C) would not hardly believe their eyes
(D) couldn't nearly believe their eyes
(E) couldn't hardly believe his or her eyes

1. Neither the strength of the army nor how agile they were was able to compensate for the superior strategy of its enemy.

   (A) nor how agile they were
   (B) nor their agility
   (C) nor its agility
   (D) or how agile it was
   (E) or its agility

2. Although Georgia preferred to perform with her fellow band members, they were not used by her when she sang at the opening ceremony.

   (A) they were not used by her
   (B) they were not used by she
   (C) it was her who did not use them
   (D) she had not used them
   (E) she did not use them

3. Without rehearsing at all the previous week, the troupe performed the first act of the play in full costume.

   (A) Without rehearsing
   (B) Being that they didn't rehearse
   (C) They didn't rehearse
   (D) Without having rehearsed
   (E) They hadn't even rehearsed

GO ON TO THE NEXT PAGE

9   9   9   9   9   9

4. Not since the beginning of the resistance movement <u>has the major media outlets acknowledged the scope of the opposition</u>.

(A) has the major media outlets acknowledged the scope of the opposition
(B) have the major media outlets acknowledged the scope of the opposition
(C) have the scope of the opposition been acknowledged by the major media outlets
(D) has it been acknowledged by the major media outlets what the scope is of the opposition
(E) have the major media outlets been acknowledging the scope of the opposition

5. We would be healthier today <u>if we have had to hunt and scavenge</u> for our food as our ancestors did.

(A) if we have had to hunt and scavenge
(B) having hunted and scavenged
(C) if we would have hunted and scavenged
(D) for hunting and scavenging
(E) if we had to hunt and scavenge

6. <u>Against popular opinion</u>, college students with strong reasoning skills are more successful than students with strong memorization skills.

(A) Against popular opinion
(B) Not what popular opinion says
(C) Contrary to popular opinion
(D) Opposite to what popular opinion says
(E) Contrary to what popular opinion says

7. The school renovations should be planned <u>so as to minimize disruption and inconvenience to teachers and students</u>.

(A) so as to minimize disruption and inconvenience to teachers and students
(B) for the minimizing of disruptions and inconvenience to teachers and students
(C) so that teachers and students have minimum disruptions and inconvenience
(D) to minimize disruption and inconvenience on the part of teachers and students
(E) in order for the minimization of disruption and inconvenience to teachers and students

8. Dina, having struggled for months <u>to find a job as a writer; she finally</u> took a position at a local advertising agency.

(A) to find a job as a writer; she finally
(B) to find a job as a writer, finally
(C) for finding a job as a writer, finally
(D) finding a job as a writer, finally
(E) to find a job as a writer, so she finally

9. The fall of the Roman Empire was precipitated not so much by foreign invaders as <u>by the delusions and indulgences of its ruling class</u>.

(A) by the delusions and indulgences of its ruling class
(B) because of the delusions and indulgences of their ruling class
(C) the delusions and indulgences of its ruling class did
(D) it was by the delusions and indulgences of its ruling class
(E) the delusions and indulgences of its ruling class

10. If the preliminary sales numbers are reliable, then Hannigan's first book appears <u>like it is a success</u>.

(A) like it is a success
(B) like a success
(C) a success
(D) to be a success
(E) as a success

11. The response to the revised proposal has been much more favorable than <u>the original one</u>.

(A) the original one
(B) the original one was
(C) the response to the original one
(D) to the one that was originally given
(E) to the original one

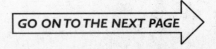

GO ON TO THE NEXT PAGE

9   9   9   9   9   9

12. The discovery was made by a team of <u>scientists trying to locate a gene responsible for producing a particular enzyme, but they found instead</u> a set of genetic triggers for a predisposition to heart disease.

(A) scientists trying to locate a gene responsible for producing a particular enzyme, but they found instead

(B) scientists; trying to locate a gene responsible for producing a particular enzyme, but they found instead

(C) scientists who, trying to locate a gene responsible for producing a particular enzyme, instead found

(D) scientists that tried to locate a gene responsible for producing a particular enzyme, instead finding

(E) scientists who instead, in trying to find a gene responsible for producing a particular enzyme, found

13. The strongest opposition to the sale of alcohol in the United States came in the late nineteenth century, <u>and this is the time when religious movements</u> preaching temperance were sweeping the nation.

(A) and this is the time when religious movements

(B) when religious movements were

(C) and this is when religious movements

(D) at the time in which religious movements were

(E) when religious movements

14. Professor Angleton valued conciseness highly, telling his students to edit their papers thoroughly <u>for eliminating any extra superfluous</u> information in the text.

(A) for eliminating any extra superfluous

(B) to eliminate any extra superfluous

(C) and eliminate any superfluous

(D) having eliminated any superfluous

(E) in eliminating any superfluous

STOP

If you finish before time is called, you may check your work on this section only. Do not turn to any other section of the test.

ANSWER KEY

Critical Reading

Section 3

	COR. ANS.	DIFF. LEV.		COR. ANS.	DIFF. LEV.
1.	A	1	13.	D	3
2.	D	2	14.	E	2
3.	B	3	15.	A	4
4.	C	3	16.	B	5
5.	C	3	17.	A	4
6.	E	4	18.	C	3
7.	B	4	19.	E	3
8.	D	4	20.	B	2
9.	B	4	21.	D	3
10.	D	2	22.	E	5
11.	B	1	23.	B	4
12.	A	3	24.	C	4

Number correct

Number incorrect

Section 6

	COR. ANS.	DIFF. LEV.		COR. ANS.	DIFF. LEV.
1.	B	1	13.	B	4
2.	D	1	14.	E	4
3.	C	3	15.	C	3
4.	A	4	16.	A	4
5.	A	5	17.	A	4
6.	B	3	18.	C	3
7.	D	2	19.	D	3
8.	C	4	20.	B	1
9.	E	4	21.	A	3
10.	E	2	22.	C	3
11.	C	3	23.	E	3
12.	A	3	24.	C	4

Number correct

Number incorrect

Section 8

	COR. ANS.	DIFF. LEV.		COR. ANS.	DIFF. LEV.
1.	E	1	11.	A	3
2.	B	3	12.	D	4
3.	B	2	13.	C	3
4.	D	4	14.	D	5
5.	D	5	15.	D	3
6.	A	5	16.	C	4
7.	D	4	17.	E	3
8.	A	3	18.	A	5
9.	C	2	19.	E	4
10.	C	3			

Number correct

Number incorrect

Math

Section 2

	COR. ANS.	DIFF. LEV.		COR. ANS.	DIFF. LEV.
1.	C	1	11.	D	4
2.	D	1	12.	B	3
3.	A	2	13.	C	3
4.	D	2	14.	B	4
5.	B	2	15.	E	4
6.	D	2	16.	B	3
7.	E	2	17.	E	5
8.	D	3	18.	A	4
9.	C	3	19.	C	5
10.	C	3	20.	C	4

Number correct

Number incorrect

Section 5

Multiple-Choice Questions

	COR. ANS.	DIFF. LEV.
1.	B	1
2.	A	2
3.	D	3
4.	E	3
5.	D	3
6.	C	4
7.	C	4
8.	B	5

Student-produced Response questions

	COR. ANS.	DIFF. LEV.
9.	135	2
10.	104	2
11.	30	2
12.	3	3
13.	18	3
14.	28	4
15.	45	4
16.	22.5	4
17.	12	4
18.	37.5	5

Number correct

Number incorrect

Number correct (9–18)

Section 7

	COR. ANS.	DIFF. LEV.		COR. ANS.	DIFF. LEV.
1.	B	1	10.	D	3
2.	D	2	11.	D	4
3.	A	2	12.	D	3
4.	C	3	13.	A	4
5.	C	3	14.	B	5
6.	A	3	15.	B	5
7.	C	3	16.	A	5
8.	C	3			
9.	D	3			

Number correct

Number incorrect

Writing

Section 4

	COR. ANS.	DIFF. LEV.		COR. ANS.	DIFF. LEV.		COR. ANS.	DIFF. LEV.		COR. ANS.	DIFF. LEV.
1.	B	1	11.	A	4	21.	C	4	31.	C	3
2.	A	1	12.	B	1	22.	B	4	32.	D	3
3.	E	2	13.	D	3	23.	D	5	33.	E	3
4.	D	2	14.	E	3	24.	E	4	34.	A	3
5.	D	4	15.	B	3	25.	B	3	35.	D	3
6.	A	2	16.	B	3	26.	C	4			
7.	C	3	17.	D	4	27.	C	4			
8.	D	3	18.	D	5	28.	A	5			
9.	B	3	19.	B	3	29.	D	4			
10.	E	3	20.	E	3	30.	B	4			

Number correct

Number incorrect

Section 9

	COR. ANS.	DIFF. LEV.		COR. ANS.	DIFF. LEV.
1.	C	1	8.	B	4
2.	E	2	9.	A	4
3.	D	2	10.	D	3
4.	B	3	11.	C	4
5.	E	4	12.	C	4
6.	C	3	13.	E	3
7.	A	3	14.	C	5

Number correct

Number incorrect

NOTE: Difficulty levels are estimates of question difficulty that range from 1 (easiest) to 5 (hardest).

SCORE CONVERSION TABLE

How to score your test

Use the answer key on the previous page to determine your raw score on each section. **Your raw score on each section except Section 5 is simply the number of correct answers minus ¼ of the number of wrong answers. On Section 5, your raw score is the sum of the number of correct answers for questions 1–18 minus ¼ of the number of wrong answers for questions 1–8.** Next, add the raw scores from Sections 3, 6, and 8 to get your Critical Reading raw score, add the raw scores from Sections 2, 5, and 7 to get your Math raw score, and add the raw scores from Sections 4 and 9 to get your Writing raw score. Write the three raw scores here:

Raw Critical Reading score: _____   Raw Math score: _____   Raw Writing score: _____

Use the table below to convert these to scaled scores.

Scaled scores: Critical Reading: _____   Math: _____   Writing: _____

Raw Score	Critical Reading Scaled Score	Math Scaled Score	Writing Scaled Score	Raw Score	Critical Reading Scaled Score	Math Scaled Score	Writing Scaled Score
67	800			32	520	570	610
66	800			31	510	560	600
65	790			30	510	550	580
64	780			29	500	540	570
63	770			28	490	530	560
62	750			27	490	520	550
61	740			26	480	510	540
60	730			25	480	500	530
59	720			24	470	490	520
58	700			23	460	480	510
57	690			22	460	480	500
56	680			21	450	470	490
55	670			20	440	460	480
54	660	800		19	440	450	470
53	650	800		18	430	450	460
52	650	780		17	420	440	450
51	640	760		16	420	430	440
50	630	740		15	410	420	440
49	620	730	800	14	400	410	430
48	620	710	800	13	400	410	420
47	610	710	800	12	390	400	410
46	600	700	790	11	380	390	400
45	600	690	780	10	370	380	390
44	590	680	760	9	360	370	380
43	590	670	740	8	350	360	380
42	580	660	730	7	340	350	370
41	570	650	710	6	330	340	360
40	570	640	700	5	320	330	350
39	560	630	690	4	310	320	340
38	550	620	670	3	300	310	320
37	550	620	660	2	280	290	310
36	540	610	650	1	270	280	300
35	540	600	640	0	250	260	280
34	530	590	630	−1	230	240	270
33	520	580	620	−2 or less	210	220	250

SCORE CONVERSION TABLE FOR WRITING COMPOSITE
[ESSAY + MULTIPLE CHOICE]

Calculate your Writing raw score as you did on the previous page and grade your essay from a 1 to a 6 according to the standards that follow in the detailed answer key.

Essay score: _____   Raw Writing score: _____

Use the table below to convert these to scaled scores.

Scaled score: Writing: _____

Raw Score	Essay Score 0	Essay Score 1	Essay Score 2	Essay Score 3	Essay Score 4	Essay Score 5	Essay Score 6
−2 or less	200	230	250	280	310	340	370
−1	210	240	260	290	320	360	380
0	230	260	280	300	340	370	400
1	240	270	290	320	350	380	410
2	250	280	300	330	360	390	420
3	260	290	310	340	370	400	430
4	270	300	320	350	380	410	440
5	280	310	330	360	390	420	450
6	290	320	340	360	400	430	460
7	290	330	340	370	410	440	470
8	300	330	350	380	410	450	470
9	310	340	360	390	420	450	480
10	320	350	370	390	430	460	490
11	320	360	370	400	440	470	500
12	330	360	380	410	440	470	500
13	340	370	390	420	450	480	510
14	350	380	390	420	460	490	520
15	350	380	400	430	460	500	530
16	360	390	410	440	470	500	530
17	370	400	420	440	480	510	540
18	380	410	420	450	490	520	550
19	380	410	430	460	490	530	560
20	390	420	440	470	500	530	560
21	400	430	450	480	510	540	570
22	410	440	460	480	520	550	580
23	420	450	470	490	530	560	590
24	420	460	470	500	540	570	600
25	430	460	480	510	540	580	610
26	440	470	490	520	550	590	610
27	450	480	500	530	560	590	620
28	460	490	510	540	570	600	630
29	470	500	520	550	580	610	640
30	480	510	530	560	590	620	650
31	490	520	540	560	600	630	660
32	500	530	550	570	610	640	670
33	510	540	550	580	620	650	680
34	510	550	560	590	630	660	690
35	520	560	570	600	640	670	700
36	530	560	580	610	650	680	710
37	540	570	590	620	660	690	720
38	550	580	600	630	670	700	730
39	560	600	610	640	680	710	740
40	580	610	620	650	690	720	750
41	590	620	640	660	700	730	760
42	600	630	650	680	710	740	770
43	610	640	660	690	720	750	780
44	620	660	670	700	740	770	800
45	640	670	690	720	750	780	800
46	650	690	700	730	770	800	800
47	670	700	720	750	780	800	800
48	680	720	730	760	800	800	800
49	680	720	730	760	800	800	800

Detailed Answer Key

Section 1

Consider carefully the issue discussed in the following passage, then write an essay that answers the question posed in the assignment.

> We like to believe that physical phenomena, animals, people, and societies obey predictable rules, but such rules, even when carefully ascertained, have their limits. Every rule has its exceptions.

Assignment: **What is one particularly interesting "exception" to a rule?** Write an essay in which you answer this question and discuss your point of view on this issue. Support your position logically with examples from literature, the arts, history, politics, science and technology, current events, or your experience or observation.

The following essay received 12 points out of a possible 12. This means that it demonstrates clear and consistent competence in that it

- develops an insightful point of view on the topic
- demonstrates exemplary critical thinking
- uses effective examples, reasons, and other evidence to support its thesis
- is consistently focused, coherent, and well organized
- demonstrates skillful and effective use of language and sentence structure
- is largely (but not necessarily completely) free of grammatical and usage errors

One particularly interesting exception to a rule is the orbit of Mercury. For hundreds of years, Sir Isaac Newton's laws of motion and gravity stood as a testament to the power of mathematics to describe the universe. Newton's equations showed that the moon did not revolve around the earth because the gods willed it to, or because of the abstract perfection of a circular orbit. Rather, it circled the earth because doing so obeyed a simple mathematical formula: Newton's Universal Law of Gravitation. It was a singular achievement in the history of science.

The equation was not only elegant, but enormously powerful. It was used to predict the existence of two new planets before they were even seen: Neptune and Pluto. Astronomers actually began to doubt the power of the Universal Law of Gravitation when they noticed that Uranus was not behaving the way the equation said it should. Its orbit was wobblier than Newton's law predicted. Could the law be incorrect? A few careful scientists noticed that the law could still be correct if another planet, further from the sun, were tugging at Uranus. Indeed, astronomers looked carefully and found a planet they called Neptune. As even further confirmation of Newton's law, irregularities in Neptune's orbit led astronomers to find Pluto exerting yet another tiny gravitational tug at the edge of the solar system. It seemed that Newton's equation could do no wrong.

But it was wrong. When astronomers began to notice irregularities in Mercury's orbit, they surmised, naturally, that another planet must be near the sun tugging at Mercury. They even went so far as to call the undiscovered planet Vulcan. But even the most careful observations revealed no such planet. How could this equation, so powerful and elegant, be wrong? It turned out that Newton's equation broke down a bit as gravitational force became great, as it did near the sun. It wasn't until the 20th century that Einstein's theory of General Relativity tweaked Newton's equation to make it explain the precession of Mercury's orbit.

The value of Mercury's orbit, in fact, lies not so much in its ability to "prove" Einstein's theory as in its ability to disprove Newton's. It was the exception to a very powerful rule. It seems to suggest that, in science, nothing is truly sacred; everything must be examined. If one of the most powerful and elegant equations in all of science—one that had been "proven" time and again by rigorous experiment—could turn out to be wrong (albeit only by a tiny bit, in most ordinary circumstances), how much can we trust our own beloved "truths" about our universe? So many of us believe we know at least a few things that are "absolutely true." But can we say that we are more insightful, intelligent, or rigorous than Isaac Newton? Perhaps we should be more like the scientists, and look for the holes in our theories.

The following essay received 8 points out of a possible 12, meaning that it demonstrates *adequate competence* in that it

- develops a point of view on the topic
- demonstrates some critical thinking, but perhaps not consistently
- uses some examples, reasons, and other evidence to support its thesis, but perhaps not adequately
- shows a general organization and focus but shows occasional lapses in this regard
- demonstrates adequate but occasionally inconsistent facility with language
- contains occasional errors in grammar, usage, and mechanics

When we are children, everyone—parents, teachers and friends—tells us that we should never lie. It's even one of the ten commandments in the Bible. This is a rule that many believe should have no exceptions. It is just something you should not do. Lying is bad, and being truthful is good. End of story.

But I believe that this rule has its exceptions, as many rules do. Sometimes lying can even be considered the right thing to do. It's obviously not good to lie just because you don't feel like telling the truth or just because you might look better if you lie. There has to be a good reason to deceive someone in order for it to be a valid action.

For instance, sometimes telling the truth can really hurt a situation more than it helps. For example, my friend is in a dance company, and I went to see her in the Nutcracker dance performance this past weekend. Even though she was pretty good, the whole thing was long, boring, and a lot of the dancers were not very good. I know that she would not want to hear that. So instead of telling her the truth, I lied and told her how great it was. This is what is called a 'white lie.' Yes, I was deceiving her, but there was really very little to come from telling her the truth that the show was a disaster. What is the point of telling the truth there if it is only going to hurt everyone involved?

Recently, I watched a documentary about the Vietnam War. The documentary focused on a troop of 25 soldiers and their experience in the war and how they grew closer together as a group as the time went by. One of the soldiers, a 16 year old boy who had lied about his age so that he could fight, died because he made a bad decision and chased after a Vietnamese soldier into the woods without anyone else to back him up. Part of the reasoning behind this action, they explained, was because he spent his entire life trying to prove to his parents that he was not a failure at everything and that he could be a hero. A fellow troopmate knew what he had done, knew the struggle for respect he was going through at home, and wrote the formal letter home to the family telling them how their son had died in an honorable fashion saving several members of the troop with his heroism. Some might argue that it was bad to lie about his death, but I would argue that this was a valiant thing done by the soldier who wrote the letter because it allowed the family to feel better about the death of their young son in a war so many miles away.

To summarize, in general, it is best not to lie. But there are in fact situations where it is better to tell partial truths than the whole truth. It is important to avoid lying whenever possible, but it is also important to know when it is OK to tell a slight variation to the truth.

> The following essay received 4 points out of a possible 12, meaning that it demonstrates *some incompetence* in that it
>
> - has a seriously limited point of view
> - demonstrates weak critical thinking
> - uses inappropriate or insufficient examples, reasons, and other evidence to support its thesis
> - is poorly focused and organized and has serious problems with coherence
> - demonstrates frequent problems with language and sentence structure
> - contains errors in grammar and usage that seriously obscure the author's meaning

A lot of rules have exceptions because there are different circumstances for everybody and also people grow up and the old rules don't apply anymore. One afternoon back in elementary school, I got in trouble when I took my friend's Capri-Sun drink out of his lunchbox and took a sip without asking his permission. My teacher caught me in the act and yelled at me reciting the "Golden Rule." She said: How would you feel if he took your drink and had some without asking you? I guess I would have been pretty annoyed. I hate it when people drink from the same glass as me. It seemed like a pretty fair rule that I should only do things to other people that I would be OK with them doing to me.

This interaction with my 3rd grade teacher stuck with me throughout my education experience and I heard her voice in my head many times as I was about to perform questionable acts upon others around me. It kept me from doing a lot of pranks like I used to do like tie Eric's shoelaces together and putting hot pepper flakes in Steve's sandwich one afternoon while he went off to get himself another cup of water.

But this rule seemed to get a bit more difficult to follow as I got older and found myself in more complex relationships. Sometimes I wanted to be treated in ways that my friends did not want to be treated. I wanted my friends to call me each night so that we could talk and catch up on the day's events so I would call each of them every night to chat. This annoyed my friends though who did not like talking on the phone. Or, I would always point out to my friends when something they were wearing did not look good because I wanted to be told such things so that I did not embarrass myself. This made a LOT of my friends very angry at me and cost me a few good friendships.

"Do unto others" is a rule that requires a bit of thought and a lot of good judgment. Doing unto others things that I was hoping they would do to me sometimes cost myself friendships. I think it is better to reserve that rule for things that I might consider negative rather than positive.

Section 2

1. C It does not matter how big each station is. All that matters is the total area and *how many* stations there are.

$$\text{average} = \frac{\text{total}}{\text{pieces}} = \frac{3{,}600 \text{ ft}^2}{6 \text{ stations}} = 600 \text{ ft}^2$$

2. D Solve for a and b:　　　　　　$3a = 15$

Divide by 3:　　　　　　　　　$a = 5$

　　　　　　　　　　　　　　　$4b = 10$

Divide by 4:　　　　　　　　　$b = 2.5$

Plug in a and b:　　　　$\dfrac{a}{b} = \dfrac{5}{2.5} = 2$

3. A Pick the employee whose line has the largest positive slope. This is Employee 1. Her line has the largest "rise over run." Her salary increases approximately $20,000 in 8 years, or roughly $2,500 per year.

4. D Use unit analysis and solve:

$$100 \text{ children} \times \frac{1 \text{ bucket}}{5 \text{ children}} = 20 \text{ buckets}$$

$$60 \text{ adults} \times \frac{1 \text{ bucket}}{3 \text{ adults}} = 20 \text{ buckets}$$

Total number of buckets $= 20 + 20 = 40$

5. B　　　　　　　$(5x - 3x + 4)(3x + 6x - 2)$

Combine like terms:　　$(2x + 4)(9x - 2)$

FOIL:　　　　　　　$(18x^2 - 4x + 36x - 8)$

Combine like terms:　　$18x^2 + 32x - 8$

6. D

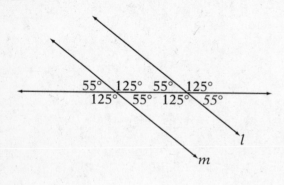

Linear pair:　　　$z + x = 180$

Substitute:　　　$55 + x = 180$

Subtract 55:　　　$x = 125$

Since lines l and m are parallel:

Corresponding:　　　$z = d = 55$

　　　　　　　　　$x = c = 125$

Alternate interior:　　$z = a = 55$

　　　$x = c = 125$

$a + b + c = 55 + 125 + 125 = 305$

7. E　　　　　　　$7\sqrt{x} + 16 = 79$

Subtract 16:　　　　$7\sqrt{x} = 63$

Divide by 7:　　　　$\sqrt{x} = 9$

Square both sides:　　$x = 81$

8. D Work backwards with this problem. Each term, starting with the second, is 2 less than the square root of the previous term. So to work backwards and find the previous term, add 2 and then square the sum:　　　2nd term $= (1 + 2)^2 = 3^2 = 9$

1st term $= (9 + 2)^2 = 11^2 = 121$

9. C Before trying to solve this with geometrical formulas, analyze the figure. The rectangle is divided into 15 squares. Each of the 15 squares is split into 2 identical triangles, which means there are 30 triangles total. Of those 30 triangles, 15 of them are shaded in, or *half* of the figure. This means that half of the area, or 45, is shaded.

10. C The long way:

$\bigstar{16} = 15 + 14 + 13 + 12 + 11 + 10 + 9 + 8 + 7 + 6 + 5 + 4 + 3 + 2 + 1 = 120$

$\bigstar{13} = 12 + 11 + 10 + 9 + 8 + 7 + 6 + 5 + 4 + 3 + 2 + 1 = 78$

$\bigstar{16} - \bigstar{13} = 120 - 78 = 42$

More simply, this can be solved without actually calculating the sums. Just focus on the terms in the sum of

$\bigstar{16}$ that are not "cancelled" by the terms in $\bigstar{13}$:

$\bigstar{16} - \bigstar{13} = 15 + 14 + 13 = 42$

11. **D** Look at the right (units) column first.
$$Y + X = X$$
Subtract X: $Y = 0$
Look at the 10s column: $3 + Y = 3$
Because $Y = 0$, we know there is no carried digit.
Look at the left (1,000s) column:
$$X + 5 = 13$$
Subtract 5: $X = 8$

12. **B** Write out an equation given the average:

$$\frac{x + y + 3y}{3} = 3x$$

Multiply by 3: $x + y + 3y = 9x$
Combine like terms: $x + 4y = 9x$
Subtract x: $4y = 8x$
Divide by 4: $y = 2x$

13. **C**

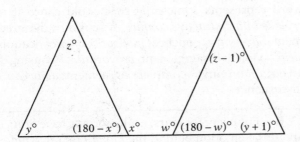

The simplest method is to use the Triangle External Angle theorem, which says that the measure of an "exterior angle" of a triangle equals the sum of the measures of the two "remote interior angles," so $x = y + z$ and $w = (z - 1) + (y + 1) = y + z$. Therefore, $w = x$.

Another, more involved method is to write an equation for each triangle:
Triangle on left: $y + z + (180 - x) = 180$
Subtract 180: $y + z - x = 0$
Add x: $y + z = x$
Triangle on right: $(y + 1) + (z - 1) + (180 - w) = 180$
Subtract 180 and simplify: $y + z - w = 0$
Add w: $y + z = w$
Substitute w for $y + z$: $w = x$

14. **B** Pick a value for r, like 19, that makes this statement true. (r must be 9 more than some multiple of 10.) If r is 19, then $r + 2$ is 21. When 21 is divided by 5, it leaves a remainder of 1.

15. **E**

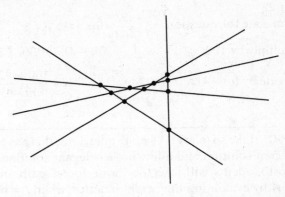

The best way to solve this problem is to draw the lines. With each line you draw, attempt to create as many intersection points as possible. The maximum number of intersection points possible with 5 lines is 10, as shown above.

16. **B** The probability of selecting a king is 1/4, and the probability of selecting a queen is 2/7. To find the probability of randomly choosing a jack, add up the probabilities of choosing a king and a queen and subtract that sum from 1. $\frac{1}{4} + \frac{2}{7}$
Find a common denominator: $\frac{7}{28} + \frac{8}{28} = \frac{15}{28}$
Subtract from 1: $1 - \frac{15}{28} = \frac{13}{28}$

17. **E**

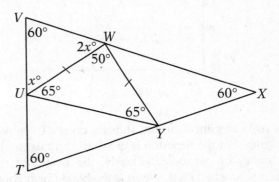

Since $\triangle VXT$ is equilateral, its angles all measure 60°. Mark the diagram as shown.
If $WU = WY$, then $\angle WUY = \angle WYU = 65°$.
$\angle VWU$ ($2x°$) is twice as large as $\angle VUW$ ($x°$).

There are 180 degrees in a triangle: $x + 2x + 60° = 180°$
Combine like terms: $3x + 60° = 180°$
Subtract 60°: $3x = 120°$
Divide by 3: $x = 40°$
The angles on one side of a line add up to 180°:
$$40° + 65° + \angle TUY = 180°$$
Combine like terms: $105° + \angle TUY = 180°$
Subtract 105°: $\angle TUY = 75°$

18. A The question asks: what percent of $m - 4$ is $n + 2$?

Translate the question: $\dfrac{x}{100} \times (m - 4) = n + 2$

Multiply by 100: $x(m - 4) = 100(n + 2)$

Divide by $(m - 4)$: $x = \dfrac{100(n + 2)}{m - 4}$

19. C Like so many SAT math questions, this has an elegant solution and a few not-so-elegant solutions. Most students will take the "brute force" path and start by evaluating the height function when $t = 10$: $h(10) = -5(10)^2 + 120(10) + m = 700 + m$. Then they will try to find the other solution to the equation:

$$700 + m = -5t^2 + 120t + m$$

Subtract $700 + m$: $0 = -5t^2 + 120t - 700$

Factor the quadratic
(the tricky step): $0 = -5(t - 10)(t - 14)$

Apply the 0 product property: $t = 10$ or 14

Obviously, factoring a quadratic can be a pain, but in this problem you can make it easier by remembering that the equation must be true for $t = 10$, which means that you already know one of the factors: $t - 10$.

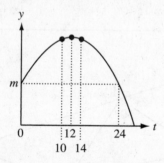

The truly elegant solution, though, comes from recognizing that the function is quadratic and using the symmetry of parabolas. Clearly, the height of the rocket is m when $t = 0$. When is the height next equal to m? The next time that $-5t^2 + 120t$ is equal to 0. This is a much easier quadratic to solve:

$$-5t^2 + 120t = 0$$

Factor: $-5t(t - 24) = 0$

Apply the 0 product property: $t = 0$ or 24

Since these two values of t give the same height, they must be reflections of each other over the parabola's axis of symmetry. The axis of symmetry is therefore halfway between $t = 0$ and $t = 24$, at $t = 12$. (This is when the rocket is at its maximum height.) So when is the rocket at the same height as it is at $t = 10$? At $t = 14$, since 10 and 14 are both the same distance from 12.

20. C Work month by month with the price:

Start of Jan: d
After Jan: $d - .2d = .8d$
After Feb: $.8d + (.4)(.8d) = 1.12d$
After Mar: $1.12d - (.25)(1.12d) = .84d$
After Apr: $.84d + (.25)(.84d) = 1.05d$

Or, more simply, remember that each percent change is a simple multiplication: $d(.8)(1.4)(.75)(1.25) = 1.05d$.

Section 3

1. A The bistro is world-renowned, so it is famous and successful. Both words should be positive. *delectable* = pleasing to the taste; *scrumptious* = delicious; *unpalatable* = bad tasting; *tantalizing* = exciting because kept out of reach; *debilitating* = sapping energy; *savory* = pleasing to the taste

2. D The first word represents something that could put a country on the *brink of war*. The second word represents something that could cause it to *explode into destructive conflict*. *dissension* = disagreement; *harmony* = concord; *instigation* = provocation; *strife* = violent disagreement; *provocation* = rousing of anger; *unanimity* = complete agreement; *agitation* = disturbance

3. B For over 500 years, art historians have argued about the emotion behind the *Mona Lisa*'s *enigmatic* (mysterious) smile. This would make the painting the source of much *debate* or *discussion*. *assent* = agreement; *deliberation* = discussion of all sides of an issue; *concurrence* = agreement; *remuneration* = payment for goods or services; *reconciliation* = the act of resolving an issue

4. C Every year, crowds of people travel to Elvis's hometown to pay *tribute* (respect). Therefore, he was a very *well-respected* or *admired* musician. *satirized* = made fun of, mocked; *unexalted* = not praised; *revered* = respected, worshipped; *despised* = hated; *shunned* = avoided

5. C The poker player uses *tactics* (strategies) to *out-think* his opponents, so his tactics must be intellectual. This is why he is called "the professor." *obscure* = not well understood; *cerebral* = using intellect; *transparent* = easily understood; *outlandish* = bizarre, unusual

6. E   Detractors are critics who would likely say something negative about the aesthetics of the building, whereas its developers would likely claim that the project would be a *great success. adversary* = opponent; *enhancement* = something that improves the appearance or function of something else; *gratuity* = tip; *embellishment* = decoration or exaggeration; *windfall* = unexpected benefit; *defacement* = act of vandalism; *calamity* = disaster; *atrocity* = horrific crime; *boon* = benefit

7. B   Poe wrote tales of cruelty and torture, so they must have been *horrific.* His tales mesmerized his readers, so they must have been *hypnotizing. tenuous* = flimsy; *spellbinding* = mesmerizing; *grotesque* = distorted, horrifying, outlandish; *enthralling* = captivating; *interminable* = never-ending; *sacrilegious* = grossly disrespectful; *eclectic* = deriving from a variety of sources; *sadistic* = taking pleasure in others' pain; *chimerical* = unrealistically fanciful, illusory; *mundane* = everyday, common

8. D   The DNA evidence was vital to proving the defendant's innocence. The missing word should mean to *prove innocent* or *free from blame. perambulate* = walk through; *expedite* = speed up; *incriminate* = accuse of a crime; *exculpate* = free from blame; *equivocate* = avoid telling the whole truth

9. B   Debussy is said to have started the *breakdown of the old system* (line 3) and then to have been the *first . . . who dared to make his ear the sole judge of what was good harmonically* (lines 6–7). Therefore, the old system did not allow this and was a rigid method for writing harmonies.

10. D   The passage as a whole describes Debussy's inventiveness as a composer of musical harmony.

11. B   The hot-air balloon trip is an analogy for the difficulties involved in exploring the ocean.

12. A   These are examples of the *limited and relatively ineffective methods* (lines 15–16) that make ocean exploration *a difficult and expensive task* (lines 18–19).

13. D   This *primal concept* is revealed by the fact that the paintings of Stone Age artists are charged with *magical strength* and *fulfilled . . . other functions beyond the mere representation of the visible* (lines 8–10).

14. E   To be *charged with magical strength* is to be *filled with magical strength.*

15. A   The *stylistic change* was from the *naturalism based on observation and experience* to a *geometrically stylized world of forms discoverable . . . through thought and speculation* (lines 45–48). In other words, artists were depicting ideas rather than just objects and animals.

16. B   The sculptures are said to be *ample witnesses* (line 63) to the fact that art of this period contained *elements of naïveté . . . side by side with . . . formalized compositions* (lines 59–62).

17. A   The passage states that Renaissance art is characterized by the *discovery of linear and aerial perspective* (lines 80–81), that is, the ability to imply depth in painting, while the earlier *art of the period of the catacombs* (line 71) *was averse to any spatial illusions* (line 74) and contained action *pressed onto the holy, two-dimensional surface* (lines 75–76).

18. C   *Transitional forms* (line 9) are described as fossils that gradualists would cite as *evidence for their position* (line 8), which is that evolution proceeds gradually.

19. E   This case is mentioned as an illustration of the theory of *punctuated equilibrium* (lines 11–12).

20. B   The passage says that *one explanation for the extinction of the dinosaurs* is that a meteorite created a *cloud of gas and dust* that destroyed *most plants and the chain of animals that fed on them* (lines 42–48).

21. D   This sentence is discussing fossil evidence. The supportive structures are those bones that support the weight of the body.

22. E   The passage states in lines 35–38 that the biggest mass extinction in history happened between the Paleozoic era and the Mesozoic era, thereby implying that there were far fewer species in the early Mesozoic era than there were in the late Paleozoic era.

23. B   In lines 66–71, the passage states that *the probable key to the rapid emergence of Homo erectus was a dramatic change in adaptive strategy: greater reliance on hunting through improved tools and other cultural means of adaptation.*

24. C   The author presents several examples of mass extinctions and environmental changes that would likely lead to punctuated evolution but also describes species like *Homo erectus,* which *remained fairly stable for about 1 million years* (lines 72–73).

Section 4

1. B The original phrasing is a fragment. Choice (B) completes the thought clearly and concisely.

2. A The original phrasing is best.

3. E This phrasing is concise, complete, and in the active voice.

4. D The original sentence and choice (E) are both guilty of a *number shift:* the sentence describes three examples of sciences, not *an example* or *a science.* In choices (B) and (C), the pronoun *where* is illogical, because sciences are not places.

5. D The original phrasing contains a comparison error, comparing *his speech* to the *candidates.* Choice (D) best corrects the mistake.

6. A The original sentence is best. Choices (B), (C), and (E) are unidiomatic, and choice (D) is not a modifying phrase, and so does not coordinate with the clause that follows.

7. C The original sentence lacks parallel phrasing. Choice (C) is the only choice with consistent parallel phrasing.

8. D The pronoun *their* does not agree with its antecedent, *student.* Choice (C) is close, but including the word *also* implies that the tests do indicate academic skill.

9. B The original phrasing is a sentence fragment. Choices (C) and (D) are incorrect because semicolons must separate independent clauses.

10. E The phrase *requested that* indicates that the idea to follow is **subjunctive.** The correct subjunctive form here is *be.*

11. A The original sentence is best. Choices (B), (D), and (E) use awkward or illogical verbs, and choice (C) uses the illogical phrase *have distributed by allocating.*

12. B The verb *had sang* is incorrect because it does not use the correct past participle form of *to sing.* It should be changed to *had sung.*

13. D The phrase *from those to choose from* is redundant. It should be changed to a phrase such as *of them* or *from the group.*

14. E The sentence is correct.

15. B This phrase lacks parallel structure. A good revision is *a charismatic leader.*

16. B Both idiom and parallel structure require changing the gerund *focusing* to the infinitive *to focus.*

17. D The use of *either* requires the use of *or,* not *nor.*

18. D *Eluded* means *evaded,* so this is a diction error. The correct word here is *alluded,* meaning *hinted at.*

19. B The pronoun *his or her* does not agree with the plural antecedent, *members,* and should be changed to *their.*

20. E The sentence is correct as written.

21. C This sentence contains an illogical comparison: one scientist's *theoretical work* is not logically comparable to *the greatest scientists,* but rather to *the work of the greatest scientists.*

22. B Both the *emissary* and the *committee* are singular, so the pronoun *their* should be changed to *its* (if it refers to the committee) or *his* or *her* (if it refers to the emissary).

23. D The verb *require* does not agree in number with its singular subject *each,* and should be changed to *requires.*

24. E The sentence is correct.

25. B The subject of this sentence is *genre,* so the correct conjugation of the verb is *encompasses.*

26. C The proper idiom is *method of channeling* or *method for channeling.*

27. C The sentence does not make a comparison, but rather indicates a result, so the word *as* should be replaced with *that.*

28. A The word *perspective* is a noun meaning point of view. In this context, the proper word is *prospective,* which is an adjective meaning *having the potential to be.*

29. D The list of camp activities should be parallel. The verbs should consistently be in the present tense, so *will write* should be changed to *write.*

30. B This phrasing is concise and parallel and makes a logical comparison.

31. C Chaplin's mother's mental illness is not pertinent to the main ideas of paragraph 1.

32. D In the original phrasing, the opening modifiers are left dangling. Choice (D) corrects this problem most concisely.

33. E This choice is most parallel.

34. A Sentence 11 introduces the idea that some were interested in more than Chaplin's art. Sentence 9 expands on this fact with the specific example of Senator McCarthy's interest in Chaplin's political beliefs. Sentence 10 extends the ideas in sentence 9.

35. D This sentence provides the best transition from the idea that Chaplin's films contained political messages to a discussion of their specific messages about domestic and international issues.

Section 5

1. B Eric earns a 5% commission on each $200 stereo, so he makes ($200)(.05) = $10 per stereo. So if he makes $100 on x stereos, $10x = 100$
Divide by 10: $x = 10$

2. A Fill in the table:

Jane's Discount Music Superstore
Holiday Sales

	CDs	DVDs	Total
New	3,000	4,500	7,500
Used	4,000	**2,500**	6,500
Total	7,000	7,000	14,000

Since 7,000 out of the total of 14,000 items sold were CDs, 14,000 − 7,000 = 7,000 were DVDs. Since 4,500 of these DVDs were new, 7,000 − 4,500 = 2,500 were used.

3. D Set up a ratio:
$$\frac{5 \text{ pounds}}{\$4.00} = \frac{x \text{ pounds}}{\$20.00}$$
Cross-multiply: $4x = 100$
Divide by 4: $x = 25$

$$25 \text{ pounds} \times \frac{16 \text{ ounces}}{1 \text{ pound}} = 400 \text{ ounces}$$

Set up a proportion:
$$\frac{1 \text{ bag}}{40 \text{ ounces}} = \frac{x \text{ bags}}{400 \text{ ounces}}$$

Cross-multiply: $40x = 400$
Divide by 40: $x = 10$ bags

4. E Divide this complex-looking shape into a square and two right triangles.

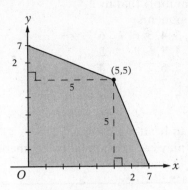

$\text{Area}_{\text{square}} = (5)(5) = 25$
$\text{Area}_{\text{triangle}} = \frac{1}{2}(2)(5) = 5$

Total shaded area = $\text{Area}_{\text{square}} + \text{Area}_{\text{triangle}} + \text{Area}_{\text{triangle}} = 25 + 5 + 5 = 35$

5. D If each of the small cubes has a volume of 8 cubic inches, then each side of the smaller cubes must be 2 inches long. So the dimensions of the box are 6, 4, and 4. To find the surface area, use the formula:

$$SA = 2lw + 2lh + 2wh$$

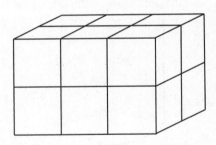

Plug in values: $SA = 2(6)(4) + 2(6)(4) + 2(4)(4)$
Simplify: $SA = 48 + 48 + 32 = 128$

6. C Don't waste time doing the calculation: −15 + −14 + −13 + −12 + −11 + −10 + −9 + −8 + −7 + −6 + −5 + −4 + −3 + −2 + −1 + 0 + 1 + 2 + 3 + 4 + 5 + 6 + 7 + 8 + 9 + 10 + 11 + 12 + 13 + 14 + 15 + 16 + 17 + 18 + 19. Instead, think logically. The sum of the numbers from −15 to +15 is 0. They cancel out completely: −15 + 15 = 0, −14 + 14 = 0, −13 + 13 = 0, etc. Therefore, y must be greater than 15. With a little checking, it's easy to see that 16 + 17 + 18 + 19 = 70, so $y = 19$. The total number of integers from −15 to 19, inclusive, is 19 − (−15) + 1 = 35.

7. **C**   The general strategy is to find out how many matches there are if each plays every other player once and multiply that by 2.

                    Opponents:
Player 1: 2, 3, 4, 5, 6, 7   6
Player 2: 3, 4, 5, 6, 7   5
Player 3: 4, 5, 6, 7   4
Player 4: 5, 6, 7   3
Player 5: 6, 7   2
Player 6: 7   1
Total head to-head-matchups: 21

Since they play each opponent twice, there is a total of $21 \times 2 = 42$ matches.

---

8. **B**   The area of the base of the prism is 12.5π. Since this is one-quarter of a circle, the entire circle has an area of $4(12.5\pi) = 50\pi$.

                    $\pi r^2 = $ area
Substitute: $\pi r^2 = 50\pi$
Divide by π: $r^2 = 50$

Take square root: $r = \sqrt{50}$

You are told that the volume of the prism is 300π. Since this is ¼ of a cylinder, the entire cylinder would have a volume of $4(300\pi) = 1{,}200\pi$.

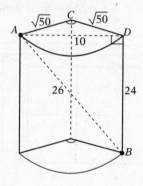

                    $\pi r^2 h = $ volume of a cylinder
Substitute: $\pi r^2 h = 1{,}200\pi$
Divide by π: $r^2 h = 1{,}200$

Substitute $r = \sqrt{50}$: $\left(\sqrt{50}\right)^2 h = 1{,}200$
Simplify: $50h = 1{,}200$
Divide by 50: $h = 24$

Finally, to find the distance from point A to point B, notice that AB is the hypotenuse of a right triangle with legs AD and DB. First you must find the value of AD:

$$\left(\sqrt{50}\right)^2 + \left(\sqrt{50}\right)^2 = (AD)^2$$

Simplify: $50 + 50 = 100 = (AD)^2$
Take square root: $10 = AD$
Solve for AB: $(AD)^2 + (DB)^2 = (AB)^2$
Substitute: $(10)^2 + (24)^2 = (AB)^2$
Simplify: $100 + 576 = (AB)^2$
Combine like terms: $676 = (AB)^2$
Take square root: $26 = AB$

---

9. **135**   Set up an equation: $x + (3y + 3) = 180°$
Substitute $y + 1$ for x: $y + 1 + 3y + 3 = 180°$
Combine like terms: $4y + 4 = 180°$
Subtract 4: $4y = 176°$
Divide by 4: $y = 44°$
Solve for $3y + 3$: $3(44) + 3 = 135°$

---

10. **104**   Quadrilateral $ABCD$ is composed of two identical triangles, each with an area of 240 square inches.

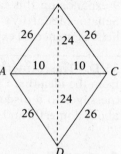

Area of $\triangle ABC = \frac{1}{2}bh$
$240 = \frac{1}{2}(20)(h)$
$h = 24$ inches

To solve for side BC, set up the Pythagorean theorem:
                            $10^2 + 24^2 = (BC)^2$
Simplify: $100 + 576 = (BC)^2$
Combine like terms: $676 = (BC)^2$
Take the square root: $26 = BC$
(Or simply notice that each right triangle is a classic 5-12-13 triangle times 2: 10-24-26.)

The perimeter of quadrilateral $ABCD =$
                    $26 + 26 + 26 + 26 = 104$

---

11. **30**   If two things are equal, you can substitute either one for the other. Since $g(x) = x^2 - 5$,
                    $f(g(x)) = f(x^2 - 5)$
Plug $x^2 - 5$ into $f(x)$ and simplify:
                    $f(x) = 7(x^2 - 5) + 2$
Distribute: $7x^2 - 35 + 2$
Plug in 3 for x: $7(3)^2 - 35 + 2$
Simplify: $63 - 35 + 2 = 30$

---

12. **3**   Start by simplifying the expression:

$$\frac{6x - 9}{5} - \frac{x + 6}{5} = \frac{6x - 9 - x - 6}{5}$$

Combine like terms: $\dfrac{5x - 15}{5}$

Simplify: $x - 3$
This expression is 3 less than x.

---

13. **18**   Approach this problem logically, but keep the restrictions in mind. If we want the *largest* possible value of a and $a + b < 20$, try $a = 19$. But that is not a possibility, because b is a positive integer and so can be no less than 1, and $19 + 1$ is equal to, not less than 20. Therefore, the largest value of a that fits the restriction is 18. If $a = 18$ and $b = 1$, then $ab = (18)(1) = 18$, an even number.

14. 28   Since rectangle *U* and rectangle *V* share a side with integer length, this length must be a common factor of 18 and 21. Similarly, the side that rectangle *U* and rectangle *W* share must be a common factor of 18 and 12. Therefore, the common side between *U* and *V* is 3, and the common side between *U* and *W* is 6. So *U* is a 6-by-3 rectangle, *V* is a 7-by-3 rectangle, and *W* is a 6-by-2 rectangle, which means rectangle *X* must have an area of 14. The sum of the areas of those four rectangles is $18 + 21 + 12 + 14 = 65$. The area of the entire rectangle is given as 117. Thus, the area of rectangles *Y* and *Z* together must be $117 - 65 = 52$. Set up an equation:

$$6x + 7x = 52$$

Combine like terms: $13x = 52$

Divide by 13: $x = 4$

If $x = 4$, then the area of rectangle *Z* is $4 \times 7 = 28$.

	6		7
U		3	*V*
W 6		2	*X* 7
Y 6		x	*Z* 7

15. 45   Begin by finding the amount the class would spend on 55 regular-price tickets: $55 \times \$15 = \$825$. Then calculate how much 60 discounted tickets cost: $60 \times \$13 = \$780$. Then subtract to find the amount saved: $\$825 - \$780 = \$45$.

16. 22.5

W ————— 15 ————— Y

The length of $\overline{WY}$, as shown above, is 15.

W — 7.5 — X — 7.5 — Y ——— 15 ——— Z

Point *X* is the midpoint of $\overline{WY}$, so $WX = XY = 7.5$. $YZ = 2WX = 2(7.5) = 15$. So $XZ = 22.5$.

17. 12

$$r \,\square\, s = \frac{rs^2}{r - s}$$

Solve for *x*: $3 \,\square\, 2 = \dfrac{(3)(2^2)}{3 - 2} = \dfrac{12}{1} = 12 = x$

$$x \,\square\, 3 = 12 \,\square\, 3 = \frac{(12)(3^2)}{12 - 3} = \frac{108}{9} = 12$$

18. 37.5

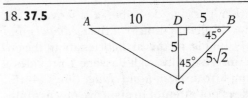

Since $\overline{DC} \perp \overline{AB}$, angle *CDB* is a right angle, so $\triangle CDB$ is a 45°-45°-90° right triangle. Therefore, $DB = DC = 5$. Since $AD = 2DB$, $AD = (5)(2) = 10$.

The area of $\triangle ABC = \frac{1}{2}(b)(h) = \frac{1}{2}(15)(5) = 37.5$.

Section 6

1. B   The reflex produces an *immediate* (or *instantaneous*) response. *transient* = short-lived; *stagnant* = not moving; *revitalized* = filled with new life and energy

2. D   Although the cats are *emaciated* (excessively thin) and *starved for food*, summoning energy would help them to fight *hard* or *aggressively* for the scraps. *humanely* = with mercy; *vigilantly* = in a watchful way; *fluently* = smoothly; *ferociously* = fiercely

3. C   Jennifer *irritated* her peers with her *supercilious* (overly proud) and *pretentious* (haughty) remarks. These are characteristic of an arrogant or showy demeanor. *reticent* = reserved, unwilling to speak; *belligerent* = warlike; *lofty* = pompous; *self-effacing* = modest; *discomfited* = uneasy, uncomfortable

4. A   The first part of the sentence indicates that a sushi master's work is not easily learned. Therefore, much *training* and *studying* are required to become a master chef. *Apprenticeship, tutelage,* and *cultivation* are all good choices for the first word. This training will give someone the *autonomy* to create his or her own work. *apprenticeship* = working as a beginner under the assistance of an instructor; *autonomy* = independence; *tutelage* = instruction; *ineptitude* = lack of skill; *dormancy* = lack of activity; *sovereignty* = supreme authority; *cultivation* = the act of improving; *boorish* = rude, lacking manners; *quiescent* = not active

5. A   The journalist had a reputation for breaking news early, almost as if she were *able to see the future*. Later she admitted that she had privileged sources and did not use *prophecy* at all. *prophetic* = able to tell the future; *prescience* = knowledge of future events; *premeditated* = planned ahead of time; *predilection* = preference; *dismissive* = indifferent; *omniscience* = total knowledge; *preeminent* = superior; *reluctance* = resistance; *insolvent* = bankrupt; *foresight* = thinking ahead

6. B Neither passage describes a discovery, but rather the *world picture* (line 5) of the *medieval mind* (lines 26–27), that is, medieval theories about the nature of the universe. Although Passage 1 provides a counterexample to an *often-heard charge* (lines 14–15), Passage 2 does not attempt to disprove any assumptions. Neither passage questions the medieval theories presented. Instead, the passages merely describe those theories. Lastly, neither passage discusses the everyday life in medieval Europe.

7. D The passage states that where our universe is thought to be dark, the other one was presumed to be illuminated, which means that the medieval universe was perceived to be full of light, unlike our modern universe.

8. C Pascal is said to be *disturbed by the silence of the vast spaces between the stars* (lines 10–11), in contrast to the medieval thinkers who *formerly thought* that the universe produced *the "music of the spheres"* (lines 12–13).

9. E Dante's theory is described in Passage 1 to counter the charge that medieval thinkers were focused on *man's sense of self-importance* (lines 16–17), but Hildegard's theory presented in the final sentence of Passage 2 is clearly anthropocentric, or human-centered. The world views of both Dante and Hildegard are focused on religion and an ordered hierarchy, but neither addresses scientific methods. Lastly, Passage 1 does not discuss the public acceptance of Dante's theory.

10. E This passage is concerned primarily with describing the relationships among the plants, animals, and climate of the Serengeti. Therefore, it is describing how a particular ecosystem works. Although the passage mentions human intervention tangentially in the last paragraph, where it refers to badly drawn park boundaries, it is not a central focus of the passage. Although it does mention individual plants, the passage as a whole does not focus on them, but instead shows how they play a role in a larger ecosystem. It does not mention natural disasters, and only mentions the distinction between grazers and browsers as a minor point.

11. C These sentences suggest that the variety in the diet of grazers increases with the length of the grass. When the grass is short, all the animals apparently eat much the same sort of grass, but when it is long, they diversify their diets.

12. A Browsers are said to *feed on shrubs or the leaves of trees* (lines 15–16), as opposed to the grazers, which eat *the abundant grass that springs up like a well-mown lawn* (lines 9–11).

13. B The passage states that *unlike all the other grazers on the plain,* (zebras) *have teeth in both jaws* (lines 27–28). *All the rest* (besides the zebras) *are various species of antelope* (lines 30–31), which have *toothless upper palates* (lines 32–33).

14. E The second paragraph states that *where the grass is all short . . . all the animals apparently eat the same sort of grass . . . but where the grass is of varied lengths . . . each animal copes differently with the available fodder* (lines 19–24). This difference is then described in the third paragraph, where the grazing sequence is specified.

15. C The rains are said to bring on *fresh growth* (line 53), encouraging the grazers to return to old grazing lands.

16. A This paragraph states that if the *migrant herds . . . were confined* (lines 63–64), they would *so weaken the grass that it would die out* (lines 67–68). So maintaining the grasslands requires that the animals not be confined.

17. A The thesis of the passage is that *men come greatly to desire that these capricious gifts of Nature* (that is, the natural resources that are hard for some and easy for others to find , by luck alone) *might be intercepted by some agency having the power and the goodwill to distribute them justly. . . . This desire is Socialism* (lines 41–47).

18. C This primitive cultivator is a person who tries to stick a spade into the earth and make wheat and other edible matters spring from it. This is a farmer. Although the author uses figurative and metaphorical language throughout the passage, this particular phrase is being used literally.

19. D The *astronomer* is said to regard the earth as simply *a ball . . . without ulterior motives* (lines 3–4), while the *foolish spendthrift . . . suddenly realizes that the earth is offering him gold* (lines 21–24). Therefore, the astronomer regards the earth as impersonal, while the spendthrift regards it as generous.

20. B The *closed hand* represents the tendency of the Earth to hide its *diamonds* and *good red wheat* (line 31).

21. A The author is discussing how capricious nature is in revealing its resources, and suggests that anyone trying to harvest the earth's resources must become a *gambler* (line 33), and scoff at theorists who prate (speak inconsequentially) of moral virtues such as industry and honesty and equality. Therefore, the author is suggesting that these virtues are not as valuable as many people claim they are.

22. **C**   This fate is the fate of the *gambler* (line 33), who is at the whim of mother earth.

23. **E**   The author states that the *Social Democratic State . . . remains to be tried* (lines 51–52).

24. **C**   The author states that *our own choice* (that is, the choice of his society) *is shown by our continual aspiration to possess property* (lines 59–60).

Section 7

1. **B**
$$3x + 5x + 8x = 32$$
Combine like terms: $16x = 32$
Divide by 16: $x = 2$

2. **D**
$$\left(\frac{1}{x}\right)\left(\frac{x}{3}\right)(6x) = 8$$
Simplify: $2x = 8$
Divide by 2: $x = 4$

3. **A**
$$5b - 10 \geq 15$$
Add 10: $5b \geq 25$
Divide by 5: $b \geq 5$

4. **C**   First find 30% of 50: $(.3)(50) = 15$
$t\%$ of 60 is 15
Set up the equation: $\dfrac{t}{100} = \dfrac{15}{60}$
Cross-multiply: $60t = 1,500$
Divide by 60: $t = 25$

5. **C**   First convert 8 hours into minutes:

$$\frac{8 \text{ hours}}{x \text{ minutes}} = \frac{1 \text{ hour}}{60 \text{ minutes}}$$

Cross-multiply: $x = 480$ minutes
Then set up a ratio to answer the question:

$$\frac{480 \text{ minutes}}{y \text{ cards}} = \frac{40 \text{ minutes}}{h \text{ cards}}$$

Cross-multiply: $40y = 480h$
Divide by 40: $y = 12h$

6. **A**   First find the product of -1.5×1.25: -1.875. Point A is closest to -1.875 on the number line presented.

7. **C**   If the four people must each have a different positive number of cards, then the least that three may have is one, two, and three cards. This leaves a maximum of $100 - 6 = 94$ for the remaining person.

8. **C**   A quick plot of the data listed in the table will point you to answer choice (C). Since the miles per gallon are decreasing as the age increases, you can eliminate choice (A). There is no point where the data levels out, which eliminates answer choice (D). Finally, because it is not decreasing at a constant rate, you can eliminate choices (B) and (E).

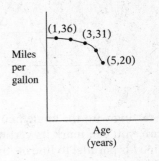

9. **D**   If the question is *at most* how many of these integers *could* be odd, begin by imagining that ALL of them are odd. The integers may be the same, so imagine that they are all 1: $1 + 1 + 1 + 1 + 1 + 1 + 1 = 7$. But 7 is odd, so try 6 odds and 1 even: $1 + 1 + 1 + 1 + 1 + 1 + 2 = 8$. Therefore, the most that could be odd is 6.

10. **D**   You can write out a quick calendar for yourself to track the days:

Su	M	T	**W**	Th	F	Sa
			1	2	3	4
5	6	7	8	9	10	11
12	13	14	15	16	17	18
19	20	21	**22**	23	24	25
26	27	28	29	30	31	

If you do this problem too quickly, you might assume that since the fourth Wednesday is the 22nd, the fourth Monday would be the 20th. But the first Monday comes after the first Wednesday, which makes the fourth Monday the 27th.

11. **D**   Be careful with this question. Make sure you understand the chart before choosing an answer. The question asks about teachers who use gas heat. There are $60 + 13 = 73$ teachers who use gas heat, and 60 of these live in a house.

12. **D**   "Stack" the equations: $5x + 7y = 18$
                                         $\underline{2x - 4y = 6}$
Add straight down: $7x + 3y = 24$

13. A

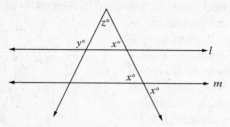

Starting with the angle marked $x°$ in the original figure, you can mark its vertical angle $x°$ as well. Since line l is parallel to line m, the corresponding angle in the top triangle is also $x°$. Set up an equation for the triangle:

$$x + z + (180 - y) = 180$$
Subtract 180:　$x + z - y = 0$
Add y:　　　　$x + z = y$

(You might also simply notice that the angle marked $y°$ is an "exterior" angle to the triangle, so its measure is equal to the sum of the two "remote interior" angles: $y = x + z$.)

Subtract z:　　　　　　　　　$x = y - z$

---

14. B　This problem involves rates, so it helps to recall the rate equation: $d = rt$.

Because she travels home *along the same route*, you can use d for the distance both to and from work. Because she spends a total of 2 hours in the car, if she spends t hours on the way to work, she will spend $2 - t$ hours on the way home from work.

Set up rate equations for both legs of the trip:

To work:　　　　　　　　$d = 40(t)$
From work:　　　　　　　$d = 24(2 - t)$
Set the expressions equal:　$40t = 24(2 - t)$
Distribute:　　　　　　　$40t = 48 - 24t$
Add $24t$:　　　　　　　$64t = 48$
Divide by 64:　　　　　　$t = .75$

Plug 0.75 in for t and solve for d:　$d = 40(.75) = 30$
Check by confirming that plugging $t = .75$ into the other rate equation gives the same distance from home to work.

---

15. B　The graph of the original function will be shifted up 4 and right 2. Answer choice (B) shows the proper representation of the new graph.

---

16. A

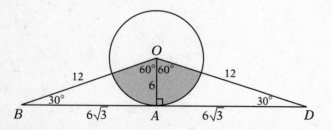

Line segment $\overline{BD}$ is tangent to the circle at point A, so angles BAO and DAO are right angles. This means that both $\triangle DAO$ and $\triangle BAO$ are 30°-60°-90° triangles.

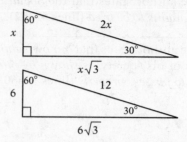

Using the 30°-60°-90° reference information at the beginning of this section, you can find the values of the remaining sides of the triangles.

Find the area of $\triangle BOD$:　Area $= \dfrac{1}{2}$(base)(height)

Plug in values:　Area $= \dfrac{1}{2}(12\sqrt{3})(6) = 36\sqrt{3}$

The radius of the circle is 6, so the area of the entire circle can be found using the equation Area $= \pi r^2 = \pi(6)^2 = 36\pi$.

The shaded region of the circle makes up 120°, or ⅓ of the circle. Therefore, the area of the shaded region is equal to ⅓(πr^2) = ⅓$(36\pi) = 12\pi$.

The area of the unshaded region of the triangle can be found by subtracting the area of the shaded region from the total area of the triangle: $36\sqrt{3} - 12\pi$.

Section 8

1. E　If businesses are having a hard time staying current, their equipment must be *old* or *outdated* because technology is advancing at a *fast rate*. *urgency* = pressing importance; *progressive* = advancing forward; *conventional* = standard; *torpidity* = lethargy; *antiquated* = outdated; *lassitude* = lack of energy; *innovative* = inventive, novel

---

2. B　The sentence states that one feature of Joyce's work *gave way* to another, suggesting that the first missing word is a noun that directly contrasts the adjective in the second blank. The second word is paired with *arcane*, which means *secret* or *little-understood*. This word must also describe works that feature *neologisms* (invented words) and *obscure literary tricks*. Therefore the first word should mean something like *clarity* and the second phrase should include an adjective like *hard to understand*. *lucidity* = clarity; *opaque* = very difficult to understand or translate; *concise* = brief and to the point; *anachronism* = quality of being out of place in time; *derivative* = copied from others

3. B Churchill was known to *choose his strategies arbitrarily* (without logical reason), so he was *whimsical* or *impulsive*. *diligent* = working with great effort; *impulsive* = acting without thought; *vicious* = evil, harsh; *malevolent* = wishing harm, malicious

4. D If the king executed those who acted irreverently (without respect), he must have demanded *utmost respect*. *insolence* = brazen rudeness; *impudence* = disrespect; *truculence* = inclination to pick fights; *deference* = respect; *ignominy* = humiliation

5. D Since Galileo contradicted church teachings, he was a *heretic*. *ostracized* = cut off from society; *hermit* = one who seeks solitude; *venerated* = worshipped; *demagogue* = powerful leader; *hallowed* = respected as holy; *revisionist* = one who rethinks or reshapes a commonly accepted view; *denounced* = accused or condemned for being a villain; *heretic* = one who holds controversial opinions; *reviled* = attacked with harsh language; *luminary* = one who inspires others

6. A The Senator is known for her *iconoclastic* views, which means that she goes against the party line. Because of this, she would have a tough time getting *traditional* party members to support her. *contentious* = quarrelsome; *orthodox* = traditional; *litigious* = prone to bringing lawsuits; *disingenuous* = insincere; *vituperative* = using harsh censure or condemnation; *dissident* = disagreeing; *heretical* = going against standard beliefs; *polemical* = pertaining to a highly controversial political or intellectual position

7. D This is an address to the Atlanta Exposition (as the introduction indicates), and the author is clearly addressing those in *the commercial world* (lines 26–27) and entreating ex-slaves and Southern whites to work together for their mutual benefit.

8. A The author does not directly address those in the antislavery movement but does address (B) *those of the white race who look to the incoming of those of foreign birth . . . for the prosperity of the South* (lines 45–48), (C) *those of my race who depend upon bettering their condition* (lines 12–14), (D) those for whom African Americans have *tilled your fields, cleared your forests . . .* (lines 56–57), and (E) those African Americans who *underestimate the importance of cultivating friendly relations with the Southern white man* (lines 14–16).

9. C The captain did not heed the first, second, or third call but heeded the fourth call *at last* (line 9), suggesting that he did not believe the responses were helpful at first.

10. C The phrase *this chance* refers to the *man's chance* (that African Americans can have) *in the commercial world* (lines 26–27).

11. A In saying that *there is as much dignity in tilling a field as in writing a poem* (lines 40–41), the author is saying that such manual labor is valuable work.

12. D These indicate the thoughts of a *Negro who has given earnest thought to the situation of his people in America* (lines 68–70).

13. C In saying that because of *incessant self-questioning* (line 83) . . . *the best energy of the Negro people cannot be marshalled to do the bidding of the race* (lines 89–91), the author means that introspection keeps African Americans from organizing themselves to meet the needs of their race.

14. D Such people are said to *make room for every rascal and demagogue who chooses to cloak his selfish deviltry under the veil of race pride* (lines 91–93); that is, they allow themselves to be influenced by selfish and evil people.

15. D *That point* refers to the point *farther than* (which) *our Americanism does not go* (lines 121–122). In other words, this is the point up to which African Americans share much in common with all Americans but beyond which they are a unique people.

16. C This *broader humanity* is that which *freely recognizes differences in men, but sternly deprecates* (disapproves of) *inequality in their opportunities of development* (lines 139–141). In other words, its members value equal opportunity for all races.

17. E Passage 1 focuses on the manual labor that African Americans have performed in tilling fields, clearing forests, building railroads and cities, etc., while the author of Passage 2 emphasizes contributions like *the subtle sense of song that has given America its only American music, its only American fairy tales, its only touch of pathos and humor . . .* (lines 130–133).

18. A The *black tomorrow* in Passage 2 is the influence of African Americans in softening *the whiteness of the Teutonic today* (line 129), which suggests a change in the dominant culture. Passage 1, on the other hand, envisions a future in which African Americans make *friends in every manly way of the people of all races by whom we are surrounded* (lines 19–20) and incorporate themselves into the existing dominant industries of *agriculture, mechanics, . . . commerce, . . .* (and) *domestic service* (lines 21–22).

19. E   Passage 1 indicates that the dominant culture can give the African American *a man's chance in the commercial world* (lines 26–27) and contains many *opportunities* (line 44). Passage 2 is more assertive in suggesting that African Americans have changed and will continue to change the dominant culture: *We are the first fruits of this new nation, the harbinger of that black tomorrow which is yet destined to soften the whiteness of the Teutonic today* (lines 126–129).

Section 9

1. C   The parallel idiom *neither . . . nor* requires that the phrase following *neither* and the phrase following *nor* have the same grammatical form. The only choice that maintains proper idiom and parallelism is (C).

2. E   This sentence contains three clauses, each of which has the same subject, *Georgia*. The underlined clause, however, is in the passive voice, unlike the other two. It should be changed to the active voice like the others.

3. D   Since any rehearsal would have been completed before the performance, the participle in the underlined phrase should be in the perfect form *having rehearsed*. Choice (B) also uses the nonstandard phrase *being that*, and choices (C) and (E) create run-on sentences.

4. B   In the original sentence, the subject *outlets* does not agree with the verb *has acknowledged*. In choice (C), the subject *scope* disagrees with the verb *have been acknowledged*. Choice (D) is awkward and choice (E) uses an illogical verb tense. Choice (B) conveys the idea clearly and grammatically.

5. E   The original verb *have had* is in the imperative mood, but should be in the subjunctive mood because it conveys a hypothetical condition. Choice (E) conveys the mood correctly.

6. C   The statement made in the main clause is not *against* popular opinion, but rather is *contrary* to it. Although choice (E) uses the proper modifier, it illogically suggests that an opinion can *say* something.

7. A   The original sentence is the most logical and effective option.

8. B   The original phrase misuses the semicolon, because the phrase preceding it is not an independent clause. Similarly, choice (E) uses the conjunction *so* to join two clauses, but the first is not independent, so the sentence is ungrammatical. Choices (C) and (D) use the unidiomatic phrases *struggled for finding* and *struggled finding*. Choice (B) avoids these problems, and is clear and effective.

9. A   The original phrasing is best. It provides the parallel form required by the comparative idiom *not so much by . . . as by . . .*, whereas the others violate parallel form.

10. D   The original phrasing is unidiomatic. The correct idiom is *A appears to be B*.

11. C   The comparison is logically between the *response* to the revised proposal and the *response* to the original proposal. Choice (C) is the only one that makes the correct logical and parallel comparison.

12. C   The original phrasing breaks the idea into two independent clauses. But since it conveys one central idea, it is more effectively phrased with a single independent clause and a modifying phrase. Choice (C) does this effectively, idiomatically, and concisely.

13. E   The original phrasing is unnecessarily wordy and does not effectively coordinate the ideas in the sentence. Choice (C) has the same problem. Choices (B) and (D) create clauses with uncoordinated verbs. Only choice (E) conveys the idea concisely and effectively.

14. C   The phrase *extra superfluous* is redundant, and the phrase *to edit for eliminating* is unidiomatic. Choice (C) is clear and concise.

PRACTICE PSAT

ANSWER SHEET

Last Name:_____   First Name:_____

Date:_____   Testing Location:_____

Administering the Test

- **Remove this answer sheet** from the book and use it to record your answers to this test.
- This test will require **2 hours and 10 minutes** to complete. Take this test in one sitting.
- Use a stopwatch to time yourself on each section. The time limit for each section is written clearly at the beginning of each section. The first four sections are 25 minutes long, and the last section is 30 minutes long.
- Each response must **completely fill the oval. Erase all stray marks completely**, or they may be interpreted as responses.
- **You must stop ALL work on a section when time is called**.
- If you finish a section before the time has elapsed, check your work on that section. **You may NOT move on to the next section until time is called**.
- Do not waste time on questions that seem too difficult for you.
- Use the test book for scratchwork, but you will only receive credit for answers that are marked on the answer sheets.

Scoring the Test

- Your scaled score, which will be determined from a conversion table, is based on your raw score for each section.
- You will receive one point toward your raw score for every correct answer.
- You will receive no points toward your raw score for an omitted question.
- For each wrong answer on a multiple-choice question, your raw score will be reduced by 1/4 point. For each wrong answer on a numerical "grid-in" question (Section 4, questions 29–38), your raw score will receive no deduction.

SECTION 1 — Critical Reading — 25 minutes

Questions 1–24, each with answer choices (A) (B) (C) (D) (E)

Time: 25 minutes
Start: _____
Stop: _____

SECTION 2 — Math — 25 minutes

Questions 1–20, each with answer choices (A) (B) (C) (D) (E)

Time: 25 minutes
Start: _____
Stop: _____

SECTION

3

Critical
Reading
25 minutes

25. Ⓐ Ⓑ Ⓒ Ⓓ Ⓔ
26. Ⓐ Ⓑ Ⓒ Ⓓ Ⓔ
27. Ⓐ Ⓑ Ⓒ Ⓓ Ⓔ
28. Ⓐ Ⓑ Ⓒ Ⓓ Ⓔ
29. Ⓐ Ⓑ Ⓒ Ⓓ Ⓔ
30. Ⓐ Ⓑ Ⓒ Ⓓ Ⓔ
31. Ⓐ Ⓑ Ⓒ Ⓓ Ⓔ
32. Ⓐ Ⓑ Ⓒ Ⓓ Ⓔ

33. Ⓐ Ⓑ Ⓒ Ⓓ Ⓔ
34. Ⓐ Ⓑ Ⓒ Ⓓ Ⓔ
35. Ⓐ Ⓑ Ⓒ Ⓓ Ⓔ
36. Ⓐ Ⓑ Ⓒ Ⓓ Ⓔ
37. Ⓐ Ⓑ Ⓒ Ⓓ Ⓔ
38. Ⓐ Ⓑ Ⓒ Ⓓ Ⓔ
39. Ⓐ Ⓑ Ⓒ Ⓓ Ⓔ
40. Ⓐ Ⓑ Ⓒ Ⓓ Ⓔ

41. Ⓐ Ⓑ Ⓒ Ⓓ Ⓔ
42. Ⓐ Ⓑ Ⓒ Ⓓ Ⓔ
43. Ⓐ Ⓑ Ⓒ Ⓓ Ⓔ
44. Ⓐ Ⓑ Ⓒ Ⓓ Ⓔ
45. Ⓐ Ⓑ Ⓒ Ⓓ Ⓔ
46. Ⓐ Ⓑ Ⓒ Ⓓ Ⓔ
47. Ⓐ Ⓑ Ⓒ Ⓓ Ⓔ
48. Ⓐ Ⓑ Ⓒ Ⓓ Ⓔ

Time: 25 minutes

Start: _____

Stop: _____

SECTION

4

Math
25 minutes

21. Ⓐ Ⓑ Ⓒ Ⓓ Ⓔ
22. Ⓐ Ⓑ Ⓒ Ⓓ Ⓔ
23. Ⓐ Ⓑ Ⓒ Ⓓ Ⓔ
24. Ⓐ Ⓑ Ⓒ Ⓓ Ⓔ

25. Ⓐ Ⓑ Ⓒ Ⓓ Ⓔ
26. Ⓐ Ⓑ Ⓒ Ⓓ Ⓔ
27. Ⓐ Ⓑ Ⓒ Ⓓ Ⓔ
28. Ⓐ Ⓑ Ⓒ Ⓓ Ⓔ

Time: 25 minutes

Start: _____

Stop: _____

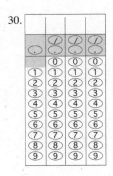

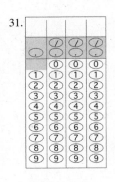

29. 30. 31. 32. 33.

34. 35. 36. 37. 38.

SECTION

5

Writing
Skills
30 minutes

1. Ⓐ Ⓑ Ⓒ Ⓓ Ⓔ
2. Ⓐ Ⓑ Ⓒ Ⓓ Ⓔ
3. Ⓐ Ⓑ Ⓒ Ⓓ Ⓔ
4. Ⓐ Ⓑ Ⓒ Ⓓ Ⓔ
5. Ⓐ Ⓑ Ⓒ Ⓓ Ⓔ
6. Ⓐ Ⓑ Ⓒ Ⓓ Ⓔ
7. Ⓐ Ⓑ Ⓒ Ⓓ Ⓔ
8. Ⓐ Ⓑ Ⓒ Ⓓ Ⓔ
9. Ⓐ Ⓑ Ⓒ Ⓓ Ⓔ
10. Ⓐ Ⓑ Ⓒ Ⓓ Ⓔ
11. Ⓐ Ⓑ Ⓒ Ⓓ Ⓔ
12. Ⓐ Ⓑ Ⓒ Ⓓ Ⓔ
13. Ⓐ Ⓑ Ⓒ Ⓓ Ⓔ

14. Ⓐ Ⓑ Ⓒ Ⓓ Ⓔ
15. Ⓐ Ⓑ Ⓒ Ⓓ Ⓔ
16. Ⓐ Ⓑ Ⓒ Ⓓ Ⓔ
17. Ⓐ Ⓑ Ⓒ Ⓓ Ⓔ
18. Ⓐ Ⓑ Ⓒ Ⓓ Ⓔ
19. Ⓐ Ⓑ Ⓒ Ⓓ Ⓔ
20. Ⓐ Ⓑ Ⓒ Ⓓ Ⓔ
21. Ⓐ Ⓑ Ⓒ Ⓓ Ⓔ
22. Ⓐ Ⓑ Ⓒ Ⓓ Ⓔ
23. Ⓐ Ⓑ Ⓒ Ⓓ Ⓔ
24. Ⓐ Ⓑ Ⓒ Ⓓ Ⓔ
25. Ⓐ Ⓑ Ⓒ Ⓓ Ⓔ
26. Ⓐ Ⓑ Ⓒ Ⓓ Ⓔ

27. Ⓐ Ⓑ Ⓒ Ⓓ Ⓔ
28. Ⓐ Ⓑ Ⓒ Ⓓ Ⓔ
29. Ⓐ Ⓑ Ⓒ Ⓓ Ⓔ
30. Ⓐ Ⓑ Ⓒ Ⓓ Ⓔ
31. Ⓐ Ⓑ Ⓒ Ⓓ Ⓔ
32. Ⓐ Ⓑ Ⓒ Ⓓ Ⓔ
33. Ⓐ Ⓑ Ⓒ Ⓓ Ⓔ
34. Ⓐ Ⓑ Ⓒ Ⓓ Ⓔ
35. Ⓐ Ⓑ Ⓒ Ⓓ Ⓔ
36. Ⓐ Ⓑ Ⓒ Ⓓ Ⓔ
37. Ⓐ Ⓑ Ⓒ Ⓓ Ⓔ
38. Ⓐ Ⓑ Ⓒ Ⓓ Ⓔ
39. Ⓐ Ⓑ Ⓒ Ⓓ Ⓔ

Time: 30 minutes

Start: _____

Stop: _____

SECTION I
Time—25 minutes
24 questions (1–24)

| Turn to Section I of your answer sheet to answer the questions in this section. |

Directions: For each question in this section, select the best answer from among the choices given and fill in the corresponding circle on the answer sheet.

Each sentence below has one or two blanks, each blank indicating that something has been omitted. Beneath the sentence are five words or sets of words labeled A through E. Choose the word or set of words that, when inserted in the sentence, best fits the meaning of the sentence as a whole.

EXAMPLE:

Rather than accepting the theory unquestioningly, Deborah regarded it with -----.

(A) mirth
(B) sadness
(C) responsibility
(D) ignorance
(E) skepticism

 Ⓐ Ⓑ Ⓒ Ⓓ ●

---

1. The lawyer was ------- in her cross-examination; her aggressive questioning continued for what seemed like days.

   (A) unrelenting
   (B) sympathetic
   (C) casual
   (D) reflective
   (E) stagnant

2. A disaster was ------- by the quick-thinking helmsman, who steered the ship away from the rocks that had ------- emerged from the ocean.

   (A) predicted . . permanently
   (B) forestalled . . reluctantly
   (C) averted . . suddenly
   (D) dispelled . . passively
   (E) avoided . . serenely

3. The ------- decline in the price of the stock caught many investors unprepared; they had expected its value to remain ------- for many months, if not years.

   (A) unexpected . . volatile
   (B) gradual . . low
   (C) improvised . . uniform
   (D) cumbersome . . liquid
   (E) precipitous . . stable

4. Unlike our previous manager, who often made sudden decisions without thinking carefully about them, the new one is far more ------- and deliberate.

   (A) capricious
   (B) pensive
   (C) remorseful
   (D) intolerant
   (E) inexorable

5. When spending long periods of time among the tribal peoples whose cultures they are studying, ------- should be careful not to introduce harmful germs or disruptive technologies into those societies.

   (A) herpetologists
   (B) oncologists
   (C) ornithologists
   (D) agronomists
   (E) anthropologists

GO ON TO THE NEXT PAGE →

6. Alicia's ------- performance in the company play astonished those who were familiar with her ------- demeanor at work.

(A) fearless . . intrepid
(B) emotional . . stolid
(C) inspiring . . meticulous
(D) stable . . attentive
(E) amusing . . flippant

7. In an industry in which truthfulness is too often an impediment to success, many salespeople have had to become masters of ------- in order to advance their careers.

(A) prevarication
(B) timidity
(C) certitude
(D) perseverance
(E) consumption

8. Gina considered her thousands of hours of volunteer work to be selfish rather than -------; she simply enjoyed working with people and did not consider herself a paragon of -------.

(A) altruistic . . magnanimity
(B) egotistical . . placidity
(C) generous . . diversity
(D) reassuring . . distortion
(E) desperate . . obsession

The passages below are followed by questions based on their content and the relationship between the passages. Answer each question based on what is stated or implied in the passages and in any introductory material that may be provided.

Questions 9–12 are based on the following passage.

PASSAGE 1

Reasoning is a vital human activity. For
Line unlike some animals that function instinctively, we need knowledge in order to survive.
5 Some knowledge can be gained directly. In
this way we know, for example, that an object
in front of us looks orange and tastes sweet.
But we cannot know that it is edible and
nutritious, or that it contains vitamin C,
10 which prevents scurvy, without a process of
reasoning. The vast bulk of human
knowledge is based on reasoning. Indeed, our
knowledge can be described as a pyramid, in
which what is directly evident provides the
15 foundation on which all other beliefs are
based.

PASSAGE 2

Believe nothing. The less we believe, the less
likely we are to believe something false.
When arguing, we must always assume that
20 our opposers are both sharp-minded and
low-minded, so that we never underrate their
ability. Since many argument maneuvers are
not made *consciously*, the simple fact that
people are sincere does not mean that we can
25 trust their arguments (though we might be
able to trust them). Furthermore, some
people who believe in a position also believe
that anything furthering their position is
acceptable. This is the attitude that "the end
30 justifies the means." But while they are
already convinced, we should not be.

GO ON TO THE NEXT PAGE ⟶

Passage 1: Reproduced courtesy of Prentice-Hall. Wayne A. Davis, *An Introduction to Logic* © 1986 Prentice-Hall
Passage 2: Michael A. Gilbert, *How to Win an Argument* © 1965 McGraw-Hill

9. Which of the following pairs of adjectives best characterizes the perspectives of Passage 1 and Passage 2, respectively, on the topic of human reasoning?

   (A) humorous versus solemn
   (B) resigned versus hopeful
   (C) analytical versus celebratory
   (D) literary versus scientific
   (E) descriptive versus prescriptive

10. The author of Passage 2 would most likely qualify the claim in Passage 1 that "the vast bulk of human knowledge is based on reasoning" (lines 10–11) by

   (A) asserting that human knowledge comes directly from the senses
   (B) cautioning that such reasoning is often dubious
   (C) disputing the suggestion that humans are capable of reasoning
   (D) arguing that people respond more to logic than to emotion
   (E) stressing that most people tend to resist making illogical arguments

11. Unlike Passage 1, Passage 2 is primarily concerned with describing

   (A) the biases of debaters
   (B) the nature of knowledge
   (C) the process of reasoning
   (D) the various types of logical proof
   (E) the use of deception to bolster an argument

12. In Passage 2, the sentence "Believe nothing" (line 16) primarily suggests that we should

   (A) assume that our opponents are insincere
   (B) rely exclusively on our senses to ascertain the truth
   (C) be skeptical of the claims others make to support their arguments
   (D) remember that "the end justifies the means"
   (E) regard knowledge as having a hierarchical structure

Questions 13–24 are based on the following passages.

The following passages discuss the moral and social value of capital punishment.

PASSAGE 1

Reverence for human life is part of the moral foundation of a just society. The only justifi-
Line cation for causing death is to prevent the deaths of others. Thus, individuals have the
5 right to use deadly force to save their own lives from criminal aggressors, and countries have the right to wage war to prevent their own destruction. Likewise, a community can and should use capital punishment to protect
10 the lives of its members. Saint Thomas Aquinas wrote: "The slaying of an evildoer is lawful inasmuch as it is directed to the welfare of the whole community."

When judiciously applied as a punishment
15 for the willful killing of innocents, the death penalty serves to deter those who would murder and to protect society from those who have murdered. By reserving the ultimate penalty of death for those who
20 wantonly kill, we are clearly proclaiming our special reverence for life. It is society's ultimate means of self-defense.

The death of a criminal can certainly be justified if it prevents the future deaths of
25 innocent victims. Since death is the greatest punishment a society can impose, it stands to reason that it is the most powerful way to deter those who would commit a crime.

Economist Isaac Ehrlich compared the
30 murder rate in the United States with the rate of executions between 1933 and 1967. His conclusion: "The trade-off between the execution of an offender and the lives of potential victims it might have saved was of
35 the order of magnitude of 1 for 8." In other words, each use of the death penalty seems to have deterred the killing of eight potential victims. Homicides decreased by almost 36 percent immediately following a well-
40 publicized execution, according to the research of sociologist David Phillips.

GO ON TO THE NEXT PAGE ⟹

The absence of a death threat encourages crime. In 1950, when 82 criminals were executed, there were 7,020 homicides. In
45   1980, after a decade of virtual abandonment of the death penalty, there were 22,958 homicides, a 300 percent increase. As society became more concerned with the life of the criminal, lives of innocent victims became
50   cheaper.

Another value of the death penalty is one that has been unfairly disparaged in the softhearted modern era; punishment for the sake of doing justice. Some attack this notion
55   by labelling it retribution, and argue that our system should seek only deterrence and rehabilitation. Deterrence is important, but it is a practical and utilitarian consideration rather than a moral and just one. Rehabilitation
60   is a worthy ideal, but justice demands more. Without punishment for the sake of punishment, the age-old notion of justice falters.

One clear way we show our respect for life is to decree that those who unjustly take a life
65   should forfeit their own. The crime of murder is so horrendous, so irrevocable, that it demands a commensurate punishment. Those who blithely dismiss retribution as barbaric are the ones who in fact demean the
70   value of human life. As philosopher Ernest van den Haag says: "Life becomes cheaper as we become kinder to those who wantonly take it."

PASSAGE 2

Reverence for human life is part of the moral
75   foundation of a just society. That is why no one can justly kill another; just as it is wrong for an individual to do so, it is wrong for the state to do so.

There is simply no convincing evidence
80   that executions deter potential murders. In the reams of studies on the issue, only one se-rious work, that of economist Isaac Ehrlich, showed a correlation, and his analysis was soundly refuted by investigations into his
85   procedures. The most thorough research is that of Professor J. Thorsten Sellin of the University of Pennsylvania, who compared the murder rate in similar communities that have and do not have the death penalty. His
90   conclusions: "Capital executions have no

demonstrable effect on homicide rates. Police are killed as frequently in death penalty states as in abolitionist states...abolition or restoration of the death penalty has no
95   demonstrable effect on the rate of subsequent homicides."

There is no logical reason to believe that capital punishment will deter murder any more effectively than a life prison term will.
100   Murder is an irrational act, often a crime of passion. Those who kill tend not to balance the possible penalties against their desires.

The fact that capital punishment violates our ideal of rehabilitation is even more
105   apparent, for the death penalty is absolute and irrevocable. It could permit the greatest injustice of all, the murder of an innocent person. Human beings are fallible, which is one reason they should not have power of life
110   and death over each other. The number of murder convictions that have been discov-ered to be in error is a powerful argument against the death penalty.

Fundamentally, the argument boils down
115   to the just role of the state. As part of the social contract, people surrender some of their natural rights to the state. But the state has no right to take an individual's life, just as no individual has that right over another.
120   Most murders are committed for reasons of vengeance. We should not legitimize murderous vengeance by making it part of our system of justice.

GO ON TO THE NEXT PAGE

Reprinted from *Pro and Con* © 1983 by Walter Issacson and The Stonesong Press and used with permission of The Stonesong Press, LLC.

13. The first paragraph of Passage 1 suggests that individuals, communities, and countries

(A) must categorically denounce violence
(B) are using outdated theories of morality
(C) each have different priorities
(D) all have similar rights of self-protection
(E) do not adequately punish criminals

14. Passage 1 mentions Saint Thomas Aquinas as one who

(A) denounces war
(B) values the rights of individuals over those of society
(C) supports the death penalty
(D) was a former criminal
(E) shares a common misconception

15. According to Passage 1, a society can proclaim its "special reverence for life" (line 21) by

(A) abstaining from declarations of war
(B) protecting those who are accused of crimes from physical retribution
(C) severely punishing those who kill others
(D) providing for the needs of the poor
(E) protecting children from abusive adults

16. Which of the following, if true, would most directly undermine the argument made in the fifth paragraph of Passage 1 (lines 42–50)?

(A) Most Americans favor the death penalty.
(B) Executions have always been highly publicized events.
(C) In 1950, the electric chair was more widely used than lethal injection.
(D) Most criminals come from low-income families.
(E) Far fewer murder weapons were available and the population was much lower in 1950 than in 1980.

17. Which of the following best characterizes Ernest van den Haag's attitude toward those who commit homicide, as it is presented in Passage 1?

(A) utilitarian and practical
(B) harsh and uncompromising
(C) sympathetic
(D) scientifically analytical
(E) indifferent

18. The author of Passage 2 mentions "reams" (line 81) in order to emphasize

(A) the dramatic effect of capital punishment in deterring crime
(B) the amount of legislation pertaining to capital punishment
(C) the many cases in which an innocent person has been executed for a crime
(D) the quantity of research that demonstrates no relationship between executions and future murder rates
(E) the extent to which the public disapproves of capital punishment

19. It can be inferred that "abolitionist states" (line 93) are those that

(A) have eliminated the death penalty
(B) have more severe penalties for those who kill police officers than for those who kill non-officers
(C) use capital punishment intermittently
(D) use executions solely to deter future crimes
(E) do not have coherent laws regarding the punishment of those who commit homicide

GO ON TO THE NEXT PAGE

20. In saying that "the death penalty is absolute" (line 105), the author of Passage 2 indicates that execution is

(A) endorsed by legislative bodies
(B) supported by a majority of the population
(C) a deterrent for potential criminals
(D) an act that cannot be reversed
(E) foreign to most systems of morality

21. Which of the following topics does the author of Passage 2 discuss in both the first paragraph and the final paragraph?

(A) revenge
(B) the social contract
(C) a just society
(D) rehabilitation
(E) motives for killing

22. Which of the following best characterizes the attitudes of the two passages toward the work of Isaac Ehrlich?

(A) Both passages praise it, but also indicate minor flaws.
(B) Passage 1 cites it uncritically, but Passage 2 dismisses it.
(C) Both passages use it to support their theses.
(D) Passage 1 criticizes it on moral grounds, while Passage 2 criticizes it on scientific grounds.
(E) Passage 1 praises it highly, but Passage 2 abstains from evaluating it.

23. Which of the following best summarizes the position of each passage on the death penalty?

(A) Both passages claim that it is ineffective.
(B) Passage 1 claims that it is a moral duty, while Passage 2 claims that it is a practical necessity.
(C) Passage 1 claims that it should be used only as a deterrent, while Passage 2 claims that it can be used for strictly punitive purposes.
(D) Passage 1 claims that it is necessary to a just society, while Passage 2 claims that it is antithetical to a just society.
(E) Passage 1 claims that it demeans life, while Passage 2 claims that it honors life.

24. Those who "attack this notion" (line 54) are most likely to include which of the following?

(A) Saint Thomas Aquinas
(B) The author of Passage 1
(C) David Phillips
(D) The author of Passage 2
(E) Isaac Ehrlich

STOP

If you finish before time is called, you may check your work on this section only. Do not turn to any other section of the test.

2   2   2   2   2   2

SECTION 2
Time—25 minutes
20 questions (1–20)

Turn to Section 2 of your answer sheet to answer the questions in this section.

Directions: For this section, solve each problem and decide which is the best of the choices given. Fill in the corresponding circle on the answer sheet. You may use any available space for scratchwork.

Notes

1. The use of a calculator is permitted.

2. All numbers used are real numbers.

3. Figures that accompany problems in this test are intended to provide information useful in solving the problems. They are drawn as accurately as possible EXCEPT when it is stated in a specific problem that the figure is not drawn to scale. All figures lie in a plane unless otherwise indicated.

4. Unless otherwise specified, the domain of any function f is assumed to be the set of all real numbers x for which $f(x)$ is a real number.

Reference Information

   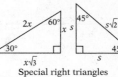

$A = \pi r^2$ $A = \ell w$ $A = \frac{1}{2} bh$ $V = \ell wh$ $V = \pi r^2 h$ $c^2 = a^2 + b^2$ Special right triangles

$C = 2\pi r$

The number of degrees of arc in a circle is 360.

The sum of the measures in degrees of the angles of a triangle is 180.

---

1. Which of the following integers, when doubled, produces a number that is 2 greater than a multiple of 6?

   (A) 5
   (B) 6
   (C) 7
   (D) 8
   (E) 9

2. What is the circumference, in inches, of a circle with an area of 16π square inches?

   (A) 2π
   (B) 4π
   (C) 8π
   (D) 16π
   (E) 32π

3. If 4.5 zots are equivalent to 1 zat, how many zats are equivalent to 36 zots?

   (A)   8
   (B)   9
   (C) 12
   (D) 16
   (E) 81

GO ON TO THE NEXT PAGE

2   **2**   2   **2**   **2**   **2**

1, 2, 1, 2, 1, 2 . . .

4. If the sequence above continues as shown, what is the sum of the first 20 terms?

(A) 20
(B) 30
(C) 40
(D) 45
(E) 60

5. Tom's weight is 20 pounds less than twice Carl's weight. If together Tom and Carl weigh 340 pounds, how much does Tom weigh?

(A) 120 pounds
(B) 160 pounds
(C) 180 pounds
(D) 200 pounds
(E) 220 pounds

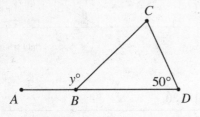

Note: Figure not drawn to scale.

6. In the figure above, if $BC = BD$, what is the value of y?

(A) 100
(B) 120
(C) 125
(D) 130
(E) 140

7. For all integers n, if $*n$ is defined by the equation

$$*n = \begin{cases} \dfrac{n}{3} & \text{if } n \text{ is divisible by 3} \\ 3n & \text{if } n \text{ is not divisible by 3} \end{cases}$$

which of the following is equivalent to $*10$?

(A) $*3$
(B) $*9$
(C) $*20$
(D) $*30$
(E) $*90$

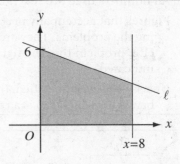

Note: Figure not drawn to scale.

8. In the figure above, if line l has a slope of $-\dfrac{1}{2}$, what is the area of the shaded region, in square units?

(A) 28
(B) 32
(C) 36
(D) 40
(E) 42

9. If each box of pencils contains x pencils, and if 10 boxes of pencils cost d dollars, how many dollars should it cost to buy $50x$ pencils?

(A) $\dfrac{d}{5x}$

(B) $\dfrac{x}{5d}$

(C) $\dfrac{5}{dx}$

(D) $5d$

(E) $5dx$

GO ON TO THE NEXT PAGE

2   2   2   2   2   2   2

10. Beth had planned to run an average of 6 miles per hour in a race. She had a very good race and actually ran at an average speed of 7 miles per hour, finishing 10 minutes sooner than she would have if she had averaged 6 miles per hour. How long was the race?

(A)   6 miles
(B)   7 miles
(C)   18 miles
(D)   60 miles
(E)   70 miles

11. On a certain map that is drawn to scale, 1.5 centimeters is equivalent to 2 miles. If two cities are 35 miles apart, how many centimeters apart should they be on this map?

(A)   24.75
(B)   26.00
(C)   26.25
(D)   45.00
(E)   46.33

12. Jose needs a $\frac{5}{8}$ meter length of copper pipe to complete a project. Which of the following lengths of pipe can be cut to the required length with the least length of pipe left over?

(A) $\frac{9}{16}$ meter

(B) $\frac{3}{5}$ meter

(C) $\frac{3}{4}$ meter

(D) $\frac{4}{5}$ meter

(E) $\frac{5}{6}$ meter

13. If $\frac{1}{2}a = 2b = 4c = 24$, what is the value of $a+b+c$?

(A)   24
(B)   40
(C)   42
(D)   64
(E)   66

14. If $x^2 > 6$, which of the following statements must be true?

   I. $|x| > 3$
   II. $(x-2)(x+2) > 2$
   III. $x + 1{,}000 > 0$

(A)   II only
(B)   I and II only
(C)   I and III only
(D)   II and III only
(E)   I, II, and III

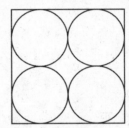

15. Each of the four circles in the figure above is tangent to two sides of the square and also tangent to two of the other circles. If each circle has a circumference of 4π inches, what is the area, in square inches, of the square?

(A)   4
(B)   16
(C)   24
(D)   32
(E)   64

$$abc + df + g$$

16. If the expression above is an odd number, then at most how many of the integers a, b, c, d, f, and g could be even?

(A)   Two
(B)   Three
(C)   Four
(D)   Five
(E)   Six

GO ON TO THE NEXT PAGE

2   **2**   2   2   **2**   **2**

17. The average (arithmetic mean) of six integers is 32. If the numbers are all different, and if none is less than 10, what is the greatest possible value of any of these integers?

 (A)   127
 (B)   132
 (C)   137
 (D)   142
 (E)   147

18. If $\left(\dfrac{1}{4}\right)^{n} = 2^{-3}$, then $n =$

 (A) $-\dfrac{3}{2}$

 (B) $-\dfrac{2}{3}$

 (C) $\dfrac{2}{3}$

 (D) $\dfrac{3}{2}$

 (E)   3

19. How many integers from 100 to 1,000 contain NO repeated digits? (Numbers like 252 and 991 are considered to have repeated digits.)

 (A)   632
 (B)   648
 (C)   720
 (D)   810
 (E)   900

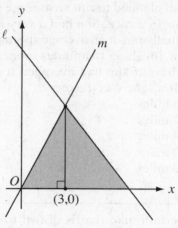

Note: Figure not drawn to scale.

20. If line m in the figure above has a slope of 2 and the shaded triangle has an area of 24 square units, what is the slope of line ℓ?

 (A) -6

 (B) $-\dfrac{6}{5}$

 (C) $-\dfrac{5}{6}$

 (D) $-\dfrac{2}{3}$

 (E) $-\dfrac{1}{3}$

STOP

If you finish before time is called, you may check your work on this section only. Do not turn to any other section of the test.

3   3   3   3   3   3

SECTION 3
Time—25 minutes
24 questions (25–48)

Turn to Section 3 of your answer sheet to answer the questions in this section.

Directions: For each question in this section, select the best answer from among the choices given and fill in the corresponding circle on the answer sheet.

Each sentence below has one or two blanks, each blank indicating that something has been omitted. Beneath the sentence are five words or sets of words labeled A through E. Choose the word or set of words that, when inserted in the sentence, <u>best</u> fits the meaning of the sentence as a whole.

EXAMPLE:

Rather than accepting the theory unquestioningly, Deborah regarded it with -----.

(A) mirth
(B) sadness
(C) responsibility
(D) ignorance
(E) skepticism

25. Since the publisher had only allotted 250 pages to the book, the author's 400-page manuscript had to be drastically -------.

   (A) enhanced
   (B) pursued
   (C) accelerated
   (D) abridged
   (E) conducted

26. The critics agreed that the first film was ------- and artistically daring; but that its sequel, in direct contrast, was bland and -------.

   (A) enchanting . . conventional
   (B) dull . . innovative
   (C) humorous . . unique
   (D) tedious . . pedestrian
   (E) trite . . foreign

27. For an inveterate gambler, even ------- rewards reinforce the obsession, disproving the assumption that payoffs must be consistent to support an addiction.

   (A) luxurious
   (B) steadfast
   (C) sporadic
   (D) placid
   (E) continual

28. Those who denied a ------- between exercise and ------- were suprised by the finding that those who walked at least 10 miles per week lived an average of 7 years longer than those who were sedentary.

   (A) causation . . exhaustion
   (B) relationship . . diet
   (C) dispute . . fulfillment
   (D) mediation . . prosperity
   (E) correlation . . longevity

29. Even to physicists who study it for decades, subatomic physics is -------; to laypeople, then, it is downright -------.

   (A) forthcoming . . responsive
   (B) daunting . . fallow
   (C) cryptic . . routine
   (D) challenging . . inscrutable
   (E) fatuous . . singular

GO ON TO THE NEXT PAGE

3   **3**   3   3   **3**   **3**

Each passage below is followed by one or two questions based on its content. Answer each question based on what is stated or implied in the passage that precedes it.

Questions 30–31 are based on the following passage.

Media is a term that describes a variety of people, structures, technologies, and
Line relationships. Traditional definitions of media focus on messages that originate from
5 some institutional source, travel through some channel, and reach a large, anonymous audience. Although these basic components of media are present today, their nature has changed with the advent of new electronic
10 forms of communication. The current media environment does not always fit this description. Although previously constrained by cost, individuals can now offer messages inexpensively via the internet. Audiences for
15 media messages are sometimes small and on occasion make themselves known to the producers of the messages.

30. The passage suggests that, unlike traditional media, many new forms of media

(A) originate from institutions
(B) are anonymous
(C) focus exclusively on selling products or services
(D) are difficult to understand
(E) are more accessible to users

31. The tone of this passage is best described as

(A) pleading
(B) humorous
(C) objective
(D) skeptical
(E) indignant

Questions 32–33 are based on the following passage.

When mathematicians speak frankly about their discipline, they tend to circle
Line around a fundamental question: are the ideas of mathematicians discovered or invented?
5 Mathematicians speak of proofs as "elegant" or "beautiful," praising work for its aesthetic nature. Dr. Mina Rees, a logician, wrote, "Mathematics is both inductive and deductive, needing, like poetry, persons who are
10 creative and have a sense of the beautiful for its surest progress." But, even so, most mathematicians say that the great ideas of mathematics exist independently of them. Dr. John Conway, for one, cannot imagine he is doing
15 anything but discovering results that exist without him. Why? "Because they couldn't be otherwise than what they are," he said. "Two and two might be five and pigs might fly. But in the world I come from, two and two are
20 four and pigs don't fly."

32. The quotation in lines 8–11 ("Mathematics is both...its surest progress") suggests that

(A) mathematicians are often very good writers
(B) aesthetic sense is an asset to mathematical thought
(C) many mathematical claims cannot be proved
(D) mathematical truths are discovered, not invented
(E) poets have made many contributions to mathematical progress

33. The quotation in lines 17–20 ("Two and two...don't fly") is intended to refute the idea that

(A) mathematical discoveries do not require intuition
(B) mathematical proofs are beautiful
(C) mathematicians do not require formal education to make profound discoveries
(D) logic is never violated in mathematics
(E) mathematical truths are open to interpretation

First passage: Timothy A. Borchers, *Persuasion in the Media Age.* © 2002 McGraw-Hill
Second passage: *Scientists at Work,* Science Times. © 2000 McGraw-Hill

GO ON TO THE NEXT PAGE ⟩

3　　　**3**　　　**3**　　　**3**　　　**3**　　　**3**

Questions 34–40 are based on the following passage.

The following is an excerpt from a book about American journalism that was written in 1939.

It is singular that newspapers, seldom bashful
about their virtues, have made so little to-do
Line about their achievements in crusading. As
champions of reforms, as defenders of individ-
5　uals, as protagonists of their communities,
they have exercised influences quite as important as the transmission of information and the
expression of opinion.
　　Yet this has been written only in fragmen-
10　tary form. Historians of daily journals, biogra-
phers of newspaper publishers and editors,
and occasionally an instructor in a school of
journalism, have dealt with it in particular,
sometimes in its larger aspects, but not sweep-
15　ingly. A treatment at once minute and comprehensive, indeed, is impossible within the
scope of a single volume, such is the wealth of
material available. What is presented here
must attempt a representative selection.
20　　More than once a newspaper, at the conclusion of a successful campaign, has preened
itself or has paid tribute to a fellow. Yet by and
large our most articulate institution, sometimes almost as vainglorious as politics, has
25　been surprisingly reticent about one of its
primary responsibilities. It has nevertheless
recognized crusading as a natural function
and as a responsibility, and has discharged it
for the most part admirably, sometimes at
30　severe sacrifice. That there has been default in
certain areas none can deny, but the account
balances heavily to the credit of the press and
to the benefit of the public.
　　Here lies the best argument for newspaper
35　freedom not only from governmental interference but from the coercion of a capitalist economy. The history of our press since colonial days
is shot through with the struggle for unre-
stricted capital activity and the right to crusade.
40　Every crusade implies, to be sure, the expression of opinion or of an attitude, but it involves
more than that. It means also a willingness to
fight if need be. It means, according to my dictionary, "to contend zealously against any evil,
45　or on behalf of any reform."
　　To contend zealously must mean surely to
struggle with ardent devotion. The zeal which

fires a crusading editor may bring him to the
boiling point of fanaticism, and has done it
50　time and again. None who has undertaken a
campaign in the certainty that it would entail
loss of circulation and advertising, perhaps
permanently, was not a fanatic, just on the
sunny side of lunacy. Skeptics who deny that
55　campaigns are ever undertaken for other
than sordid motives may disabuse their
minds by examining the record. If newspapers have faced actual losses in the discharge
of their duties as public servants, then they
60　have an unmistakable claim to the guarantee
of the First Amendment.

34.　The author's attitude toward newspapers is
　　best described as

　　(A)　laudatory
　　(B)　objectively analytical
　　(C)　exasperated
　　(D)　jocular
　　(E)　harshly critical

35.　In the first paragraph, the author indicates
　　surprise at the fact that newspapers

　　(A)　are still profitable
　　(B)　are not more widely read
　　(C)　transmit so little information that is
　　　　worthy of notice
　　(D)　do not exercise more influence in their
　　　　communities
　　(E)　have not acknowledged one of their virtues

36.　The "wealth of material" (lines 17–18) is infor-
　　mation about

　　(A)　the means by which reporters get their
　　　　information
　　(B)　the corporate structure of certain
　　　　newspapers
　　(C)　the reading practices of Americans
　　(D)　the ability of newspapers to effect
　　　　change in their communities
　　(E)　the relationship between newspapers
　　　　and other media

Silas Bent, *Newspaper Crusaders: A Neglected Story* © 1939
McGraw-Hill

GO ON TO THE NEXT PAGE →

37. As it is used in line 28, "discharged" most nearly means

(A) electrified
(B) dismissed
(C) accomplished
(D) emitted
(E) refused

38. The "skeptics" (line 54) believe that newspapers

(A) are becoming less popular
(B) are fundamentally self-serving
(C) are fanatical about political causes
(D) do not take advantage of the First Amendment
(E) should be replaced by other forms of media

39. As it is used in line 48, "fires" most nearly means

(A) destroys
(B) dismisses
(C) initiates
(D) stimulates
(E) interrogates

40. The final paragraph suggests that crusading poses a potential danger to newspapers by

(A) causing a loss of revenue
(B) increasing competition with other newspapers
(C) encouraging reporters to abandon journalistic principles
(D) restricting the freedom of journalists
(E) spurring good journalists to quit their jobs

Questions 41–48 are based on the following passage.

The following passage discusses some of the work of Henri Matisse, an influential twentieth-century French artist.

Henri Matisse wrote in a 1948 letter:

I have always tried to hide my own efforts
Line *and wished my work to have the lightness and*
joyousness of a springtime which never lets
5 *anyone know the labors it has cost. So I am*
afraid the young, seeing in my work only the
apparent facility and negligence in the drawing,
will use this as an excuse for dispensing with
certain efforts I believe necessary.

10 Matisse's *The Flowing Hair*, made of cut and
pasted paper, appears so unlabored that one
might misunderstand all that is behind and
went before it. Few would guess that a work as
lively and energetic as *The Flowing Hair* was
15 executed by a man eighty-three years old.
Moreover, *The Flowing Hair* is just one work in
an entire cut paper series of joyous, colorful
pieces suggesting dance and music.
   The Flowing Hair shows no three-
20 dimensional modeling of the forms or shadows.
The female form is depicted as an intense
blue shape of flowing curves, a graceful rhyth-
mic arabesque. The whole figure—arms, legs,
torso, even the hair—seems to be in motion.
25 The footless legs have strength, and the arms
have almost become wings. One feels that at
any moment the figure might dance off the
paper.
   How did Matisse, as an old man, come to
30 create such vital works? One answer is his
development of a new art form: cut paper, or
as it is called in French, *Papier collé, Papier
découpé,* or *découpage.* Partly crippled by illness
and repeated surgery in 1941, Matisse came to
35 rely on the less strenuous medium of cut paper,
rather than oil painting, as his major art form.
He could work in the new art form lying down
in his bed or from his chair. He had studio assistants paint expanses of paper in brilliant hues of
40 gouache, an opaque watercolor paint, to his
requirements. The old master then cut shapes

GO ON TO THE NEXT PAGE →

3   3   3   3   3   3

directly out of the paper without any preparatory drawings. He felt he was drawing with
scissors. He loved the directness of the process
45 of cutting. After the shapes were cut, Matisse
instructed his assistants to pin the pieces onto
his studio wall. The many tiny pinholes in the
paper show that Matisse had his helpers adjust
the arrangement of the cutouts numerous times
50 until the most expressive spatial relationship
had been achieved.

    Out of the painted, cut, and pasted papers
arose a self-sufficient medium of great
pictorial strength. Cutting paper with scissors
55 gave him a very strong feeling for line and
enabled him to develop forms of great simplicity and economy. Yet Matisse did not use his
scissors to declare war on drawing and painting. Rather, his scissors were an extension of
60 pencil, charcoal stick, and paintbrush. "My
découpages," he stated, "do not break away
from my former pictures. It is only that I have
achieved more completely and abstractly a
form reduced to the essential, and have
65 retained the object, no longer in the complexity of its space, but as the symbol which is
both sufficient and necessary to make the
object exist in its own right, as well as for the
composition in which I have conceived it."
70   Old and crippled, Matisse could have rested
on the laurels of his past accomplishments.
But not Matisse. He truly enjoyed the
challenge, the directness, the intimacy of his
new approach to collage. He relished the
75 opportunity to select, place, and reposition the
cut paper shapes. His habit of hard work in
the studio was so deeply rooted and his
creative vitality was so strong that he let
nothing, not even bad health, interrupt his art.
80 In the end, Matisse came to esteem his cut
paper works as the high point of his creative
career.

Robert Bersson, *Responding to Art: Form, Content, and
Context.* © 2004 McGraw-Hill

41. The central purpose of this passage is to

(A) contrast the artistic works of Henri
Matisse with those of his contemporaries
(B) enumerate the merits of *The Flowing
Hair*
(C) analyze a controversy regarding the life
of Henri Matisse
(D) describe the development of a new art
form
(E) examine several artistic movements of
the early twentieth century

42. The quotation in lines 5–9 ("So I am . . . I believe
necessary") suggests that Matisse was con-
cerned about people thinking that his work

(A) was created in an inferior medium
(B) required less effort than it actually did
(C) evoked dark themes
(D) was not valuable
(E) too closely imitated the work of other
artists

43. The author mentions that Matisse was "eighty-
three years old" (line 15) primarily in order to

(A) emphasize the influence Matisse had on
the art world in general
(B) indicate that Matisse had begun his
artistic career late in life
(C) refute the misconception that Matisse
died young
(D) contrast Matisse's artistic style with that
of the younger generation of artists
(E) contrast the litheness of Matisse's work
with his physical condition

44. In line 39, the word "brilliant" most nearly
means

(A) intelligent
(B) flimsy
(C) celebrated
(D) shining
(E) intimidating

GO ON TO THE NEXT PAGE ⇒

3   **3**   **3**   **3**   **3**   **3**

45. The quotation from Matisse in lines 60–69 emphasizes which of the following qualities of découpage?

   (A) pictorial simplicity
   (B) changeability
   (C) vividness
   (D) three-dimensionality
   (E) transparency

46. The "intimacy" mentioned in line 73 characterizes the relationship between Matisse and

   (A) his critics
   (B) his fellow artists
   (C) his medium
   (D) his philosophy
   (E) his assistants

47. The passage indicates that the medium of cut paper provided Matisse with all of the following EXCEPT

   (A) ease of use
   (B) the ability to manipulate forms
   (C) pictorial strength
   (D) the feeling of depth
   (E) vitality

48. The final paragraph characterizes Matisse primarily as

   (A) weak and ineffective
   (B) popular and outgoing
   (C) enthusiastic and diligent
   (D) sober and intellectual
   (E) critical and irascible

If you finish before time is called, you may check your work on this section only. Do not turn to any other section of the test.

SECTION 4
Time—25 minutes
18 questions (21–38)

Turn to Section 4 of your answer sheet to answer the questions in this section.

Directions: This section contains two types of questions. You have 25 minutes to complete both types. For questions 21–28, solve each problem and decide which is the best of the choices given. Fill in the corresponding circle on the answer sheet. You may use any available space for scratchwork.

Notes

1. The use of a calculator is permitted.
2. All numbers used are real numbers.
3. Figures that accompany problems in this test are intended to provide information useful in solving the problems. They are drawn as accurately as possible EXCEPT when it is stated in a specific problem that the figure is not drawn to scale. All figures lie in a plane unless otherwise indicated.
4. Unless otherwise specified, the domain of any function f is assumed to be the set of all real numbers x for which $f(x)$ is a real number.

Reference Information

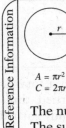   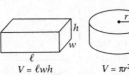 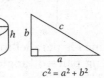 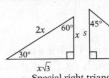

$A = \pi r^2$ $A = \ell w$ $A = \frac{1}{2} bh$ $V = \ell wh$ $V = \pi r^2 h$ $c^2 = a^2 + b^2$ Special right triangles
$C = 2\pi r$

The number of degrees of arc in a circle is 360.
The sum of the measures in degrees of the angles of a triangle is 180.

21. If, $\dfrac{18}{15} = \dfrac{x}{5}$, then $x =$

   (A) $\dfrac{6}{5}$

   (B) 3

   (C) $\dfrac{75}{18}$

   (D) 6

   (E) 54

22. What is the height of a triangle with a base of 6 inches and an area of 24 square inches?

   (A) 12 inches
   (B) 8 inches
   (C) 6 inches
   (D) 4 inches
   (E) 2 inches

Copies of *Artist's World* Magazine Sold

= 20,000 copies

23. According to the chart above, how many more copies of *Artist's World* were sold in 2003 than in 2002?

   (A) 2,500
   (B) 5,000
   (C) 25,000
   (D) 50,000
   (E) 250,000

GO ON TO THE NEXT PAGE ▷

4   **4**   **4**   **4**   **4**   **4**

24. What number is 24 less than 3 times itself?

(A) 12
(B) 24
(C) 36
(D) 48
(E) 72

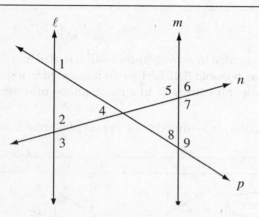

25. In the figure above, line l is parallel to line m. Which of the following pairs of angles must have equal measures?

    I.   1 and 9
   II.   2 and 8
  III.   5 and 7

(A) I only
(B) II only
(C) III only
(D) I and II only
(E) I and III only

26. The average (arithmetic mean) of 0, a, and b is $2a$. What is the value of b in terms of a?

(A) a
(B) $2a$
(C) $3a$
(D) $4a$
(E) $5a$

27. If a, b, and c are integers greater than 1, and if $ab = 21$ and $bc = 39$, which of the following must be true?

(A) $a < b < c$
(B) $a < c < b$
(C) $b < a < c$
(D) $b < c < a$
(E) $c < a < b$

28. David, Charlene, and Rudy earned a total of $22.00 yesterday. If Charlene earned three times as much as David did, and Rudy earned $2.50 less than Charlene did, then how much money did Rudy earn?

(A) $3.50
(B) $5.50
(C) $8.00
(D) $10.50
(E) $11.00

GO ON TO THE NEXT PAGE ⟹

4   4   4   4   4   4

Directions: For student-produced response questions 29–38, use the grids at the bottom of the answer sheet page on which you have answered questions 21–28.

Each of the remaining ten questions requires you to solve the problem and enter your answer by marking the circles in the special grid, as shown in the examples below. You may use any available space for scratchwork.

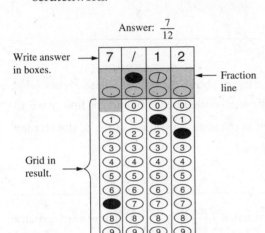

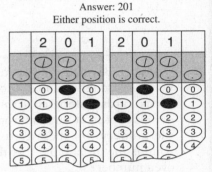

Note: You may start your answers in any column, space permitting. Columns not needed should be left blank.

- Mark no more than one circle in any column.

- Because the answer sheet will be machine-scored, **you will receive credit only if the circles are filled in correctly.**

- Although not required, it is suggested that you write your answer in the boxes at the top of the columns to help you fill in the circles accurately.

- Some problems may have more than one correct answer. In such cases, grid only one answer.

- No question has a negative answer.

- **Mixed numbers** such as $3\frac{1}{2}$ must be gridded as

  3.5 or 7/2. (If $\boxed{3\ 1\ /\ 2}$ is gridded, it will be

  interpreted as $\frac{31}{2}$ not $3\frac{1}{2}$.)

- **Decimal Answers:** If you obtain a decimal answer with more digits than the grid can accommodate, it may be either rounded or truncated, but it must fill the entire grid. For example, if you obtain an answer such as 0.6666..., you should record your result as .666 or .667. **A less accurate value such as .66 or .67 will be scored as incorrect.**

  Acceptable ways to grid $^2/_3$ are:

---

29. The ratio of 2.5 to 16 is the same as the ratio of .25 to what number?

30. For all real numbers x and y, let $x \, \Delta \, y$ be defined by the equation
$x \, \Delta \, y = (xy) - (x + y)$. What is the value of $12 \, \Delta \, 6$?

> **GO ON TO THE NEXT PAGE**

4   **4**   **4**   **4**   **4**   **4**

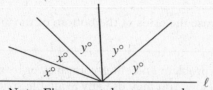

Note: Figure not drawn to scale.

31. In the figure above, if $x = 24$, what is the value of y?

32. One deck of cards consists of six cards numbered 1 through 6, and a second deck consists of six cards numbered 7 through 12. If one card is chosen at random from each deck, and the numbers on these cards are multiplied, what is the probability that this product is an even number?

33. When an integer m is divided by 5, the remainder is 3. When m is divided by 7, the remainder is 1. If m is greater than 40 but less than 80, what is one possible value of m?

34. If $(2x^2 + 5x + 3)(3x + 1) = ax^3 + bx^2 + cx + d$ for all values of x, what is the value of c?

35. In a sequence of numbers, each term except the first is 4 less than 4 times the previous term. If the fourth term in this sequence is 12, what is the first term?

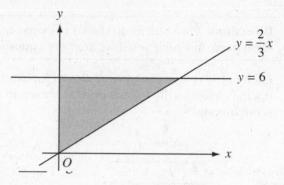

36. In the figure above, the shaded triangle is bounded by the y-axis, the line $y = 6$, and the line $y = \frac{2}{3}x$. What is the area, in square units, of the shaded triangle?

37. The value of $\dfrac{2x+10}{5} + \dfrac{3x-2}{5}$ is how much greater than the value of x?

38. If $9\left(\dfrac{1}{3}\right)^n = 3^m$, what is the value of $m + n$?

If you finish before time is called, you may check your work on this section only. Do not turn to any other section of the test.

5   **5**   **5**   **5**   **5**   **5**

SECTION 5
Time—30 minutes
39 questions (1–39)

Turn to Section 5 of your answer sheet to answer the questions in this section.

Directions: For each question in this section, select the best answer from among the choices given and fill in the corresponding circle on the answer sheet.

The following sentences test correctness and effectiveness of expression. Part of each sentence or the entire sentence is underlined; beneath each sentence are five ways of phrasing the underlined material. Choice A repeats the original phrasing; the other four choices are different. Select the choice that completes the sentence most effectively.

In making your selection, follow the requirements of standard written English; that is, pay attention to grammar, choice of words, sentence construction, and punctuation. Your selection should result in the most effective sentence—clear and precise, without awkwardness or ambiguity.

EXAMPLE:

The children couldn't hardly believe their eyes.

(A) couldn't hardly believe their eyes
(B) could hardly believe their eyes
(C) would not hardly believe their eyes
(D) couldn't nearly believe their eyes
(E) couldn't hardly believe his or her eyes

Ⓐ ● Ⓒ Ⓓ Ⓔ

1. As a young boy, was when Francis discovered that he could spend his life exploring the ocean he loved so much.

(A) was when Francis discovered that he could spend his life
(B) that was when Francis discovered that he could spend his life
(C) Francis discovered then that his life could be spent
(D) Francis discovered that he could spend his life
(E) Francis discovered the spending of his life

2. Paleontologists disputed the authenticity of the discovery, it was believed rather that it was an elaborate hoax.

(A) discovery, it was believed rather that
(B) discovery; they believed that
(C) discovery; but instead they believed that
(D) discovery in believing that
(E) discovery, it being believed that

3. Although the race was only five minutes long, James climbed out of the pool feeling as if swimming across the English Channel.

(A) swimming
(B) having swam
(C) he had swum
(D) he were swimming
(E) in swimming

4. People often sign life insurance contracts even before the provisions and contingencies of their policies are known by them.

(A) the provisions and contingencies of their policies are known by them
(B) the provisions and contingencies of their policies being known by them
(C) the provisions of their policies are known by them, or the contingencies
(D) they know the provisions and contingencies of their policies
(E) they know neither the provisions nor the contingencies of their policies

GO ON TO THE NEXT PAGE

5. A major hurdle to educational reform is parents expect the school experience to be the same as it was decades ago.

   (A) parents expect the school experience to be
   (B) parents that are expecting the school experience being
   (C) parents are expecting that the school experience be
   (D) that parents expect the school experience being
   (E) that parents expect the school experience to be

6. Perelman was an essayist and travel writer and many generations of humorists were inspired by him, such as Woody Allen.

   (A) and many generations of humorists were inspired by him, such as Woody Allen
   (B) who inspired many generations of humorists such as Woody Allen
   (C) that inspired many generations, such as Woody Allen, of humorists
   (D) by whom many generation of humorists, like Woody Allen, were inspired
   (E) of whom many generations of humorists, such as Woody Allen, were inspired

7. The fact is every human language shares a basic underlying structure, this a discovery of Noam Chomsky.

   (A) The fact is every human language shares a basic underlying structure, this a discovery of Noam Chomsky.
   (B) Noam Chomsky having discovered that every human language shares a basic underlying structure.
   (C) Every human language shares a basic underlying structure and this Noam Chomsky discovered.
   (D) The fact of every human language sharing a basic underlying structure was discovered by Noam Chomsky.
   (E) Noam Chomsky discovered that every human language shares a basic underlying structure.

8. We would not be such an obese nation if we had to hunt and gather our food as our ancestors did.

   (A) we had to hunt and gather our food as our ancestors did
   (B) hunting and gathering of our food was required of us as our ancestors
   (C) we had to hunt and gather our food as our ancestors were doing
   (D) our hunting and gathering of food was as required of us as our ancestors
   (E) we had to be hunting and gathering our food like our ancestors

9. When your body is more erect, one's mind is more alert.

   (A) one's mind is more alert
   (B) your mind is more alert
   (C) your mind's alertness is greater
   (D) the alertness of one's mind increases
   (E) the mind is alerter

10. The reason the tent fell over was that we did not anchor the center pole.

   (A) that we did not anchor the center pole
   (B) because we did not anchor the center pole
   (C) we did not anchor the center pole
   (D) for our not anchoring the center pole
   (E) because of our not anchoring the center pole

11. Unable to meet all of its costs with such meager revenue, bankruptcy could not be avoided by the small company.

   (A) bankruptcy could not be avoided by the small company
   (B) the small company's bankruptcy could not be avoided
   (C) the small company could not avoid bankruptcy
   (D) it was not possible for the small company to avoid bankruptcy
   (E) the bankruptcy of the small company could not be avoided

GO ON TO THE NEXT PAGE

5   5   5   5   5   5

12. The medium of watercolor requires precise brushwork, <u>careful timing and planning must be meticulous</u>.

(A) careful timing and planning must be meticulous
(B) the timing careful, and the planning meticulous
(C) care in the timing, and meticulous planning
(D) careful timing, and meticulous planning
(E) care in the timing, and meticulousness in the planning

13. Many visitors were impressed by the monument's sheer <u>size, but for others it was</u> its solemn gravity.

(A) size, but for others it was
(B) size; but others thought it was
(C) size, others were impressed by
(D) size and not, like for others,
(E) size; others by

14. Finding the mountain pass treacherous, <u>the safest thing, the expedition leader decided, was to stay in camp another night</u>.

(A) the safest thing, the expedition leader decided, was to stay in camp another night
(B) the expedition leader decided that it would be safest to stay in camp another night
(C) staying in camp another night was the safest thing, the expedition leader decided
(D) the expedition leader, deciding that the safest thing to do was to stay in camp another night
(E) it was safest to stay in camp another night, the expedition leader decided

15. Most educators believe <u>peers teach students more values than their</u> school curricula.

(A) peers teach students more values than their
(B) it's more their peers that teach students values than their
(C) that students learn more about values from their peers than from their
(D) values are taught more by their peers than from a student's
(E) that students learn more from their peers about values than their

16. The scientists decided to shut down the robot <u>to conserve its energy while they worked to fix</u> its processor.

(A) to conserve its energy while they worked to fix
(B) for conserving its energy while they worked on fixing
(C) to conserve its energy and working to fix
(D) in conserving its energy and in order to work on fixing
(E) with regards to conserving its energy as they were working to fix

17. Those critics who deny that films ever do justice to literary <u>masterpieces, often failing</u> to recognize the unique limitations of each art form.

(A) masterpieces, often failing
(B) masterpieces in often failing
(C) masterpieces often fail
(D) masterpieces, and so often fail
(E) masterpieces would nevertheless often fail

GO ON TO THE NEXT PAGE

18. The professor asserted that, although ancient hominids were likely very intelligent, there is little hard evidence <u>of its being true</u>.

   (A) of its being true
   (B) of its truth
   (C) that it is the truth
   (D) of support to the claim
   (E) supporting this claim

19. I sometimes prefer <u>making a selection based on the advice of a friend over</u> my own analysis.

   (A) making a selection based on the advice of a friend over
   (B) to base a selection on the advice of a friend rather than on
   (C) basing a selection on the advice of a friend more than
   (D) making a selection based rather on the advice of a friend instead of
   (E) to make a selection based on what a friend says rather than

20. Marcus, who threw a remarkable pass to Reggie for a touchdown, <u>could not have completed the play if Doug had not made a stunning block</u>.

   (A) could not have completed the play if Doug had not made a stunning block
   (B) would not complete the play if Doug did not make a stunning block
   (C) if it was not Doug's stunning block, then could not have completed the play
   (D) didn't complete the play if not for Doug's stunning block
   (E) would not have completed the play but Doug made a stunning block

GO ON TO THE NEXT PAGE →

5   **5**   **5**   **5**   **5**   **5**

The following sentences test your ability to recognize grammar and usage errors. Each sentence contains either a single error or no error at all. No sentence contains more than one error. The error, if there is one, is underlined and lettered. If the sentence contains an error, select the one underlined part that must be changed to make the sentence correct. If the sentence is correct, select choice E. In choosing answers, follow the requirements of standard written English.

EXAMPLE:

By the time <u>they reached</u> the halfway point
            A

<u>in the race</u>, <u>most of the runners</u> <u>hadn't hardly</u>
   B   C   D

begun to hit their stride. <u>No error</u>
                E

Ⓐ Ⓑ Ⓒ ● Ⓔ

---

21. <u>In the basket</u> <u>was</u> several savory treats <u>that</u>
      A   B   C
Helene knew her friends <u>would enjoy</u>.
                 D

<u>No error</u>
  E

22. Our girl scout troop <u>has already raised</u> twice
                A
<u>as much</u> money <u>for the children's hospital</u>
  B   C
this year as <u>last year</u>. <u>No error</u>
        D   E

23. Since she was <u>committed to</u> becoming a great
           A
stage <u>performer</u>, Noelle <u>studied</u> not only
      B   C
voice and acting, <u>and</u> dancing and stage
             D
combat as well. <u>No error</u>
          E

24. <u>Never seeing</u> a giraffe before, even
    A
<u>in a picture book</u>, Dina <u>was astonished</u> to
    B   C
come face to face with <u>one of these</u> magnificent
               D
creatures at the city zoo. <u>No error</u>
                 E

25. <u>Having injured herself</u> in an unfortunate
          A
stage accident during the opening act, the

lead actress could no longer <u>precede</u> in her
                 B

role, and <u>had to be</u> replaced
        C
<u>by her understudy</u>. <u>No error</u>
    D   E

26. Ricardo, <u>like</u> so many other freshmen
         A
<u>on the varsity team</u>, <u>were intimidated</u> by
   B   C
both the size and the <u>aggressiveness</u> of his
               D
teammates. <u>No error</u>
        E

27. <u>Having spent</u> enormous sums on
    A
infrastructure, many new companies

<u>must operate</u> successfully for many years
  B
<u>before</u> they <u>can recover</u> their initial
  C   D
investments. <u>No error</u>
        E

28. As a former lead researcher

<u>at a major observatory</u>, <u>our professor</u> is able
      A   B
<u>to provide</u> many <u>insights on</u> the most current
  C   D
astronomical research. <u>No error</u>
             E

GO ON TO THE NEXT PAGE ⟶

5   **5**   **5**   **5**   **5**   **5**

29. We were surprised at how <u>close</u> the two
                                  A

    sisters resembled <u>each other</u>, even though
                              B

    they <u>were</u> actually fraternal,
             C

    <u>rather than identical</u>, twins. <u>No error</u>
             D   E

30. The <u>inspiring</u> movies of Frank Capra, unlike
          A

    <u>many modern directors</u>, <u>capture</u> the most
            B   C

    hopeful <u>aspects</u> of American life. <u>No error</u>
          D   E

31. Such tragedies <u>as</u> the tsunami of December 2004
              A

    <u>show</u> the extent <u>to which</u> nature can devastate
     B   C

    <u>vast areas</u> in a very brief time. <u>No error</u>
      D   E

32. Although they often roam in packs <u>in which</u>
                          A

    they must <u>cooperate</u>, <u>the hyena employs</u>
             B   C

    subtle signs of dominance and submission

    <u>within</u> their groups. <u>No error</u>
      D   E

33. <u>When examining</u> the letters and tape
         A

    recordings from the Oval Office, the extent

    <u>of the deception</u> and <u>illicit</u> behavior of the
       B   C

    President <u>becomes</u> obvious. <u>No error</u>
           D   E

34. Meryl Streep <u>has avoided</u> vocal stereotyping,
             A

    so common <u>among</u> famous actors,
           B

    <u>by adapting</u> her voice with uncanny fluency
      C

    <u>to fit characters</u> with many different
          D

    nationalities. <u>No error</u>
           E

Directions: The following passage is an early draft of an essay. Some parts of the passage need to be rewritten.

Read the passage and select the best answers for the questions that follow. Some questions are about particular sentences or parts of sentences and ask you to improve sentence structure or word choice. Other questions ask you to consider organization and development. In choosing answers, follow the requirements of standard written English.

Questions 35–39 pertain to the following passage.

(1) When buying consumer goods, we rarely think beyond what we want and what they cost. (2) But there are two other important questions we should be asking: where did they come from? and where are they going? (3) Unlike long ago, when our consumer goods were usually made locally, we usually don't know the history of the things we buy. (4) And then, when we throw it out, or its packaging, we put it out of our minds.

(5) The manufacturers of some products, like paper and wood, employ unsustainable methods that destroy forests irrevocably. (6) This provides income for local workers, but then soon they must move on because they have rendered the environment unlivable.

(7) Other manufacturers employ slave labor, prison labor, or child labor to create cheap products like clothing or electronic equipment. (8) Some believe that producers should be permitted to search for the cheapest possible labor to make a good profit, but not if it means being inhumane to workers.

(9) Many consumer items contain dangerous chemicals that end up poisoning streams and groundwater. (10) In order to turn a short-term profit, manufacturers sometimes sacrifice whole ecosystems for generations to come.

(11) We cannot afford to be ignorant of where our consumer goods come from or where they are going. (12) As cogs in the machine of consumerism, we are as much responsible as the manufacturers themselves for the pollution and injustices that these items may cause.

GO ON TO THE NEXT PAGE →

35. Which of the following is the best revision of the underlined portion of sentence 3 (reproduced below)?

Unlike long ago, when our consumer goods were usually made locally, we usually don't know the history of the things we buy.

(A) we don't hardly
(B) today we rarely
(C) the consumers of today don't usually
(D) it's less likely today that we
(E) it's not as likely to

36. In context, which of the following is the best revision of sentence 4 (reproduced below)?

And then, when we throw it out, or its packaging, we put it out of our minds.

(A) We also rarely give much thought to where these items, or their packaging, will go when we discard them.
(B) Nevertheless, we also rarely think of where these items or their packaging will end up when we throw them out.
(C) We also rarely think about where it, or its packaging, goes when we throw it out.
(D) Then, when we throw them out, it's out of our minds.
(E) Throwing them out is what simply puts them out of our minds.

37. In context, which of the following is the best revision of the underlined portion of sentence 6 (reproduced below)?

This provides income for local workers, but then soon they must move on because they have rendered the environment unlivable.

(A) (as it is now)
(B) This is good for some local workers in providing income, but bad in making them move because they have rendered
(C) Which provides income for local workers, but forces them to move because it has rendered
(D) Although providing income for local workers, it forces them to move by rendering
(E) Although such methods provide income for local workers, they also soon force the workers to move on by rendering

GO ON TO THE NEXT PAGE →

5   5   5   5   5   5

38. In context, which of the following is the best revision of the underlined portion of sentence 8 (reproduced below)?

Some believe that producers should be permitted to search for the cheapest possible labor to make a good profit, but not if it means being inhumane to workers.

(A) (as it is now)
(B) but even though that means being inhumane to workers
(C) but sometimes this search leads to inhumane practices
(D) and that means being inhumane to workers
(E) but it shouldn't mean being inhumane to workers

39. Which of the following sentences, if placed before sentence 9 to begin the fourth paragraph, would provide the most logical transition?

(A) The low prices of such items hardly seem worth it.
(B) It really doesn't take much effort to become aware of some of the problems in manufacturing.
(C) Some consumers are becoming aware of these problems and changing their buying habits.
(D) We should consider not only the manufacture of consumer goods, but their disposal as well.
(E) Many manufacturers, however, are more responsible in their practices.

STOP

If you finish before time is called, you may check your work on this section only. Do not turn to any other section of the test.

ANSWER KEY

Critical Reading

Section 1

	COR. ANS.	DIFF. LEV.		COR. ANS.	DIFF. LEV.
1.	A	1	13.	D	1
2.	C	2	14.	C	2
3.	E	3	15.	C	3
4.	B	3	16.	E	3
5.	E	3	17.	B	4
6.	B	4	18.	D	3
7.	A	4	19.	A	3
8.	A	4	20.	D	5
9.	E	3	21.	C	3
10.	B	1	22.	B	3
11.	A	4	23.	D	4
12.	C	3	24.	D	4

Number correct _____

Number incorrect _____

Section 3

	COR. ANS.	DIFF. LEV.		COR. ANS.	DIFF. LEV.
25.	D	3	37.	C	1
26.	A	2	38.	B	3
27.	C	3	39.	D	2
28.	E	4	40.	A	3
29.	D	4	41.	D	3
30.	E	5	42.	B	4
31.	C	4	43.	E	3
32.	B	3	44.	D	4
33.	E	2	45.	A	3
34.	A	4	46.	C	3
35.	E	4	47.	D	3
36.	D	2	48.	C	3

Number correct _____

Number incorrect _____

Math

Section 2

	COR. ANS.	DIFF. LEV.		COR. ANS.	DIFF. LEV.
1.	C	1	11.	C	4
2.	C	2	12.	C	3
3.	A	2	13.	E	3
4.	B	3	14.	A	4
5.	E	2	15.	E	4
6.	A	2	16.	D	3
7.	E	3	17.	B	5
8.	B	3	18.	D	4
9.	D	3	19.	B	4
10.	B	3	20.	B	5

Number correct _____

Number incorrect _____

Section 4

Multiple-Choice Questions

	COR. ANS.	DIFF. LEV.
21.	D	1
22.	B	3
23.	D	3
24.	A	3
25.	E	3
26.	E	4
27.	C	5
28.	C	5

Student-produced Response questions

	COR. ANS.	DIFF. LEV.
29.	1.6 or 8/5	2
30.	54	2
31.	44	2
32.	3/4 or .75	3
33.	43 or 78	3
34.	14	4
35.	1.5 or 3/2	4
36.	27	4
37.	8/5 or 1.6	4
38.	2	5

Number correct _____

Number incorrect _____

Number correct _____ (29–38)

Writing

Section 5

	COR. ANS.	DIFF. LEV.		COR. ANS.	DIFF. LEV.		COR. ANS.	DIFF. LEV.		COR. ANS.	DIFF. LEV.
1.	D	1	11.	C	3	21.	B	3	31.	E	3
2.	B	1	12.	D	1	22.	D	3	32.	C	3
3.	C	2	13.	E	3	23.	D	4	33.	A	4
4.	D	2	14.	B	3	24.	A	4	34.	E	3
5.	E	3	15.	C	3	25.	B	4	35.	B	3
6.	B	2	16.	A	4	26.	C	3	36.	A	3
7.	E	3	17.	C	3	27.	E	4	37.	E	3
8.	A	3	18.	E	2	28.	D	4	38.	C	3
9.	B	4	19.	B	3	29.	A	5	39.	D	3
10.	A	3	20.	A	3	30.	B	3			

Number correct _____

Number incorrect _____

NOTE: Difficulty levels are estimates of question difficulty that range from 1 (easiest) to 5 (hardest).

SCORE CONVERSION TABLE

How to score your test

Use the answer key on the previous page to determine your raw score on each section. Your raw score on any section is equal to the number of correct answers on that section minus 1/4 of the number of wrong answers, with the exception of the mathematical "grid-in" section, on which wrong answers are not deducted from your score. Remember to add the raw scores from Sections 1 and 3 to get your Critical Reading raw score, and to add the raw scores from Sections 2 and 4 to get your Math raw score. Write the three raw scores here:

Raw Critical Reading score (Section 1 + Section 3): _____

Raw Math score (Section 2 + Section 4): _____

Raw Writing score (Section 5): _____

Use the table below to convert these to scaled scores.

Scaled scores: Critical Reading: _____   Math: _____   Writing: _____

Raw Score	Critical Reading Scaled Score	Math Scaled Score	Writing Scaled Score	Raw Score	Critical Reading Scaled Score	Math Scaled Score	Writing Scaled Score
48	80			20	49	52	54
47	80			19	48	51	52
46	78			18	47	50	51
45	76			17	46	48	50
44	74			16	45	47	49
43	72			15	44	46	48
42	71			14	43	45	46
41	69			13	42	44	45
40	68			12	41	43	44
39	67		80	11	40	42	43
38	66	80	80	10	39	41	41
37	64	77	78	9	38	40	40
36	63	74	77	8	37	39	39
35	62	72	76	7	36	38	37
34	62	70	74	6	34	36	36
33	61	68	73	5	33	35	35
32	60	66	71	4	32	34	33
31	59	65	69	3	30	32	32
30	58	64	68	2	29	30	31
29	57	62	66	1	27	29	30
28	56	61	65	0	25	26	29
27	55	60	63	-1	22	23	28
26	54	59	62	-2	20	20	27
25	54	58	60	-3	20	20	25
24	54	57	59	-4	20	20	24
23	52	55	57	-5	20	20	22
22	51	54	56	-6	20	20	21
21	50	53	55	-7 or less	20	20	20

Detailed Answer Key

Section I

1. **A** If she was *aggressive* for *what seemed like days,* she must have been quite *tenacious. unrelenting* = stubbornly persistent; *reflective* = pensive, thoughtful; *stagnant* = showing no movement or progress for a long period of time.

2. **C** If the helmsman *steered the ship away from the rocks,* then clearly the disaster was *avoided.* If he had to be *quick-thinking,* the rocks must have emerged *suddenly. forestalled* = put off until a later time; *averted* = prevented; *dispelled* = halted the spread of a wrong idea; *passively* = without effort or action; *serenely* = calmly.

3. **E** If investors *expected [the stock's] value to remain [steady] for many months,* they would be surprised by a *rapid* decline. *volatile* = explosive, prone to rapid change; *improvised* = performed quickly and without planning; *uniform* = having a consistent, monotonous quality; *cumbersome* = burdensome; *liquid* = quickly convertible to cash; *precipitous* = steep and rapid.

4. **B** If the new manager does not make *sudden decisions without thinking,* she must be more *thoughtful. capricious* = inclined to act on a whim; *pensive* = thoughtful; *inexorable* = unstoppable

5. **E** Those who study human cultures are *anthropologists. herpetologists* = scientists who study reptiles; *oncologists* = physicians specializing in cancer; *ornithologists* = scientists who study birds; *agronomists* = scientists who study farming.

6. **B** If *those who were familiar with* Alicia's demeanor were *surprised* by something she did, then she must have done something out of character. Look for the word pair that describes opposite kinds of behaviors. *intrepid* = fearless; *stolid* = unemotional; *meticulous* = paying close attention to details; *flippant* = inappropriately jocular, prone to making jokes at the wrong times.

7. **A** If *truthfulness* is . . . *an impediment to success* in a certain field, then to be successful in that field one must learn to *avoid the truth. prevarication* = willful avoidance of the truth; *timidity* = shyness;

certitude = certainty; *perseverance* = ability to remain committed to a task.

8. **A** Most people would consider *thousands of hours of volunteer work* to be *selfless* rather than *selfish,* but Gina obviously thinks differently. She does not consider herself a *paragon* (prime example) of *generosity. altruistic* = selfless; *magnanimity* = generosity; *egotistical* = self-centered; *placidity* = calmness; *diversity* = variation within a population.

9. **E** Passage 1 focuses on describing how *what is directly evident provides the foundation on which all other beliefs are based* (lines 13–15), that is, that most of human knowledge derives from reasoning about our direct sensory experience. Passage 2, in contrast, focuses on cautioning the reader against trusting the arguments of other people. Hence Passage 1 is *descriptive* while Passage 2 is *prescriptive.*

10. **B** The author of Passage 2 cautions us to *believe nothing* (line 16) about the claims of others because we cannot trust their arguments. Therefore, the author would most likely *qualify* (add reservations to) the claim that *the vast bulk of human knowledge is based on reasoning* (lines 10–11) by *cautioning that such reasoning is often dubious.* The author of Passage 2 does not *assert that human knowledge comes directly from the senses;* that is what the author of Passage 1 does. He also does not *dispute the suggestion that humans are capable of reasoning,* and to the contrary suggests that we *assume that our opposers are...sharp-minded* (lines 18–19). The author of Passage 2 also does not mention *emotion* or imply that *most people tend to resist making illogical arguments.*

11. **A** The author of Passage 2 is primarily concerned with *the biases of debaters,* while the author of Passage 1 is not. The use of terms like *arguing* (line 18), *opposers* (line 19), *argument maneuvers* (lines 21), and *arguments* (line 24) make it clear that this passage is focused on the topic of debate, and how debaters are biased to believe *that anything furthering their position is acceptable* (lines 27–28). Although Passage 2 does mention *the process of reasoning,* this is clearly the focus of Passage 1 as well. Also, Passage 2 does not suggest *the use of deception to bolster an argument,* but merely suggests that we *assume our opposers are...low-minded* (line 18–20).

12. C The sentence *Believe nothing* (line 16) primarily suggests that we should *be skeptical of the claims others make to support their arguments* because our opponents frequently use *maneuvers* and are likely to *believe that anything furthering their position is acceptable* (lines 27–28). Since the author indicates that *many argument maneuvers are not made consciously* (lines 21–22), and that *we might be able to trust [our opponents]* (lines 24–25), he is not asking us to *assume that our opponents are insincere.*

13. D The first paragraph states that *individuals have the right . . . to save their own lives . . . and countries have the right . . . to prevent their own destruction* (lines 4–8).

14. C By saying that *the slaying of an evildoer is lawful,* Aquinas clearly supports the death penalty.

15. C The passage states that we proclaim our special reverence for life by *reserving the ultimate penalty of death for those who wantonly kill* (lines 18–20).

16. E The argument being made here is that the increase in homicides between 1950 and 1980 was due to the *abandonment of the death penalty;* yet no alternative explanations for such a rise are considered. A refutation, then, would cite other possible reasons for this rise, such as a rise in population and the availability of weapons.

17. B Mr. van den Haag says that *life becomes cheaper as we become kinder to those who wantonly take it* (lines 71–73), thereby suggesting that life is honored as we become less kind to killers. Therefore, his attitude toward killers is harsh and uncompromising.

18. D These reams are the many *studies on the issue [of whether executions deter potential murders]* (lines 79–81). The author then goes on to say that these studies, save one that was *soundly refuted* (line 84), show that no correlation exists.

19. A The *abolitionist states* (line 93) are contrasted directly with those that have capital executions; therefore abolitionst states are those that have abolished the death penalty.

20. D The author of Passage 2 states that *the death penalty is absolute and irrevocable.* This means that it cannot be taken back if it is rendered in error, as the author fears it may be.

21. C The author discusses the *moral foundation of a just society* (lines 74–75) in the first paragraph and the *just role of the state* (line 115) in the final paragraph.

22. B Passage 1, in lines 29–41, uses Ehrlich's research to support the thesis that executions are effective. Passage 2, however, states that this research was *soundly refuted* (line 84).

23. D The two passages take clearly opposing views on the necessity of the death penalty to a just society. Passage 1 regards the death penalty as *clearly proclaiming our special reverence for life* (lines 20–21), while Passage 2 regards it as *murderous vengeance* (line 122) that must not be legitimized.

24. D The author of Passage 2 clearly would *attack this notion [of employing execution as sheer retribution]* and in fact does so by criticizing it as *murderous vengeance* (line 122).

Section 2

1. C This one is pretty straightforward. Simply double each number given in the choices. This gives 10, 12, 14, 16, and 18. The right answer will be a number that is two more than a multiple of 12, so subtract 2 from each one, getting 8, 10, 12, 14, and 16, and choose the multiple of 12, which is given in (C).

2. C If the circle has an area of 16π square inches, just use the area formula for a circle (remember, it's in the reference information on every test) to find the radius:

$$16\pi = \pi r^2$$

Divide by π: $\quad\quad 16 = r^2$

Take the square root: $\quad 4 = r$

Then use the circumference formula to find the circumference: $c = 2\pi r = 2\pi(4) = 8\pi.$

3. A Write the equation: 4.5 zots = 1 zat
Divide by 4.5:   1 zot = 2/9 zat
Multiply by 36:   36 zots = 72/9 zats = 8 zats

4. B Think of the sequence of 20 terms as being 10 sets of 2 terms (1, 2). Since each set has a sum of $1 + 2 = 3$, the sum of the 20 terms is $3(10) = 30$.

5. E This one is best done algebraically, although you can work backward from the answer choices, as well. If you do it algebraically, start by saying that Tom weighs t pounds and Carl weighs c pounds. If Tom weighs 20 pounds less than twice Carl's weight, then $t = 2c - 20$. If together they weigh 340 pounds, then $t + c = 340$. Since you are looking for Tom's weight, eliminate c from the system through substitution:

$$t + c = 340$$

Subtract t: $\qquad\qquad\qquad\qquad c = 340 - t$

Substitute $340 - t$ for c in the
first equation ($t = 2c - 2$): $\qquad t = 2(340 - t) - 20$
Distribute: $\qquad\qquad\qquad\qquad t = 680 - 2t - 20$
Simplify: $\qquad\qquad\qquad\qquad\quad t = 660 - 2t$
Add $2t$: $\qquad\qquad\qquad\qquad\quad 3t = 660$
Divide by 3: $\qquad\qquad\qquad\qquad t = 220$

Don't forget to check your answer. If they weigh 340 pounds altogether, then Carl must weigh $340 - 220 = 120$ pounds. Check that this satisfies the first condition, namely, that Tom weighs 20 pounds less than twice Carl's weight: $220 = 2(120) - 20$. Yes!

6. A As always, be sure to mark up the diagram with the information you are given or can figure out.

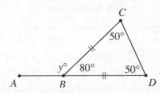

Since $BC = BD$, the two angles opposite those sides must be equal also, so $\angle BCD = 50°$. Since the sum of the angles in a triangle is always 180°, $\angle CBD = 180 - 50 - 50 = 80°$. Since $\angle ABC$ is supplementary to $\angle CBD$ because they form a straight angle, then $y = 180 - 80 = 100$.

7. E First evaluate *10. Since 10 is not a multiple of 3, *10 = 3(10) = 30. Now check to see which choice is also equivalent to 30. [Be careful not to jump right to choice (D) just because it contains a 30!] Following the instructions gives (A) *3 = 3/3 = 1, (B) *9 = 9/3 = 3, (C) *20 = 3(20) = 60, (D) *30 = 30/3 = 10, and (E) *90 = 90/3 = 30.

8. B First notice that the shaded region consists of a right triangle and a rectangle, the areas of which you can find easily once you know the base and height of each. As always, mark up the diagram.

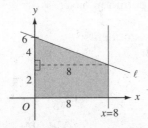

Remember that the slope of the line is simply the "rise" between two points divided by the "run" between those same two points. Consider line ℓ between the y-axis and the line $x = 8$. Clearly, the "run" here is 8. Since the slope of line ℓ is $-1/2$, rise/8 $= -1/2$.
Multiply by 8: $\qquad\qquad$ rise $= -4$
So line ℓ descends 4 units between the y-axis and the line $x = 8$, as shown in the diagram. Since line ℓ intercepts the y-axis at 6, the height of the rectangle must be $6 - 4 = 2$. The area of the rectangle, then, is $(8)(2) = 16$, and the area of the right triangle is $(\frac{1}{2})(8)(4) = 16$. The area of the shaded region, then, is $16 + 16 = 32$.

9. D You can use simple algebra or plug in simple values for x and d, whichever is easier. If each box contains x pencils, then 10 boxes contain $10x$ pencils, which you are told cost d dollars. Simply multiplying by 5 shows that $50x$ pencils cost $5d$ dollars.
Alternatively, you could just pick simple values like $x = 20$ and $d = 6$. This would mean that 10 boxes of 20 pencils cost 6 dollars, or $10 \times 20 = 200$ pencils cost 6 dollars. The question now becomes: how much do $50x = (50)(20) = 1,000$ pencils cost? A proportion might be handy:

$$\frac{200 \text{ pencils}}{6 \text{ dollars}} = \frac{1,000 \text{ pencils}}{y \text{ dollars}}$$

Cross-multiply: $\qquad 200y = 6,000$
Divide by 200: $\qquad\quad y = 30$

Now, if you plug $x = 20$ and $d = 6$ into the answer choices, you will see that only choice (D) gives the value of 30.

10. B First notice that this is a rate problem and remember the rate formula: *distance = rate × time*. Compare the real race with the "planned" race. Beth had planned to run at 6 mph and finish in t hours. Therefore, using the rate formula, you can express the distance of the race as $6t$ miles. But she actually ran the race at 7 mph and finished in $t - 1/6$ hours. (Remember that 10 minutes is $10/60 = 1/6$ of an hour.) So the race distance can also be expressed as $7(t - 1/6)$. Since the distance is the same in either case,

$$7(t - 1/6) = 6t$$

Distribute: $\qquad\qquad 7t - 7/6 = 6t$
Subtract $6t$: $\qquad\qquad\quad t - 7/6 = 0$
Add $7/6$: $\qquad\qquad\qquad\qquad t = 7/6$
Therefore, the distance is $6t = 6(7/6) = 7$ miles.

11. C Since the map is drawn to scale, you can set up a proportion:

$$\frac{1.5 \text{ cm}}{2 \text{ miles}} = \frac{x \text{ cm}}{35 \text{ miles}}$$

Cross-multiply: $\qquad 52.5 = 2x$
Divide by 2: $\qquad\quad 26.25 = x$

12. C Since comparing decimals is easier than comparing fractions, it's probably best to convert all the fractions to decimals with your calculator. Since the project requires $5/8 = .625$ meter of pipe, the correct answer must be no less than .625. To minimize the waste, we must find the smallest length that is greater than .625. "Decimalizing" the choices gives (A) .5625, (B) .6, (C) .75, (D) .8, and (E) .83. The smallest length greater than .625 is (C) .75.

13. E Just focus on one equation at a time to find the values of the unknowns:

$$4c = 24$$
Divide by 4: $$c = 6$$
$$2b = 24$$
Divide by 2: $$b = 12$$
$$\left(\frac{1}{2}\right)a = 24$$
Multiply by 2: $$a = 48$$
Therefore $a + b + c = 48 + 12 + 6 = 66$.

14. A Think about the statement $x^2 > 6$. Notice that both positive values, like $x = 5$, and negative values, like $x = -5$, satisfy this inequality. (Try them and see!) The square root of 6 is $+2.449...$, so if x^2 is greater than 6, x must be either greater than 2.449... or less than $-2.449...$. Therefore x could equal 2.5, which shows that statement I is not necessarily true (because $|2.5|$ is not greater than 3). Also, x could be $-1,000,000$, because anything less than $-2.449...$ will work, so statement III is not necessarily true (because $-1,000,000 + 1,000$ is not greater than 0). Now, if you simply eliminate all of the answer choices containing statement I or statement III, you are left only with (A). So statement II must be true. If you want to be sure, a little algebra will show that statement II is equivalent to the given statement and therefore must be true.

$$(x - 2)(x + 2) > 2$$
FOIL: $$x^2 + 2x - 2x - 4 > 2$$
Simplify: $$x^2 - 4 > 2$$
Add 4: $$x^2 > 6$$

15. E As always, mark up the diagram with the information as you get it.

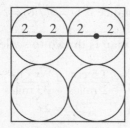

You are given the circumference of the circles, and asked to find the area of the square. So, you must find the relationship between the circles and the square. You can use the circumference formula to find the radius of each circle:
$$4\pi = 2\pi r$$
Divide by 2π: $$2 = r$$
Now notice that one side of the square has the length of 4 radii, as shown in the diagram. So the length of one side of the square is $(4)(2) = 8$. The area of the square is found by squaring the length of one side: $s^2 = 8^2 = 64$.

16. D Since your task is to *maximize* the number of evens in this set, it is best to first ask whether they can *all* be even. Notice that this gives (even)(even)(even) + (even)(even) + (even). Remember that the product of an even number and any other integer is always even, and that the sum of two even numbers is always even. Therefore this expression reduces to (even) + (even) + (even), which necessarily yields an even number. This can't be, though, because we are told that the result must be odd. To get an odd result, all we would have to do is change the last number, g, to an odd number. (Check it and see!) Therefore, the maximum number of evens in this set is five.

17. B If the average of six numbers is 32, then their sum is $(6)(32) = 192$. Since this sum is fixed, then to maximize one of the numbers, you must *minimize* the sum of the other five. You are told that the numbers are *different integers*, none of which is less than 10, implying that the least the other five can be is 10, 11, 12, 13, and 14. Therefore, if x is the greatest possible value of any of the numbers,
$$10 + 11 + 12 + 13 + 14 + x = 192$$
Simplify: $$60 + x = 192$$
Subtract 60: $$x = 132$$

18. D If you are comfortable using your rules of exponents, you can probably solve the equation for n algebraically. If not, you can just "test" the choices by plugging them in for n until you find one that makes the equation true. Here's one of many ways to solve agebraically:

$$(1/4)^n = 2^{-3}$$
Simplify: $$(1/4)^n = 1/8$$
Cross-multiply: $$4^n = 8$$
Write with common base: $$(2^2)^n = 2^3$$
Simplify: $$2^{2n} = 2^3$$
Equate the exponents: $$2n = 3$$
Divide by 2: $$n = 3/2$$

19. B   Looking at the choices makes it pretty clear that writing out all of the possible numbers is going to take a while. To simplify the counting, use the fundamental counting principal. First, notice that all of the integers between 100 and 1,000 have three digits, so "choosing" one of these integers involves specifying three digits. There are only nine choices for the first digit, since it can't be 0. Once that first digit is chosen, there are nine digits remaining for the second digit. (Remember that you can use 0 as the second digit, but you can't use the first digit again.) Then, since you can't use either of the first two digits again, there are only eight digits remaining for the last digit. This give a total of $9 \times 9 \times 8 = 648$ such integers.

20. B   Be sure to mark up the diagram with any given information and any information you can deduce:

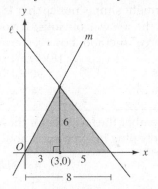

If line m has a slope of 2, then when the "run" is 3 (as it is from the origin to the point where the lines intersect), then "rise" must be $(2)(3) = 6$. Notice that this is also the height of the triangle. Since the area of the triangle is 24, you can use the triangle area formula to find the length of the base:

$$24 = (1/2)b(6)$$
Simplify: $24 = 3b$
Divide by 3: $8 = b$

Since the base is 8 units, the other part of the base is $8 - 3 = 5$, as shown in the diagram. This gives a "rise" and "run" for line ℓ, so the slope is $-6/5$.

Section 3

25. D   Editing a manuscript from 400 pages down to 250 pages is quite a *reduction*. *enhanced* = improved; *abridged* = shortened a text

26. A   The sentence contains a parallel structure that indicates that the first missing word should contrast *bland* and the second missing word should contrast *artistically daring*. *enchanting* = charming and delightful; *conventional* = ordinary; *innovative* = new and inventive; *tedious* = difficult to tolerate; *pedestrian* = ordinary; *trite* = overused

27. C   An *inveterate gambler* is one who gambles habitually. To disprove the assumption that *payoffs must be consistent* to support an addiction, one must show that the payoffs might be *given at irregular intervals*. *steadfast* = fixed or unchanging; *sporadic* = occurring at irregular intervals; *placid* = peaceful

28. E   If one is *surprised* by the finding that walking prolongs life, that person must have *denied a relationship between exercise and long life*. *mediation* = the act of resolving a dispute between two or more other parties; *prosperity* = flourishing success; *correlation* = relationship; *longevity* = length of life

29. D   The phrase *even to* suggests an element of surprise. Those who study something for a long time are expected to know a lot about it. It would be surprising, therefore, if they still found that subject *difficult to understand*. It would logically be *even more difficult to understand* for someone who did not study the subject. *forthcoming* = frank and honest; *daunting* = intimidating; *fallow* = unproductive; *cryptic* = hard to decipher; *inscrutable* = incapable of being comprehended; *fatuous* = foolishly stupid; *singular* = unique

30. E   The passage states that the *current media environment* allows individuals to *offer messages inexpensively over the internet* so that they are no longer *constrained by cost*. In other words, the new media are more accessible to users.

31. C   The passage does not take any controversial or emotional stance on the topic, mentioning only objective facts.

32. B   This quotation states that *mathematics [needs] persons who...have a sense of the beautiful*. Therefore, an aesthetic sense is helpful to mathematical thought.

33. E   John Conway is mentioned because he *cannot imagine he is doing anything but discovering* rather than inventing mathematical results. His quotation reinforces that point, saying that mathematical truths are as closed to interpretation as the truth that *pigs don't fly*.

34. A   This passage, as a whole, praises newspapers for *their achievements in crusading*. Therefore, its overall tone is *laudatory*.

35. E   The author states that it is *singular* (surprising and unique) *that newspapers . . . have made so little to-do about their achievements in crusading* (lines 1–3). In other words, the newspapers are not acknowledging one of their virtues.

36. D   This *wealth of material* refers to the information about how newspapers have acted as *champions of reform...[and] protagonists of their communities* (lines 4–5). This means that they have acted to change their communities.

37. C   In saying that the institution of newspapers *has discharged it [that is, crusading] for the most part admirably,* the passage is saying that it has *performed or accomplished* this task well.

38. B   The skeptics *deny that campaigns are ever undertaken for other than sordid motives.* In other words, they believe that newspapers only "crusade" for selfish purposes.

39. D   In saying that *zeal . . . fires a crusading editor,* the author means that this zeal *inspires* or stimulates the editor.

40. A   The final paragraph indicates that some campaigns result in a *loss of circulation and advertising* (line 52), which are the only sources of revenue for a newspaper.

41. D   The overall purpose of the passage is to examine the art form of *cut and pasted paper* (lines 10–11) which was pioneered by Henri Matisse. Notice that every paragraph refers to *cut and pasted paper, collage,* or *decoupage,* which all refer to the same art form.

42. B   The quotation indicates that Matisse was *afraid the young . . . will . . . [dispense] with certain efforts* (lines 6–9) because Matisse has tried to *never let . . . anyone know the labors* of his art. In other words, he is concerned that younger artists will think that his art is easier to make than it really is.

43. E   This comment is made in the context of a discussion of how *lively and energetic* Matisse's art is, so the comment about Matisse's advanced age serves as a stark contrast.

44. D   The *brilliant hues* of the paper are its *vibrant colors.* Therefore, *shining* is the best choice.

45. A   Matisse is quoted to say that he has achieved a form that is *reduced to the essential* (line 64) and is *no longer in the complexity of its space* (lines 65–66), in other words, his decoupage is pictorially simple.

46. C   This *intimacy* describes the relationship between Matisse and the medium of decoupage, in which he is able to *select, place, and reposition the cut paper shapes* (lines 75–76).

47. D   In lines 19–20, the passage states that Matisse's most famous work of decoupage shows *no three-dimensional modeling of the forms or shadows.* Elsewhere in the passage, however, the author describes the medium's relative ease of use (*less strenuous,* line 35), manipulability (*select, place, and reposition,* line 75), *pictorial strength* (line 54), and vitality (*lively and energetic,* line 14).

48. C   The final paragraph states that Matisse *truly enjoyed,* indeed *relished,* his challenges, suggesting that he was enthusiastic. It also states that he had the *habit of hard work* (line 76), indicating that he was diligent.

Section 4

21. D   You might simply notice that 18/15 reduces to 6/5, making the answer obvious. If you want to use the "brute force" method, however, cross-multiply:
$$(18)(5) = 15x$$
Simplify: $90 = 15x$
Divide by 15; $6 = x$

22. B   Remember the formula for the area of a triangle, and simply plug in what you know:

$$A = \frac{1}{2}bh$$

Substitute: $24 = \frac{1}{2}(6)h$
Simplify: $24 = 3h$
Divide by 3: $8 = h$

23. D   Read the chart carefully and notice that each book represents 20,000 copies. Since the sales in 2003 are 2.5 "books" more than in 2002, the difference in copies is $2.5 \times 20,000 = 50,000$ copies.

24. A   What number is 24 less than 3 times itself?
Translate: $x = 3x - 24$
Subtract $3x$: $-2x = -24$
Divide by -2: $x = 12$

25. E   You need to know the Parallel Lines theorem for this one. Because the two lines are parallel, angles 1 and 9 must be equal because they are "corresponding" angles. Angles 5 and 7 must be equal because they are "vertical" angles. Therefore, statements I and III are true. The only answer choice containing both I and III is (E), so that must be the correct answer. As to statement II, angles 2 and 8 are not necessarily equal, because they do not share any common lines.

26. **E**   The average of 0, a, and b is $\dfrac{0+a+b}{3}$.

$$\dfrac{0+a+b}{3}=2a$$

Multiply by 3: $a+b=6a$

Subtract a: $b=5a$

---

27. **C**   The prime factorization of 21 is 3×7, and the prime factorization of 39 is 3×13. Since b represents a common factor of 21 and 39 that is greater than 1, it must be 3. This means that a is 7 and c is 13. Therefore $b < a < c$.

---

28. **C**   You can solve this one algebraically or just test the choices. Recall that when you test the choices, it's usually best to start with (C) because it's the "middle" value. Begin by guessing that Rudy earns $8. Since Rudy earned $2.50 less than Charlene did, Charlene must have earned $8.00 + $2.50 = $10.50. If Charlene earned three times as much as David did, then David must have earned $10.50 ÷ 3 = $3.50. Check this by seeing if the total is $22.00, as the problem says: $8.00 + 10.50 + $3.50 = $22.00. Bingo! Here we got lucky because the first choice we checked happened to be correct. The drawback to testing the choices is that you may need to do it more than once. To avoid this, you can set up an equation and solve directly. If Rudy earned r dollars, then Charlene must have earned $r + 2.50$ dollars, and David must have earned $(r + 2.50)/3$ dollars. Set up the equation:

$$r+(r+2.50)+\dfrac{r+2.50}{3}=22$$

Multiply by 3: $3r + 3r + 7.50 + r + 2.50 = 66$

Simplify: $7r + 10 = 66$

Subtract 10: $7r = 56$

Divide by 7: $r = 8$

---

29. **1.6 or 8/5**   that two-part ratios can be treated as fractions: $2.5/16 = .25/x$

Cross-multiply: $2.5x = 4$

Divide by 2.5: $x = 1.6$ or $8/5$

---

30. **54**   Simply substitute the given numbers using the definition of the new symbol. Since $x \, \Delta \, y = (xy) - (x + y)$, then $12 \, \Delta \, 6 = (12 \times 6) - (12 + 6) = 72 - 18 = 54$.

---

31. **44**   Because the sum of the five angles is a straight angle, which measures $180°$, $x + x + y + y + y = 180$

Simplify: $2x + 3y = 180$

Substitute 24 for x: $2(24) + 3y = 180$

Simplify: $48 + 3y = 180$

Subtract 48: $3y = 132$

Divide by 3: $y = 44$

---

32. **3/4 or .75**   To simplify the problem, first notice that half of the cards in each deck are odd and half are even. Therefore, you only need to consider four possible outcomes from multiplying a number from one deck and a number from the other: (even)(even), (even)(odd), (odd)(even), and (odd)(odd). Each of these outcomes is equally likely, and the first three produce an even product. Therefore, the probability that the product is even is 3/4.

---

33. **43 or 78**   Since you only need to look at the integers between 40 and 80, listing them isn't so difficult. Since the number you want gives a remainder of 1 when it is divided by 7, start by listing the integers between 40 and 80 that are 1 more than a multiple of 7: $42 + 1 = 43$, $49 + 1 = 50$, $56 + 1 = 57$, $63 + 1 = 64$, $70 + 1 = 71$, and $77 + 1 = 78$. The only numbers in this set that give a remainder of 3 when divided by 5 are 43 and 78.

---

34. **14**   This question tests your ability to use the Distributive law to multiply polynomials:

$$(2x^2 + 5x + 3)(3x + 1)$$
$$(3x)(2x^2 + 5x + 3) + (1)(2x^2 + 5x + 3)$$
$$(3x)(2x^2) + (3x)(5x) + (3x)(3) + 2x^2 + 5x + 3$$
$$6x^3 + 15x^2 + 9x + 2x^2 + 5x + 3$$

Combine like terms: $6x^3 + 17x^2 + 14x + 3$

Since c represents the coefficient of the "x" term, $c = 14$.

---

35. **1.5 or 3/2**   It may help to write out blank spaces to represent the unknown terms in the sequence. Since the fourth term is 12, the sequence looks like ------, ------, ------, 12. Now you need to "work backwards" to find the first term. Since each term is 4 less than 4 times the previous term, then each term must by 1/4 of the number that is 4 *greater* than the *next* term. (If this makes your brain hurt a bit, try it out and check.) In other words, the third term must be $(1/4)(12 + 4) = 4$. (Now check: notice that if you follow the rule to get the next term, you get 12!) Continuing gives you $(1/4)(4 + 4) = 2$ for the second term, and $(1/4)(2 + 4) = 1.5$ for the first term. Check one more time that the sequence follows the rule *forward*: 1.5, 2, 4, 12.

36. 27 One way to analyze this problem is to find the point where the two lines cross. This is the same as solving the system $y = 6$ and $y = (2/3)x$.

Set the y equal: $6 = (2/3)x$

Multiply by 3/2: $= x$

So the point of intersection is $(9, 6)$, which means that the triangle has a "base" of 6 and a "height" of 9. (You might turn the diagram 90° to get a clearer picture.)

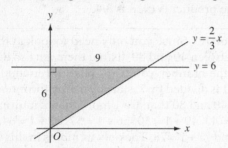

Therefore, it has an area of $(1/2)(9)(6) = 27$.

37. 8/5 or 1.6 $\dfrac{2x+10}{5} + \dfrac{3x-2}{5}$

Add fractions: $\dfrac{(2x+10)+(3x-2)}{5}$

Simplify: $\dfrac{5x+8}{5}$

Distribute: $\dfrac{5x}{5} + \dfrac{8}{5}$

Simplify: $x + \dfrac{8}{5}$

Therefore, this expression is 8/5 greater than x.

38. 2 $9\left(\dfrac{1}{3}\right) = 3^m$

Simplify: $9\left(\dfrac{1}{3^n}\right) = 3^m$

Multiply by $3n$: $9 = 3^m \times 3^n$
Simplify: $9 = 3^{m+n}$
Write with common base: $3^2 = 3^{m+n}$
Equate exponents: $2 = m + n$

Section 5

1. D The modifying phrase at the beginning of the sentence must be followed by the noun it modifies, *Francis*. Choice (C) uses *then* redundantly, and choice (E) is illogical.

2. B This is a run-on sentence because it joins two independent clauses with only a comma. The second clause is also unnecessarily vague. It uses the passive voice to obscure the subject, which should be the same as that in the previous clause—*paleontologists*. Choice (B) joins the clauses appropriately with a semicolon, and clarifies the subject of the second clause.

3. C The phrase *as if* should be followed by an independent clause that describes a hypothetical condition. The original sentence, however, follows it with an incomplete thought. Choice (C) provides the most logical phrasing. The past perfect subjunctive *had swum* must be used because the statement is hypothetical (or subjunctive), and because the action would have been completed before James got out of the pool, and so is a "perfect" action.

4. D The original sentence lacks parallel form and therefore reads awkwardly. The two clauses have the same subject and so should both be in the active voice. Choice (D) accomplishes this most concisely.

5. E The subject and verb of the sentence are *a hurdle is*. What follows should be a noun (predicate nominative) that is equivalent to the *hurdle*. In the original phrasing, what follows is an independent clause rather than a noun phrase. Choices (B), (D), and (E) are all noun phrases, but (B) is illogical, and (D) uses the unidiomatic *expect being* instead of the correct *expect to be*.

6. B The original phrasing is redundant and contains two problems: a lack of parallelism and a misplaced modifier. The two clauses have the same subject, so they should both be in the active voice. Also, the phrase *such as Woody Allen* should be closer to the noun it modifies, *humorists*. Choice (B) corrects both problems most concisely and effectively.

7. E The original phrasing is awkward, wordy, and unclear. The subject and verb *the fact is* do not convey the central idea of the sentence, and the modifying phrase at the end of the sentence is nonstandard. Choice (E) uses a much more effective and meaningful subject and verb: *Noam Chomsky discovered*.

8. A The original phrasing is the most concise and logical.

9. B The original sentence uses pronouns inconsistently. Since the first clause, uses *your*, the second clause should, also. Choice (B) is better than (C) because its phrasing is parallel with that of the first clause.

10. A The original phrasing is best. The subject and verb of the sentence are *the reason was*. Therefore, what follows should be a noun phrase that describes the *reason*. Choice (B) is not a noun phrase, and it uses the nonstandard construction *the reason was because*. The other choices are also not noun phrases.

11. C The modifying phrase at the beginning of the sentence should be followed by the noun that it modifies, *the small company*. Choice (C) is the only one that repairs the dangling modifier.

12. D The phrasing in the original sentence is not parallel. Since it contains a list, the phrasing of the items should be similar. Choice (D) puts all three items in the same form: *adjective noun*.

13. E In the original sentence, the phrasing of the two clauses is not parallel, and the pronoun *it* has no clear antecedent. Choice (E) might sound odd at first reading, because it uses *ellipsis*, that is, the omission of a phrase that is implied by the parallelism in the sentence. In other words, the sentence is equivalent to *Many visitors were impressed by the monument's sheer size; others [were impressed] by its solemn gravity.* The phrase in brackets can be omitted because it is implied by the parallel clause that came before.

14. B The participial phrase beginning with *finding* should be followed by the noun it modifies, *the expedition leader*, since it was he who did the finding. Choice (D) appears to repair the dangling participle, but it does not create a complete sentence.

15. C The original sentence phrases the comparison awkwardly. It is not clear what is being compared. Furthermore, the subject and verb of the sentence are *educators believe*, so what follows should be a noun phrase that describes what they believe. Choices (C) and (E) are both noun phrases, but only choice (C) shows a clear and logical comparison.

16. A The original phrasing is correct.

17. C The original phrasing is only a sentence fragment, because the main "clause" contains no verb. Choices (C) and (E) are the only ones that form complete sentences, but choice (E) is illogical.

18. E The pronoun *its* has no clear antecedent in the sentence. Choices (D) and (E) clarify the noun by specifying it as *the claim*, but choice (D) uses the unidiomatic phrasing *of support to*.

19. B The original comparison is illogical and not parallel. Choice (B) makes the comparison clearer and more logical through parallel phrasing—*based on the advice of a friend* parallels *based on my own analysis*.

20. A This sentence is correct. It must use the subjunctive verbs *could not have completed* and *had not made* because it describes a hypothetical situation.

21. B The subject of the verb is *treats*, so the verb should be conjugated for a plural subject: *were*. This is a bit tricky because the sentence is "inverted"; that is, the subject comes *after* the verb.

22. D This is an illogical comparison. The comparison should be between the *money* collected this year and the *money* collected last year, so the correct phrasing in (D) is *we collected last year*.

23. D The idiomatic phrasing here should be *not only A but B as well*. Therefore (D) should be changed to *but*.

24. A The word *before* indicates that the *seeing* would have been completed before the *being astonished*. To show the correct time sequence, choice (A) should use the perfect participle *never having seen*.

25. B *Precede* means *come before*. This usage is illogical here. The sentence clearly implies that the actress could not *proceed* (continue).

26. C The subject of the sentence is *Ricardo*. Since this is a singular subject, the verb conjugation should be *was*.

27. E The sentence is correct.

28. D This phrase is not idiomatic. The correct idiom is *insights into*.

29. A This modifies the verb *resembled*, so it should be the adverb *closely*.

30. B This comparison is illogical. It should compare the *movies of Frank Capra* to the *movies of many modern directors*.

31. E The sentence is correct.

32. C The pronoun *they* requires a plural antecedent, so this phrase should read *hyenas employ*.

33. A The participle *examining* dangles in the original sentence since its subject never appears. The best way to correct this problem is to rephrase it as *when one examines*.

34. E The sentence is correct.

35. B The word *unlike* indicates a comparison between *long ago* and some other time. This "other time" must be indicated for the comparison to be logical. Choice (B) corrects this problem by comparing *long ago to today*.

36. **A**   The pronoun *it* does not have a proper antecedent. It seems to refer to *the things we buy* in sentence 3, but this is plural, not singular. Choices (A), (B), and (E) avoid this problem, but (B) shows an illogical contrast and (E) is awkward and vague.

37. **E**   The pronoun *this* has no clear antecedent, and the pronoun *they* is used to refer to two different antecedents, *workers* and *methods*. Choice (E) clarifies these references most effectively.

38. **C**   The clause *it means being inhumane* is extremely vague. Choice (C) clarifies the subject and verb and conveys the idea logically.

39. **D**   Choice (D) provides the most logical transition because it mentions the previous discussion about *the manufacture of consumer goods* and introduces a new, but related, discussion about *their disposal*.